Information and Decisions

Accounting and Other Issues for Managers

Edited by James L. Jaffe

Beth Walston-Dunham
Midland Lutheran College
Fremont, Nebraska

Bruce A. Baldwin
Arizona State University
West

Carl S. Warren
University of Georgia, Athens
Professor of Accounting

Earl K. Stice
PricewaterhouseCoopers
Professor of Accounting
Brigham Young University

Eugene F. Brigham
University of Florida

Frank B. Cross
Associate Director, Center for
Legal and Regulatory Studies
University of Texas at Austin

Gaylord A. Jentz
Herbert D. Kelleher
Professor in Business Law
University of Texas at Austin

James D.Stice
Brigham Young University

James M. Reeve
University of Tennessee,
Knoxville
Professor of Accounting

Jeff Madura
Florida Atlantic University

Jeffrey F. Beatty
Boston University

Joel F. Houston
University of Florida

John W. Hill
Indiana University

Kenneth W. Clarkson
University of Miami

Kevin E. Murphy
Oklahoma State University

Mark Higgins
University of Rhode Island

Michael A. Diamond
University of Southern
California

Philip E. Fess
University of Illinois,
Champaign-Urbana
Professor Emeritus of
Accounting

Robert W. Ingram
University of Alabama

Roger LeRoy Miller
Institute for University
Studies Arlington, Texas

Scott Besley
University of South Florida

Susan S. Samuelson
Boston University

Thomas L. Albright
University of Alabama

THOMSON LEARNING™
CUSTOM PUBLISHING

Printed in the United States of America

Thomson Learning Custom Publishing
5191 Natorp Boulevard
Mason, OH 45040
USA

For information about our products, contact us:
1-800-355-9983
http://www.custom.thomsonlearning.com

International Headquarters
Thomson Learning
International Division
290 Harbor Drive, 2nd Floor
Stamford, CT 06902-7477
USA

UK/Europe/Middle East/South Africa
Thomson Learning
Berkshire House
168-173 High Holborn
London WCIV 7AA

Asia
Thomson Learning
60 Albert Street, #15-01
Albert Complex
Singapore 189969

Canada
Nelson Thomson Learning
1120 Birchmount Road
Toronto, Ontario MIK 5G4
Canada
United Kingdom

ISBN 0-324-21307-7

Custom Contents

Chapter 2 Organizational Structure 31

Chapter 3 Choice of Business Entity - General Tax and Nontax Factors/ Formation 57

Glossary 629

Glossary 641

1

Selecting a Form of Business Ownership

When entrepreneurs establish a business, they must decide on the form of business ownership. The choice of a specific form of business ownership can affect various business characteristics, which influence the firm's value.

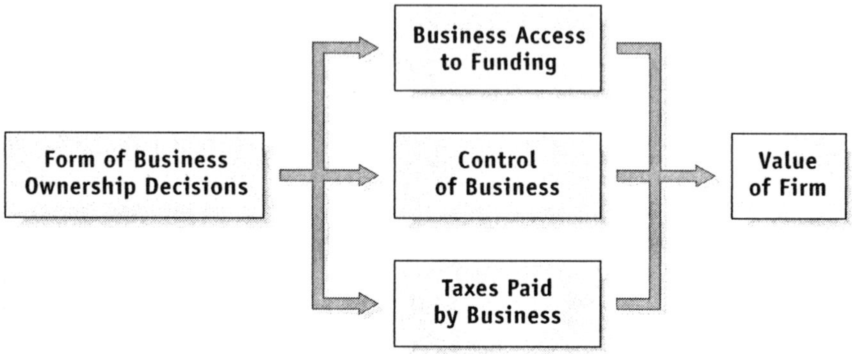

Consider the case of Outback Steakhouse, which has more than 235 restaurants spread from California to New Jersey. Outback's sales have recently grown at an annual rate of 114 percent. What is the ideal form of business ownership for Outback? What factors did Outback consider when it selected a form of business ownership? What are the risks of Outback from the perspective of its owners? This chapter provides a background on business ownership, which can be used to address these questions.

The **Learning Goals** of this chapter are to:

1. Explain how business owners select a form of business ownership.
2. Describe methods of owning existing businesses.
3. Explain how business owners can measure their business performance.

POSSIBLE FORMS OF BUSINESS OWNERSHIP

1 **Explain how business owners select a form of business ownership.**

Entrepreneurs choose one of three possible forms of business ownership:

- Sole proprietorship
- Partnership
- Corporation

Sole Proprietorship

sole proprietorship a business owned by a single owner

sole proprietor the owner of a sole proprietorship

A business owned by a single owner is referred to as a **sole proprietorship.** The owner of a sole proprietorship is called the **sole proprietor.** A sole proprietor may obtain loans from creditors to help finance the firm's operations, but these loans do not represent ownership. The sole proprietor is obligated to cover any payments resulting from the loans, but does not need to share the business profits with creditors.

Typical examples of sole proprietorships include a local restaurant, a local construction firm, a barber shop, a laundry service, and a local clothing store. About 70 percent of all firms in the United States are sole proprietorships. But because these firms are relatively small, they generate less than 10 percent of all business revenue. The earnings generated by a sole proprietorship are considered as personal income received by the proprietor and are subject to personal income taxes imposed by the Internal Revenue Service (IRS).

CHARACTERISTICS OF SUCCESSFUL SOLE PROPRIETORS Sole proprietors must be willing to accept full responsibility for the firm's performance. The pressure of this responsibility can be much greater than any employee's responsibility. Sole proprietors must also be willing to work flexible hours. They are on call at all times and may even have to substitute for a sick employee. Their responsibility for the success of the business encourages them to continually monitor business operations. They must exhibit strong leadership skills, be well organized, and communicate well with employees.

Many successful sole proprietors had previous work experience in the market in which they are competing, perhaps as an employee in a competitor's firm. For example, restaurant managers commonly establish their own restaurants. Experience is critical to understanding the competition and behavior of customers in a particular market.

ADVANTAGES OF A SOLE PROPRIETORSHIP The sole proprietor form of ownership has the following advantages over other forms of business ownership:

1 *All Earnings Go to the Sole Proprietor* The sole proprietor (owner) does not have to share the firm's earnings with other owners. Thus, the rewards of establishing a successful firm come back to the owner.

2 *Easy Organization* Establishing a sole proprietorship is relatively easy. The legal requirements are minimal. A sole proprietorship need not establish a separate legal entity. The owner must register the firm with the state, which can normally be done by mail. The owner may also need to apply for an occupational license to conduct a particular type of business. The specific license requirements vary with the state and even the city where the business is located.

3 *Complete Control* Having only one owner with complete control of the firm eliminates the chance of conflicts during the decision-making process. For example, an owner of a restaurant can decide on the menu, the prices, and the salaries paid to employees.

4 *Lower Taxes* The earnings in a proprietorship are considered as personal income, and may be subject to lower taxes than some other forms of business ownership, as will be explained later in this chapter.

DISADVANTAGES OF A SOLE PROPRIETORSHIP Along with its advantages, the sole proprietorship has the following disadvantages:

1 *The Sole Proprietor Incurs All Losses* Just as sole proprietors do not have to share the profits, they are unable to share any losses that the firm incurs. For example, assume you invested $10,000 of your funds in a lawn service and borrowed an additional $8,000 that was invested in the business. Assume that the revenue was barely sufficient to pay salaries to your employees, which caused you to terminate the firm. You not only lost all of your $10,000 investment in the firm but also are liable for the $8,000 that you borrowed. Since you are the sole proprietor, no other owners are available to help cover the losses.

unlimited liability no limit on the debts for which the owner is liable

2 *Unlimited Liability* A sole proprietor is subject to **unlimited liability,** which means there is no limit on the debts for which the owner is liable. If a sole proprietorship is sued, the sole proprietor is personally liable for any judgment against that firm.

3 *Limited Funds* A sole proprietor may have limited funds available to invest in the firm. Thus, sole proprietors have difficulty engaging in airplane manufacturing, shipbuilding, computer manufacturing, and other businesses that require substantial funds. Sole proprietors have limited funds to support the firm's expansion or to absorb temporary losses. A poorly performing firm may improve if given sufficient time. But if this firm cannot obtain additional funds to make up for its losses, it may not be able to continue in business long enough to recover.

4 *Limited Skills* A sole proprietor has limited skills and may be unable to control all parts of the business. For example, a sole proprietor may have difficulty running a large medical practice because different types of expertise may be needed.

Partnership

partnership a business that is co-owned by two or more people

partners co-owners of a business

general partnership all partners have unlimited liability

limited partnership a firm that has some limited partners

limited partners partners whose liability is limited

general partners partners who manage the business, receive a salary, share the profits or losses of the business, and have unlimited liability

A business that is co-owned by two or more people is referred to as a **partnership.** The co-owners of a business are called **partners.** The co-owners must register the partnership with the state and may need to apply for an occupational license. About 10 percent of all firms are partnerships.

In a **general partnership,** all partners have unlimited liability. That is, these partners are personally liable for all obligations of the firm. Conversely, a **limited partnership** is a firm that has some **limited partners,** or partners whose liability is limited to the cash or property they contributed to the partnership. Limited partners are only investors in the partnership and do not participate in the management of the business. Yet, because they invested in the business, they share the profits or losses of the business. A limited partnership has one or more **general partners,** or partners who manage the business, receive a salary, share the profits or losses of the business, and have unlimited liability. The earnings distributed to each partner represent personal income and are subject to personal income taxes imposed by the IRS.

ADVANTAGES OF A PARTNERSHIP The partnership form of ownership has three main advantages:

While most of the work of a physician is done on an individual basis, physicians commonly form partnerships to share the basic administrative responsibilities and expenses of running an office.

1 *Additional Funding* An obvious advantage of a partnership over sole proprietorships is the additional funding that one or more partners can provide. Therefore, more money may be available to finance the business operations.
2 *Losses Are Shared* Any business losses that the partnership incurs do not have to be absorbed by a single person. Each owner will absorb only a portion of the loss.
3 *More Specialization* A partnership can allow partners to focus on their respective specializations and serve a wide variety of customers. For example, an accounting firm may have one accountant who specializes in personal taxes for individuals and another who specializes in business taxes for firms. A medical practice partnership may have doctors with various types of expertise.

DISADVANTAGES OF A PARTNERSHIP Along with its advantages, the partnership has the following disadvantages:

1 *Control Is Shared* The decision making in a partnership must be shared. Partners may disagree about how a business should be run, which may destroy business and personal relationships. For example, about 53 percent of Kiwi International Air Lines was owned by employees (primarily pilots). Many of the owners were good pilots but poor managers. Kiwi experienced major financial problems in 1995 because of poor management.
2 *Unlimited Liability* General partners in a partnership are subject to unlimited liability, just like sole proprietors.
3 *Profits Are Shared* Any profits that the partnership generates must be shared among all partners.

S-CORPORATIONS A partnership that has thirty-five owners or less and satisfies other criteria may choose to be a so-called **S-corporation.** The earnings of an S-corporation are distributed to the owners and taxed at the respective personal income tax rate of each owner. Thus, the owners are only subject to limited liability (like owners of corporations), but are taxed as if the firm was a partnership. Some state governments impose a corporate tax on S-corporations.

S-corporation a partnership that has thirty-five owners or less and satisfies other criteria. The earnings are distributed to the owners and taxed at the respective personal income tax rate of each owner

limited liability company (LLC) a firm that has all the favorable features of a typical general partnership but also offers limited liability for the partners

LIMITED LIABILITY COMPANY (LLC) A type of general partnership called a **limited liability company (LLC)** has become popular in recent years. An LLC is a firm that has all the favorable features of a typical general partnership but also offers limited liability for the partners. It typically protects a partner's personal assets from the negligence of other partners in the firm. This type of protection is highly desirable for partners, given the high frequency of liability lawsuits. The assets of the company (such as the property or machinery owned by the company) are not protected. While S-corporations may also provide liability protection, various rules may restrict some partners of S-corporations from limited liability. The LLC does not impose such stringent rules.

The LLC must be created according to the laws of the state where the business is located. The precise rules on liability protection vary among states. Most states either allow for the creation of LLCs or have enacted legislation to allow them in the future. Numerous general partnerships (including many accounting firms) have converted to LLCs to capitalize on the advantages of a partnership, while limiting liability for their owners.

COMPARISON OF A PROPRIETORSHIP WITH A PARTNERSHIP A general comparison of a proprietorship with a partnership can be illustrated by considering how your earnings and losses would be affected by the form of business you choose. Exhibit 2.1 shows the earnings of your business over four years if you were the sole proprietor, versus those if you were a co-owner (partner) in a partnership. In the first two years when the business incurred losses, your loss would be larger if you were the sole owner of the business rather than a co-owner. However, in the next two years when the business generated positive earnings, your gain would be larger if you were the sole owner of the business. The comparison illustrates the relative advantage of being the sole owner when the business performs well, but the relative disadvantage when the business incurs losses.

Corporation

corporation a state chartered entity that pays taxes and is legally distinct from its owners

A third form of business is a **corporation,** which is a state-chartered entity that pays taxes and is legally distinct from its owners. About 20 percent of all firms are corporations. Yet, corporations generate almost 90 percent of all business revenue. Exhibit 2.2 compares the relative contributions of sole proprietorships, partnerships, and corporations.

charter a document to incorporate a business; the charter describes important aspects of the corporation

bylaws general guidelines for managing the firm

An individual or group must adopt a corporate **charter,** or a document to incorporate a business, and file it with the state government. The charter describes important aspects of the corporation such as the name of the firm, information about the stock issued, and a description of the firm's operations. The people who organize the corporation must also establish **bylaws,** which are general guidelines for managing the firm.

Since the shareholders of the corporation are legally separated from the entity, they have limited liability, meaning they are not held personally responsible for the firm's actions. The most that the stockholders of a corporation can lose is the amount of money they invested.

The stockholders of a corporation elect the members of the board of directors, who are responsible for establishing the general policies of the firm. One of the board's responsibilities is to elect the president and other key officers (such as vice-presidents), who are then given the responsibility of running the business on a day-to-day basis.

Exhibit 2.1
Your Portion of Earnings (or Losses) on a Proprietorship Versus a Partnership

Year	Total Business Earnings (or Loss)	Earnings to a Sole Owner	Earnings to One Partner
1	−$40,000	−$40,000	−$20,000
2	−$20,000	−$20,000	−$10,000
3	+$40,000	+$40,000	+$20,000
4	+$80,000	+$80,000	+$40,000

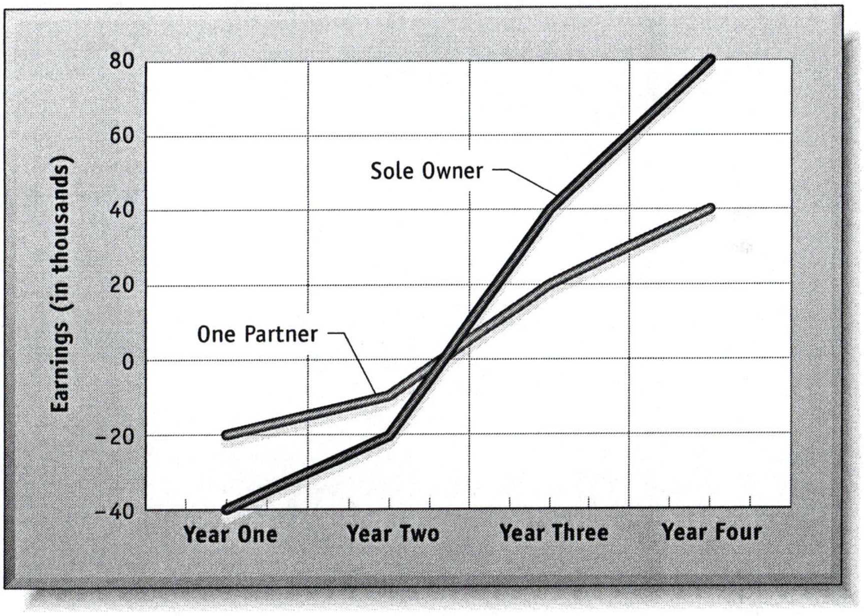

Lou Gerstner, chief executive officer and chairman of the board, speaks at IBM's annual meeting of shareowners.

If the board of directors becomes displeased with the performance of the key officers, the board has the power to replace them. Similarly, if the stockholders become displeased with the performance of members of the board, the stockholders can replace the directors in the next scheduled election. In some corporations, one or a few individuals may serve as a stockholder, as a member of the board of directors, and as a key officer of the firm. For example, Louis Gerstner is the chief executive officer of IBM, is the chairman of the board, and holds more than eighty thousand shares of IBM stock.

HOW STOCKHOLDERS EARN A RETURN ON THEIR INVESTMENT Stockholders can earn a return on their investment in a firm in two different ways. First, they may receive dividends from the firm, which represent a portion of recent earnings of the firm over the last three months that are distributed to stockholders. Second, the stock they hold may increase in value. When the firm becomes more profitable, the value of its stock tends to rise, meaning the value of stock maintained by owners has increased. Thus, they can benefit by selling that stock for a much higher price than they paid for it. In the 1994–1996 period, stock prices of many well-known firms such as the Coca-Cola Company, Eastman Kodak, IBM, and PepsiCo more than doubled. The stock price of Netscape increased by more than 500 percent during 1995.

Exhibit 2.2
Relative Contributions of Sole Proprietorships, Partnerships, and Corporations

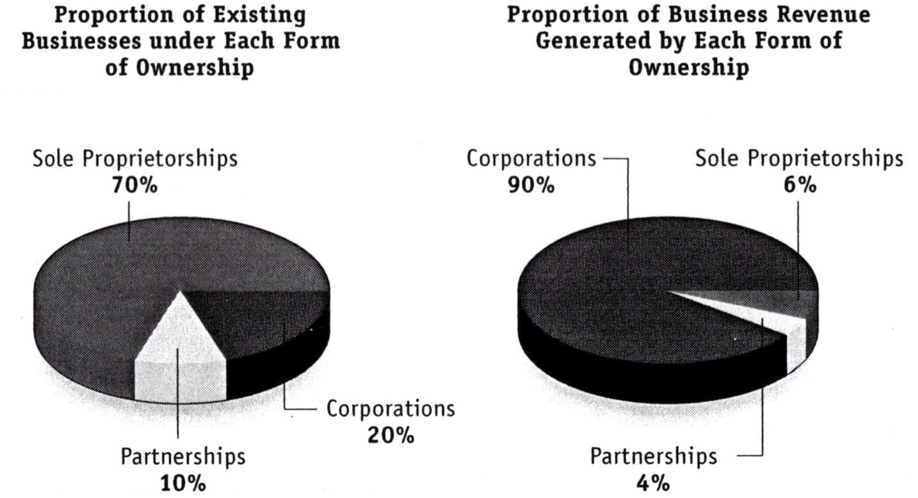

PRIVATELY HELD VERSUS PUBLICLY HELD CORPORATIONS People become owners of a corporation by purchasing shares of stock. Many small corporations are **privately held,** meaning that ownership is restricted to a small group of investors. Some of the more well-known privately held firms include L L Bean, Enterprise Rent-A-Car, Polo Ralph Lauren, Rand McNally and Company, and United Parcel Service. Most large corporations are **publicly held,** meaning that shares can be easily purchased or sold by investors.

privately held ownership is restricted to a small group of investors

publicly held shares can be easily purchased or sold by investors

Stockholders of publicly held corporations can sell their shares of stock when they need money, are disappointed with the performance of the corporation, or simply expect that the stock price will not rise in the future. Their stock can be sold (with the help of a stockbroker) to some other investor who would like to invest in that corporation.

Netscape founder Marc Andreessen helped make Netscape one of the hottest public stock offerings of 1995.

While virtually all firms (even Ford Motor Company) were privately held when they were created, some of these firms became publicly held when they needed funds to support large expansion. The act of initially issuing stock to the public is called **going public.**

going public the act of initially issuing stock to the public

Publicly held corporations can obtain additional funds by issuing new common stock. This means that either their existing stockholders could purchase more stock, or other investors could become stockholders by purchasing the corporation's stock. By issuing new stock, corporations may obtain whatever funds are needed to support any business expansion. Corporations that wish to issue new stock must be able to convince investors that the funds will be utilized properly, resulting in a reasonable return for the investors.

ADVANTAGES OF A CORPORATION A corporate form of ownership has the following advantages:

1 *Limited Liability* Owners of a corporation have limited liability (as explained earlier), whereas sole proprietors and general partners typically have unlimited liability.
2 *Access to Funds* A corporation can easily obtain funds by issuing new stock (as explained earlier). This allows corporations the flexibility to grow and to engage in new business ventures. Sole proprietorships and partnerships have less access to funding when they wish to finance expansion. To obtain more funds, they may have to rely on their existing owners or on loans from creditors.
3 *Transfer of Ownership* Investors in large, publicly traded companies can normally sell their stock in minutes by calling their stockbrokers. Conversely, owners of sole proprietorships or partnerships may have some difficulty in selling their share of ownership in the business.

DISADVANTAGES OF A CORPORATION Along with its advantages, the corporate form of ownership has the following disadvantages:

1 *High Organizational Expense* The expense of organizing a business normally is greater for the corporate form of business than for the other forms. The higher expense results from the necessity of creating a corporate charter and filing it with the state. Some expense also may be incurred in establishing bylaws.
2 *Financial Disclosure* When the stock of a corporation is traded publicly, the investing public has the right to inspect the company's financial data, within certain limits. As a result, firms may be obligated to publicly disclose more about their business operations and employee salaries than they would like. Privately held firms are not forced to disclose financial information to the public.
3 *Agency Problems* Publicly held corporations are normally run by managers who are responsible for making decisions for the business that will serve the interests of the owners. Managers may not always act in the best interests of stockholders. For example, managers may attempt to take expensive business trips that are not necessary to manage the business. These types of actions may increase the expenses of running a business, reduce business profits, and therefore reduce the returns to stockholders. When managers do not act as responsible agents for the shareholders who own the business, this results in a so-called **agency problem.** Such a problem does not normally occur with proprietorships, because the sole owner may also serve as the sole manager and make most or all business decisions.

agency problem when managers do not act as responsible agents for the shareholders who own the business

4 *High Taxes* Since the corporation is a separate entity, it is taxed separately. The annual taxes paid by a corporation are determined by applying the corporate tax rate to the annual earnings. The corporate tax rate is different from the personal tax rate.

Corporations, just like individuals, have to pay taxes. PepsiCo pays hundreds of millions of dollars in taxes each year.

Consider a corporation that earns $10 million in earnings this year. Assume that the corporate tax rate applied to earnings of corporations is 30 percent this year (the corporate tax rates can be changed by law over time). Thus, the taxes and after-tax earnings of the corporation are shown here:

Earnings before Tax = $10,000,000
Corporate Tax = $ 3,000,000 (computed as 30% of $10,000,000)
Earnings after Tax = $ 7,000,000

If any of the after-tax earnings are paid to owners as dividends, the dividends represent personal income to stockholders. Thus, the stockholders will pay personal income taxes on the dividends. Continuing with our example, assume that all of the $7 million in after-tax earnings is distributed to the stockholders as dividends. Assume that the personal tax rate is 20 percent for all owners who will receive dividends (personal tax rates depend on the person's income level and can be changed by law over time). The actual dividend income received by stockholders after paying income taxes is as follows:

Dividends Received = $7,000,000
Taxes Paid on Dividends = $1,400,000 (computed as 20% of $7,000,000)
Earnings after Tax = $5,600,000

Since the corporate tax was $3,000,000 and the personal tax was $1,400,000, the total tax paid as a result of the corporation's profits was $4,400,000. This total tax amount represents 44 percent of the $10,000,000 profit that was earned by the corporation.

This example shows how owners of corporations are subject to double taxation, because the corporation's entire profits from their investment are first subject to corporate taxes. Then, any profits distributed as dividends to individual owners are subject to personal income taxes. Exhibit 2.3 shows the flow of funds between owners and the corporation to illustrate how owners are subject to double taxation.

To recognize the disadvantage of double taxation, consider what the taxes would have been for this business if it was a sole proprietorship or partnership rather than a

Exhibit 2.3
Illustration of Double Taxation

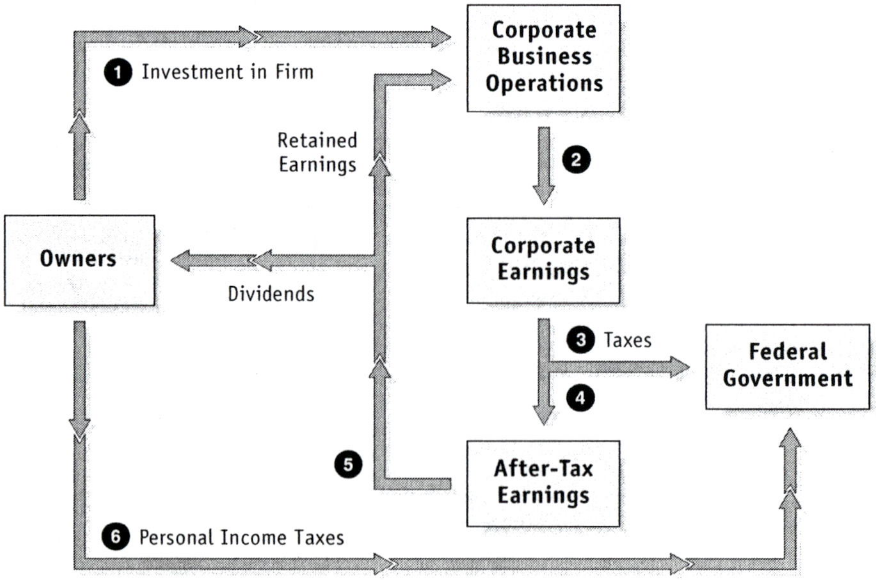

Exhibit 2.4
Comparison of Tax Effects between Corporations and Sole Proprietorships

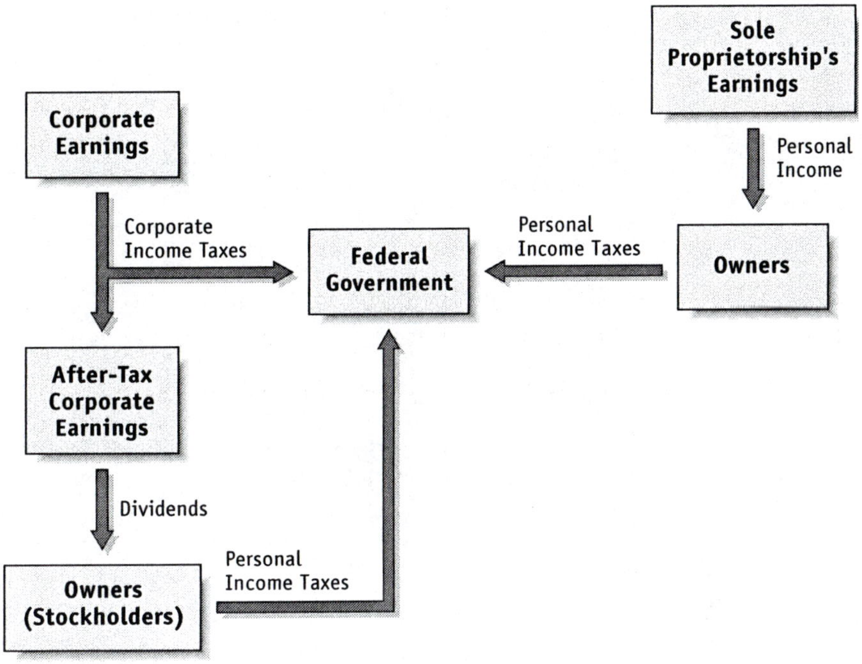

corporation. The $10,000,000 profit would have been considered personal income to a sole proprietor or to partners, which would be subject to personal taxes. If the personal tax rate was 20 percent, the total tax amount would be $2,000,000 (computed as 20 percent of $10,000,000). This tax amount is less than half of what would be paid out by a corporation that earned the same profit. Even if the personal income tax rate of a sole proprietor or a partner was higher than 20 percent, the taxes paid by a corporation would probably still be higher. A comparison of the tax effects between corporations and sole proprietorships is provided in Exhibit 2.4.

One way in which the corporation may reduce the taxes paid by owners is to reinvest its earnings (called "retained earnings") rather than pay the earnings out as dividends. If owners do not receive dividends from a corporation, they would not be subject to personal taxes on the profits earned by the corporation. This strategy makes sense only if the corporation can put the retained earnings to good use.

When stockholders of a corporation sell their stocks for more than they paid for them, they earn a **capital gain,** which represents the price received from the sale of stock minus the price they paid for the stock. The stockholders would pay a so-called capital gains tax on the capital gain. Whether stockholders receive income from selling the stock at a gain or from receiving dividend payments, they are subject to taxes.

capital gain the price received from the sale of stock minus the price paid for the stock

Comparing Forms of Business Ownership

No single form of business ownership is ideal for all business owners. An individual setting up a small business may choose a sole proprietorship. Some people who decide to co-own a small business may choose a partnership. However, if they would prefer to limit their liability, they may decide to establish a privately held corporation. If this corporation grows substantially over time and needs millions of dollars to support additional business expansion, it may convert to a publicly held corporation so that it can obtain funds from stockholders.

SMALL BUSINESS SURVEY

Key Concerns about Business Ownership

A survey by the consulting firm Arthur Andersen and Company and a lobbying group (National Business United) asked business owners their main concerns about their businesses. Multiple answers were allowed. Some of the key results are summarized in the following table:

Concerns about Business Ownership	Percentage of Respondents
Identifying a successor	35%
Handling nonfamily key employees	32%
Management training for family members	31%
Financing	28%
Estate-tax problems	27%
Employee morale	9%

These results suggest that owners have a wide variety of concerns, most of which are related to management or to financing.

METHODS OF OWNING EXISTING BUSINESSES

2 **Describe methods of owning existing businesses.**

Many people become sole owners of businesses by starting their own business. However, some people become the sole owners without starting the business. The following are common methods by which people become owners of existing businesses:

- Assuming ownership of a family business
- Purchasing an existing business
- Franchising

Assuming Ownership of a Family Business

Many people work in a family business and after a period of time assume the ownership of it. This can be an ideal way to own a business because its performance may be somewhat predictable as long as the key employees continue to work there. Major decisions regarding the production process and other operations of the firm have been predetermined. If the business has historically been successful, a new owner's main function may be to ensure that the existing operations continue to run efficiently. Alternatively, if the business is experiencing poor performance, the new owner may have to revise management, marketing, and financing policies.

Purchasing an Existing Business

Businesses are for sale on any given day in any city. They are often advertised in the classified ads section of local newspapers. Businesses are sold for various reasons, including financial difficulties and death or retirement of an owner.

People who consider purchasing an existing business must determine whether they have the expertise to run the business or at least properly monitor the managers. Then they must compare the expected benefits of the business with the initial outlay that would be required to purchase it. Historical sales volume may be provided by the seller of a business and can be used to estimate the future sales volume. However, the prospective buyer must be cautious when using these figures. In some businesses such as dentistry and hair styling, personal relationships between the owner and customers are critical. Many customers may switch to competitors if the ownership changes. For these types of businesses, the historical sales volume may substantially overestimate future sales. For some other less personalized businesses such as grocery stores, a change of ownership is not likely to have a significant effect on customer preferences (and therefore on sales volume).

Franchising

franchise arrangement whereby a business owner allows others to use its trademark, trade name or copyright, under specific conditions

franchisor firm that allows others to use its trade name of copyright, under specified conditions

franchisee firm that is allowed to use the trade name or copyright of a franchise

A **franchise** is an arrangement whereby a business owner (called a **franchisor**) allows others (the **franchisee**) to use its trademark, trade name or copyright, under specified conditions. Each individual franchise operates as an independent business and is typically owned by a sole proprietor.

Franchises in the United States number over five hundred thousand, and they generate more than $800 billion in annual revenue. Some of the more well-known franchises include Hardees, Thrifty Rent-a-Car System, Mail Boxes Etc., Dairy Queen, Super 8 Motels Inc., TGI Fridays, Pearle Vision Inc., and Baskin-Robbins. The ten fastest growing franchises are identified on Exhibit 2.5.

To gain more insight on the costs and potential benefits of franchising, consider the following examples. A franchise called Kid to Kid Franchise System sells used clothing for children. This franchise can be purchased for about $90,000. A Wendy's restaurant franchise can be purchased for $25,000, but the building costs over $500,000 and the equipment costs about $200,000. The costs of purchasing a franchise can vary significantly, depending on the specific trademarks, technology, and services provided to the franchises.

McDonald's is probably the most successful franchise in the world. Starting at this original location in DesPlaines, Illinois, McDonalds has 18,000 locations in more than 90 countries.

Exhibit 2.5
Fastest Growing Franchises

Firm	Number of Franchises	Percentage of Growth in Franchises over 1991–1994
Snap on Tools	2,922	1,298%
GNC Franchising	608	533%
Play It Again Sports	495	450%
Tower Cleaning Systems	1,095	213%
Jackson Hewitt Tax	916	125%
Mail Boxes Etc.	2,441	69%
Coverall North America	3,083	66%
Blimpie	691	63%
O.P.E.N. Cleaning	807	59%
Miracle Ear	963	58%

TYPES OF FRANCHISES Most franchises can be classified as a distributorship, a chain-style business, or a manufacturing arrangement.

distributorship a firm in which a dealer is allowed to sell a product produced by a manufacturer

chain-style business a firm that is allowed to use the trade name of a company and follows guidelines related to the pricing and sales of the product

manufacturing arrangement a firm that is allowed to manufacture a product using the formula provided by another company

A **distributorship** is a firm in which a dealer is allowed to sell a product produced by a manufacturer. For example, Chrysler and Ford dealers are distributorships.

A **chain-style business** is a firm that is allowed to use the trade name of a company and follows guidelines related to the pricing and sales of the product. Some examples are Dunkin' Donuts, CD Warehouse, Holiday Inn, Subway, and Pizza Hut.

A **manufacturing arrangement** is a firm that is allowed to manufacture a product using the formula provided by another company. For example, Microsoft may allow a foreign company to produce its software, as long as the software is sold only in that country. Microsoft would receive a portion of the revenue generated by that firm.

ADVANTAGES OF A FRANCHISE The typical advantages of a franchise are as follows:

1 *Proven Management Style* Franchisees look to the franchisors for guidance in production and management. McDonald's provides extensive training to its franchisees. The management style of a franchise is already a proven success. A franchise's main goal is to duplicate a proven business in a particular location. Thus, the franchise is a less risky venture than a new type of business, as verified by a much higher failure rate for new businesses.

2 *Name Recognition* Many franchises are nationally known because of advertising by the franchisor. This provides the franchisee with name recognition, which can significantly increase the demand for the product. Therefore, owners of Holiday Inn, Pizza Hut, and other franchises may not need to spend money on advertising because the franchises are already popular with consumers.

3 *Financial Support* Some franchisees receive some financial support from the franchisor, which can ensure sufficient start-up funds for the franchisee. For example, some McDonald's franchisees can receive funding from McDonald's. Alternatively, franchisees can purchase materials and supplies from the franchisor on credit, which represents a form of short-term financing.

DISADVANTAGES OF A FRANCHISE Two common disadvantages of franchising are as follows:

SPOTLIGHT ON TECHNOLOGY

Organizing Your Business by Using the Internet

The decision on the form of business ownership can have long-term implications for taxes, liability, and control of the business. For these reasons, it should not be made lightly and will usually require a lawyer. Unfortunately, good legal advice does not come cheap. Therefore, entrepreneurs should familiarize themselves with the issues involved in organizing their businesses prior to retaining legal counsel. In recent years, the Internet has become an excellent place for finding out about such issues.

Perhaps the best starting point for learning more about business organization is the Small Business Administration (SBA). The SBA's home page (http://www.sbaonline.sba.gov/), pictured in Exhibit 2.6, represents an excellent starting point for further research. Among the resources offered:

- Information on local SBA offices.
- Access to the Service Corps of Retired Executives (SCORE), consisting of over ten thousand retired businesspeople who have volunteered to help small businesses for free.
- SBA publications. As illustrated (Exhibit 2.7), the range of topics covered by the publications is enormous, and each can be copied directly to the entrepreneur's computer at no charge.

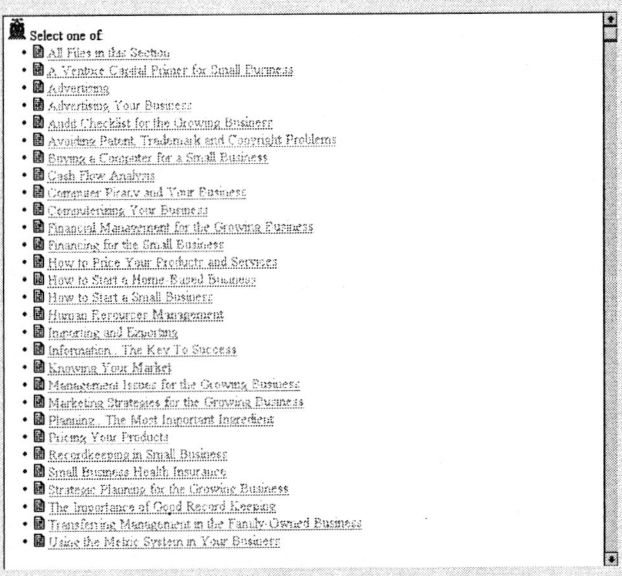

Exhibit 2.7 List of SBA Publications on the Internet

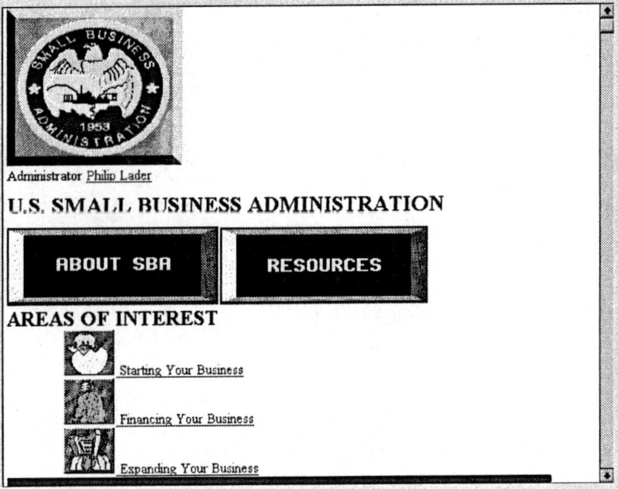

Exhibit 2.6 The Small Business Administration's Home Page

While all of these services are also available through local SBA offices, the entrepreneur can reach them far more quickly over the Internet.

In addition to government agencies, such as the SBA, many private organizations provide information and services to small businesses just getting set up. Many of these, such as the Company Corporation (Exhibit 2.8), allow corporations and other forms of businesses to be set up entirely over the Internet. Such services are made particularly attractive by their low cost—often hundreds or thousands of dollars less than using a lawyer. The entrepreneur is cautioned, however, that "undoing" the wrong form of ownership can often be expensive. Therefore, unless the entrepreneur has extensive knowledge of various forms of ownership, establishing a long-term relationship with a local attorney is generally prudent.

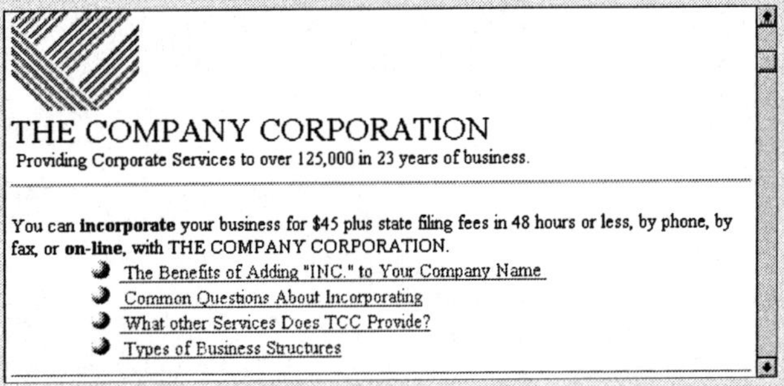

Exhibit 2.8 The Company Corporation Home Page

1 *Sharing Profits* In return for services provided by the franchisor, the franchisee must share profits with the franchisor. Annual fees paid by the franchisee may be 8 percent or more of the annual revenue generated by the franchise.

2 *Less Control* The franchisee must abide by guidelines regarding product production and pricing, and possibly other guidelines as well. Consequently, the franchisee's performance is dependent on these guidelines. Owners are not allowed to revise some of the guidelines.

While decision making is limited, owners of a franchise still make some critical decisions. They must decide whether a particular franchise can be successful in a particular location. In addition, even though the production and marketing policies are somewhat predetermined, the owners are responsible for managing their employees. They must provide leadership and motivation to maximize production efficiency. Thus, a franchise's performance is partially dependent on its owners and managers.

RECEIVING ASSISTANCE AS A NEW BUSINESS

When new businesses are established, they are relatively small. These businesses may be assisted by the Small Business Administration (SBA), which was established by Congress in 1953 to encourage entrepreneurship. The SBA attempts to enhance the managerial capabilities of small business owners through counseling, workshops, and free brochures. In addition, retired business executives offer free assistance to business owners through the SBA. These executives have varied backgrounds and periodically conduct workshops in local communities for people planning to begin their own businesses.

In recognition of the relatively small proportion of minority-owned businesses, the SBA has offered much assistance to minorities that considered establishing their own businesses. Special financing assistance has also been available. Some universities maintain small business development centers that can help small business owners or people planning to start a business.

The degree of government assistance offered to small businesses frequently changes in response to the funds allocated for this purpose in the federal budget. When pressure to reduce government spending exists, the funding for small business assistance may be reduced.

HOW OWNERS MEASURE BUSINESS PERFORMANCE

3 **Explain how business owners can measure their business performance.**

Owners who invest in a firm focus on two key criteria to measure a firm's performance: (1) return on their investment and (2) risk of their investment. These two criteria are discussed now, because the business strategies that managers implement should be intended to satisfy the business owners. Managers must determine how various business strategies will affect the firm's return on investment and risk.

Return on Investment

The return on investment in a firm is derived from the firm's profits (also called "earnings" or "income"). As a firm produces income, a portion of these earnings is paid to the Internal Revenue Service as income taxes. The remaining (after-tax) earnings represent the return (in dollars) to the business owners. However, dollar value of a firm's after-tax earnings is not necessarily a useful measure of the firm's perfor-

equity the total investment by the firm's stockholders

return on equity (ROE) earnings as a proportion of the equity

mance unless it is adjusted for the amount of firm's **equity,** which is the total investment by the firm's stockholders. For this reason, business owners prefer to measure the firm's profitability by computing its **return on equity (ROE),** which is the earnings as a proportion of the equity:

$$\text{Return on Equity} = \frac{\text{Earnings after Tax}}{\text{Equity}}$$

For example, if a firm was provided with $1,000,000 by stockholders, and if its after-tax earnings last year were $150,000, its return on equity last year was:

$$\text{ROE} = \frac{\$150{,}000}{\$1{,}000{,}000}$$

$$= .15, \text{ or } 15\%.$$

Thus, the firm generated a return equal to 15 percent of the owner's investment in the firm.

To recognize why a "return" measurement such as ROE is more useful than the dollar value of profits, consider the following situation for Firms A and B in a particular industry:

	Firm A	Firm B
Earnings after Tax Last Year	$15 million	$15 million
Stockholders' Equity	$100 million	$300 million
Return on Equity	15%	5%

Notice that each firm had the same dollar value of earnings after taxes. However, it took three times the investment in Firm B to achieve the same level of annual profit. Therefore, the return on equity (measured as earnings after taxes divided by stockholders' equity) is much higher for Firm A than for Firm B. Thus, Firm A is apparently making better use of the funds invested by stockholders.

As a realistic application, the return on investment for Campbell Soup Company last year is derived in Exhibit 2.9. Notice that Campbell generated an earnings before taxes of $1,042 million. Of this amount, $344 million was used to pay corporate taxes. The remaining $698 million represents after-tax earnings. Given the total investment (equity) of $2,468 million, the after-tax earnings represent a return of 28 percent (computed as $698 million divided by $2,468 million).

Risk

risk the degree of uncertainty about the firm's future earnings

The **risk** of a firm represents the degree of uncertainty about the firm's future earnings, which reflects an uncertain return to the owners. A firm's future earnings are dependent on its future revenue and its expenses. Firms could experience losses if the revenue is less than expected, or if the expenses are more than expected. Some firms that experience severe losses ultimately fail. In these cases, the owners may lose most or all of the funds they invested in the firms. Also, creditors may not be repaid for the loans that they provided to the firms.

To illustrate the risk of a business, consider the uncertainty of the future revenue and expenses of a lawn service firm. Revenue generated by the firm could be less than expected if unusually cold weather prevents grass and shrubs from growing. In addition, other lawn service firms may be created, which will compete for any avail-

Exhibit 2.9
Annual Profits for Campbell Soup Company

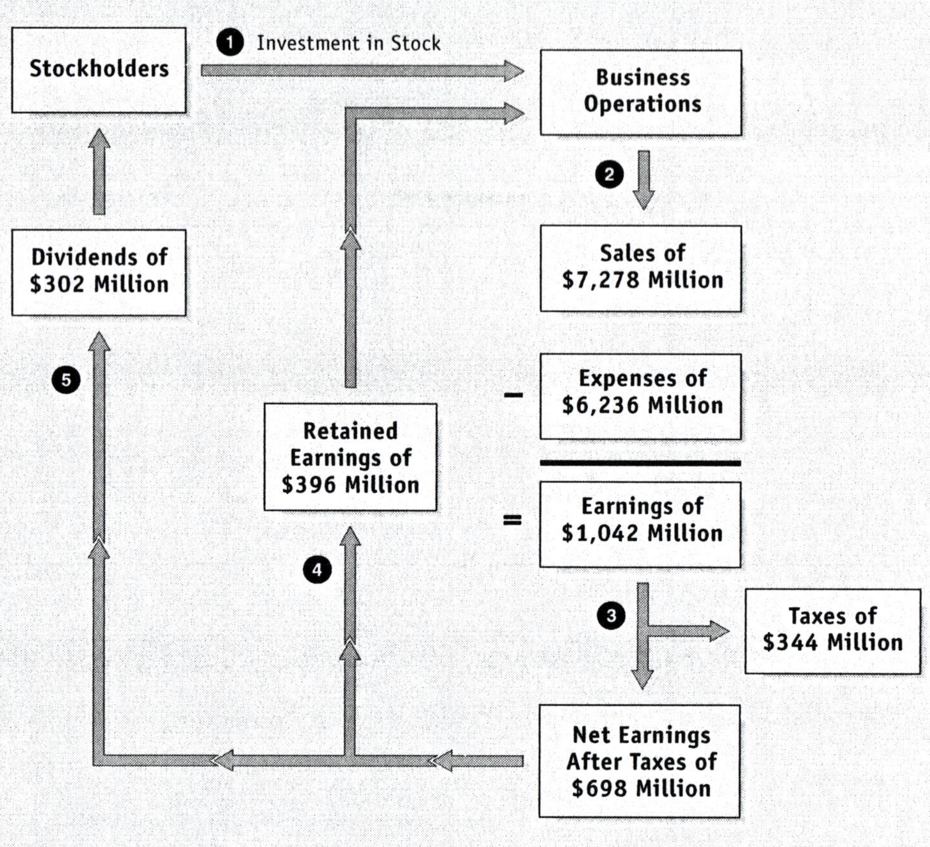

Return on Equity (ROE)
Given that Campbell's equity was about $2,468 million, its ROE was:

$$\text{ROE} = \frac{\text{Earnings after Taxes}}{\text{Equity}}$$

$$= \frac{\$698 \text{ Million}}{\$2{,}468 \text{ Million}}$$

$$= 28\%$$

able business. Given a limited number of lawns in a community, any lawn jobs done by new lawn service firms take away the business that was previously provided by this firm. The expenses of a lawn service may be higher than expected if lawn mowers break down or if the cost of hiring employees rises.

Exhibit 2.10 illustrates how business risk applies to the lawn service. This exhibit shows that the owner of the lawn service anticipated the firm's earnings to be $30,000 in one year. However, since actual revenue was $40,000 less than expected, and expenses were $4,000 more than expected, the firm incurred a loss of $14,000. Large firms such as KMart and Smith Corona (typewriters) have experienced losses following a decline in the demand for their products.

Firms cannot control some factors that may affect their revenue or expenses. However, firms should recognize how possible adverse conditions can affect demand,

Exhibit 2.10
Example of Business Risk

	Expected	Actual
Revenue	$90,000	$50,000
Expenses	60,000	64,000
Earnings	$30,000	−$14,000

so that they can develop a realistic forecast of revenue. In addition, to create a more realistic expectation of the total expenses, they should anticipate that some repairs on their machinery may be needed.

To prepare for potential problems, the risks of each business should be recognized. While many success stories are created in business, many failures occur as well. Some new businesses fail simply because the entrepreneur did not recognize the risks. The Self-Scoring Exercise offers a self-test for assessing your own skills to succeed in business. However, recognize that some people may be successful as managers but not as entrepreneurs because they do not recognize the risks involved in establishing a new business.

SELF-SCORING EXERCISE

Do You Have Necessary Skills to Succeed in Business?

According to the U.S. Department of Labor, achieving success in the workplace, now and in the future, will require that a person possess three enabling skills as a foundation for the five functional skills required in the business environment. Answer each of these three basic questions.

1. Do you believe you possess the basic reading, speaking, listening, and mathematics skills required for future learning?
2. Do you believe you possess the intellectual skills for effective-decision making and problem solving?
3. Do you believe you possess the affective skills required for you to cooperate with others and achieve effective sociability?

If you answered each question yes, you have the needed basic skills to enable you to master five functional skills in the business environment. How do you rate yourself now in each of these five functional skill areas? In the blank before each skill, place the number from 1 (very good) to 5 (needs improvement) that reflects your self-rating.

____ 1. Resource management skills, such as human resource management, time management, and financial resources management.

____ 2. Information management skills, such as identifying and interpreting information.

____ 3. Personal interaction skills, such as teamwork, negotiation, and working with customers.

____ 4. Systems behavior and performance skills, such as anticipating consequences of behavior and cause-effect relationships.

____ 5. Technology utilization skills, such as selecting, using, maintaining, and/or troubleshooting technology.

If you rated yourself a 4 or 5 on any one of the five functional skills, you may want to talk with your instructor or the university's career and counseling office about specific opportunities that will enable you to strengthen those skills.

CROSS-FUNCTIONAL TEAMWORK

Sources of Risk Across Business Functions

A firm relies on the management of resources (including human resources and other resources such as machinery), marketing, and finance functions to perform well. Poor performance can normally be attributed to poor management of resources, poor marketing, or poor financing, as explained next.

If resources are not properly managed, the firm will incur excessive expenses. The following are typical mistakes that can cause excessive production expenses:

1. Hiring more employees than necessary, which results in high operating expenses
2. Hiring fewer employees than necessary, which prevents the firm from achieving the desired volume or quality of products
3. Hiring employees who lack proper skills or training
4. Investing in more equipment or machinery than necessary, which results in high operating expenses
5. Investing in less equipment or machinery than necessary, which prevents the firm from achieving the desired volume or quality of products

The following are typical marketing mistakes that can cause poor performance:

1. Excessive spending on marketing programs
2. Ineffective marketing programs, which do not enhance the firm's revenue

The following are typical finance mistakes that can cause poor performance:

1. Borrowing too much money, which results in a high level of interest expenses incurred per year
2. Not borrowing enough money, which prevents a firm from investing the necessary amount of funds to be successful

Since business decisions are related, a poor decision in one department can affect other departments. For example, Compaq Computer's production volume is based on the forecasted demand for computers by the marketing department. When the marketing department underestimates the demand, Compaq experiences shortages.

RELATIONSHIP BETWEEN RISK AND RETURN Some firms have a much higher degree of risk than others when the demand for their products is highly uncertain. Potential owners will support these high-risk firms only if they are expected to provide a higher return. For example, people may be willing to become owners of an exotic jewelry store only if they expect the store to generate high profits. The people could have used their money to invest in a less risky business, such as a retail bookstore or a grocery store, but investing in the exotic jewelry store offers the possibility of earning a higher return on their investment.

Like business investors, creditors will provide funds to a risky firm only if they have the potential to earn a relatively high return on the funds provided. The return to creditors is the interest rate charged on the loans they provide. To compensate for the higher risk, creditors charge a higher rate of interest when lending funds to a risky business.

RISK OF SMALL BUSINESSES Small businesses tend to be riskier than larger businesses because small businesses have neither the managerial expertise nor the funds to diversify into other businesses. Thus, if their single line of business experiences problems, they are highly susceptible to failure. Any event that affects the single industry they have entered (such as a workers' strike in a supplier firm or reduced demand for the type of products they produce) can result in failure. In addition, the death or retirement of a key manager can have a greater impact on a small business. Larger businesses typically employ several employees for high-level positions to make key decisions, so that no one person is irreplaceable.

Investors recognize the higher risk of small businesses and will invest in them only if the potential for high profitability outweighs the risk involved. Creditors will lend to small businesses only if they will receive a higher return (higher interest rate) that properly reflects the risk. Consequently, the cost of financing for a small business is generally higher than for a large corporation.

GLOBAL BUSINESS

Ownership of Foreign Businesses

Opportunities in foreign countries have encouraged many entrepreneurs in the United States to establish foreign businesses in recent years. A common method for an entrepreneur to establish a foreign business is to purchase a franchise created by a U.S. firm in a foreign country. For example, McDonald's, Pizza Hut, and KFC have franchises in numerous foreign countries. The potential return on these franchises may be higher than in the United States if there is less competition.

Another popular method for U.S. entrepreneurs to own a foreign business is to purchase a business that is being sold by the foreign government. During the 1990s, many foreign governments in Eastern Europe and Latin America sold a large number of businesses that they had owned. They also encouraged more competition among firms in each industry. Entrepreneurs recognized that many businesses previously owned by the government were not efficiently managed. Consequently, many businesses were perceived as having relatively low values, thus enabling some entrepreneurs to purchase the businesses at low prices. However, these businesses were subject to a high degree of risk because the foreign environment was so uncertain. Since most of the businesses in these countries had been managed by their respective governments, the rules for privately owned businesses were not completely established. The tax rates that would be imposed on private businesses were uncertain. The degree of competition was also uncertain, as firms were now allowed to enter most industries.

Given the uncertainty for businesses that were just established in these foreign countries, some entrepreneurs made agreements with existing foreign firms rather than establishing their own business. For example, an entrepreneur may recognize that various household products would be popular in some Latin American countries, but may prefer not to establish a firm there because of uncertainty about tax rates and other government policies. The entrepreneur may make an agreement with an existing firm that distributes related products to retail stores throughout Latin America. This firm would earn a fee for selling the household products produced by the entrepreneur. This example is just one of many possible arrangements that allow U.S. entrepreneurs to capitalize on situations in a foreign country without owning a business there.

BUSINESS DILEMMA

Ownership Decision at College Health Club

Sue Kramer has completed her business plan for College Health Club (CHC), as explained in Chapter 1, in which she would be sole proprietor. She believes that she is well prepared to run her own health club. She submits the plan along with a request for a business loan from her local bank. Shortly after submitting her plan, she notices that a national health club chain is planning to establish a health club franchise near a huge corporate office complex at the other end of town. This franchise is not perceived as a competitor to CHC because it is far away from the campus and is targeted at employees who work in the office complex. However, the franchise is of interest to Sue because it is searching for someone to purchase it. Sue decides to consider purchasing the franchise. The franchisee would be trained by the national chain on how to run the health club and would receive a fraction of the revenue earned by the franchise. While similar types of health clubs are in the area, the national chain believes that room exists for at least one more competitor.

Dilemma

Sue has to decide whether to purchase the franchise or establish CHC. For this reason, she needs to consider the advantages of purchasing the franchise health club versus establishing CHC. What are the advantages of each alternative? Which alternative should Sue select?

Solution

One advantage of the franchise health club is that it would offer training. Second, it has a well-established plan for managing health clubs. Third, the club has a national name that potential customers recognize.

However, an advantage of owning CHC is that it would be less expensive than the franchise health club. Second, CHC would allow Sue to capitalize on her specific idea of targeting college students. Third, Sue would be able to manage CHC without any interference, whereas the franchise would need to be managed in a manner dictated by the national chain. Fourth, Sue would not have to pay any fraction of her revenue to the national chain if she establishes her own health club.

Given the balanced advantages of each alternative business opportunity, the choice is dependent on personal preferences and abilities. Since Sue feels that she has the skills to run her own health club, she decides to do it on her own rather than purchase a franchise.

Additional Issues for Discussion

1 Sue could also have considered purchasing one of the existing health clubs that are for sale in the area. What do you think is an advantage of purchasing an existing health club? What is a disadvantage?

2 One advantage of a partnership is that it allows partners to focus on their respective specializations. Should this advantage cause Sue to search for a partner for her health club business?

3 How will CHC be taxed given that Sue plans to be the sole owner?

SUMMARY

1 When starting a new business, entrepreneurs must select from among three forms of ownership:

- a sole proprietorship, owned by a single person who often manages the firm as well.
- a partnership, composed of two or more co-owners who may manage the firm as well. A partnership can allow for more financial support by owners than a sole proprietorship, but it also requires that control and profits of the firm be shared among owners.
- a corporation, which is an entity that is viewed as separate from its owners. Owners of a corporation have limited liability, while owners

of sole proprietorships and partnerships have unlimited liability.

2 The common methods by which people become owners of existing businesses are as follows:

- assuming ownership of a family business
- purchasing an existing business
- franchising

Assuming the ownership of a family business is desirable because a person can normally learn much about that business before assuming ownership. Yet, many people are not in a position to assume the family business. To purchase an existing business, one must estimate future sales and expenses to determine whether making the investment is feasible. Franchising may be desirable for people who will need some guidance in running the firm. However, the franchisee must pay annual fees to the franchisor.

3 A firm's performance is measured by its owners using two criteria: return on the owner's investment (equity) and risk. Owners of a business commonly assess the return on their investment by measuring the firm's return on equity (ROE), which represents a firm's after-tax earnings as a percentage of the total investment by owners.

The risk of a business represents the uncertainty about its future earnings. Firms that have more uncertain revenue or expenses will have more uncertain earnings, and therefore higher risk. The owners and creditors require a higher return when providing funds to firms whose future earnings are more uncertain.

KEY TERMS

agency problem
bylaws
capital gain
chain-style business
charter
corporation
distributorship
equity
franchise
franchisee
franchisor
general partners
general partnership
going public
limited liability company (LLC)
limited partners
limited partnership
manufacturing arrangement
partners
partnership
privately held
publicly held
return on equity (ROE)
risk
S-corporation
sole proprietor
sole proprietorship
unlimited liability

REVIEW QUESTIONS

1 Compare a sole proprietorship with a partnership and a corporation.
2 Discuss the advantages and disadvantages of a sole proprietorship.
3 Distinguish between a general partnership and a limited partnership.
4 Identify and explain the differences between an S-corporation and a limited liability company.
5 How can stockholders earn a return on their investment?
6 Identify and explain the differences between privately held and publicly held corporations.
7 Identify the advantages of an S-corporation.
8 Explain why stockholders are concerned that managers do not always act in their best interests.
9 Identify and explain the advantages and disadvantages of a franchise.
10 Explain the difference between the corporate tax rate and the personal tax rate.

DISCUSSION QUESTIONS

1 For the following situations, recommend an appropriate form of business ownership:

a. Four physicians wish to start a practice together, and each wants to have limited liability.

b. A friend wants to start her own convenience store.

c. An entrepreneur wants to

acquire a large U.S. steel business.

d. Five friends want to build an apartment complex and are not concerned about limited liability.

2 Discuss the basic steps that should be undertaken to organize a corporation in your state.

3 Discuss and give examples of what you believe is the most common form of business ownership in your hometown.

4 Assume you are creating your own business. What decisions have to be made for you to consider the type of ownership and control of your business?

5 Identify a fast-food franchise that experienced growth in the 1970s and compare it with a fast-food franchise that experienced growth in the 1990s.

RUNNING YOUR OWN BUSINESS

1 Describe whether your business will be a sole proprietorship, a partnership, or a corporation. Why did you make this decision?

2 Describe the risk of your business. That is, explain what conditions could result in lower revenue than what you expect or in higher expenses than what you expect.

INVESTING IN THE STOCK OF A BUSINESS

Using the annual report of the firm in which you would like to invest, complete the following:

1 Each annual report contains an income statement, which discloses the firm's earnings before taxes, its taxes, and its earnings after taxes over the most recent year. Search for the table called "Income Statement" and determine your firm's earnings before taxes, taxes paid, and earnings after taxes last year. What proportion of your firm's earnings were eventually paid as tax expense?

2 Is your firm involved in franchising? If so, describe the details on its franchises. Write the company and ask for information on opening a franchise.

3 Describe any conditions mentioned in the annual report that expose the firm to risk.

CASE 1 Deciding the Type of Business Ownership

Paul Bazzano and Mary Ann Boone are lifelong friends and have decided to go into business. They are not sure of the form of business ownership and control. Paul has stated he would like to invest his savings of $25,000, but does not want to take an active role in managing the day-to-day operations of the business. Mary Ann, on the other hand, is a self-starter, enjoys cooking and baking, and has a vast number of pizza recipes. An existing pizza business is for sale for $50,000. Paul and Mary Ann both like the idea of getting into a business investment. Mary Ann has $5,000 she would like to contribute and believes that buying an existing business has certain advantages. She likes the idea that Paul will not be an active owner and that she will have full control of the pizza operation.

The existing business has sales of $150,000 and generates earnings after taxes of $32,500. Mary Ann believes the business can be expanded and foresees future growth to expand into different locations throughout the Boston area. She projects two more stores in the next five years. The only problem is that she and Paul would take out of the business any profits that are made.

Questions

1 What form of business ownership would you recommend for this business?

2 Would Mary Ann's form of ownership be any different from Paul's?

3 As the business expands, what recommendations would you give Mary Ann?

CASE 2 The Franchising Decision

In recent years the growth of franchises in the United States has slowed. Many franchises are shutting their doors because of saturation in business communities and neighborhoods around the country. Franchisees are also concerned about new economic development, such as food courts appearing in shopping malls.

The franchise contract, an agreement between the franchisor and the franchisee, must detail the exact conditions under which the franchise will operate. Franchise contracts are often lengthy, with few obligations placed on the franchisor. The franchisee must heed the warning "Let the buyer beware." Franchisees must also be acutely aware of everything that is put into writing because the contract generally favors the franchisor's rights. "Franchise contracts are inordinately one-sided. I'd never sign one again unless I could make major revisions," says Greg Johns, a franchisee with American Fastsigns.

The initial costs to get into a franchise are high, often ranging from $5,000 to $35,000. An exception is McDonald's, which costs $500,000 or more. When franchisees open for business, they often pay monthly royalties (from 2 percent to 8 percent of gross sales), plus another 1 or 2 percent for advertising. In addition to advertising fees and royalties, the costs of getting into a franchise are often initially higher than starting a small business. However, the profits and success rate for the franchise are still higher than they are for small businesses.

Questions

1 Distinguish a franchisor from a franchisee.

2 Discuss some of the problems confronting franchisees.

3 What is the meaning of the statement "Let the buyer beware"?

4 Are the costs of getting into a franchise higher than starting a small business? Explain.

VIDEO CASE A Business Ownership Dilemma

Douglas Bagley's moving company called A-1 Pioneer of Salt Lake City, Utah, lost so much ground years ago that it almost failed. But Bagley reversed its direction quickly. It has been moving forward ever since.

The business piled up debt in 1988, and the debt load became heavier when a tractor-trailer carrying $150,000 worth of furniture was lost in a fire. Insurance didn't cover all the loss.

In April, 1988, the partner died. His widow struggled to run the business until the life insurance proceeds were paid; that took six months. And A-1 Pioneer's debt was so heavy that it couldn't meet all its obligations on time.

Bagley filed for bankruptcy protection in January, 1989. The company recovered in less than 12 months.

What made that rapid recovery possible? The key was to obtain funds, or at least retain the funds previously borrowed from creditors. While Bagley may have been able to obtain funds by taking on a new partner, he decided to focus on working with his creditors. First, Bagley assured creditors that they would be paid and gained their confidence by outlining plans for his company. Then he visited his longtime clients and pledged that A-1 Pioneer would do a good job for them. Although some clients took their business elsewhere, most did not.

Today, Bagley has 37 employees—up from eight in 1989. He also has the revenue to justify the rise in payroll. Annual sales have increased year by year and now exceed $1.5 million.

Questions

1 When Douglas Bagley, owner of A-1 Pioneer Moving & Storage, needed to improve the firm's financial condition, he decided to negotiate with his existing creditors. What is an advantage of this strategy over finding a partner who would be willing to invest in the firm:? What is a disadvantage?

2 Assume that Bagley needs about $100,000 of additional support for his firm. Do you think that his firm is in a position to offer stock to the public and become a publicly traded corporation?

3 Assume that Bagley expects that he will earn a return of 20 percent annually on his investment in his moving and storage firm. He based this estimate on the firm's earnings in the last few years. Given the recent population growth in the local area, he expects that the demand for his firm's moving and storage services will increase. Gasoline expenses incurred in the moving business have not risen much because gasoline prices have been stable. Furthermore, wages in the moving business have not risen much, so that the labor expenses incurred by the firm have been stable. Offer some reasons why the return on investment may not be as high as expected.

THE Coca-Cola COMPANY ANNUAL REPORT PROJECT

The following questions apply concepts learned in this chapter to The Coca-Cola Company. Read from Reality #1 on page 3 up to Reality #4 (on page 6) in The Coca-Cola Company annual report before answering these questions.

1 Why do you think The Coca-Cola Company is organized as a corporation rather than a sole proprietorship or a partnership?

2 The annual report suggests that The Coca-Cola Company's economic values added (EVA) influences the return on the investment by shareholders. What does this mean?

3 What challenges does The Coca-Cola Company face?

IN-TEXT STUDY GUIDE

Answers are in an appendix at the back of the book.

True or False

1 A sole proprietor may obtain loans from creditors to help finance the firm's operations, which constitutes ownership.

2 The legal requirements for establishing a sole proprietorship are very difficult.

3 When stockholders of a corporation sell their stocks for more than what they paid for them, they can be subject to a capital gain.

4 If the board of directors becomes displeased with the performance of the key officers, the board has the power to replace them.

5 Publicly held corporations can obtain additional funds by issuing new common stock.

6 Publicly held corporations are not obligated to periodically disclose financial information to the public.

7 To incorporate a business, one must adopt a corporate charter and file it with the state government where it is to be located.

8 The limited liability feature is an advantage in owning a sole proprietorship.

9 A limited liability company must be created according to the laws of the state where the business is located.

10 Limited partners are investors in the partnership and participate in the management of the business.

Multiple Choice

11 People become owners of a corporation by purchasing:
a) shares of stock.
b) corporate bonds.
c) retained earnings.
d) inventory.
e) accounts receivable.

12 The following are possible forms of business ownership except for a:
a) sole proprietorship.
b) partnership.
c) bureaucracy
d) corporation.

13 The return on investment in a firm is derived from the firm's ability to earn:
a) assets.
b) liabilities.
c) profits.
d) expenses.

14 What percentage of all firms in the United States are sole proprietorships?
a) 10 percent
b) 20 percent
c) 30 percent
d) 50 percent
e) 70 percent

15 A partnership that has thirty-five owners or less and meets other criteria may choose to be a so-called:
a) cooperative.
b) proprietorship.
c) joint venture.
d) S-corporation.
e) bureaucracy.

16 A sole proprietorship has the following disadvantages except for:
a) unlimited liability.
b) complete control.
c) limited skills.
d) limited funds.

17 Sharing profits and less control of the business ownership are two common disadvantages of:
a) sole proprietorships.
b) downsizing.
c) divestiture.
d) franchising.

18 Partners have unlimited liability in a:
a) general partnership.
b) corporation.
c) limited partnership.
d) cooperative.

19 An arrangement whereby business owners allow others to use their trademark, trade name, or copyright under specified conditions is a:
a) franchise.
b) labor union.
c) bureau.
d) joint venture.
e) cartel.

20 The degree of uncertainty about future earnings, which reflects an uncertain return to the owners, is known as:
a) certainty.
b) profits.
c) risk.
d) equity.
e) dividends.

21 Stockholders of a corporation elect the members of the:
a) organization.
b) labor union.
c) business trust.
d) board of directors.
e) project team.

22 Stockholders can earn a return on their investment if the stock they hold increases in value over time or through:
a) interest payments.
b) divestiture.
c) dividends.
d) bank notes.
e) conservation.

23 A business that is allowed to use the trade name of a company and follows guidelines related to the pricing and sales of the products is a:
a) joint venture.
b) monopoly.
c) chain-style business.
d) sole proprietorship.

24 General guidelines for the management of a company are called:
a) rules.
b) bylaws.
c) procedures.
d) standards.
e) controls.

25 A general partnership that protects a partner's personal assets from the firm is a:
a) limited liability company.
b) sole proprietorship.
c) cooperative.
d) nonprofit institution.

26 A state-chartered entity that is legally distinct from its owners and pays taxes is a:
a) sole proprietorship.
b) corporation.
c) partnership.
d) limited partnership.
e) joint venture.

27 When ownership of a small corporation is restricted to a small group of investors, it is:
a) publicly held.
b) government owned.
c) bureaucratic.
d) privately held
e) perfectly competitive.

28 Most franchises can be classified as the following except for:
a) business agent.
b) chain-style business.
c) manufacturing arrangement.
d) distributorship.

29 Small businesses are riskier than larger businesses because small businesses lack :
a) enthusiasm.
b) managerial expertise.
c) better service.
d) creativity.
e) innovativeness.

30 A business owned by a single owner is referred to as a:
a) partnership.
b) sole proprietorship.
c) limited partnership.
d) corporation.
e) subchapter S-corporation.

31 The following are disadvantages of a partnership except for:
a) control is shared.
b) losses are shared.
c) unlimited liability.
d) profits are shared.

32 When a corporation's shares can be easily purchased or sold by investors, it is:
a) publicly held.
b) privately held.
c) institutionalized.
d) monopolized.
e) franchised.

33 Important aspects of the corporation, such as the name of the firm, information about the stock issued, and a description of the firm's operations, are contained in a:
a) mission.
b) policy.
c) charter.
d) plan.
e) venture.

34 When two or more people, having complementary skills, agree to co-own a business, this agreement is referred to as a:
a) partnership.
b) sole proprietorship.
c) cooperative.
d) corporation.
e) joint venture.

35 When entrepreneurs establish a business, they must first decide on the form of:
a) divestiture.
b) global expansion.
c) joint ventures.
d) ownership.

What is the World Wide Web?

The Internet evolved primarily as a U.S. network. It became more popular to established and new businesses as a result of a new application, referred to as the World Wide Web (WWW). Today, the WWW has become nearly synonymous with the Internet in the minds of most users.

What makes the WWW different from other Internet applications is its user-friendly graphic interface. Organizations and individuals create web pages, such as the University of Central Arkansas' web page (Exhibit 2.11), using a document format called hypertext markup language (HTML). Web pages can incorporate both

Exhibit 2.11
The University of Central Arkansas' Web Page
http://www.sbaer.uca.edu/

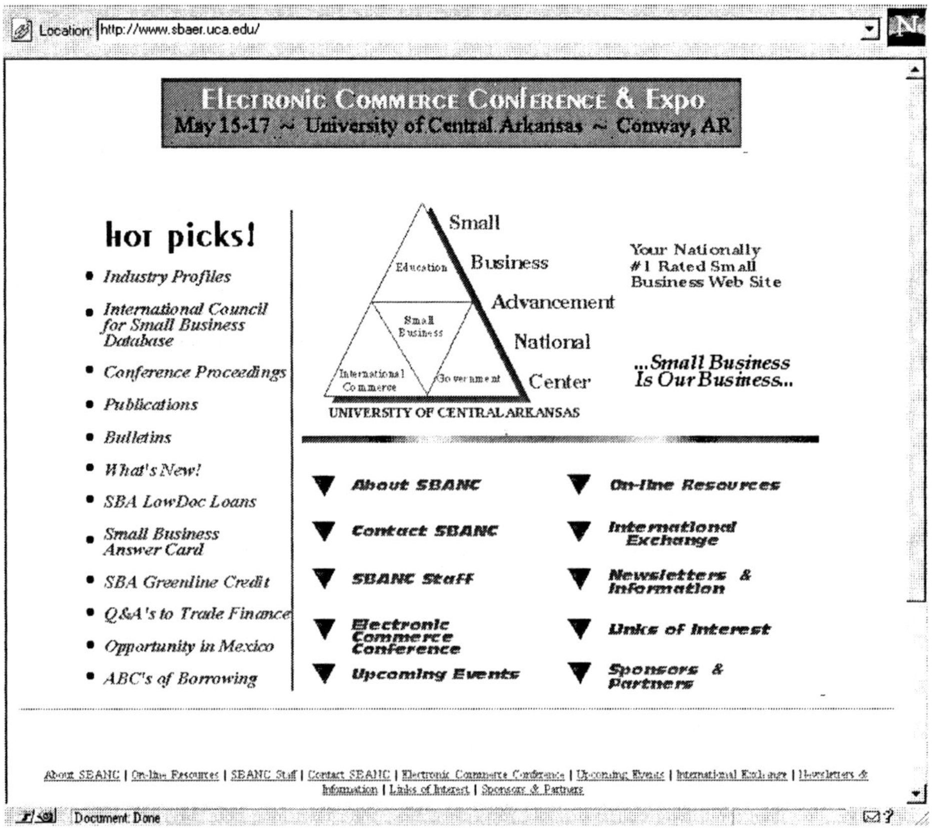

Exhibit 2.12
Popular Web Browsers

	e-mail
Netscape Navigator	http://home.netscape.com/
Microsoft Explorer	http://www.inet.fi/microsoft/
NCSA Mosaic	webdev@ncsa.uiuc.edu
Lynx (text-based only)	grobe@ukans.edu
America On-Line	info@aol.com

text and graphics. Features such as on-line questionnaires, polls, and even product ordering screens can also be incorporated into HTML documents. Today's most advanced web pages go even further, and are now delivering multimedia effects including sound and animation.

Once a web page has been developed, it is then placed on a web server, a computer running special software that is directly connected to the Internet. Each server has its own Uniform Resource Locator (URL), which normally begins with http: (for example, http://www.sbaer.uca.edu/). The web page that is called up when the site is accessed is sometimes referred to as the site's home page. To access web pages, a user needs a connection to the Internet and a program called a web browser. Examples of such browsers include Mosaic, Netscape, and America Online (Exhibit 2.12). The purpose of the browser is to take a copy of the web page sent by the web server and display it on the user's screen. The site featured above is one of the top resources for small business information on the web. Through this site an entrepeneur can gather information on many topics related to starting and running a small business, including advice on selecting a form of business ownership.

Probably the key factor in the rapid acceptance of the WWW is the ability to establish linkages between web pages. Using URLs and HTML document file names makes it possible to reference any other WWW site in the world. On the user's screen, these linkages typically appear as underlined text, although buttons and images may contain linkages to other sites as well (such as the Links of Interest icon within the graphic image in the illustration). To jump to these references, all the user has to do is click on the text. The page from the new site is then automatically sent to the browser, where it is displayed on the user's screen. Conceptually, then, the WWW can be viewed as a giant web of connected documents, and "surfing the net" is the process of jumping from site to site using these connections.

For an explanation of the language commonly used in reference to the World Wide Web, see Exhibit 2.13: "The Lingo to Know".

Exhibit 2.13

"The Lingo to Know"

By Leslie Miller
USA TODAY

Business conversation—even cocktail chatter—is getting tough these days without a grasp of cyberspeak. Webs, home pages, on line, long strings of codes beginning with h-t-t-p-colon-slash-slash. . . . Language skills suddenly fail you.

Here's a concise phrasebook to help you talk like a local.

- **Bulletin board system (BBS).** A computer service similar to an on-line service, usually smaller (and cheaper) with fewer users, fewer features and a narrow focus. A bulletin board is also any on-line or Internet area for posting messages.
- **Bits per second (bps).** How fast modems send and receive data. A 14.4 modem moves 14,400 bits per second; a 28.8 modem, also known as a V.34 (say it V-dot-three-four) is twice as fast. An earlier term, baud, is considered archaic.
- **Browser.** Software to view the graphical "pages" on the World Wide Web.
- **Chat rooms.** Areas on an on-line service, BBS or the Internet that allow real-time, typed-in communication with other people.
- **Cyberspace.** The metaphoric space where electronic communication takes place. Everything in cyberspace is "virtual"—not physically real perhaps but a shared experience nonetheless.
- **Download.** To electronically copy a file to your computer from another computer.
- **E-mail.** Electronic mail, messages from one user to another (or to a group).
- **Emoticons,** also called smileys or winkies, are little punctuation faces to add body language to cybercommunication. A smiley looks like this :) or, with a nose, like this :^) and a winky is this ;).
- **Flame.** Noun or verb; a nasty on-line message or personal attack, often sent in response to a posting the flamer disagrees with.
- **Forum.** An on-line area on a particular topic; the new-age forum on CompuServe has bulletin boards, a chat room and a library.
- **FTP.** File transfer protocol. A way to download remote files over the Internet.
- **GIF** (pronounced *jif*). A format for transmitting photos. A newer photo format: JPEG (say it *JAY-peg*).
- **Gopher.** A way to search for information on the 'Net with a program that lets you burrow into a remote computer's files through on-screen menus. Also the mascot at University of Minnesota, where the program was born.
- **Home page.** A main page on the Web. Companies and organizations have home pages that serve as virtual brochures; individual home pages often share personal passions.
- **Hypertext.** Hidden codes that let users click on a highlighted word or phrase to automatically access a related site. Hypertext markup language (HTML) is the language in which Web pages are written and linked; hypertext transfer protocol (http) is how information is sent over the Web.
- **IMHO.** In my humble opinion. Often appended to opinionated posted views.
- **Snail mail.** U.S. Postal Service, disparagingly.
- **Surfing the 'Net.** Navigating the Internet, usually random Web browsing.
- **Sysop.** The system operator of a BBS, a forum or area on an on-line service (pronounced *SIS-op*).
- **Upload.** To send a copy of a file from your computer to another computer.
- **Usenet newsgroups.** More than 15,000 Internet bulletin boards on a huge variety of topics. Each line of discussion is called a thread.
- **URL.** Uniform Resource Locator (pronounced *you-are-el,* not *earl*) is the address of an Internet site; all Web URLs start with http://.
- **World Wide Web.** the fastest-growing part of the 'Net. It's multimedia-capable, intricately interlinked and set up for viewing in colorful magazine-style "pages" containing text, photos and sounds.

2

Organizational Structure

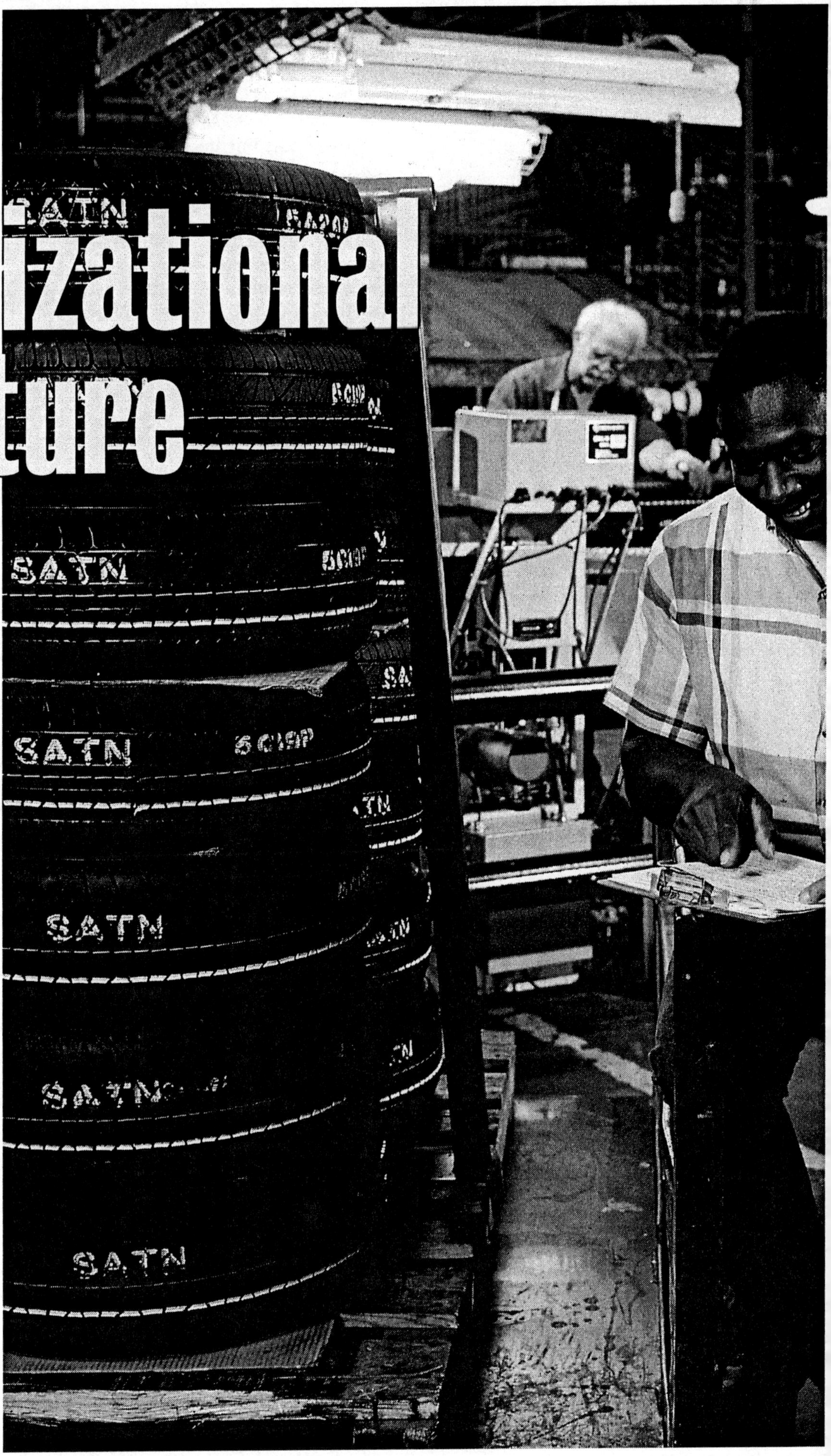

Each firm should have a strategic plan that identifies the future direction of its business. The responsibilities of its managers should be organized to achieve the strategic plan.

Each firm establishes an organizational structure, or the structure within the firm that identifies responsibilities for each job position and the relationships among those positions. An organizational structure also indicates how all the job responsibilities fit together. The organizational structure affects the efficiency with which a firm produces its product, and therefore affects a firm's value.

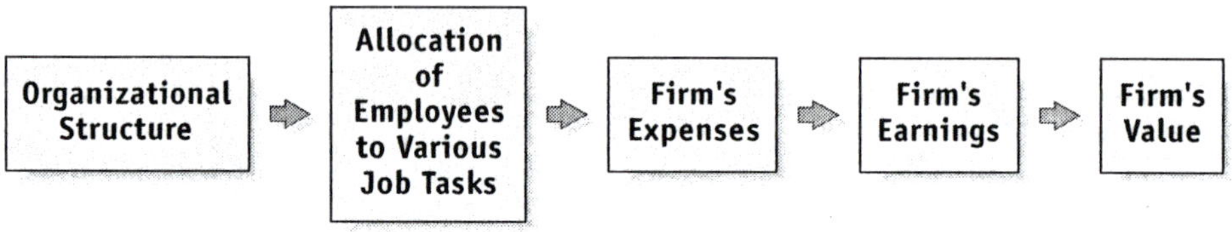

Consider the case of Heinz, which manufactures hundreds of different products. Should a different manager be responsible for overseeing the operations of each product? How much responsibility should Heinz assign to those employees who produce Heinz products? What factors should Heinz consider when determining how much authority to assign to its employees? This chapter provides a background on organizational structure, which can be used to address these questions.

The **Learning Goals** of this chapter are to:

1. Explain how an organizational structure may be used by a firm to achieve its strategic plan.
2. Identify methods that can be used to departmentalize tasks.

HOW A FIRM'S ORGANIZATIONAL STRUCTURE ACHIEVES ITS STRATEGIC PLAN

1 **Explain how an organizational structure may be used by a firm to achieve its strategic plan.**

organizational structures the structure within the firm that identifies responsibilities for each job position and the relationship among those positions

organization chart a diagram that shows the interaction among employee responsibilities

chain of command identifies the job position to which each type of employee must report

No one specific **organizational structure** is optimal for all firms. The means by which responsibilities are organized for a large multinational manufacturing firm such as DuPont may not necessarily be appropriate for a small firm such as Starbucks.

A firm's organizational structure can be illustrated with an **organization chart,** which is a diagram that shows the interaction among employee responsibilities. Exhibit 8.1 provides an example of an organization chart.

Chain of Command

The organizational structure indicates the **chain of command,** which identifies the job positions to which all types of employees must report. The chain of command also indicates who is responsible for various activities. Since employees often encounter problems that require communication with other divisions, it helps to know who is responsible for each type of task.

Heinz needs an organizational structure that can manage the production of all its products that are produced for sale in numerous countries.

Exhibit 8.1
Example of an Organization Chart

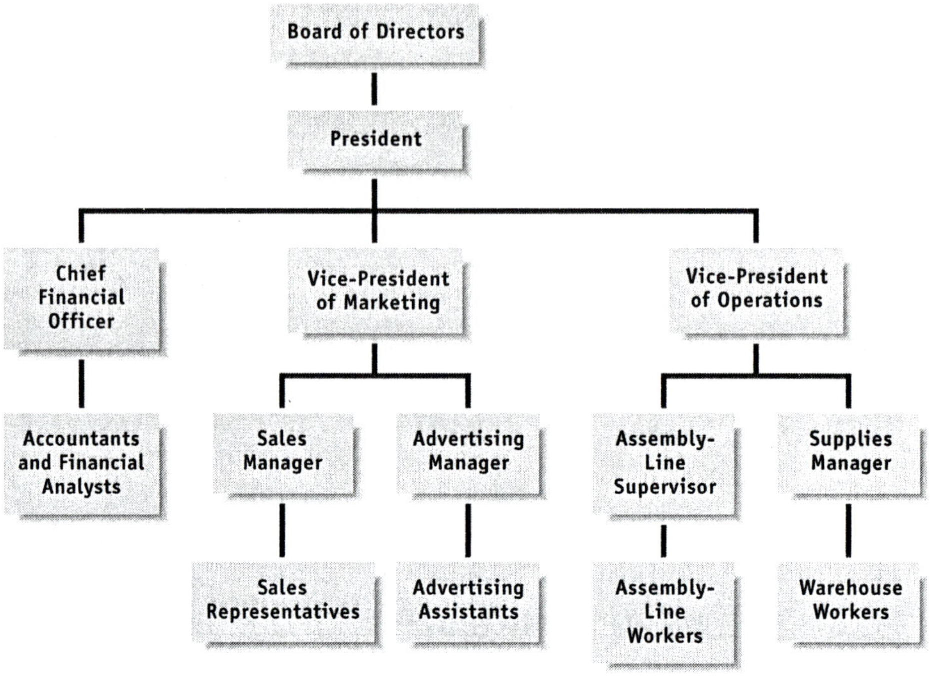

The president (who also typically holds the position of chief executive officer) has the ultimate responsibility for the success of a firm. The president normally attempts to coordinate all divisions and provide direction for the firm's business. For most firms, many managerial duties are delegated to other managers. Vice-presidents normally oversee specific divisions or broad functions of the firm and report to the president.

Authority of the Board of Directors

board of directors a set of executives that is responsible for monitoring the activities of the firm's president and other high-level managers

Each firm has a **board of directors,** or a set of executives that is responsible for monitoring the activities of the firm's president and other high-level managers. Directors are selected by shareholders; they serve as representatives for the shareholders, as confirmed by a recent quote from Sears' annual report:

> *The board of directors regularly reviews the corporation's structure to determine whether it supports optimal performance and thus serves the best interests of shareholders by delivering shareholder value.*

inside board members board members who are also managers of the same firm

outside board members board members who are high-level managers of other firms

Directors have the authority to approve or disapprove key business proposals made by a firm's managers, such as acquisitions or layoffs. For example, IBM's decision to acquire Lotus and Boeing's decision to lay off workers required board approval. Those board members who are also managers of the same firm (such as the chief executive officer) are referred to as **inside board members.** Board members who are high-level managers of other firms are referred to as **outside board members.** In general, the board focuses only on key decisions and is not normally involved in the day-to-day activities of the firm. Board members attend a board meeting that is generally scheduled every few months or are called when their input is needed regarding a key business decision.

SMALL BUSINESS SURVEY

Who Are the Board Members of Small Firms?

A recent survey asked the chief executive officers (CEOs) of small firms (with less than $50 million in annual sales) about the background of their outside board members. The results of the survey follow.

Background	Percentage of Firms Whose Board Members Have That Background
Executives of other firms	69%
Major investors in the firm	36%
Retired business executives	30%
Attorneys	29%
Accountants	22%
Bankers	18%
Business consultants	13%
Customers	2%
Others	3%

The results suggest that these firms rely heavily on either executives or major investors to serve as their outside board members. The attorneys, accountants, and business consultants that are hired as outside board members typically also perform other duties (such as legal or banking duties) for the firm.

The largest one thousand U.S. firms have about twelve directors on their board on average. The average annual compensation to directors for serving on the boards of the largest industrial firms in the United States is about $68,000. Some firms, such as General Electric and PepsiCo, provide the directors with their stock as partial compensation. This type of compensation may motivate the directors to serve the interests of the firm's shareholders, because the board members will benefit if the firm's stock price rises. Some firms, such as Travelers Group, pay their board members entirely with stock so that they can ensure that the board members will focus on decisions that may boost the stock's price for shareholders.

Directors not only oversee the key decisions of managers but may also initiate changes in a firm. For example, the board may decide that the firm's chief executive officer needs to be replaced or that the firm's businesses should be restructured. The boards of numerous well-known firms such as American Express, W. R. Grace, Honeywell, IBM, and KMart have recently initiated major changes. In many cases, the board becomes more involved after a period of poor performance by the firm. Board members of numerous firms have become more active in recent years as a result of pressure from shareholders.

A board of directors may be more willing to take action if most of its members are outside members (and therefore are not employees of the firm). The outside board members may suggest policies that will benefit shareholders, even if the policies are not supported by the firm's top managers. For example, they may suggest that the salaries of some high-level managers be reduced. Such a policy is less likely

The gentleman pictured above may not be a household name, but major U.S. corporations make a point to meet him. As CEO of CalPERS (the California Public Employees' Retirement System), James E. Burton oversees the management of $100 billion investment dollars.

to be suggested by those inside board members who are also employed by the firm as high-level managers.

Monitoring by Institutional Investors

The high-level managers of a firm are monitored not only by the board of directors, but also by institutional investors (such as life insurance companies and pension plans) that hold a large amount of the firm's shares. The institutional investors do not have direct control over the firm, but may publicly criticize any major decisions of high-level managers that are not intended to increase the value of the firm's stock. They may also inform the firm's board members of their views. Board members may listen to those institutional investors that are major shareholders of the firm. Large shareholders can influence the composition of the board because shareholders are allowed to vote for board members.

Span of Control

span of control the number of employees managed by each manager

Top management determines the firm's **span of control,** or the number of employees managed by each manager. When an organizational structure is designed to have each manager supervise just a few employees, it has a narrow span of control. Conversely, when it is designed to have each manager supervise numerous employees, it has a wide span of control. For a firm with numerous employees who perform similar tasks, a wide span of control is used, since these employees can be more easily managed by one or a few managers. However, for a firm with highly diverse tasks, more managers with various skills may be needed to manage the different tasks, resulting in a narrow span of control.

Exhibit 8.2 illustrates how the span of control can vary among firms. The organizational structure on the left reflects a narrow span of control. Each employee oversees only one other employee. The nature of the business may require highly specialized skills in each position, so that employees may focus more on their own tasks and do not have to monitor a large set of employees. The organizational structure on the right reflects a wide span of control. The president directly oversees all other employees. Such a wide span of control is more typical of firms in which many employees have similar positions that can be easily monitored by a single person.

Organizational Height

The organizational structure can also be described by its height. A tall organizational structure implies that there are many layers from the bottom of the structure to the top of the structure. Conversely, a short (or flat) organizational structure implies that there is not much distance from the bottom of the structure to the top, because there are not many layers of employees between the bottom and top. Many firms that are able to use a wide span of control tend to have a flat organizational structure, as they do not require as many layers. Conversely, firms that need to use a narrow span of control tend to have a tall organizational structure with many layers. Notice that in Exhibit 8.2, the organizational structure with the narrow span of control is tall, while the organizational structure with the wide span of control is flat.

Centralization

centralization an effort to maintain most authority among the high-level managers

Some firms make an effort to maintain most authority among the high-level managers, which is referred to as **centralization.** For these firms, middle and supervisory

Exhibit 8.2
Distinguishing between a Narrow and a Wide Span of Control

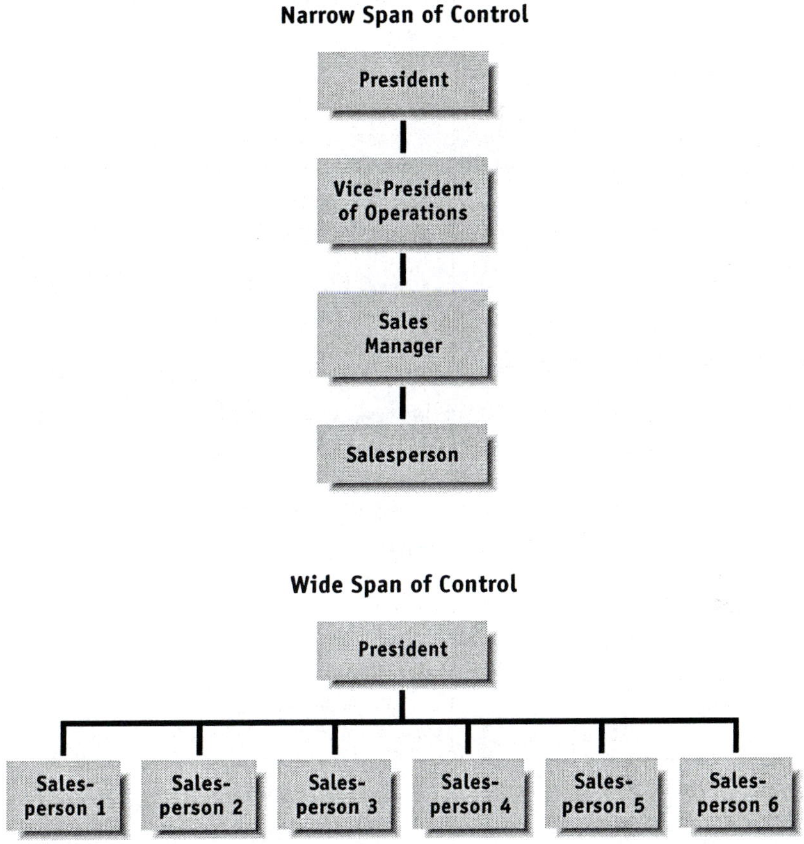

managers are more responsible for day-to-day tasks and for reporting to the top managers, but are not allowed to make many decisions.

Decentralization

decentralized authority is spread among several divisions or managers

autonomy divisions can make their own decisions and act independently

In recent years, many firms have **decentralized,** meaning that authority is spread among several divisions or managers. An extreme form of decentralization is **autonomy,** in which divisions can make their own decisions and act independently. The trend by firms to decentralize is due to its potential advantages. The delegation of authority can improve the morale of the employees, who may have more enthusiasm if the firm assigns them more responsibilities. In addition, these managers become more experienced in decision making. Therefore, they will be more qualified for high-level management positions in the future. Many technology firms have been innovative as a result of being decentralized, as more managers have become more creative.

Decentralization can be useful in accelerating the decision-making process. Decisions are made more quickly if they are not stalled while waiting for approval from top managers. Many firms, including IBM, have decentralized to accelerate their decision making.

Johnson and Johnson is a prime example of a firm that has benefited from decentralization. It has 168 operating divisions scattered among 53 countries, and most of the decision making is done by the managers at those divisions. This has enabled each of Johnson and Johnson's units to make quick decisions in response to local market conditions.

SELF-SCORING EXERCISE

How Decentralized Is Your Company?

Decentralization is one of the key design dimensions in an organization. It is closely related to several behavioral dimensions of an organization, such as leadership style, degree of participative decision making, teamwork, and the nature of power and politics within the organization.

The following questionnaire allows you to get an idea about how decentralized your organization is. (If you do not have a job, have a friend who does work complete the questionnaire to see how decentralized his or her organization is.) Which level in your organization has the authority to make each of the following eleven decisions? Answer the questionnaire by circling one of the following:

0 = The board of directors makes the decision.
1 = The CEO makes the decision.
2 = The division/functional manager makes the decision.
3 = A sub-department head makes the decision.
4 = The first-level supervisor makes the decision.
5 = Operators on the shop floor make the decision.

Decision Concerning:	Circle Appropriate Level					
a. The number of workers required.	0	1	2	3	4	5
b. Whether to employ a worker.	0	1	2	3	4	5
c. Internal labor disputes.	0	1	2	3	4	5
d. Overtime worked at shop level.	0	1	2	3	4	5
e. Delivery dates and order priority.	0	1	2	3	4	5
f. Production planning.	0	1	2	3	4	5
g. Dismissal of a worker.	0	1	2	3	4	5
h. Methods of personnel selection.	0	1	2	3	4	5
i. Method of work to be used.	0	1	2	3	4	5
j. Machinery or equipment to be used.	0	1	2	3	4	5
k. Allocation of work among workers.	0	1	2	3	4	5

Add up all your circled numbers. Total = ______ . The higher your number (for example, 45 or more), the more decentralized your organization. The lower your number (for example, 25 or less), the more centralized your organization.

ADVANTAGES The decentralized organizational structure can improve the firm's performance for the following reasons. First, it reduces operating expenses because salaries of some employees who are no longer needed are eliminated. Second, it accelerates the decision-making process, as lower-level employees are assigned more power. Third, it motivates some employees by assigning them more responsibilities. Fourth, it allows those employees who are closely involved in the production of a particular product to offer their input.

DISADVANTAGES A decentralized organizational structure could force some managers who do not have sufficient experience to make major decisions. Also, if middle and supervisory managers are assigned an excessive amount of responsibilities, they may be unable to complete all of their tasks.

PROPER DEGREE OF DECENTRALIZATION The proper degree of decentralization for any firm is dependent on the skills of managers who could be assigned more responsibilities. Decentralization can be beneficial when the managers who are given more power are capable of handling their additional responsibilities. For example, assume that historically, top managers determined annual raises for all assembly-line workers, but decided to delegate this responsibility to supervisors who monitor those workers. The supervisors are closer to the assembly line and are possibly in a better position to assess worker performance. Therefore, this type of decentralization may be appropriate. The top managers may still have final approval of the raises that supervisors propose for their workers.

As a second example, assume that top managers allow supervisors of assembly lines to decide the price to bid for a specific business that is presently for sale. Assembly-line supervisors are not normally trained for this type of task and should not be assigned such a task. The proper price to bid for a business requires a strong financial background and should not be delegated to managers without the proper skills.

The two examples demonstrate that high-level managers should retain authority for those tasks that require the specialized skills of high-level managers, but should delegate authority when the tasks can be handled by other managers. Routine decisions should be made by the employees who are closely involved with the tasks of concern. This may improve decision making, since other managers are closer to the routine tasks and may have greater insight than top managers on these matters.

Some degree of centralization is necessary when determining how funds should be allocated to support various divisions of a firm. If managers of each division were given the authority to make this decision, they might request more funds to expand even if there was no reason for the divisions to expand. Centralized management of funds can prevent division managers from making decisions that conflict with the goal of maximizing the firm's value.

EFFECT OF DOWNSIZING ON DECENTRALIZATION As firms expanded during the 1980s, additional management layers were created resulting in taller organization charts. However, in the 1990s, many firms attempted to cut expenses by eliminating job positions. This so-called **downsizing** has resulted in flatter organization charts with fewer layers of managers. Notice from Exhibit 8.3 how Continental Airlines, IBM, General Motors, and Sears have downsized in recent years.

downsizing an attempt by a firm to cut expenses by eliminating job positions

Exhibit 8.3
Downsizing by Four Different Firms

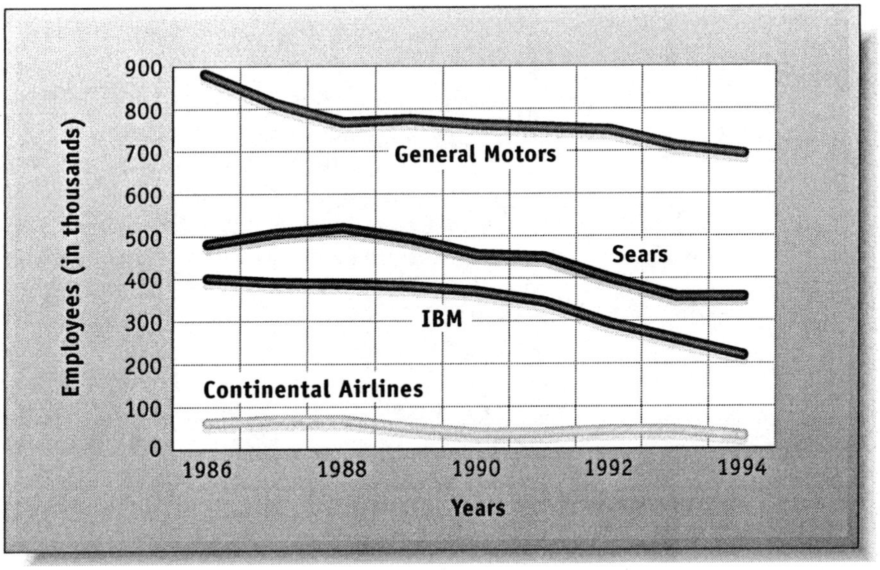

Exhibit 8.4
Effect of Downsizing on Span of Control

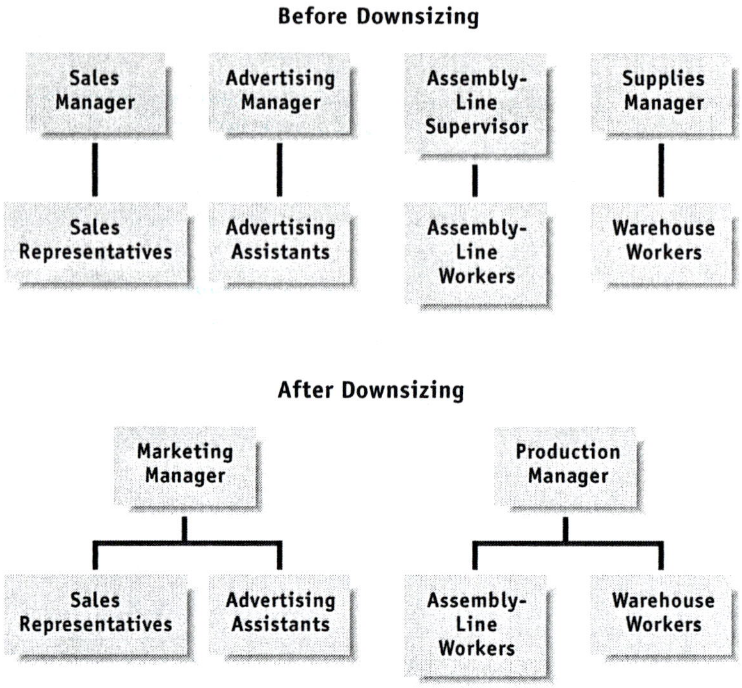

As some management positions were eliminated, many of those responsibilities were delegated to employees who previously reported to the managers whose positions were eliminated. For example, Amoco eliminated a middle layer of its organizational structure. When managers in the middle of the organization chart are removed, other employees must be assigned more power to make more decisions. That is, downsizing has resulted in a greater degree of decentralization.

Downsizing has also affected each manager's span of control. The decentralization caused by eliminating many middle managers resulted in more diverse responsibilities to the remaining managers. Consequently, the organizational structure of many firms was revised to reflect a wider span of control, as illustrated in Exhibit 8.4.

Downsizing not only has removed some management layers and created a wider span of control, but also has combined various job responsibilities within the organizational structure. While job assignments have traditionally focused on production tasks, more attention is now given to customer satisfaction. Many firms recognize that they rely on the same customers for additional business in the future, and have revised their strategic plan to focus more on achieving repeat business from their customers. In many cases, customers would prefer to deal with a single employee rather than several different employees. Consequently, employees are not as specialized because they must have diverse skills to accommodate the customers.

Line Versus Staff Positions

The job positions in an organizational structure can be classified as line positions or staff positions. **Line positions** are established to make decisions that achieve specific business goals. Conversely, **staff positions** are established to support the efforts of line positions, rather than to achieve specific goals of the firm. For example, managers at Black and Decker who are involved in the production of power tools are in line positions. Employees in staff positions at Black and Decker offer support to the

line positions established to make decisions that achieve specific business goals

staff positions established to support the efforts of line positions managers who are in line positions. The staff positions provide assistance to the line positions, while the authority to make decisions is still assigned to line positions.

An organization chart that contains only line positions and no staff positions is referred to as a **line organization.** This type of organizational structure may be appropriate for businesses that cannot afford to hire staff for support.

line organization an organization chart that contains only line positions and no staff positions

Most firms need some staff positions to provide support to the line positions. An organizational structure that includes line positions and staff positions and assigns authority from higher-level management to employees is referred to as a **line-and-staff organization.**

line-and-staff organization an organizational structure that includes line positions and staff positions and assigns authority from higher-level management to employees

Exhibit 8.5 illustrates a comparison between a line organization and a line-and-staff organization. The line-and-staff organization in this exhibit contains a director of computer systems, who oversees the computer system, and a director of legal ser-

Exhibit 8.5
Comparison of a Line Organization with a Line-and-Staff Organization

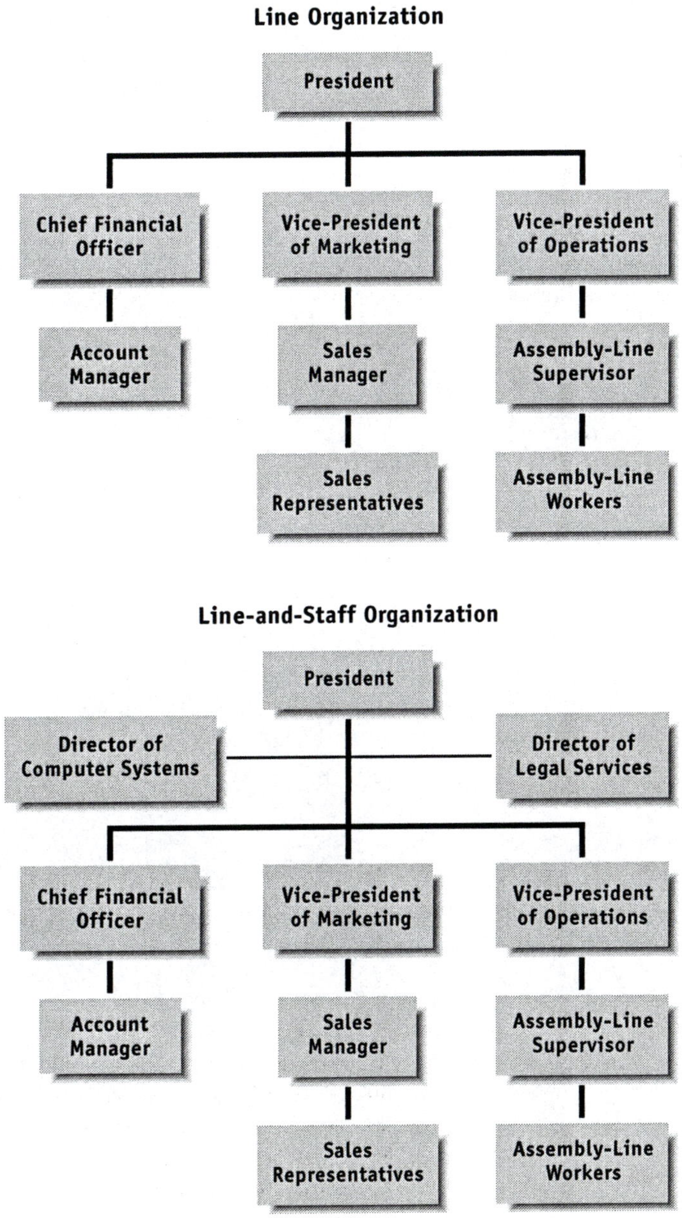

vices, who is involved with hiring and training employees. These two positions are staff positions because they can assist the finance, marketing, and production departments, but do not have the authority to make decisions that achieve specific business goals.

Creating a Structure that Allows More Employee Input

Firms commonly rely on the input of employees from various divisions for special situations. For this reason, they may need to temporarily adjust their formal organizational structure so that some extra responsibilities may be assigned. The following are two common methods for revising the organizational structure to obtain employee input:

- Matrix organization
- Intrapreneurship.

Each of these methods is discussed in turn.

matrix organization the interaction among various parts of the firm to focus on specific projects

MATRIX ORGANIZATION Firms are often confronted with special circumstances that require input from their employees. A **matrix organization** represents the interaction among various parts of the firm to focus on specific projects. Because the projects may take up only a portion of the normal workweek, participants can continue to perform their normal tasks and are still accountable to the same boss for those tasks. For example, a firm that plans to install a new computer system may need input from each division on the specific functions of the system that are necessary. This example is illustrated in Exhibit 8.6. The team of employees periodically works on any assigned project until the project is completed. Some employees may be assigned to two or more projects during the specific period. Exhibit 8.6 shows that one representative was chosen from the finance, marketing, and production divisions; each representative can offer insight from the perspective of his or her respective division. The horizontal thin line in Exhibit 8.6 shows the interaction among the representatives from different divisions. A computer systems employee is the manager of this

Louisville Slugger bat makers bring a significant amount of individual skill to their jobs. The production process benefits from input by employees directly involved in the production.

Exhibit 8.6
A Matrix Organization for a Special Project to Design a New Computer System

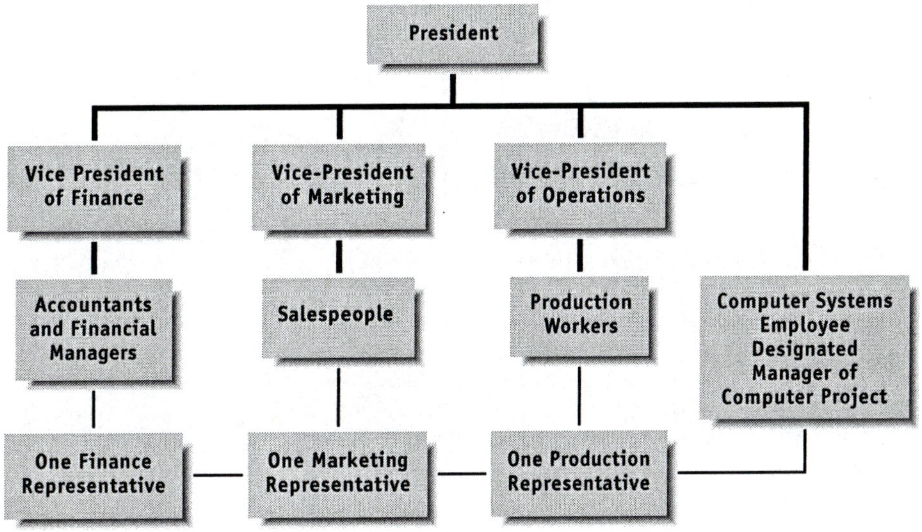

project; this person would report the recommendations of the matrix organization to the president or to some other top manager.

An advantage of the matrix approach is that it involves employees who can offer insight from different perspectives. Each participant who has been assigned to a specific group (or team) has particular skills that are used to contribute to the project. This teamwork involves all participants in decision making, which may provide more employee satisfaction than typical day-to-day assignments. Firms such as Intel, IBM and Boeing have commonly used teams of employees to complete specific projects.

One possible disadvantage of a matrix organization is that no employee may feel responsible because responsibilities are assigned to teams of several employees. Therefore, a firm that uses teams to complete various tasks may designate one job position with the responsibility of organizing the team and ensuring that the team assignment is completed before the deadline. The person designated as project manager (or team leader) of a specific project does not necessarily have authority over the other participants for any other tasks.

Another disadvantage of the matrix organization is that any time used to participate in projects reduces the time allocated for normal tasks. In some cases, ultimate responsibility is not clear, causing confusion. Digital Equipment Corporation eliminated its matrix structure for this reason.

INTRAPRENEURSHIP Some firms not only require input from employees on specific issues but also encourage employees to offer ideas for revising operations that would enhance the firm's value. These firms may even create a special subsidiary within their organizational structure in which particular employees are given the responsibilities of innovation. In this way, the costs and benefits of innovation can be estimated separately from the rest of the business operations.

Particular employees of a firm can be assigned to create ideas, as if they were entrepreneurs who were running their own firms. This process is referred to as **intrapreneurship,** as employees are encouraged to think like entrepreneurs within the firm. However, they differ from entrepreneurs in that they are employees rather than owners of the firm. Some employees may even be assigned responsibilities to develop new products or ideas for improving existing products. Intrapreneurship can pull employees away from normal, day-to-day production tasks. However, it can also allow firms to be more innovative because employees are encouraged to search for

intrapreneurship assignment of particular employees of a firm to create ideas, as if they were entrepreneurs who were running their own firms

SPOTLIGHT ON TECHNOLOGY

How Information Systems Enhance Organizational Structures

Information technology has allowed greater flexibility in the organizational structure of firms. An excellent example is the U.S. property and casualty (P&C) insurance industry. The traditional structure for P&C companies consists of a central headquarters, which performs high-level management activities, and a national network of local agents, who are owned either by the company or by many independent agents. Within the P&C industry it is the network of agents who provide the critical link between customers and the P&C headquarters.

One exception to this typical P&C structure is United Services Automobile Association (USAA), which services all customers directly from its San Antonio, Texas, headquarters.

USAA's highly centralized structure might lead one to conclude that its customer service suffers in comparison with other P&C companies, whose local agents get to know customers and establish personal relationships. The opposite is true, however. Historically, USAA ranks at the top of P&C companies for service and commitment to customers.

Computers are present in every aspect of USAA's P&C business. Incoming correspondence is immediately scanned to optical disks and indexed into a document processing system that was the most advanced in the world when it was constructed. All information relating to a given USAA member is indexed by member number so that customer service representatives can instantly access the information when a customer calls. A USAA customer service representative can access specific information on a particular customer's policy or claim, along with copies of relevant correspondence, in less time than it takes the local agent to walk across the room to the file cabinet. USAA has also made extensive use of computers to eliminate the need for space to maintain hard copies of all documents. Becoming the industry leader in information technology has enabled USAA to prosper.

new ideas. Many firms, including Apple Computer and 3M Company, have used intrapreneurship to encourage new ideas.

Intrapreneurship is likely to be more successful if employees are rewarded with some type of bonus for innovations that are ultimately applied by the firm. The firm should also attempt to ensure that any ideas that employees develop are seriously considered. If managers shoot down ideas for the wrong reasons (jealousy, for instance), employees may consider leaving the firm and implement their ideas (by starting their own business).

Informal Organizational Structure

informal organizational structure an informal communications network among a firm's employees

All firms have both a formal organizational structure and an informal organizational structure. An **informal organizational structure** represents an informal communications network among a firm's employees. The network (sometimes called a "grapevine") is developed as a result of employee interaction that occurs over time. Some employees interact because they work on a similar task. Interaction among employees in unrelated divisions often occurs in a common lunch area, at social events, or even as a result of a decision that requires input from two different divisions.

ADVANTAGES The informal organizational structure can benefit a firm in the following ways. Employees that need help in performing a task may benefit from others. If employees had to use the formal structure to seek help, they would require assistance from the person to whom they report. This may be inconvenient when that particular person is not available, and can slow the production process. An informal structure may also allow employees to substitute for one another, which can ensure that a task will still be completed on time. An informal structure can reduce the amount of manager involvement.

Self-directed work team members at the Bristol Myers Squibbs ConvaTec plant in Deeside, Wales, set their own schedules and allocate resources. Most workers enjoy having this control and involvement.

Another advantage of an informal structure is that friendships result from it. Friendships with other employees is a common reason for employee satisfaction with their jobs. It could be the major factor that discourages them from looking for a new job. This is especially true of lower-level jobs that pay low wages. Because friendship can strongly influence employee satisfaction, firms commonly encourage social interaction by organizing social functions.

Informal communication can occur among employees on different levels. This allows for information to travel informally from the top down or from the bottom up throughout the organization.

DISADVANTAGES Along with the advantages just described, an informal structure also has some disadvantages. Perhaps the main disadvantage is that employees obtain unfavorable information about the firm through the informal structure. Whether the information is true or is a gross exaggeration, it can have a major impact on employee morale. Unfavorable information that would have an adverse impact tends to travel faster and further throughout an informal structure. Second, some employees may have some influence over others in an informal structure. If any poor employees have an influence over others, the firm would be adversely affected.

METHODS OF DEPARTMENTALIZING TASKS

departmentalize assign tasks and responsibilities to different departments

When developing or revising an organizational structure, high-level management must first identify all the different tasks and responsibilities that the firm performs. The next step is to **departmentalize** those tasks and responsibilities, which means to assign tasks and responsibilities to different departments. The manner by which to departmentalize tasks and responsibilities is dependent on the characteristics of the business. Four of the more popular methods of departmentalizing are as follows:

- By function
- By product
- By location
- By customer

Exhibit 8.7
Departmentalizing by Function

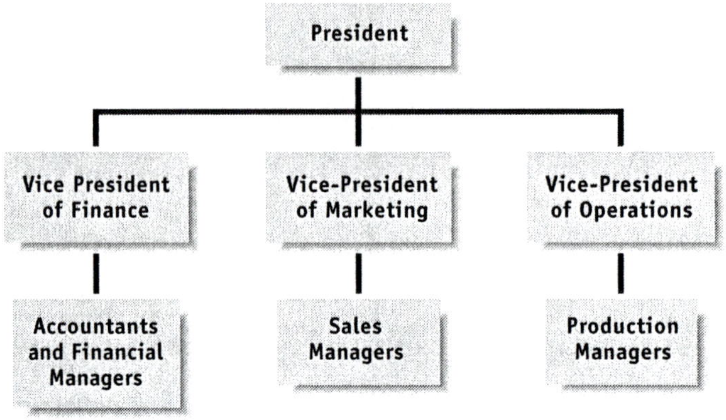

Departmentalize by Function

Many small firms departmentalize by function, meaning that tasks and responsibilities are allocated according to employee functions. The organization chart shown in Exhibit 8.7 is departmentalized by function. The finance, marketing, and production divisions are separated. This system works well when the firm is engaged in the production of just one or a few products.

Departmentalize by Product

For larger firms with many products, departmentalizing by product is common. The allocation of tasks and responsibilities is separated according to the type of product produced. The organization chart shown in Exhibit 8.8 is departmentalized by product (soft drink, food, and restaurant). This type of organizational structure is used by General Motors, which has created divisions for Buick, Cadillac, Oldsmobile, and Chevrolet.

Many large firms departmentalize by both product and function, as shown in Exhibit 8.9. The specific divisions are separated by product and each product division is departmentalized by function. Thus, each product division may have its own marketing, finance, and production divisions. It may appear that this system is inefficient because of the need for several divisions. Yet, if the firm is large enough, a single division would need to hire as many employees as are needed for several divisions. Separation by product allows employees to become more familiar with a single product rather than having to keep track of several different products.

When a firm is departmentalized by product, the expenses involved in the production of each product can be more easily estimated. Therefore, the firm can be viewed as a set of separate business divisions (separated by product) and each divi-

Exhibit 8.8
Departmentalizing by Product

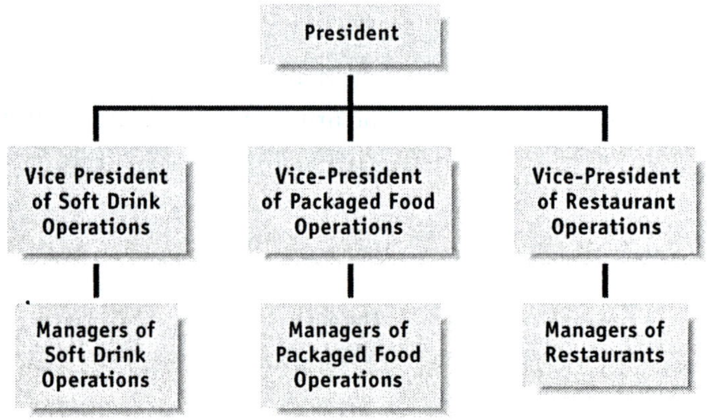

Exhibit 8.9
Departmentalizing by Product and Function

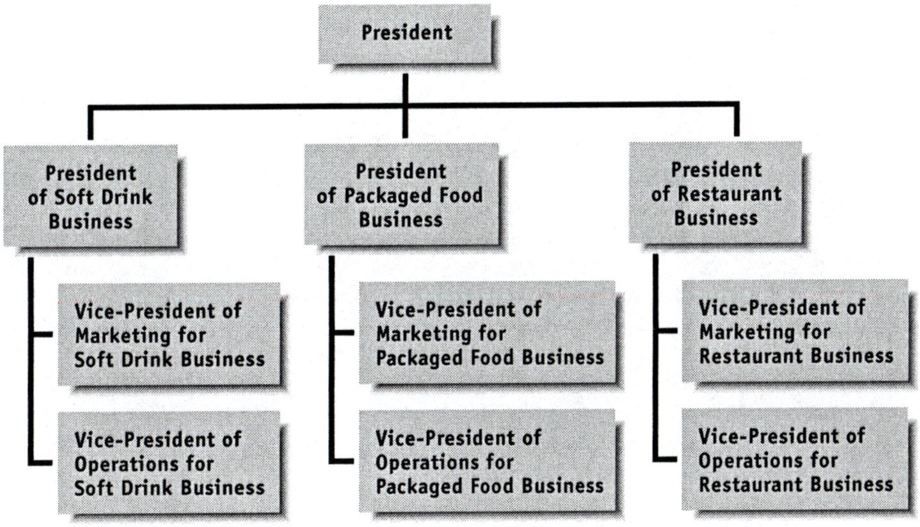

sion's profits can be determined over time. This allows the firm to determine the contribution of each business division to its total profits, which is useful when the firm is deciding which divisions should be expanded.

For a small or medium-sized firm with just a few products, departmentalizing by product would cause an inefficient use of employees, resulting in excessive expenses. A single financial manager should be capable of handling all financial responsibilities, and a single marketing manager should be capable of handling all marketing responsibilities. Thus, there is no reason to departmentalize by product.

Departmentalize by Location

Another method of separating tasks and responsibilities is to departmentalize by location. Regional offices could be established to cover specific geographical regions. This system may be appealing if corporate customers in particular locations frequently purchase a variety of the firm's products. Such customers would be able to contract the same regional office to place all of their orders. Large accounting firms departmentalize by location in order to be close to their customers.

When a firm is departmentalized by location, its expenses involved in each location can be more easily estimated. Therefore, the firm can be viewed as a set of divisions separated by location, with each location generating its own profits. This allows the firm to identify the locations that have been performing well, which may help determine which locations should attempt to expand their business.

Departmentalize by Customer

Some firms have separated divisions according to the type of customer. For example, some airlines have a separate reservations division to focus exclusively on group trips. Computer firms such as IBM have designated some salespeople to focus exclusively on selling computers to school systems. They also have some divisions that focus on retail stores, while others focus on large corporate customers.

Departmentalize by Various Characteristics

Some large firms use more than one method to departmentalize tasks. For example, they may departmentalize some tasks by location and others by product. Other firms

CROSS-FUNCTIONAL TEAMWORK

Interaction Among Departments

While the organizational structure formally indicates to whom each employee reports, it still allows interaction among different departments. For example, a firm may departmentalize by function, so that one executive is responsible for the management of operations, a second executive is responsible for the marketing function, and a third executive is responsible for the financing function.

While each function appears independent of the others on the organization chart, executives in charge of their respective functions must interact with the other departments. Exhibit 8.10 shows how the marketing, production, and finance departments rely on each other for information before making decisions. The marketing department needs to be aware of any changes in the production of a product and the volume of the product that will be available before it finalizes its marketing strategies. The production department needs customer satisfaction information as it considers redesigning products. It also needs to receive forecasts of expected sales from the marketing department, which affects the decision of how much to produce. The marketing and production departments provide the finance department with their forecasts of funds needed to cover their expenses. The finance department uses this information along with other information to determine whether it needs to obtain additional financing for the firm.

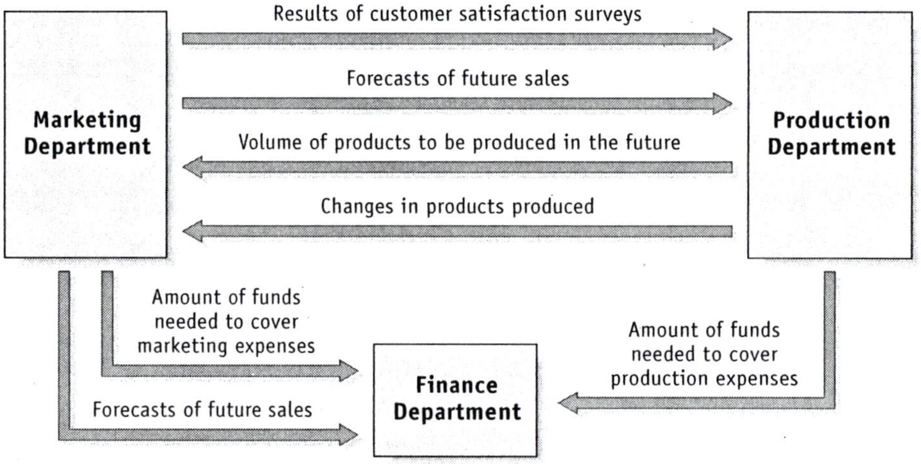

Exhibit 8.10
Flow of Information across Departments

departmentalize by location and product. Their offices are geographically distributed so that salespeople are easily accessible to local customers. In addition, their operating units are separated by product so that each unit can specialize in the production of a specific product.

GLOBAL BUSINESS

Organizational Structure of a Multinational Corporation

The organizational structure of a multinational corporation is complex because responsibilities must be assigned not only to U.S. operations but also to all foreign operations. To illustrate, consider General Motors, which has facilities in Europe, Canada, Asia, Latin America, Africa, and the Middle East. It has departmentalized by location, so either a president or a vice-president is in charge of each foreign region. Specifically, it has a president assigned to GM of

Mexico, a president assigned to GM of Brazil, a vice-president of Asian and Pacific operations, a president assigned to GM of Canada Limited, and a vice-president assigned to Latin American, African, and Middle East operations. In Europe, it has a vice-president assigned to sales and marketing and a second vice-president assigned to Europe's manufacturing plants. That is, the European operations are also departmentalized by function.

Even when firms departmentalize their U.S. operations by product or by function, they commonly departmentalize their foreign operations by location. Since some foreign operations are distant from the firm's headquarters, departmentalizing operations in any foreign country by product or function would be difficult. If the foreign operations were departmentalized by product, an executive at the U.S. headquarters would have to oversee each product produced in the foreign country. If the operations were departmentalized by function, an executive at the U.S. headquarters would have to oversee each function conducted at the foreign facility. Executives at the U.S. headquarters are not normally capable of monitoring the foreign operations because they are not there on a daily or even a weekly basis. Consequently, it is more appropriate to assign an executive at the foreign facility with the responsibility of overseeing a wide variety of products and functions at that facility.

In recent years, some multinational corporations have begun to develop a board of directors that has international business experience. In this way, the board is more capable of monitoring the firm's foreign operations. Furthermore, some multinational corporations are more willing to promote managers within the firm who have substantial experience in international business. Thus, they sometimes assign employees to their foreign facilities so that they can gain that experience.

BUSINESS DILEMMA

Organizational Structure Of College Health Club

When Sue Kramer created College Health Club (CHC), the organizational structure consisted of only herself and one part-time employee. However, she is planning to establish a second health club near a college campus about sixty miles away from the club she presently owns.

Sue recognizes that an organizational structure could be created by departmentalizing by (1) function, (2) product (service), or (3) location. Sue must decide whether to departmentalize by function, by product (service), or by location. These characteristics are summarized next.

Function

1. Marketing: To attract more members.
2. Production: To produce the services for its members.

Product (Service) Offered

1. Ensure that weight machines are working properly.
2. Provide aerobics classes.

Location

1. First health club located next to a local college.
2. Second health club to be located next to a college sixty miles away.

Dilemma

Another way of describing Sue's dilemma is as follows. Should Sue departmentalize responsibilities according to function so that one person conducts the marketing and another manages the production? Or should Sue departmentalize responsibilities by service so that one person focuses on tasks related to the weight machines while another focuses on tasks related to aerobics classes? Or should Sue departmentalize responsibilities by location so that one person manages all functions and services of the health club at the local college campus, while another person manages all functions and services of the health club at the campus sixty miles away?

Solution

Given that the two health clubs are sixty miles apart, Sue may prefer to departmentalize by location. She could focus on the duties at the new health club and allow one or more employees to manage the existing health club. There is no reason to departmentalize by service because it would force one person to manage the weight machines at both clubs (which are sixty miles apart) and another to manage aerobics classes at both clubs. It would be more efficient if the two tasks were performed at each health club by one person. This method avoids travel time between the two clubs. Even if Sue allows someone to perform the key functions at one of the health clubs, she would still have the authority as president to oversee or change any major decisions at that club.

Additional Issues for Discussion

1 As the memberships at CHC increase, Sue Kramer will hire some college students on a part-time basis. Would most of these positions be line positions or staff positions? Why?

2 Sue Kramer considered hiring a college student for an intrapreneurship position for the summer months only. How could this student be beneficial to CHC?

3 If Sue Kramer hires employees at CHC, what types of jobs would possibly be needed? To whom would these employees report?

SUMMARY

1 The organizational structure of a firm identifies responsibilities for each job position within a firm and the relationships among those positions. The structure enables employees to recognize which job positions are responsible for the work performed by other positions.

Most firms use a line-and-staff organizational structure. However, they may also use a matrix organization to obtain employee input on various projects. They may also encourage intrapreneurship in which some employees are assigned to create new products or ideas.

2 The main methods of departmentalizing are by:

- Function, in which tasks are separated according to employee functions;
- Product, in which tasks are separated according to the product produced;
- Location, in which tasks are concentrated in a particular division to serve a specific area; and
- Customer, in which tasks are separated according to the type of customer that purchases the firm's products.

KEY TERMS

autonomy
board of directors
centralization
chain of command
decentralized
departmentalize
downsizing
informal organizational structure
inside board members
intrapreneurship
line organization
line positions
line-and-staff organization
matrix organization
organization chart
organizational structure
outside board members
span of control
staff positions

REVIEW QUESTIONS

1 Explain why no one specific organizational structure is optimal for all firms.
2 Define organizational structure and how it can affect the value of the firm.
3 In operating a global business, explain why the organizational structure of a multinational corporation is so complex.
4 Describe the different spans of control you would use for a firm with numerous employees who perform similar tasks and for a firm with highly diverse tasks.
5 Assume you are creating a new organizational structure for your firm that allows more employee input. Identify and explain the two common methods you could implement.
6 Explain the difference between line positions and staff positions within an organization and cite examples of each.
7 Explain the advantages and disadvantages of an informal organizational structure.
8 Define inside board members and outside board members. What type of compensation may motivate these directors to serve the interests of the firm's shareholders?
9 Explain how cross-functional teamwork interacts among departments.
10 Define and explain the advantages and disadvantages of decentralization of management.

DISCUSSION QUESTIONS

1 Assume you are high-level management and you are revising the organizational structure of your firm. Identify and explain the main methods for departmentalizing the tasks and responsibilities to the different departments.
2 Assume you have just been named the project manager for a firm. You must bring together line-and-staff personnel in formulating a temporary organizational structure for this project. What type of organizational structure would you recommend and why?
3 In your opinion, describe how departmentalization would become the building block for organizational structure.
4 As a manager, why must you distinguish delegation from accountability for your employees?
5 Express your opinion of the informal organization. Is it the same as the "grapevine"? Should a manager ever use the "grapevine" with employees?

RUNNING YOUR OWN BUSINESS

1 Describe the organizational structure of your business.
2 Provide an organization chart and describe the responsibilities of any employees that you plan to hire.
3 How might this structure change as the business grows?

INVESTING IN THE STOCK OF A BUSINESS

Using the annual report of the firm in which you would like to invest, complete the following:

1. Describe the organizational structure of the firm.
2. Does it appear that there are many high-level managers in the firm?
3. Has the firm downsized in recent years by removing middle managers from its organizational structure?

CASE 1 Creating An Organizational Structure

Janet Shugarts is president of a barbecue sauce manufacturer in Austin, Texas. A manager in production has come up with a new barbecue recipe that he claims will be the best on the market because it's hot and spicy and has a flavor that the competition cannot match.

Janet has just received new marketing research information. The research indicates that the taste and preference of most Europeans is for a hot and spicy barbecue sauce. The marketing manager is excited about this new product and believes it can be exported into Western Europe.

Janet has just come out of a meeting with her four managers. They have decided to create a sales office in Paris, France. The plan is to create a project team to establish a production facility within a year in this country. The marketing manager will head up this project team and has requested that this subsidiary be decentralized, to provide him with an opportunity to make timely decisions in this local market.

Because of this expansion, Janet is planning to increase her work force by 20 percent based on an already existing work force of 120 employees. She has recently hired a human resource manager to take charge of the recruiting and selection function. The "grapevine" is circulating a rumor around the plant. The rumor hints that employees may attempt to bring in a union. The human resource manager is alarmed because of his position on the organization chart. His position is listed as a support position, and thus he can only advise and make recommendations to a line manager concerning issues relating to recruiting and selection.

Questions

1. Has Janet created an organizational structure? If so, how?
2. Why would the marketing manager request decentralization of authority in Paris, France?
3. Does this organization reflect a line-and-staff organizational structure? If so, explain.

CASE 2 Restructuring at Apple Computer

With its cash flow problems and loss of market share, will Apple Computer be able to survive this latest knockdown? Gilbert Amelio, the new CEO of Apple, believes these troubles are fixable and that this is an organizational problem of arranging resources to achieve goals. Some people believe, however, that Apple's problems will continue. Apple has been unable to market enough innovative and snazzy machines to justify higher prices and maintain a significant chunk of the personal computer (PC) market. Its global PC share dropped to 7.8 percent, down from 8.3 percent a year earlier.

Apple must develop a new strategy in which it should consider merging with a strong partner. Amelio's rescue plan includes the development of new products and eliminating the "dogs" within its product line. This would require intrapreneurship to create new products or ideas.

The issue of downsizing is prevalent because of Apple's streamlining of the Macintosh product line, and Apple's EWorld, its on-line service, may be axed. This may follow massive across-the-board layoffs.

Apple needs to restructure its organization. It will create new departments such as research and development and new job descriptions to meet the high technological demands of the computer industry. The R&D department will be a support function and advise the marketing department with regard to new products.

Questions

1. Explain how Apple's problems relate to its organization.
2. Define intrapreneurship and indicate what it means for Apple.
3. Should the research and development department be a line or staff function at Apple? Explain.

VIDEO CASE Reorganizing to Achieve Business Success

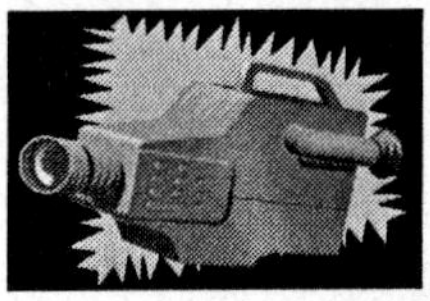

The healthy growth and profits it had enjoyed for sixty-three years were rudely interrupted in 1986 at Bradbury and Stamm Construction Company (BSC), one of New Mexico's largest private contractors.

A disastrous energy market in neighboring Texas, traditional source of most capital for New Mexican development, and passage of the Tax Reform Act of 1986, which removed significant investment incentives, sent New Mexico's building industry into a tailspin. Hundreds of companies declared bankruptcy.

Under Jim King, a fourteen-year employee who became BSC's third president that year, the Albuquerque firm acted to ensure that it wouldn't have to follow suit.

Next, responsibility was spread across a wider spectrum of the company. The tall organization chart was eliminated, and four self-sufficient teams were created to handle large projects and smaller projects. Each team had its own manager.

Three women were promoted to team technician slots and eventually became project managers—first of their gender in so high a position among New Mexican contractors.

Today BSC, which has 198 employees—30 more than three years ago, but half the number it had before 1986—is doing well. Annual sales are at the $65 million to $70 million level.

"We're a whole lot leaner, smarter, and more customer-oriented than just a few years ago," says Jim King. "We've learned to respond positively to obstacles, and we've thrown away the panic button."

Questions

1 Bradbury and Stamm Construction (BSC) originally used a tall organizational structure, with several layers of management. Describe how it changed its organizational structure. How do you think BSC may benefit from the change in the organizational structure?

2 What is a potential disadvantage of the new organizational structure used by BSC, as compared with its original organizational structure?

3 Should BSC also allow its production workers to make decisions normally made by its executives, such as where to expand, how much to pay when acquiring another company, and how much money to borrow?

THE Coca-Cola COMPANY ANNUAL REPORT PROJECT

The following questions apply concepts in this chapter to The Coca-Cola Company. Read the first two paragraphs of page 3 and the organization chart on page 72 in The Coca-Cola Company annual report before answering these questions.

1 Explain how The Coca-Cola Company changed its management structure in 1996.

2 Review The Coca-Cola Company's organizational structure on page 72. Why do you think The Coca-Cola Company has an organizational structure that is divided (decentralized) in geographic divisions?

3 **a.** How many of the individuals on the board of directors are company employees? (See page 73)

b. Why do you think few Company employees are on the board?

c. There are at least two famous individuals on the board; can you name them? (See page 73)

d. The Coca-Cola Company employed 32,000 people in 1996. Based on the Company's net operating revenues, how much revenue did each employee generate?

IN-TEXT STUDY GUIDE

Answers are in an appendix at the back of the book.

True or False

1 When a firm is departmentalized by location, its expenses involved in each location can be more easily estimated.

2 The organization chart indicates the reports to and interaction among employee responsibilities.

3 The organization chart ensures that each employee is directly accountable to a member who sits on the board of directors.

4 Most firms departmentalize their foreign operations by function.
5 Authority is always maintained at the highest level of management.
6 An organizational structure indicates how all the job responsibilities fit together.
7 An informal organizational structure (also called the "grapevine") represents a formal communications network among employees of a firm.
8 Job positions in an organizational structure can be classified as line or staff positions.
9 Departmentalization by function works well when the firm is engaged in the production of many different products.
10 An organizational structure that is designed to have each manager supervise just a few employees has a narrow span of control.

Multiple Choice

11 When the managers of a financing function rely on the marketing managers to make decisions, this is an example of:
a) contingency planning.
b) autocratic leadership.
c) departmentalization.
d) board of directors.
e) cross-functional teamwork.

12 An example of a firm that would departmentalize by type of customer is a(n):
a) airline industry.
b) candy store.
c) large accounting firm.
d) food distributor.
e) newspaper.

13 An organizational structure that includes line positions and staff positions and assigns authority from higher-level management to employees is referred to as a:
a) line organization.
b) staff organization.
c) customer organization.
d) line-and-staff organization.
e) product organization.

14 Many staff positions serve the line function in a(n):
a) command role.
b) assistance role.
c) direct authority role.
d) responsibility center.
e) line organization.

15 Some management layers have been removed and a wider span of control has been created through:
a) unity of command.
b) downsizing.
c) division of work.
d) specialization.
e) contingency planning.

16 An organization that represents the interaction between various parts of the firm to come together on specific projects is a:
a) matrix organization.
b) functional organization.
c) product organization.
d) geographic organization.
e) customer orientation.

17 It is common for larger firms with many products to departmentalize by:
a) function.
b) customer.
c) manufacturing process.
d) geographic area.
e) product.

18 A tall organizational structure reflects:
a) many layers.
b) one owner.
c) one manager.
d) numerous stockholders.
e) numerous board members.

19 The responsibilities of a firm's managers should be organized to achieve the:
a) grapevine.
b) formal contingency.
c) strategic plan.
d) chain of command.
e) bureaucratic organization.

20 The process that identifies responsibilities for each job position and the relationships among those positions is the:
a) organizational structure.
b) planning function.
c) leadership application.
d) job description.
e) control cycle.

21 Jobs that are established to make decisions that achieve specific business goals are:
a) staff positions.
b) line positions.
c) line-and-staff functions.
d) temporary jobs.
e) job placement.

22 An organizational structure that includes only line positions and no staff positions is referred to as a:
a) product organization.

b) line organization.
c) single position organization.
d) supportive organization
e) single linear organization.

23 In recent years many firms have decided to spread authority among several divisions or managers; this is called:
a) centralization.
b) decentralization.
c) chain of command.
d) intrapreneurship.
e) authority.

24 The ultimate responsibility for the success of a firm lies with the:
a) president.
b) employee.
c) customer.
d) competition.
e) labor union.

25 The board of directors serve as representatives of the:
a) employees.
b) customers.
c) shareholders.
d) competition.
e) labor unions.

26 According to the text, large accounting firms departmentalize by:
a) decentralizing.
b) centralization.
c) location.
d) customer.
e) specialization.

27 Downsizing results in:
a) autocratic management.
b) centralization.
c) decentralization.
d) a matrix organization.
e) intrapreneurship.

28 Board members who are managers of the same firm (such as the chief executive officer) are referred to as:
a) chain of command.
b) organization chart.
c) outside board members.
d) centralized authority.
e) inside board members.

29 A set of executives that is responsible for monitoring the activities of the firm's president and other high-level managers is called a(n):
a) board of directors.
b) chain of command.
c) span of control.
d) unity of command.
e) organization chart.

30 An extreme form of decentralization in which divisions can make their own decisions and act independently is called:
a) centralization.
b) autonomy.
c) span of control.
d) span of management.
e) departmentalization.

31 Span of control is determined by:
a) consultants.
b) staff.
c) top management.
d) employees.
e) customers.

32 Assigning tasks and responsibilities to different departments means to:
a) specialize.
b) decentralize.
c) downsize.
d) departmentalize.
e) autonomize.

33 A diagram that shows the formal structure of the firm is a(n):
a) organization chart.
b) chain of command.
c) corporate charter.
d) strategic plan.
e) organization.

34 Board members who are high-level managers of other firms are called:
a) board leaders.
b) inside board members.
c) outside board members.
d) institutional investors.
e) creditors.

35 A process whereby particular employees of a firm can be assigned to create ideas, as if they were entrepreneurs, is referred to as:
a) staff organization.
b) intrapreneurship.
c) co-ownership.
d) leadership.
e) line organization.

Surfing the Net

Managing by Telecommuting

Many of today's organizational structures are based upon the notion of a "place of business." What happens to such structures if the place of business disappears? One major long-term impact of the Internet will be to increase our ability to work out of our homes. But working at home using a computer to communicate, often referred to as telecommuting, brings with it many challenges. How do home-based workers prevent distractions from interfering with their work? How can a manager monitor a home-based employee's productivity? Many sites on the WWW address these problems. A good place to start is *HomeWorker* magazine's home page (Exhibit 8.11), which features articles on many of these subjects as well as links to other telecommuting sites.

Exhibit 8.11
Home Worker Magazine Web Site
http://www.homeworker.com/

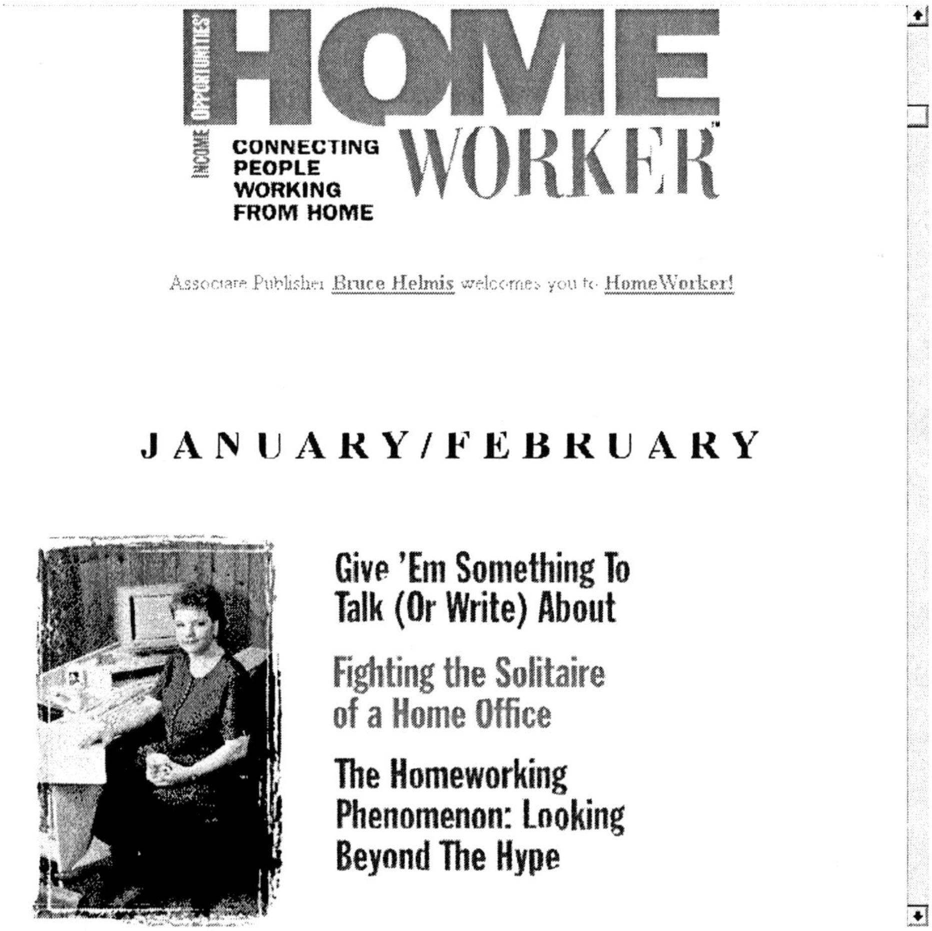

3

Choice of Business Entity—General Tax and Nontax Factors/Formation

CHAPTER LEARNING OBJECTIVES

- Discuss the nontax characteristics that affect the choice of business entity.
- Compare the nontax characteristics of sole proprietorships, partnerships, corporations, S corporations, limited liability companies, limited liability partnerships, and personal service corporations, and explain the effects of their characteristics on the choice of business entity.
- Explain the general income tax characteristics of the various entities, including the incidence of taxation, double taxation, and the status of an owner as an employee of the entity.
- Show how general income tax provisions can affect the choice of business entity.
- Discuss differences in treatment of items that occur at the formation of an entity, including transfers to the entity and how they affect the basis of the entity and its owners.
- Explain the treatment of start-up and organizational costs.
- Compare accounting method and accounting period choices among the various entities.

▲ CONCEPT REVIEW ▲

Accounting method A taxpayer must adopt an accounting method that clearly reflects income.

Annual accounting period All entities must report the results of their operations on an annual basis (the tax year). Each tax year stands on its own, apart from other tax years.

Basis The amount of unrecovered investment in an asset. As amounts are expended and/or recovered relative to an asset over time, the basis is adjusted in consideration of such changes. The **adjusted basis** of an asset is the original basis, plus or minus the changes in the amount of unrecovered investment.

Business purpose To be deductible, an expenditure or a loss must have a business or other economic purpose that exceeds any tax avoidance motive. The primary motive for the transaction must be to make a profit.

Capital recovery No income is realized until the taxpayer receives more than the amount invested to produce the income. The amount invested in an asset represents the maximum amount recoverable.

Conduit entity An entity for which the tax attributes flow through to its owners for tax purposes.

Entity All items of income, deductions, and so on are traced to the tax unit responsible for the item.

Legislative grace Any tax relief provided is the result of a specific act of Congress that must be strictly applied and interpreted. All income received is taxable unless a specific provision in the tax law excludes the income from taxation. Deductions must be approached with the philosophy that nothing is deductible unless a provision in the tax law allows the deduction.

Realization No income or loss is recognized until it has been realized. A realization involves a change in the form and/or the substance of a taxpayer's property rights that results from an arm's-length transaction.

Related party Family members and corporations that are owned by family members are considered related parties, as are certain other relationships between entities in which the power to control the substance of a transaction is evidenced through majority ownership.

Substance-over-form doctrine Transactions are to be taxed according to their true intention rather than some form that may have been contrived.

INTRODUCTION

Although individuals are the largest group of taxpaying entities (discussed in Chapter 8) and generally the principal focus of an entry-level tax course, many different legal, natural, economic, social, and cultural entities exist. Not all entities pay income tax. Because of legislative grace, only three types of entities are taxed on their income: individuals, corporations, and fiduciaries (trusts and estates). All other entities are either exempt or are considered conduit entities. Whether an entity is taxable, tax-exempt, or a conduit can depend on practical considerations or the theoretical foundation of the entity. For example, organizations whose primary function is charity are not required to pay tax on the income generated by their charitable function. This exemption from tax is based on the premise that such organizations are not formed for a business purpose and that the proceeds are to be used to promote the charitable function. Because most of these organizations perform functions that would fall to the government if they did not exist, extracting revenue from these entities is neither practical nor desirable.

Taxpayers often need to choose a form for a business entity. Because simple formulas for deciding the correct form for conducting a business do not exist, this chapter and Chapters 14 and 15 address many factors that affect the choice of business entity. Both tax and nontax factors must be considered. Accordingly, these three chapters compare the consequences of events during an entity's life cycle from the viewpoints of sole proprietors, partnerships, corporations, and S corporations.

These chapters do not discuss trusts and estates. Their purpose generally is to preserve assets rather than to conduct a trade or business. Therefore, they are not a consideration in choosing a business entity.

This chapter begins with a discussion of the nontax factors that can affect the choice of business entity. It then reviews each entity in relation to these factors and compares the general income tax factors for each business form. A discussion of issues that arise at the formation of an entity begins the life-cycle explanation of factors that affect the choice of business entity.

Chapter 14 concludes the life cycle entity discussion by examining the differences in the calculation of taxable income for the various entity forms, the effects of income calculations on an owner's basis, and the tax treatment of distributions received from an entity. Chapter 15 discusses special topics affecting the various entity forms. These topics include types of compensation plans available to owners of various entity types, tax credits available for businesses, the effect of the alternative minimum tax on entities and their owners, and the impact of multinational operations on the choice of business entity.

NONTAX FACTORS

Income taxation is only one factor to consider when an economic decision must be made. Often, taxation is not as significant as nontax factors in the choice of business form. The number of owners, limiting personal liability, freedom to choose how to transfer ownership, anticipated life of the enterprise, ability to participate in business management, costs of organizing the entity, and ability to raise capital are some of the nontax factors.

The number of owners can restrict the choice of entity. For example, a one-owner business cannot use the partnership form of ownership because a partnership must have more than one owner. Similarly, if the number of owners is large, use of an S corporation may be prohibited. Therefore, the number of current and potential future owners affects the choice of entity used to conduct a business.

Limited liability means that investors are not risking more of their personal assets than the amount they paid for their investment interest. That is, an investor's personal assets are not at risk to cover liabilities incurred by the entity. Limiting personal liability is often the most important factor for investors choosing a legal form for operating their businesses.

The **transferability of ownership interest** refers to the ease with which ownership can be transferred. In certain situations, restricting the buying and selling of an ownership interest may be desirable. Common restrictions include those that keep an investor from selling to anyone other than a current owner and/or require the ownership group to vote on the acceptance of any new owners. Such restrictions generally occur with closely held businesses. In contrast, companies trading on the major public stock exchanges offer free transferability of ownership interests. The ability to restrict the transfer of ownership interests is often an important factor in choosing the form for doing business.

Businesses that have frequent changes in ownership must consider the continuity of an entity's life when choosing a business form. **Continuity of life** refers to whether an entity continues to operate or technically dissolves and ceases to exist in its present form when a change occurs in the ownership structure. State law dictates whether an entity continues or technically dissolves if its ownership structure changes. Continuity of life is an attribute of corporations that ensures that a corporate business will continue to exist, regardless of which shareholders trade their stock. Under most state laws, partnerships technically dissolve when ownership changes.

The degree of management control also can vary across entities. Corporations use **centralized management** structures, which ensure the existence of a corporation even when managers and owners come and go. General partnerships allow broad-based management: All partners have the right to participate in management decisions. However, the nature of a partnership lets the partners define each partner's role in managing the business.

The cost of organizing each entity varies according to legal requirements. In general, corporations are more costly to organize than are sole proprietorships; partnerships cost more than sole proprietorships but less than corporations. In addition, each entity has legal characteristics that can affect the ability of the entity to raise additional capital should the need arise.

▲ **EXAMPLE 1** Barbara is planning to open a travel agency. Her father died recently, and she inherited property and cash worth several hundred thousand dollars. Barbara has spent the past 18 years as a high school social studies teacher and wants to change careers. She is single and has 3 children: Catrina, 23; Niki, 21; and Patrick, 19. Barbara wants to know the proper form for her business entity. Should she incorporate her new business?

Discussion: The initial answer is, "It depends. . . ." There is no simple cookie-cutter answer to this question. Many factors, both tax and nontax, affect the choice. Barbara should conduct a comparative analysis of forming a sole proprietorship, partnership, corporation, and S corporation and focus on the nontax and tax factors of each entity.

This section discusses the nontax factors associated with each of the four types of entity. Special entities such as limited liability companies, limited liability partnerships, and personal service corporations are also addressed.

The nontax factors arise primarily because of the legal differences in the various entity forms. This section also discusses the legal aspects and their effect on the nontax factors for each entity.

Sole Proprietorship

A **sole proprietorship** is a business owned by one individual. It is the most common business form in the United States. Individuals need do nothing formal to establish a sole proprietorship. A sole proprietorship is easy to form because the business is not separate from the individual owner from both a legal and a tax perspective. The only restriction is that the business can have only one owner, who must be an individual. This makes the sole proprietorship the least costly form of business to organize.

State law does not treat the sole proprietorship as an entity that owns property separately from the individual entrepreneur. Business debts are directly attributable to the individual business owner. Thus, the sole proprietor is personally liable for all debts of the business. This factor often discourages use of the sole proprietorship in a business that has a substantial risk of lawsuits involving product liability or malpractice.

Sometimes the separation issue becomes blurred because of financial accounting rules that require proprietors to exclude reporting of nonbusiness items (e.g., personal expenses or nonbusiness income) from proprietorship financial reports. Schedule C of Form 1040 is the vehicle for reporting the proprietorship income and expenses. This reporting mechanism appears to separate the proprietor from the proprietor's business. Yet this reporting procedure reinforces the conduit nature of the sole proprietorship. The net operating income flows directly to the individual proprietor's Form 1040 as an item of gross income.

▲ **EXAMPLE 2** Refer to the facts in example 1. Assume that Barbara wants to use the sole proprietorship for her business. What are the legal effects of running her travel agency as a sole proprietorship?

Discussion: There are no formal requirements to meet when starting a business that will operate as a sole proprietorship. Barbara will not have to spend a great deal of money to organize the business. However, any business debts resulting from either contractual obligations of the business (e.g., loans or accounts payable) or tort claims resulting from operating malfeasance can be collected from her family's personal assets, which are fairly extensive. Barbara needs to assess the vulnerability of her personal assets, given the level of risk in operating a travel agency. For example, she could have liability exposure if she books tickets for clients on an airplane that subsequently has an accident or for a vacation tour to Hawaii that is ruined by a hurricane. Purchasing insurance can mitigate some of her liability, but it may not be economically feasible to purchase insurance that will adequately cover all her personal wealth.

As the only owner of the business, the sole proprietor has the freedom to transfer ownership at any time and in any manner. When a sole proprietor dies, the business becomes part of the owner's estate and can be passed on to a spouse, children, or others, according to the owner's desires. The sole proprietorship also enjoys complete management control. One limitation of being the sole owner is that it is often difficult to raise large amounts of capital if the need arises.

Partnership

Most states declare that a **partnership** exists when two or more individuals engage collectively in an activity with the expectation of generating profits. A partnership is a flexible business form because the arrangement is purely consensual. Any individual owner in the partnership may dissolve the partnership at any time and depart with her or his share of the assets. Partnerships, like sole proprietorships, usually have no special state reporting requirements other than tax returns that report the results of operations.

Each general partner is personally responsible for any partnership obligations that arise during the existence of the partnership—similar to a sole proprietorship. Also, general partners legally have equal abilities to contribute to management decision-making.

Although partnerships are considered conduits for the purpose of income taxation, they are treated as separate entities under local law. Thus, partnerships can transact business and own property in their names, separate from the partners. This characteristic is a major difference between sole proprietorships and partnerships. The legal characteristics of partnerships are common and similar to those for other statutory business forms, such as corporations.

Partnerships give owners the ability to raise capital more easily than a sole proprietor because of the greater number of owners. Also, the costs of raising additional capital are relatively low when compared with those of corporations, which have fairly high costs for issuing stocks and bonds. However, the inability to issue stocks and bonds to the general public limits the amount of capital a partnership can raise. Even though it is relatively easy to form a partnership, the costs of ending the partnership and winding up its affairs may be costly. A tax is borne by the partners in the form of liquidating distributions that may have built up over the years as a profitable partnership. The partners will pay a tax on the difference between their basis in the partnership and the value of the partnership interest. Some of this difference may be treated as ordinary income, and some may be treated as capital gain. Liquidating distributions are covered in more detail in Chapter 14.

Certain types of partnerships can take on the corporate characteristic of limited liability to make the acquisition of capital easier. A **limited partnership** has at least one partner whose liability is limited to the amount of his or her investment in the partnership. This attribute provides a measure of safety for a limited partner's personal assets. To obtain the limited liability attribute, a limited partner gives up any right to participate in the management of the business. Management is left to at least one general partner, whose liability is not limited and who is responsible for the ongoing activities of the business. The limited partnership has been a popular medium for investors in risky activities, such as mining or oil and gas exploration.

▲ **EXAMPLE 3** Refer to example 1. Can Barbara operate the travel agency as a partnership?

Discussion: Barbara's business is hers alone. She needs at least one other person as an owner to establish a partnership. Because Barbara apparently does not need additional capital for her business, she does not need partners as additional investors. Barbara could bring one or more of her children into the business and form a partnership if she determined that it was the best form after considering all other factors. She might want to form a partnership if she needed additional capital or expertise. In that case, Barbara could offer either general or limited partnership ownership interests in her travel agency to obtain these assets. Transactions costs for exchanges like these are minimal. Preparation of a partnership agreement is generally the only expense. Barbara is not constrained to a maximum number of partners. She can add any number of partners to the ownership group and still maintain her individual management role by creating limited partnership interests. Only general partners are allowed to participate in day-to-day business decisions. Unlike limited partnership interests, adding general partnership interests spreads the business liability risks among more people. Of course, Barbara can offer a mixture of general and limited partnership interests in exchange for additional capital.

Corporation

A **corporation** is an artificial entity created under the auspices of state law. As a separate statutory entity, a corporation can enter into contracts in its name, own property, and be sued, and it must pay income tax based on its taxable income.

Attaining corporate status is fairly simple. Articles of incorporation are drafted and filed with the appropriate state agency (e.g., the Division of Corporations and Commercial Code of the state of Utah). Then the state grants a charter, and the corporation issues stock to shareholders. Once the corporation is formed and operating, it must follow a myriad of formal rules. The corporation must hold stockholder meetings and record the minutes of each meeting. Also, it must maintain stock transfer records and file annual reports with the appropriate state agency. All these requirements are costly, both in terms of time and actual money spent. For example, legal fees, charter and franchise fees, underwriter fees, and other organizational costs can be extensive.

Adhering to all the rules required by the state of incorporation gives the entity a separate legal identity that has the nontax attributes of limited liability, unlimited life, free transferability of ownership, and centralized management. These nontax factors are often the impetus for operating a business in the corporate form.

The attribute of limited liability can be misleading for small-business owners. That is, most shareholders of closely held corporations are required to personally guarantee loans to the corporation. Bankers and other creditors want assurance that the corporate debts are secured. Therefore, shareholders of closely held corporations often have only partial limited liability. However, this attribute still protects the personal assets of corporate shareholders from product liability or malpractice judgments brought against the business.

Limited liability is not available in most states for professional service (e.g., accounting, law, health-care, and architecture) corporations. This incorporated entity loses the traditional corporate protection for shareholders' personal assets. Customers and clients retain recourse against professionals when malpractice is a factor.

▲ **EXAMPLE 4** Return to example 1. If Barbara incorporates her business, what will be its legal characteristics?

Discussion: Barbara is not constrained by a number-of-owners requirement if she chooses the corporate form of business. One shareholder is generally enough to form a corporation. However, some states require a minimum of 2 or 3 members for the board of directors. Barbara can attain this by naming as a director the attorney who helps her with the filing requirements or by using 1 or more of her children as directors without effectively diluting her ownership control. If she needs additional equity in the future, she can have her corporation sell more shares of stock. The corporate attribute of free transferability of ownership interests permits the corporation or the shareholders to transfer ownership interests without jeopardizing the existence of the entity. Corporate status for Barbara's business will give her the key attribute of limited liability. This characteristic will shield her personal assets from creditors' claims. Given Barbara's financial position, limited liability is a characteristic that should be important to her and her family.

S Corporation

An **S corporation** is a regular corporation with special tax attributes. Corporations, chartered under the laws of one of the 50 states, may obtain conduit entity tax status by making a valid election per Subchapter S of the Internal Revenue Code of 1986.[1] The S corporation retains the legal characteristics of the corporate form (limited liability, free transferability of interests, continuity of life, and centralized management) while obtaining taxation characteristics similar to those of a partnership.

S corporation status is attained when a qualified corporation elects this status. The election is effective for the current tax year if the election is filed at any time during the preceding year or on or before the 15th day of the third month of the current year. Therefore, a calendar-year corporate taxpayer desiring S corporation status for

2001 must file the election at any time from January 1, 2000, through March 15, 2001. To qualify as an S corporation, a corporation

- Must be a domestic corporation
- May not have more than 75 shareholders. (Married individuals who are both shareholders are deemed to be one shareholder for S corporation status.)
- Must have as its shareholders only individuals, estates, tax-exempt organizations, and certain trusts
- Cannot have a nonresident alien as a shareholder
- Must have only one class of stock outstanding
- Must have the consent of all shareholders to the election of S corporation status[2]

Unlike partnerships and regular corporations, the number and type of owners in an S corporation are limited. No more than 75 shareholders may participate in ownership, and only individuals, estates, and certain trusts can be shareholders. The election is only for federal tax purposes. Certain states do not recognize this election for state income tax purposes. You should consult the state taxing authority to determine whether the S corporation election is valid for your state's income tax system.

▲ **EXAMPLE 5** Refer to example 4. Barbara wants to incorporate her business to get limited liability while retaining the benefits of conduit tax treatment. What are the key entity attributes if she makes the S corporation election?

Discussion: If Barbara incorporates her business and elects S corporation status, she converts a taxable entity to a conduit entity. Operating losses often result in the early years of a new business, and flow-through tax treatment lets Barbara deduct the losses on her personal tax return. Barbara's corporation retains the corporate characteristics of limited liability, free transferability of interests, continuity of life, and centralized management.

Every qualifying requirement must be met at the time of the election and at all times thereafter. The S corporation election terminates immediately when one or more of the qualifying characteristics ceases to exist. As of the date of termination, the corporation becomes a taxable corporate entity.

▲ **EXAMPLE 6** Assume that Barbara makes a valid S corporation election in 2000. On April 1, 2002, she sells 100 shares of her stock to Holder LTD, a limited partnership. Does this transaction affect the status of Barbara's corporation?

Discussion: Barbara's S corporation election terminates on April 1, 2002. Partnerships may not be shareholders in S corporations. Therefore, Barbara's corporation is an S corporation through March 31 and a taxable corporation from April 1 through December 31. NOTE: If the termination of the election is inadvertent, the S status may continue uninterrupted if the corporation corrects the disqualifying action. Therefore, if Barbara becomes aware of the implications of her action and can revoke the sale of the stock to the limited partnership, her corporation will not lose S corporation status.

An S corporation may forfeit its election voluntarily. If holders of more than 50 percent of the total shares of stock consent to revoke the S status, the revocation is effective for the current year if made on or before the 15th day of the third month of the year.

▲ **EXAMPLE 7** Assume that Barbara owns 70% of the S corporation and that each of her 3 children owns a 10% interest. In 2001, Barbara no longer desires S status, and on June 30, she files an intent to terminate. Is the termination valid? If it is, when is it effective?

Discussion: The termination is valid because Barbara owns more than 50% of the shares of the S corporation. The earliest effective date for the termination of S status is January 1 of the next tax year because the termination was not made on or before the 15th day of March during the current year.

Once an election is terminated, the corporation may not make a new election for five years without special consent of the commissioner of the IRS.[3]

Limited Liability Company

The limited liability company is a relatively new and unique form of business organization created under state laws. The **limited liability company (LLC)** combines the corporate characteristic of limited liability with the conduit tax treatment of partnerships. This form of business organization developed because of the growth of international trade. U.S. businesses were dealing with German and Latin American entities with management and earnings-sharing agreements that were more flexible than those afforded U.S. corporations. These foreign organizations had the basic corporate attributes of limited liability and recognition as a separate legal entity, as well as the partnership characteristics of dissolution on an owner's death and controlled admission of new owners. To satisfy the need of these foreign entities to know whether they would be treated as conduits or taxable entities, the IRS followed the tests contained in the regulations for determining whether an entity is a corporation or a partnership.[4]

When they saw the advantages of LLC entities, U.S. businesses began lobbying state legislatures to enact laws allowing similar structures. Today all states legally recognize or are considering recognition of LLCs. Although an LLC resembles a corporation in many respects, it accommodates more flexible business arrangements. Like a corporation, an LLC is created by following the requirements of state law. It is treated as a legal entity, separate from its individual owners, and is recognized as the owner of the trade or business property. The members of an LLC, like shareholders of a corporation, have limited liability: Members' personal assets are not at risk for the entity's liabilities. Beginning in 1997, owners of noncorporate entities will choose whether to be taxed as a corporation or to receive conduit tax treatment, without regard to the corporate attribute test.[5] This will greatly enhance the ability of a business to limit its liability without resorting to the use of a corporation.

Whereas corporations are created by filing articles of incorporation, LLCs file articles of organization. The entity must have two or more members, have an objective to carry on a business, and establish a specific method for dividing the profits and losses from the business. The ability to create special allocations of profits and losses is an attribute of partnerships and LLCs not permitted to corporations. Corporate shareholders receive their shares of an entity's earnings based on the percentage of stock owned. Also, similar to a partnership, LLC members are allowed to control who owns an interest; the corporate characteristic of free transferability of interests does not exist for these conduit entities.

LLC members have great flexibility in organizing the entity's management structure. Unlike a limited partnership, all members of an LLC may be involved in the enterprise's operating decisions. For example, members can choose a centralized management group while retaining the right to contribute to company decision-making in a manner similar to a corporate board of directors.

▲ **EXAMPLE 8** Recalling the facts in example 1, Barbara is planning to open a travel agency with money that she inherited from her father. She has three children and would like to change careers from being a high school teacher to running the business full-time. Is a limited liability company an appropriate business form for Barbara?

Discussion: Unless Barbara acquires at least one co-owner, the choice of an LLC will not provide the conduit tax treatment of a partnership. Although some state laws allow single-member LLCs, the IRS regulations classify these entities as either a corporation or a sole proprietorship. At best, the travel agency would be considered a separate entity with limited liability for Barbara, and she would gain nothing over using the corporate form.

Limited Liability Partnership

Another new form of organization that is growing in popularity is the limited liability partnership. The **limited liability partnership (LLP)** is a general partnership with the added characteristic of limited liability for owners. States allowing this type of entity are responding to concerns about the traditional concepts of partner liability: General partners are unconditionally liable for partnership debts. Accordingly, an LLP permits the usual partnership conduit tax treatment but limits the liabilities of partners. Under state partnership laws, partners in an LLP are liable for their acts and acts of individuals under their direction and control but not for negligence or misconduct by other partners. This characteristic differentiates an LLP from an LLC. In an LLC, no single owner has unlimited liability. A partner in an LLP has limited liability for business contractual obligations but can have unlimited liability for personal acts of malfeasance. Thus, an organization that seeks conduit tax treatment and limited personal liability for business obligations for all owners has two options that provide virtually the same tax treatment—LLPs and LLCs.

Certain states restrict the types of business entities that can choose either LLP or LLC status. For example, certain states allow professional service businesses (i.e., law firms, accounting firms, and health-care businesses) only LLP status; they cannot elect LLC status. Because the LLC and the LLP have identical tax results, nontax factors determine whether the entity should be an LLC or an LLP.

▲ **EXAMPLE 9** Refer to example 8. Is a limited liability partnership an appropriate business form for Barbara?

Discussion: Barbara cannot qualify for LLP status because she is the sole owner of her business. Like any partnership, at least 2 owners are necessary for this special type of limited liability entity. If Barbara brings in at least 1 partner and organizes her business as an LLP, her liability is limited for the contractual legal obligations of her business. However, she remains liable for any personal acts. Because her travel agency is not a professional service business, state law does not require her to choose an LLP if she desires a limited liability entity.

Planning Commentary

Table 13–1 summarizes the nontax factors for each entity type. Ease of formation and low organizational costs are the primary nontax attributes of sole proprietorships. In addition, sole proprietors can freely transfer their interests and have complete management control. However, the proprietor is personally liable for all the liabilities of the business entity and has limited ability to raise additional capital. The lack of limited liability is the main factor discouraging the use of the sole proprietorship.

At least two owners are necessary to form a partnership. General partners have the ability to determine the management structure and can restrict the transfer of ownership interests. General partners are personally liable for the obligations of the entity. Limited partners bring in capital without being exposed to the liabilities of the business. If the business creates high liability exposure for the owners, using an LLC or LLP can limit personal liability while retaining the desirable conduit entity characteristics.

The primary advantage of the corporate form is limited liability for the owners. Corporations also have the greatest ability to raise additional capital, although incorporating and raising capital are more costly than with the other entity forms. Continuity of life of the entity and free transferability of ownership are attributes that can be positive or negative, depending on the owner's desires.

The S corporation is an income tax election. It is useful when owners desire the limited liability protection of the corporate form and the taxation characteristics of a conduit entity. However, the limited liability protection may be reduced initially because creditors may require the owners to provide personal assets as collateral for loans to the business.

General Income Tax Factors

The main income tax item of interest in choosing a business form is the total tax liability (entity tax plus owner's tax). This section discusses general income tax factors that affect the total tax liability of an entity. Differences in total tax liability are due to the incidence of taxation, double taxation of corporate dividends, and the question of whether an owner can be an employee of the entity.

▲ **Table 13-1**

Comparison of Nontax Factors among Business Forms

Factor	Sole Proprietorship	Partnership	Limited Liability Company	Limited Liability Partnership	Corporation	S Corporation
Number of owners is restricted	Yes, restricted to 1	No, except there must be more than 1	No, generally more than 1	No, except there must be more than 1	No, certain states may have minimums	Yes, 75 owners maximum
Entity recognized as separate	No	Yes	Yes	Yes	Yes	Yes
Owners have limited liability	No	No, except for limited partners	Yes	Yes, except for personal acts of malfeasance by an individual partner	Yes, except for professional service corporations	Yes
Owners have the right to direct participation in management	Yes	Yes for general partners; no for limited partners	Yes	Yes	No	No
Entity continues regardless of ownership changes	No	No	No	No	Yes	Yes
Free transferability of ownership interests	Yes	No	No	No	Yes	Yes
Level of difficulty to form	Low	Low	Low	Low	Relatively high	Relatively high
Organizational costs	None	Moderate	Moderate	Moderate	Relatively high	Relatively high
Ability to raise capital	Limited	Good, better for limited partnerships	Good	Good	Excellent	Excellent

Incidence of Income Taxation

Corporation and individuals are the two primary taxpaying entities. Conduit entities do not pay tax; their income flows through to the owners of the entity for taxation. Therefore, the **incidence of taxation** rests with either incorporated taxable entities or owners of conduit entities. Because the tax rate schedules differ for individuals and corporations, proper entity selection offers opportunities to minimize income taxes. However, the tax law contains provisions that limit this ability when the corporation's primary income source is the personal service of the owner(s) or consists primarily of passive forms of income. The incidence of taxation for each entity form is the starting point for determining the entity that provides the most favorable income tax treatment in a given situation. This section provides an overview of the taxation of each entity.

Sole Proprietorship. Sole proprietorships operate as conduits and tax the individual owner on the income of the business. The net operating income of a trade or business flows directly into the individual proprietor's gross income. The mechanism for accomplishing this is Schedule C of Form 1040. Individuals are subject to four tax rate schedules.[6] Each schedule is based on filing status. The schedules for all taxable entities appear in Appendix A. Each individual schedule has a five-step progression for taxing taxable income. The first four rates are 15 percent, 28 percent, 31 percent, and 36 percent; the top rate for all remaining taxable income is 39.6 percent. The amounts of taxable income at which the tax rates change (i.e., from 15 percent to 28 percent) vary according to the individual's filing status.

Because sole proprietorships are not separate taxable entities, they may not deduct owner-employee salaries and owner-employee fringe benefits. In addition, a cash withdrawal from a sole proprietorship has no tax consequences because the only entity involved is the individual. Proprietorship cash draws are analogous to taking money from one pocket and putting it into another pocket in the same pair of pants.

▲ **EXAMPLE 10** Monte, who is married and has 3 children, owns and operates a chain of gas stations. In 2001, he draws a salary of $60,000. The income from the gas stations before payment of the salary has consistently been $150,000 a year. What is Monte's income tax liability in 2001 if he operates the business as a sole proprietorship? For illustrative purposes, assume that Monte and his wife have other income that exactly offsets their allowable deductions.

Discussion: The taxable income for the business is $150,000. Monte's salary is not a deductible expense of the sole proprietorship. He is taxed on the earnings of the business, $150,000. Because Monte is married, his filing status is married, filing jointly, giving him a tax liability of $37,347 {$24,714.00 + [31% × ($150,000 − $109,250)]} in 2001.

Partnership. Like sole proprietors, partners pay tax on their share of the partnership income. A partnership is a conduit entity that does not pay tax.[7] Income is taxed at the owner level rather than at the entity level. However, partnerships are still required to annually report the results of their operations. Form 1065 for partnerships is analogous to an individual taxpayer's Schedule C of Form 1040.

As discussed in Chapters 3 and 5, because taxation takes place at the partner level, any items that receive special treatment at the individual level (e.g., capital gains, investment expenses) must be reported separately to each partner. Therefore, partners must be provided with the items and amounts to be reported on their individual tax returns. This is accomplished by Schedule K-1 of Form 1065.

Partners generally have significant flexibility when allocating percentages of income, gains, losses, expenses, and credits. Unlike other entity forms, partnerships can specially allocate certain types and amounts of income, gains, losses, and the like among partners. As long as the allocations are economically realistic, partners with different marginal tax rates can receive allocations that provide relatively advantageous benefits.

Partners may take cash withdrawals from their businesses, but, as with a sole proprietorship, these payments are not going from one taxable entity to another. Unless the withdrawals represent guaranteed payments, the partnership may not deduct them and they are not taxable to the partner. They are nontaxable returns of capital. Therefore, partners are not subject to double taxation when earnings are distributed as cash withdrawals.

▲ **EXAMPLE 11** Assume the same facts as in example 10, except that Monte's cousin Beau manages 1 station and receives a salary of $40,000. Monte and Beau organize the gas station enterprise as a partnership called M&B Company. Monte owns a 70% interest and Beau owns a 30% interest. Monte is paid a salary of $60,000. Beau is single and has other income equal to his allowable deductions. How does this affect the total tax liability of the business income?

Discussion: The partnership cannot deduct the salaries paid to Monte and Beau, resulting in partnership income of $150,000. The salaries are nontaxable returns of capital. Monte's share of the partnership income, $105,000 ($150,000 × 70%), flows through to him for inclusion on his personal tax return. His income tax liability is $23,524 {$6,780.00 + [28% × ($105,000 − $45,200)]}. Beau's share of income, $45,000 ($150,000 × 30%), flows to him, and he pays $9,084 {$4,057.50 + [28% × ($45,000 − $27,050)]} of tax. The total tax liability of both partners is $32,608. Bringing in Beau as a partner and splitting the business income between Monte and Beau reduces the total tax liability by $4,739 ($37,347 − $32,608) compared with operating the business as a sole proprietorship.

General partnerships, limited partnerships, limited liability companies, and limited liability partnerships are treated as partnerships for tax purposes. Therefore, the results discussed in example 11 would be the same for those entity types.

Corporation. Corporations are taxable entities that are separate and distinct from their owners. A corporation pays tax on its income.[8] The results of corporate operations are reported on Form 1120, which is analogous to an individual's Form 1040. The owners (shareholders) are taxed on distributions of money (dividends), which are reported on their individual returns. For example, individual taxpayers report their dividend income on Schedule B of Form 1040.

Because the corporation is separate from its shareholders, it can employ shareholders and pay them salaries or wages. The ability to pay deductible salaries to owners, combined with the differences in the individual and corporate tax rate schedules, provides an opportunity to lower the total tax liability of the business.

The corporate tax rate schedule appears in Appendix A. There is only one corporate tax rate schedule, which is not subject to inflation indexing. The corporate schedule has six rates:

Taxable Income	Marginal Tax Rate (%)
$ -0- to 50,000	15%
50,001 to 75,000	25
75,001 to 100,000	34
100,001 to 335,000	39
335,001 to 10,000,000	34
10,000,001 to 15,000,000	35
15,000,001 to 18,333,333	38
18,333,334 to . . .	35

This somewhat-convoluted rate schedule stems from Congress's desire to take the benefits of the lower (15-percent and 25-percent) tax rate brackets away from higher-income corporations. Accordingly, a 5-percent surtax is levied on corporate taxpayers with income greater than $100,000 and less than $335,000. Therefore, a marginal tax rate of 39 percent exists for income between $100,000 and $335,000. The effect of this surtax is to tax corporations with incomes greater than $335,000 and less than $10 million at a flat rate of 34 percent. As with the 15- and 25-percent rates, the benefit of the 34-percent rate is phased out with a 3 percent surtax on taxable income in excess of $15 million. The tax law adds a marginal tax rate of 38 percent for income between $15 million and $18,333,333. The effect is to tax corporations with incomes greater than $18,333,333 at a flat rate of 35 percent.

The top individual income tax rate of 39.6 percent lets business owners use a corporation to shelter income when taxable income exceeds $297,350. Also, when taxable income is between $45,200 and $75,000, a corporation is taxed at a lower rate than a married couple filing jointly. Therefore, under the right circumstances, business owners can lower their income tax liabilities by incorporating. However, if the corporation distributes dividends to the individual owner-shareholder, the individual incurs additional income taxes. This situation is a classic case of double taxation, which may mitigate the tax advantage of incorporating.

▲ **EXAMPLE 12** Recall the facts from example 11 in which Monte's cousin Beau manages one of the gas stations and is paid a salary of $40,000. Monte is to get a salary of

$60,000. Assume Monte and Beau incorporate the business as M&B Company. Monte owns 70% of the stock of the corporation, and Beau owns 30%. Monte and Beau are employees of the business. The business has operating income of $150,000 before considering salary payments to Monte ($60,000) and Beau ($40,000). What is the total tax liability using the corporate form of business operation?

Discussion: Because Monte and Beau can be employees of their corporation, their salaries are deductible in calculating taxable income. M&B's taxable income is $50,000 ($150,000 − $60,000 − $40,000), and it pays a tax of $7,500 ($50,000 × 15%). Monte pays a tax of $10,924 {$6,780.00 + [28% × ($60,000 − $45,200)]} on his $60,000 salary, and Beau pays a tax of $7,684 {$4,057.50 + [28% × ($40,000 − $27,050)]} on his $40,000 salary. The total tax liability is $26,108 compared with $32,608 when the business is operated as partnership, a savings of $6,500 ($32,608 − $26,108). This is accomplished by shifting $50,000 of Monte and Beau's partnership income, which was taxed at 28%, to the corporation, where it is taxed at 15%.

As example 12 illustrates, because a corporation is taxed at a lower rate than are married individuals filing jointly for taxable incomes between $45,200 and $75,000, taxable incomes of up to $75,000 produce lower taxes for corporations than individuals. The first $50,000 of a corporation's income is taxed at 15 percent, whereas a married couple filing jointly is taxed at 15 percent up to only $45,200. Therefore, corporations receive the benefit of an additional $4,800 ($50,000 − $45,200) taxed at 15 percent. A corporation's next $25,000 is taxed at only 25 percent, whereas a married individual is taxed at 28 percent for the same taxable income level. Thus, using a corporation to split the income of a business between a corporation and its owners can result in significant tax savings.

Personal Service Corporation. The purpose of the personal service corporation rules is to deny the benefit of the graduated corporate tax rates to individuals who attempt to lower their tax on personal services income by using a corporation. It does this by taxing the income of a personal service corporation at a flat rate of 35 percent. A **personal service corporation (PSC)** is a corporation in which

- The performance of personal services is the principal activity
- The services are performed by owner-employees
- The owner-employees together own 95 percent or more of the stock[9]

▲ **EXAMPLE 13** Assume M&B Company in example 12 is a petroleum consulting business. Monte and Beau perform all the consulting work that the operation is contracted to do. How does this affect the total tax liability?

Discussion: M&B is a personal service corporation, and its $50,000 taxable income is taxed at 35%, resulting in a tax of $17,500 ($50,000 × 35%). Monte and Beau's tax liabilities remain at $10,924 and $7,684, respectively, for a total tax liability of $36,108. The personal service corporation tax results in an additional $10,000 in tax ($36,108 − $26,108) over what a corporation would pay. However, this arrangement still yields a tax savings of $1,239 ($37,347 − $36,108) over the use of a sole proprietorship though it costs $3,500 ($36,108 − $32,608) more in taxes than the partnership form.

The flat 35-percent tax rate encourages owner-employees of PSCs to take corporate earnings out of the corporation as salary.

▲ **EXAMPLE 14** Assume the same facts as in example 13, except that Monte's salary is $105,000 and Beau's salary is $45,000. How does this affect the total tax liability?

Discussion: The deduction of Monte and Beau's salaries reduces M&B's taxable income to zero; it pays no tax. Monte and Beau's tax on their salaries totals $32,608, the same tax paid if M&B were organized as a partnership. The elimination of the PSC tax through payment of the income as salaries saves $3,500 in taxes.

Example 14 shows that a PSC is still a viable option when the owners of the entity seek the limited liability protection of the corporation. As long as the salary income paid to owner-employees of a PSC is taxed at a rate lower than 35 percent, the PSC offers a tax advantage over the sole proprietorship. When all the income is distributed as salaries in proportion to the owners' interests, the total tax liability is equivalent to that of a partnership.

S Corporation. An S corporation is a corporation with tax characteristics similar to those of a partnership. S corporations are conduit entities that do not pay tax.[10] Form 1120S is used to report operating results to the government. The income of an S corporation flows through to its shareholders for taxation. As with a partnership, taxation at the individual owner level requires that items that receive special treatment at the individual level be reported separately so that shareholders can prepare their returns properly. Schedule K-1 of Form 1120S provides shareholders with their proportionate share of entity income, deductions, and credits to include on their personal tax return. As with partnerships, distributions (dividends) paid to shareholders are nontaxable recoveries of capital. Because of the separate entity status of the corporation, S corporation shareholders can be employees of the business entity.

▲ **EXAMPLE 15** Assume the same facts as in example 12, except that Monte and Beau make the election to have M&B Company treated as an S corporation. What is the total tax liability?

Discussion: Because Monte and Beau can be employees of the S corporation, their salaries are deductible in calculating taxable income. M&B's taxable income is $50,000 ($150,000 − $60,000 − $40,000). Monte is taxed on his $35,000 ($50,000 × 70%) share of the corporate income and his $60,000 salary. His tax liability is $20,724 {$6,780.00 + [28% × ($95,000 − $45,200)]}. Beau pays a tax of $11,884 {$4,057.50 + [28% × ($55,000 − $27,050)]} on his $55,000 ($40,000 + $15,000) in salary and his share of corporate income. The total tax liability of $32,608 is greater than the $26,108 tax on a corporation because the $50,000 in corporate income is taxed at the higher individual rates. The S corporation and the partnership have identical tax liabilities because Monte and Beau are in the same marginal tax bracket even though total taxable income allocated to each is different than the allocation from a partnership.

Double Taxation

Obtaining cash or other property distributions is generally the ultimate objective of corporate owners. In addition to paying salaries to shareholder-employees, corporations distribute cash to shareholders via dividends. Salaries are deductible expenses; dividend payments are not. Dividends are considered distributions of corporate earnings (which have already been taxed). When shareholders receive the dividends, the dividends are taxed again. Because the corporation and its shareholders are recognized as separate taxpaying entities, corporate earnings are subject to **double taxation** when paid to shareholders as dividends.

▲ **EXAMPLE 16** Assume that in example 12, M&B Company distributes the $50,000 in corporate earnings as a dividend. What is the effect of paying dividends on the total tax liability?

Discussion: Dividends are not a deductible expense. Therefore, M&B pays a tax of $7,500 ($50,000 × 15%) on its $50,000 taxable income. Monte receives $35,000 of the dividend, which increases his tax liability to $20,724 on his $95,000 in income. Beau receives a $15,000 dividend and pays a tax of $11,884 on his $55,000 in income. The total tax liability of $40,108 is $14,000 ($40,108 − $26,108 from example 12) more than when no dividends are paid. This occurs because the $50,000 in corporate earnings is taxed twice: first at the corporate level and again at the individual stockholder level.

Double taxation occurs only with the use of a corporation. One way to avoid double taxation is to pay salaries to owner-employees equal to the corporate income. This eliminates taxation at the corporate level but negates the tax savings that can be obtained from income splitting. In example 16, payment of salaries of $95,000 and $55,000 would yield a total tax liability of $32,608, identical to that of an S corporation. In addition, if the salary amounts are not reasonable, the portion of the salary that isn't reasonable will be recast as a dividend, and no savings will result. Choosing a conduit entity rather than an incorporated taxable entity eliminates the double taxation problem when reasonable salaries cannot be paid to achieve the desired tax result.

▲ **EXAMPLE 17** Assume that in example 16, Monte and Beau make a valid S corporation election for M&B Company, effective for the current year. How does this affect the total tax liability?

Discussion: As a conduit entity, M&B pays no income tax. The $50,000 in corporate income passes through to Monte and Beau, who include it in their taxable income. The S corporation election eliminates the $7,500 corporate tax. Distributions paid to S corporation shareholders are nontaxable returns of capital and do not affect Monte and Beau's taxable income. Their tax liabilities remain at $20,724 and $11,884, respectively, for a total tax liability of $32,608. By using a conduit entity, Monte and Beau have eliminated the double taxation of the earnings of the corporation without increasing their salaries to a point that may be considered unreasonable.

Employee versus Owner

Owners participating in the operation of their entity may or may not be treated as employees for tax purposes, depending on the business entity. If an owner is classified as an employee, the owner can receive a salary and fringe benefits, and can have access to company retirement plans (discussed in Chapter 15). These types of compensation potentially reduce the entity's taxable income and can minimize the effects of double taxation on corporations and their shareholders. The payment of tax-deductible salaries to owner-employees can be a planning tool for income splitting, which is used to decrease the total tax liability of the entity and its owners. The ability to provide nontaxable fringe benefits to owner-employees also reduces the total tax liability and can be an important factor in the choice of entity.

Unincorporated entities cannot have owner-employees. Because a sole proprietor is not legally an entity separate and apart from the business, the sole proprietor cannot be an employee of the business. (Individuals cannot hire themselves.) Therefore, the tax benefits of salaries or fringe benefits are not available to sole proprietors. The business is not allowed a deduction for these items, and fringe-benefit recipients are not permitted exclusions for the value of fringe benefits received.

▲ **EXAMPLE 18** Recall the facts in example 10, in which Monte owns and operates a chain of gas stations. He draws a salary of $60,000. The income from the gas stations before payment of the salary has been consistently $150,000 a year. Assume that Monte's business provides him with $10,000 in otherwise-nontaxable fringe benefits. How are the salary and fringe benefits treated for tax purposes, and what is the total tax liability when the business is operated as a sole proprietorship?

Discussion: Monte and his business are not considered separate entities. The business cannot deduct Monte's salary and fringe-benefit payments. The $150,000 taxable income is reported on Monte's individual return, resulting in a tax of $37,347 (see example 10).

As with sole proprietorships, partnerships are not considered entities separate from their owners (partners), and the partners cannot be employees of the entity. Partners cannot receive deductible salaries. Partners often receive guaranteed payments for rendering services to or on behalf of the business. A **guaranteed payment** is a payment made to a partner for specific services performed by the partner and is made without regard to the income of the partnership. These payments are compensation to the partner but are treated as though they are paid to a self-employed individual, separate from the partnership. Unlike other payments made to partners, a guaranteed payment is deductible in determining a partnership's operating income.

▲ **EXAMPLE 19** Recall from the facts in example 11 that Monte and Beau formed a partnership with Monte owning a 70% interest and Beau owning a 30% interest. Monte is paid a salary of $60,000, and Beau is paid a salary of $40,000. Assume that the salaries paid to Monte and Beau are guaranteed payments. How does this affect the total tax liability?

Discussion: The guaranteed payments are deductible by the partnership, reducing operating income to $50,000. Monte includes in his taxable income the $60,000 guaranteed payment and his $35,000 ($50,000 × 70%) share of partnership income. His taxable income is $95,000. Beau's $55,000 of taxable income consists of his $40,000 guaranteed payment and his $15,000 ($50,000 × 30%) share of partnership income. Monte's tax liability is $20,724 (example 15), and Beau's tax liability is $11,884 (example 15). Note that the total tax liability with the guaranteed payments is the same as that for an S corporation (example 15).

Partners can receive certain fringe benefits from the partnership. The cost of the fringe benefits is considered a guaranteed payment to the partner. As a guaranteed payment, the cost of the fringe benefits received is taxable to the partner and deductible by the partnership.

▲ **EXAMPLE 20** Assume that M&B Company is operated as a partnership. Monte owns a 70% interest, and Beau owns a 30% interest. M&B provides Monte and Beau with $10,000 each in nontaxable fringe benefits. Partnership income is $150,000 before consideration of Monte and Beau's salaries (which are not guaranteed payments) and fringe benefits. How does this affect the total tax liability?

Discussion: Because partners cannot be employees of the partnership, M&B cannot deduct the salary it pays to the partners. The partnership can deduct the fringe-benefit payments it makes to the partners, but the partners must include the fringe-benefit payments in their gross income. Partnership taxable income is reduced to $130,000 by the fringe benefit-payments. Monte must include his share of the partnership income, $91,000 ($130,000 × 70%), on his individual return. In addition, the fringe benefit payments are included in his taxable income. Monte's taxable income is $101,000 ($91,000 + $10,000), and he pays $22,404 {$6,780.00 + [28% × ($101,000 − $45,200)]} in income tax. Beau's taxable income is $49,000 [($130,000 × 30%) + $10,000], and he pays $10,204 {$4,057.50 + [28% × ($49,000 − $27,050)]} in income tax.

The entity concept drives the ability of owners to be corporate employees for income tax purposes. Corporations are deemed separate entities, taxable on their income. Accordingly, corporate owners (shareholders) can be employees of their corporation(s). As described in Chapter 6, attempts to reduce corporate taxable income through the use of the owner-employee status can have pitfalls. The substance-over-form doctrine, dealing with the issues of lack of business purpose, unreasonableness of salary, and discriminatory fringe benefits, is the usual focus of IRS scrutiny. Closely held businesses are often objects of concern on these issues. Yet, when these pitfalls are avoided, benefits do accrue to owner-employees who take advantage of the corporate form of business.

▲ **EXAMPLE 21** Assume the same facts as in example 20, except that M&B Company is organized as a corporation. The salaries are reasonable based on the services performed for the corporation, and the fringe benefits do not discriminate in favor of Monte or Beau. How does this affect the total tax liability?

Discussion: Because the corporation is viewed as a separate legal entity, it can employ Monte and Beau, pay them tax-deductible salaries, and provide them with nontaxable fringe benefits. After deduction of the salaries and the cost of the fringe benefits, the corporation's taxable income is $30,000 ($150,000 − $100,000 − $20,000), and it pays $4,500 ($30,000 × 15%) in income tax. Monte and Beau include their salaries in their taxable income and pay $10,924 and $7,684 (example 12), respectively, in income tax. In addition, the provision of nontaxable fringe benefits has lowered the overall tax liability by $3,000 ($20,000 × 15%) through deduction by the corporation and exclusion from Monte and Beau's income tax.

Because corporate entities can have owner-employees, an S corporation can pay tax-deductible salaries to its owners. However, the S corporation election generally results in the treatment of owner-employees as partners for fringe-benefit purposes. Although certain fringe benefits can be provided to partners and S corporation owner-employees, the value of the fringe benefits is included in the owner's taxable income. The corporation can deduct the cost of the fringe benefits.

▲ **EXAMPLE 22** Assume the same facts as in example 21, except that M&B Company makes a valid S corporation election for the current year. How does the S corporation election affect the total tax liability?

Discussion: M&B Company deducts the salary payments and the cost of the fringe benefits provided to Monte and Beau, reducing its income to $30,000. Monte's taxable income consists of his $60,000 salary, his $21,000 share of M&B income, and the $10,000 in fringe benefits. The tax on his $91,000 of income is $19,604. Beau's tax on his $59,000 ($40,000 + $9,000 + $10,000) in income is $13,004. The total tax liability of $32,608 is greater than that of a corporation ($26,108) because the $30,000 of corporate income is taxed at Monte and Beau's higher marginal tax rates and Monte and Beau cannot exclude the fringe benefits from taxation.

Fringe Benefits

Another consideration in choosing the appropriate entity for conducting business is the tax treatment of fringe benefits paid to employees. This is especially important for an individual who is also an owner of the business. These owners generally participate in the day-to-day activities of the business and have owner-employee status. Because a corporation is considered a separate entity and its income is taxable, the corporate owners (shareholders) can be employees of the corporation. Recall from the discussion in Chapter 4 that, because of legislative grace, certain employee benefits are excluded from taxation. The provision of tax-free fringe benefits is a key element in designing a compensation plan to attract and retain qualified employees. The following benefits are generally not included in an employee's gross income.

- Employer-provided term life insurance up to $50,000 coverage
- Employer-sponsored accident and health-care plans
- Meals and lodging furnished for the convenience of the employer
- Cafeteria plans
- Employer-provided educational assistance
- Dependent-care programs
- No additional-cost services
- Qualified employee discounts
- Working-condition fringe benefits
- De minimis fringe benefits

Because of related party concerns with owner-employees and the legislative grace afforded fringe benefits, Congress has established a set of nondiscriminatory rules. That is, historically some employers have provided tax-free fringe benefits to only a few highly compensated employees or to corporate officers. Therefore, companies must offer most types of fringe benefits of at least equal value to nonshareholder employees to retain the exclusion status for the recipients.

A corporation can deduct the cost of providing these fringe benefits to an employee, although the value of these benefits is not income to the employee. Thus, fringe benefits are an excellent compensation and tax savings tool for an owner-employee.

▲ **EXAMPLE 23** The Golic Group, a corporation, has a company health-care plan for all employees. Miguel, an employee, owns 15% of the corporate stock, and Roberto, also an employee, owns 1%. The cost of Miguel's health plan is $4,800, and Roberto's plan costs $4,200. How are the costs of these benefits treated by each shareholder-employee and by the corporation?

Discussion: The cost of the health benefits provided to Miguel and Roberto is excluded from their gross income. The $9,000 cost of the health benefits is a deductible business expense for the corporation.

A sole proprietorship is not a separate taxable entity. Because sole proprietors cannot be employees of their business, the salaries paid and fringe benefits provided to the owner are not deductible by the business. Likewise, the theoretical construct of the conduit entity provides that an employer-employee relationship cannot exist between a partnership and its partners. Unlike pension plans, which require that a partner own more than a 10-percent interest in the partnership to be considered an owner-partner, all partners are treated as owner-partners for fringe-benefit purposes. The partnership is allowed to deduct the cost of certain fringe benefits as a guaranteed payment, and the partners are required to include the guaranteed payment as income on their tax return. Only employer-provided group term life insurance coverage, employer-sponsored accident and health-care plans, cafeteria plans, and meals and lodging furnished for the convenience of the employer are subject to this treatment. Because the tax law mentions only these fringe benefits, all other fringe benefits appear to be deductible by the partnership as an ordinary business expense and are not income to the partner. As a self-employed taxpayer, a partner can deduct 60 percent of the cost of health-care premiums for adjusted gross income. The remaining 40 percent of the cost is treated as an itemized medical expense deduction.

▲ **EXAMPLE 24** Return to example 23. Assume that the Golic Group is a partnership and that both Miguel and Roberto are partners, owning 15% and 1%, respectively, in the partnership. How is the cost of the health-care plan treated by each partner and by the partnership?

Discussion: The cost of both health plans is deductible as a guaranteed payment from the partnership to the partner. Both Miguel and Roberto must include in their income the cost of the health plan provided to them. Each is allowed a deduction for the cost of the health plan. Because they are self-employed, each may take a 60% deduction for adjusted gross income and 40% as an itemized medical expense deduction.

Generally, shareholder-employees of an S corporation are treated the same as employees of regular corporations. Shareholder-employees must include their salary in gross income, and the S corporation can deduct the salary expense and the related payroll taxes. However, the tax treatment of fringe benefits paid by an S corporation to an employee-shareholder depends on the employee's ownership percentage. If an employee-shareholder owns 2 percent or less of an S corporation, the fringe benefits are deductible by the corporation and are not included in the employee's gross income. If a shareholder owns more than 2 percent of the S corporation stock, the tax treatment of the fringe benefits is similar to the tax treatment for a partner. The cost of the fringe benefit is deductible by the S corporation as salary expense, and the owner-employee must include the cost of the fringe benefit as income.[33] The owner-employee can deduct 60 percent of the cost of health care premiums for adjusted gross income. The remaining 40 percent of the cost is treated as an itemized medical expense deduction. As with a partnership, only employer-provided term life insurance coverage, employer-sponsored accident and health-care plans, cafeteria plans, and meals and lodging furnished for the convenience of the employer are subject to this treatment. As with a partnership, because the tax law mentions only these fringe benefits, all other fringe benefits appear to be deductible by an S corporation as an ordinary business expense and are not income to the owner-employee.

▲ **EXAMPLE 25** Return to example 23. Assume that Golic Group is an S corporation. How is the cost of the health-care plan treated by each shareholder-employee and by the S corporation?

Discussion: Because Roberto owns less than 2% of Golic, the corporation can take as a deductible business expense the $4,200 paid for his health-care plan, and the cost is excluded from his gross income. Because Miguel owns more than 2% of the corporate stock, the corporation can deduct the $4,800 paid for his health plan, but Miguel must include it in his gross income. Miguel is allowed a deduction for adjusted gross income for 60% of the medical premiums. The remaining 40% of the premiums is an itemized medical expense deduction.

Finally, in determining the total value of fringe benefits provided to an employee, a business needs to consider the cost of employment taxes. The two major employment taxes are Social Security and federal and state unemployment compensation (FUTA and SUTA). All entities are liable for the payment of these taxes on the salaries of their employees. Therefore, a business pays up to an additional 13.85 percent (7.65 percent for Social Security and a maximum 6.2 percent for FUTA and SUTA) of an employee's salary for these taxes.

Social Security Taxes

The Social Security tax is imposed on the wages of employees and the net self-employment income of self-employed individuals. For self-employed individuals, the Social Security tax is referred to as the **self-employment tax.** These terms are used interchangeably throughout the rest of this chapter. Employers are required to match the amount contributed by the employee. Employees pay 7.65 percent of their salary into the Social security system; this percentage has two components: Old Age, Survivors, and Disability Insurance (OASDI) at a rate of 6.2 percent, and Medical Health Insurance (MHI) at a rate of 1.45 percent of an individual's wages. For 2001, the maximum amount of earnings subject to the OASDI tax is $80,400. The MHI tax is levied on all wages or net self-employment income. The net operating income earned by a sole proprietor or a partner is considered self-employment income. A guaranteed payment to a partner is also self-employment income. A self-employed individual is considered both an employee and the employer and must pay 15.3 percent (7.65% × 2) in self-employment tax. To reduce this additional tax burden, a self-employed individual can deduct for adjusted gross income one-half of the amount of self-employment taxes paid. In determining self-employment income, the net earnings from self-employment are reduced by one-half of the self-employment tax paid. The effect of this provision is that only 92.35 percent [100% − (50% × 15.3%)] of the net earnings from self-employment are subject to self-employment tax.

▲ **EXAMPLE 26** Yari and Sven are partners in the Coffee Bean, a local cafe. Yari owns 75% of the business, and Sven owns 25%. The net operating income from the business is $120,000. Who is responsible for paying the Social Security taxes on the income Yari and Sven receive? Who is allowed a deduction for the Social Security taxes paid?

Discussion: Because the Coffee Bean is a partnership, the individual partners cannot be employees of the entity. Therefore, each partner, and not the Coffee Bean, must pay the self-employment tax on his pro rata share of the income. Each is allowed a deduction for AGI for one-half of the self-employment taxes paid. Yari reports $90,000 ($120,000 × 75%) as self-employment income, and his net self-employment income is $83,115 ($90,000 × 92.35%). Sven reports $30,000 ($120,000 × 25%) as self-employment income, and his net self-employment income is $27,705 ($30,000 × 92.35%). Yari and Sven's self-employment tax and their deduction for self-employment taxes are as follows:

Yari:	
Tax on $80,400 of net self-employment income:	
$80,400 × 15.3%	$12,301
Tax on net self-employment income in excess of $80,400	
$83,115 − $80,400 = $2,715 × 2.9%	79
Self-employment tax	$12,380
Deduction for one-half of self-employment taxes paid	$ 6,190
Sven:	
Tax on $27,705 of net self-employment income:	
$27,705 × 15.3%	$ 4,239
Deduction for one-half of self-employment taxes paid	$ 2,120

The total amount of self-employment taxes paid by Yari and Sven is $16,619 ($12,380 + $4,239).

A corporation is a separate taxable entity. As a result, it can employ shareholders and deduct the salary or wages paid to them in arriving at the corporation's taxable income. The corporation must match the amount of Social Security taxes paid by an employee. The corporation is allowed to deduct its share of the Social Security taxes paid in calculating its taxable income.

▲ **EXAMPLE 27** Assume the same facts as in example 26, except that the Coffee Bean is a corporation and pays Yari and Sven salaries of $90,000 and $30,000, respectively. Who is responsible for paying the Social Security taxes on the salaries paid to Yari and Sven? Who is allowed a deduction for the Social Security taxes paid?

Discussion: Each employee is responsible for paying Social Security taxes on her or his salary. Because Yari's salary exceeds the 2001 maximum of $80,400, he will pay a tax of 6.20% on the first $80,400 of his salary and 1.45% on his entire $90,000 salary. Because Sven's salary is below the maximum amount, he pays Social Security tax at a rate of 7.65% on his salary of $30,000. The Coffee Bean is responsible for matching the amount of the Social Security taxes paid by each employee. The company can deduct the amount it pays in Social Security taxes. The amount Yari and Sven pay in Social Security taxes is not deductible.

Yari:	
Tax on $80,400 of salary income:	
$80,400 × 7.65%	$6,151
Tax on salary income in excess of $80,400:	
$90,000 − $80,400 = $9,600 × 1.45%	139
Social Security tax	$6,290
Sven:	
Tax on $30,000 of salary income:	
$30,000 × 7.65%	$2,295
Coffee Bean: ($6,290 + $2,295)	$8,585

The total amount of Social Security tax paid by the Coffee Bean, Yari, and Sven is $17,170 ($8,585 + $6,290 + $2,295). The total Social Security tax paid using the corporate form of organization is $551 ($17,170 − $16,619) more than the tax paid using a partnership.

Although an S corporation is a conduit entity, it can employ shareholders and deduct the salary or wages paid to them in determining the corporation's ordinary income. Unlike a partnership, the income that flows through to the owner of an S corporation is not subject to Social Security tax. Only the wages received by an owner-employee of an S corporation are subject to Social Security tax. An S corporation is required to match the amount contributed by the employee and receives a deduction for the amount paid.

▲ **EXAMPLE 28** Assume the same facts as in example 26, except that the Coffee Bean is an S corporation. Who is responsible for paying the Social Security taxes on the income Yari and Sven receive? Who is allowed a deduction for the Social Security taxes paid?

Discussion: The amount of income that flows through to Yari and Sven is not subject to self-employment tax. Therefore, neither Yari nor Sven pays Social Security tax on his income. The use of an S corporation represents a tax savings of $17,170 ($17,170 − $0) over the partnership form and a savings of $16,619 ($16,619 − $0) over the corporate form.

As the examples in this section illustrate, the use of an S corporation saves a substantial amount in Social Security taxes over other forms of organization. However, caution should be exercised in adopting the no-salary, all-flow-through approach used in example 28. The IRS would probably argue that the salary paid to Yari and Sven is not reasonable (i.e., the amount is too low). Therefore, a conservative yet effective tax-planning technique is to pay each owner-employee a moderate salary commensurate with the work performed.

In deciding whether to operate a business as a partnership, corporation, or S corporation, the employee-owner needs to consider the total tax liability of operating the business. Therefore, the employee-owner must combine the tax on the entity and the employee-owner's individual tax liabilities with the Social Security and self-employment taxes to determine the entity's total tax liability.

▲ **EXAMPLE 29** Return to the facts of example 26. Compare the total tax liability of operating the Coffee Bean as a partnership, corporation, or an S corporation. Assume that Yari and Sven are both single and have other income that exactly offsets their itemized deductions and their personal exemption.

Discussion: The total tax liability of operating the business includes the tax on the entity, the individual tax liability of the employee-owner, and the Social Security and any self-employment tax liability on the entity and the employee-owner.

Partnership:
Because a partnership is a flow-through entity, it pays no tax. In calculating his individual tax liability, each partner can deduct one-half of the self-employment taxes paid. Yari's taxable income is $83,810 ($90,000 − $6,190 from example 26) and Sven's taxable income is $27,880 ($30,000 − $2,120 from example 26). The total tax liability of operating the business is $41,407:

Yari's income tax liability: $14,837.50 + [($83,810 − $65,550) × 31%] =	$20,498
Sven's income tax liability: $4,057.50 + [($27,880 − $27,050) × 28%] =	4,290
Social Security tax (from example 26)	16,619
Total tax liability	$41,407

Corporation:
Because all of the corporation's revenue is paid to Yari and Sven in salary, the corporation has no tax liability. In fact, the corporation has a net operating loss carryforward of $8,585—the amount of Social Security taxes paid by the corporation. Yari and Sven cannot deduct the Social Security taxes they have paid; therefore their taxable income is equal to their salary.

Yari's income tax liability: $14,837.50 + [($90,000 − $65,550) × 31%] =	$22,417
Sven's income tax liability: $4,057.50 + [($30,000 − $27,050) × 28%] =	4,884
Social Security tax (from example 27)	17,170
Total tax liability	$44,471

S Corporation:
Because an S corporation is a flow-through entity, it pays no tax. In addition, because the income that flows through to the individual owners is not subject to self-employment tax, neither the corporation nor the owner-employees pay Social Security taxes. As with the corporate form of organization, the taxable income of the owner-employees is equal to their salary.

Yari's income tax liability: $14,837.50 + [($90,000 − $65,550) × 31%] =	$22,417
Sven's income tax liability: $4,057.50 + [($30,000 − $27,050) × 28%] =	4,884
Social Security tax (from example 28)	-0-
Total tax liability	$27,301

Using an S corporation represents a total tax savings of $14,106 ($41,407 − $27,301) over the partnership form and a savings of $17,170 ($44,471 − $27,301) over the corporate form.

CONCEPT CHECK

<u>CONCEPT CHECK</u> The tax treatment of fringe benefits provided to employees and employee/owners of entities is based on the *legislative grace concept.* With the exception of a sole proprietorship, all entities may deduct certain fringe benefits in arriving at the entities' taxable income. The *entity concept* requires each entity to report the income and deductions applicable to that entity. Because an owner may be an employee in either a corporation or an S corporation, the value of the fringe benefits are generally excluded from the recipient's income. However, partners and more than 2-percent S corporation shareholders are not separate entities and therefore must include the value of fringe benefits in income under the *conduit entity* construct.

Planning Commentary

Even at a basic level, the total tax liability of a particular entity form is the result of a complex interaction between the incidence of taxation and how payments to or on behalf of an owner-employee are treated for tax purposes. The choice of an entity form that minimizes the total tax liability in a given situation may conflict with other objectives of the owner(s). For example, the owner(s) of a business often need the limited liability feature of the corporation. However, the corporate form does not minimize the total tax liability in all cases. Therefore, other options, such as the use of an S corporation, LLC, or LLP, must be considered. Often these alternate forms can give equivalent tax results. In other situations, higher total taxes may have to be paid to achieve the nontax objectives of the owner(s). No two business situations are alike, and all factors, tax and nontax, must be analyzed carefully to determine the best entity form in a given situation.

Generally, the fringe benefits paid to an employee of a corporation are deductible by the corporation and are not taxable income for the employee. This is true even if the employee is an owner of the corporation. However, an individual who is a partner or an employee of an S corporation who owns more than 2 percent of the entity must include the cost of certain fringe benefits as income: employer-provided term life insurance coverage, employer-sponsored accident and health-care plans, cafeteria plans, and meals and lodging furnished for the convenience of the employer. Both a partnership and an S corporation can deduct the cost of the fringe benefits as compensation expenses. The fringe benefits paid to an owner of a sole proprietorship are not deductible. However, 60 percent of the cost of health insurance premiums paid by a sole proprietor, partner, or an owner-employee of an S corporation who holds more than 2 percent of the entity are deductible for AGI on the individual's tax return.

A sole proprietor is subject to self-employment taxes on the net income of the business. Partners are subject to self-employment taxes on their pro rata share of the ordinary income of the partnership. Guaranteed payments received by a partner also are subject to self-employment tax. Because sole proprietors and partners are deemed to be both an employee and an employer for Social Security/self-employment tax purposes, each is responsible for both the employer's share (7.65%) and the employee's share (7.65%) of self-employment taxes. To offset this additional tax liability, sole proprietors and partners are allowed a deduction for adjusted gross income for one-half of the self-employment taxes paid.

An owner-employee of a corporation is responsible for Social Security taxes on only the amount of salary received. Dividends paid to an owner-employee are not subject to Social Security taxes. However, the dividends are subject to double taxation (i.e., at the corporate and individual levels). As a separate taxpaying entity, the corporation is required to match the Social Security tax paid by the owner-employee and receives a deduction for the amount of Social Security tax it pays.

The income from an S corporation that flows through to an owner-employee is not subject to self-employment tax. Only the salary received by an owner-employee is subject to Social Security tax. The S corporation must match the amount of Social Security tax paid by the employee and receives a deduction for the amount of Social Security tax it pays. Therefore, because the income that flows through to an owner-employee of an S corporation is not subject to Social Security tax, the use of this form of organization can significantly reduce an owner-employee's total tax liability.

FORMATION

A number of tax issues arise at the formation of a business entity. In forming the entity, the owner(s) typically contribute cash or other assets in exchange for an ownership interest. The entity incurs costs before it begins operations. Once the entity begins operations, it must select an accounting period and an accounting method. The taxability of transfers of property to an entity and the effects on the bases of the owner and the entity are important factors that can affect the choice of entity. The proper treatment of costs incurred before the business begins operations and the selection of accounting periods and methods are important tax issues that must be resolved at the beginning. This section discusses each of these factors and how they differ for each entity.

Transfers to an Entity

In general, any exchange of property is a taxable event. As described in Chapter 11, when the amount realized from an exchange is greater than the adjusted basis of the property exchanged, a gain is realized on the transaction. Absent legislative grace, realized gains are recognized.

Congress has granted tax deferral status to certain transfers of property in exchange for an ownership interest in a business entity. In general, no gain or loss is recognized when taxpayers contribute property solely in exchange for an ownership interest in a business. The underlying rationale for this treatment is that the transferors are merely exchanging direct ownership of property for indirect ownership through their ownership interest in the entity. This is an application of the substance-over-form doctrine. In addition, even though a gain may be realized on such exchanges, such transfers do not provide the transferors with the wherewithal to pay the tax on the gain. Therefore, the tax treatment of the transfers parallels the tax treatment of like-kind exchanges. Consistent with the taxation of gains on like-kind exchanges, gains on exchanges of property for ownership interests are recognized to the extent that the transferor receives boot in the transaction.

Sole Proprietorship. A sole proprietorship is not an entity that is separate from the owner. Transferring property to a sole proprietorship does not result in a realization because a second party is not involved in the transaction. Therefore, no tax effects arise when an individual contributes property to be used in a sole proprietorship.

Partnership. No gain or loss is recognized when property is contributed to a partnership solely in exchange for a partnership ownership interest.[11] Direct ownership of the property is being replaced by an ownership interest in the property. The tax law permits partners to defer taxes on contributions associated with formation of a partnership and on contributions throughout the life of the entity. Services rendered are not considered property. Services exchanged for a partnership ownership interest do not represent a transformation of the ownership of property from direct to indirect. Under the all-inclusive income concept, the receipt of an ownership interest in exchange for services rendered to a partnership constitutes gross income.

▲ **EXAMPLE 30** Bonita and Chin plan to open a restaurant near the new airport in their community. Bonita owns a parcel of land that she inherited from her uncle when it was worth $100,000. She will contribute the land, now valued at $180,000, cash of $75,000, and her management skills to the business and receive a 90% ownership interest in Bonchin Restaurant. In return for her part of the ownership interest, Bonita will provide services valued at $15,000 while the business is in its developmental stage (e.g., negotiating loans, arranging for suppliers, and hiring employees). Chin will contribute $20,000 in cash and his personal recipe collection with an agreed-upon value of $10,000, and he will be the head chef for the restaurant. He will receive a 10% ownership interest in the restaurant. Both owners will receive $50,000 annually for the services they will contribute to the business operations. Bonita and Chin agree to form a partnership and share business profits and losses in a 90:10 ratio. What are the tax consequences of the transfers to the business in exchange for ownership interests in the partnership?

Discussion: Neither the partners nor the partnership will recognize a gain or loss on the transfer of property solely in exchange for ownership in the restaurant. Both partners will provide services to the business in the future. They will recognize the income received for those services when they receive it. Bonita is to provide $15,000 in services for the entity while it is being organized. The value of those services is income to Bonita in the year rendered.

Corporation. Deferral provisions for contributions of property to a corporation in exchange for ownership interest are more restrictive than for a partnership. The exchange of property must be solely for stock of the corporation, and the shareholder(s) must control the corporation immediately after the transfer.[12] For deferral purposes, the shareholders must own at least 80 percent of the stock to control the corporation. Transfers qualifying for deferral may be made to existing corporations as well as newly created corporations. The shareholder recognizes as income stock received for services rendered to the corporation. Because the S corporation election relates primarily to the incidence of taxation, transfers to S corporations follow the same rules as for contributions of property to corporations.

▲ **EXAMPLE 31** Assume the same facts as in example 30, except that the two owners want to incorporate their business to limit their liability. Bonita will receive 900 shares of stock for her contributions to the business, and Chin will receive 100 shares of stock for his contributions. What are the tax consequences of the exchange?

Discussion: Because Bonita will own at least 80% of the stock of the entity (actually, 90%), she will control the corporation immediately after the exchange of her property for the corporate stock. She recognizes no gain. Bonita will include in her gross income for the year the $15,000 she receives for her services. Chin's exchange also qualifies for deferral because it is concurrent with Bonita's, and he will not recognize any gain on the exchange transaction. All that is necessary to satisfy the control requirement is that the transferor-shareholders together own at least 80% of the stock. NOTE: The same result occurs even if Bonita and Chin make an S corporation election.

Basis Considerations

In forming an entity or purchasing an interest in an entity, the owner(s) obtain a basis for their investment. Basis is established when an investor purchases an ownership interest (e.g., shares of corporate stock or a partnership interest). The cost of the investment is the initial basis amount.[13] When an owner contributes property in exchange for an ownership interest, two assets are created. The owner has a basis in her or his investment, and the entity has a basis in the property it receives. Following the underlying rationale for gain deferral—that in substance, nothing is changed regarding ownership of property—the adjusted basis of the property exchanged is substituted for the basis of the ownership interest received. The entity receiving the property has a basis in the property equal to the owner's adjusted basis. If gain recognition occurs, the basis of the ownership interest and the entity's basis are increased by the gain recognized. The usual result is that both bases are equal to fair market value. An exception occurs when personal use property is contributed to the business entity. In this situation, the split-basis rule for personal property converted to business use applies (see Chapter 9), and the entity's basis in the property is the lower of the fair market value or the adjusted basis as of the contribution date.

Sole Proprietorship. Because the ownership of property contributed to a sole proprietorship does not change hands, the sole proprietor remains the owner of the property. The owner's basis remains unchanged unless the property is personal use property converted to business.

▲ **EXAMPLE 32** Assume that in example 30, Bonita will be the sole owner of the restaurant. The restaurant will purchase Chin's recipes for $10,000, and Chin will lend $20,000 to the business. What is the basis of the property Bonita contributes to the business?

Discussion: Bonita's sole proprietorship will use the land she contributes to the business operation. She still owns the land as an individual because she is not separate from her business, and her ownership interest does not change. The land retains the $100,000 basis established when Bonita inherited it from her uncle. Bonita also obtains a $10,000 basis in the recipe collection she purchases from Chin.

▲ **EXAMPLE 33** Return to example 32, and assume that the land's value at the date it is placed in service of the business is $180,000 and Bonita's basis is $200,000. What is the basis of the land?

Discussion: Because the value of the land is less than Bonita's basis at the date it is converted to business use, the split-basis rules apply. The land is not depreciable. Therefore, basis will not be determined until the land is sold. Bonita's gain basis is her $200,000 basis. Her loss basis is the $180,000 fair market value at the date of conversion to business use.

Partnership. Basis in a conduit entity may be the most critical attribute for owners. Basis establishes the amount of unrecovered investment in the conduit entity. Basis does more than establish the realized gain or loss upon disposition of the investment through application of the capital recovery concept; it also determines the taxability of distributions from the conduit entity to owners. Also, an owner must have an adequate amount of basis before the owner can recognize losses flowing from the conduit entity.

When a partner contributes property in exchange for a partnership interest, the general basis rules apply. The partner's basis in the partnership interest is equal to the basis of the property contributed.[14] The partnership's basis in the property is equal to the contributing partner's basis in the property.[15] When a partnership interest is received in exchange for services, the income recognized by the partner is added to the basis of the partnership interest. The partnership either deducts the cost of the services, if they are for current period expenses, or capitalizes the costs if they have a benefit that extends substantially beyond the end of the tax year (capital expenditure).

▲ **EXAMPLE 34** Recall the original facts from example 30 in which Bonita and Chin agree to form a partnership. Bonita contributes land worth $180,000, cash of $75,000, and services valued at $15,000 for a 90% interest in the partnership. Chin will contribute $20,000 in cash and a recipe collection valued at $10,000 for a 10% interest in the partnership. The land has a basis of $100,000 to Bonita. Both owners will receive $50,000 annually for the services they will contribute toward the business operation. What are Bonita's and Chin's bases in the partnership? What is the partnership's basis in the property contributed by Bonita and Chin.

Discussion: Because the contribution of property was tax-free, Bonita and Chin will have bases in the partnership equal to the basis in the property each contributed. Bonita's basis is $190,000, consisting of her $100,000 basis in the land, the $75,000 in cash she contributed, and the $15,000 in fees received for organizing the partnership. Because she received part of her ownership for organizing the partnership, the income she recognizes becomes part of her ownership basis. Chin's basis is limited to his $20,000 cash contribution. Because he does not have a basis in the recipe collection, there is no basis to transfer to his ownership interest. The partnership has $95,000 in cash, and its basis in the land is equal to Bonita's $100,000 basis. Because Chin had no basis in the recipes, the partnership has a zero basis in the recipes. The partnership must also capitalize the $15,000 Bonita receives for services in organizing the partnership. (See the discussion of organization costs later in this chapter.)

PARTNERSHIP DEBT EFFECTS. Recall that basis begins with a person's contribution of assets or services in exchange for an ownership interest. However, doing business as a partnership adds a unique complexity to basis calculations. Unlike corporate shareholders, partners are liable for the debts of the partnership. Because of this liability feature, **partnership debt** assumed by a partner and the partner's share of partnership debt are deemed to be additional cash contributions to the partnership by the partner.[16] Accordingly, any partnership debt assumed by the partner and the partner's share of partnership liabilities increase the partner's basis. Decreases in debts of a partner or a partnership are deemed cash distributions to partners.[17] Therefore, any partner's debt that is assumed by the partnership and any decreases in the partner's share of partnership liabilities decrease the partner's basis.

▲ **EXAMPLE 35** Assume the same facts as in example 34, except that Bonita's land is encumbered by a $20,000 mortgage that the partnership assumes. What effect does this have on Bonita's and Chin's bases?

Discussion: Bonita adds her $18,000 ($20,000 × 90%) share of mortgage debt to her basis and subtracts the $20,000 in debt relief that she receives when the partnership assumes the mortgage on her land. Chin adds his $2,000 ($20,000 × 10%) share of the mortgage debt to his basis. Bonita's basis is $188,000, and Chin's basis is $22,000:

	Bonita	Chin
Basis of property or cash contributed	$190,000	$20,000
Plus: Debt assumed by partnership		
Mortgage loan	18,000	2,000
Less: Debt relief	(20,000)	
Basis of ownership interest	$188,000	$22,000

RECOURSE AND NONRECOURSE LOANS. Chapter 7 introduced the at-risk potential of loans. A **recourse debt** is a loan for which the debtor remains liable until repayment occurs. If the borrower defaults on repayment, the creditor has recourse; the creditor may obtain a judgment against the borrower, who must personally make up the amount of default. Because partners are liable for the liabilities of the partnership, individual partners have a potential risk of loss from partnership debts. Accordingly, partners are permitted to increase the basis of their partnership interest by their share of the potential loss from partnership debts. Partnership debt created before January 30, 1989, is allocated to partners by using the loss-sharing percentage.[18] Partnership debt created after January 29, 1989, is allocated by using what is called the economic risk of loss scenario.[19] The basic thrust of this approach is to determine the cash contribution each partner would have to make to pay off partnership liabilities if all the partnership assets became worthless. This can result in partners' allocations of liabilities in ratios different than their loss-sharing ratios. The rules for this approach are very complex and beyond the scope of this text. However, in many instances, the application of these rules provides results similar to those obtained by using the old liability-sharing rules. Therefore, to make it easier to understand adjustments to bases that are made for partnership debts, in our examples, we use the approach for debts created before January 30, 1989.

▲ **EXAMPLE 36** Return to example 34, and assume that Bonita and Chin agree to share profits and losses differently. Bonita will have a 90% interest in entity profits and an 80% interest in entity losses. Chin's ownership interests are 10% in profits and 20% in losses. The partnership obtains a loan to use for operating expenses. The loan is a $50,000, 3-year, 10% recourse loan with only the interest payable until maturity. What are the partners' bases in their ownership interests?

Discussion: Bonita and Chin will add their respective shares of the loan to the bases they receive for their contributions of cash and other property. Because the loan is a recourse loan, the loss-sharing percentage is used to determine each partner's share of the debt. Bonita's basis is increased to $230,000 by her $40,000 ($50,000 × 80%) share of the partnership debt. Chin's $10,000 ($50,000 × 20%) share of the debt increases his basis to $30,000.

	Bonita	Chin
Basis of property or cash contributed	$190,000	$20,000
Plus: Recourse debt assumed by partnership		
80%	40,000	
20%		10,000
Basis of ownership interest	$230,000	$30,000

A **nonrecourse debt** is a liability that is secured only by the underlying property; the borrower is not personally liable for the debt. In the case of a loan default, the creditor has no recourse against the borrower for liability amounts greater than the value of the property that secures the debt instrument. Nonrecourse debts are common when financing real estate and the creditor expects the property to increase in value. Borrowers repay nonrecourse loans from entity profits, and the property securing the loans aids in earning these profits. Therefore, partnerships with nonrecourse liabilities have the risk of losing profits if the property is lost in a loan default judgment. Accordingly, partners are allowed to increase the bases of their partnership interests by their share of nonrecourse partnership debt. As with recourse debt, the rules for allocating nonrecourse debt created before January 30, 1989, are straightforward: Nonrecourse debt is allocated by using the partners' profit-sharing percentages.[20] Nonrecourse debt created after January 29, 1989, also uses a complex set of rules to determine each partner's share of the debt; discussion of those rules is beyond the scope of this text.[21] As with the new rules for recourse debt, applying the new rules for nonrecourse debts often provides results similar to the old rules, and we use the rules for nonrecourse debt created before January 30, 1989, to illustrate the adjustments made to partners' bases for nonrecourse debt.

▲ **EXAMPLE 37** Assume the same facts as in example 36. To construct the restaurant building, the partnership obtains a $200,000, 15-year nonrecourse mortgage loan. How does the loan affect the partners' bases?

Discussion: Bonita and Chin will add their respective shares of the loan liability to their bases. Because the loan is nonrecourse, the profit-sharing percentage is used to determine each partner's share of the debt. Bonita adds $180,000 ($200,000 × 90%) to her basis, and Chin adds $20,000 ($200,000 × 10%) to his basis. Bonita's basis is $410,000, and Chin's basis is $50,000:

	Bonita	Chin
Basis of property or cash contributed	$190,000	$20,000
Plus: Debt assumed by partnership		
Operating loan	40,000	10,000
Mortgage loan	180,000	20,000
Basis of ownership interest	$410,000	$50,000

Note that the overall effect of a partnership's incurring debt is to increase the partners' basis in the partnership. When partnership operating losses flow through to the partners, the partners cannot deduct losses in excess of their bases. The increase in basis for debt of the partnership makes the partnership a desirable entity form for business ventures that finance their operations with substantial amounts of debt, thus allowing greater loss deductions by the partners.

Corporation. When shareholders contribute property solely in exchange for stock in a tax-free transaction, the shareholders' bases in the property become their bases in the stock received.[22] The corporation uses the shareholders' bases in the property as its basis in the property.[23] As discussed earlier, receipt of stock for services constitutes income to a shareholder. The income recognized from such services is added to the shareholder's basis. The corporation either expenses the cost of the services or capitalizes the cost, depending on the life of the asset created by the services.

▲ **EXAMPLE 38** Return to example 31. Recall that Bonita and Chin wish to incorporate the business and contribute property in exchange for stock. What is the basis of the corporate stock in the hands of shareholders, and what is the basis of the property for the corporation?

Discussion: Because the exchange of property for stock does not result in gain or loss recognition, Bonita's basis is $190,000 ($100,000 land basis + $75,000 cash + $15,000 for services) for her 900 shares of stock. Chin's basis is $20,000 ($20,000 cash + zero basis for the recipes) for his 100 shares of stock. The corporation has land with a basis of $100,000; the services provided by Bonita are capitalized at their $15,000 cost; and the recipes have a zero basis.

Consistent with the wherewithal-to-pay concept and parallel to the treatment of like-kind exchanges, if the shareholder receives boot in a property-for-stock transaction, any gain realized on the exchange is recognized to the extent of the boot received. In recognizing gains on transfers of property to a corporation, a liability of the shareholder assumed by the corporation is not considered boot, and the shareholder is not taxed on the liability assumption.[24] To avoid double taxation of any gains recognized, the shareholder and the corporation increase their bases by the amount of gain recognized by the shareholder. Any liability of the shareholder assumed by the corporation reduces the shareholder's basis.

▲ **EXAMPLE 39** Bonita and Chin incorporate their restaurant business. Assume that Bonita's land is encumbered by a $20,000 mortgage that the corporation assumes. How does the assumption of the $20,000 mortgage on Bonita's land affect the taxability of the transaction and the bases of Bonita and Chin?

Discussion: Because the corporation's assumption of Bonita's $20,000 mortgage is not considered boot received for purposes of the property-for-stock deferral, Bonita does not recognize a gain on the transaction. Since she has received debt relief without income recognition, Bonita must reduce the basis in her stock by the $20,000 mortgage assumption. Bonita's basis is $170,000 ($100,000 + $75,000 + $15,000 − $20,000). The corporation's basis in the land is $100,000, and it has a liability with a basis of $20,000.

Because of the 80-percent control requirement, taxpayers contributing appreciated property to a corporation after formation usually recognize gains.

▲ **EXAMPLE 40** Assume that after several years of operating their business as a corporation, Bonita and Chin decide to expand their restaurant business by adding a delivery service. Reggie will manage the operation of the new service. He owns 3 delivery vans worth $30,000 that have an adjusted basis of $12,000. Reggie exchanges the delivery vans for 100 shares of corporate stock. What are the tax effects of this transaction?

Discussion: Although the transfer is solely in exchange for stock in the corporation, Reggie does not control the corporation immediately after the transfer, and he cannot defer gain on the transaction. Reggie must recognize an $18,000 gain ($30,000 − $12,000) on the exchange. His basis in the stock is $30,000 ($12,000 basis + $18,000 gain recognized). The corporation's basis in the delivery vans is $30,000.

CORPORATION DEBT EFFECTS. Shareholders of corporations do not adjust their basis for increases and decreases in the liabilities of the corporation. A corporation is an entity that is separate from its owners, and therefore it is liable for its debts. Because the shareholders do not have any personal liability for corporate debts, they are not at risk, and a basis adjustment is not necessary.

▲ **EXAMPLE 41** Assume the same facts as in example 39, except that the corporation obtains a loan of $50,000 to use for operating expenses. What is the effect on Bonita and Chin's bases of the corporation's $50,000 loan?

Discussion: Shareholders do not adjust their basis when the corporation borrows money or incurs other liabilities. Bonita and Chin's bases are unaffected by the corporation's $50,000 loan.

As with the requirements for a tax-free exchange of property between a corporation and a shareholder, an S corporation is subject to the same basis rules as a corporation. Even though the incidence of taxation of an S corporation is similar to that of a partnership, S corporation shareholders are not allowed to add debt of the corporation to their basis. This follows from the limited liability feature of the corporation, which is retained by an S corporation.

▲ **EXAMPLE 42** Assume that in example 41, Bonita and Chin make an S corporation election for their business. How will this affect Bonita's and Chin's bases?

Discussion: S corporation shareholders do not adjust their basis when the corporation borrows money or incurs liabilities. Bonita's and Chin's bases are unaffected by the corporation's $50,000 loan.

<u>CONCEPT CHECK</u> The tax law allows tax-free transfers of property solely in exchange for an ownership interest. This is in part because of the *wherewithal-to-pay concept.* The transferor is giving up direct control of assets in exchange for an ownership interest that provides indirect control of the same assets. Economically, the transferor is still in the same position as before the exchange. Further, if the transferor receives something in addition to the ownership interest (e.g., cash), the transferor must recognize gain to the extent of the

CONCEPT CHECK

(continued)
additional amount received. When an entity assumes debt of a transferor, gain or loss is generally not recognized because of the *wherewithal-to-pay concept*. A partner's share of partnership debt increases the partner's basis to reflect the personal exposure to the liability that partners face. Corporate shareholders are not personally liable for the debt, and therefore, their basis in the stock they hold is not increased for debt. The *capital recovery concept* allows the recovery of capital investment before gain is recognized on a disposition. Because partners and S corporation shareholders pay tax on their share of the entity's income, the owners' basis is increased to avoid double taxation of the earnings. Similarly, partnership and S corporation losses and withdrawals from the entity reduce the owner's basis in the partnership interest to prevent a double tax benefit. These adjustments ensure that proper capital recovery is achieved when a partnership or S corporation interest is sold or otherwise disposed of. Because corporations and shareholders are separate entities, adjustments for the income of the corporation and dividends received from the corporation are not made to the shareholders' basis.

Organizational Costs

The business purpose concept allows deduction of the ordinary and necessary expenses of a business. A business cannot expense immediately those business expenditures with a life that extends substantially beyond the end of the tax year. These expenses are capitalized and deducted over their useful or statutory life. A business incurs **start-up costs** (discussed in Chapter 5) before it begins operations. Other costs that pertain to getting the entity ready to operate are referred to as **organizational costs.** Typical organizational costs include

- Legal services relating to drafting organizational documents and agreements
- Accounting services incident to the organization of the business
- Fees paid to the state in which the business is organized
- Expenses of temporary directors or management team

Costs that are incurred before the entity starts its business activities do not have a business purpose and cannot be deducted as operating expenses. Therefore, start-up and organizational costs must be capitalized, and the business can elect to amortize them over at least 60 months, beginning with the month the enterprise begins business operations.[25] If an election to amortize is not made, the entity cannot deduct start-up and/or organizational expenditures until it is liquidated or sold. The treatment of start-up and organizational costs applies to all business entities.

▲ **EXAMPLE 43** Return to example 30. How should the partnership account for the $15,000 interest Bonita receives for management services related to the organization of the partnership? Assume that the partnership begins operation on September 1, 2001.

Discussion: Because the management services are performed before the business begins operations, the partnership must capitalize the $15,000 as an organizational cost. It can elect to amortize the cost over a period of at least 60 months, beginning on September 1, 2001. The maximum 2001 deduction is $1,000 [($15,000 ÷ 60) × 4 months].

Expenses that are not considered organizational expenditures include those for the issue, or sale, of shares of corporate stock (e.g., commissions, printing costs).[26] These are selling expenses and reduce the amount of stockholders equity that results from the sale of the stock.

▲ **EXAMPLE 44** Return to example 31. In addition to the stock issued for Bonita's services in organizing the corporation, the corporation pays $4,200 to attorneys, accountants, and state regulatory agencies to organize the corporation. Commissions and printing costs related to the stock issuance are $200. How should the corporation treat these costs? Assume that the corporation begins business operations on September 1, 2001.

Discussion: The value of the stock Bonita receives for organizing the corporation and the $4,200 paid to organize the corporation must be capitalized. If an election to amortize is made, the maximum 2001 deduction is $1,280 {$1,000 + [($4,200 ÷ 60) × 4 months]}.

The $200 in costs related to the issuance of the stock is not an organizational cost. It is treated as a reduction of stockholders' equity from the issuance of the shares.

Accounting Periods

The annual accounting period concept requires all entities to report the results of operations on an annual basis. The period for which an entity reports is referred to as the **taxable year.** A taxable year may be either a calendar year (ending on December 31) or a fiscal year.[27] A **fiscal year** is defined as

1. A period of 12 months ending on the last day of any month other than December.
2. A 52- to 53-week taxable year. The 52- to 53-week fiscal year ends on the same day of the week each year. The year must end either the last time a particular day occurs during the month (e.g., the last Wednesday in October) or the day that occurs closest to the end of a particular month (e.g., the Friday closest to March 31, even if that Friday happens to be April 2).

An entity establishes a taxable year by keeping its books on the basis of that year and filing its first tax return based on that taxable year.[28] This requires the entity to formally close its books on that date and file a timely tax return for the tax year selected. If the entity does not close its books on that date or if it does not keep formal books, it must use a calendar year. In addition, if the entity closes its books on a date that does not qualify as a fiscal year (e.g., November 15), it must use a calendar year for tax purposes.

Taxpayers are generally free to choose which accounting period they will use as their taxable year. However, the tax law limits the choices for partnerships and S corporations. A sole proprietorship is not an entity separate and apart from its owner and therefore must use the same tax year as its owner. Because of the record-keeping requirement, most individuals (who do not keep formal books for personal income and expenses) use calendar years. Corporations are separate legal and taxable entities and have extensive flexibility in their choice of accounting periods. Without any restrictions on the selection of a taxable year, owners of conduit entities could obtain a tax deferral benefit by having the entity select a taxable year different from that of the owners.

▲ **EXAMPLE 45** Mark, Suzanne, and Tim own Driveway Barbequers. Driveway is organized as a partnership and keeps its books on the basis of a fiscal year ending March 31. The owners, who receive the bulk of their income from the partnership, use a calendar year to report their incomes. What tax benefit will Mark, Tim, and Suzanne receive if the partnership is allowed to report its results to the government using the March 31 fiscal year?

Discussion: If Driveway were allowed to use a March 31 fiscal year, Mark, Suzanne, and Tim would receive a 9-month deferral on the reporting of their income from Driveway. This would happen because income from a conduit entity is deemed to be earned on the last day of the entity's tax year. Because the owners would receive their income from Driveway on March 31, they would not report it on their individual returns until December 31, resulting in a 9-month deferral of income.

Because of this potential deferral, the tax law contains a set of rules that limits the choice of taxable years for partnerships and S corporations.

Partnership. A partnership tax year is selected on a hierarchical basis that attempts to match the tax year of the partnership to those of the partners.[29] First, the partnership must use the tax year used by those partners having a majority interest (more than 50 percent) in partnership profits and capital, called the **majority-interest tax year.**

▲ **EXAMPLE 46** Return to the facts of example 45, and assume that all the partners use calendar years. What taxable year must Driveway use?

Discussion: Because more than 50% of the partnership interests use a calendar year, Driveway must also use a calendar year. The effect of this rule is to have the partnership's taxable year end match the year end of the majority of the partners.

▲ **EXAMPLE 47** Assume that in example 46, Mark owns 60% of Driveway and Suzanne and Tim each own a 20% interest. Mark validly establishes a January 31 fiscal year. What taxable year must Driveway use?

Discussion: Because Mark owns more than 50% of Driveway, Driveway must use the same fiscal year as Mark, January 31. As with example 46, the effect of this rule is to match 60% of the partnership's profits to Mark's taxable year, with only 40% subject to deferral.

If the majority-interest partners do not have the same tax year, the partnership must use the tax year of its principal partners, referred to as the **principal partner tax year.** A principal partner is a partner with at least a 5-percent interest.[30]

▲ **EXAMPLE 48** Assume that in example 46, Driveway Barbequers is operated as a limited partnership with 38 limited partners each owning a 2% interest. The remaining 24% is owned equally by Mark, Suzanne, and Tim, each of whom uses a March 31 fiscal year. The tax years of the 38 limited partners are diverse; there is no majority-interest tax year. What tax year must Driveway use?

Discussion: Because there is no majority-interest tax year, the partnership must use the tax year of the principal partners. In this case, none of the limited partners qualifies as a principal partner because each owns less than 5% of the partnership. Mark, Suzanne, and Tim are the only principal partners. Because the 3 principal partners have the same tax year, the partnership must use that tax year—a fiscal year ending March 31.

When the principal partners do not have the same tax year, the partnership must use the tax year that results in the least aggregate deferral of income for the partners.[31] Because the purpose of the partnership limitations is to effect the least amount of deferral, under this rule, a partnership will always use the tax year of at least one partner. The rules for applying this technique are beyond the scope of this text.

A partnership can use a taxable year other than that prescribed by the hierarchical rules if it can establish to the IRS's satisfaction that a valid business purpose exists for having a different tax year.[32] To establish a **business purpose tax year,** the partnership must obtain permission from the IRS by proving that the year selected does not create for either the partnership or its partners significant deferral of income or shifting of deductions. The type of business purpose tax year granted most frequently is the natural business tax year. The natural business year test (discussed next) also applies to S corporations.

S Corporation. In general, an S corporation must use a calendar year.[33] However, it can choose an alternate year under the ownership tax year or the natural business year exceptions. An **ownership tax year** is the tax year of more than 50 percent of the owners of the corporation.[34] Thus, the ownership tax year is similar in concept to the majority-interest tax year of a partnership.

▲ **EXAMPLE 49** Assume that Mark, Suzanne, and Tim incorporate Driveway Barbequers with Mark owning 45%, Suzanne owning 35%, and Tim owning 20% of the stock. Mark uses a fiscal year that ends July 31. Suzanne and Tim use a fiscal year ending October 31. They make a valid S corporation election. What is the ownership tax year?

Discussion: Suzanne and Tim have the same tax year and own more than 50% of the corporation. Therefore, the ownership tax year is Suzanne and Tim's tax year—the fiscal year ending October 31. Driveway can use either a calendar year or a fiscal year ending October 31.

A **natural business year** is defined as "the annual accounting period encompassing all related income and expenses."[35] To establish a natural business year, an S corporation (or a partnership) must have peak and off-peak business periods. The natural business year is the end of the peak business period. A mechanical test determines a natural business year.[36] Under this test, an annual accounting period qualifies as a natural business year if the gross receipts from sales or services for the final two months of the current year and each of the two preceding years equal or exceed 25 percent of the gross receipts for the entire 12-month period.

▲ **EXAMPLE 50** Assume the same facts as in example 49. Driveway's heaviest sales period occurs during July and August, when demand is greatest for carryout barbecue. Gross sales for July and August and the 12-month period ending on August 31 of the current year and each of the 2 preceding years are as follows:

	July and August	12-Month Period
Current year	$35,000	$125,000
Preceding year 1	31,250	120,000
Preceding year 2	25,000	100,000

Does August 31 qualify as a natural business year under the gross receipts test?

Discussion: To qualify under the gross receipts test, the gross receipts for the last 2 months of the fiscal year (July and August) must equal or exceed 25% of the gross receipts of the current year and the 2 preceding years. Here is the calculation of the gross receipt percentages for the 3 applicable periods:

Current year	$35,000 ÷ $125,000 = 28%
Preceding year 1	$31,250 ÷ $120,000 = 26%
Preceding year 2	$25,000 ÷ $100,000 = 25%

Because the gross receipts for July and August for the current year and the 2 preceding years equal or exceed 25% in each of those years, August 31 qualifies as a natural business year.

Accounting Methods

Taxpayers are required to maintain the accounting records necessary to enable them to file their annual tax returns. To properly characterize income and deduction items, taxpayers must select an accounting method. The three acceptable accounting methods are the cash method, the accrual method, and the hybrid method.

In selecting a method of accounting, taxpayers are required to use for taxable income computation the method of accounting that they regularly use for their books. The method must be used consistently from period to period and must clearly reflect the income of the taxpayer. Once adopted, the taxpayer must use the accounting method consistently from one period to the next.

We have already discussed the general application of the accounting methods and applications of the methods to income and deductions. This section discusses the selection of an accounting method by the various entities. As with accounting periods, entities have a significant degree of latitude in selecting their accounting method. However, certain provisions restrict the choice for certain types of taxpayers. For example, a basic restriction imposed on entities that have inventories of goods is that they must use the accrual method to account for sales and cost of goods sold. This requires entities with inventories to select either the accrual or hybrid method to compute taxable income.

Partnership. A partnership can generally elect to use any accounting method. The election is made at the partnership level and is independent of the method(s) of accounting used by the partners. For example, a partnership electing the accrual method forces its partners to report income of the partnership on the accrual method, even if the partners use the cash method.[37]

A partnership that has at least one corporate partner must use the accrual method. This restriction is an extension of the corporate restriction (discussed next) to prevent using a partnership to defer taxes through use of the cash method.

▲ **EXAMPLE 51** Jackamani Company is organized as a partnership. Jack owns a 20% interest, and Aman owns 60%. IM Corporation owns the remaining 20%. What accounting methods may Jackamani select if Jackamani is in the financial consulting business and does not have inventories?

Discussion: Because a corporation is a partner, Jackamani must use the accrual method of accounting, unless one of the exceptions (discussed next) applies.

Corporation. A corporation is generally required to use the accrual method of accounting.[38] Any method that accounts for some but not all items on the cash basis (i.e., the hybrid method) is considered a cash method. The restriction on the use of the cash method is designed to prevent a corporation from manipulating its cash receipt-and-disbursement policies to obtain a tax advantage.

Corporations and partnerships in which a corporation is a partner may still elect to use the cash method (if they are otherwise eligible to do so) if the average gross receipts for the three previous years are $5 million or less.

▲ **Example 52** Assume the same facts as in example 51, except that Jackamani Company's average sales for the previous 3 years are $3,600,000. What accounting methods may Jackamani select?

Discussion: Because Jackamani's average annual gross receipts for the previous 3 years are less than $5,000,000, Jackamani is exempted from the restriction on accounting methods that applies to a partnership with a corporation as a partner. Therefore, Jackamani can use either the cash method or the accrual method. NOTE: If Jackamani were organized as a corporation, the exception would also apply and Jackamani could use either method.

▲ **EXAMPLE 53** Assume the same facts as in example 52, except that Jackamani is a manufacturer of tack for racehorses.

Discussion: Although Jackamani meets the $5,000,000 average annual gross receipts exception, it must use the accrual method because it has inventories. NOTE: Jackamani also may elect to use the hybrid method and use the accrual method only to account for sales and cost of goods sold.

A second exception allows a corporation or a partnership with a corporate partner that is engaged in farming to use the cash method, regardless of the amount of its gross receipts. However, if the entity is also engaged in a separate nonfarming business, it must account for that portion of its business by using the accrual method, unless the exception for average annual gross receipts applies.

S Corporation. An S corporation is allowed to use either the cash method or the accrual method. No restrictions on the use of the cash method apply to S corporations, other than the general restriction regarding inventories.

▲ **EXAMPLE 54** Return to the facts of example 51. Assume that Jackamani is organized as a corporation and makes an S corporation election. If average annual sales for the last 3 years total $8,000,000, what methods of accounting may Jackamani select?

Discussion: As an S corporation, Jackamani is not subject to the corporate restriction on the use of the cash method. It may elect to use either the cash or accrual method in accounting for its operations.

Planning Commentary

Table 13–2 summarizes the major tax aspects to consider at the formation of a business entity. Although many tax treatments are identical for all entity forms, significant differences do exist. These differences should be considered when choosing an entity. As with the nontax and tax factors discussed earlier, no one factor will drive the choice of entity. All factors must be considered in determining the appropriate entity to use in a given situation.

All entities are allowed tax-free transfers of property solely in exchange for an ownership interest. Whenever an owner provides services or receives boot in the ownership exchange, the owner must recognize income. The corporate deferral provisions require that the transferors control the corporation immediately after the transfer. Thus, it is important that all owners of a new corporate entity make their transfers to the entity simultaneously to meet this requirement. Piecemeal transfers to a corporation may result in taxation of any unrealized gain on the property being transferred.

The most significant difference is the basis treatment of entity liabilities. Partners are allowed to add their share of partnership debt to their basis. This treatment allows a greater deduction of losses to flow from the partnership to the partners. This

▲ **Table 13–2**

TAX FACTORS AT FORMATION OF A BUSINESS ENTITY

Factor	Sole Proprietorship	Partnership	Corporation	S Corporation
Contribution of property to the entity	Not a taxable transaction	Generally, not a taxable transaction	A taxable transaction unless the transferors control the corporation immediately after the transfer	A taxable transaction unless the transferors control the corporation immediately after the transfer
Basis of ownership interest	Adjusted basis of property contributed	Adjusted basis of property contributed plus gain recognized plus share of partnership liabilities minus liabilities assumed by the partnership	Adjusted basis of property contributed plus gain recognized	Adjusted basis of property contributed plus gain recognized
Basis of property contributed to the entity	Adjusted basis of property contributed	Adjusted basis of property contributed plus gain recognized	Adjusted basis of property contributed plus gain recognized	Adjusted basis of property contributed plus gain recognized
Basis treatment of entity liabilities	Not applicable	Included in partners' bases	Cannot be included in shareholders' bases	Cannot be included in shareholders' bases
Start-up and organizational costs	Amortizable over 60 months	Amortizable over 60 months	Amortizable over 60 months	Amortizable over 60 months
Accounting periods	Same tax year as owner's	Restricted to tax year of majority-interest partner, principal partners, least aggregate deferral of partners' income, or natural business year	Unrestricted	Must use a calendar year or ownership tax year unless qualified for a natural business year
Accounting methods	Same accounting method as owner's	Generally unrestricted; cash method not available if a corporation is a partner unless the partnership's average annual gross receipts for last 3 years are $5 million or less, or it is engaged in farming	Restricted to accrual method unless average annual gross receipts for last 3 years are $5 million or less, or it is engaged in farming	Unrestricted

makes a partnership a desirable entity to use in a business that expects large operating losses in the early years of operations. This choice is enhanced when the business also uses large amounts of debt to finance its operations.

Partnerships and S corporations are restricted in their choice of an accounting period. These restrictions are intended to reduce the deferral advantage that can be obtained by a conduit entity that selects a tax year different from that of its owners. Partnerships that have a corporate partner are generally restricted to the accrual method of accounting, as are corporations. S corporations may select any method of accounting.

CONCEPT CHALLENGE

http://murphy.swcollege.com

Reinforce the concepts covered in this chapter by completing the on-line tutorials located at the *Concepts in Federal Taxation* website.

SUMMARY

This chapter introduced the basic factors that must be considered when choosing a business entity. Many factors affect the choice of entity. Nontax factors such as limited liability, transferability of interest, continuity of life, centralized management, and the cost of organizing various entity forms are often more important than the income tax factors in determining the appropriate entity for a given business. Even so, the tax aspects of an entity are an important consideration in choosing a business entity.

Basic income tax factors that affect the choice of business entity are the incidence of taxation (who pays the tax), double taxation of corporate dividends, and the status of an owner as an employee (the deductibility of salaries paid to owner-employees). The owners of sole proprietorships, partnerships, and S corporations pay tax on the income of the entity. A corporation pays tax on its income, and shareholders pay tax on dividends received from a corporation. This allows taxpayers to use a corporation to split income between the corporation and owner-employees but also results in double taxation of dividends. A sole proprietor or a partner cannot be an employee of the business. Owners of corporations and S corporations can be employed by the corporation.

Partnerships and S corporations can deduct the cost of fringe benefits provided to owner-employees or owner-partners. However, the payment of these benefits is treated as compensation to the recipient. Only employer-provided group term life insurance coverage, employer-sponsored accident and health-care plans, cafeteria plans, and meals and lodging furnished for the convenience of the employer are subject to this treatment. Employees of a corporation or an S corporation are required to pay Social Security tax on their compensation. The corporation matches the amount paid by the employee. Partners must pay self-employment tax on their net self-employment income. A guaranteed payment from a partnership is also treated as self-employment income. The net income from a sole proprietorship is subject to self-employment tax. Both a partner and a sole proprietor can deduct one-half of the self-employment taxes paid as a deduction for adjusted gross income. Unlike a partnership, the income that flows through to the individual owner of an S corporation is not subject to self-employment tax.

Several tax issues arise at the formation of an entity. The transfer of property in exchange for an ownership interest is generally nontaxable, although the requirements for a tax-free transfer to a corporation (and S corporation) are more restrictive than those for a partnership. When property is transferred to an entity in a nontaxable transaction, the owner and the entity receiving the property receive a basis equal to the adjusted basis of the property transferred. Because partners are liable for debts of a partnership, they are allowed to add their proportionate share of any partnership debt to their basis in the partnership.

All entities must capitalize and amortize start-up and organizational costs. At formation, an entity must select an accounting period and an accounting method.

Partnerships and S corporations face restrictions on the selection of their annual accounting period. Corporations and partnerships with a corporation as a partner generally cannot use the cash method of accounting.

Key Terms

business purpose tax year (p. 580)
centralized management (p. 552)
continuity of life (p. 552)
corporation (p. 555)
double taxation (p. 563)
fiscal year (p. 579)
guaranteed payment (p. 564)
incidence of taxation (p. 559)
limited liability (p. 552)
limited liability company (LLC) (p. 557)
limited liability partnership (LLP) (p. 557)
limited partnership (p. 554)
majority-interest tax year (p. 579)
natural business year (p. 580)
nonrecourse debt (p. 575)
organizational costs (p. 578)
ownership tax year (p. 580)
partnership (p. 554)
partnership debt (p. 574)
personal service corporation (PSC) (p. 562)
principal partner tax year (p. 580)
recourse debt (p. 575)
S corporation (p. 555)
self-employment tax (p. 568)
sole proprietorship (p. 553)
start-up costs (p. 578)
taxable year (p. 579)
transferability of ownership interest (p. 552)

Primary Tax Law Sources

[1] Sec. 1362—Discusses the rules for election, disqualification, and revocation of S status.

[2] Sec. 1361—Provides the qualifying characteristics of corporations making the S election.

[3] Reg. Sec. 1.1372-5—Provides the circumstances under which an S corporation may retain that status without a five-year wait once that election is terminated.

[4] Reg. Sec. 301.7701-2—Lists the characteristics that are determinative in defining whether an entity is considered a corporation for tax purposes.

[5] Reg. Sec. 301.7701-1—Permits most noncorporate entities to elect whether to be treated as a corporation or a partnership for federal income tax purposes.

[6] Sec. 1—Imposes income tax on all individuals and other noncorporate entities; provides the tax rate schedules for noncorporate taxpayers.

[7] Sec. 701—States that a partnership is not subject to income tax and that partners are liable for taxes only on their individual shares.

[8] Sec. 11—Imposes income tax on corporate entities and provides the tax rates.

[9] Reg. Sec. 1.448-1T—Describes the criteria that establish a personal service corporation.

[10] Sec. 1363—Explains that S corporations are not subject to income tax and states that the S corporation computes its taxable income in a manner similar to that used by an individual taxpayer, except for the items that are subject to separate statement.

[11] Sec. 721—States that no gain or loss is recognized by the contributing partner or by the partnership upon the contribution of property to a partnership solely in exchange for a partnership interest.

[12] Sec. 351—States that no gain or loss is recognized on the transfer of property to a corporation solely in exchange for stock of the corporation if the transferees control the corporation immediately after the exchange.

[13] Sec. 1012—Defines basis of property: The general rule for the initial basis of a property is its cost.

[14] Sec. 722—States that partners' basis in their partnership interest is the adjusted bases of the property contributed to attain the partnership interest.

[15] Sec. 723—States that the basis of property contributed to a partnership by a partner is the adjusted basis of the property at the time of the contribution.

[16] Sec. 752—Describes the effect of partnership debt on a partner's basis.

[17] Reg. Sec. 1.752-1—Details how liabilities affect the basis of a partner's interest in a partnership.

[18] Reg. Sec. 1.752-1(e) before removal by TD 8237, 12/29/88—Partnership recourse debts incurred before January 30, 1989, are allocated among the partners according to the partners' loss-sharing percentages.

[19] Reg. Sec. 1.752-2—Describes the allocation to partners of partnership recourse debt incurred after January 29, 1989.

[20] Reg. Sec. 1.752-1(e) before removal by TD 8237, 12/29/88—Nonrecourse debt of a partnership incurred before January 30, 1989, is allocated among the partners according to the partners' profit-sharing percentages.

[21] Reg. Sec. 1.752-3—Provides the procedure for allocating to the partners any partnership nonrecourse debt incurred after January 29, 1989.

[22] Sec. 358(a)—States that the basis of a shareholder in stock received in exchange for property in a nontaxable exchange is equal to the basis of the property given in the exchange.

[23] Sec. 362(a)—States that the basis of property received by a corporation for stock of the corporation in a nontaxable exchange is equal to the transferor's basis in the property.

[24] Sec. 357(a)—Provides that liabilities of a shareholder assumed by a corporation in a nontaxable exchange of stock for property are not treated as boot received by the shareholder.

[25] Sec. 248—Permits the amortization and deduction of organizational expenses over a period of not less than 60 months at the election of the corporation.

[26] Reg. Sec. 1.248-1—Gives examples of items that are considered organizational expenditures and examples of items that are not considered organizational expenditures.

[27] Sec. 441—Allows taxpayers to use either a calendar year or a fiscal year to compute taxable income. Defines *fiscal year.*

[28] Reg. Sec. 1.441-1T—Explains how to establish a tax year.

[29] Sec. 706—Provides the rules for selecting a partnership tax year.

[30] Reg. Sec. 1.706-1—Defines a principal partner for purposes of selecting a partnership tax year and illustrates the *principal partner tax year.*

[31] Reg. Sec. 1.706-1T—Explains the computation of the *least aggregate deferral tax year* for a partnership.

[32] Rev. Rul. 87-57—Explains the factors necessary for a partnership to establish a business purpose tax year.

[33] Sec. 1378—Defines the tax years that an S corporation can use.

[34] Rev. Proc. 87-32—Explains the ownership tax year test and how to adopt an ownership tax year.

[35] Reg. Sec. 1.706-1—Defines *natural business year.*

[36] Rev. Proc. 87-32—Provides examples of the test for a natural business year.

[37] Sec. 703—States that elections related to the computation and reporting of partnership items are made at the partnership level and not by the individual partners.

[38] Sec. 448—Disallows the use of the cash method of accounting by corporations and partnerships in which a corporation is a partner. Provides exceptions for corporations and partnerships with a corporate partner with average annual gross receipts of $5 million or less for the last three years and for corporations and partnerships with a corporate partner engaged in farming activities.

Discussion Questions

1. What are the primary nontax factors to consider when choosing a form for doing business?

2. Compare and contrast the characteristics of sole proprietorships, partnerships, corporations, S corporations, limited liability companies, and limited liability partnerships.

3. Discuss the comparative advantages and disadvantages of general partnerships and limited partnerships.

4. Limiting the liability of the owner(s) of a business is often the primary motive for using the corporate form. Under what circumstances may the use of a corporation not shield the owner(s) from all liabilities of the business?

5. What are the nontax differences between a corporation and an S corporation?

6. What are the requirements to qualify for the S corporation election?

7. How is a limited liability company different from a corporation?

8. How is a limited liability partnership different from a partnership?

9. Compare the incidence of taxation for each of the following entities:

a. Sole proprietorship
b. Partnership
c. Corporation
d. S corporation

10. What are the tax differences between a corporation and a personal service corporation?

11. Armand is an owner of Content Company. During the current year, he receives a $15,000 cash distribution from Content. What is the tax effect of the receipt of the $15,000 if Content is organized as
    a. A partnership?
    b. A limited liability company?
    c. A corporation?
    d. An S corporation?
12. Which entity(ies) is/are subject to double taxation?
13. Why is it important for an owner to also be classified as an employee of the business for tax purposes?
14. Which entity form(s) recognize owners as employees of the business?
15. What is the tax treatment for a guaranteed payment?
16. Compare the tax treatment of fringe benefits provided to an owner of a corporation with the treatment of fringe benefits provided to an owner of
    a. A sole proprietorship
    b. A partnership
    c. An S corporation
17. Is all compensation that is paid to an employee deductible? Discuss the circumstances in which employee compensation cannot be deducted.
18. What is the tax treatment of health insurance premiums paid on behalf of
    a. A sole proprietor?
    b. A partner?
    c. An owner-employee of a corporation?
    d. An owner-employee of an S corporation?
19. What is the rationale for not taxing transfers of property in exchange for an ownership interest?
20. What are the tax consequences of receiving an ownership interest in an entity in exchange for services rendered to the entity?
21. Compare the requirements for a tax-free exchange of property for an ownership interest in a partnership with the requirements for a corporation.
22. Discuss the basis of an ownership interest received in exchange for property and the basis of the property received in exchange for an ownership interest in the hands of the entity.
23. How do liabilities affect the basis of a partner's interest in a partnership?
24. Explain the difference between a recourse debt and a nonrecourse debt.
25. Why are partners allowed to add their share of partnership debts to their bases?
26. What is the tax effect of a corporation's assuming the debt of a shareholder on property that is exchanged for an ownership interest in the corporation?
27. Why might a shareholder recognize a gain on an exchange of property for an ownership interest when a partner making the same exchange with a partnership would not recognize a gain?
28. How do S corporation liabilities affect the basis of an S corporation shareholder's stock?
29. Which of the following are organizational costs?
    a. State fees for incorporation
    b. Legal and accounting fees incident to organization
    c. Expenses for the sale of stock
    d. Organizational meeting expenses
30. What is the difference between a calendar year and a fiscal year?
31. Why are restrictions placed on the selection of a tax year by partnerships and S corporations?
32. Which types of tax entities generally cannot elect to use the cash method of accounting?

PROBLEMS

COMMUNICATION

33. Herman, who is unmarried and has 2 dependent children, owns and operates a used car lot as a sole proprietorship. The net income from the business is consistently $120,000 annually. Herman's friends have told him that he should incorporate his business, but he does not understand how this would give him any advantage. He has come to you for advice. Write Herman a letter explaining the advantages and disadvantages of incorporating his business.

34. Lydia and Paulo agree to become equal owners in a pizza delivery business. Lydia will manage the delivery side of the business, and Paulo will be in charge of kitchen operations. They will borrow most of the money they need to get the business started. Considering only the nontax factors associated with the business, what business entity(ies) would be appropriate for the new business? Discuss the positive and negative factors of each business entity that would be appropriate.

35. Rollo and Andrea are equal owners of Gosney Company. During the current year, Gosney's taxable income before considering salaries paid to Andrea and Rollo is $140,000. Rollo is single, his salary is $30,000, and he has net taxable income of $20,000 from other sources. Andrea is also single, her salary is $40,000, and she has net taxable income of $30,000 from other sources. What is the total income tax liability if Gosney is organized as
    a. A partnership?
    b. A corporation?
    c. An S corporation?

36. Return to the facts of problem 33. Compare the total income tax liability of Herman's incorporating his business versus operating it as a sole proprietorship. Assume that he is paid a $60,000 salary and has income from other sources that is $14,000 more than his allowable deductions.

37. Polly owns CopyEdit, a sole proprietorship. The net income from CopyEdit is consistently around $200,000. Polly is considering making Kevin, one of her employees, an owner of the business. He would continue to be paid his $40,000 salary and own a 25% interest in the business. Polly would receive a salary of $100,000 from the new entity. She has asked you to determine the total income tax liability for each of the entities listed below. Assume that both Polly and Kevin have income from other sources that offset their allowable deductions, and that they are both single.
    a. Partnership
    b. Corporation
    c. S corporation

COMMUNICATION

38. Return to the facts of problem 37. Upon giving your tax calculation results to Polly, you learn that CopyEdit's primary business is the provision of copyediting services to corporate clients. Polly and Kevin perform all the work. Write a letter to Polly explaining the effect of this information on the calculations you performed in problem 37.

39. Kelly, Gwen, and Tuoi incorporated their accounting business and own all its outstanding stock. During the current year, the corporation's taxable income is $300,000 after deducting salaries of $60,000 for each shareholder-employee. Assume all three owners are single and that each of them has other income that offsets their allowable deductions.
    a. What is the corporate income tax liability?
    b. What could the shareholders do to lower the corporate income tax liability in the future?

40. Drew is the sole owner of Morris, Inc., a corporation. Morris's net income for the current year is $150,000 before considering Drew's $85,000 salary. Assume Drew is single and has income from other sources that is $30,000 more than his allowable deductions. What is the total income tax liability if Morris is
    a. A corporation?
    b. An S corporation?

41. Return to the facts of problem 40. Assume that late in the year, Drew needs extra cash to pay off gambling debts and has the corporation declare a $25,000 dividend to provide the cash. What is the effect of the dividend payment on the total income tax liability if Morris is
    a. A corporation?
    b. An S corporation?

42. In January of the current year, Josh purchases all the stock of Ballpark Corporation for $100,000. Ballpark's taxable income for the current year is $200,000, and it pays $61,250 in income tax. None of the earnings is distributed as dividends. Josh believes that if he sells his stock two years later for $238,750, he will avoid double taxation. Write a memo to Josh explaining why he is not avoiding double taxation just because he receives no dividends.

43. Antonio and Michaela are equal partners in A&M Booking Services. Antonio manages the business and receives $40,000 per year for his management services. He and Michaela each withdraw $30,000 in cash during the current year. A&M's ordinary income is $80,000 before considering any payments to the partners. How much income do Michaela and Antonio have from A&M during the current year?

44. Estel and Raymond own the GoalLine Partnership. Estel owns 70% of the business. She provided the capital for it and consults with Raymond on overall business strategy. Raymond is responsible for the daily operation of the business and owns the remaining 30%. The business consistently produces net income of $200,000 per year. Each year, Estel withdraws $30,000 from the partnership and Raymond withdraws $70,000. Although Estel believes that Raymond is entitled to receive more cash each year because of his daily involvement in the business, she is concerned that she is taxed on 70% of the income. Estel has come to your firm for advice on how to improve their situation. Leonard, your supervisor, has assigned you the task of coming up with a strategy that will result in Estel's having less income from GoalLine. Write Leonard a memorandum explaining a strategy that GoalLine can use to reduce the income taxed to Estel without altering the current profit-sharing ratio.

45. Artis owns 40% of the Rhode Island Chile Parlor (RICP). During the current year, Rhode Island gives Artis fringe benefits worth $4,000 in addition to his $30,000 salary. RICP's net taxable income before considering the payments to Artis is $160,000. Assume Artis is single and has income from other sources that offsets his allowable deductions. What are Artis's taxable income and income tax liability if RICP is organized as

a. A partnership, and the salary is a guaranteed payment?
b. A partnership, and the salary is not a guaranteed payment?
c. A corporation?
d. An S corporation?

46. Enterprise Business Systems pays the $5,000 health and accident insurance policy of its owner, Gena. The business's net operating income for the year is $60,000 before considering Gena's benefit. Determine the business's net income for the year and the tax effects for Gena for each of the following entities:

a. A sole proprietorship
b. A partnership
c. A corporation
d. An S corporation

47. Colleen, Rosemary, and Suzanne own a software development firm. Colleen owns 45% of the business, Rosemary 30%, and Suzanne 25%. The net operating income from the business is $220,000. Assume Suzanne is paid a salary of $45,000. For each of the following situations, determine who is responsible for paying the Social Security and self-employment taxes on the income from the business and who is allowed a deduction for the Social Security and self-employment taxes paid:

a. The business is formed as a partnership. Suzanne's salary is not a guaranteed payment.
b. The business is formed as a corporation.
c. The business is formed as an S corporation.

48. Natalie operates her bookkeeping service as a corporation. She is the sole shareholder and is an employee functioning as the chief operating officer. The corporation employs several other individuals and offers them good fringe benefits: group term life insurance, health insurance, disability insurance, and a 12% qualified pension plan. Natalie's good friend, Ricci, operates a custom software development company. The business is an S corporation, and Ricci is the sole shareholder. She is also an employee who serves as the manager. Upon Natalie's recommendation, Ricci copies the fringe benefit package of Natalie's corporation. Assume both businesses are quite profitable.

a. How do the employee benefits affect the tax bills of Natalie and her corporation?
b. How do the employee benefits affect the tax bills of Ricci and her corporation?
c. Write letters to both Natalie and Ricci explaining these tax ramifications.

49. Billy Bob is employed by Pony Ranch Corporation and owns 1% of the corporation's stock. The corporation provides excludable meals and lodging for Billy Bob at a cost of $12,000 annually.

a. Can Pony Ranch Corporation deduct the costs of the meals and lodging provided to Billy Bob?

b. How are the meals and lodging treated for tax purposes if Pony Ranch is an S corporation?

c. Assume the same facts as in part b, except that Billy Bob owns 5% of Pony Ranch Corporation.

50. Miko and Mona form M&M Beverages in the current year. Miko contributes $20,000 in cash and delivery trucks worth $70,000 for 30% interest. Miko's basis in the delivery trucks is $80,000. Mona contributes $30,000 and land worth $130,000 (basis = $100,000) and provides services in organizing the business worth $20,000 in exchange for her 70% interest. What are the tax effects of the transfers and the bases of the owners and the entity if M&M is organized as

a. A partnership?

b. A corporation?

c. An S corporation?

51. John and Katerina form JK Enterprises in the current year. John contributes $200,000 in cash for a 40% interest. Katerina contributes real estate valued at $480,000 and encumbered by a mortgage of $180,000 that is assumed by the business. Katerina's basis in the real estate is $100,000. She receives a 60% interest in the business. What is each owner's basis in his or her interest and the entity's basis in the assets acquired if JK Enterprises is organized as

a. A partnership?

b. A corporation?

c. An S corporation?

52. Emmon and Darcy are equal owners of Golf Instruction Academy (GIF). The business has been profitable, and they would like to expand their operations. Tiger owns Power Golf. Emmon and Darcy will make Tiger an equal owner of GIF (i.e., each will have a 1/3 interest) in exchange for Tiger's business assets. Tiger's business assets are worth $100,000 and have an adjusted basis of $70,000. What are the tax effects of Tiger's exchange of assets for the ownership interest if GIF is organized as

a. A partnership?

b. A corporation?

53. Toby exchanges property worth $80,000 (basis of $55,000) for a 20% interest in Landscape Developers. What are the tax effects of the exchange if Landscape is organized as

a. A partnership?

b. A corporation?

c. An S corporation?

54. Return to the facts of problem 53. Assume that the property Toby contributes is encumbered by a $20,000 mortgage that is assumed by Landscape Developers. How does this affect the tax results for each of the entity forms?

55. Myron, Al, and Janda make the following transfers from their sole proprietorships to a newly formed business, each receiving a 1/3 ownership interest.

Owner	Asset Transfers	Basis of Property Transferred	Fair Market Value of Property/Services Transferred	Liabilities Assumed by Business
Myron	Building	$60,000	$110,000	$30,000
Al	Equipment	90,000	80,000	-0-
Janda	Vehicles	30,000	60,000	10,000
	Legal services		30,000	

In addition, the business borrows $60,000 from a local bank for working capital. The loan is a nonrecourse debt. Determine the gain or loss the owners must recognize from the transfers and their basis in the ownership interest received under the assumptions set forth here. Also, determine any gain or loss recognized by the business entity from the transfers and its basis in the property received:

a. The business is organized as a partnership.
b. The business is organized as a corporation.
c. The business is organized as an S corporation.

56. Big C Corporation, a calendar-year corporation, is formed during the current year and begins business operations on September 1. Big C pays $8,000 to attorneys, accountants, and state regulatory agencies to organize the corporation. Big C also pays $6,000 in commissions on the sale of corporate stock. Write a letter to Big C Corporation's controller explaining how much of the $14,000 expenditure is deductible.

COMMUNICATION

57. Shree is considering opening a travel agency. She spends $20,000 investigating the profitability of the business and potential locations and $5,000 for legal and other fees incident to the organization of the business. Although the costs are high, Shree believes that she will recover them quickly. What is the proper treatment of the costs? Will the treatment be different if she organizes the business as a sole proprietorship or a corporation?

58. What tax year must each of the following taxpayers use? Explain.

a. Brayanth works for Gippsland Corporation. His income for the year includes salary, interest, dividend income, and a long-term capital gain. Although he itemizes his deductions, he keeps no formal books or records, relying instead on his wage statement, canceled checks, and other formal documents furnished to him for preparing his tax return.
b. Assume the same facts as in part a, except that Brayanth is self-employed as a plumber and keeps meticulous books and records.
c. Cindy and Derek are partners in a pet shop. Cindy owns 55%, and Derek owns 45%. Cindy reports her income using a July 31 fiscal year, whereas Derek uses a calendar year.
d. Syme, Inc., is an S corporation wholly owned by Jeremiah. He uses a calendar year to report his income.
e. Assume the same facts as in part d, except that Syme, Inc., is a corporation.

59. Determine the tax year(s) each of the following S corporations must use. Explain.

a. Will, Dan, and Tom are equal owners of Rheen Corporation, and each has a different fiscal year. Will has a fiscal year that ends April 30, Dan's ends May 31, and Tom's ends November 30.
b. Assume the same facts as in part a, except that Tom and Dan each own a 20% interest in Rheen and Will owns the remaining 60%.
c. Assume the same facts as in part b. Rheen's business is seasonal; the heaviest revenue months are July and August. Revenues for 3 years are as follows:

	July and August	12-Month Period
Current year	$90,000	$300,000
1st preceding year	80,000	260,000
2nd preceding year	60,000	230,000

60. Which accounting method must each of the following taxpayers use?

a. Fax, Inc., is an S corporation wholly owned by Helena. She uses a calendar year to report her income.
b. Assume the same facts as in part a, except that Fax, Inc., is a corporation. Its annual revenues have never exceeded $1,000,000.
c. Assume the same facts as in part b, except that Fax's annual revenues usually are between $7,000,000 and $8,000,000.
d. Spoke and Pedal Cyclery is organized as a partnership. It is owned by John and Gloria as equal partners.

COMMUNICATION

61. Kim and Brendan, who are longtime friends, have decided to buy a golf equipment store and go into business together as equal partners. Kim reports his income by calendar year, and Brendan uses a fiscal year that ends September 30. One attraction of owning the golf equipment store is that the business is seasonal and will let them take long vacations. The peak revenue months are June and July. The owner gives them the following information:

	June and July	12-Month Period
Current year	$200,000	$500,000
1st preceding year	280,000	700,000
2nd preceding year	325,000	850,000

Write a memo to Kim and Brendan discussing each alternative below:

a. If Kim and Brendan form a corporation, what options, if any, do they have in choosing their tax year and method of accounting?

b. If Kim and Brendan form a partnership, what options, if any, do they have in choosing their tax year and method of accounting?

c. If Kim and Brendan form an S corporation, what options, if any, do they have in choosing their tax year and method of accounting?

Issue Identification Problems

In each of the following problems, identify the tax issue(s) posed by the facts presented. Determine the possible tax consequences of each issue that you identify.

62. A former clergyman with a degree in counseling decides to go into business for himself. He contracts with four large corporations to provide alcohol, drug, and psychological analysis for their employees. The contracts require him to be available on a weekly basis to see employees who need help. He also contracts with other organizations to provide therapy for patients in hospitals and members of churches and other non-profit organizations. He anticipates that he will need two offices and will need to hire staff to help with phone calls, appointments, and other administrative functions.

63. Raquel is an employee of Jones Company and owns a 30% interest in the company. Her salary is $44,000. She also receives a $10,000 cash distribution from Jones. During the current year, Jones' operating income is $130,000.

64. Rolf owns 20% of Chaminade Corporation. During the current year, Chaminade reports operating income of $240,000 and pays $60,000 in cash dividends.

65. Miriam is a self-employed computer consultant. Her business nets $120,000 annually, and she takes $85,000 of the earnings in salary. Miriam is considering incorporating her computer consulting business.

66. Robbie is the vice president of Mailer Corporation. He owns 40% of Mailer, which is organized as an S corporation. Robbie's salary is $75,000, and he receives group-term life insurance and health and accident insurance that costs $3,000. Mailer's operating income without considering any payments or benefits that Robbie receives is $180,000.

67. Rikki and Rhonda are equal owners of LilMark Corporation. To expand their operations, Marsha will contribute a building worth $80,000 for which she will receive a one-third ownership interest in the corporation. Marsha's basis in the building is $30,000.

68. Ben and Pete form a corporation to run a real estate investment management company. Ben contributes cash of $40,000 to the corporation in exchange for 50% of its stock. Pete obtains his 50% ownership interest by contributing land with a fair market value of $40,000 and a basis of $60,000. The land has the potential to be more valuable to the business in the future. Ben is aware of the nonrecognition rules for contributions to corporations and wants to use the corporate form. Pete realizes that if he contributes the land, he will not be able to recognize the unrealized loss.

69. Ariel and Mia agree to combine their business assets to form the A&M corporation. Ariel's business assets are worth $135,000 and have a basis of $80,000. Mia's business assets are worth $200,000, have a basis of $165,000, and are encumbered by a $90,000 mortgage, which A&M will assume. Mia will also contribute $25,000 in cash to equalize their contributions.

Technology Applications

70. **INTERNET ASSIGNMENT** The IRS has established procedures to simplify taxpayers' choice of entity for tax purposes. The procedures are referred to as the "check-the-box" regulations. Use the Internet to find articles or discussions about these new rules and how they are applied. Trace the steps you use in locating such sources (search engine, tax directory, or website, etc.). Write a summary of the information you find, including the URL of the World Wide Web site that contains the information you use for your summary.

71. **INTERNET ASSIGNMENT** Recently, there has been a lot of discussion about what is commonly referred to as "corporate tax shelters" as a means of corporations' avoiding paying income tax. Discussions in Congress may lead to legislation aimed at closing corporate "loopholes" in the tax system. Using the Internet, locate articles and discussions regarding this issue. Trace the steps you use in locating such sources (search engines, tax directory, or website, etc.). Write a summary of the information you find and specifically identify the issues you find associated with "corporate tax shelters."

72. **RESEARCH PROBLEM** Ruiz and his two brothers founded a social club called the Last Snake Inn in 1983. They want to take advantage of a new state law that lets them serve beer, liquor, and wine to their patrons on Sundays. To do so, the club must obtain a special liquor license that is required of all retail businesses wishing to serve alcohol on Sundays. Ruiz and his brothers want to incorporate the club specifically to acquire the special license. The club will continue to be operated by the three brothers as before, with each paying for supplies and other materials as needed out of his own pocket. The three brothers will serve as the corporation's officers. Ruiz is designated as the president. He has learned that to form a corporation, it must have a clear business purpose, and wonders whether forming a corporation merely to acquire a special liquor license satisfies the business purpose requirement. Write a letter to Ruiz that addresses his concern about having sufficient business purpose for his planned incorporation of the club.

73. **RESEARCH PROBLEM** Shirley and Roseann form Rosa Corporation with each contributing assets and cash in exchange for all of the corporation's stock. Shirley and Roseann each own 50% of the stock immediately after the exchange. Shortly thereafter, Shirley sells all her stock to Don per a written agreement executed before the formation of Rosa Corporation. Prepare a memorandum discussing the effect of this prearranged agreement.

Discussion Cases

74. Jacqui and Joanne plan to buy a bed-and-breakfast inn for $200,000. Jacqui will contribute $20,000 toward the purchase and operate the enterprise. Joanne's primary role is that of investor. She will contribute $100,000. However, she will be an active participant because of her involvement in management decisions. They will borrow the balance of the purchase price from a local bank. Advise Jacqui and Joanne on a choice of business form. Consider that the enterprise is expected to realize operating losses of $50,000 annually for the first 3 years. During the 4th year, the inn should realize a meager profit.

75. Nan wants to incorporate her sole proprietorship and will transfer cash of $5,000 and property with a fair market value of $60,000 and a basis of $20,000. The corporation will assume the $55,000 mortgage on the property. Nan will be paid a salary of $40,000. She has been advised by her cousin that she might want to be a corporation for tax purposes because its income is taxed at a lower rate and her salary can be deducted as a business expense to lower overall taxes. However, she recently read an article in a small business owners' journal extolling the virtues of using an S corporation. Discuss the income tax consequences for Nan if she structures her business as an S corporation versus a corporation.

Tax Planning Cases

76. Tony and Susan are starting a retail business selling formal wear for men and women. They estimate profits and losses for the next five years to be: ($20,000), ($10,000), ($5,000), $10,000, and $50,000 respectively. Susan will work full time in the store while Tony will be involved in managing the operations. Susan is married to Tom and is in the 31% marginal tax bracket. Tony is single and has other sources of income that put him in the 31% marginal tax bracket. Susan will be paid a salary of $30,000 for the first five years, after which her compensation will be reviewed. Tony and Susan each contribute $50,000 to get the business started. The remaining question facing Tony and Susan is which business form to use for the business. They believe they should operate as a partnership but have been informed that forming a corporation might be a better option since it would limit their liability. Prepare an analysis to determine whether Tony and Susan should operate their business as a partnership or a corporation.

77. Tory, Becky, Hal, and Jere form TBHJ Partnership as equal owners. TBJH Partnership rents heavy tools and equipment. Becky and Hal are married to each other while Tory and Jere are brothers but are not related to Becky or Hal. Because Becky and Hal have other jobs, Tory and Jere are to be the full-time managers of the business. Although Tory and Jere will run the business full-time, Becky will help in the store on weekends and some evenings. Hal will lend his financial expertise to the firm by doing the bookkeeping and preparing the tax returns. Even though the four have equal ownership interests, it is not clear how each owner is to be compensated so that there is equity among the partners yet rewards for those engaged in specific tasks. Hal has told the others that they cannot receive deductible salaries. However, he suggests that guaranteed payments be made to each partner/employee for an agreed-upon amount based on the value of the services each provides and/or the time spent at the store. Discuss the ramifications of employing this plan and whether this is an equitable way to allocate compensation among the partners. What are the implications of this arrangement for the partners and the partnership?

Ethics Discussion Case

78. Assume that you are a CPA and a tax specialist. Your clients include Ale and Grains, Inc., an S corporation, and Gustav and Heidi Lager, a married couple who are shareholders and the operators of Ale and Grains. The S corporation has expanded to include 75 qualified shareholders this year. Gustav and Heidi have told you that they have just obtained a divorce. Both individuals will continue to operate Ale and Grains for the ownership group, and neither party plans to dispose of her or his ownership interest. They know that certain rules govern the number of shareholders allowed in an S corporation, but they tell you not to be concerned because only their mailing addresses will change. They refer to the doctrine of substance over form and how it fits this situation. Write a letter to Gustav, Heidi, and the other shareholders offering your advice. Refer to the AICPA Code of Professional Conduct and the Statements on Standards for Tax Services where necessary.

COMMUNICATION

4

Business Ethics and Social Responsibility

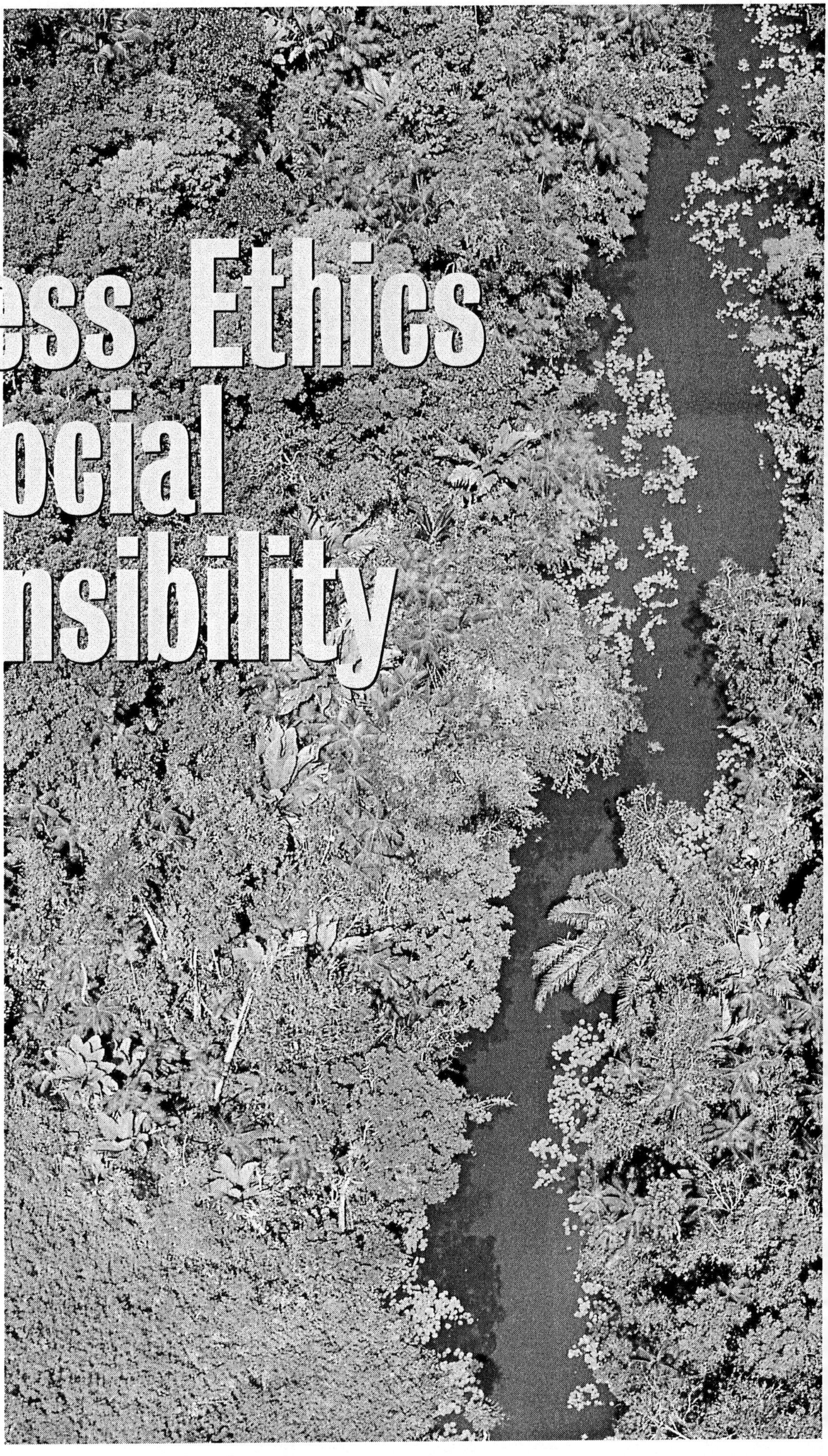

A firm's employees should practice business ethics, which is a set of principles that should be followed when conducting business. Each firm has a social responsibility, which is the firm's recognition of how its business decisions can affect society. The term *social responsibility* is sometimes used to describe the firm's responsibility to its community and to the environment. However, it may also be more broadly used to include the firm's responsibility to its customers, employees, and creditors. While a firm makes business decisions that are intended to increase its value, its decisions must not violate its ethics and social responsibilities.

Business Ethics and Social Responsibility → **Business Decisions** → **Firm's Earnings** → **Value of Firm**

To illustrate how business ethics can affect the value of a business, consider the case of Homestake Mining Company, which focuses on gold mining in the United States, Canada, and other countries. What responsibilities does Homestake have toward its employees who are involved in mining? What responsibilities does Homestake have toward the environment in which it conducts mining operations? What responsibilities does Homestake have toward the stockholders who have invested their funds in the firm? Can Homestake satisfy all of these responsibilities simultaneously? This chapter provides a background on a firm's social responsibilities, which can be used to address these questions.

The Learning Goals of this chapter are to:

1. Describe the responsibilities of firms to their customers.
2. Describe the responsibilities of firms to their employees.
3. Describe the responsibilities of firms to their stockholders and creditors.
4. Describe the responsibilities of firms to the environment.
5. Describe the responsibilities of firms to their communities.
6. Explain the costs that firms incur in achieving their social responsibilities.

RESPONSIBILITY TO CUSTOMERS

1 Describe the responsibilities of firms to their customers.

social responsibility firm's recognition of how its business decisions can affect society

A firm's responsibility to customers goes beyond the provision of products or services. Firms have a **social responsibility** when producing and selling their products, as discussed next.

Responsible Production Practices

Products should be produced to ensure customer safety. Proper warning labels should be attached to products to prevent accidents that could result from misuse. For some products, proper information on possible side effects should be provided. For example, Tylenol gelcaps, Nyquil cough syrup, and Coors beer all have warning labels about possible adverse effects.

Responsible Sales Practices

When employees are hired to sell a firm's products, they usually receive a commission or bonus based on sales volume. Employees of some firms may attempt to maximize their product sales, even when they recognize that the product is not appropriate for particular customers. For example, to increase commissions some insurance salespeople sell more insurance than customers need. Furthermore, some firms falsely advertise their products. Firms need guidelines that discourage employees from using overly aggressive sales strategies or deceptive advertising.

How Firms Ensure Responsibility toward Customers

A firm can ensure responsibility toward its customers by following these steps:

business ethics a set of principles that should be followed when conducting business

1 *Establish a Code of Ethics* Firms can establish a code of **business ethics** that sets guidelines for product quality, as well as guidelines for how employees, customers, and owners should be treated. The pledge (from an annual report) by Bristol-Myers Squibb Company in Exhibit 3.1 is an example of a code of ethics. Many firms have a booklet on ethics that is distributed to all employees.

2 *Monitor Complaints* Firms should make sure that customers have a phone number that they can call if they have any complaints about the quality of the product or about how they were treated by employees. The firm can attempt to determine the source of the complaint and ensure that such a complaint does not occur again. Many firms have a department that receives the complaints and attempts to resolve them. This step may involve assessing different parts of the production process to ensure that the product is produced properly. Or it may require an assessment of particular employees who may be violating the firm's code of responsibility to its customers.

3 *Customer Feedback* Firms can ask customers for feedback on the products or services they recently purchased, even if the customers did not call in to complain. This process may detect some other problems with the product's quality or with the way customers were treated. For example, automobile dealers such as Saturn send a questionnaire to customers to determine how they were treated by salespeople. They may also be asked whether they have any complaints about the automobile they recently purchased. Once the firm is informed of problems with either production defects or customer treatment, it should take action to correct these problems.

Exhibit 3.1
Excerpts from a Pledge of Ethics and Responsibility by Bristol-Myers Squibb Company

THE BRISTOL-MYERS SQUIBB PLEDGE

TO THOSE WHO USE OUR PRODUCTS . . .
We affirm Bristol-Myers Squibb's commitment to the highest standards of excellence, safety and reliability in everything we make. We pledge to offer products of the highest quality and to work diligently to keep improving them.

TO OUR EMPLOYEES AND THOSE WHO MAY JOIN US . . .
We pledge personal respect, fair competition and equal treatment. We acknowledge our obligation to provide able and humane leadership throughout the organization, within a clean and safe working environment. To all who qualify for advancement, we will make every effort to provide opportunity.

TO OUR SUPPLIERS AND CUSTOMERS . . .
We pledge an open door, courteous, efficient and ethical dealing, and appreciation of their right to a fair profit.

TO OUR SHAREHOLDERS . . .
We pledge a companywide dedication to continued profitable growth, sustained by strong finances, a high level of research and development, and facilities second to none.

TO THE COMMUNITIES WHERE WE HAVE PLANTS AND OFFICES . . .
We pledge conscientious citizenship, a helping hand for worthwhile causes, and constructive action in support of civic and environmental progress.

TO THE COUNTRIES WHERE WE DO BUSINESS . . .
We pledge ourselves to be a good citizen and to show full consideration for the rights of others while reserving the right to stand up for our own.

ABOVE ALL, TO THE WORLD WE LIVE IN . . .
We pledge Bristol-Myers Squibb to policies and practices which fully embody the responsibility, integrity and decency required of free enterprise if it is to merit and maintain the confidence of our society.

How Consumerism Ensures Responsibility toward Customers

consumerism the collective demand by consumers that businesses satisfy their needs

The responsibility of firms toward customers may be enforced not only by the firms but also by specific groups of consumers. **Consumerism** represents the collective demand by consumers that businesses satisfy their needs. Consumer groups became popular in the 1960s and have become increasingly effective as a result of their growth.

How the Government Ensures Responsibility toward Customers

In addition to the codes of responsibility by firms and the wave of consumerism, the government attempts to ensure responsibility to customers with various laws on product safety, advertising, and industry competition.

GOVERNMENT REGULATION OF PRODUCT SAFETY The government protects consumers by regulating the quality of some products produced by firms. For example, the Food and Drug Administration (FDA) is responsible for testing food products to determine whether they meet specific requirements. The FDA also examines new drugs that firms have recently manufactured. Because the potential side effects may not be known immediately, some drugs are continually tested by the FDA for several years.

GOVERNMENT REGULATION OF ADVERTISING The federal government also has established laws against deceptive advertising. Yet, it may not be able to prevent all unethical business practices. Numerous examples of advertising could be called deceptive. It is difficult to know if a product is "new and improved." In addition, the use of a term such as "lowest price" may have different meanings or interpretations.

GOVERNMENT REGULATION OF INDUSTRY COMPETITION Another way in which the government ensures that consumers are treated properly is to promote competition in most industries. Competition between firms is beneficial to consumers, because firms that charge excessive prices or whose goods are of unacceptable quality will not survive in a competitive environment. Because of competition, consumers can avoid a firm that is using deceptive sales tactics.

monopoly sole provider of goods or services

A firm has a **monopoly** if it is the sole provider of goods or services. It can set prices without concern about competition. However, the government regulates those firms that have a monopoly. For example, it regulates utility firms that have monopolies in specific locations and can control the pricing policies of these firms.

In some industries, firms created various agreements to set their prices and avoid competing with each other. The federal government has attempted to prevent such activity by enforcing antitrust laws. Some of the more well-known antitrust acts are summarized in Exhibit 3.2. All of these acts share the objective of promoting competition. Yet, each act focuses on particular aspects that can influence the degree of competition within the industry.

The trucking, railroad, airlines, and telecommunications industry have been deregulated, allowing more firms to enter the industry. In addition, banks and other financial institutions have been deregulated since 1980 and now have more

Exhibit 3.2
Key Antitrust Laws

Sherman Antitrust Act (1890)	Encouraged competition and prevented monopolies.
Clayton Act (1914)	Reinforced the rules of the Sherman Antitrust Act and specifically prohibited the following activities because they reduced competition: *Tying agreements* Forced firms to purchase additional products as a condition to purchase the products desired. *Binding contracts* Prevented firms from purchasing products from a supplier's competitors. *Interlocking directorates* Prohibited the same person from serving on the board of directors of two competing firms.
Federal Trade Commission Act (1914)	Prohibited unfair methods of competition; also called for the establishment of the Federal Trade Commission (FTC) to enforce antitrust laws.
Robinson-Patman Act (1936)	Prohibited price policies or promotional allowances that reduce competition within an industry.
Celler-Kefauver Act (1950)	Prohibited mergers between firms that reduce competition within an industry.

flexibility on the types of deposits and interest rates to offer. They also have more freedom to expand across state lines. In general, deregulation results in lower prices for consumers.

RESPONSIBLITY TO EMPLOYEES

2 **Describe the responsibilities of firms to their employees.**

Firms also have a responsibility toward their employees to ensure safety, proper treatment by other employees, and equal opportunity.

Employee Safety

Firms ensure that the workplace is safe for employees by closely monitoring the production process. Some obvious safety precautions are to check machinery and equipment for proper working conditions, require safety glasses or any other equipment that can prevent injury, and emphasize any special safety precautions in training seminars.

Firms that create a safe working environment prevent injuries and improve the morale of their employees. Many firms, such as Allied Signal, now identify workplace safety as one of their main goals. Levi Strauss and Company imposes safety guidelines not only on its U.S. facilities but also on Asian factories where some of its clothes are made. Starbucks Coffee Company has developed a code of conduct in an attempt to improve the quality of life in coffee-producing countries.

Proper Treatment by Other Employees

Firms are responsible for ensuring that employees are treated properly by other employees. Two of the key issues regarding the treatment of employees are diversity and the prevention of sexual harassment, which are discussed next.

DIVERSITY In recent years, the work force has become much more diverse. More women have entered the job market, and more minorities now have the necessary

In Bangladesh, garment factories were forced to respond to the Levi Strauss Company's demand to stop employing child labor. In a deal to keep the children from being put out on the street, Levi's pays their full salary while they attend school.

Starbuck's has been proactive in monitoring working conditions in coffee-producing countries. A portion of their statement of beliefs reads, "We respect human rights and dignity. We believe that people should work because they want or need to, but not because they are forced to do so. We believe that people have the right to freely associate with whichever organizations or individuals they choose. We believe that children should not be unlawfully employed as laborers."

sexual harassment unwelcome comments or actions of a sexual nature

skills and education to qualify for high-level jobs. Exhibit 3.3 discloses the proportions of various job categories held by women, Blacks, and Hispanics.

Many firms have responded to the increased diversity among employees by offering diversity seminars. These seminars are normally intended to inform employees about cultural diversity. Such information can help employees recognize that certain statements or behavior may be offensive to other employees.

The following statement from a recent annual report of General Motors reflects the efforts that have been made by many firms to encourage diversity:

> ***"Internally, we are working to create an environment where diversity thrives. We are trying to remove barriers that separate people and find new ways to engage teams to maximize productivity and profitability. This is being done through communication, teamwork, mutual support, and pulling together to achieve common objectives. Our challenge is to seek a diverse population in leadership roles with a wide range of backgrounds, views, and experiences to ensure we capture diverse perspectives to meet and exceed customer expectations."***

Firms such as Johnson and Johnson, MCI, the Coca-Cola Company, IBM, Merrill Lynch, Sara Lee Corporation and many other firms have made major efforts to promote diversity. Rockwell International has a diversity task team that developed guidelines for work force diversity planning in each of its businesses. Xerox has improved its workplace diversity in recent years. About 32 percent of its employees are women, and 26 percent of its employees are minorities.

PREVENTION OF SEXUAL HARASSMENT In addition to diversity in the workplace, another issue is **sexual harassment,** which represents unwelcome comments or actions of a sexual nature. For example, one employee might make unwelcome sexual advances toward another and use personal power within the firm to threaten the

Exhibit 3.3
Proportion of Women and Minorities in Various Occupations

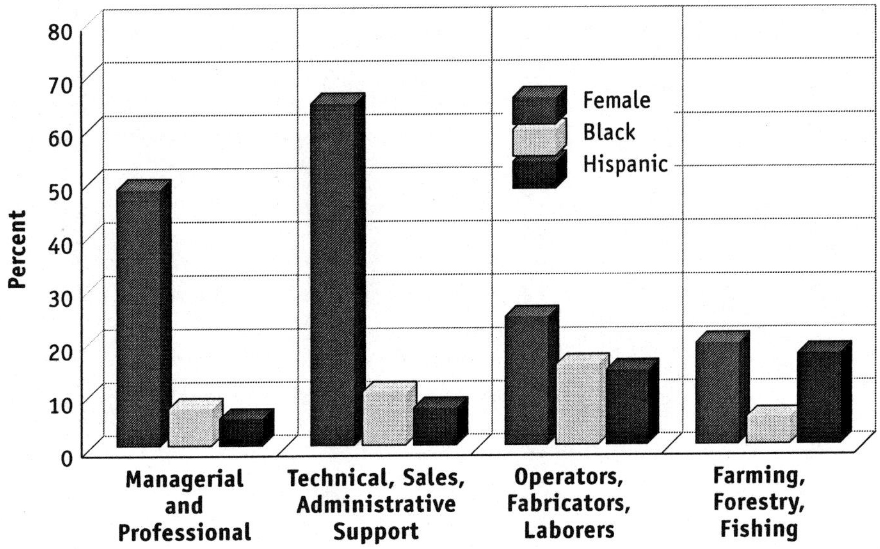

Denny's has taken many positive steps to overcome claims of racial bias in their restaurant operation.

other employee's job status. Firms attempt to prevent sexual harassment by offering seminars on the subject. Like the diversity seminars, these seminars can help employees recognize how some statements or behavior may be offensive to other employees. These seminars are not only an act of responsibility to employees but also can improve a firm's productivity by helping employees get along.

Equal Opportunity

Employees who apply for a position at a firm should not be subjected to discrimination because of their national origin, race, gender, or religion. The Civil Rights Act of 1964 prohibits such forms of discrimination. The act is enforced by a federal agency known as the Equal Employment Opportunity Commission (EEOC). Beyond the federal guidelines, many firms attempt to ensure equal treatment among applicants for a position by assigning someone to monitor the hiring process. The concept of equal treatment applies not only to the initial hiring of an employee but also to annual raises and promotions within the firm.

affirmative action a set of activities intended to increase opportunities for minorities and women

Many firms and government agencies implement **affirmative action** programs. Some people expect affirmative action programs to ensure equal treatment among prospective and existing employees. Other people expect these programs to establish quotas, which would designate specific positions for minorities or women. Most people would agree that affirmative action programs have good intentions, but quotas may be viewed as a form of reverse discrimination.

Denny's (a restaurant business) was charged with racial discrimination in 1993. In 1993, it began implementing a program to promote diversity. It increased minority management from 18 percent in 1993 to 24 percent in 1996. It also increased African-American owned franchises from one in 1993 to twenty-seven in 1996.

How Firms Ensure Responsibility toward Employees

To ensure that employees receive proper treatment, many firms establish a grievance procedure for employees who believe they are not being given equal opportunity. A specific person or department is normally assigned to address such complaints. This method of addressing employee complaints is similar to that of addressing customer complaints. By recognizing the complaints, the firm attempts both to resolve them and to revise its procedures to prevent further complaints.

A good example of a firm's effort to resolve employee complaints is Marriott, which implemented three strategies. First, it created a mediation process, in which a neutral person outside the firm (called a mediator) assesses the employee complaint and suggests a solution. The mediator does not have the power to enforce a final judgement but may help the employee and the firm resolve the conflict.

Second, Marriott offers a toll-free number for employees to call if they believe they were subjected to discrimination, harassment, or improper firing. Marriott begins to investigate the complaint within three days of the call.

Third, Marriott allows the employee to voice complaints in front of a panel of other employees who determine whether the employee's complaints are valid, based on Marriott's existing guidelines.

Since Marriott began its procedure for resolving employee complaints, EEOC complaints against Marriott by its employees declined by 50 percent in the following year and by 83 percent in the year after. Since more employee complaints were resolved within the firm, employees were more satisfied with their jobs, which allowed them to focus on satisfying customers.

The cost to a firm that attempts to listen to every employee complaint can be substantial. Furthermore, some of the complaints may not be valid. Firms must attempt to distinguish between complaints that are valid and those that are not, and then focus on resolving the valid complaints.

Conflict with Employee Layoffs

Some business decisions are controversial because they may adversely affect employees in the local community despite their improving the firm's performance. Consider the following example, which reflects a common dilemma that many firms face. As your firm's business grew, you hired more employees. However, because of the recent decline in demand for your product, you no longer need twenty of the employees that you hired over the last two years. If you lay off twenty employees, you will reduce your expenses substantially and satisfy your stockholders. However, you may be criticized for not serving employee interests. This situation is unpleasant because the layoffs may be necessary (to cut expenses) for your firm to survive. If your firm fails, all your other employees will also be out of work as well.

This dilemma has no perfect solution. Many firms may do what's best for the business, while attempting to reduce the adverse effects on their employees. For example, they may help those employees find employment elsewhere, or may even attempt to retrain them for jobs that will be available within the firm.

GLOBAL BUSINESS

Global Ethics

U.S. firms typically have a code of ethics that provides guidelines to the employees. However, these guidelines may be much more restrictive than those generally used in some foreign countries. Consider a U.S. firm that sells supplies to manufacturers. The employees of this firm may be subject to rules that prevent them from providing payoffs ("kickbacks") to any employees of the manufacturing companies that order the firm's supplies. Yet, other competitors may provide payoffs to employees of the manufacturing companies ordering supplies from their company. In some countries, this type of behavior is acceptable. Thus, the U.S. supplier is at a disadvantage because its employees are required to follow a stricter code of ethics. This is a common ethical dilemma that U.S. firms face in a global environment. The employees of U.S. firms must either ignore their ethical guidelines or be at a disadvantage in specific foreign countries.

Another ethical dilemma that U.S. firms face in some foreign countries is their relationship with foreign governments. Firms that conduct business in foreign countries are subject to numerous rules enforced by the local government. Officials of some foreign governments commonly accept bribes from firms that need approval for various business activities. For example, a firm may need to have its products approved for safety purposes, or its local manufacturing plant may need to be approved for environmental purposes. The process of approving even minor activities could take months and prevent the firm from conducting business. Those firms that pay off government officials may receive prompt attention from the local governments. Employees of Lockheed were charged with bribing Egyptian government officials to win a contract to build new aircraft. Executives of IBM's Argentina subsidiary were charged with bribing Argentine government officials to generate business from the government.

A recent assessment of foreign countries by the U.S. Commerce Department and intelligence agencies detected more than one hundred deals in 1994 in which foreign firms used bribes to win business contracts over U.S. competitors. Many of these foreign firms are located in France, Germany, and Japan, as well as in some less-developed countries.

Many U.S. firms attempt to follow a worldwide code of ethics that is consistent across countries. This type of policy reduces the confusion that could result from using different ethical standards in different countries. While a worldwide code of ethics may place the U.S. firm at a disadvantage in some countries, it may also enhance the credibility of that firm.

RESPONSIBILITY TO STOCKHOLDERS

3 **Describe the responsibilities of firms to their stockholders and creditors.**

Firms are responsible for satisfying their owners (or stockholders). Employees may be tempted to make decisions that satisfy their own interests rather than those of the owners. For example, some employees may use the firm's money to purchase personal computers for their personal use rather than for the firm.

How Firms Ensure Responsibility

Managers of a firm monitor employee decisions to ensure that they are made in the best interests of the owners. Employee salaries may be directly tied to the firm's performance. In this way, employees stay focused on maximizing the firm's value.

Owners of a firm recognize that the firm will incur costs in meeting responsibilities such as employee safety and prevention of pollution. The firm's efforts to provide a safe and pollution-free environment represent a necessary cost of doing business.

How Stockholders Ensure Responsibility

shareholder activism the active role that stockholders take to influence a firm's management policies

In recent years, there has been much **shareholder activism,** which represents the active role that stockholders take to influence a firm's management policies. Stock-

Ben and Jerry, shown here, have been recognized nationally for their focus on employees, the community in which they operate, and society as a whole. No employee of Ben & Jerry's can receive more than eight times the salary of the lowest paid employee.

holders have been especially active when they are dissatisfied with the firm's executive salaries or other policies.

institutional investors financial institutions that purchase large amounts of stock

The stockholders who have been most active are **institutional investors,** or financial institutions that purchase large amounts of stock. For example, insurance companies invest a large portion of the insurance premiums that they receive in stocks. If institutional investors invest a large amount of money in a particular stock, the return on their investment is highly dependent on how that firm performs. Since many institutional investors commonly invest $10 million or more in a single firm's stock, they pay close attention to the performance of any firm in which they invest.

If an institutional investor believes the firm is poorly managed, it may attempt to meet with the firm's executives and express its dissatisfaction. It may even attempt to team up with other institutional investors who also own a large proportion of the firm's stock. This gives them more negotiating power because the firm's executives are more likely to listen to institutional investors who collectively hold a large proportion of the firm's stock. The institutional investors do not attempt to dictate how the firm should be managed. Instead, they attempt to ensure that the firm's managers make decisions that are in the best interests of all stockholders.

Conflict with Excessive Executive Compensation

A firm's managers can attempt to satisfy its stockholders by ensuring that funds invested by the stockholders are put to good use. If these funds are used to cover unnecessary expenses, the firm's profits are reduced, which reduces the return that stockholders receive on their investment. A major concern of stockholders is the salaries provided to the firm's chief executive officer (CEO) and other executives. The potential effect of excessive executive salaries on a firm's performance (and therefore on the returns to stockholders) is illustrated with the following example.

Consider two firms called Firm C and Firm D, which are in the same industry and have similar revenue and expenses, as shown in Exhibit 3.4. Assume that the only difference is that Firm C pays its top five executives a total of $30 million in annual salary, while Firm D pays its top five executives a total of $5 million. As shown in Exhibit 3.4, the annual profits of Firm D are $25 million above those of

Exhibit 3.4
Impact of Executive Salaries on a Firm's Performance

	Firm C	Firm D
Revenue	$200,000,000	$200,000,000
− Expenses (except executive salaries)	−$150,000,000	−$150,000,000
− Executive Salaries Expense	− $30,000,000	− $5,000,000
= Profits	= $20,000,000	= $45,000,000

Firm C. This difference is attributed to Firm C's higher executive salary expenses. Thus, the return to the stockholders of Firm C is smaller than the return to stockholders of Firm D.

Exhibit 3.5 discloses the salary, bonus, and other forms of long-term compensation of the top ten highest-paid CEOs in 1995. The total annual pay (including other compensation) exceeds $16 million for each of these CEOs. High compensation is also provided to other executives. Each of the top ten highest-paid executives who are not CEOs received more than $11 million during 1995.

Some customers and stockholders may argue that firms paying executives such high salaries are not meeting their social responsibilities. These firms may be serving the interests of the executives, and not the stockholders who own the firm. However, the counterargument is that these executives deserve high salaries because their contribution to the value of the firm exceeds the amount of their compensation.

RESPONSIBILITY TO CREDITORS

Firms are responsible for meeting their financial obligations to their creditors. If firms are experiencing financial problems and are unable to meet their obligations, they should inform creditors. Sometimes creditors are willing to extend payment deadlines and may even offer advice to firms on how to improve their financial condition. A

Exhibit 3.5
Highest Paid CEOs

CEO	Firm	Annual Salary (in thousands)	Other Compensation (in thousands)	Total Annual Compensation (in thousands)
Lawrence Coss	Green Tree Financial	$65,580	$0	$65,580
Sanford Weill	Travelers Group	5,607	44,233	49,840
John Welch Jr.	General Electric	5,321	16,741	22,060
Gordon Binder	Amgen	1,513	19,992	21,505
James Donald	DSC Communications	5,595	13,588	19,183
Casey Cowell	U.S. Robotics	2,799	15,770	18,569
Floyd English	Andrew Corp.	1,739	15,927	17,666
Howard Solomon	Forest Laboratories	611	16,416	17,026
Stanley Gault	Goodyear Tire & Rubber	2,207	14,343	16,550
Edward Brennan	Sears, Roebuck	3,098	13,252	16,350

Note: Amounts reflect compensation during 1995.

firm has a strong incentive to satisfy its responsibility to creditors. If the firm does not pay what is owed to creditors, it may be forced into bankruptcy by them.

RESPONSIBILITY TO THE ENVIRONMENT

4 **Describe the responsibilities of firms to the environment.**

The production processes that firms use, as well as the products they produce, can be harmful to the environment. The most common abuses to the environment are discussed next, along with recent actions that firms have taken to improve the environment.

Air Pollution

Some production processes cause air pollution, which is harmful to society because it inhibits breathing. For example, the production of fuel and steel, as well as automobile use, increases the amount of carbon dioxide in the air.

HOW FIRMS PREVENT AIR POLLUTION Automobile and steel firms have reduced air pollution by revising their production processes so that less carbon dioxide escapes into the air. For example, firms such as Allied Signal and Inland Steel spend substantial funds to prevent pollution.

HOW THE GOVERNMENT PREVENTS AIR POLLUTION The federal government has also become involved by enforcing specific guidelines for firms to limit the amount of carbon dioxide caused by the production process. In 1970, the Environmental

Don Laskowski (an engineer and farmer) and Dan Tekulve (a designer of motorized hospital beds) had no experience in the sawmill industry. That didn't stop them from designing a product that can extract 30% more useable lumber from trees, minimizing waste and pollution. The partners didn't stop there. They seeded the business by donations—10% of profits and 300 sawmills to third world countries. Sales at Wood-Mizer now top $50 million.

Inland Labs uses rare toxic substances from tropical rain forests (left) to produce a new cancer treatment called Ricin D (right). If these rain forests are destroyed, the promise of these treatments are lost forever.

Protection Agency (EPA) was created to develop and enforce pollution standards. In recent years, pollution control laws have become more stringent.

Land Pollution

Land has been polluted by toxic waste resulting from some production processes. A related form of land pollution is solid waste, which does not deteriorate over time. As a result of waste, land not only looks less attractive but also may no longer be useful for other purposes, such as farming.

HOW FIRMS PREVENT LAND POLLUTION Firms have revised their production and packaging processes to reduce the amount of waste. They now store toxic waste and deliver it to specified toxic waste storage sites. They also recycle plastic and limit their use of materials that would ultimately become solid waste.

Many firms have environmental programs that are designed to reduce damage to the environment. For example, Homestake Mining Company recognizes that its mining operations disturb the land, and it spends money to minimize any effect on the environment. PPG Industries restructured its production processes to generate about six thousand fewer tons of waste in a single year. Kodak recycles more than a half-billion pounds of material a year, and also supports a World Wildlife Fund environmental education program. IBM typically spends more than $30 million a year for environmental assessments and cleaning. Rockwell International has reduced its hazardous waste by more than 50 percent in recent years.

To appreciate the efforts that some firms have made to protect the environment and the costs of these efforts, consider the following statement from a recent annual report of DuPont:

> *The company operates about 150 manufacturing facilities, five petroleum refineries, 20 natural gas processing plants and numerous product-handling and distribution facilities around*

the world, all of which are significantly affected by a broad array of laws and regulations relating to the protection of the environment. It is the company's policy to comply fully with or exceed all legal requirements worldwide . . . About $400 million was spent for capital projects related to environmental requirements in 1994 . . . environmental expenses charged to current operations totalled about $950 million in 1994, as compared to $1 billion in 1993, and $900 million in 1992.

Conflict with Environmental Responsibility

While most firms agree that a clean environment is desirable, they may disagree on how much responsibility they have in improving the environment. Consider two firms called Firm A and Firm B, which have similar revenue and expenses. Firm A, however, makes a much greater effort to clean up the environment; it spends $10 million, while Firm B spends $2 million. The profit of each firm is shown in Exhibit 3.6. Firm A has an annual profit of zero, while Firm B has an annual profit of $8 million. If you could invest in the stock of either Firm A or Firm B, where would you invest your money? Most investors desire to earn a high return on their money. While they recognize that a firm may have some environmental cleanup expenses, they would not want those expenses to be excessive. Therefore, most investors would prefer to invest in Firm B rather than Firm A.

Firm A could attempt to recapture its high environmental cleanup expenses by charging a higher price for its product. In this way, it may be able to spend heavily on the environment, while still generating a reasonable return to its stockholders. This strategy makes the customers pay for its extra environmental cleanup. However, if Firm A charges a higher price than Firm B, many customers would switch to Firm B in order to pay a lower price.

This example illustrates that there is a limit to which firms can use funds toward improving the environment. Firms have a responsibility to avoid damaging the environment. However, if they spend excessively on environmental improvement, they will not satisfy most of their customers or owners.

While firms have increased their efforts to clean up the environment, they do not necessarily agree with the guidelines enforced by the government. Oil refineries that are losing money remain open to avoid the cleanup that the EPA would enforce if they were closed down. Some refineries would pay about $1 billion for cleanup costs because of the EPA's strict guidelines. Firms have questioned many other environmental guidelines imposed by the EPA.

Exhibit 3.6
Effect of Environmental Expenses on Business Performance

	Firm A	Firm B
Revenue	$90,000,000	$90,000,000
Total Operating Expenses	−$80,000,000	−$80,000,000
Environmental Cleanup Expenses	−$10,000,000	− $2,000,000
Profit	0	$8,000,000

RESPONSIBILITY TO THE COMMUNITY

5 **Describe the responsibilities of firms to their communities.**

When firms establish a base in a community, they become part of that community and rely on it for customers and employees. Firms demonstrate their concern for the community by sponsoring local events or donating to local charities. For example, SunTrust Bank, IBM, and many other firms have donated funds to universities. NationsBank has provided loans to low-income neighborhoods and minority communities.

Conflict with Maximizing Social Responsibility

The decisions of a firm's managers that maximize social responsibility could conflict with maximizing firm value. The costs involved in achieving such a goal would have to be passed on to consumers. Thus, the attempt to maximize responsibility to the community may reduce the firm's ability to provide products at a reasonable price to consumers.

Many companies support charitable organizations that promote nutrition, education, performing and visual arts, and amateur athletics. Even though this social support requires a considerable financial commitment, the firm can gain from an enhanced image in the eye of the consumer to whom it sells its products. In a sense, the charitable support not only can help society but also can be a valuable marketing tool to create a desired image for the firm. Consequently, society and stockholders can benefit from the charitable support. If a company properly identifies a char-

Apple Computer invests substantially in local education programs. The investment is helpful to local communities but also helps increase sales to schools and individuals.

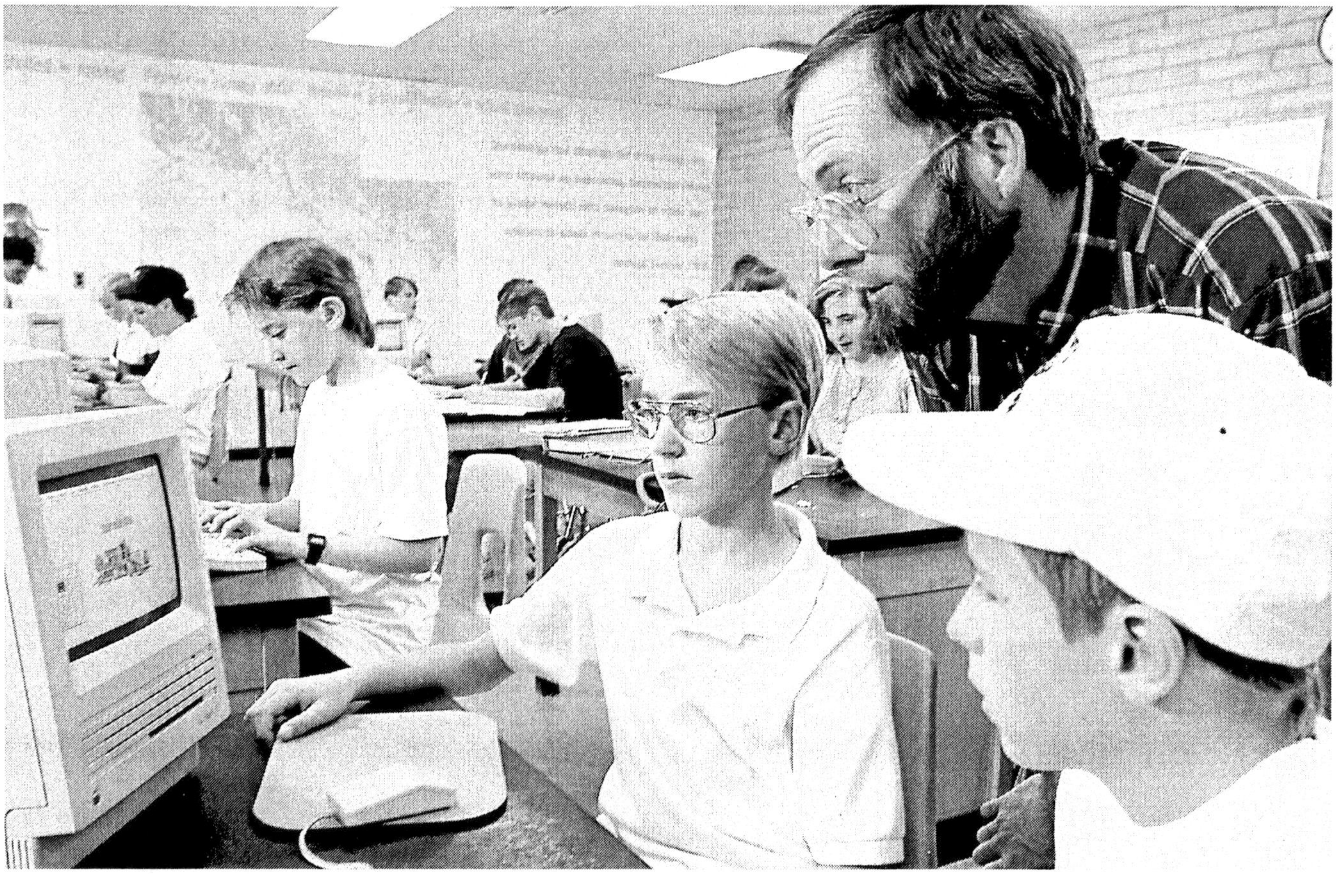

SPOTLIGHT ON TECHNOLOGY

When Does Tough Competition Become Unethical?

As more and more business is conducted over shared information networks, distinguishing between tough competition and unethical behavior frequently becomes difficult. The airline reservation systems are a case in point. Originally established in the mid-1960s as internal information systems, several of these systems (most notably American Airline's SABRE system and United Airline's Apollo system) were made available to travel agents in the mid-1970s. Using these systems, travel agents were able to book flights for their customers without calling the airlines. Early adoption of these systems by travel agents was slow, however. Because airline schedules and prices were regulated, there was no great benefit (aside from slightly greater convenience) to booking reservations electronically versus booking them by phone.

In the late 1970s, however, airline deregulation changed the situation dramatically. Suddenly, fares could change from minute to minute and routes could change in as little as thirty days. In addition, airlines were free to offer fares with complex restrictions. These changes made it necessary for travel agents to be on-line. They simply couldn't service their customers adequately with the paper-based schedules they had used in the past.

Deregulation proved to be a major boon for the airlines that had reservation systems in place, particularly American Airlines and United Airlines, which jointly accounted for about 75 percent of the reservation system market. Airlines that did not own their own reservation systems had to pay to become "co-hosts" on systems such as SABRE and Apollo. Even after paying to become co-hosts, however, these airlines argued they were being treated unfairly by system owners.

Among their complaints were the following:

- *Exclusion of carriers:* Where a carrier was in direct competition with a system owner, the carrier might be denied the right to become a co-host. Frontier Airlines, for example, claimed that United Airlines repeatedly refused to allow it to become a co-host because they were fierce competitors in Frontier's Denver hub.
- *Screen bias:* The reservation systems normally displayed flights on a separate screen page for each airline. Carriers directly competing with a system owner in a particular hub might find that their page was strategically placed at the end of all the pages, meaning that it could take the agent several minutes to reach the page. Such a delay was disastrous from a business standpoint, as 70 to 80 percent of all reservations were made from flights on the first page displayed by the system.
- *Unfair access to information:* The systems owners were instantly aware of any changes to routes or fares that their competitors made. The co-hosts did not have comparable access to such information from the reservation systems.
- *Unfair communications to agents:* The reservations systems provided a direct pipeline from owners to agents, which was sometimes used to send messages disparaging other airlines. For example, United Airlines was accused of making critical comments about a Frontier Airline rate reduction over Apollo. In Dallas, American Airlines was accused of sending messages to agents relating to the precarious financial state of Braniff Airlines over SABRE, and urging them to purchase tickets from American to protect their customers! (Both Frontier and Braniff ultimately went bankrupt).
- *Anticompetitive practice:* System owners employed a wide variety of techniques to ensure they were used exclusively by travel agents. Particular pressure was placed on agents located in competitive market areas. For example, in Denver, where United competed head-to-head with Frontier airlines, an estimated 75 percent of agents used United's Apollo system to book reservations.

One could easily argue that these techniques employed by system owners were simply tough competition, and ethics weren't really involved. However, system co-hosts such as Frontier and Braniff, had, in good faith, paid to be included on the systems. As a result, they were customers of the system owners, as well as being competitors. Was it ethical for the system owners to take money from their co-hosts while manipulating the systems to put them at a competitive disadvantage?

itable cause that is related to its business, it may be able to simultaneously contribute to society and maximize the firm's value. For example, a running shoe manufacturer may sponsor a race, or a tennis racket manufacturer may sponsor a tennis tournament.

Apple and IBM invest substantial funds in local education programs. This investment not only is helpful to the communities but also results in computer sales to schools. Home Depot donated $8 million to community programs in 1995. About 45 percent of the money was used for housing projects. Many Checkers restaurants have been targeted for locations in inner-city areas. They not only provide jobs to many minorities but also have been profitable.

SUMMARY OF BUSINESS RESPONSIBILITIES

Firms have many responsibilities toward customers, employees, the environment, the community, stockholders, and creditors that must be recognized when doing business. The general concern of firms about ethics and social responsibility can be illustrated with the quotations from recent annual reports on the next two pages.

SELF-SCORING EXERCISE

Assessing the Ethical Standards of the Firm Where You Work

Think about the organization you currently work for or one you know something about and complete the following Ethical Climate Questionnaire.

Please use the scale below and write the number that best represents your answer in the space next to each item.

To what extent are the following statements true about your company?

Completely false	Mostly false	Somewhat false	Somewhat true	Mostly true	Completely true
0	1	2	3	4	5

____ 1. In this company, people are expected to follow their own personal and moral beliefs.

____ 2. People are expected to do anything to further the company's interests.

____ 3. In this company, people look out for each other's good.

____ 4. It is very important here to follow strictly the company's rules and procedures.

____ 5. In this company, people protect their own interests above other considerations.

____ 6. The first consideration is whether a decision violates any law.

____ 7. Everyone is expected to stick by company rules and procedures.

____ 8. The most efficient way is always the right way in this company.

____ 9. Our major consideration is what is best for everyone in the company.

____ 10. In this company, the law or ethical code of the profession is the major consideration.

____ 11. It is expected at this company that employees will always do what is right for the consumer and the public.

To score the questionnaire, first add up your responses to questions 1, 3, 6, 9, 10, and 11. This is subtotal number 1. Next, reverse the scores on questions 2, 4, 5, 7, and 8 (5 = 0, 4 = 1, 3 = 2, 2 = 3, 1 = 4, 0 = 5). Add the reverse scores to form subtotal number 2. Add subtotal number 1 to subtotal number 2 for an overall score.

Subtotal 1 ______ + Subtotal 2 ______ = Overall Score ______ .

Overall scores can range from 0 to 55. The higher the score, the more the organization's culture encourages ethical behavior.

SELF-SCORING EXERCISE

Assessing Whether Specific Situations Are Ethical

The purpose of this exercise is to explore your opinions about ethical issues faced in organizations. The class should be divided into twelve groups. Each group will randomly be assigned one of the following issues:

1. Is it ethical to take office supplies from work for home use? Make personal long-distance calls from the office? Use company time for personal business? Or do these behaviors constitute stealing?
2. If you exaggerate your credentials in an interview, is it lying? Is lying to protect a co-worker acceptable?
3. If you pretend to be more successful than you are to impress your boss, are you being deceitful?
4. How do you differentiate between a bribe and a gift?
5. If there are slight defects in a product you are selling, are you obligated to tell the buyer? If an advertised "sale" price is really the everyday price, should you divulge the information to the customer?
6. Suppose you have a friend who works at the ticket office for the convention center where Garth Brooks will be appearing. Is it cheating if you ask the friend to get you tickets so that you won't have to fight the crowd to get them? Is buying merchandise for your family at your company's cost cheating?
7. Is it immoral to do less than your best in work performance? Is it immoral to accept worker's compensation when you are fully capable of working?
8. What behaviors constitute emotional abuse at work? What would you consider an abuse of one's position of power?
9. Are high-stress jobs a breech of ethics? What about transfers that break up families?
10. Are all rule violations equally important? Do employees have an ethical obligation to follow company rules?
11. To what extent are you responsible for the ethical behavior of your co-workers? If you witness unethical behavior and don't report it, are you an accessory?
12. Is it ethical to help one work group at the expense of another group? For instance, suppose one group has excellent performance and you want to reward its members with an afternoon off. The other work group will have to pick up the slack and work harder if you do this. Is this ethical?

Once your group has been assigned its issue, you have two tasks:

1. First, formulate your group's answer to the ethical dilemmas.
2. After you have formulated your group's position, discuss the individual differences that may have contributed to your position. You will want to discuss the individual differences presented in this chapter as well as any others that you believe affected your position on the ethical dilemma.

Your instructor will lead the class in a discussion of how individual differences may have influenced your positions on these ethical dilemmas.

> ***A comprehensive annual ethics training program heightens the awareness of our employees and provides guidelines to resolve issues responsibly.***
>
> **—Rockwell International**

CROSS-FUNCTIONAL TEAMWORK

Ethical Responsibilities Across Business Functions

The perception of a firm's ethical standards is dependent on its team of managers. The ethical responsibilities of a firm's managers vary with their specific job assignments. Production managers are responsible for producing a product that is safe. They should also ensure that the production process satisfies environmental standards.

Marketing managers are responsible for marketing a product in a manner that neither misrepresents the product's characteristics nor misleads consumers or investors. Marketing managers must communicate with production managers to ensure that product marketing is consistent with the production. Any product promotion by marketing managers that makes statements about quality should be assessed by production managers to ensure accuracy.

Financial managers are responsible for providing accurate financial reports to creditors or investors who may provide financial support to the firm. They rely on information from production and marketing managers when preparing their financial reports.

A firm earns a reputation for being ethical by ensuring that ethical standards are maintained in all business functions. If a part of the team of managers is unethical, the entire firm will be viewed as unethical.

"Boise Cascade is committed to protecting the health and safety of our employees, being a responsible corporate citizen in the communities in which we operate, and providing active stewardship of the timberlands under our management."

—Boise Cascade

"We . . . believe that to create long term value for shareholders, we must also create value in our relationships with customers, employees, suppliers and the communities in which we operate."

—Briggs & Stratton

Most firms have procedures in place to ensure that these social responsibilities are satisfied. They also enforce codes that specify their responsibilities. Prudential Securities has created a new position called "Corporate Values Officer," to ensure that its social responsibilities are satisfied.

Some firms may make more of an effort to follow ethical standards than others. The first Self-Scoring Exercise allows you to assess the ethical standards of the firm where you work. Employees may vary in their perception of what behavior is ethical. The second Self-Scoring Exercise provides a variety of situations which would probably be perceived as unethical behavior by some people but as acceptable behavior by others.

THE COST OF ENSURING SOCIAL RESPONSIBILITIES

6 **Explain the costs that firms incur in achieving their social responsibilities.**

A summary of possible expenses incurred as a result of social responsibilities is provided in Exhibit 3.7. Some firms incur large expenses in all areas of social responsibility. For example, automobile manufacturers such as Ford Motor Company and General Motors must ensure that their production of automobiles does not harm the environment. Second, they must ensure proper treatment of employees because of

Exhibit 3.7
Possible Expenses Incurred as a Result of Social Responsibilities

Responsibility to:	Expenses Incurred as a Result of:
Customers	Establishing program to receive and resolve complaints Conducting surveys to assess customer satisfaction Lawsuits by customers (product liability)
Employees	Establishing program to receive and resolve complaints Conducting surveys to assess employee satisfaction Lawsuits by employees based on allegations of discrimination
Stockholders	Disclosing financial information periodically Lawsuits by stockholders based on allegations that the firm's managers are not fulfilling their obligations to stockholders
Environment	Complying with governmental regulations on environment Complying with self-imposed environmental guidelines
Community	Sponsoring community activities

their massive work force. Third, they must ensure that they deliver a safe and reliable product to their customers.

In recent years, many new government regulations have been imposed to create a cleaner environment and ensure other social responsibilities. Normally, all the firms in the industry will raise their prices to cover the expenses associated with following new government regulations. For example, restrictions on cutting down trees resulted in higher expenses for paper companies. These companies raised their prices to cover these higher expenses. Maintaining social responsibilities is necessary but costly, and customers indirectly pay the expenses involved.

Cost of Lawsuits

When assessing the expense involved in dealing with customer or employee complaints, firms will normally consider the cost of hiring people to resolve the complaints. However, they must also consider the cost of defending against possible lawsuits by customers and employees. Customers suing firms for product defects or deceptive advertising and employees suing their firms for discrimination are common practices today.

Some obvious expenses associated with a lawsuit are as follows. First, the court may fine a firm that is found guilty. Some fines imposed by the court have amounted to several million dollars. Second, some lawsuits are settled out-of-court but commonly require firms to make some payment to customers or employees. Third, a firm may incur substantial expenses when hiring an attorney. Many lawsuits continue for several years, and the expenses of the attorney (or a law firm) for a single case may exceed \$1 million. Fourth, an indirect cost of a lawsuit is the decline in demand for a firm's product because of bad publicity associated with the lawsuit. This results in less revenue to the firm.

Even when firms establish and enforce a comprehensive code of social responsibility, they do not necessarily avoid lawsuits. They must recognize this when estimating the expenses involved in social responsibility. Consider the situation in June 1993, when the media announced that some customers had found syringes in their Pepsi cans. After this announcement, other customers reported similar findings. This

The cost of double hulling—creating a protective layer between the outside of the ship and the oil—leads to increased ship building costs, the increased cost of fueling a heavier vessel, and lost transport volume. This cost must be balanced against the costs of a spill to commercial fishermen, recreational fishermen, and beach visitors.

not only caused potential product liability lawsuits but also caused some consumers to switch to other soft drinks. Within two weeks of the first claim, several people were arrested for false tampering charges. One person placing a syringe in a Pepsi can was even caught on videotape. It became clear that the product was not defective but that people were claiming a defect to win large cash settlements through lawsuits. While the conclusion in this case was favorable, PepsiCo spent millions of dollars attempting to determine whether the claims were valid and then convincing the public that the claims were false.

Firms must recognize that they will incur some expenses arising out of customer or employee claims (whether the claims are valid or not). They may also incur expenses from purchasing product liability insurance to cover potential lawsuits. In some businesses (such as specific medical fields), a major expense to the firm is liability insurance. The threat of liability lawsuits may even discourage entrepreneurs from establishing some types of businesses.

BUSINESS DILEMMA

COLLEGE HEALTH CLUB

Social Responsibility At College Health Club

As a college student, Sue Kramer always had an interest in the social responsibility of businesses. Now that she is establishing the College Health Club (CHC), she can apply her beliefs about social responsibility to her own business.

Dilemma

Sue recognizes that being socially responsible might either reduce her firm's earnings or result in higher prices to her customers because expenses are incurred as a result of many social responsibilities. Sue's goal is to develop strategies for satisfying CHC's social responsibilities in a manner that could still maximize the value of CHC. What responsibilities should Sue have toward her customers? Employees? Community? Environment?

Solution

Sue identifies specific responsibilities of CHC to her customers, employees, and environment, as explained next:

- *Responsibility to Customers* Sue plans to spend some of her time talking with customers at the health club to determine whether the customers (members) are satisfied with the facilities that CHC offers. She also plans to send out a survey to all the members to obtain more feedback. Furthermore, she offers a money-back guarantee if the customers are not satisfied after a two-week trial period.

  Sue's efforts are intended not only to fulfill a moral responsibility but also to increase the firm's memberships over time. In the health club business, the firm's reputation for satisfying the customer is important. Many customers choose a health club because of referrals by other customers. Therefore, Sue hopes that her efforts will identify ways in which she can make CHC more appealing to potential members. She also wants to show her interest in satisfying the existing members.
- *Responsibility to Employees* Sue started the business with herself as the only full-time employee. However, she has one part-time employee (Lisa Lane) and expects to hire more employees over time as the number of memberships increases. Sue plans to pay employees wages that are consistent with other health clubs in the area. She also plans to have employees that are diverse in gender and race. Her goal is not just to demonstrate her willingness to seek diversity but also to attract diversity among customers as well. For example, she wants her health club to have a somewhat even mix of males and females, and believes that an even mix of employees over time might attract an even mix of customers.
- *Responsibility to the Community* Sue feels a special allegiance to the local college she has attended over the last four years. She volunteers to offer a free seminar for the college students on health issues. She believes that this service would not only fulfill her moral responsibility but also allow her to promote her new health club located next to the college campus. Therefore, her community service could ultimately enhance the value of CHC.
- *Responsibility to the Environment* Since the health club is a service, no production process is involved that could damage the environment. However, Sue will establish recycling containers for cans of soft drinks consumed at CHC.
- *Summary of CHC's Social Responsibilities* In general, Sue develops strategies that not only would satisfy social responsibilities but also would retain existing customers and attract new customers.

Additional Issues for Discussion

1 Sue was recently asked if she wanted to sell aerobics clothing in her health club. A clothing firm has the clothing produced in Asia and would sell it to Sue at low prices. Sue could then sell it to her customers at reasonable prices and still earn a profit. This would be beneficial to the customers and to CHC. Sue has heard that the clothing in some Asian countries is sometimes produced by young children under poor working conditions. Should Sue purchase the clothing?

2 Based on the information in the previous question, what is Sue's social responsibility (if any) toward preventing improper treatment of employees in other countries?
3 Recently, several college students have asked Sue for jobs at CHC. While Sue would like to help the students out, she does not need any more employees at this time. Should she hire them anyway?

SUMMARY

1 The behavior of firms is molded by business ethics, which represent a set of moral values. Firms have a responsibility to produce safe products and to sell their products without misleading the customers. They ensure social responsibility toward customers by establishing a code of ethics, monitoring customer complaints, and asking customers for feedback on products they recently purchased.

2 Firms have a responsibility to safety, proper treatment, and equal opportunity for employees. They can ensure responsibility toward employees by enforcing safety guidelines, by offering seminars on diversity, and by establishing a grievance procedure that allows employees to state any complaints.

3 Firms have a responsibility to satisfy the owners (or stockholders) who provided funds. They attempt to ensure that managers make decisions that are in the best interests of stockholders.

4 Firms have a responsibility to maintain a clean environment when operating their businesses. However they incur expenses when attempting to fulfill their environmental responsibility.

5 Firms have a social responsibility to the local communities in which they attract customers and employees. They provide donations and other benefits to local communities.

6 When firms ensure their social responsibilities, they may incur substantial expenses. These expenses are ultimately incurred by the customers, since the prices of products charged by firms are influenced by the expenses incurred.

KEY TERMS

affirmative action
business ethics
consumerism
institutional investors
monopoly
sexual harassment
shareholder activism
social responsibility

REVIEW QUESTIONS

1 Define business ethics and describe an ethical situation in which you had to decide right from wrong.
2 Describe a firm's social responsibility to its community and the environment.
3 Identify and explain the major areas of social responsibility with which a business should be concerned.
4 Identify the steps a firm develops to ensure social responsibility to its customers.
5 How can a business ensure social responsibility to its customers and still have a right to earn a profit?
6 Explain how the government becomes socially responsible to consumers.
7 Describe the most common abuses to the environment and how businesses can prevent them.
8 How does a business's environmental responsibility impact product prices?
9 Identify and explain the conflicting objectives that often challenge a manager's responsibility.
10 Identify expenses that a firm may incur when assuming social responsibility for customers and employees.

DISCUSSION QUESTIONS

1 Assume you are a manager. How would your firm's business ethics and social responsibility impact your decision making, and what effect would these issues have on the organization's bottom line (earnings)?

2 Assume you are a manager. What are your ethical responsibilities to the following: (a) employees (b) stockholders (c) customers, and (d) suppliers.

3 Assume you are a salesperson on commission. How would you react if you just came out of a meeting in which the sales manager had stated: "Sales are down. I want you to sell at all costs"?

4 You are an advertising manager. You have just left a meeting having been made aware of truth in labeling laws. Would you be obligated to disclose the ingredients in your product, especially if that product has a potential side effect?

5 Discuss the pros and cons of affirmative action programs and how they impact business in their recruiting and selection efforts. Do they constrain or aid business?

RUNNING YOUR OWN BUSINESS

1 Describe the ethical dilemmas (if any) that you might face in your business. How do you plan to handle these situations?

2 What types of social responsibilities would your business have toward your employees, customers, or community? What, if any, special policies would you set to take better care of your employees, customers, or community?

INVESTING IN THE STOCK OF A BUSINESS

Using the annual report of the firm in which you would like to invest, complete the following:

1 Many firms disclose their policies on ethics and social responsibilities within their annual reports. Does your firm mention any specific policies that encourage employees' ethical behavior? Does the firm give any specific examples of how it accomplishes these goals?

2 Describe your firm's policies on its social responsibility toward its community and the environment. Does the firm give any specific examples of how it accomplishes these goals?

CASE 1 E-Mail and Ethics

The use of e-mail has become an ethical issue for many on-line computer services such as CompuServe, where fraud was committed by individuals who seized opportunities to sell illegal cellular phone devices to interested buyers. An engineer at AT&T Corporation's wireless unit was monitoring CompuServe's commercial on-line service when he came across an illegal advertisement, which permitted millions to view and purchase such equipment.

The illegal advertisements included a cellular phone that can eavesdrop on calls placed by other cellular phone users; a small, easily concealed device that steals legitimate users' phone numbers by taking them off the airwaves; and several phones that can be programmed with up to ninety-nine stolen phone numbers, instead of using a separate personal computer.

The wireless industry says it loses about $500 million in revenue each year to these individuals, but independent observers estimate the loss is closer to $1 billion. The industry must get a grip on this advancing technology. With the boom in wireless services expected to continue into the twenty-first century, current crimes are adding urgency to the industry's effort to crack down on fraud.

Questions

1 Explain whether e-mail is legal or illegal to advertise over telephone lines.

2 Do you believe there is an ethical issue in this case? If so, what is the issue?

3 Is fraud being committed over the airwaves?

4 Do sellers have a social responsibility in marketing cellular phones?

CASE 2 Social Responsibilities to Employees

David Thomas, a supervisor in the bearings department at the ABC Corporation, a rollerblade manufacturer, manages a nonunion plant where the work atmosphere appears to be a "good ol' boy" system. He desires to give preference to males by giving them the better jobs and newer equipment, and favoritism is often extended to them. Currently there are no females in management positions throughout the plant. Females tend to occupy token positions, often starting out as clerk-typists or file clerks, and few female employees advance into higher positions. Presently twenty people work in Mr. Thomas's department; only two are female. All perform the same job; skills, responsibility, and authority are the same. Males are paid $10.50 per hour; females with the same seniority earn $7.50 per hour. Working conditions throughout the department are often unsanitary, and neglect on the supervisor's part has made the department unsafe. Recently, many complaints have been made from Mr. Thomas's employees concerning the poor working conditions. Mr. Thomas is a profit maximizer with a bottom-line orientation and often ignores any safety policy directive that comes from top management.

In his office, Mr. Thomas has pinups on every wall. On his desk are sexually explicit slogans that some females have found offensive. His language tends to be off-color and is often upsetting to many people throughout the plant.

Mr. Thomas has just received a memo. He has been asked by the company president to attend a meeting on social responsibility. The memo reads, "The company is going in a new direction. We would like your input on social responsibility issues that this company should adopt." Mr. Thomas's immediate reaction is, "This company has always been a profit-maximizing firm and should not concern itself with any social issues because they constrain and impact the bottom line of the company's operations." Thus, he refuses to attend the meeting.

Questions

1. Is Mr. Thomas ignoring any social responsibility issues in his department operations?
2. Is Mr. Thomas correct in saying that the ABC Corporation should be a profit-maximizing firm at all costs?
3. Is Mr. Thomas discriminating against females and, if so, in what areas?
4. What are the potential costs to the firm as a result of Mr. Thomas's actions?

VIDEO CASE Payback for Social Responsibility

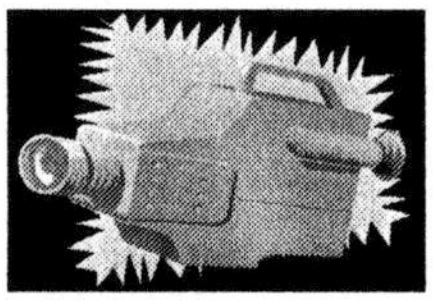

One of a retailer's worst nightmares turned into reality for Alton Bankston when the principal supplier of his primary wares, paints, opened a company outlet a few blocks away and called on his customers, offering lower prices on the same paint he had been selling.

The big company thought Bankston might close up shop. But he wasn't going to give up a business he's put 10 years of his life into. He fought back.

The first thing Alton Bankston had to do to stay in business was choose a new paint line. He quickly got it in stock and informed his customers about it. (His new supplier didn't make marine paint, a necessity for a Gulf Coast paint retailer, so he found a supplier for that, too.)

To counter efforts to woo away his customers, he emphasized personalized treatment. He established a file of custom colors clients used. And customers began receiving Bankston's thank-you, get-well, and congratulations cards.

Believing that "people buy from people they know," he says, he and his staff became heavily involved in community affairs, joining civic, charitable, and service organizations. Bankston's sponsored Little League basketball, baseball, football, and soccer teams, and employees sometimes coached.

Paint sales increased 31 percent in a year. "We were a tired bunch of folks but very happy and thankful," Bankston says.

Then the street in front of the store was torn up in a major construction project, which was supposed to take six months but lasted 18.

If customers couldn't get to the store, it would go to them. It delivered and not just during normal business hours. "Each night our employees loaded up their cars and delivered on the way home and in the early morning," Bankston says.

The demand for Bankston's products increased over time in response to its efforts to satisfy the community. The community service not only was in the form of social responsibility, but also resulted in a continual demand by customers for its products.

Questions

1 Was it unethical for Bankston's supplier to open a paint store just a few blocks away and try to lure Bankston's customers to its new store?

2 Why might some firms benefit more than others as a result of social responsibility? To answer this question, consider whether a paint supplier that focuses on supplying paint to several paint stores around the country would benefit as much as Bankston's from serving the local community.

3 If you owned a store, how could you discourage one of your suppliers from opening a retail store nearby that would directly compete with your store?

THE Coca-Cola COMPANY ANNUAL REPORT PROJECT

The following questions apply concepts learned in this chapter to The Coca-Cola Company. Read the section called "Environmental Statement" on page 74 in The Coca-Cola Company annual report before answering these questions

1 Do you think The Coca-Cola Company has an advantage over other large companies with respect to its impact on the environment?

2 What is the focus of the Company's environmental efforts?

3 How can you obtain more information about The Coca-Cola Company's environmental efforts?

IN-TEXT STUDY GUIDE

Answers are in an appendix at the back of the book.

True or False

1 The responsibility of firms toward customers can be enforced by specific groups of consumers.

2 The government protects consumers by regulating the quality of some products that firms produce.

3 Deregulation results in lower prices for consumers.

4 Marketing managers are primarily responsible for providing accurate financial information to creditors or investors who may provide financial support to the firm.

5 In 1970, the Environmental Protection Agency was created to develop and enforce pollution standards.

6 Employees commonly sue firms for product defects or deceptive advertising.

7 Firms have a social responsibility when producing and selling their products.

8 An attempt by a firm to maximize social responsibility to the community may reduce the firm's ability to provide products at a reasonable price to consumers.

9 U.S. firms that conduct business in foreign countries are not subject to the rules enforced by the local government.

10 The Clayton Act prevents competition.

Multiple Choice

11 The act that prohibits unfair methods of competition is the:
a) Humphrey Act.
b) Civil Rights Act of 1964.
c) Federal Trade Commission Act.
d) Garn Act.
e) Reagan Antitrust Act.

12 An active role by stockholders in influencing a firm's management policies is called:
a) empowerment.
b) reengineering.
c) self-managed teams.
d) quality circles.
e) shareholder activism.

13 Tying agreements, binding contracts, and interlocking directorates are prohibited by the:
a) Clayton Act.
b) Sherman Antitrust Act.
c) Robinson-Patman Act.
d) Celler-Kefauver Act.
e) Federal Trade Commission Act.

14 Many U.S. firms provide guidelines of behavior to employees through a code of:
a) reciprocity.
b) cartel arrangements.

c) kickback arrangements.
d) technical production manuals.
e) ethics.

15 Compensation that is based on the volume of an employee's sales of the firm's products is called:
a) share of stock.
b) stock certificate.
c) corporate bond.
d) promotion.
e) commission or bonus.

16 To ensure that employees receive proper treatment if they believe they are not being given equal opportunity, the firm's management establishes a:
a) labor contract. b) strike.
c) grievance procedure. d) walkout.
e) lockout.

17 ______________________ of a firm can monitor any employee decisions to ensure that the decisions are made in the best interests of the owners.
a) Unions b) Customers
c) Creditors d) Managers
e) Business agents

18 The act that prohibits mergers between firms that reduce competition within an industry is the:
a) Robinson-Patman Act.
b) Celler-Kefauver Act.
c) Federal Trade Commission Act.
d) Clayton Act.
e) Sherman Antitrust Act.

19 Programs intended to prevent discrimination against minorities and women are:
a) affirmative action.
b) American disability.
c) equal say.
d) minimum wage.
e) age discrimination and employment.

20 The recognition of how a firm's business decisions can affect society is its:
a) moral code.
b) social responsibility.
c) conservation policies.
d) recycling program.
e) consumer bill of rights.

21 The decisions of a firm's managers that maximize social responsibility could conflict with maximizing:
a) cartels.
b) union gains.
c) economic forecast.
d) firm value.
e) interest payments.

22 In some industries, firms created various agreements to set prices and avoid competition, which the federal government has attempted to prevent by enforcing:
a) business trust.
b) regulated monopolies.
c) antitrust laws.
d) consumerism.
e) conservationism.

23 If a firm is the sole provider of goods or services, it has a(n):
a) oligopoly.
b) monopsony.
c) partnership.
d) sole proprietorship.
e) monopoly.

24 Managers who are responsible for marketing a product in a manner that neither misrepresents the product's characteristics nor misleads consumers or investers are:
a) finance managers.
b) sales managers.
c) marketing managers.
d) human resource managers.
e) production managers.

25 Shareholder activism is most commonly practiced by:
a) customers.
b) chief executive officers.
c) institutional investors.
d) managers.
e) the government.

26 ______________________ represents the collective consumer demand that businesses satisfy their needs.
a) Conservationism
b) Consumerism
c) Social responsibility
d) Business ethics
e) Recycling

27 Managers responsible for producing a safe product are called:
a) marketing managers.
b) finance managers.
c) sales managers.
d) human resource managers.
e) production managers.

28 Most firms have procedures in place as well as codes to ensure individual employee accountability. This is a part of their:
a) program network.
b) division of work.
c) local area network.
d) social responsibility.
e) recycling program.

29 Firms are responsible to their creditors by meeting their:
a) dividend payments.
b) financial obligations.
c) retained earnings.
d) stockholder's equity.
e) treasury stock.

30 A set of principles that deal with the right and wrong issues pertaining to business decisions are:
a) business policies.
b) procedures.
c) rules.
d) business ethics.
e) work standards.

31 The act that prohibits discrimination due to national origin, race, gender, or religion is the:
a) Clayton Act.
b) Sherman Antitrust Act.
c) Federal Trade Commission Act.
d) Civil Rights Act of 1964.
e) Robinson-Patman Act.

32 The following industries have been deregulated, allowing more firms to enter the industry, except for:
a) trucking.
b) railroads.
c) airlines.
d) boating.
e) telecommunications.

33 The firm's management is responsible for satisfying their:
a) union demands.
b) owners or stockholders.
c) business agents.
d) competition.
e) friends.

34 The act that prohibits price differences on promotional allowances that reduce competition within an industry is the:
a) Celler-Kefauver Act.
b) Robinson-Patman Act.
c) Clayton Act.
d) Sherman Antitrust Act.
e) Federal Trade Commission Act.

35 The act that encourages competition and prevents monopolies is the:
a) Deregulation Act.
b) Federal Trade Commission Act.
c) Robinson-Patman Act.
d) Celler-Kefauver Act.
e) Sherman Antitrust Act.

Finding Information About Firms on the Internet

The Internet, particularly the World Wide Web (WWW), represents a tremendous source of firm and industry information. Tens of thousands of companies have placed information about themselves (including their social responsibilities and their products) on the WWW, information that is freely accessible to those who know where to look. Unfortunately, knowing where to look can be challenging. To aid users in that task, three different types of tools are available: directories, search engines, and metasearch engines.

DIRECTORIES In the past few years, a number of companies have undertaken the task of trying to catalog useful sites on the WWW. Yahoo! (Exhibit 3.8) whose mission is "To be the world's best guide for information and online discovery," is a prime example of a company that attempts to provide such a service. Using the service begins by accessing Yahoo!'s home page using a WWW browser such as Mosaic, Netscape, or the America Online browser (pictured). From that page, the search can then begin.

Suppose, for example, we are interested in finding out about participants in the brewery industry. We would begin by choosing "Business and Economy." A new win-

Exhibit 3.8
Yahoo! Home Page
http://www.yahoo.com/

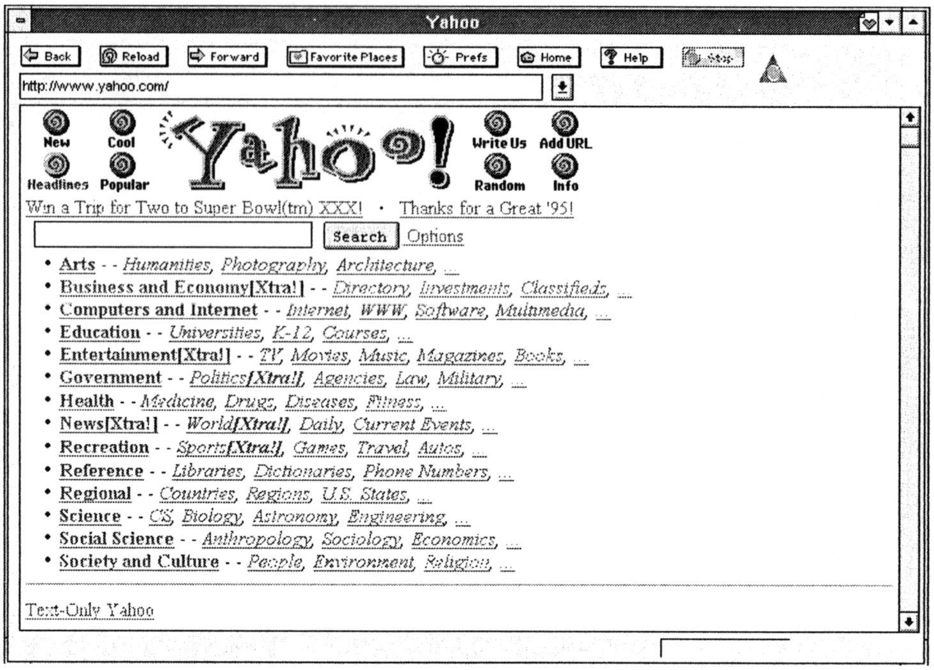

dow appears, which displays a list of different topics to choose from (Exhibit 3.9). Since we are interested in brewery industry participants, the most appropriate selection would be "Companies."

The company page is then displayed, which organizes companies according to the industry in which they are located (Exhibit 3.10). By clicking the mouse on "Breweries," we are then presented with a list of breweries that have established WWW sites (Exhibit 3.11). By clicking on individual sites, access to the information provided by the company is then made visible.

Exhibit 3.9
Topics in Yahoo!'s "Business and Economy" Page

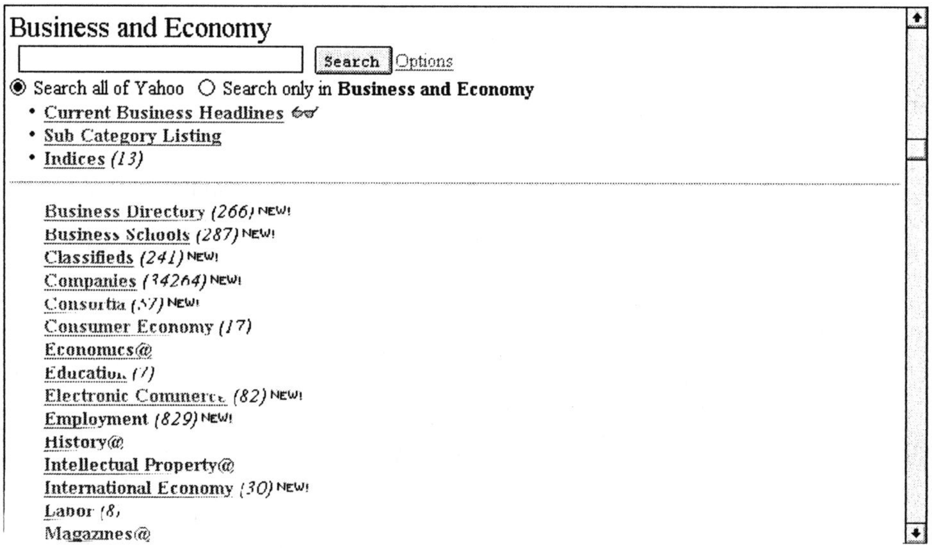

Exhibit 3.10
Yahoo! Links to Companies, by Industry

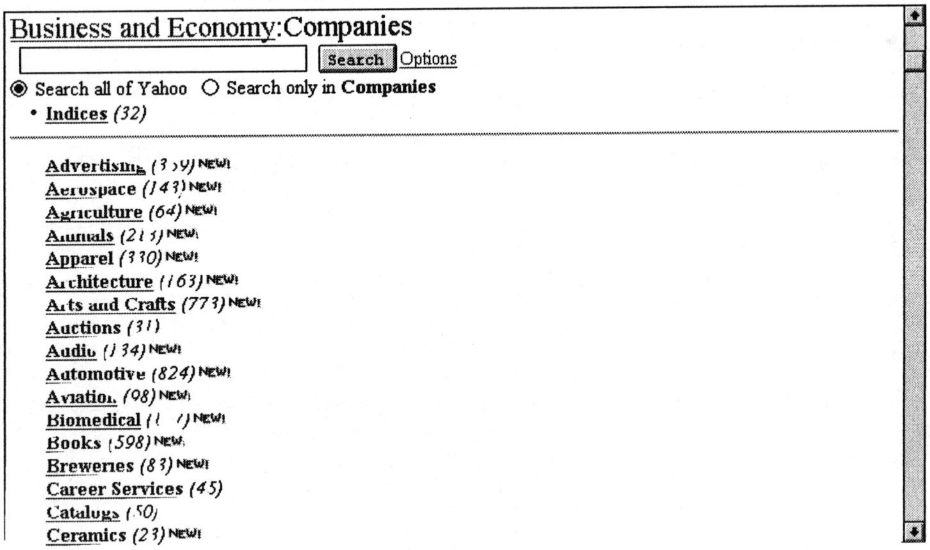

SEARCH ENGINES In addition to searching by navigating through the menus, searching is also possible by using keywords (Exhibit 3.12). Yahoo! for example, offers keyword searches for sites contained in the Yahoo! system. Such searches are accompanied by entering the desired information in a search box, then pressing the search button (see figure). Other sites, such as Lycos and WebCrawler, continually search the web for new home pages and index them in a database that can then be searched. As of the end of 1995, both sites had over a million pages indexed. They are also easily accessible; for example, both are available for use in Yahoo! itself.

METASEARCH ENGINES Metasearch engines are sites or software that automatically invoke other search engines to find user-specified keywords. In other words, when you type in your keyword, the metasearch site automatically contacts other search sites and returns the results of all searches. An example of such a site is SavvySearch (Exhibit 3.13). The advantage of such engines is that they free the user from worry-

Exhibit 3.11
Listing of Individual Breweries with WWW Sites

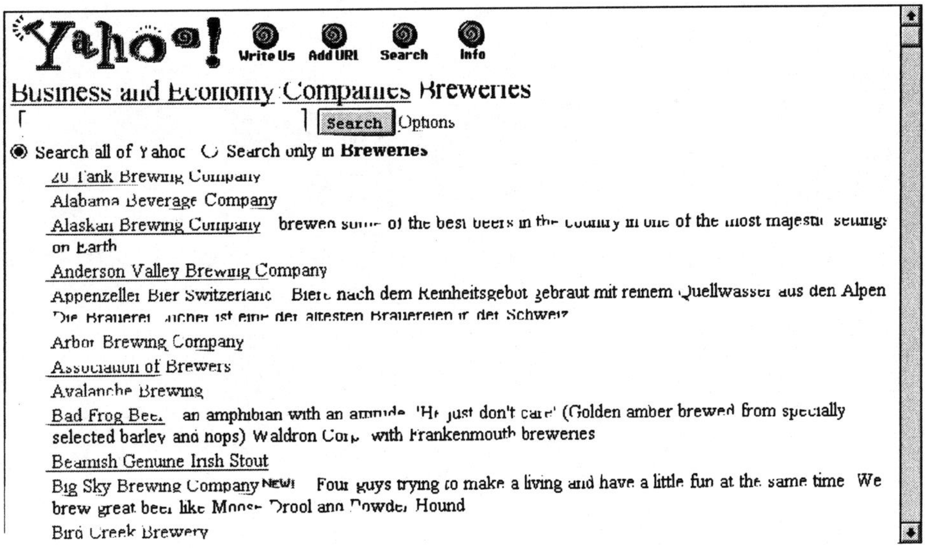

Exhibit 3.12
Major Search Resources

Search tools are accessed by plugging their address into a web browser. Below are the addresses for some of the most powerful search resources.

Search Engines	
Open Text Index	http://www.opentext.com:8080/
Info Seek	http://www.infoseek.com/
Alta Vista (digital)	http://altavista.digital.com
Lycos	http://www.lycos.com/
Web Crawler	http://www.webcrawler.com/
World Wide Web Worm	http://wwww.cs.colorado.edu/wwww
Harvest	http://harvest.cs.colorado.edu/
Aliweb	http://www.nexor.co.uk/public/aliweb/aliweb.html
Deja News	http://www.dejanews.com/
Magellan	http://www.mckinley.com/
Yellow Pages	http://www.mcp.com/
Metasearch Engines	
Search Savvy	http://guaraldi.cs.colostate.edu:2000/
Starting Point	http://www.stpt.com/

ing about the specifics of a search. PC-based software, such as Quarterdeck's Compass, is also capable of performing such searches. For an excellent review of using search engines for business purposes, see the Luckman Home Page (http://www.luckman.com).

Exhibit 3.13
Savvy Search

http://www.cs.colostate.edu/~dreiling/smartform.html

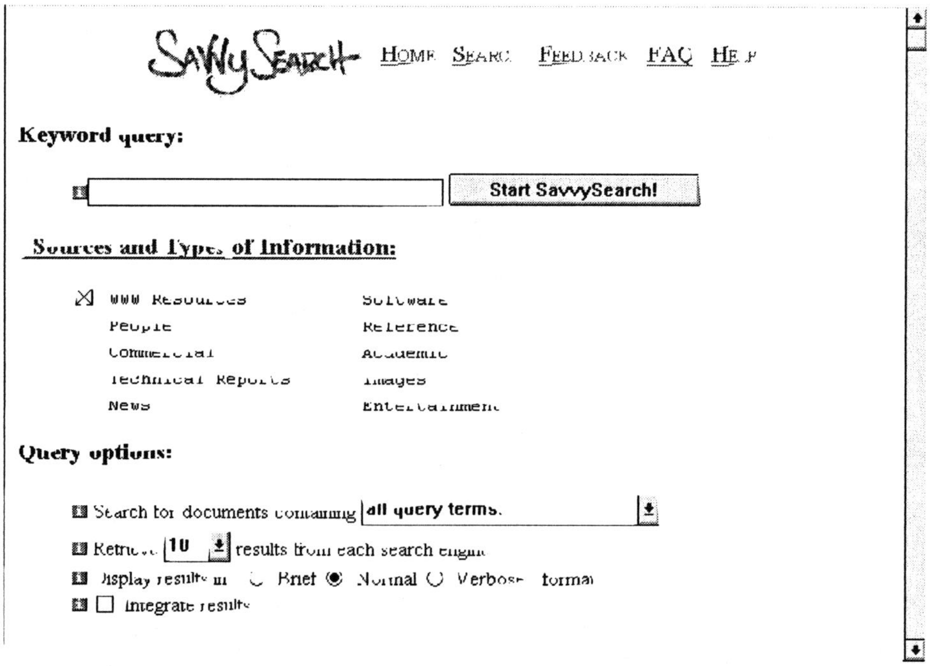

ETHICS There are many ethical issues related to the use of the Internet. Because there is no governing body for much of the Internet, the system is self-monitoring and dependent on the ethical behavior of the users. A list of behaviors to avoid follows:

- Profanity should be confined to appropriate locations and audiences.
- It is unethical and illegal to distribute copyrighted materials.
- Users should minimize the use of blank space and excessively long messages. Overuse creates system delays for all users.
- There are many marketplace sites and websites that allow product ordering; however users should not be sent unsolicited sales and marketing materials by e-mail.
- Personal records and information should not be distributed without the person's consent.
- A variety of software programs screen websites for graphic material. Most sites willingly participate in these ratings to assist parents and users with locking out violent images or pornography.

SUMMARY OF PART I

The success of a business may depend on the initial decisions that are made by its owners when it is established. The first set of decisions is made within the business plan (Chapter 1), which requires management, marketing and financial plans. The management plan consists of decisions about production, organizational structure, and employee job descriptions. Management policies are discussed in more detail in Parts II and III. The marketing plan consists of pricing, distribution, and promotion decisions, and is discussed in more detail in Part IV. The financial plan consists of financing decisions and business investment decisions, which are discussed in detail in Part V.

In addition to the business plan, owners who establish a new business must select the proper form of ownership (Chapter 2). The possible forms of ownership are sole proprietorships, partnerships, and corporations. This decision is based on various characteristics of the business, such as the potential liability of the business and the amount of funds needed to support the business.

Owners of a new business also need to establish ethical and social responsibilities (Chapter 3), which provide guidelines for proper treatment of its customers, employees, stockholders, and creditors. Overall, the business plan, form of business ownership, and ethical guidelines establish a foundation which can be used by the firm's managers to make future decisions.

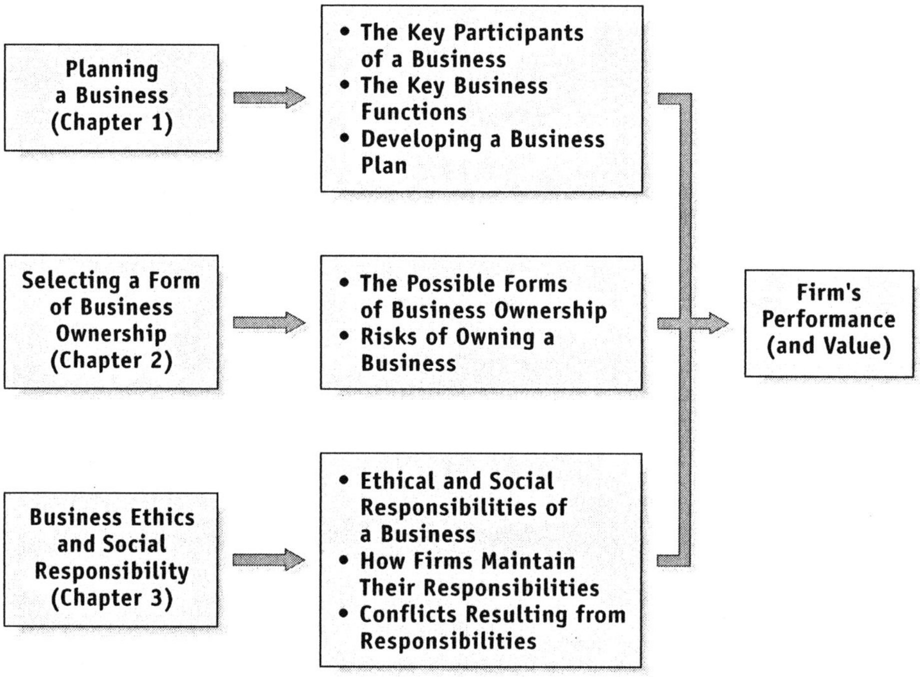

5

Accounting and Organizations

OVERVIEW

This book introduces basic concepts of accounting. It will help you understand why accounting information is important, how accounting information is produced, and how you can use this information in making decisions about organizations. Accounting describes economic events that occur in organizations. Therefore, to understand accounting, you need to understand organizations. This chapter will introduce the purposes of organizations, how they achieve their purposes, the types of decisions made in organizations, and the role of accounting information in making these decisions. **Once you have completed this chapter, you should understand that accounting is a system that produces information for making decisions about organizations.**

Major topics covered in this chapter include:

- An illustration of the accounting process
- The purposes and functions of organizations
- Decisions made in organizations
- The role of accounting in making decisions about organizations

The Accounting Information System

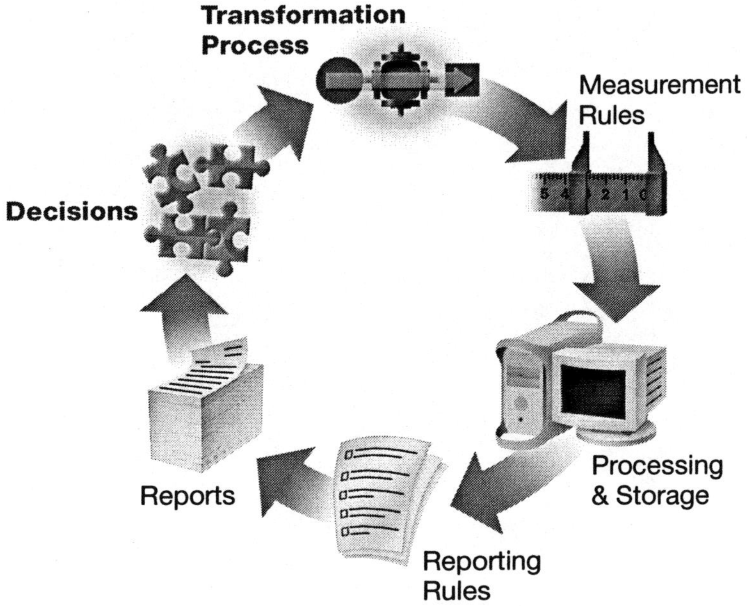

OBJECTIVES

Once you have completed this chapter, you should be able to:

1. Identify how accounting information helps decision makers.
2. Explain why accounting is an information system.
3. Compare major types of organizations and explain their purpose.
4. Explain why owners invest in businesses.
5. Explain why accounting information is useful to investors.
6. Identify financing activities and the types of decisions they require.
7. Identify investing activities and the types of decisions they require.
8. Identify operating activities and the types of decisions they require.
9. Describe the steps in an organization's transformation process.
10. Define accounting.

INFORMATION FOR DECISIONS

OBJECTIVE 1

Identify how accounting information helps decision makers.

All of us make decisions, and we use information to help us make our decisions. ***Information* includes facts, ideas, and concepts that help us understand the world.** To use information, we must be able to interpret it and understand its limitations. Poor information or the improper use of information often leads to poor decisions.

As an example, assume you wish to drive from Sevierville to Waynesville. The drive will take several hours and require several turns on unfamiliar secondary roads. Therefore, you use a map to provide information to help guide you along the way (Exhibit 1).

Exhibit 1

Map from Sevierville to Waynesville

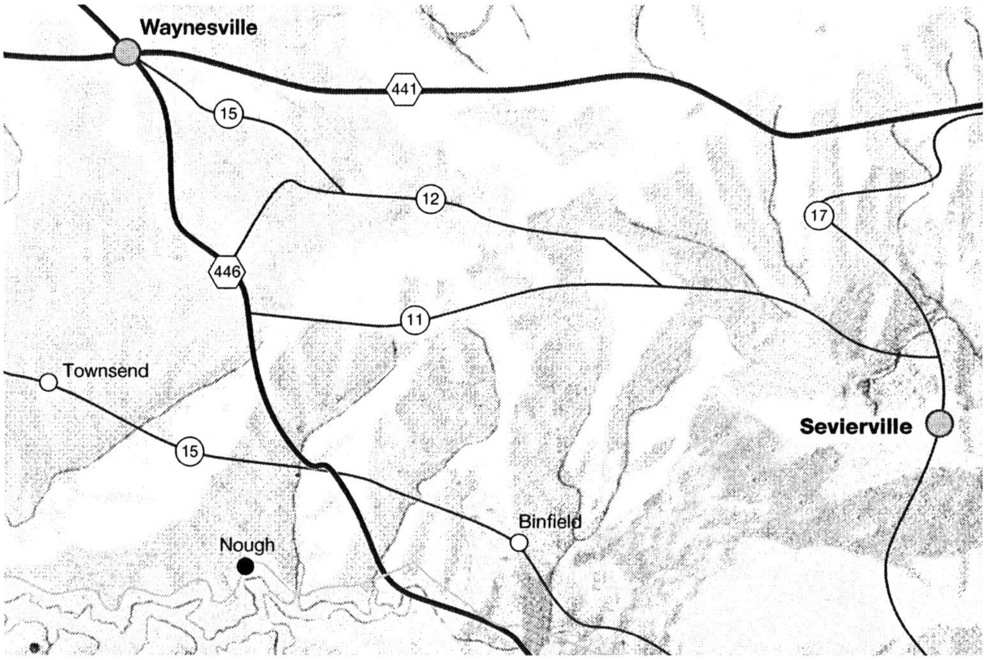

Why is the map useful? The map can help you plan your trip. You have selected a primary goal: arrive at Waynesville. You may have other goals as well, such as getting there as quickly as possible. Or, perhaps you wish to stop at various points along the way. The map provides information about alternative routes so that you can select the one that is shortest, fastest, or most scenic. Using the map along the way helps you make decisions about where to turn or stop. It helps you determine how far you have traveled and how far you have left to go. It helps you decide whether you are on the right road or where you made a wrong turn. It helps you decide where you are, how you got there, and where you are going.

Accounting provides information to help in making decisions. This information is like a map of one or more organizations. **Accounting information helps decision makers determine where they are, where they have been, and where they are going.** Rather than measuring distances in miles or kilometers, accounting measures an organization's activities by the dollar amounts associated with these activities. The primary measurement unit for accounting information is dollars in the United States or the local currency for other countries.

To illustrate, suppose you decide, as a summer job, to start a business at the beach selling sunglasses, hats, and suntan products. You will operate out of a small stand, appropriately named The Beach Shack, which you can rent from a nearby hotel that owns the beach property. Important questions you might ask include: Is this a good business opportunity? How much money should you expect to make? Are you making as much money as you expected?

Consider the primary components of your business. What will you need to start and run a business? You will need merchandise to sell. Therefore, you will have to purchase this merchandise from suppliers. You will need a place to operate your business and someone to sell the merchandise. You will need money to pay for your merchandise, the rent for your stand, wages, and any miscellaneous costs such as a business license and advertising.

As an initial step in deciding whether to start the business, you might consider how much you can expect to sell. You discuss the venture with some other business operators and determine that a small stand such as yours usually will sell about $8,000 of merchandise each month for June, July, and August.

Next, you consider how much money you will need to operate your business. Assume you determine that each month the merchandise you can sell for $8,000 will cost you $4,000. You plan to work 50 hours per week. However, you decide you will need some part-time helpers to keep the stand open ten hours a day, seven days a week. Therefore, you calculate that your costs each month will be:

Merchandise to sell	$4,000
Rent for stand	500
Wages	1,300
Miscellaneous	200
Total	$6,000

Also, you consider how much you expect to make from the business. As shown in Exhibit 2, if you expect each month to sell merchandise for $8,000 and your costs will be $6,000, you should expect to make $2,000 profit from the business, or $6,000 (3 × $2,000) for the summer. **Profit is the amount left over after the cost of doing business is subtracted from the sales amount.**

Exhibit 2

Expected Earnings from The Beach Shack

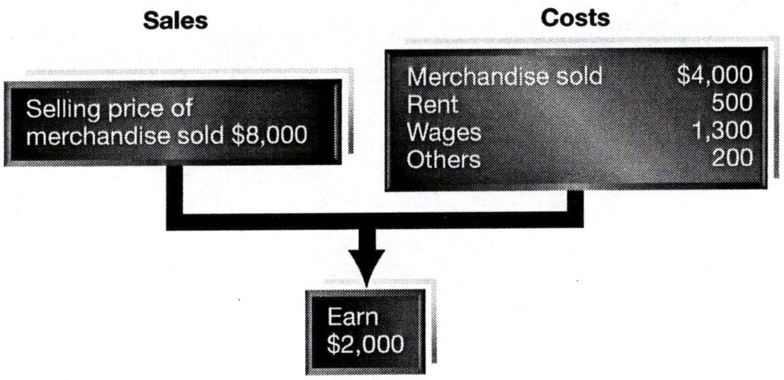

Does this appear to be a good business for you? Suppose you have $5,000 to invest in the business. You use this money to purchase an initial stock of merchandise and to pay June's rent, a portion of June's wages, and the miscellaneous costs for the month. Would investing your money in the business be a good idea?

If you don't start the business, you could work at some other job. For example, you might work at a fast-food restaurant that pays $6 an hour. If you worked 50 hours a week at the restaurant, you could earn $3,600 ($6 × 50 hours × 12 weeks) for the summer. In addition, you would not be risking your $5,000 investment and could earn some interest from investing your $5,000 in a savings account.

The information about costs and earnings cannot make your decision for you. You must consider whether you want to work on the beach instead of in a restaurant, how certain you are about the amount you can earn from your business, and how much risk you are willing to take. Investing in a business is always risky. *Risk* **is uncertainty about an outcome,** such as the amount of profit you will earn. Suppose the summer turns out to be unusually cold and wet. If you sell less than you expect, your earnings also will be less. You could even lose money. Are you willing to take the risk? Accounting can help with these decisions by providing information about what you should expect. You have to evaluate the information and make a decision.

Accounting is a way of looking at a business. It measures the activities of a business by the dollars it receives and spends. It helps decision makers determine where they started: For example, you will start by investing $5,000. It helps determine where you should end up: You expect to earn $6,000 from your investment. It helps determine whether your expectations are being met: For example, suppose you sold $7,000 of merchandise during June instead of the $8,000 you expected to sell. Like a map, accounting can help you determine that you are not where you want to be. It can help you determine what went wrong and, in some cases, what you might change to get back on the proper route.

Accounting provides a model of a business by measuring the business activities in dollar amounts. Underlying this model is an information system. This system provides a process for obtaining facts that can be converted into useful information. Understanding the system and its processes will help you understand the information provided by accounting.

The purpose of accounting is to help people make decisions about economic activities. Economic activities involve the allocation of scarce resources. People allocate scarce resources any time they exchange money, goods, or services. These activities are so common that almost every person in our society uses the accounting process to assist in decision making.

LEARNING NOTE

The terms *money* and *cash* often are used interchangeably. In everyday speech, money refers specifically to paper bills and coins. Cash is a broader term that includes checks, bank accounts, and other resources that are easily converted to money. A general term for money and items easily converted to money is *financial resources.*

THE ACCOUNTING PROCESS

OBJECTIVE 2

Explain why accounting is an information system.

To illustrate a simple accounting system, we can examine a checking account. Suppose you decide to invest in The Beach Shack. You open a checking account for the business at First Beach Bank and deposit $5,000 in the account.

Exhibit 3 The Beach Shack Check Register

Date	Check Number	Activity	Deposits	Checks	Balance
June 1		Deposit by owner	5,000.00		5,000.00
1	1	Beach Supply Company (merchandise)		3,500.00	1,500.00
1	2	Beach Hotel (rent)		500.00	1,000.00
1	3	Sun City (license)		100.00	900.00
7		Sales receipts	1,500.00		2,400.00
7	4	Wages		300.00	2,100.00
		(Other transactions for June are omitted.)			

With your checks and deposit slips, you have a check register similar to the example in Exhibit 3. (This exhibit reflects actual transactions. Do not confuse these with the expected amounts shown in Exhibit 2.) The register helps you manage and control your money by keeping track of amounts you deposit or withdraw, the source of the deposits, the recipients of the checks, the dates of these events, and the amount available in your account.

Summary Reports

If you wanted to know how much you spent in June for your business and for what purposes, you could summarize the information from the check register to help you understand these activities. For example, you might prepare a summary similar to Exhibit 4.

Exhibit 4

Summary of Deposits and Payments for June

The Beach Shack Checking Account
Summary of Deposits and Payments
For June

Beginning cash balance			$ 0
Cash deposits:			
Deposit by owner	$5,000		
Sales receipts	7,800		
Total cash deposited		$12,800	
Cash payments:			
Merchandise	$5,200		
Rent	500		
Wages	1,200		
License	100		
Total cash paid		7,000	
Excess of deposits over payments			5,800
Ending cash balance			$5,800

Note, the summary of deposits and payments provides information about cash received and paid in June. For example, you can determine that $5,200 was paid for merchandise and that $7,800 was received from customers in June. However, you cannot determine from this information if all of the merchandise purchased in June was sold to customers in June. Also, you cannot determine if customers owe you money for merchandise they bought but have not paid for.

The bank provides you with a statement that reports your checking account activities for the month. The statement lists deposits you made with the bank and checks you wrote that the bank paid during the month. The bank provides this report so that you can verify the accuracy of the information you have recorded in your check register and the accuracy of the bank's information about your account. You verify the accuracy by comparing your check register with the bank statement.

Steps in the Accounting Process

Some of the most important steps in the accounting process occur in this example of a checking account. In a checking account, you are accounting for money held by a bank for your use. The basic information unit in an accounting system is an account. **An *account* is a record of increases and decreases in the dollar amount associated with a specific resource or activity.** All information you record in your check register involves one account: your cash account with the bank. The register helps you keep track of the increases, decreases, and balance in your checking account.

The information in your check register summarizes the activities of your checking account. You record information in the register when an event occurs that increases or decreases the money in your account. **A *transaction* is an event that increases or decreases an account balance.** Transactions identify changes in resources and activities that affect resources. For example, when you write a check to pay for merchandise, you exchange money from your checking account for the merchandise. This event is a transaction, and you record it in your check register by noting the amount of the check and the reduction in your cash balance.

The bank maintains an account for each of its customers. Each time a customer deposits money or writes a check, the bank records the transaction in the customer's account. The account balance is the amount available for use by the customer. The monthly bank statement summarizes the transactions recorded by the bank for the customer's account.

The activities associated with a checking account provide an example of a typical accounting process. Exhibit 5 illustrates the four basic steps included in the process.

Exhibit 5

The Four Steps of a Typical Accounting Process

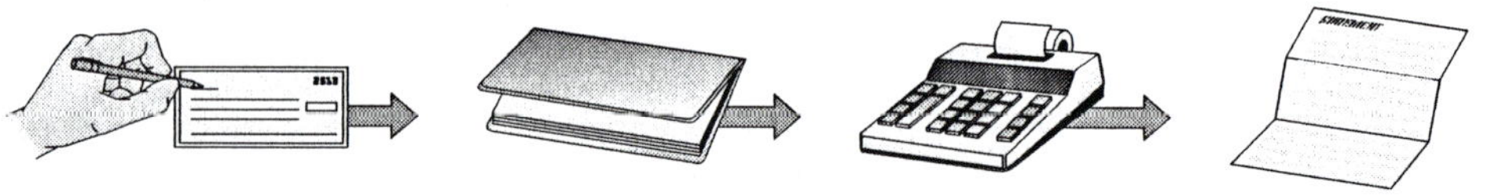

Step	Example
1. A transaction occurs.	1. Purchase mercandise.
2. Record the transaction in the proper accounts.	2. Record the payment in the check register.
3. Calculate the account balance.	3. Subtract the check amount from the balance.
4. Summarize and report transactions periodically to serve a specific need.	4. Prepare a summary of checking account activities for the month.

A *system* is a set of interrelated activities or processes that work together to achieve a goal. Because accounting involves recording, summarizing, and reporting economic information used in making decisions, it is an information system.

Uses of Accounting Information

The decisions made by users of an accounting information system determine the type of information reported by the system. A check register and a bank statement are examples of accounting information. They exist to help the depositor. Information about your checking account can help you understand how you have used your money: How much did you spend for rent last month? It can help you plan for future expenditures: Can you afford to purchase additional merchandise? It can provide assurance that you have the amount of money you think you have. Accounting information helps people make decisions.

Accounting provides information for managers, owners, members, and other stakeholders who make decisions about organizations. ***Stakeholders* include those who have an economic interest in an organization and those who are affected by its activities. An *organization* is a group of people who work together to develop, produce, and/or distribute goods or services.**

The next section of this chapter discusses the purpose of organizations and the role of accounting in organizations. Before proceeding, test your understanding of what you have read by solving the following self-study problem.

Self-Study Problem 1

The following list contains transactions for the checking account of Garcia's Deli at the Central National Bank for April 2000:

April	1	Paid rent of $800 to Northside Real Estate Company.
	5	Deposited customer receipts of $1,000.

7 Withdrew $70 for miscellaneous supplies from an automatic teller machine.
12 Purchased food for $300 from Miller's Wholesale Grocery.
14 Deposited customer receipts of $950.
17 Withdrew $50 for miscellaneous supplies from an automatic teller machine.
20 Paid the company's car payment of $200 to Citizens Loan Company.
21 Deposited customer receipts of $725.
25 Paid utility bill of $160 to City Light and Water.
27 Purchased food for $340 from Wang's Grocery.
28 Purchased supplies for $280 from Restaurant Supply Company.
28 Deposited customer receipts of $875.
30 Transferred $500 (by check) to savings account at First Savings and Loan.

The beginning balance in Garcia's Deli's checking account was $1,450. Check numbers should be recorded sequentially beginning with 346.

Required

A. Record each transaction as it would appear in Garcia's Deli's check register. Use the format provided below.

Date	Check Number	Checks Issued, Withdrawals, and Deposits	Amount of Deposit	Amount of Check/ Withdrawal	Balance

B. Prepare a summary report of cash deposits and payments for April.
C. List the steps in the accounting process associated with the checking account.

The solution to Self-Study Problem 1 appears at the end of the chapter.

THE PURPOSE OF ORGANIZATIONS

OBJECTIVE 3

Compare major types of organizations and explain their purpose.

Many types of organizations exist to serve society. Why do these organizations exist? Most exist because people need to work together to accomplish their goals. The goals are too large, too complex, or too expensive to be achieved without cooperation. All organizations provide goods and/or services. By working together, people can produce more and better goods and services.

Organizations differ as to the types of goods or services they offer (Exhibit 6). *Merchandising* **(or** *retail***)** *companies* **sell to consumers goods that are produced by other companies.** Grocery, department, and hardware stores are examples. The Beach Shack is a merchandising company. It purchases merchandise from a supplier and sells the merchandise to customers. *Manufacturing companies* **produce goods that they sell to consumers, to merchandising companies, or to other manufacturing companies.** Examples include automobile manufac-

Exhibit 6

Types of Organizations

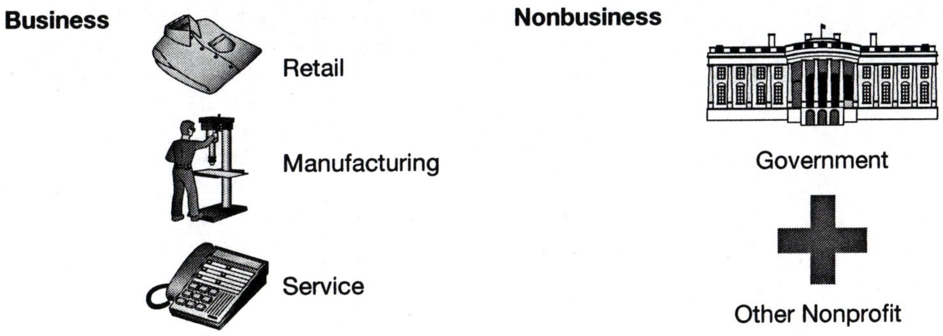

turers, petroleum refineries, furniture manufacturers, computer companies, and paper companies. *Service companies* **sell services rather than goods.** These companies include banks, insurance companies, hospitals, colleges, law firms, and accounting firms. Some companies may be a combination of types. For example, gas stations are both retail and service companies. Restaurants are both manufacturing and service companies.

Organizations may be classified by whether or not they attempt to earn a profit. Profits result from selling goods and services to customers at prices greater than the cost of the items sold. **Organizations that sell their goods and services to make a profit are** *business organizations*. *Governmental and nonprofit organizations*, **sometimes referred to as nonbusiness organizations, provide goods or, more typically, services without the intent of making a profit.** Nonbusiness organizations include civic, social, and religious organizations. Some types of services, such as education and health-care services, are provided by both business and nonbusiness organizations. Though the products are similar, the goals of the organizations providing these services are different. Nevertheless, all organizations need accounting information for decision making. This book focuses primarily on accounting for business organizations.

Transformation of Resources

A common purpose of organizations is to transform resources from one form to a different, more valuable, form to meet the needs of people. Resources include natural resources (such as minerals and timber), physical resources (such as buildings and equipment), management skills, labor, financial resources, legal rights (such as patents and trademarks), information, and the systems that provide information. The transformation process combines these resources to create goods and services (Exhibit 7). Transformation may involve making goods or services easier or less expensive for customers to obtain, as in most merchandising and service companies. Or it may involve physically converting resources by processing or combining them, as in manufacturing companies. The Beach Shack transforms resources by obtaining merchandise and making it available to customers when they need it while they are on the beach.

Exhibit 7

Transformation of Resources

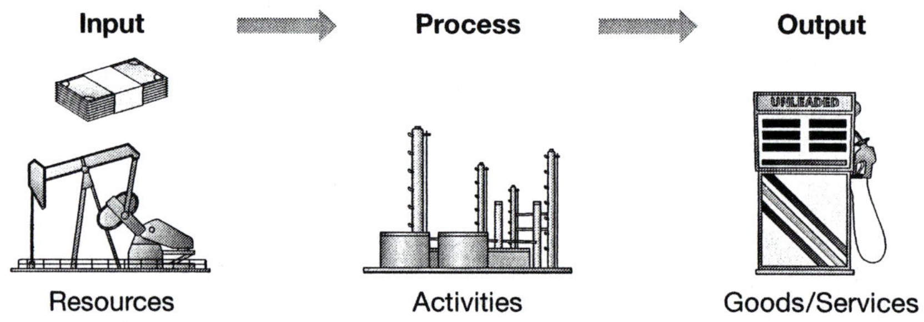

Organizations are created because many transformations are too difficult or too expensive for individuals to accomplish without working together. By combining their managerial skills, labor, and money, individuals create organizations to provide benefits that otherwise would be unavailable. These benefits occur when an organization transforms resources from a less desirable form or location to a more desirable form or location. **The transformation, if it meets a need of society, creates value because people are better off after the transformation than before.** For example, a company that manufactures shirts creates value because the shirts are more useful to those who purchase them than the material from which the shirts are made or the cotton or synthetic fibers used to make the material.

To improve its welfare, a society must encourage organizations to increase the value they create. Because resources are in scarce supply, a society should attempt to use its resources wisely. **A major purpose of accounting information is to help decide how to get the most value from scarce resources.**

Creation of Value

How can society determine how to use its resources? Decisions about using scarce resources wisely are not easy. Because society is made up of many individuals, disagreement often exists as to how resources should be used. In our society and many others, markets are the means used to promote the wise use of many resources.

Markets exist to allocate scarce resources used and produced by organizations. **A *market* is any location or process that permits resources to be bought and sold.** Competition in a market determines the amount and value of resources available for exchange. The more valuable a resource is in meeting your needs, the more you are willing to pay for it as a buyer, or the more you want for it as a seller.

The price paid for a resource in a competitive market is an indication of the value assigned to it at the particular time the buyer and seller negotiate an exchange. For example, when you buy a car, you exchange money for the car. The amount of money is a measure of the value you place on the car. Thus, the price of goods and services in a market is a basis for measuring value. **Accounting measures the increase in value created by a transformation as the difference between the total price of goods and services sold and the total cost of resources consumed in developing, producing, and selling the goods and services.**

LEARNING NOTE

Distinguish between prices charged by a business to its customers and prices paid by a business for resources it consumes. A price charged by a business is a **sales price.** A price paid by a business to purchase resources that will be consumed in providing goods and services is a **cost** to the business.

What value results when you purchase a car? The amount you pay for the car is an indication of the value you expect to receive from owning it. However, resources were consumed in producing the car and making it available to you (Exhibit 8).

The total cost of these resources (such as metals, plastics, rubber, fabric, machinery, and labor used in the manufacturing process) plus the cost of money to acquire other resources, and the cost of transportation to the dealer, is the cost of resources consumed in making the car available to you. The increase in value from the transformation that produced the car is the difference between the price you pay and the total cost of the resources consumed.

Exhibit 8

Value Created by Transformation

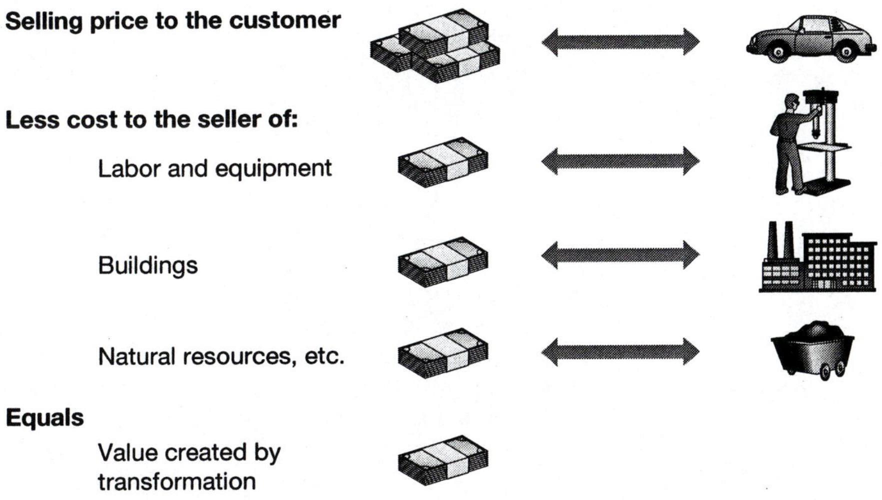

For example, if you pay $15,000 for a car and the total cost of producing the car and making it available to you is $12,000, the value added by the transformation is $3,000. The difference between the price you pay and the total cost of the car to the seller is profit for the automobile manufacturer and the dealership, or, more precisely, for the owners of those firms. ***Profit* is the difference between the price a seller receives for goods or services and the total cost to the seller of all resources consumed in developing, producing, and selling these goods or services during a particular period.** Thus, profits are the net resources generated by the sales events (resources received from the sales minus resources used in making the sales).

LEARNING NOTE

A "period" is an important concept in accounting. A period may be any length of time used to measure the effects of transactions. Common periods include months, quarters, and years. An accounting period often is called a fiscal period, because it may not coincide with a calendar period. For example, a company's fiscal year might begin on July 1.

Several types of markets are important in our economy. Markets exist for resources used by organizations. Organizations compete in **financial markets** for financial resources. Investors choose where to put their money to work by selecting among competing organizations. Organizations compete in **supplier markets** for other resources needed to produce goods and services. Competition in these markets determines the costs of materials, labor, equipment, and other resources available to organizations. Organizations compete in **product markets** (markets for goods and services). These markets determine the prices of goods and services available to customers. From the perspective of organizations, financial and supplier markets are input markets; product markets are output markets. All of these markets allocate scarce resources.

An Illustration of Creating Value

Exhibit 9 reports profit earned by The Beach Shack in June. Profit of $2,100 represents the difference between the amount of resources created by selling goods to customers and the total cost of resources consumed in providing those goods.

Exhibit 9

Profit Statement for June

The Beach Shack
Profit Earned
For June

Resources created		$7,800
Resources consumed:		
Merchandise sold	$3,900	
Rent	500	
Wages	1,200	
License	100	
Total resources consumed		5,700
Profit		$2,100

Of course, a business venture may not produce a profit. It may produce a loss by consuming more resources than it creates.

Observe that Exhibit 9 reports the cost of resources consumed, not resources purchased. Only part of the merchandise purchased was sold during June. The cost of merchandise sold during June was $3,900, though $5,200 of merchandise was purchased (see Exhibit 4). The Beach Shack still had $1,300 of unsold merchandise on hand at the end of June. Also, observe that the exhibit includes only resources earned. The Beach Shack earned the $7,800 of sales it made to customers during June. It did not earn the initial $5,000 investment by the owner. It is important to distinguish between resources earned and consumed and other amounts received or paid. This exhibit reports results of activities that occurred during June. These results can be compared with expected results. Thus, The Beach Shack had sales of $7,800, compared with expected sales of $8,000. The cost of merchandise sold during June was $3,900, rather than the expected amount of $4,000 (see Exhibit 2).

Investment by Owners

OBJECTIVE 4

Explain why owners invest in businesses.

Businesses earn profits by providing goods and services demanded by society. **Owners invest in a business to receive a return on their investments from profits earned by that business.** By investing in a business, owners are forgoing the use of their money for other purposes. In exchange, they expect to share in a business's earnings. *Return on investment (ROI)* **is the amount of profits earned by a business that could be paid to owners.** Return on investment often is expressed as a percentage: Profit ÷ amount invested.

Profits represent net resources that have been earned through sales transactions. A business may distribute profits to its owners. Alternatively, owners (or managers acting on their behalf) may decide to reinvest profits in a business to acquire additional resources. The business can use the additional resources to earn more profits by expanding its size or by expanding into new locations or product lines. Either way, the owners are better off. They receive cash from their investments if profits are withdrawn, or they own a business that is more valuable if profits are reinvested.

As shown in Exhibit 9, The Beach Shack earned $2,100 during June. As the owner, you may choose to withdraw some or all of this amount for personal use. It is your return on investment. Alternatively, you might choose to reinvest a portion of this profit to enlarge your company by buying a larger amount of merchandise for sale in July. Or, you might decide to open a second store if you are optimistic about future sales.

Your return on investment for June was $2,100, or 42% ($2,100 ÷ $5,000) relative to your initial investment. If you withdraw more than $2,100 from your business, the additional amount withdrawn is a return *of* investment, not a return *on* investment. It is a return of a portion of the amount you originally invested. **For a company to maintain its capital (the amount invested by its owners), it must pay a return to owners from profits the company has earned. Otherwise, the company is reducing its capital by returning a portion of owners' investments to them.**

The amount of return you receive from a company depends on the company's success in earning a profit. If you are the primary owner of a business, its success depends primarily on your ability and effort. If you invest in a large company, its success depends largely on the abilities and efforts of those who manage the business. When you invest in a business, you have no guarantee that it will be successful. You are taking a risk that you may not receive a return on your investment, that the return may be smaller than you expected, or even that you might lose your investment.

Why invest in a business if the investment is risky? If a business is successful, its owners can expect to earn a higher rate of return on their investments than they could earn on a safer alternative such as a savings account. By investing $5,000 in The Beach Shack, you expect to earn $6,000 from your investment. If you invested your money in a savings account, you might expect to earn $75 for the same 3-month period (assuming an annual interest rate of 6%).

To earn profits and pay returns to owners, businesses must operate effectively and efficiently. **An *effective business* is one that is successful in providing goods and services demanded by customers.** Effective management involves identifying the right products and putting them in the right locations at the right times. **An *efficient business* is one that provides goods and services at low costs relative to their selling prices.** Managers must control costs by using the proper mix, qualities, and quantities of resources to avoid waste and to reduce costs. The risk of owning a business is lower if the business is effective and efficient than if it is ineffective or inefficient. Efficient and effective businesses are competitive in financial, supplier, and product markets.

The Beach Shack will be effective if you select merchandise desired by customers and if your location is one that places you near your customers. The company will be efficient if you can purchase merchandise at a low enough cost so that you can sell it profitably and also pay rent, wages, and other costs.

The Market for Investors

OBJECTIVE 5

Explain why accounting information is useful to investors.

Businesses must compete not only for resources and customers, but also for investors. Business owners expect to receive a return on their investments. Investors choose among alternative investments by evaluating the amount, timing, and uncertainty of the returns they expect to receive. Businesses that earn high profits and are capable of paying returns have less difficulty in obtaining investors than other businesses. A business that cannot earn sufficient profits will be forced to become more effective and efficient or to go out of business.

The accounting information system is a major source of the information investors use in deciding about their investments. **Accounting information helps investors assess the effectiveness and efficiency of businesses.** It helps them estimate the returns that can be expected from investing in a business and the amount of risk associated with their investments.

Financial, supplier, and product markets create incentives for businesses to provide products that society demands. These markets help ensure that scarce resources are used to improve society's welfare. Markets help allocate scarce resources to those organizations that can best transform them to create value.

You will profit from your investment in The Beach Shack if you provide products demanded by customers and provide them at competitive prices that are sufficient to cover your costs. If you believe you will be unable to create a profit from your investment, you will choose to invest in an alternative rather than in The Beach Shack. Thus, as a part of society, you make a decision to invest when you believe the return will be sufficient to compensate you for your investment. Your decision depends on whether you believe you can provide society (your customers) with products it wants at prices it is willing to pay.

Self-Study Problem 2

John Bach owns a music store in which he sells and repairs musical instruments and sells sheet music. The following transactions occurred for Bach's Music Store during December 2000:

1. Sold $8,000 of musical instruments that cost the company $4,300.
2. Sold $1,400 of sheet music that cost the company $870.
3. The price of repair services provided during the month was $2,200.
4. Rent on the store for the month was $650.
5. The cost of supplies used during the month was $250.
6. The cost of advertising for the month was $300.
7. The cost of utilities for the month was $200.
8. Other miscellaneous costs for December were $180.

Required

A. Determine the profit earned by Bach's Music Store for December.
B. Explain how profit measures the value created by Bach's Music Store.

The solution to Self-Study Problem 2 appears at the end of the chapter.

DECISIONS IN ORGANIZATIONS

Many types of decisions are made in organizations. Accounting provides important information to make these decisions. In this section, we will consider three types of organizational activities that use accounting information for decision making: financing, investing, and operating activities.

Financing Activities

OBJECTIVE 6

Identify financing activities and the types of decisions they require.

Organizations require financial resources to obtain other resources used to produce goods and services. They compete for these resources in financial markets. *Financing activities* **are the methods an organization uses to obtain financial resources from financial markets and how it manages these resources.** Primary sources of financing for most businesses are owners and creditors. The following sections consider these sources.

Business Ownership. Businesses may be classified into two categories: those that are distinct legal entities apart from their owners and those that are not distinct legal entities. **A** *corporation* **is a legal entity with the right to enter into contracts, the right to own, buy, and sell property, and the right to sell stock.** Resources are owned by the corporation, rather than by individuals.

Corporations may be very large or fairly small organizations. Small corporations often are managed by their owners. The owners of most large corporations do not manage their companies. Instead, they hire professional managers. These owners have the right to vote on certain major decisions, but they do not control the operations of their corporations on a day-to-day basis. One reason most large businesses are organized as corporations is that they typically have greater access to financial markets than other types of organizations.

Corporations often are owned by many investors who purchase shares of stock (certificates of ownership) issued by corporations. **Each share of *stock* represents an equal share in the ownership of a corporation.** An investor who owns 10% of the shares of a corporation owns 10% of the company and has a right to 10% of the return available to stockholders. ***Stockholders*, or shareholders, are the owners of a corporation.**

Percentage of Companies and Volume of Sales by Type of Organization

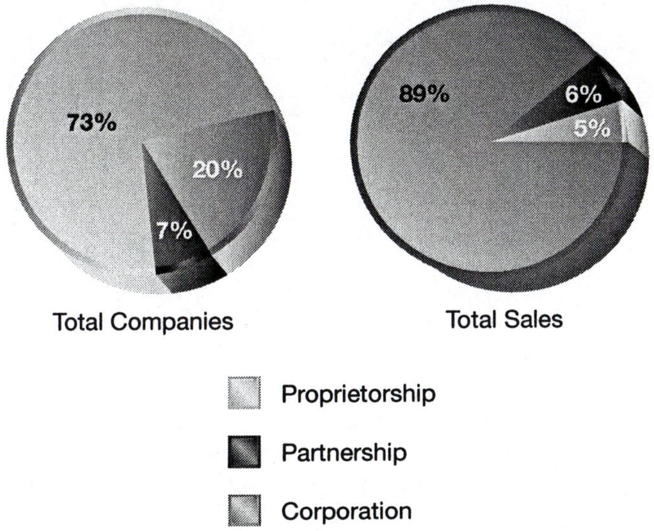

Data Source: 1998 Statistical Abstract of the United States

Shares of stock often are traded in stock markets, such as the New York, London, and Tokyo stock exchanges, that are established specifically for this purpose. These markets facilitate the exchange of stock between buyers and sellers. Therefore, unlike other businesses, ownership in many corporations changes frequently as stockholders buy or sell shares of stock. Major corporations, such as **General Motors, Exxon,** or **IBM,** have received billions of dollars from stockholders.

***Proprietorships* and *partnerships* are business organizations that do not have legal identities distinct from their owners. Proprietorships have only one owner; partnerships have more than one owner.** For most proprietorships and partnerships, owners also manage the business. Owners have a major stake in the business because often much of their personal wealth is invested in it. The amount of a proprietor's personal wealth and his or her ability to borrow limits the size of a proprietorship. If a proprietorship is profitable, profits earned by the proprietor can be reinvested and the business can become fairly large.

Partnerships can include several partners; therefore, the money available to finance a partnership depends on the money available from all the partners. New partners can be added, making new money available to the business. While most partnerships are small, large businesses (with as many as a thousand or more owners) sometimes are organized as partnerships.

Management of Corporations. Exhibit 10 describes the organizational structure of a typical corporation.

A **board of directors** oversees the decisions of management and is responsible for protecting the interests of stockholders. Normally, the board is appointed by management with the approval of stockholders. Top managers often serve on the board along with outside directors who are not part of the corporation's management. The **chairman of the board** often holds the position of **chief executive officer** (CEO) with the ultimate responsibility for the success of the business. The **president,** as **chief operating officer** (COO), is responsible for the day-to-day management of a corporation. In some cases, the president also may be the CEO. The company may appoint any number of **vice presidents,** who are responsible for various functions in the organization. The titles and roles of these managers will vary from corporation to corporation. Along with the CEO and the president, the vice presidents constitute the top management of a corporation. Together, they make planning decisions and develop company goals and policies.

Functions performed within a corporation may be separated into support functions and primary functions. Support functions assist the primary functions by providing information and other resources necessary to produce and sell goods and services. Primary functions are those actually involved in producing and selling goods and services. These functions include distribution of goods and services to customers and servicing the goods and services to meet customer needs.

Exhibit 10

Corporate Management Functions

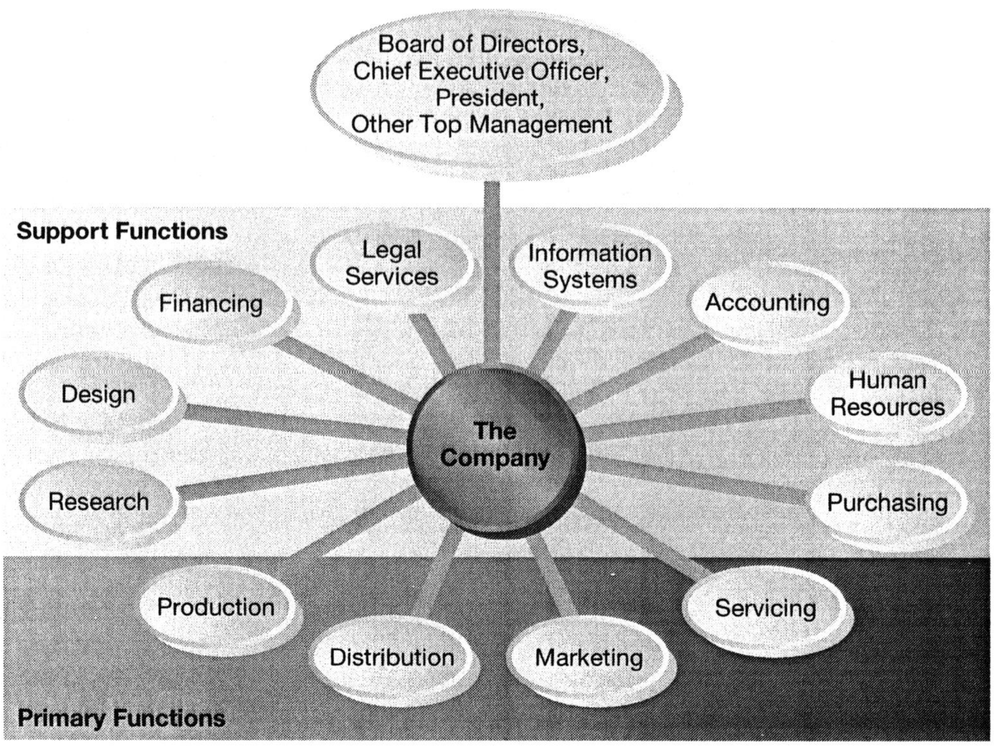

Among the support functions are research and development, product and production design, finance, legal services, accounting, purchasing, and human resources. The **chief financial officer** (CFO), who also may be the **treasurer,** is responsible for obtaining financial resources and managing a corporation's cash. The **controller,** as the chief accounting officer, is responsible for accounting and financial reporting, developing and maintaining the accounting information system, and reporting to tax and regulatory authorities.

M

Primary functions involve production, distribution, sales, and service. Plant managers oversee production for specific product lines or geographical locations. These managers often have their own staffs at the divisional or plant level. For example, divisional or plant level controllers exist in many corporations. Research, design, and development staffs also exist at the divisional or plant level in some organizations.

Corporations may be organized by functions such as those described in Exhibit 10. Other corporations are organized primarily by region or product line. For example, multinational companies may be organized into North American, European, and Pacific divisions. Functional areas, such as development and production, report to regional or product managers. Many corporations are finding advantages in changing from a traditional organization structure to teams of managers working together on specific projects. Thus, the idea for a new product may be the responsibility of a team of employees from a company's functional areas,

CASE IN POINT

ON THE INTERNET

http://www.ingram@swcollege.com

Visit International Paper's web site.

International Paper Company divides its operations by geography and product line. Geographical divisions include the United States, Europe, and the Pacific Rim. Product lines include printing papers, packaging, specialty products, and forest products.

such as engineering, accounting, and marketing. Together, the team decides on a design for the product and on a production process to create efficiency and product quality.

Advantages of Corporations. A corporate form of organization has several advantages over proprietorships or partnerships. Corporations have **continuous lives** apart from those of their owners. If a proprietor or partner sells her or his share of a business or dies, the business ceases to exist as a legal entity. The new owner of the business must reestablish the business as a new legal entity. Most corporations, however, continue unchanged if current owners sell their stock, donate it to charity, give it to relatives, or otherwise dispose of their shares.

Shareholders normally are not liable personally for the debts of a corporation. This is a characteristic known as **limited liability.** If a corporation defaults on debt or enters bankruptcy, its owners may lose a portion or all of their investments in the company. But they are not obligated to use their personal wealth to repay creditors for losses the creditors incurred. In many cases, proprietors and partners are personally liable for the debts of their companies and can be required to use their personal wealth to repay their creditors. Some partnerships are organized as limited liability partnerships (LLP).

Shareholders of most corporations do not manage the company. They elect members of the board of directors, who then hire **professional managers** to run the corporation. Investors can own part of a corporation or parts of many corporations without having to participate in the day-to-day decisions of running those companies. Many Americans own stock in corporations through personal investments and retirement plans, but they are not required to commit large amounts of their personal time to corporate concerns.

Shareholders cannot enter into contracts or agreements that are binding on a corporation unless they are managers or directors. Therefore, investors in a corporation do not have to be concerned about the abilities of other stockholders to make good business decisions. In contrast, bad decisions by one partner can result in the personal bankruptcy of all partners in a partnership. This problem arises because partners normally are in a mutual agency relationship. *Mutual agency* **permits a partner to enter into contracts and agreements that are binding on all members of a partnership.**

By selling shares to many investors, a corporation can obtain a large amount of financial resources. The ability to **raise large amounts of capital** permits corporations to become very large organizations. Thus, corporations can invest in plant facilities and undertake production activities that would be difficult for proprietorships or partnerships.

Disadvantages of Corporations. There are several disadvantages to the corporate form of ownership. Most **corporations must pay taxes on their incomes.** Corporate taxes are separate from the taxes paid by shareholders on dividends received from the company. (Some corporations, however, especially smaller ones, are not taxed separately.) Another disadvantage is that **corporations are regulated** by various state and federal government agencies. These regulations require corporations to comply with many state and federal rules concerning business practices and reporting of financial information. Corporations must file many reports with government agencies and make public disclosure of their business activities. **Compliance with these regulations is costly.** Also, some of the **required disclosures may be helpful to competitors.** Partnerships and proprietorships are regulated also, but the degree of regulation normally is much less than for corporations.

Owners of corporations usually do not have access to information about the day-to-day activities of their companies. They depend on managers to make decisions that will increase the value of their investments. However, managers' personal interests sometimes conflict with the interests of stockholders. This problem produces a condition known as moral hazard. Moral hazard arises when one group, known as agents (such as managers), is responsible for serving the needs of another group, known as principals (such as investors). *Moral hazard* **is the condition that exists when agents have superior information to principals and are able to make decisions that favor their own interests over those of the principals.**

Without disclosure of reliable information, corporations would have difficulty in selling stock, and investors would be unable to determine whether managers were making decisions that increased stockholder value or were making decisions that took advantage of the stockholders. Accounting reports are major sources of information to help stockholders assess the performance of managers. For example, an income statement helps owners evaluate how well managers have used owners' investments to earn returns for the owners. **Moral hazard imposes costs on corporations because managers must report to stockholders and, generally, these reports are audited.** An audit verifies the reliability of reported information.

The size of many corporations makes them difficult to manage. An individual manager cannot be involved directly with all the decisions made in operating a large organization. Top-level managers depend on lower-level managers to make decisions and to keep them informed about a corporation's operations. This process is costly because coordination among managers may be difficult to achieve. Moral hazard also exists among managers and employees, not just between managers and investors. Corporate goals and policies provide guidance for manager decisions, but communicating goals and policies and providing incentives for managers to implement them often is difficult and expensive. Employees and lower-level managers may not report reliable information about their activities to higher-level managers if the information is not in their best interests. Multinational corporations, in particular, are complex and difficult to manage. Distant locations for facilities and differences in language and local custom can cause special problems.

Creditors. In addition to money provided by owners, businesses (and other organizations) may borrow money. Money may be obtained from banks and other financial institutions, or it may be borrowed from individual lenders. **A lender or *creditor* is someone who loans financial resources to an organization.**

Most organizations depend on banks and similar institutions to lend them money. Corporations often borrow money from individuals or other companies. Exhibit 11 describes the amount of money several large corporations have received from owners and creditors. The amounts and proportions of financing from owners and creditors vary greatly across companies.

Exhibit 11

Sources of Financing for Selected Corporations

Data source: 1998 annual reports.

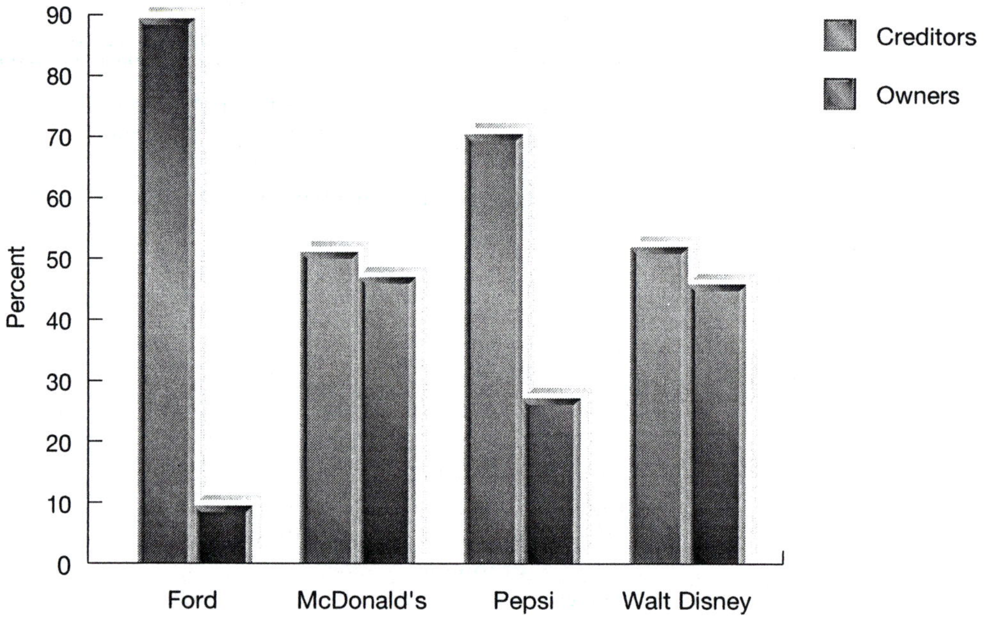

Creditors loan money to organizations to earn a return on their investments. They usually loan money for a specific period and are promised a specific rate of return on their investments. Usually, this is a fixed rate (say 10%). In contrast, owners invest for a nonspecific period (until they decide to sell their ownership rights) and receive a return that depends on the profits earned by the business.

The success of a business determines whether or not creditors will receive the amount promised by the borrower. When a business fails to generate sufficient cash from its revenues to pay its expenses and to pay its creditors, the creditors may not receive the amount promised. Therefore, creditors evaluate the probability that an organization will be able to repay debt and interest. Risk is a concern of both creditors and owners. Exhibit 12 illustrates financing activities.

Exhibit 12

Components of Financing Activities

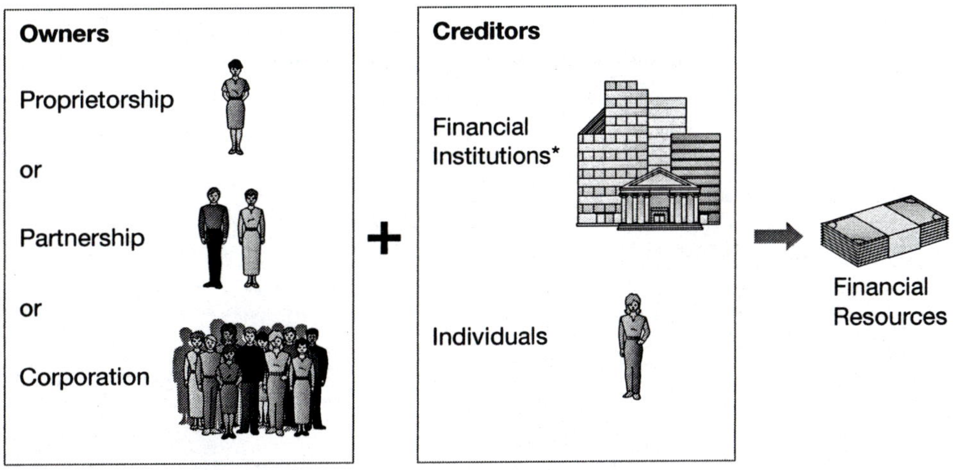

*The term "financial institutions" refers to banks, savings and loans, and similar companies.

Financing Decisions. Financing decisions involve choices about when and where to obtain financial resources and about the amount needed. A corporation must decide how much stock and debt to issue, when they should be issued, and to whom they should be issued to obtain favorable prices. These decisions depend on the business's need for money and on its ability to repay owners and creditors for their investments.

Financing decisions are made by owners, creditors, and managers. Owners and creditors need to know how managers are using their money and how much risk they are taking. Managers decide how much money a business needs, how much return they will pay to investors, how they will invest capital, and the probable effect of financing arrangements on the profitability and survival of an organization. Questions answered by financing decisions include:

How much financing does an organization need?
Where should an organization obtain its financing?
When should an organization obtain financing?
What effect will financing have on profitability and survival?

As owner of The Beach Shack, you must decide how much money you will need for your business and how to obtain the money. If you have sufficient money to start the business, you may decide not to borrow. If you decide to borrow, you will have to make enough money to repay your loan and interest.

Investing Activities

OBJECTIVE 7

Identify investing activities and the types of decisions they require.

Managers use capital from financing activities to acquire other resources used in the transformation process. Having the right mix of resources is essential to efficient and effective operations.

Investing activities **involve the selection and management (including disposal and replacement) of long-term resources that will be used to develop, produce, and sell goods and services.** Resources include land and natural resources, buildings, equipment, legal rights such as patents and trademarks, and other resources necessary for an organization to produce goods and services. Organizations compete in supplier markets for these resources. Exhibit 13 illustrates some components of investing activities.

LEARNING NOTE

Don't confuse investments made by owners and creditors (financing activities) with investments made by managers (investing activities).

Managers decide how much to invest in resources and the types of resources to acquire. Often these decisions involve large amounts of money and have a major effect on the future of an organization. These decisions affect future profitability, future supply of goods and services, and future return to owners and creditors.

In making investing decisions, managers need information for predicting the demand for goods and services. They need to know which products will be demanded, when they will be demanded, how much will be demanded, and the prices customers are willing to pay. This information is useful for determining the types of resources

Exhibit 13

Components of Investing Activities

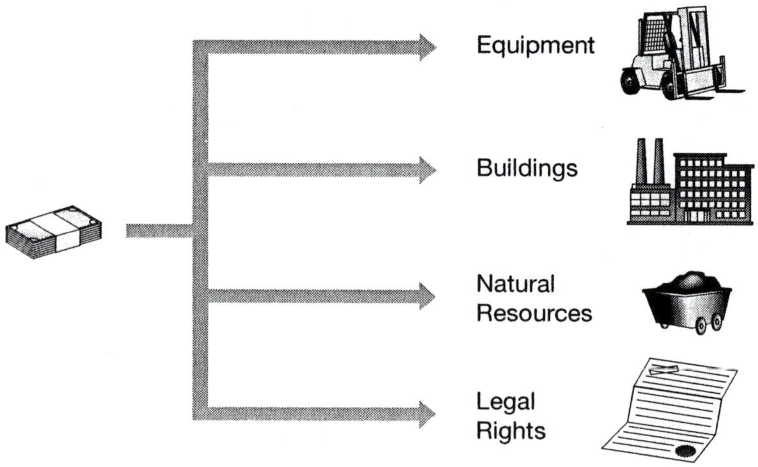

needed to produce the goods and services demanded by customers. In addition, managers need information about the current availability of resources and how resources are being used. They need to know what can be produced, how much can be produced, when and where it can be produced, and how costly it is to produce. Managers evaluate alternative ways of acquiring resources; for example, resources may be purchased or they may be leased or rented.

Examples of questions answered by investing decisions include:

What long-term resources should an organization acquire?
How much of each type of resource should be acquired?
When should resources be acquired, sold, or replaced?
Where should resources be placed?

LEARNING NOTE

Though most investing activities involve long-term resources, exceptions exist for certain short-term resources that will be considered later in the book.

One of your tasks as owner and manager of The Beach Shack is to determine the types and amounts of resources your company will need.

Operating Activities

OBJECTIVE 8

Identify operating activities and the types of decisions they require.

Operating activities **involve the use of resources to design, produce, distribute, and market goods and services.** Operating activities include research and development, design and engineering, purchasing, human resources, production, distribution, marketing and selling, and servicing. Organizations compete in supplier and labor markets for resources used in these activities. Also, they compete in product markets to sell the goods and services created by operating activities. Exhibit 14 features key components of operating activities.

Exhibit 14 Components of Operating Activities

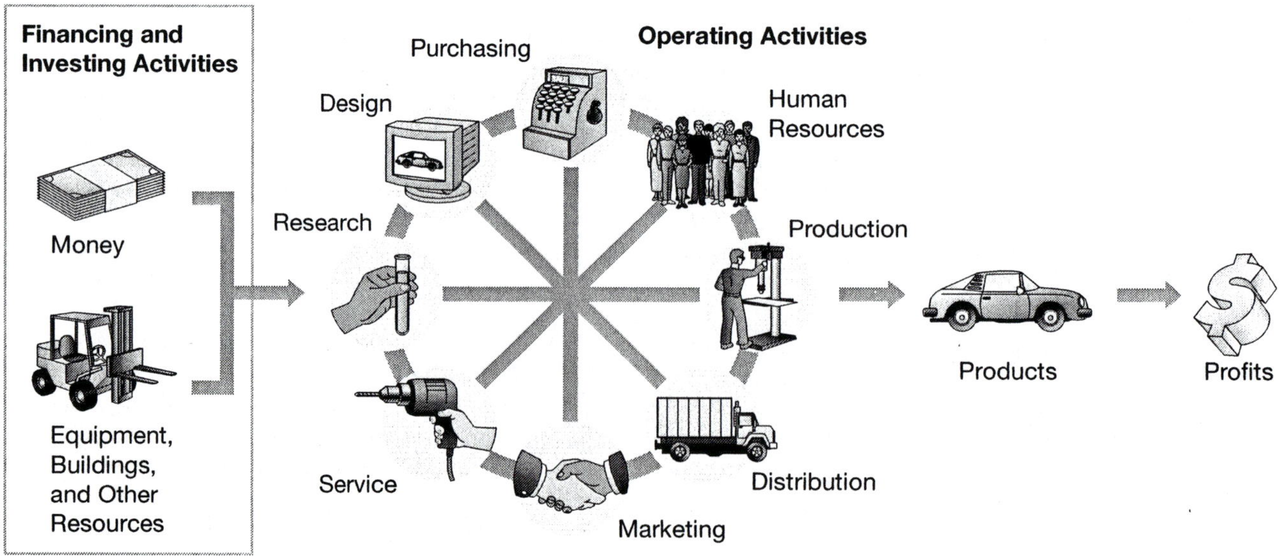

These activities are often performed by individual departments or divisions of an organization. Each division may have its own manager, who is responsible for decisions in that division. Not every organization needs each of these activities. For example, merchandising and service organizations generally do not require engineering and production. Often, some activities are combined in a division. For example, distribution, marketing, and servicing may be combined in a single division with one manager.

Exhibit 15 summarizes key components of a company's operating activities. Questions answered by operating decisions include:

Research and Development: How can new products be made or existing ones be improved?
Design and Engineering: How should products be designed and produced?
Purchasing: What quantity and types of materials and supplies that will be used to produce goods and services should an organization acquire?
Human Resources: How many and what types of employees are needed? What kind of training do employees need? How should employees be compensated?
Production: How should production activities be scheduled? Should production occur in domestic or foreign locations?
Distribution: How should goods be shipped and stored so that they are available to customers when needed?
Marketing and Selling: What activities are necessary to promote and sell goods and services?
Servicing: What types of installation, repair, and maintenance services should be provided to customers for the goods they purchase?

As owner, you will have to make operating decisions for The Beach Shack. Among these are where to get merchandise at the best price, what kind of merchandise to sell, how to handle defective merchandise, how to advertise or promote your business, whom to hire to assist in selling your goods, and how much to charge for your products.

The profitability of a company depends on its success in selling its products and controlling its costs. Profits are a measure of a company's ability to manage its capital and resources.

Exhibit 15 A Summary of Operating Activities

***Research and Development.* Research and development activities create new products and update old products or production processes.** Many companies operate in a highly competitive environment and must keep up with rapidly changing technology and consumer preferences. Examples include pharmaceutical and computer manufacturers. This environment demands that organizations search continuously for ways to improve their products and for new products that meet consumer needs.

***Design and Engineering.* Design and engineering activities determine the design of products, production facilities, production processes, and distribution systems.** Equipment and labor requirements, manufacturing and assembly processes, and other features of the way goods are produced and distributed have a major effect on product costs and marketability.

***Purchasing.* Purchasing activities involve acquiring and managing the materials and supplies needed for production or sale.** Materials used in manufacturing must be purchased in the appropriate amounts and at the right times to ensure availability. This function also is important in merchandising and service companies. Purchasing controls the selection and acquisition of goods that are available for use or sale.

Human Resources. In addition to materials, labor is a primary factor in producing and selling goods and services. **Human resource activities involve obtaining the needed amount of human resources with the appropriate skills.** Primary functions involve hiring, firing, and training employees, as well as coordination of payroll and employee benefits such as retirement and health care.

***Production.* Production activities involve the manufacture and assembly of goods for sale.** Decisions must be made to schedule the production process so that labor, materials, and equipment are available when needed. The appropriate mix of these factors is necessary to ensure that the required quantity and quality of goods can be produced.

Distribution. **Distribution activities involve getting the right goods to the right location at the right time.** Because transportation is costly, decisions must be made about how goods will be shipped, when they will be shipped, and how much will be shipped. Distribution activities are especially important for companies that operate in global markets. Goods often must be shipped from countries where they are produced to other countries where they are sold.

Marketing and Selling. **Marketing and selling activities involve pricing products, making potential buyers aware of products, and selling products to customers.** Managers decide how to reach buyers effectively and how to present the company's products to create sales. Decisions include the amount and type of advertising and sales force to use, the types and amounts of credit and discounting to give to different buyers, and the determination of consumer needs and demands. Therefore, selling involves more than the actual sale of goods and services. It involves careful monitoring of consumer needs and tastes. This information, in turn, is important in guiding the company's research and manufacturing efforts to produce the amount and types of goods and services demanded by customers.

Servicing. **Servicing products often continues after the sale.** Servicing activities involve the assistance provided to buyers after goods have been sold. Companies provide warranties on many products that require the company to repair and replace defective merchandise. Some organizations provide installation and training for products they sell. For example, computer companies often contract to install computer systems and to train employees to use them. Computers, automobiles, and other high-technology products require periodic maintenance after the sale.

SUMMARY OF THE TRANSFORMATION PROCESS

OBJECTIVE 9

Describe the steps in an organization's transformation process.

Decisions concerning financing, investing, and operating activities require information. The accounting information system is designed to meet certain information needs, particularly those involving the financial effects of the transformation process. **The *transformation process*** is a cycle that begins with the **acquisition of capital from owners and creditors.** This capital is **invested in facilities, equipment, and other resources** needed to create goods and services. Organizations use these resources in **developing, producing, distributing, and selling goods and services.** Selling goods and services results in the **inflow of additional financial resources** so that the cycle can continue.

While the flow of resources typically is from financing to investing and operating decisions, information often follows the reverse path. For example, decisions about what kind of products are demanded by customers and how much to produce are necessary before products can be designed. These decisions are necessary to plan production and distribution activities. The number of units produced affects the need for materials, labor, and equipment used in the production process. The need for materials, labor, and equipment determines the need for financing to provide money for these resources. Thus, planning often begins with expectations about the sale of goods and services and works backward to determine the resources and activities needed to produce the goods and services. Make sure you have a good understanding of how organizations transform resources into goods and services as illustrated in Exhibit 16.

Exhibit 16

A Summary of the Transformation Process

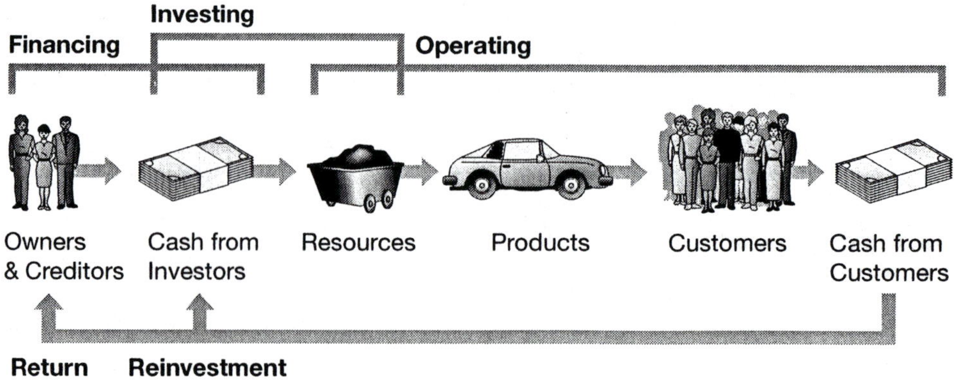

DEFINITION OF ACCOUNTING

OBJECTIVE 10

Define accounting.

What role does accounting play in an organization's transformation process? ***Accounting*** **is an information system for the measurement and reporting of the transformation of resources into goods and services and the sale or transfer of these goods and services to customers.** Accounting uses the prices and costs of resources to measure value created by the transformation process and to trace the flow of resources through the transformation process. By tracing the flow of resources, managers and other decision makers can determine how efficiently and effectively resources are being used.

This chapter began by illustrating the accounting process as one of identifying, measuring, recording, summarizing, and reporting transactions. The accounting system in organizations also contains these steps. Transactions occur any time an organization acquires financial or other resources, uses the resources, or sells goods and services. The effects of these transactions are measured by their prices (or costs) and are recorded in individual accounts for each type of resource or activity. The account balances are summarized periodically and are reported to owners, creditors, managers, and others who make decisions about an organization. Accounting for organizations is much more complex than keeping a checking account because the number of events and accounts is much larger. Also, decisions about when to record events in a checking account are fairly simple: You should record a check when you write it. Decisions about when to record events in an organization's accounts are not so simple, as we will see in later chapters.

This book emphasizes accounting and financial reporting for corporations. Moral hazard resulting from the separation of owners and managers has led to the creation of a strong regulatory environment for corporations. This environment oversees the development of accounting and reporting requirements for corporations. We will examine this environment and the resulting requirements. While accounting is important in other forms of organizations, owners normally manage these organizations; therefore, the formal regulation of reporting by managers to owners is unnecessary. Accounting information reported by managers to owners and other external decision makers is the subject of financial accounting. This information also is used by managers. Though managers have access to information that extends beyond that reported to external decision makers, internal and external decisions are related. Therefore, this book will consider internal and external decisions that rely on accounting information.

The modern multinational corporation is a complex entity. Many familiar corporations—**Coca-Cola, IBM,** and **McDonald's** to name a few—maintain headquarters in the United States. They rely on U.S. markets for a major portion of their financing, but their production, marketing, and distribution facilities are spread throughout the world. These companies compete in a global market. Information is a critical resource for internal and external decision makers in both U.S. and foreign economies.

Accounting serves the information needs of a wide variety of decision makers who are internal and external to organizations. Chapter 2 will examine the accounting information system and how it provides information to decision makers. Appendix A, at the end of this book, summarizes some important sources of accounting information about various companies and industries.

Self-Study Problem 3

G. Galileo, a manufacturer of small optical instruments, owns Galileo Glassware. Galileo invested $7,500 in the business and borrowed $2,500 from a local bank. With this investment, he purchased a small building and some equipment. He develops and designs the instruments he sells, purchases materials from local hardware and specialty stores, and has two assistants to help him fabricate and assemble the instruments. Galileo advertises in professional journals. He produces most of his instruments to fill special orders from customers to whom he ships the products.

Required

A. Identify each stage of the transformation process that occurs for Galileo Glassware.
B. What prices and costs are likely to be associated with each stage of the transformation?

The solution to Self-Study Problem 3 appears at the end of the chapter.

Accounting As a Profession

A profession is a group of individuals who share specific skills and training. This group is accepted by society as being qualified to engage in certain services or activities that serve the public need. Most professions require their members to meet licensing requirements and often are regulated by governmental authorities. The accounting profession includes those who have attained a high level of knowledge of accounting through education and experience. These individuals use their skills to develop accounting systems, to prepare and evaluate accounting information, and to assist decision makers with the analysis and interpretation of this information. Some of these responsibilities require accountants to be licensed to perform certain services. To acquire a license, an accountant generally must complete a college degree with a specified number of business and accounting courses, pass a qualifying examination administered by the profession, and obtain experience in accounting practice.

The accounting profession encompasses accountants who work in businesses, public accounting firms, governmental and nonprofit organizations, and educational institutions.

Management Accounting

Management accounting includes all accounting functions within business organizations. These functions include:

Information Systems Development. Many organizations maintain an information systems department for designing and implementing information systems for accounting, production, purchasing, and customer orders. Typically, these systems are computerized.

Accounting System Management. Accountants oversee the processing of accounting information. While entering transactions in the accounting system is primarily a clerical activity, accountants are responsible for managing this activity to ensure that information from the accounting system meets the needs of other managers.

Financial Reporting. Accountants prepare financial statements and other reports for distribution to owners, creditors, employees, and regulatory authorities.

Financial Planning and Analysis. Accountants analyze and interpret financial statements and other accounting reports to determine how well a company is performing. This information is used by managers in planning future operations and in making strategic decisions about obtaining and using resources.

Cost Accounting and Management. Cost accounting includes those functions necessary to accumulate and report a company's costs. Cost management includes strategies and methods to reduce costs and increase competitiveness.

Internal Auditing. Internal auditing is the process of evaluating a company's activities to assess whether appropriate procedures are being used and whether management policies are being implemented. Internal auditors identify ways for departments to improve their operations.

Public Accounting

Accountants provide services to the public as auditors, tax advisers, and consultants.

Independent auditing services are provided in the United States by certified public accountants (CPAs). A CPA is an individual who has met education, examination, and experience requirements imposed by a state government.

Auditing. An audit involves a detailed, systematic investigation of a company's accounting records. To provide auditing services, external auditors must be independent, in fact and appearance, of the organizations they audit. Therefore, they are referred to as independent auditors or independent accountants. An external financial audit provides assurance to owners, creditors, governmental authorities, and others who rely on a company's financial reports that they are faithful representations of the company's economic activities.

Tax Advising. Public accountants work with individuals and businesses to prepare tax returns and to help with tax planning.

Consulting. Public accountants assist businesses in designing and implementing information systems, understanding financial information, and planning their business activities.

Governmental and Nonprofit Accounting

Accounting activities in federal, state, and local governments and in nonprofit organizations, such as nonprofit hospitals and universities, are similar to those of businesses. These nonbusiness organizations require accounting systems, prepare financial reports, and analyze financial information for decision purposes.

Education

Accounting is taught in high schools and colleges. Accounting faculty are educated as accountants, as educators, and as researchers. Many have been employed in the practice of accounting.

APPENDIX: A SHORT INTRODUCTION TO EXCEL™

This introduction summarizes some of the primary operations and functions of a spreadsheet. It is intended to get you started if you have not had previous experience with Excel. There are many operations and functions in addition to those mentioned here.

Identifying and Selecting Cells

A spreadsheet consists of rows and columns. Rows are identified by numbers, and columns are identified by letters. An intersection of a row and column is a cell. A cell is identified by the column letter and row number that intersect at that cell.

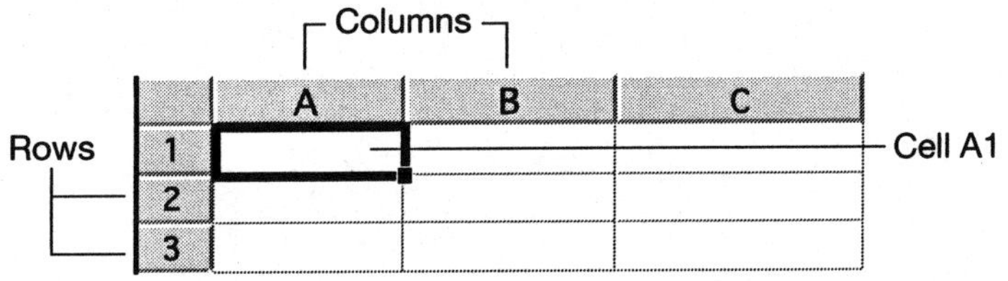

To select a cell, click on the cell using the left mouse button. A cell must be selected before you can enter data or format the cell. Enter data by typing numbers, words, or characters. Enter numbers without commas. Commas can be added using formatting procedures described later. An entire row or column can be selected by clicking on the row or column header. The row header is the leftmost cell in a row that contains the row number. A column header is the topmost cell in a column that contains the cell letter. A group of neighboring cells can be selected by clicking with the left mouse button on the cell in the upper, left corner of the group, then dragging the cursor over all the cells to be selected.

Referencing and Mathematical Operations

The contents of one or more cells can be referenced in another cell. To reference a cell, enter the equal sign followed by the cell being referenced. For example, entering =A1 in cell B1 will copy the contents of cell A1 in cell B1. If the contents of cell A1 are changed, these changes also will appear in cell B1. A common use of cell referencing is to calculate totals from data in a series of cells. For example, the following spreadsheet contains sales data for the first three months of a year. The total appears in cell B5. To calculate the total, you would enter a formula in cell B5. The formula would be =B2+B3+B4.

	A	B
1		Sales
2	January	3,457.38
3	February	3,892.90
4	March	3,204.07
5	Total	10,554.35

Normal mathematical operations can be entered in a cell:

=B2+B3 adds the contents of cells B2 and B3.
=B2–B3 subtracts the contents of cell B3 from cell B2.
=B2*B3 multiplies the contents of cell B2 by the contents of cell B3.
=B2/B3 divides the contents of cell B2 by the contents of cell B3.
=B2^B3 raises the number in cell B2 to the power of the number in cell B3.

Copying Cell Contents

The contents (including a formula) can be copied from one cell or group of cells to another cell or group of cells. To copy the contents, select the cells containing the data to be copied and click on Edit/Copy. Then select the cell you want to copy to (or the upper, left cell of a group of cells) and click Edit/Paste.

The contents of a cell also can be copied to a neighboring cell using a shortcut procedure. In the following example, we want to copy the contents of cell B4 to cell C4. Cell B4 contains the formula =B2+B3. To copy the contents, we select cell B4 and drag the cursor over the box in the lower, right corner of cell B4. The cursor changes shape and appears as crosshairs (+). If we click on the left mouse button while the cursor is in this shape, we can drag the contents of cell B4 to cell C4. The formula =B2+B3 is copied to cell C4, except that the references are automatically adjusted for the new column, and the formula appears as =C2+C3.

	A	B	C
1		Cash	Merchandise
2	Store 1	1,543.02	16,794.23
3	Store 2	4,587.45	24,586.50
4	Total	6,130.47	

Box

When you enter a formula in a cell, such as =B2+B3, the cell addresses are relative addresses. When the formula is copied to another cell, the relative addresses change. Copying the contents of cell B4 above to cell C4 results in an adjustment in the formula so that =B2+B3 is changed to =C2+C3. You can also enter absolute addresses. An absolute address results from entering a dollar sign ($) before a cell address. For example, if you enter =$B2+$B3 in cell B4 and then copy cell B4 to cell C4, the formula in C4 remains =$B2+$B3. You can use absolute addresses for the column (=$B2), the row (=B$2) or both (=B2).

Changing Column Widths

You can make a column wider or narrower using the Format/Column/Width menu. A simpler approach is to move the cursor to the right-hand side of the column header of the column you wish to adjust. The cursor changes to appear as ↔. Click and drag the cursor to the right or left to adjust the column width. The same procedure can be used for row height adjustments.

Menus

The top of an Excel spreadsheet contains menus. A brief description of the menu items you are likely to use on a regular basis follows.

File. Use the File menu to open a **New** spreadsheet, to **Open** an existing spreadsheet, to **Save** a spreadsheet, to **Print** a spreadsheet, and to **Close** the Excel program.

Edit. Use the Edit menu to **Delete** a row, column, or cell. Select the row, column, or cell and click Edit/Delete. You can delete the contents of a particular cell by selecting the cell and pressing the Backspace or Delete key.

View. Use the View menu to select which Toolbars appear on the spreadsheet. The Header and Footer command permits you to add titles and comments to spreadsheets that will appear on printed output. The Zoom command allows spreadsheets to be resized as they appear on the monitor to make them easier to see. This command does not affect printed output.

Insert. Use the Insert menu to insert **Rows, Columns,** and **Cells.** To enter a new row, select the row *above* the row you wish to add and click on Insert/Row. To enter a new column, select the column to the *left* of the column you want to add and click on Insert/Column. To enter a new cell, click on the cell where you want to add a new cell and click on Insert/Cell. A dialog box will ask whether you want the existing cell moved to the right or down. When you enter a new cell, all existing cells to the right or below the entered cell will be moved to make room for the new cell.

Format. Use the Format menu to format **Cells.** Select the cells and click on Format/Cells. A dialog box provides options. The **Number** tab provides various formatting options. The **Alignment** tab provides options for how numbers or text will be aligned. The Wrap text box can be checked (click on the box) to allow for more than one line of text to appear in a particular cell.

Tools. Use the Tools menu to check your **Spelling.**

Data. Use the Data menu to **Sort** data. To sort, select all the columns in the spreadsheet and click Data/Sort. A dialog box lets you select the column or columns you want to use to sort the data.

Help. Use the Help menu to get additional directions about using Excel. Click on Help/Contents and Index. Select a topic from the **Contents** tab or click on the **Index** tab. Type the keyword for an item to get additional information and click on the Display button.

Buttons

Several of the buttons under the menu are particularly useful. The identity of each button and its use are described below.

 **Save.** Click to save your spreadsheet. **Save your work often.**

 **Copy.** Copies the contents of a selected cell or group of cells.

 **Paste.** Pastes the contents of a copied cell or group of cells into a selected cell or group.

 **Format Painter.** Copies the format of a selected cell into another cell or group of cells. Select the cell with the format to be copied and click the button. Then click on the cell or click and drag over the cells where the format will be copied.

 **AutoSum.** Select a cell to contain the sum of a neighboring set of cells (above or to the left of the selected cell). For example, we want to sum the contents of cells E10 and E11 into cell E12. Select cell E12 and click on the AutoSum button. The =Sum formula appears in cell

E12 as shown below. You can change the cells to be included in the sum by clicking on the top cell to be included and dragging the cursor over the cells to be added as part of the sum.

Once the sum formula is correct, click on the checkmark in the selection box at the top of the spreadsheet:

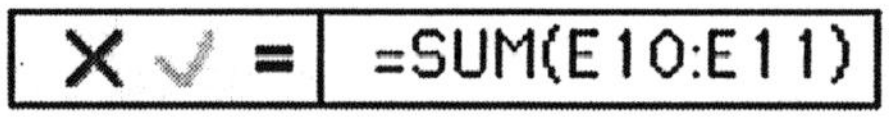

Click on the green checkmark to accept the cell contents. Click on the red X to remove the cell contents.

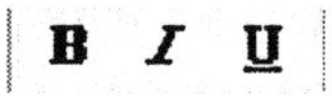

Format. Select a cell or group of cells and click on B for bold, I for italics, and U for underline.

Align. Select a cell or group of cells and click on a button to align the cell contents to the left, center, or right of the cell.

Merge and Center. Select two or more neighboring cells in a row and click on the button to merge the cells into a single cell and center the cell contents. For example, the caption (The Book Wermz) in the following example was created by selecting cells B1 and C1 and clicking on the Merge and Center button.

	A	B	C
1		The Book	Wermz
2	Store 1	1,543.0	Merchandise
3	January	4,528.23	145,360.98

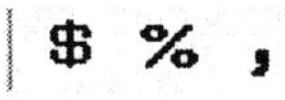

Number Formatting. Select a cell or group of cells and click on a button to include a dollar sign in the cell(s), to convert from decimals to percentages, or to add comma separators between thousands' digits in numbers.

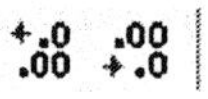

Decimal Places. Select a cell or group of cells and click on a button to increase or decrease the number of decimal places showing in the cell(s).

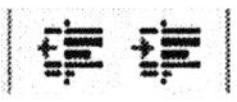

Indent. Select a cell or group of cells and click on a button to indent the cell contents or to remove the indentation.

Borders. Select a cell or group of cells and click on the down arrow. Select the type of border you want for the cell(s) from the options provided. If the option you want is already showing on the button, click on the button to select that option.

Review

SUMMARY of IMPORTANT CONCEPTS

1. The accounting process provides information about business activities.
   a. Accounting is an information system for recording, summarizing, and reporting the financial effects of economic events to help in making decisions.
   b. The account is the basic unit of accounting information. The effects of transactions are recorded in accounts.
   c. The typical accounting process includes: (1) the occurrence of an event to be accounted for, (2) the recording of the effects of the event in accounts, (3) the calculation of account balances, and (4) the summary of the recorded events of a period and the reporting of those summaries.

2. Organizations serve the needs of society.
   a. Organizations exist to benefit society by transforming resources from one form to another form that is more valuable in meeting the needs of people.
   b. Because most resources are in scarce supply, society attempts to use its resources to create the greatest benefit for its members.
   c. Markets provide a way for people to express their perceptions of the value of goods and services by the products they purchase and the prices they pay. The increase in value created by a transformation process can be measured by the total price of the goods and services sold less the total cost of resources consumed to produce them.
   d. Owners invest in a business to receive a return on their investments from business profits. Businesses that operate effectively and efficiently normally will earn greater profits.
   e. Businesses that are not profitable will have difficulty attracting investors and will be forced to change their behavior or to go out of business. Therefore, markets make financial and other scarce resources available to organizations that can best transform them to maximize their value for society.

3. Organizational decisions are made by those who have a stake in an organization.
   a. Managers, owners, and creditors require information in order to assess the effectiveness and efficiency of an organization, to ensure the protection of their interests, and to evaluate investment risk and return on investment.
   b. The transformation process involves the conversion of financial and other resources into goods and services. This process can be divided into financing, investing, and operating activities.
   c. Financing decisions are decisions an organization makes about how it will obtain, manage, and repay financial resources. Businesses obtain capital from owners (proprietors, partners, or stockholders) and from creditors.
   d. Investing decisions involve choices managers make about long-term resources an organization uses to produce goods and services for its customers.
   e. Operating decisions involve choices managers make about how resources will be transformed into goods and services. Decisions are made about the development and design of products, the purchase of materials, the selection and training of employees, the production process, and the distribution, marketing, and servicing of products.

4. Accounting plays a major role in decision making.
   a. Accounting is an information system for measuring and reporting the transformation of resources into goods and services.
   b. Accounting information is used by internal and external decision makers who have a stake in an organization's activities.

5. The accounting profession includes those who work in public accounting firms, other businesses, governmental and nonprofit organizations, and educational institutions.
   a. Management accountants work for businesses and provide services that include the development and management of information systems, financial reporting, financial planning and analysis, cost accounting, and internal auditing.
   b. Public accountants work for accounting firms that provide auditing, tax advice, and consulting services to businesses, nonprofit organizations, and individuals.
   c. Governmental and nonprofit accountants provide management accounting services to their organizations.
   d. Accounting educators teach in high schools and colleges.

Define

TERMS and CONCEPTS DEFINED in This CHAPTER

account (F6)
accounting (F22)
business organization (F9)
corporation (F13)
creditor (F17)
effective business (F12)
efficient business (F12)
financing activities (F13)
governmental and nonprofit organizations (F9)
information (F3)
investing activities (F18)
manufacturing companies (F8)
market (F10)
merchandising companies (F8)
moral hazard (F16)
mutual agency (F16)
operating activities (F19)
organization (F7)
partnerships (F14)
profit (F10)
proprietorships (F14)
retail companies (F8)
return on investment (ROI) (F11)
risk (F5)
service companies (F9)
stakeholders (F7)
stock (F14)
stockholders (F14)
system (F7)
transaction (F6)
transformation process (F21)

Self-Study Problem SOLUTIONS

1 A. Check Register

Date	Check Number	Checks Issued, Withdrawals, and Deposits	Amount of Deposit	Amount of Check/ Withdrawal	Balance
April 1		Balance			1,450
1	346	Northside Real Estate Company		800	650
5		Customer receipts	1,000		1,650
7		Cash withdrawn		70	1,580
12	347	Miller's Wholesale Grocery		300	1,280
14		Customer receipts	950		2,230
17		Cash withdrawn		50	2,180
20	348	Citizens Loan Company		200	1,980
21		Customer receipts	725		2,705
25	349	City Light and Water		160	2,545
27	350	Wang's Grocery		340	2,205
28	351	Restaurant Supply Company		280	1,925
28		Customer receipts	875		2,800
30	352	First Savings and Loan		500	2,300

B.

Garcia's Deli
Summary of Cash Deposits and Payments
For April 2000

Beginning cash balance			$1,450
Deposits:			
Customer receipts		$3,550	
Cash payments:			
Rent	$800		
Food	640		
Car payment	200		
Supplies	400		
Utilities	160		
Transfer to savings	500		
Total cash paid		2,700	
Increase in cash for April			850
Ending cash balance			$2,300

C. The steps in the accounting process include: (1) Garcia receives money or checks and deposits them in his account. He writes checks to exchange money for goods and services. (2) Each transaction is recorded in Garcia's check register. (3) Garcia's cash balance is calculated by adding or subtracting the effect of each transaction. (4) The transactions are summarized and a report is prepared to tell Garcia how he spent his money during April and how much money he has at the end of the month.

2 A.

Bach's Music Store
Profit Earned
For December 2000

Resources created from goods and services sold:		
Musical instruments	$8,000	
Sheet music	1,400	
Repair of instruments	2,200	
Total resources created		$11,600
Resources consumed:		
Cost of instruments sold	$4,300	
Cost of sheet music sold	870	
Rent	650	
Supplies used	250	
Advertising	300	
Utilities	200	
Miscellaneous	180	
Total resources consumed		6,750
Profit		$4,850

B. The value created by a transformation of resources is the difference between the total price of the goods and services sold and the total cost of the resources consumed in producing these goods and services. This difference is profit for the seller.

3 A. The stages of the transformation process are:
1. Galileo financed his business by investing his own money and by borrowing from a bank.

2. Financial resources were invested in a building and equipment and used to acquire other resources the business needed in order to operate.
3. Galileo operates the business. Operations involve:
   (a) Development of instruments.
   (b) Design of the instruments.
   (c) Purchase of materials and supplies for manufacturing the instruments.
   (d) Hiring of employees to help with production.
   (e) Manufacture of instruments.
   (f) Marketing and sale of instruments.
   (g) Distribution of instruments to customers.

B. The prices and costs associated with the transformation include:
   1. A cost is incurred in borrowing money for use in the business.
   2. A cost is incurred in the purchase of buildings and equipment.
   3. Operating costs include materials; wear on building and equipment used in development, engineering, and production activities; wages of assistants; advertising; and distribution of products.
   4. The price of the instruments sold provides income for Galileo.

Questions

1-1 *Obj. 1* What is meant by risk and why is it an important concept for decision makers to understand? What is the relationship between risk and accounting?

1-2 *Obj. 2* What is the purpose of accounting? How does accounting accomplish that purpose?

1-3 *Obj. 2* Accounting is often referred to as an information system. In general, what is a system and why does accounting qualify to be referred to as an information system?

1-4 *Obj. 3* How does the purpose of merchandising, manufacturing, and service companies differ? How do they each create value?

1-5 *Obj. 3* List an example of each of the following types of organization. Describe how each type of organization differs from each of the others.
a. Merchandising
b. Manufacturing
c. Service
d. Governmental
e. Nonprofit

1-6 *Obj. 4* Why do owners invest in businesses even though such an investment is more risky than investing in U.S. Savings Bonds? If you had $3,000 to invest, how would you decide whether to invest it in businesses or whether to invest it in U.S. Savings Bonds?

1-7 *Obj. 4* Phillip invested $3,000 in a business at the beginning of the year. By the end of the year, the value of this investment had risen to $4,100. Near year-end, the business announced that it would reduce in size and sent Phillip a check for $2,000. Describe the difference between a return on investment and a return of investment. What portion of the $2,000 is return on investment and what portion is return of investment?

1-8 *Obj. 5* How are effectiveness, efficiency, rate of return on investment, and accounting interrelated? Be specific.

1-9 *Obj. 6* Joan Hoyt is considering opening a small retail store to sell knives and other kitchen utensils. She has a small amount of money to invest and wants to maintain as much control over the business as she can. She has asked you to help her decide how to finance her business. Describe the primary issues you would suggest Joan consider.

1-10 *Obj. 6* Hardly Moving and Storage Corporation needs an additional $1,000,000 in financing to build new facilities. What are the major sources of financing available to Hardly? What issues should company management consider in deciding on the type of financing to use?

1-11 *Obj. 7* Felicia Ferrari has $8,000 available from personal savings to start an automobile garage. Identify the types of resources she will need for her business. How might she pay for all the necessary resources?

1-12 *Obj. 8* What is the essential characteristic of an operating activity? That is, what do all operating activities have in common? Select a company from your local community and identify 5 different examples of its operating activities.

1-13 *Obj. 9* Sandy Dune overheard some friends from your accounting class discussing the "transformation process." She is curious about what this term means and how it applies to organizations and accounting. Explain to Sandy your understanding of the transformation process and why it is an important concept in accounting.

1-14 *Obj. 10* Accounting is an information system that measures and reports the value created by a company's transformation process. Is there a transformation process related to the accounting system itself? That is, does an accounting system itself create value? If so, how? If not, why do companies have them?

Exercises

1-1 Write a short definition for each of the terms listed in the *Terms and Concepts Defined in This Chapter* section.

1-2 *Obj. 2* At the beginning of August, Freddy had $400 in his checking account. The following events occurred during August:

a. Wrote a check for payment on auto loan, $180.
b. Deposited payroll check from employer, $650.
c. Wrote a check for groceries, $100.
d. Wrote a check for rent, $375.
e. Wrote a check for clothing, $60.

Set up a table using the following format and record each event. Afterward, prepare a report (similar to Exhibit 4) describing the changes in Freddy's cash account during August.

Transaction	Amount of Check	Amount of Deposit	Balance
Balance on August 1			$400
a.			
b.			

1-3 *Obj. 2* Leonardo has started a small business making sundials. He has asked you to help him design a system to record cash received and paid by his business. Cash receipts are deposited daily in a bank account, and payments are made by checks written against the account. Develop an accounting information system you would recommend to Leonardo. (Hint: You may wish to refer to Exhibit 3.) Demonstrate how the system functions using the following transactions:

April 1	Cash balance	$500
3	Cash received from customers	300
4	Cash paid for rent	450
5	Cash paid for supplies	225
7	Cash received from customers	670
8	Cash paid for taxes	180

1-4 *Obj. 2* Bea Taylor owns a small business selling homemade pickles. She maintains a checking account with a local bank and keeps a record of her deposits and checks in a check register. Each month Bea receives a bank statement describing the transactions in her account. She looks at the statements and then throws them away each month. She thinks it is a waste of the bank's money to prepare and mail the statements each month, since she already has a record of her checking account transactions in her check register. She asks you why the bank goes to the trouble of sending her the statements. How would you respond?

1-5 *Obj. 2* Assume you have a friend, Edwina Polinder, who has no knowledge of accounting. She asks you to explain the purpose of accounting and to provide a brief description that will help her understand the accounting process. Draft a short memo to Edwina that will help her understand the purpose of accounting and the accounting process.

DATE:	(today's date)
TO:	Edwina Polinder
FROM:	(your name)
SUBJECT:	Inquiry about accounting.

(your response)

1-6 *Obj. 3* Fashion Threads Company uses the following four steps to make a particular pair of cotton slacks:

a. Cotton is planted, grown, harvested, and shipped to a textile manufacturer. The cost of the cotton associated with the slacks is $5. This amount of cotton is sold to the manufacturer for $5.50.
b. Raw cotton is processed into cotton fabric. The cost of producing the fabric for the slacks, including the cost of the raw cotton, is $13.25. This fabric is sold to a garment manufacturer for $17.
c. Cotton fabric is cut and sewn to produce a pair of slacks. The cost of making the slacks, including the cost of the fabric, is $25. The slacks are sold to a retailer for $30.
d. The cost to the retailer of making the slacks available for sale, including the cost of the slacks, is $34. The retailer sells the slacks for $56.

Use Exhibits 8 and 9 to help you answer the following questions. How much profit is earned at each step in the production and selling process? How much total profit is earned by those involved in making and selling the slacks? Why are customers willing to pay the costs and profits earned by those involved in this process?

1-7 *Obj. 3* Alexander makes baseball gloves by hand. He buys leather for $80 a yard. Padding costs $6 a pound; thread and other materials cost $16 for a month's supply. He pays $500 a month rent for a small shop, and utilities average $150 a month. Shipping costs are about $4.50 per glove. In an average month, Alexander produces and sells 8 gloves. Each glove requires a half yard of leather and a half pound of padding. What is the average cost of a glove made by Alexander? How much profit does Alexander earn on each glove if he sells them for $475 each? How much profit does Alexander earn each month, on average? Exhibits 8 and 9 will help you answer these questions.

1-8 *Obj. 3* Mario's is a restaurant specializing in Italian food. During February, Mario's recorded the following sales to customers and costs of doing business:

Sales to customers	$19,500
Cost of food products used	5,750
Cost of rented building and equipment	4,376
Cost of employee labor services used	3,750
Maintenance and utilities used	2,000

Prepare a schedule that shows the amount of profit (or loss) experienced by Mario's Restaurant during February. (Hint: See Exhibit 9.)

1-9 *Obj. 3* The Quick Stop is a fast-food restaurant. During March, Quick Stop recorded the following sales to customers and costs of doing business:

(Continued)

Sales to customers	$4,400
Cost of food products used	2,100
Cost of rented building and equipment	1,250
Cost of employee labor services used	1,000
Maintenance and utilities used	600

Prepare a schedule that shows the amount of profit (or loss) experienced by Quick Stop during March. (Hint: See Exhibit 9.)

1-10 *Obj. 3* Pam Lucas is a high school student who delivers papers to earn spending money. During May, she received $450 from customers in payment for their subscriptions for the month. She paid $300 for the papers she delivered. In addition, she paid $45 to her parents for use of their car to deliver the papers, and she paid $30 for gas. Prepare a statement to compute the amount of profit Pam earned from her paper route in May. (Hint: See Exhibit 9.)

1-11 *Obj. 4* On January 1, 2002, Alicia invested $4,000 in a savings account. At the end of January, the account balance had increased to $4,020. The balance at the end of February was $4,040.10. The balance at the end of March was $4,060.30. The increases occurred because of interest earned on the account. What was Alicia's return on investment, in dollars and cents, for each of the three months? What was the total return for the three months taken together?

1-12 *Obj. 4* Davy Crockett invested $15,000 in Mike Fink Rafting Company. At the end of the year, Crockett's investment was worth $17,250 because of earnings during the year. Fink paid Crockett $3,000 at the end of the year. What was Crockett's return on investment (in dollars) for the year? What was his return of investment (in dollars) for the year? Did Mike Fink Rafting maintain its capital as a result of these events? Explain.

1-13 *Obj. 5* Flick and Flack are two companies that are identical with respect to the products they sell. They are owned by various individuals and are located in different parts of the same city. During September, Flick sold $24,000 of goods, while Flack sold $18,000. Flick produced $8,000 of profit, and Flack produced $2,000. Compare the efficiency and effectiveness of the two companies.

1-14 *Obj. 5* Rogers and Hornsby are two companies that compete in the same market with the same product, a brand of steak sauce. The companies are the same size and sell to the same grocery retailers. Both products are sold by the retailers at the same price. During 2002, Rogers sold 500,000 bottles of its sauce at a profit of 10 cents per bottle. Hornsby sold 425,000 bottles at a profit of 15 cents a bottle. Which company was more effective? Which was more efficient? Which company was more profitable?

1-15 *Obj. 5* You have a choice of investing in either of two companies, Lewis or Clark. Both companies make the same products and compete in the same markets. Over the last five years, the operating results for the two companies have been:

	Lewis	Clark
Sales to customers	$4,500,000	$5,625,000
Profit	$412,500	$675,000
Return on investment per dollar invested	$.045	$.075

Which company is more efficient? Which is more effective? In which company would you invest? State the reasons for your answers.

1-16 *Objs. 3, 5* Soft Light Company produces specialty lamps and sells them to retail stores. During the latest year, the company sold 40,000 lamps at an average price of $70 per lamp. The production and distribution costs per lamp were $25, on average. Other expenses for management salaries and facilities were $1,200,000 for the year. Total investment in the company is $3,000,000. How much profit did Soft Light earn for the year? Describe the steps you went through to get your answer. Suggest some changes that Soft Light could make to improve its profitability. (Hint: See Exhibit 9.)

1-17 *Obj. 6* Identify each of the following as describing corporations, proprietorships, and/or partnerships. Some items have more than one answer.

a. Distinct legal entity separate from its owners.
b. More than one owner.
c. Ownership by stockholders.
d. Controlled by a board of directors.
e. Change of legal identity when a company is sold.
f. Limited liability.
g. Mutual agency.
h. Access to large amounts of capital.
i. Direct taxation of profits.
j. Moral hazard usually not a major problem.

1-18 *Objs. 6, 7, 8* Leonetta Garcetti owns and manages a large construction company. This morning she is faced with the following issues.

1. The office manager just submitted his resignation and the search for a replacement must be organized.
2. A loan officer from the company's bank just phoned saying that the company's application for a 5-year, $400,000 loan had been approved at a favorable interest rate.
3. Bids from several vendors have been received regarding installation of a new computerized information system. One of the proposals must be selected.
4. Because the new bank loan has been approved, two short-term loans at high interest rates can be paid off.
5. Old office furniture is awaiting disposal.
6. A long-time customer is unhappy with the firm's latest architectural drawings for a new shopping center complex.
7. A new construction crane is being purchased. Leonetta has not yet approved the transaction because she is unhappy with the trade-in price offered for the older and smaller crane being replaced.
8. An investor has approached Leonetta offering to purchase 20% of her company in exchange for a sizeable infusion of cash.
9. The firm is considering the purchase of exclusive regional rights to a newly patented construction process.
10. One of the company's customers is behind on scheduled payments. The amounts are large and Leonetta must decide whether to suspend construction on the project involved.

Identify each of the issues above as involving a financing activity, an investing activity, or an operating activity.

1-19 *Obj. 8* Prepare a table to describe the major operating activities you would expect in each of the following organizations: (a) **Ford Motor Company,** (b) **Wal-Mart,** (c) **Humana,** a for-profit community hospital. The table should be organized so that it is easy to understand.

1-20 *Obj. 9* The three general types of business—merchandising, manufacturing, and service—are based on differing transformation processes. Some possible activities in the transformation process include: (1) financing, (2) investing, (3) research and development, (4) design and engineering, (5) purchasing, (6) personnel, (7) production, (8) distribution, (9) marketing, and (10) servicing.

For each of the three types of business, indicate which of the activities above are likely to be included in its transformation process. If you exclude a specific activity for a given type of business, explain why.

1-21 *Obj. 9* For each of the following items, identify which part of the transformation process is involved. Use (F) to indicate a financing activity, (I) to indicate an investing activity, or (O) to indicate an operating activity.

(Continued)

a. ____ New manufacturing equipment was purchased for installation in the factory.
b. ____ Three new salespersons were hired.
c. ____ A short-term loan was obtained from a local bank.
d. ____ A $500 down payment was received from a customer on goods sold.
e. ____ The Human Resources department hired three new employees.
f. ____ The company's worn-out delivery truck was sold to the junk yard for $400.
g. ____ The owner contributed more cash to the business.
h. ____ Refunds totaling $450 were given to several customers.
i. ____ Goods were shipped to a customer in a neighboring state.
j. ____ The remaining balance of a long-term loan was repaid in full.

Problems

Tips and hints for selected problems and cases are available on the Ingram WebTutor for WebCT site.

PROBLEM 1-1 Developing a Cash Plan

Objs. 1,2

Myrla Rhyman is planning to start a new business as a systems consultant. She has saved $7,000 to invest in the business. She expects to receive $3,800 each month, on average, from sales to customers. She expects that she will need cash to pay the following items each month, on average: rent, $900; supplies, $500; utilities, $100; other, $250. She will need to purchase $13,000 of equipment to start the business; in addition, she thinks she will need $3,000 to cover initial operating costs. A local bank has agreed to consider a loan to help Myrla start her business and has asked her to develop a plan that describes her expected cash receipts and payments for the first year. The plan should show how much cash she will need for the business, how much she will need to borrow, and how she expects to pay back the loan. Monthly payments will be required to pay off the loan and interest. The bank will charge $10 per year in interest for each $100 borrowed until the loan is repaid at the end of the year. Myrla has asked you to prepare a plan for her to submit to the bank.

Required Prepare a plan for Myrla. Describe any assumptions you make. (Hint: See Exhibit 4.)

PROBLEM 1-2 Developing and Using Accounting Information

Obj. 2

Amelia is the proprietor of Computer Consultant Company, a firm with a variety of business and individual customers. During May 2002, the following transactions were entered into the check register of the business's checking account. Unless noted otherwise, all expenditures were made by check.

May 1 Paid $53 to Giant Supply Store for office supplies such as copier paper and floppy disks.
3 Made the $389 lease payment on the company car to Wheels-4-Lease, Inc.
6 Transferred $700 into the business's checking account from the business's savings account.
7 Paid the $525 monthly rent for the office to Landlord Company.
9 Received and deposited checks totaling $1,350 from customers.

13 Paid $41 to Good Impressions, Inc. for copies of a proposal of services to a potential new client. (Amelia viewed this as advertising and promotion of her business.)
16 Withdrew $50 from the ATM machine and took a potential new client to lunch. (Amelia viewed this as advertising and promotion of her business.)
18 Received and deposited checks from customers totaling $1,900.
22 Paid $182 for a display ad that ran last week in *Local Business News.*
24 Sent a check in the amount of $88 to Com.com, the Internet service provider.
25 Paid $134 to Citizen's Power Company for electricity.
29 Deposited checks from customers totaling $875.
30 Sent $1,403 to MasterCard for business expenses incurred at an out-of-town training conference attended early in the month.

The checks written during May were numbered consecutively starting with check #933.

Required

A. Record each transaction as it would appear in Amelia's business check register. Use the format shown below. The May 1 opening balance is already shown.

Date	Check Number	Checks Issued, Withdrawals, and Deposits	Amount of Deposit	Amount of Check/ Withdrawal	Balance
May 1		Opening balance			784

B. Prepare a summary report of the cash deposits and payments for the month of May.
C. List the steps in the accounting process associated with the checking account.
D. Amelia's goal is to have her business earn a profit each month of $2,500. Explain whether you believe her goal was met during May.

PROBLEM 1-3 *Objs. 1, 2, 5*

Summary Information About a Checking Account

T. Edison had the following checking account activity during September: Edison made deposits of $2,000 from salary and $600 from royalties on inventions. He wrote checks of $525 for house payment, $300 for food, $124 for clothing, $100 for entertainment, $90 for utilities, $74 for flying lessons, $200 for insurance, and $250 for car payment, and transferred $500 to savings. The beginning balance in his checking account was $580.

Required

A. Prepare a report in good form, following the example of Exhibit 4, to describe Edison's financial activities for September.
B. What would be the source of the information described in this report?
C. Why might this information be useful for Edison?
D. Describe some decisions Edison might make using this information.

PROBLEM 1-4 *Objs. 1, 2, 5*

Information from a Bank Statement

At the end of September, T. Edison received the following statement from his bank:

(Continued)

T. Edison
Bank Statement
For September

Beginning balance		$ 700
Deposits received:		
Sept. 17	$2,000	
Sept. 24	600	
Total deposits		2,600
Checks paid:		
Sept. 2	$120	
Sept. 5	500	
Sept. 8	300	
Sept. 9	124	
Sept. 13	100	
Sept. 16	44	
Sept. 19	74	
Sept. 22	200	
Sept. 25	250	
Total checks		(1,712)
Ending balance		$1,588

Required

A. What information is contained in the bank statement that is not available to Edison from his summary in Problem 1-3?
B. Why are some of the numbers in the bank statement different from those in Edison's summary in Problem 1-3?
C. Why is this information useful to him?

PROBLEM 1-5 Developing and Evaluating a Cash Plan

Objs. 1, 4, 5

Through hard work and careful saving, Hans and his family have $10,000 to start a small specialty foods business. The family estimates sales to customers will be about $5,500 per month during the first year, but 5% of those sales will be uncollectible. On the average, expected cash payments per month are budgeted as follows:

Wages for occasional labor	$ 700	Utilities	100
Rent on land and buildings	1,200	Advertising	300
Supplies	75	Delivery costs	225

The cost of equipment necessary to operate the business is expected to be about $15,000 and another $3,000 will be needed to cover one-time start-up expenses. A wealthy elderly relative (and experienced businessperson) has offered to provide a loan to get started but only if Hans can present a detailed plan that describes expected cash receipts and disbursements the first year. The plan must show how much cash will be needed for the business, how much must be borrowed, and how Hans and family expect to pay back the loan. The relative requires that Hans and family make monthly repayments and will charge $12 interest per year for each $100 borrowed until the loan is completely paid off. Hans seeks your assistance in preparing the needed plan.

Required

A. Prepare a plan, in a neat and organized fashion, so that Hans and his family can impress the elderly relative.
B. If you were the elderly relative, what questions would you have for Hans after reviewing his plan?
C. If you were the elderly relative, would you make the loan to Hans and his family? Why or why not?

PROBLEM 1-6 Accounting Information and the Transformation Process

Objs. 2, 6, 7, 8

Mustafa is the proprietor of Buildings-R-Us, an architectural firm located in Feelgood City. The firm has a wide variety of business clients. During October 2001, the following transactions were entered into the check register of the business's checking account. Unless noted otherwise, all expenditures were made by check.

Oct 1 Paid $95 to Architect's Supply for drawing instruments and CAD-CAM software.
3 Paid the $137 due annually for a city business license.
4 Contributed $2,500 to the company from his own personal funds.
7 Paid the $1,050 monthly office rent to Business Park, Inc.
10 Borrowed $500 on a short-term loan from Happytown National Bank.
14 Paid $350 to Jon Upgood, a professional colleague, to perform one-time drawing and design services.
17 Withdrew $100 from an ATM machine and took a potential new client to lunch.
18 Received and deposited checks from customers totaling $1,500.
22 Paid $400 annual dues to the National Architects' Society, a professional organization.
24 Sent a $42 check to Feelgood Company for water and garbage service.
26 Paid the monthly electricity bill, $102, to Low Tension Power Company.
29 Deposited checks from customers totaling $465.
30 Paid the company's only employee, Jenice Howard, $1,233 for half-time work.
31 Purchased office furnishings from Pleasant Furniture Company for $759.

The checks written during October were numbered consecutively starting with check #1007.

Required

A. Record each transaction as it would appear in Mustafa's business check register. Use the format shown below. The October 1 opening balance is already shown.

Date	Check Number	Checks Issued, Withdrawals, and Deposits	Amount of Deposit	Amount of Check/ Withdrawal	Balance
Oct 1		Opening balance			387

B. Prepare a summary report of the cash deposits and payments for the month of October.
C. Identify each transaction above as being a financing, investing, or operating activity.

PROBLEM 1-7 A Basic Accounting System

Obj. 2

Dream Maker Finance Company is a financial institution that lends money to individuals to purchase personal items, such as furniture, appliances, and vacations. Once a loan application is processed, a check is written to approved applicants. The loan recipient then makes a payment to the company each month to repay the loan and to pay interest.

Required Describe an accounting system that Dream Maker might use to keep track of its financial activities with its customers. Include in your description a discussion of the accounts, events, and reports that would be included. What would be the primary purpose served by accounting reports prepared by the company? Illustrate your accounting system with sample transactions for a customer. Prepare a sample report that would be sent to the customer.

PROBLEM 1-8 Choosing a Form of Business Organization

Obj. 3

Below are three independent situations.

A. Larry, Ulysses, and Irene are three college student friends planning to set up a summer business at a nearby resort to sell T-shirts, souvenirs, and novelties to tourists. While they have no assets (to speak of) of their own, Larry's uncle has agreed to finance them with upfront capital to acquire inventory and so on. They plan to operate for only one summer as all expect to graduate soon and take permanent jobs in a nearby state.
B. Murine and Visine are twin sisters who have decided to start a computer software consulting firm. Murine is the "techie," and a bit of a flake. (Murine prefers the term "visionary.")

(Continued)

Visine is a highly successful manager gifted with organizational and business skills. Between the two, they believe they can attract and serve a profitable clientele. In fact, they envision rapid expansion of their practice and diversification into a variety of related business activities. Between them they have only enough liquid capital to start a small operation.

C. Reginald and Ruth Ann are ne'er-do-well offspring of a deceased industrialist who left them each $400 million—most of which they still have. Ever the optimists, they think there is money to be made in the steel business. A friend they met at the country club has persuaded them to provide $10 million to set up a business that would manufacture and distribute a line of lightweight-steel kites. Operations would be located in a nearby state.

Required For each of the three independent situations, recommend the form of business organization that you believe would be most appropriate. Explain your reasoning in each case, both in favor of your selection and why the other options are not appropriate.

PROBLEM 1-9 Determining Profit and Return on Investment

Objs. 3, 4

Harry Honda owns a small car dealership. He rents the property he uses, buys cars from a manufacturer, and resells them to customers. During July, Harry sold 14 cars that cost him a total of $189,000. The total amount he received from the sale of these cars was $224,000. Other costs incurred by Harry for the month included rent, $2,550; utilities, $800; insurance, $825; maintenance of property and cars, $500; advertising, $1,000; and property taxes and business license, $200.

Required Prepare a profit report that calculates the amount of profit earned during July. What can Harry do with the profit he earned? Assuming he invested $1,200,000 in the dealership, what was the return on his investment for July expressed as a percentage of his investment?

PROBLEM 1-10 Determining Prices and Return on Investment

Obj. 4

Tesla Electric Company produces electricity. It is investor-owned, is the only electric utility in the geographic area that it serves, and is regulated by a public service commission. The commission has determined that the rate the company should charge its customers should be sufficient for investors to earn a 10% return on investment. At the end of 2001, the total investment in the company was $1,000,000. The commission considers rate requests from the company each January based on prior year costs and anticipated levels of production. The company expects to produce 20,000,000 kilowatt-hours of electricity during 2002, at a cost of $2,000,000.

Required

A. What amount of profit should Tesla be permitted to earn during 2002?
B. How much total revenue would the company require to earn the profit?
C. What amount would the company charge its customers per kilowatt-hour in order to earn the revenue and profit? Show all work in good form.

PROBLEM 1-11 The Relationship between Profit and Value Created

Objs. 4, 5

Marty and Judi own and operate Tender Sender Company, a store providing private mail boxes, contract shipping services on commission, and a wide variety of gift and novelty items. The following transactions occurred during the month of February 2002.

1. Sold $6,000 of gift items for which the company had paid $3,100.
2. Advertising, both newspaper and radio, was $1,500.
3. Rent received from mail box customers totaled $1,640.
4. The monthly rent for the store location was $2,200.
5. The cost of utilities for the month was $475.
6. Commissions earned from shipping services totaled $1,588.
7. Sold $3,200 of novelty items that had cost the company $1,450.
8. The cost of supplies used during the month was $384.
9. Other miscellaneous costs for the month of February totaled $250.

Required

A. Prepare a schedule that shows the amount of profit earned by the company during the month of February.
B. Has the company created value? Explain your answer.

PROBLEM 1-12 Using Accounting Information to Make Decisions

Objs. 3, 4, 5

Albright Manufacturing produces small refrigerators and distributes them through a network of independent retail stores. During the current year, the company expects to manufacture and sell 20,000 refrigerators at an average price of $105 each. The expected cost of producing and distributing these refrigerators is approximately $30 each. In addition, other expenses for management salaries and facilities are budgeted at $1,500,000. Total investment in the company is $2,800,000.

Required Your supervisor has asked you to provide her with your best estimate of the following information. Each estimate is independent of the others. Part A is completed as an example.

A. Current year profit.

Resources created from sales (20,000 × $105)		$2,100,000
Resources consumed:		
Production and distribution (20,000 × $30)	$ 600,000	
Salaries and facilities	1,500,000	2,100,000
Expected profit this year		0

B. Current year profit if:
   1. the average selling price had been $2 higher per unit.
   2. sales volume had been 10% higher.
   3. average production and distribution costs had been $1 less per unit.

C. Assuming that it is equally difficult to raise prices, raise sales, or lower costs by the amounts suggested in part (B) above, which of the three strategies would you suggest the company pursue?

D. Would you be willing to invest in this company in its current situation or if any of the three new strategies is adopted? Why or why not?

PROBLEM 1-13 Making Financing Decisions and Maintaining a Check Register

Objs. 1, 6

Part A. Betsy wants to start a business making flags. She has calculated that she will need $62,500 to start the business. The money will be used to rent a building, purchase equipment, hire workers, and begin production and sales. Betsy has $12,500 in savings she can invest in the business.

Required What alternatives might Betsy have for obtaining the additional $50,000 she needs for her business? What information about her business will potential providers of capital want to have? What decisions will Betsy have to make in deciding on which sources of financing to use?

Part B. Betsy started the Betsy's Flag Co. on September 1 with an investment of $12,500 from savings and $50,000 borrowed from Independence Bank. The money was deposited in a checking account in the name of the company. During September, Betsy wrote checks for the following purchases for the company:

Date	Check	Amount	Payee
9/3	101	$ 625	Gina Washington (for rent)
9/5	102	15,000	SingSong Sewing Machine Co.
9/12	103	28,750	Fulton Fabric Co.
9/18	104	500	City (for business license)
9/22	105	250	City (deposit on utilities)
9/25	106	4,500	Franklin Construction Co.
9/30	107	2,500	Tyler Jefferson (for wages)
9/30	108	625	Independence Bank (for interest)

Required Complete the check register for Betsy's Flag Co. for September using the following format. Remember to record the deposits.

(Continued)

CHECK REGISTER BETSY'S FLAG CO.					
Date	Check Number	Checks Issued/ Deposit Received	Amount of Deposit	Amount of Check	Balance

PROBLEM 1-14 *Obj. 6*

Ethics and Moral Hazard

You are the manager of a retail electronics store. Recently, you purchased 200 What-A-Sound portable CD players from a wholesaler in a going-out-of-business sale. These units cost you $80 each, about half of the normal cost of other brands that you sell for $260. You expected to sell these units at the regular price and earn an above-normal profit. After your purchase, you discovered that the units were poorly constructed and would probably last about a third as long as other major brands.

Customers often ask you for a recommendation when considering the purchase of a portable CD player. If you tell them the truth about the What-A-Sound model, you may have difficulty in selling these units, even if you offer a steep discount.

Required What will you tell a customer who asks about these units? What are the short-run and long-run implications for your company's profits if (a) you conceal the quality of the units and sell them at their regular price or (b) reveal the quality problem? If you were to choose alternative b, what options might you consider in an effort to minimize the effect of these units on your profits?

PROBLEM 1-15 *Obj. 6*

Ethics and Moral Hazard

You manage an auto service store. One of your major services is brake replacement. You purchase replacement parts at an average cost of $30 per set. Each set contains parts for four wheels and will repair one car. You charge an average of $100 per car for replacing worn brakes, including an average labor cost of $40. Your current volume for brake replacements is about 700 jobs per month. A new vendor has contacted you with an offer to sell you replacement parts at an average cost of $22.50 per set. After checking on the quality of these parts, you find that their average life is about two-thirds that of the parts you are currently using.

Required What are the short-run profit implications of using the $22.50 brakes instead of the $30 brakes? What are the long-run profit implications? What ethical issues should be considered in choosing which brakes to use?

PROBLEM 1-16 *Objs. 5, 6, 7, 8*

Budgeting and the Transformation Process

The chief financial officer (CFO) of Flash Bulb and Seed Company has prepared the following projection of cash for the month of August.

Projected cash collections:		
Cash sales to customers		$385,000
Cash collections from prior sales on credit		186,500
		571,500
Projected cash payments for monthly expenses:		
Rent	$ 85,000	
Utilities	2,900	
Wages	274,000	
Advertising	115,000	
Supplies	2,500	479,400
		92,100
Other projected cash payments:		
Remodeling of seed storage facility	$ 12,000	
Repayment of loan to major creditor	30,000	
Purchase of new production machinery	128,000*	170,000
Projected cash shortage for the month		$(77,900)

**The market for the company's products is expanding rapidly and the firm desperately needs new production capacity.*

Required

A. Why is it important that the CFO prepare a document like this?
B. Identify which of the amounts on the cash projection are financing activities, investing activities, or operating activities.
C. If the company came to your bank requesting a loan, how would you respond? From the data given, does the firm appear that it is likely or unlikely to be able to repay a loan? Why?

PROBLEM 1-17 Identifying Financing, Investing, and Operating Activities and Reporting Cash

Objs. 6, 7, 8

Surf-The-Net.com had the following events occur during October:

1. Paid $5,800 for utilities.
2. Collected $89,460 from customers.
3. Paid $28,600 for new equipment.
4. Paid $4,900 on loan principal.
5. Borrowed $65,000 from local bank.
6. Paid $59,430 to employees for salaries.
7. Paid $11,900 for maintenance and repair.
8. Received $48,600 in new capital from investors.
9. Received $18,000 from sale of old equipment used by the firm.
10. Paid $3,750 for supplies.

Required

A. Identify each event as being a financing, investing, or operating activity.
B. What issues must a manager consider before making a specific financing decision? Before making a specific investing decision?
C. Prepare a schedule reporting the company's cash received and paid in October. Assume the cash balance at the beginning of the month was $14,500.

PROBLEM 1-18 The Transformation Process

Objs. 3, 6, 7, 8, 9

You are considering opening a shop in a nearby mall that will sell specialty T-shirts. T-shirts will be produced for customers on order, containing designs and words selected by customers. You will need $10,000 to acquire materials and supplies and $15,000 for equipment and facilities to begin operations. You have accumulated $5,000 in savings and will need to borrow the remainder. A local bank has agreed to consider a loan and has asked for a summary plan to demonstrate the performance you expect from your company and your ability to repay the loan. You will pay $5.50 for T-shirts and will sell them for $15. The cost of paint and supplies will be $0.50 per shirt. An examination of similar stores at other malls indicates that you should be able to sell an average of 1,000 shirts per month. Rent for your store will be $800 per month. Utilities

(Continued)

will be $150 per month, on average. Wages will be $2,800 per month. Interest on the loan will average $180 per month. The loan will be repaid in monthly installments of $400. All transactions are for cash. (Note: Payment of interest on the loan is an operating activity.)

Required

A. Identify the major financing, investing, and operating activities that will be part of your business. (Note: Interest payment is an operating activity.)
B. Develop a financial plan describing the expected profit performance of your company for the first year of operation. The plan should show the initial financing and investing activities that will be needed, and it should show the expected results of operating activities.

PROBLEM 1-19 *Objs. 6, 7, 8, 9*

Tracing Cash Flows through the Transformation Process

Quality Homebuilders, Inc. was organized on January 2 and stock was sold to the public. Construction equipment and a small parcel of land (with buildings) was purchased for cash to support sales, construction activities, and equipment storage. A tract of land was acquired on credit and became the company's first subdivision. Payment on the land is due in one year. The subdivision is underway with the first 20 houses complete and sold to customers. Another 50 houses have been sold and are under construction; 400 lots are still available. Customers make a substantial down payment before construction begins and make progress payments as construction proceeds. The firm employs a complete staff of sales and construction personnel and uses a major advertising campaign to generate sales. Late in the year, the company obtained a loan from a regional bank. About this time, management determined that it had overestimated the amount of construction equipment needed and sold off four large items. The company was profitable during the first year and paid dividends to its stockholders.

Required

A. Identify which of the events described above are financing activities, which are investing activities, and which are operating activities.
B. For each set of activities (financing, investing, operating), indicate whether you believe those activities caused a cash inflow to the company during the year or a cash outflow. Explain your reasoning.
C. Prepare a diagram showing the three major components of the transformation process. Use arrows to show the flow of cash among the three major components. Identify the external parties (people or institutions outside the company) that the company dealt with at each stage of the transformation process. Use arrows to show the exchange of cash with external parties at each stage.

PROBLEM 1-20

Excel in Action

Millie and Milo Wermz are the owners and managers of a small bookstore, The Book Wermz, near a college campus. The store specializes in rare and out-of-print books. The store maintains a checking account with the Second State Bank. At the end of August 2001, the balance in the checking account was $3,476.82. During the first week of September, Millie and Milo made deposits and wrote checks as follows:

September 1	Check 1237 was written for $1,250.00 to Aldos Real Estate for building rent.
September 2	Check 1238 was written for $292.44 to People's Power Co. for electricity.
September 2	A deposit of $1,381.90 was made from sales receipts.
September 3	Check 1239 was written for $487.65 to Prairie Publishing for books purchased by the store.
September 3	Check 1240 was written for $78.27 to Bud's Office Supplies for supplies.
September 4	Check 1241 was written for $237.08 to June Mars for books purchased by the store.
September 5	A deposit of $790.33 was made from sales receipts.
September 5	Check 1242 was written for $412.89 to Mary Speers for wages.
September 6	Check 1243 was written for $84.56 to Mobile Parcel Service for delivery charges.

Required Use a spreadsheet to prepare a check register for The Book Wermz. The spreadsheet should contain six columns: Date, Check Number, Description, Deposit Amount, Check Amount, and Balance. Use the check register to record the beginning balance and the checking account transactions for the first week of September. Your spreadsheet should appear similar to the following example. Use the formatting instructions that follow the example for this purpose.

	A	B	C	D	E	F
1	Date	Check Number	Description	Deposit Amount	Check Amount	Balance
2						
3						

The register should automatically calculate the account balance after each transaction is recorded. Enter =F2+D3−E3 in cell F3 to calculate the balance that appears in this cell, for example. The contents of cell F3 can be copied to cells F4, F5, and so on to calculate balances after each transaction. Use the Format menu to wrap text in cells B1, D1, and E1. Select the appropriate cell and click on Format/Cells. Then click on the Alignment tab and click on the Wrap text box. Use the Comma button , to format columns D, E, and F beginning with row 2 to display two decimal places and include commas to separate thousands from hundreds. Draw a line to separate headings from entries in the register. Select cells A1 to F1 and click on the borders button. Use the drop down arrow to select the line style from the options provided. Align text on the left hand side of each column and align numbers on the right hand side by selecting the appropriate cells and clicking on the alignment buttons.

Your spreadsheet can be modified as needed by inserting or deleting rows, columns, or cells. To insert a row, column, or cell, select the row above the row to be added, the column to the left of the column to be added, or the cell(s) where you want the new cell(s) to appear. Click on the Insert menu and select the appropriate item. To delete a row, column, or cell, select that row, column, or cell(s) and click on the Edit menu. Then click on Delete.

It is important to **save your work on a regular basis.** Save your work before you make any major changes so that mistakes will not require you to redo a lot of work.

PROBLEM 1-21 Multiple-Choice Overview of the Chapter

1. The basic purpose of accounting is to:
   a. minimize the amount of taxes a company has to pay.
   b. permit an organization to keep track of its economic activities.
   c. report the largest amount of net income to stockholders.
   d. reduce the amount of risk experienced by investors.

2. The four primary steps in the accounting process are listed below in random order.
   A. A summary is prepared of the events of the period.
   B. A transaction occurs.
   C. An account balance is increased or decreased.
   D. The effect of an event is recorded.

   In what chronological order do these steps really occur?
   a. C, B, D, A
   b. A, B, C, D
   c. D, C, B, A
   d. B, D, C, A

3. A primary purpose of all organizations in our society is to:
   a. make a profit.
   b. minimize the payment of taxes.
   c. provide employment for the largest number of workers possible.
   d. transform resources from one form to another.

4. Value is created when organizations:
   a. raise capital by borrowing funds from banks, individuals, or other businesses.
   b. pay cash to suppliers, employees, owners, and government.
   c. sell products or services at prices that exceed the value of resources consumed.
   d. invest in machinery.

5. Which of the following are features of the corporate form of business organization?

	Mutual agency	Limited liability
a.	Yes	Yes
b.	Yes	No
c.	No	Yes
d.	No	No

6. Tammy Faye invested $2,000 in a partnership. One year later, the partnership was sold and cash from the sale was distributed to the partners. On that date, Tammy received a check for her share of the company in the amount of $2,250. What was Tammy's return on investment?
   a. $0
   b. $250
   c. $2,000
   d. $2,250

7. Sternberg Enterprises developed a new type of roller skate that is very popular because of its high quality and reasonable price. Sternberg is losing money on the product, however, because several key production personnel recently resigned and replacements are not as skilled. Which of the following terms properly describes the firm?

	Effective	Efficient
a.	Yes	Yes
b.	Yes	No
c.	No	Yes
d.	No	No

8. Which of the following is an investing activity?
   a. A manufacturer borrows from creditors.
   b. A service firm pays a return to its stockholders.
   c. A retailer sells goods to a not-for-profit agency at cost.
   d. A government agency purchases a new mainframe computer system.

9. Which of the following is *not* an operating activity?
   a. Merchandise is sold to customers.
   b. Utility bills are paid.
   c. Merchandise is shipped to customers.
   d. Equipment is purchased for use in manufacturing.

10. The term *transformation process* refers to:
    a. a repetitive cycle of financing, investing, and operating activities.
    b. the conversion of materials into goods for sale.
    c. procedures designed to reduce a company's risk.
    d. training methods by which unskilled workers become efficient and effective.

Cases

CASE 1-1 Understanding the Transformation Process

Obj. 9

Environmental Housing Company designs and builds log homes. Financing is provided by owners and creditors, primarily banks. The company owns buildings and equipment it uses in the management, design, transportation, and construction process. It purchases logs and other building materials from other companies. These materials are shipped by the sellers. Homes are designed for customers. Logs are cut to the dimensions called for in a design and shipped to the customer's building site with other materials for assembly. Environmental Housing employs design engineers, construction and assembly workers, maintenance personnel, and marketing and service personnel, in addition to its management and office staff. The company is in charge of the construction process until the home is completed and ready for occupancy. The company gives warranties that for one year after completion the completed home is free of defects from materials or construction.

Required Identify the three basic stages of Environmental Housing transformation process and describe what happens in each stage. Construct a diagram showing the flow of resources through each of the three major stages. On the diagram, list the events in each stage of the transformation process that will result in money flowing into or out of the company in exchange for other resources.

CASE 1-2 Financing, Investing, and Operating Activities as Part of the Transformation Process

Obj. 9

Refer to the information provided in Case 1–1.

Required List decisions involving the acquisition, use, or disposal of resources that Environmental Housing's managers would make at each stage of the transformation process.

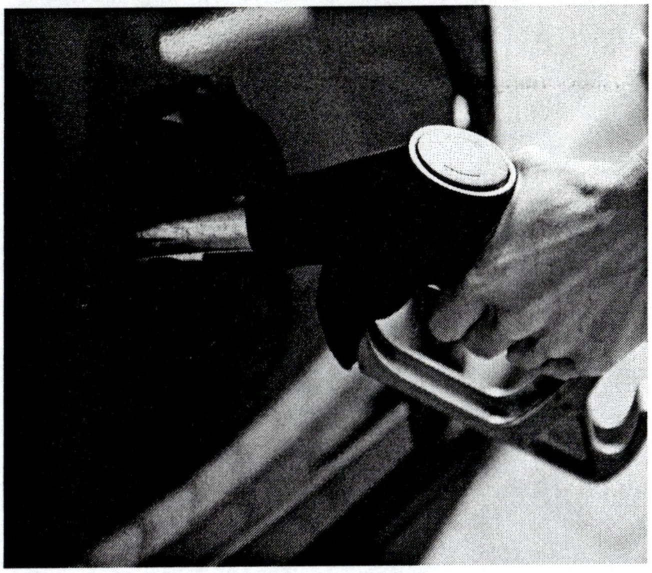

6

OVERVIEW

This chapter discusses the reporting phase of the accounting information system. The output of the accounting system consists of reports and schedules. For these outputs to be useful to decision makers, the reports must accurately summarize the transactions in the transformation process. Therefore, the system must measure the effects of transactions accurately. It must process transactions to produce reliable information. And, it must summarize the information in a form that is understandable to users.

This chapter discusses stages 4 and 5 of the accounting information system, reporting rules and reports.

Reporting rules define how data are combined and summarized in preparing reports and schedules. Reports present information in a form consistent with reporting rules.

The form and content of reports from the accounting system depend on the needs of users. This chapter describes some of the most common accounting reports, financial statements. The purpose of this chapter is to explain how financial statements report transactions that occur in an organization's transformation process. Once you have completed this chapter, you should understand the purpose of financial statements.

Major topics covered in this chapter include:

- The purpose and content of financial statements
- Reporting rules used in preparing financial statements
- Special attributes and limitations of financial statements

Reporting Accounting Information

The Accounting Information System

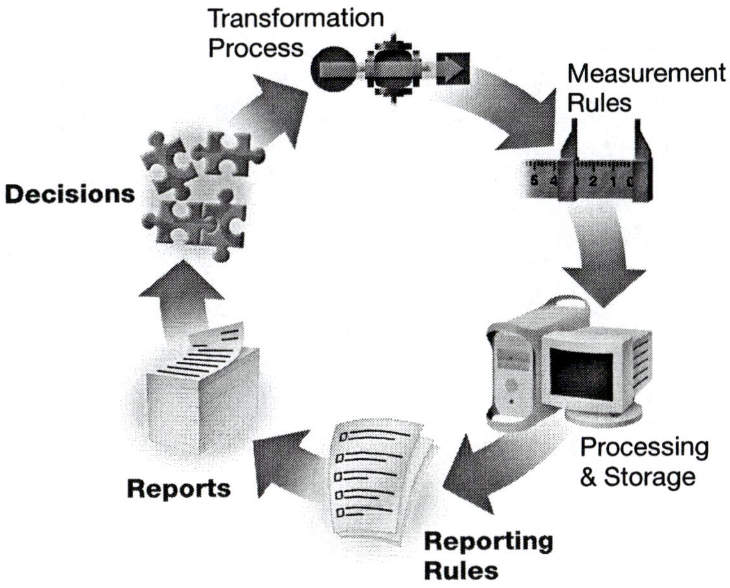

OBJECTIVES

1. Identify the primary financial statements issued by businesses.
2. Summarize the reporting rules and the information presented on a company's income statement.
3. Summarize the reporting rules and the information presented on a company's statement of stockholders' equity.
4. Summarize the reporting rules and the information presented on a company's balance sheet.
5. Discuss how financial statements work together to present a picture of a company for a fiscal period and the purpose of consolidated financial statements.
6. Identify some of the primary limitations of financial statements.
7. Identify the purpose and basic concepts of an audit report.

THE PURPOSE OF FINANCIAL STATEMENTS

OBJECTIVE 1

Identify the primary financial statements issued by businesses.

Accounting information may serve general and specific purposes. Financial statements are the primary means organizations use to report general-purpose accounting information to external decision makers. Most business organizations prepare three financial statements:

1. **An income statement**
2. **A balance sheet**
3. **A statement of cash flows**

Many corporations prepare a fourth statement also, *a statement of stockholders' equity*, because of the variety and complexity of their ownership transactions. The following sections examine the purpose and content of the income statement, the statement of stockholders' equity, and the balance sheet. Chapter F6 examines the statement of cash flows. Information contained in financial statements and information accompanying the statements are a primary concern of financial accounting. Specific-purpose accounting reports and other information used by internal decision makers are subjects of managerial accounting.

The form and content of financial statements evolved throughout the twentieth century and continue to change to meet user needs. Financial statements are used by internal and external decision makers. The format and content of the statements used by managers to make financing, investing, and operating decisions often follow those of statements prepared for external users. Statements for internal use may be prepared in any form and with any content desired by management, however.

For many years the balance sheet was the primary financial statement reported to external users. It was designed to meet the needs of creditors, who want information about resources and claims to these resources. The income statement developed to meet the needs of corporate investors, who want information about earnings. Earnings information is useful for evaluating management decisions that affect dividends and stock values. The statement of stockholders' equity describes transactions affecting stock and the amount and use of retained earnings. A recent addition to external reports, the statement of cash flows provides information that enables creditors, investors, and other users to assess a company's ability to meet its cash requirements.

Financial statements for general-purpose external reporting normally are prepared according to generally accepted accounting principles (GAAP). GAAP specify the format and content of the statements, though they permit managers to choose among alternative procedures in reporting some transactions.

Income Statement

An income statement (sometimes called an earnings statement or a profit and loss [P&L] statement) reports an organization's revenues and expenses for a fiscal period. The income statement presents operating results on an accrual basis. It measures the amount of goods and services provided to customers and resources consumed in providing these goods and services.

Revenues and expenses result from the sale and consumption of resources for a fiscal period. Therefore, the income statement reports the results of these operating activities for a particular period, such as a month, quarter, or fiscal year. For example, the income statement might report operating results for the month of July, the first quarter ending September 30, or the fiscal year ending June 30.

Statement of Stockholders' Equity

A *statement of stockholders' equity* **reports changes in a corporation's stockholders' equity for a fiscal period.** These changes result from profits earned during a period, from dividends paid to owners, and from the sale or repurchase of stock by a corporation. This statement links the income statement to the balance sheet because it describes how much net income was reinvested as part of stockholders' equity.

Balance Sheet

A balance sheet reports the balances of the asset, liability, and owners' equity accounts at a particular date. Other names for the balance sheet are **statement of financial position** and **statement of financial condition.** These names are good descriptions of the statement because it reports the cost of resources available to an organization at a particular date and the sources of financing used to acquire those resources. In combination, the resources and financing are the financial position, or condition, of the organization at the report date.

FINANCIAL STATEMENT CONTENT AND PRESENTATION

Financial statements summarize account balances. This section illustrates financial statements that report typical business transactions. Assume that you manage a company, Rockyfellow, Inc., that operates a small chain of gas stations. Exhibit 1, on page F198, lists account balances for Rockyfellow, Inc. at December 31, 2001, the end of the fiscal year. The following sections illustrate how these data are reported in the company's financial statements.

The Income Statement

OBJECTIVE 2

Summarize the reporting rules and the information presented on a company's income statement.

The income statement reports the revenue and expense account balances and the net income for the period, as illustrated in Exhibit 2.

In interpreting the income statement, it is important to remember that revenues and expenses are measured on an *accrual basis.* Revenues indicate the sales price of goods and services sold during a period. They do *not* indicate how much cash was received from the sales during a current fiscal period. Expenses identify the cost of resources consumed in producing and selling goods and services sold during a period. They do *not* identify how much cash was paid for resources during a period. **Net income is not cash flow.**

As shown on the income statement for Rockyfellow, Inc., an income statement normally is divided into several sections. The usual sections are shown in Exhibit 3.

LEARNING NOTE

Columns are used on financial statements to make addition and subtraction easier. The goal is clear presentation of the information. The format of financial statements varies considerably in practice.

Exhibit 1

Rockyfellow, Inc. Account Balances December 31, 2001	
Account	**Balance**
Cash	$ 15,600
Accounts receivable	22,430
Merchandise inventory	43,500
Supplies	12,670
Prepaid insurance	8,290
Equipment	93,070
Allowance for depreciation—equipment	22,350
Buildings	275,000
Allowance for depreciation—buildings	83,510
Land	36,810
Patents	32,000
Accounts payable	24,790
Wages payable	4,100
Interest payable	11,250
Income taxes payable	2,400
Notes payable, current portion	14,400
Notes payable, long-term	177,600
Investment by owners	125,000
Retained earnings, 1/1/01	62,700
Dividends	5,000
Sales revenue	186,230
Cost of goods sold	73,350
Wages expense	42,700
Utilities expense	6,430
Depreciation expense	9,650
Insurance expense	3,420
Supplies expense	8,390
Interest expense	10,300
Advertising expense	7,120
Patent expense	3,000
Income tax expense	5,600
Other Information: Shares of stock	12,500

Exhibit 2

Rockyfellow, Inc.
Income Statement
For the Year Ended December 31, 2001

Sales revenue		$186,230
Cost of goods sold		73,350
Gross profit		112,880
Operating expenses:		
Wages	$42,700	
Utilities	6,430	
Depreciation	9,650	
Insurance	3,420	
Supplies	8,390	
Advertising	7,120	
Patent	3,000	
Total operating expenses		80,710
Operating income		32,170
Interest expense		10,300
Pretax income		21,870
Income tax expense		5,600
Net income		$ 16,270
Earnings per share of common stock ($16,270 ÷ 12,500 shares)		$1.30

Exhibit 3

Typical Income Statement Sections

1		Revenues from Sales of Goods and Services
	−	Cost of Resources Consumed in Producing Goods and Services Sold
	=	Gross Profit
2	−	Operating Expenses: Other Resources Consumed by Operating Activities
	=	Operating Income
3	+	Other (Nonoperating) Revenues
	−	Other (Nonoperating) Expenses
	=	Pretax Income
4	−	Income Taxes
5	=	Net Income
6	=	Earnings per Share (Net Income ÷ Shares of Stock)

Gross Profit. The income statement reports *gross profit,* **which is the difference between the selling price of goods or services sold to customers during a period and the cost of the goods or services sold.** For a merchandising company, the cost of goods sold is the cost of the merchandise inventory sold during a period. For a manufacturing company, cost of goods sold includes the dollar amounts of materials, labor, and other resources that are consumed directly in producing the goods sold during a period. As explained in Chapter F3, these costs are product costs. Product costs are recorded as an asset (Inventory) until goods are sold. Then the costs are matched against the revenues generated from the sale by recording an expense (Cost of Goods Sold) during the same fiscal period as the sale.

Cost of services, rather than cost of goods, is important for service companies. **The** *cost of services sold* **is the cost of material, labor, and other resources consumed directly in producing services sold during a period.** For example, in a hospital, the cost of nursing and other patient care costs are costs of services. These costs cannot be inventoried and, therefore, are expensed in the period in which the services are provided.

Other Operating Expenses and Operating Income. The second section of an income statement lists operating expenses other than cost of goods sold or cost of services sold. *Operating expenses* **are costs of resources consumed as part of operating activities during a fiscal period that are not directly associated with specific goods or services. Most operating expenses are period costs because they are recognized in the fiscal period in which they occur.** Operating expenses include administrative and selling expenses incurred during a period. Salaries for managers and their support staffs who are not involved directly in producing goods and the cost of resources used by managers are operating expenses. These expenses include depreciation, taxes, and insurance on office buildings and equipment, and the costs of supplies and utilities consumed in operating these facilities. GAAP require most marketing and selling costs and research and development costs incurred during a fiscal period to be reported as operating expenses of the period in which they occur. Because identifying how much of these costs is associated with benefits of future periods is difficult, GAAP require that these amounts be expensed to avoid an overstatement of profits during the current fiscal period.

The excess of gross profit over operating expenses is *income from operations*, or *operating income*. If operating expenses are greater than gross profit, a loss from operations results.

Other Revenues and Expenses. Revenues and expenses may occur that are not directly related to a company's primary operating activities. These are reported separately. The item listed in this category most often is interest expense. Borrowing money frequently is necessary for an organization's operations; however, except for financial institutions, it is not part of its primary operating activities. Accordingly, other expenses and revenues are reported on the income statement after operating income. This separate listing distinguishes them from revenues and expenses that result from operating activities.

Income Taxes. Most corporations pay income taxes on their earnings. **The amount of income tax expense is determined by applying tax rates required by current tax laws and regulations to the income earned by a company during a fiscal period.** Exhibit 2 reports that Rockyfellow, Inc. incurred income taxes of $5,600 on pretax income of $21,870 in 2001.

Proprietorships and partnerships do not pay income taxes on their profits directly. Instead, those profits are treated as personal income of the owners. An owner pays income tax on a proprietorship's profits or on his or her share of the profits of a partnership.

LEARNING NOTE

Not all U.S. corporations pay income taxes on profits. Certain small corporations, known as Subchapter S corporations in the tax laws, are treated like partnerships for tax purposes. Each stockholder is taxed on his or her share of the corporation's profits.

Special Items. The revenues and expenses described to this point are common to most corporations. Occasionally, however, companies must account for special revenues and expenses. Those special items are reported separately from other items and require special disclosure because they affect net income during the current fiscal period but will not affect net income in future periods. Decision makers should evaluate special items differently from activities that are expected to affect income in future periods, especially when forecasting income. There are three types of special items: discontinued operations, extraordinary items, and accounting changes.

A company expects to derive income from its continuing operations in future years. In contrast, ***discontinued operations*** **are product lines or segments from which a company will no longer derive income** because it has sold or closed (or is in the process of selling or closing) that product line or segment of its operations. Discontinued operations differ in size and type of activity from restructurings, which are reported as operating revenues or expenses. Discontinued operations involve large segments of a company's operations, such as a major product line or geographic region. Discontinued operations are rare events because a company cannot close many major segments and remain in business.

A gain or loss from the sale or closing of a discontinued operation is reported on the income statement net of income taxes. Like the gain or loss from discontinued operations, the related income tax effect is a one-time event.

LEARNING NOTE

Income taxes reported as a separate line item on the income statement are taxes on pretax income and do not include the tax effects of items reported below that line. Items reported below income taxes are reported net of their income tax effects. That is, the taxes are subtracted from the total amount of gain or loss associated with these special items to give a net gain or loss amount.

CASE IN POINT

ON THE INTERNET

http://www.ingram@swcollege.com

Learn more about PepsiCo's financial information

PepsiCo Inc. reported the following income statement items in its 1998 annual report:

(in millions)	1998	1997	1996
Income from continuing operations	1,993	1,491	942
Discontinued operations, net of income taxes	—	651	207

Gains and losses that are both unusual and infrequent are reported as *extraordinary items.* *Unusual* and *infrequent* are defined by the individual company. What is unusual and infrequent for one company may not be unusual or infrequent for another. GAAP require that certain items, such as gains or losses from the early retirement of debt, always be reported as extraordinary items. Extraordinary items are reported separately on the income statement (net of taxes) to call attention to their special nature. A specific extraordinary item is not expected to recur in future years.

CASE IN POINT

Revlon Inc. reported the following income statement items in its 1998 annual report:

(in millions)	1998	1997	1996
Income (loss) before extraordinary item	(91.5)	58.5	24.8
Extraordinary loss on retirement of debt, net of income tax	(51.7)	(14.9)	(6.6)
Net (loss) income	(143.2)	43.6	18.2

Accounting changes **are the effects on income caused by changes in the application of accounting principles from one fiscal period to another.** Companies must report material effects on their income when they adopt new accounting standards or change from one accounting method to another. In most cases, when a change in accounting methods is made, the income that has been reported differs from that which would have been reported in earlier periods if the new method had been used. The cumulative effect of the accounting change on income of earlier periods is reported on the income statement.

An accounting change is reported as a separate item on the income statement, net of taxes. This reporting requirement calls attention to the change. Remember that consistency is an important characteristic of accounting methods. A company should not change accounting methods unless that change is justified by the company's economic circumstances or the need to adopt a new accounting standard. A change in accounting method generally alters the way income or expense is calculated. Net income computed using a particular accounting method in one year is not comparable with income computed using a different method in the next year. Accordingly, companies must disclose the effects of the changes and restate, when possible, previous financial statement amounts that are affected by the change so that they are comparable to those reported in the current year.

A change in accounting method is different from a change in accounting estimate. Many transactions require a company to make estimates. For example, when a company records

CASE IN POINT

Amcast Corp. reported the following income statement items in its 1998 annual report:

(in thousands)	1998	1997	1996
Income Before Cumulative Effect of Accounting Change	16,765	12,983	15,926
Cumulative Effect of Accounting Change	(8,588)	—	—
Net Income	$ 8,177	$12,983	$15,926

The cumulative effect resulted from adoption of a new accounting standard. Amcast disclosed the following information in notes to its financial statements:

> In April 1998, the American Institute of Certified Public Accountants issued Statement of Position (SOP) No. 98-5, "Reporting on the Costs of Start-Up Activities." SOP No. 98-5 provides guidance on the financial reporting of start-up and organization costs and requires such costs to be expensed as incurred, with the effect of initial adoption reported as a cumulative effect of a change in accounting principle. The Company has adopted SOP No. 98-5 retroactively to the first quarter of 1998 as required under the SOP.

depreciation expense, it must estimate the remaining useful lives of its plant assets. Estimates are likely to change from time to time as new information becomes available to managers or as conditions change. Companies are not required to report or disclose changes in estimates.

For example, suppose Raider Co. changes its estimate of the remaining useful life of some of its plant assets from five years to three years. If the book value of the assets is $30,000, the company would record $10,000 ($30,000 ÷ 3 years), instead of $6,000 ($30,000 ÷ 5 years), of depreciation expense each year over the remaining life of those assets. No adjustments would be made to amounts recorded in previous periods.

Net Income. Net income is the amount of profit earned by a company during a fiscal period. It is the amount reported after special items have been added or subtracted. It represents an increase in owners' or stockholders' equity, and it can be either distributed to owners or reinvested in the company. Dividends are not an expense. They are a deduction from net income representing a transfer to stockholders of a portion of a company's earnings. Undistributed earnings are included in retained earnings on a company's balance sheet.

LEARNING NOTE

It is important to note that cash dividends and cash withdrawals are paid out of cash. Therefore, a company must have either current or past undistributed profits and sufficient cash available before it can pay dividends or before owners can withdraw money. Remember that net income does not guarantee that a company will have favorable cash flows during a period.

Comprehensive Income. For many decades there has been controversy among accountants concerning whether certain items should be reported as part of a company's net income. Recently, the FASB introduced a new reporting requirement that goes beyond net income. In addition to net income, all firms must report comprehensive income. *Comprehensive income* **is the change in a company's equity during a period resulting from all nonowner transactions and activities.** It includes any event that changes equity except those arising from dealings with the company's own stockholders. Accordingly, it excludes events such as selling stock or paying dividends.

Under the new requirements, three items that are not included in net income are included as part of comprehensive income: (a) gains or losses from holding certain marketable securities, (b) certain gains or losses from foreign currency effects on foreign subsidiaries, and (c) certain changes in the minimum liability for employee pensions. Gains and losses from holding marketable securities are discussed in Chapter 10. The other two topics are beyond the scope of this text. Items affecting comprehensive income, but not affecting net income, are reported either on the income statement in a section following net income or in a separate statement of comprehensive income.

Earnings Per Share. GAAP require that corporate income statements prepared for distribution to shareholders and other external users present earnings per share as part of the statement. *Earnings per share* **is a measure of the earnings performance of each share of common stock during a fiscal period. In general, it is computed by dividing net income by the average number of shares of common stock outstanding during a fiscal period.** By multiplying earnings per share times the number of shares they own, stockholders can identify the amount of profit or loss associated with their individual investments. Many companies calculate net income per share by dividing net income available to common stockholders by the average common shares outstanding during a fiscal period. That average is weighted by the number of months shares of common stock were outstanding during a fiscal period.

For example, suppose that Marble Slab Corporation has 2 million shares of common stock outstanding at the beginning of 2001. On October 1, 2001, the company issues an additional 1 million shares. The weighted average number of shares would be 2.25 million [(2,000,000 × 9 ÷ 12) + (3,000,000 × 3 ÷ 12)]. If Marble Slab reports net income of $5 million for 2001, its earnings per share would be $2.22 ($5,000,000 ÷ 2,250,000).

When a company reports discontinued operations, extraordinary items, or accounting changes, it also must report earnings per share separately for those items. These items are reported net of tax effects.

For some companies, earnings per share is complicated by stock options, stock warrants, convertible bonds, or convertible preferred stock—instruments that can be exchanged for shares of common stock. When an exchange is made, additional shares of common stock are issued, reducing earnings per share. These companies report two sets of earnings per share numbers, basic and diluted earnings per share. **Basic earnings per share** (as described above) is calculated without considering the impact of current stock options or warrants or convertible stocks or bonds. **Diluted earnings per share** is adjusted for the effects of new shares that would be issued if options or warrants were exercised or if convertible bonds or preferred stock were converted to common shares. Diluted earnings per share is never greater than basic earnings per share. It is a more conservative measure of earnings during a period.

M

Internal and External Uses. Income statements for internal use may be prepared for different divisions of a company, for different product lines, or for different regions. The type and amount of information included in a statement will depend on the needs of the managers who use it. The format and content of such statements are not governed by GAAP.

Income statements for external use, especially those of large corporations, may be more or less complex than the one presented in Exhibit 2. Most corporations report income statements for the most recent 3 fiscal years in their annual reports. Some income statement information for the latest 5- or 10-year period often is reported in schedules accompanying the financial statements.

Exhibit 4 shows the relationships of several income statement categories to total revenues for four large corporations.

Exhibit 4

Expenses and Net Income as a Percentage of Total Revenues for Selected Corporations

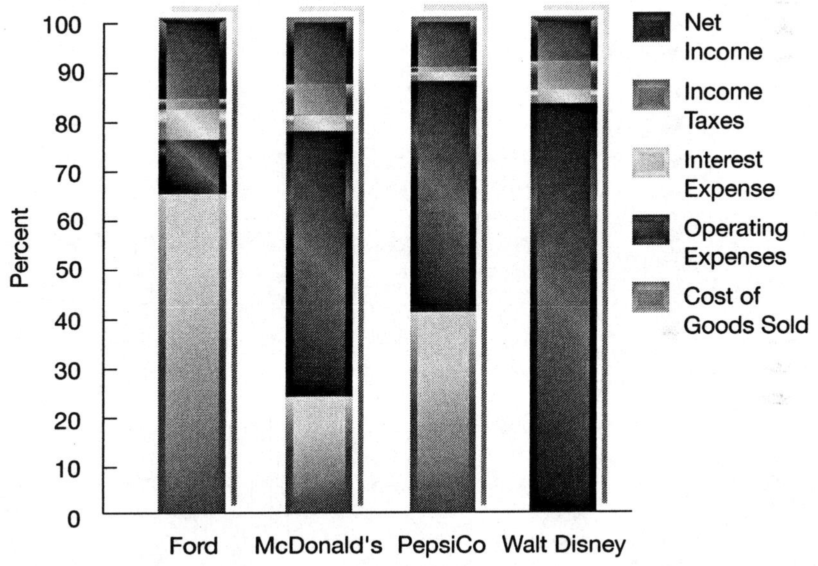

Data source: 1998 annual reports. Slight modifications in classification have been made to the original.

Self-Study Problem 1

ON THE INTERNET

http://www.ingram@swcollege.com

Visit IBM's home page.

An income statement for **IBM Corporation** for a recent fiscal year is provided on page F204. Use this statement to answer the following questions:

1. How much revenue did IBM earn from selling computers?
2. How much revenue did it earn from other operating activities?
3. How much revenue did it earn from nonoperating activities?
4. How much gross profit did IBM earn?
5. How much expense did it incur for nonoperating activities?
6. Approximately how many shares of stock did IBM have outstanding during the year?
7. What were IBM's total product costs on the income statement?
8. How much operating income and net income did IBM earn during the fiscal year?
9. How much cash did IBM receive from its operating activities during the year?

International Business Machines Corporation
Income Statement
For the Year Ended December 31, 1998

(Dollars in millions except per share amounts)		
Revenue:		
Hardware sales	$35,419	
Services	28,916	
Software	11,863	
Financing and other	5,469	
		$81,667
Cost of goods and services sold:		
Hardware sales	24,214	
Services	21,125	
Software	2,260	
Financing and other	3,196	
		50,795
Gross profit		30,872
Operating expenses:		
Selling, general, and administrative	16,662	
Research, development, and engineering	5,046	
		21,708
Operating income		9,164
Other income, principally interest		589
Interest expense		(713)
Earnings before income taxes		9,040
Income taxes		(2,712)
Net income		$ 6,328
Earnings per share		$6.57

Data source: IBM, 1998 Annual Report. Slight modifications in format have been made to the original.

The solution to Self-Study Problem 1 appears at the end of the chapter.

The Statement of Stockholders' Equity

OBJECTIVE 3

Summarize the reporting rules and the information presented on a company's statement of stockholders' equity.

Recall that the statement of stockholders' equity provides information about changes in owners' equity for a corporation during a fiscal period. Exhibit 5 provides an example of this statement for Rockyfellow, Inc.

Stockholders' equity consists of two major divisions: contributed capital and retained earnings. *Contributed capital* **is the amount of direct investment by owners in a corporation.** It is the amount paid in to the corporation by stockholders for the ownership shares at the time the stock was sold by the corporation. The balance of contributed capital changes during a fiscal period when a corporation sells additional shares of stock. The balance also

Exhibit 5

Rockyfellow, Inc.
Statement of Stockholders' Equity
For the Year Ended December 31, 2001

	Contributed Capital	Retained Earnings	Total
Balance at December 31, 2000	$100,000	$62,700	$162,700
Common stock issued	25,000		25,000
Net income		16,270	16,270
Dividends declared		(5,000)	(5,000)
Balance at December 31, 2001	$125,000	$73,970	$198,970

changes when the company buys its own shares back from stockholders and retires those shares so that they cannot be resold.

Retained earnings is the cumulative amount of net income earned that has been reinvested in the corporation. It is the amount of profit that has not been paid out as dividends to stockholders. During a fiscal period, retained earnings increases by the amount of net income. It decreases by the amount of any net loss and by the amount of dividends paid or promised (declared) during the period.

Dividends are not reported on the income statement because they are not expenses. They are a distribution of net income to owners. Dividends are a reduction in retained earnings and are reported on the statement of stockholders' equity.

The statement of stockholders' equity provides a link between the income statement and the balance sheet, as illustrated in Exhibit 6. The ending balances from the statement of stockholders' equity are the amounts reported as stockholders' equity on the balance sheet. Corporations typically provide a statement of stockholders' equity for the most recent three fiscal years in their annual reports.

LEARNING NOTE

Corporations sometimes report an abbreviated version of the statement of stockholders' equity that contains only the retained earnings section of Exhibit 5. Accountants refer to this abbreviated version as a **statement of retained earnings.** Some corporations combine the statement of retained earnings with the income statement.

Exhibit 6
The Role of the Statement of Stockholders' Equity as a Link Between the Income Statement and Balance Sheet

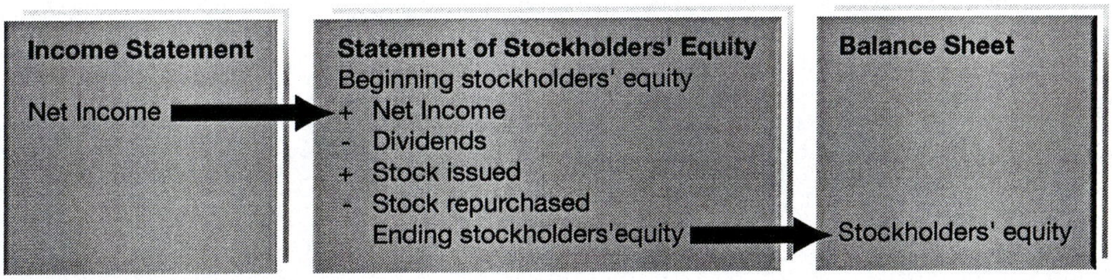

The Balance Sheet

OBJECTIVE 4

Summarize the reporting rules and the information presented on a company's balance sheet.

A balance sheet reports the asset, liability, and owners' equity account balances for a company at the end of a fiscal period. Exhibit 7, on page F206, provides a balance sheet for Rockyfellow, Inc.

Recall that the total amount of assets reported on the balance sheet at the end of a fiscal period must be equal to the total amount of liabilities and owners' equity (after revenues and expenses have been transferred to owners' equity). This relationship, assets = liabilities + owners' equity, is the fundamental balance sheet equation.

Exhibit 7 provides a **classified balance sheet** in which assets and liabilities are separated by type. Also, the exhibit illustrates a **comparative balance sheet** because it provides information for more than one fiscal period. A balance sheet provides information for a particular date; thus, information for the beginning and ending dates of a fiscal period is useful for determining changes in balance sheet accounts during that period. GAAP require classified and comparative balance sheets in reports to external users. Supplemental schedules may disclose some balance sheet information for the most recent 5 or 10 years.

A balance sheet can be classified into eight primary sections, as illustrated in Exhibit 8, on page F207.

LEARNING NOTE

An organization's operating cycle is the period from the time cash is used to acquire or produce goods until these goods are sold and cash is received. The operating cycles of most organizations are less than 12 months. A fiscal year is the primary reporting period for these companies. Occasionally, a company's operating cycle is longer than 12 months. In such cases, which are rare, current assets are defined as those that a company expects to convert to cash or consume during the next operating cycle.

Current Assets. *Current assets* **are cash or other resources that management expects to convert to cash or consume during the next fiscal year.** Some current assets are liquid assets. *Liquid assets* **are resources that can be converted to cash in a relatively short period.** In

Exhibit 7

Rockyfellow, Inc.
Balance Sheet
December 31, 2001

	2001	2000
Assets		
Current assets:		
Cash	$ 15,600	$ 11,700
Accounts receivable	22,430	13,850
Merchandise inventory	43,500	44,450
Supplies	12,670	9,920
Prepaid insurance	8,290	5,950
Total current assets	102,490	85,870
Property, plant, and equipment:	2001	2000
Equipment	93,070	79,570
Buildings	275,000	235,000
	368,070	314,570
Less: Accumulated depreciation	105,860	96,210
	262,210	218,360
Land	36,810	45,000
Total property, plant, and equipment	299,020	263,360
Other assets:		
Patents	32,000	35,000
Total assets*	$433,510	$384,230
Liabilities		
Current liabilities:		
Accounts payable	$ 24,790	$ 22,630
Wages payable	4,100	5,510
Interest payable	11,250	9,920
Income taxes payable	2,400	3,000
Notes payable, current portion	14,400	9,320
Total current liabilities	56,940	50,380
Long-term liabilities:		
Notes payable, long-term	177,600	171,150
Total liabilities	234,540	221,530
Stockholders' Equity		
Contributed capital	125,000**	100,000
Retained earnings	73,970**	62,700
Total stockholders' equity	198,970**	162,700
Total liabilities and stockholders' equity	$433,510	$384,230

**Total assets = total current assets + total property, plant, and equipment + other assets*

***From Exhibit 5*

addition to cash, current assets include (1) accounts receivable for which a company expects to receive cash during the next fiscal year, (2) inventory a company expects to sell during the next fiscal year, and (3) resources a company expects to consume during the next fiscal year, such as supplies and prepaid insurance.

Long-Term Investments. *Long-term investments* **occur when one company purchases the stock or bonds of another company.** Companies often invest in other companies to share in their earnings or to obtain access to resources, management skills, technology, and markets available to other companies. If management expects to hold these investments beyond the next fiscal year, they are classified as long-term investments.

Exhibit 8

Primary Balance Sheet Classifications

Assets:

1 Current Assets
2 Long-Term Investments
3 Property, Plant, and Equipment
4 Other Long-Term Assets

Liabilities:

5 Current Liabilities
6 Long-Term Liabilities

Stockholders' Equity:

7 Contributed Capital
8 Retained Earnings

Property, Plant, and Equipment. *Property, plant, and equipment,* **often called fixed or plant assets, are long-term, tangible assets that are used in a company's operations.** Unlike inventory, these assets are not intended for resale. U.S. GAAP require fixed assets, other than land, to be depreciated over their estimated useful lives. Depreciation allocates the cost of these assets to the fiscal periods that benefit from their use as a means of matching expenses with revenues. GAAP in some countries permit the immediate expensing of plant assets.

Other Long-Term Assets. *Other assets* **include noncurrent receivables, fixed assets held for sale, prepaids not expected to be consumed in the next fiscal year, and long-term legal rights such as patents, trademarks, and copyrights.** These types of assets may be listed on the balance sheet under separate headings if they constitute a significant portion of a company's assets.

Accounts and notes receivable that a company does not expect to collect during the next fiscal year (or longer operating cycle) are not included among current assets. These items are reported in the Other Assets category. Property, plant, and equipment items that a company is not using currently but is holding for future use, disposal, or sale also are included in this category. For example, land held for a future factory site would be listed here.

Long-term legal rights resulting from the ownership of patents, copyrights, trademarks, and similar items are known as *intangible assets,* in contrast to tangible assets such as property, plant, and equipment. The cost of these assets is allocated over their estimated useful lives in a manner similar to the allocation of fixed asset costs. *Amortization* **is the process of systematically allocating a cost to expense over a period of time.** Intangible assets usually are amortized on a straight-line basis. That is, the cost of the assets is allocated to expense equally over the fiscal periods management expects will benefit from their use. This allocation attempts to match expense with revenue. Patent Expense, reported on the income statement in Exhibit 2, is the amortization expense for patents. For intangibles, unlike fixed assets, an accumulation account, such as Accumulated Depreciation, normally is not used to record the cumulative amortization. The amortization expense for a period is subtracted directly from the appropriate intangible asset account when the expense is recorded.

To illustrate, assume that on January 1, 2001 a company purchased a patent, giving that company the exclusive right to produce a product. The cost of the patent was $10,000, and it was expected to have a useful life for the company of 10 years. The amount of amortization expense for the patent would be $1,000 per year for the 10-year period. The balance of the patent account reported on the company's December 31, 2001, balance sheet would be $9,000. The balance on December 31, 2001, would be $8,000, and so forth.

Exhibit 9 shows the relationship of three different asset categories to total assets for four large corporations.

Exhibit 9 Current, Plant, and Other Assets as a Percent of Total Assets for Selected Corporations

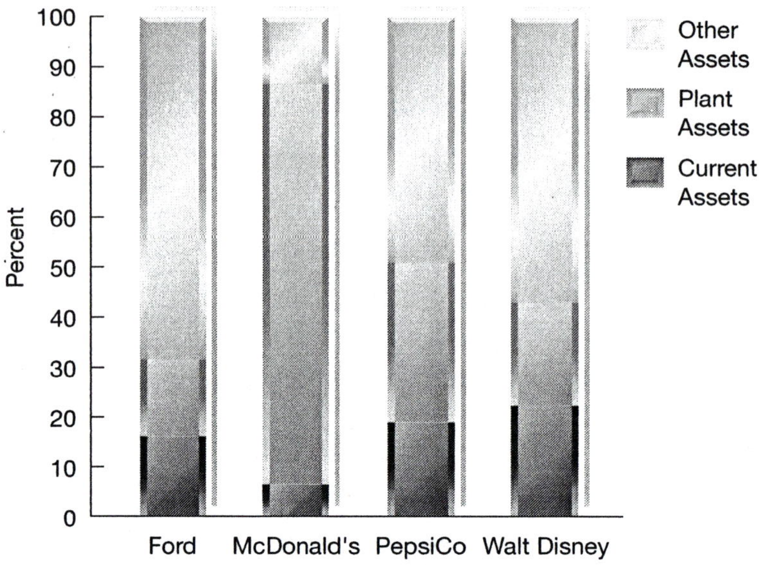

Data source: 1998 annual reports

Liabilities. A balance sheet separates liabilities into current and long-term categories. *Current liabilities* **are those obligations that management expects to fulfill during the next fiscal year (or longer operating cycle).** *Long-term liabilities* **are those obligations not classified as current liabilities.**

When long-term debt is paid in installments, the amount that will be paid during the next year is a current liability (such as Notes Payable, Current Portion in Exhibit 7). For example, assume that a company issues $20,000 in long-term notes payable on January 1, 2001. The principal is to be paid in four equal annual installments. Therefore, $5,000 of the notes would be reported as a current liability on a balance sheet prepared for December 31, 2001. The remaining unpaid balance would be reported as a long-term liability.

Exhibit 10 shows the relationship of two liability and two equity categories to total assets for four large corporations.

Exhibit 10 Liabilities and Stockholders' Equity as a Percent of Total Assets for Selected Corporations

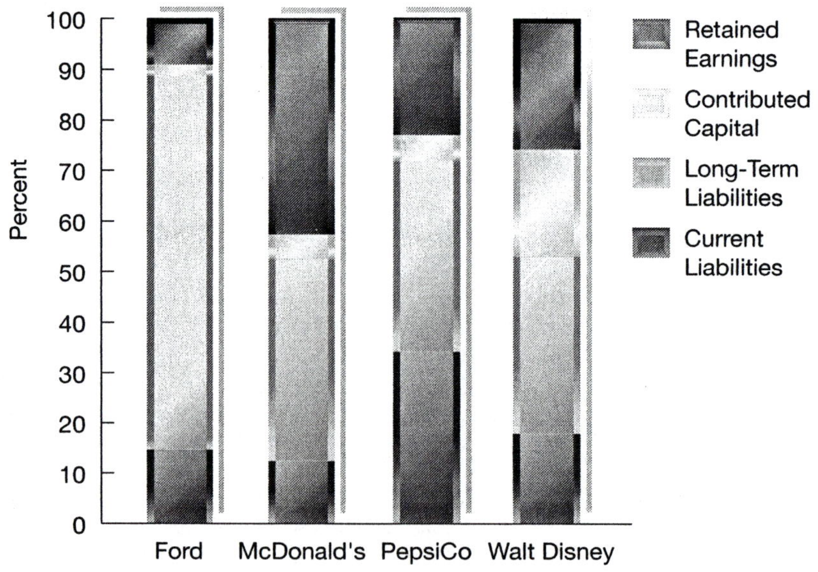

Working Capital. Financial statement users often are interested in the relationship between an organization's current assets and current liabilities. *Working capital* **is the amount of current assets minus the amount of current liabilities.** For Rockyfellow, Inc., working capital for 2001 is $45,550 ($102,490 of current assets − $56,940 of current liabilities). Working capital often is expressed as a ratio. **The** *working capital ratio,* **or** *current ratio,* **is the amount of current assets divided by the amount of current liabilities.** Rockyfellow's working capital ratio for 2001 is 1.8 ($102,490 ÷ $56,940). Working capital is a commonly used measure of a company's *liquidity* **(having sufficient liquid assets to cover current obligations).** A large amount of working capital, or a high working capital ratio, often means that a company will be able to meet its current obligations on a timely basis.

Stockholders' Equity. The balances of stockholders' equity accounts on the balance sheet are the ending balances reported for these accounts on the statement of stockholders' equity (see Exhibit 5). These balances normally include the cumulative amount of contributed capital and retained earnings created by a corporation since its beginning. A later chapter examines stockholders' equity in greater detail.

Other Balance Sheet Formats. Like the income statement, the balance sheet may appear in a variety of formats in practice. Companies may use reporting rules that differ from those previously described. Some types of companies—many utilities, for example—report fixed assets prior to current assets and report stockholders' equity prior to liabilities. Foreign companies often use formats that differ from those used in the United States.

Self-Study Problem 2

Listed below are account balances, cash receipts and payments, and other data for Lewy Pasture, Inc., a company that distributes pharmaceutical supplies, for the fiscal year ended October 31, 2001:

Accounts payable	$ 22,000
Accounts receivable	11,000
Accumulated depreciation	164,000
Buildings	412,000
Cash	16,000
Contributed capital	300,000
Cost of goods sold	146,000
Dividends (declared and paid)	17,000
Equipment	245,000
General and administrative expenses	96,000
Income tax expense	14,000
Income tax payable	6,000
Interest expense	25,000
Interest payable	14,000
Land	35,000
Long-term investments	35,000
Merchandise inventory	62,000
Notes payable, current portion	10,000
Notes payable, long-term	278,000
Prepaid insurance	7,000
Retained earnings, October 31, 2000	25,000
Sales revenue	357,000
Selling expenses	47,000
Supplies	13,000
Trademarks	13,000
Wages payable	18,000
Shares of common stock: 10,000	

Required From the data presented above, determine the amount of each of the following items for Lewy Pasture's financial statements:

1. Gross profit
2. Income from operations
3. Net income
4. Earnings per share
5. Current assets
6. Property, plant, and equipment
7. Other assets
8. Total assets
9. Current liabilities
10. Working capital and working capital ratio
11. Total liabilities
12. Retained earnings, October 31, 2001
13. Total stockholders' equity
14. Total liabilities and stockholders' equity

The solution to Self-Study Problem 2 appears at the end of the chapter.

USE OF FINANCIAL STATEMENTS

OBJECTIVE 5

Discuss how financial statements work together to present a picture of a company for a fiscal period and the purpose of consolidated financial statements.

Financial statements are a primary source of accounting information for external decision makers. External users analyze statements to evaluate the ability of an organization to use its resources effectively and efficiently. By comparing changes in assets, liabilities, earnings, and cash flows over time, users form expectations about return and risk. Comparisons across companies help determine which companies are being managed effectively and provide the best investment opportunities.

Section 2 of this book describes methods of analyzing and interpreting financial statements in detail. The remainder of this chapter considers attributes of financial statements that decision makers should understand when interpreting them.

Interrelationships among Financial Statements

Taken as a whole, the financial statements describe the economic events that changed the financial condition of a company from the beginning to the end of a fiscal period. Information on the income statement and statement of cash flows explains changes in balance sheet accounts during a period.

The summary information presented in financial statements does not always provide sufficient detail to explain the change in every balance sheet account. Access to individual account balances would be necessary to provide a complete explanation. Nevertheless, the relationships among the financial statements are important. Balance sheets for the beginning and ending of a fiscal period reveal changes in a company's resources and finances. The company's income statement and statement of cash flows reveal major events that caused these changes. **The relationship among financial statements in which the numbers on one statement explain numbers on other statements is called** *articulation.* You should remember that a company's financial statements are not independent of each other. They work together to explain the events that changed the company's financial condition:

Amounts on the Balance Sheet Beginning of Fiscal Period	±	Changes Reported on the Income Statement and Statement of Cash Flows	=	Amounts on the Balance Sheet End of Fiscal Period

Consolidated Financial Statements

Most large corporations publish consolidated financial statements. *Consolidated financial statements* **report the combined economic activities of two or more corporations owned by the same stockholders.** Most major corporations own a controlling interest in other corporations. If one corporation owns a sufficient number of shares of another corporation (generally more than 50%), it is able to control the management of the corporation it owns. **A corporation that controls another corporation is known as a** *parent corporation.* **A corporation controlled by another corporation is a** *subsidiary.* A subsidiary may be wholly owned (100% owned by a parent) or partially owned (less than 100%). Consolidated financial statements report the activities of a parent and its subsidiaries as though they were one company. A parent and its subsidiaries are sometimes referred to as a group. This term is particularly common in financial reports of European corporations. These reports refer to "group accounts" or "group financial statements" when referring to consolidated statements.

Consolidated statements combine the accounts of a parent and its subsidiaries for reporting purposes. Assume that Push Automotive Company owns Slick Tire Company and Sticky Brakes Company. At the end of fiscal 2001, the cash accounts for the three companies appear as follows:

Push Automotive	$180,000
Slick Tire	60,000
Sticky Brakes	40,000
Total cash	$280,000

The consolidated balance sheet for Push Automotive for 2001 would report a cash balance of $280,000.

Not all accounts can be combined in the same way as cash, however. For example, assume sales revenue for the three companies was as follows:

Push Automotive	$1,400,000
Slick Tire	500,000
Sticky Brakes	300,000
Total revenue	$2,200,000

The combined total represents the consolidated revenues of Push Automotive and its subsidiaries only if no sales were made *among* the three companies. Assume that Slick Tire sold goods to Push that amounted to $300,000 of its sales, and Sticky Brakes sold goods to Push Automotive that amounted to $180,000 of its sales. Consolidated revenues would be:

Push Automotive		$1,400,000
Slick Tire	$500,000	
Less intercompany sales	300,000	200,000
Sticky Brakes	300,000	
Less intercompany sales	180,000	120,000
Total consolidated revenue		$1,720,000

Intercompany sales must be eliminated from total revenues because these sales are not transactions with customers outside the consolidated business. Cost of Goods Sold would have to be adjusted, as well, for the costs associated with intercompany sales. Other accounts that require adjustments include intercompany payables and receivables. In addition, subsidiary stockholders' equity is eliminated because it is owned by the parent.

The consolidated statements represent the economic activities of a parent and its subsidiaries as though they were one business organization. Owners of a parent firm are also owners of the subsidiaries controlled by the parent. Therefore, consolidated statements provide information about the activities of a group of companies owned by particular stockholders. The stockholders should be concerned about the activities of both parent and subsidiaries because the value of the stockholders' investments is determined by the value of the consolidated business.

Some countries do not require consolidation of parent and subsidiary financial statements. Each company reports its own statements. When statements are not consolidated, investors have more difficulty in assessing the performance of a parent company.

Limitations of Financial Statements

OBJECTIVE 6

Identify some of the primary limitations of financial statements.

In spite of the abundant information financial statements provide, their usefulness is limited by certain constraints of the reporting process. Some of these limitations include:

1. Use of estimates and allocations
2. Use of historical costs
3. Omission of transactions
4. Omission of resources and costs
5. Delay in providing information

These constraints result primarily from costs associated with the reporting process. Information is a resource, and it is costly to provide. Its value is determined by the benefits derived by those who use the information. For information to be valuable, its cost must be less than the benefits it provides to users. Therefore, the amount and type of reported information are constrained by costs and benefits.

The following sections consider these limitations. Users should keep these limitations in mind when interpreting financial statement information.

Use of Estimates and Allocations. **Many of the numbers reported in financial statements result from estimates and allocations.** For example, depreciation and amortization represent allocations of asset costs to expenses over the estimated lives of the assets. These estimates often are not exact because the amount of the asset consumed in a particular fiscal period is difficult to determine. Decisions about when to recognize revenues and expenses frequently require management judgment. These subjective decisions and estimates mean that accounting numbers are not as precise as they might appear.

Use of Historical Costs. **Financial statements report primarily the historical cost of assets and liabilities.** ***Historical cost*** **is the purchase or exchange price of an asset or liability at the time it is acquired or incurred.** The recorded values of many assets are reduced over time by depreciation and amortization. They are not adjusted for changes in the purchasing power of money or for changes in the current value of the assets or liabilities, however. The purchasing power of money changes over time because of inflation; for example, a dollar in 2001 buys less than a dollar would buy in 1981. The current value of an asset is the amount at which that asset, in its current condition, could be bought or sold at the present time.

Certain assets and liabilities, particularly financial securities such as investments in stocks or bonds, are reported at market value in the United States. We will examine these reporting rules in a later chapter. Some countries, such as the United Kingdom and the Netherlands, permit plant assets and other items to be reported using current values. Assets and liabilities are restated to approximate their market values at the end of a fiscal period.

Omission of Transactions. Financial statements include the primary transactions that occur as part of a company's transformation process. Nevertheless, **there is no guarantee that all important transactions are fully reported in a company's financial statements.** Some transactions do not result from specific exchanges. They result when revenues or expenses are allocated to fiscal periods. Accountants and managers sometimes disagree about when certain activities should be recognized. Also, they may disagree about the amount that should be reported in the financial statements for these activities. The accounting profession has debated extensively issues such as how to recognize the costs of employee retirement benefits. Today, companies report certain liabilities, assets, and expenses associated with these items that were not reported 10 years ago. Undoubtedly, other issues will arise that will alter information reported in the financial statements.

The importance of information changes over time. Companies develop new financing and compensation arrangements. Reporting rules for these arrangements may not be covered by existing GAAP. If the arrangements become common and new reporting rules would increase the benefits of information for users, GAAP may be created for transactions involving these new arrangements. GAAP are dynamic. They change as the needs of users and economic activities of organizations change.

Omission of Resources and Costs. **Certain types of resources and costs are not reported in the financial statements.** The value of employees is not an asset listed on most balance sheets. Nevertheless, a well-trained and stable workforce and skilled managers may be the resource that adds the most to the value of many companies. Without skilled labor and management, the remaining resources of a company often would have little value. Financial statements do not report these human resources. They are not owned by a company, and their values are difficult and costly to determine. A major portion of the value of many companies derives from their research and development activities, which create new and improved products. The costs of these efforts are expensed when they are incurred each fiscal period even though they may have a major effect on the future earnings of a company. Such costs are expensed because of the difficulty and cost of identifying the timing and amount of future benefits a company will receive from these efforts. Nevertheless, the economic value of a company differs from the amount reported on its financial statements because of these measurement limitations.

Delay in Providing Information. **Financial statement information is not always timely.** Annual financial statements may lag actual events by a year or more; even monthly statements may lag events by several weeks. While such delays may not be a major problem for certain types of decisions, they may be critical for others. Users often need more timely sources. Managers, in particular, may need information on an ongoing basis in order to make effective decisions. Traditional financial statements are only one type of accounting information. Because financial statements are costly to produce and distribute, external reporting is limited to distinct fiscal periods. In addition to annual financial reports, major corporations provide quarterly reports to stockholders. As information technology reduces the cost of reporting, more frequent reporting to external users may become feasible.

Usefulness of Financial Statements

Though a variety of problems impair their usefulness, financial statements continue to be a primary source of information for managers and external users about a company's activities. But these problems mean that considerable care is needed to understand accounting information and to use it correctly in making decisions. Careful analysis of the information is necessary.

FINANCIAL STATEMENTS AND THE TRANSFORMATION PROCESS

The first five chapters of this book have examined the purpose and function of business organizations and the role of the accounting information system. Organizations transform resources into goods and services. The accounting information system identifies events associated with the transformation process. It includes these events in financial statements that can be summarized and reported to decision makers.

Exhibit 11 illustrates financial statement representation of the transformation process. Financial statements and individual accounts originate within the transformation process. The balance sheet identifies sources of financing for a company and how the financing was invested in resources available to the company. The income statement identifies operating activities that provide additional financial resources and equity. These operating activities also require the consumption of resources. Their consumption is measured by expenses. Both investments by owners and reinvestment of profits affect stockholders' equity. These events are identified in the statement of stockholders' equity.

Exhibit 11 Accounting Information and the Transformation Process

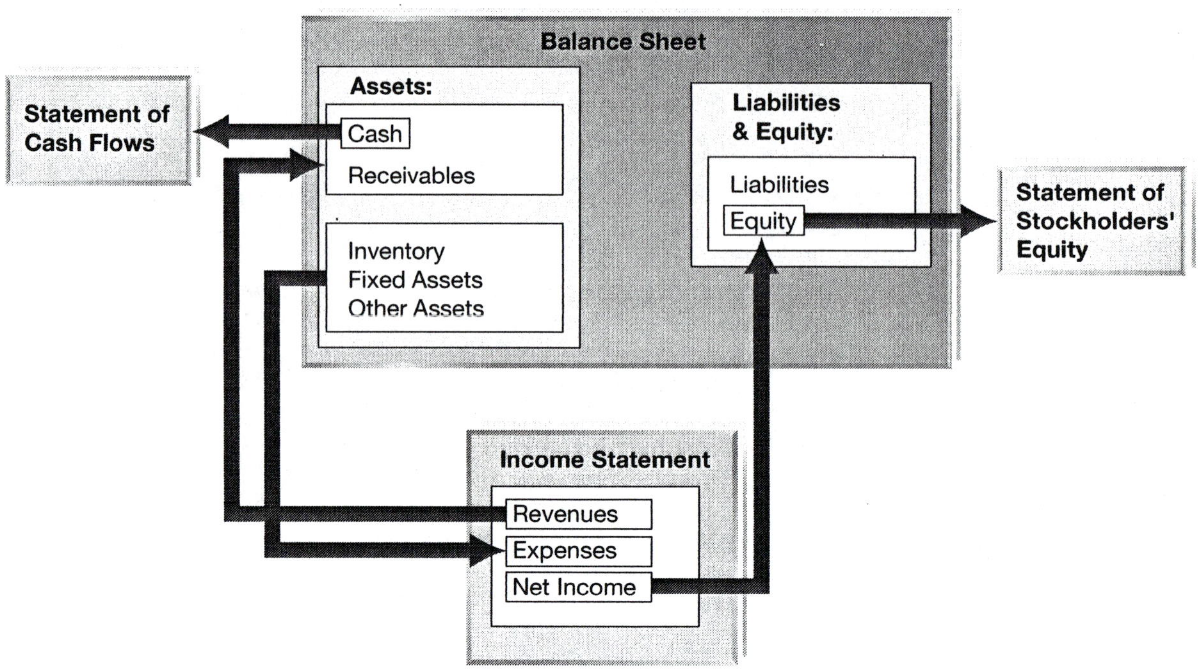

Other Information Accompanying Financial Statements

OBJECTIVE 7

Identify the purpose and basic concepts of an audit report.

In addition to financial statements, companies include other information in their reports to external users. Corporate annual reports usually include a letter from the president or chief executive officer of the company, a description of the company's products and business activities, a discussion of the company's performance by management, notes to the financial statements, and an audit report. Notes to the financial statements are important for helping readers interpret the statements. They describe how some of the numbers were computed and provide additional information about some items reported in the statements. We will examine some of these notes in future chapters.

The audit report is an important item accompanying a company's financial statements. Auditors issue an audit report upon completion of their audit work. An audit involves a detailed, systematic investigation of a company's accounting records. The auditor attempts to verify that the numbers and disclosures made by management in its financial reports are consistent with the company's actual financial position and operating results. Records, operating procedures, contracts, resources, and management policies and decisions are examined to provide evidence of the fairness of financial report information. Auditors determine if internal control procedures exist and are being used. They compare the information in financial reports with information from prior years and other sources to confirm the fairness of the reports.

Attestation **occurs when an auditor affirms the fairness of financial statements by signing an audit report. The** ***audit report,*** **or** ***audit opinion,*** **provides public notice of the auditor's belief about the fairness of the accompanying financial information.** Exhibit 12 provides an example of an auditor's report.

An audit report usually is addressed to the shareholders of the company. Normally, an audit is performed on behalf of the shareholders and other external parties. Audits may be requested for special purposes also—for example, to secure a bank loan or as part of merger negotiations.

The first paragraph of the audit report identifies the statements and fiscal periods covered by the audit. A typical audit will cover all the primary financial statements: income statement, balance sheet, and statement of cash flows. The audit normally covers the most recent three years of operations. For most large corporations, the audited financial statements are the consolidated statements of the parent and its subsidiaries.

Exhibit 12

Example of an Auditor's Report

The Shareholders
Rockyfellow, Inc.

We have audited the accompanying balance sheets of Rockyfellow, Inc., as of December 31, 2001 and 2000, and the related statements of income, retained earnings, and cash flows for the year ended December 31, 2001. These financial statements are the responsibility of the company's management. Our responsibility is to express an opinion on these financial statements based on our audits.

We conducted our audits in accordance with generally accepted auditing standards. Those standards require that we plan and perform the audit to obtain reasonable assurance about whether the financial statements are free of material misstatement. An audit includes examining on a test basis evidence supporting the amounts and disclosures in the financial statements. An audit also includes assessing the accounting principles used and significant estimates made by management, as well as evaluating the overall financial statement presentation. We believe that our audits provide a reasonable basis for our opinion.

In our opinion, the financial statements referred to above present fairly, in all material respects, the financial position of Rockyfellow, Inc., as of December 31, 2001 and 2000, and the results of its operations and its cash flows for the year ended December 31, 2001, in conformity with generally accepted accounting principles.

Hedgehog and Hammer
500 Main St.
Anytown, USA
February 26, 2002

The first paragraph also describes the responsibilities of auditors and management. Management is responsible for preparing the statements. Auditors are responsible for competently using the technology available to them to confirm (or disconfirm) the assertions of management.

The second paragraph of the audit report summarizes the audit process. *Generally accepted auditing standards (GAAS)* **include procedures used in conducting an audit to help auditors form an opinion about the fairness of the audited statements.** GAAS are developed in the United States by the Auditing Standards Board (ASB). The ASB is a division of the American Institute of Certified Public Accountants (AICPA). Auditing standards are published and updated periodically by the AICPA. Failure to conform with GAAS in an independent audit is a major violation of a CPA's responsibilities.

From evidence collected from using GAAS, auditors assert that the financial statements are free of material misstatement. Materiality is a criterion for establishing the importance of a potential misstatement in audited financial statements. Financial statements contain estimates and allocations that depend on management judgement. In addition to finding errors in accounting records, auditors may disagree with managers about their estimates and allocations. Unless these errors and disagreements are material (important) to the overall amounts reported on the financial statements, however, auditors are not required to take action on these issues.

Auditors examine accounting records on a "test basis." Auditors do not examine 100% of a company's transactions. Instead, they use sampling techniques to select representative transactions. By verifying these transactions, auditors form an opinion about the financial statements as a whole. Sampling is necessary because the cost of auditing all of a company's records generally would be prohibitive.

The third paragraph of the audit report states the auditor's opinion. Most audit reports provide an **unqualified opinion.** Such an opinion states that the auditor believes that the financial statements fairly present the company's actual economic events for the period covered by the audited statements. Fair presentation means that the financial statements are prepared in conformity with GAAP and are free from material omissions and misstatements.

The first three paragraphs are standard for most corporate audit reports. A fourth paragraph is included only if the auditor believes that additional information that is not contained in the earlier paragraphs should be noted in the opinion.

Audit reports must be signed by the public accounting firm that performed the audit, thus indicating its responsibility. The date of the audit report is the date on which all audit work was completed for the periods covered by the report. The auditor is responsible for disclosing any material information that might affect a decision maker's interpretation of the financial statements through the date of the audit report.

Audit reports for foreign corporations differ from those for U.S. corporations. Different countries establish their own auditing and accounting standards. The format of the audit report depends on the auditing standards of the country in which a company has its principal operations.

Self-Study Problem 3

A series of financial statement items is listed below:

1. Accounts receivable
2. Merchandise
3. Supplies
4. Prepaid insurance
5. Buildings
6. Patents
7. Accounts payable
8. Wages payable
9. Interest payable
10. Notes payable
11. Contributed capital
12. Retained earnings
13. Dividends
14. Sales revenue
15. Cost of goods sold
16. Depreciation expense
17. Wages expense
18. Interest expense
19. Amount of stock issued
20. Amount of stock repurchased

Required For each account, indicate the financial statement (income statement, balance sheet, or statement of stockholders' equity) on which the account would appear. Then identify the information provided by the account. Use the format shown below. The first item is provided as an example:

Item	Financial Statement	Information Provided
1. Accounts receivable	Balance sheet	Cash to be received in the future from prior sales

The solution to Self-Study Problem 3 appears at the end of the chapter.

Creating Accounting Standards

Accounting standards are important to protect the interests of investors, managers, and the general public. Therefore, the standards must be perceived as being reasonable and responsive to the needs of different constituents. Arbitrary and unnecessary standards do not serve the needs of society. For these reasons, accounting standards are established through a political process. This process gives interested parties an opportunity to express their opinions and to provide information that may have a bearing on prospective standards. The fact that accounting standards are referred to as *generally accepted* accounting principles (GAAP) is not accidental. To serve the needs of society, accounting standards must be accepted by those who are affected by them.

The process used by the FASB (introduced in Chapter F4) is typical of that used by other organizations, such as the GASB and the IASC. The process consists of the following steps:

1. Accounting issues are identified and evaluated for consideration.
2. A discussion memorandum is issued and responses are solicited.
3. Public hearings are held.
4. An exposure draft is issued and responses are solicited.
5. Additional public hearings are held as needed.
6. A standard is issued.
7. Existing standards are reviewed and modified as needed.

Accounting issues may be identified by the accounting profession, managers, investors, or the FASB staff. The staff evaluates the issues, and the board determines those issues that appear to be important for it to address.

A discussion memorandum is a document that identifies accounting issues and alternative approaches to resolving the issues. All interested parties are encouraged to respond to a discussion memorandum. The board develops a proposed standard after reviewing responses to a discussion memorandum and issues its proposal in the form of an exposure draft. An exposure draft is a document that describes a proposed accounting standard. It identifies requirements that may be contained in an actual standard. Responses again are solicited, and public hearings sometimes are held.

Once the board reviews responses to an exposure draft, it may modify and reissue the exposure draft or issue a standard. An accounting standard is an official pronouncement establishing acceptable accounting procedures or financial report content. FASB standards are known as Statements of Financial Accounting Standards. To be issued, a standard must be agreed to by at least five of the seven members of the board. Once a standard has been issued, it becomes part of GAAP. Standards can be reviewed at any time to determine if they are serving their intended purposes and can be modified or replaced if they are found to be ineffective.

Review

SUMMARY of IMPORTANT CONCEPTS

1. Financial statements report activities in the transformation process.
   a. Financial statements include the balance sheet, the income statement, the statement of cash flows, and the statement of stockholders' equity.
   b. The income statement reports on the accrual basis the results of a company's operations for a fiscal period. It reports information about the creation and consumption of resources in producing and selling goods and services, not about actual cash flows.
   c. Corporations often report a statement of stockholders' equity. It describes the results of transactions that have changed the amount of contributed capital and retained earnings of a company during a fiscal period.
   d. A balance sheet identifies asset, liability, and owners' equity account balances at the end of a fiscal period. Balance sheets often classify accounts into current and long-term asset and liability categories. Comparative balance sheets report account balances for more than one fiscal period.
   e. Two essential concepts describe the information reported by financial statements: (1) Financial statements represent the transformation process of an organization for a fiscal period, and (2) financial statements report the effects of transactions for specific periods.
2. The interrelated financial statements, as a set, describe the financial effects of economic events of a company from the beginning to the end of a fiscal period.
3. Consolidated financial statements report the economic activities of a parent and its subsidiaries as though they were one business entity.
4. Financial statements have limitations that affect the usefulness of the information the statements report. These limitations include the need for estimates of financial results, the use of historical costs for representing asset values, and incomplete measures for some resources or transactions that might affect a company's value.
5. Other information usually is reported along with financial statements. This information includes notes to help decision makers interpret the statements and an auditor's report.
6. The FASB and other organizations that set accounting standards use a political process in establishing these standards.

Define

TERMS and CONCEPTS DEFINED in This CHAPTER

accounting changes (F201)
amortization (F207)
articulation (F210)
attestation (F214)
audit report (audit opinion) (F214)
comprehensive income (F202)
consolidated financial statements (F211)
contributed capital (F204)
cost of services sold (F199)
current assets (F205)
current liabilities (F208)
current ratio (F209)
discontinued operations (F200)
earnings per share (F202)
extraordinary items (F201)
generally accepted auditing standards (GAAS) (F215)
gross profit (F199)
historical cost (F212)
income from operations (F200)
intangible assets (F207)
liquid assets (F205)
liquidity (F209)
long-term investments (F206)
long-term liabilities (F208)
operating expenses (F199)
operating income (F200)
other assets (F207)
parent corporation (F211)
property, plant, and equipment (F206)
statement of stockholders' equity (F197)
subsidiary (F211)
working capital (F209)
working capital ratio (F209)

Self-Study Problem SOLUTIONS

1 (Answers in millions)

1. Revenue from sale of computers	$35,419
2. Other operating revenue:	
Services	$28,916
Software	11,863
Financing and other	5,469
Total	$46,248
3. Other income	$ 589
4. Gross profit	$30,872
5. Interest expense	$ 713
6. Number of shares outstanding ($4,178,000,000 net income ÷ $7.23 earnings per share) = 578 million shares	
7. Cost of goods and services sold	$50,795
8. Operating income	$ 9,164
Net income	$ 6,328
9. Net cash from operations cannot be determined from the income statement.	

2

1. Gross profit:		
Sales revenue		$357,000
Cost of goods sold		146,000
Gross profit		$211,000
2. Income from operations:		
Gross profit		$211,000
General and administrative expenses	$96,000	
Selling expenses	47,000	
Total operating expenses		143,000
Income from operations		$ 68,000
3. Net income:		
Income from operations		$ 68,000
Interest expense	$25,000	
Income tax expense	14,000	39,000
Net income		$ 29,000

4. Earnings per share:
Net income ÷ shares of common stock ($29,000 ÷ 10,000) = $2.90

5. Current assets:	
Cash	$ 16,000
Accounts receivable	11,000
Merchandise inventory	62,000
Supplies	13,000
Prepaid insurance	7,000
Current assets	$109,000

6. Property, plant, and equipment:

Land	$ 35,000
Buildings	412,000
Equipment	245,000
Accumulated depreciation	(164,000)
Property, plant, and equipment	$528,000

7. Other assets:

Long-term investments	$ 35,000
Trademarks	13,000
Other assets	$ 48,000

8. Total assets:

Current assets	$109,000
Property, plant, and equipment	528,000
Other assets	48,000
Total assets	$685,000

9. Current liabilities:

Accounts payable	$ 22,000
Wages payable	18,000
Interest payable	14,000
Income tax payable	6,000
Notes payable, current portion	10,000
Current liabilities	$ 70,000

10. Working capital and working capital ratio:

Current assets	$109,000
Current liabilities	70,000
Working capital	$ 39,000

Working capital ratio ($109,000 ÷ $70,000) = 1.557

11. Total liabilities:

Current liabilities	$ 70,000
Notes payable, long-term	278,000
Total liabilities	$348,000

12. Retained earnings, October 31, 2001:

Retained earnings, October 31, 2000	$ 25,000
Net income	29,000
Dividends	(17,000)
Retained earnings, October 31, 2001	$ 37,000

13. Total stockholders' equity:

Contributed capital	$300,000
Retained earnings	37,000
Stockholders' equity	$337,000

14. Total liabilities and stockholders' equity:

Total liabilities	$348,000
Stockholders' equity	337,000
Total liabilities and stockholders' equity	$685,000

3

Item	Financial Statement	Information Provided
1. Accounts receivable	Balance sheet	Cash to be received in the future from prior sales
2. Merchandise	Balance sheet	Cost of resources acquired in the past to be used in future operations
3. Supplies	Balance sheet	Cost of resources acquired in the past to be used in future operations
4. Prepaid insurance	Balance sheet	Cost of resources acquired in the past to be used in future operations
5. Buildings	Balance sheet	Cost of resources acquired in the past to be used in future operations
6. Patents	Balance sheet	Cost of resources acquired in the past to be used in future operations
7. Accounts payable	Balance sheet	Cash to be paid in the future for resources acquired in the past
8. Wages payable	Balance sheet	Cash to be paid in the future for services used in past operations
9. Interest payable	Balance sheet	Cash to be paid in the future for the use of money borrowed in the past
10. Notes payable	Balance sheet	Cash borrowed in the past, to be repaid in the future
11. Contributed capital	Balance sheet and stockholders' equity	Cash or other resources received in the past from owners
12. Retained earnings	Balance sheet and stockholders' equity	Profits earned from operations that have been reinvested
13. Dividends	Stockholders' equity	Cash paid and/or promised to owners from results of operations
14. Sales revenue	Income statement	Cash received or to be received from past operations
15. Cost of goods sold	Income statement	Cost of resources consumed in past operations
16. Depreciation expense	Income statement	Cost of resources consumed in past operations
17. Wages expense	Income statement	Cost of services consumed in past operations
18. Interest expense	Income statement	Cost of debt used in past operations
19. Stock issued	Stockholders' equity	Cash or other resources received from investors
20. Stock repurchased	Stockholders' equity	Cash paid to investors to acquire stock

Questions

5-1 *Obj. 1* How do the purpose of the income statement, the purpose of the balance sheet, and the purpose of the statement of stockholders' equity differ?

5-2 *Obj. 1* Why are account balances summarized into financial statements? Why don't companies simply distribute a list of year-end account balances?

5-3 *Obj. 2* A friend says, "The income statement doesn't reveal anything about the amount of cash that was received from sales during a fiscal period." Do you agree with this statement? Why or why not?

5-4 *Obj. 2* Why are there so many different sections of information on an income statement?

5-5 *Obj. 3* The statement of stockholders' equity can be thought of as a bridge between the income statement and the balance sheet. Why?

5-6 *Obj. 3* Are dividends an expense? Sometimes? Always? Never? Explain.

5-7 *Objs. 3, 4* If all of the stockholders' equity accounts are reported on the balance sheet, why is the statement of stockholders' equity necessary?

5-8 *Obj. 4* Explain the difference between a classified balance sheet and a comparative balance sheet.

5-9 *Obj. 4* In what way are the depreciation of plant, property, and equipment and the amortization of intangible assets alike? In what way are they different?

5-10 *Obj. 5* Identify three questions that can be answered by reviewing a firm's income statement but that cannot be answered by reviewing the firm's balance sheet or statement of stockholders' equity. Be specific.

5-11 *Obj. 5* Identify three questions that can be answered by reviewing a firm's balance sheet but that cannot be answered by reviewing the firm's income statement or statement of stockholders' equity. Be specific.

5-12 *Obj. 5* Why does a parent company prepare consolidated financial statements?

5-13 *Obj. 6* Why is the use of historical cost information a limitation of financial statements?

5-14 *Obj. 7* What is an audit and why is it important?

5-15 *Obj. 7* A friend has been reviewing the annual report of a firm in which he has invested. He says, "I'm worried because the auditors gave an unqualified opinion on the financial statements. You'd think a big company like this would have auditors that were qualified." Clear up your friend's misunderstanding.

Exercises

5-1 Write a short definition for each of the terms listed in the *Terms and Concepts Defined in This Chapter* section.

5-2 *Obj. 1* Listed below are typical accounts or titles that appear on financial statements. For each item, identify the financial statement(s) on which it appears.

a. Wages expense
b. Wages payable
c. Cost of goods sold
d. Common stock
e. Current assets
f. Accounts receivable
g. Sales revenue
h. Gross profit
i. Earnings per share
j. Inventory
k. Net income
l. Retained earnings
m. Contributed capital
n. Operating income
o. Common stock issued during year

5-3 *Obj. 1* A list of information contained in financial statements is provided below. For each item, indicate which financial statement provides the information.

a. Changes in a corporation's stockholders' equity for a fiscal period
b. The dollar amount of resources available at a particular date
c. The amount of credit sales not yet collected
d. Accrual-based operating results for a fiscal period

e. The cost of resources consumed in producing revenues for a period
f. The sources of finances used to acquire resources
g. The effect of issuing stock on the amount of contributed capital during a period
h. The amount of profit earned by each share of stock
i. Revenues generated during a fiscal period

5-4 *Objs. 1, 6* For each of the items listed below, indicate the financial statement (or statements) for which the information is true. Use (I) to indicate income statement, (B) to indicate balance sheet, and (SE) to indicate statement of stockholders' equity. If the item below is not true for any of the three financial statements, indicate with an (N).

1. The statement provides information about resources consumed during an accounting period.
2. The portion of profits that were distributed to owners of the firm is disclosed.
3. The current market value of the firm's resources is reported.
4. The statement is dated as of a specific point in time.
5. The amounts that are owed to other organizations or individuals are reported.
6. The total amount of capital that has been contributed to the organization is reported.
7. The amount of capital that has been contributed to the organization during the accounting period just ended is reported.
8. Information is reported regarding the rewards that have been earned from serving customers during the accounting period just ended.
9. The statement is not as of a specific date, but covers a period of time.
10. Reports information that has been developed on the accrual basis.
11. The statement contains information about the financial sacrifices that were made to acquire resources.
12. The statement contains information concerning contributed capital.
13. The statement contains information concerning depreciation.
14. The amount of stock that has been sold during the accounting period just ended is disclosed.
15. The amount of profit that was earned by each share of common stock is disclosed.

5-5 *Obj. 2* Slotnick Company sells, rents, and services ski equipment. Information about the company's financial performance for a recent fiscal period is provided below.

Average shares outstanding	$20,000
Cost of goods sold	$34,000
Debt outstanding	$65,000
General and administrative expenses	$12,000
Income tax expense	$20,000
Interest expense	$ 8,000
Payments to owners	$30,000
Rental revenue	$45,000
Sales revenue	$79,000
Selling expense	$27,000
Service revenue	$23,000

From the information provided, compute the following amounts for the period:

a. Gross profit
b. Operating expenses
c. Income from operations
d. Pretax income
e. Net income
f. Earnings per share

5-6 *Obj. 2* Flowers by Freddie presented the income statement on page F224 for its most recent fiscal year. The items have been numbered for convenience in analysis.

(Continued)

(1) Sales revenue	$371,923
(2) Cost of goods sold	201,668
(3) Gross profit	170,255
(4) Operating expenses	72,853
(5) Operating income	97,402
(6) Other revenues	538
(7) Other expenses	(13,227)
(8) Pretax income	84,713
(9) Income taxes	29,650
(10) Net income	$ 55,063

Answer the following questions. Be specific. Give examples to clarify.

a. What is the difference between the revenue listed in item 1 and that listed in item 6?
b. What does item 3 represent, and why is it important?
c. What do items 2, 4, and 7 have in common?
d. How are items 2, 4, and 7 different from one another?
e. How is item 9 similar to items 2, 4, and 7?
f. Why do you think items 2, 4, 7, and 9 are listed separately on an income statement rather than being lumped together as one item?

5-7 *Obj. 2* An income statement for **Delta Airlines** for a recent fiscal year is provided below:

Consolidated Statement of Income
For the Year Ended June 30, 1998

	(In millions, except per share amounts)
Operating revenues:	
Passenger	$12,976
Cargo	582
Other	580
Total operating revenues	14,138
Operating expenses:	
Salaries and employee costs	4,850
Aircraft fuel	1,507
Passenger commissions	980
Depreciation and amortization	861
Aircraft rent	552
Passenger service	450
Aircraft maintenance materials and repairs	495
Landing fees	649
Other	2,101
Total operating expenses	12,445
Operating income	1,693
Other income (expense):	
Interest expense	(186)
Less: Interest capitalized	38
Interest and other income	103
	(45)
Income before income taxes	1,648
Provision for income taxes	(647)
Net income	$ 1,001
Earnings per share	$12.68

Note: Modifications have been made to the statement for the purposes of simplifying the presentation.

Use this income statement to answer the following questions:

a. What was Delta's primary source of revenue?
b. What percentage of Delta's revenue came from this source?
c. What were its largest expenses?
d. How much revenue did Delta earn from transporting passengers?
e. How much revenue did it earn from operating activities other than transporting passengers?
f. How much revenue did it earn from nonoperating activities?
g. How much operating income did Delta earn (or lose)?
h. How much expense did it incur for nonoperating activities?
i. Approximately how many shares of stock did Delta have outstanding during the year?
j. How much profit did Delta earn during the fiscal year?

5-8 *Obj. 2* A recent income statement for **Applebees International** (a restaurant chain) is provided below. Use this financial statement to answer the questions that follow. It operates both company-owned and franchised restaurants.

Applebees International, Inc.
Income Statement
For the Year Ended December 28, 1997

(Dollars in thousands except per share amounts)		
Revenue:		
Company restaurant sales	$452,173	
Franchise income	63,647	
Total operating revenues		$515,820
Cost of company restaurant sales:		
Food and beverage	$124,469	
Labor	145,165	
Direct and occupancy	114,196	
Pre-opening expense	3,661	
Total cost of company restaurant sales		387,491
Gross profit		$128,329
Operating expenses:		
General and administrative expenses	$ 52,579	
Amortization of intangible assets	3,258	
Loss on disposition of restaurants and equipment	1,209	
Total operating expenses		57,046
Operating earnings		$ 71,283
Other income (expense):		
Other income, principally investment		2,223
Interest expense		(1,705)
Earnings before income taxes		$ 71,801
Income taxes		(26,710)
Net earnings		$ 45,091
Basic net earnings per common share		$1.44

1. How much revenue did Applebees earn from food and drinks?
2. How much revenue did it earn from other operating activities?
3. How much revenue did it earn from nonoperating activities?
4. What amount of gross profit did Applebees earn? Express your answer both in dollars and as a percentage of total revenues.
5. How much expense did it incur for nonoperating activities?
6. Approximately how many shares of stock did Applebees have outstanding during the year?

(Continued)

7. How much operating income and net income did Applebees earn during the fiscal year? Express your answers both in dollars and as a percentage of total revenues.
8. Can the amount of cash Applebees received from its operating activities during the year be determined from the income statement? If so, what is that amount? If not, why not?

5-9 *Obj. 2* SuperQuick Computer Corporation reported the following income statement for a recent quarter:

Consolidated Statement of Income
For the Quarter Ended December 31, 2001

Sales	$719,150
Cost of sales	549,313
	169,837
Research and development costs	16,900
Selling, general, and administrative expense	83,771
Other income and expense, net	7,685
	108,356
Income before income taxes	61,481
Provision for income taxes	15,451
Net income	$ 46,030
Earnings per share	$0.93

Assume that Other Income and Expense are nonoperating.

a. What was the company's gross profit for the year?
b. What was the amount of the company's product costs expensed during the year?
c. What was the amount of its operating expenses?
d. What was the amount of its operating income?
e. What was the amount of its nonoperating income or expense?

5-10 *Obj. 2* Alex didn't study very hard when he took accounting because he thought he wouldn't ever use it on the job at Valentine Company. Yesterday, after preparing all end-of-the-month adjusting entries, both of the company's accounting staff became ill. The company owner, knowing that Alex had taken accounting as part of his college major, asked him to finish the job by preparing the financial statements. The owner needs the statements tomorrow to present to her banker. Alex isn't sure that his income statement is prepared properly.

Valentine Company
Income Statement
at September 30, 2001

Sales revenue	$48,500
Wages expense	11,369
Operating income	**37,131**
Operating expenses:	
Advertising	3,133
Cost of goods sold	30,070
Insurance	670
Interest expense	240
Utilities	1,250
Gross profit	**1,768**
Depreciation expense	282
Pretax income	**1,486**
Income tax expense	519
Net income	$ 967

Alex is confident that each revenue account and expense account balance is correct because those were determined by the accounting staff. He is unsure, however, that he has organized them properly on the income statement. Therefore, he is unsure about the summary amounts listed in bold-faced print on the statement.

Rearrange the accounts into proper income statement format. Be sure to date the statement correctly.

5-11 *Obj. 3* Crane Pool Corporation reported the following selected information for its 2001 fiscal year:

Contributed capital at June 30, 2000	$ 657
Retained earnings at June 30, 2000	1,536
Dividends	222
Net income	953
Common stock issued	243

Use this information to prepare a statement of stockholders' equity for Crane Pool for the year ended June 30, 2001.

5-12 *Objs. 2, 3* The accounting staff at Moonbeam Enterprises prepares monthly financial statements. At the end of April, the company's ledger accounts have the following balances. All adjusting entries have been made and the next step is to prepare the financial statements. The company has 18,200 shares of stock outstanding.

Accounts payable	$17,000	Land	$45,000
Accounts receivable	14,700	Long-term notes payable	33,000
Accumulated depreciation	13,100	Merchandise inventory	12,480
Buildings	50,000	Notes payable, current portion	15,100
Cash	10,360	Patents	3,300
Contributed capital	38,770	Prepaid insurance	1,100
Copyrights and trademarks	5,000	Retained earnings, March 31	8,400
Cost of goods sold	15,050	Sales revenue	26,000
Depreciation expense	1,100	Supplies	3,570
Dividends declared	1,200	Supplies expense	1,300
Income tax expense	1,060	Wage expense	1,500
Insurance expense	550	Wages payable	17,700
Interest expense	900		

(1) Prepare an income statement in good form. (2) Prepare a statement of stockholders' equity in good form. (Hint: There was no change in contributed capital during the month.) For each statement, use a three-line heading on the statement that includes (a) the name of the company, (b) the name of the statement, and (c) the appropriate time period or date.

5-13 *Obj. 4* Listed below are selected account balances for Hemmingway Company for June 30, 2001.

Accounts payable	$95,300	Land	$250,000
Accounts receivable	$78,100	Merchandise inventory	$390,000
Accumulated depreciation	$318,000	Notes payable, current portion	$50,000
Buildings	$750,000	Notes payable, long-term	$571,300
Cash	$34,500	Prepaid insurance	$38,000
Contributed capital	$700,000	Retained earnings	$279,000
Cost of goods sold	$840,000	Supplies on hand	$52,000
Equipment	$450,000	Trademarks	$45,000
Interest payable	$38,000	Wages expense	$375,000
		Wages payable	$36,000

Determine each of the following amounts. (Hint: Not all items will be used.)

a. Current assets
b. Current liabilities

(Continued)

c. Property, plant, and equipment
d. Total assets
e. Long-term liabilities
f. Total liabilities
g. Stockholders' equity
h. Total liabilities and stockholders' equity
i. Working capital

5-14 *Obj. 4* Styles Unlimited reported the following information at January 31:

Accounts payable	$ 250
Accounts receivable	1,057
Accrued expenses (current)	348
Cash and equivalents	321
Contributed capital	319
Deferred income taxes (liabilities)	275
Income taxes payable (current)	93
Inventories	734
Long-term debt	650
Other current assets	109
Other current liabilities	16
Other long-term assets	248
Other long-term liabilities	61
Property and equipment, net (of depreciation)	1,667
Retained earnings, net of adjustments	2,124

Accrued expenses are current liabilities. Deferred income taxes are long-term liabilities.

Use the information provided to prepare a balance sheet for Styles Unlimited in good form.

5-15 *Obj. 4* Use the information provided in Exercise 5-12.

Prepare a classified balance sheet in proper format. Use a three-line heading on the statement that includes (1) the name of the company, (2) the name of the statement, and (3) the appropriate date.

5-16 *Obj. 4* Jenny didn't study very hard when she took accounting because she thought she would never use it on the job at Tech-Noid Company. Yesterday, after preparing all end-of-the-month adjusting entries, the company's accountant became ill. The company asked Jenny to finish the job by preparing the financial statements. The owner needs the statements tomorrow to present to his banker. Jenny is having trouble getting the balance sheet to balance.

Tech-Noid Company
Balance Sheet
January 31, 2002

Assets		Liabilities and Stockholders' Equity	
Current assets:		**Current liabilities:**	
Inventory	1,121	Accounts payable	$231
Interest payable	100	Accounts receivable	691
Land	2,200	Wages payable	636
Noncurrent assets:		**Long-term liabilities:**	
Buildings and equipment	4,990	7%, 10-year note payable	2,000
Retained earnings	1,398	Accumulated depreciation	531
Total assets	$9,809	**Stockholders' equity:**	
		Contributed capital	4,230
		Cash	124
		Total liabilities and equity	$8,443

(a) Help Jenny by making a list of the five account categories that are printed in bold-faced type on the balance sheet. Leave 3 lines between each category listed. For each category, write the names of Tech-Noid's accounts that should be reported under it on the balance sheet. (b) Determine the correct balance sheet amounts for:

1. total current assets
2. total noncurrent assets
3. total assets
4. total current liabilities
5. total long-term liabilities
6. total stockholders' equity
7. total liabilities and equity

5-17 *Objs. 2, 4* Listed below are account balances and other data for Hands & Eyes, Inc., a company that sells crafts and decorative supplies, for the fiscal year ended December 31, 2002.

Accounts payable	$ 41,000	Land	$ 65,000
Accounts receivable	29,000	Long-term investments	46,000
Accumulated depreciation	180,000	Merchandise inventory	79,000
Buildings	430,000	Notes payable, current portion	25,000
Cash	35,000	Notes payable, long-term	307,000
Contributed capital	315,000	Prepaid insurance	22,000
Cost of goods sold	130,000	Retained earnings,	
Dividends (declared and paid)	22,000	Dec. 31, 2000	19,000
Equipment	262,000	Sales revenue	373,000
General and administrative		Selling expenses	34,000
expenses	98,000	Supplies	25,000
Income tax expense	8,000	Trademarks	31,000
Income tax payable	22,000	Wages payable	36,000
Interest expense	33,000	Interest payable	31,000
Shares of common stock outstanding:	20,000		

From the data presented above, determine the amount of each of the items that follow. (Hint: Pretax income for the year 2002 = $78,000.)

1. Gross profit
2. Operating income
3. Net income
4. Earnings per share
5. Current assets
6. Property, plant, and equipment
7. Other assets
8. Total assets
9. Current liabilities
10. Working capital and working capital ratio
11. Total liabilities
12. Retained earnings, December 31, 2001
13. Total stockholders' equity
14. Total liabilities and stockholders' equity

5-18 *Objs. 2, 3, 4* A list of financial statement items is given below:

1. Accounts receivable
2. Rent payable
3. Retained earnings
4. Cost of sales
5. Prepaid rent
6. Supplies expense

(Continued)

7. Equipment
8. Dividends
9. Depreciation expense
10. Copyrights
11. Accrued liabilities
12. Wages payable
13. Land
14. Notes payable
15. Service revenue
16. Inventory
17. Advertising expense
18. Treasury stock
19. Common stock

Use the format shown below. (a) For each account, indicate the financial statement on which the account would appear. (b) Identify the information provided by the account. The first item is completed as an example:

Item	Financial Statement	Information Provided
1. Accounts receivable	Balance sheet	Cash to be received in the future from prior sales

5-19 *Obj. 5* Listed below are financial statements for the Sunflower Company.

Income Statement
For the Year Ended December 31, 2001

Sales revenue	$20,000
Cost of sales	(12,000)
Gross profit	8,000
Operating expenses	(4,000)
Selling and administrative expenses	(3,000)
Net income	$ 1,000

Statement of Stockholders' Equity
For the Year Ended December 31, 2001

	Contributed Capital	Retained Earnings	Total
Balance at December 31, 2000	$5,000	$13,000	$18,000
Common stock issued	2,000		2,000
Net income		1,000	1,000
Dividends		(4,000)	(4,000)
Balance at December 31, 2001	$7,000	$10,000	$17,000

Balance Sheet
as of December 31, 2001

Assets:		Liabilities and Stockholders' Equity	
Cash	$ 9,000	Accounts payable	$ 5,000
Accounts receivable	3,000	Notes payable	8,000
Inventory	2,000	Common stock	7,000
Land	16,000	Retained earnings	10,000
Total	$30,000	Total	$30,000

(a) Describe what is meant by the term *articulation.* (b) What evidence of articulation is there in this set of financial statements?

5-20 *Obj. 5* Nairobi Company and Tripoli Enterprises are subsidiaries of Africa, Incorporated. It is the end of the fiscal year of each firm and each firm has prepared its own *separate* financial statements. Selected end-of-the-year ledger account balances for each of the three firms is shown below in columns.

Item	Africa Incorporated	Nairobi Company	Tripoli Enterprises
Cash	$ 33,100	$ 9,500	$ 13,800
Sales	960,000	325,000	470,000

Additional information:

1. One-half of Nairobi's sales were to Africa, Inc.
2. One-tenth of Africa, Inc.'s sales were to Tripoli Enterprises.
3. One-fourth of Tripoli's sales were to Nairobi Company.

(a) Determine the proper amounts that Africa, Inc. should report in its consolidated financial statements for consolidated cash and for consolidated sales. (b) List four other accounts that must be adjusted for intercompany transactions when preparing consolidated financial statements.

5-21 *Obj. 6* U.S. GAAP require that companies report their plant assets at historical cost less accumulated depreciation. GAAP of other countries sometimes allow a different basis. For example, the 1997 annual report of SmithKline Beecham, a British company, disclosed:

> The financial statements are prepared under the historical cost convention, modified for the revaluation of land and buildings. Such assets are revalued from time to time based on a professional appraisal of the open market value for their existing use.

Using this method, SmithKline Beecham reported land and buildings on its balance sheet at 1,096 million British pounds. In the notes to the financial statements it was disclosed that the book value using historical cost (i.e., cost minus accumulated depreciation) would have been 479 million British pounds.

a. Which information do you believe is more relevant and useful to financial statement users, the market values or the historical cost numbers? Why?
b. How does the use of market value numbers affect SmithKline Beecham's return on total assets (net income ÷ total assets) and return on stockholders' equity (net income ÷ total stockholders' equity)?

5-22 *Obj. 7* Bill's grandparents have been buying shares of stock for his college education fund since the day he was born. Yesterday, Bill received the annual report of Thompson Consolidated Shoulderpads, Inc. and is telling you about it. Bill says:

> "I feel really good about the company because its financial statements were prepared and audited by a well-known national accounting firm. Not only that, but the firm received an unqualified audit report. This means that the auditor checked out all the company's transactions and that the company is healthy. Since the auditors think the company is doing well, I think I'll invest some of my summer job savings in it."

How would you respond to your friend? Do you believe he has a good understanding of what information is conveyed by an auditor's report? Discuss.

Problems

Tips and hints for selected problems and cases are available on the Ingram WebTutor for WebCT site.

PROBLEM 5-1 *Obj. 1*

Identifying the Purpose of Financial Statements

Assume you are a financial manager with a U.S. corporation. A. Suliman is a recently employed manager in the Middle Eastern division of your corporation and a visitor to the United States. He has little familiarity with U.S. financial reporting practices. Your boss has given you the responsibility of explaining financial reports to Mr. Suliman.

Required Write a short report describing each of the four basic corporate financial statements for Suliman. Make sure you are clear about the purpose of each statement, its contents, and its relationships to the other financial statements.

PROBLEM 5-2 *Obj. 2*

Evaluating Financing Arrangements

Selected financial statement information is presented below for two companies, High Flyer Company and Conservative Company. The companies are in the same industry, and both have fiscal years ending March 31. All amounts are in millions.

	High Flyer Company	Conservative Company
Current assets	$ 8	$ 8
Total assets	20	20
Total liabilities	16	2
Interest expense	2.4	.4
Operating expenses	3.2	3.2

Cost of goods sold is 40% of sales revenue for both companies. Income taxes are 30% of pretax income for both companies. High Flyer Company has 500,000 shares of stock outstanding. Conservative Company has 2,000,000 shares outstanding.

Required

A. Prepare an income statement (including earnings per share) for each company assuming sales revenues are:
   1. $12 million
   2. $10 million
   3. $8 million

   (Note: Be aware that if a company shows a loss before taxes, it can obtain a refund of prior income taxes that were paid on prior profits.)
B. Explain what causes net income and earnings per share to change for the two companies when the amount of sales revenues fluctuates.
C. If you had $100,000 to invest in either of these companies and this amount would purchase the same number of shares in either, in which would you buy stock? Why?

PROBLEM 5-3 *Obj. 2*

Identifying and Correcting Errors in an Income Statement

Just after preparing the adjusting entries for the year, the long-time controller at Parrot Company suffered a massive heart attack and died instantly. Her inexperienced assistant did his best to prepare financial statements from the information the controller had left behind. He had particular difficulty with the income statement.

The item labeled sales expense is the sum of the amounts charged customers during the year for goods and services provided.

Income Statement December 31, 2002		
Sales expense		$260,722
Cost of goods sold		102,690
Net profit		$158,032
Operating expenses:		
Wages	$59,780	
Utilities	9,002	
Interest	14,420	
Depreciation	13,510	
Total operating expense		97,712
Operating income		$ 60,320
Advertising expense		9,968
Pretax income		$ 50,352
Income tax expense		13,150
Net income		$ 63,502
Earnings per share of common stock ($64,502 ÷ 15,000 shares)		$4.30

Required

A. Identify and list the errors in the income statement above.
B. Prepare a corrected income statement.

PROBLEM 5-4 Interpreting an Income Statement

Obj. 2

Microsoft Corporation's 1998 annual report included the following income statement information:

Microsoft			
In millions, except earnings per share			
Year Ended June 30	**1996**	**1997**	**1998**
Revenue	$8,671	$11,358	**$14,484**
Operating expenses:			
Cost of revenue	1,188	1,085	**1,197**
Research and development	1,432	1,925	**2,502**
Acquired in-process technology	—	—	**296**
Sales and marketing	2,657	2,856	**3,412**
General and administrative	316	362	**433**
Other expenses	19	259	**230**
Total operating expenses	5,612	6,487	**8,070**
Operating income	3,059	4,871	**6,414**
Interest income	320	443	**703**
Income before income taxes	3,379	5,314	**7,117**
Provision for income taxes	1,184	1,860	**2,627**
Net income	2,195	3,454	**4,490**
Earnings per share	$ 0.86	$ 1.32	**$ 1.67**

Required Ratios often are used to assess changes in financial statement information over time. Use Microsoft's income statements to answer the following questions. Express your answers as percentages.

(Continued)

A. What was the ratio of net income to net revenues each year?
B. What was the ratio of cost of revenues (cost of goods sold) to net revenues each year?
C. What was the ratio of operating expenses to net revenues each year?
D. What was the percentage change in net income between 1996 and 1997, and between 1997 and 1998? (Hint: Divide the increase in net income from 1996 to 1997 by the net income for 1996.)
E. Did Microsoft's operating results improve between 1996 and 1997? Between 1997 and 1998? Explain your answers.

PROBLEM 5-5 Special Items and Earnings Per Share

Obj. 2

Garzarelli Enterprises reported the following income statement information for the year 2001. All amounts are before taxes or tax effects have been applied.

Income from continuing operations, before taxes	$912,000
Current year loss from discontinued operations	(43,000)
Gain from sale of discontinued operations	11,000
Loss from damages caused by earthquake	(90,000)
Gain from change of depreciation method	24,000
Tax rate, applicable to all income statement items	30%
Number of shares of common stock outstanding on January 1, 2001	150,000
Additional shares issued on September 1, 2001	30,000

Required

A. Beginning with the Income from continuing operations, before taxes, prepare the remaining sections of the income statement. (Hint: Discontinued operations are reported before extraordinary items which are reported before changes in accounting principle.)
B. Determine the weighted-average number of shares outstanding during the year.
C. Calculate earnings per common share for all sections of the income statement.

PROBLEM 5-6 Comprehensive Income

Obj. 2

The Lo Company imports and sells Chinese furniture in the U.S. Its new accountant has been assigned the task of preparing the income statement. She knows that the FASB is now requiring that certain unrealized gains and losses be reported as part of comprehensive income. She has the following information available for the year just ended.

1. Loss on cumulative effect of change of depreciation method, net of tax	$ 840
2. Gain from disposal of discontinued operations, net of tax	3,500
3. Cost of goods sold	180,000
4. Revenue received in advance	2,500
5. Work in process inventory	135,000
6. Interest expense	4,000
7. Provision for income tax	11,700
8. Sale of treasury stock at a price greater than cost	5,050
9. Sales revenue	250,000
10. Unrealized gain on increase of market value of investment	1,240
11. Sale of stock to investors	60,300
12. General and administrative expense	27,000
13. Extraordinary gain on retirement of debt, net of tax	4,200
14. Unrealized loss on foreign currency translation (regarding foreign subsidiary)	3,600
15. Cash received from customers	75,000
16. Dividends paid to shareholders	8,000

Required

A. From the information given on page 234, decide which items should appear in the income statement, which would appear on a separate statement of comprehensive income, and which would not appear on either. If an item does not appear on either statement, indicate where it would be found. Also indicate which are transactions with owners.
B. Using the information above, prepare an income statement and a separate statement of comprehensive income.

PROBLEM 5-7 Information in the Statement of Stockholders' Equity

Obj. 3

A recent annual report for Wal-Mart Stores, Inc., and its subsidiaries is provided below:

Consolidated Statements of Shareholders' Equity
(In millions)

	# shares	Common Stock	Capital in Excess of Par	Retained Earnings	Other Adjustments	Total
Balance, 1-31-1995	2,297	$230	$539	$12,213	$(256)	$12,726
Net income				2,740		2,740
Cash dividends				(458)		(458)
Treasury stock	(5)		(4)	(101)		(105)
Other	1	(1)	10		(156)	(147)
Balance, 1-31-1996	2,293	229	545	14,394	(412)	14,756
Net income				3,056		3,056
Cash dividends				(481)		(481)
Treasury stock	(8)		(7)	(201)		(208)
Other		(1)	9		12	20
Balance, 1-31-1997	2,285	228	547	16,768	(400)	17,143
Net income				3,526		3,526
Cash dividends				(611)		(611)
Treasury stock	(47)	(5)	(48)	(1,516)		(1,569)
Other	3	1	86		(73)	14
Balance, 1-31-1998	2,241	$224	$585	$18,167	$(473)	18,503

Note: Slight modifications have been made to the statement for the purposes of simplifying the presentation.

Required From the information provided, answer the following questions:

A. What is the total amount of contributed capital as of January 31, 1995?
B. Did total contributed capital increase or decrease between January 31, 1995 and January 31, 1998? By what amount?
C. How much profit has been distributed to owners in cash during the three years covered by this statement?
D. Has stockholders' equity increased or decreased over the three years and what is the main reason?
E. Compute the ratio of cash dividends to net income for each year. Did the portion of profits paid out in dividends each year increase, decrease, or stay about the same?
F. Compute the percentage change in net income between 1996 and 1997, and between 1997 and 1998. (Hint: Divide the increase in net income from 1996 to 1997 by the net income for 1996.) Do you believe this is an encouraging sign or a discouraging sign?
G. Compute the percentage change in dividends between 1996 and 1997, and between 1997 and 1998. Is the rate of dividend increase greater or smaller than the rate of profit increase?

PROBLEM 5-8 *Obj. 4*

Reading and Interpreting a Balance Sheet

A recent balance sheet for **Walt Disney Company** is provided below.

Consolidated Balance Sheet
(Walt Disney Company and Subsidiaries)

at September 30 (in millions)	1998	1997
Assets		
Cash	$ 127	$ 317
Receivables	3,999	3,329
Inventories	899	853
Film and television costs (current)	3,223	2,186
Other	1,127	968
Total current assets	9,375	7,653
Film and television costs	2,506	2,215
Investments	1,814	1,914
Theme parks, resorts, and other property, at cost		
Attractions, buildings, and equipment	14,037	11,787
Accumulated depreciation	(5,382)	(4,857)
	8,655	6,930
Intangible assets, net	15,769	16,011
Other assets	3,259	3,774
	$41,378	$38,497
Liabilities and stockholders' equity		
Accounts and taxes payable and other accrued liabilities	$4,767	$4,748
Current portion of borrowings	2,132	897
Unearned royalties and other advances	635	631
Total current liabilities	7,525	6,276
Borrowings	9,562	10,171
Other noncurrent liabilities	4,903	4,765
Stockholders' equity		
Common stock	8,995	8,548
Retained earnings	10,981	9,543
Adjustments	(588)	(806)
	19,388	17,285
	$41,378	$38,497

Note: Slight modifications have been made to the format of the statement for purposes of simplifying the presentation.

Required Respond to the following questions.

A. Do you agree that Disney's balance sheet is both classified and comparative? Explain why or why not.
B. At year-end 1998, what percentage of total assets was composed of current assets? Did this percentage increase or decrease since year-end 1997?
C. What was Disney's amount of working capital at year-end 1998? Did it change significantly from year-end 1997?

D. Compute the working capital ratio at year-end 1998 and year-end 1997. Did it improve or deteriorate between 1997 and 1998?
E. Film and television costs is the amount paid to produce movies or television shows. Explain why it appears in two places on the balance sheet.
F. What were the amounts of total assets, total liabilities, and stockholders' equity at year-end 1998 and year-end 1997?
G. As of year-end 1998, what percentage of Disney's assets were financed with capital provided by stockholders? What percentage was financed with capital provided by creditors? Is the stockholders' portion increasing or decreasing?
H. Did Disney's overall financial position improve between 1997 and 1998? Explain.

PROBLEM 5-9 Identifying and Correcting Errors in a Balance Sheet

Obj. 4

Ceramics, Inc. reported the following balance sheet for the year 2001.

Balance Sheet
For the year ending December 31, 2001

Assets:	
Cash	$ 2,000
Accounts payable	500
Inventory	900
Equipment	1,000
Land	1,500
Total assets	$6,000
Liabilities:	
Accounts receivable	$3,000
Accrued liabilities	1,000
Total liabilities	4,000
Stockholders' equity:	
Common stock	1,800
Retained earnings	5,100
Total stockholders' equity	6,900
Total liabilities and stockholders' equity	$10,900

Required

A. Identify and list the errors in the balance sheet above.
B. Prepare a corrected balance sheet.

(Continued)

PROBLEM 5-10
Preparing Financial Statements

Objs. 2, 4

Argyle Company has the following account balances at December 31, 2001. During the year, Argyle had 10,000 shares of stock outstanding.

Argyle Company
Account Balances
at December 31, 2001

Account	Balance
Cash	$ 4,650
Accounts receivable	16,350
Inventory	30,500
Supplies	7,700
Prepaid insurance	3,550
Equipment	42,500
Accumulated depreciation—equipment	17,500
Buildings	170,000
Accumulated depreciation—buildings	105,000
Land	10,000
Patents	3,000
Accounts payable	18,250
Wages payable	3,450
Interest payable	1,700
Income taxes payable	4,050
Notes payable, current portion	2,500
Notes payable, long-term	37,500
Owners' investment	25,000
Retained earnings, December 31, 2000	60,150
Dividends	15,000
Sales revenue	130,000
Cost of goods sold	62,500
Wages expense	16,000
Utilities expense	2,000
Depreciation expense	1,050
Insurance expense	1,500
Supplies expense	2,300
Interest expense	3,650
Advertising expense	1,450
Patent expense	400
Income tax expense	11,000

Required From this information

A. Prepare an income statement in good form, and
B. Prepare a classified balance sheet for the fiscal year. Include appropriate headings and subheadings.

PROBLEM 5-11
Preparing Financial Statements

Objs. 2, 4

The following account balances are provided for Rustic Company at December 31, 2001. Revenues and expense accounts cover the fiscal year ending on that date. All numbers are dollars except shares outstanding.

Account	Amount
Accounts payable	$ 14,000
Accounts receivable	18,000
Accumulated depreciation	30,000
Cash	6,000
Common stock, par value	20,000
Cost of goods sold	35,000
Current portion of long-term debt	2,000
Income taxes	6,000
Interest expense	4,000
Interest payable	500
Inventory	34,000
Long-term debt	40,000
Net income	12,000
Paid-in capital in excess of par	30,000
Patents and trademarks	4,000
Prepaid insurance	2,500
Property, plant, and equipment, cost	150,000
Retained earnings	78,000
Sales revenues	110,000
Selling, general, and administrative expenses	65,000
Service revenues	12,000
Supplies	3,000
Wages payable	3,000
Shares outstanding	20,000

Required From these data

A. Prepare an income statement in good form.
B. Prepare a classified balance sheet.

PROBLEM 5-12 *Obj. 5*

Consolidated Financial Statements

Recreation Inc., a manufacturer of metal and plastic components, is the parent company of Boats Galore and Camp Trailer International. Both are 100% owned by Recreation, Inc. Because of the nature of each company's business, there are substantial interrelated activities among the three firms. The following table of selected information is available for the year ended December 31, 2002.

	Recreation Incorporated	Boats Galore	Camp Trailer International	Unaffiliated Companies	Total
Sales:					
Recreation, Inc. sales to	-0-	$1,455	$2,715	$7,456	$11,626
Boats Galore sales to	-0-	-0-	281	1,938	2,219
Camp Trailer sales to	$331	212	-0-	877	1,420
Total sales					$15,265
Accounts receivable:					
Recreation, Inc. due from	-0-	$155	$305	$714	$1,174
Boats Galore due from	-0-	-0-	33	202	235
Camp Trailer due from	$25	38	-0-	95	158
Total accounts receivable					$1,567
Accounts payable:					
Recreation, Inc. owes to	-0-	$400	$275	$1,100	$1,775
Boats Galore owes to	$50	-0-	40	142	232
Camp Trailer owes to	85	29	-0-	37	151
Total accounts payable					$2,158

Recreation, Inc. had a gross profit percentage for the year of 18%. For Boats Galore, the gross profit percentage was 22%, and for Camp Trailer International it was 28%.

(Continued)

Required Answer the following questions.

A. What is the purpose of preparing consolidated financial statements?

B. Why can't the accounts receivable (or accounts payable) of these three companies just be added together to obtain consolidated receivables (or consolidated payables)? Be specific.

C. Determine the proper amounts that should be reported for:

1. Consolidated sales
2. Consolidated cost of goods sold
3. Consolidated accounts receivable
4. Consolidated accounts payable

PROBLEM 5-13 The Transformation Process as Reported in Financial Statements

Obj. 5

Far East Specialties is an import company, financed primarily by stockholders and bank loans. It imports handmade goods from Central and East Asia to the United States, where they are sold to retail stores. The company's buyers contract with small companies for goods, which the buyers ship to a central location in the United States. The goods are inventoried and then redistributed as orders are received from retailers. The company receives a bill from the manufacturers along with the goods it receives. Payment is made each month. Bills are sent to retailers along with orders. Most retailers pay their bills each month, as well. It can be several months from the time goods are shipped to the United States until cash is received from retailers.

Required

A. Explain how the various aspects of Far East Specialties' transformation process are reported in its financial statements. That is, consider the events described above and identify where information about each event is reported in the financial statements. In particular, consider the relationship the company has with its investors, suppliers, and customers.

B. Why is it important that time, and the timing of events, be considered in reporting accounting information?

PROBLEM 5-14 Ethical Issues in Financial Reporting

Obj. 5

Flower Childs is a regional sales manager for Green-Grow, Inc., a producer of garden supplies. The company's fiscal year ends on April 30. In mid-April, Flower is contacted by the president of Green-Grow. He indicates that the company is facing a financial problem. Two years ago, the company borrowed heavily from several banks to buy a competitor company and to increase production of its primary products: insecticides and fertilizers. As a part of the loan agreement, Green-Grow must maintain a working capital ratio of 1.5 to 1 and earn a net income of at least $2 per share. If the company fails to meet these requirements, as reflected in its annual financial statements, the banks can restrict future credit for the company or require early payment of its loans, potentially forcing the company into bankruptcy.

The president explains that this fiscal year has been a difficult one for Green-Grow. Sales have slipped because of increased competition, and the rising prices of chemicals have increased the company's production costs. The company is in danger of not meeting the loan requirements. The company could be forced to make drastic cuts or to liquidate its assets. The president informs Flower that her job could be in danger. The president asks her to help with the problem by dating all sales invoices that clear her office during the first half of May as though the sales had been made in April. May is a month of heavy sales volume for the company as retail stores stock up for the coming season. The president believes that the added sales would be sufficient to get the company past the loan problem. He explains that this procedure will be used only this one time. By next year, the company will be in better shape because of new products it is developing. Also, he reminds Flower that her bonus for the year will be higher because of the additional sales that will be recorded for April. He points out that the company is fundamentally in sound financial shape, and that he would hate to see its future jeopardized by a minor bookkeeping problem. He is asking for the cooperation of all of the regional sales managers. He argues that the stockholders, employees, and managers will all be better off if the sales are predated. He wants Flower's assurance that she will cooperate.

Required A. What effect will predating the sales have on Green-Grow's balance sheet, income statement, and statement of cash flows? Be specific about which accounts will be affected and why. B. How will this practice solve the company's problem with the banks? C. What would be the appropriate behavior for the company president under the circumstances the company is facing? D. What would be the appropriate behavior for Flower?

PROBLEM 5-15 *Obj. 5*

Using Interrelationships among Financial Statements

Corey Issacson is an investor in Stone Cold Enterprises. Last week he received the company's most recent financial statements but some of the numbers were smudged and unreadable. Each of the unreadable numbers is represented below with a letter.

Stone Cold Enterprises
Comparative Balance Sheet (in thousands)
December 31, 2001 and 2002

	December 31, 2002	December 31, 2001
Assets		
Cash	$ 2,940	$ 1,020
Accounts receivable	1,850	1,225
Merchandise	2,855	1,000
Prepaid insurance	*(a)*	3,000
Plant, property, and equipment	25,000	*(b)*
Accumulated depreciation	*(c)*	(6,250)
Other assets	8,400	3,000
Total assets	$35,545	$ *(d)*
Liabilities and equity:		
Accounts payable	$ 1,580	$ 950
Wages payable	125	700
Rent payable	500	500
Long-term notes payable (8%)	12,000	12,000
Common stock	*(e)*	*(f)*
Retained earnings	*(g)*	10,845
Total liabilities and equity	$ *(h)*	$ *(i)*

Stone Cold Enterprises
Statement of Stockholders' Equity
Year Ended December 31, 2002

	Common Stock	Retained Earnings	Total
Balance, December 31, 2001	$3,000	$ *(j)*	$ *(k)*
Issued common stock	*(l)*		*(m)*
Net income		$14,495	14,495
Dividends paid		(9,000)	(9,000)
Balance, December 31, 2002	$5,000	$ *(n)*	$21,340

Stone Cold Enterprises
Income Statement
Year Ended December 31, 2002

Sales revenue		$103,000
Cost of goods sold		66,000
Gross profit		37,000
Operating expenses:		
Wages	$5,490	
Interest	*(o)*	
Rent	*(p)*	
Insurance	1,000	
Depreciation	1,250	
Total operating expenses		*(q)*
Pretax income		*(r)*
Income taxes (35%)		*(s)*
Net income		*(t)*

Additional information:

1. No items of plant, property, and equipment were purchased or sold during the year.
2. The prepaid insurance account represents the remaining portion of a 4-year policy purchased on January 1, 2001.
3. The rent payable account at year end (both years) represents December's rent that had not yet been paid.

Required Use your knowledge regarding the interrelationships among financial statements to determine each of the missing amounts.

PROBLEM 5-16 *Objs. 2, 3, 4, 5*

Estimating Future Activities

Van Gogh is considering a business opportunity selling artificial flowers, especially irises and lilies. He needs $25,000 in financing to begin operations. He has $15,000 in savings that he can invest. He has spoken with a local bank about borrowing the additional $10,000 he needs. The bank has indicated that it will consider the loan but has asked for a set of financial statements that describes what Van believes the company's financial condition will look like at the end of the first three months of operations. Van has asked for your assistance in preparing the financial statements. He has provided you with the following expectations:

A. Plant assets costing $22,500 will be needed.
B. Inventory of $5,000 will be purchased for the first month. The inventory will be paid for in the month following purchase. The amount of inventory purchased each month will equal the amount sold in the prior month.
C. Average monthly sales should be about $7,500. Two-thirds of the sales will be for cash each month, and one-third will be for credit. Credit sales will be collected in the month following sale.
D. The cost of the inventory sold will be $4,000 each month.
E. The interest on the loan will require a payment of $125 at the end of each month. An additional $100 will be paid to the bank each month to repay the loan.
F. Operating expenses, other than depreciation, each month should be $1,000. These will be paid in cash. Depreciation should be $200 each month.
G. Van expects to withdraw $1,000 from the business each month for living expenses.

In addition, he has provided the following work sheet, completed for the first month of operations:

	First Month	Second Month	Third Month
Sales revenues	$7,500		
Cost of goods sold	(4,000)		
Gross profit	3,500		
Depreciation	(200)		
Other operating expenses	(1,000)		
Income from operations	2,300		
Interest expense	(125)		
Net income	$2,175		
Cash	$5,275		
Accounts receivable	2,500		
Inventory	1,000		
Plant assets, net of depreciation	22,300		
Total assets	$31,075		
Accounts payable	5,000		
Notes payable	9,900		
Investment by owner	15,000		
Retained earnings	1,175		
Total liabilities & owners' equity	$31,075		

Required Complete the work sheet for the second and third months.

PROBLEM 5-17 Limitations of Financial Statements

Obj. 6

Markus O'Realius is considering the purchase of Caesar Company. The potential seller has provided Markus with a copy of the business's financial statements for the last three years. The financial statements reveal total assets of $350,000 and total liabilities of $150,000. The seller is asking $300,000 for the business. Markus believes that the business is worth only about $200,000, the amount of owners' equity reported on the balance sheet. He has asked your assistance in determining a price to offer for the business.

Required Write a memo to Markus explaining why he should not interpret the balance sheet as an accurate measure of the value of the business. Describe limitations of financial statements that might mean that the market value of the business was higher (or lower) than the financial statement amounts.

PROBLEM 5-18 Limitations of Financial Statements

Obj. 6

Limits, Ltd. had the following financial statements and auditors report for the fiscal year ending December 31, 2002 (the statement of stockholders' equity and the statement of cash flows are not shown).

Limits, Ltd.
Income Statement
For the Year Ending December 31, 2002

Sales revenue		$20,000
Operating expenses:		
Cost of sales	$1,000	
Wages expense	800	
Advertising expense	100	
Depreciation expense	300	
Research and development expense	300	
Total operating expense		2,500
Operating income		17,500
Other expenses:		
Interest expense		500
Income before taxes		17,000
Income tax		5,100
Net income		$11,900

Limits, Ltd.
Balance Sheet
as of December 31, 2002

Assets		*Liabilities and stockholders' equity*	
Current assets:		Current liabilities:	
Cash	$ 2,300	Accounts payable	$ 3,000
Accounts receivable	8,000	Wages payable	7,600
Inventory	15,000	Interest payable	900
Current assets	$25,300	Current liabilities	$11,500
Property, plant, and equipment:		Notes payable, long-term	9,000
Equipment	$21,000	Total liabilities	20,500
Accumulated depreciation	(8,000)	Stockholders' equity:	
Buildings	90,000	Owners' investment	9,700
Accumulated depreciation	(85,000)	Retained earnings	13,100
PP&E	18,000	Total stockholders' equity	22,800
Total assets	$43,300	Total liabilities and stockholders' equity	$43,300

(Continued)

Independent Auditors' Report

The Shareholders
Limits, Ltd.

We have audited the accompanying balance sheet of Limits, Ltd., as of December 31, 2002, and the related statements of income, stockholders' equity, and cash flows for the year ended December 31, 2002. These financial statements are the responsibility of the company's management. Our responsibility is to express an opinion on these financial statements based on our audits.

We conducted our audits in accordance with generally accepted auditing standards. Those standards require that we plan and perform the audit to obtain reasonable assurance about whether the financial statements are free of material misstatement. An audit includes assessing the accounting principles used and significant estimates made by management as well as evaluating the overall financial statement presentation. We believe that our audits provide a reasonable basis for our opinion.

In our opinion, the financial statements referred to above present fairly, in all material respects, the financial position of Limits, Ltd., as of December 31, 2002, and the results of its operations and cash flows for the year ended December 31, 2002 in conformity with generally accepted accounting principles.

Grinn and Barrett
100 Maple Street
Townville, USA
March 15, 2003

Required The text lists several limitations of financial statements. Using the financial statements and audit report given here, identify as many examples of limitations or items that relate to limitations of financial statements as you can.

PROBLEM 5-19 *Objs. 2, 3, 4, 6*

Preparing Financial Statements

ABC, Inc. has the following account balances at December 31, 2001.

Accounts payable	$17,080	Income tax expense	$ 1,300
Accounts receivable	9,400	Land	50,000
Accumulated depreciation	26,100	Notes payable	30,000
Buildings	60,000	Retained earnings,	
Cash	20,880	December 31, 2000	17,000
Contributed capital	31,000	Sales revenue	26,000
Cost of goods sold	15,600	Supplies	7,500
Depreciation expense	2,200	Wages expense	3,000
Dividends paid	1,200	Wages payable	23,900

During the year 2001, the company issued $6,000 of new common stock.

Required From this information, prepare (A) an income statement, (B) a statement of stockholders' equity, and (C) a classified balance sheet. (D) Show how the three financial statements articulate. (Note: In parts (A), (B), and (C), include appropriate headings and subheadings in the financial statements that you prepare.)

PROBLEM 5-20 *Objs. 2, 3, 4, 6, 7*

Understanding the Information in Financial Statements

Today is April 1 and Dale has just received the annual report of Clam Chowder Company, in which she owns stock. Displayed on page F245 are the comparative balance sheet and income statement that have drawn her attention.

Balance Sheet	Dec. 31, 2002	Dec. 31, 2001
Cash	$ 1,244	$ 1,512
Accounts receivable	6,914	5,886
Inventory	11,211	9,099
Buildings and equipment	49,900	46,500
Accumulated depreciation	(5,319)	(2,497)
Land	22,000	22,000
Total assets	$85,950	$82,500
Accounts payable	$ 2,313	$ 1,988
Interest payable	-0-	2,563
Wages payable	7,364	6,327
7%, 10-year note payable	20,000	20,000
Contributed capital	42,300	42,300
Retained earnings	13,973	9,322
Total liabilities and equity	$85,950	$82,500

Income Statement	For Year 2002
Sales revenue	$485,000
Cost of goods sold	300,700
Gross profit	$184,300
Operating expenses:	
Advertising	31,330
Depreciation	2,822
Utilities	19,200
Wages	113,698
Operating income	17,250
Interest expense	2,400
Pretax income	14,850
Income tax expense	5,200
Net income	$ 9,650
Earnings per share	$ 3.86

After reviewing this information, Dale makes the following comments.

1. I'm surprised that the value of the company's land has not increased. Prices have been increasing rapidly in the area the company is located.
2. I'm sure that I received a dividend from this company, but they don't report that they paid any.
3. I don't see how the company's cash balance could have declined when it took in $485,000 in cash from sales to customers.
4. Since these financial statements received an unqualified report from the outside auditors, I can be confident that every transaction was looked at and that every event was recorded without error.
5. I see that the value of the buildings and equipment declined by $2,822. That seems about right.
6. I don't understand why the company's highly trained workforce is not listed as an asset. It is one of the most important resources that the company has.
7. One thing I really like about this company is the up-to-the-minute financial reports it provides.
8. It's good to see that the value of the inventory has increased since last year.

Required

A. Help Dale better understand these financial statements by responding to each of her comments. Explain whether you agree or disagree with each comment and why.
B. Did the company declare and pay cash dividends during the year just ended? If so, what total amount was distributed?
C. Approximately how many shares of stock does the company have outstanding?

PROBLEM 5-21 Excel in Action

Listed on page F246 are account balances and other data for The Book Wermz at the close of November 30, 2001. Revenue and expense account balances are for the month of November. All amounts are dollars except shares of common stock. The Book Wermz operates as a corporation.

(Continued)

Accounts payable	$ 6,131.77
Accounts receivable	375.00
Accumulated depreciation	13,891.82
Cash	12,307.99
Contributed capital	100,000.00
Cost of goods sold	30,937.32
Depreciation expense	817.20
Dividends paid	1,500.00
Equipment	57,650.00
Income tax expense	897.45
Interest expense	932.03
Inventory	235,255.06
Notes payable, current portion	1,122.77
Notes payable, long-term	120,084.57
Rent expense	1,738.15
Sales	43,312.25
Service revenues	1,566.23
Shares of common stock	1,000
Supplies	2,130.12
Supplies expense	2,411.53
Wages expense	4,697.35
Wages payable	1,150.68

Required Use the account balances to produce an income statement, a statement of stockholders' equity, and a balance sheet for The Book Wermz in a spreadsheet. The financial statements should follow the examples illustrated in Chapter F5. The balance sheet should contain columns for November and October. October 31 balances should be obtained from data provided in the Chapter F3 spreadsheet problem.

Enter account titles in column A. Use columns B, C, and D as necessary for amounts. Use the Borders button to produce single and double lines by selecting the cell to be formatted, using the button down arrow to select the proper line type, and clicking on the button. Use the Indent button to indent titles and captions as needed by selecting the cell and clicking on the button. Use the Comma and Currency buttons to format amounts by selecting the cell and clicking on the appropriate buttons. The Comma button also formats numbers so that negative amounts appear in parentheses. The first and last amounts in a column of numbers should include dollar signs as illustrated in the chapter. Set column widths by placing the cursor at the right edge of a column header so the Change Width cursor appears, clicking and dragging the column to the right or left as needed. Use functions to sum subtotals and totals, =SUM(B5:B8) for example, so the spreadsheet will automatically recalculate any changes in account numbers. Use the Merge Cells button to merge adjacent cells for titles by selecting the cells to be merged and clicking on the Merge Cells button. Put titles in bold type by selecting the cell containing the title and clicking on the Bold Type button **B**.

Suppose sales for November had been $45,000 and the cash balance at November 30 had been $13,995.74. How much net income would the company report for November? How much total assets and stockholders' equity would it report at November 30?

PROBLEM 5-22 Multiple-Choice Overview of the Chapter

1. Which of the following is not a statement you would expect to find in a corporate annual report?
   a. Statement of financial position
   b. Statement of earnings
   c. Statement of stockholders' equity
   d. Statement of accounts receivable

2. The following information was reported on the income statement of Wagon Wheel Company:

Sales revenues	$450,000
Cost of goods sold	200,000
Selling, general, and administrative expenses	150,000
Interest expense	30,000

Wagon Wheel's gross profit and operating income would be:

	Gross profit	Operating income
a.	$300,000	$70,000
b.	$250,000	$70,000
c.	$250,000	$100,000
d.	$100,000	$70,000

3. Which of the following is a *false* statement regarding the statement of stockholders' equity?
   a. It lists changes in contributed capital and retained earnings for a fiscal period.
   b. It contains information about net income and dividends for a fiscal period.
   c. It reports the net change in stockholders' equity for a fiscal period.
   d. It reports increases or decreases in stocks and bonds for a fiscal period.

4. The following assets appear on the balance sheet for Astroid Company:

Accounts receivable	$50,000
Accumulated depreciation	160,000
Cash	20,000
Intangible assets	60,000
Inventory	100,000
Plant assets	400,000

The amount of current assets reported by Astroid is:
   a. $170,000
   b. $150,000
   c. $230,000
   d. $470,000

5. A balance sheet that provides information for more than one fiscal period is:
   a. a classified balance sheet.
   b. a comparative balance sheet.
   c. a consolidated balance sheet.
   d. a combined balance sheet.

6. Working capital is the amount of:
   a. cash and cash equivalents available to a company at the end of a fiscal period.
   b. long-term investments available at the end of a fiscal period less long-term debt at the end of the period.
   c. current assets available at the end of a fiscal period less current liabilities at the end of the period.
   d. total assets available at the end of a period that can be converted to cash.

7. Orange Bowl Company reported plant assets for the latest fiscal year of $5 million, net of accumulated depreciation. From this information, which of the following is an accurate statement about the company?
   a. The book value of the company's plant assets at the end of the fiscal year was $5 million.
   b. The company would have to pay $5 million to replace its assets if they were replaced at the end of the fiscal year.
   c. The amount the company would receive if it sold its plant assets at the end of the fiscal year would be $5 million.
   d. The amount the company paid for the plant assets it controlled at the end of the fiscal year was $5 million.

8. A consolidated financial statement is one in which:
   a. more than one year's financial data is included.
   b. the personal financial activities of the owner are combined with those of the company.
   c. the income statement and the balance sheet are combined into a single statement.
   d. the financial information of multiple corporations is reported as if they were a single firm.

9. Which of the following is *false?*
   a. Financial statement information is not always presented in a timely manner.
   b. The purpose of a balance sheet is to report the market value of assets and liabilities.
   c. Certain types of resources and costs are not reported in financial statements.
   d. Many of the numbers reported in financial statements result from estimates and allocations.

10. The purpose of an audit report is to show that:
    a. a CPA has prepared the company's financial statements.
    b. all of the company's transactions have been inspected for accuracy.
    c. an independent party believes that the financial statements do not contain any significant errors.
    d. the company is healthy, profitable, and likely to remain that way into the foreseeable future.

Cases

CASE 5-1 Comparing Financial Statement Information

Obj. 5

Selected financial statement information for 1997 is provided below for **Coca-Cola Company** and **PepsiCo, Inc.** The data are expressed in millions of dollars.

	Coke	Pepsi
Sales revenue	$18,868	$20,917
Cost of goods sold	6,015	8,525
Operating expenses	7,852	9,241
Net income	4,129	2,142
Cash from operating activities	4,033	3,419
Cash from (for) investing activities	(500)	(4,164)
Cash from (for) financing activities	(3,095)	(5,962)
Current assets	5,969	2,883
Plant assets, net	5,771	6,261
Total assets	16,940	20,101
Current liabilities	7,379	4,257
Long-term liabilities	2,250	8,908
Stockholders' equity	7,311	6,936

Required Compare the results of the operating, investing, and financing activities of the two companies from the information provided. Use any comparisons you believe are useful. (Hint: Comparisons can be made by converting income statement numbers to percentages by dividing by sales revenues. Divide balance sheet numbers by total assets. Divide cash flow numbers by cash from operating activities. Also, you may wish to compare income and cash flow numbers to balance sheet numbers, such as net income to total assets.) Identify and comment on any significant differences that you find. How do the firms compare regarding effectiveness and efficiency?

CASE 5-2 *Objs. 2, 4, 5*

Analysis of Corporate Financial Statements

Financial statements for **McDonald's Corporation** from a recent annual report are provided below. Examine these statements and answer the questions that follow the statements.

Consolidated Statement of Income
For the Year Ended December 31

(In millions of dollars, except per common share data)	1997	1996	1995
Revenues			
Sales by company-operated restaurants	$ 8,136.5	$ 7,570.7	$ 6,863.5
Revenues from franchised restaurants	3,272.3	3,115.8	2,931.0
Total revenues	11,408.8	10,686.5	9,794.5
Operating costs and expenses			
Company-operated restaurants			
Food and packaging	2,772.6	2,546.6	2,319.4
Payroll and other employee benefits	2,025.1	1,909.8	1,730.9
Occupancy and other operating expenses	1,851.9	1,706.8	1,497.4
	6,649.6	6,163.2	5,547.7
Franchised restaurants—occupancy expenses	613.9	570.1	514.9
General, administrative, and selling expenses	1,450.5	1,366.4	1,236.3
Other operating income	(113.5)	(45.8)	(105.7)
Total operating costs and expenses	8,600.5	8,053.9	7,193.2
Operating income	$ 2,808.3	$ 2,632.6	$ 2,601.3
Interest expense	364.4	342.5	340.2
Other nonoperating expense	36.6	39.1	92.0
Income before provision for income taxes	2,407.3	2,251.0	2,169.1
Provision for income taxes	764.8	678.4	741.8
Net income	$ 1,642.5	$ 1,572.6	$ 1,427.3
Net income per common share	$ 2.35	$ 2.21	$ 1.97
Dividends per common share	$ 0.32	$ 0.29	$ 0.26

(Continued)

Consolidated Balance Sheet

(In millions of dollars)	December 31, 1997	1996
Assets		
Current assets		
Cash and equivalents	$ 341.4	$ 329.9
Accounts and notes receivable	483.5	495.4
Inventories	70.5	69.6
Prepaid expenses and other current assets	246.9	207.6
Total current assets	1,142.3	1,102.5
Other assets		
Notes receivable due after one year	67.0	85.3
Investments in and advances to affiliates	634.8	694.0
Intangibles and miscellaneous	1,436.0	1,152.1
Total other assets	2,137.8	1,931.4
Property and equipment		
Property and equipment, at cost	20,088.2	19,133.9
Accumulated depreciation and amortization	(5,126.8)	(4,781.8)
Net property and equipment	14,961.4	14,352.1
Total assets	$18,241.5	$17,386.0
Liabilities and shareholders' equity		
Current liabilities		
Notes payable	$ 1,293.8	$ 597.8
Accounts payable	650.6	638.0
Income taxes	52.5	22.5
Other taxes	148.5	136.7
Interest payable	107.1	121.7
Other liabilities	396.4	523.1
Current maturities of long-term debt	335.6	95.5
Total current liabilities	2,984.5	2,135.3
Long-term debt	4,834.1	4,830.1
Other long-term liabilities	427.5	726.5
Deferred income taxes	1,063.5	975.9
Shareholders' equity		
Common stock	616.5	747.3
Retained earnings	12,569.0	11,173.0
Adjustments	(4,253.6)	(3,202.1)
Total shareholders' equity	8,931.9	8,718.2
Total liabilities and shareholders' equity	$18,241.5	$17,386.0

Note: Slight modifications have been made to the format of the statements for purposes of simplifying the presentation.

Required Use McDonald's financial statements to answer each of the following questions.

A. You have been requested to compare McDonald's 1997 accrual basis operating results to its 1996 accrual basis operating results. Which financial statement would you inspect, and which numbers would you use? Justify use of the numbers you selected over other numbers on that statement. How do 1997 operating results compare to 1996?

B. How has the percentage of operating revenues from company-owned restaurants, as compared to operating revenues from franchised restaurants, changed over the last three years? What might this imply about the company's new-store strategy? Show your work.

C. Compare the company's percentage return on total assets (net income ÷ total assets) for 1997 and 1996. Also compare the company's percentage return on stockholders' equity (net income ÷ total stockholders' equity) for 1997 and 1996. Did the measures improve or deteriorate?

D. If you owned 10,000 shares of the company's stock, what was your claim on the company's earnings for 1997? How much cash would you have received from the company during 1997?

E. As of year-end 1997, what have been the two most important sources of capital for McDonald's? What percentage of assets have been financed by these two sources alone?

F. Which category (or categories) of assets has the company invested most heavily in? Describe.

G. What assets may be important to the company that are not reported on its balance sheet?

7

Key Points Covered in This Chapter

1 Net income is typically viewed as the fundamental measure of a company's profitability, but there are also a variety of other measures of "income." The best measure of sustainable profitability is income from continuing operations.

2 The primary categories of income statement items are revenues, expenses, gains, and losses. Income statement items that do not relate to a company's continuing operations are income from discontinued operations, extraordinary items, and the cumulative effect of accounting changes.

3 Income statements are prepared in a variety of formats. One useful format is the multiple-step income statement.

4 Revenue should be recognized only after the required work has been performed and after collectibility of cash is reasonably assured. The matching concept has traditionally been used to decide when to recognize expenses.

5 Individual transactions impacting income can be analyzed using the expanded accounting equation, which is:

Assets = Liabilities + Paid-in Capital + (Revenues – Expenses – Dividends)

6 An important use of an income statement is to forecast income in future periods. Good forecasting requires an understanding of what underlying factors determine the level of a revenue or an expense.

The Income Statement

General Motors is the brainchild of William Durant and was formed through the acquisition of a number of preexisting car makers. Buick and Oldsmobile were acquired in 1908, and Cadillac and Pontiac (originally called Oakland) were added in 1909. General Motors made so many acquisitions in those early years that financing quickly ran out and Durant lost control of his company. After some dizzying dealing, Durant found himself back in charge in 1916. Things were so crazy during the time Durant was fighting to regain the reins of GM that, at one point, Chevrolet Motor Company (another Durant creation) owned a majority of General Motors stock, but then, presto, Chevrolet became a subsidiary of General Motors in 1918.

An economic slowdown following the end of World War I stretched Durant's financial resources past the breaking point, and in 1920 he lost control of General Motors for good. The new president of GM was Pierre S. du Pont who had been a GM investor since 1914. In addition to bringing the financial resources and business connections associated with his own family's chemical empire, du Pont also was instrumental in instituting the du Pont style of management and control. This system, implemented at General Motors by

Alfred P. Sloan (who later went on to head GM until 1956), emphasized decentralized decision making with managers of autonomous divisions being evaluated based on meeting specific financial targets. This "DuPont" system of evaluation was discussed in Chapter 3.

Under Alfred P. Sloan's leadership, General Motors became the dominant car maker in the world, a position it still holds. In addition to implementing the DuPont system of evaluation and control, Sloan also formalized the caste system among GM's different automobile lines. For example, Chevrolets were targeted at the lower end of the market while Cadillacs were aimed at the higher end. Sloan was also instrumental in creating the annual ritual of the "car model year" to encourage owners of old models to trade them in on cars incorporating the latest innovations.

Although GM's global market share has declined in the face of stiff competition from Japanese and European companies, as well as from its domestic competitors, Ford and Chrysler, General Motors still sells more cars and trucks than any other company in the world. In 1996, GM sold 8.4 million vehicles comprising 16.2 percent of the worldwide total. In addition, GM remains one of the largest private employers in the United States, ranking second behind Wal-Mart in the 1998 Fortune 500 listing (see Exhibit 5-1).

EXHIBIT 5-1 U.S. Companies with the Most Employees

BIGGEST EMPLOYERS AMONG U.S. COMPANIES
1997

Company	Number of Employees
Wal-Mart	825,000
General Motors	**608,000**
Ford Motor	363,892
United Parcel Service	331,000
Sears Roebuck	296,000

Source: 1998 Fortune 500 listing available at **www.fortune.com**.

In addition to being the most prolific car maker in the world, General Motors has the unenviable distinction of having posted the world record for largest annual net loss of all time. In 1992, GM reported a loss for the year of $23.5 billion. This record loss followed losses of $2.0 billion in 1990 and $4.5 billion in 1991.

How was General Motors able to stay in business while reporting these large losses? Well, it may surprise you to learn that during the same period GM was reporting large losses on its income statement, it was reporting healthy cash from operations in its cash flow statement. In fact, in 1992, the year of the record loss, General Motors' positive cash from operations was $9.8 billion. This strong cash flow enabled GM to continue normal operations, pay its suppliers, repay its loans, and maintain investor confidence even while reporting large losses.

So, where did these large losses come from if they weren't the result of a shortfall in cash from operations? The losses came from business expenses that General Motors had incurred as part of its operations but which have not yet had to be paid in cash. For example, the record $23.5 billion loss was primarily due to GM's recording its large business expense related to post-retirement medical benefits that have been promised to GM employees. General Motors won't actually have to make the cash payments related to these benefits until the employees retire in the future. However, the GM employees have already earned the benefits, so the estimated cost of the benefits should be reported as a cost of business now. The art of accounting involves recording all business expenses—both those expenses that are paid in cash and those expenses that involve promises of payment in the future. And as GM's $23.5 billion loss illustrates, those promises of future payment can really add up.

The income statement was introduced in Chapter 2. As stated in that chapter, the income statement describes a company's financial performance for a period of time and is, in the minds of many, THE premier financial statement. The purpose of the income statement is to provide financial statement users with information concerning the profitability of a company for a particular period of time. The income statement lists all of the revenues, expenses, gains, and losses that the company earned or incurred during the accounting period. The difference between the total of revenues plus gains and the total of expenses plus losses is either net income or net loss.

Income measurement is much more than merely tabulating cash receipts and cash payments. A proper measure of economic performance requires judgment in estimating the value of work completed during a year, along with an estimate of the economic value of resources consumed in doing that work. And since investors, creditors, and other financial statement users want frequent income reports, these estimates must be made when many business deals are still in the middle of being completed.

Accrual accounting is the process that accountants use in adjusting raw transaction data into refined measures of a firm's economic performance. For example, imagine that you have just completed a $20,000 consulting contract but so far have only collected $3,000 of your fee in cash. To state that you made $3,000 on the contract is very misleading since you fully expect to collect the additional $17,000 in the future. The practice of accrual accounting requires that a company's performance be measured based on all of the cash flows—past, present, and future—that will result from the company's actions undertaken during the current period. Thus, according to accrual accounting your income on the consulting contract is $20,000 whether you have collected that amount in cash already or whether you expect to collect the cash in the future. Obviously, the practice of accrual accounting requires one to exercise judgment in estimating the future cash flows that will result from current actions. One of the important economic contributions made by accountants is the collection of accrual accounting rules which, when applied to a company's raw cash flow data, result in a superior measure of that company's economic performance.

The difficulty in using accrual accounting to generate a performance measure is represented in Exhibit 5-2. Each horizontal bar in the exhibit represents a business deal such as the production and sale of a car, the delivery of legal services for a specific lawsuit, or the development, delivery, and support of a piece of software. Some deals last less than a day from start to finish, such as when a barber provides a haircut in exchange for cash. The obligations and responsibilities associated with other deals can stretch on for years. For example, when you buy a GM car, the deal is not done from your standpoint until four or five years later after you have received all of the GM warranty services promised to you. And, from GM's standpoint, the deal is not done until 40 or 50 years later after GM has paid the assembly line workers all of the pension benefits they earned through the labor hours spent assembling your car. In spite of the fact that the economic loose ends of some business deals extend for years, financial statement users still require periodic reports about a company's operating performance. As you can see in Exhibit 5-2, the beginning and the end of a year are arbitrary breaks in the life of an ongoing business. The job of accountants is to consider all business deals that were at least partly completed during a year and to measure the profit associated with those deals. This profit is then reported as net income for the year. As you can see, income measurement is much more than mere "bean counting."

EXHIBIT 5-2 The Problem of Income Measurement

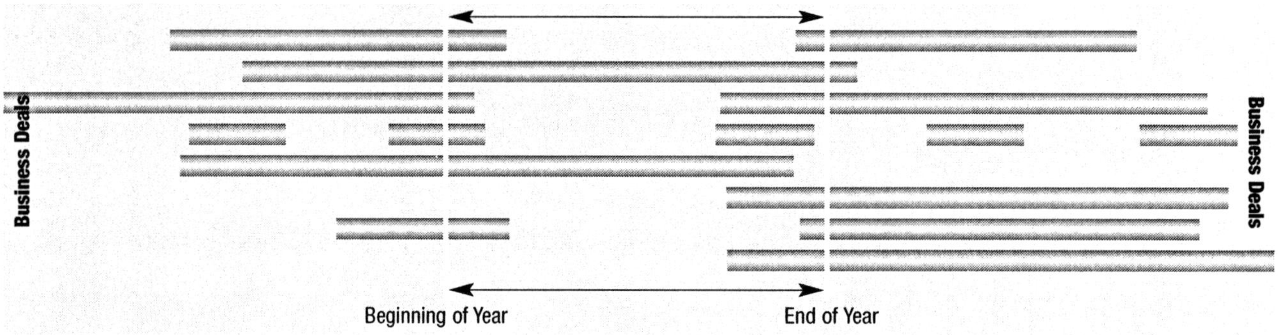

This chapter includes an explanation of the items commonly found in an income statement. The chapter also outlines the conceptual issues involved with the timing of revenue and expense recognition. The process of analyzing operating transactions is also introduced in this chapter. Finally, the chapter demonstrates how one can generate forecasts of income for future years.

Different Measures of Income

(Key Point #1)

What is income? A simple, intuitive definition is that income is the increase in an individual's or a company's wealth during a period. A quick example will demonstrate that this intuitive definition is difficult to apply in practice. Assume the following:

- You bought a house for $200,000 on January 1. This house is your primary residence.
- You sold the house on December 31 for $220,000.
- General price level inflation for the year was 3%.

Now, did you have income during the year in association with this house and, if so, how much? There are several possible answers to this question.

- *Income of $20,000.* Many would say that you obviously had income of $20,000 because you sold the house for $20,000 more than you bought it for at the beginning of the year. Your dealings with the house have caused your financial resources to increase from $200,000 to $220,000.
- *Income of $14,000.* You have $220,000 at the end of the year, but the 3 percent inflation for the year means that the $200,000 you had at the beginning of the year is the equivalent of $206,000 ($200,000 × 1.03) in inflated dollars by year-end. Thus, the inflation-adjusted income is $14,000 ($220,000 – $206,000). Computation of income in the United States usually ignores inflation adjustments.

- *No income.* Where will you live after you sell your house? If you expect to live in a house comparable to the one you sold, the replacement house will cost you $220,000. As a result, you have no real income since it will take your entire $220,000 to put you into the same type of house that you had at the beginning of the year. This concept, termed **physical capital maintenance**, states that income is earned only when one experiences an increase in actual physical resources.

The approach that accountants typically use in computing a company's income is the first option described above in which inflation is ignored and a company is said to have income when its financial resources increase. This approach is called the **financial capital maintenance** concept and states that income exists when the dollar amount of a company's net assets (assets − liabilities, or owners' equity) increases during the year, after excluding the effects of new owner investment or payment of dividends to owners.

Much attention is focused on a company's bottom-line net income. In fact, prior to the advent of large corporations, owners would often summarize their results from operations into one net income number and disclose, when required, only that one number. These days, a variety of different measures of income can be extracted from a company's income statement. These income measures are summarized in Exhibit 5-3 and are briefly discussed below.

EXHIBIT 5-3 Different Measures of Income

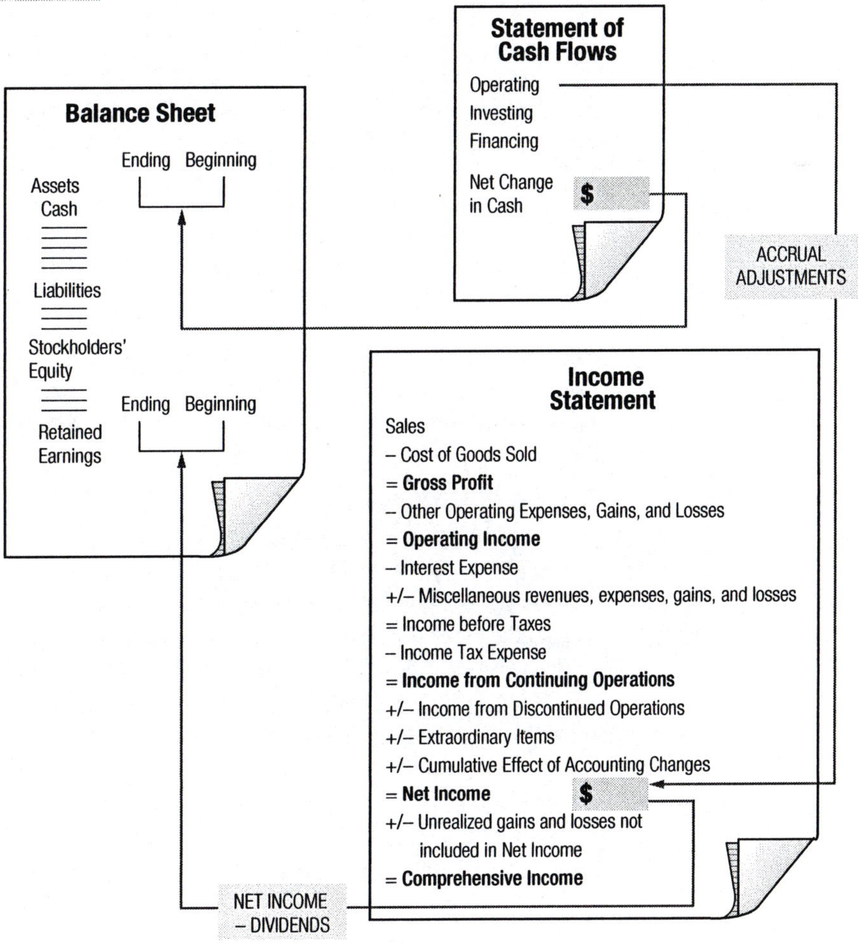

FYI

Accountants in the United States experimented with inflation-adjusted income computations in the late 1970s and early 1980s. The low level of inflation in recent years has caused the business community to lose interest in these adjustments.

Gross Profit

For a company selling a product, **gross profit** is the difference between the selling price of the product and the cost of the product. For General Motors, gross profit is the difference between the cost to manufacture a car and the price GM charges to dealers who buy cars. In a supermarket, gross profit is the difference between the retail selling price and wholesale cost.

Gross profit is an important number. If a company is not generating enough from the sale of a product or service to cover the costs directly associated with that product or service, that company will not be able to stay in that line of business for long. For example, if GM sells a truck for $26,000 and the materials, labor, and overhead costs associated with producing that truck are $29,000, the gross profit of $(3,000) suggests that GM is in serious difficulty. After all, with a negative gross profit, how would GM then be able to pay for advertising, executive salaries, interest expense, and the like?

Note that not all companies structure their income statement to report gross profit. For example, the General Motors income statement illustrated later in the chapter does not explicitly report the gross profit earned by GM from the sale of its manufactured products. However, gross profit, if it is not presented directly, can usually be computed by reformatting the income statement or by accessing detailed information contained in the notes to the financial statements.

Operating Income

Operating income measures the performance of the fundamental business operations conducted by a company and is computed as gross profit minus operating expenses. A general rule of thumb is that all expenses are operating expenses *except* interest expense and income tax expense. Accordingly, another name for operating income is EBIT, or earnings before interest and taxes.

Operating income tells users how well a business is performing in the activities unique to that business, separate from the financing and income tax management policies that are handled at the corporate headquarters level. For example, operating income allows you to evaluate Wal-Mart's overall ability to choose store locations, establish pricing strategies, train and retain workers, and manage relations with its suppliers. Operating income does not tell you anything about the interest cost of Wal-Mart's loans or how successful Wal-Mart's tax planners have been at structuring and locating operations to minimize income taxes.

Income from Continuing Operations

A key purpose of financial accounting is to provide interested parties with information that can be used to predict how a company will perform in the future. Therefore, financial statement users desire an income number that reflects the aspects of a company's performance that are expected to continue into the future. This number is labeled "Income from Continuing Operations." **Income from continuing operations** is computed by subtracting interest expense, income tax expense, and other miscellaneous items from operating income. Income from continuing operations is significant because of the three categories of items that it ***excludes***:

- *Income from Discontinued Operations.* On occasion, a company elects to dispose of a major business segment. After such a decision is made, the results of the discontinued segment are reported separately, along with any costs of disposing of the segment. For example, in 1991 when Winnebago Industries disposed of its Commercial Vehicle Division and lost $13 million in the process, all financial information relating to that division was summarized in the income statement after income from continuing operations.

- *Extraordinary Gains and Losses.* For accounting purposes, extraordinary items are defined as events or transactions that are unusual in nature and infrequent in occurrence. For example, a company suffering a large uninsured loss from an earthquake would report the loss as an extraordinary item. The effect of an extraordinary item is disclosed separately after income from continuing operations. In 1995, Sprint, the telecommunications giant, reported an extraordinary loss of $565 million. This loss arose because deregulation removed Sprint's legal right to earn a minimum return on its assets. Accordingly, Sprint was forced to make a one-time adjustment to its assets reflecting the fact that those assets would not generate the return that had previously been expected.
- *Cumulative Effect of Accounting Changes.* On occasion, accounting standard setters revise the accounting rules or make new ones. If these rules require a retroactive catch-up adjustment as a result of a company's having accounted for things differently in the past, the catch-up adjustment is usually required to be disclosed separately after income from continuing operations. The world record cumulative adjustment was reported in 1992 by General Motors when it recorded a $33 billion one-time adjustment relating to a change in the accounting standard concerning postretirement medical benefits.

The items excluded from the computation of income from continuing operations are collectively called "below-the-line" items. In this phrase, "the line" is income from continuing operations, and items falling in one of these three categories are reported "below the line." A more complete description of these three categories is given later in the chapter.

Net Income

Net income is the accountant's attempt to summarize in one number the overall economic performance of a company for a given period. Since net income is an overall summary number, it includes items from the three "below-the-line" categories mentioned above. In the absence of any irregular items, net income is the same as income from continuing operations.

From the discussion above, you can see that when people make a reference to a company's "income" or "profit," they could be referring to any one of a host of numbers—gross profit, operating income, income from continuing operations, or net income. It is important to learn to be very specific when discussing a company's income. After all, comparing one company's net income to another company's operating income would be like comparing apples to oranges.

Comprehensive Income

Recall from the beginning of this section that a general definition of "income" is the increase in a company's wealth during a particular period. The wealth of a company is impacted in a variety of ways that have nothing to do with the business operations of the company. For example, changes in exchange rates can cause the U.S. dollar value of a company's foreign subsidiaries to increase or decrease. **Comprehensive income** is the number used to reflect an overall measure of the change in a company's wealth during the period. In addition to net income, comprehensive income includes items that, in general, arise from changes in market conditions unrelated to the business operations of a company. The most common of these items are:

Business Context 5.1

Net Income vs. EVA®

As mentioned earlier in the chapter, accountants are proud of the set of accrual accounting rules that they have developed over the years. According to accountants, when these rules are applied to raw cash flow data, the resulting net income number provides a superior measure of a company's performance. Some financial analysts and many finance professors have long been skeptical about the value of accrual accounting. These skeptics contend that an investor is better off analyzing a company using cash flow data because the accounting rules distort a company's reported performance.

Recently, accrual accounting has been attacked from another direction. Stern Stewart & Company has marketed an alternative measure of financial performance that it claims is superior to the net income number computed by accountants. The Stern Stewart measure is called Economic Value Added, or EVA®. Many prominent companies, including Coca-Cola, AT&T, and Sprint, have paid Stern Stewart for the right to use EVA® as an internal performance measure. Stern Stewart claims that EVA® is "almost 50 percent better than its closest accounting-based competitor in explaining changes in shareholder wealth."

Three accounting professors decided to test the validity of these challenges to the usefulness of accrual accounting. Professors Biddle, Bowen, and Wallace constructed statistical tests to determine which performance measure—accrual accounting net income, EVA®, or cash flow from operations—is most closely associated with the ultimate performance measure, the annual change in the market value of a company. Using data for 773 U.S. companies for 11 years, Professors Biddle, Bowen, and Wallace computed a statistic called "adjusted R^2," which reflects the degree of association between a performance measure number for a given company in a given year and the company's market value change in the same year. The higher the adjusted R^2 value, the closer the association between the performance measure and the company's change in market value. The computed adjusted R^2 values were:

Net income (excluding extraordinary items)	12.8%
EVA®	6.5%
Cash flow from operations	2.8%

So, accrual accounting is still the undisputed champion of performance measures.

Questions

1. What conclusion would we have been forced to draw if cash flow from operations had yielded a higher adjusted R^2 number than did net income?
2. If net income is a better performance measure, why do you think that companies pay for the right to implement the EVA® system as an internal performance measure?

Source: Gary C. Biddle, Robert M. Bowen, and James S. Wallace. "Does EVA® Beat Earnings? Evidence on Associations with Stock Returns and Firm Values." *Journal of Accounting and Economics*, December 1997, p. 301.

- Changes in the U.S. dollar value of foreign subsidiaries, caused by changes in foreign currency exchange rates
- Changes in the value of investment securities that are not held for active trading purposes
- Changes in the value of certain derivative instruments

These items are excluded from net income because they are viewed as yielding little information about the economic performance of a company's business operations. However, they are reported as part of comprehensive income because they do impact the value of assets and liabilities reported in the balance sheet. These items are explained in more detail later in the chapter.

This section has provided an overview of the major parts of the income statement. A detailed discussion of individual items is covered in the next section.

FYI

The requirement to report comprehensive income is very recent. The requirement was issued by the FASB in June 1997.

Individual Income Statement Items

(Key Point #2)

To illustrate the individual accounts found in many income statements, we will reference General Motors' 1997 income statement (reproduced in Exhibit 5-4). Companies that fall under SEC jurisdiction are required to provide income statement numbers for three years. Hence, for comparability purposes, GM's 1997 income statement includes numbers for 1995, 1996, and 1997.

Revenues

The reported amount of **revenue** represents the value of the goods and services provided by a company in its business operations. In exchange for providing goods and services, a company receives cash, promises of future payment (accounts receivable), or other items of value. For example, a company would report $5,000 in revenue if it provided a service to a lender in lieu of repaying a $5,000 loan from that lender. Thus, revenue is anything of value generated through business operations.

Sales Revenue Revenue can be generated by a business in a variety of ways, some of which are illustrated in General Motors' income statement contained in Exhibit 5-4. The most common type of revenue is **sales** and reflects the aggregate selling price of goods sold during the period. In 1997, General Motors generated revenue of $153.7 billion from sales of manufactured products. Consistent with our view of General Motors as primarily a manufacturer, sale of manufactured products is GM's primary source of revenue. By comparison, Ford reported 1997 sales of $122.9 billion.

Service Revenue Another common source of revenue for companies is the fees charged for services. Service fees are the primary source of revenue for law firms, plumbers, investment banks, CPAs, and all other businesses that provide services instead of goods. Fee revenue differs from sales revenue in that fees are earned in exchange for services whereas sales revenue is earned in exchange for goods. In Exhibit 5-4, General Motors reports financial services revenue of $12.8 billion in 1997. This revenue is generated primarily by General Motors Acceptance Corporation (GMAC) and consists, in large part, of lease revenue from the increasingly popular practice of leasing a GM vehicle through GMAC rather than buying the vehicle outright. Ford also reports financial services revenue, which totaled $30.7 billion in 1997.

FYI

As of December 31, 1997, Chase Manhattan is the only one of the largest 20 banks in the world, ranked in terms of total assets, based in the United States. Eight are Japanese banks and three are French banks.

Interest Revenue Another source of revenue is interest revenue. In the notes to its financial statements, General Motors discloses that of the $11.7 billion in "other income" reported in its income statement (see Exhibit 5-4), $2.1 billion is interest revenue. For most companies, interest revenue is only a small part of total revenue because the interest is earned on temporary investments of excess cash and is not a part of the primary business operations. For other businesses, such as banks, interest revenue is the primary source of revenue. In 1997, Chase Manhattan Bank (the largest U.S. bank in terms of total assets) reported total revenue of $30.4 billion, of which $21.8 billion was interest revenue.

Other Revenue Of course, there are thousands of different labels that can be attached to specific types of revenue because there are thousands of different ways for businesses to make money. Some additional examples are as follows:

- Universities report tuition revenue. For example, Rice University (a private university located in Houston, Texas) disclosed that 15 percent of its 1996–97 operating budget of $217 million was met through tuition and fee revenue from students.
- Professional sports teams report licensing revenue for the fees they earn by allowing apparel manufacturers to use the teams' names and logos.
- McDonald's reports franchising revenue for the fees it receives from companies and individuals who have contracted for the right to use the McDonald's name and system of food preparation. In Appendix A, it can be seen that McDonald's franchising revenue in 1997 was $3.3 billion.

EXHIBIT 5-4 Income Statement for General Motors

GENERAL MOTORS CORPORATION AND SUBSIDIARIES CONSOLIDATED STATEMENTS OF INCOME

	Years Ended December 31		
	1997	**1996**	**1995**
(dollars in millions)			
Net Sales and Revenues			
Manufactured products	$153,683	$145,341	$143,666
Financial services	12,762	12,674	11,664
Other income	11,729	5,998	4,924
Total Net Sales and Revenues	178,174	164,013	160,254
Costs and Expenses			
Cost of sales and other operating charges, exclusive of items listed below	130,028	123,195	121,300
Selling, general and administrative expenses	16,192	14,580	12,550
Depreciation and amortization expenses	16,616	11,840	11,213
Interest expense	6,113	5,695	5,182
Other deductions	1,511	2,083	1,678
Total Costs and Expenses	170,460	157,393	151,923
Income from Continuing Operations before Income Taxes and Minority Interests	7,714	6,620	8,331
Income taxes	1,069	1,723	2,316
Minority interests	53	56	18
Income from Continuing Operations before Cumulative Effect of Accounting Change	6,698	4,953	6,033
Income from discontinued operations	-0-	10	900
Cumulative effect of accounting change	-0-	-0-	(52)
Net Income	$ 6,698	$ 4,963	$ 6,881
Basic Earnings per Share	$8.70	$6.06	$7.28
Diluted Earnings per Share	8.62	6.02	7.21

Large multinational corporations often generate significant amounts of revenue from several different sources. This fact is illustrated in the income statement of IBM, a portion of which is shown in Exhibit 5-5. Note that hardware sales, for which IBM is primarily known, accounted for less than half of total revenue in 1997.

FYI

IBM reports $12.8 billion in software sales in 1997. We all know that Microsoft dominates the software industry, and yet total revenue for Microsoft in 1997 was just $11.4 billion.

EXHIBIT 5-5 Different Sources of Revenue for IBM

IBM

Revenue (dollars in millions)

For the year ended December 31:	**1997**	**1996**	**1995**
Revenue:			
Hardware sales	$36,229	$36,316	$35,600
Services	19,302	15,873	12,714
Software	12,844	13,052	12,657
Maintenance	6,402	6,981	7,409
Rentals and financing	3,731	3,725	3,560
Total revenue	$78,508	$75,947	$71,940

Expenses

The recorded amount of **expenses** represents the value of resources used in generating the reported revenue. Expenses are incurred in anticipation that they will generate revenues. For example, companies buy inventory in hopes that they can sell it. Companies buy advertising in hopes that it will generate sales. Companies hire employees in hopes that they can produce products for sale to customers or provide services that can be billed to clients. As illustrated in General Motors' income statements, there are various types of expenses. The major categories of expenses are discussed below.

Cost of Goods Sold When a business sells goods to customers, the cost of the goods sold is recorded as an expense called **cost of goods sold**, or cost of sales. For a retailer, cost of goods sold is merely the wholesale cost paid to purchase the item. For a manufacturer, cost of goods sold is the total cost of labor, materials, and overhead used to produce the item sold. As seen in Exhibit 5-4, the manufactured goods that General Motors sold for $153.7 billion in 1997 cost GM $130.0 billion to make.

As mentioned earlier in the chapter, the difference between sales and cost of goods sold is called gross profit and represents the margin between the cost of a product to a company and the price for which the company sells that product. An important relationship is the gross profit percentage, which is computed as gross profit divided by sales and is interpreted as the number of pennies of gross profit made from each dollar of sales. The gross profit percentages for several large U.S. companies are given in Data Mining 5.1.

Test Your Intuition

Aside from simplifying the report, why else would companies sometimes group expenses under the summary heading of "selling, general, and administrative expenses"?

Selling, General, and Administrative Expense The heading "selling, general, and administrative expense" is often used as an overall label for a wide variety of operating expenses. For example, General Motors reports selling, general, and administrative expense of $16.2 billion in 1997 (see Exhibit 5-4). In the notes to its financial statements, GM reveals that this amount includes advertising expense of $4.1 billion and research and development expense of $8.2 billion. Included in this total would also be the cost of running the corporate offices and the salaries of the executives and staff working in company headquarters. Below is a brief description of some of the items that can be classified under selling, general, and administrative expense. Note that these items can also be reported separately in the income statement.

Data Mining 5.1

Gross Profit Percentage

1997

(dollars in billions)	Sales	Cost of Goods Sold	Gross Profit Percentage
Ford (manufacturer)	$122.9	$108.9	11.4
General Motors (manufacturer)	153.7	130.0	15.4
Wal-Mart (general retailer)	118.0	93.4	20.8
Safeway (supermarket)	22.5	16.1	28.4
Merck (pharmaceuticals)	23.6	11.8	50.0
McDonald's (fast food)	8.1	2.8	65.4
Microsoft (software)	11.4	1.1	90.4

Questions

1. How does the composition of cost of goods sold for General Motors differ from that for Wal-Mart?
2. When the retail price for a supermarket item is $1.00, what is the approximate wholesale cost of that item?
3. Occasionally, McDonald's sponsors a 2-for-1 promotion. Does McDonald's lose money when a thrifty customer refuses to buy anything except the promotion item?
4. What important costs do you think are excluded from Microsoft's cost of goods sold?

FYI

The international standard for R&D accounting differs from the U.S. standard in requiring some R&D to be recorded as an asset rather than as an expense. This same approach is also applied to some computer software R&D in the U.S. Chapter 10 has the details.

Research and Development Expense Companies perform research and development (R&D) in hopes of discovering new products or processes that will generate profits in the future. This description sounds suspiciously like the definition of an asset that was given in Chapter 2—"probable future economic benefit." The case of R&D illustrates that there is sometimes a fine line between spending money to buy an asset, which provides probable future economic benefit, and spending money that will be reported as an expense, which has helped generate revenue in the past but has no future economic benefit. With R&D, meticulous application of theoretical accounting concepts would require accountants to evaluate each individual R&D expenditure to determine whether it has created future economic benefit and therefore should be recorded as an asset rather than an expense. To avoid this potentially chaotic and time-consuming accounting exercise, the FASB has issued a blanket rule stating that U.S. companies should report all R&D expenditures as expenses in the income statement. The magnitude of R&D expense for selected U.S. companies is illustrated in Exhibit 5-6.

EXHIBIT 5-6 Research and Development Expense for Selected U.S. Companies

RESEARCH AND DEVELOPMENT EXPENSE

1997

(dollars in billions)	Research and Development Expense	As a Percentage of Sales
Microsoft	$1.9	16.9%
Intel	2.3	9.4%
Merck	1.7	7.1%
General Motors	8.2	5.3%
Ford	6.3	5.1%
DuPont	1.1	2.4%

CAUTION

For a service or a retail business, wages are reported as a separate expense. For a manufacturer, such as General Motors, wages are included in the computation of the cost of the products manufactured and sold.

Wages and Salaries Expense For many businesses, particularly service providers, wages and salaries constitute a major expense. In McDonald's 1997 income statement (included in Appendix A), we can see that payroll costs consume 24.9 cents of every McDonald's sales dollar. Typically, the expense reported for wages and salaries includes the cost of all employee benefits, such as pensions, employer-paid health care, etc.

Bad Debt Expense When a company extends credit to customers, there is always the risk that some customers will never pay. The amount of these uncollectible accounts is reported as bad debt expense. As illustrated in Chapter 8, the difficulty in accounting for bad debts is that at the end of each year the accountant must estimate the amount of new bad debts created that year, even though the ultimate collectibility of individual accounts may not be known for several years. In 1997, Chase Manhattan estimated that it suffered $804 million in new bad debts as part of its loan operations.

This section has given a sampling of expenses that are sometimes classified under "selling, general, and administrative expenses." To illustrate the wide variety of expenses one might see, a few additional examples from recent annual reports are listed below:

- In 1997, Consolidated Edison recorded a $47 million expense to represent the expected future cost of decontaminating and storing nuclear waste created in its power plants during that year.
- For the year ended February 2, 1997, Home Depot reported a $54.7 million expense called "pre-opening costs." This expense represents the cost associated with opening new stores during the year.
- In 1997, Philip Morris reported an expense of $1.457 billion called "settlement charges." This expense is related to the payouts Philip Morris is anticipating it will be required to make in connection with government litigation about the health effects of cigarettes.
- Sears reported a $475 million "reaffirmation charge" in 1997. This is the estimated cost Sears will have to bear in settling lawsuits claiming that the company violated the United States Bankruptcy Code in trying to collect from credit customers.

Depreciation Long-lived assets, such as buildings and equipment, are used up gradually by business operations over the course of years. Proper income measurement for a year requires a company to record some amount of depreciation expense to represent the wear and tear on long-lived assets during the year. For example, in 1997 General Motors reported depreciation expense of $16.6 billion. An important thing to remember about depreciation expense is that it doesn't involve any cash outflow—the amount of depreciation is only an accountant's estimate of wear and tear. As a result, companies with large amounts of building and equipment frequently report net income (which includes a large deduction for depreciation) that is much less than cash flow from operations. For example, 1997 cash flow from operations for General Motors was $16.5 billion, much greater than the $6.7 billion reported amount of net income.

Interest Expense Interest is the rent paid to use someone else's money. To accurately reflect the interest expense associated with a given year, accrual accounting requires that a company report the entire amount of interest that has accumulated for the year, whether that interest has been paid in cash or not. For example, if a company has a $1,000 loan outstanding for a year, and the interest rate on the loan is 10%, then interest expense for the year is $100 ($1,000 × 0.10)—and the same amount of interest expense is reported whether the $100 interest is paid in cash at the end of the year or is not paid until sometime the following year.

As mentioned earlier, interest expense is not considered to be an operating expense. Operating expenses relate to the unique nature of a particular business—the business processes and associated expenses at General Motors differ dramatically from those at Wal-Mart or at Microsoft. However, the process of borrowing money and paying interest is essentially the same in all businesses. Thus, interest expense has little to do with the essential character of a company's operations and is not classified as an operating expense.

In Exhibit 5-4, you can see that 1997 interest expense for General Motors was $6.1 billion. In its financial statement notes, General Motors reveals that this amount of interest accumulated on loans totaling $93.0 billion with interest rates ranging from 5.2 percent to 7.5 percent.

FYI

The bulk of GM's loans are denominated in U.S. dollars. However, General Motors has also borrowed significant quantities of Canadian dollars, Deutsche marks, British pounds sterling, and Australian dollars.

Income Tax Expense Income tax expense is the sum of all the income tax consequences of all transactions undertaken by a company during a year. Some of those tax consequences may occur in the current year, and some may occur in future years. For example, in 1997 General Motors generated enough taxable income to require it to pay $3.3 billion in income taxes for the year—$1.3 billion to the U.S. federal government, $0.2 billion to U.S. state and local governments, and $1.8 billion to foreign governments. However, in 1997 General Motors also entered into transactions creating tax deductions that GM can use in future years to reduce the income tax it must pay by $2.2 billion. So, as seen in Exhibit 5-4, General Motors reports income tax expense for 1997 of $1.1 billion ($3.3 billion payable during the year less $2.2 billion in tax reductions in future years), which represents the net tax effects of all transactions entered into during the year.

Gains and Losses

Revenues and expenses are created by activities undertaken in the normal course of business. When a company makes or loses money on activities that are peripheral to its primary operations, the amount is classified as a **gain** or a **loss** instead of as a revenue or an expense.

The most common source of gains and losses is a company selling a long-term asset for more or less than the recorded cost of the asset. For example, in 1997 General Motors sold its Hughes Defense division to Raytheon, a large defense contractor. GM made the sale for $4.3 billion more than the amount at which the Hughes Defense division assets were recorded in GM's books, so a $4.3 billion gain was recognized on the sale. This gain is included as part of "other income" in General Motors' 1997 income statement (see Exhibit 5-4).

Restructuring Charges A particularly controversial type of loss arises when companies propose a restructuring of their operations. A restructuring typically causes some assets to lose value because they no longer fit in a company's strategic plans. A restructuring also creates additional costs associated with the termination or relocation of employees. For example, in the notes to its financial statements, General Motors disclosed that its operating expenses for 1997 include a restructuring charge of $6.4 billion resulting from a series of three "Competitiveness Studies" that suggested a refocus of some operations.

FYI

In a speech given on September 28, 1998, Arthur Levitt, chairman of the SEC, identified five popular areas of "Accounting Hocus-Pocus" used by companies to manipulate reported earnings. Number one on that list was big bath restructuring charges.

The controversy over **restructuring charges** stems from the fact that companies exercise considerable discretion in determining the amount of a restructuring charge. The fear is that companies can use this discretion as a tool for manipulating the amount of reported net income. For example, companies that are already faced with the prospect of poor reported performance for a year may intentionally OVERestimate the cost of a restructuring. The motivation for this so-called big bath approach is that if a company is going to report poor results anyway, it makes sense to gather up all the bad news in the company and report it at the same time, thus diluting the effect of any single bad news item. If this big bath approach is followed, reported performance in the years following the big bath year will appear much improved, in large part because the big bath restructuring charge resulted in many expenses of future years being estimated and reported as one lump sum in the big bath year. Examples of companies taking restructuring charges in recent years include Eastman Kodak ($1.290 billion in 1997), AT&T ($3.023 billion in 1995), and IBM ($445 million in 1997, $1.491 billion in 1996, and $2.119 billion in 1995).

"Below-the-Line" Items

As mentioned earlier in the chapter, "below-the-line" items are excluded from income from continuing operations because they are unlikely to recur in the future. Each of the three categories of below-the-line items is discussed below.

Income from Discontinued Operations Occasionally a company makes a decision to simply get out of a certain line of business completely. For example, on June 7, 1996, General Motors split off the operations of its Electronic Data Systems (EDS) division. After June 7, 1996, any financial statement user attempting to forecast GM's future performance must be careful to exclude the historical results of the **discontinued operations** of EDS. The solution is to report the EDS results in a separate category called income from discontinued operations. In GM's income statement in Exhibit 5-4 it can be seen that income from the discontinued EDS operations was $900 million in 1995 and $10 million in the first five months of 1996. The effect of this segregation of the EDS results is that GM's income from continuing operations for 1995, 1996, and 1997 contains the results of only those business segments that are still part of GM's future plans as of the end of 1997.

In some cases, the disposal of a business segment may require several years to actually complete. In the year that the initial decision is made to dispose of the segment, company management must estimate two things:

- income (or loss) from continuing to operate the segment until it is finally disposed, and
- the gain (or loss) to be realized upon sale of the assets of the segment.

Test Your Intuition

In what way does conservatism result in biased financial statements? In what way does conservatism improve the quality of financial statement information?

If the net of these two items is a projected loss, that loss is reported in its entirety in the year that the disposal decision is made. If the net result is a projected gain, that gain is not recognized until the years in which it actually occurs. This practice is an example of accounting conservatism, meaning that accounting rules frequently result in the reporting of losses (bad news) as soon as they can be estimated whereas gains (good news) are not reported until they actually occur.

Extraordinary Items **Extraordinary items** are gains and losses that result from transactions that are both unusual in nature and infrequent in occurrence. Because these transactions are unusual and infrequent, they need to be separated from continuing operations so that investors can better use the income statement to predict future income. The criteria for classifying an item as extraordinary are quite restrictive in order to prevent companies from selectively classifying all losses as extraordinary in an attempt to remove them from the computation of income from continuing operations. An unusual event or transaction is one that is highly abnormal or is clearly only incidentally related to a company's ordinary and typical activities. To be infrequent in occurrence, an event should be of a type that would not reasonably be expected to recur in the foreseeable future.

FYI

Because of a provision in the accounting rules, all gains and losses that result when a company pays off a loan early must be reported as extraordinary items. These early extinguishment gains and losses comprise the bulk (over 90%) of reported extraordinary items.

In Exhibit 5-4, you can see that General Motors reports no extraordinary items in the period from 1995 through 1997. In fact, examples of extraordinary items are, by their very nature, difficult to find. In 1996, Chrysler reported an extraordinary loss of $191 million resulting from its early repayment of a $550 million debt.

Cumulative Effect of a Change in Accounting Principle In accounting for some items, a company has a choice among acceptable accounting methods. As you will see throughout this book, there are different methods of determining bad debts, cost of goods sold, and depreciation expense. Once a particular method is chosen, accountants feel that it should be consistently used unless a change to a different method is preferable, or unless revision of a particular accounting standard mandates the change. When there is a change in accounting method, a company is required to compute how much net income would have been different in past years if the new accounting method had been used all along. These differences are summed and the total difference is reported in the current year's income statement as a **cumulative effect of a change in accounting principle.** Because this cumulative effect yields no information about a company's continuing profit potential, it is excluded from the computation of income from continuing operations.

Test Your Intuition

Can you think of a better way to appropriately reflect the effects on past years of a change in accounting principles this year? Describe your superior method.

In Exhibit 5-4, you can see that in 1995 General Motors reported a decrease in income of $52 million from the cumulative effect of an accounting change. This particular change involved a revision in the way that GM accounts for its sales of cars to rental car companies. General Motors also has the distinction of having reported the largest cumulative effect of all time—a $20.8 billion reduction in net income in 1992 stemming from a change in the way GM accounts for its obligation to pay for the health care of retired workers. By the way, as with most accounting principle changes made by companies, both of these accounting changes made by General Motors were made in response to accounting rule changes by the standard setters. Accordingly, GM had no choice but to make the changes.

FYI

Because all below-the-line items are reported net of taxes, the income tax expense reported in the income statement is actually the tax expense associated with income from continuing operations.

Reporting Net of Taxes Note that the $20.8 billion number given for GM's 1992 cumulative effect does not match the $33 billion number used earlier in the chapter to describe the same cumulative effect. The difference stems from the fact that the $20.8 billion amount is the net effect of the accounting change, after taking account of the offsetting tax effect. Specifically, the fact that GM is required to report an additional expense of $33 billion also means that GM's income taxes should decrease. Therefore, the total impact of the $33 billion expense increase is only $20.8 billion after subtracting the estimated tax benefit of $12.2 billion. Similarly, the $10 million amount of income from discontinued operations reported in GM's 1996 income statement in Exhibit 5-4 actually represents $24 million in income less $14 million in income taxes related to the discontinued operation. Extraordinary items are also reported net of taxes in the income statement.

Comprehensive Income

As mentioned earlier, comprehensive income reflects the overall change in a company's wealth during a period and includes items that, in general, arise from changes in market conditions unrelated to the business operations of a company. Three items that are excluded from the computation of net income but that are included in comprehensive income are discussed below.

Foreign Currency Translation Adjustment During 1997, there was a decline in the value of the currencies in the countries where General Motors has foreign subsidiaries. Thus, the U.S. dollar value of the net assets of those subsidiaries declined by $775 million during the year. This decline was not the result of poor business performance by General Motors; it was simply a function of the ebb and flow of the worldwide economy. This "loss" is not reported as part of net income but is included in the computation of comprehensive income. Ford was exposed to the same market conditions during the year and reported a reduction in comprehensive income for foreign currency changes of $1.038 billion.

Unrealized Gains and Losses on Available-For-Sale Securities In order to maintain a liquid reserve of assets that can be converted into cash if needed, most companies purchase an investment portfolio of stocks and bonds. For example, as of December 31, 1997, General Motors owned $1.7 billion in bonds issued by the U.S. government, $1.6 billion in bonds issued by state and local governments, and $4.5 billion in other corporate bonds and stocks. For accounting purposes, GM classified the securities in this investment portfolio as "available for sale," meaning GM does not intend to actively trade the securities in this portfolio but they are available to be sold if the need for cash arises. These securities are reported in the balance sheet at their current market value. As the market value of these securities fluctuates, GM experiences "unrealized" gains and losses. An "unrealized" gain or loss is the same as what is sometimes called a paper gain or loss, meaning that because the security has not yet been sold, the gain or loss is only on paper. Because available-for-sale securities are not part of a company's operations, the associated unrealized gains and losses are excluded from the computation of net income and are instead reported as part of comprehensive income. During 1997, GM recorded an $81 million gain on its available-for-sale portfolio; this amount was reported as an increase in comprehensive income. Berkshire Hathaway has a very large investment portfolio and reported an unrealized gain on available-for-sale securities of $6.054 billion in 1997 as part of comprehensive income.

Deferred Gains and Losses on Derivative Instruments Companies frequently use derivative instruments in order to hedge their exposure to risk stemming from changes in prices and rates. As price and rate change, the value of a derivative based on that price or rate also changes. As with available-for-sale securities, these value changes give rise to unrealized gains and losses. In some cases, these unrealized gains and losses on derivatives are included in net income and are offset against gains on losses on the items that were being hedged. In other cases, the reporting of the unrealized gains and losses on derivatives in net income is delayed until a subsequent year; in the meantime, the unrealized gains and losses are reported as part of comprehensive income. A further discussion of derivatives is given in Chapter 12.

CAUTION

Remember that the comprehensive income items do not appear on the income statement and are explicitly *excluded* from the computation of net income.

A few other comprehensive income items exist in addition to the three described above. For example, in 1997 General Motors reports a reduction in comprehensive income of $572 million stemming from an increase that was made to GM's reported pension liability. The key point to remember is that these items represent changes in assets and liabilities reported in the balance sheet that are not deemed to reflect a company's own economic performance and are therefore excluded from the computation of net income.

Earnings per Share

An individual shareholder is interested in how much of a company's net income is associated with his or her ownership interest. As a result, the income statement reports **earnings per share (EPS)**, which is the amount of net income associated with each share of stock. For example, in Exhibit 5-4 it can be seen that EPS for GM in 1997 was $8.70. This means that an owner of 100 shares of GM stock has claim on $870 ($8.70 EPS × 100 shares) of the $6.7 billion in GM net income for 1997.

Companies often disclose two earnings per share numbers. Basic EPS reports earnings based solely on shares actually outstanding during the year. In Exhibit 5-4 you can see that GM's basic EPS in 1997 was $8.70. Basic earnings per share is computed by dividing income available to common shareholders (net income less dividends paid to or promised to preferred shareholders) by the average number of shares outstanding during the period.

Diluted earnings per share reflect the existence of stock options or other rights that can be converted into shares in the future. For example, in addition to having shares outstanding, a company can also have granted stock options that allow the option holders to buy shares of stock at some predetermined price. At present, the option holders don't own shares of stock, but they can acquire them from the company at any time. In other cases, a company might borrow money but also give the right to the lender to exchange the loan for shares of stock at some predetermined price. Diluted EPS is computed to give financial statement users an idea about the potential impact on EPS of the exercise of existing stock options or other rights to acquire shares.

General Motors reports basic earnings per share and diluted earnings per share in 1997 of $8.70 and $8.62, respectively (see Exhibit 5-4). If all the options and other convertible items that are likely to be converted were in fact converted into shares of GM stock, the effect on GM's earnings per share would be to reduce it by $0.08. A small difference of $0.08 (less than 1 percent of basic EPS) indicates that General Motors does not have a lot of options and convertible securities outstanding. On the other hand, Intel reported basic and diluted EPS in 1997 of $4.25 and $3.87, respectively. The difference of $0.38 (or almost 9 percent of basic earnings per share) indicates that Intel has a lot of securities outstanding that could possibly dilute earnings per share.

Historically, the accounting rules in the United States governing the computation of EPS have been unnecessarily complex. In the mid 1990s, the FASB initiated a project, in conjunction with the IASC, to both improve U.S. accounting practice with respect to EPS and to increase international agreement on this important accounting issue. In 1997, the FASB and IASC issued almost identical standards prescribing the methods of computing the basic and diluted EPS numbers outlined above. Not only did this represent a big improvement in U.S. accounting practice, but it also was a milestone in that it was the first time that the FASB and the IASC worked jointly to issue an accounting standard.

Format of the Income Statement

(Key Point #3)

As with the balance sheet, management has considerable discretion over the exact format of the income statement. The format used by General Motors in Exhibit 5-4 is called a **single-step income statement.** With this format, all revenues are grouped together, all expenses are grouped together, and net income is computed as the difference between total revenues and total expenses. Note that income tax expense is shown separately, to emphasize the fact that the amount of income tax expense depends on the amount of income before taxes.

The single-step format is simple, but it does not highlight the different measures of "profit" or "income" discussed earlier in the chapter. An alternate format is called the **multiple-step income statement.** With a multiple-step income statement, the revenue and expense items are arranged to highlight important profit relationships and income numbers such as gross profit and operating income. The income statement for General Motors is rearranged into a multiple-step format in Exhibit 5-7.

EXHIBIT 5-7 Multiple-Step Income Statement for General Motors

GENERAL MOTORS CORPORATION AND SUBSIDIARIES
CONSOLIDATED STATEMENTS OF INCOME
MULTIPLE-STEP FORMAT

	Years Ended December 31		
	1997	**1996**	**1995**
(dollars in millions)			
Net sales of manufactured products	$153,683	$145,341	$143,666
Cost of sales and other operating charges, exclusive of items listed in operating expenses	130,028	123,195	121,300
Gross profit	$ 23,655	$ 22,146	$ 22,366
Operating expenses:			
Selling, general, and administrative expenses	16,192	14,580	12,550
Depreciation and amortization expenses	16,616	11,840	11,213
Operating income (loss)	$ (9,153)	$ (4,274)	$ (1,397)
Financial services revenue	12,762	12,674	11,664
Other income	11,729	5,998	4,924
Interest expense	(6,113)	(5,695)	(5,182)
Other deductions	(1,511)	(2,083)	(1,678)
Total nonoperating revenues and expenses	16,867	10,894	9,728
Income from Continuing Operations before Income Taxes and Minority Interests	7,714	6,620	8,331
Income taxes	(1,069)	(1,723)	(2,316)
Minority interests	53	56	18
Income from Continuing Operations before Cumulative Effect of Accounting Change	6,698	4,953	6,033
Income from discontinued operations	-0-	10	900
Cumulative effect of accounting change	-0-	-0-	(52)
Net Income	$ 6,698	$ 4,963	$ 6,881

FYI

Ford presents its income statement in a format that reports the revenues and expenses associated with manufacturing operations and financial operations separately.

The format of a multiple-step income statement emphasizes the presentation of gross profit and operating income. The objective of the multiple-step format is to make it easier for financial statement users to see key relationships. For example, in GM's case the multiple-step format highlights the importance of nonmanufacturing activities to GM's overall profitability. In fact, with the simple reformatting performed here, it appears that GM's core manufacturing operations lose money every year. This is somewhat misleading because undoubtedly some of the selling, general, and administrative expense is actually associated with nonmanufacturing activities. Nonetheless, you can see that, in GM's case, the multiple-step format brings out relationships among income statement items that aren't apparent when the data are presented in a single-step format.

Revenue Recognition and Matching

(Key Point #4)

An important function of accrual accounting is making sure that revenues and expenses are reported during the correct time period. If an income statement is to accurately reflect a company's performance during a certain year, then it is crucial that only revenues and expenses associated with that year be reported. The issue of when revenues and expenses should be recognized is covered in this section.

Revenue Recognition

Revenue recognition was discussed in Chapter 2. To review, accountants use the following two criteria to determine when revenue should be recognized:

1. The promised work must be done before revenue is recognized.
2. Cash collectibility should be reasonably assured before revenue is recognized.

The application of these two criteria is illustrated with the following examples:

- *Milk.* When a supermarket, such as Safeway, sells a gallon of milk for cash, the work (delivery of the milk to the customer) and cash collection are both completed at the time of the sale. Thus, revenue is recognized immediately.
- *Furniture.* Furniture retailers, such as Sears, often offer special deals in which a customer can take furniture home immediately and not make any payments until, say, six months in the future. From the standpoint of Sears, the work (delivery of the furniture to the customer) is done at the time of sale. If Sears is reasonably sure, based on historical experience, that the customer will ultimately pay for the furniture, then revenue should be recognized immediately at the time of the sale. If cash collection is not reasonably assured (such as is the case for some rent-to-own companies that sell to customers with a past history of credit problems), then revenue should be recognized gradually as the cash is collected.
- *Airline ticket.* Cash collection is not an issue for airline companies because passengers are required to pay for their tickets in advance. However, the airline company does not recognize the ticket proceeds as revenue until after the work (providing air transportation) is completed.
- *Football season ticket.* Fans lucky enough to have season tickets to Green Bay Packers games are required to pay for their tickets before the season even begins. However, the work (providing football entertainment) is done only gradually as the season progresses. Thus, the Packers recognize revenue from their season ticketholders proportionately, depending on the fraction of the games that have been played.
- *Software.* When you buy Microsoft software, you actually buy both the software and technical support. Thus, Microsoft recognizes a portion (80 percent for

the Office 97 software) of the software price as revenue immediately upon delivery of the software to you. The rest of the software price is recognized as revenue gradually over time as the technical support service is provided.

Expense Recognition

The concept typically used in practice to determine when an expense should be recognized is the **matching** concept. The idea behind matching is that an expense should be recognized in the same period in which the revenue it was used to generate is recognized. For example, if General Motors recognizes revenue from the sale of a car, then the cost of that car should be recognized as an expense in the same period. If McDonald's recognizes revenue from the sale of fast food, then the labor cost associated with the sale of that fast food should be presented in McDonald's income statement during the same period.

Some expenses are associated more with a time period than they are with a specific revenue-generating activity. For example, depreciation expense associated with the wear and tear on a factory building is related more to the passage of time than to the production of a particular group of products. Similarly, insurance expense is associated with reducing a company's risk for a certain period and cannot be matched with specific products or activities. With these types of expenses, the most reasonable approach is to systematically allocate the total cost over the periods expected to be benefited. Thus, the cost of a building expected to be in service for 30 years is recognized as depreciation expense systematically over those 30 years.

FYI

For advertising costs associated with direct mail campaigns to targeted customers, specific advertising expenses can be linked with specific sales, so the direct matching approach is used.

Some expenses are extremely difficult to match with specific revenues and even with specific time periods. For example, advertising is expected to increase future sales, but it is usually impossible to link a specific sale with a specific piece of advertising. In cases such as these, no attempt is made to match the expense with an associated revenue. Instead, the expense is recognized immediately in the period in which it is incurred. Other examples of expenses that are recognized immediately are research and development and the salaries of top executives.

In summary, the three methods used to determine when to recognize an expense are:

1. Direct matching, as with cost of goods sold
2. Systematic allocation, as with depreciation
3. Immediate recognition, as with advertising

Transaction Analysis
(Key Point #5)

Transaction analysis was introduced in Chapter 4. The accounting equation was used to critically and systematically analyze the impact of business events on a company's reported financial performance and position. The analysis of transactions undertaken on the first day of business for the hypothetical company Veda Landscape Solutions is summarized in Exhibit 5-8 (which is a duplication of Exhibit 4-11).

Notice from the transactions in Exhibit 5-8 that Veda hasn't actually done any business yet. All of the transactions considered thus far have just been in preparation for doing business. As a result, no sales have yet been made and no expenses have been incurred.

Analysis of revenue and expense transactions requires the use of the **expanded accounting equation:**

Assets = Liabilities + Paid-in Capital + (Revenues – Expenses – Dividends)

Business Context 5.2

Why Doesn't the U.S. Government Use Accrual Accounting?

In February 1993, the Office of Management and Budget forecast that the budget deficit for the U.S. government for fiscal 1993 would total $332 billion. The deficit was projected to decrease to only $205 billion in 1996. This inability of the federal government to balance its budget prompted a flood of proposals, accusations, campaign slogans, and TV infomercials. At the time, no one imagined that there would be a budget surplus by 1998.

In the midst of the budget deficit despair years, one suggested remedy was that the U.S. government adopt accrual accounting. The cash basis used by the federal government makes no attempt to differentiate between operating expenditures, such as current-period salaries, and capital expenditures, such as amounts spent on interstate highway construction. All cash expenditures are lumped together, the total is subtracted from total cash receipts, and the difference is called the deficit or the surplus. Accrual accounting, it is claimed, would yield a more accurate picture of the government's financial health.

This call for accrual accounting by the federal government was not a new one. In 1975, Arthur Andersen, the public accounting firm, assisted the U.S. government in preparing a prototype set of financial statements using accrual accounting. These financial statements are still prepared annually but are not widely disseminated by the government. A look at the 1991 balance sheet reveals why this might be so. Total reported assets were $1.394 trillion while total liabilities were $4.540 trillion, resulting in a negative equity of $3.146 trillion. Thus far, the only national government to adopt the accrual basis for its official accounting system is New Zealand.

Some claim that the use of accrual accounting would make the reported federal budget numbers less subject to manipulation. One of the most blatant acts of manipulation occurred in 1987 when Congress ordered the Department of Defense to change its payday from the last day in September, which is the last day in the federal government's fiscal year, to the first day in October. Since the cash basis requires that expenditures be recognized in the period they are paid instead of when they are incurred, this simple delay in mailing out the paychecks reduced the reported deficit for fiscal 1987 by $1 billion.

The cash basis is certainly subject to some manipulation, but the same can be said of the accrual basis. If the federal government were to adopt the accrual basis, cash outlays would then have to be classified as capital expenditures or operating expenditures. For capital expenditures, lawmakers would be required to estimate depreciable lives, among other important variables. Imagine a Congress empowered to make accounting judgments—scary.

Questions

1. The "equity" in the 1991 prototype balance sheet of the U.S. federal government was a negative $3.146 trillion. What aspects of the historical cost accounting model might have caused this prototype balance sheet to look worse than it really is?
2. How can Congress take advantage of cash-basis accounting to manipulate the reported deficit? How could Congress use accrual accounting to manipulate the reported deficit?

Sources: "Clinton's Budget at a Glance," *The Wall Street Journal*, February 19, 1993, p. A4.

"Balancing the Government's Books," *The Economist*, January 25, 1992.

Charles A. Bowsher, "Commentary on the Federal Budget: Presenting and Facing the Facts," *Accounting Horizons*, June 1990, p. 96.

web search

The Congressional Budget Office (CBO) is charged with providing the U.S. Congress with the information and estimates necessary to manage the federal budget. Access the CBO's Web site at www.cbo.gov and find out whether the CBO is currently forecasting a budget surplus or a budget deficit.

EXHIBIT 5-8 Spreadsheet for Analysis of Initial Transactions of Veda Landscape Solutions

	Cash	Inventory	Prepaid Insurance	Land	Buildings	Equipment	Total Assets	Accounts Payable	Bank Loan Payable	Mortgage Payable	Paid-In Capital	Total Liabilities & Equity
1. Initial investment	$700,000						$700,000				$700,000	$700,000
2. Bank loan	300,000						300,000		$300,000			300,000
3. Purchased warehouse	(100,000)			$50,000	$400,000		350,000			$350,000		350,000
4. Purchased equipment	(650,000)					$650,000	0					0
5. Hired employees							0					0
6. Leased truck							0					0
7. Purchased inventory	(10,000)	$90,000					80,000	$80,000				80,000
8. Paid for insurance	(15,000)		$15,000				0					0
	$225,000	$90,000	$15,000	$50,000	$400,000	$650,000	$1,430,000	$80,000	$300,000	$350,000	$700,000	$1,430,000

The insight behind this expanded accounting equation is that equity can be decomposed into paid-in capital and retained earnings and that revenues, expenses, and dividends are just temporary subcategories of retained earnings. This expanded accounting equation will be used to analyze the following additional events during the first year of business for Veda Landscape Solutions. [*Note*: The list starts with Item 9 because Items 1 through 8 were analyzed in Chapter 4.]

January 1, 2001, through December 31, 2001:

1–8. See page 132 in Chapter 4.

9. Purchased additional inventory items for retail resale for a total of $1,300,000. The entire amount was put on suppliers' accounts, so no cash was paid at the time of purchase.
10. Sold inventory costing $800,000 to retail customers for $1,100,000. The customers paid $200,000 in cash and the remaining $900,000 was put on the customers' accounts.
11. Performed landscaping consulting services for several large clients. Billed these clients $200,000 for services.
12. Collected cash of $160,000 for the consulting services billings. Veda expects to collect the remainder early next year.
13. Provided landscaping work for a variety of customers. The total fees for these services were $500,000, of which the entire amount was collected in cash. As part of the landscaping work, used some of the retail inventory (mulch, fertilizer, etc.). The total cost of the inventory used was $100,000.
14. Collected $820,000 cash from customers as payment on their accounts.
15. Paid a total of $1,200,000 cash to suppliers as payment on account for the inventory purchases.
16. Paid employees a total of $460,000 cash for wages. As of the end of the year, employees had earned an additional $40,000, which Veda will not pay until the first week in January 2002.
17. Paid $9,600 cash in lease payments for a large truck.
18. Cash paid for advertising, utilities, and office supplies totaled $150,000.
19. During the year, Veda developed a reputation for doing high-quality work. In fact, Veda's reputation and method of business were attractive enough that a landscaping business in another city asked for permission to use Veda's name and operating methods. A franchise agreement was signed on December 1. Veda received $50,000 cash and agreed to help the franchisee open its store and get its systems up and running. After that, Veda will have no direct involvement in the operation of the franchise store. The franchise store will open in early March of next year.

20. On December 31, Veda calculated how much interest has accumulated on its loans during the year. Interest on its $300,000 bank loan is $30,000 [$300,000 × 0.10] and interest on its $350,000 mortgage loan is $28,000 [$350,000 × 0.08]. Interest on both of these loans will be paid on January 1, 2002.
21. On December 31, Veda noted that the $15,000 one-year insurance policy purchased on the first day of the year had expired.
22. On December 31, Veda estimated how much wear and tear had occurred on its warehouse and equipment during the year. The estimate of $150,000 was computed as follows:

	Cost	Estimated Useful Life	Depreciation for the Year
Buildings	$400,000	20 years	$ 20,000
Equipment	650,000	5 years	130,000
			$150,000

Veda also has land costing $50,000. Veda has assumed that this land will not depreciate.

23. On December 31, Veda paid a $5,000 cash dividend to the investors.

Analyzing the Impact of Transactions on the Income Statement

The impact of each of these events on Veda's income statement and balance sheet is illustrated in the spreadsheet contained in Exhibit 5-9. A description of the analysis of each item is given below.

1–8. See page 133 in Chapter 4.
9. The Inventory account is increased by $1,300,000 because Veda has more inventory. Also, because the Inventory was purchased entirely on account, the amount of Accounts Payable has also increased by $1,300,000.
10. As a result of this business transaction, Veda has added to two asset accounts—an increase in Cash of $200,000 and an increase in the asset Accounts Receivable of $900,000. These assets were not borrowed and they were not invested; instead, they were generated in the course of doing business. When assets come into a business in this way, their source is recorded as revenue. In this case, the account Sales Revenue is increased by $1,100,000. The Sales Revenue account is a subcategory of Retained Earnings and represents an increase in the equity of the business that has occurred because of conducting business operations.

    In exchange for the Cash and Accounts Receivable, Veda gave up Inventory costing $800,000. This is reflected by reducing the asset Inventory by $800,000. This asset was consumed in the course of business operations, so it is also reflected as the expense Cost of Goods Sold. The $800,000 amount under Cost of Goods Sold is shown as a subtraction because it represents a reduction in equity. As with the Sales Revenue account, the Cost of Goods Sold expense account is a subcategory of Retained Earnings. When put together, the $1,100,000 equity increase recorded as Sales Revenue and the $800,000 equity decrease recorded as Cost of Goods Sold mean that this operating transaction increased the equity of the business by $300,000 ($1,100,000—$800,000).

11. The landscaping consulting services represent another operating transaction. The asset Accounts Receivable is increased by $200,000 because Veda expects to collect this much from clients as a result of the services performed. Equity is also increased by this transaction and is shown as Consulting Revenue of $200,000. This source of revenue is given a different name from the Sales Revenue recorded in (10) so that Veda can tabulate the amount of revenue earned by each different type of business activity.
12. Veda collected $160,000 of the $200,000 earned in (11). This collection is recorded as an increase in Cash and a decrease in Accounts Receivable. Note that no additional revenue is recorded; revenue is recorded when work is done, not when cash is collected.

EXHIBIT 5-9 Spreadsheet for Transaction Analysis

	Cash	Accounts Receivable	Inventory	Prepaid Insurance	Land	Buildings	Equipment	TOTAL ASSETS
Balance, January 1	225,000		90,000	15,000	50,000	400,000	650,000	1,430,000
9. Purchased inventory			1,300,000					1,300,000
10. Sold inventory	200,000	900,000	(800,000)					300,000
11. Consulting services		200,000						200,000
12. Collected consulting	160,000	(160,000)						0
13. Landscaping work	500,000		(100,000)					400,000
14. Collected retail	820,000	(820,000)						0
15. Paid suppliers	(1,200,000)							(1,200,000)
16. Paid employees	(460,000)							(460,000)
17. Paid lease	(9,600)							(9,600)
18. Paid SG&A	(150,000)							(150,000)
19. Franchise	50,000							50,000
20. Accrued interest								0
21. Insurance expired				(15,000)				(15,000)
22. Depreciation						(20,000)	(130,000)	(150,000)
23. Dividends	(5,000)							(5,000)
Balance, December 31	135,400	120,000	490,000	0	50,000	380,000	520,000	1,690,400

	Accounts Payable	Wages Payable	Unearned Franchise Revenue	Interest Payable	Bank Loan Payable	Mortgage Payable	Paid-In Capital	Sales Revenue
Balance, January 1	80,000				300,000	350,000	700,000	
9. Purchased inventory	1,300,000							
10. Sold inventory								1,100,000
11. Consulting services								
12. Collected consulting								
13. Landscaping work								
14. Collected retail								
15. Paid suppliers	(1,200,000)							
16. Paid employees		40,000						
17. Paid lease								
18. Paid SG&A								
19. Franchise			50,000					
20. Accrued interest				58,000				
21. Insurance expired								
22. Depreciation								
23. Dividends								
Balance, December 31	180,000	40,000	50,000	58,000	300,000	350,000	700,000	1,100,000

13. The landscaping work is a third source of revenue for Veda. Cash is increased by $500,000 and Landscaping Revenue of $500,000 is recorded. Again, the $500,000 in revenue represents an increase in equity through business operations. As part of the landscaping work, $100,000 in inventory was used. Note that this inventory was not sold as it was in transaction (10). Therefore, to distinguish this use of inventory from the Cost of Goods Sold recorded earlier, the $100,000 reduction in inventory is recorded as Landscaping Supplies Expense. This distinction between Cost of Goods Sold and Landscaping Supplies Expense allows Veda to match expenses with the revenue they were used to generate. This matching of revenues and expenses enables Veda to analyze the profitability of each of its different business activities.
14. As in (12), Cash is increased and Accounts Receivable is decreased when cash is collected from customers who had previously purchased a product or service on account.
15. When Veda makes payments on its own accounts, Cash is decreased and the amount of Accounts Payable is also decreased. Note that Veda records an expense when inventory is used in business operations, not when cash is paid to purchase inventory.
16. Employees earned a total of $500,000 in wages during the year; this amount is reported as Wages Expense. As with other expenses, Wages Expense is a subcategory of Retained Earnings and reflects a decrease in equity because resources were consumed in the course of business. Cash is reduced by $460,000, and the liability account Wages Payable is increased by $40,000. Note that Veda records Wages Expense for the amount of wages earned by employees during the year, not for the amount of cash actually paid. This aspect of accrual accounting results in reported expenses being the accountant's estimate of the economic value of resources used in generating revenue rather than a mere tabulation of the cash paid during the year.
17. The $9,600 cash paid for the use of the truck is reported as a reduction in Cash and as part of the general expense total titled Selling, General, and Administrative Expense (SG&A Expense).

RETAINED EARNINGS									
Consulting Revenue	**Landscaping Revenue**	**Cost of Goods Sold**	**Landscaping Supplies Expense**	**Wages Expense**	**SG&A Expense**	**Interest Expense**	**Depreciation Expense**	**Dividends**	**TOTAL LIABILITIES & EQUITY**
									1,430,000
									1,300,000
		(800,000)							300,000
200,000									200,000
									0
	500,000		(100,000)						400,000
									0
									(1,200,000)
				(500,000)					(460,000)
					(9,600)				(9,600)
					(150,000)				(150,000)
									50,000
						(58,000)			0
					(15,000)				(15,000)
							(150,000)		(150,000)
								(5,000)	(5,000)
200,000	500,000	(800,000)	(100,000)	(500,000)	(174,600)	(58,000)	(150,000)	(5,000)	1,690,400

18. The $150,000 cash paid for advertising, utilities, and office supplies is also reported as part of Selling, General, and Administrative Expense.
19. Veda entered into a franchise agreement and received $50,000 cash, so the account Cash is increased by $50,000. However, this amount is NOT reported as Franchising Revenue because Veda has not yet done the work promised in the franchise agreement. In other words, Veda has not earned the $50,000 yet. Accordingly, a liability, Unearned Franchise Revenue, of $50,000 is reported, representing Veda's obligation to provide service in the future in connection with the franchise agreement.
20. As of December 31, 2001, Veda owes $58,000 ($30,000 + $28,000) in interest. Accordingly, a $58,000 liability called Interest Payable is recorded. This $58,000 represents the interest charge associated with Veda's use of borrowed money during the year. This interest is a cost of doing business for the year and is recorded as Interest Expense. Note that the expense is recorded even though the interest has not yet been paid in cash. To repeat, accrual accounting seeks to report an estimate of the economic value of services consumed during the year, not simply a list of cash paid.
21. The $15,000 insurance policy, recorded as an asset when it was initially purchased at the beginning of the year, has been used during the year. Thus, the $15,000 cost should be recorded as Insurance Expense for the year. In addition, the $15,000 Prepaid Insurance asset is reduced by $15,000 because the policy has now expired and has no further value.
22. Veda roughly estimates that $150,000 worth of the service potential of the buildings and equipment has been consumed during the year. This amount is recorded as Depreciation Expense and also as a reduction in the recorded amounts of the Buildings and Equipment. As illustrated later, when a balance sheet is prepared, these reductions are shown under the label "Accumulated Depreciation."
23. Cash dividends are *not* considered to be an expense of doing business. Therefore, they are *never* shown on the income statement. Veda's payment of cash dividends is shown as a $5,000 reduction in Cash, along with a $5,000 reduction in equity under the Dividends account. Like revenues and expenses, the Dividends account is a subcategory of Retained Earnings. Unlike revenues and expense, the amount of dividends is not shown in the income statement.

The key points to remember concerning the recording of revenues and expenses is that revenues increase and expenses decrease the Retained Earnings portion of equity. Dividends also decrease Retained Earnings. As illustrated in Chapter 7, part of the end-of-year bookkeeping process is that all of the revenue, expense, and dividend accounts are summarized and formally transferred to the Retained Earnings balance.

The revenue and expense data from the spreadsheet in Exhibit 5-9 can be used to construct an income statement for Veda Landscape Solutions for the year 2001. The income statement in Exhibit 5-10 is a single-step statement since all revenues are grouped together and all expenses are grouped together.

EXHIBIT 5-10 Income Statement for the Year 2001 for Veda Landscape Solutions

VEDA LANDSCAPE SOLUTIONS INCOME STATEMENT For the Year Ended December 31, 2001	
Sales Revenue	$1,100,000
Consulting Revenue	200,000
Landscaping Revenue	500,000
Total Revenues	$1,800,000
Expenses:	
Cost of Goods Sold	$800,000
Landscaping Supplies Expense	100,000
Wages Expense	500,000
Selling, General, and Administrative Expense	174,600
Interest Expense	58,000
Depreciation Expense	150,000
Total Expenses	1,782,600
Net Income	$ 17,400

Forecasting The Future

(Key Point #6)

Financial statements report past results, but financial statement users are often interested in what will happen in the future. Therefore, an important skill for financial statement users to develop is using past financial statements to predict the future. This section gives a simple demonstration of how to use historical financial statement information to forecast a future income statement and balance sheet.

The key to a good financial statement forecast is identifying which underlying factors determine the level of a certain revenue or expense. For example, the level of cost of goods sold is closely tied to the level of sales, whereas the level of interest expense is only weakly tied to sales and is instead a direct function of the level of interest-bearing debt.

Most forecasting exercises start with a forecast of sales. The sales forecast indicates how fast the company is expected to grow and represents the general volume of activity expected in the company. This expected volume of activity influences the amount of assets that are needed to do business, which in turn determines the level of financing required. In short, for the resulting forecasted financial statements to be reliable, an accurate projection of sales is critical. The starting point for a sales forecast is last year's sales, with an addition for expected year-to-year growth based on the average sales growth experienced in previous years. This initial crude sales forecast should then be refined using as much company-specific information as is available. For example, in forecasting McDonald's sales, one should try to determine how many new outlets McDonald's expects to open during the coming year. The resulting sales forecast is the basis on which to forecast the remainder of the balance sheet, income statement, and statement of cash flow information.

Exhibit 5-11 contains financial statement information for the hypothetical Derrald Company. This information will be used as the basis for a simple forecasting exercise. The 2001 information for Derrald Company is historical information.

Analysis of Derrald's past history of sales growth, combined with a consideration of Derrald's strategic plans for 2002, suggests that sales for 2002 are likely to rise 40 percent to $1,400.

EXHIBIT 5-11 Historical Financial Data for Derrald Company

Balance Sheet	**2001**
Cash	10
Other current assets	250
Property, plant, and equipment, net	300
Total assets	560
Accounts payable	100
Bank loans payable	300
Total stockholders' equity	160
Total liabilities and equities	560

Income Statement	
Sales	1,000
Cost of goods sold	700
Gross profit	300
Depreciation expense	30
Other operating expenses	170
Operating profit	100
Interest expense	30
Income before taxes	70
Income taxes	30
Net income	40

Forecast of Balance Sheet Accounts

Not all balance sheet accounts change according to the same process. Some items increase naturally as sales volume increases. Others increase only in response to specific long-term expansion plans. And other balance sheet items change only in response to specific financing choices made by management. Below is outlined how these different processes impact the forecast of a balance sheet.

Natural Increase If Derrald Company plans to increase its sales volume by 40 percent in 2002, it seems logical to assume that Derrald will need about 40 percent more cash with which to handle this increased volume of business. In other words, the increased level of activity itself will create the need for more cash. The same is true of other current assets such as accounts receivable and inventory and of current operating liabilities such as accounts payable and wages payable. In short, a planned 40 percent increase in the volume of Derrald's business means that, in the absence of plans to significantly change its methods of operation, Derrald will also experience a 40 percent increase in the levels of its current operating assets and liabilities. These forecasted natural increases are reflected in the forecasted balance sheet contained in Exhibit 5-12.

Long-Term Planning Long-term assets, such as property, plant, and equipment, do not increase naturally as sales volume increases. Instead, the addition of a new factory building, for example, only occurs as the result of a long-term planning process. Thus, a business anticipating an increase of sales in the coming year of only 10 percent may expand its productive capacity by 50 percent as part of its long-term strategic plan. Similarly, a business forecasting 25 percent sales growth may plan to use existing excess capacity to handle the entire sales increase without any increase in long-term assets. In short, forecasting future levels of long-term assets requires some knowledge of a company's strategic expansion plan. For Derrald Company, it is assumed that we know that Derrald plans to increase its property, plant, and equipment from $300 in 2001 to $500 in 2002. This forecasted increase is reflected in Exhibit 5-12.

EXHIBIT 5-12 Forecasted Balance Sheet and Income Statement for Derrald Company

Balance Sheet	2001	2002 Forecasted	Basis for Forecast
Cash	10	14	40% natural increase
Other current assets	250	350	40% natural increase
Property, plant, and equipment, net	300	500	
Total assets	560	864	
Accounts payable	100	140	40% natural increase
Bank loans payable	300	524	
Total stockholders' equity	160	200	
Total liabilities and equities	560	864	

Income Statement	2001	2002 Forecasted	
Sales	1,000	**1,400**	**40% increase**
Cost of goods sold	700	980	70% of sales, like last year
Gross profit	300	420	
Depreciation expense	30	50	10% of PPE, like last year
Other operating expenses	170	238	17% of sales, like last year
Operating profit	100	132	
Interest expense	30	52	10% of bank loan, like last year
Income before taxes	70	80	
Income taxes	30	34	43% of pre-tax, like last year
Net income	40	46	

Financing Choices The level of long-term debt and of stockholders' equity is determined by management's decisions on how to best obtain financing. In fact, management often uses forecasted financial statements, prepared under a variety of different financing scenarios, to help determine what financing choices to make. Because detailed treatment of the field of corporate finance is beyond the scope of this discussion, we will merely assume that Derrald is planning to finance its operations in 2002 by increasing its bank loans payable from $300 to $524 and by increasing stockholders' equity from $160 to $200. These forecasted increases are shown in Exhibit 5-12. Notice that the forecasted balance sheet for 2002 has total assets of $864 and total liabilities and equities of $864. The numerical discipline imposed by the structure of the balance sheet ensures that the forecasted asset increases are consistent with Derrald Company's plans for additional financing.

Forecast of Income Statement Accounts

The amount of some expenses is directly tied to the amount of sales for the year. Derrald Company's sales are forecasted to increase by 40 percent in 2002, so it is reasonable to predict that cost of goods sold will increase by the same 40 percent. Another way to perform this calculation is to assume that the ratio of cost of goods sold to sales remains constant from year to year. Thus, since cost of goods sold was 70 percent of sales in 2001 ($700/$1,000 = 70%), cost of goods sold should increase to $980 ($1,400 × 0.70) in 2002, as shown in Exhibit 5-12. Similarly, other operating expenses, such as wages and shipping costs, are also likely to maintain a constant relationship with the level of sales.

The amount of a company's depreciation expense is determined by how much property, plant, and equipment the company has. In 2001, Derrald Company had $30 of depreciation expense on $300 of property, plant, and equipment, meaning that depreciation was equal to 10% ($30/$300) of the amount of property, plant, and equipment. If the same relationship holds in 2002, Derrald can expect to report depreciation expense of $50 ($500 × 0.10) for the year.

Interest expense depends on how much interest-bearing debt a company has. In 2001, Derrald Company reported interest expense of $30 with a bank loan payable of $300. These numbers imply that the interest rate on Derrald's loan is 10 percent ($30/$300). Since the bank loan payable is expected to increase to $524 in 2002, Derrald can expect interest expense for the year of $52 ($524 × 0.10 = $52, rounded).

As seen in Exhibit 5-12, the assumptions made so far imply that Derrald's income before taxes in 2002 will total $80. Income tax expense is determined by how much pretax income a company has. And the most reasonable assumption to make is that a company's tax rate, equal to income tax expense divided by pretax income, will stay constant from year to year. Derrald's tax rate in 2001 was 43 percent ($30/$70) which, when applied to the forecasted pretax income for 2002 of $80, implies that income tax expense in 2002 will total $34 ($80 × 0.43, rounded).

The complete forecasted income statement for 2002 is shown in Exhibit 5-12 and indicates that Derrald Company's income for the year will be $46. The quality of this forecast is only as good as the assumptions that underlie it. In order to determine how much impact the assumptions can have, it is often useful to conduct a sensitivity analysis. This involves repeating the forecasting exercise using a set of pessimistic and a set of optimistic assumptions. Thus, one can construct a worst-case, standard-case, and best-case scenario to use in making decisions with the forecasted numbers.

Financial statement forecasting is used to construct an estimate of how well a company will perform in the future. This forecasting exercise is useful for bankers worried about whether they can recover their money if they make a loan to a company and for investors who want to determine how much they should pay to invest in a company. Forecasted financial statements are also useful for company management in evaluating alternate strategies and determining whether the planned operating, investing, and financing activities appropriately mesh together. The Derrald Company example used in this chapter will also be used in Chapter 6 to illustrate how to forecast a company's statement of cash flows.

Review of Key Points

1. **Net income is typically viewed as the fundamental measure of a company's profitablity, but there are also a variety of other measures of "income." The best measure of sustainable profitability is income from continuing operations.**
Five key measures of income are as follows:

- Gross profit: the difference between the selling price of a product and the cost of the product.
- Operating income: gross profit minus all other expenses except for interest and taxes. Operating income measures the performance of the fundamental business operations conducted by a company.
- Income from continuing operations: operating income minus interest expense, minus income tax expense, and plus or minus other miscellaneous revenue and expense items. Income from continuing operations is the best baseline from which to forecast a company's income for the following year.
- Net income: income from continuing operations plus or minus the results of discontinued operations, extraordinary items, and the cumulative effect of any changes in accounting principles. Net income includes all revenues, expenses, gains, and losses.
- Comprehensive income: net income plus or minus adjustments for changes in company wealth stemming from changes in certain exchange rates, interest rates, or financial instruments' values.

2. **The primary categories of income statement items are revenues, expenses, gains, and losses. Income statement items that do not relate to a company's continuing operations are income from discontinued operations, extraordinary items, and the cumulative effect of accounting changes.**

   Some of the types of activities through which a company can generate revenue are: selling of goods, providing of services, and earning of interest through loaning money to others. The key expense items are cost of goods sold; selling, general, and administrative expense; depreciation expense; interest expense; and income tax expense. Gains and losses arise from activities that are peripheral to a company's main operations. Income from discontinued operations, extraordinary items, and the cumulative effect of accounting changes are collectively referred to as the below-the-line items. Earnings per share (EPS) is the amount of net income associated with each share of stock. In addition to basic EPS, computation of diluted EPS adds information about the potential impact on EPS of the exercise of stock options and other rights to acquire shares.

3. **Income statements are prepared in a variety of formats. One useful format is the multiple-step income statement.**

   A single-step income statement merely groups all of the revenues and all of the expenses, and reports the overall difference as net income. A multiple-step income statement emphasizes the presentation of gross profit and operating income.

4. **Revenue should be recognized only after the required work has been performed and after collectibility of cash is reasonably assured. The matching concept has traditionally been used to decide when to recognize expenses.**

   In order for revenue to be recognized, the promised work must be done and cash collection must be reasonably assured. A useful concept in recognizing expenses is that of matching, which states that an expense should be recognized in the same period in which the revenue it was used to generate is recognized. When direct matching is not possible, expenses are recognized using either systematic allocation or immediate expensing.

5. **Individual transactions impacting income can be analyzed using the expanded accounting equation which is:**

   Assets = Liabilities + Paid-in Capital + (Revenues – Expenses – Dividends)

   The insight behind the expanded accounting equation is that equity can be decomposed into paid-in capital and retained earnings and that revenues, expenses, and dividends are just temporary subcategories of retained earnings. Revenues increase equity; and expenses and dividends represent a reduction in equity.

6. **An important use of an income statement is to forecast income in future periods. Good forecasting requires an understanding of what underlying factors determine the level of a revenue or an expense.**

   Most financial statement forecasting exercises start with a forecast of sales, which establishes the expected scale of operations in future periods. Some balance sheet items increase naturally as the level of sales increases; examples of such accounts are cash, accounts receivable, inventory, and accounts payable. Other balance sheet items, such as property, plant, and equipment, change in response to a company's long-term strategic plans. Finally, the amounts of the balance sheet items associated with financing, such as long-term debt and paid-in capital, are determined by the financing decisions made by a company's management.

   Some income statement items, such as cost of goods sold, maintain a constant relationship with sales. Depreciation expense is more likely to be related to the amount of a company's property, plant, and equipment. Interest expense is tied to the balance in interest-bearing debt. Finally, income tax expense is typically a relatively constant percentage of income before taxes.

Key Terms

accrual accounting (166)
comprehensive income (170)
cost of goods sold (174)
cumulative effect of a change in accounting principle (179)
discontinued operations (178)
earnings per share (EPS) (181)
expanded accounting equation (184)
expenses (174)
extraordinary items (178)
financial capital maintenance (168)
gain (177)
gross profit (169)
income from continuing operations (169)
loss (177)
matching (184)
multiple-step income statement (182)
net income (170)
operating income (169)
physical capital maintenance (168)
restructuring charges (178)
revenue (172)
revenue recognition (183)
sales (172)
single-step income statement (182)

Questions

1. In measuring income, the concept of financial capital maintenance is employed by businesses. Explain what this concept means.
2. Identify the various measures of income. What information does each different measure contain?
3. What is the most common type of revenue?
4. For a manufacturing company, what would represent the largest expense?
5. What types of expenses are included under the heading "selling, general, and administrative expense"?
6. What does depreciation expense represent?
7. What is the difference between a revenue and a gain? Between an expense and a loss?
8. What are restructuring charges and why do they generate controversy?
9. Identify the three categories of "below-the-line" items. Why are these items disclosed separately rather than as part of income from continuing operations?
10. What are the criteria for determining whether an item should be classified as extraordinary?
11. What does it mean when an item is disclosed "net of taxes"?

12. What is the difference between net income and comprehensive income? What items are included in comprehensive income?
13. Identify the two earnings per share figures. Which one is based solely on things that have already happened?
14. Give an example of something that results in a diluted EPS computation. Explain how this item affects the EPS computation.
15. Of the two common formats for an income statement, which highlights the computation of gross profit and operating income?
16. In order for a business to recognize revenue, two things must occur—what are they?
17. Identify the three different methods for recognizing expenses. Which method is the most theoretically correct? Why isn't it used in all cases?
18. What is the expanded accounting equation?
19. What is the starting point for the preparation of forecasted financial statements?
20. Describe the process one should use in forecasting depreciation expense.
21. What can be done to assess the magnitude of the impact that assumptions have on forecasted financial statements?

Exercises

E5-1 *Identifying Income Statement Items*

A summary of Lee Corporation's transactions during March is reproduced below.

a. The owners needed additional funds, and they borrowed $200,000 from the bank.
b. A dividend of $500 was declared and paid in March.
c. The company collected $20,000 from a sale made on account in February.
d. The company made sales on account in March totaling $7,500.
e. Cash sales during March totaled $5,000.
f. The company received its March utility bill of $75.
g. The company paid its February utility bill of $40.

Required State which of the events would be recorded in the income statement for March.

E5-2 *Income Statement Classification*

Below are classifications commonly found in an income statement.

a. Revenues
b. Cost of goods sold
c. Selling, general and administrative expenses
d. Other income statement items
e. Not an income statement item

Required In the space next to each of the numbered items, write the letter that best indicates to which classification it belongs.

1. Sales
2. Taxes payable
3. Supplies on hand
4. Gain on sale of land
5. Dividends paid
6. Interest payable
7. Depreciation expense
8. Sales commissions paid
9. Restructuring charge
10. President's salary
11. Income tax expense
12. Delivery expense
13. Interest expense
14. Advertising expense
15. Prepaid insurance

E5-3 *Operating Income*

Rambo Adventures Inc. provides guided adventures for those individuals seeking extreme thrills. They offer such adventures as climbing Mount Everest, navigating the crocodile-infested Nile, touring the remotest jungles of Africa, and driving in Los Angeles' rush hour traffic. Demand for its services has been so great that management is considering borrowing money to expand the extreme offerings. You are a bank loan officer and have received the following information relating to the company's financial performance for the past year.

RAMBO ADVENTURES
INCOME STATEMENT
For the Year Ended December 31, 2001

Revenues from services	$1,550,000
Expenses:	
Salaries and wages	625,000
Supplies	375,000
Transportation	78,000
Insurance	115,000
General and administrative	130,000
Settlement from recent lawsuit	250,000
Income taxes	17,000
Net income	$ (40,000)

Required Analyze this information to determine the following:

1. What is the company's operating income?
2. What additional information would you request in order to properly evaluate the company's loan application?

E5-4 *Measuring Income*

Kevin Stocks buys and sells cars as a hobby. He purchases used cars at wholesale, makes minor repairs, and then resells them. At the start of the month he had two vehicles on hand: a 1978 Ford truck (cost $700) and a 1990 Honda Civic (cost $2,200). During the month, he purchased (paying cash) and used $100 worth of parts for each vehicle and then sold the truck for $1,300 and the car for $3,200. On the last day of the month he purchased (paying cash) two more vehicles: a 1981 Chevrolet truck (cost $1,350) and a 1991 Toyota Corolla (cost $3,450).

Required

1. Compute Kevin's income for the month.
2. Compute Kevin's net cash flow for the month.
3. Why are the two numbers different?
4. Kevin is thinking about finding a different hobby because he doesn't seem to be making much money at this one. How could you convince Kevin to change his thinking?

E5-5 *Income Statement*

The Furillo Company makes both cash and credit sales. You have obtained the following data from the company's records:

Credit sales for November	$230,000
Cash received in November	
From October credit sales	90,000
From November credit sales	45,000
From November cash sales	76,000
Gross profit (as a percentage of sales)	32%
Net income (as a percentage of sales)	16%
Income tax rate (tax expense as a percentage of pretax income)	30%

Selling expenses are one-third of general and administrative expenses.

Required Prepare an income statement for the month ended November 30, 2001.

E5-6 *Income Statement*

The university bookstore has just completed its busy fall season and reports the following summary of transactions:

a. Sales, both cash and on account, totaled $2,000,000.
b. Salary and wages equaled 9 percent of sales.
c. All items were priced to sell at 1.25 times their cost.
d. Insurance expense for the period was $5,000.
e. Miscellaneous expense equaled 1.5 percent of cost of goods sold.
f. Advertising expense was 4 percent of sales.
g. Income tax expense is 30 percent of pretax income.

Required Construct an income statement (using a single-step format) for the month ending September 30.

E5-7 *Income Statement*

Jeff Didericksen wants to know the bottom line from his 2001 operations and provides the following information:

a. Salaries and wages expense was $152,000.
b. Equipment rental revenue came to $544,000.
c. Insurance expense was $6,400.
d. Interest earned on invested cash was $1,600.
e. Rental revenue from renting idle storage space totaled $35,000.
f. Fuel costs and other expenses totaled $43,600.
g. Advertising expense totaled $5,800.
h. Income taxes totaled 25 percent of income before taxes. (*Hint*: Income before taxes equals revenues minus all expenses other than taxes.)

Required Prepare an income statement (using a single-step format).

E5-8 *Income Statement*

Iyengar Corporation provides the following information relating to 2001:

Rent expense	$12,000	Cost of goods sold	$46,000
Taxes expense	2,250	General and administrative expense	3,000
Sales	82,000		
Interest expense	6,000		

Required Prepare an income statement (using a multiple-step format) for the year ended December 31, 2001.

E5-9 *Income Statement*

You have obtained the following information for the Ponce Pickle Factory.

Sales	$250,000	Delivery expense	$ 1,500
Depreciation expense	28,000	Cost of goods sold	110,000
Insurance expense	8,500	Interest expense	5,000
Salaries expense	52,000	Rental income	1,000

Required Prepare two income statements for the year ended December 31, 2001. The first should be prepared using the single-step format and the second should use the multiple-step format. Assume a tax rate of 30 percent of income before taxes.

E5-10 *Income Statement*

You have obtained the following data for Cardinal Company:

Sales	$200,000
Gross profit percentage	40%
Return on sales	5%
Income tax rate	20%

Required

1. Based on the above data, determine the following:
   a. Cost of goods sold
   b. Net income
   c. Income taxes
   d. Operating expenses (assume that there are no "other expenses and revenues")
2. Prepare a single-step income statement.

E5-11 *Extraordinary Items*

During a very eventful year, the following happened to the Bacuall Corporation:

1. The first hurricane in 100 years occurred in the area where the corporation's headquarters were located, and its headquarters building was completely destroyed.
2. The company recorded a loss on the abandonment of some equipment formerly used in the business.
3. A customer that owed Bacuall $20,000 declared bankruptcy. Because Bacuall knows that it will never collect the loan, it has decided to write off the loan receivable and consider the $20,000 a loss.

4. One of the company's major employee unions went on strike, and the firm was shut down for several weeks. Management estimates that profits of $500,000 were lost.

Required Which of the above items should be classified as extraordinary, and why?

E5-12 *Below-the-Line Items*

The controller of Moreno Technical Systems gave you the following information for the year ended December 31, 2001:

Sales	$4,000,000	Loss on disposal of discontinued operations	$40,000
Cost of goods sold	2,800,000	Extraordinary loss from earthquake damage	70,000
Interest expense	500,000	Tax rate on all items	30%
General and administrative expenses	200,000		
Income from discontinued operations	100,000		

Required Prepare a multiple-step income statement for the year ended December 31, 2001.

E5-13 *Revenue Recognition*

Consider the following independent transactions and events:

a. On February 1, 2001, Tolkien Consulting signed a contract for $12,000 to provide consulting services for Ironcrown Inc. for the period of one year. The services are to be provided evenly throughout the contract period.
b. Charlie Johnson owns several condominiums in Salt Lake City, Utah. Because of the Winter Olympics being held in Salt Lake City in 2002, demand for Charlie's condos has skyrocketed. He recently rented one condo for two weeks during 2002 for $10,000 per week and has already received the cash.
c. Concepts, Inc. owes a supplier $20,000 due in 30 days. Because of the supplier's cash flow difficulties, the supplier has agreed to accept $17,500 immediately as payment in full.
d. Silverado Ranch owns land that increased in value during the past year by $125,000.

Required Indicate whether any revenue should be recognized in 2001 and, if so, how much. Provide support for your answer.

E5-14 *Expense Recognition*

Consider the following independent items:

a. Johnson & Smith, Inc., conducts cancer research. The company's hope is to develop a cure for the deadly disease. To date, its efforts have proven unsuccessful. They are testing a new drug, Ebzinene, which has cost $400,000 to develop.
b. Williams Coal and Lumber warranties many of the products it sells. Although the warranty periods range from days to years, Williams can reasonably estimate warranty costs.
c. Stocks Company recently signed a two-year lease agreement on a warehouse. The entire cost of $15,000 was paid in advance.
d. John Clark assembles chairs for the Stone Furniture Company. The company pays Clark on an hourly basis.
e. Hardy Company recently purchased a fleet of new delivery trucks. The trucks are each expected to last for 100,000 miles.
f. Taylor Manufacturing Inc. regularly advertises in national trade journals. The objective is to acquire name recognition, not to promote a specific product.

Required For each of the preceding items, indicate whether the expense should be recognized using (1) direct matching, (2) systematic allocation, or (3) immediate recognition. Provide support for your answer.

E5-15 *Income Statement Items*

As the accountant for Jimbo Company, you have prepared the following income statement:

JIMBO COMPANY
INCOME STATEMENT
For the Year Ended December 31, 2001

Revenues:	
Cash sales	$160,000
Sales on account	240,000
Total revenues	$400,000
Expenses:	
Cost of goods sold	$190,000
Salary expense	60,000
Advertising expense	50,000
Rent expense	30,000
Interest expense	10,000
Total expenses	340,000
Income before taxes	$ 60,000
Income tax expense	5,000
Net income	$ 55,000

Required

1. One of the directors of the company, an engineer by training, knows only a little about accounting. She asks you the following questions, to which you should make a brief response:
   a. How does one determine when a sale on account should be recognized as revenue?
   b. Since advertising is intended to boost future sales, shouldn't it be recorded as an asset rather than as an expense?
   c. Why aren't equipment purchases reported in the income statement?
   d. Why aren't dividend payments reported in the income statement?
2. Redo this income statement using the multiple-step format.

E5-16 *Expanded Accounting Equation*

Cottrell Corporation began business at the start of 2001. The following transactions occurred during the first month of operations:

a. Dave Cottrell invested $10,000 and became the sole shareholder.
b. Purchased inventory on account for $21,000.
c. Sold $17,000 of inventory for $28,000. Seventy-five percent of the sales were on account.
d. Paid $15,000 of accounts payable.
e. Collected $18,000 on account.
f. Paid $10,000 in operating expenses.

Required

1. Use a worksheet format similar to that illustrated in Exhibit 5-9 to analyze the effect of each transaction on the expanded accounting equation.
2. Determine the ending balance in each account.
3. Does the expanded accounting equation balance?
4. Prepare a single-step income statement for Cottrell's first month of operations.

E5-17 *Expanded Accounting Equation*

Soelberg Enterprises began the year with the following account balances:

Cash	$ 5,000
Accounts receivable	14,000
Inventory	11,000
Accounts payable	8,000
Shareholders' equity	22,000

During the year, Soelberg had the following transactions:

a. Sales of $225,000, 90 percent on account.
b. Cash collections of accounts receivable, $200,000.

c. Purchased inventory on account, $180,000.
d. Cost of inventory sold, $175,000.
e. Paid accounts payable, $173,000.
f. Paid miscellaneous expenses, $37,000.

Required

1. Use a worksheet format similar to that illustrated in Exhibit 5-9 to analyze the effect of each transaction on the expanded accounting equation.
2. Prepare an income statement for the year and a balance sheet as of the end of the year.

E5-18 *Forecasted Income Statement*

Han Company wishes to forecast its net income for the year 2002. Han has assembled balance sheet and income statement data for 2001 and has also done a forecast of the balance sheet for 2002. In addition, Han has estimated that its sales in 2002 will rise to $2,200. This information is summarized below:

Balance Sheet	2001	2002 Forecasted
Cash	20	22
Other current assets	500	550
Property, plant, and equipment, net	600	800
Total assets	1,120	1,372
Accounts payable	200	220
Bank loans payable	600	500
Total stockholders' equity	320	652
Total liabilities and equities	1,120	1,372

Income Statement	2001	2002 Forecasted
Sales	2,000	**2,200**
Cost of goods sold	700	
Gross profit	1,300	
Depreciation expense	120	
Other operating expenses	1,010	
Operating profit	170	
Interest expense	90	
Income before taxes	80	
Income taxes	30	
Net income	50	

Required Prepare a forecasted income statement for 2002. Clearly state what assumptions you make.

E5-19 *Forecasted Balance Sheet and Income Statement*

Ryan Company wishes to prepare a forecasted income statement and a forecasted balance sheet for 2002. Ryan's balance sheet and income statement for 2001 are given on the next page:

	2001
Balance Sheet	
Cash	10
Other current assets	250
Property, plant, and equipment, net	800
Total assets	1,060
Accounts payable	100
Bank loans payable	700
Total stockholders' equity	260
Total liabilities and equities	1,060

	2001
Income Statement	
Sales	1,000
Cost of goods sold	750
Gross profit	250
Depreciation expense	40
Other operating expenses	80
Operating profit	130
Interest expense	70
Income before taxes	60
Income taxes	20
Net income	40

In addition, Ryan has assembled the following forecasted information regarding 2002:

a. Sales are expected to increase to $1,500.
b. Ryan expects to become more efficient at utilizing its property, plant, and equipment in 2002. Therefore, Ryan expects that the sales increase will not require any increase in property, plant, and equipment. Accordingly, the year 2002 property, plant, and equipment balance is expected to be $800.
c. Ryan's bank has approved a new long-term loan of $200. This loan will be in addition to the existing loan payable.

Required Prepare a forecasted balance sheet and a forecasted income statement for 2002. Clearly state what assumptions you make.

Problems

P5-20 ***Different Measures of Income***

On January 1, 2001, Stanley Gifford purchased some land for $400,000. In December, Stanley sold the land for $450,000. On December 31, Stanley found another piece of land, identical in all respects to the first, and purchased it for $430,000.

Required

1. Using the financial capital maintenance concept of income, compute Stanley Gifford's land-related income for 2001.
2. Using the physical capital maintenance concept of income, compute Stanley Gifford's land-related income for 2001.
3. **ANALYSIS:** What factors would cause Stanley Gifford to pay $430,000 to buy a piece of land in December when he was able to buy an identical piece of land for just $400,000 at the beginning of the year? What factors would cause Stanley to be able to sell a piece of land for $450,000 and then immediately replace the land with an identical piece for just $430,000?

P5-21 *Elements of the Income Statement*

In the space in front of each of the items below, indicate whether the item is a revenue, expense, gain, or loss.

____ 1. Interest earned on short-term investments
____ 2. The sale of a delivery truck for more than its purchase price
____ 3. The destruction of a warehouse in a fire
____ 4. The estimated amount of accounts receivable created this year that ultimately will be uncollectible
____ 5. Fees received in exchange for providing a service
____ 6. Retail price of goods sold
____ 7. Wholesale cost of goods sold
____ 8. The sale of land for less than its purchase price

P5-22 *Below-the-Line Items*

During 2001, the Fullerton Manufacturing Company sold its carpet manufacturing division because of its consistently poor performance. In addition, you obtained the following information about the events that affected the firm during 2001:

	Continuing Operations	Discontinued Operations
Sales	$4,500,000	$1,800,000
Cost of goods sold	3,000,000	1,500,000
Operating expenses	500,000	500,000
Loss on disposal of discontinued operations		(300,000)
Gain on recovery of assets expropriated by foreign country	300,000	
Gain on sale of building	100,000	
Cumulative effect (gain) of change of depreciation method	50,000	

All of the above items are shown prior to any tax effect. Assume that a tax rate of 30 percent applies to all items.

Required

1. Prepare an income statement for the year ended December 31, 2001.
2. ANALYSIS: In the absence of any additional information, what is your best guess of what Fullerton Manufacturing's net income will be in 2002? Explain your answer.

P5-23 *Income Statement Preparation*

The following items were taken from the records of Lily Company for 2001:

Sales	$620,000
Salaries expense	80,000
Prepaid expense	140,000
Cost of goods sold	335,000
Interest revenue	55,000
Interest expense	45,000
Repairs and maintenance expense	54,000
Retained earnings, January 1, 2001	230,000
Unearned revenue	40,000
Income tax expense	30,000
Dividends declared and paid	100,000

Required

1. Prepare a multiple-step income statement for 2001. *Note:* Not all of the items belong on the income statement.
2. During the year, the company made sales of $100,000 on credit, which have not yet been collected in cash. Why are these sales included in the 2001 income statement?
3. ANALYSIS: Judging from the size of the dividend paid during the year, relative to income for the year, do you think Lily Company is an old, established company or a new, start-up company? Explain.

P5-24 *Income Statement Preparation*

The revenue, expense, and related accounts of Weiss Company for the year ended June 30, 2001 are as follows.

Advertising expense	$ 2,500
Beginning retained earnings	50,000
Cost of goods sold	40,000
Delivery expense	6,000
Depreciation expense	5,000
Insurance expense	1,000
Interest expense	200
Repairs and maintenance expense	2,500
Sales	90,000
Salaries expense*	5,000
Supplies expense	750
Income tax rate	25%

*Included in the salaries expense of $5,000 is $1,000 of dividends paid to the owner, E. Weiss.

Required

1. Prepare an income statement for the year ended June 30, 2001. Use the multiple-step format.
2. Assuming that the company has paid-in capital in the amount of $75,000, what is the total of stockholders' equity at June 30, 2001?
3. **ANALYSIS:** Currently, Weiss Company has a very high markup percentage; goods are marked up to sell at 125 percent above cost ($90,000 = $40,000 + [1.25 × $40,000]). What would Weiss Company's net income be if goods were marked up only 75 percent?

P5-25 *Revenue and Expense Recognition*

On December 31, 2001, The Hadley Company provides the following pre-audit income statement for your review:

Sales	$185,000
Cost of goods sold	(94,000)
Gross profit	$ 91,000
Rent expense	(18,000)
Advertising expense	(6,000)
Warranty expense	(8,000)
Other expenses	(20,000)
Net income	$ 39,000

The following information is also available:

a. Many of Hadley's customers pay for their orders in advance. At year-end, $18,000 of orders paid for in advance of shipment have been included in the sales figure.
b. Hadley introduced and sold several products during the year with a 30-day, money-back guarantee. During the year, customers seldom returned the products. Hadley has not included in revenue or in cost of goods sold those items sold within the last 30 days that included the guarantee. The revenue is $16,000, and the cost associated with the products is $7,500.
c. On January 1, 2001, Hadley prepaid its building rent for 18 months. The entire amount paid, $18,000, was charged to Rent Expense.
d. On July 1, 2001, Hadley paid $24,000 for general advertising to be completed prior to the end of 2001. Hadley's management estimates that the advertising will benefit a two-year period and, therefore, has elected to charge the costs to the income statement at the rate of $1,000 a month.
e. In past years, Hadley has estimated warranty expense using a percentage of sales. Hadley estimates future warranty costs relating to 2001 sales will amount to 5 percent of sales. However, during 1999, Hadley elected to charge costs to warranty expense as costs were incurred. Hadley spent $8,000 during 2001 to repair and replace defective inventory sold in current and prior periods.

Required

1. For each item of additional information, identify the revenue or expense recognition issue.
2. Prepare a revised income statement using the information provided.
3. **ANALYSIS:** Assume that Hadley issued a press release announcing that its preliminary earnings calculations indicated that net income for the year would be $39,000, as reported in the income statement presented above.

   After you make your revisions and Hadley announces the revised income number (as computed in part 2), what do you think will happen to Hadley's stock price? Explain. *Note*: Think about what the necessity for the release of revised income numbers tells the market about Hadley's management.

P5-26 *Expanded Accounting Equation*

Nielsen Company began business at the start of 2001. The following transactions occurred during the first year of operations:

a. Shareholders invested $20,000 in cash.
b. Borrowed $50,000 from the bank on a long-term loan.
c. Purchased inventory on account for $57,000.
d. Paid wages of $65,000. In addition, wages earned by employees during the year but not yet paid total $7,000.
e. Sold inventory costing $48,000 for $128,000. Received cash of $30,000 and the remainder was on account.
f. Paid $45,000 of accounts payable.
g. Collected $60,000 on account.
h. Paid $10,000 in dividends.

Required

1. Use a worksheet format similar to that illustrated in Exhibit 5-9 to analyze the effect of each transaction on the expanded accounting equation.
2. Prepare an income statement for 2001 for Nielsen Company.
3. Prepare a balance sheet as of December 31, 2001 for Nielsen Company.
4. **ANALYSIS:** Comment on the amount of the cash dividend. In particular, comment on whether you think the dividend was financially advisable and legally allowable.

P5-27 *Expanded Accounting Equation*

Deedle Company began the year with the following account balances:

Cash	$15,000
Accounts receivable	42,000
Inventory	33,000
Accounts payable	24,000
Paid-in capital	45,000
Retained earnings	21,000

During the year, Deedle had the following transactions:

a. Borrowed $30,000 on a long-term loan.
b. Interest expense for the year was $3,000. This amount has not yet been paid in cash.
c. Sales for the year were $500,000, all on account.
d. Cash collections of accounts receivable, $280,000.
e. Purchased inventory on account, $380,000.
f. Cost of inventory sold was $350,000.
g. Paid accounts payable, $173,000.
h. Paid wage expense, $137,000.

Required

1. Use a worksheet format similar to that illustrated in Exhibit 5-9 to analyze the effect of each transaction on the expanded accounting equation.
2. Prepare an income statement for the year and a balance sheet as of the end of the year.
3. **ANALYSIS:** Look at item (g). Why do you think Deedle chose to pay such a small fraction of its total outstanding amount of accounts payable?

P5-28 *Forecasted Balance Sheet and Income Statement*

Lorien Company wishes to prepare a forecasted income statement and a forecasted balance sheet for 2002. Lorien's balance sheet and income statement for 2001 are given below:

	2001
Balance Sheet	
Cash	40
Other current assets	350
Property, plant, and equipment, net	1,000
Total assets	1,390
Accounts payable	100
Bank loans payable	1,000
Paid-in capital	100
Retained earnings	190
Total liabilities and equities	1,390

	2001
Income Statement	
Sales	1,000
Cost of goods sold	350
Gross profit	650
Depreciation expense	200
Other operating expenses	250
Operating profit	200
Interest expense	120
Income before taxes	80
Income taxes	20
Net income	60

In addition, Lorien has assembled the following forecasted information regarding 2002:

a. Sales are expected to increase to $1,200.
b. Lorien does not expect to buy any new property, plant, and equipment during 2002. *Hint*: Think about how depreciation expense in 2002 will affect the reported amount of property, plant, and equipment.
c. Because of adverse banking conditions, Lorien does not expect to receive any new bank loans in 2002.
d. Lorien plans to pay cash dividends of $15 in 2002.

Required

1. Prepare a forecasted balance sheet and a forecasted income statement for 2002. Clearly state what assumptions you make.
2. **ANALYSIS:** If you construct your forecasted balance sheet in (1) correctly, total forecasted paid-in capital for 2002 should be negative. Is this possible? Explain.

Applications and Extensions

Deciphering Actual Financial Statements

Deciphering 5-1 *McDonald's*

The 1997 annual report for McDonald's is included in Appendix A. Locate that annual report and consider the following questions:

1. What are the two primary sources of revenue for McDonald's? Does the mix between the two revenue sources change from 1995 to 1997? Explain.
2. Has McDonald's operating income as a percentage of total revenues changed from 1995 to 1997? Explain.

3. Compute the percentage increase in net income for 1996 and 1997. For example, the 1997 percentage increase is computed as follows:

   (1997 net income–1996 net income)/1996 net income

   Compute the percentage increase in basic earnings per share for the same period. Why aren't the net income and EPS growth percentages the same?
4. Does McDonald's generate most of its revenue within the United States or outside the United States? *Note*: Look for the note on Segment and Geographic Information.
5. How does the company expense its advertising costs and the costs of its property and equipment: direct matching, systematic and rational allocation, or immediate recognition? *Note*: Look at the note giving the Summary of Significant Accounting Policies.

Deciphering 5-2 *Wells Fargo & Company*

Wells Fargo & Company's consolidated statement of income is shown below:

WELLS FARGO & COMPANY AND SUBSIDIARIES
CONSOLIDATED STATEMENT OF INCOME

(dollars in millions)	Year ended December 31, 1997	1996	1995
Interest Income			
Federal funds sold and securities purchased under resale agreements	$ 18	$ 29	$ 4
Investment securities	732	779	599
Mortgage loans held for sale	-0-	-0-	76
Loans	6,094	5,688	3,403
Other	60	27	3
Total interest income	6,904	6,523	4,085
Interest Expense			
Deposits	1,703	1,586	997
Federal funds purchased and securities sold under repurchase agreements	154	92	199
Commercial paper and other short-term borrowings	17	16	32
Senior and subordinated debt	315	302	203
Guaranteed preferred beneficial interests in Company's subordinated debentures	101	6	—
Total interest expense	2,290	2,002	1,431
Net interest income	4,614	5,521	2,654
Provision for loan losses	615	105	—
Net interest income after provision for loan losses	3,999	4,416	2,654
Noninterest income			
Fees and commissions	946	740	433
Service charges on deposit accounts	861	868	478
Trust and investment services income	450	377	241
Investment securities gains (losses)	20	10	(17)
Sale of joint venture interest	—	—	163
Other	427	205	26
Total noninterest income	2,704	2,200	1,324
Noninterest Expense			
Salaries	1,269	1,357	713
Incentive compensation	195	227	126
Employee benefits	332	373	187
Equipment	385	399	193
Net occupancy	388	366	211

Goodwill	326	250	35
Core deposit intangible	255	243	42
Operating losses	320	145	45
Other	1,079	1,277	649
Total noninterest expense	4,549	4,637	2,201
Income before income tax expense	2,154	1,979	1,777
Income tax expense	999	908	745
Net income	$1,155	$1,071	$1,032
Net income applicable to common stock	$1,130	$1,004	$ 990
Earnings per common share	$12.77	$12.21	$20.37
Earnings per common share—assuming dilution	$12.64	$12.05	$20.06

Using the Wells Fargo income statement information, answer the following questions:

1. How is this income statement different from all the income statements illustrated in the chapter?
2. For a merchandising firm, gross margin represents sales less cost of goods sold. For Wells Fargo, what component of the income statement would be similar to gross margin?
3. The market value per share of Wells Fargo's stock at the end of each year was $339.44, $269.75, and $216.00 for the years 1997, 1996, and 1995, respectively. Compute the firm's price earnings ratio for each year. Is the PE ratio increasing or decreasing over time? What might cause a company's PE ratio to change?

Deciphering 5-3 *The Reader's Digest Association, Inc.*

Reader's Digest is the most widely read monthly magazine in the world. But the Reader's Digest Association does more than just sell a monthly magazine. Information relating to the company's business segments can be found in the company's annual report, an excerpt of which is reprinted below:

BUSINESS SEGMENT FINANCIAL INFORMATION

	Years ended June 30,		
in millions	**1998**	**1997**	**1996**
Revenues			
Reader's Digest magazine	$ 712.3	$ 729.2	$ 739.8
Books and home entertainment products	1,635.0	1,850.5	2,099.4
Special interest magazines	97.0	81.9	91.9
Other businesses	193.1	181.0	170.6
Intersegment	(3.7)	(3.6)	(3.6)
	$2,633.7	$2,839.0	$3,098.1
Operating profit			
Reader's Digest magazine	$ 16.7	$ 42.7	$ 11.2
Books and home entertainment products	37.9	175.6	192.0
Special interest magazines	1.7	0.4	(21.1)
Other businesses	19.9	22.5	(9.9)
Corporate expense	(46.0)	(48.4)	(62.9)
	$ 30.2	$ 192.8	$ 109.3
Identifiable assets			
Reader's Digest magazine	$ 380.4	$ 410.4	$ 358.3
Books and home entertainment products	853.6	881.8	981.1
Special interest magazines	75.0	76.4	66.4
Other businesses	70.8	75.1	76.9
Corporate	184.2	200.1	421.4
	$1,564.0	$1,643.8	$1,904.1

1. How does *Reader's Digest* generate most of its revenues? Operating profits?
2. By dividing revenues by assets, we can obtain a measure of the efficiency with which assets are being employed. Compute each segment's asset turnover ratio.
3. The profitability of each sales dollar is indicated by computing the ratio of operating profit divided by revenue. By this measure, which of *Reader's Digest*'s segments is the most profitable?
4. Based on your answers to questions 1, 2, and 3, how critical is the *Reader's Digest* magazine to the firm's overall success? Before you answer this question, think about how the company is able to sell all of its books and home entertainment products.

Deciphering 5-4 *Ford Motor Company*

A partial consolidated statement of income for Ford Motor Company is presented below:

FORD MOTOR COMPANY AND SUBSIDIARIES
CONSOLIDATED STATEMENT OF INCOME
For the Years Ended December 31, 1997, 1996 and 1995
(in millions)

	1997	1996	1995
Automotive			
Sales (Note 1)	$122,935	$118,023	$110,496
Costs and expenses (Notes 1 and 15):			
Costs of sales	108,907	108,882	101,171
Selling, administrative and other expenses	7,082	6,625	6,044
Total costs and expenses	115,989	115,507	107,215
Operating income	6,946	2,516	3,281
Interest income	1,116	841	800
Interest expense	788	695	622
Net interest income	328	146	178
Equity in net loss of affiliated companies (Note 1)	(88)	(6)	(154)
Net expense from transactions with Financial Services (Note 1)	(104)	(85)	(139)
Income before income taxes—Automotive	7,082	2,571	3,166
Financial Services			
Revenues (Note 1)	30,692	28,968	26,641
Costs and expenses (Note 1):			
Interest expense	9,712	9,704	9,424
Depreciation	7,645	6,875	6,500
Operating and other expenses	6,621	6,217	5,499
Provision for credit and insurance losses	3,230	2,564	1,818
Asset write-downs and dispositions (Note 15)	—	121	—
Total costs and expenses	27,208	25,481	23,241
Net revenue from transactions with Automotive (Note 1)	104	85	139
Gain on sale of Common Stock of a subsidiary (Note 15)	269	650	—
Income before income taxes—Financial Services	3,857	4,222	3,539
Total Company			
Income before income taxes	10,939	6,793	6,705
Provision for income taxes (Note 6)	3,741	2,166	2,379
Income before minority interests	7,198	4,627	4,326
Minority interests in net income of subsidiaries	278	181	187
Net income	$ 6,920	$ 4,446	$ 4,139

Use the Ford Motor income statement information to answer the following questions:

1. What is the first thing you notice about the way revenues and expenses are partitioned? Why do you think Ford has partitioned its income statement in this way?

2. For 1995, 1996, and 1997, compute the pretax profit percentage (pretax income divided by sales or revenues) for the automotive and financial services divisions of Ford.
3. Which of the company's two divisions seems to be performing better over time?
4. Is Ford a car company that finances automobiles or a finance company that makes cars?

International Financial Statements

Nestlé

Nestlé calls itself the world's leading food company. Nestlé is Switzerland's largest industrial company and, as of June 30, 1998, the company had a market value of $84 billion, making it the 27th most valuable company in the world (right behind DuPont). Nestlé dates back to 1867 when Henri Nestlé created the first commercially sold infant formula. Nestlé's income statement for 1997 is reproduced below (amounts are in millions of Swiss francs):

	1997	1996
Sales to customers	69,998	60,490
Cost of goods sold	(35,981)	(31,495)
Distribution expenses	(4,713)	(4,037)
Marketing and administration expenses	(21,147)	(18,027)
Research and development costs	(777)	(710)
Restructuring costs	(360)	(257)
Amortization of intangible assets	(140)	(102)
Trading profit	6,880	5,862
Net financing costs	(1,056)	(915)
Net non-trading items	(63)	(9)
Profit before taxation	5,761	4,938
Taxation	(1,842)	(1,552)
Net profit of consolidated companies	3,919	3,386
Share of profit attributable to outside interests	(170)	(218)
Share of results of associated companies	256	233
Net profit for the year	4,005	3,401

Using the income statement data for Nestlé, answer the following questions:

1. Nestlé uses the term "trading profit" in its income statement. From the items included in the computation of "trading profit," what term did we use in the chapter to describe the same concept?
2. Nestlé reported sales of 69.998 billion Swiss francs in 1997. How much is this in U.S. dollars? For simplicity, use the current exchange rate rather than going back to find out what the U.S. dollar/Swiss franc exchange rate was in 1997.
3. At what rate is Nestlé taxed? What factors would cause this rate to differ from the overall Swiss corporate tax rate?
4. Speculate on what you think is represented by the following two items from Nestlé's income statement:
   a. Share of profit attributable to outside interests (a subtraction)
   b. Share of results of associated companies (an addition)
5. A large can (64 oz.) of Nestlé's Quik chocolate powder mix has a retail selling price of about $6. What is your estimate of this item's production cost?
6. Overall, what significant differences do you see between Nestlé's income statement and the U.S. income statements that you have seen thus far in this textbook?

Business Memo

Recognizing Holding Gains

Historically, accounting standards in the United States have not allowed companies to recognize the increases in value that occur while a company holds an asset while awaiting the asset's sale or use. However, in a pronouncement released in 1993 (FASB Statement No. 115), the FASB allowed companies to recognize gains stemming from increases in the value of investment securities that are held for the purpose of earning a short-term return. The increases in value of these securities are reported in the current period's income. Holding gains for securities expected to be held for a longer period are excluded from the computation of net income but are disclosed as part of comprehensive income.

Write a one-page memo explaining why, after all these years, accounting-standard setters have decided to require the recognition of holding gains on investment securities. Your memo should cover the following issues:

1. Why have accounting-standard setters been reluctant to allow firms to recognize holding gains?
2. Why would the FASB now allow investment securities held for trading purposes to be valued at fair market value?
3. Why are some holding gains included in the computation of net income while some are only disclosed as part of comprehensive income?
4. If the FASB allows holding gains to be recognized for certain investment securities, why doesn't the Board move to fair-value accounting on other assets such as equipment, patents, and land?

Research

Reviewing Actual Income Statements and Associated Footnotes

Your group is to obtain the annual reports of five companies. The easiest way to obtain these annual reports is to download them from the companies' Web sites. Alternatively, you can download Form 10-K from the SEC archives (at www.sec.gov); Form 10-K includes a company's annual financial statements. Using these annual reports, your group is to report (either orally or in writing) the answers to the following questions:

1. What format of the income statement is used by the five companies—single-step, multiple-step, or some combination thereof?
2. Each income statement should have three years' worth of information. Compute the percentage increase in revenues for the two most recent years (for example, [(2001 revenues—2000 revenues)/2000 revenues]) and compare these percentages with the percentage increases in net income for the same periods of time. Search the income statements for possible explanations of why net income is growing at a different rate than revenue.
3. Review each company's revenue recognition footnote. Do the companies' revenue recognition policies make sense given the nature of their operations?
4. Determine whether each annual report provides additional breakdown of revenues and net income. Common breakdowns are by business segment and by geographical location. Are the companies you are reviewing becoming more or less diversified in terms of sources of revenue and income? Are the companies becoming more or less international in terms of the revenue and income obtained from outside the United States?
5. Do any of the annual reports contain a below-the-line item? That is, are there any companies with discontinued operations, extraordinary items, or cumulative changes in accounting principles? Review the footnotes to the annual reports to obtain detailed information as to the nature of these items.

Ethics Dilemma

How Flexible Are Income Statement Estimates?

Far from being an exact science, accounting involves estimation and judgment. Consider the case of Dwight Nelson, chief financial officer of Pilot Enterprises. Pilot is a relatively young, privately held company with thoughts of going public in the near future. The owners of the business would like to include in the prospectus (a document containing information about the company and its past performance) financial statements that support their assertion that Pilot is a successful company with a bright future.

The problem is this: the income statement for the past year shows a slight decrease in income from the prior period. When Dwight presented this information to the board of directors of Pilot, he was told that the income statement would have to be revised. He was specifically counseled to review his estimates associated with bad debt expense, warranty expense, and estimated useful life of depreciable assets. He was invited to present his "revised" income statement to the board of directors when it showed a 5 percent increase over last period's net income—anything less would not do.

After reviewing the assumptions made regarding uncollectibles, warranties, and depreciation, Dwight found that he could revise his estimates and obtain the 5 percent target increase in income. But he did not feel that the revised income statement properly reflected the performance of Pilot for the period.

1. What are the risks to Dwight of revising the income statement to meet the target figure?
2. What are the risks to Dwight of not revising the income statement to meet the target figure?

The Debate

What Is Accrual-Basis Income?

Most people understand the purpose of a balance sheet—it reports a company's resources and claims to those resources. Most people understand a statement of cash flows—it reports where a firm's cash comes from and where the cash goes. The concept of "income" is a little more difficult for many people to get a handle on. Is it cash? Is it retained earnings? Just what is it and what does it measure?

Divide your group into two teams.

- One team represents cash-basis income. You contend that instead of measuring revenues, we should measure cash collected from customers. Instead of measuring cost of goods sold, we should measure cash paid for inventory, and so on.
- The other team represents accrual-basis income. You believe that the accrual accounting rules developed by accountants over the years provide a superior measure of income.

In preparing your debate positions, consider things such as:

- Which measure of income would better predict the future performance of a company and why?
- Which measure of income is easier to understand for the users of financial information?

Note: Your teams are NOT to make even-handed, reasonable arguments. Each team is an advocate for a position and should do everything possible (short of lying, of course) to present a convincing case.

Cumulative Spreadsheet Project

This spreadsheet assignment is a continuation of the spreadsheet assignments given in earlier chapters. If you completed those spreadsheets, you have a head start on this one.

1. Refer back to the financial statement numbers for Handyman Company for 2001 (given in part (1) of the Cumulative Spreadsheet Project assignment in Chapter 2). Using the balance sheet and income statement created with those numbers, create spreadsheet cell formulas to compute and display values for the following ratios:
   a. gross profit percentage (gross profit/sales)
   b. operating income percentage (operating income/sales)
   c. return on sales (net income/sales)
   d. asset turnover (sales/total assets)
   e. return on assets (net income / total assets)
2. Determine the impact of each of the following transactions on the ratio values computed in (1). Treat each transaction independently, meaning that before determining the impact of each new transaction you should reset the financial statement values to their original amounts. Each of the hypothetical transactions is assumed to occur on the last day of the year.
   a. Collected $20 cash from customer receivables.
   b. Purchased $100 in property, plant, and equipment. The entire amount of the purchase was financed with new stockholder investment.
   c. Sold goods costing $50 for $75, all on account.
   d. Sold property, plant, and equipment costing $100 for $100 cash. The cash was then used to repay long-term debt.
   e. Incurred additional operating expenses of $20, all on account.
3. Review the transactions in (2). Should any of these transactions have impacted income tax expense? Explain.
4. Handyman wishes to prepare a forecasted balance sheet and a forecasted income statement for 2002. Use the original financial statement numbers for 2001 (given in part (1) of the Cumulative Spreadsheet Project assignment in Chapter 2) as the basis for the forecast, along with the following additional information:
   a. Sales in 2002 are expected to increase by 40 percent over 2001 sales of $700.

b. In 2002, Handyman expects to acquire new property, plant, and equipment costing $80.
c. The $160 in operating expenses reported in 2001 breaks down as follows: $5 depreciation expense, $155 other operating expenses.
d. No new long-term debt will be acquired in 2002.
e. No cash dividends will be paid in 2002.
f. New short-term loans payable will be acquired in an amount sufficient to make Handyman's current ratio in 2002 exactly equal to 2.

CLEARLY STATE ANY ADDITIONAL ASSUMPTIONS THAT YOU MAKE.

Internet Search

We opened this chapter with a brief history of General Motors. To find out a little more about General Motors, access General Motors' Web site at www.gm.com. Once you've gained access to General Motors' Web site, answer the following questions:

1. In what year was the first American car to be manufactured in large quantities produced? (See the Company Overview site.)
2. Locate GM's financial statements and create a graph that charts the following numbers over the most recent three-year period: (a) net sales and revenues, (b) income from continuing operations, and (c) net income. What conclusions can you draw from this simple graph?
3. Locate GM's financial statement footnote on revenue recognition. How does the company recognize revenue for its various revenue sources?
4. What is GM's policy regarding the treatment of product-related expenses? How does the company depreciate its property?

8

Introduction to Business Expenses

CHAPTER LEARNING OBJECTIVES

- Introduce the reporting of allowable deductions by individuals, corporations, and conduit entities.
- Describe the classification of expenditures as those that are related to a taxpayer's trade or business, those for the production of income, and those for personal use.
- Discuss the criteria for distinguishing a trade or business from a production-of-income activity.
- Describe mixed-purpose assets and mixed-use expenditures and discuss the tax treatment of such assets and expenditures.
- Explain the ordinary, necessary, and reasonable requirements for the deduction of trade or business and production-of-income expenses.
- Discuss the general classes of expenditures for which a deduction is not allowed.
- Explain the potential for abuse and the consequent tax treatment of three mixed-use expenditures: hobby expenses, vacation home expenses, and home office expenses.
- Explain the general rules for deducting expenses under the cash and the accrual methods of accounting and the specific requirements for related party accrued expenses.

▲ CONCEPT REVIEW ▲

Ability to pay A tax should be based on the amount that the taxpayer can afford to pay, relative to other taxpayers.

Accounting method A taxpayer must adopt an accounting method that clearly reflects income.

Administrative convenience Those items for which the cost of compliance would exceed the revenue generated are not taxed.

Annual accounting period All entities report the results of their transactions on an annual basis (the tax year). Each tax year stands on its own, apart from other tax years.

Arm's-length transaction A transaction in which all parties to the transaction have bargained in good faith and for their individual benefit, not for the benefit of the transaction group.

Basis This is the amount of unrecovered investment in an asset. As amounts are expended and/or recovered relative to an asset over time, the basis is adjusted in consideration of such changes. The **adjusted basis** of an asset is the original basis, plus or minus the changes in the amount of unrecovered investment.

Business purpose To be deductible, an expenditure or a loss must have a business or other economic purpose that exceeds any tax avoidance motive. The primary motive for the transaction must be to make a profit.

Capital recovery No income is realized until the taxpayer receives more than the amount invested to produce the income. The amount invested in an asset represents the maximum amount recoverable.

Entity All items of income, deduction, and so on are traced to the tax unit responsible for the item.

Legislative grace Any tax relief provided is the result of a specific act of Congress that must be strictly applied and interpreted. All income received is taxable unless a specific provision in the tax law excludes the income from taxation. Deductions must be approached with the philosophy that nothing is deductible unless a provision in the tax law allows the deduction.

Related party Family members and corporations that are owned by family members are considered related parties, as are certain other relationships between entities in which the power to control the substance of a transaction is evidenced through majority ownership.

Tax benefit rule Any deduction taken in a prior year that is recovered in a subsequent year is income in the year of recovery, to the extent that a tax benefit was received from the deduction.

Wherewithal to pay Income is recognized in the period in which the taxpayer has the means to pay the tax on the income.

INTRODUCTION

Chapter 1 pointed out that deductible expenditures are grouped into three broad categories: business expenses, losses, and other itemized deductions. This chapter focuses on the general requirements for deducting business expenses. Specific business-expense deductions are the topic of Chapter 6, deductions for losses are discussed in Chapter 7, and itemized deductions that are specific to individual taxpayers are fully discussed in Chapter 8.

Tax **deductions** are a matter of legislative grace. As a result, two restrictions immediately apply to deductions. First, only deductions allowed by the tax law may be subtracted to compute taxable income. The deduction provisions are part of Congress's approach to implementing the ability-to-pay concept. By allowing deductions, Congress is, in effect, recognizing the inequity that could result from imposing a tax on gross income rather than taxable income. Therefore, Congress allows deductions for the costs of earning income and certain other expenditures. Second, a deduction is allowed for an item only if all the requirements for the deduction are satisfied. Because deductions are intended to provide relief from tax, the deduction rules are strictly interpreted and applied. Thus, a deduction is not allowed merely because a taxpayer thinks it is fair or equitable to use the expenditure to reduce income.

▲ EXAMPLE 1 Joan earns $25,000 in wages as a county property tax assessor. John owns and operates his own business selling Slippery Oil. John's Slippery Oil sales are $60,000, the cost of the oil sold is $25,000, and he has other business expenses of $10,000.

Discussion: Joan should report $25,000 in wages as gross income. Because the tax law allows a deduction for the cost of sales and business expenses, John has a gross income of $35,000 ($60,000 − $25,000) and reports $25,000 in taxable income from his business ($35,000 − $10,000). After recovering his expenses, John pays tax on his increase in wealth according to the ability-to-pay concept. Compared with Joan's tax treatment, it is inequitable to tax John on his gross income and deny him a deduction to recover the amounts he invests to earn a profit.

▲ **EXAMPLE 2** Randy and Cindy are both practicing CPAs, specializing in tax. Randy enrolls in law school so he can take tax courses. He intends to get a law degree. Cindy enrolls in a master's program in tax to improve her skills as a tax accountant. Eventually, Cindy hopes to earn the master's degree.

Discussion: Both Randy and Cindy have incurred expenses to improve or maintain their skills as practicing tax accountants. However, Randy cannot deduct his expenses. Educational expenses that qualify a person for a new profession (the practice of law) are not deductible. Cindy's expenses are deductible because they relate to her job and do not qualify her for a new profession.[1] Although treating Randy differently than Cindy seems unfair, Randy did not satisfy all the requirements of the tax law to claim an educational expense deduction.

To deduct a **business expense,** the expenditure must have a business purpose that is unrelated to its tax effect. Under the business purpose concept, there must be a business purpose for the expenditure that exceeds any tax-avoidance motive. Failure to establish a business purpose for the expense can result in the loss of the deduction. In most instances, a business purpose can be established by showing that the expense was related to a profit-motivated transaction. When the taxpayer has both business and personal reasons for an expenditure, the taxpayer risks losing the deduction. For these expenditures, the taxpayer will need to show that the business purpose was the primary or dominant motive for the transaction.

▲ **EXAMPLE 3** Zoltan is a physician who has not seen his sister for more than 10 years because she lives in Kenya. He would like to visit her and write a book about his experiences. He has never written a book. Because his trip has a business purpose—to write a book—Zoltan intends to deduct the full cost of his trip as a business expense. Has Zoltan met the dominant motive requirement for deducting the cost of the trip?

Discussion: Because Zoltan has several motives for making the trip, he will have to prove that the dominant motive is a business purpose. Based on the facts, it would appear that Zoltan is not entitled to a deduction because the primary purpose of his trip is a personal reason (to visit his sister). Because Zoltan has no experience in writing travel books, he would have a hard time proving that writing the book is his dominant motive.

Gross income has been defined to include only the excess of an individual's capital investment. As a result, the expenditure or consumption of capital to earn income results in a tax deduction. The capital recovery concept limits the amount of a deduction to the amount of the expenditure or the taxpayer's investment in an asset. As a result of this concept, the deduction for an item may not exceed the taxpayer's cost. For example, the payment of a $500 business expense is limited to a $500 deduction. In this chapter, basis is used to identify the amount that can be deducted under the capital recovery concept. *Basis* is a technical term that was introduced as a construct in Chapter 2 and is discussed in detail in Chapter 9. For discussion purposes, think of basis as the cost of an asset or the dollar amount of a specific expenditure. Thus, basis represents the maximum amount of an expenditure that can be deducted as a recovery of capital.

The accounting concepts discussed in Chapter 2 influence the tax treatment of deductions. Although a deduction of basis is allowed under the capital recovery concept, the entity concept requires the taxpayer claiming the deduction to own the capital being deducted as a recovery. Thus, the entity concept prevents one taxpayer from deducting another taxpayer's expenditures.

▲ **EXAMPLE 4** Miranda is a public accountant and is required by state law to have a license to practice public accounting. When the state license renewal fee comes due, Miranda is short of money and cannot renew her license. Miranda's mother pays the license renewal fee for her so she can continue working as a public accountant. Can Miranda deduct the fee as a business expense?

Discussion: The license renewal fee is Miranda's business expense, and only she can deduct the payment of the fee. Because Miranda does not pay the license renewal fee, she is not allowed a deduction for the business expense. Because the license renewal fee is not Miranda's mother's expense, her mother cannot deduct the payment of the expense. Based on these facts, neither Miranda nor her mother can deduct the payment of the license renewal fee.

Note that the bad tax result here can be avoided if Miranda's mother either gifts or makes a valid loan to Miranda of the money necessary to pay the licensing fee and Miranda makes the payment from her own funds.

The annual accounting period concept requires the taxpayer to use an acceptable accounting method to determine the year in which a deduction should be reported. Once an accounting method is adopted, it should be used as the basis for the systematic and consistent allocation of expenses to the proper tax years. Failure to claim an expense in the correct year can result in loss of the deduction. If an expenditure, such as utilities or office supplies, benefits only one tax year, it is allowed as a deduction in the year benefited. When an expenditure benefits more than one accounting period, the expenditure is usually allocated, based on the annual accounting period concept, to the proper tax years by using an acceptable accounting method. Examples of expenses that may need to be allocated are prepaid rent, prepaid interest, and prepaid insurance as well as depreciation on buildings and equipment. If the expenditure has an indefinite life, it is normally not deducted until the accounting period in which the asset is disposed of, abandoned, or proved to have lost its value. Thus, assets such as securities and land that do not have definite useful lives are not subject to amortization or depreciation for tax purposes.

As deductions are more closely examined in the rest of this chapter, the concepts discussed in Chapter 2 will be related to the specific rules and requirements for a deduction. The discussion and examples throughout this chapter consider deduction issues from the points of view of individuals, corporations, and conduit entities (partnerships and S corporations). Situations in which a tax rule applies only to individual taxpayers will be pointed out.

Reporting Deductions

The phrases **deductions for adjusted gross income** and **deductions from adjusted gross income** identify where in the tax computation an individual taxpayer deducts an allowable expense. Because all of a corporation's expenses are related to a business purpose, it is not necessary to use these two phrases when discussing its deductions; a corporation does not have personal expenses similar to those of an individual, which are deducted from adjusted gross income. Thus, the term **adjusted gross income** is unique to the individual tax computation.

Chapter 1 introduced an income tax computational framework as an overview of the federal income tax computation. At this point, we expand the framework for computing an individual's income tax (see Exhibit 5–1) to illustrate how individuals deduct various expenses. This chapter discusses the distinctions among *trade or business, production of income,* and *personal expenses.* Note in Exhibit 5–1 that trade or business expenses are deducted *for* adjusted gross income, whereas production-of-income expenses are subtracted as a deduction *from* adjusted gross income.[2] Recall that amounts deducted for adjusted gross income are always deductible, but deductions from adjusted gross income are subject to various limitations.

Trade or business expenses, expenses related to the production of rent and royalty income, losses on sales of property used in a trade or business, and capital losses (limited to $3,000) are deducted from gross income to compute adjusted gross income. As a result of legislative grace, these deductions receive more favorable treatment than deductions from adjusted gross income. Unless the passive activity rules discussed in Chapter 7 apply, trade or business expenses and losses and rent expenses are fully allowed as deductions for adjusted gross income in computing taxable income.

The allowable deduction from adjusted gross income is the greater of the taxpayer's standard deduction amount or allowable itemized deductions.[3] **Itemized deductions** consist of allowable personal expenditures[4] and miscellaneous itemized

▲ **Exhibit 5–1**

INDIVIDUAL INCOME TAX COMPUTATION FRAMEWORK

Income "broadly defined"
(includes income from all sources)
Minus: **Excluded sources of income**
Equals: **Gross income**
Minus: **Deductions for adjusted gross income**
- Trade or business expenses
- Rent or royalty expenses
- Trade or business losses
- Capital loss deduction ($3,000 maximum)
- Other specifically allowable deductions

Equals: **Adjusted gross income**
Minus: **Deductions from adjusted gross income**
The greater of:
1. Standard deduction

or

2. Allowable itemized deductions:
   - Deductible personal expenditures
     - Medical expenses
     - Home mortgage interest/investment interest
     - Property taxes/state income taxes
     - Charitable contributions
     - Personal casualty losses
   - Other miscellaneous itemized deductions
     - Investment expenses for the production of income
     - Expenses related to tax return preparation and compliance
     - Unreimbursed employee business expenses

Minus: **Personal and dependency exemptions**
Equals: **Taxable income**

deductions. Most itemized deductions are subject to income limitations. For example, investment expenses are deductible as miscellaneous itemized deductions. However, miscellaneous itemized deductions must be reduced by 2 percent of adjusted gross income in calculating the amount of the total expense that can be deducted.[5] In addition, total itemized deductions are reduced for high-income taxpayers. As a result, deductions from adjusted gross income receive less favorable treatment than deductions for adjusted gross income. Except for rent and royalty expenses deducted for adjusted gross income and investment interest, all expenses for the production of income are deductible as miscellaneous itemized deductions, subject to the 2 percent of adjusted gross income limitation. The computation of allowable personal itemized deductions and the applicable limitations are discussed in Chapter 8. If the taxpayer uses the predetermined standard deduction, all tax benefits available from an itemized deduction for investment expenses are lost.

▲ **EXAMPLE 5** Jennifer owns a dress shop. During the current year, she incurs $43,000 in valid expenses related to the dress shop. In addition, Jennifer incurs $6,000 in expenses related to production-of-income activities. If Jennifer's adjusted gross income is $83,000 without considering either of these expenses, how much expense can she deduct?

Discussion: Trade or business expenses are deductions for adjusted gross income. The $43,000 in trade or business expenses reduces her adjusted gross income to $40,000 ($83,000 − $43,000). Production-of-income expenses are deductible as miscellaneous itemized deductions, subject to the 2% of adjusted gross income limitation. Therefore, Jennifer is allowed to deduct only $5,200 [$6,000 − ($40,000 × 2%)] of the production-of-income expenses.

Note another advantage of the deductions for adjusted gross income: By reducing adjusted gross income, the amount of any deduction from adjusted gross income that is subject to a limitation increases. In this case, the $43,000 in business expenses allows Jennifer an extra $860 ($43,000 × 2%) deduction of her production-of-income expenses. Thus, correct classification of a deduction as for adjusted gross income or from adjusted gross income is critical in the calculation of an individual's taxable income.

Conduit Entity Reporting

Conduit entities (partnerships and S corporations) are not subject to tax. Rather, the taxable income from the conduit flows through to each owner, and each is taxed on his or her individual tax return. As discussed in Chapter 3, a conduit entity reports some items separately to the partner or shareholder, because certain income items (such as capital gains) are subject to special tax rules; they are not included in the calculation of a conduit entity's ordinary taxable income or loss.[6] Certain deductions are also subject to special tax rules—typically limitations on the amount that can be deducted by the owners—and must be reported separately. For example, investment expenses of individuals are miscellaneous itemized deductions that must be reduced by 2 percent of adjusted gross income. Therefore, as with some income items, not all deductions of a conduit entity are used in calculating ordinary taxable income or loss.

▲ **EXAMPLE 6** The Hackett Group (HG), a partnership, operates a management consulting firm; it consists of three equal partners, Mark, Nancy, and Ahmed. HG's taxable income for the year is $255,000, consisting of the following:

Sales revenues	$1,500,000
Short-term capital gain	27,000
Trade and business expenses	(1,260,000)
Investment expenses	(12,000)
Taxable income	$ 255,000

How must the Hackett Group report its results to Mark, Nancy, and Ahmed for tax purposes?

Discussion: Because the Hackett Group must report each partner's share of short-term capital gain and investment expenses, the Hackett Group cannot divide the partnership's taxable income of $255,000 equally and report ordinary taxable income of $85,000 ($255,000 ÷ 3) to each partner. Rather, the Hackett Group uses only the partnership's sales revenue and business expenses to calculate the ordinary taxable income for each partner. As a result, each partner's share of the ordinary taxable income is $80,000 [($1,500,000 − $1,260,000 = $240,000) ÷ 3]. The Hackett Group must report to each partner $9,000 ($27,000 ÷ 3) of short-term capital gain and $4,000 ($12,000 ÷ 3) of investment expenses.

Because investment expenses must be reduced by 2 percent of adjusted gross income, investment expenses are not included in calculating the conduit's ordinary taxable income or loss. Otherwise, each partner is able to deduct the full amount of the investment expenses.

▲ **EXAMPLE 7** Assume the same facts as in example 6. Ahmed is single; his adjusted gross income for the year is $25,000, and his total itemized deductions are $12,000 (before considering the information in example 6). What is the effect on Ahmed's taxable income of stating the investment expenses separately?

Discussion: If the Hackett Group did not report both investment income and expenses separately, Ahmed's ordinary taxable income from the Hackett Group would be $85,000 ($255,000 ÷ 3). He would have an adjusted gross income of $110,000 ($25,000 + $85,000), itemized deductions of $12,000, and taxable income of $95,100 ($110,000 – $12,000 – $2,900).

Because the capital gains and investment expenses receive special tax treatment, HG must report these items separately. Ahmed's share of the ordinary income is $80,000, and his adjusted gross income is $114,000 ($25,000 + $80,000 + $9,000). The $4,000 of investment expenses is a miscellaneous itemized deduction, which is reduced by 2% of adjusted gross income.

Investment expenses	$4,000
Limitation: 2% × $114,000	(2,280)
Investment expense deduction	$1,720

Ahmed's itemized deductions total $13,720 ($12,000 + $1,720), and his taxable income is $97,380 ($114,000 − $13,720 − $2,900). Because HG reports these items separately, Ahmed's taxable income increases by $2,280 ($97,380 − $95,100).

In essence, the owner and not the conduit entity is subject to tax. The conduit is viewed as only a form of organization, with the income and deductions flowing through to each owner. This ensures that income and deductions of a conduit are treated similarly to income and deductions incurred by an individual taxpayer. As example 7 illustrates, it is important that a conduit entity report separately any deduction that receives special tax treatment. The following is a list of commonly incurred deductions that a conduit entity must report separately:

- Charitable contributions
- Investment interest expense
- Investment expenses
- Section 179 expense
- Nondeductible expenses

Classification of Deductions

Proper application of the ability-to-pay and legislative grace concepts requires the separation of expenditures that qualify for deduction from those that are not allowed by the tax law. The basic test to be applied to obtain the initial classification of expenditures is whether the expenditure is related to a profit-motivated transaction or is motivated by personal needs and wants. Thus, expenditures are initially classified as profit-motivated or personal expenditures. Figure 5–1 illustrates this classification scheme.

Profit-Motivated Expenditures

As discussed in Chapter 1, a taxpayer may legitimately plan transactions to avoid the payment of tax. Because business profits reflect tax costs and savings, the tax effect of a transaction is an important planning consideration. A legitimate business reason for entering a transaction is to save taxes. However, the tax law prohibits deductions that are motivated solely by the expected tax benefits (savings). To be deductible, the business purpose concept requires an expenditure to have a bona fide

▲ **Figure 5–1**

Classification of Deductions of an Individual

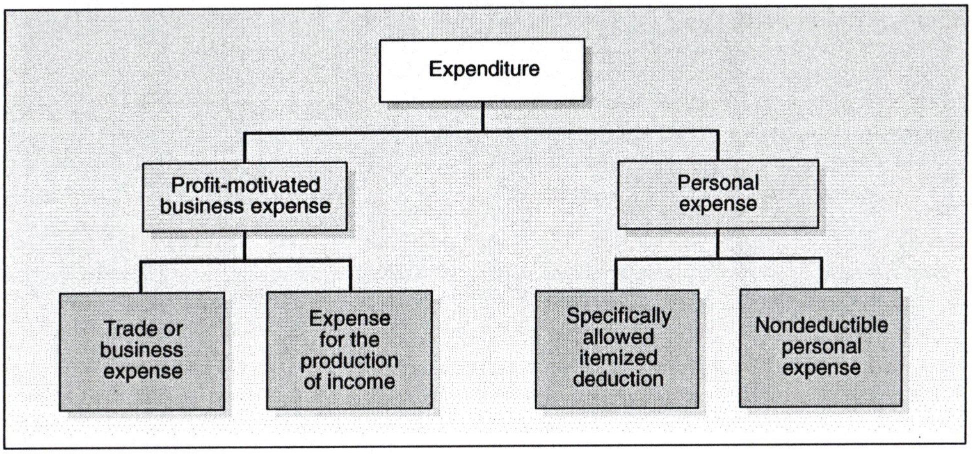

business reason other than tax avoidance. If the sole purpose of a transaction is tax savings, it will not be allowed as a deduction.

The courts maintain that the presence of a business purpose does not always require that a transaction be recognized. Where objective evidence indicates no potential for economic profit apart from tax savings, a transaction can be disregarded.[7] Thus, to be deductible, the dominant motive for incurring a business expense must be to earn a profit that is independent of any tax savings. Therefore, only expenses that satisfy the requirement that profit be the **dominant motive** are classified as business expenses.

▲ **EXAMPLE 8** Harry's son Junior wants to open a motorcycle dealership. Because Junior is short of funds, Harry purchases a building for the dealership and leases it to Junior. No lease is signed, but Harry tells Junior not to worry about paying rent until the dealership begins to show a profit. In addition, Harry agrees not to sell the building without Junior's approval. Is Harry's dominant motive in acquiring the building to obtain a profit?

Discussion: On the facts presented, Harry's dominant motive in acquiring the building is to help his son get his business established. Because there is no formal rental agreement and Harry will not sell the building without Junior's approval, the purchase of the building and the payment of costs related to the building are in the nature of a gift. Harry is not attempting to profit from either rental payments or potential appreciation in the value of the business. Therefore, any expenditures Harry makes regarding the building are not classified as business expenses. As personal expenses, only those personal expenses specifically allowed by the tax law (property taxes) are deductible.

Recall from Chapter 2 that the business purpose concept means that the taxpayer's dominant motive for an expenditure is to earn an economic benefit (profit) before considering the effects of tax savings. Thus, profit-motivated expenses, or expenses related to a business purpose, are deductible as business expenses. Throughout the remainder of this text, reference to a *business expense* means that the expenditure satisfies the dominant profit-motive requirement.

Based on the legislative grace concept, business expenses are grouped into two main categories:

- Trade or business expenses
- Expenses for the production of income

Both classifications apply to individuals and certain conduit entities (partnerships, S corporations, etc.). However, production-of-income expenses do not apply to corporations. A corporation's expenses are always classified as trade or business expenses, regardless of the underlying business purpose. The deductions allowed under these two provisions of the tax law are the types of expenses that you would expect to find on a typical income statement. For example, on an income statement, you expect to find employee wages, depreciation expense, advertising, and similar items subtracted from income to determine net income. Thus, you are already familiar with several types of expenses that are allowed as business deductions.

Trade or Business or Production-of-Income Expenses?

Because business expenses are classified either as related to a trade or business or for the production of income, it is necessary to look at these two classifications more closely. Although many of the same kinds of expenses can be deducted in these two categories, the tax result can be significantly different. As explained later, classification of an activity as either a trade or business or for the production of income depends on the facts related to the particular activity. No single definition applies to all situations. Because both types of activities must be profit-motivated, a trade or business will most likely be identified by the extent of the taxpayer's involvement and whether the intent is to earn a living from the activity.

Trade or Business Expenses. If a taxpayer's activities qualify as a trade or business, the related expenses are fully deductible. As you can see from the following excerpt from the tax law, **trade or business expenses** is broadly defined:

> SEC. 162. TRADE OR BUSINESS EXPENSES
> (A) IN GENERAL—There shall be allowed as a deduction all the ordinary and necessary expenses paid or incurred during the taxable year in carrying on any trade or business, including—
> (1) a reasonable allowance for salaries or other compensation for personal services actually rendered;
> (2) traveling expenses (including amounts expended for meals and lodging other than amounts that are lavish or extravagant under the circumstances) while away from home in the pursuit of a trade or business; and
> (3) rentals or other payments required to be made as a condition to the continued use or possession, for purposes of the trade or business, of property to which the taxpayer has not taken or is not taking title or in which he has no equity.

A taxpayer may deduct "all the ordinary and necessary expenses" of operating a "trade or business." But what is a trade or business? The Internal Revenue Code contains at least 50 references to a trade or business without defining the phrase. The Treasury regulations are also silent on the definition of a trade or business. Therefore, the task has been left to the courts. One interpretation observed for many years was that taxpayers who held themselves out as engaged in the selling of goods or services were engaged in a trade or business. Although noting that a person selling goods or services would usually be engaged in a trade or business, in 1987 the Supreme Court rejected these activities as the single appropriate test for a trade or business. Instead, the Court took a broader view of what constituted a trade or business.

The Court has stated that to be engaged in a trade or business, a taxpayer must meet the following requirements:

- Profit motivation—The primary purpose for engaging in the activity must be to earn income or a profit.
- Continuous and regular activity—There must be continuity and regularity in the taxpayer's involvement in the activity.
- Livelihood, not a hobby—The activity must not be sporadic, a hobby, or an amusement diversion.[8]

The Court went on to say that whether an activity meets these tests must be determined by examining the facts in each case. In this regard, the Court noted that taxpayers meeting the prior "holding out as a seller of goods and services" test would normally meet the requirements for being engaged in a trade or business.

As a general rule, an employee is usually engaged in the trade or business of rendering services to the employer. The most common problem encountered in delineating a trade or business activity from a production-of-income activity involves dealings in securities. A person who transacts business in securities may be an active investor, an active trader, or a dealer in securities. Unlike active traders and dealers, active investors are not considered to be in a trade or business.

An **active investor** is a person who continually, regularly, and extensively manages her or his own portfolio with a view toward long-term appreciation in the portfolio's value and not short-term profit. An active investor's income is earned from interest, dividends, and gains from long-term holdings of securities, and the investment expenses are deductible only as miscellaneous itemized deductions. An active investor is never deemed to be engaged in a trade or business.

An **active trader** earns a livelihood buying and selling securities for personal profit. The main source of an active trader's income is from selling securities for more than they cost to make a profit. The securities are typically held for a short time before they are sold, with the active investor trying to capture the short-term swings in the market. Thus, an active trader may be distinguished from the active investor by the nature of the investing activities and the source of income. If the trader's activities are frequent and substantial, the trader will be deemed to be engaged in a trade or business, and the expenses will be deductible for adjusted gross income.

Distinguishing a trader from an active investor is often quite difficult. The determination of whether a taxpayer should be classified as a trader or an active investor is best left to a tax expert.

A **securities dealer** purchases a security expecting to realize a profit from selling it to a customer for a fee or commission. The dealer acts as an agent who performs the services of a wholesaler or retailer in bringing together a buyer and a seller. Dealers have customers with whom they deal to earn a profit. Dealers are deemed to be engaged in a trade or business.

Expenses for the Production of Income. If the taxpayer's business activity fails to qualify as a trade or business, expenses related to the production of income may still be deductible under Section 212 of the Internal Revenue Code. Although the formal tax term for these deductions is *nonbusiness expenses*, we will refer to these items as **investment expenses,** consistent with the terminology used by most taxpayers. The tax law provides a broad definition of **production-of-income expenses** that an individual taxpayer can deduct:

> SEC. 212. EXPENSES FOR THE PRODUCTION OF INCOME.
> In the case of an individual there shall be allowed as a deduction all the ordinary and necessary expenses paid or incurred during the taxable year—
> (1) for the production or collection of income;
> (2) for the management, conservation, or maintenance of property held for the production of income, or
> (3) in connection with the determination, collection, or refund of any tax.

The objectives of Section 212 are to tax the net profits of income-motivated transactions and to allow individuals a deduction for costs of complying with the tax law. However, expenses deducted under this provision receive less-favorable treatment than trade or business expenses. Generally, expenses related to earning rent and royalty income are treated the same (as deductions for adjusted gross income), whether they are considered to be for the production of income or trade or business expenses. However, as shown in Exhibit 5–1, other investment and tax-related expenses allowed by Section 212 are deducted from adjusted gross income as "other miscellaneous itemized deductions." In addition, total itemized deductions are often subject to special adjustments (discussed in Chapter 8) that reduce the amount allowed as a deduction for computing taxable income.

▲ **EXAMPLE 9** Grady owns a large portfolio of stocks, bonds, and other securities. What is the treatment of Grady's securities activities in each of the following cases?

Case A

Grady spends all his time managing his portfolio. He continually trades securities to obtain a profit from short-term price increases. Grady rarely holds a security for the dividend or interest income it may produce or for long-term appreciation in value. He has no other job and receives the bulk of his income from his securities dealings.

Case B

Grady is employed as a chemist for Dough Company. He spends an average of five hours per week studying investment materials and making investment decisions. Grady primarily invests in securities for their dividend and interest income and long-term appreciation potential. Because his portfolio is quite extensive, more than half his income comes from his security investments.

Discussion: In case A, Grady's activities constitute a trade or business. His primary motive is profit, he engages in the activity on a continual and regular basis, and his securities activities are his livelihood. Grady's business expenses are deductible for adjusted gross income. In addition, gains and losses from his securities dealings are considered gains and losses from a trade or business.

In case B, Grady's security dealings are a production-of-income activity. He receives a substantial portion of his income from his securities, but they are not his livelihood, nor does he engage in the activity with the continuity and regularity of a trade or business.

Therefore, Grady's expenses are deductible as miscellaneous itemized deductions. In addition, gains and losses Grady incurs from selling the securities are capital gains and losses.

To be deductible, investment expenses must bear a reasonable and proximate (close) relationship to the earning of taxable income. That is, the expenses must have a business purpose. Deductible investment expenses may relate to income earned in a prior year, the current year, or in a future year. In addition, the expenses may relate to a single transaction, such as the sale of a security, as well as to recurring transactions, such as the collection of interest or dividends. For example, the cost of a safe deposit box used to store stocks and bonds is an investment expense. The securities stored in the box may have paid interest and dividends in a prior year but not the current year. On the other hand, they may be paying income in the current year but may not have paid interest and dividends in prior years. Alternatively, they may never have paid interest or dividends, but they are being held for sale when their market value increases. Regardless of which situation applies, the safe deposit box rent is deductible. Other deductible investment expenses include employee wages, depreciation, advertising, advisory fees, office rent, and subscriptions to financial publications.

Rental Activity

Depending on the extent of the taxpayer's activities related to renting out real estate, the activity could be deemed either a trade or business or an investment activity. For many years, the mere rental of a single piece of improved real estate was considered a trade or business, whereas the rental of unimproved real estate was subject to an "all the facts and circumstances" test to determine the classification of the rental activity.[9] Improved real estate is land that has a building or other capital improvement on it. Unimproved real estate is raw land without a building or other structure on it. In recent years, several courts have begun to apply a facts-and-circumstances test to both improved and unimproved real estate to determine whether rental property is a trade or business or an investment asset. The courts have looked to the scope of the rental activities and the extent of the taxpayer's involvement with the rental operations to classify the property.

For example, the U.S. Tax Court considered whether a rental activity was a trade or business for purposes of the home office deduction.[10] The court indicated that, as a matter of law, a rental activity is not automatically a trade or business. Classification as a trade or business depends on the facts related to the taxpayer's activities. In examining the facts, the Tax Court looked at the scope of ownership and management activities in classifying a rental activity as a trade or business instead of an investment activity. The IRS has stated that rental property must produce income from an active trade or business, as opposed to income that would be earned on portfolio investments (e.g., stocks, bonds), to qualify as property used in a trade or business.

▲ **EXAMPLE 10** Frank agrees to lease land in downtown Chicago to Sleepytime Motels for 99 years. Under the lease, Sleepytime has the right to construct a motel on the land. Sleepytime is responsible for all expenses, claims, and liabilities related to the property. In the event of default on the lease, Frank has the right to assume ownership of the building and possession of the property. Is Frank's rental activity a trade or business or a production-of-income activity?

Discussion: Because Frank is not actively involved in the management of the property, the income earned is similar to the income that is earned by an investor in stocks or bonds. Thus, the lease described does not constitute a trade or business. Frank's rental activity is considered a production-of-income activity.

▲ **EXAMPLE 11** Yolanda owns two rental properties. She obtains tenants for the properties, makes repairs, provides maintenance, pays expenses related to the properties, and is subject to claims and liabilities arising from the rental properties. Is Yolanda's rental activity a trade or business or a production-of-income activity?

Discussion: Because Yolanda actively manages the two properties, pays expenses related to them, and is liable for claims on the properties, she is deemed to be engaged in a trade or business.

Note in Exhibit 5–1 that rental expenses are deductible for adjusted gross income. This is true whether the rental activity is classified as a trade or business or for the production of income. Therefore, the proper classification of rental deductions is not an issue in preparing a taxpayer's return. However, when the taxpayer decides to sell the property, the classification becomes important. Disposal of rental property at a gain results in similar tax treatment whether the property is classified as a trade or business or an investment asset. However, if the rental property is disposed of at a loss, the full amount of the loss can be deducted in the year of the sale only if the property is used in a trade or business (Exhibit 5–1). Investment property sold at a loss is classified as a capital loss. Although net capital losses are also deducted for adjusted gross income, a capital loss may be limited to a $3,000 deduction each year until it is fully used. Because of the limitation on capital losses, classification of rental real estate as an investment asset is usually less desirable than classification as a trade or business asset when the property is sold at a loss.

▲ **EXAMPLE 12** Frank sells the property in example 10 at a $10,000 loss during 2001. How much of the loss can Frank deduct?

Discussion: Because Frank's rental activity is a production-of-income activity, the $10,000 is a capital loss. The $10,000 loss would be included in the 2001, capital gain-and-loss netting. If Frank had no other capital gains and losses during 2001, he could deduct only $3,000 of the loss in 2001, with the remaining $7,000 of loss carried forward to 2002.

▲ **EXAMPLE 13** Assume that Yolanda sells one of her rental properties in example 11 at a $10,000 loss during 2001. How much of the loss can Yolanda deduct?

Discussion: Because Yolanda's rental activities constitute a trade or business, the $10,000 loss on the sale of the rental property is deducted in full in 2001 as a trade or business loss.

The trade or business versus investment characterization of rental real estate is also important if the taxpayer wants to claim deductions or credits, such as home office expenses, that are available only to a trade or business activity.

Personal Expenditures

An individual's personal expenditures are also grouped into two categories: allowable personal itemized deductions and nondeductible personal expenses. In contrast to expenditures for a business purpose in which all ordinary and necessary expenses are deductible, the tax law severely limits deductions for personal expenditures. As shown in Exhibit 5–1, allowable personal expenses are deductible from adjusted gross income. In addition, most personal itemized deductions are subject to a limit based on the taxpayer's adjusted gross income. A major problem in determining an individual's personal itemized deductions is that many assets and expenses are used for both business and personal purposes. Proper accounting for such assets and expenses requires segregation of the business portion from the personal portion.

Mixed Business and Personal Expenditures

These categories of expenditures, *mixed-use assets* and *mixed-use expenditures*, present special problems for individual taxpayers. A person's expenses related to mixed-use assets and mixed-use expenditures must be analyzed and allocated between profit-motivated and personal expenditures. To the extent an expense is related to a profit-motivated transaction, it is treated as a business expense. Unless the personal expenditure qualifies as an itemized deduction, it is not deductible.

Mixed-Use Assets. A **mixed-use asset** is an asset that is used both to earn income and for personal purposes. For tax purposes, the single asset is effectively treated as two separate assets. One is a business asset, and the other is a personal use asset. For example, a taxpayer may own one car that he uses to travel for his business and to provide local transportation for his family. To deny a deduction for the business use of the car would violate both the ability-to-pay and capital recovery concepts. Because the income earned using the car is taxable, a deduction is allowed for the expense related to the business use of the car. The cost of using the car to provide local transportation for the family is a personal expense that is not deductible. Thus, an expense that is related to using a mixed-use asset must be reasonably allocated between business and personal use. The portion of the expense reasonably allocated to business use is treated the same as other expenses that are related to the profit-motivated activity. An expense allocated to personal use cannot be deducted unless it qualifies as a specifically allowed itemized deduction.

▲ **EXAMPLE 14** Aaron purchases a computer in 2000 at a cost of $8,000. He uses the computer in his dry-cleaning business and for personal purposes after work and on weekends. During 2000, Aaron's records indicate that 75% of the computer's use is for business purposes and 25% for personal purposes. How should Aaron treat the computer for tax purposes?

Discussion: Aaron must treat the computer as two separate assets for tax purposes. For purposes of computing depreciation on the computer, only $6,000 ($8,000 × 75%) of the cost can be depreciated for tax purposes. The remaining $2,000 of cost is considered a personal use asset. Depreciation is not allowed on personal use assets.

▲ **EXAMPLE 15** Aaron sells the computer in 2002 for $4,000. His business use remains at 75% for 2001 and 2002. Aaron properly deducts $2,400 in depreciation on the computer for 2000 through 2002. What is Aaron's taxable gain or loss on the sale of the computer?

Discussion: Aaron must treat the sale of the computer as the sale of two assets—one a business asset and one a personal asset. The $4,000 sales price and the $8,000 purchase price must be allocated between business and personal use:

		Business	Personal
Selling price—$4,000 × 75%		$3,000	
$4,000 × 25%			$ 1,000
Less: Adjusted basis			
Original cost—$8,000 × 75%	$6,000		
$8,000 × 25%			(2,000)
Less: Depreciation	(2,400)	(3,600)	
Loss on sale		$ (600)	$(1,000)

The $600 loss on the business portion of the computer is deductible as a business loss. However, the $1,000 loss on the personal use portion is a nondeductible personal use loss.

Mixed-Use Expenditures. Mixed-use expenditures are also subject to special treatment. **Mixed-use expenditures** are expenses that are incurred for both profit and personal reasons. As with mixed-use assets, these expenditures must be allocated between business and personal use and deducted according to the rules for each use. In addition, certain types of mixed-use expenditures (e.g., hobby and vacation home expenses, which are discussed later in this chapter) are subject to special rules designed to prevent taxpayer abuse by disallowing all or part of an otherwise-deductible expenditure.

▲ **EXAMPLE 16** Pam travels to San Diego for 4 days primarily for business reasons. Her air fare costs $800, and she incurs expenses of $200 a day for lodging and incidentals. Because Pam has never been to San Diego, she stays 2 extra days to visit the zoo and to tour the city. How much of her costs can be deducted as a business expense?

Discussion: Pam has incurred mixed-use expenditures. The expense relates to a business trip and a personal vacation. Because the primary motive for making the trip (as evidenced by spending more days on business than for personal purposes) was to conduct business, Pam can deduct the full $800 air fare. She can also deduct $200 for each day she was in San Diego to conduct business. Pam cannot deduct any part of the $200 per day for lodging and incidentals for the 2 extra days she stayed for personal reasons.

CONCEPT CHECK For an expense to be deductible under the *business purpose concept*, it must have a business or other economic purpose that exceeds any tax avoidance motive. The primary motive for the transaction must be to make a profit. In addition, the *legislative grace concept* requires that any tax relief provided is the result of a specific act of Congress that must be strictly applied and interpreted. Deductions must be approached with the philosophy that nothing is deductible unless a provision in the tax law allows the deduction. Under the *entity concept*, all items of income and deduction are traced to the tax unit responsible for the item. Therefore, a taxpayer who uses an asset for both business and personal use (i.e., a mixed-use asset) or has expenses that are incurred for both business and personal reasons (i.e., mixed-use expenses) must separate the business portion from the personal portion. The *capital recovery concept* limits the deduction to the amount invested in the asset. The *annual accounting period concept* requires all entities to report the results of their operations on an annual basis. As a result, if an asset has a tax life that extends substantially beyond the end of the tax year, this concept requires the taxpayer to recover the cost of the asset over its tax life.

Tests for Deductibility

In classifying expenditures, only expenses that have a business purpose are treated as deductible trade or business and investment expenses. In addition to having a business purpose, these expenses must also be

- Ordinary
- Necessary
- Reasonable in amount

Note that all three requirements must be met to deduct a trade or business or an investment expense. Deductible trade or business and investment expenses may *not* be any of the following:

- A personal expense
- A capital expenditure
- A payment that frustrates public policy
- An expense related to tax-exempt income
- Another person's expense

The discussion that follows examines each requirement for determining deductible business and investment expenses.

Ordinary, Necessary, and Reasonable in Amount

Trade or business and investment-related activities are allowed a deduction for the ordinary and necessary expenses of earning income. In addition, the tax law provides that a trade or business can deduct reasonable salaries. According to the IRS and the courts, an expense must be reasonable in amount to be ordinary and necessary.[11] Thus, the portion of an expense that is not reasonable in amount will not be deductible because it is not ordinary or necessary. Because of their importance in identifying deductible business expenses, these terms need further consideration.

Ordinary Expense. An expenditure must qualify as an ordinary expense to be deductible. The term *ordinary* is generally interpreted to have two meanings. First, the expense must be of a kind commonly incurred in the particular income-earning activity.[12] Thus, the expense is said to be customary or usual in the activity. An **ordinary expense** is one that is normal, common, and accepted under the circumstances of the business community. In addition, although the expense must be common to the income-earning activity, it does not have to be a regularly recurring item for the taxpayer.

▲ **EXAMPLE 17** Kara owns and operates a pet shop. One day, a customer is bitten by a snake. Although the accident is the customer's fault, he sues Kara for $25,000. After Kara pays her lawyer $2,500 to defend her, the customer drops the suit. Are the legal fees an ordinary expense for Kara?

Discussion: Lawsuits by customers are a common occurrence in today's business environment. The cost of defending the business against the disgruntled customer is a normal cost of doing business, although it is not a recurring expense. The legal fees satisfy the ordinary test.

▲ **EXAMPLE 18** The Russo Company, which raises hogs, enters into a contract with the local feed mill to buy hog feed. Under the terms of the agreement, Russo agrees to purchase a quantity of grain and pay for it in advance. The mill agrees to deliver the feed as needed and to charge the deliveries against Russo's advance payment at the lower of the market price on delivery or the maximum price in the contract. Is the advance payment for the hog feed an ordinary expense?

Discussion: The payment for the grain qualifies as an ordinary expense. The advance purchase of the grain for feeding livestock is the normal way farmers conduct their business. By ensuring that the grain is available, Russo can better plan the scope of its farm operations for the coming months.

As these examples illustrate, an ordinary expense may or may not occur frequently. Also, the determination of what is usual or customary depends on the nature of the taxpayer's business. A typical expense for a pet shop (bird seed) is not a typical expense for an auto mechanic (repair parts).

The second meaning of *ordinary* is that the expenditure is an expense that is assignable to the current accounting period. A capital expenditure that provides future benefits cannot be deducted now.[13] Capital expenditures that benefit more than one tax year are allocated by means of a depreciation, depletion, or amortization deduction to the accounting periods receiving benefit from the use of the asset.

▲ **EXAMPLE 19** Gustav Brothers, a partnership, buys a $20,000 machine in the current year to use in its business. The machine has a 7-year tax life. When can the partnership deduct the cost of the machine?

Discussion: The machine is to be used to earn income during several tax years. As a result, its cost must be capitalized and allocated to the years benefited by the use of the machine. The deductions allowed for depreciation are discussed in Chapter 10.

Necessary Expense. An expense must also be necessary to be deductible. The courts have defined a **necessary expense** as one that is "appropriate and helpful" to the taxpayer's income activity.[14] An expense will be considered necessary if a reasonable and prudent businessperson would incur the expense in a similar situation. It is important to note that the term *necessary* does not mean that the expense must be essential to the continued existence of the income activity to be deductible. In most cases, the courts have tended to accept the taxpayer's judgment of the business necessity of the expenditure rather than attempt to determine the commercial value of the expenditure.

▲ **EXAMPLE 20** A tax lawyer purchases a large red, white, and blue flag with the numerals 1040 for his yacht. While using his yacht, many people inquire about the flag, and the tax attorney obtained a few customers as a result of such contact. Can the lawyer deduct the cost of operating his yacht as a promotional expense?

Discussion: On similar facts, the Tax Court determined that operating the yacht is not the ordinary method of promoting the taxpayer's business. Further, the court determined that the expenses of the yacht were so personal in nature that they could not be necessary in the common sense of the word.

▲ **EXAMPLE 21** Buster, Inc., is a women's clothing store in Fashion City. One day a year, the company pays $500 to publish a full-page advertisement in the town newspaper to announce its annual clothing sale. Is the cost of the advertisement deductible?

Discussion: The $500 paid for the sale advertisement is deductible. The expense satisfies both the ordinary and necessary tests. It is customary for clothing retailers to advertise their merchandise. In addition, the advertisement helps the business because it both promotes the store to the public and attracts the attention of customers, and gives them an incentive to shop at the store—to take advantage of the sale prices.

Reasonable in Amount. An expense must also be reasonable in amount to be deductible. An expense does not satisfy the ordinary and necessary tests unless it is reasonable in amount. The reasonableness test most often becomes an issue in transactions involving related parties. When unrelated parties are dealing at arm's length in their own best interests, the result of the negotiations will normally be a fair market value. However, related parties have incentives to shift income by charging prices higher or lower than what would be paid in an arm's-length transaction, so these costs would not constitute **reasonable expenses.**

▲ **EXAMPLE 22** Tara operates a shoe store in a building she rents from her father for $1,000 per month. Comparable store space is readily available for rent at $400 per month. Is the rental payment reasonable?

Discussion: Tara is allowed a $400 rent expense deduction unless she can establish that the location or other unique features of her father's building justify a higher rent than other, comparable store space. Unless Tara can prove otherwise, the $600 excess payment is considered a nondeductible payment to her father (a gift).

▲ **EXAMPLE 23** Roy pays Sally $100 per week to clean his medical office. When Sally became ill, he hired his daughter, Janice, to fill in and keep the office tidy. Roy pays Janice $300 a week. How much of the $300 payment is reasonable?

Discussion: Of the $300 per week paid Janice, he is allowed to deduct only $100, because that is the amount he pays Sally. Unless Roy can prove otherwise, Janice's $300 weekly salary is considered excessive because he normally pays $100 a week for the same services.

NOTE: In each of these examples, the apparently unreasonable compensation is paid to a related party. It is unlikely that the taxpayers in these examples would pay the same amounts had the transaction been with an unrelated party.

Not a Personal Expense

The tax law specifically disallows a deduction for personal, living, and family expenses.[15] Because deductions are a matter of legislative grace, this rule eliminates deductions for expenditures that do not have a business purpose, such as

- Premiums the insured taxpayer pays for life insurance
- Insurance premiums paid on the taxpayer's home and personal property
- Expenses of maintaining a home such as rent, utilities, and maintenance
- Losses from disposing of property held for personal, living, or family purposes
- The cost of transportation, meals, or lodging unless they are related to a trade or business, the production of income, charitable contributions, or medical expenses; the personal cost of commuting to work and back is not deductible
- Legal fees and costs of obtaining a divorce; the portion of the attorney's fee paid to obtain alimony or other taxable income is allowed as a deduction for the production of income
- The costs of obtaining an education to meet the minimum requirements of the taxpayer's trade or business or that are part of a program that qualifies the taxpayer to enter a new business or profession

Frequently, an expense is incurred for both business and personal reasons. Does the business purpose automatically qualify the expense for deduction? According to the IRS and the courts, the answer is no. To be deductible, the expense must bear a proximate relationship to the income-producing activity.[16] In addition, the primary or dominant motivation for incurring the expense must be the business purpose. A significant business motivation is not enough.

▲ **EXAMPLE 24** Atman and Sarita are good friends. Atman also supplies Sarita with artwork that she sells to customers in her interior decorating business. Atman takes Sarita to dinner at the Greyhouse. During the meal, they discuss business, and Sarita agrees to buy several pieces of art. Atman pays for the meal. Is the cost of the meal a business expense or a personal expense?

Discussion: If Atman takes Sarita to dinner just to spend time with a friend, the fact that the conversation drifts to business does not result in a business deduction for the meal. Because the dominant motive for the expense is personal, the expense is not deductible.

If Atman takes Sarita to dinner so he can discuss his artwork and to solicit an order for paintings and the event centered on a business discussion, Atman can deduct the cost of the meal as a business expense because the dominant motive is business.

Not a Capital Expenditure

A **capital expenditure** that results in an asset that benefits future accounting periods is not allowed as a current deduction because the useful life extends beyond the end of the tax year.[17] Capital expenditures include the cost of acquiring land, buildings, machinery, equipment, furniture, and fixtures; the cost of perfecting or defending title to property; and purchased goodwill. Amounts paid for freight and installation charges related to getting an asset to the taxpayer's location and set up are included in the asset's basis. If the taxpayer constructs an asset for his or her own business, the property's basis includes both the direct and indirect costs of production. If an asset has a useful life that extends substantially beyond the end of the tax year of the expenditure, its immediate deduction is generally not allowed.

▲ **EXAMPLE 25** Paula buys Colleen's advertising agency. As part of the purchase price, she pays Colleen $12,000 not to open another advertising agency in the area for 3 years. Can Paula deduct the $12,000 as a current business expense?

Discussion: The $12,000 payment (known as a *covenant not to compete*) will benefit Paula's business for 3 years by not having Colleen as a competitor during that period. Thus, the benefit of the payment extends substantially beyond the end of the tax year and must be capitalized and amortized as an intangible asset.

The capital recovery and the accounting period concepts require deduction of an asset's basis through depreciation, amortization, depletion, or as a reduction in the amount realized on the asset's disposition. For example, assets with a limited life, such as buildings and equipment, are subject to a depreciation expense deduction. The cost of assets with an indefinite useful life, such as land, are permanently capitalized until the asset's disposition. Based on the administrative convenience concept, tools that wear out and are thrown away within one year can be deducted in the year of purchase. Contrary to the general rule, by legislative grace, Congress lets taxpayers take a current deduction for certain long-lived assets. For example, a taxpayer can elect to expense certain depreciable business assets (Section 179 election).

The commission paid on the acquisition of a security is not a current deduction. When a commission is paid on the purchase of a security, it is considered part of the cost of buying the asset and is added to the security's basis. When the security is sold, the basis is deducted from the sale price as a capital recovery. The commission paid on the sale of a security is a reduction in the amount realized on the sale.

▲ **EXAMPLE 26** Connie purchases 100 shares of Calvinator Corporation stock for $100 per share. She also pays a commission on the purchase of $400. What is the basis of the 100 shares of stock?

Discussion: The basis of the stock is the cost of obtaining it. Because the commission is part of the cost of acquiring the stock, it is added to basis; commissions are not current period expenses. Therefore, the cost of the 100 shares of stock is $10,400 [(100 × $100) + $400].

▲ **EXAMPLE 27** Connie sells the 100 shares of stock purchased in example 26 for $130 per share. She pays a commission of $600 on the sale. What is Connie's gain or loss on the sale of the stock?

Discussion: Connie has a gain of $2,000 on the sale. The $600 commission is a reduction of the amount realized on the sale; it is not a current period expense:

Selling price (100 × $130)	$13,000
Less: Commissions	(600)
Amount realized from sale	$12,400
Less: Basis of shares sold	(10,400)
Gain on sale	$ 2,000

Repair-and-Maintenance Expense. The difference between a capital expenditure that results in an asset and a **repair-and-maintenance expense** is important. Repair-and-maintenance expenses are allowed as a deduction in the current accounting period.[18] Repairs include repainting an office, fixing a leaking water or gas line, patching a roof, and replacing a broken glass in a window. These expenses generally include the costs of keeping business assets in normal operating condition. Unlike improvements and replacements, repairs do not appreciably extend an asset's useful life or materially add to its value. **Improvements,** such as rewiring or putting a new roof on a building, should be capitalized, because they either extend useful life or add to the value of the property. A **replacement,** such as a major overhaul of a machine, that extends the life of an asset should also be capitalized. In addition, expenditures made as part of a plan to recondition, improve, or alter an asset (called *betterments*) should be capitalized as assets, although if considered separately, the individual expenditures might qualify as repairs.[19] The costs of improvements, replacements, and betterments should be deducted in the accounting periods benefited by their use, based on an acceptable depreciation or amortization method.

Start-up Costs. Capital expenditures can also include start-up costs. **Start-up costs** are related to investigating and creating a new active trade or business. The start-up costs to be capitalized are the expenses incurred before the new business begins its activities. Start-up costs could include

- Surveys and analyses of markets, facilities, and labor force
- Travel to develop the business and locate potential customers and suppliers
- Advertising the new business
- Salaries to train employees
- Salaries for executives and consultants
- Other expenses such as legal and accounting fees

The items included as capitalized start-up costs must be similar to expenses that would be deductible in expanding an existing business.

A taxpayer who begins a new business can amortize the start-up costs over 60 months or longer.[20] The amortization deduction is allowed starting in the month the new business begins its operations. If the taxpayer does not elect to amortize the start-up costs, they become locked in and can be deducted only upon disposition of the business. If the taxpayer does not enter the new business, expenses related to investigating it are not deductible.[21] The transaction is given this treatment because the taxpayer's motivation is deemed to be primarily personal before a new business is begun. A taxpayer's efforts to investigate a business do not establish a business purpose for the expenditures.

It is important to note that a taxpayer operating an existing trade or business can claim a current deduction for the cost of investigating, expanding, or establishing new locations for the same line of business. The investigation costs are considered an ordinary and necessary expense of the existing trade or business and therefore fully deductible when incurred. However, an existing business entering an unrelated trade or business is subject to the same capitalization rules as a new business.[22] If the unrelated business is not acquired, the investigation expenses are nondeductible.

▲ **EXAMPLE 28** Jason has operated Main Street Cafe for 15 years. He would like to branch out by opening another cafe in a nearby city. Can Jason deduct the costs of investigating the feasibility of opening the second cafe?

Discussion: Whether Jason decides to expand his business and open a second cafe or not, he can deduct the costs of investigating a location for a second cafe as a current deduction. Because the expenses are related to opening a business that is related to Jason's existing business, they are allowed as a current deduction, no matter what he decides.

▲ **EXAMPLE 29** What would happen if Jason, in example 28, investigates opening a retail store selling speedboats?

Discussion: The retail speedboat store would be a new business because it is unrelated to his cafe business. If Jason decides not to enter the retail boat business, he cannot deduct any investigation expenses. They are considered nondeductible personal expenses. If Jason acquires the retail store, he will have to capitalize the investigation expenses and amortize them over 60 months, starting with the month the new business started.

The costs of organizing a corporation or partnership must also be capitalized. Organization costs are those costs incurred to organize a corporation or a partnership. Such costs include legal, accounting, filing, and other fees and costs incidental to the start-up of a corporation or a partnership. They are similar to start-up costs in that they are incurred before the entity is legally organized. As such, they are subject to the same election as start-up costs and are amortized over a minimum of 60 months.[23]

Not Frustrate Public Policy

In a long series of cases before 1970, the courts disallowed deductions (usually for fines and penalties) for expenditures that the courts thought were frustrating public policy by encouraging unlawful conduct.[24] The courts' rationale was that it was neither ordinary nor necessary to violate the law. In 1969, Congress preempted the court battles by amending Section 162 to disallow certain categories of payments. The following payments are explicitly stated in the tax law as nondeductible expenditures:

- Direct or indirect illegal bribes or kickbacks to government officials and employees, including payments to federal, state, local, and foreign government officials and employees as well as officials and employees of a government agency
- Direct or indirect payments to any person of an amount that constitutes an illegal bribe, kickback, or other illegal payment under federal or state law (if the state law is generally enforced)
- Bribes, kickbacks, or rebates by a provider of services, supplier, physician, or other persons who furnish items or services under Medicare or Medicaid
- Fines, penalties, or similar payments to a governmental unit for the violation of any law
- Certain damage payments for violation of the antitrust laws

▲ **EXAMPLE 30** Rapid Trucking Company incurred several weight overload fines. Although Rapid took reasonable precautions to avoid violating the overall weight limit, loads that shifted during transit resulted in violations of the axle-weight limit. Can Rapid deduct the overload fines?

Discussion: Even if Rapid Trucking Company had exercised all due care and incurred the overweight fines without willful intent, the fines would not be allowed as a deduction. A deduction for fines is specifically disallowed as being in violation of public policy.

▲ **EXAMPLE 31** Chitsa is a tax return preparer. She forgot to sign tax returns she prepared for her clients. As a result, she was fined $50 for each unsigned return. Can Chitsa deduct the fines as a cost of doing business?

Discussion: The tax law requires a return preparer to sign each return prepared for a fee. A $50 penalty is assessed for each return not properly signed. The penalties paid by Chitsa are not deductible as an expense related to her tax return preparation business.

Expenses of an Illegal Business. Although the tax law specifically denies a deduction for the listed expenditures on the basis that they are illegal payments, a taxpayer can deduct the legal ordinary and necessary expenses related to carrying on an illegal trade or business.[25]

▲ **EXAMPLE 32** Bert is engaged in the business of illegally trafficking in liquor, gambling, and betting on horse races. The business is operated out of the Overflow Club. Under state law, the activities are illegal. What expenses may Bert deduct against his illegal income?

Discussion: Bert's income from the illegal activities is taxable under the all-inclusive income concept. The payment of fines for breaking the law and bribes paid to protect the business from raids and arrests by state and county law officers are not deductible. However, legitimate expenses incurred in the illegitimate business are deductible. Among the allowable expenses are rent, utilities, and employee wages.

A special provision in the tax law denies all deductions other than cost of goods sold for individuals engaged in the illegal trafficking of controlled substances (drugs).[26]

Lobbying Expenses and Other Political Activities. Relying on the ordinary and necessary requirement for deducting business expenses, in 1918 the Treasury Department promulgated regulations that denied deductions for expenditures for the promotion or defeat of legislation, and political contributions. With minor changes in language, these restrictions have been retained. The denial of such deductions has been upheld by the courts on the grounds that money was an "insidious influence" on politics.

Contributions to political campaigns and expenditures to influence public opinion about legislation, a referendum, or how to vote in an election are not deductible. This denial of deductions extends to advertising in a political party's convention program, admission to political fund-raising dinners, and events such as an inaugural ball, parades, and concerts.

▲ **EXAMPLE 33** The accounting firm of Williams, Daniels, and Thomas contributes $100 to a political campaign fund. The objective of the group managing the fund is to defeat a senator who has proposed legislation unfavorable to CPAs and to support candidates who favor CPAs' positions. Can the firm deduct the $100 payment?

Discussion: The firm's political contribution is not allowed as a deduction because the fund supports the election of a candidate and attempts to influence public opinion concerning the suitability of the senator to hold office.

LOBBYING EXPENSES. Before 1994, costs incurred for lobbying in favor of or against legislation of direct interest to the taxpayer's trade or business were deductible. Under this exception to the general rule disallowing political expenditures, the taxpayer was allowed to deduct **lobby expenses** such as traveling, preparing testimony, and communicating the taxpayer's view directly to legislators or the legislative body. The taxpayer was also permitted to deduct membership dues paid to lobbying organizations. For tax years after 1993, no deduction is generally allowed for expenses incurred in connection with influencing federal or state legislation or for expenses (including dues to lobbying organizations) associated with attempting to influence officials in the federal executive branch.[27] These rules do not apply to attempts to influence a local legislative body (i.e., town council) or to the cost associated with monitoring federal or state legislation, unless the taxpayer then attempts to influence the same or similar legislation.

▲ **EXAMPLE 34** Kathleen, a Realtor, testified before a state legislative committee, explaining how the new building code requirements will affect housing starts. She incurs $2,500 in costs to prepare her testimony and to travel to and stay in the state capital. Are these expenses deductible?

Discussion: Because the purpose of the expenses is to influence the legislative process, these expenses are not deductible. However, if Kathleen had gone to the legislative meetings only to listen and to monitor the legislation—as opposed to presenting her views—her expenses would have been deductible.

Not Related to Tax-Exempt Income

Expenses incurred to earn tax-exempt income are not allowed as a deduction.[28] Allowing the deduction of these expenses would violate the ability-to-pay concept by giving the taxpayer the double benefit of excluding income while deducting the related expenses. Frequently, taxpayers have to allocate investment expenses to both taxable and tax-exempt income. When making the allocation, expenses directly related to a class of income are allocated to that income. Expenses indirectly related to more than one class of income are allocated among the various classes of income by using a reasonable accounting method. One reasonable method of allocating indirect expenses is by total investment income.

▲ **EXAMPLE 35** Clemons incurs $5,000 in investment expenses related to earning $3,000 in interest on taxable bonds and $3,600 in interest on tax-exempt bonds. The expenses are not directly allocable to either class of income. How much of the $5,000 in investment expenses can Clemons deduct as a production-of-income expense?

Discussion: Clemons can deduct only the portion of the expenses that is incurred to produce taxable income. The portion attributable to the production of tax-exempt income is not deductible. The investment expenses are allocated to the classes of interest income as follows:

Bonds	Total Investment Income	% of Total Income	Investment Expenses
Taxable interest income	$3,000	45.5%	$2,273
Tax-exempt interest income	3,600	54.5	2,727
Totals	$6,600	100.0%	$5,000

Clemons is allowed a deduction for the expenses related to the taxable bonds ($2,273). The investment expenses related to tax-exempt bonds ($2,727) are not deductible.

Expenditure Must Be for Taxpayer's Benefit

To be deductible, an expenditure must be for the taxpayer's benefit or be a payment of the taxpayer's obligation. A payment of another person's obligation does not result in a tax deduction for either person. The person making the payment cannot deduct an expense that is not related to her or his business because the payment lacks a business purpose.[29] The person for whom the debt is paid is not entitled to another entity's deduction for a capital recovery.

▲ **EXAMPLE 36** Marty's mother, Mary, owes $5,000 in back property taxes. To help her out of financial difficulty, Marty pays the property taxes. Can either Marty or Mary take a deduction for the property taxes paid by Marty?

Discussion: Although property taxes are allowed as a personal itemized deduction, Marty may not claim a deduction for payment of his mother's obligation. The property taxes were not Marty's obligation, and he did not benefit from the use of the property subject to the taxes. Mary may not deduct the payment of taxes because she did not pay the expense.

To make sure that a deduction is allowed for the taxes, Marty could have made a gift of the $5,000 to Mary and had her pay the taxes directly.

An exception to the disallowance of the payment of another's expenses is made in the case of medical expenses of a dependent. All medical expenses paid on behalf of a taxpayer's dependent are deductible by the taxpayer, subject to the limitations on medical expense deductions.

LIMITED MIXED-USE EXPENSES

As indicated earlier in the chapter, mixed-use expenses and expenses related to using mixed-use assets must be analyzed and allocated between business and personal expenses. The discussion that follows examines the three areas that Congress has determined have the greatest potential for abuse: hobby, vacation home, and home office expenses. The common thread among all three activities is that they are entered into by individuals who have an incentive to attempt to convert personal expenditures within the activity to deductible business expenses. Thus, detailed rules have been written to prevent this from happening. The legislative grace, ability-to-pay, business purpose, and capital recovery concepts all apply to these deductions and indicate that these expenses should be allowed to the extent they are incurred to earn income. As these topics are discussed, note the similarities in the calculation of the deductions and how the income from the mixed activity limits the amount deductible. The common denominator among all three mixed-use activities is that business expenses in excess of income earned in a hobby, vacation home, or home office activity are not deductible because they lack a business purpose.

Hobby Expenses

A taxpayer may engage in an income-earning activity primarily for personal reasons that prevents its qualifications as a trade or business or an investment activity. The activity may be carried on mainly for recreation and personal enjoyment, with profitability a secondary concern. In tax law jargon, this type of activity is referred to as a **hobby,** because it lacks a business purpose. However, the legislative grace, ability-to-pay, and capital recovery concepts all indicate that hobby income should be taxed only to the extent it exceeds the related expenses.

The hobby rules apply when a taxpayer has income and expenses in an activity without a predominant profit motive. The tax law considers nine factors in determining whether an activity that earns income is profit-motivated and should be treated as a business or is subject to the hobby rules. These factors are

- Whether the taxpayer carries on the activity in a businesslike manner
- Expertise of the taxpayer or the taxpayer's reliance on advice of experts
- Time and effort the taxpayer spends to carry on the activity
- Expectation that the assets used in the activity will appreciate in value
- Taxpayer's success in similar activities
- Taxpayer's history of income or losses in the activity
- Amount of occasional profits, if any
- Taxpayer's financial status
- Elements of personal pleasure or recreation in the activity[30]

The courts consider and weigh all these factors in determining whether a taxpayer's activity constitutes a hobby. An activity's classification as a hobby is based on all the facts and circumstances presented by the taxpayer. Thus, the classification is subjective and is not determined by a single factor or by the presence of more factors indicating a hobby than a profit objective. The courts also will consider other factors relevant to the taxpayer's situation that may indicate a profit motive. In many situations, the determination of whether an activity is a hobby is best left to a tax expert.

A taxpayer's deductible hobby expenses cannot exceed the gross income from the hobby.[31] The expenses in excess of income are referred to as **hobby losses.** Hobby losses are not deductible. Hobby deductions must be computed in a specific order. First the deductions are grouped into three categories:

1. Expenses that could be deducted as either business expenses or itemized deductions (e.g., home mortgage interest and property taxes)
2. Expenses related to the hobby that would be deductible if the hobby had qualified as a business (e.g., supplies, utilities, repairs, auto expenses)
3. Depreciation on assets used to carry on the hobby activity

Category 1 expenses are deducted from hobby income first. If any income remains, category 2 expenses are deducted. Category 3 expenses can then be deducted to the extent that any income remains after deducting categories 1 and 2. In addition, hobby expenses in categories 2 and 3 must be reported as miscellaneous itemized deductions. Recall that miscellaneous itemized deductions (discussed in depth in Chapter 8) are subject to a 2 percent of adjusted gross income limitation. Because hobby expenses are classified as miscellaneous itemized deductions, a taxpayer might not be allowed a deduction for part or all of the hobby expenses. Thus, the benefit of hobby deductions is limited in two ways: The expenses are allowed only to the extent of hobby income, and the actual amount deductible is limited as an itemized deduction. If a taxpayer uses the standard deduction instead of listing the actual itemized deductions, all benefit from the hobby deduction is lost.

▲ **EXAMPLE 37** Barclay is a physician. As a hobby, Barclay operates a farm where she raises exotic animals. During the year, Barclay has gross income of $18,000 from the farm and pays the following expenses:

Property taxes on the farm	$ 6,000
Labor, feed, and veterinary costs	10,000
Depreciation on farm building and equipment	4,000

How much of the $20,000 that Barclay incurs as expenses can she deduct?

Discussion: Barclay's deductions are limited to the $18,000 from the farm for the year. Her deductible expenses are determined as follows:

Gross income	$18,000
Less: Category 1 expenses that are allowed as either personal or business deductions (e.g., itemized property tax).	(6,000)
Balance of income	$12,000
Less: Category 2 expenses of operating the farm that are deductible in a trade or business (e.g., labor, feed, vet).	(10,000)
Balance of income	$ 2,000
Less: Depreciation expense. The $4,000 expense for this category cannot exceed the balance of income before the deduction.	(2,000)
Balance of income	$ -0-

Barclay should report $18,000 in gross income. She can deduct $6,000 in taxes as an itemized deduction and $12,000 as miscellaneous itemized deductions. She cannot deduct as a hobby expense the $2,000 in depreciation deductions in excess of income, a sum that is referred to as the *nondeductible hobby loss.*

Discussion: On the surface, it appears that Barclay's hobby has no effect on her income. However, $12,000 in hobby expenses is subject to the 2% of adjusted gross income limitation for miscellaneous itemized deductions. For example, if Barclay's adjusted gross income were $100,000 and she had no other miscellaneous itemized deductions, her deduction for hobby expenses would be limited to $16,000 ($10,000 + $6,000):

Total allowable miscellaneous itemized deductions	$12,000
Less: 2% of AGI ($100,000 × 2%)	(2,000)
Miscellaneous hobby expense deductions	$10,000
Property taxes	6,000
Total hobby expense deduction	$16,000

Therefore, although hobby expenses technically are limited to hobby income, the net effect is that Barclay reports $2,000 in income ($18,000 − $16,000) from the hobby.

Vacation Home Expenses

A **vacation home** can be a house, apartment, condominium, mobile home, boat, or similar property. A taxpayer who owns a vacation home that is used for family vacations and then rented to unrelated people during the remainder of the year is subject to special rules. The deductibility of vacation home rental expenses depends on the rental income and the extent of the taxpayer's personal use of the home.

Table 5–1 summarizes the treatment of vacation home expenses.[32] As the table shows, if the taxpayer rents out the vacation home for a minimal period during the year (14 days or fewer), the dwelling is not considered to have been used for business purpose and is treated as a personal residence. For administrative convenience, the rental income is not reported and rent expenses are not deducted. As discussed in Chapter 8, home mortgage interest and property taxes on the property can be deducted as a personal itemized deduction.

▲ **EXAMPLE 38** Amber owns a summer cabin that she and her family use for personal purposes from May through August of each year. In August, Expando Corporation pays Amber $1,000 to rent her cabin for 5 days. Amber's expenses related to the cabin include $5,000 in taxes and interest and $2,000 in utilities and maintenance for the year. What is the proper treatment of the summer cabin income and expense?

Discussion: Because the cabin is rented for 14 days or fewer, Amber does not have to report the $1,000 received from Expando Corporation as rental income. The cabin is considered a personal residence, and Amber may not deduct any expense related to the rental use of the vacation home by Expando. She can deduct the property taxes and interest as personal itemized deductions.

If the home is rented for more than 14 days and used for personal use for a minimal length of time (the greater of 14 days or 10 percent of the days rented), the property is treated the same as investment rental property. Expenses allocable to the personal use of the dwelling are not deductible. Expenses related to rental use that have a business purpose are deducted just as they would be for any other profit-motivated transaction.

As the third row of Table 5–1 shows, using the vacation home for more than 14 days as rental property and using it for more than 14 days as a personal vacation home limits the deduction for expenses to the amount of the rental income. Expenses that have a business purpose are deducted in the same order as for hobby expenses. But unlike a hobby loss, vacation home expenses in excess of current income can be carried forward indefinitely for use in a later year in which there is enough rental income to offset them. The IRS requires that the taxpayer allocate vacation home ex-

▲ **Table 5–1**

SUMMARY OF VACATION HOME USE TESTS

Rent Period	Personal Use Period	Tax Result
14 days or fewer	Remainder of year.	A personal residence. Do not report income and do not deduct rent expenses.
More than 14 days	14 days or fewer, or 10% or less of the number of days rented at a fair rental price, whichever is longer.	A rental property. Report like any other rental property. Expenses must be allocated between rental and personal use.
More than 14 days	More than 14 days, or more than 10% of the number of days rented at a fair rental price, whichever is longer.	A vacation home. Report rental income and allocate rental expenses using specified priority. Expenses are limited to gross rental income. A loss cannot be deducted.

penses between personal and rental by using the ratio of personal days to total days of use (sum of personal days and rental days).[33]

▲ **EXAMPLE 39** Latoya owns a cabin that she uses 20 days for her family's vacation during the current year. The cabin is rented to others for 40 days, for which she receives gross rental income of $5,500. Her total expenses of maintaining the cabin are

Interest and property taxes	$6,000
Utilities, insurance, and repairs	1,500
Depreciation expense	4,500

What are Latoya's allowable deductions on the cabin?

Discussion: Because Latoya uses the property for personal use for more than 14 days, the total deductions allocable to the rental are limited to rental income. The first step is to allocate the expenses to rental use and personal use.

			Amount Allocated to	
	Total Cost	Rent Use Ratio	Rental Use	Personal Use
Interest and property taxes	$6,000	40/60	$4,000	$2,000
Utilities, insurance, repairs	1,500	40/60	1,000	500
Depreciation expense	4,500	40/60	3,000	1,500

Latoya's deductions for the rental are limited to the $5,500 in gross rental income. Further, the $5,500 in deductions must be taken from the expenses in the same order as deductions for hobby expenses:

Gross rental income	$5,500
Less: Deductions allowable as either itemized deductions or as rental expenses (interest and property taxes).	(4,000)
Balance of income	$1,500
Less: Deductions allowable only as a rental expense (utilities, insurance, repairs).	(1,000)
Balance of income	$ 500
Less: Depreciation. Limited to the balance of income after other expenses.	(500)
Balance of income	$ -0-

The $2,500 ($3,000 − $500) in depreciation that is disallowed because of the income limitation is carried into future years for deduction if there is enough rental income to absorb the expense. In addition, Latoya can deduct the $2,000 of personal interest and property taxes as a personal itemized deduction. Assuming that Latoya itemizes deductions, the net effect of the cabin on her income is a reduction of $2,000 because of the deductions for personal itemized interest and property taxes.

Home Office Expenses

A taxpayer who operates a trade or business from home can claim a deduction for expenses related to its business use. Expenses such as mortgage interest, real property taxes, insurance, utilities, repairs, and depreciation can be allocated on a reasonable basis to the area of the home used for a business purpose. This deduction is commonly referred to as the **home office deduction.** To claim a deduction, strict tests must be satisfied.

A specific part of the home must be used exclusively for carrying on a trade or business. A taxpayer who does not have another business location can deduct the cost of using an area in the home for storing inventory on a regular basis. If a room is used for a trade or business and is also used for investing or personal activities, the exclusive use test is not met and no deduction for home office expenses is allowed.

The home office area must also be regularly used as the principal place to conduct a trade or business belonging to the taxpayer or as a place to meet or deal with patients, clients, or customers in the normal course of the trade or business.[34] If the portion of the home used for business is a separate structure, the taxpayer needs only to show that it was used in connection with a trade or business. If these tests are met, the taxpayer can deduct expenses related to using part of the home for business.

In addition, a taxpayer who uses a home office to conduct substantial administrative or management activities and has no other fixed location to conduct these activities is allowed to deduct the cost of a home office. The taxpayer must still use the home office exclusively and on a regular basis in carrying on a trade or business.[35]

Employees who use an office in their home to conduct business for their employer must meet an additional test. Employee use must be "for the convenience of the employer" and "required as a condition of employment" before any deductions for a home office may be taken.[36] Because most employee use of a home office is for the convenience of the employee (i.e., people work at home because they want to, not because they are required to), most employee situations will not result in a deduction for home office expenses.

▲ **EXAMPLE 40** Reginald is an engineer for Arclight Petroleum Company. Rather than work late at the office, he often takes home Arclight work, which he works on in an office in his home. Reginald prefers to bring work home so that he can have dinner with his family and not have to return to his office late at night or on weekends. Can Reginald deduct any of the costs of maintaining the home office?

Discussion: Because Reginald's use of the office is related to his employment with Arclight, he must prove that the use of the home office is for Arclight's convenience and that it is required as a condition of his employment. Under the facts as given, Reginald's use is for his convenience, not Arclight's. Thus, the deduction would not be allowed. In addition, it is doubtful that Arclight requires Reginald to maintain an office in his home to maintain employment, which is also required for deductibility.

Expenses of maintaining the home are allocated between the home office and the areas used as a residence. The expenses may be allocated on the basis of the number of rooms or on the basis of square footage of floor space in the home. The method chosen should reasonably reflect the area used as an office. The home office deduction follows the same computational pattern as the hobby and vacation home deductions discussed earlier. However, the income limitation is based on income earned from the home office activity after deducting all other business expenses that are unrelated to the use of the home office. If the home office deductions exceed the income limitation, the excess may be carried forward and used to reduce income in a later year.

▲ **EXAMPLE 41** Kendall uses 1 room in her home as the primary location for her business. Her home has 6 rooms and is 2,500 square feet. The office area is 300 square feet or 12% of the total area. For the current year, she has $15,000 in mortgage interest and real estate taxes and $8,000 in insurance, repairs, and maintenance related to her home. Kendall determines that depreciation on the house for the current year is $4,000. She has $21,000 in income and $17,800 in other business expenses. What is Kendall's allowable home office deduction for the current year?

Discussion: Kendall's home office deduction cannot exceed her income from the home office activity after deducting all other business expenses that are unrelated to the home office. Thus, her maximum home office deduction is $3,200 ($21,000 − $17,800). The amounts that Kendall can deduct for her home office are

Income limitation on home office expenses ($21,000 − $17,800)	$3,200
1. Deduct expenses otherwise allowed as a deduction under other tax rules:	
Interest and taxes ($15,000 × 12%)	(1,800)
Balance of income	$1,400
2. Deduct office expenses not otherwise allowed as a deduction:	
Insurance, repairs, and other expenses ($8,000 × 12%)	(960)
Balance of income	$ 440

3. Deduct depreciation on office portion of residence:		
Current-year depreciation	$4,000	
Business percentage	× .12	
Depreciation on office	$ 480	
Deduction limited to balance of income		(440)
Balance of income		$ -0-

The $40 ($480 − $440) in depreciation that was not allowed as a deduction in the current year because of the income limitation can be carried forward to next year.

You should be aware of two important points concerning the operation of a business from home. First, the expenses of operating the business that are not related to the home office are allowed as a deduction, even if the home office expense is disallowed because of the income limitation. Second, to deduct telephone expenses relating to a home office, the taxpayer must have a separate phone line (i.e., phone number) for the business. If the taxpayer has only one phone, the basic phone charge cannot be deducted; only long distance business-related phone calls are allowed as a deduction.

▲ **EXAMPLE 42** Alvin operates his business from home. His sales for the year total $50,000. He incurs $55,000 in travel expenses, employee wages, depreciation on equipment, and other expenses unrelated to his home office. The residence expenses allocated to the home office using the approach illustrated total $2,000. What are Alvin's allowable deductions?

Discussion: Alvin's deductible loss from his business before considering a home office deduction is $5,000 ($50,000 − $55,000). He cannot deduct any of his home office expense in the current year because of the income limitations. However, the $2,000 in home office expenses can be carried forward to next year and deducted if he has enough income.

CONCEPT CHECK For an expense to be deductible under the *business purpose concept* it must have a business or other economic purpose that exceeds any tax avoidance motive. The primary motive for the transaction must be to make a profit. Under the *entity concept*, all items of income and deduction are traced to the tax unit responsible for the item. Therefore, taxpayers that use an asset for both business and personal use (e.g., vacation home, home office) must allocate the expenses associated with the asset between business use and personal use. Under the *ability to pay concept*, a taxpayer's tax liability must be based on the amount the taxpayer can afford to pay, relative to other taxpayers. The *legislative grace concept* requires that any tax relief provided is the result of a specific act of Congress that must be strictly applied and interpreted. Therefore, losses must be approached with the philosphy that a loss is not deductible unless a provision in the tax law allows it. Through these two concepts Congress allows deductions for expenses of hobbies, vacation homes, and home offices, but specifically limits the deductions to the income generated from the activity.

Timing of Deductions—Effect of Accounting Method

The annual accounting period concept requires taxpayers to determine the expenses that can be deducted for each tax year. To assign expenses to the correct year, the tax law requires the taxpayer to adopt an accounting method that clearly reflects income. A taxpayer's **accounting method** refers to the overall method used to compute income and deductions belonging to the tax year. It also refers to the method used to compute the amount of particular income or deduction items. For example, the taxpayer may determine net income for a business using either the cash or the accrual method. In addition, to calculate the deduction for automobile expenses, the taxpayer must elect to use either the actual cost method or the standard rate method (discussed in Chapter 6).

If the taxpayer adopts a method of accounting that does not fairly reflect income (such as accrual method for expense and the cash method for income), the IRS can designate the method to be used by the taxpayer.[37] The accounting method adopted by the taxpayer is important because it controls the timing of a deduction. Deduction of an expense in the wrong accounting period is not allowed.

▲ **EXAMPLE 43** Craig pays $100 for supplies on December 28, 2001. His taxable income for 2001 is the lowest it has ever been, and he does not need more deductions for the year. Although he uses the cash method of accounting and normally expenses supplies when he buys them, he decides to save the $100 deduction until 2002. He reasons that his actions are proper because he has not used the supplies. When should Craig deduct the cost of the supplies?

Discussion: Given his accounting method, Craig must deduct the expenses in 2001. He must use a method of accounting that fairly reflects income and apply that method on a consistent basis. As a cash basis taxpayer, Craig must deduct the $100 supplies expense in 2001. Under the cash method, he cannot take the deduction in 2002.

Cash Method

A cash basis taxpayer may claim a deduction in the year an expense is paid. The basic question to be answered then is when does payment occur? If a check is honored when it is taken to the bank for deposit, an expense is generally considered paid on the date the taxpayer gives or mails the check to the creditor. If the check is not honored when presented for payment, the timing of the deduction is not clear. Depending on the facts that caused the check to be dishonored, the deduction could be delayed until the check is made good. If the check is intended as payment of the debt but is not honored because of clerical errors, the deduction is allowed when the check is mailed if it is promptly paid. If the taxpayer does not have the funds to pay the check and intends for the check to be a promise to pay in the future (i.e., a note), the deduction is allowed in the year the check (note) is paid.

▲ **EXAMPLE 44** On December 31, 2001, Elvira, a cash basis taxpayer, mails a $500 check to her attorney to pay for legal fees related to her business. The attorney receives the check on January 2 and deposits it in her account. When can Elvira deduct the legal fees?

Discussion: If the check is honored by the bank when it is presented for payment, Elvira can claim the deduction when she mailed it—in 2001—although the check was not cashed until 2002.

If the check bounces because Elvira does not have sufficient funds for the check to clear, the deduction is not allowed until sufficient funds are deposited and the check clears or Elvira makes some other form of payment to the lawyer.

When a property or service is used to pay an expense, payment occurs when the taxpayer gives the property or renders the service to the creditor. If property or services are used to pay an expense, the amount deductible is generally the fair market value of the property or services given the creditor. However, a cash basis taxpayer will have to recognize the fair market value of services used to pay an expense as income and then deduct the expense incurred in providing the service. When the fair market value of an asset is more or less than its basis, the transfer of property will result in a realized gain or loss.

▲ **EXAMPLE 45** Sandra has worked out an agreement with a local radio station for advertising. The radio station will run 30-second commercials in exchange for interior decorating services offered by her business. During the current year, she provides enough interior decorating services to compensate the radio station for $2,500-worth of advertising. Her expenses related to performing the services total $1,200. How should Sandra treat this arrangement?

Discussion: Sandra should deduct $2,500 in advertising expense and report $2,500 in service sales related to the advertising contract. Her $1,200 in expenses related to doing the work for the radio station are deductible as normal business expenses.

Payment of an expense by charging it to a credit card is treated as payment on the date the transaction is charged to the card.[38] It does not matter when the taxpayer pays the credit card company. If a taxpayer gives his or her own note payable to a creditor, or the creditor charges an item on an open account, the expense is not considered paid until the note or open account is paid off. On the other hand, a taxpayer may go to the bank and borrow money, give the bank a note for the loan, and then use the money to pay expenses. Expenses paid with borrowed money are allowed as a deduction regardless of when the loan is repaid.

▲ **EXAMPLE 46** Laval owes $3,000 in expenses that are tax deductible. However, he does not have the cash to write a check. How can Laval obtain a current deduction for the expenses?

Discussion: If Laval charges the expenses to a credit card, he is deemed to have paid the expense on the date of the charge and can take a deduction on the charge date. He can pay the credit card balance when he has the money.

If the expenses are not payable by credit card, Laval could borrow the money from a friend or a bank and give his note in return. He could use the cash to pay the expense and claim a deduction on the payment date. He could repay the note when he has the funds.

If Laval pays the expense by giving a note directly to the creditor, the expense is not deductible until the note is paid.

A cash basis taxpayer may deduct prepaid expenses in the year paid if the prepayment does not create an asset that extends substantially beyond the year of payment. Thus, the late 2001 purchase of office supplies to be used in January 2002 is deducted when the supplier is paid in 2001. However, the IRS has said that if $1,000 in business insurance is prepaid for one year on July 1, 2001, the expense must be allocated by charging $500 to 2001 and $500 to 2002. The courts differ with the IRS on this issue. The courts have held that a prepayment of an expense that will be used up before the end of the tax year following the year of prepayment can be deducted when paid.[39] That is, such prepayments are deemed not to extend substantially beyond the tax year. This is referred to as the **one-year rule for prepaid expenses.** To qualify a prepaid expense under the one-year rule, the taxpayer must show that the payment is required by the creditor and that the payment does not distort income.

▲ **EXAMPLE 47** Woody rents his office building. According to his 15-year lease, he is required to pay the $12,000 rent in advance on August 1 for the period September 1 through August 31. Woody has complied with the lease terms for the last 3 years. Can he deduct the $12,000 in the year it is paid?

Discussion: Woody can deduct the $12,000 annual rent when paid. Because the terms of the lease require the prepayment, the deduction will not distort income, and because it is used up before the end of the tax year following the year of prepayment, he will not need to amortize the expense. Note that a prepayment that extends beyond 1 year (e.g., a 2-year rent prepayment) is allocated to the periods benefited by the expense.

Prepaid taxes are deductible in the year paid, even if the prepayment results in a refund in a later year. Under the tax benefit rule, the tax refund is reported as income.

▲ **EXAMPLE 48** Plain County assesses property taxes annually on December 1. The taxes are not due until March 1. Hortense always pays her property taxes before December 31. When can Hortense deduct the tax payments?

Discussion: Although Hortense is not under a legal obligation to pay the taxes until March 1, the taxes are deductible when paid in December under the one-year rule.

▲ **EXAMPLE 49** Charles has $2,200 in state income taxes withheld from his paycheck during 2001. How much of the $2,200 can Charles deduct in 2001?

Discussion: State income taxes are deductible as a personal itemized deduction. Assuming that Charles itemizes his deductions on his 2001 tax return, he can deduct the $2,200 in state income taxes paid during 2001.

▲ **EXAMPLE 50** Assume that after deducting the $2,200 in state income taxes, Charles files his state tax return and receives a refund of $300. How should Charles treat the $300 refund?

Discussion: Under the tax benefit rule, the $300 refund is a recovery of an expense deducted in a prior year. Therefore, Charles must include the $300 in his gross income in the year of receipt, 2002. NOTE: The $300 is not a reduction of 2002 state taxes paid. Also, if Charles does not itemize his deductions in 2001, the refund in 2002 is not included in his gross income, because he receives no tax benefit from the state income tax deduction.

Prepaid interest is not generally deductible under the one-year rule. The tax law effectively requires all interest to be accounted for with the accrual method.[40] In essence, prepaid interest is payment for the use of money over time. As a result, it is allocated to the periods in which the money is used. The only exception to this rule is the payment of "points" on a loan used to purchase or construct a principal residence. The treatment of points is discussed further in Chapter 8.

▲ **EXAMPLE 51** On April 1, 2001, Tasi borrows $10,000 from his bank. The $10,000, 10%-interest, 1-year note is due on March 31, 2002. To increase his expenses for 2001, Tasi prepays the $1,000 in interest on the note on December 31, 2001. How much of the $1,000 of prepaid interest is deductible in 2001?

Discussion: Because interest expense is a charge for the use of money over a period of time, Tasi must allocate the prepaid interest to the time period in which the money is used. Tasi may deduct only the interest related to the period of April 1 through December 31, 2001, $750 [$1,000 × (9 ÷ 12)] in 2001. The remaining $250 in prepaid interest is not allowed as a deduction until it accrues in 2002.

Accrual Method

An accrual basis taxpayer may deduct expenses in the year in which two tests are met. The first test is called the *all-events test.* The **all-events test** is met when all the events have occurred that determine that a liability exists and the amount of the liability can be determined with reasonable accuracy.

▲ **EXAMPLE 52** Hunter manufactures and sells electronic components for radar. The electronic components are fully warranted against defects for 3 years from the date of sale. Based on experience, Hunter knows that 5% of the components will be returned under the terms of the warranty. He estimates warranty costs related to 2001 sales at $15,000. Does Hunter satisfy the all-events test with regard to the $15,000 of estimated warranty expense?

Discussion: Although Hunter can reasonably anticipate $15,000 in warranty costs for 2001, the liability does not satisfy the all-events test. Because the actual payee and the nature of the claim are unknown, the amount of the warranty expense must be estimated. Thus, the warranty liability is not fixed, and it is not determinable with reasonable accuracy. None of the estimated warranty expenses is allowed as a tax deduction until the parts are actually returned and the warranty obligation becomes certain. NOTE: This treatment differs from financial accounting. In financial accounting, reasonable estimates of expenses are sufficient to fix the liability for the expense. Tax accounting differs in the requirement that the payee be known before an amount is considered fixed.[41]

The second test requires economic performance to have occurred with regard to the liability. Economic performance occurs when services or property are provided to the taxpayer or when the taxpayer uses property. Table 5–2 summarizes when economic performance is considered to have occurred for several commonly accrued expenses. For example, interest accrues with the passage of time, and compensation of employees accrues as workers perform services. Only when the all-events test and the **economic performance test** have been met can an expense be accrued and deducted for tax purposes.

▲ **EXAMPLE 53** Assume in example 52 that in 2002, customers return defective components sold in 2000 and 2001. It costs Hunter $4,000 to replace the defective parts. When can Hunter deduct the $4,000?

Discussion: When the defective components are returned and they are replaced or the sale price is refunded, Hunter has satisfied the all-events test and economic performance has occurred. He may deduct the $4,000 in warranty expenses in 2002.

The purpose of the economic performance test is to disallow a current deduction for costs that will not be paid in the near future. This contrasts with financial accounting for such costs, where an accrual is necessary to properly match expenses to the revenues being generated. In working with the income tax accrual method, you should keep in mind that matching expenses to revenues is not a general criterion that must always be satisfied. Rather, income tax accounting is designed to implement the ability-to-pay and wherewithal-to-pay concepts that assess the tax according to the amount available in the current period to pay taxes.

▲ **EXAMPLE 54** Big Oil Company enters into an offshore oil- and gas-drilling lease in 2001. In 2002, Big installs a platform and commences drilling. The terms of the lease obligate Big to remove its offshore platform and well fixtures upon abandonment of the well or termination of the lease. Based on past experience, Big estimates that the well will be productive for 10 years, after which it will cost $2,000,000 to remove the platform and fixtures. When can Big deduct the cost of removing the platform and fixtures for financial accounting purposes? for income tax purposes?

Discussion: Proper matching of expenses to revenues for financial accounting purposes requires Big to accrue a portion of the estimated cost of removing the platform and fixtures over the life of the well. Therefore, Big will expense $200,000 ($2,000,000 ÷ 10 years) per year beginning in 2002. For income tax purposes, the cost of removing the platform and fixtures is not deductible until economic performance of the liability occurs. Thus, Big will not be able to deduct any of the costs until it begins removal and incurs costs related to the removal.

▲ **EXAMPLE 55** Janson Corporation runs charter aircraft services. In 2001, Janson enters into a lease agreement with Dana Airlines to lease one of its aircraft for the next 4 years. The lease obligates Janson to pay Dana a base rental of $500,000 per year. In addition, Janson must pay $25 to a repair escrow account for each hour flown. The amounts in the escrow account are to be used by Dana to make necessary repairs to the aircraft. At the end of the lease, any amount remaining in the escrow account is to be returned to Janson. In 2001, the aircraft flies 1,000 hours, and Janson pays $25,000 into the escrow account. Repairs to the plane in 2002 cost $20,000. In 2003, $20,000 is released from the escrow account to pay Dana for the repairs. When can Janson deduct the costs associated with the lease?

Discussion: Janson can deduct the $500,000 rental payment each year, because both the all-events and economic performance tests are met as Janson uses the plane. However, the $25,000 paid into the escrow account for repairs is not deductible until economic performance occurs. Economic performance occurs when the repair service is rendered. Janson must wait until the repairs are made in 2002 to deduct the $20,000. Note that under financial accounting rules the amounts paid into the escrow fund would be deducted as they are paid as a cost of using the plane that year.

An exception to the economic performance test permits a taxpayer to take a current deduction for an item even if economic performance has not yet occurred. This is known as the *recurring item exception.* Use of this exception requires all of the following:

▲ **Table 5–2**

SUMMARY OF ECONOMIC PERFORMANCE TESTS

Source of Expense	When Economic Performance Occurs
Taxpayer is to receive property or services from others	As taxpayer receives property or services
Taxpayer is to use property owned by others	As property is used by taxpayer
Taxpayer is to provide property or services to others	As taxpayer provides property or services to others
Taxpayer owes interest expense	With passage of time, as taxpayer uses money borrowed
Taxpayer owes compensation to employees	As employees render services
Taxpayer owes vacation pay to employees	When paid by taxpayer, or when accrued if paid within 2½ months after close of year
Payments required ■ Under workers' compensation laws ■ As payment of liability for tort	As payments are made by taxpayer
Payments for accrued recurring items ■ Sales commissions ■ Shipping costs	When paid by taxpayer if immaterial *or* for a material item if it is treated the same for financial purposes
Prepaid items ■ Insurance ■ Warranty contracts ■ Service contracts	When paid only if immaterial *and* service is provided in a reasonable time after close of year

- That the all-events test is met without regard to economic performance
- That economic performance occurs within the shorter of
  a. 8½ months after the close of the year
  b. A reasonable time after the close of the year
- That the taxpayer consistently treats the item as incurred in the year the all-events test is met
- That the expense either is not material or the accrual of the expense results in a better matching of income and expense than accruing the expense in the year in which economic performance occurs[42]

Congress intended this exception to apply primarily to accrued expenses—those that have not yet been paid but that meet the all-events test and will be paid within a reasonable time after the close of the year.

▲ **EXAMPLE 56** Arturo has a commission agreement with his sales force. Under the agreement, he is to pay his salespeople a percentage of their net sales for 2001. Because of accounting requirements, he pays the salespeople their commissions in February 2002. When can Arturo deduct the commissions?

Discussion: Under the matching exception, Arturo can deduct the accrued commissions in 2001. Although economic performance (payment of commissions) does not occur until 2002, deducting the payment in 2001 results in a better match of sales income and commission expense.

Prepaid expenses qualify under the recurring item exception only if the expense is not material. A material prepaid expense (e.g., insurance) cannot qualify for the recurring item exception because deducting the total amount of the expense in the current period does not result in a better match of the expense with income. If an item is considered material for financial accounting purposes, it is treated as material for tax purposes. However, if an item is immaterial for financial purposes, it is not necessarily immaterial for tax purposes. For an item to qualify as immaterial for tax purposes, the actual amount of the item *and* its relationship to other items of income and expense for the entity must be immaterial.

▲ **EXAMPLE 57** Robin enters into a 1-year maintenance contract on July 1, 2001, by paying $12,000. The cost of the maintenance contract is a large expense relative to the total expenses of her business. For financial reporting, the expense is prorated, $6,000 to 2001 and $6,000 to 2002. When can Robin deduct the $12,000 cost of the maintenance contract?

Discussion: Robin should deduct $6,000 in 2001 and $6,000 in 2002. Robin does not qualify for the recurring item exception because the item is material. She does not qualify under the matching criteria because taking a current deduction for the expense does not result in a better match of the expense with income.

▲ **EXAMPLE 58** Robin enters into a 1-year maintenance contract on July 1, 2001, by paying $12,000. The cost of the contract is a minor expense relative to the total expenses of her business for both financial and tax purposes. For financial reporting, the expense is prorated, $6,000 to 2001 and $6,000 to 2002. When can Robin deduct the $12,000 cost of the maintenance contract?

Discussion: Robin can deduct $12,000 in 2001. She qualifies for the recurring item exception because the item is immaterial. NOTE: Robin's prorating the expense for financial purposes does not affect her tax treatment.

▲ **EXAMPLE 59** Claudio begins carrying a new line of clothing in his men's shop in 2001. He pays $5,000 for advertising the introduction of the new line in 2001. Claudio does not expect to have to run the advertising campaign in the future. When can he deduct the cost of the advertising?

Discussion: Under the matching exception, Claudio should deduct $5,000 for advertising in 2001. According to the IRS, expenses such as advertising, which cannot be practically associated with income of a particular period, should be assigned to the period in which the costs are incurred. The matching requirement is satisfied if the taxpayer reports the advertising expense in the same accounting period for both financial and tax reporting.

Related Party Accrued Expenses

The tax law limits the timing of the deduction of accrued expenses payable to a related cash basis taxpayer. **Related parties** are members of an individual's family and business entities in which the person directly or constructively owns more than a 50-percent interest. The arm's-length transaction and business purpose concepts require that related party transactions be scrutinized closely to discourage unwarranted tax avoidance. The ownership of a controlling interest in a business entity permits the taxpayer to exert significant control over the timing of transactions between the business and the taxpayer. The objective of the related party limitations is to defer accrued expenses from transactions that lack economic substance. For example, an accrual basis corporation and a cash basis related party could time a transaction to permit a deduction for the corporation in one year with the income reported by the related party in a later year. Thus, the taxpayers would receive benefit from the interest-free use of the deferred tax payment. (The benefit is the interest related to the present value of the deferred tax.)

▲ **EXAMPLE 60** Kool Corporation, an accrual basis taxpayer, accrues a $10,000 bonus payable to Ivan for its year ending December 31, 2001. Kool pays the bonus to Ivan on February 28, 2002. Ivan owns 90% of Kool Corporation. Ivan reports his income on the cash basis. What tax savings might Ivan realize from the accrual?

Discussion: Assuming a 31% marginal tax rate and an 8% interest rate (the present value factor for one year is 0.926), Ivan could save $229 by structuring the transaction to accelerate the deduction while deferring the income. The tax savings are solely the result of the timing of the transaction [($10,000 × 31%) − ($10,000 × 31% × 0.926)]. However, the related party rules discussed next prevent this result.

The related party rules prevent the abuse in example 60 by requiring an accrual basis taxpayer to use a cash method of accounting for expenses that are paid to a cash basis related party. If an accrual basis taxpayer accrues an expense payable to a cash basis related party, the expense is not deductible until it is paid in cash and included in the related cash basis taxpayer's gross income.[43] Thus, the tax law requires a matching of the deduction with the related reporting of income to avoid potential tax avoidance. If both parties are accrual basis taxpayers, the problem does not arise. The accrual accounting method results in the transaction being recognized by the related parties at the same date.

▲ **EXAMPLE 61** What is the proper treatment of the bonus in example 60?

Discussion: Kool Corporation may not deduct the accrued bonus for tax purposes until the cash is paid to Ivan and included in his taxable income. Thus, Ivan reports the $10,000 bonus as income in 2002 when it is received, and Kool Corporation deducts the expense in 2002. The related party rules require both parties to recognize the transaction on the same date.

If Ivan and Kool Corporation are both accrual basis taxpayers, they would both accrue the transaction for the year ended December 31, 2001, regardless of when the cash was paid. Ivan would report income, and Kool would claim a deduction for the expense in 2001.

Financial and Taxable Income Differences

Financial accounting rules place a strong emphasis on the matching of expenses to the income generated during the period. In addition, conservatism dictates that expenses and losses be recognized for financial accounting purposes before they are actually incurred. As a result, financial accounting promotes the use of reasonable estimates of the expenses incurred to earn income. However, tax accounting rules emphasize objectivity in measuring taxable income to be sure the proper tax is collected each year. The tax law's objectivity is essential to protecting revenue collection. Because of the time value of money, deducting an expense too early reduces the time value of tax collections. Deducting an expense in the wrong year to receive the benefit of a higher marginal tax rate will also reduce the tax collections. Thus, the timing of deductions is a critical issue.

The all-events and economic performance tests create temporary differences between financial (book) and taxable income. For example, the tax law generally requires the use of the specific charge-off method (discussed in Chapter 6) for computing a bad debt deduction. Financial accounting requires the use of the allowance method, which uses a reasonable estimate of the current year's bad debt deduction to be charged against income.

▲ **EXAMPLE 62** For financial reporting, Press Corporation estimates its bad debt expense to be 2% of credit sales. For 2001, Press records $500,000 in credit sales and $10,000 (2% × $500,000) in bad debt expense. However, a review of individual accounts receivable indicates that on the specific charge-off method, actual bad debts for 2001 total $6,000. How much can Press deduct for bad debts for tax purposes?

Discussion: Although the allowance method is used to estimate bad debt expense for financial reporting, the specific charge-off method must be used for tax reporting. As a result, Press should deduct $10,000 in bad debt expense for financial income reporting and $6,000 in bad debt expense for tax income. The difference in the book and tax deductions results in a $4,000 temporary difference.

For financial accounting, vacation pay accrues as it is earned by the employees. The economic performance requirement allows vacation pay as a deduction when paid or when accrued if payment occurs within 2½ months after the close of the year. Similar rules apply to allowances for warranties. Warranty repair allowances are estimated and deducted as sales are made for financial accounting, but tax accounting allows a deduction only when the taxpayer performs warranty services.

Other tax laws, which are discussed in this and later chapters in the text, also create differences between book and taxable income. These differences are temporary differences in some instances and permanent differences in others. For example, capital expenditures benefiting future tax years are not currently deductible. However, the tax law makes several exceptions to this requirement to promote economic and social objectives. Chapter 10 discusses a special provision that lets a business expense $24,000 of the cost of new equipment in the year it is purchased. For a small business, these expenditures could be a significant drain on working capital. Allowing an immediate tax deduction for the expenditure takes into account two concepts: The immediate tax reduction recognizes that an investment in capital expenditures may reduce the taxpayer's wherewithal to pay, and the election to expense assets adds administrative convenience by eliminating the need to make annual depreciation calculations and keep detailed records for small investments in business assets.

Other temporary differences are caused by the tax law calculation of depreciation. For example, current tax depreciation rules ignore an asset's salvage value and compute depreciation over a predefined statutory life instead of the asset's useful life. These tax rules have the effect of allowing deductions for tax purposes before they are allowed for book income. Because the capital recovery concept limits the total depreciation deduction to the investment in the asset for both book and tax purposes, the difference is in the timing of deductions.

The tax laws also create permanent differences between book and taxable income. Provisions in the tax law that disallow 50 percent of the cost of business meals and entertainment, limit the deduction of business gifts to $25 per donee, deny a deduction for excessive compensation paid to employees, and the federal income tax expense are examples of expenses that do not reduce taxable income but are deducted for financial reporting. As a result, these expenses create permanent differences between book and taxable income. On the other hand, the tax law allows deductions that are not recognized as expenses for financial reporting.

As discussed in Chapter 1, the personal and dependency exemptions and the standard deduction are tax accounting constructs. These constructs make the tax rate structure more progressive and enhance administrative convenience, which makes the tax law easier to enforce. The use of exemptions and standard deductions is foreign to financial reporting. Further, the tax law allows a percentage depletion deduction for certain natural resources. Percentage depletion is a tax deduction based on a percentage of income from the mineral source. The deduction is allowed even if the taxpayer has fully recovered the capital invested in the asset. This deduction violates both the capital recovery concept and financial reporting's cost depletion rules. However, Congress, in its exercise of legislative grace, has decided that it is desirable to violate the concept to provide tax incentives to promote the economic objective of developing natural resources. In doing so, the tax law has again introduced permanent differences between book and taxable income.

CONCEPT CHECK

CONCEPT CHECK The *annual accounting period concept* requires taxpayers to adopt an accounting method that clearly reflects income. Once an accounting method is adopted, it must be used as the basis for the systematic and consistent allocation of expenses to the proper tax years. Therefore, the taxpayer cannot choose to use the cash basis to report income and the accrual basis to report deductions. Alternatively, the taxpayer cannot report expenses on the cash basis in the current year and then switch to the accrual basis in the following year.

CONCEPT CHALLENGE

http://murphy.swcollege.com

Reinforce the concepts covered in this chapter by completing the on-line tutorials located at the *Concepts in Federal Taxation* website.

SUMMARY

Tax deductions are a matter of legislative grace. Therefore, expenses incurred in a trade or business or for the production of income that have a business purpose are allowed as deductions. Personal expenditures are not deductible unless they are specifically allowed itemized deductions. A conduit entity is not subject to tax. Rather, deductions flow through to each owner and are treated similarly to deductions incurred by an individual taxpayer. Mixed-use expenditures and expenses related to using mixed-use assets must be analyzed to determine the business deductions allowed for such expenditures.

An activity will generally be considered a trade or business if it is profit-motivated and the taxpayer is regularly and continually involved in the activity to earn a livelihood. A profit-motivated activity that does not satisfy the continual and regular involvement or the livelihood requirements will usually be considered an income-producing activity. Trade or business expenses receive preferential treatment compared with expenses for the production of income in the individual income tax calculation. Trade or business expenses and losses, rent and royalty expenses, and capital losses of individuals (subject to the $3,000 annual limitation) are deducted for adjusted gross income. As a result, they are fully deductible unless the passive activity loss limitations apply. Expenses for the production of income are generally deductions from adjusted gross income (miscellaneous itemized deductions) and generally are subject to an income limitation.

To be deductible, a business expense must be ordinary, necessary, and reasonable in amount. A deductible expense may not be

- A personal living expense
- A capital expenditure
- An expenditure that frustrates a public policy
- Related to earning tax-exempt income
- An expenditure for another person's benefit

The deduction for hobby, vacation home, and home office expenses is limited to the amount of income earned from the activity. If these mixed-use expenses exceed the related income, the excess expenses are not allowed as a deduction from other sources of income such as wages, dividends, and interest. Taxpayers claiming deductions for a hobby, vacation home, or home office must observe strict requirements to be able to deduct the expenses.

The year in which a deduction is taken is determined by the taxpayer's accounting method. A cash basis taxpayer may deduct expenses when paid. An accrual basis taxpayer may deduct expenses when the all-events test is met and economic performance has occurred. Both cash and accrual basis taxpayers generally must allocate prepaid expenses and capital expenditures to the accounting period benefiting from the use of the asset. Accrued expenses owed to a related cash basis taxpayer are not allowed as a deduction until the item is paid and included in the cash basis taxpayer's income. Temporary and permanent differences between financial reporting income and taxable income arise from the tax law's emphasis on the accounting period concept and objectivity in measuring and reporting allowable deductions.

Key Terms

accounting method (p. 198)
active investor (p. 180)
active trader (p. 180)
adjusted gross income (p. 175)
all-events test (p. 201)
business expense (p. 174)
capital expenditure (p. 188)
conduit entity (p. 177)
deductions (p. 173)
deductions for adjusted gross income (p. 175)
deductions from adjusted gross income (p. 175)
dominant motive (p. 179)
economic performance test (p. 201)
hobby (p. 193)
hobby loss (p. 193)
home office deduction (p. 196)
improvements (p. 189)
investment expense (p. 181)
itemized deduction (p. 175)
lobbying expense (p. 191)
mixed-use asset (p. 183)
mixed-use expenditure (p. 184)
necessary expense (p. 186)
one-year rule for prepaid expenses (p. 200)
ordinary expense (p. 185)
production-of-income expense (p. 181)
reasonable expense (p. 187)
related party (p. 204)
repair-and-maintenance expense (p. 189)
replacement (p. 189)
securities dealer (p. 181)
start-up costs (p. 189)
trade or business expense (p. 180)
vacation home (p. 195)

Primary Tax Law Sources

[1] Reg. Sec. 1.162-5—Allows the deduction of education expenses that maintain or improve skills required in the taxpayer's employment or that meet the express requirements of the taxpayer's employer or applicable laws in order to retain employment.

[2] Sec. 62—Defines *adjusted gross income* for individual taxpayers and specifies the deductions allowed as deductions for adjusted gross income.

[3] Sec. 63—Defines *taxable income;* allows individual taxpayers to deduct the greater of their allowable itemized deductions or the standard deduction. Standard deduction amounts are specified and are required to be adjusted annually for inflation.

[4] Sec. 211—Generally allows specific personal expenditures as itemized deductions of individuals.

[5] Reg. Sec. 1.212-1—Requires investment-related expenses of individuals to be deducted as miscellaneous itemized deductions, subject to the 2% of adjusted gross income reduction rule.

[6] Sec. 703(a)—Requires that the taxable income of a partnership be computed in a manner similar to an individual's. However, certain deductions are not allowed, and the items listed in Sec. 702(a)(1) through 702(a)(7) must be reported separately. Likewise, Sec. 1363(b) requires that the taxable income of an S corporation be computed in a manner similar to an individual's. Also, certain deductions are not allowed [Sec. 703(a)], and the items listed in Sec. 1366(a) must be reported separately.

[7] Knetsch v. U.S., 348 F.2d 932 (Cl. Ct. 1965)—Disallowed deductions from an investment in which the sole anticipated gain was the tax savings from the investment.

[8] Comm. v. Groetzinger, 480 U.S. 23 (1987)—Provides the current criteria for determining what constitutes a trade or business.

[9] Hazard v. Comm., 7 T.C. 372 (1946)—Held that the rental of a single parcel of improved property constituted a trade or business.

[10] Curphrey v. Comm., 73 T.C. 766 (1980)—Held that the ownership and rental of real property does not automatically constitute a trade or business, that the ultimate determination is based on the facts and circumstances of each taxpayer, and that the scope of ownership and management activities is an important consideration.

[11] Comm. v. Lincoln Electric Co., 176 F.2d 815 (6th Cir. 1949)—Held that the reasonableness of a payment is an element to con-

sider in determining whether the payment is ordinary and necessary.

[12] Deputy v. DuPont, 308 U.S. 488 (1940)—Held that an ordinary expense is one that is normal, usual, or customary in the particular business of the taxpayer.

[13] Comm. v. Tellier, 383 U.S. 687 (1966)—Held that the term *ordinary* distinguishes those expenditures that are currently deductible from those that are capital in nature.

[14] Welch v. Helvering, 290 U.S. 111 (1933)—Defines what constitutes an ordinary and necessary expense.

[15] Sec. 262—Provides the general rule for the disallowance of deductions for personal expenditures by individuals.

[16] U.S. v. Gilmore, 372 U.S. 39 (1963)—Held that the origin of an expense determines its deductibility.

[17] Sec. 263—Provides the general rule that disallows current period deductions for capital expenditures.

[18] Reg. Sec. 1.162-4—Allows the deduction as an ordinary and necessary business expense of incidental repairs that do not add to the value of the property or that do not appreciably prolong the life of the property.

[19] Reg. Sec. 1.263(a)-1—Defines the characteristics of a capital expenditure.

[20] Sec. 195—Provides the rules for amortization of start-up costs of a new business.

[21] Rev. Rul. 72-254—States that the expenses related to a general search for a new business are not deductible.

[22] The Colorado Springs National Bank v. U.S., 505 F.2d 1185 (10th Cir. 1974)—Held that the deductibility of the costs of investigating a new business depends on whether the business being investigated is in the same or a similar line of business in which the taxpayer is already engaged.

[23] Sec. 248—Allows a corporation to amortize over 60 months the costs of organizing the corporation. For partnerships, similar rules are found in Sec. 709.

[24] Hoover Motor Express Co. Inc. v. U.S., 356 U.S. 38 (1958)—Held that payments contrary to public policy are not ordinary and necessary.

[25] Max Cohen v. Comm., 176 F.2d 394 (10th Cir. 1949)—Held that expenses related to an illegal business are deductible as ordinary and necessary business expenses.

[26] Sec. 280E—Specifically disallows the deduction of business expenses of drug dealers. (Cost of goods sold is not a business expense.)

[27] Sec. 162(e)—Disallows the deduction for certain lobbying and political expenditures.

[28] Sec. 265—Disallows the deduction of expenditures related to the production of tax-exempt income.

[29] Reg. Sec. 1.162-1—Disallows deductions for expenses that are not related to a taxpayer's own trade or business or production-of-income activities.

[30] Reg. Sec. 1.183-2—Sets forth the criteria for determining when an activity constitutes a hobby.

[31] Sec. 183—Limits the deductions allowed for hobbies.

[32] Sec. 280A—Limits the allowable deductions on home offices and vacation homes; defines requirements for home office expense deduction and what constitutes a vacation home.

[33] Prop. Reg. Sec. 1.280A-3—Requires that all expenses related to a vacation home be allocated between rental use and personal use on the basis of the number of days of total use of the vacation home.

[34] Comm. v. Soliman, 113 S. Ct. 701 (1993)—Held that for purposes of determining what constitutes a principal place of business for purposes of the home office deduction, the home office must be the focal point of the taxpayer's business.

[35] Sec. 280A(c)(1)—A taxpayer is allowed a home office deduction if the taxpayer conducts substantial administrative or management duties in the office and has no other location available to perform these duties.

[36] Sec. 280A—See note 32.

[37] Sec. 446—Provides the general rules for methods of accounting, including what constitutes a permissible method.

[38] Rev. Rul. 73-39—States than an expense of a cash basis taxpayer is deductible in the year in which it is charged to a credit card, not the year in which the credit card payment is made.

[39] Martin J. Zaninovich v. Comm., 616 F.2d 429 (9th Cir. 1980)—Allowed the deduction of prepaid expenses by a cash basis taxpayer when the expense would expire before the end of the tax year following the year of the payment and the payment was required. This is the one-year rule for prepaid expenses by cash basis taxpayers.

40 Sec. 461—Provides the general rules for determining the year in which a deduction may be taken, provides the criteria for the all-events and economic performance tests, disallows the current deduction of prepaid interest.

41 Hughes Properties Inc. v. U.S., 106 S. Ct. 2092 (1986)—Held that a liability must be fixed and determinable in that the payee is known before an expense can be accrued.

42 Reg. Sec. 1.461-4—Explains the economic performance test and the application of the exception for recurring items.

43 Sec. 267—Defines related parties and disallows accrual of deductions to a cash basis related party.

Discussion Questions

1. All allowable deductions of individual taxpayers are classified as either for adjusted gross income or from adjusted gross income. Why are deductions for adjusted gross income usually more advantageous than deductions from adjusted gross income?
2. Why does the computation of adjusted gross income apply only to individual taxpayers and not to other tax entities such as corporations?
3. What is the fundamental requirement that must be satisfied to deduct a business expense?
4. What are the two primary categories of business expense? Why is it necessary to classify business expenses in these two categories?
5. Why must a conduit entity report certain deductions separately?
6. What is the effect on a partner's individual tax return if a partnership does not report separately the partner's pro rata share of investment expenses and instead includes these expenses in determining the partnership's ordinary taxable income?
7. The rules for deducting business expenses assure that virtually all expenses related to a trade or business or a production-of-income activity are deductible at some time during the life of the activity. However, few personal expenditures are deductible. Why is there such a difference in treatment of the expenses?
8. Discuss how well the rules for deducting expenses implement the ability-to-pay concept.
9. How are mixed-use expenditures and expenses related to mixed-use assets treated for tax reporting?
10. What is the difference between a trade or business and a production of income activity and why is it important to distinguish between these two types of activities?
11. What requirements must be met to deduct a trade or business expense? an expense related to the production of income?
12. When are capital expenditures deductible?
13. How do you distinguish a currently deductible expenditure from a capital expenditure? Give examples of each type of expenditure.
14. Why are start-up costs related to the investigation of a business opportunity treated differently depending on the current trade or business of the taxpayer?
15. Explain the rationale for not allowing a deduction for political and lobbying expenditures.
16. Explain why the income tax concepts support a deduction for some expenses of an illegal business.
17. Why are expenses related to the production of tax-exempt income not deductible?
18. Explain the rationale for the treatment of deductions related to hobbies, vacation homes, and home offices.
19. What is/are the requirement(s) for determining whether a residence used for personal purposes is a vacation home or a true rental property?
20. Under what circumstances can a taxpayer deduct the costs of a home office?
21. What is/are the criterion (criteria) for the deduction of an expense by a cash basis taxpayer?
22. What constitutes the payment of an expense by a cash basis taxpayer?

23. What are the criteria for the current deduction of a prepaid expense by a cash basis taxpayer?

24. What tests must be met for an accrual basis taxpayer to deduct an expense?

25. What is the general purpose of the economic performance test?

PROBLEMS

26. Alexandra is a veterinarian employed by Fast Vet Services. Susan is a self-employed veterinarian. During the current year, Alexandra and Susan have the same amounts of income and deductions. Why might a deductible expense paid by Susan affect her taxable income differently from the payment of the same expense by Alexandra?

27. Discuss how an individual would deduct each of the following expenditures. If more than one treatment is possible, discuss the circumstances under which each type of deduction would be obtained:
   a. Amos purchased 500 shares of Lietzke stock for $50 per share. He also paid $1,200 in commissions on the purchase.
   b. Dandy owns an optical store. She paid $2,000 in medical insurance premiums on her employees and $1,400 on a medical policy covering herself and her family.
   c. Oscar is a finance professor at State University. He purchased professional journals costing $400 which he uses to keep current on the latest developments in finance.
   d. Gerry is a nurse. He paid $350 for nursing uniforms.
   e. Edgar owns a rental property. His rental income for the year was $13,000, and his allowable expenses were $9,000.

28. Determine how each of the following expenses would be deducted for tax purposes. If the expense is not deductible, explain why not.
   a. Chander paid $500 in interest on a loan he used to purchase equipment for his retail business.
   b. Peter paid $500 in interest on a loan he used to purchase 1,000 shares of Pickled Pepper stock.
   c. Portia paid $500 in interest on a loan she used to purchase her personal automobile.
   d. Jordan's primary source of income is his wholesale warehousing business. During the current year, he paid $8,000 in state income taxes.
   e. Alphonse is a professional golfer who likes to race cars in his spare time. He spent $60,000 on expenses related to racing cars during the current year.
   f. Barry is an insurance agent. He bought a golf cart and had his insurance company logo put on the golf cart to attract customers while he played golf.

29. Andy, Azim, and Ashwin operate the Triple-A Steak House, a popular restaurant and bar. The three, who have been friends since childhood, are equal partners in the establishment. For the year, Triple-A reports the following:

Sales revenues	$800,000
Short-term capital gains	24,000
Short-term capital losses	(12,000)
Business expenses	(560,000)
Investment expenses	(6,000)
Taxable income	$246,000

How must the Triple-A Steak House report its results to each partner for tax purposes?

30. Manuel and Fernando own and operate an electronics store, Electronica, as an S corporation. Manuel owns 70%, and Fernando owns 30%. For the current year, the store reports the following:

Sales revenue	$1,000,000
Long-term capital gains	8,000
Business expenses	(840,000)
Charitable contributions	(9,000)
Non-deductible expenses	(4,000)
Short-term capital losses	(15,000)
Operating income	$ 140,000

a. How must Electronica report its results to Manuel and Fernando for tax purposes?

b. In addition to the income and deductions from Electronica, Manuel has interest and dividend income of $3,500, long-term capital gains of $1,500, and other itemized deductions of $14,500. He is married and has two children. What is his taxable income and his income tax liability?

31. Fernando is a retired auto mechanic. Since retiring four years ago, he has made stained glass windows. Because he has only occasional sales, Fernando treats this activity as a hobby. A friend of Fernando's recommends him to a local merchant who is renovating her office and needs someone to make and install 15 new windows. The job takes Fernando a month to complete, and he is paid $3,000. In preparing his tax return, Fernando is unsure whether the $3,000 is subject to self-employment tax. The instructions accompanying his federal income tax return indicate that a payment is subject to self-employment tax only if an individual is engaged in a trade or business. Write a letter to Fernando explaining whether he is engaged in a trade or a business. COMMUNICATION

32. Max owns an office building that he rents for $750 a month. Under the terms of the lease, the tenant is responsible for paying all property taxes and costs related to the building's operation and maintenance. The only cost to Max in relation to the lease is an annual legal fee for renewing the lease. Is Max engaged in the trade or business of renting real estate? How would you classify his deduction for the attorney's fee?

33. Don was a senior vice president of a bank until its officials found he had embezzled more than $1,000,000. Don had set up fictitious checking accounts and deposited the funds into the accounts. He then created fictitious loans to himself. The embezzled money was used for personal purposes and to keep the fictitious loan payments current. Thus, he created fictitious loans to make payments on prior fictitious loans. Don worked hard to keep the loans current so he would not be detected. Because of a tax audit, he is seeking your advice. If his embezzlement activity is a trade or business, he claims he should be able to deduct as an ordinary and necessary expense the payments on the loans to keep his actions secret. What advice would you give Don concerning his business and deductions? Explain.

34. Hamid owns and lives in a duplex. He rents the other unit to an unrelated married couple for $850 per month. During the current year, he incurs the following expenses related to the duplex:

Mortgage interest		$7,500
Property taxes		1,100
Utilities		1,450
Repairs		
Paint exterior of duplex	$2,200	
Fix plumbing in rental unit	320	
Shampoo carpet in both units	290	
Fix dishwasher in Hamid's unit	120	2,930
Homeowner's association fee		480
Insurance		800
Special property tax assessment to pave sidewalks		3,100
Depreciation (both units)		4,200

How should Hamid treat the expenditures related to the duplex? Explain.

35. In 2001, RayeAnn acquires a car for $14,000. She uses the car in her advertising business and for personal purposes. Her records indicate the car is used 70% for business and that her total annual operating expenses, including depreciation, are $3,800.

a. How should RayeAnn treat the operating costs of the car for tax purposes?

b. In 2004, RayeAnn sells the car for $6,500. Her business use for 2002 through 2004 remains at 70%, and she properly deducted $5,880 in depreciation. What is her taxable gain or loss from the sale of the car?

36. Big Star Auto regularly advertises on local television. Carla, the owner of Big Star, pays her 6-year-old grandson $250 for each commercial in which he appears for Big Star. During the current year, the grandson appeared in 100 commercials. Big Star wants to deduct the full $25,000 as a business expense. The grandson will report the $25,000 as income. Write a letter to Carla explaining whether Big Star can deduct the advertising fee paid to her grandson. COMMUNICATION

37. Discuss whether the following expenditures meet the ordinary, necessary, and reasonable requirements:
    a. Sadie owns 5 shares of Megaconglomerate stock. She spent $4,000 to attend the annual shareholders' meeting.
    b. Sam runs a successful medical practice. Because he has a substantial investment portfolio, he spent $3,000 to attend a seminar on investing strategies.
    c. Alana is a self-employed tax attorney. She spent $3,000 to attend the American Institute of Certified Public Accountants' annual conference on income tax developments.
    d. Kevin owns a large ranching operation. He is deeply religious and feels it is important that his employees have access to religious counseling. He hired an ordained minister to live on the ranch and be available to counsel his employees on any religious problems they might have.

38. Discuss whether the following expenditures meet the ordinary, necessary, and reasonable requirements:
    a. The Brisbane Corporation is being sued in connection with allegations that it produced a faulty product. Brisbane has hired an expert witness to testify that the product was not faulty. The expert's standard fee is $200 per day plus expenses. Brisbane has agreed to pay her standard fee plus expenses and a bonus of $5,000 if the company wins the lawsuit.
    b. Shannon is a professor who teaches film study at Burwood College. Her annual salary is $45,000. She maintains an extensive library of films and books at her home. During the year, she spends $15,000 on new material for her library. Most of the material is available at the university library.
    c. Francis operates a video store and rents the building from his aunt Shirley, who acquired it last year. He paid the previous owner $600 a month in rent. When Francis's lease expires, his aunt increases the rent to $750. Rent for a comparable building in the area is $850.
    d. Max owns a dairy farm in Wisconsin. During the year, he makes 10 phone calls to his sister Ruby, who is an accountant. The calls, which total $150, are for financial and business advice. Ruby prepares Max's business and personal tax returns.

39. For each of the following situations, discuss whether the expense is currently deductible or must be capitalized:
    a. The Mickleham Hotel installs a $125,000 sprinkler system to comply with recently enacted fire regulations.
    b. The Healesville Corporation pays a real estate commission of $35,000 in acquiring its new office building.
    c. The Doverson Company pays $25,000 to repave its parking lot.
    d. The Watsonia Company pays $56,000 to add an air-conditioning system to its warehouse. The company had agreed to air condition the warehouse as part of a three-year labor agreement with its employees.
    e. Hua pays $600 to repair the walls and ceiling of his rental property after his tenant moves out.

COMMUNICATION

40. Rebecca is the head chef at a local restaurant and is exploring the possibility of leaving her current job and opening her own restaurant in a nearby town. She has spent $1,600 investigating potential locations for the restaurant and $1,400 on an analysis of the demand for a restaurant specializing in Asian cuisine. Write a letter to Rebecca explaining the proper tax treatment of the investigation expenses.

41. Neal and Ned spend $4,500 on travel, surveys, and financial forecasts to investigate the possibility of opening a bagel shop in the city. Because their suburban bagel shop has been so successful, they would like to expand their operations. What is the proper treatment of their expenditures if
    a. They open a bagel shop in the city?
    b. They decide not to open a bagel shop in the city?
    c. Answer a and b assuming they are investigating opening a computer store in the city and they operate a bagel shop in the suburbs.

42. What is the proper tax treatment for each of the following expenses?
    a. All apartment house construction in Sandy Beach must comply with local and state building codes. To ensure that these codes are observed, Rex, a city building inspector, regularly visits construction sites. Shoddy Construction deposits $20,000 in a fund to provide a scholarship for Rex's son to attend college. The payment is in appreciation for Rex's help in getting around a building code violation.

b. Rachel operates a pharmacy. She pays a 10% commission on all Medicare and Medicaid business and a 5% commission on all other business sent her way by the Last Stop Nursing Home.

c. Kelly is a registered nurse. She receives a $1,750-per-month salary working for a local clinic. Because Kelly is five minutes late to work two days in a row, the clinic fines her $25. Thus, her salary for the current month is $1,725.

43. What is the proper tax treatment for each of the following expenses?

a. Bernilyn, a commercial real estate broker, is late for a meeting with her boss when she is stopped and ticketed $150 for speeding. She is using a company car when she receives the ticket.

b. Russell is an employee of the Dinsmore Corporation, a small plumbing repair business. He learns that his boss Simon, the sole owner of the business, was arrested twenty years ago for burglary. Because Simon needs access to homes and businesses to do his work, he pays Russell $100 per month for his silence.

c. Anastasia owns a travel agency. The daughter of the president of her largest corporate client is getting married, and Anastasia insists on paying for her bridal shower at a local restaurant.

d. The San Martin Construction Company pays local union officers $20,000 to ensure that San Martin continues to receive construction contracts. The payments are standard practice in the area.

44. Are the following payments deductible?

a. A contribution to a fund to finance Honest Abe's campaign for mayor.

b. A contribution to the Hardcore Gamblers' Association to fund efforts to persuade the public to vote for pari-mutuel betting on licensed turtle races.

c. Joyce, who is in the import-export business, sends an employee to Washington, D.C., to monitor current legislation. The expenses for the one-week trip are $1,500.

d. Ruth, a small business owner, incurs $3,000 in travel, lodging, and meal expenses to testify in Washington, D.C., on the effect on small business of new environmental regulations.

45. During the current year, the Fremantle Corporation, a real estate development firm, incurs $2,200 of expenses lobbying and testifying before the city council to change the zoning rules. The firm also spends $3,500 testifying before the state legislature and lobbying to modify the existing law that restricts commercial building in areas that are classified as wetlands. Can Fremantle deduct the cost of these lobbying efforts?

46. During the current year, Maureen pays Universal Bank and Trust $1,600 for investment advice. The fee is not directly related to any particular investment owned by Maureen. The company provides her with the following summary of her investments:

COMMUNICATION

Type of Security	Fair Market Value of Securities	Income Earned
Taxable	$72,000	$7,300
Tax-exempt	$48,000	$2,700

Write a letter to Maureen explaining the proper tax treatment of the $1,600 she paid for investment advice.

47. Ying pays an adviser $300 to help manage her investments and provide investment advice. The adviser's fee is not directly related to any particular investment owned by Ying. She owns $40,000 worth of municipal bonds that pay her $2,400 in interest and $20,000 worth of bonds that pay her taxable interest of $2,000. What is the proper tax treatment of the $300 fee for investment advice?

48. Tracy and Brenda are equal partners in Crescent Home Furniture, which is organized as an S corporation. For the year, the company reports sales revenue of $330,000 and business expenses of $195,000. Crescent also earns $15,000 in taxable interest and dividend income and $3,700 in tax-exempt interest on its investments. The investment portfolio consists of $35,000 in tax-exempt securities and $100,000 in taxable securities. Not included in the business expenses is a $3,400 fee Crescent paid for investment advice. As the staff accountant in charge of taxes for Crescent Home Furniture, write a memo to Judy, the accounting manager, explaining how the company must report its results to Tracy and Brenda.

COMMUNICATION

49. Determine the current tax deduction allowed in each of the following situations:
  a. Doug, John's son, buys a new car that is titled in Doug's name. John pays for Doug's auto license tag. The tag costs $220: $40 for registration plus $180 in property taxes based on the value of the auto. Doug qualifies as John's dependent for tax purposes. Doug uses the auto for personal transportation.
  b. Elvis owns Ace Auto Repair. His head mechanic is arrested for drunken driving. Because Elvis needs the mechanic back at work as soon as possible, he pays the $500 bail to get the mechanic out of jail. To keep him out of jail, he pays $450 in attorney's fees and the $500 fine the court imposes on the mechanic.

50. Determine the current tax deduction allowed in each of the following situations:
  a. Sam owns and operates SoftPro, a software programming business. In June, the firm files for bankruptcy. Eighteen months earlier, Sam's attorney, Karl, had recommended SoftPro as a good investment to his clients. Three of Karl's clients each loaned SoftPro $40,000 at 12% interest. To avoid losing his three clients, Karl repays the $40,000 each client had loaned to SoftPro.
  b. During the year, Susan's mother is hospitalized for 3 weeks and incurs $36,000 of medical costs. Her mother's insurance company pays only $22,000 of the medical expenses. Because her mother could pay only $4,000 of the remaining medical costs, Susan pays the remaining $10,000. Susan's mother does not qualify as her dependent.

51. As a hobby, Jane creates and sells oil paintings. During the current year, her sales total $8,000. How is the tax treatment of her hobby different from the treatment of a trade or business, if
  a. Her business expenses total $5,600?
  b. Her business expenses total $10,000?
  c. Assume that Jane itemizes her deductions and that she has an adjusted gross income of $42,000 before considering the effect of the hobby. Discuss the actual amount of the deduction Jane would receive in parts a and b.

52. Sharon is single and a data-processing manager for the phone company. She also owns and operates a sports memorabilia store. Sharon goes to shows, subscribes to numerous magazines on sports memorabilia, and maintains a Web page on the Internet. She has been engaged in the activity for the last 5 years. During that time, she reported a net loss in two of the years and net income in the other three. Overall, her sports memorabilia activity has shown a slight loss, but the value of her collection over the 5 years has increased by 20%. Sharon rents a 600-square-foot storefront for $500 a month. Although the store is open only on Saturdays, she is usually in her office at the store 2 or 3 nights a week buying and selling sports memorabilia on the Internet. For the current year, she has an adjusted gross income of $42,000 before considering the following income and expenses related to her sports memorabilia activity:

Sale of memorabilia	$11,500
Cost of items sold	3,725
Cost of new memorabilia acquired	1,500
Registration and booth fees	750
Transportation to memorabilia shows	600
Meals attending shows	250
Cost of magazines	280
Cost of Internet connection	240
Office utilities	800
Phone	400
Depreciation on computer	200

  a. What is the proper tax treatment of these items if Sharon is engaged in a trade or business?
  b. What is the proper tax treatment of these items if she is engaged in a hobby?
  c. What factors (e.g., facts, aspects) of Sharon's sports memorabilia activity indicate that it is a hobby? a trade or business?

53. Lee and Sally own a winter retreat in Harlingen, Texas, that qualifies as their second home. This year they spent 40 days in their cabin. Because of its ideal location, it is easy to rent at $120 a day and was rented for 80 days this year. The total upkeep costs of the cabin for the year were as follows:

Mortgage interest	$9,000
Real and personal property taxes	1,200
Insurance	750
Utilities	600
Repairs and maintenance	1,000
Depreciation (unallocated)	2,500

What is the proper treatment of this information on Lee and Sally's tax return?

54. Mel and Helen own a beachfront home in Myrtle Beach, S.C. During the year, they rented the house for 5 weeks (35 days) at $800 per week and used the house for personal purposes 65 days. The costs of maintaining the house for the year were:

Mortgage interest	$5,500
Real property taxes	4,500
Insurance	650
Utilities	1,000
Repairs and maintenance	480
Depreciation (unallocated)	3,500

a. What is the proper tax treatment of this information on their tax return?
b. What is the proper tax treatment if Helen and Mel rented the house for only 2 weeks (14 days)?

55. Matilda owns a condominium on the beach in Rehoboth, Delaware. During the current year, she incurs the following expenses related to the property:

Mortgage interest	$8,000
Property taxes	1,750
Utilities	1,050
Maintenance fees	600
Repairs	350
Depreciation (unallocated)	3,200

Determine the amount of Matilda's deductions in each of the following cases:

Case	Rental Income	Rental Days	Personal Use Days
A	$12,000	365	0
B	$ 3,800	80	20
C	$ 600	14	86
D	$ 9,050	275	25

56. Hassad owns a rental house on Lake Tahoe. He uses a real estate firm to screen prospective renters, but he makes the final decision on all rentals. He also is responsible for setting the weekly rental price of the house. During the current year, the house rents for $1,500 per week. Hassad pays a commission of $150 and a cleaning fee of $75 for each week the property is rented. During the current year, he incurs the following additional expenses related to the property:

Mortgage interest	$12,000
Property taxes	2,700
Utilities	1,400
Landscaping fees	900
Repairs	450
Depreciation (unallocated)	7,500

a. What is the proper tax treatment if Hassad rents the house for only 1 week (7 days) and uses it 50 days for personal purposes?
b. What is the proper tax treatment if Hassad rents the house for 8 weeks (56 days) and uses it 44 days for personal purposes?
c. What is the proper tax treatment if Hassad rents the house for 25 weeks (175 days) and uses it 15 days for personal purposes?

COMMUNICATION

57. Ray, 83, is a used car dealer. He lives in a rural community and operates the business out of his home. One room in his 6-room house is used exclusively for his business office. He parks the cars in his front yard, and when customers come along, they sit on the front porch and negotiate a sale price. The income statement for Ray's auto business is as follows:

Sales		$110,000
Cost of cars sold		(78,000)
Gross profit		$ 32,000
Interest expense on cars	$4,200	
Property tax on cars	700	
Gas, oil, repairs	1,200	
Loan fees	3,200	
Depreciation on equipment	1,800	(11,100)
Net profit		$ 20,900

If Ray's home were rental property, the annual depreciation would be $2,900. The utilities and upkeep on the home cost Ray $6,400 for the year. Ray's mortgage interest for the year is $2,400. When asked about the loan fees, Ray bitterly responds that Jim, the bank loan officer, charges him 10% of his gross profit on cars financed through the bank. Ray says, "The money is under the table, and if I don't shell out the cash, Jim won't loan the money to my customers to buy my cars. Everybody goes to Jim—he's got the cash."

Write a letter to Ray explaining the proper treatment of this information on his tax return.

58. Hromas uses a separate room in his home as an office. The room is 500 square feet of the total 2,000 square feet in the house. During the current year, Hromas incurs the following household expenses:

Mortgage interest		$12,000
Property taxes		1,400
Insurance		450
Utilities		
Gas and electric	$2,100	
Cable TV	280	
Phone ($15 per month for a separate phone number for the office)	450	2,830
House cleaning		1,820
Long-distance phone calls (business-related)		670
Depreciation (unallocated)		5,600

How much of a deduction is Hromas allowed for the cost of the home office in each of the following situations?

a. Hromas is an independent salesperson who uses the room exclusively to call customers who buy goods from him. During the current year, his sales total $83,000, cost of goods sold is $33,000, and he incurs other valid business expenses unrelated to the office of $25,000.

b. Hromas is an employee of Ace Computer Company. He uses the office primarily when he brings work home at nights and on weekends. He occasionally uses the office to pay personal bills and to study the stock market so he can make personal investments. His salary at Ace is $80,000 per year. He is not paid extra for the time he spends working at home.

59. Charlotte owns a custom publishing business. She uses 500 square feet of her home (2,000 square feet) as an office and for storage. All her business has come from telemarketing (telephone sales), direct mailings, or referrals. In her first year of operation, she has revenues of $37,000, cost of goods sold of $25,900, and other business expenses of $8,100. The total expenses related to her home are:

Home mortgage interest	$6,400
Real property taxes	2,100
Insurance	560
Utilities	800
Repairs and maintenance	600
House cleaning	960
Depreciation (unallocated)	5,000

What amount can Charlotte deduct for her home office?

60. The Adelaide Advertising Agency, a cash basis taxpayer, bills its clients for services it renders and any out-of-pocket expenses it pays to third parties on behalf of its clients. For example, in creating a television commercial for a client, Adelaide charges the client for its staff time in creating the commercial and the third-party costs of filming and editing the commercial. During the year, Adelaide bills its clients $2,800,000. Of this amount, $600,000 is for expenses it pays to third parties. On December 31, the accounts receivable ledger shows a balance due to Adelaide of $400,000, $35,000 of which is for third-party expenses. How much of the third-party expenses can Adelaide deduct during the current year?

61. On July 1, 2001, Andaria borrows $30,000 from the First Financial Bank. The loan is for 1 year at an annual interest rate of 10%. How much interest can Andaria deduct under each of the following situations?
    a. The bank deducts the interest from the loan proceeds.
    b The $30,000 loan proceeds are due at the end of the loan, but Andaria pays interest on the loan each month.
    c. The interest and loan proceeds are due June 30, 2002.

62. The Kane Corporation is an accrual basis taxpayer. State law requires that Kane acquire workers' compensation insurance from a third-party carrier or maintain a self-funded workers' compensation insurance plan. Kane has decided to create a self-funded workers' compensation plan and pay $6 per month (the state minimum) into the fund for each of its 800 employees. During the year, the corporation pays $52,500 in workers' compensation benefits to its employees. How much can Kane deduct as workers' compensation expense for the year? Discuss.

63. Appliance Sales Corporation sells all types of appliances. In addition, it offers purchasers of its appliances the option of purchasing repair contracts. During the current year, Appliance estimates that repairs totaling $13,100 will be made under the contracts sold during the current year. Actual repair costs are $7,500 related to last year's contracts and $2,450 on contracts sold during the contract year. How much repair cost can Appliance deduct during the current year?

64. Gonzo Company is an accrual basis taxpayer. It provides medical insurance for its employees through a self-insured reimbursement plan. Gonzo pays $150 per month per employee into the plan fund. The fund is then used to reimburse employees' medical expenses. During the current year, Gonzo pays $90,000 into the fund and pays medical reimbursement claims totaling $78,300. How much can Gonzo deduct for the provision of employee medical coverage? Discuss.

65. Damon's Lawn and Garden Supply, an accrual basis taxpayer, is the exclusive dealer for Tru-Cut lawn mowers. In 2001, Damon's agrees to pay the Dash Corporation, the manufacturer of Tru-Cut, an additional $15 per lawn mower. In exchange, the Dash Corporation will provide advertising and promotion to Damon's for a 2-year period. Damon's purchases and pays for 200 lawn mowers in 2001 and 350 lawn mowers in 2002. The Dash Corporation pays $2,750 for advertising and promotion in 2001 and $5,500 in 2002. How much of the amount paid to the Dash Corporation for advertising and promotion can Damon's deduct in 2001? in 2002?

66. Joy incurs the following expenses in her business. When can she deduct the expenses if she uses the accrual method of accounting? the cash method?
    a. Joy rents an office building for $750 a month. Because of a cash-flow problem, she is unable to pay the rent for November and December 2001. On January 5, 2002, Joy pays the $2,250 rent due for November, December, and January.
    b. Joy borrows $60,000 on a 1-year note on October 1, 2001. To get the loan, she has to prepay $6,200 in interest.
    c. Joy owes employees accrued wages totaling $20,000 as of December 31, 2001. The accrued wages are paid in the regular payroll in January 5, 2002.
    d. Joy purchases $2,400-worth of supplies from a local vendor. The supplies are delivered on January 29, 2001. They are fully used up on December 30, 2001. Because of unusual circumstances, a bill for the supplies arrives from the vendor on January 10, 2002, and is promptly paid.
    e. While at a trade convention, Joy purchases some pens and paperweights to send out as holiday gifts to her clients. She charges the $700 cost to her credit card in December 2001. She pays the credit card bill in January 2002.

67. The Parr Corporation incurs the following expenses. When can it deduct the expenses if it uses the accrual method of accounting? the cash method?
    a. Parr Corporation mails a check for $5,000 to the United Way on December 26, 2001. The company's canceled check shows that the United Way did not deposit the check until January 16, 2002.
    b. For 2001, Parr Corporation estimates its warranty expense to be 1.5% of sales. The company's sales for 2001 were $2,100,000. The actual warranty costs paid in 2001 were $40,000.
    c. On August 1, 2001, Parr Corporation borrows $225,000 on a 1-year note. Because the company is experiencing a cash-flow problem, the bank agrees to let Parr pay the interest when the note matures. In exchange, the interest rate on the note is 10%—3% above the current market rate.
    d. Parr Corporation advertises on radio and in the newspaper. During the year, the company is billed $16,500 for advertising. The beginning balance in the advertising payable account on January 1, 2001, is $2,500, and the ending balance on December 31, 2001, is $3,300.
    e. On August 1, 2001, Parr Corporation pays $3,200 for a 1-year fire insurance policy for the period August 1, 2001, through July 31, 2002. Parr's insurance company requires the 1-year prepayment, which the company makes every year.
68. Kai, a cash basis taxpayer, is a 75% owner and president of Finnigan Fish Market. Finnigan, an S corporation, uses the accrual method of accounting. On December 28, 2001, Finnigan accrues a bonus of $40,000 to Kai. The bonus is payable on February 1, 2002. When is the bonus deductible? How would your answer change if Finnigan is a cash basis taxpayer?
69. Lonnie owns 100% of Quality Company's common stock. Lonnie, the president of Quality, is a cash basis taxpayer. Quality is short of cash as of December 31, 2001, the close of its tax year. As a result, it is necessary to accrue a $50,000 bonus payable to Lonnie. As soon as the cash becomes available on January 15, 2002, Quality pays Lonnie the bonus in cash. When is the bonus deductible for the accrual basis corporation? How would your answer change if Lonnie is an accrual basis taxpayer?
70. During the current year, Covino Construction makes $5,000 in political contributions to ten political candidates. What amount can Covino deduct for financial accounting purposes? for tax purposes?
71. The Martin Corporation is an accrual basis taxpayer that manufactures cellular phones. The company provides a 5-year limited warranty on its phones and estimates that warranty expenses will be 1.5% of sales. During the current year, Martin has sales of $12,000,000 and incurs $149,000 of warranty expenses. What amount can Martin deduct for financial accounting purposes? for tax purposes?

Issue Identification Problems

In each of the following problems, identify the tax issue(s) posed by the facts presented. Determine the possible tax consequences of each issue that you identify.

72. Shuana works as a lawyer for a large law firm where professional dress is expected. Her friend, Carissa, is a nurse at a local hospital. Shuana spends $1,500 a year on clothing, shoes, and accessories that she wears to work. Carissa spends $500 on uniforms and shoes for her job.
73. Angela owns a duplex. She rents out one unit and lives in the other. During the current year, she pays $4,500 in interest on the loan she used to buy the duplex, $900 in property taxes on the duplex, and $1,200 in dues to the duplex association which maintains the grounds and the swimming pool.
74. Harry and Sydney each inherited 50% of the stock in their father's corporation when he died. Harry had been working for his father and wanted to retain control of the business. Sydney was not really interested in the family business and wanted to sell her stock to outsiders. To retain control of the corporation, Harry made Sydney a vice president of the corporation with an annual salary of $200,000. The only requirements of the position were that Sydney not sell her stock and that she let Harry run the business.

75. Leonard owns an apartment complex. During the current year, he pays $14,000 to have all the apartments painted and recarpeted. Gena purchases an apartment complex during the current year. Before she can rent out the apartments, she pays $14,000 to have them painted and recarpeted.

76. In auditing the Philbin Corporation's repair expense account, Sara finds a $28,000 entry. Since the amount is so large, she obtains supporting documentation. The invoice lists the Fradin Roofing Company as providing the service, but no description of the work the company performed is attached to the invoice. However, a notation on the check says "office roof."

77. Trevor and Sandy operate three electronics stores that sell televisions, VCRs, stereo equipment, and computers. Recently, they spent $4,000 for market and demographic surveys, financial projections, and real estate appraisals to help them decide whether to open a new store.

78. Marcus is the vice president of human resources for Griffin Industries. He spent one week testifying before Congress on the impact health care legislation will have on small business. His trip cost $2,750.

79. Russell is employed as a prosecutor for the town of Swansee. He also works 15–20 hours a week raising purebred Labradors. Over the last 7 years, he has reported an average net income from this activity of $7,000 per year. However, in two of those years, he had losses of $3,000 and $4,000. He believes he could make more money from the activity if he kept better records, was less stubborn, and listened more to the advice of his cousin who has won national awards in dog breeding.

80. Chin, a cash basis taxpayer, borrows $25,000 on a 2-year loan from State Bank to purchase business equipment. Under the terms of the loan, State Bank deducts $4,500 in interest on the loan and gives Chin the $20,500 net proceeds. Chin will repay State Bank $25,000 in 2 years.

81. The Showgate Hotel Casino is an accrual basis taxpayer and maintains its records on a calendar year. It has 3,000 slot machines, one of them a progressive machine whose jackpot increases based on the amount wagered. The casino guarantees that a person who hits the jackpot will receive the lesser of 5% of the amount wagered to date or $250,000. On December 1, 2001, the progressive slot machine reaches the $250,000 maximum payoff. The following January, a hotel guest wins the $250,000 jackpot.

Technology Applications

82. **INTERNET ASSIGNMENT** Many legislative, administrative, and judicial resources are available on the Internet. Court cases can be located using a search engine provided by your browser or a tax directory site on the Internet. Using a search engine or one of the tax directory sites provided in Exhibit 16–6 (Chapter 16), find the 1987 Supreme Court decision that provides the current criteria for determining what constitutes a trade or business. Trace the process you used to find this case (search engine or tax directory used and key words). Describe the facts that led to this decision.

83. **INTERNET ASSIGNMENT** Articles on tax topics are often useful in understanding the income tax law. One journal that is free and accessible through the Internet is the *CPA Journal*. Go to the *CPA Journal* web page (http://www.cpajournal.com/) and find an article discussing the tax deductibility of environmental cleanup costs. Summarize the information in the article.

84. **RESEARCH PROBLEM** Spencer and Richard own S&R Sports, a regional chain of 15 sporting goods stores. They decide to expand their business by opening three new stores. The stores will employ 90 people, most of whom will work part-time. Over the years, S&R Sports has been able to keep its employee turnover lower than the competition by having its new employees attend a three-day training seminar. The cost of training the new employees will be $45,000. Explain whether S&R Sports can deduct the cost of training the new employees in the current year.

85. **RESEARCH PROBLEM** Calvin and Lorna live in Nebraska and own rental property in the Ozark Mountains. They have always prepared their own tax return and have allocated their rental expenses including their mortgage interest and property taxes using the ratio of personal days to total days of use. During the year, they rent the property for 75 days and use it for 25 days. They receive $8,500 in rental income and incur the following expenses:

Mortgage interest	$7,500
Property taxes	1,800
Insurance	500
Maintenance	400
Utilities	650
Depreciation (unallocated)	4,200

One of Calvin's neighbors tells him that there is a better way to deduct the mortgage interest and property taxes on the rental that results in a greater tax deduction. Find authority for a different method for deducting mortgage interest and property taxes on Calvin and Lorna's rental property, and calculate the effect of that method on their taxable income.

86. **SPREADSHEET PROBLEM** Teresa owns a condominium in Florida. During the current year, she incurs the following expenses related to the property:

Mortgage interest	$10,200
Property taxes	1,500
Utilities	800
Maintenance fees	1,000
Repairs	600
Depreciation (unallocated)	5,000

Prepare a spreadsheet calculating Teresa's rental income or loss for each of the following cases. The spreadsheet should be prepared so that it will calculate the rental income or loss by changing the number of rental and personal days.

Case	Rental Income	Rental Days	Personal Use Days
A	$9,000	40	10
B	$9,000	40	20
C	$1,000	12	48

Comprehensive Problem

87. Carol is a single mother who owns a wholesale auto parts distributorship. The business is organized as a sole proprietorship. Her business has advanced, and she can no longer devote the time necessary to do her own tax return. Because she always has prepared her own return, Carol is familiar with most tax rules applicable to her business and personal affairs. However, she has come to you for advice with respect to a number of items she paid during the current year. You are to determine whether she can take a deduction for the expenditures in the current year.
    a. Carol purchased a small building on March 2 to use as a warehouse for her auto parts inventory. To purchase the building, she borrowed $180,000 on a 30-year loan and paid $20,000 in additional cash. Carol also incurred $3,200 in legal and other fees to purchase the building. The bank charged her $3,600 in points (prepaid interest) to obtain the loan. After acquiring the building, Carol spent an additional $25,000 to renovate it for use as a warehouse. The $25,000 included $8,000 for painting.
    b. Carol had her office building painted at a cost of $14,000 and paid $6,000 to have it landscaped. She paid for the building renovation in part a and the office building work by borrowing $60,000 on April 1 at 7% interest. (See part f for details of the interest payments.)
    c. On April 1, Carol prepaid a 1-year fire insurance policy on her 2 buildings. The policy cost $1,500, and the insurer required the prepayment. On September 1, Carol prepaid a $5,000, 2-year maintenance contract on the buildings.
    d. Carol started a self-insured medical reimbursement plan for her employees this year. Based on actuarial assumptions, she deposited $13,500 in a fund to pay employees' medical expenses. Actual payments from the fund totaled $11,200.

e. Carol purchased a new automobile costing $32,000. She can document that her business use of the automobile came to 90% and that her out-of-pocket operating costs totaled $3,600.
f. Carol paid the following interest on business-related loans:

Warehouse	$15,300
Office building	4,000
Renovation loan	5,400

The renovation loan was for $60,000. Because she spent only $45,000 renovating the new building and painting and landscaping the old one, she used the additional $15,000 to purchase city of Seattle bonds with a yield of 6%.
g. Carol became active in politics and contributed $1,000 to the presidential campaign of an independent candidate. She made the contribution because she believed that, if elected, the candidate would institute policies beneficial to her business. The candidate lost the election and immediately started a grassroots lobbying organization. The purpose of the organization is to keep track of elected officials' campaign promises and report to the public when they vote contrary to their stated campaign promises. Carol paid $1,600 in dues to join the lobbying organization.
h. Carol's oldest son began college during the current year. She paid his tuition and living expenses, a total of $13,300, out of the company's checking account. During the summer, her son worked for the business, and Carol paid him $4,300, the same amount she paid other college students working during the summer. Because she consults her son from time to time on the operation of the business, she thinks that at least some of the $13,300 should be deductible.
i. Carol has always itemized her deductions. This year, her mother and father retired and could no longer afford the mortgage interest and property taxes on their home. Rather than have them sell the house, Carol made the payments for them. They received a statement from their bank indicating that a total of $8,125 in mortgage interest and taxes were paid in the current year. Carol knows that mortgage interest and property taxes are deductible as itemized deductions and would like to add them to her personal interest and property tax payments.
j. Because of the success of her business, Carol has received many offers to invest in various business ventures. One offer was to establish a chain of nursing homes in Florida. Carol spent two weeks in Florida evaluating the prospects of the proposed venture and incurred costs of $2,100. After careful consideration, she decided the venture was too risky and decided not to expand into the health-care business.

Discussion Cases

88. Malloy Industries manufactures air conditioners. The machines used to manufacture the air conditioners usually are insulated with asbestos. Because of health risks associated with asbestos, the Occupational Safety and Health Administration (OSHA) lowered the permissible level of asbestos fibers in the air. In addition, employers who have asbestos-insulated buildings or machines are required to monitor the amount of asbestos fibers in the air to ensure that they do not exceed the permissible level. Malloy Industries, a leader in providing its employees with a safe and healthy work environment, decided to remove the asbestos insulation from its 45 machines and replace it with another insulation material. The company determined that it would be less expensive to remove the asbestos insulation from its machines than to monitor asbestos levels on a daily basis. The company has found that the replacement material is 10% less efficient than the asbestos insulation. Should Malloy Industries capitalize or deduct the expense of replacing the asbestos insulation? Explain.

89. Conrad purchases a condominium in Aspen, Colorado. Because of his hectic work schedule, Conrad is unsure how much he will be able to use the condo over the next few years. A friend of his who has a condo in Aspen tells him that the condominium is both a great investment and an excellent tax shelter. Conrad's friend has been able to rent his condominium for $1,000 per week. Conrad expects to incur the following expenses related to the condominium:

Home mortgage interest	$16,000
Real property taxes	5,500
Insurance	825
Utilities	2,150
Condominium fee	2,400
Maintenance	300
Depreciation (unallocated)	6,500

Conrad is somewhat hesitant to rent his new condo out for the entire year, just in case he can sneak away from work for a few days. Therefore, he wants to explore all his options. Explain the different tax treatments of his condominium expenses depending on the number of days he uses it.

90. During the current year, Benjamin and Valerie were notified that their 1999 tax return was being audited. The IRS commissioner has disallowed all the losses attributable to Valerie's cattle breeding and showing.

Valerie was raised on a small ranch where her family raised commercial cattle. When she was 18, she left to attend college, where she obtained an accounting degree. Valerie is now employed as a full-time accountant by Veltkamp, Stannebein & Bateson, a local accounting firm, and receives an annual salary of $45,000. Ben, a full-time househusband, takes care of their children, Kody and Jaycee.

In 1995, Valerie purchased 10 impregnated purebred Maine Anjou heifers, an exotic breed of cattle from France, for a total price of $16,375. She entered into a contract with a local farmer to obtain pastureland for her herd. The contract requires a payment of $20 a month from April through October for each cow and calf. From November through March, the cost of feeding each cow and calf is $1.50 per day. In February 1997, Valerie purchased a bull with an exceptional pedigree for $7,500 to improve the quality of her calves.

She sells any inferior animals to the meat market, keeps her best heifers for breeding, and shows her best bull calves in livestock shows. The livestock shows provide her with the opportunity to show and sell her exotic cattle. Until 1999, Valerie had been responsible for getting the animals ready to show, which requires approximately 4 hours per day from November through January. Unfortunately, Valerie was injured while working with one of her bulls and was forced to pay someone to finish breaking and showing the bulls. During the summer months, Valerie pays someone to watch the cattle so she can spend time with her family.

In 1995 and 1996, Valerie realized losses of $4,125 and $1,894, respectively. In 1997 and 1998, she realized gains of $3,000 and $750, respectively. For 1999, Valerie realized an operating loss of $1,200 and a casualty loss of $7,500 because her new bull was struck by lightning and killed. Valerie has maintained adequate records for all tax years since she began the cattle venture.

Explain whether Valerie's ranching activity is a trade or business.

Tax Planning Cases

91. Rosita's grandmother dies in November 2000 and leaves her an investment portfolio worth $180,000. In January 2001, when Rosita receives ownership of the investments, the portfolio consists of $112,000 in tax-exempt securities and $68,000 in taxable securities. Her grandmother's accountant estimated that the tax-exempt securities would earn $8,175 in interest and the taxable securities would pay $7,140 in dividends in 2001. The management expenses were estimated at $2,100. Rosita is single, has no other investments, and earns $42,000 as an engineer. She expects that her itemized deductions, not including the management expenses, will include state income taxes of $2,800, real estate taxes of $1,600, and home mortgage interest of $4,000.

a. What is Rosita's projected taxable income for 2001?

b. Assume that Rosita switches $40,000 from tax-exempt securities to taxable securities and the rate of return on both portfolios remains the same. In switching the securities, Rosita has a $10,000 gain on the sale of the tax-exempt securities and pays $2,000 in tax. Instead of reducing the value of her portfolio, she pays the tax from her other income. All the other information would remain unchanged, except that state income taxes would increase by $500. What is the effect on her taxable income of changing her investment strategy?

c. Should Rosita switch $40,000 in her portfolio from tax-exempt securities to taxable securities? Explain.

COMMUNICATION

92. Allison and Paul are married and have no children. Paul is a lawyer who earns a salary of $80,000. In November 2000, Allison quit her job as a copy editor and began exploring the possibility of breeding and showing horses. She would run the business on their property. Allison expects to travel to nine or ten horse shows during the year. While researching the activity, she came across an article entitled: "IRS Cracking Down on Horse Breeding—Is It Really a Business or Is It a Hobby?" She is unsure of the tax ramifications discussed in the article and has come to you for advice on whether her activity will be considered a business or a hobby. Allison provides you with the following projections of the 2001 income and expense items for the horse breeding and showing activity:

Revenue:	
Sale of horses	$13,500
Prizes	4,200
Expenses:	
Hay	7,200
Veterinarian fees	3,100
Utilities	880
Property taxes	470
Registration and papers for horses	2,100
Interest expense on the barn	1,230
Depreciation	6,000

Paul and Allison expect to receive $6,000 in interest and dividend income, they will have an $8,000 net long-term capital gain, and their other itemized deductions will total $16,300 in 2001. Write a letter to Allison explaining the factors the IRS will use to determine whether she is engaged in a trade or business or a hobby. You should also provide her with a calculation of their taxable income and tax liability and explain the difference(s) caused by the classification of the horse breeding and showing activity as a business or as a hobby.

ETHICS DISCUSSION CASE

93. Dan owns a successful sports bar in downtown Providence. The state is considering legislation that would restrict the sale of alcohol in restaurants and bars on Saturdays and Sundays until after 7 P.M. The association of Providence restaurant owners is thinking about hiring a lobbyist to fight the legislation. The lobbyist has told the association that the lobbying effort would cost each owner $6,000. Dan's accountant has informed him that his $6,000 contribution would not be deductible for tax purposes. Dan has told his 30 employees, most of whom are students at a local college, that if the legislation passes, he will have to lay off employees. In addition, he told them that most local restaurant owners cannot afford to pay a lobbyist $6,000 to fight the legislation, because it is not tax deductible. Ann, one of Dan's employees and an accounting major, suggests that Dan pay each employee an extra $200 dollars in salary (30 × $200 = $6,000) and that they forward the payments to the lobbyist. That way, Ann reasons, the cost will be deductible as salary expense. Dan tells his accountant about Ann's idea, and his accountant thinks it is great. In fact, he is so impressed with the idea that he has offered Ann a job when she graduates next spring. Do you think Ann's idea is a legal way to deduct the lobbying expenses? What ethical standards has Dan's accountant violated? (Refer to the Statements on Standards for Tax Services.)

9

Statement of Cash Flows

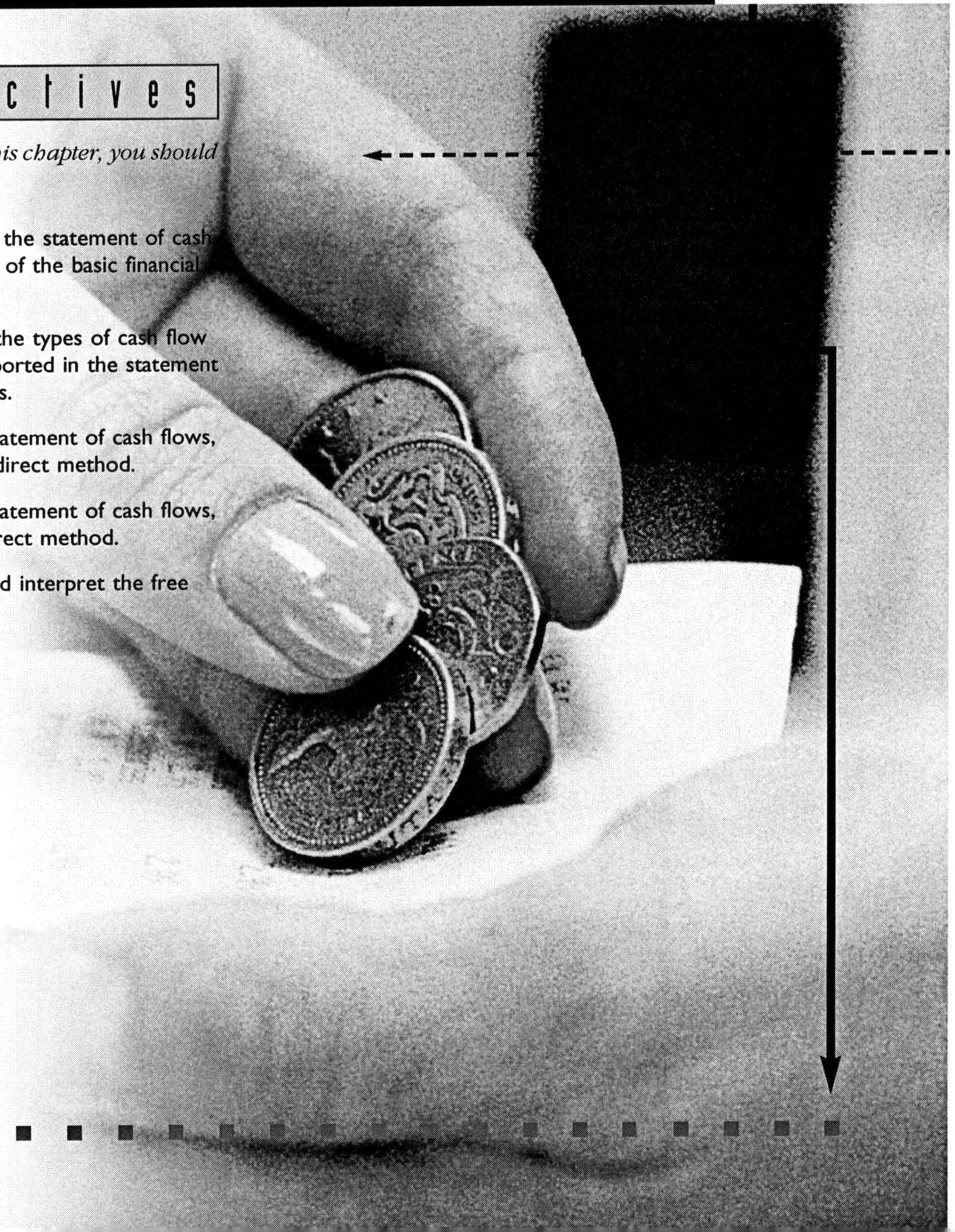

objectives

After studying this chapter, you should be able to:

1. Explain why the statement of cash flows is one of the basic financial statements.
2. Summarize the types of cash flow activities reported in the statement of cash flows.
3. Prepare a statement of cash flows, using the indirect method.
4. Prepare a statement of cash flows, using the direct method.
5. Calculate and interpret the free cash flow.

Setting the Stage

How much cash do you have in the bank or in your wallet or purse? How much cash did you have at the beginning of the month? The difference between these two amounts is the net change in your cash during the month. Knowing the reasons for the change in cash may be useful in evaluating whether your financial position has improved and whether you will be able to pay your bills in the future.

For example, assume that you had $200 at the beginning of the month and $550 at the end of the month. The net change in cash is $350. Based on this net change, it appears that your financial position has improved. However, this conclusion may or may not be valid, depending upon how the change of $350 was created. If you borrowed $1,000 during the month and spent $650 on living expenses, your cash would have increased by $350 by living off borrowed funds. On the other hand, if you earned $1,000 and spent $650 on living expenses, your cash would have also increased by $350, but your financial position is improved compared to the first scenario.

In previous chapters, we have used the income statement, balance sheet, and retained earnings statement and other information to analyze the effects of management decisions on a business's financial position and operating performance. In this chapter, we present how to prepare and use the statement of cash flows.

Purpose of the Statement of Cash Flows

objective 1

Explain why the statement of cash flows is one of the basic financial statements.

The **statement of cash flows** reports a firm's major cash inflows and outflows for a period.[1] It provides useful information about a firm's ability to generate cash from operations, maintain and expand its operating capacity, meet its financial obligations, and pay dividends.

The statement of cash flows is one of the basic financial statements. It is useful to managers in evaluating past operations and in planning future investing and financing activities. It is useful to investors, creditors, and others in assessing a firm's profit potential. In addition, it is a basis for assessing the firm's ability to pay its maturing debt.

Reporting Cash Flows

objective 2

Summarize the types of cash flow activities reported in the statement of cash flows.

The statement of cash flows reports cash flows by three types of activities:

1. **Cash flows from operating activities** are cash flows from transactions that affect net income. Examples of such transactions include the purchase and sale of merchandise by a retailer.
2. **Cash flows from investing activities** are cash flows from transactions that affect the investments in noncurrent assets. Examples of such transactions include the sale and purchase of fixed assets, such as equipment and buildings.

[1] As used in this chapter, cash refers to cash and cash equivalents. Examples of cash equivalents include marketable securities, certificates of deposit, U.S. Treasury bills, and money market funds.

3. **Cash flows from financing activities** are cash flows from transactions that affect the equity and debt of the business. Examples of such transactions include issuing or retiring equity and debt securities.

The statement of cash flows reports cash flows from operating, investing, and financing activities.

The cash flows from operating activities is normally presented first, followed by the cash flows from investing activities and financing activities. The total of the net cash flow from these activities is the net increase or decrease in cash for the period. The cash balance at the beginning of the period is added to the net increase or decrease in cash, resulting in the cash balance at the end of the period. The ending cash balance on the statement of cash flows equals the cash reported on the balance sheet.

Exhibit 1 shows common cash flow transactions reported in each of the three sections of the statement of cash flows. By reporting cash flows by operating, investing, and financing activities, significant relationships within and among the activities can be evaluated. For example, the cash receipts from issuing bonds can be related to repayments of borrowings when both are reported as financing activities. Also, the impact of each of the three activities (operating, investing, and financing) on cash flows can be identified. This allows investors and creditors to evaluate the effects of cash flows on a firm's profits and ability to pay debt.

Exhibit 1 Cash Flows

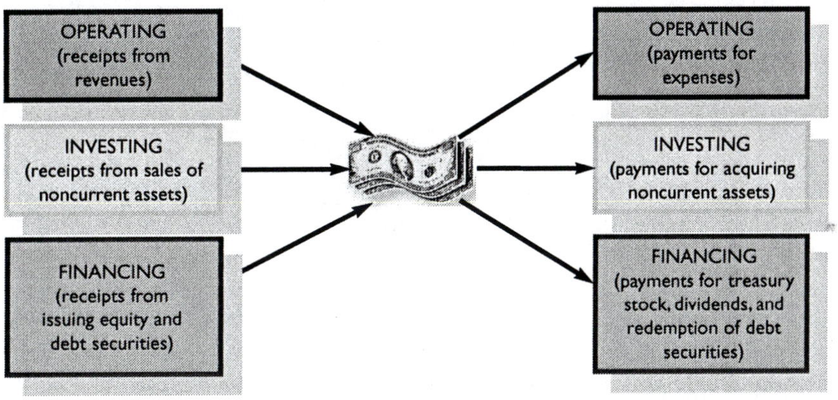

BUSINESS ON STAGE

Focus on Cash Flow

In the past, investors and creditors have relied heavily on a company's earnings information in judging the company's performance. Now, more and more investors and creditors are also focusing on cash flows for providing additional information, as described below.

As the term suggests, cash flow is basically a measure of the money flowing into—or out of—a business. If large companies were run, like lemonade stands, on a cash basis, earnings and cash flow would be identical.

Every major corporation, however, keeps its books on an accrual basis. . . . [This] can give a truer picture of corporate profitability, but sometimes it obscures important developments.

Take a company that spent $140 million on new machinery last year. If it depreciates the equipment over a seven-year period, it will be subtracting $20 million from reported profits each year.

But if the machines will stay up to date and useful for 25 years, the company's reported earnings may understate its true strength. . . .

Sometimes the reverse is true. If a company has been neglecting capital spending, its earnings may look good. But on a cash-flow basis, it will look no better . . . than its competitors. ■

Source: John R. Dorfman, "Stock Analysts Increase Focus on Cash Flow," *The Wall Street Journal,* February 17, 1987, Section 2, p. 1.

Cash Flows from Operating Activities

The most important cash flows of a business often relate to operating activities. There are two alternative methods for reporting cash flows from operating activities in the statement of cash flows. These methods are (1) the direct method and (2) the indirect method.

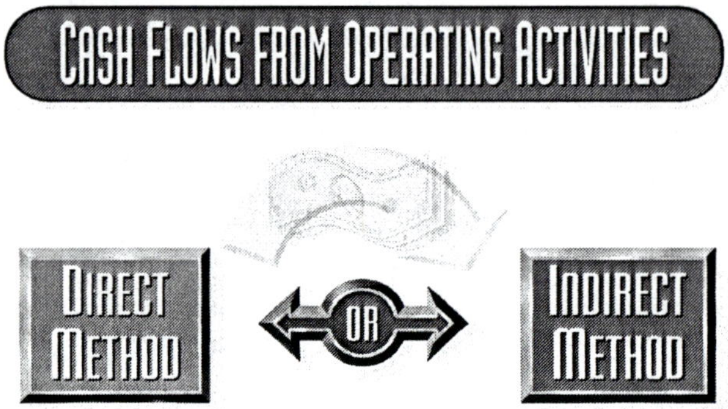

The **direct method** reports the sources of operating cash and the uses of operating cash. The major source of operating cash is cash received from customers. The major uses of operating cash include cash paid to suppliers for merchandise and services and cash paid to employees for wages. The difference between these operating cash receipts and cash payments is the net cash flow from operating activities.

The primary advantage of the direct method is that it reports the sources and uses of cash in the statement of cash flows. Its primary disadvantage is that the necessary data may not be readily available and may be costly to gather.

The **indirect method** reports the operating cash flows by beginning with net income and adjusting it for revenues and expenses that do not involve the receipt or payment of cash. In other words, accrual net income is adjusted to determine the net amount of cash flows from operating activities.

A major advantage of the indirect method is that it focuses on the differences between net income and cash flows from operations. In this sense, it shows the relationship between the income statement, the balance sheet, and the statement of cash flows. Because the data are readily available, the indirect method is normally less costly to use than the direct method. Because of these advantages, most firms use the indirect method to report cash flows from operations.

Exhibit 2 illustrates the cash flow from operating activities section of the statement of cash flows under the direct and indirect methods. Both statements are for NetSolutions for the month ended November 2002. Both methods show the same amount of net cash flow from operating activities, regardless of the method. We will illustrate both methods in detail later in this chapter.

Real World

Which U.S. industrial companies have the largest cash balances? A recent list is as follows:

	In millions
Ford Motor Co.	$24,773
General Motors	20,024
Microsoft	13,927
Intel	7,626
IBM	5,768

These companies have had substantial cash flows from operations over the past 3–5 years, and as a result, have been able to build large cash balances (in the billions!). These balances can be used to cushion future business downturns, as would be the case for businesses subject to boom and bust cycles, such as Ford and GM. Alternatively, the cash can be used to expand the business or move into new markets, as would be the case for technology companies, such as Microsoft, Intel, and IBM.

NET SOLUTIONS

Cash Flows from Investing Activities

Cash inflows from investing activities normally arise from selling fixed assets, investments, and intangible assets. Cash outflows normally include payments to acquire fixed assets, investments, and intangible assets.

Cash flows from investing activities are reported on the statement of cash flows by first listing the cash inflows. The cash outflows are then presented. If the inflows

Exhibit 2 Cash Flow from Operations: Direct and Indirect Methods

Direct Method	
Cash flows from operating activities:	
Cash received from customers	$7,500
Deduct cash payments for expenses and payments to creditors	4,600
Net cash flow from operating activities	$2,900

Indirect Method	
Cash flows from operating activities:	
Net income, per income statement	$3,050
Add increase in accounts payable	400
	$3,450
Deduct increase in supplies	550
Net cash flow from operating activities	$2,900

Real World

The Walt Disney Company recently invested $3.3 billion to develop new action and animated films and $2.3 billion to design and develop new theme park attractions and resort properties, such as Disney's California Adventure and the Disney Cruise Line.

are greater than the outflows, **net cash flow provided by investing activities** is reported. If the inflows are less than the outflows, **net cash flow used for investing activities** is reported.

The cash flows from investing activities section in the statement of cash flows for NetSolutions is shown below.

Cash flows from investing activities:	
Cash payments for acquiring land	$(20,000)

Cash Flows from Financing Activities

Cash inflows from financing activities normally arise from issuing debt or equity securities. Examples of such inflows include issuing bonds, notes payable, and preferred and common stocks. Cash outflows from financing activities include paying cash dividends, repaying debt, and acquiring treasury stock.

Cash flows from financing activities are reported on the statement of cash flows by first listing the cash inflows. The cash outflows are then presented. If the inflows are greater than the outflows, **net cash flow provided by financing activities** is reported. If the inflows are less than the outflows, **net cash flow used for financing activities** is reported.

The cash flows from financing activities section in the statement of cash flows for NetSolutions is shown below.

Real World

Intel Corp. plans to keep enough cash on hand to build two computer chip factories and to repurchase common stock (treasury stock).

Cash flows from financing activities:	
Cash received as owner's investment	$25,000
Deduct cash withdrawal by owner	2,000
Net cash flow from financing activities	$23,000

Noncash Investing and Financing Activities

A business may enter into investing and financing activities that do not directly involve cash. For example, it may issue common stock to retire long-term debt. Such a transaction does not have a direct effect on cash. However, the transaction does eliminate the need for future cash payments to pay interest and retire the bonds. Thus, because of their future effect on cash flows, such transactions should be reported to readers of the financial statements.

When noncash investing and financing transactions occur during a period, their effect is reported in a separate schedule. This schedule usually appears at the bottom of the statement of cash flows. For example, in such a schedule, **Amazon.com** disclosed the issuance of $217 million in common stock for Internet acquisitions. Other examples of noncash investing and financing transactions include acquiring fixed assets by issuing bonds or capital stock and issuing common stock in exchange for convertible preferred stock.

BUSINESS ON STAGE

Seasonal Cash Management

A business must manage its cash position so that there is enough cash on hand to pay bills and other liabilities. Cash management is particularly important for seasonal businesses, which use cash in one part of the year and generate it in another. For example, consider this assumed cash position from operations for Smart Toys, Inc., a toy retailer:

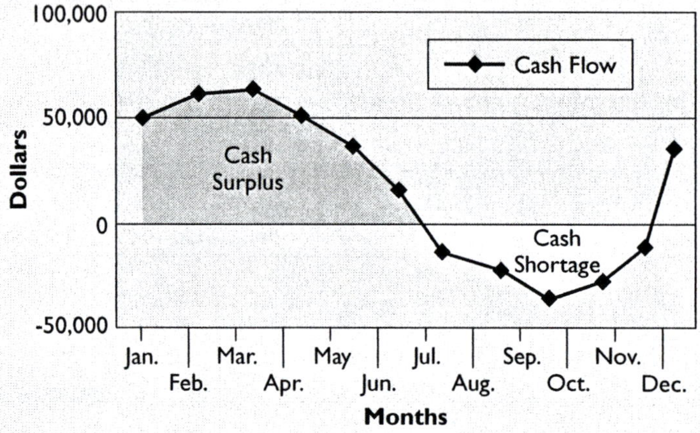

Smart Toys uses cash to purchase inventory prior to the winter holiday season. It is able to generate surplus cash by selling its inventory throughout the holiday season and into the early part of the calendar year.

If the cash required to purchase inventory exceeds Smart Toys' ability to generate operating cash flow, it may experience a cash shortage. In such a case, it must obtain short-term credit, which may be structured as a line of credit from a bank. A line of credit is an agreement that allows the business to borrow an unsecured amount of money up to some stated limit. For example, Smart Toys has a line of credit of $60,000, of which $40,000 was used during the year. Amounts drawn on a line of credit must usually be paid back within a year.

Seasonal businesses must be careful to avoid overextending their cash position during the "down cycle." For example, if Smart Toys purchases items that do not sell, a cash surplus will not be generated during the selling season. ■

No Cash Flow per Share

The term *cash flow per share* is sometimes reported in the financial press. Often, the term is used to mean "cash flow from operations per share." Such reporting may be misleading to users of the financial statements. For example, users might interpret cash flow per share as the amount available for dividends. This would not be the case if most of the cash generated by operations is required for repaying loans or for reinvesting in the business. Users might also think that cash flow per share is equivalent or perhaps superior to earnings per share. For these reasons, the financial statements, including the statement of cash flows, should not report cash flow per share.

Statement of Cash Flows—The Indirect Method

objective 3

Prepare a statement of cash flows, using the indirect method.

The indirect method of reporting cash flows from operating activities is normally less costly and more efficient than the direct method. In addition, when the direct method is used, the indirect method must also be used in preparing a supplemental reconciliation of net income with cash flows from operations. The 1999 edition of *Accounting Trends & Techniques* reported that 99% of the companies surveyed used the indirect method. For these reasons, we will discuss first the indirect method of preparing the statement of cash flows.

To collect the data for the statement of cash flows, all the cash receipts and cash payments for a period could be analyzed. However, this procedure is expensive and time-consuming. A more efficient approach is to analyze the changes in the noncash balance sheet accounts. The logic of this approach is that a change in any balance sheet account (including cash) can be analyzed in terms of changes in the other balance sheet accounts. To illustrate, the accounting equation is rewritten below to focus on the cash account:

Assets = Liabilities + Stockholders' Equity
Cash + Noncash Assets = Liabilities + Stockholders' Equity
Cash = Liabilities + Stockholders' Equity − Noncash Assets

Any change in the cash account results in a change in one or more noncash balance sheet accounts. That is, if the cash account changes, then a liability, stockholders' equity, or noncash asset account must also change.

Additional data are also obtained by analyzing the income statement accounts and supporting records. For example, since the net income or net loss for the period is closed to *Retained Earnings*, a change in the retained earnings account can be partially explained by the net income or net loss reported on the income statement.

There is no order in which the noncash balance sheet accounts must be analyzed. However, it is usually more efficient to analyze the accounts in the reverse order in which they appear on the balance sheet. Thus, the analysis of retained earnings provides the starting point for determining the cash flows from operating activities, which is the first section of the statement of cash flows.

The comparative balance sheet for Rundell Inc. on December 31, 2003 and 2002, is used to illustrate the indirect method. This balance sheet is shown in Exhibit 3. Selected ledger accounts and other data are presented as needed.[2]

Retained Earnings

The comparative balance sheet for Rundell Inc. shows that retained earnings increased $80,000 during the year. Analyzing the entries posted to the retained earnings account indicates how this change occurred. The retained earnings account for Rundell Inc. is shown below.

ACCOUNT ***Retained Earnings*** **ACCOUNT NO.**

Date		Item	Debit	Credit	Balance Debit	Balance Credit
2003 Jan.	1	Balance				202,300
Dec.	31	Net income		108,000		310,300
	31	Cash dividends	28,000			282,300

The retained earnings account must be carefully analyzed because some of the entries to retained earnings may not affect cash. For example, a decrease in retained earnings resulting from issuing a stock dividend does not affect cash. Such transactions are not reported on the statement of cash flows.

[2] An appendix that discusses using a work sheet as an aid in assembling data for the statement of cash flows is presented at the end of this chapter. This appendix illustrates a work sheet that can be used with the indirect method and a work sheet that can be used with the direct method of reporting cash flows from operating activities.

Exhibit 3 Comparative Balance Sheet

Rundell Inc.
Comparative Balance Sheet
December 31, 2003 and 2002

Assets	2003	2002	Increase Decrease*
Cash	$ 97,500	$ 26,000	$ 71,500
Accounts receivable (net)	74,000	65,000	9,000
Inventories	172,000	180,000	8,000*
Land	80,000	125,000	45,000*
Building	260,000	200,000	60,000
Accumulated depreciation—building	(65,300)	(58,300)	(7,000)
Total assets	$618,200	$537,700	$ 80,500
Liabilities			
Accounts payable (merchandise creditors)	$ 43,500	$ 46,700	$ 3,200*
Accrued expenses payable (operating expenses)	26,500	24,300	2,200
Income taxes payable	7,900	8,400	500*
Dividends payable	14,000	10,000	4,000
Bonds payable	100,000	150,000	50,000*
Total liabilities	$191,900	$239,400	$ 47,500*
Stockholders' Equity			
Common stock ($2 par)	$ 24,000	$ 16,000	$ 8,000
Paid-in capital in excess of par	120,000	80,000	40,000
Retained earnings	282,300	202,300	80,000
Total stockholders' equity	$426,300	$298,300	$128,000
Total liabilities and stockholders' equity	$618,200	$537,700	$ 80,500

For Rundell Inc., the retained earnings account indicates that the $80,000 change resulted from net income of $108,000 and cash dividends declared of $28,000. The effect of each of these items on cash flows is discussed in the following sections.

Cash Flows from Operating Activities

The net income of $108,000 reported by Rundell Inc. normally is not equal to the amount of cash generated from operations during the period. This is because net income is determined using the accrual method of accounting.

Under the accrual method of accounting, revenues and expenses are recorded at different times from when cash is received or paid. For example, merchandise may be sold on account and the cash received at a later date.

Likewise, insurance expense represents the amount of insurance expired during the period. The premiums for the insurance may have been paid in a prior period. Thus, the net income reported on the income statement must be adjusted in determining cash flows from operating activities. The typical adjustments to net income are summarized in Exhibit 4.[3]

[3] Other items that also require adjustments to net income to obtain cash flow from operating activities include amortization of bonds payable discounts (add), losses on debt retirement (add), amortization of bonds payable premium (deduct), and gains on retirement of debt (deduct).

Exhibit 4 Adjustments to Net Income—Indirect Method

Net income, per income statement		$XX	
Add: Depreciation of fixed assets and amortization of intangible assets	$XX		
Decreases in current assets (receivables, inventories, prepaid expenses)	XX		
Increases in current liabilities (accounts and notes payable, accrued liabilities)	XX		
Losses on disposal of assets	XX	XX	
Deduct: Increases in current assets (receivables, inventories, prepaid expenses)	$XX		
Decreases in current liabilities (accounts and notes payable, accrued liabilities)	XX		
Gains on disposal of assets	XX	XX	
Net cash flow from operating activities			$XX

Some of the adjustment items in Exhibit 4 are for expenses that affect noncurrent accounts but not cash. For example, depreciation of fixed assets and amortization of intangible assets are deducted from revenue but do not affect cash.

Some of the adjustment items in Exhibit 4 are for revenues and expenses that affect current assets and current liabilities but not cash flows. For example, a sale of $10,000 on account increases accounts receivable by $10,000. However, cash is not affected. Thus, the increase in accounts receivable of $10,000 between two balance sheet dates is deducted from net income in arriving at cash flows from operating activities.

Cash flows from operating activities should not include investing or financing transactions. For example, assume that land costing $50,000 was sold for $90,000 (a gain of $40,000). The sale should be reported as an investing activity: "Cash receipts from the sale of land, $90,000." However, the $40,000 gain on the sale of the land is included in net income on the income statement. Thus, the $40,000 gain is deducted from net income in determining cash flows from operations in order to avoid "double counting" the cash flow from the gain. Losses from the sale of fixed assets are added to net income in determining cash flows from operations.

The effect of dividends payable on cash flows from operating activities is omitted from Exhibit 4. Dividends payable is omitted because dividends do not affect net income. Later in the chapter, we will discuss how dividends are reported in the statement of cash flows. In the following paragraphs, we will discuss each of the adjustments that change Rundell Inc.'s net income to "Cash flows from operating activities."

Depreciation

The comparative balance sheet in Exhibit 3 indicates that Accumulated Depreciation—Building increased by $7,000. As shown below, this account indicates that depreciation for the year was $7,000 for the building.

ACCOUNT ***Accumulated Depreciation—Building*** **ACCOUNT NO.**

Date		Item	Debit	Credit	Balance Debit	Balance Credit
2003 Jan.	1	Balance				58,300
Dec.	31	Depreciation for year		7,000		65,300

Net income was $45,000 for the year. The accumulated depreciation balance increased by $15,000 over the year. There were no sales of fixed assets or changes in noncash current assets or liabilities. What is the cash flow from operations?

$60,000 ($45,000 + $15,000)

The $7,000 of depreciation expense reduced net income but did not require an outflow of cash. Thus, the $7,000 is added to net income in determining cash flows from operating activities, as follows:

Cash flows from operating activities:		
Net income	$108,000	
Add depreciation	7,000	$115,000

Current Assets and Current Liabilities

As shown in Exhibit 4, decreases in noncash current assets and increases in current liabilities are added to net income. In contrast, increases in noncash current assets and decreases in current liabilities are deducted from net income. The current asset and current liability accounts of Rundell Inc. are as follows:

	December 31		Increase
Accounts	2003	2002	Decrease*
Accounts receivable (net)	$ 74,000	$ 65,000	$9,000
Inventories	172,000	180,000	8,000*
Accounts payable (merchandise creditors)	43,500	46,700	3,200*
Accrued expenses payable (operating expenses)	26,500	24,300	2,200
Income taxes payable	7,900	8,400	500*

In a recent year, Cablevision Systems had a net loss of $449 million, but a positive cash flow from operating activities of $456 million. This difference was mostly due to $734 million in depreciation and amortization expenses. Younger companies in industries requiring huge infrastructure investments, such as cable or cellular systems, will often have net losses coupled with positive cash flows from operations during the early years of operations.

The $9,000 increase in **accounts receivable** indicates that the sales on account during the year are $9,000 more than collections from customers on account. The amount reported as sales on the income statement therefore includes $9,000 that did not result in a cash inflow during the year. Thus, $9,000 is deducted from net income.

The $8,000 decrease in **inventories** indicates that the merchandise sold exceeds the cost of the merchandise purchased by $8,000. The amount deducted as cost of merchandise sold on the income statement therefore includes $8,000 that did not require a cash outflow during the year. Thus, $8,000 is added to net income.

The $3,200 decrease in **accounts payable** indicates that the amount of cash payments for merchandise exceeds the merchandise purchased on account by $3,200. The amount reported on the income statement for cost of merchandise sold therefore excludes $3,200 that required a cash outflow during the year. Thus, $3,200 is deducted from net income.

The $2,200 increase in **accrued expenses payable** indicates that the amount incurred during the year for operating expenses exceeds the cash payments by $2,200. The amount reported on the income statement for operating expenses therefore includes $2,200 that did not require a cash outflow during the year. Thus, $2,200 is added to net income.

The $500 decrease in **income taxes payable** indicates that the amount paid for taxes exceeds the amount incurred during the year by $500. The amount reported on the income statement for income tax therefore is less than the amount paid by $500. Thus, $500 is deducted from net income.

Net income was $36,000 for the year. Accounts receivable increased $3,000, and accounts payable increased $5,000. What is the cash flow from operations?

$38,000 ($36,000 − $3,000 + $5,000)

Gain on Sale of Land

The ledger or income statement of Rundell Inc. indicates that the sale of land resulted in a gain of $12,000. As we discussed previously, the sale proceeds, which include the gain and the carrying value of the land, are included in cash flows from investing activities.[4] The gain is also included in net income. Thus, to avoid double

[4] The reporting of the proceeds (cash flows) from the sale of land as part of investing activities is discussed later in this chapter.

reporting, the gain of $12,000 is deducted from net income in determining cash flows from operating activities, as shown below.

Cash flows from operating activities:	
Net income	$108,000
Deduct gain on sale of land	12,000

Reporting Cash Flows from Operating Activities

We have now presented all the necessary adjustments to convert the net income to cash flows from operating activities for Rundell Inc. These adjustments are summarized in Exhibit 5 in a format suitable for the statement of cash flows.

Exhibit 5 Cash Flows from Operating Activities—Indirect Method

Cash flows from operating activities:			
Net income		$108,000	
Add: Depreciation	$ 7,000		
Decrease in inventories	8,000		
Increase in accrued expenses	2,200	17,200	
		$125,200	
Deduct: Increase in accounts receivable	$ 9,000		
Decrease in accounts payable	3,200		
Decrease in income taxes payable	500		
Gain on sale of land	12,000	24,700	
Net cash flow from operating activities			$100,500

Cash Flows Used for Payment of Dividends

According to the retained earnings account of Rundell Inc., shown earlier in the chapter, cash dividends of $28,000 were declared during the year. However, the dividends payable account, shown below, indicates that dividends of only $24,000 were paid during the year.

ACCOUNT *Dividends Payable* ACCOUNT NO.

Date		Item	Debit	Credit	Balance Debit	Balance Credit
2003 Jan.	1	Balance				10,000
	10	Cash paid	10,000		—	—
June	20	Dividends declared		14,000		14,000
July	10	Cash paid	14,000		—	—
Dec.	20	Dividends declared		14,000		14,000

The $24,000 of dividend payments represents a cash outflow that is reported in the financing activities section as follows:

Cash flows from financing activities:	
Cash paid for dividends	$24,000

Common Stock

The common stock account increased by $8,000, and the paid-in capital in excess of par—common stock account increased by $40,000, as shown below. These increases result from issuing 4,000 shares of common stock for $12 per share.

eToys, Inc. has had a negative cumulative cash flow from operations from its inception until recently. However, eToys has been able to grow by obtaining cash from the sale of common stock. Investors are willing to purchase the common stock on the belief that eToys will have a very profitable future as e-commerce matures.

ACCOUNT ***Common Stock*** **ACCOUNT NO.**

Date		Item	Debit	Credit	Balance Debit	Balance Credit
2003 Jan.	1	Balance				16,000
Nov.	1	4,000 shares issued for cash		8,000		24,000

ACCOUNT ***Paid-In Capital in Excess of Par—Common Stock*** **ACCOUNT NO.**

Date		Item	Debit	Credit	Balance Debit	Balance Credit
2003 Jan.	1	Balance				80,000
Nov.	1	4,000 shares issued for cash		40,000		120,000

This cash inflow is reported in the financing activities section as follows:

Cash flows from financing activities:
Cash received from sale of common stock $48,000

Bonds Payable

The bonds payable account decreased by $50,000, as shown below. This decrease results from retiring the bonds by a cash payment for their face amount.

ACCOUNT ***Bonds Payable*** **ACCOUNT NO.**

Date		Item	Debit	Credit	Balance Debit	Balance Credit
2003 Jan.	1	Balance				150,000
June	30	Retired by payment of cash at face amount	50,000			100,000

This cash outflow is reported in the financing activities section as follows:

Cash flows from financing activities:
Cash paid to retire bonds payable $50,000

Building

The building account increased by $60,000, and the accumulated depreciation—building account increased by $7,000, as shown below.

ACCOUNT *Building*					ACCOUNT NO.	
					Balance	
Date		Item	Debit	Credit	Debit	Credit
2003 Jan.	1	Balance			200,000	
Dec.	27	Purchased for cash	60,000		260,000	

ACCOUNT *Accumulated Depreciation—Building*					ACCOUNT NO.	
					Balance	
Date		Item	Debit	Credit	Debit	Credit
2003 Jan.	1	Balance				58,300
Dec.	31	Depreciation for the year		7,000		65,300

Q&A *A building with a cost of $145,000 and accumulated depreciation of $35,000 was sold for a $10,000 gain. How much cash was generated from this investing activity?*

$120,000 ($145,000 – $35,000 + $10,000)

The purchase of a building for cash of $60,000 is reported as an outflow of cash in the investing activities section, as follows:

Cash flows from investing activities:
Cash paid for purchase of building $60,000

The credit in the accumulated depreciation—building account, shown earlier, represents depreciation expense for the year. This depreciation expense of $7,000 on the building has already been considered as an addition to net income in determining cash flows from operating activities, as reported in Exhibit 5.

Land

The $45,000 decline in the land account resulted from two separate transactions, as shown below.

ACCOUNT *Land*					ACCOUNT NO.	
					Balance	
Date		Item	Debit	Credit	Debit	Credit
2003 Jan.	1	Balance			125,000	
June	8	Sold for $72,000 cash		60,000	65,000	
Oct.	12	Purchased for $15,000 cash	15,000		80,000	

The first transaction is the sale of land with a cost of $60,000 for $72,000 in cash. The $72,000 proceeds from the sale are reported in the investing activities section, as follows:

Cash flows from investing activities:
Cash received from sale of land (includes $12,000 gain reported in net income) $72,000

The proceeds of $72,000 include the $12,000 gain on the sale of land and the $60,000 cost (book value) of the land. As shown in Exhibit 5, the $12,000 gain is also deducted from net income in the cash flows from operating activities section. This is necessary so that the $12,000 cash inflow related to the gain is not included twice as a cash inflow.

The second transaction is the purchase of land for cash of $15,000. This transaction is reported as an outflow of cash in the investing activities section, as follows:

Cash flows from investing activities:	
Cash paid for purchase of land	$15,000

Preparing the Statement of Cash Flows

The statement of cash flows for Rundell Inc. is prepared from the data assembled and analyzed above, using the indirect method. Exhibit 6 shows the statement of cash flows prepared by Rundell Inc. The statement indicates that the cash position increased by $71,500 during the year. The most significant increase in net cash flows, $100,500, was from operating activities. The most significant use of cash, $26,000, was for financing activities.

Exhibit 6 Statement of Cash Flows—Indirect Method

Rundell Inc.
Statement of Cash Flows
For the Year Ended December 31, 2003

Cash flows from operating activities:			
Net income		$108,000	
Add: Depreciation	$ 7,000		
Decrease in inventories	8,000		
Increase in accrued expenses	2,200	17,200	
		$125,200	
Deduct: Increase in accounts receivable	$ 9,000		
Decrease in accounts payable	3,200		
Decrease in income taxes payable	500		
Gain on sale of land	12,000	24,700	
Net cash flow from operating activities			$100,500
Cash flows from investing activities:			
Cash from sale of land		$ 72,000	
Less: Cash paid to purchase land	$15,000		
Cash paid for purchase of building	60,000	75,000	
Net cash flow used for investing activities			(3,000)
Cash flows from financing activities:			
Cash received from sale of common stock		$ 48,000	
Less: Cash paid to retire bonds payable	$50,000		
Cash paid for dividends	24,000	74,000	
Net cash flow used for financing activities			(26,000)
Increase in cash			$ 71,500
Cash at the beginning of the year			26,000
Cash at the end of the year			$ 97,500

Statement of Cash Flows—The Direct Method

objective 4

Prepare a statement of cash flows, using the direct method.

As we discussed previously, the manner of reporting cash flows from investing and financing activities is the same under the direct and indirect methods. In addition, the direct method and the indirect method will report the same amount of cash flows from operating activities. However, the methods differ in how the cash flows from operating activities data are obtained, analyzed, and reported.

To illustrate the direct method, we will use the comparative balance sheet and the income statement for Rundell Inc. In this way, we can compare the statement of cash flows under the direct method and the indirect method.

Exhibit 7 shows the changes in the current asset and liability account balances for Rundell Inc. The income statement in Exhibit 7 shows additional data for Rundell Inc.

Exhibit 7 Balance Sheet and Income Statement Data for Direct Method

Rundell Inc.
Schedule of Changes in Current Accounts

Accounts	December 31 2003	December 31 2002	Increase Decrease*
Cash	$ 97,500	$ 26,000	$71,500
Accounts receivable (net)	74,000	65,000	9,000
Inventories	172,000	180,000	8,000*
Accounts payable (merchandise creditors)	43,500	46,700	3,200*
Accrued expenses payable (operating expenses)	26,500	24,300	2,200
Income taxes payable	7,900	8,400	500*
Dividends payable	14,000	10,000	4,000

Rundell Inc.
Income Statement
For the Year Ended December 31, 2003

Sales		$1,180,000
Cost of merchandise sold		790,000
Gross profit		$ 390,000
Operating expenses:		
Depreciation expense	$ 7,000	
Other operating expenses	196,000	
Total operating expenses		203,000
Income from operations		$ 187,000
Other income:		
Gain on sale of land	$ 12,000	
Other expense:		
Interest expense	8,000	4,000
Income before income tax		$ 191,000
Income tax expense		83,000
Net income		$ 108,000

The direct method reports cash flows from operating activities by major classes of operating cash receipts and operating cash payments. The difference between the major classes of total operating cash receipts and total operating cash payments is the net cash flow from operating activities.

Cash Received from Customers

The $1,180,000 of sales for Rundell Inc. is reported by using the accrual method. To determine the cash received from sales to customers, the $1,180,000 must be adjusted. The adjustment necessary to convert the sales reported on the income statement to the cash received from customers is summarized below.

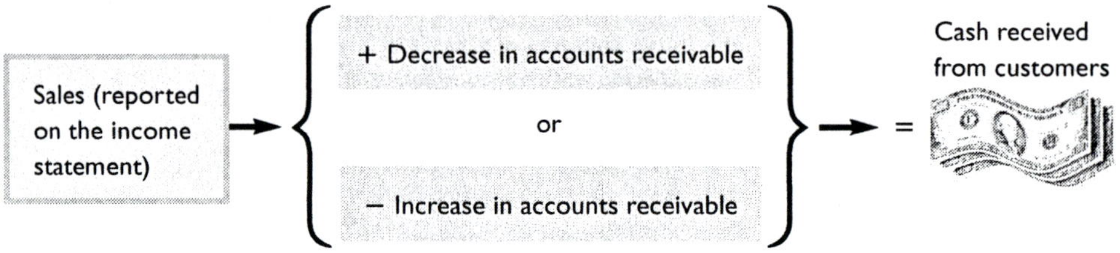

For Rundell Inc., the cash received from customers is $1,171,000, as shown below.

Sales	$1,180,000
Less increase in accounts receivable	9,000
Cash received from customers	$1,171,000

Q&A: Sales reported on the income statement were $350,000. The accounts receivable balance declined $8,000 over the year. What was the amount of cash received from customers?

$358,000 ($350,000 + $8,000)

The additions to **accounts receivable** for sales on account during the year were $9,000 more than the amounts collected from customers on account. Sales reported on the income statement therefore included $9,000 that did not result in a cash inflow during the year. In other words, the increase of $9,000 in accounts receivable during 2003 indicates that sales on account exceeded cash received from customers by $9,000. Thus, $9,000 is deducted from sales to determine the cash received from customers. The $1,171,000 of cash received from customers is reported in the cash flows from operating activities section of the cash flow statement.

Cash Payments for Merchandise

The $790,000 of cost of merchandise sold is reported on the income statement for Rundell Inc., using the accrual method. The adjustments necessary to convert the cost of merchandise sold to cash payments for merchandise during 2003 are summarized below.

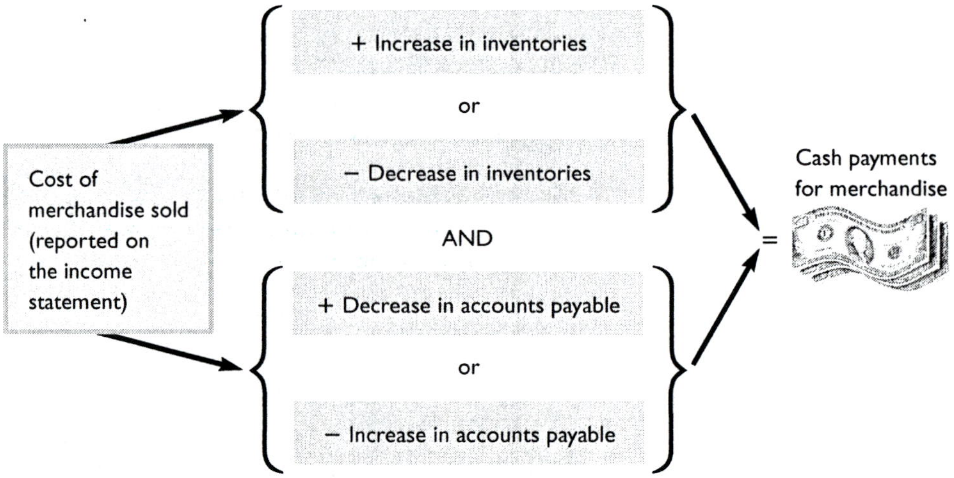

For Rundell Inc., the amount of cash payments for merchandise is $785,200, as determined below.

Cost of merchandise sold	$790,000
Deduct decrease in inventories	(8,000)
Add decrease in accounts payable	3,200
Cash payments for merchandise	$785,200

The $8,000 decrease in **inventories** indicates that the merchandise sold exceeded the cost of the merchandise purchased by $8,000. The amount reported on the income statement for cost of merchandise sold therefore includes $8,000 that did not require a cash outflow during the year. Thus, $8,000 is deducted from the cost of merchandise sold in determining the cash payments for merchandise.

The $3,200 decrease in **accounts payable** (merchandise creditors) indicates a cash outflow that is excluded from cost of merchandise sold. In other words, the decrease in accounts payable indicates that cash payments for merchandise were $3,200 more than the purchases on account during 2003. Thus, $3,200 is added to the cost of merchandise sold in determining the cash payments for merchandise.

Cash Payments for Operating Expenses

The $7,000 of depreciation expense reported on the income statement did not require a cash outflow. Thus, under the direct method, it is not reported on the statement of cash flows. The $196,000 reported for other operating expenses is adjusted to reflect the cash payments for operating expenses, as summarized below.

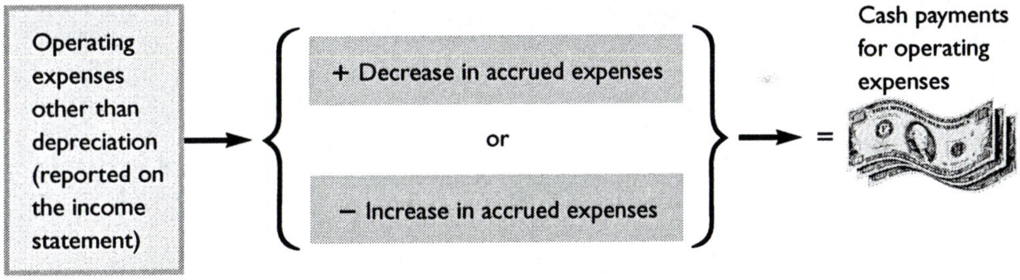

For Rundell Inc., the amount of cash payments for operating expenses is $193,800, determined as follows:

Operating expenses other than depreciation	$196,000
Deduct increase in accrued expenses	2,200
Cash payments for operating expenses	$193,800

The increase in **accrued expenses** (operating expenses) indicates that operating expenses include $2,200 for which there was no cash outflow (payment) during the year. In other words, the increase in accrued expenses indicates that the cash payments for operating expenses were $2,200 less than the amount reported as an expense during the year. Thus, $2,200 is deducted from the operating expenses on the income statement in determining the cash payments for operating expenses.

Gain on Sale of Land

The income statement for Rundell Inc. in Exhibit 7 reports a gain of $12,000 on the sale of land. As we discussed previously, the gain is included in the proceeds from the sale of land, which is reported as part of the cash flows from investing activities.

Interest Expense

The income statement for Rundell Inc. in Exhibit 7 reports interest expense of $8,000. The interest expense is related to the bonds payable that were outstanding during the year. We assume that interest on the bonds is paid on June 30 and December 31. Thus, $8,000 cash outflow for interest expense is reported on the statement of cash flows as an operating activity.

If interest payable had existed at the end of the year, the interest expense would be adjusted for any increase or decrease in interest payable from the beginning to the end of the year. That is, a decrease in interest payable would be added to interest expense and an increase in interest payable would be subtracted from interest expense. This is similar to the adjustment for changes in income taxes payable, which we will illustrate in the following paragraphs.

Cash Payments for Income Taxes

The adjustment to convert the income tax reported on the income statement to the cash basis is summarized below.

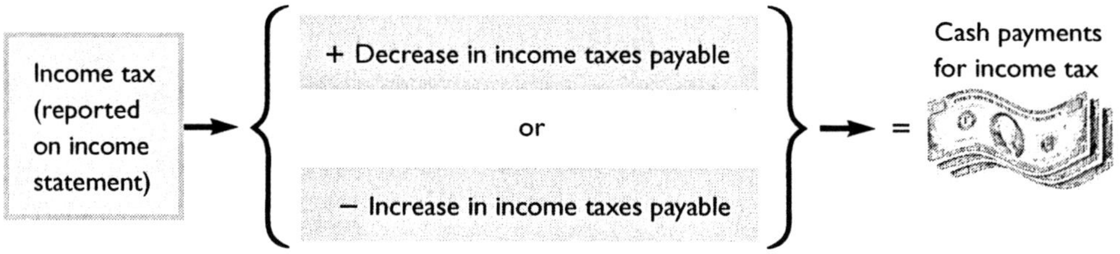

For Rundell Inc., cash payments for income tax are $83,500, determined as follows:

Income tax	$83,000
Add decrease in income taxes payable	500
Cash payments for income tax	$83,500

Real World Dell Computer Corporation is one of the few companies that has a *negative cash conversion cycle*. This means that Dell receives payment for a computer before it pays for the parts that went into that computer. This can only be done by collecting the sale with a credit card, maintaining very little inventory, and holding accounts payable open for 30 days.

The cash outflow for income taxes exceeded the income tax deducted as an expense during the period by $500. Thus, $500 is added to the amount of income tax reported on the income statement in determining the cash payments for income tax.

Reporting Cash Flows from Operating Activities—Direct Method

Exhibit 8 is a complete statement of cash flows for Rundell Inc., using the direct method for reporting cash flows from operating activities. The portions of this statement that differ from the indirect method are highlighted in color. Exhibit 8 also includes the separate schedule reconciling net income and net cash flow from operating activities. This schedule must accompany the statement of cash flows when the direct method is used. This schedule is similar to the cash flows from operating activities section of the statement of cash flows prepared using the indirect method.

Exhibit 8 Statement of Cash Flows—Direct Method

Rundell Inc.
Statement of Cash Flows
For the Year Ended December 31, 2003

Cash flows from operating activities:			
Cash received from customers		$1,171,000	
Deduct: Cash payments for merchandise	$785,200		
Cash payments for operating expenses	193,800		
Cash payments for interest	8,000		
Cash payments for income taxes	83,500	1,070,500	
Net cash flow from operating activities			$100,500
Cash flows from investing activities:			
Cash from sale of land		$ 72,000	
Less: Cash paid to purchase land	$ 15,000		
Cash paid for purchase of building	60,000	75,000	
Net cash flow used for investing activities			(3,000)
Cash flows from financing activities:			
Cash received from sale of common stock		$ 48,000	
Less: Cash paid to retire bonds payable	$ 50,000		
Cash paid for dividends	24,000	74,000	
Net cash flow used for financing activities			(26,000)
Increase in cash			$ 71,500
Cash at the beginning of the year			26,000
Cash at the end of the year			$ 97,500

Schedule Reconciling Net Income with Cash Flows from Operating Activities:

Net income, per income statement		$108,000
Add: Depreciation	$ 7,000	
Decrease in inventories	8,000	
Increase in accrued expenses	2,200	17,200
		$125,200
Deduct: Increase in accounts receivable	$ 9,000	
Decrease in accounts payable	3,200	
Decrease in income taxes payable	500	
Gain on sale of land	12,000	24,700
Net cash flow from operating activities		$100,500

FINANCIAL ANALYSIS AND INTERPRETATION

objective 5

Calculate and interpret the free cash flow.

A valuable tool for evaluating the cash position of a business is free cash flow. **Free cash flow** is a measure of operating cash flow available for corporate purposes after providing sufficient fixed asset additions to maintain current productive capacity and dividends. Thus, free cash flow can be calculated as follows:

	Cash flow from operating activities
Less:	Cash used to purchase fixed assets to maintain productive capacity used up in producing income during the period
Less:	Cash used for dividends
	Free cash flow

Real World

Many high technology firms must aggressively reinvest in new technology to remain competitive. This can reduce free cash flow. For example, **Motorola's** free cash flow is less than 10% of the cash flow from operating activities. In contrast, **Coca-Cola's** free cash flow is approximately 75% of the cash flow from operating activities.

To illustrate, assume that O'Brien Company had cash flow from operating activities of $1,400,000. O'Brien Company invested $450,000 in fixed assets to maintain productive capacity, and another $300,000 to expand capacity. Dividends were $100,000. Thus, free cash flow is as follows:

Cash flow from operating activities		$1,400,000
Less: Cash invested in fixed assets to maintain productive capacity	$450,000	
Cash for dividends	100,000	550,000
Free cash flow		$ 850,000

A company that has free cash flow is able to fund internal growth, retire debt, and enjoy financial flexibility. A company with no free cash flow is unable to maintain current productive capacity or dividend payouts to stockholders. Lack of free cash flow can be an early indicator of liquidity problems. Indeed, as stated by one analyst, "Free cash flow gives the company firepower to reduce debt and ultimately generate consistent, actual income."[5]

ENCORE

Cash Is King for the Pack

The **Green Bay Packers** is the only team in the NFL to be owned by the fans (over 109,000 of them). Indeed, over 10,000 fans show up in early July at Lambeau Field for the shareholders' meeting, the largest shareholders' meeting in corporate America. Unfortunately, the recent financial news has not been good. Although the club had a profit of $1 million, it had a negative cash flow of $10.7 million (excluding a one-time expansion team payment). Why did the cash decline in the face of positive earnings? The answer is simple. The Packers have paid over $32 million in player-signing bonuses, while continuing to make improvements to Lambeau Field. John Underwood, treasurer, stated, "We really need to focus our attention on generating higher levels of cash. In the business we're in, cash is king. And every dollar we make in this franchise goes to only one of two purposes: the football team or the facilities." While the Packers place 15th out of 31 teams in total revenue, the president predicts that they will fall to last place by 2003 if Lambeau Field is not renovated. A stadium renovation will allow the Packers to:

- expand the concourse for additional retail shops and concession space.
- build a stadium club that can be used for banquets and events.
- expand Lambeau's rather small 61,000-seat capacity by 8,000 seats.
- rebuild the luxury boxes.

The added cash flow from stadium improvements is the key to financial success in professional football. The question is how to come up with $150 million for stadium renovations. The team is presently considering a one-time, $1,000 per-seat user fee to be assessed to the season ticket holders to cover part of it. Apparently, if you're a stockholder who also holds season tickets, the news is doubly bad. ■

[5] Jill Krutick, *Fortune*, March 30, 1998, p. 106.

APPENDIX: WORK SHEET FOR STATEMENT OF CASH FLOWS

A work sheet may be useful in assembling data for the statement of cash flows. Whether or not a work sheet is used, the concepts of cash flow and the statements of cash flows presented in this chapter are not affected. In this appendix, we will describe and illustrate the use of work sheets for the indirect method and the direct method.

Work Sheet—Indirect Method

We will use the data for Rundell Inc., presented in Exhibit 3, as a basis for illustrating the work sheet for the indirect method. The procedures used in preparing this work sheet, shown in Exhibit 9, are outlined at the top of the next page.

Exhibit 9 Work Sheet for Statement of Cash Flows—Indirect Method

Rundell Inc.
Work Sheet for Statement of Cash Flows
For the Year Ended December 31, 2003

	Accounts	Balance Dec. 31, 2002	Transactions		Balance Dec. 31, 2003	
			Debit	Credit		
1	Cash	26,000	(o) 71,500		97,500	1
2	Accounts receivable (net)	65,000	(n) 9,000		74,000	2
3	Inventories	180,000		(m) 8,000	172,000	3
4	Land	125,000	(k) 15,000	(l) 60,000	80,000	4
5	Building	200,000	(j) 60,000		260,000	5
6	Accumulated depreciation—building	(58,300)		(i) 7,000	(65,300)	6
7	Accounts payable (merchandise creditors)	(46,700)	(h) 3,200		(43,500)	7
8	Accrued expenses payable (operating expenses)	(24,300)		(g) 2,200	(26,500)	8
9	Income taxes payable	(8,400)	(f) 500		(7,900)	9
10	Dividends payable	(10,000)		(e) 4,000	(14,000)	10
11	Bonds payable	(150,000)	(d) 50,000		(100,000)	11
12	Common stock	(16,000)		(c) 8,000	(24,000)	12
13	Paid-in capital in excess of par	(80,000)		(c) 40,000	(120,000)	13
14	Retained earnings	(202,300)	(b) 28,000	(a) 108,000	(282,300)	14
15	Totals	0	237,200	237,200	0	15
16	Operating activities:					16
17	Net income		(a) 108,000			17
18	Depreciation of building		(i) 7,000			18
19	Decrease in inventories		(m) 8,000			19
20	Increase in accrued expenses		(g) 2,200			20
21	Increase in accounts receivable			(n) 9,000		21
22	Decrease in accounts payable			(h) 3,200		22
23	Decrease in income taxes payable			(f) 500		23
24	Gain on sale of land			(l) 12,000		24
25	Investing activities:					25
26	Sale of land		(l) 72,000			26
27	Purchase of land			(k) 15,000		27
28	Purchase of building			(j) 60,000		28
29	Financing activities:					29
30	Issued common stock		(c) 48,000			30
31	Retired bonds payable			(d) 50,000		31
32	Declared cash dividends			(b) 28,000		32
33	Increase in dividends payable		(e) 4,000			33
34	Net increase in cash			(o) 71,500		34
35	Totals		249,200	249,200		35

1. List the title of each balance sheet account in the Accounts column. For each account, enter its balance as of December 31, 2002, in the first column and its balance as of December 31, 2003, in the last column. Place the credit balances in parentheses. The column totals should equal zero, since the total of the debits in a column should equal the total of the credits in a column.
2. Analyze the change during the year in each account to determine the net increase (decrease) in cash and the cash flows from operating activities, investing activities, financing activities, and the noncash investing and financing activities. Show the effect of the change on cash flows by making entries in the Transactions columns.

Analyzing Accounts

An efficient method of analyzing cash flows is to determine the type of cash flow activity that led to changes in balance sheet accounts during the period. As we analyze each noncash account, we will make entries on the work sheet for specific types of cash flow activities related to the noncash accounts. After we have analyzed all the noncash accounts, we will make an entry for the increase (decrease) in cash during the period. These entries, however, are not posted to the ledger. They only aid in assembling the data on the work sheet.

The order in which the accounts are analyzed is unimportant. However, it is more efficient to begin with the retained earnings account and proceed upward in the account listing.

Retained Earnings. The work sheet shows a Retained Earnings balance of $202,300 at December 31, 2002, and $282,300 at December 31, 2003. Thus, Retained Earnings increased $80,000 during the year. This increase resulted from two factors: (1) net income of $108,000 and (2) declaring cash dividends of $28,000. To identify the cash flows by activity, we will make two entries on the work sheet. These entries also serve to account for or explain, in terms of cash flows, the increase of $80,000.

In closing the accounts at the end of the year, the retained earnings account was credited for the net income of $108,000. The $108,000 is reported on the statement of cash flows as "cash flows from operating activities." The following entry is made in the Transactions columns on the work sheet. This entry (1) accounts for the credit portion of the closing entry (to Retained Earnings) and (2) identifies the cash flow in the bottom portion of the work sheet.

(a)	Operating Activities—Net Income	108,000	
	Retained Earnings		108,000

In closing the accounts at the end of the year, the retained earnings account was debited for dividends declared of $28,000. The $28,000 is reported as a financing activity on the statement of cash flows. The following entry on the work sheet (1) accounts for the debit portion of the closing entry (to Retained Earnings) and (2) identifies the cash flow in the bottom portion of the work sheet.

(b)	Retained Earnings	28,000	
	Financing Activities—Declared Cash Dividends		28,000

The $28,000 of declared dividends will be adjusted later for the actual amount of cash dividends paid during the year.

Other Accounts. The entries for the other accounts are made in the work sheet in a manner similar to entries (a) and (b). A summary of these entries is as follows:

(c)	Financing Activities—Issued Common Stock	48,000	
	Common Stock		8,000
	Paid-In Capital in Excess of Par—Common Stock		40,000

(d)	Bonds Payable	50,000	
	Financing Activities—Retired Bonds Payable		50,000
(e)	Financing Activities—Increase in Dividends Payable	4,000	
	Dividends Payable		4,000
(f)	Income Taxes Payable	500	
	Operating Activities—Decrease in Income Taxes Payable		500
(g)	Operating Activities—Increase in Accrued Expenses	2,200	
	Accrued Expenses Payable		2,200
(h)	Accounts Payable	3,200	
	Operating Activities—Decrease in Accounts Payable		3,200
(i)	Operating Activities—Depreciation of Building	7,000	
	Accumulated Depreciation—Building		7,000
(j)	Building	60,000	
	Investing Activities—Purchase of Building		60,000
(k)	Land	15,000	
	Investing Activities—Purchase of Land		15,000
(l)	Investing Activities—Sale of Land	72,000	
	Operating Activities—Gain on Sale of Land		12,000
	Land		60,000
(m)	Operating Activities—Decrease in Inventories	8,000	
	Inventories		8,000
(n)	Accounts Receivable	9,000	
	Operating Activities—Increase in Accounts Receivable		9,000
(o)	Cash	71,500	
	Net Increase in Cash		71,500

Completing the Work Sheet

After we have analyzed all the balance sheet accounts and made the entries on the work sheet, all the operating, investing, and financing activities are identified in the bottom portion of the work sheet. The accuracy of the work sheet entries is verified by the equality of each pair of the totals of the debit and credit Transactions columns.

Preparing the Statement of Cash Flows

The statement of cash flows prepared from the work sheet is identical to the statement in Exhibit 6. The data for the three sections of the statement are obtained from the bottom portion of the work sheet.

In the cash flows from operating activities section, the effect of depreciation is normally presented first. The effects of increases and decreases in current assets and current liabilities are then presented. The effects of any gains and losses on operating activities are normally reported last. The cash paid for dividends is reported as $24,000 instead of the amount of dividends declared ($28,000) less the increase in dividends payable ($4,000). Any noncash investing and financing activities are usually reported in a separate schedule at the bottom of the statement.

Work Sheet—Direct Method

As a basis for illustrating the direct method work sheet, we will use the balance sheet data for Rundell Inc. in Exhibit 3 and the income statement data in Exhibit 7. The procedures used in preparing the work sheet are outlined following Exhibit 10.

1. List the title of each balance sheet account in the Accounts column. For each account, enter its balance as of December 31, 2002, in the first column and its balance as of December 31, 2003, in the last column. Place the credit balances in parentheses. The column totals should equal zero, since the total of the debits in a column should equal the total of the credits in a column.

Exhibit 10 Work Sheet for Statement of Cash Flows—Direct Method

Rundell Inc.
Work Sheet for Statement of Cash Flows
For the Year Ended December 31, 2003

Accounts	Balance Dec. 31, 2002	Transactions Debit	Transactions Credit	Balance Dec. 31, 2003
Balance Sheet				
Cash	26,000	(t) 71,500		97,500
Accounts receivable (net)	65,000	(s) 9,000		74,000
Inventories	180,000		(r) 8,000	172,000
Land	125,000	(q) 15,000	(e) 60,000	80,000
Building	200,000	(p) 60,000		260,000
Accumulated depreciation—building	(58,300)		(c) 7,000	(65,300)
Accounts payable (merchandise creditors)	(46,700)	(o) 3,200		(43,500)
Accrued expenses payable (operating expenses)	(24,300)		(n) 2,200	(26,500)
Income taxes payable	(8,400)	(m) 500		(7,900)
Dividends payable	(10,000)		(l) 4,000	(14,000)
Bonds payable	(150,000)	(k) 50,000		(100,000)
Common stock	(16,000)		(j) 8,000	(24,000)
Paid-in capital in excess of par	(80,000)		(j) 40,000	(120,000)
Retained earnings	(202,300)	(i) 28,000	(h) 108,000	(282,300)
Totals	0	237,200	237,200	0
Income Statement				
Sales			(a) 1,180,000	
Cost of merchandise sold		(b) 790,000		
Depreciation expense		(c) 7,000		
Other operating expenses		(d) 196,000		
Gain on sale of land			(e) 12,000	
Interest expense		(f) 8,000		
Income taxes		(g) 83,000		
Net income		(h) 108,000		
Cash Flows				
Operating activities:				
Cash received from customers		(a) 1,180,000	(s) 9,000	
Cash payments:				
Merchandise		(r) 8,000	(b) 790,000	
			(o) 3,200	
Operating expenses		(n) 2,200	(d) 196,000	
Interest			(f) 8,000	
Income taxes			(g) 83,000	
			(m) 500	
Investing activities:				
Sale of land		(e) 72,000		
Purchase of land			(q) 15,000	
Purchase of building			(p) 60,000	
Financing activities:				
Issued common stock		(j) 48,000		
Retired bonds payable			(k) 50,000	
Declared cash dividends			(i) 28,000	
Increase in dividends payable		(l) 4,000		
Net increase in cash			(t) 71,500	
Totals		2,506,200	2,506,200	

2. List the title of each income statement account and "Net income" on the work sheet.
3. Analyze the effect of each income statement item on cash flows from operating activities. Beginning with sales, enter the balance of each item in the proper Transactions column. Complete the entry in the Transactions columns to show the effect on cash flows.
4. Analyze the change during the year in each balance sheet account to determine the net increase (decrease) in cash and the cash flows from operating activities, investing activities, financing activities, and the noncash investing and financing activities. Show the effect of the change on cash flows by making entries in the Transactions columns.

Analyzing Accounts

Under the direct method of reporting cash flows from operating activities, analyzing accounts begins with the income statement. As we analyze each income statement account, we will make entries on the work sheet that show the effect on cash flows from operating activities. After we have analyzed the income statement accounts, we will analyze changes in the balance sheet accounts.

The order in which the balance sheet accounts are analyzed is unimportant. However, it is more efficient to begin with the retained earnings account and proceed upward in the account listing. As each noncash balance sheet account is analyzed, we will make entries on the work sheet for the related cash flow activities. After we have analyzed all the noncash accounts, we will make an entry for the increase (decrease) in cash during the period.

Sales. The income statement for Rundell Inc. shows sales of $1,180,000 for the year. Sales for cash provide cash when the sale is made. Sales on account provide cash when customers pay their bills. The entry on the work sheet is as follows:

(a)	Operating Activities—Receipts from Customers	1,180,000	
	Sales		1,180,000

Cost of Merchandise Sold. The income statement for Rundell Inc. shows cost of merchandise sold of $790,000 for the year. The cost of merchandise sold requires cash payments for cash purchases of merchandise. For purchases on account, cash payments are made when the invoices are due. The entry on the work sheet is as follows:

(b)	Cost of Merchandise Sold	790,000	
	Operating Activities—Payments for Merchandise		790,000

Depreciation Expense. The income statement for Rundell Inc. shows depreciation expense of $7,000. Depreciation expense does not require a cash outflow and thus is not reported on the statement of cash flows. The entry on the work sheet to fully account for the depreciation expense is as follows:

(c)	Depreciation Expense	7,000	
	Accumulated Depreciation—Building		7,000

Other Accounts. The entries for the other accounts are made on the work sheet in a manner similar to entries (a), (b), and (c). A summary of these entries is as follows:

(d)	Other Operating Expenses	196,000	
	Operating Activities—Paid Operating Expenses		196,000

(e)	Investing Activities—Sale of Land	72,000	
	Land		60,000
	Gain on Sale of Land		12,000
(f)	Interest Expense	8,000	
	Operating Activities—Paid Interest		8,000
(g)	Income Taxes	83,000	
	Operating Activities—Paid Income Taxes		83,000
(h)	Net Income	108,000	
	Retained Earnings		108,000
(i)	Retained Earnings	28,000	
	Financing Activities—Declared Cash Dividends		28,000
(j)	Financing Activities—Issued Common Stock	48,000	
	Common Stock		8,000
	Paid-In Capital in Excess of Par—Common Stock		40,000
(k)	Bonds Payable	50,000	
	Financing Activities—Retired Bonds Payable		50,000
(l)	Financing Activities—Increase in Dividends Payable	4,000	
	Dividends Payable		4,000
(m)	Income Taxes Payable	500	
	Operating Activities—Cash Paid for Income Taxes		500
(n)	Operating Activities—Cash Paid for Operating Expenses	2,200	
	Accrued Expenses Payable		2,200
(o)	Accounts Payable	3,200	
	Operating Activities—Cash Paid for Merchandise		3,200
(p)	Building	60,000	
	Investing Activities—Purchase of Building		60,000
(q)	Land	15,000	
	Investing Activities—Purchase of Land		15,000
(r)	Operating Activities—Cash Paid for Merchandise	8,000	
	Inventories		8,000
(s)	Accounts Receivable	9,000	
	Operating Activities—Cash Received from Customers		9,000
(t)	Cash	71,500	
	Net Increase in Cash		71,500

Completing the Work Sheet

After we have analyzed all the income statement and balance sheet accounts and have made the entries on the work sheet, all the operating, investing, and financing activities are identified in the bottom portion of the work sheet. The mathematical accuracy of the work sheet entries is verified by the equality of each pair of the totals of the debit and credit Transactions columns.

Preparing the Statement of Cash Flows

The statement of cash flows prepared from the work sheet is identical to the statement in Exhibit 8. The data for the three sections of the statement are obtained from the bottom portion of the work sheet. Some of these data may not be reported exactly as they appear on the work sheet. The cash paid for dividends is reported as $24,000 instead of the amount of dividends declared ($28,000) less the increase in the dividends payable ($4,000).

KEY POINTS

1 Explain why the statement of cash flows is one of the basic financial statements.

The statement of cash flows reports useful information about a firm's ability to generate cash from operations, maintain and expand its operating capacity, meet its financial obligations, and pay dividends. This information assists investors, creditors, and others in assessing the firm's profit potential and its ability to pay its maturing debt. The statement of cash flows is also useful to managers in evaluating past operations and in planning future operating, investing, and financing activities.

2 Summarize the types of cash flow activities reported in the statement of cash flows.

The statement of cash flows reports cash receipts and cash payments by three types of activities: operating activities, investing activities, and financing activities.

Cash flows from operating activities are cash flows from transactions that affect net income. There are two methods of reporting cash flows from operating activities: (1) the direct method and (2) the indirect method.

Cash inflows from investing activities are cash flows from the sale of investments, fixed assets, and intangible assets. Cash outflows generally include payments to acquire investments, fixed assets, and intangible assets.

Cash inflows from financing activities include proceeds from issuing equity securities, such as preferred and common stock. Cash inflows also arise from issuing bonds, mortgage notes payable, and other long-term debt. Cash outflows from financing activities arise from paying cash dividends, purchasing treasury stock, and repaying amounts borrowed.

Investing and financing for a business may be affected by transactions that do not involve cash. The effect of such transactions should be reported in a separate schedule accompanying the statement of cash flows.

Because it may be misleading, cash flow per share is not reported in the statement of cash flows.

3 Prepare a statement of cash flows, using the indirect method.

To prepare the statement of cash flows, changes in the noncash balance sheet accounts are analyzed. This logic relies on the fact that a change in any balance sheet account can be analyzed in terms of changes in the other balance sheet accounts. Thus, by analyzing the noncash balance sheet accounts, those activities that resulted in cash flows can be identified. Although the noncash balance sheet accounts may be analyzed in any order, it is usually more efficient to begin with retained earnings. Additional data are obtained by analyzing the income statement accounts and supporting records.

4 Prepare a statement of cash flows, using the direct method.

The direct method and the indirect method will report the same amount of cash flows from operating activities. Also, the manner of reporting cash flows from investing and financing activities is the same under both methods. The methods differ in how the cash flows from operating activities data are obtained, analyzed, and reported. The direct method reports cash flows from operating activities by major classes of operating cash receipts and cash payments. The difference between the major classes of total operating cash receipts and total operating cash payments is the net cash flow from operating activities.

The data for reporting cash flows from operating activities by the direct method can be obtained by analyzing the cash flows related to the revenues and expenses reported on the income statement. The revenues and expenses are adjusted from the accrual basis of accounting to the cash basis for purposes of preparing the statement of cash flows.

When the direct method is used, a reconciliation of net income and net cash flow from operating activities is reported in a separate schedule. This schedule is similar to the cash flows from operating activities section of the statement of cash flows prepared using the indirect method.

5 Calculate and interpret the free cash flow.

Free cash flow is the amount of operating cash flow remaining after replacing current productive capacity and maintaining current dividends. Free cash flow is the amount of cash available to reduce debt, expand the business, or return to shareholders through increased dividends or treasury stock purchases.

ILLUSTRATIVE PROBLEM

The comparative balance sheet of Dowling Company for December 31, 2004 and 2003, is as follows:

Dowling Company
Comparative Balance Sheet
December 31, 2004 and 2003

	2004	2003
Assets		
Cash	$ 140,350	$ 95,900
Accounts receivable (net)	95,300	102,300
Inventories	165,200	157,900
Prepaid expenses	6,240	5,860
Investments (long-term)	35,700	84,700
Land	75,000	90,000
Buildings	375,000	260,000
Accumulated depreciation—buildings	(71,300)	(58,300)
Machinery and equipment	428,300	428,300
Accumulated depreciation—machinery and equipment	(148,500)	(138,000)
Patents	58,000	65,000
Total assets	$1,159,290	$1,093,660
Liabilities and Stockholders' Equity		
Accounts payable (merchandise creditors)	$ 43,500	$ 46,700
Accrued expenses (operating expenses)	14,000	12,500
Income taxes payable	7,900	8,400
Dividends payable	14,000	10,000
Mortgage note payable, due 2004	40,000	0
Bonds payable	150,000	250,000
Common stock, $30 par	450,000	375,000
Excess of issue price over par—common stock	66,250	41,250
Retained earnings	373,640	349,810
Total liabilities and stockholders' equity	$1,159,290	$1,093,660

The income statement for Dowling Company is shown below.

Dowling Company
Income Statement
For the Year Ended December 31, 2004

Sales		$1,100,000
Cost of merchandise sold		710,000
Gross profit		$ 390,000
Operating expenses:		
Depreciation expense	$ 23,500	
Patent amortization	7,000	
Other operating expenses	196,000	
Total operating expenses		226,500
Income from operations		$ 163,500
Other income:		
Gain on sale of investments	$ 11,000	
Other expense:		
Interest expense	26,000	(15,000)
Income before income tax		$ 148,500
Income tax expense		50,000
Net income		$ 98,500

An examination of the accounting records revealed the following additional information applicable to 2004:

a. Land costing $15,000 was sold for $15,000.
b. A mortgage note was issued for $40,000.
c. A building costing $115,000 was constructed.
d. 2,500 shares of common stock were issued at 40 in exchange for the bonds payable.
e. Cash dividends declared were $74,670.

Instructions

1. Prepare a statement of cash flows, using the indirect method of reporting cash flows from operating activities.
2. Prepare a statement of cash flows, using the direct method of reporting cash flows from operating activities.

Solution

1.

Dowling Company
Statement of Cash Flows—Indirect Method
For the Year Ended December 31, 2004

Cash flows from operating activities:			
Net income, per income statement		$ 98,500	
Add: Depreciation	$23,500		
Amortization of patents	7,000		
Decrease in accounts receivable	7,000		
Increase in accrued expenses	1,500	39,000	
		$137,500	
Deduct: Increase in inventories	$ 7,300		
Increase in prepaid expenses	380		
Decrease in accounts payable	3,200		
Decrease in income taxes payable	500		
Gain on sale of investments	11,000	22,380	
Net cash flow from operating activities			$115,120
Cash flows from investing activities:			
Cash received from sale of:			
Investments	$60,000		
Land	15,000	$ 75,000	
Less: Cash paid for construction of building		115,000	
Net cash flow used for investing activities			(40,000)
Cash flows from financing activities:			
Cash received from issuing mortgage note payable		$ 40,000	
Less: Cash paid for dividends		70,670	
Net cash flow used for financing activities			(30,670)
Increase in cash			$ 44,450
Cash at the beginning of the year			95,900
Cash at the end of the year			$140,350

Schedule of Noncash Investing and Financing Activities:

Issued common stock to retire bonds payable	$100,000

2.

Dowling Company
Statement of Cash Flows—Direct Method
For the Year Ended December 31, 2004

Cash flows from operating activities:			
Cash received from customers[1]		$1,107,000	
Deduct: Cash paid for merchandise[2]	$720,500		
Cash paid for operating expenses[3]	194,880		
Cash paid for interest expense	26,000		
Cash paid for income tax[4]	50,500	991,880	
Net cash flow from operating activities			$115,120
Cash flows from investing activities:			
Cash received from sale of:			
Investments	$ 60,000		
Land	15,000	$ 75,000	
Less: Cash paid for construction of building		115,000	
Net cash flow used for investing activities			(40,000)
Cash flows from financing activities:			
Cash received from issuing mortgage note payable		$ 40,000	
Less: Cash paid for dividends[5]		70,670	
Net cash flow used for financing activities			(30,670)
Increase in cash			$ 44,450
Cash at the beginning of the year			95,900
Cash at the end of the year			$140,350

Schedule of Noncash Investing and Financing Activities:

Issued common stock to retire bonds payable	$100,000

Computations:

[1]$1,100,000 + $7,000 = $1,107,000
[2]$710,000 + $3,200 + $7,300 = $720,500
[3]$196,000 + $380 − $1,500 = $194,880
[4]$50,000 + $500 = $50,500
[5]$74,670 + $10,000 − $14,000 = $70,670

SELF-EXAMINATION QUESTIONS

Answers at End of Chapter

Matching

Match each of the following statements with its proper term. Some terms may not be used.

A. **cash flows from financing activities**
B. **cash flows from investing activities**
C. **cash flows from operating activities**
D. **decrease in accounts payable**
E. **decrease in accounts receivable**

___ 1. An addition to sales under the direct method for determining cash flows from operating activities.

___ 2. A statement of cash flows disclosure item.

___ 3. The section of the statement of cash flows that reports cash flows from transactions affecting the equity and debt of the business.

___ 4. A financing activity that increases cash.

___ 5. An addition to net income under the indirect method for determining cash flows from operating activities.

___ 6. The section of the statement of cash flows that reports cash flows from transactions affecting investments in noncurrent assets.

F. direct method
G. dividends declared
H. free cash flow
I. loss on sale of land
J. indirect method
K. issuance of common stock
L. purchase of land with common stock
M. sale of land
N. statement of cash flows

___ 7. A summary of the major cash receipts and cash payments for a period.

___ 8. A deduction from net income under the indirect method for determining cash flows from operating activities.

___ 9. A method of reporting the cash flows from operating activities as the difference between the operating cash receipts and the operating cash payments.

___ 10. The section of the statement of cash flows that reports the cash transactions affecting the determination of net income.

___ 11. A method of reporting the cash flows from operating activities as the net income from operations adjusted for all deferrals of past cash receipts and payments and all accruals of expected future cash receipts and payments.

___ 12. An investing activity.

___ 13. The amount of operating cash flow remaining after replacing current productive capacity and maintaining current dividends.

Multiple Choice

1. An example of a cash flow from an operating activity is:
   A. receipt of cash from the sale of stock
   B. receipt of cash from the sale of bonds
   C. payment of cash for dividends
   D. receipt of cash from customers on account

2. An example of a cash flow from an investing activity is:
   A. receipt of cash from the sale of equipment
   B. receipt of cash from the sale of stock
   C. payment of cash for dividends
   D. payment of cash to acquire treasury stock

3. An example of a cash flow from a financing activity is:
   A. receipt of cash from customers on account
   B. receipt of cash from the sale of equipment
   C. payment of cash for dividends
   D. payment of cash to acquire land

4. Which of the following methods of reporting cash flows from operating activities adjusts net income for revenues and expenses not involving the receipt or payment of cash?
   A. Direct method
   B. Purchase method
   C. Reciprocal method
   D. Indirect method

5. The net income reported on the income statement for the year was $55,000, and depreciation of fixed assets for the year was $22,000. The balances of the current asset and current liability accounts at the beginning and end of the year are as follows:

	End	Beginning
Cash	$ 65,000	$ 70,000
Accounts receivable	100,000	90,000
Inventories	145,000	150,000
Prepaid expenses	7,500	8,000
Accounts payable (merchandise creditors)	51,000	58,000

The total amount reported for cash flows from operating activities in the statement of cash flows, using the indirect method, is:
   A. $33,000
   B. $55,000
   C. $65,500
   D. $77,000

CLASS DISCUSSION QUESTIONS

1. What is the principal disadvantage of the direct method of reporting cash flows from operating activities?
2. What are the major advantages of the indirect method of reporting cash flows from operating activities?
3. A corporation issued $200,000 of common stock in exchange for $200,000 of fixed assets. Where would this transaction be reported on the statement of cash flows?
4. a. What is the effect on cash flows of declaring and issuing a stock dividend?
   b. Is the stock dividend reported on the statement of cash flows?
5. A retail business, using the accrual method of accounting, owed merchandise creditors (accounts payable) $290,000 at the beginning of the year and $315,000 at the end of the year. How would the $25,000 increase be used to adjust net income in

determining the amount of cash flows from operating activities by the indirect method? Explain.

6. If salaries payable was $75,000 at the beginning of the year and $65,000 at the end of the year, should $10,000 be added to or deducted from income to determine the amount of cash flows from operating activities by the indirect method? Explain.
7. A long-term investment in bonds with a cost of $75,000 was sold for $80,000 cash. (a) What was the gain or loss on the sale? (b) What was the effect of the transaction on cash flows? (c) How should the transaction be reported in the statement of cash flows if cash flows from operating activities are reported by the indirect method?
8. A corporation issued $5,000,000 of 20-year bonds for cash at 105. How would the transaction be reported on the statement of cash flows?
9. Fully depreciated equipment costing $55,000 was discarded. What was the effect of the transaction on cash flows if (a) $5,000 cash is received, (b) no cash is received?
10. For the current year, Accord Company decided to switch from the indirect method to the direct method for reporting cash flows from operating activities on the statement of cash flows. Will the change cause the amount of net cash flow from operating activities to be (a) larger, (b) smaller, or (c) the same as if the indirect method had been used? Explain.
11. Name five common major classes of operating cash receipts or operating cash payments presented on the statement of cash flows when the cash flows from operating activities are reported by the direct method.
12. In a recent annual report, PepsiCo, Inc., reported that during the year it issued stock of $438 million for acquisitions. How would this be reported on the statement of cash flows?

Real World

Warren Reeve Fess

RESOURCES FOR YOUR SUCCESS ONLINE AT

http://warren.swcollege.com

Remember! If you need additional help, visit South-Western's Web site.
See page 26 for a description of the online and printed materials that are available.

EXERCISES

Exercise 15–1
Cash flows from operating activities—net loss
Objective 2

Real World

On its income statement for a recent year, Amazon.com, Inc. reported a net loss of $124 million from operations. On its statement of cash flows, it reported $31 million of cash flows from operating activities.

Explain this apparent contradiction between the loss and the positive cash flows.

Exercise 15–2
Effect of transactions on cash flows
Objective 2

✓ b. Cash payment, $501,000

State the effect (cash receipt or payment and amount) of each of the following transactions, considered individually, on cash flows:

a. Purchased a building by paying $30,000 cash and issuing a $90,000 mortgage note payable.
b. Retired $500,000 of bonds, on which there was $2,500 of unamortized discount, for $501,000.

c. Paid dividends of $1.50 per share. There were 30,000 shares issued and 5,000 shares of treasury stock.
d. Sold a new issue of $100,000 of bonds at 101.
e. Purchased 5,000 shares of $30 par common stock as treasury stock at $50 per share.
f. Purchased land for $120,000 cash.
g. Sold equipment with a book value of $42,500 for $41,000.
h. Sold 5,000 shares of $30 par common stock for $45 per share.

Exercise 15–3
Classifying cash flows
Objective 2

Identify the type of cash flow activity for each of the following events (operating, investing, or financing):

a. Issued bonds.
b. Issued common stock.
c. Sold long-term investments.
d. Paid cash dividends.
e. Redeemed bonds.
f. Issued preferred stock.
g. Net income.
h. Sold equipment.
i. Purchased treasury stock.
j. Purchased buildings.
k. Purchased patents.

Exercise 15–4
Cash flows from operating activities—indirect method
Objective 3

Indicate whether each of the following would be added to or deducted from net income in determining net cash flow from operating activities by the indirect method:

a. Loss on disposal of fixed assets
b. Decrease in accounts payable
c. Decrease in salaries payable
d. Depreciation of fixed assets
e. Amortization of patent
f. Decrease in accounts receivable
g. Gain on retirement of long-term debt
h. Increase in merchandise inventory
i. Decrease in prepaid expenses
j. Increase in notes receivable due in 90 days from customers
k. Amortization of goodwill
l. Increase in notes payable due in 90 days to vendors

Exercise 15–5
Cash flows from operating activities—indirect method
Objectives 2, 3

✓ a. Cash flows from operating activities, $196,150

The net income reported on the income statement for the current year was $167,900. Depreciation recorded on equipment and a building amounted to $41,300 for the year. Balances of the current asset and current liability accounts at the beginning and end of the year are as follows:

	End of Year	Beginning of Year
Cash	$ 27,900	$ 30,900
Accounts receivable (net)	75,100	70,250
Inventories	120,400	110,900
Prepaid expenses	5,800	6,000
Accounts payable (merchandise creditors)	67,200	65,300
Salaries payable	7,150	7,950

a. Prepare the cash flows from operating activities section of the statement of cash flows, using the indirect method.
b. If the direct method had been used, would the net cash flow from operating activities have been the same? Explain.

Exercise 15–6
Cash flows from operating activities—indirect method
Objective 3

The net income reported on the income statement for the current year was $489,000. Depreciation recorded on store equipment for the year amounted to $135,700. Balances of the current asset and current liability accounts at the beginning and end of the year are as follows:

✓ Cash flows from operating activities, $657,200

	End of Year	Beginning of Year
Cash	$420,400	$509,000
Accounts receivable (net)	625,100	693,200
Merchandise inventory	724,600	704,700
Prepaid expenses	32,000	30,500
Accounts payable (merchandise creditors)	432,700	452,500
Wages payable	40,600	35,000

Prepare the cash flows from operating activities section of the statement of cash flows, using the indirect method.

Exercise 15–7
Determining cash payments to stockholders
Objective 3

The board of directors declared cash dividends totaling $280,000 during the current year. The comparative balance sheet indicates dividends payable of $60,000 at the beginning of the year and $70,000 at the end of the year. What was the amount of cash payments to stockholders during the year?

Exercise 15–8
Reporting changes in equipment on statement of cash flows
Objective 3

An analysis of the general ledger accounts indicates that office equipment, which had cost $200,000 and on which accumulated depreciation totaled $95,000 on the date of sale, was sold for $125,000 during the year. Using this information, indicate the items to be reported on the statement of cash flows.

Exercise 15–9
Reporting changes in equipment on statement of cash flows
Objective 3

An analysis of the general ledger accounts indicates that delivery equipment, which had cost $50,000 and on which accumulated depreciation totaled $23,000 on the date of sale, was sold for $24,000 during the year. Using this information, indicate the items to be reported on the statement of cash flows.

Exercise 15–10
Reporting land transactions on statement of cash flows
Objective 3

On the basis of the details of the following fixed asset account, indicate the items to be reported on the statement of cash flows:

ACCOUNT *Land* ACCOUNT NO.

Date		Item	Debit	Credit	Balance Debit	Balance Credit
2003						
Jan.	1	Balance			400,000	
Feb.	5	Purchased for cash	200,000		600,000	
Oct.	30	Sold for $105,000		80,000	520,000	

Exercise 15–11
Reporting stockholders' equity items on statement of cash flows
Objective 3

On the basis of the following stockholders' equity accounts, indicate the items, exclusive of net income, to be reported on the statement of cash flows. There were no unpaid dividends at either the beginning or the end of the year.

ACCOUNT *Common Stock, $10 Par* ACCOUNT NO.

Date		Item	Debit	Credit	Balance Debit	Balance Credit
2003						
Jan.	1	Balance, 50,000 shares				500,000
Feb.	11	6,000 shares issued for cash		60,000		560,000
June	30	2,750-share stock dividend		27,500		587,500

ACCOUNT ***Paid-In Capital in Excess of Par—Common Stock*** **ACCOUNT NO.**

Date		Item	Debit	Credit	Balance Debit	Balance Credit
2003						
Jan.	1	Balance				90,000
Feb.	11	6,000 shares issued for cash		240,000		330,000
June	30	Stock dividend		137,500		467,500

ACCOUNT ***Retained Earnings*** **ACCOUNT NO.**

Date		Item	Debit	Credit	Balance Debit	Balance Credit
2003						
Jan.	1	Balance				475,000
June	30	Stock dividend	165,000			310,000
Dec.	30	Cash dividend	180,000			130,000
	31	Net income		450,000		580,000

Exercise 15–12
Reporting land acquisition for cash and mortgage note on statement of cash flows
Objective 3

On the basis of the details of the following fixed asset account, indicate the items to be reported on the statement of cash flows:

ACCOUNT ***Land*** **ACCOUNT NO.**

Date		Item	Debit	Credit	Balance Debit	Balance Credit
2003						
Jan.	1	Balance			450,000	
Feb.	10	Purchased for cash	210,000		660,000	
Nov.	20	Purchased with long-term mortgage note	250,000		910,000	

Exercise 15–13
Determining net income from net cash flow from operating activities
Objective 3

Tiger Golf Inc. reported a net cash flow from operating activities of $93,200 on its statement of cash flows for the year ended December 31, 2003. The following information was reported in the cash flows from operating activities section of the statement of cash flows, using the indirect method:

Decrease in income taxes payable	$ 1,600
Decrease in inventories	7,400
Depreciation	12,500
Gain on sale of investments	2,350
Increase in accounts payable	3,200
Increase in prepaid expenses	1,500
Increase in accounts receivable	4,850

Determine the net income reported by Tiger Golf Inc. for the year ended December 31, 2003.

Exercise 15–14
Cash flows from operating activities
Objective 3

Real World

Selected data derived from the income statement and balance sheet of **Intel Corp.** for a recent year are as follows:

Income Statement Data (dollars in millions)	
Net earnings	$6,068
Depreciation	2,807
Loss on sale of property, plant, and equipment	282
Other noncash expenses	242

✓ Cash flows from operating activities, $9,191

Balance Sheet Data (dollars in millions)

Increase in accounts receivable	$ 38
Decrease in inventories	167
Decrease in other operating assets	37
Decrease in accounts payable and accrued expenses	163
Decrease in income tax payable	211

Prepare the cash flows from operating activities section of the statement of cash flows (using the indirect method) for Intel Corp., for the year.

Exercise 15–15
Cash flows from operating activities—direct method
Objective 4

✓ a. $723,000

The cash flows from operating activities are reported by the direct method on the statement of cash flows. Determine the following:

a. If sales for the current year were $685,000 and accounts receivable decreased by $38,000 during the year, what was the amount of cash received from customers?
b. If income tax expense for the current year was $72,000 and income tax payable decreased by $4,500 during the year, what was the amount of cash payments for income tax?

Exercise 15–16
Cash paid for merchandise purchases
Objective 4

Real World

The cost of merchandise sold for Toys 'R' Us, Inc., for a recent year was $8,191 million. The balance sheet showed the following current account balances (in millions):

	Balance, End of Year	Balance, Beginning of Year
Merchandise inventories	$1,902	$2,464
Accounts payable	1,415	1,280

Determine the amount of cash payments for merchandise.

Exercise 15–17
Determining selected amounts for cash flows from operating activities—direct method
Objective 4

✓ b. $87,500

Selected data taken from the accounting records of Zippy Electronics Company for the current year ended December 31 are as follows:

	Balance December 31	Balance January 1
Accrued expenses (operating expenses)	$ 5,800	$ 6,200
Accounts payable (merchandise creditors)	35,700	39,100
Inventories	25,000	27,400
Prepaid expenses	3,000	3,500

During the current year, the cost of merchandise sold was $315,000 and the operating expenses other than depreciation were $87,600. The direct method is used for presenting the cash flows from operating activities on the statement of cash flows.

Determine the amount reported on the statement of cash flows for (a) cash payments for merchandise and (b) cash payments for operating expenses.

Exercise 15–18
Cash flows from operating activities—direct method
Objective 4

✓ Cash flows from operating activities, $51,800

The income statement of Tender Memories Greeting Card Company for the current year ended June 30 is as follows:

Sales		$358,000
Cost of merchandise sold		163,400
Gross profit		$194,600
Operating expenses:		
Depreciation expense	$ 32,500	
Other operating expenses	142,600	
Total operating expenses		175,100
Income before income tax		$ 19,500
Income tax expense		7,300
Net income		$ 12,200

Changes in the balances of selected accounts from the beginning to the end of the current year are as follows:

	Increase Decrease*
Accounts receivable (net)	$17,000*
Inventories	5,300
Prepaid expenses	3,100*
Accounts payable (merchandise creditors)	13,600*
Accrued expenses (operating expenses)	8,300
Income tax payable	2,400*

Prepare the cash flows from operating activities section of the statement of cash flows, using the direct method.

Exercise 15–19
Cash flows from operating activities—direct method
Objective 4

✓ Cash flows from operating activities, $130,100

The income statement for Wholly Donut Company for the current year ended June 30 and balances of selected accounts at the beginning and the end of the year are as follows:

Sales		$935,600
Cost of merchandise sold		534,200
Gross profit		$401,400
Operating expenses:		
Depreciation expense	$ 54,200	
Other operating expenses	195,700	
Total operating expenses		249,900
Income before income tax		$151,500
Income tax expense		65,300
Net income		$ 86,200

	End of Year	Beginning of Year
Accounts receivable (net)	$ 96,500	$ 93,000
Inventories	143,200	132,700
Prepaid expenses	7,500	8,900
Accounts payable (merchandise creditors)	102,300	98,400
Accrued expenses (operating expenses)	12,400	14,000
Income tax payable	2,000	2,000

Prepare the cash flows from operating activities section of the statement of cash flows, using the direct method.

Exercise 15–20
Analysis of statement of cash flows
Objectives 3, 5

Real World

The financial statements for **Cisco Systems, Inc.**, are presented in Appendix G at the end of the text.

a. From Cisco Systems' statement of cash flows, determine the free cash flow for 1999 and 2000. Assume that 40% of the acquisition of property and equipment and 20% of the acquisition of technology licenses are used to maintain productive capacity. The remaining 60% and 80%, respectively, add to productive capacity.

b. What conclusions can you draw from your analysis?

Exercise 15–21
Statement of cash flows
Objective 3

The comparative balance sheet of Maria's Memories Inc. for December 31, 2003 and 2002, is as follows:

✓ Net cash flow from operating activities, $22

	Dec. 31, 2003	Dec. 31, 2002
Assets		
Cash	$ 54	$ 34
Accounts receivable (net)	23	27
Inventories	16	14
Land	20	30
Equipment	26	12
Accumulated depreciation—equipment	(8)	(5)
Total	$131	$112
Liabilities and Stockholders' Equity		
Accounts payable (merchandise creditors)	$ 17	$ 18
Dividends payable	8	6
Common stock, $1 par	3	2
Paid-in capital in excess of par—common stock	15	10
Retained earnings	88	76
Total	$131	$112

The following additional information is taken from the records:

a. Land was sold for $17.
b. Equipment was acquired for cash.
c. There were no disposals of equipment during the year.
d. The common stock was issued for cash.
e. There was a $25 credit to Retained Earnings for net income.
f. There was a $13 debit to Retained Earnings for cash dividends declared.

Prepare a statement of cash flows, using the indirect method of presenting cash flows from operating activities.

Exercise 15–22
Statement of cash flows
Objective 3

What's Wrong With This?

List the errors you find in the following statement of cash flows. The cash balance at the beginning of the year was $70,700. All other figures are correct, except the cash balance at the end of the year.

Cyber-Master Games Inc.
Statement of Cash Flows
For the Year Ended December 31, 2003

Cash flows from operating activities:			
Net income, per income statement		$100,500	
Add: Depreciation	$ 49,000		
Increase in accounts receivable	11,500		
Gain on sale of investments	7,000	67,500	
		$168,000	
Deduct: Increase in accounts payable	$ 4,400		
Increase in inventories	18,300		
Decrease in accrued expenses	1,600	24,300	
Net cash flow from operating activities			$143,700
Cash flows from investing activities:			
Cash received from sale of investments		$ 85,000	
Less: Cash paid for purchase of land	$ 90,000		
Cash paid for purchase of equipment	150,100	240,100	
Net cash flow used for investing activities			(155,100)
Cash flows from financing activities:			
Cash received from sale of common stock		$107,000	
Cash paid for dividends		36,800	
Net cash flow provided by financing activities			143,800
Increase in cash			$132,400
Cash at the end of the year			105,300
Cash at the beginning of the year			$237,700

PROBLEMS SERIES A

Problem 15–1A
Statement of cash flows—indirect method
Objective 3

✓ Net cash flow from operating activities, $139,800

The comparative balance sheet of Everlast Flooring Co. for June 30, 2003 and 2002, is as follows:

	June 30, 2003	June 30, 2002
Assets		
Cash	$124,200	$ 67,900
Accounts receivable (net)	102,400	97,600
Inventories	142,700	123,500
Investments	0	58,000
Land	124,000	0
Equipment	373,400	201,400
Accumulated depreciation	(79,400)	(58,900)
	$787,300	$489,500
Liabilities and Stockholders' Equity		
Accounts payable (merchandise creditors)	$ 93,200	$ 84,600
Accrued expenses (operating expenses)	13,000	12,300
Dividends payable	15,000	12,500
Common stock, $10 par	120,000	80,000
Paid-in capital in excess of par—common stock	310,000	130,000
Retained earnings	236,100	170,100
	$787,300	$489,500

The following additional information was taken from the records of Everlast Flooring Co.:

a. Equipment and land were acquired for cash.
b. There were no disposals of equipment during the year.
c. The investments were sold for $50,000 cash.
d. The common stock was issued for cash.
e. There was a $126,000 credit to Retained Earnings for net income.
f. There was a $60,000 debit to Retained Earnings for cash dividends declared.

Instructions

Prepare a statement of cash flows, using the indirect method of presenting cash flows from operating activities.

Problem 15–2A
Statement of cash flows—indirect method
Objective 3

SPREADSHEET

✓ Net cash flow from operating activities, $151,800

The comparative balance sheet of Bon Voyage Luggage Company at December 31, 2003 and 2002, is as follows:

	Dec. 31, 2003	Dec. 31, 2002
Assets		
Cash	$ 155,400	$ 134,600
Accounts receivable (net)	192,400	176,400
Inventories	287,500	312,300
Prepaid expenses	8,500	6,000
Land	100,000	100,000
Buildings	550,000	415,000
Accumulated depreciation—buildings	(201,500)	(176,000)
Machinery and equipment	295,700	295,700
Accumulated depreciation—machinery & equipment	(119,800)	(84,600)
Patents	37,400	40,000
	$1,305,600	$1,219,400

(continued)

	Dec. 31, 2003	Dec. 31, 2002
Liabilities and Stockholders' Equity		
Accounts payable (merchandise creditors)	$ 131,400	$ 146,700
Dividends payable	12,000	10,000
Salaries payable	10,500	12,800
Mortgage note payable, due 2004	50,000	—
Bonds payable	—	164,000
Common stock, $1 par	19,000	15,000
Paid-in capital in excess of par—common stock	210,000	50,000
Retained earnings	872,700	820,900
	$1,305,600	$1,219,400

An examination of the income statement and the accounting records revealed the following additional information applicable to 2003:

a. Net income, $99,800.
b. Depreciation expense reported on the income statement: buildings, $25,500; machinery and equipment, $35,200.
c. Patent amortization reported on the income statement, $2,600.
d. A building was constructed for $135,000.
e. A mortgage note for $50,000 was issued for cash.
f. 4,000 shares of common stock were issued at $41 in exchange for the bonds payable.
g. Cash dividends declared, $48,000.

Instructions

Prepare a statement of cash flows, using the indirect method of presenting cash flows from operating activities.

Problem 15–3A
Statement of cash flows—indirect method
Objective 3

✓ Net cash flow from operating activities, ($1,500)

The comparative balance sheet of Union Wholesale Supply Co. at December 31, 2003 and 2002, is as follows:

	Dec. 31, 2003	Dec. 31, 2002
Assets		
Cash	$ 24,900	$ 27,400
Accounts receivable (net)	113,100	94,600
Inventories	194,000	176,500
Prepaid expenses	3,400	4,000
Land	60,000	80,000
Buildings	265,000	155,000
Accumulated depreciation—buildings	(55,800)	(43,500)
Equipment	195,600	185,600
Accumulated depreciation—equipment	(71,500)	(74,500)
	$728,700	$605,100
Liabilities and Stockholders' Equity		
Accounts payable (merchandise creditors)	$140,000	$143,700
Income tax payable	4,000	3,800
Bonds payable	50,000	—
Common stock, $1 par	26,000	25,000
Paid-in capital in excess of par—common stock	350,000	280,000
Retained earnings	158,700	152,600
	$728,700	$605,100

The noncurrent asset, the noncurrent liability, and the stockholders' equity accounts for 2003 are as follows:

ACCOUNT ***Land*** **ACCOUNT NO.**

Date		Item	Debit	Credit	Balance Debit	Balance Credit
2003						
Jan.	1	Balance			80,000	
April	20	Realized $34,000 cash from sale		20,000	60,000	

ACCOUNT ***Buildings*** **ACCOUNT NO.**

Date		Item	Debit	Credit	Balance Debit	Balance Credit
2003						
Jan.	1	Balance			155,000	
April	20	Acquired for cash	110,000		265,000	

ACCOUNT ***Accumulated Depreciation—Buildings*** **ACCOUNT NO.**

Date		Item	Debit	Credit	Balance Debit	Balance Credit
2003						
Jan.	1	Balance				43,500
Dec.	31	Depreciation for year		12,300		55,800

ACCOUNT ***Equipment*** **ACCOUNT NO.**

Date		Item	Debit	Credit	Balance Debit	Balance Credit
2003						
Jan.	1	Balance			185,600	
	26	Discarded, no salvage		30,000	155,600	
Aug.	11	Purchased for cash	40,000		195,600	

ACCOUNT ***Accumulated Depreciation—Equipment*** **ACCOUNT NO.**

Date		Item	Debit	Credit	Balance Debit	Balance Credit
2003						
Jan.	1	Balance				74,500
	26	Equipment discarded	30,000			44,500
Dec.	31	Depreciation for year		27,000		71,500

ACCOUNT ***Bonds Payable*** **ACCOUNT NO.**

Date		Item	Debit	Credit	Balance Debit	Balance Credit
2003						
May	1	Issued 20-year bonds		50,000		50,000

ACCOUNT ***Common Stock, $1 Par*** **ACCOUNT NO.**

Date		Item	Debit	Credit	Balance Debit	Balance Credit
2003						
Jan.	1	Balance				25,000
Dec.	7	Issued 1,000 shares of common stock for $71 per share		1,000		26,000

ACCOUNT ***Paid-In Capital in Excess of Par—Common Stock*** **ACCOUNT NO.**

Date		Item	Debit	Credit	Balance Debit	Balance Credit
2003						
Jan.	1	Balance				280,000
Dec.	7	Issued 1,000 shares of common stock for $71 per share		70,000		350,000

ACCOUNT ***Retained Earnings*** **ACCOUNT NO.**

Date		Item	Debit	Credit	Balance Debit	Balance Credit
2003						
Jan.	1	Balance				152,600
Dec.	31	Net income		12,100		164,700
	31	Cash dividends	6,000			158,700

Instructions

Prepare a statement of cash flows, using the indirect method of presenting cash flows from operating activities.

Problem 15–4A
Statement of cash flows—direct method
Objective 4

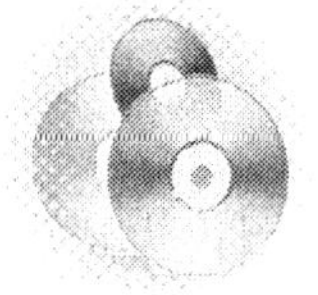

GENERAL LEDGER
SPREADSHEET

✓ Net cash flow from operating activities, $99,900

The comparative balance sheet of Green Thumb Nursery Inc. for December 31, 2003 and 2004, is as follows:

	Dec. 31, 2004	Dec. 31, 2003
Assets		
Cash	$ 154,700	$176,500
Accounts receivable (net)	261,300	243,200
Inventories	317,800	303,300
Investments	—	65,000
Land	95,000	—
Equipment	365,000	275,000
Accumulated depreciation	(123,700)	(103,200)
	$1,070,100	$959,800
Liabilities and Stockholders' Equity		
Accounts payable (merchandise creditors)	$ 248,300	$235,700
Accrued expenses (operating expenses)	10,900	12,500
Dividends payable	24,000	20,000
Common stock, $1 par	15,000	12,000
Paid-in capital in excess of par—common stock	185,000	110,000
Retained earnings	586,900	569,600
	$1,070,100	$959,800

The income statement for the year ended December 31, 2004, is as follows:

Sales		$1,250,000
Cost of merchandise sold		759,000
Gross profit		$ 491,000
Operating expenses:		
Depreciation expense	$ 20,500	
Other operating expenses	284,500	
Total operating expenses		305,000
Operating income		$ 186,000
Other income:		
Gain on sale of investments		14,000
Income before income tax		$ 200,000
Income tax expense		85,000
Net income		$ 115,000

The following additional information was taken from the records:

a. Equipment and land were acquired for cash.
b. There were no disposals of equipment during the year.
c. The investments were sold for $79,000 cash.
d. The common stock was issued for cash.
e. There was a $97,700 debit to Retained Earnings for cash dividends declared.

Instructions

Prepare a statement of cash flows, using the direct method of presenting cash flows from operating activities.

Problem 15–5A
Statement of cash flows—direct method applied to Problem 15–1A
Objective 4

✓ Net cash flow from operating activities, $139,800

The comparative balance sheet of Everlast Flooring Co. for June 30, 2003 and 2002, is as follows:

	June 30, 2003	June 30, 2002
Assets		
Cash	$124,200	$ 67,900
Accounts receivable (net)	102,400	97,600
Inventories	142,700	123,500
Investments	0	58,000
Land	124,000	0
Equipment	373,400	201,400
Accumulated depreciation	(79,400)	(58,900)
	$787,300	$489,500
Liabilities and Stockholders' Equity		
Accounts payable (merchandise creditors)	$ 93,200	$ 84,600
Accrued expenses (operating expenses)	13,000	12,300
Dividends payable	15,000	12,500
Common stock, $10 par	120,000	80,000
Paid-in capital in excess of par—common stock	310,000	130,000
Retained earnings	236,100	170,100
	$787,300	$489,500

The income statement for the year ended June 30, 2003, is as follows:

Sales		$543,800
Cost of merchandise sold		198,200
Gross profit		$345,600
Operating expenses:		
Depreciation expense	$ 20,500	
Other operating expenses	110,300	
Total operating expenses		130,800
Operating income		$214,800
Other expenses:		
Loss on sale of investments		8,000
Income before income tax		$206,800
Income tax expense		80,800
Net income		$126,000

The following additional information was taken from the records:

a. Equipment and land were acquired for cash.
b. There were no disposals of equipment during the year.
c. The investments were sold for $50,000 cash.
d. The common stock was issued for cash.
e. There was a $60,000 debit to Retained Earnings for cash dividends declared.

Instructions

Prepare a statement of cash flows, using the direct method of presenting cash flows from operating activities.

PROBLEMS SERIES B

Problem 15–1B
Statement of cash flows—indirect method
Objective 3

✓ Net cash flow from operating activities, $368,900

The comparative balance sheet of Idaho Al's Golf Shops Co. for December 31, 2003 and 2002, is as follows:

	Dec. 31, 2003	Dec. 31, 2002
Assets		
Cash	$ 524,300	$ 313,400
Accounts receivable (net)	132,500	126,700
Inventories	342,600	332,100
Investments	0	90,000
Land	125,000	0
Equipment	755,000	535,000
Accumulated depreciation—equipment	(189,000)	(158,000)
	$1,690,400	$1,239,200
Liabilities and Stockholders' Equity		
Accounts payable (merchandise creditors)	$ 85,200	$ 80,300
Accrued expenses (operating expenses)	4,300	7,400
Dividends payable	24,000	20,000
Common stock, $10 par	80,000	50,000
Paid-in capital in excess of par—common stock	335,000	200,000
Retained earnings	1,161,900	881,500
	$1,690,400	$1,239,200

The following additional information was taken from the records:

a. The investments were sold for $114,000 cash.
b. Equipment and land were acquired for cash.
c. There were no disposals of equipment during the year.
d. The common stock was issued for cash.
e. There was a $376,400 credit to Retained Earnings for net income.
f. There was a $96,000 debit to Retained Earnings for cash dividends declared.

Instructions

Prepare a statement of cash flows, using the indirect method of presenting cash flows from operating activities.

Problem 15–2B
Statement of cash flows—indirect method
Objective 3

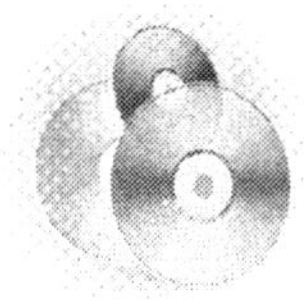

SPREADSHEET

✓ Net cash flow from operating activities, $262,100

The comparative balance sheet of Gold Medal Athletic Apparel Co. at December 31, 2003 and 2002, is as follows:

	Dec. 31, 2003	Dec. 31, 2002
Assets		
Cash	$ 232,500	$ 257,900
Accounts receivable (net)	497,800	532,500
Merchandise inventory	635,200	621,300
Prepaid expenses	17,000	15,000
Equipment	720,000	600,000
Accumulated depreciation—equipment	(265,000)	(297,500)
	$1,837,500	$1,729,200
Liabilities and Stockholders' Equity		
Accounts payable (merchandise creditors)	$ 423,100	$ 397,600
Mortgage note payable	0	205,000
Common stock, $10 par	120,000	70,000
Paid-in capital in excess of par—common stock	820,000	620,000
Retained earnings	474,400	436,600
	$1,837,500	$1,729,200

Additional data obtained from the income statement and from an examination of the accounts in the ledger for 2003 are as follows:

a. Net income, $125,800.
b. Depreciation reported on the income statement, $92,000.
c. Equipment was purchased at a cost of $244,500, and fully depreciated equipment costing $124,500 was discarded, with no salvage realized.
d. The mortgage note payable was not due until 2006, but the terms permitted earlier payment without penalty.
e. 5,000 shares of common stock were issued at $50 for cash.
f. Cash dividends declared and paid, $88,000.

Instructions

Prepare a statement of cash flows, using the indirect method of presenting cash flows from operating activities.

Problem 15–3B
Statement of cash flows—indirect method
Objective 3

✓ Net cash flow from operating activities, ($131,800)

The comparative balance sheet of Handyman's Helper Hardware Company at December 31, 2003 and 2002, is as follows:

	Dec. 31, 2003	Dec. 31, 2002
Assets		
Cash	$ 263,400	$ 275,400
Accounts receivable (net)	375,200	356,800
Inventories	543,200	512,400
Prepaid expenses	8,500	9,000
Land	95,000	120,000
Buildings	470,000	350,000
Accumulated depreciation—buildings	(182,300)	(170,000)
Equipment	198,700	185,500
Accumulated depreciation—equipment	(44,000)	(48,000)
	$1,727,700	$1,591,100
Liabilities and Stockholders' Equity		
Accounts payable (merchandise creditors)	$ 367,900	$ 377,100
Bonds payable	60,000	0
Common stock, $1 par	90,000	70,000
Paid-in capital in excess of par—common stock	450,000	250,000
Retained earnings	759,800	894,000
	$1,727,700	$1,591,100

The noncurrent asset, the noncurrent liability, and the stockholders' equity accounts for 2003 are as follows:

ACCOUNT *Land* ACCOUNT NO.

Date		Item	Debit	Credit	Balance Debit	Balance Credit
2003						
Jan.	1	Balance			120,000	
April	20	Realized $38,000 cash from sale		25,000	95,000	

ACCOUNT *Buildings* ACCOUNT NO.

Date		Item	Debit	Credit	Balance Debit	Balance Credit
2003						
Jan.	1	Balance			350,000	
April	20	Acquired for cash	120,000		470,000	

ACCOUNT *Accumulated Depreciation—Buildings* ACCOUNT NO.

Date		Item	Debit	Credit	Balance Debit	Balance Credit
2003						
Jan.	1	Balance				170,000
Dec.	31	Depreciation for year		12,300		182,300

ACCOUNT *Equipment* ACCOUNT NO.

Date		Item	Debit	Credit	Balance Debit	Balance Credit
2003						
Jan.	1	Balance			185,500	
	26	Discarded, no salvage		45,000	140,500	
Aug.	11	Purchased for cash	58,200		198,700	

ACCOUNT *Accumulated Depreciation—Equipment* ACCOUNT NO.

Date		Item	Debit	Credit	Balance Debit	Balance Credit
2003						
Jan.	1	Balance				48,000
	26	Equipment discarded	45,000			3,000
Dec.	31	Depreciation for year		41,000		44,000

ACCOUNT *Bonds Payable* ACCOUNT NO.

Date		Item	Debit	Credit	Balance Debit	Balance Credit
2003						
May	1	Issued 20-year bonds		60,000		60,000

ACCOUNT *Common Stock, $1 Par* ACCOUNT NO.

Date		Item	Debit	Credit	Balance Debit	Balance Credit
2003						
Jan.	1	Balance				70,000
Dec.	7	Issued 20,000 shares of common stock for $11 per share		20,000		90,000

ACCOUNT *Paid-In Capital in Excess of Par—Common Stock* ACCOUNT NO.

Date		Item	Debit	Credit	Balance Debit	Balance Credit
2003						
Jan.	1	Balance				250,000
Dec.	7	Issued 20,000 shares of common stock for $11 per share		200,000		450,000

ACCOUNT *Retained Earnings* ACCOUNT NO.

Date		Item	Debit	Credit	Balance Debit	Balance Credit
2003						
Jan.	1	Balance				894,000
Dec.	31	Net loss	114,200			779,800
	31	Cash dividends	20,000			759,800

Instructions

Prepare a statement of cash flows, using the indirect method of presenting cash flows from operating activities.

Problem 15–4B
Statement of cash flows—direct method
Objective 4

The comparative balance sheet of Nature's Bounty Markets, Inc., for December 31, 2004 and 2003, is as follows:

SPREADSHEET

GENERAL LEDGER

✓ Net cash flow from operating activities, $70,900

	Dec. 31, 2004	Dec. 31, 2003
Assets		
Cash	$ 65,800	$ 83,500
Accounts receivable (net)	101,200	95,800
Inventories	132,400	125,700
Investments	—	45,000
Land	70,500	—
Equipment	300,500	210,500
Accumulated depreciation	(65,900)	(45,600)
	$604,500	$514,900
Liabilities and Stockholders' Equity		
Accounts payable (merchandise creditors)	$ 93,500	$ 86,700
Accrued expenses (operating expenses)	10,200	12,000
Dividends payable	6,000	4,000
Common stock, $1 par	17,000	15,000
Paid-in capital in excess of par—common stock	200,000	150,000
Retained earnings	277,800	247,200
	$604,500	$514,900

The income statement for the year ended December 31, 2004, is as follows:

Sales		$545,000
Cost of merchandise sold		294,000
Gross profit		$251,000
Operating expenses:		
Depreciation expense	$ 20,300	
Other operating expenses	152,500	
Total operating expenses		172,800
Operating income		$ 78,200
Other expense:		
Loss on sale of investments		4,000
Income before income tax		$ 74,200
Income tax expense		20,500
Net income		$ 53,700

The following additional information was taken from the records:

a. Equipment and land were acquired for cash.
b. There were no disposals of equipment during the year.
c. The investments were sold for $41,000 cash.
d. The common stock was issued for cash.
e. There was a $23,100 debit to Retained Earnings for cash dividends declared.

Instructions

Prepare a statement of cash flows, using the direct method of presenting cash flows from operating activities.

Problem 15–5B

Statement of cash flows—direct method applied to Problem 15–1B

Objective 4

The comparative balance sheet of Idaho Al's Golf Shops Co. for December 31, 2003 and 2002, is as follows:

✓ Net cash flow from operating activities, $368,900

	Dec. 31, 2003	Dec. 31, 2002
Assets		
Cash	$ 524,300	$ 313,400
Accounts receivable (net)	132,500	126,700
Inventories	342,600	332,100
Investments	0	90,000
Land	125,000	0
Equipment	755,000	535,000
Accumulated depreciation—equipment	(189,000)	(158,000)
	$1,690,400	$1,239,200
Liabilities and Stockholders' Equity		
Accounts payable (merchandise creditors)	$ 85,200	$ 80,300
Accrued expenses (operating expenses)	4,300	7,400
Dividends payable	24,000	20,000
Common stock, $10 par	80,000	50,000
Paid-in capital in excess of par—common stock	335,000	200,000
Retained earnings	1,161,900	881,500
	$1,690,400	$1,239,200

The income statement for the year ended December 31, 2003, is as follows:

Sales		$1,096,500
Cost of merchandise sold		401,200
Gross profit		$ 695,300
Operating expenses:		
Depreciation expense	$ 31,000	
Other operating expenses	163,400	
Total operating expenses		194,400
Operating income		$ 500,900
Other income:		
Gain on sale of investments		24,000
Income before income tax		$ 524,900
Income tax expense		148,500
Net income		$ 376,400

The following additional information was taken from the records:

a. The investments were sold for $114,000 cash.
b. Equipment and land were acquired for cash.
c. There were no disposals of equipment during the year.
d. The common stock was issued for cash.
e. There was a $96,000 debit to Retained Earnings for cash dividends declared.

Instructions

Prepare a statement of cash flows, using the direct method of presenting cash flows from operating activities.

SPECIAL ACTIVITIES

Activity 15–1
Fine Fashions Inc.
Ethics and professional conduct in business

Toni Lance, president of Fine Fashions Inc., believes that reporting operating cash flow per share on the income statement would be a useful addition to the company's just completed financial statements. The following discussion took place between Toni Lance and Fine Fashions' controller, Tom Kee, in January, after the close of the fiscal year.

Toni: I have been reviewing our financial statements for the last year. I am disappointed that our net income per share has dropped by 10% from last year. This is not going to look good to our shareholders. Isn't there anything we can do about this?

Tom: What do you mean? The past is the past, and the numbers are in. There isn't much that can be done about it. Our financial statements were prepared according to generally accepted accounting principles, and I don't see much leeway for significant change at this point.

Toni: No, no. I'm not suggesting that we "cook the books." But look at the cash flow from operating activities on the statement of cash flows. The cash flow from operating activities has increased by 20%. This is very good news—and, I might add, useful information. The higher cash flow from operating activities will give our creditors comfort.

Tom: Well, the cash flow from operating activities is on the statement of cash flows, so I guess users will be able to see the improved cash flow figures there.

Toni: This is true, but somehow I feel that this information should be given a much higher profile. I don't like this information being "buried" in the statement of cash flows. You know as well as I do that many users will focus on the income statement. Therefore, I think we ought to include an operating cash flow per share number on the face of the income statement—someplace under the earnings per share number. In this way users will get the complete picture of our operating performance. Yes, our earnings per share dropped this year, but our cash flow from operating activities improved! And all the information is in one place where users can see and compare the figures. What do you think?

Tom: I've never really thought about it like that before. I guess we could put the operating cash flow per share on the income statement, under the earnings per share. Users would really benefit from this disclosure. Thanks for the idea—I'll start working on it.

Toni: Glad to be of service.

How would you interpret this situation? Is Tom behaving in an ethical and professional manner?

Activity 15–2
VideoToGo.com Inc.
Using the statement of cash flows

You are considering an investment in a new start-up Internet company, VideoToGo.com Inc. A review of the company's financial statements reveals a negative retained earnings. In addition, it appears as though the company has been running a negative cash flow from operating activities since the company's inception.

How is the company staying in business under these circumstances? Could this be a good investment?

Activity 15–3
Biltmore Company
Analysis of cash flow from operations

The Retailing Division of Biltmore Company provided the following information on its cash flow from operations:

Net income	$ 450,000
Increase in accounts receivable	(340,000)
Increase in inventory	(300,000)
Decrease in accounts payable	(90,000)
Depreciation	100,000
Cash flow from operating activities	$(180,000)

The manager of the Retailing Division provided the accompanying memo with this report:

From: Senior Vice President, Retailing Division

I am pleased to report that we had earnings of $450,000 over the last period. This resulted in a return on invested capital of 10%, which is near our targets for this division. I have been aggressive in building the revenue volume in the division. As a result, I am happy to report that we have increased the number of new credit card customers as a result of an aggressive marketing campaign. In addition, we have found some excellent merchandise opportunities. Some of our suppliers have made some of their apparel merchandise available at a deep discount. We have purchased as much of these goods as possible in order to improve profitability. I'm also happy to report that our vendor payment problems have improved. We are nearly caught up on our overdue payables balances.

Comment on the senior vice president's memo in light of the cash flow information.

Activity 15–4
Elite Cabinets, Inc.
Analysis of statement of cash flows

Alan Hart is the president and majority shareholder of Elite Cabinets, Inc., a small retail store chain. Recently, Hart submitted a loan application for Elite Cabinets, Inc., to Montvale National Bank. It called for a $200,000, 11%, ten-year loan to help finance the construction of a building and the purchase of store equipment, costing a total of $250,000, to enable Elite Cabinets, Inc., to open a store in Montvale. Land for this purpose was acquired last year. The bank's loan officer requested a statement of cash flows in addition to the most recent income statement, balance sheet, and retained earnings statement that Hart had submitted with the loan application.

As a close family friend, Hart asked you to prepare a statement of cash flows. From the records provided, you prepared the following statement.

Elite Cabinets, Inc.
Statement of Cash Flows
For the Year Ended December 31, 2003

Cash flows from operating activities:			
Net income, per income statement		$ 86,400	
Add: Depreciation	$31,000		
Decrease in accounts receivable	11,500	42,500	
		$128,900	
Deduct: Increase in inventory	$12,000		
Increase in prepaid expenses	1,500		
Decrease in accounts payable	3,000		
Gain on sale of investments	7,500	24,000	
Net cash flow from operating activities			$104,900
Cash flows from investing activities:			
Cash received from investments sold		$ 42,500	
Less: Cash paid for purchase of store equipment		31,000	
Net cash flow from investing activities			11,500
Cash flows from financing activities:			
Cash paid for dividends		$ 40,000	
Net cash flow used for financing activities			(40,000)
Increase in cash			$ 76,400
Cash at the beginning of the year			27,500
Cash at the end of the year			$103,900

Schedule of Noncash Financing and Investing Activities:

Issued common stock at par for land	$ 40,000

After reviewing the statement, Hart telephoned you and commented, "Are you sure this statement is right?" Hart then raised the following questions:

1. "How can depreciation be a cash flow?"
2. "Issuing common stock for the land is listed in a separate schedule. This transaction has nothing to do with cash! Shouldn't this transaction be eliminated from the statement?"
3. "How can the gain on sale of investments be a deduction from net income in determining the cash flow from operating activities?"
4. "Why does the bank need this statement anyway? They can compute the increase in cash from the balance sheets for the last two years."

After jotting down Hart's questions, you assured him that this statement was "right." However, to alleviate Hart's concern, you arranged a meeting for the following day.

a. How would you respond to each of Hart's questions?
b. Do you think that the statement of cash flows enhances the chances of Elite Cabinets, Inc., receiving the loan? Discuss.

Activity 15–5
Into the Real World
Statement of cash flows

This activity will require two teams to retrieve cash flow statement information from the Internet. One team is to obtain the most recent year's statement of cash flows for **Philip Morris Companies**, and the other team the most recent year's statement of cash flows for **Loral Space & Communications, LTD.**, a satellite-based mobile phone company.

The statement of cash flows is included as part of the annual report information that is a required disclosure to the Securities and Exchange Commission (SEC). The SEC, in turn, provides this information online through its EDGAR service. EDGAR (Electronic Data Gathering, Analysis, and Retrieval) is the electronic archive of financial statements filed with the Securities and Exchange Commission (SEC). SEC documents can be retrieved using the EdgarScan service from **PricewaterhouseCoopers** at **edgarscan.pwcglobal.com**.

To obtain annual report information, type in a company name in the appropriate space. EdgarScan will list the reports available to you for the company you've selected. Select the most recent annual report filing, identified as a 10-K or 10-K405. EdgarScan provides an outline of the report, including the separate financial statements. You can double-click the income statement and balance sheet for the selected company into an Excel™ spreadsheet for further analysis.

As a group, compare the two statements of cash flows. How are Philip Morris and Loral Space & Communications similar or different regarding cash flows?

ANSWERS TO SELF-EXAMINATION QUESTIONS

Matching

1. E	3. A	5. I	7. N	9. F	11. J	13. H
2. L	4. K	6. B	8. D	10. C	12. M	

Multiple Choice

1. **D** Cash flows from operating activities affect transactions that enter into the determination of net income, such as the receipt of cash from customers on account (answer D). Receipts of cash from the sale of stock (answer A) and the sale of bonds (answer B) and payments of cash for dividends (answer C) are cash flows from financing activities.
2. **A** Cash flows from investing activities include receipts from the sale of noncurrent assets, such as equipment (answer A), and payments to acquire noncurrent assets. Receipts of cash from the sale of stock (answer B) and payments of cash for dividends (answer C) and to acquire treasury stock (answer D) are cash flows from financing activities.
3. **C** Payment of cash dividends (answer C) is an example of a financing activity. The receipt of cash from customers on account (answer A) is an operating activity. The receipt of cash from the sale of equipment (answer B) is an investing activity. The payment of cash to acquire land (answer D) is an example of an investing activity.

4. **D** The indirect method (answer D) reports cash flows from operating activities by beginning with net income and adjusting it for revenues and expenses not involving the receipt or payment of cash.

5. **C** The cash flows from operating activities section of the statement of cash flows would report net cash flow from operating activities of $65,500, determined as follows:

Net income		$55,000
Add: Depreciation	$22,000	
Decrease in inventories	5,000	
Decrease in prepaid expenses	500	27,500
		$82,500
Deduct: Increase in accounts receivable	$10,000	
Decrease in accounts payable	7,000	17,000
Net cash flow from operating activities		$65,500

OVERVIEW

10

This chapter looks at the role of budgeting in decision making. Budgeting is an important tool in managing a company's financial performance. The discussion of budgeting includes the development of the master budget, which is a widely-used concept in budgeting. Standard costs and quantities as an important part of budgeting are introduced. The current chapter presents the development of both operating and financial budgets and explains the concept of flexible budgets. Standard costs and flexible budgets are important because they help managers understand what costs should be, given different levels of sales and production. Finally, this chapter deals with how the company's budgeting culture, important considerations when budgeting, and the behavioral aspects of budgeting affect decision making.

The Role of Budgets in Decision Making

Major topics covered in this chapter include:

- An overview of the master budget process
- Development of a master budget
- Basic analysis of budget data
- Development of a sound budgeting culture in companies
- How some companies construct effective budgets
- Implications of budgets for management behavior

Accounting and Management Decisions

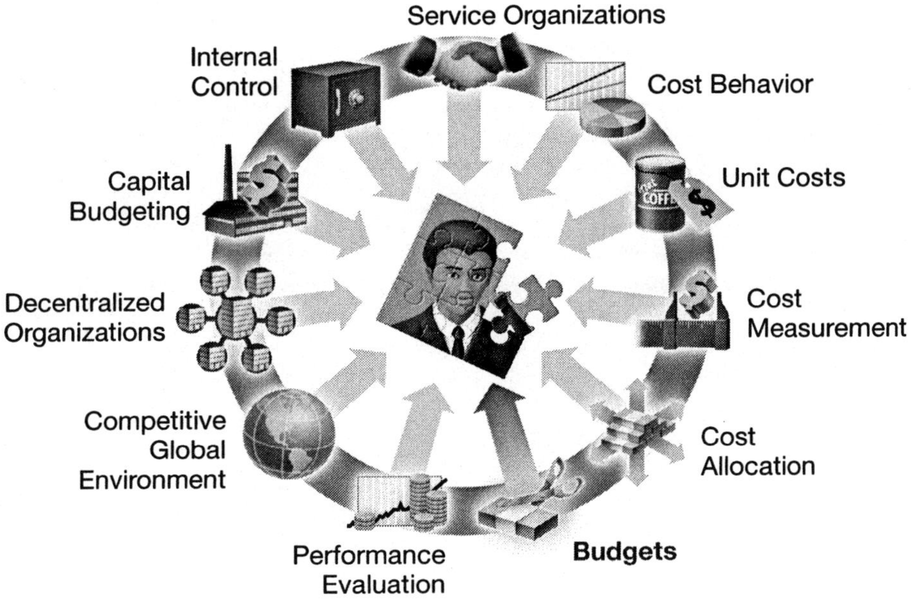

OBJECTIVES

Once you have completed this chapter, you should be able to:

1. Define and describe budgets.
2. Identify the steps in preparing a master budget.
3. Explain the difference between static and flexible budgets.
4. Describe the elements of a sound budgeting culture in companies.
5. Describe the influence of inflation and foreign operations on budgeting.
6. Identify how budgets affect management behavior.
7. Describe how budgets influence strategic decisions.
8. Explain the role of budgets in service organizations.

OVERVIEW OF THE MASTER BUDGET

OBJECTIVE 1

Define and describe budgets.

ON THE INTERNET

http://www.ingram.swcollege.com

Learn about some of the commercial software for budgeting that's available.

A *budget* **is a detailed plan describing the use of financial and operating resources over a specific period.** Companies set goals in order to guide decisions. Measures are often necessary to determine whether goals are being achieved. One way of measuring goal achievement is through budgets. A budget describes management's expectations for the company's future in terms of numbers and dollars. It contains specific details about management's financial goals and expectations for future resource requirements. It provides a means for managers to measure a company's progress toward specific financial goals. Consequently, managers in both manufacturing and service companies use budgets to monitor and control their operations. A budget is prepared for a specific period, typically a year for operating budgets. Some companies budget for longer periods.

A *master budget* **is a collection of related budgets covering sales, production, purchasing, labor, manufacturing overhead, administrative expenses, and financing activities.** Together, these individual budgets provide a strategic summary of a company's financial plans and goals. The master budget results in a set of pro forma financial statements. Pro forma means "before the fact." **Pro forma financial statements** identify expected, rather than actual, financial performance. Pro forma financial statements are prepared at the end of the budget process and include (1) a pro forma income statement giving the expected profit or loss for the budget period, (2) a pro forma balance sheet giving the anticipated levels of assets, liabilities, and equity at the end of the budget period, and (3) a pro forma cash flow statement (called a cash budget) giving the expected cash flows.

The master budget is a collection of several budgets, each of which provides financial details about part of a company's activities. Exhibit 1 illustrates the sequence in which the various budgets that form the master budget are prepared. These budgets can be separated into two subgroups, operating budgets and financial budgets. *Operating budgets* **describe revenues, production costs, and general and administrative costs** and are shown with darker shading in Exhibit 1, on page M208. *Financial budgets* **describe cash flows and financial position, including assets, liabilities, and owners' equity.** Financial budgets are developed after and rely on operating budgets and are shown with lighter shading in Exhibit 1. The financial requirements of a company's operations determine the expected amounts of assets and liabilities and the cash requirements.

Exhibit 1

Components of a Master Budget

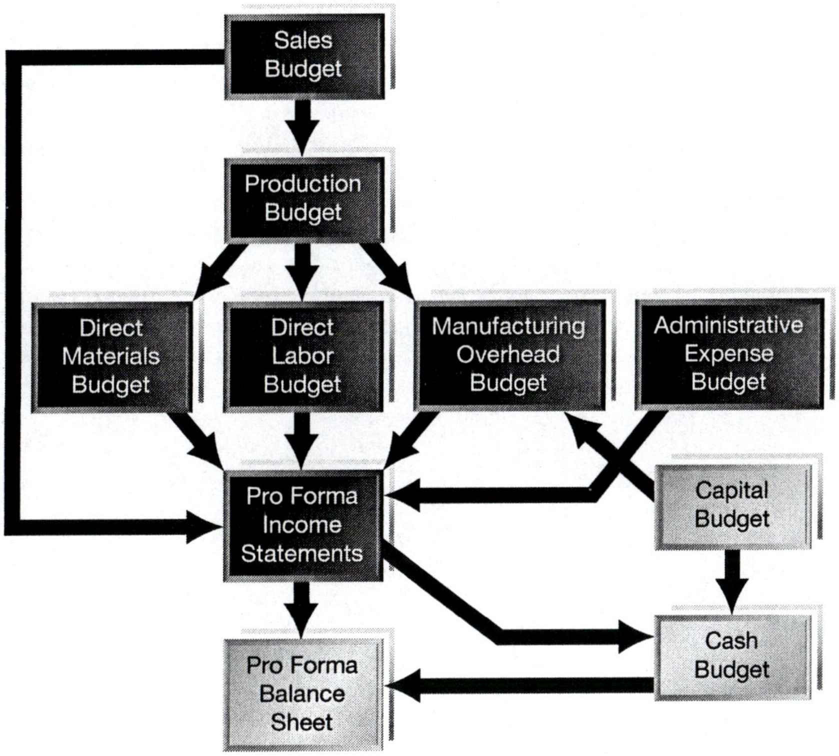

DEVELOPING THE MASTER BUDGET

OBJECTIVE 2

Identify the steps in preparing a master budget.

The components of the master budget referred to in Exhibit 1 are developed sequentially, beginning with the sales budget. Demand for a company's products is the driving force for production, and production creates production costs, such as the purchase of materials. This section examines each of the various master budget components.

LEARNING NOTE

This chapter does not cover **capital budgets,** which involve the acquisition of land, buildings, and equipment for plant expansion or replacement. Capital budgets are part of strategic planning and are covered in Chapter M10.

A company normally develops a master budget for each month or quarter of the coming year. The Kirkland Company serves as an example of budget preparation in Exhibits 2 through 11. The company produces and sells gourmet chocolates that are marketed exclusively through fine-quality department stores. Kirkland prepares the following budgets on a quarterly basis:

1. A sales budget, including a schedule of expected cash collections
2. A production budget
3. A direct materials budget, including expected payments for raw materials
4. A direct labor budget
5. A manufacturing overhead budget
6. A selling and administrative expense budget
7. A cash budget
8. A pro forma budgeted income statement
9. A pro forma budgeted balance sheet

Several calculations used in the development of the master budget for Kirkland require standard costs and quantities. *Standards* **identify the quantity and cost of inputs, such as materials and labor, expected for a single unit of product.**

Sales Budget

The *sales budget* **projects revenues from sales of a company's products or services.** It is prepared from a sales forecast developed by marketing managers. Sales forecasts are based on various factors such as past sales experience, pricing policies, unfilled orders, market research, general economic conditions, industry economic conditions, advertising and promotion plans, and competition. The sales budget is the starting point in preparing the master budget. Nearly all the other items in the master budget, including production requirements, purchases, and operating expenses, depend on the sales budget. Thus, it is important that the sales budget be as accurate as possible. Sales budget accuracy depends on an accurate sales forecast. Management sometimes sets unrealistic sales goals in the belief that these goals will inspire salespeople to sell more. Unrealistic sales forecasts, however, can lead to budgets that do not reflect the market for a company's products. Management accountants should work closely with sales and marketing personnel to ensure that the sales budget is realistic.

The sales budget is prepared by multiplying the expected sales in units by the unit sales price.

Expected sales dollars = expected sales (in units) × selling price (per unit)

If a company makes more than one product, this procedure is repeated for each product, and the dollar sales for all products are added together to calculate a total sales figure.

Generally, the sales budget is accompanied by a Schedule of Expected Cash Collections for the budgeted period. This schedule is needed for preparation of the cash budget. It is prepared along with the sales budget because the sales department generally controls the credit terms offered to customers. Expected cash collections for any given quarter are the sum of (1) expected cash sales during the quarter and (2) cash payments received for credit sales made in previous quarters. Exhibit 2 contains the sales budget and expected collection schedule for Kirkland.

Exhibit 2 A Sales Budget and Expected Cash Collections Schedule

Kirkland Company
Sales Budget
For the Year Ended December 31, 2001

	Quarter				
	1	**2**	**3**	**4**	**Year**
Expected sales in units	1,000	3,000	4,000	2,000	10,000
Selling price per unit	$ 20	$ 20	$ 20	$ 20	$ 20
Total sales	$20,000	$60,000	$80,000	$40,000	$200,000

Schedule of Expected Cash Collections

Accounts receivable, 12/31/00*	$ 9,000				$ 9,000
First-quarter sales†	14,000	$ 6,000			20,000
Second-quarter sales		42,000	$18,000		60,000
Third-quarter sales			56,000	$24,000	80,000
Fourth-quarter sales‡				28,000	28,000
Total cash collections	$23,000	$48,000	$74,000	$52,000	$197,000

* *Assumed.*

† *Cash collections from sales are expected as follows: 70% in the quarter of sale, 30% in the following quarter. Note that the uncollected portion of sales at 12/31/00 was $9,000.*

‡ *The uncollected portion of fourth-quarter cash sales appears as Accounts Receivable on the year-end pro forma balance sheet.*

CASE IN POINT

To a bank, loans to customers are like sales to manufacturers or retailers. Banks often use sophisticated forecasting models to project demand for loans. Some of the factors banks may consider in forecasting loans are economic growth, changes in interest rates, trends in consumer spending, and competition from other banks. A bank may develop a sales forecasting model that contains these and other variables. The expected values of each of these variables is inserted into the model to arrive at an estimate of future loan demand.

Production Budget

After the sales budget has been prepared, production requirements for the period can be calculated from existing inventories and expected sales, and a production budget can be prepared. **The *production budget* identifies the amount of a product that must be produced to meet a company's needs for sales and inventory.** In preparing the production budget, management must consider the amount of inventory needed for production requirements. Many companies prefer to keep some inventory of raw materials and finished goods on hand in case actual demand is greater than expected. Such inventories often are referred to as "just in case" inventories. In addition to producing enough units to meet sales demand, a company also must produce enough units to provide for the desired ending inventory levels. A portion of the production requirements will exist already in beginning finished goods inventory (last period's ending inventory).

Exhibit 3 shows a production budget for Kirkland. The production budget is developed by adding expected sales units to the desired ending inventory level and then subtracting the beginning inventory to arrive at the total number of units the company needs to produce.

Production budget = expected sales in units + desired ending inventory units − beginning inventory units

This process begins with the first quarter and moves sequentially to the fourth quarter. The ending inventory for each quarter becomes the beginning inventory for the following quarter. If a company manufactures more than one product, a production budget is developed for each product.

Recall that keeping inventory on hand is costly. Proper inventory planning is essential in order to avoid unnecessary inventory cost. The cost of keeping inventory should be compared with the possible loss of sales due to an inability to meet customer demand. Consequently, the amount of inventory kept on hand by a company will be determined by several factors, including (1) the ordering patterns of the company's customers, (2) the time required to produce and ship products, (3) the availability of raw materials, and (4) the reliability of suppliers of raw materials.

Exhibit 3 A Production Budget

Kirkland Company
Production Budget
For the Year Ended December 31, 2001

	Quarter				
	1	**2**	**3**	**4**	**Year**
Expected sales (from Exhibit 2)	1,000	3,000	4,000	2,000	10,000
Add desired ending inventory*†	600	800	400	300	300
Total needs	1,600	3,800	4,400	2,300	10,300
Less: Beginning inventory of finished goods‡	200	600	800	400	200
Units to produce	1,400	3,200	3,600	1,900	10,100

* *Twenty percent of the following quarter sales (e.g., in the first quarter, 600 = 20% × 3,000 units that are expected to be sold in Quarter 2).*

† *Note that Quarter 4 ending inventory is also the expected ending inventory for the year and is used when preparing the annual pro forma balance sheet.*

‡ *Beginning inventory is the assumed ending inventory from the prior quarter.*

Once a company's expected production requirements are known, resources used in production can be budgeted. The direct materials, direct labor, and manufacturing overhead budgets are based on the units forecast in the production budget.

Direct Materials Budget

The *direct materials budget* **identifies the amount of materials that will be required to support a company's total production needs.** The company will need enough materials to produce units for the period and to provide for the desired ending inventory levels of raw materials. Some raw materials will exist already in the form of beginning raw materials inventory. The remainder will be purchased from suppliers. For each successive period, the previous period's ending inventory becomes the beginning inventory for the period. If more than one material is required to manufacture a product, a separate schedule is developed for each material and the costs are combined to obtain a total cost of direct materials.

When this budget is constructed, generally a Schedule of Expected Cash Disbursements for materials also is prepared. This schedule is based on the credit terms the purchasing department anticipates receiving from its suppliers. The Schedule of Cash Disbursements is needed in preparing the cash budget. Exhibit 4 provides a direct materials budget for Kirkland. The number of units of product to be produced during each quarter is multiplied by the standard amount of raw materials needed to make a unit to determine the amount of raw materials required for production. The desired ending inventory of raw materials is added to this amount to obtain the total amount of raw materials needed. The beginning raw materials inventory is subtracted from the total amount needed to determine the amount the company needs to purchase. (See the equation at the top of page M212.)

Exhibit 4 A Direct Materials Budget

Kirkland Company
Direct Materials Budget
For the Year Ended December 31, 2001

	Quarter				
	1	**2**	**3**	**4**	**Year**
Units to be produced (from Exhibit 3)	1,400	3,200	3,600	1,900	10,100
Raw materials per unit (lbs.)	5	5	5	5	5
Production needs (lbs.)	7,000	16,000	18,000	9,500	50,500
Add desired ending inventory (lbs.)*	1,600	1,800	950	**750**	**750**
Total needs (lbs.)	8,600	17,800	18,950	10,250	51,250
Less: Beginning raw materials inventory (lbs.)†	**700**	1,600	1,800	950	**700**
Raw materials to be purchased	7,900	16,200	17,150	9,300	50,550
Cost of material purchases ($.60/lb.)	$4,740	$ 9,720	$10,290	$ 5,580	$30,330

* *Ten percent of the following quarter production needs are desired as ending inventory each quarter (e.g., for Quarter 1, Quarter 2's production needs of 16,000 lbs. × 0.1 = 1,600 lbs.).*
† *Beginning inventory is the assumed ending inventory of the prior quarter.*

Schedule of Expected Cash Disbursements

	1	2	3	4	Year
Accounts payable 12/31/00‡	$2,580				$2,580
First-quarter purchases§	2,370	$2,370			4,740
Second-quarter purchases		4,860	$4,860		9,720
Third-quarter purchases			5,145	$5,145	10,290
Fourth-quarter purchases¶				2,790	2,790
Total cash disbursements	$4,950	$7,230	$10,005	$7,935	$30,120

‡ *Assumed.*
§ *Cash payments are expected to total 50% in quarter of purchase, and 50% in quarter following purchase.*
¶ *The unpaid portion of the fourth-quarter purchases appears in Accounts Payable on the year-end pro forma balance sheet.*

Direct materials budget = (units to be produced × standard amount of raw materials per unit) + desired ending raw materials inventory − beginning raw materials inventory

Direct Labor Budget

Management also prepares the direct labor budget from the production budget. **The *direct labor budget* identifies the labor resources required to meet production needs.** Labor requirements can be predicted, and an organization can plan labor needs based on the direct labor budget. Failure to plan labor needs may result in labor shortages, unnecessary overtime, or unexpected layoffs. These results can affect employee morale and lead to high turnover. A direct labor budget also is necessary to project the total expected cost of direct labor.

Direct labor requirements are based on the number of units to be produced during a period, as determined in the production budget, multiplied by the number of direct labor hours required to produce one unit of product. The total direct labor hour requirements then are converted into expected direct labor costs. Though a company may face a wide range of labor costs due to different employees having different wage rates, an average rate often is used to compute direct labor costs. Some companies develop a separate schedule for each type of labor when rates vary across the types. A separate labor schedule must be developed for each product because different products consume different quantities of labor.

In some instances, organizations have contracts or employment policies that prevent them from laying off and rehiring workers. These commitments must be considered in calculating expected direct labor costs. Assume that Kirkland is able to adjust labor to its actual needs in Exhibit 5.

Exhibit 5 A Direct Labor Budget

Kirkland Company
Direct Labor Budget
For the Year Ended December 31, 2001

	Quarter				
	1	**2**	**3**	**4**	**Year**
Units to be produced (from Exhibit 3)	1,400	3,200	3,600	1,900	10,100
Direct labor time per unit (hours)	0.8	0.8	0.8	0.8	0.8
Total hours of direct labor required	1,120	2,560	2,880	1,520	8,080
Direct labor cost per hour	$7.50	$7.50	$7.50	$7.50	$7.50
Total direct labor costs	$8,400	$19,200	$21,600	$11,400	$60,600

Kirkland's requirements for labor are least in quarter 1, when only 1,400 units are expected to be produced. The requirements are greatest in quarter 3, when 3,600 units are to be produced. Notice that the direct labor cost per hour remains constant at $7.50. If Kirkland had to use overtime to meet its labor requirements instead of hiring additional workers, this figure would increase because of the need to pay an overtime premium.

Manufacturing Overhead Budget

The *manufacturing overhead budget* **provides a schedule of all costs of production other than direct materials and direct labor.** Fixed and variable costs are separated for budgeting purposes. This separation permits actual and expected costs to be compared. From the manufacturing overhead budget, a predetermined overhead rate is developed by dividing the amount of expected overhead by the expected level of the activity base used to apply overhead.

Predetermined overhead rate = expected overhead ÷ expected activity base

Exhibit 6 illustrates the manufacturing overhead budget, by quarter, and the related expected cash disbursements, by quarter. Kirkland applies manufacturing overhead based on direct labor hours. From the total expected overhead cost and the number of labor hours expected, the company computes a variable rate of $2 per direct labor hour. Total fixed costs are budgeted at $6,060 per quarter, of which $1,500 represents noncash expense for depreciation. Further assume that all expenses will be paid in the quarter in which the expenses are incurred.

Variable manufacturing overhead costs can be determined by multiplying the variable overhead rate by the activity base (units produced, direct labor hours, machine hours, and so on).

Variable manufacturing overhead = variable overhead rate × activity base

For example, in Exhibit 6, variable overhead for the first quarter of 2001 is determined by multiplying the 1,120 budgeted direct labor hours by the variable overhead rate of $2.00 per direct labor hour to determine the budgeted variable overhead of $2,240.

Fixed manufacturing overhead remains constant over a wide range of activity levels and does not change based on production requirements. Fixed overhead is added to variable overhead to arrive at the total expected manufacturing overhead cost.

Exhibit 6 A Manufacturing Overhead Budget

Kirkland Company
Manufacturing Overhead Budget
For the Year Ended December 31, 2001

	Quarter				
	1	**2**	**3**	**4**	**Year**
Budgeted direct labor hours (from Exhibit 5)	1,120	2,560	2,880	1,520	8,080
Variable overhead rate	$2	$2	$2	$2	$2
Budgeted variable overhead	$2,240	$ 5,120	$ 5,760	$3,040	$16,160
Budgeted fixed overhead	6,060	6,060	6,060	6,060	24,240
Total budgeted manufacturing overhead	8,300	11,180	11,820	9,100	40,400
Less: Noncash expenses	1,500	1,500	1,500	1,500	6,000
Cash disbursements for manufacturing overhead	$6,800	$ 9,680	$10,320	$7,600	$34,400

Selling and Administrative Expense Budget

The *selling and administrative expense budget* **contains a list of anticipated expenses for the period for activities other than manufacturing.** This budget generally is made up of many individual budgets prepared by managers with responsibilities for various functions. The number of items that compose this portion of the master budget can be quite large, depending on the size and complexity of an organization, and will include activities such as marketing, accounting and finance, and human resources.

The selling and administrative expense budget is based on the number of units expected to be sold, which is derived from the sales budget. Selling expenses, in particular, depend on the number of units sold, and many administrative functions also support the sales effort. The selling and administrative expense budget in Exhibit 7, on page M214, for Kirkland identifies variable- and fixed-cost components. The exhibit assumes that variable selling and administrative expenses are expected to be $1.80 per unit sold. Fixed costs of advertising, insurance, executive salaries, and property taxes will be paid in the quarter in which they are incurred. Also, when preparing the selling and administrative expense budget, noncash expenses such as depreciation need to be identified for omission from the cash budget.

As shown in Exhibit 7, total variable expenses of $1,800 for quarter 1 are determined by multiplying the 1,000 units to be sold by the $1.80 expected variable cost of sales for each unit. The $8,000 fixed selling and administrative expenses are added to the variable component to arrive at total budgeted selling and administrative expenses of $9,800. Noncash expenses for depreciation of $500 are then deducted to arrive at the cash expenditure for selling and administrative activity.

Note that the fixed expense varies from quarter to quarter even though it does not vary with the volume of production. This can result from factors such as changes in depreciation due to the addition and retirement of equipment during the year.

Exhibit 7 A Selling and Administrative Expense Budget

Kirkland Company
Selling and Administrative Expense Budget
For the Year Ended December 31, 2001

	Quarter				
	1	**2**	**3**	**4**	**Year**
Budgeted sales in units (from Exhibit 2)	1,000	3,000	4,000	2,000	10,000
Variable selling and administrative expenses per unit	$1.80	$1.80	$1.80	$1.80	$1.80
Budgeted variable expenses	1,800	5,400	7,200	3,600	18,000
Budgeted fixed selling and administrative expenses	8,000	8,190	11,775	9,815	37,780
Total budgeted selling and administrative expenses	9,800	13,590	18,975	13,415	55,780
Less: Noncash expenses	500	500	500	500	2,000
Cash expenditures for selling and administrative expenses	$9,300	$13,090	$18,475	$12,915	$53,780

Self-Study Problem 1

Bluffton Industries manufactures one product, a leather portfolio that sells for $20 per unit. This item is manufactured from a single raw material, tanned leather, that costs $2.00 a yard. It takes 1.5 yards of leather to produce a finished product. Each unit produced by Bluffton requires 0.25 hour of direct labor, which costs Bluffton $16 per hour. Variable overhead to produce a unit of product totals $3 per unit. Fixed overhead for the coming year, 2001, is expected to be:

Depreciation	$25,000
Insurance	10,000
Property taxes	6,000
Supervision	35,000

Selling and administrative expenses for the coming year are expected to be $2 per unit sold plus the following fixed expenses:

Depreciation	$15,000
Sales salaries	30,000
Advertising	10,000
Office clerk	18,000
President's salary	60,000

At the beginning of 2001, Bluffton had 500 units of finished goods in inventory. The company wants to end the year with 2,500 units of finished goods in inventory. The company also requires 1,000 yards of raw material at year-end and began the year with 5,000 yards of material in inventory. A sales forecast indicates that 100,000 units will be sold during 2001.

Required For 2001:

1. Prepare a sales budget.
2. Prepare a production budget.
3. Prepare a direct materials budget.
4. Prepare a direct labor budget.
5. Prepare a manufacturing overhead budget.
6. Prepare a selling and administrative expense budget.

The solution to Self-Study Problem 1 appears at the end of the chapter.

Pro Forma Budgeted Income Statement

The **pro forma budgeted income statement** is a projected income statement prepared from information developed in the budget process. The pro forma income statement is a key schedule in the master budget. It provides an estimate of an organization's profitability during a future period and often is the primary benchmark against which a company's performance during the period will be assessed. Exhibit 8 contains a pro forma income statement for Kirkland.

Exhibit 8 A Pro Forma Budgeted Income Statement

Kirkland Company
Pro Forma Budgeted Income Statement
For the Year Ended December 31, 2001

Sales (from Exhibit 2)	$200,000
Less: Cost of goods sold*	130,000
Gross margin	70,000
Less: Selling and administrative expenses (from Exhibit 7)	55,780
Net operating income	14,220
Less: Interest expense	1,400‡
Income before income taxes	12,820
Less: Income taxes (from tax return)	7,200‡
Net income	$ 5,620

* *Based on the cost per unit as follows:*

Exhibit	*Description*	*Quantity*	*Cost*	*Total*
4	*Direct materials*	*5 lbs.*	*$ .60/lb.*	*$ 3.00*
5	*Direct labor*	*0.8 hr.*	*$7.50/hr.*	*6.00*
6	*Manufacturing overhead*	*0.8 hr.*	*$5.00/hr.†*	*4.00*
	Total			*13.00*
2	*Units sold*			*× 10,000*
	Budgeted cost of goods sold			*$130,000*

† *$40,400 total budgeted manufacturing overhead ÷ 8,080 budgeted direct labor hours = $5.00 per hour.*
‡ *Assumed.*

Flexible Budget Approach

OBJECTIVE 3

Explain the difference between static and flexible budgets.

Exhibit 8 illustrates a pro forma income statement for a single level of activity developed using absorption costing. This statement is based on a *static budget* **because it identifies the income that would be earned at a predetermined level of sales activity.** Because the static budget reflects only one level of activity, it is unable to provide information about other levels of activity. Many companies, however, are unable to project exactly how many units of products will be produced and what sales will be. Flexibility budgeting permits these companies to see how budgets differ using different assumptions about future sales and production.

Stated differently, flexible budgets allow managers to observe how sensitive budgets are to changes in production and sales. This is one form of sensitivity analysis, which is discussed later in this chapter.

Exhibit 9 illustrates a flexible pro forma income statement for Kirkland using the variable-costing approach. The *flexible budget* **enables a company to examine projected income over a *range* of sales levels.** Flexible budgets are best developed using the variable-costing format because this format separates the variable costs, which change with different levels of sales activity, from fixed costs, which remain constant over a wide range of sales and manufacturing activity.

Exhibit 9 A Pro Forma Flexible Budget Income Statement

Kirkland Company
Pro Forma Flexible Income Statement
Variable-Costing Format
For the Year Ended December 31, 2001

	Budget Formula (per unit)	Sales in units 9,000	10,000*	11,000	12,000
Sales	$20.00	$180,000	$200,000	$220,000	$240,000
Less variable expenses:					
Direct materials (from Exhibit 8)	3.00	27,000	30,000	33,000	36,000
Direct labor (from Exhibit 8)	6.00	54,000	60,000	66,000	72,000
Variable overhead†	1.60	14,400	16,000	17,600	19,200
Variable selling (from Exhibit 7)	1.80	16,200	18,000	19,800	21,600
Total variable expenses	12.40	111,600	124,000	136,400	148,800
Contribution margin	$ 7.60	68,400	76,000	83,600	91,200
Less fixed expenses:					
Manufacturing overhead (from Exhibit 6)		24,240	24,240	24,240	24,240
Selling and administrative (from Exhibit 7)		37,780	37,780	37,780	37,780
Taxes and interest‡		8,600	8,600	8,600	8,600
Total fixed expenses		70,620	70,620	70,620	70,620
Net income (loss)		$ (2,220)	$ 5,380§	$ 12,980	$ 20,580

* *Projected sales in the static budget.*
† *See Exhibits 5 and 6: $2 variable overhead rate per direct labor hour × 0.8 direct labor hour per unit = $1.60 variable overhead rate per unit.*
‡ *For simplicity, taxes and interest are the same at all levels.*
§ *The $240 difference between the variable-costing income of $5,380 and the absorption-costing income of $5,620 from Exhibit 8 can be explained as follows:*

Increase in finished goods inventory (see Exhibit 3: 10,100 − 10,000 units)	*100 units*
Fixed manufacturing costs deferred in ending inventory (fixed costs of $24,240 ÷ 10,100 units = $ 2.40 per unit) ×	*$ 2.40 per unit*
Difference	*$240.00*

Cash Budget

The *cash budget* **describes cash requirements for the budget period.** The basic sources and uses of cash are shown in Exhibit 10.

Exhibit 10 Cash Budget

Kirkland Company
Cash Budget
For the Year Ended December 31, 2001

	Quarter 1	Quarter 2	Quarter 3	Quarter 4	Year
Cash balance, beginning	**$ 4,250***	$ 4,000	$ 4,000	$ 4,050	**$ 4,250***
Add receipts:					
Collections on account (from Exhibit 2)	23,000	48,000	74,000	52,000	197,000
Total cash available	27,250	52,000	78,000	56,050	201,250
Less disbursements:					
Direct materials (from Exhibit 4)	4,950	7,230	10,005	7,935	30,120
Direct labor (from Exhibit 5)	8,400	19,200	21,600	11,400	60,600
Manufacturing overhead (from Exhibit 6)	6,800	9,680	10,320	7,600	34,400
Selling and administrative (from Exhibit 7)	9,300	13,090	18,475	12,915	53,780
Income taxes (from Exhibit 8)*	1,800	1,800	1,800	1,800	7,200
Equipment purchases	3,000	2,000			5,000
Dividends	1,000	1,000	1,000	1,000	4,000
Total disbursements	35,250	54,000	63,200	42,650	195,100
Excess (deficiency) of cash	(8,000)	(2,000)	14,800	13,400	6,150
Financing:					
Borrowings	12,000	6,000			18,000
Repayments			(10,000)	(8,000)	(18,000)
Interest			(750)†	(650)‡	(1,400)
Total financing	12,000	6,000	(10,750)	(8,650)	(1,400)
Cash balance, ending	$ 4,000	$ 4,000	$ 4,050	**$ 4,750**	**$ 4,750**

* *Assumed.*

† *Interest relates to $10,000 of the $12,000 borrowed in the first quarter: $10,000 × 0.1 × 3/4 = $750.*

‡ *Interest relates to $2,000 borrowed in the first quarter and $6,000 borrowed in the second quarter:*

$2,000 × 0.1 × one year =	*$200*
$6,000 × 0.1 × 3/4 =	*450*
Total interest	*$650*

The cash budget has four major sections:

1. cash receipts,
2. cash disbursements,
3. cash excess or deficiency, and
4. financing requirements.

The receipts section of the cash budget combines the beginning cash balance with expected cash receipts for the period. Generally, the major source of cash receipts is collections of accounts receivable and cash sales. Other cash receipts, such as interest from investments, also are included in this section.

The disbursements section of the cash budget contains all cash payments expected for the budget period. These payments include disbursements for raw materials, labor, manufacturing overhead, and administrative expenses as contained in these budgets. Other cash disbursements, such as income taxes, capital equipment purchases, and dividend payments, also are included.

The cash excess or deficiency section identifies the difference between cash receipts and cash disbursements. This section is important because it reveals the amount a company needs to borrow if a deficiency exists. If an excess exists, a company should plan for investment of its excess cash.

The financing section of the cash budget identifies amounts to be borrowed or repaid during the budget period. Also, it identifies interest to be paid on borrowings. This section of the cash budget allows an organization to work with lenders to ensure that cash is available when needed. Often, organizations have lines of credit available through banks to meet short-term needs. The financing section will assist managers in determining whether any special borrowing arrangements are necessary in addition to existing lines of credit.

Exhibit 10 provides a cash budget for Kirkland on a quarterly basis. The exhibit assumes that all borrowing takes place at the beginning of a quarter in which cash is needed and all repayments are made at the end of the quarter.

Additional information to complete the cash budget includes:

1. The company expects to pay $3,000 and $2,000 for equipment in the first and second quarters, respectively.
2. Dividends of $1,000 are planned for each quarter.
3. The company must maintain a minimum balance of $4,000 at the bank.
4. Interest is paid at the time of principal repayment.
5. No loans are outstanding at the beginning of the budget period.
6. The company must pay interest at an annual rate of 10% on any borrowed funds.

The cash budget is an important part of the master budget. Even if a company generates net income, it can experience serious difficulties if it does not have the cash it needs for day-to-day operations. For example, a company that cannot pay its accounts payable on a timely basis often loses discounts and may incur penalties for late payment. In extreme cases, suppliers may refuse additional credit to a company that does not pay on a timely basis. Consequently, planning for a company's cash needs is necessary for sound financial management.

Pro Forma Budgeted Balance Sheet

The **pro forma budgeted balance sheet** identifies the expected amount of assets, liabilities, and owners' equity at the end of the budget period. Exhibit 11 presents a comparative balance sheet showing actual beginning-of-year and pro forma end-of-year amounts for Kirkland.

The December 31, 2001, balance sheet figures are derived as follows. The ending cash balance (a) is projected in the cash budget, Exhibit 10. Accounts receivable (b) are projected as 30% of fourth-quarter sales from Exhibit 2 ($40,000 × 30%). Based on Exhibit 4, the ending raw materials inventory (c) was $420 (700 lbs. at $.60 per lb.) for 2000 and is projected to be $450 (750 lbs. at $.60 per lb) for 2001. Budgeted finished goods inventory (d) is projected from Exhibit 3 to be 300 units. Each unit is costed at $13 (see Exhibit 8) per unit (300 units × $13 = $3,900). Equipment purchases (e) will total $5,000 during the year as reflected on the cash budget (Exhibit 10). Accumulated depreciation is determined by the expected increase in total depreciation for the year. Depreciation charges (f) for the year are $6,000 (Exhibit 6) and $2,000 (Exhibit 7), for a total increase of $8,000 from the beginning of the year. Accounts payable (g) is forecast as one-half of the fourth-quarter raw materials purchases ($5,580) from Exhibit 4. Retained earnings is projected as shown below:

December 31, 2000 balance	$44,990
Add net income (from Exhibit 8)	5,620
	50,610
Less dividends paid (from Exhibit 10)	(4,000)
Balance at December 31, 2001	$46,610

A pro forma balance sheet provides information about expected assets and liabilities. This information can be useful for a variety of reasons. For example, management may want to determine if ending working capital (the difference between current assets and current liabilities) is sufficient for planned operations. Managers can use the pro forma statement to assess expected performance. Measures such as expected return on assets, expected return on equity, and expected debt to equity ratios involve balance sheet amounts.

Exhibit 11 A Pro Forma Budgeted Balance Sheet

Kirkland Company
Pro Forma Budgeted Balance Sheet
at December 31, 2000 and 2001

	2000 (Actual)	2001 (Pro forma)
Assets		
Current assets:		
Cash	$ 4,250*	$ 4,750 (a)
Accounts receivable	9,000	12,000 (b)
Raw materials inventory	420	450 (c)
Finished goods inventory	2,600*	3,900 (d)
Total current assets	16,270	21,100
Plant and equipment:		
Land	8,000*	8,000*
Buildings and equipment	70,000	75,000 (e)
Accumulated depreciation	(29,200)*	(37,200) (f)
Plant and equipment, net	48,800	45,800
Total assets	$65,070	$66,900
Liabilities and Stockholders' Equity		
Current liabilities:		
Accounts payable (raw materials)	$ 2,580	$ 2,790 (g)
Stockholders' equity:		
Common stock	17,500*	17,500*
Retained earnings	44,990*	46,610 (h)
Total stockholders' equity	62,490	64,110
Total liabilities and stockholders' equity	$65,070	$66,900

* *Assumed.*

Sensitivity Analysis in Budgeting

Although the budgeting process may seem mechanical, forecasting financial information accurately is as much art as science. Usually, the farther in the future a forecast is made, the less reliable it is. This is because there are often many uncertainties involved in forecasting financial information that require budget forecasters to make many assumptions. It is common for at least some of these assumptions to be wrong. For example, the sales forecast may be based upon the assumption that a new product will be introduced six months into the forecast period. If unforeseen product development difficulties arise, the introduction of the product may be delayed. This could mean that actual sales are lower than expected. Likewise, the actual manufacturing costs may also be lower than expected due to fewer resources being used and development costs may be higher than expected due to delayed production and difficulties associated with product development.

Because assumptions can be wrong, it is often desirable to determine how sensitive budget outcomes are to the assumptions used in developing the budget. This is called **sensitivity analysis.** A useful approach to determining budget sensitivity to budget assumptions is to modify flexible budgeting techniques to develop different budgets based upon different scenarios. This allows managers to see what financial results would look like under each scenario.

In performing sensitivity analysis, some firms develop three budget scenarios: best-case, worst-case, and most-likely-case. The best-case scenario is normally developed using the best outcomes for each assumption. The result of aggregating all of the best outcomes for each assumption is the best-case scenario. The worst-case and most-likely-case scenarios are similarly developed. Managers can then use these forecasts to establish a range of financial outcomes.

Consider the following example. The assumptions that must be made to develop the budgeted income statement for BloomingWorld, Inc., a commercial landscaping company, are shown in Exhibit 12. Taxes are assumed to be constant at 35%. Since all of BloomingWorld's business is performed under contract, there are no beginning and ending inventories.

Exhibit 12 Assumptions Necessary to Develop an Income Statement for BloomingWorld, Inc.

BloomingWorld, Inc. Budgeted Income Statement Assumptions

	Worst Case	**Most Likely Case**	**Best Case**
Sales	$10,000,000	$12,000,000	$13,000,000
Materials cost as a percentage of sales	57%	55%	53%
Average labor cost per hour	$9.75	$9.65	$9.50
Labor hours per $1 sales	.025	.024	.023
Overhead costs (variable and fixed)	$950,000	$915,000	$895,000
Variable selling expenses as a percentage of sales	6%	5%	4.5%
Fixed selling and administrative expenses	$500,000	$500,000	$500,000

Using the assumptions in Exhibit 12, BloomingWorld's budgeted income sensitivity analysis is shown in Exhibit 13:

Exhibit 13 Income Sensitivity Analysis for BloomingWorld, Inc.

BloomingWorld, Inc. Budgeted Income Statement

	Worst Case	**Most Likely Case**	**Best Case**
Sales	$10,000,000	$12,000,000	$13,000,000
Less: Cost of goods sold			
Materials	5,700,000	6,600,000	6,890,000
Labor	2,437,500	2,779,200	2,840,500
Overhead	750,000	915,000	895,000
Gross margin	$ 1,112,500	$ 1,705,800	$ 2,374,500
Less: Selling and administrative expenses			
Variable	500,000	600,000	650,000
Fixed	500,000	500,000	500,000
Net income before taxes	$ 112,500	$ 605,800	$ 1,224,500
Less: Taxes at 35%	39,375	212,030	428,575
Net income after taxes	$ 73,125	$ 393,770	$ 795,925

The sensitivity analysis in Exhibit 13 indicates that BloomingWorld's income is highly sensitive to the assumptions in Exhibit 12. Under the worst case scenario, BloomingWorld's profits are only slightly better than breakeven. Using the best case scenario, BloomingWorld would have net profits of approximately 6% of sales. This shows BloomingWorld's management the range of possible outcomes with respect to the coming year's profits.

The use of electronic spreadsheets has made sensitivity analysis much easier. This is because electronic spreadsheets permit cross-coding of cells so that the entire master budget can be adjusted instantly for changes in assumptions. For example, if assumptions about the price of raw materials are changed, this would likely affect such items as cost of goods sold, net income, inventory, and accounts payable. By using electronic spreadsheets to perform sensitivity analysis, managers can instantly observe the effects of a change in an assumption on the entire budget.

DEVELOPING A SOUND BUDGETING CULTURE

OBJECTIVE 4

Describe the elements of a sound budgeting culture in companies.

The budgeting methods adopted by a company will greatly influence how successful the budgeting process will be.

The culture of a business is the way people in the business think and behave. A sound budget culture relies on establishing a process that encourages participation by key employees in the development of budgets. Key employees are those charged with making critical decisions about sales, production, and expenditures. Key employees include top managers and others who are held accountable for critical decisions. Companies can undertake a variety of activities to develop such a culture. These activities include directing attention to the budget, educating participants in the budget process, ensuring availability of information necessary to develop the budget, evaluating actual versus budgeted results, and motivating management to be active in the budget process.

Some companies use **continuous** or **perpetual budgets,** which are updated each month or each quarter so that a full year of budgeted activity is always available. This approach is preferable to preparing and evaluating a budget only on an annual basis, because it requires managers to keep the budget and planning process always in their minds.

Preparation of the master budget requires the involvement of managers throughout an organization. Each department or manager who participates in the planning process should understand the goals of the budget and the methods used to develop it. Therefore, a company should educate managers about the goals and procedures of the budgeting process.

To create an accurate budget, a thorough understanding of an organization's cost structure is required. Managers must understand costs that affect their particular department or function. In addition, managers must understand the accounting methods a company uses in measuring costs and accumulating data in their area of responsibility. ***Responsibility accounting* assigns responsibility for the performance of a company's departments to department managers.** It requires that each manager's performance be evaluated on the basis of costs or revenues that are directly under the manager's control. Responsibility accounting reports are produced periodically for the purpose of evaluating a department manager's effectiveness in generating revenues or controlling costs.

Coordination is needed to bring the various components of the master budget together. In many organizations, a standing **budget committee** is responsible for the coordination of the master budget. This committee generally consists of the president and vice presidents in charge of various departments, such as sales, production, administration, and finance. One role of the budget committee is to resolve disputes or misunderstandings among those involved in budget preparation.

Generally, the most successful budget processes are those that permit managers to participate in developing the budgets. ***Participative budgeting* (or bottom-up budgeting) is a process that allows individuals at various levels of a company to participate in determining the company's goals and the plans for achieving those goals.** It signals that senior managers value employee judgment and this generally results in a greater degree of employee acceptance of the budget than if the budget is dictated by senior managers. Senior managers often are not in a position to know the details of day-to-day operations as well as employees involved in these operations. Therefore, participation by employees can result in more accurate and achievable budgets. Further, employees who are involved in the development of a budget are more likely to work toward achieving the budget goals. Participative budgeting will be discussed in detail later in this chapter along with other behavioral implications of budgeting.

CONSIDERATIONS IN IMPLEMENTING BUDGETS

Once an appropriate culture exists for budgeting, a formal budgeting process is necessary. This process is influenced by several factors. These include the scope of the budget, the existence of foreign operations, inflation, and the possible need to revise the budget because of changes that take place in the company's operations or costs.

Scope of the Budget

A company determines which activities to include in its budget. For example, some companies develop budgets for desired inventory levels, the levels at which inventory will be reordered, and the timing and size of inventory purchases. Some budgets may be prepared casually, whereas others require greater detail depending on the emphasis the company places on them.

Foreign Operations, Currency Fluctuation, and Inflation

OBJECTIVE 5

Describe the influence of inflation and foreign operations on budgeting.

The marketplace in which companies trade is becoming more global. Many companies own foreign subsidiaries. Multinational companies face special budget problems because they operate in an international environment. Two of these problems are foreign currency exchange rates and inflation.

Foreign currency exchange rates refer to the relative values of the currencies of different countries. A U.S. company must translate the results of foreign operations into dollars. Consequently, its results are influenced by currency fluctuations, over which managers have no control. Foreign currency fluctuation presents a special risk when transactions, such as sales, are stated in a currency other than U.S. dollars. For example, suppose that the exchange rate on March 1 is 0.65 British pound sterling (£) for one U.S. dollar. U.S. Products Co., a U.S. company, agrees to sell furniture to England Imports, Ltd., a British company, for £65,000. The equivalent U.S. dollar value on March 1 is $100,000. Delivery and payment are to be made on April 1. If the value of the pound is £.70 for one U.S. dollar on the delivery date, the £65,000 that U.S. Products receives can be exchanged for only $92,857 (£65,000 ÷ £.70 per dollar). Consequently, U.S. Products Co. will have sustained a foreign currency exchange loss of $7,143 ($100,000 − $92,857). Such a loss is impossible to budget because the value of the dollar relative to the pound is not known until after the transaction is completed.

Inflation in some countries exceeds 100% annually. High inflation rates, called **hyperinflation,** create significant problems for budget preparation for multinational companies. Hyperinflation greatly reduces the ability of managers to compare budgets from period to period because it reduces the buying power of the foreign currency.

In addition to exchange rates and inflation, multinational companies must be sensitive to government laws and policies in the countries in which they operate when they set budgets. These laws and policies might affect labor costs, equipment purchases, cash management, or other budgeted items. For example, changes in tariffs and fees on imported raw materials will affect raw material costs.

Budget Revisions

Budgets forecast the future costs of inputs, such as raw materials and labor. These forecasts are not always accurate. Substantial differences between a company's actual costs and those assumed in developing the budget make the budget less useful. For example, a large increase in raw materials prices can cause the raw materials budget to be grossly understated in terms of actual raw materials costs. Evaluating personnel responsible for raw materials purchases against such a budget would be unrealistic and probably would be unfair. Consequently, companies may find it necessary to revise the original budget if there are unforeseen changes in costs.

Inaccurate forecasts raise two concerns. First, when is the forecast inaccurate enough to justify a change in the budget? If budgets are changed frequently because of minor differences in costs, they soon will lose meaning because managers will not view the budget as a goal to be achieved. Second, is the difference between the forecast and the actual cost due to a bad forecast or to the failure of the responsible managers to control costs? If managers are allowed to escape responsibility too easily, the budget again will lose its value. In deciding whether to permit a budget revision, senior management must weigh these concerns against the concern that the budget is inaccurate. Often, the decision will depend on the extent of the inaccuracy.

BEHAVIORAL CONCERNS IN BUDGETING

During the 1920s, a series of studies were conducted at the Hawthorne plant of the **Western Electric Company** to determine whether various elements of the physical environment in the plant affected employee efficiency and output. The experimenters varied employee work en-

OBJECTIVE 6

Identify how budgets affect management behavior.

vironments and measured resulting employee performance. At first, the researchers believed that increasing the levels of light had a positive effect on productivity. They later discovered that productivity increased whenever the researchers measured employees' work, regardless of the change in the environment. The Hawthorne studies provide evidence that observing and measuring human behavior can alter that behavior. Budgets provide benchmarks for measuring performance. By observing and measuring performance, companies hope to improve the performance of their workers.

Changing Behavior

Changing the way the score is kept in a basketball game can change the strategy with which the game is played and the behavior of players. The three-point rule offers evidence of such changes. An extra point for longer shots has resulted in more outside shooting. Consequently, the rule has changed the way many coaches and players view the game and prepare for it. This was the intent behind the three-point rule. How we measure performance affects behavior.

Budgeting measures actual outcomes and compares these to expected outcomes. Budgets measure employee performance and are a means of keeping score of both the managers' and the company's performance. Well-designed budgets lead to desired changes in behavior and minimize any undesired behavior that results from the measurement process. For example, bank branch managers' performance often is measured against budgeted loan and deposit volume goals. These goals, when set properly, encourage branch mangers to solicit business from current and potential customers and result in greater loan and deposit growth. The bank benefits because its increased financial resources lead to higher profits.

Participation in the Budget Process

Different leadership styles on the part of top management can lead to different types of budgeting. Budgets can be described as either top-down or bottom-up, as shown in Exhibit 14. *Top-down budgets* **are budgets that are established by management and then provided to lower levels of an organization for compliance.** *Bottom-up budgets* **involve all levels of an organization working to achieve the organization's goals.** Top-down, nonparticipative budget setting is indicated by the one-way arrows in the left-hand figure in Exhibit 14.

For a bottom-up budget, the department managers usually submit proposed budgets and then negotiate with senior managers to create a master budget. This budget then is used to evaluate the departments' performance. There is two-way communication in bottom-up budgeting, as shown by the arrows in the right-hand portion of Exhibit 14. In bottom-up,

Exhibit 14 Nonparticipative and Participative Budgeting

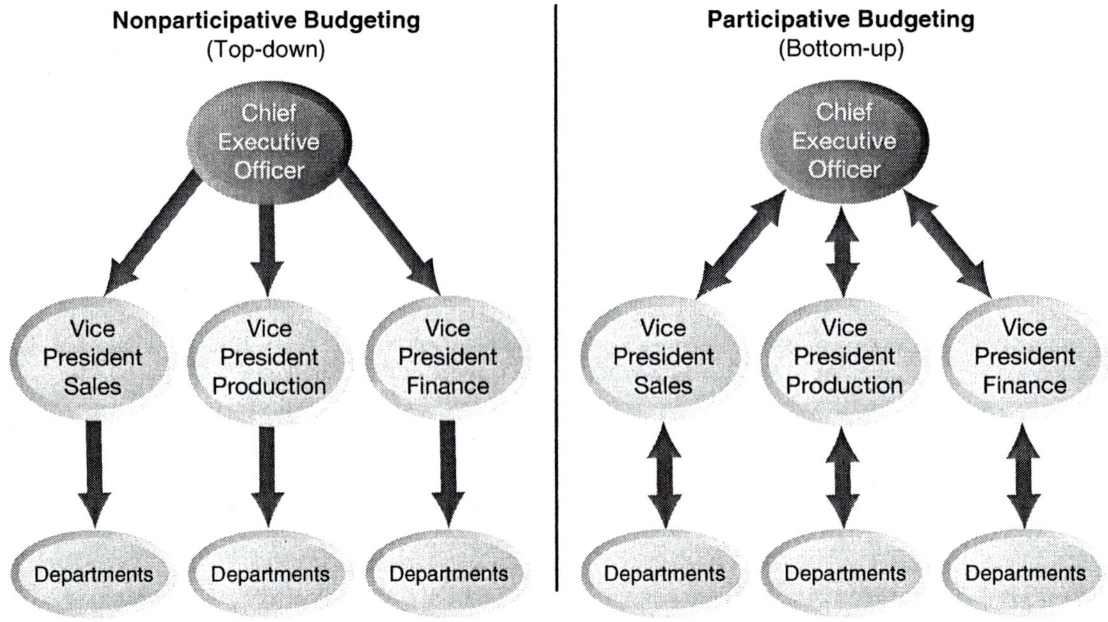

participative budget setting, the chief executive officer might direct that the vice president of sales solicit information on budget goals for the coming year from the regional sales offices or departments. After reviewing the goals submitted by the regional sales offices and negotiating any desired changes with regional sales managers, the vice president of sales would present a consolidated sales budget for the company to the chief executive. If the chief executive accepts the proposed sales budget, no further action is required. If the chief executive does not accept the budget, the vice president of sales renegotiates the regional sales budgets with the regional sales offices until an acceptable budget is reached.

Resources are necessary to meet objectives, but resources usually are limited. In many companies, departments compete with one another for a greater share of available resources. Sound planning requires decisions about the allocation of limited resources. Middle and lower-level managers tend to accept these decisions about the allocations of limited resources more readily if they have an active role in planning and setting budget goals. Participative budgeting helps encourage the acceptance of resource allocation decisions by creating a budget culture in which subordinates have a voice in these decisions.

Although it is a leader's responsibility to establish the overall mission, vision, and goals of a company, the leader affects the budgeting environment through his or her leadership style. Top managers can be responsive to new ideas and establish an environment of trust and openness by empowering managers at every level of the organization, or they can discourage involvement in the budgeting process. Usually it is better to develop an open and participative environment for the budgeting process because people make budgets work, and they usually will work harder to achieve goals that they had a role in setting.

CASE IN POINT

The **National Bank of Georgia** conducted an annual budgeting process that included loan and deposit goals for each of its branches. Top management established budget targets for the entire bank and for the branch division as a whole. Branch managers participated in this process by developing budgets for their branches and submitting these budgets to Branch Administration. Branch administrators reviewed the budgets and compared them to the targets set for the division. If the branch budgets were not as aggressive as the targets set by top management, branch administrators negotiated with individual branch managers in an attempt to get them to increase their budget targets so that the sum of the individual branches' goals was equal to the division's goal.

Slack in Budgets

When budgets are prepared, department managers have incentives to build slack into the budgets to make performance goals easier to achieve. Slack results in performance goals that are lower than what managers believe they can realistically achieve. This process of building slack into budgets is called **padding.** Budgets that have little or no slack are referred to as **tight budgets.** Research has shown that managers perform best when faced with moderately difficult but achievable goals. Not all factors that affect department performance are under the control of department managers. While managers have little control over external variables, such as the general economy, they should understand the effect those variables will have on their department's performance. Examples of external factors that should be considered in the budgeting process include economic forecasts related to a particular product, market conditions that affect a particular industry, and interest rates.

Because these external factors affect performance, even if managers run their departments well, department performance may not reflect their efforts. Budgetary slack reduces the risk that factors beyond the control of department managers will cause them to fail to meet their budget goals. On the other hand, if budgets contain too much slack, department managers can perform at a less than optimal level. Top or senior managers and department managers must work together to create budgets that will lead to satisfactory performance.

Budgets and Undesirable Behavior

Managers also should be aware that budget goals sometimes can cause subordinate managers to make decisions that are not in the best interest of the company as a whole. For example, suppose that a plant's maintenance costs are high relative to budget and the end of the budget year is approaching. Further assume that the plant manager expects to be promoted to supervisor of several plants if his particular plant's performance is superior to that of other plants. The plant manager may be tempted to defer needed maintenance in the hope of meeting the plant's budget targets and winning the promotion. The downside of such a decision, however, will be higher maintenance costs in the future because delaying necessary maintenance leads to abnormal wear of the plant's equipment.

Another example of budgets potentially leading to undesirable behavior was discussed in an earlier chapter. Absorption costing gives managers an incentive to over-produce inventory because fixed overhead costs are deferred in inventory, and so the department shows higher profits for the period. This excess inventory is costly for a company, although the costs are not fully captured in the current period's budget.

Managers need to be aware of the behavioral effects of budgeting and consider them in the budget process. With proper planning, managers can reduce behavior problems. For example, some slack can be included in the budget to reduce incentives for undesirable behavior. Companies can also attempt to detect behavior problems. As an example, a company can monitor unusual increases in inventories just prior to the end of budget periods to make sure a department is not producing unneeded inventory.

Self-Study Problem 2

Southeastern Bank owns a network of 60 branches. Each branch and branch manager is evaluated on the basis of performance relative to an annual budget. Growth in loans, deposits, and net income are the three principal measures on which managers are evaluated. The annual budget, for the fiscal year ending in December, is developed through a process of negotiation in a well-developed budget culture.

The process begins with senior managers providing general budget guidance to the branch managers. This guidance contains the branch's financial goals for the year. Each branch manager then develops a branch budget and submits this budget to senior management for approval. Branch managers know that they generally are expected to show positive growth in loans, deposits, and net income. However, since branch managers want to look as good as possible when their performance is compared against budget, they often try to pad their budgets by setting targets lower than what they actually believe they can achieve. Senior managers are aware of this tendency and frequently will not accept the budgets without an effort to get branch managers to accept higher targets.

Once the budgets are accepted, managers are provided with monthly reports that compare actual results to the budget targets. The results also are presented at quarterly meetings attended by branch and senior managers. If a branch manager is failing to meet budget targets, senior managers will ask the manager to explain why. At the end of the year, branch managers are given a performance appraisal. If the managers have met or exceeded their budgets, they are awarded a salary increase. If the managers have substantially exceeded their targets, they may receive a bonus in addition to a raise, unless the bank has had a bad year overall.

Occasionally, a manager who already has exceeded the loan growth goal for the year will wait until January to send in the paperwork on loans made in December. These loans then show up in the branch's January loan figures, rather than in the December figures. Deferring recognition of the loans enables the manager to get a head start on meeting next year's loan goals. Delays in recording a loan in the bank's accounting records do not affect the bank's cash flows. The bank loses no interest on the loans.

Required Evaluate the strengths and weaknesses of this budget process from a behavioral standpoint. How well does the bank's budget process encourage managers to strive to meet its goals? What budgeting and ethical problems does the delay in recording loans present?

The solution to Self-Study Problem 2 appears at the end of the chapter.

STRATEGIC CONSIDERATIONS IN BUDGETING

OBJECTIVE 7

Describe how budgets influence strategic decisions.

Budgets affect strategic marketing decisions. Recall that products have *life cycles* that consist of the following stages: (1) introduction of a new product, (2) building market share in preparation for future profits, (3) holding market share to ensure current profits on mature products, (4) maximizing available return while sales of a product are declining, and (5) eliminating the product when it is no longer sufficiently profitable.

Each stage has implications for the use and importance of budgets in marketing decisions. There is usually less reliance on budgets for decision-making purposes during the introduction and building stages because of uncertainty about financial performance. During these stages, little experience exists on which to base financial forecasts. Therefore, budgets tend to be less reliable during these stages and are used primarily as a short-term planning tool. Revisions to budgets are more likely to occur during the building stage because of changing information as the company gains experience with the product.

Managers of products in the introduction and building stages often have more input into the budget than managers of products in the holding and return-maximizing stages. Managers of products in the introduction and building stages operate in rapidly changing environments and have better knowledge of these changes than senior managers. In the holding and return-maximizing stages, sales tend to be more stable, and senior management can look to the company's prior experience with the product to set budget targets.

The frequency of contact between product managers and senior managers on strategic issues tends to be greater in the earlier stages of a product's life. Decisions about how to advertise the product, what markets to focus expenditures on, and how to respond to changing demand are more common in early stages than in the holding and harvesting stages. In contrast, there is more contact between product managers and senior managers on day-to-day operational issues during the later stages because of the need to manufacture the product at an economical cost.

During the earlier stages of product life, less importance is attached to meeting budget goals because these goals are not especially reliable and may need to be changed frequently. Holding product managers to tight budget targets during the building stage can result in poor decisions. For example, a manager concerned about making budget might prematurely discontinue a profitable product because it is less profitable than expected.

A company also must ensure that cash flows generated from products in the holding and profit-maximizing stages will be sufficient to support those products that are in the introduction and building stages. Meeting budget targets for products in the later stages is important if a company is to generate the cash needed to produce and market new products. Therefore, budgets are important for strategic planning.

BUDGETING IN SERVICE COMPANIES

OBJECTIVE 8

Explain the role of budgets in service organizations.

Service companies use budgets similarly to manufacturing companies. The preparation of budgets in service companies, however, can differ from budget preparation in manufacturing companies because service companies do not manufacture goods. Although service companies do not have to develop production and raw materials budgets, some aspects of budgeting can be more difficult in service organizations because it is often harder to trace costs to a particular service than to manufactured goods. In service companies, workers may be involved in the delivery of several different types of services during the same time period. In manufacturing companies, workers usually manufacture only one type of product at a time. When workers are involved with several different types of services at the same time, it is much more difficult to determine how much time (and therefore labor cost) is associated with providing one particular service. This makes it more difficult to develop budgets based on the expected amounts of services to be provided.

Consider checking account services, one of many services provided by banks. One of the costs bank management must budget for is the cost of the labor directly involved in providing checking accounts. This includes the work of tellers, new account personnel, and customer service personnel. These same personnel, however, help to provide many other types of services in addition to checking accounts, often at the same time they are dealing with checking accounts. For example, a teller may process a checking transaction, a loan payment, and a savings deposit for a given customer. How much of the cost of the teller's idle time should be assigned to each type of transaction? Although these cost allocation difficulties may be present in a manufacturing company to some extent, they are present to a greater extent in banks. The result is that banks are less able to accurately budget for the costs of providing for particular services than are manufacturing companies.

Although some aspects of service companies make budgeting more difficult than in manufacturing companies, other aspects potentially make budgeting easier and more useful. For example, some service companies, such as banks and automobile rental companies, operate many offices in different locations. The similarity of these separate offices provides a basis for analyzing budgets and evaluating performance that is not present in many manufacturing companies. The information for each unit can be compared with company-wide averages. This makes determination of good and bad performers easier than with manufacturing companies.

Self-Study Problem 3

The 4 Square Corporation, a major manufacturer of carpet-related products, recently launched a new adhesive fastener that affixes carpet to flooring. The product had a development budget of $6 million. The company has a policy of budgeting future funding for all products on the basis of recent actual versus budget sales performance. Senior management believes that all products should carry their weight and feels that this policy has served the company well. In creating the 2001 budget, 4 Square reduced the budget for the adhesive fastener because sales in 2000 were lower than projected in the marketing plan. The reduced budget did not permit extensive advertising efforts to continue. As a result, the adhesive fastener's sales did not increase at all during 2001, and the decision was made to discontinue the product. A problem occurred, however, when it was discovered that substantial additional costs were necessary to cancel contracts related to the product's development. Further, shortly after 4 Square abandoned the fastener, a competitor introduced a similar product that has been very successful.

Required Evaluate the policy of tying future funding for a product to the sales performance of that product during the previous year. What recommendations would you make to 4 Square to improve its policy?

The solution to Self-Study Problem 3 appears at the end of the chapter.

Review

SUMMARY of IMPORTANT CONCEPTS

1. The master budget is a collection of related budgets.
   a. It is composed of many individual budgets.
   b. It leads to pro forma financial statements.
   c. It has both operational and financial aspects.

2. A master budget has the following components:
   a. The sales budget shows the quantity and price of goods expected to be sold during the coming period.
   b. The production budget shows the type and quantity of products expected to be produced.
   c. The direct materials budget reflects the amount of raw materials expected to be purchased and used in production.
   d. The direct labor budget indicates the expected labor requirements for production.
   e. The manufacturing overhead budget reflects anticipated overhead costs, both fixed and variable.
   f. The selling and administrative expense budget shows anticipated cost, both fixed and variable.
   g. The cash budget shows expected cash receipts and disbursements.
   h. The pro forma income statement indicates the expected net income for the period.
   i. The pro forma balance sheet indicates anticipated levels of assets, liabilities, and owners' equity.

3. Static budgets tie to one level of sales while flexible budgets cover a range of sales. Managers often modify flexible budgets for sensitivity analysis.

4. A sound budgeting culture has the following characteristics:
   a. The culture encourages participation in budgeting at all levels of management.
   b. Cross-functional coordination is required.
   c. The budget provides motivational and performance measurement tools.
   d. The budget defines responsibility for costs and activities.

5. Some considerations in the budgeting process include the following:
   a. Several budgeting methods are available, including static and flexible budgets.
   b. International and foreign activities create special concerns, such as currency exchange rates and hyperinflation.

6. A number of behavioral concerns should be taken into account in budgeting.
   a. Leadership style greatly affects the budgeting process.
   b. Budget negotiation and budget slack are important considerations in setting budget goals.
   c. External forces related to economic conditions affect the budgeting process by imposing risk on subunit managers.
   d. Subunit managers attempting to meet budget goals may make undesirable decisions.

7. There are two important strategic considerations in budgeting:
   a. Different product life cycle stages may have different implications for the use of budgets.
   b. The implications of budgeting for product managers' decisions must be considered.

8. Budgeting in service companies differs in some respects from budgeting in manufacturing companies.
   a. Workers in service companies often perform more than one type of service at the same time, making budgeting the cost of individual services more difficult.
   b. Service companies often operate many branches, providing a basis for analyzing budgets and evaluating performance that is not present in many manufacturing companies.

Define

TERMS and CONCEPTS DEFINED in This CHAPTER

bottom-up budget (M223)
budget (M207)
cash budget (M216)
direct labor budget (M212)
direct materials budget (M211)
financial budget (M207)
flexible budget (M216)
manufacturing overhead budget (M212)
master budget (M207)
operating budget (M207)
participative budgeting (M221)
production budget (M210)
responsibility accounting (M221)
sales budget (M209)
selling and administrative expense budget (M213)
standards (M208)
static budget (M215)
top-down budget (M223)

Self-Study Problem SOLUTIONS

1

Sales Budget

Expected sales in units		100,000
Selling price per unit		$20
Total sales		$2,000,000

Production Budget

Units to be sold		100,000
Add: Desired ending inventory		2,500
Total needs		102,500
Less: Beginning inventory		500
Total units to produce		102,000

Direct Materials Budget

Total units to be produced		102,000
Materials required per unit (yds.)		1.5
Total (yds.)		153,000
Add: Desired ending inventory		1,000
Total material needs		154,000
Less: Beginning inventory		5,000
Total materials to be purchased		149,000
Cost per yard		$2.00
Total material cost		$298,000

Direct Labor Budget

Units to produce		102,000
Labor hours per unit		0.25
Total labor hours required		25,500
Labor rate per hour		$16
Total labor cost		$408,000

Manufacturing Overhead Budget

Units to produce		102,000
Variable rate per unit		$3
Total variable overhead		$306,000
Fixed manufacturing overhead:		
Depreciation	$25,000	
Insurance	10,000	
Property taxes	6,000	
Supervision	35,000	
Total fixed overhead		76,000
Total manufacturing overhead		$382,000

(Continued)

Selling and Administrative Expense Budget		
Units to be sold		100,000
Variable cost per unit		$2
Total variable selling expense		$200,000
Fixed selling and administrative expenses:		
Depreciation	$15,000	
Sales salaries	30,000	
Advertising	10,000	
Office clerk	18,000	
President's salary	60,000	
Total fixed expenses		133,000
Total selling and administrative expenses		$333,000

2 The bank's budget process has several strengths. These include (1) making clear the major objectives for branch managers to focus on and therefore encouraging them to meet goals, (2) allowing branch managers to participate in setting budget goals, (3) encouraging branch managers to be aggressive in budget goals, (4) providing managers with periodic feedback, and (5) permitting some slack in the budget without allowing this slack to become too great. The negotiation process also permits the recognition in the budget of differences in opportunities of different branches. Two weaknesses are (1) the fact that high-performing managers may not receive a bonus if the bank had a bad year, and (2) distortions in the accounting system created by the late booking of loans in January. A question arises as to whether this constitutes unethical behavior. It may be argued that since the cash flows from the loans are not affected, the bank is no worse off. However, if many managers engage in this practice and the amount of loans made but not recognized at year-end is large, the bank's accounting records will be materially misstated. More likely, the underbooking of loans in December leads to an appearance of a higher loan volume in January than actually occurs and affects future budgets. The bank could institute a policy that all loans must be booked within a specified number of days after they are made.

3 4 Square may be prematurely discontinuing new products by insisting that sales performance meet budgeted targets that were based on uncertain data. By doing so, 4 Square not only is losing the research and development costs sunk in these new products but also is forgoing the opportunity to make future profits. Such opportunities apparently exist, since a competitor marketed a product similar to 4 Square's adhesive fastener once 4 Square abandoned it. 4 Square could resolve this problem by implementing a policy in which new products are allowed a greater margin of error than more mature products in terms of meeting budgeted sales growth. The company could establish a range of likely sales performances based on differing market scenarios. Then 4 Square could compare actual sales to what sales should be given the situation that actually prevails.

Questions

6-1 *Obj. 1* Paul Reynolds recently was hired as a salesman for The Rocky Company, which sells gardening tools and potting soil through retail outlets. Paul has been asked to attend a meeting next week to discuss the preparation of the master budget for the coming year. Paul has asked you to explain what is meant by a master budget so that he can prepare for the meeting. What would you tell Paul?

6-2 *Obj. 2* Susan Broyer is a marketing manager for Glow Industries, which produces lamps and lighting fixtures. Susan's department is preparing a sales budget for the company's lighting fixtures. She has issued a memo to her staff that says in part: "I expect an annual increase in sales next year of 12% across the board. Every line and product should reflect this sales increase." What budget(s) would be affected by the estimated increase in sales?

6-3 *Obj. 2* Den and Harry own a small ice cream shop in Kokomo, Indiana. They make their own ice cream, which is sold in gallons, quarts, pints, and over the counter in the form of cones. Den and Harry use a variety of information to forecast sales demand for ice cream in Kokomo each summer. Based on their forecasts, Den and Harry then prepare a sales budget for their shop. What is the difference between a sales forecast and a sales budget? Explain.

6-4 *Obj. 2* Markle Company is a *merchandising* firm that operates 26 stores. Marvle Industries is a *manufacturer* that operates a single plant. Both firms prepare detailed master budgets each year. How would the master budgets of the two firms differ?

6-5 *Obj. 2* Frank Sheffield is the vice president of finance for The Hercules Company. Recently, Hercules completed preparation of its master budget for the coming year. Frank has scheduled a meeting with the company's banker. What portions of the master budget, if any, do you believe Frank should review with the bank?

6-6 *Obj. 2* Vantage Incorporated is preparing a master budget for the coming quarter of operations. As part of the budget process, inventory policies are being reviewed at a senior management planning meeting. Which budgets would policies concerning the level of inventories affect? Why?

6-7 *Obj. 4* During a recent staff management meeting of Hoya Enterprises, a manufacturer of dog leashes, collars, and accessories, Rocky Findlayson, company controller, exclaimed, "We will never get a handle on our operating costs without responsibility accounting!" What is meant by the term *responsibility accounting?*

6-8 *Obj. 6* Carla Eubanks is a production manager for Department 1 of Graham Packaging. Graham produces plastic bottles for detergents and cleaning supplies. Its management prepares detailed budgets at the beginning of each year covering all aspects of its business. Carla is preparing for an annual performance review with her supervisor and is certain that she will receive a positive review, since her department has achieved 20% greater production than the previous year. Is Carla correct in judging actual results based on past performance? Why or why not?

6-9 *Obj. 6* Pat Houlihan is the chief executive officer of Alco Industries. Alco has business interests in many different communication fields, including publishing, television, radio, and cable. Pat has indicated that she expects 10% across-the-board cuts in operating costs in all of her company's segments in the coming year. Do you support such an approach? Why or why not?

6-10 *Obj. 6* Leroy Smith is the production manager of The Alum Company. In addition to his salary, Leroy receives bonus compensation based solely on his ability to meet the budgeted production of units. Comment on Leroy's bonus arrangement. What weaknesses might exist in this arrangement?

6-11 *Obj. 6* Discuss the implications associated with a budgetary approach in which budgetary data are imposed on managers from above. Contrast such an approach with one in which budgetary data are self-imposed in a participative manner.

6-12 *Obj. 6* Rona Abraham is the purchasing manager for Flextech Incorporated, a manufacturer of furniture and bedding. Rona knows that as part of her bonus compensation, she must meet the material purchasing budget that was established at the beginning of the year. In an effort to meet this budget, Rona has been purchasing lower-grade materials at reduced costs and is proud of her ability to spend less than the budgeted amounts on materials. What implications do Rona's actions have for Flextech as a whole?

6-13 *Objs. 4, 6* Rick Nill is the president of The Toyco Company, which produces a wide variety of action combat toys for children. For the past few years, Rick has prepared an annual business plan at the beginning of the year, detailing his expectations for sales, production, income, and expenses. He does not share these plans with his senior managers, but rather is closely involved with each operating department, monitoring its activities and issuing directives that tell how to meet his objectives. How could Rick improve his planning and budgeting process? What benefits could Rick expect from your suggested changes?

6-14 *Objs. 4, 6* A key concept underlying the budget process is that of responsibility accounting. The basic idea behind responsibility accounting is that each manager's performance should be judged by how well he or she manages those items that are directly under his or her control. Identify three possible limitations of responsibility accounting.

6-15 *Obj. 7* Lester Arbuckle is owner of Sheetco, a manufacturer of snow shovels. Lester and his managers do no budgeting or planning for Sheetco. Sheetco management does not anticipate problems that arise, and as a result, the company has slow production, missed shipment deadlines, and lost sales. Discuss the reasons why Lester should wish to engage in budgeting and planning.

6-16 *Obj. 8* Service firms do not manufacture products; therefore budgeting is not important to service firms. Do you agree? Explain your answer.

Exercises

6-1 *Obj. 1* Write a short definition of each of the terms listed in the *Terms and Concepts Defined in This Chapter* section.

6-2 *Obj. 2* Darts-R-Fun Co. manufactures dart boards, which it sells for $30 each. Cash collections from sales are expected to be 75% in the quarter of the sale and 25% in the following quarter. The uncollected portion of sales at January 1 was $2,000. The sales forecast for the next year is:

	Expected Sales in Units
Quarter 1	100
Quarter 2	200
Quarter 3	150
Quarter 4	300

Create a sales budget and a schedule of expected cash collections.

6-3 *Obj. 2* Hoop Action manufactures basketballs, which it sells for $50 each. Cash collections from sales are expected to be 80% in the quarter of the sale and 20% in the following quarter. The uncollected portion of sales at January 1 was $40,000. The sales forecast for the next year is:

	Expected Sales in Units
Quarter 1	2,000
Quarter 2	3,000
Quarter 3	5,000
Quarter 4	5,000

Create a sales budget and a schedule of expected cash collections.

6-4 Elm Company makes a product that has peak sales in September of each year. The company has prepared a sales budget for the third quarter of 2001, as shown below:
Obj. 2

	July	August	September
Budgeted sales	$500,000	$600,000	$750,000

The company is in the process of preparing a cash budget for the third quarter and must determine the cash collections by month. Collections on sales are expected to be as follows:

70% in the month of sale
20% in the month following the month of sale
8% in the second month following the month of sale
2% uncollectible

The accounts receivable balance as of June 30 is $195,000, of which $45,000 represents uncollected May sales and $150,000 represents uncollected June sales.

a. What were the total sales for May and June?
b. What are the expected cash collections for each month of the third quarter?

6-5 Beany-Toys Company makes small, bean-filled toys which it sells to retailers. The company has prepared a sales budget for the fourth quarter of 2002, as shown below:
Obj. 2

	October	November	December
Budgeted sales	$1,000,000	$2,500,000	$3,000,000

The company is in the process of preparing a cash budget for the third quarter and must determine the cash collections by month. Collections on sales are expected to be as follows:

50% in the month of the sale
40% in the month following the sale
7% in the second month following the sale
3% uncollectible

The Accounts Receivable balance as of September 30 is $500,000, of which $100,000 represents uncollected August sales and $400,000 represents uncollected September sales.

a. What were the total sales for August and September?
b. What are the expected cash collections for each month of the fourth quarter?

6-6 The Stoner Company makes a popular Halloween mask. Peak sales are in October of each year. The company's partial sales budget, in units, for 2001 is as follows:
Obj. 2

August	September	October	November
20,000	30,000	55,000	5,000

The company has an inventory policy in which the end-of-month inventory must equal 10% of the following month's sales. The inventory as of July 31 was 2,000 units.

Prepare a production budget for the three months ended October 31, 2001. In your budget, show the number of units to be produced each month and for the quarter in total.

6-7 Razor Sharp produces a hedge trimmer for personal lawn care. The company's sales budget for April through July is as follows:
Obj. 2

April	May	June	July
300,000	350,000	250,000	150,000

The company has an inventory policy in which the end-of-month inventory must equal 5% of the following month's sales. The inventory as of March 31 was 15,000 units.

Prepare a production budget for April, May, and June. In your budget, show the number of units to be produced each month and for the quarter in total.

6-8 *Obj. 2* The Young Company produces vegetable candy bars called Veggy Bars. Each six-ounce Veggy Bar contains five ounces of brussels sprouts, which Young purchases for $.05 an ounce. Budgeted production of vegetable candy bars for the first four months of 2001 is as follows:

	Units
January	100,000
February	120,000
March	110,000
April	100,000

Young has an inventory policy that ending inventory of brussels sprouts should be 10% of the following month's requirements.

Prepare a purchasing budget for the first quarter of 2001 by month and for the quarter in total. Show the amount of materials required in unit and in dollar amounts.

6-9 *Obj. 2* Refer to the data in Exercise 6-8. Each Veggy Bar requires 0.02 direct labor hour. The average labor rate is $10 per hour.

Prepare a direct labor budget for the first quarter of 2001, showing the number of hours needed and the total labor cost required by month and for the quarter in total.

6-10 *Obj. 2* The Chugalot company produces soda mugs. Each 32-ounce mug contains 1.1 pounds of glass, which Chugalot purchases for $1.05 a pound. Budgeted production of mugs for the first four months of 2002 is as follows:

	Units
January	10,000
February	12,000
March	8,000
April	10,000

Chugalot has an inventory policy that ending inventory of mugs should be 10% of the following month's requirements.

Prepare a purchasing budget for the first quarter of 2002 by month and for the quarter in total. Show the amount of materials required in unit and in dollar amounts.

6-11 *Obj. 2* Refer to the data in Exercise 6-10. Each mug requires .05 direct labor hour. The average labor rate is $20 per hour.

Prepare a direct labor budget for the first quarter of 2002, showing the number of hours needed and the total labor cost required by month and for the quarter in total.

6-12 *Obj. 2* Cross Blade manufactures pocket knifes. The activity base used to allocate overhead is machine hours. The variable overhead rate is estimated at $4 per machine hour for 2002. The fixed overhead is budgeted at $80,000 per quarter of which $10,000 represents depreciation. The budgeted machine hours are as follows:

Quarter	Machine Hours
1	5,000
2	4,000
3	4,500
4	5,000

Prepare a manufacturing overhead budget for 2002, showing the total budgeted manufacturing overhead and the cash disbursements for manufacturing overhead by quarter and for the year in total.

6-13 *Obj. 2* Sure Staple Company manufactures staplers. The activity base used to allocate overhead is direct labor hours. The variable overhead rate is estimated at $1.25 per direct labor hour for 2002. The fixed overhead is budgeted at $20,000 per quarter of which $5,000 represents depreciation. The budgeted direct labor hours are as follows:

Quarter	Direct Labor Hours
1	10,000
2	11,000
3	11,500
4	11,500

Prepare a manufacturing overhead budget for 2002, showing the total budgeted manufacturing overhead and the cash disbursements for manufacturing overhead by quarter and for the year in total.

6-14 *Obj. 2* A+ Company manufactures study guides for students. A+ sells its study guides through door-to-door sales. Its sales people receive a $20 commission per book sold. Other annual selling and administrative expenses for 2002 are estimated as follows:

Insurance	$ 200,000
Executive salaries	1,000,000
Property taxes	30,000
Depreciation	30,000

The sales for 2002 are estimated as follows:

Quarter	Unit Sales
1	5,000
2	10,000
3	20,000
4	7,000

Prepare a selling and administrative expense budget for 2002, showing the total budgeted selling and administrative expenses and the cash disbursements for selling and administrative expenses by quarter and for the year in total.

6-15 *Obj. 2* Tough Terrain Company manufactures professional quality lawn mowers. Tough Terrain incurs variable selling expenses of $15 per lawn mower. Other annual selling and administrative expenses for 2002 are estimated as follows:

Advertising	$200,000
Insurance	100,000
Executive salaries	500,000
Property taxes	20,000
Depreciation	10,000

The sales for 2002 are estimated as follows:

Quarter	Unit Sales
1	5,000
2	30,000
3	20,000
4	2,000

Prepare a selling and administrative expense budget for 2002, showing the total budgeted selling and administrative expenses and the cash disbursements for selling and administrative expenses by quarter and for the year in total.

6-16 *Obj. 2* A sales budget for the first six months of 2001 is given below for a product manufactured by Raven and Associates.

Month	Budgeted Sales (Units)
January	6,000
February	10,000
March	8,000
April	9,000
May	8,000
June	7,000

The inventory of finished goods on hand at the end of each month must equal 20% of the following month's budgeted sales. On January 1, 2001, there were 1,200 units of finished product on hand. There was no work-in-process inventory at January 1, 2001. Each unit produced requires five pounds of a product called Amco. Raven has the policy of maintaining enough Amco in stock to meet 10% of the following month's production needs. There was exactly 10% of January production needs in inventory as of January 1, 2001. The 2001 budgeted cost per pound of Amco is $3.10.

Prepare a budget showing the amount of Amco to be purchased for each of the first three months of the year and for the quarter in total.

6-17 *Obj. 2* A sales budget for the first four months of 2002 is given below for a product manufactured by Klaasen & Company.

Month	Budgeted Sales (Units)
January	10,000
February	12,000
March	8,000
April	13,000
May	14,000

The inventory of finished goods on hand at the end of each month must equal 10% of the following month's budgeted sales. On January 1, 2002 there were 1,000 units of finished product on hand. There was no work-in-process inventory at January 1, 2002. Each unit produced requires .25 pounds of finishing varnish. Klaasen has the policy of maintaining enough finishing varnish in stock to meet 15% of the following month's production needs. There was exactly 15% of January's production needs of varnish in inventory as of January 1, 2002. The 2002 budgeted cost per pound of varnish is $6.

Prepare a budget showing the amount of varnish to be purchased for each of the first three months of the year and for the quarter in total.

6-18 *Obj. 2* On April 30, Sterling Enterprises had an inventory of 38,000 units of finished goods, and it had accounts receivable totaling $85,000. Sales, in units, have been budgeted as follows for the next four months:

May	60,000
June	75,000
July	90,000
August	81,000

Sterling has a policy that 40% of the following month's sales should be maintained in ending inventory. Each unit sells for $2. All sales are on account. The budgeted cash collections anticipate that one-third of sales will be collected in the month of sale and the remainder in the following month.

a. Prepare a production budget for the months of May, June, and July.
b. Prepare a schedule of budgeted cash collections for the months of May, June, and July.

6-19 *Obj. 2* On August 31, Blake & Sons had an inventory of 50 units of finished goods, and it had accounts receivable totaling $75,000. Sales, in units, have been budgeted as follows for the next four months:

September	300
October	400
November	450
December	500

Blake has a policy that 20% of the following month's sales should be maintained in ending inventory. Each unit sells for $500. All sales are on account. The budgeted cash collections anticipate that one half of sales will be collected in the month of sale and the other half in the following month.

a. Prepare a production budget for the months of September, October, and November.
b. Prepare a schedule of budgeted cash collections from sales for the months of September, October, and November.

6-20 *Obj. 2* Specialty Products Ltd. manufactures a collectible porcelain figurine. Labor at Specialty is provided under a union contract that requires that all workers be paid for a minimum 40-hour work week with a no-layoff policy. The guaranteed number of hours that Specialty must pay for each month is 1,600. The labor agreement also states that workers will provide overtime as needed, but will be paid time and a half for any overtime worked. Accordingly, an overtime premium must be budgeted for any labor required in excess of 1,600 hours per month. The amount of labor that is required for each unit is 0.05 hour, and the budgeted labor rate is $10 per hour. Budgeted production for the second quarter of 2001 is as follows:

	April	May	June
Production in units	26,000	46,000	29,000

a. Calculate the number of labor hours that are required to meet production for each of the three months, and for the second quarter in total.
b. Calculate the total budgeted labor expense to be paid each month and for the second quarter in total.

6-21 Sky High manufactures sports shoes. Labor at Sky High is provided under a contract that requires all workers be paid for a minimum 40-hour work week with a no-layoff policy. There are 25 workers under this contract and each one of them is guaranteed 160 hours that Sky High must pay for each month. The amount of labor that is required for each pair of tennis shoes is .5 hours and the budgeted labor rate is $3 per hour. The rate for time in excess of 160 per month is $4.50 per hour. Budgeted production for the first quarter of 2002 is as follows:

	January	February	March
Production in units	10,000	7,000	8,300

a. Calculate the total number of labor hours that are required under contract per month.
b. Calculate the number of labor hours that are required to meet production for each of the three months and for the first quarter in total.
c. Calculate the total budgeted labor expense to be paid each month and for the second quarter in total.

Problems

Tips and hints for selected problems and cases are available on the Ingram WebTutor for WebCT site.

PROBLEM 6-1 Cash Budget

Obj. 2

Kim Incorporated is getting ready to put the cash budget together for 2002. Assume that $10,000 in income taxes were paid each quarter. Also assume Kim paid a dividend of $20,000 in the fourth quarter. No financing was done and no equipment was purchased. Partial schedules of cash collections and disbursements are shown below.

	Quarter 1	Quarter 2	Quarter 3	Quarter 4	Year
Schedule of Expected Cash Collections from Sales Budget					
Accounts receivable, December 31, 2001	$ 40,000				$ 40,000
First-quarter sales	80,000	$ 20,000			100,000
Second-quarter sales		120,000	$ 30,000		150,000
Third-quarter sales			200,000	$ 50,000	250,000
Fourth-quarter sales				200,000	200,000
Total cash collections	$120,000	$140,000	$230,000	$250,000	$740,000
Schedule of Expected Cash Disbursements from Direct Materials Budget					
Accounts payable December 31, 2001	$20,000				
First-quarter purchases	40,000	$10,000			$ 50,000
Second-quarter purchases		60,000	$ 15,000		75,000
Third-quarter purchases			100,000	$ 25,000	125,000
Fourth-quarter purchases				100,000	100,000
Total cash disbursements	$60,000	$70,000	$115,000	$125,000	$350,000
Direct Labor Budget					
Units to be produced	800	1,200	2,000	2,000	6000
Direct labor time per unit	2	2	2	2	2
Total hours of direct labor required	1,600	2,400	4,000	4,000	12,000
Direct labor cost per hour	$ 10	$ 10	$ 10	$ 10	$ 10
Total direct labor costs	$16,000	$24,000	$40,000	$40,000	$120,000
Manufacturing Overhead Budget					
Budgeted direct labor hours	1,600	2,400	4,000	4,000	12,000
Variable overhead rate	$ 10	$ 10	$ 10	$ 10	$ 10
Budgeted variable overhead	$16,000	$24,000	$40,000	$40,000	$120,000
Budgeted fixed overhead	20,000	20,000	20,000	20,000	80,000
Total budgeted manufacturing overhead	$36,000	$44,000	$60,000	$60,000	$200,000
Less: Noncash expenses	5,000	5,000	5,000	5,000	20,000
Cash disbursements for manufacturing overhead	$31,000	$39,000	$55,000	$55,000	$180,000
Selling and Administrative Expense Budget					
Budgeted sales in units	800	1,200	2,000	2,000	6,000
Variable selling and administrative expenses per unit	$ 5	$ 5	$ 5	$ 5	$ 5
Budgeted variable expenses	$ 4,000	$ 6,000	$10,000	$10,000	$ 30,000
Budgeted fixed selling and administrative expenses	30,000	30,000	30,000	30,000	120,000
Total budgeted selling and administrative expenses	$34,000	$36,000	$40,000	$40,000	$150,000
Less: Noncash expenses	5,000	5,000	5,000	5,000	20,000
Cash expenditures for selling and administrative expenses	$29,000	$31,000	$35,000	$35,000	$130,000

Required

A. Create a cash budget for 2002.
B. Assume that Kim has $1,000,000 of debt outstanding as of January 1, 2002. Given the cash budget should Kim borrow or repay any of the debt during 2002? Why?
C. Why is it important to create a cash budget?

PROBLEM 6-2 Cash Budget

Obj. 2

Fun Clips is getting ready to put the cash budget together for 2002. Assume that $10,000 in income taxes were paid each quarter. Also assume Kim paid a dividend of $5000 each quarter. Kim borrowed $30,000 in the first quarter and $50,000 in the third quarter. Kim has an interest payment of $900 due in the third quarter. Partial schedules of cash collections and disbursements are shown below.

	Quarter 1	Quarter 2	Quarter 3	Quarter 4	Year
Schedule of Expected Cash Collections from Sales Budget					
Accounts receivable, December 31, 2001	$ 5,000				$ 5,000
First-quarter sales	15,000	$15,000			30,000
Second-quarter sales		20,000	$20,000		40,000
Third-quarter sales			15,000	$15,000	30,000
Fourth-quarter sales				10,000	10,000
Total cash collections	$20,000	$35,000	$35,000	$25,000	$115,000
Schedule of Expected Cash Disbursements from Direct Materials Budget					
Accounts payable, December 31, 2001	$ 2,000				$ 2,000
First-quarter purchases	10,000	$ 3,000			13,000
Second-quarter purchases		7,500	$2,250		9,750
Third-quarter purchases			5,000	$1,500	6,500
Fourth-quarter purchases				5,000	5,000
Total cash disbursements	$12,000	$10,500	$7,250	$6,500	$36,250
Direct Labor Budget					
Units to be produced	1,000	750	500	500	2,750
Direct labor time per unit	1	1	1	1	1
Total hours of direct labor required	1,000	750	500	500	2,750
Direct labor cost per hour	$ 12	$ 12	$ 12	$ 12	$ 12
Total direct labor costs	$12,000	$9,000	$6,000	$6,000	$33,000
Manufacturing Overhead Budget					
Budgeted direct labor hours	1,000	750	500	500	2,750
Variable overhead rate	$ 2	$ 2	$ 2	$ 2	$ 2
Budgeted variable overhead	$2,000	$1,500	$1,000	$1,000	$ 5,500
Budgeted fixed overhead	5,000	5,000	5,000	5,000	20,000
Total budgeted manufacturing overhead	$7,000	$6,500	$6,000	$6,000	$25,500
Less: Noncash expenses	1,000	1,000	1,000	1,000	4,000
Cash disbursements for manufacturing overhead	$6,000	$5,500	$5,000	$5,000	$21,500

(Continued)

Selling and Administrative Expense Budget

Budgeted sales in units	1,000	1,200	2,000	2,000	6,200
Variable selling and administrative expenses per unit	$ 1	$ 1	$ 1	$ 1	$ 1
Budgeted variable expenses	$ 1,000	$ 1,200	$ 2,000	$ 2,000	$ 6,200
Budgeted fixed selling and administrative expenses	10,000	10,000	10,000	10,000	40,000
Total budgeted selling and administrative expenses	$11,000	$11,200	$12,000	$12,000	$46,200
Less: Noncash expenses	1,000	1,000	1,000	1,000	4,000
Cash expenditures for selling and administrative expenses	$10,000	$10,200	$11,000	$11,000	$42,200

Required

A. Create a cash budget for 2002.
B. Why is it important to create a cash budget?

PROBLEM 6-3 Pro Forma Budgeted Balance Sheet

Obj. 2

Smith & Sons is ready to put together their pro forma budgeted balance sheet. The 2001 balance sheet is:

	2001 (Actual)
Assets	
Current assets:	
Cash	$ 20,000
Accounts receivable	40,000
Raw materials inventory	20,000
Finished goods inventory	30,000
Total current assets	$110,000
Plant and equipment:	
Land	$400,000
Buildings and equipment	200,000
Accumulated depreciation	(50,000)
Plant and equipment, net	550,000
Total assets	$660,000
Liabilities and stockholders' equity	
Current liabilities:	
Accounts payable (raw materials)	$ 20,000
Stockholders' equity:	
Common stock	$500,000
Retained earnings	140,000
Total stockholders' equity	$640,000
Total liabilities and stockholders' equity	$660,000

Selected balances from the budgets are as follows:

Sales budget:	Fourth quarter sales = $100,000
Production budget:	Desired ending inventory is 5,000 units
Direct materials budget:	Desired ending inventory = 50,000 lbs.
	Cost of materials purchased in fourth quarter = $60,000
Manufacturing overhead budget:	Noncash expense (depreciation) = $6,000
Selling and administrative expense budget:	Noncash expense (depreciation) = $4,000
Pro forma income statement:	Net income = $35,000
Cash budget:	Equipment and building purchases = $0
	Dividends paid = $10,000
	Cash balance, ending = $30,000

Accounts receivable are expected to be 50% of the fourth quarter sales. Smith & Sons pays 50% of raw materials purchases in the month of purchase, and 50% the following month. The cost of raw materials is $.50 per pound. The cost of finished goods is $10 per unit.

Required

A. Create a pro forma balance sheet.
B. What is the pro forma balance sheet used for?

PROBLEM 6-4 Pro Forma Budgeted Balance Sheet

Obj. 2

The Crab Hole is ready to put together their pro forma budgeted balance sheet. The 2001 balance sheet is:

Assets	
Current assets:	
Cash	$ 10,000
Accounts receivable	10,000
Raw materials inventory	5,000
Finished goods inventory	15,000
Total current assets	$ 40,000
Plant and equipment:	
Land	$100,000
Buildings and equipment	300,000
Accumulated depreciation	(80,000)
Plant and equipment, net	$320,000
Total asssets	$360,000
Liabilities and stockholders' equity	
Current liabilities:	
Accounts payable (raw materials)	$ 20,000
Stockholders' equity:	
Common stock	$300,000
Retained earnings	40,000
Total stockholders' equity	$340,000
Total liabilities and stockholders' equity	$360,000

(Continued)

Selected balances from the budgets are as follows:

Sales budget:	Fourth-quarter sales = $24,000
Production budget:	Desired ending inventory = 700 units
Direct materials budget:	Desired ending inventory = 4,000 lbs
	Cost of materials purchased in fourth quarter = $32,000
Manufacturing overhead budget:	Noncash expense (depreciation) = $17,000
Selling and administrative expense budget:	Noncash expense (depreciation) = $3,000
Pro forma income statement:	Net income = ($8,000) loss
Cash budget:	Equipment and building purchases = $10,000
	Dividends paid = $0
	Cash balance, ending = $8,000

Accounts receivable are expected to be 50% of the fourth-quarter sales. The Crab Hole pays 50% of raw materials purchases in the month of purchase and 50% the following month. The cost of raw materials is $3 per pound. The cost of finished goods is $20 per unit.

Required

A. Create a pro forma balance sheet.
B. What are the uses of the pro forma balance sheet?

PROBLEM 6-5 Flexible Budget

Objs. 2, 3

Say Cheese Company manufactures picture frames which sell for $25 per frame. The company has fixed manufacturing overhead of $30,000 per year, of which $5,000 is depreciation, a noncash expense. The company's fixed selling and administrative expense is $40,000 per year. Assume taxes are a fixed $15,000, which does not vary on sales amount. Other expenses are as follows:

	Cost per unit
Direct materials	$5.00
Direct labor	2.00
Variable overhead	3.00
Variable selling and administrative expense	2.00

Say Cheese believes sales for 2002 will fall somewhere between 8,000 and 10,000 units.

Required

A. Create a flexible pro forma income statement for sales of 8,000, 9,000, and 10,000 units.
B. Should you subtract out noncash expenses? Why or why not?
C. When would a company want to use a flexible budget as opposed to a static budget? What are the advantages of a flexible budget?

PROBLEM 6-6 Flexible Budget

Objs. 2, 3

Light Power manufactures laptops which sell for $2,500 each. The company has fixed manufacturing overhead of $4,000,000 per year, of which $1,000,000 is depreciation, a noncash expense. The company's fixed selling and administrative expense is $3,000,000 per year. Assume taxes are a fixed $1,000,000, which does not vary on sales amount. Other expenses are as follows:

	Cost per unit
Direct materials	$1,500
Direct labor	150
Variable overhead	50
Variable selling and administrative expense	30

Light Power believes sales for 2002 will fall somewhere between 10,000 and 15,000 units.

Required

A. Create a flexible pro forma income statement for sales of 10,000, 12,500, and 15,000 units.
B. Should you subtract out noncash expenses? Why or why not?
C. When would a company want to use a flexible budget as opposed to a static budget? What are the advantages of a flexible budget?

PROBLEM 6-7 Currency Effect

Obj. 5

Trading Company sells 3,000 units of goods to Japan at $50 each on January 1, February 1, and March 1. Trading Company agrees to be paid in yen. The price in yen is set on the date of the sale and payment is due in 30 days. When Trading Company receives payment, they immediately convert the yen back to dollars.

(Therefore, if Trading Company sold $1,000 worth of merchandise on January 15 when the exchange rate was $1 = ¥95, then our customer would owe ¥95,000. Payment would be due on February 15. If the exchange rate was $1 = ¥115, then the ¥95,000 yen would get converted into $826.)

The exchange rates are as follows:

Exchange rate January 1	$1 = ¥100
Exchange rate February 1	$1 = ¥110
Exchange rate March 1	$1 = ¥105

Required

A. Calculate the agreed price in yen for the sale of goods on January 1, February 1, and March 1.
B. Calculate the amount of dollars received on February 1 and March 1 from the previous month's sales when the yen from the first two payments are converted to dollars.
C. Assuming Trading Company does not know which way the exchange rate will move, what is the expected amount of cash collections on April 1, given in dollars?
D. Can the Trading Company include these fluctuations in the budget? Explain.

PROBLEM 6-8 Currency Effect

Obj. 5

Terry Robes, Inc. sells 200 units of robes to Japan for a total amount of ¥1,000,000 on January 1, February 1, and March 1. When Terry Robes receives payment, they immediately convert the yen back to dollars.

The exchange rates are as follows:

Exchange rate January, 1	$1 = ¥120
Exchange rate February 1	$1 = ¥110
Exchange rate March 1	$1 = ¥115

Required

A. Calculate the amount of dollars received on February 1 and March 1 when the yen from the first two payments are converted to dollars.
B. Assuming Trading Company does not know which way the exchange rate will move, what is the expected amount of cash collections on April 1, given in dollars?
C. Can the Trading Company include these fluctuations in the budget? Explain.

PROBLEM 6-9 Budgeting Behavioral Implications

Objs. 4, 6

An effective budget converts the goals and objectives of management into specific performance targets. The master budget serves as a blueprint that reflects management's plans for the budgeted period. Moreover, the master budget serves as a basis for control in that performance can be evaluated by comparing actual results to budgeted or planned results.

Given the importance of budgeting within a company, the creation of an effective budget is essential for the successful operation of the company. There are several methods of generating budget information that can be employed, all of which require extensive contact with people at various operating levels within the company. The way in which people see their involvement with the budget process is important to the successful use of the budget as a management tool.

In the budget setting process, budget A was put together by lower management, including sales representatives, purchasing managers, and factory supervisors. Budget B was put together by senior management.

(Continued)

	A	B
Unit sales	10,000	15,000
Dollar sales	$2,000,000	$3,000,000
Less variable expenses:		
Direct materials	1,100,000	1,500,000
Direct labor	220,000	300,000
Variable overhead	110,000	150,000
Variable selling and administrative expense	88,000	120,000
Total variable expenses	$1,518,000	$2,070,000
Contribution margin	$ 482,000	$ 930,000
Less fixed expenses:		
Manufacturing overhead	350,000	300,000
Selling and administrative	200,000	200,000
Taxes and interest	10,000	10,000
Total fixed expenses	$ 560,000	$ 510,000
Net income (loss)	$ (78,000)	$ 420,000

Required

A. Calculate the cost per unit for the variable costs.
B. Why do you think budget A has high costs and low sales forecasts?
C. Why do you think budget B has low costs and high sales forecasts? What are the behavioral implications of this top down approach?
D. How should the two groups participate to come to a consensus on the budget? What are the advantages of this approach?

PROBLEM 6-10 Budgeting Behavioral Implications

Objs. 4, 6

Crunch Numbers is a manufacturer of calculators. In the budget-setting process, budget A was put together by lower and middle management. Budget B was put together by senior management.

	A	B
Unit sales	20,000	30,000
Dollar sales	$600,000	$900,000
Less variable expenses:		
Direct materials	260,000	360,000
Direct labor	40,000	60,000
Variable overhead	60,000	75,000
Variable selling and administrative expense	60,000	60,000
Total variable expenses	$420,000	$555,000
Contribution margin	$180,000	$345,000
Less fixed expenses:		
Manufacturing overhead	$ 60,000	$ 50,000
Selling and administrative	100,000	80,000
Taxes and interest	10,000	10,000
Total fixed expenses	$170,000	$140,000
Net income (loss)	$ 10,000	$205,000

Required

A. Calculate the cost per unit for the variable costs.
B. Why do you think budget A has high costs and low sales forecasts?
C. Why do you think budget B has low costs and high sales forecasts? What are the behavioral implications of this top-down approach?
D. How should the two groups participate to come to a consensus on the budget? What are the advantages of this approach?

PROBLEM 6-11 *Objs. 4, 6*

Budgeting Culture and Behavior

Bob Haskins is the purchasing manager for Regal Products. Each year Regal Products develops a master budget. Bob is responsible for preparing a purchasing budget, which he bases on budgeted levels of production. Bob carefully plans purchasing costs and raw material inventory levels to meet production needs.

Each year, Yvonne Lang, president of Regal Products, conducts performance evaluations, and bonuses are paid to key employees, including Bob, based on meeting budgeted results. For the past two years, Bob has received a very small bonus and has been chided by Yvonne for poor planning. Specifically, Yvonne has pointed out that the purchasing department has not maintained adequate levels of raw material inventory and is always in a rush to obtain materials, resulting in increased shipping and handling charges. Further, Regal must often pay premium amounts for immediate shipment of materials. In her most recent evaluation, Yvonne stated to Bob, "The sales department and production department are doing an excellent job. They consistently exceed their budgets by 10% or more. I just don't understand why you can't meet your numbers. Perhaps it is time for some changes around here."

After getting chided by Yvonne, Bob went back and looked at his budget. He knew he had ordered the amount required by the budget. The budget for January and February is as follows:

	January	February
Finished goods to produce	300,000	350,000
Add: Desired ending inventory	35,000	25,000
Subtotal	335,000	375,000
Less: Beginning inventory	30,000	35,000
Total	305,000	340,000
Pounds of raw materials per unit	1.1	1.1
Required pounds of raw materials	335,500	374,000
Add: Desired ending inventory of raw materials	37,400	27,500
Less: Beginning inventory of raw materials	33,550	37,400
Total raw material needs	339,350	364,100

Required

A. If sales and production levels were 10% higher than budgeted, how many pounds of raw materials would Bob need to rush order each month so he can meet demand and the required ending inventory as shown in the budget?
B. Why does it appear that the purchasing department is having trouble meeting its budget?
C. Is it appropriate to blame Bob for all of the purchasing problems?
D. If Yvonne does "make some changes," what changes would you suggest she consider?

PROBLEM 6-12 *Objs. 4, 6*

Budgeting Culture and Behavior

Sue is the purchasing manager for Paper Goods Incorporated. Sue's budget for January and February were as follows:

	January	February
Finished goods to produce	10,000	11,000
Add: Desired ending inventory	1,100	1,100
Subtotal	11,100	12,100
Less: Beginning inventory	1,000	1,100
Total	10,100	11,000
Pounds of raw materials per unit	2.0	2.0
Required pounds of raw materials	20,200	22,000
Add: Desired ending inventory of raw materials	2,200	2,200
Less: Beginning inventory of raw materials	2,020	2,200
Total raw material needs	20,380	22,000

(Continued)

At the end of February, Sue's boss asked her, "Why are you ordering so many materials? The inventory stockroom is overflowing with materials." Puzzled, Sue checked her order amounts and saw that she had ordered the exact amount as stated by the budget. Sue then spoke to the production manager who explained that the plant had only been running at 90% capacity for the past two months due to lower demand.

Required

A. If sales and production levels were 10% lower than budgeted, how many pounds of raw materials are on hand at the end of February?

B. What is the problem with this system and how would you suggest it be improved?

PROBLEM 6-13 Sales Budget, Strategic Considerations

Objs. 2, 7

A new high tech product was launched in July. This is the first product of its type in the marketplace. The budget for this product is as follows:

	July	August
Expected sales in units	2,000	3,000
Selling price per unit	$50	$50
Total sales	$100,000	$150,000

However, the actual sales were not quite as high as was anticipated. The actual sales were:

	July	August
Actual sales in units	1,000	2,500
Selling price per unit	$50	$50
Total sales	$50,000	$125,000

Mary, the vice president of finance, spoke harshly to John, the product manager, for not meeting the budgeted amounts. She threatened to kill the product if John did not meet budgeted sales for September. Mary also wants to know how much cash would have been collected if the budgeted sales had been achieved.

Required

A. Create a schedule of cash collections for the budgeted sales for July and August. Assume that 80% of sales are collected in the month of sale and the remaining 20% of sales are collected the following month.

B. What strategic considerations should Mary take into account? Explain.

PROBLEM 6-14 Purchasing Budget, Strategic Considerations

Objs. 2, 7

Noise Hollow launched a new stereo in January. The budget for the stereo is as follows:

	January	February
Product to produce	1,000	1,500
Add: Desired ending inventory	300	400
Subtotal	1,300	1,900
Less: Beginning inventory	0	300
Total	1,300	1,600
Units of materials per finished good	10	10
Required units of materials	13,000	16,000
Cost of materials per unit	5	5
Total purchasing costs	65,000	80,000

Actual units of materials required per finished good were 12 units in January and 11 units in February. Actual cost of materials was $6 per unit in January and $5.50 per unit in February.

Required

A. Show what the budget would have looked like with the actual material requirements and costs.
B. What strategic considerations should be taken into account when reviewing this product?

PROBLEM 6-15 Labor Requirement Planning, Service Provider

Objs. 2, 8

Ceco Grass Care is a small lawn maintenance service that provides a variety of landscapte services. A large part of Ceco's sales are generated through lawn maintenance. Jeff Roberts manages Ceco. Jeff has reviewed the job order log for the next 12 weeks (three months ending July 26, 2001), and the log is full. Ceco recently acquired several commercial property accounts and has plenty of work planned. A summary of accounts shows that Ceco now has 11 commercial properties and 45 residential properties to maintain on a routine basis.

Each property is scheduled for maintenance every two weeks. The commercial accounts require 16 worker-hours to service, and the residential accounts require four worker-hours.

Ceco currently has a cutting crew of three, each of whom is paid $8.50 an hour.

Required

A. Prepare a direct labor budget for Ceco covering the next three months.
B. Does the budget raise any concerns for Ceco? Explain your answer.

PROBLEM 6-16 Excel in Action

CDTech expects to sell 500,000 CDs per month, including 400,000 data CDs and 100,000 music CDs. The selling price per unit is $2.20 for data CDs and $3.20 for music CDs. The desired level of ending inventory of raw materials is 5,000 units for blank CDs, containers, and cellophane wrap. Wrap is measured in feet, and each unit requires one foot of wrap. Paper inserts are obtained as needed, and the desired ending inventory is zero for these materials. At the beginning of May, CDTech has 10,000 blank CDs, 2,000 containers, and 20,000 feet of cellophane in stock. The cost per unit of raw materials is $0.72 for CDs, $0.12 for containers, $0.07 for inserts, and $0.01 per foot of cellophane. Direct labor hours to produce each CD is .023 for copying and 0.015 for packaging. Direct labor cost is $12 per hour for copying and $8 per hour for packaging.

Required Use the data provided to prepare a (1) sales budget, (2) direct materials budget, and (3) direct labor budget for CDTech for May. Use the following format. Use cell references and formulas where possible.

(Continued)

	A	B	C	D	E	F
1	Monthly Sales Budget					
2		Data	Music	Total		
3	Expected sales in units					
4	Selling price per unit					
5	Total sales					
6						
7	Direct Materials Budget					
8		CDs	Containers	Inserts	Cellophane	Total
9	Expected sales					
10	Desired ending inventory					
11	Total needs					
12	Beginning inventory					
13	Units to purchase					
14	Cost per unit					
15	Cost of materials					
16						
17	Direct Labor Budget					
18		Copying	Packaging	Total		
19	Units to produce					
20	Direct labor hour per unit					
21	Total hours					
22	Direct labor cost per hour					
23	Total direct labor cost					

Use appropriate formatting for numbers.

If expected sales were 350,000 data CDs and 200,000 music CDs, what would be the effect on the budgets?

PROBLEM 6-17 Multiple-Choice Overview of the Chapter

1. Which of the following represents the correct order in which the budget documents for a manufacuring company would be prepared?
   a. Sales budget, cash budget, direct materials budget, direct labor budget
   b. Production budget, sales budget, direct materials budget, direct labor budget
   c. Sales budget, cash budget, production budget, direct materials budget
   d. Production budget, direct labor budget, cash budget, pro forma financial statements

2. Which of the following is not included as one of the four major sections of the cash budget?
   a. The receipts section
   b. The financing section
   c. The selling and administrative expense section
   d. The cash excess or deficiency section

3. A major advantage of budgeting is that it
   a. eliminates major uncertainties associated with the business environment.
   b. ensures that management's objectives will be met.
   c. requires managers to give priority to the planning process.
   d. eliminates the need for stringent controls.

4. Which of the following is *not* correct with respect to the manufacturing overhead budget?
   a. Total budgeted cash expenses for manufacturing overhead are equal to total budgeted variable overhead plus total budgeted fixed overhead.
   b. Manufacturing overhead should be broken down by cost behavior.
   c. The manufacturing overhead budget should include all costs of production other than direct materials and direct labor.
   d. The budgeted variable cost of manufacturing overhead is dependent on the number of units to be produced, as shown in the production budget.

5. Budgeted production needs are computed by
   a. adding budgeted sales to the desired ending inventory and deducting the beginning inventory.
   b. adding budgeted sales to beginning inventory and deducting the desired ending inventory
   c. adding budgeted sales to the desired ending inventory.
   d. deducting beginning inventory from budgeted sales.

6. Which of the following represents a problem requiring special consideration when preparing budgets for multinational companies?
   a. The country in which the company is incorporated
   b. Foreign currency exchange rates
   c. Shipping and transportation of goods
   d. Most favored nation (MFN) trade status

7. Which of the following is *not* true with respect to a participative budgeting process?
   a. Participative budgeting requires less managerial involvement.
   b. Participative budgeting motivates managers by involving them in the budget process.
   c. Participative budgeting requires greater coordination between departments and disciplines.
   d. Participative budgeting relies on a bottom-up approach.

8. Which of the following statements is *not* correct?
   a. The strategic importance of budgets in decision making is affected by product life cycle stages.
   b. Operating budgets ordinarily are prepared for a year at a time and ignore monthly or quarterly amounts.
   c. Continuous, or perpetual, budgets cover a 12-month period and constantly add a new month or quarter on the end as the current month or quarter is completed.
   d. Continuous, or perpetual, budgets require managers to constantly think and plan a full 12 months ahead.

9. Identifying the costs that are to be controlled by a specific manager is
   a. an example of a top-down approach to budgeting.
   b. referred to as responsibility accounting.
   c. a way of ensuring that organizational policies are consistent.
   d. not necessary for the budgeting process.

10. Planning involves
   a. the development of future objectives and the preparation of budgets to achieve these objectives.
   b. the steps taken to ensure that objectives set down by management are attained.
   c. the steps taken to ensure that all parts of the organization function in a manner consistent with organizational policies.
   d. comparing budgeted to actual results and investigating variations.

Cases

CASE 6-1 The Master Budget

Obj. 2

The Columbo Company manufactures a single model trench coat sold throughout the United States. Projected sales in units for the first five months of 2001 are as follows:

January	35,000
February	20,000
March	15,000
April	8,000
May	6,000

The following information relates to Columbo's production and inventory policies and balances:

1. Finished goods inventory is maintained at 80% of the following month's sales. Finished goods inventory at January 1, 2001, was 28,000 units.
2. Two materials are required for each trench coat manufactured, as follows:

Direct Materials	Yards per Unit	Cost per Yard
Polyester	5	$8
Lining material	3	2

   Raw materials inventory is maintained at 10% of the following month's production needs. Inventory at January 1, 2001, was 51,000 yards of polyester and 30,600 yards of lining.

3. Direct labor used per unit is two hours. The average rate for labor is $9.50 per hour.
4. Overhead each month is estimated using a flexible budget format, with direct labor hours as the basis for variable costs. A summary of expected overhead costs is as follows:

	Fixed-Cost Component	Variable-Cost Component
Factory supplies		$1.00
Utilities		.75
Shop maintenance	$ 3,000	.50
Supervision	4,000	
Depreciation	60,000	
Taxes	5,000	
Other	10,000	2.00
Total	$ 82,000	$4.25

5. Selling, general, and administrative expenses are also calculated on a flexible budget basis based on the number of units sold. Cost estimates are as follows:

	Fixed-Cost Component	Variable-Cost Component
Salaries	$18,000	
Commissions		$3.00
Depreciation	22,000	
Shipping		.75
Other	10,000	1.50
Total	$50,000	$5.25

6. Each trench coat sells for $85.
7. All purchases are made in cash. All sales are on account. Collection of accounts receivable is planned as follows: 90% in the month of sale; 10% in the month following the month

of sale. The accounts receivable balance at January 1, 2001, is $145,000, all of which is collectible. The cash balance at January 1, 2001, is $202,000.

Required Prepare the following portions of the operating master budget, by month, for the first quarter of 2001:

A. Sales budget
B. Production budget
C. Direct materials budget
D. Direct labor budget
E. Overhead budget
F. Selling, general, and administrative expense budget
G. Cash budget
H. Suppose Columbo's management believes that unseasonably warm weather in March and April could cause its sales in units to differ from the original projections as follows:

January	35,000
February	20,000
March	10,000
April	6,000
May	6,000

Explain how these fluctuations in sales will affect the other portions of the master budget developed in the previous requirements. What are the implications for the importance of forecasting sales accurately?

CASE 6-2 Budgeting in a Service Company

Objs. 7, 8

Juanita Testor owns and operates a hair salon under the name Clips n' Curls. There are currently seven hair stylists, including Juanita. In addition to hair styling, Clips n' Curls sells nail care, facials, skin and hair care products, fashion jewelry, and tanning bed time.

A full-time receptionist is employed to arrange appointments and perform other clerical duties, such as counter sales and record keeping. The receptionist is paid $1,500 a month.

Juanita has eight styling bays, each equipped with a sink, cabinet, and vacuum system. Each stylist provides his or her own instruments. Each stylist, including Juanita, "rents" a bay at a cost of $400 per month. Charges for all client services are billed and collected by the receptionist, who accumulates totals for each stylist. Collections for services are paid to the stylists on a weekly basis after deducting bay rent and cost of supplies. Any supplies used by the stylists must be purchased through the shop, at Juanita's cost.

Nail care and facials are offered on a limited basis three days a week by a single individual, who receives 50% of collected billings as compensation. The tanning bed is owned by the shop. All income received from the bed goes to the shop. Variable shop costs are incurred based on the number of stylists. Based on a two-year study, Juanita has assembled the following information on monthly activity and costs to operate Clip n' Curl:

Average monthly billings per stylist	$4,000
Average product sales	600
Average gross margin on product sales	55%
Average gross nail and facial billings	$1,000
Average gross tanning bed billings	450
Fixed operating costs:	
Shop rent	500
Depreciation	400
Advertising	150
Other	100
Variable operating costs	
Maintenance, utilities, and other	1,400*

**Note: Variable operating costs are incurred as follows: 50% by stylists, 30% by tanning and nails, 15% by product display, and 5% administrative.*

(Continued)

Required

A. Assume that Juanita can hire an additional stylist who can generate the same average amount of business as the other stylists. Assume also that the additional stylist would have no impact on administrative expenses. What would be the change in average monthly shop income if Juanita hires the stylist to fill the remaining open bay? (*Hint:* Compare the change in revenues with the change in costs related to the incremental increase of one stylist.)

B. What is the average total monthly income of the shop given the number of stylists currently employed?

C. Juanita is considering a change in the bay rent agreement. Instead of charging a fixed amount per month, she is thinking of charging a stylist 12% of the stylist's billings. Would Juanita be better off with this new fee arrangement? Explain your answer.

11

Working Capital Management

A MANAGERIAL PERSPECTIVE

In December 1993, Trans World Airlines (TWA) was labeled the best domestic airline for long flights and the second best for short flights by U.S. business travelers. TWA received this accolade just one month after emerging from bankruptcy. Its future seemed rosy—employees had agreed to salary concessions in exchange for an equity position in the company, the airline had restructured its liabilities and lowered its cost structure, and the employees, with their new ownership position, appeared to possess a new-found motivation and concern for company success.

Unfortunately, the nation's seventh largest airline soon discovered that its "new lease on life" was not a long-term contract. By the summer of 1994, TWA was struggling to find ways to cover a $135 million shortfall expected for the year. Many analysts believed that the company was headed toward a second—and perhaps final—bankruptcy, primarily because it was in an extremely precarious position with respect to liquidity. The company's cash reserves were not sufficient to carry TWA through the lean sales that were expected during the coming months, and analysts were very pessimistic that needed funds could be raised by issuing stock or bonds or by selling off assets. Investors also recognized TWA's liquidity problems—the company's stock price fell about 50 percent in less than four months. It was obvious that TWA needed to improve its liquidity position to ensure its survival. The answer for the firm—reducing its costs by laying off employees, eliminating some of its flights, and replacing outdated airplanes with more fuel-efficient airplanes.

TWA emerged from its second bankruptcy and regained its status as the best domestic airline for long flights, but its financial position was still very tenuous. Unforeseen circumstances, including a tragic crash and labor difficulties, resulted in large losses in the late 1990s. For instance, in 1996, TWA lost $285 million; in 1997, the firm's loss amounted to $110 million. Nevertheless, TWA took actions to improve its liquidity position. In 1998, its revenues

(Continued)

began to increase at the same time that its operating expenses decreased, which helped boost its cash and other liquid assets by nearly 33 percent. Unfortunately, the benefits of these actions were short-lived—TWA filed for bankruptcy protection again at the beginning of 2001. In April 2001, the company was acquired by American Airlines.

All firms strive to maintain a balance between current assets and current liabilities, and between sales and each category of current assets, in an effort to provide sufficient liquidity to survive—that is, to live to maximize value in the future. As long as a good balance is maintained, current liabilities can be paid on time, suppliers will continue to provide needed inventories, and companies will be able to meet sales demands. If the financial situation gets out of balance, liquidity problems surface and often multiply into more serious problems, and perhaps even bankruptcy. As you read this chapter, consider how important liquidity—and thus proper management of working capital—is to the survival of a firm. Also, consider the fact that many start-up firms never make it past the first few months of business, primarily because they lack formal working capital policies.

working capital management The management of short-term assets (investments) and liabilities (financing sources).

This chapter describes *short-term financial management,* also termed **working capital management,** which involves decisions that relate to the current (short-term) assets and current (short-term) liabilities of a firm. As you read this chapter, you will realize that a firm's value cannot be maximized in the long run unless it survives in the short run. The primary reason that firms fail is because they are unable to meet their working capital needs. Consequently, *sound working capital management is a requisite for firm survival.*

WORKING CAPITAL TERMINOLOGY

It is useful to begin the discussion of working capital policy by reviewing some basic definitions and concepts:

working capital A firm's investment in short-term assets—cash, marketable securities, inventory, and accounts receivable.

net working capital Current assets minus current liabilities; the amount of current assets financed by long-term liabilities.

working capital policy Decisions regarding the target levels for each current asset account and the way in which current assets will be financed.

1. The term **working capital,** sometimes called gross working capital, generally refers to current assets.
2. **Net working capital** is defined as current assets minus current liabilities, with the *current ratio* being calculated by dividing current assets by current liabilities. Both measures are intended to measure a firm's liquidity. Neither a high current ratio nor a positive net working capital actually ensures that a firm will have the cash required to meet its needs. If inventories cannot be sold, or if receivables cannot be collected in a timely manner, then the apparent safety reflected by these measures could be illusory. The best way to get a comprehensive picture of a firm's liquidity position is to examine its *cash budget,* which forecasts cash inflows and outflows. The cash budget focuses on the firm's ability to generate sufficient cash inflows to meet its required cash outflows. Cash budgeting was discussed in Chapter 8.
3. **Working capital policy** refers to the firm's basic policies regarding (a) its target levels for each category of current assets and (b) the way in which current assets will be financed.
4. Only those current liabilities that are specifically used to finance current assets are included in working capital decisions. Current liabilities that resulted from

past long-term debt financing decisions are not working capital decision variables in the current period. Examples include the following: (a) the current maturities of long-term debt; (b) the financing associated with a construction program that will be funded with the proceeds of a long-term security issue after the project is completed; and (c) the use of short-term debt to finance fixed assets. Although such accounts are not part of the working capital decision process, they cannot be ignored because they are *due* in the current period. As a result, they must be taken into account when managers assess the firm's ability to meet its current obligations using expected cash inflows.

SELF-TEST QUESTION

Why is it important to properly manage short-term assets and liabilities?

THE REQUIREMENT FOR EXTERNAL WORKING CAPITAL FINANCING

In this section and throughout the chapter, we will use the financial statements of Argile Textiles, the North Carolina textile manufacturer that was introduced in Chapter 7, to illustrate working capital analyses and decisions. First, we will examine balance sheets constructed for Argile at three different dates, which are given in Table 15-1. According to the definitions given earlier, Argile's December 31, 2002, working capital was $235.2 million, its net working capital was $170.2 million, and its current ratio was 3.6. Argile's operations are very seasonal, typically peaking in September and October. Thus, at the end of September, Argile's inventories are significantly higher than they are at the end of the calendar year. As a result of this sales surge, Argile's accounts receivable balance is much higher at the end of September than it is at the end of December.

Consider what is expected to happen to Argile's current assets and current liabilities from December 31, 2002, to September 30, 2003. Current assets are expected to increase from $235.2 million to $345.0 million, or by $109.8 million; this growth must be supported with new financing. The higher volume of purchases, plus labor expenditures associated with increased production, will cause the firm's accounts payable and accruals to increase spontaneously from a total of $45 million ($15 million payables and $30 million accruals) to $95 million ($45 million payables and $50 million accruals), or by only $50 million. This increase leaves a projected $59.8 million current asset financing requirement—the amount not covered by the increase in payables and accruals. Argile expects to finance this requirement primarily through a $44.5 million increase in notes payable (from $20 million to $64.5 million). Note that from December 2002 to September 2003, Argile's net working capital is expected to increase from $170.2 million to $185.5 million, but its current ratio is expected to decline from 3.6 to 2.2. This shift occurs because most, but not all, of the funds invested in current assets are expected to come from current liabilities. Thus, *when the current ratio is greater than 1.0 and current liabilities increase (decrease) by the same (or nearly the same) dollar amount as current assets, the current ratio decreases (increases).*

The fluctuations in Argile's working capital position shown in Table 15-1 result from seasonal variations. Similar fluctuations in working capital requirements, and hence in financing needs, also occur during business cycles. For example, working capital needs typically decline during recessions and increase during booms. For some companies, such as those involved in agricultural products, seasonal fluctuations are much greater than business cycle fluctuations. For other firms, such as

Table 15-1 Argile Textiles: Historical and Projected Financials ($ million)

	12/31/02 Historical	9/30/03 Projected	12/31/03 Projected
I. Balance Sheets			
Cash	$ 10.2	$ 15.0	$ 11.2
Accounts receivable	90.0	125.0	99.0
Inventories	135.0	205.0	148.5
Total current assets (CA)	$235.2	$345.0	$258.7
Net plant and equipment	190.0	205.0	209.0
Total Assets	$425.2	$550.0	$467.7
Accounts payable	$ 15.0	45.0	$ 16.5
Accruals	30.0	50.0	33.0
Notes payable	20.0	64.5	23.6
Total current liabilities (CL)	$ 65.0	$159.5	$ 73.1
Long-term bonds	152.2	152.5	157.0
Total liabilities	$217.2	$312.0	$230.1
Common stock	65.0	78.0	80.6
Retained earnings	143.0	160.0	157.0
Total owners' equity	$208.0	$238.0	$237.6
Total Liabilities and Equity	$425.2	$550.0	$467.7
Net working capital = CA − CL	$170.2	$185.5	$185.6
Current ratio = CA/CL	3.6×	2.2×	3.6×
	2002		**2003**
II. Partial Income Statements			
Sales	$750.0		$825.0
Cost of goods sold	(600.0)		(660.0)
Fixed costs	(85.0)		(93.5)
Earnings before interest and taxes	$ 65.0		$ 71.5

appliance or automobile manufacturers, cyclical fluctuations are larger. In the following sections, we will look in more detail at the requirement for working capital financing and examine some alternative working capital policies.

SELF-TEST QUESTION

Under normal circumstances, when does a firm's working capital position change? Explain why.

THE CASH CONVERSION CYCLE

To summarize the working capital management process that Argile Textiles and most other companies face, consider the following activities:

1. Argile orders and then receives materials that it needs to produce the products that its sells. The company purchases from its suppliers on credit, so an account payable is created for the credit purchase. The purchase has no immediate cash flow effect, because payment is not made until some later date.
2. Labor is used to convert the materials (cotton and wool) into finished goods (cloth products, thread, and so forth). Wages are not fully paid at the time

when the work is done, so accrued wages will build up (perhaps for a period of one or two weeks).

3. The finished products are sold, but on credit. Thus sales create receivables, not immediate cash inflows.
4. At some point during the cycle, Argile pays its suppliers and employees. If these payments are made before Argile has collected cash from its receivables, a net cash outflow will occur, and the firm must finance this outflow.
5. The cycle is completed when Argile's receivables are collected (perhaps in 30 days). At that time, the company is in a position to pay off the credit that was used to finance production of its products, and it can then repeat the cycle.

The activities outlined here give an indication of the relationships among the various working capital accounts. To illustrate these relationships, we can formalize the process Argile faces by examining its **cash conversion cycle,** which focuses on the length of time between when the company makes cash payments, or invests in the manufacture of inventory, and when it receives cash inflows, or realizes a cash return from its investment in production.[1] The following terms are used in the model:

cash conversion cycle
The length of time from the payment for the purchase of raw materials to manufacture a product until the collection of accounts receivable associated with the sale of that product.

1. The *inventory conversion period* is the average length of time required to convert materials into finished goods and then to sell those goods; it is the amount of time that the product remains in inventory in various stages of completion. The inventory conversion period is calculated as follows:

15-1

$$\text{Inventory conversion period} = \frac{\text{Inventory}}{\left(\text{Cost of goods sold per day}\right)} = \frac{\text{Inventory}}{\left(\dfrac{\text{Annual cost of goods sold}}{360}\right)}$$

Because Argile's cost of goods sold was \$600 million in 2002, its inventory conversion period would be[2]

$$\text{Argile's inventory conversion period} = \frac{\$135.0\text{ million}}{\left(\dfrac{\$600\text{ million}}{360}\right)} = \frac{\$135.0}{\$1.667}$$

$$= 81.0\text{ days}$$

Thus, in its 2002 operations, it took Argile 81 days to manufacture and sell its products.

---

[1]See Verlyn Richards and Eugene Laughlin, "A Cash Conversion Cycle Approach to Liquidity Analysis," *Financial Management,* Spring 1980, 32–38.

[2]In the computations that follow, as well as other ratio computations in this book, we assume that there are 360 days in the year. This assumption is made to simplify computations only—360 is divisible by more integer values than 365. This assumption changes neither the meaning nor the application of the computations.

2. The *receivables collection period* is the average length of time required to convert the firm's receivables into cash—that is, to collect cash following a sale. The receivables collection period is also called the days sales outstanding (DSO), and it is calculated as follows:

15-2

$$\text{Receivables collection period} = \frac{\text{Receivables}}{\text{Average daily credit sales}} = \frac{\text{Receivables}}{\left(\dfrac{\text{Annual credit sales}}{360}\right)}$$

In 2002, Argile generated \$750 million in sales, so its DSO was

$$\text{Receivables collection period} = \frac{\$90 \text{ million}}{\left(\dfrac{\$750 \text{ million}}{360}\right)} = \frac{\$90}{\$2.083}$$

$$= 43.2 \text{ days}$$

Thus, on average, the cash payments associated with credit sales were not collected until approximately 43 days after the sale.

3. The *payables deferral period* is the average length of time between the purchase of raw materials and labor and the payment of cash for them. It is computed as follows:

15-3

$$\text{Payables deferral period} = \frac{\text{Accounts payable}}{\text{Average daily credit purchases}} = \frac{\text{Accounts payable}}{\left(\dfrac{\text{Cost of goods sold}}{360}\right)}$$

Argile's payables deferral period was

$$\text{Payable deferral period} = \frac{\$15 \text{ million}}{\left(\dfrac{\$600 \text{ million}}{360}\right)} = \frac{\$15}{\$1.667}$$

$$= 9.0 \text{ days}$$

Therefore, on average, Argile paid its suppliers nine days after materials were purchased.[3]

4. The *cash conversion cycle* computation nets out the three periods just defined, resulting in a value that equals the length of time from when the firm pays for (invests in) productive resources (materials and labor) and when it receives cash (a return) from the sale of products. In summary, the cash

[3]The computation for the payables deferral period shown here is the traditional method used to determine the value used in the calculation of the cash conversion cycle. If we recognize that the intention of the computation is to determine the length of time between the purchase of raw materials *and* the labor used to produce inventory and the payment for these inputs, then the payables deferral period might more appropriately be written to include consideration of accrued wages.

conversion cycle equals the average length of time that a dollar remains tied up in current assets.

We can now use these definitions to analyze Argile's cash conversion cycle. First, the concept is diagramed in Figure 15-1. Each component is given a number, and the cash conversion cycle can be expressed by the following equation:

15-4

$$\text{Cash conversion cycle} = \left(\text{Inventory conversion period} + \text{Receivables collection period}\right) - \text{Payables deferral period}$$

$$= 81.0 \text{ days} + 43.2 \text{ days} - 9.0 \text{ days}$$

$$= 115.2 \text{ days}$$

In this case, the cash conversion cycle is approximately 115 days. The *receipt* of cash from manufacturing and selling the products will be delayed by more than 124 days because (1) the product will be "tied up" in inventory for 81 days, and (2) cash from the sale will not be received until about 43 days after the selling date. The *disbursement* of cash for the raw materials purchased will be delayed by nine days, however, because Argile does not pay cash for the raw materials when they are purchased. As a result, the net delay in cash receipts associated with an investment (cash disbursement) in inventory is 115 days, which is nearly one-third of a year.

The firm's goal should be to shorten its cash conversion cycle as much as possible without hurting operations. This effort would improve profits because the longer the cash conversion cycle, the greater the need for external financing—such as bank loans—and such financing has a cost. The firm can shorten its cash conversion cycle by (1) reducing the inventory conversion period by processing and selling goods more quickly, (2) reducing the receivables collection period by speeding up collections, and (3) lengthening the payables deferral period by slowing down payments made to suppliers. To the extent that these actions can be taken *without harming the return* associated with the management of these accounts, they should be carried out. More specific actions that can be taken to

Figure 15-1 The Cash Conversion Cycle

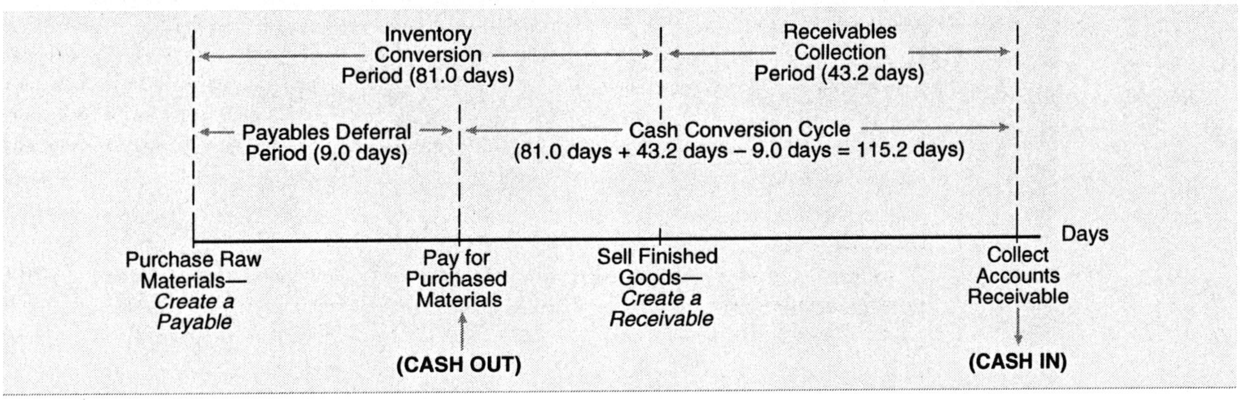

reduce the length of the cash conversion cycle are discussed later in the chapter. As you read the chapter, you should keep the cash conversion cycle concept in mind.

SELF-TEST QUESTIONS

What steps are involved in estimating the cash conversion cycle?

Define the following terms: inventory conversion period; receivables collection period; payables deferral period.

What is the cash conversion cycle model? How can it be used to improve current asset management?

WORKING CAPITAL INVESTMENT AND FINANCING POLICIES

Working capital policy involves two basic questions:

- What is the appropriate level for current assets, both in total and for specific accounts?
- How should current assets be financed?

Alternative Current Asset Investment Policies

relaxed current asset investment policy
A policy in which relatively large amounts of cash and marketable securities and inventories are carried, and sales are stimulated by a liberal credit policy that results in a high level of receivables.

restricted current asset investment policy
A policy in which holdings of cash and marketable securities, inventories, and receivables are minimized.

moderate current asset investment policy
A policy that lies between the relaxed and restrictive current asset investment policies.

Figure 15-2 depicts three alternative policies for the total amount of current assets carried. Essentially, these policies differ in that different amounts of current assets are carried to support any given level of sales. The line with the steepest slope represents a **relaxed current asset investment** (or "fat cat") **policy,** in which relatively large amounts of cash, marketable securities, and inventories are carried and sales are stimulated by the use of a credit policy that provides liberal financing to customers and a corresponding high level of receivables. With the **restricted current asset investment** (or "lean-and-mean") **policy,** the amounts of current assets are minimized. The **moderate current asset investment policy** lies between these two extremes.

The more certain a firm is about its sales, costs, order lead times, payment periods, and so forth, the lower the level of current assets it requires to support operations. If there is a great deal of uncertainty about operations, however, the firm will require some minimum amount of cash and inventories based on expected payments, expected sales, expected order lead times, and so on, plus additional amounts, or *safety stocks,* that enable it to deal with departures from the expected values. Similarly, accounts receivable levels are determined by credit terms: The tougher the credit terms, the lower the accounts receivable for any given level of sales. With a restricted current asset investment policy, the firm would hold minimal levels of safety stocks for cash and inventories, and it would have a tight credit policy even though it would mean running the risk of losing sales. A restricted, lean-and-mean current asset investment policy generally provides the highest expected return on investment, but it entails the greatest risk. The reverse is true under a relaxed policy. The moderate policy falls in between the two extremes in terms of both expected risk and return.

In terms of the cash conversion cycle, a restricted investment policy would tend to reduce the inventory conversion and accounts receivable collection periods, resulting in a relatively short cash conversion cycle. Conversely, a relaxed policy would create higher levels of inventories and accounts receivable, longer

Figure 15-2 Alternative Current Asset Investment Policies ($ million)

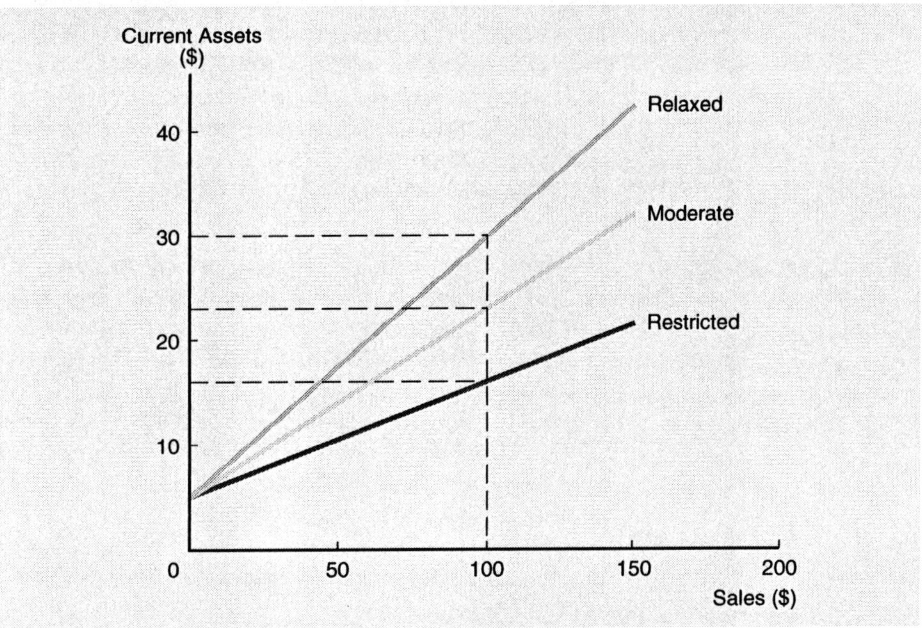

Policy	Current Assets to Support Sales of $100
Relaxed	$30
Moderate	23
Restricted	16

Note: The sales/current assets relationship is shown here as being linear, but the relationship is often curvilinear.

inventory conversion and accounts receivable collection periods, and a relatively long cash conversion cycle. A moderate policy would produce a cash conversion cycle somewhere between the two extremes.

Alternative Current Asset Financing Policies

permanent current assets
Current assets' balances that do not change due to seasonal or economic conditions. These balances exist even at the trough of a firm's business cycle.

temporary current assets
Current assets that fluctuate with seasonal or economic variations in a firm's business.

Most businesses experience seasonal fluctuations, cyclical fluctuations, or both. For example, construction firms have peaks in the spring and summer, retailers peak around Christmas, and the manufacturers that supply both construction companies and retailers follow similar patterns. Similarly, virtually all businesses must build up current assets when the economy is strong, but they then sell off inventories and have net reductions of accounts receivable when the economy slacks off. Even so, current assets rarely drop to zero, and this realization has led to the development of the idea that some current assets should be considered **permanent current assets** because their levels remain stable no matter the seasonal or economic conditions.

Temporary current assets, on the other hand, are those amounts of current assets that vary with respect to the seasonal or economic conditions of a firm. During off-season periods, temporary assets will be zero; during peak-season periods, they will be very high. Table 15-1 shows that the level of current assets for Argile Textiles is expected to be $345 million in September 2003 and only $258.7 in December 2003. Because the height of Argile's selling season occurs in the fall, most of the difference between the levels of current assets at these two dates results from changes in temporary current assets.

The manner in which the permanent and temporary current assets are financed is called the firm's *current asset financing policy.* In general, the approach that a firm uses to finance its current assets is referred to as either *maturity matching, aggressive,* or *conservative.*

maturity matching (self-liquidating) approach A financing policy that matches asset and liability maturities—considered a moderate current asset financing policy.

Maturity Matching (Self-Liquidating) Approach The **maturity matching, or "self-liquidating," approach** calls for matching asset and liability maturities. This strategy minimizes the risk that the firm will be unable to pay off its maturing obligations *if* the liquidations of the assets can be controlled to occur on or before the obligations reach maturity. At the limit, a firm could attempt to match exactly the maturity structure of its assets and liabilities. Inventory expected to be sold in 30 days could be financed with a 30-day bank loan; a machine expected to last for five years could be financed by a five-year loan; and so forth. Of course, two factors make it impossible to match maturities exactly: (1) There is uncertainty about the lives of assets, thus when cash inflows will be received; and (2) some common equity, which has no maturity, must be used to finance the firm.

aggressive approach A policy in which all of the fixed assets of a firm are financed with long-term capital, but some of the firm's permanent current assets are financed with short-term, nonspontaneous sources of funds.

Aggressive Approach A firm that follows the **aggressive approach** finances *all* of its fixed assets and some of its permanent current assets with long-term capital; the remainder of the permanent current assets and all of the temporary current assets are financed with such short-term financing as bank loans. Several different *degrees* of aggressiveness are possible. For example, one firm might finance nearly all of its permanent current assets with short-term credit, while another firm might finance relatively little of its current permanent assets with the same type of credit. The aggressive approach is riskier than either of the other two approaches because the short-term credit used to finance the permanent current assets must be renewed each time it comes due. As a consequence, the firm faces the threat of rising interest rates as well as loan renewal problems. Because short-term debt often is less expensive than long-term debt, however, some firms are willing to sacrifice safety for the chance of higher profits.

conservative approach A policy in which all of the fixed assets, all of the permanent current assets, and some of the temporary current assets of a firm are financed with long-term capital.

Conservative Approach With the **conservative approach,** permanent, or long-term, capital is used to finance all permanent asset requirements and to meet some or all of the seasonal demands, and hence to finance temporary current assets. At the extreme, a firm could finance all of its seasonal needs with long-term financing alternatives, thereby eliminating the need to use short-term financing. This would be a difficult, if not impossible, task to accomplish. Most firms that follow this approach use some amounts of short-term credit to meet financing needs during peak-season periods. Even so, they will have "extra" permanent funds during off-peak periods, which allows them to "store liquidity" in the form of short-term investments, called marketable securities, during the off-season. As its name implies, this approach is a very safe, conservative current asset financing policy, and it generally is not as profitable as the other two approaches.

SELF-TEST QUESTIONS

What two key issues does working capital policy involve?

What are three alternative current asset investment policies? Is one best?

What are three alternative current asset financing policies? Is one best?

What distinguishes *permanent current assets* from *temporary current assets*?

ADVANTAGES AND DISADVANTAGES OF SHORT-TERM FINANCING

The three different financing policies just described are distinguished by the relative amounts of short-term debt used under each policy. The aggressive policy calls for the greatest use of short-term debt, the conservative policy requires the least, and maturity matching falls in between. This section considers some of the pros and cons of short-term financing.

Speed

A short-term loan can be obtained much faster than long-term credit. Lenders will insist on a more thorough financial examination before extending long-term credit, and the loan agreement will have to be spelled out in considerable detail, because much can happen during the life of a long-term loan.

Flexibility

If the needs for funds are seasonal or cyclical, a firm might not want to commit itself to long-term debt for three reasons:

- The cost of issuing long-term debt is considerably greater than the cost of using short-term credit.
- Some long-term loans charge expensive penalties for paying off the debt prior to maturity.
- Long-term loan agreements contain provisions, or covenants, that restrict the firm's future actions, whereas short-term credit agreements usually are much less onerous in this regard.

In general, then, short-term financing alternatives are more flexible than long-term financing alternatives.

Cost of Long-Term versus Short-Term Debt

As discussed in Chapter 5, the yield curve normally is upward sloping, indicating that interest rates generally are lower on short-term debt than on long-term debt. Thus interest costs normally will be lower if the firm borrows on a short-term rather than on a long-term basis.

Risk of Long-Term versus Short-Term Debt

A disadvantage of short-term debt is that it subjects the firm to more risk than does long-term debt. This greater risk occurs for two reasons:

- If a firm borrows on a long-term basis, its interest costs will be relatively stable—perhaps even fixed—over time. If it uses short-term credit, its interest expense will fluctuate, at times reaching very high levels.
- If a firm borrows heavily on a short-term basis, it could find itself unable to repay this debt, and it might be in such a weak financial position that the lender will not extend the loan. Such an event could force the firm into bankruptcy.

SELF-TEST QUESTIONS

What are some advantages of short-term debt over long-term debt as a source of capital?

What are some disadvantages of short-term debt?

SOURCES OF SHORT-TERM FINANCING

short-term credit
Any liability originally scheduled for repayment within one year.

Statements about the flexibility, cost, and riskiness of short-term debt versus long-term debt depend, to a large extent, on the type of short-term credit used. **Short-term credit** is defined as any liability originally scheduled for payment within one year. Numerous sources of short-term funds exist. In the following section, we briefly describe five major types: accruals, accounts payable (trade credit), bank loans, commercial paper, and secured short-term loans. In addition, we discuss the cost of short-term financing.

Accruals

accruals
Continually recurring short-term liabilities; liabilities such as wages and taxes that increase spontaneously with operations.

A firm generally pays employees on a weekly, biweekly, or monthly basis, so its balance sheet typically shows some accrued wages. Similarly, the firm's own estimated income taxes, the Social Security and income taxes withheld from employee payrolls, and the sales taxes collected generally are paid on a weekly, monthly, or quarterly basis, so the balance sheet typically also shows some accrued taxes. These **accruals** increase automatically, or spontaneously, as a firm's operations expand. This type of debt generally is considered "free" in the sense that no explicit interest is paid on funds raised through accruals. Ordinarily, a firm cannot control its accruals—the timing of wage payments is set by economic forces and industry custom, whereas tax payment dates are established by law.

Accounts Payable (Trade Credit)

trade credit
The credit created when one firm buys on credit from another firm.

Most firms purchase from their suppliers on credit, recording the debt as an *account payable.*[4] Representing approximately 40 percent of the current liabilities for the average nonfinancial corporation, this type of financing—called **trade credit**—is the largest single category of short-term debt. Trade credit is a *spontaneous* source of financing in the sense that it arises from ordinary business transactions. The amount of trade credit used by a firm depends on the terms of the

[4]In a credit sale, the seller records the transaction as a receivable, and the buyer records it as a payable. We examine accounts receivable as an investment later in the chapter. Note that if a firm's accounts payable exceed its accounts receivable, it is said to be *receiving net trade credit.* If its accounts receivable exceed its accounts payable, it is *extending net trade credit.* Smaller firms frequently receive net credit; larger firms generally extend it.

credit purchase and the size of the firm's operations. For example, lengthening the credit period, as well as expanding sales and purchases, generates additional trade credit.

Short-Term Bank Loans

Commercial banks, whose loans generally appear on a firm's balance sheet as notes payable, are second in importance to trade credit as a source of short-term financing.[5] The banks' influence actually is greater than it appears from the dollar amounts they lend, because banks provide *nonspontaneous* funds. That is, as a firm's financing needs increase, it specifically requests additional funds from its bank. If the request is denied, the firm might be forced to abandon attractive growth opportunities. Bank loans include the key features described next.

Maturity Bank loans to businesses frequently are written as 90-day notes, so the loan must be repaid or renewed at the end of 90 days. Of course, if a borrower's financial position has deteriorated at that point, the bank might refuse to renew the loan.

promissory note
A document specifying the terms and conditions of a loan, including the amount, interest rate, and repayment schedule.

compensating balance (CB)
A minimum checking account balance that a firm must maintain with a bank to borrow funds—generally 10 to 20 percent of the amount of loans outstanding.

line of credit
An arrangement in which a bank agrees to lend up to a specified maximum amount of funds during a designated period.

revolving credit agreement
A line of credit in which the funds are guaranteed, or committed, by the bank or other lending institution.

commitment fee
A fee charged on the *unused* balance of a revolving credit agreement to compensate the bank for guaranteeing that the funds will be available when needed by the borrower.

Promissory Note When a bank loan is approved, the agreement is executed by signing a **promissory note** that specifies (1) the amount borrowed, (2) the interest rate, (3) the repayment schedule, (4) whether collateral, or security, is required, and (5) any other terms and conditions to which the bank and the borrower have agreed.

Compensating Balances Banks often require a firm to maintain an average checking account balance, called a **compensating balance,** as a requirement of getting a loan. The funds that are used to maintain a compensating balance, which generally equals 10 to 20 percent of the loan amount, cannot be used by the firm to pay its bills or to invest. A compensating balance does not earn interest. As a result, a compensating balance essentially represents a charge by the bank for *servicing* the loan (bookkeeping, maintaining a line of credit, and so on).

Line of Credit A **line of credit** is an agreement between a bank and a borrower indicating the maximum credit that the bank will allow the borrower to have outstanding at any point in time. For example, a bank loan officer might indicate to a financial manager that the bank regards the firm as being "good" for a maximum of $200,000 during the forthcoming year. That is, the firm can have at most a $200,000 balance of loans outstanding from this source at any time during the year. When a line of credit arrangement is *guaranteed,* it is called a **revolving credit agreement.** With a revolving credit agreement, the bank has a *legal obligation* to provide funds requested by the borrower. The bank generally charges a **commitment fee** for guaranteeing the availability of the funds. This fee is usually charged on the unused balance of the credit line because, to guarantee that the funds will be available

[5]Although commercial banks remain the primary source of short-term loans, other sources are available. For example, in 2001 GE Capital Corporation (GECC) had several billion dollars in commercial loans outstanding. Firms such as GECC, which was initially established to finance consumers' purchases of GE's durable goods, often find business loans to be more profitable than consumer loans.

when requested, the funds must be accessed very quickly; as a consequence, the bank must invest these funds in liquid instruments that provide relatively low returns. Neither the legal obligation nor the fee exists under a "regular" credit line, because this type of credit provides the funds only if they are available at the bank.

Commercial Paper

commercial paper Unsecured, short-term promissory notes issued by large, financially sound firms to raise funds.

Commercial paper is a type of unsecured promissory note *issued* by large, strong firms. It is sold primarily to other firms, insurance companies, pension funds, money market mutual funds, and banks. The use of commercial paper is restricted to a comparatively small number of firms that are *exceptionally* good credit risks. Maturities of commercial paper vary from one to nine months, with an average of about five months.[6] Using commercial paper permits a corporation to tap a wider range of credit sources, including financial institutions across the country, which can reduce interest costs. One potential problem with commercial paper is that a debtor who is in temporary financial difficulty might receive little help, because commercial paper dealings generally are less personal than are bank relationships.

Secured Loans

secured loan A loan backed by collateral. For short-term loans, the collateral often consists of inventory, receivables, or both.

pledging receivables Using accounts receivable as collateral for a loan.

factoring The outright sale of accounts receivable.

recourse A situation in which the lender can seek payment from the borrowing firm when the accounts receivable used to secure a loan are uncollectable.

Most loans can be secured, or collateralized, if it is deemed necessary or desirable. Given a choice, it is usually better to borrow on an unsecured basis because the bookkeeping costs of **secured loans** often are high. Nevertheless, weak firms might find that they can borrow only if they put up some type of security or that using security allows them to borrow at a lower rate.

Most secured short-term business loans involve the use of short-term assets, such as accounts receivable and inventories, as collateral. When receivables are used as collateral, the firm is said to be **pledging** its receivables. Sometimes, receivables are actually *sold* to financial institutions. With this arrangement, the firm is said to be **factoring** its receivables, and the buyer is called a *factor.* A principal difference between the two arrangements is that when receivables are pledged, the lender has both a claim against the receivables and **recourse** to the borrower. Thus, if one of the borrowing firm's credit customers, which represents an account receivable, does not pay, the borrowing firm rather than the lending institution takes the loss. With most factoring arrangements, the factor that buys the receivables must take the loss. Therefore, it is not uncommon for the factor to provide a credit department for the borrower to carry out the credit investigation of its customers.

A substantial amount of credit is secured by business inventories. If a firm is a relatively good credit risk, the mere existence of the inventory might be a sufficient basis for receiving an unsecured loan. If the firm is a relatively poor risk, the lending institution might insist on security in the form of a *lien* against the inventory. The three major types of inventory liens include the following:

1. A *blanket lien* gives the lending institution a lien against all of the borrower's inventories without limiting the borrower's ability to sell the inventories. This

---

[6]The maximum maturity without SEC registration is 270 days. Also, commercial paper can be sold only to "sophisticated" investors; otherwise, SEC registration would be required even for maturities of 270 days or less.

type of lien generally is used when the inventory put up as collateral is relatively low priced, fast moving, and difficult to identify individually.

2. A ***trust receipt*** is an arrangement in which the goods are held in trust for the lender, perhaps stored in a public warehouse or held on the premises of the borrower. Such an arrangement generally is used for goods that are relatively high priced, slow moving, and easy to identify individually using serial numbers or some other distinguishing characteristic. When the goods that are affected by this lien are sold, proceeds from the sale must be given to the lender. Automobile dealer financing is one of the best examples of trust receipt financing.
3. ***Warehouse receipt*** financing refers to an arrangement in which inventory used as collateral is physically separated from the borrower's other inventory and then stored in a secured site located either on the premises of the borrower (***field warehousing***) or in an independent warehouse (***terminal warehousing***). To provide inventory supervision, the lending institution employs a third party in the arrangement—a warehousing company that acts as its agent in the oversight and the sale of the inventory.

SELF-TEST QUESTIONS

What types of short-term source of funds are classified as accruals?

What is trade credit?

How does a revolving line of credit differ from a regular line of credit?

What is commercial paper? What types of companies can use commercial paper to meet their short-term financing needs?

What is a secured loan? What two types of current assets are pledged as security for short-term loans?

Differentiate between pledging accounts receivable and factoring accounts receivable.

Describe three arrangements in which inventory is used as collateral for a short-term loan.

COMPUTING THE COST OF SHORT-TERM CREDIT

For short-term financing, the percentage cost of using the funds for a given period, r_{PER}, can be computed as follows:

15-5

$$\text{Percentage cost per period} = r_{PER} = \frac{\text{Dollar cost of borrowing}}{\text{Amount of usable funds}}$$

In this equation, the numerator represents the dollar amount that must be paid for using the borrowed funds. This cost includes the interest paid on the loan, application fees, charges for commitment fees, and so forth. The denominator represents the amount of the loan that actually can be used (spent) by the borrower. This amount is not necessarily the same as the principal amount of the loan, because discounts, compensating balances, or other costs might reduce the amount of the loan proceeds that the firm can use. In this section, we will see that when loan restrictions prevent the borrower from using the entire amount of the loan, the effective annual rate paid for the loan is higher than the stated interest rate.

Using Equation 15-5 and the concepts described in Chapter 9, the effective annual rate (EAR) and the annual percentage rate (ARR) for short-term financing can be computed as follows:

15-6

$$\text{Effective annual rate} = \text{EAR} = \left[1 + r_{PER}\right]^{m} - 1.0$$

15-7

$$\text{Annual percentage rate} = \text{APR} = r_{PER} \times m = i_{SIMPLE}$$

where m is the number of borrowing periods in one year (that is, if the loan is for one month, m = 12). Recall from our discussion in Chapter 9 that the EAR incorporates interest compounding in the computation, but the APR does not. Both computations adjust the percentage cost per period so that it is stated on an annual basis. We annualize the cost to make it easier to compare short-term credit instruments with different maturities.

To illustrate the application of these equations, consider the credit terms of 2/10, net 30, which allows the firm to take a 2 percent discount from the purchase price if payment is made on or before Day 10 of the billing cycle; otherwise, the entire bill is due by Day 30. If the firm does not take the discount, it effectively pays 2¢ to borrow 98¢ for a 20-day period, so the cost of using the funds for the additional 20 days is

$$\text{Periodic rate} = r_{PER} = \frac{2¢}{98¢} = 0.020408 \approx 2.041\%$$

Because there are m = 18 20-day periods in a 360-day year, the APR, or simple interest rate, associated with the trade credit is

$$\text{APR} = i_{SIMPLE} = 0.02041 \times 18 = 0.367 = 36.7\%$$

The effective annual cost (rate), EAR, of using trade credit with these terms as a source of short-term financing is

$$\text{EAR} = (1 + 0.02041)^{18} - 1.0 = 1.439 - 1.0 = 0.439 = 43.9\%$$

According to this computation, if the firm chooses to pay its bill on Day 30, then it will "forgo" the 2 percent cash discount, which is equivalent to borrowing funds at a rate of nearly 44 percent per year.[7]

discount interest loan
A loan in which the interest, which is calculated on the amount borrowed (principal), is paid at the beginning of the loan period; interest is paid in advance.

Next, let's consider what happens when a firm finances with a **discount interest loan** from the bank. With this type of loan, the interest due is deducted "up front" so that the borrower receives less than the principal amount, or face value, of the loan. Assume that Argile Textiles received a $10,000 discount interest loan

[7] We assume that the firm pays its supplier on the last day possible. That is, if it takes the discount, payment is made on Day 10; if it doesn't take the discount, payment is made on Day 30. This pattern constitutes rational business behavior. If the firm does not take the discount, but pays on Day 20 (or any other time before the final due date), then the cost associated with using this source of financing is higher than computed here. The funds cost more because the firm uses them for a shorter period.

with a 12 percent quoted (simple) interest rate to be used for a period of nine months. The interest payment on this loan is \$10,000 × 0.12 × (9/12) = \$900. Note that interest is paid only for the portion of the year during which the loan is outstanding—nine months in this case. Because the interest is paid in advance, the Argile has only \$9,100 = \$10,000 − \$900 available for use. Thus the nine-month interest rate paid for the loan is

$$r_{PER} = \frac{\text{Nine-month}}{\text{interest rate}} = \frac{\$10{,}000 \times 0.12 \times \left(\frac{9}{12}\right)}{\$10{,}000 - \left[\$10{,}000 \times 0.12 \times \left(\frac{9}{12}\right)\right]}$$

$$= \frac{\$900}{\$9{,}100}$$

$$= 0.0989 = 9.89\%$$

The APR for the loan is

$$\text{APR} = 9.89\% \times \left(\frac{12}{9}\right) = 13.19\%$$

The EAR is

$$\text{EAR} = (1.0989)^{\left(\frac{12}{9}\right)} - 1 = 0.1340 = 13.40\%$$

What do you think the cost of the loan described here would be if Argile's bank charged a \$50 fee to cover the costs of processing the loan? To answer this question, first look at Equation 15-5 and determine whether the payment affects the numerator (that is, the dollar cost of borrowing), the denominator (that is, the amount of usable funds), or both. The general rule is that the numerator is affected by any expense associated with the loan, and the denominator is affected if funds must be put aside (for example, to satisfy a compensating balance requirement) or if costs are paid out of the proceeds at the beginning of the loan period. Thus, if Argile uses the proceeds from the loan to pay the \$50 fee, both the numerator and the denominator are affected, and the nine-month interest rate is

$$r_{PER} = \frac{\text{Nine-month}}{\text{interest rate}} = \frac{\$900 + \$50}{\$9{,}100 - \$50}$$

$$= \frac{\$950}{\$9{,}050}$$

$$= 0.1050 = 10.5\%$$

Check to see that the APR and the EAR are now 14.0 percent and 14.2 percent, respectively.

From the examples presented here, you should recognize that the percentage cost of short-term financing is higher when the dollar expenses (such as those associated with interest, clerical efforts, loan processing, and so forth) are higher or when the net proceeds from the loan are less than the principal amount. In most cases, then, the effective interest rate (cost) of short-term financing is greater than its stated (quoted) interest rate. The effective interest rate of a loan is equal to the quoted rate only when the entire principal amount borrowed can be used by the borrower for an entire year and the only dollar cost is interest charged on the outstanding balance of the loan.

SELF-TEST QUESTIONS

What is the difference between APR and EAR?

All else being equal, what causes the APR and EAR to increase?

MANAGING CASH AND MARKETABLE SECURITIES

In Chapter 10, we discovered that value, which the firm's management should want to maximize, is based on cash flows. Consequently, managing cash flows is an extremely important task for a financial manager. Part of this task involves determining how much cash a firm should have on hand at any time to ensure that normal business operations can continue uninterrupted. This section describes factors that affect the amount of cash held by firms and some of the cash management techniques currently used by businesses.

Cash Management

For the purposes of the discussion here, the term *cash* refers to the funds a firm holds that can be used for immediate disbursement—it includes the amount a firm holds in its checking account as well as the amount of actual currency it has. Cash is a "nonearning, or idle, asset" that is needed to pay bills. When possible, it should be "put to work" by investing in assets that have positive expected returns. Thus the goal of the cash manager is to minimize the amount of cash held by the firm for use in conducting its normal business activities, while simultaneously ensuring that the firm has sufficient cash to support its operations.

Firms hold cash for the following reasons:

transactions balance
A cash balance necessary for day-to-day operations; the balance associated with routine payments and collections.

precautionary balance
A cash balance held in reserve for unforeseen fluctuations in cash flows.

speculative balance
A cash balance held to enable the firm to take advantage of any bargain purchases that might arise.

1. The primary reason that firms maintain cash balances is because payments must be made in cash and receipts are deposited in a cash account. Cash balances associated with routine payments and collections are known as **transactions balances.**
2. A bank often requires a firm to maintain a *compensating balance* on deposit to help offset the costs of providing services such as check clearing, cash management advice, and so forth.
3. Because cash inflows and outflows are somewhat unpredictable, firms generally hold some cash in reserve to insure against random, unforeseen fluctuations in cash flows. These "safety stocks" are called **precautionary balances.** The less predictable the firm's cash flows, the larger such balances should be. If the firm has quick and easy access to borrowed funds, perhaps through an established line of credit, its need for precautionary balances is reduced.
4. At times, cash balances are held to enable the firm to take advantage of bargain purchases that might arise. These funds are called **speculative balances.** As with precautionary balances, firms that have easy access to borrowed funds are likely to rely on their ability to borrow quickly rather than use cash balances for speculative purposes.

Although the cash accounts of most firms can be envisioned as consisting of transactions, compensating, precautionary, and speculative balances, we cannot calculate the amount needed for each purpose, sum them, and produce a total desired cash balance, because the same money often serves more than one purpose. For instance, precautionary and speculative balances can also be used to satisfy compensating balance requirements. Firms do, however, consider all four factors when establishing their target cash positions.

In addition to the four motives given here, a firm maintains cash balances to preserve its credit rating by keeping its liquidity position in line with those of other firms in the same industry. A strong credit rating enables the firm to purchase goods from suppliers on favorable terms and to maintain an ample line of credit with its bank.

Cash Management Techniques

synchronized cash flows
A situation in which cash inflows coincide with cash outflows, thereby permitting a firm to hold low transactions balances.

float
The difference between the balance shown in a firm's (or individual's) checkbook and the balance on the bank's records.

disbursement float
The value of the checks that have been written and disbursed, but have not yet fully cleared through the banking system and thus have not been deducted from the account on which they were written.

collections float
The amount of checks that have been received and deposited, but have not yet been credited to the account in which they were deposited.

net float
The difference between disbursement float and collections float; the difference between the balance shown in the firm's (or individual's) checkbook and the balance shown on the bank's books.

Most cash management activities are performed jointly by the firm and its primary bank, but the financial manager ultimately is responsible for the effectiveness of the cash management program. Effective cash management encompasses proper management of both the cash inflows and the cash outflows of a firm, which entails consideration of the factors discussed in this section.

Cash Forecasts The most critical ingredient of proper cash management is the cash forecast, often referred to as the cash budget. A firm needs to predict the timing of its cash inflows and cash outflows to plan for its investment and borrowing activities. If a cash shortfall is projected to occur during a particular period, arrangements can be made to borrow the needed funds before a crisis erupts. At the same time, if a cash surplus is projected, the firm can plan to temporarily invest the funds rather than letting them sit idle. The cash budget is discussed in greater detail in Chapter 8.

Cash Flow Synchronization Companies try to arrange matters so that their cash inflows and cash outflows are matched as well as possible—that is, customers are billed so that their "billing cycles" will coordinate when the firm pays its own bills. Having **synchronized cash flows** enables the firm to reduce its cash balances, decrease its bank loans, lower its interest expenses, and boost its profits. The more predictable the timing of the cash flows, the greater the synchronization that can be attained. Notably, utilities and credit card companies generally have a high degree of cash flow synchronization.

Float **Float** is defined as the difference between the balance shown in a firm's (or individual's) checkbook and the balance on the bank's records. For example, suppose a firm writes checks in the amount of $5,000 each day, and it normally takes six days from the time the check is mailed until it is cleared and deducted from the firm's bank account. This particular delay causes the firm's own checkbook to show a balance $30,000 = ($5,000 × 6 days) smaller than the balance on the bank's records; this difference is called **disbursement float.** Now suppose the firm receives checks in the amount of $6,500 daily, but it loses four days while the checks are being deposited and cleared. This delay results in $26,000 = ($6,500 × 4 days) of **collections float.** Together, the firm's **net float**—the difference between the $30,000 positive disbursement float and the $26,000 negative collections float—will be $4,000. Thus the net balance that the bank shows in the firm's checking account is $4,000 greater than the balance that the firm shows in its own checkbook.

Delays that cause float arise because it takes time for checks to (1) travel through the mail (*mail delay*), (2) be processed by the receiving firm (*processing delay*), and (3) clear the banking system (*clearing, or availability, delay*). Basically, the size of a firm's net float is a function of its ability to speed up collections on checks received and to slow down collections on checks written. Efficient firms go to great lengths to speed up the processing of incoming checks, thereby putting the funds to work more quickly, and they try to delay their own payments for as long as possible.

Acceleration of Receipts A firm cannot use customers' payments until they are received *and* converted into a spendable form, such as cash or an increase in a checking account balance. Not surprisingly, it would benefit the firm to accelerate the collection of customers' payments and the conversion of those payments into cash.

Although the firm cannot directly control some of the delays that cause float, it can use the following techniques to manage collections:

lockbox arrangement
A technique used to reduce float by having payments sent to post office boxes located near the customers.

1. A **lockbox arrangement** requires customers to send their payments to a post office box located in the area near where they live rather than directly to the firm. The firm arranges for a local bank to collect the checks from the post office box, perhaps several times each day, and to immediately deposit them into the company's checking account. Float is reduced in two ways. First, the mail delay is less than if the payment had to travel farther. Second, checks are cleared more rapidly because the banks on which the checks are written are located in the same Federal Reserve district.

preauthorized debit system
A system that allows a customer's bank to periodically transfer funds from its account to a selling firm's bank account for the payment of bills.

concentration banking
A cash management technique in which funds from many bank accounts are moved to a more central cash pool so as to more effectively manage cash.

2. If a firm receives regular, repetitious payments from its customers, then it might want to establish a **preauthorized debit system** (sometimes called preauthorized payments). With this arrangement, the collecting firm and its customer (paying firm) enter into an agreement whereby the paying firm's bank periodically transfers funds from the paying firm's account to the collecting firm's account, even if that account is located at another bank. The transfer of funds is accelerated because mail and check-clearing delays are eliminated and the processing delay generally is reduced significantly.
3. **Concentration banking** is a cash management arrangement used to mobilize funds from decentralized collection locations, whether they are lockboxes or decentralized company locations, into one or more central cash pools. The cash manager then uses these pools for short-term investing or reallocation of funds among the firm's banks. By pooling its cash, the firm can take maximum advantage of economies of scale in cash management and investment. For example, commissions are often less per dollar on large investments, and investments of larger dollar amounts sometimes earn higher returns than do smaller investments.

Disbursement Control Accelerating collections represents one side of cash management, and controlling funds outflows, or disbursements, represents the other side. Three methods are commonly used to control disbursements:

1. Centralizing the processing of accounts payable permits the financial manager to evaluate the payments coming due for the entire firm and to schedule the

availability of funds so as to meet these needs on a companywide basis. It also permits more efficient monitoring of accounts payable and the effects of float. A disadvantage associated with centralized disbursement systems is that regional offices might not be able to make prompt payments for services rendered, which can create ill will and raise the company's operating costs. As payment systems become more electronically advanced, the centralization of disbursements can be coordinated more effectively, and such situations should occur much less often.

zero-balance account (ZBA) A special checking account used for disbursements that has a balance equal to zero when no disbursement activity occurs.

controlled disbursement account (CDA) A checking account in which funds are not deposited until checks are presented for payment, usually on a daily basis.

2. A **zero-balance account (ZBA)** is a special disbursement account that has a balance equal to zero when no disbursement activity occurs. Typically, a firm establishes several ZBAs in its concentration bank and funds them from a master account. As checks are presented to a ZBA for payment, funds are automatically transferred from the master account.
3. Whereas ZBAs are typically established at concentration banks, **controlled disbursement accounts (CDAs)** can be set up at any bank. These accounts are not funded until the day's checks are presented against the account. The firm relies on the bank that maintains the CDA to provide information in the morning (generally before 11 A.M., New York time) concerning the total amount of the checks that will be presented for payment that day. This notification permits the financial manager to (a) transfer funds to the controlled disbursement account to cover the checks presented for payment or (b) invest excess cash at midday, when money market trading is at its peak.

Marketable Securities

Realistically, the management of cash and marketable securities cannot be separated. Management of one implies management of the other, because the amount of marketable securities held by a firm depends on its short-term cash needs.

marketable securities Securities that can be sold on short notice without loss of the principal or original investment.

Marketable securities, or *near-cash* assets, are extremely liquid, short-term investments that permit the firm to earn positive returns on cash that is not needed to pay bills immediately, but will be needed sometime in the near term, perhaps in a few days, weeks, or months. Although such investments typically provide much lower yields than do operating assets, nearly every large firm has them. Firms cite two basic reasons for owning marketable securities:

1. Marketable securities serve as a *substitute for cash balances.* Firms often hold portfolios of marketable securities, liquidating part of the portfolio to increase the cash account when cash is needed, because the *marketable securities offer a place to temporarily put cash balances to work earning a positive return.* In such situations, the marketable securities could be used as a substitute for transactions balances, precautionary balances, speculative balances, or all three.
2. Marketable securities are used as a *temporary investment* (a) to finance seasonal or cyclical operations and (b) to amass funds to meet financial requirements in the near future. For example, if the firm has a conservative financing policy (as discussed earlier), then its long-term capital will exceed its permanent assets, and marketable securities will be held when inventories and receivables are low.

Because marketable securities are temporary investments, financial assets that are considered appropriate investments include those sold in the money markets.

Examples of such securities (as described in Chapter 2) include Treasury bills, commercial paper, negotiable certificates of deposit, and Eurodollar time deposits. Depending on how long these instruments will be held, the financial manager decides on a suitable set of securities, and a suitable maturity pattern, to hold as *near-cash reserves* in the form of marketable securities. Long-term securities are not appropriate investments for marketable securities as described in this section. Instead, safety—especially maintenance of principal—should be the paramount concern when putting together a marketable securities portfolio.

SELF-TEST QUESTIONS

Why is cash management important?

What are the motives for holding cash?

What is float? How do firms use float to increase cash management efficiency?

What are some methods that firms can use to accelerate receipts?

What are some techniques employed for controlling disbursements?

Why do firms hold marketable securities?

CREDIT MANAGEMENT

Firms prefer to sell for cash only, because payment is certain and immediate. Why, then, do firms sell for credit? The primary reason is because their competitors offer credit. Consider what you would do if you had the opportunity to purchase the same product for the same price from two different firms, but one firm required cash payment at the time of the purchase whereas the other firm allowed you to pay for the product one month after the purchase without any additional cost. From which firm would you purchase the product? Like you, firms prefer to delay their payments, especially if no additional costs are associated with the delay.

Effective credit management is extremely important because too much credit is very costly in terms of the investment in, and maintenance of, accounts receivable. Conversely, too little credit might result in the loss of profitable sales. Carrying accounts receivable has both direct and indirect costs, but it also provides an important benefit—granting credit should increase profits. Thus, to maximize shareholders' wealth, a financial manager needs to understand how to effectively manage the firm's credit activities.

This section describes the factors considered important when determining the appropriate credit policy for a firm, procedures for monitoring the credit policy to ensure that it is being administered properly, and ways to evaluate whether credit policy changes will benefit the firm.

credit policy
A set of decisions that includes a firm's credit standards, credit terms, methods used to collect credit accounts, and credit monitoring procedures.

credit standards
Standards that indicate the minimum financial strength a customer must have to be granted credit.

Credit Policy

The major controllable variables that affect demand for a company's products are sales prices, product quality, advertising, and the firm's **credit policy.** The firm's credit policy, in turn, includes the following factors:

1. **Credit standards** refer to the financial strength and creditworthiness that a customer must exhibit to qualify for credit. The firm's credit standards are applied to determine which customers qualify for the regular credit terms and how much credit each customer should receive. Major factors considered

when setting credit standards relate to the likelihood that a given customer will pay slowly or perhaps even end up as a bad debt loss. Determining the credit quality—that is, creditworthiness—of a customer is probably the most difficult part of credit management. Nevertheless, credit evaluation is a well-established practice and a good credit manager can make reasonably accurate judgments of the probability of default exhibited by different classes of customers by examining a firm's current financial position and evaluating factors that might affect this position in the future.

terms of credit
The payment conditions offered to credit customers. The terms include the length of the credit period and any cash discounts offered.

credit period
The length of time for which credit is granted. After that time, the credit account is considered delinquent.

cash discount
A reduction in the invoice price of goods offered by the seller to encourage early payment.

collection policy
The procedures followed by a firm to collect its accounts receivable.

receivables monitoring
The process of evaluating the credit policy to determine whether a shift in customers' payment patterns has occurred.

days sales outstanding (DSO)
The average length of time required to collect accounts receivable; also called the *average collection period.*

aging schedule
A report showing how long accounts receivable have been outstanding. The report categorizes receivables into specified periods, which provides information about the proportion of receivables that are current and the proportion that are past due for given lengths of time.

2. **Terms of credit** are the conditions of the credit sale. The most important aspect of the terms of credit deals with the payment arrangements. Firms need to determine when the **credit period** will begin, how long the customer will have to pay for credit purchases before the account is considered delinquent, and whether a cash discount for early payment should be offered. An examination of the credit terms offered by firms in the United States shows great variety across industries—credit terms range from cash before delivery (CBD) and cash on delivery (COD) to **cash discounts** offered for early payment. Because of the competitive nature of trade credit, most financial managers follow the norm of the industry in which they operate when setting credit terms.
3. The **collection policy** refers to the procedures followed by the firm to collect its credit accounts. The firm needs to determine when, and how, notification of the credit sale will be conveyed to the buyer. The more quickly a customer receives an invoice, the sooner the bill *can* be paid. In today's world, many firms have begun to use electronic methods to "send" invoices to customers.

Receivables Monitoring

Once a firm sets its credit policy, it must operate within that policy's limits. To ensure that the firm adheres to this policy, it must examine its receivables periodically to determine whether customers' payment patterns have changed to the extent that credit operations are outside the credit policy limits. **Receivables monitoring** refers to the process of evaluating the credit policy to determine whether a shift in customers' payment patterns has occurred.

Traditionally, firms have monitored accounts receivable by using methods that measure the length of time credit remains outstanding. Two such methods are the *days sales outstanding (DSO)* and the *aging schedule:*

1. The **days sales outstanding (DSO),** also called the *average collection period,* represents the average time it takes to collect credit accounts. Equation 15-2 shows the computation for DSO (average collection period). Recall that we found that the DSO for Argile was 43.2 days in 2002. If Argile's credit terms are 2/10, net 30, then we know that some customers are delinquent when paying their accounts. In fact, if many customers are paying within 10 days to take advantage of the cash discount, the others would, on average, have to be taking much longer than 43.2 days. One way to check for this possibility is to use an aging schedule.
2. An **aging schedule** is a breakdown of a firm's receivables by age of account. Table 15-2 shows the December 31, 2002, aging schedule for Argile Textiles. The standard format for an aging schedule generally includes age categories

Table 15-2 Argile Textiles: Receivables Aging Schedule for 2002

Age of Account (days)	Net Amount Outstanding	Fraction of Total Receivables	Average Days
0–30	$36.0	40%	18
31–60	45.0	50	55
61–90	5.4	6	77
Over 90	3.6	4	97
	$90.0	100%	

DSO = 0.40(18 days) + 0.50(55 days) + 0.06(77 days) + 0.04(97 days)
= 43.2 days

broken down by month. Even more precision, and hence better monitoring information, can be attained by using narrower age categories (for example, one or two weeks).

According to Argile's aging schedule, only 40 percent of the firm's credit sales are "current" because they have been outstanding for 30 days or less; 60 percent of the credit sales collections are delinquent. Some of the payments are delinquent by only a few days, whereas others are delinquent by three to four times the 30-day credit period.

Management should constantly monitor the DSO and the aging schedule to detect trends; this information can be used to see how the firm's collection experience compares with its credit terms as well as how effectively the credit department is operating in comparison with other firms in the industry. If the DSO starts to lengthen or if the aging schedule begins to show an increasing percentage of past-due accounts, then the firm might need to tighten its credit policy.

You must use care when interpreting changes in the DSO or the aging schedule. If a firm experiences sharp seasonal variations, or if it is growing rapidly, then both measures could be distorted. Recall that Argile's peak selling season occurs in the summer. Table 15-1 shows that forecasted receivables are expected to be high ($125 million) in September 2003, but much lower ($99 million) at the end of December 2003. Because sales are expected to amount to $825 million in 2003, Argile's DSO will be 54.5 days = $125/($825/360) on September 30, but only 43.2 days = $99/($825/360) on December 31, 2003. This decline in DSO would not indicate that Argile had tightened its credit policy, but merely that its sales had declined due to seasonal factors. Similar problems arise with the aging schedule when sales fluctuate widely.

A change in either the DSO or the aging schedule should be taken as a signal to investigate further, but not necessarily as a sign that the firm's credit policy has weakened. If a firm generally experiences widely fluctuating sales patterns, some type of modified aging schedule should be used to account for these fluctuations.[8] Even with this caveat, the DSO measure and the aging schedule still represent useful tools for evaluating credit customer's payment behavior.

---

[8]See Eugene F. Brigham and Phillip R. Daves, *Intermediate Financial Management,* 7th ed. (Cincinnati, OH: South-Western College Publishing, 2002), Chapter 20, for a more complete discussion of the problems with the DSO and aging schedule and how to correct for them.

Analyzing Proposed Changes in Credit Policy

The key question when deciding on a proposed credit policy change is this: How will the change affect the firm's value? If the added benefits expected from a credit policy change do not exceed the added costs on a present value basis, then the firm should *not* make the policy change.

To illustrate how to evaluate whether a proposed change in a firm's credit policy is appropriate, let's examine what would happen if Argile Textiles makes changes to reduce its average collection period. The company's financial manager has proposed that this task be accomplished in 2003 by taking two steps: (1) billing customers sooner and exerting more pressure on delinquent customers to pay their bills on time, and (2) examining the accounts of existing credit customers and suspending the credit of those who are considered "habitually delinquent." Clearly, these actions will increase the costs associated with Argile's credit policy. At the same time, even though Argile has an extremely loyal customer base, it is expected that some sales will be lost to competitors as the result of some customers having their credit eliminated. Because the credit policy changes will have little, if any, effect on the "good" credit customers, the financial manager does not expect a change in the payments of those customers who currently take advantage of the cash discount. If the proposed credit policy changes are approved, the average collection period (DSO) for receivables is expected to be reduced from 43.2 days to 34.9 days, which is more in line with the credit terms offered by Argile (2/10, net 30) and closer to the industry average of 32 days. Also, if the average collection period is reduced, the amount "carried" in accounts receivable will be reduced, which means that fewer funds will be "tied up" in receivables.

Table 15-3 provides information relating to Argile's existing credit policy and the financial manager's proposed changes. According to the table, if the company changes its credit policy, its sales will drop by $2 million per year, or $5,556 per day. Notice that only the amount paid by customers who do not currently take the cash discount will be affected by this decrease. This group of customers includes the "habitually delinquent" payers, which is the category of customers that the credit policy change is intended to affect. As a result, on a daily basis, the amount paid by the nondiscount customers will decrease by $5,556, from $1.9021 million to $1.8965 million, if the proposed credit policy is adopted; the amount paid by the discount customers, however, will remain $0.3818 million.

To determine whether Argile should adopt the financial manager's proposal, we need to evaluate how the proposed changes will affect the value of the firm. Thus we must compare the net present values (NPV) of the two credit policies. To complete the analysis, we make two simplifying assumptions:

- Sales occur evenly throughout the year.
- Each production/selling cycle is constant such that cash inflows and cash outflows occur at the same point in time relative to the credit sale, no matter what time of the year is examined.

These assumptions allow us to evaluate the cash inflows and cash outflows associated with credit sales for one day to determine whether the proposed credit policy change should be made.

Table 15-3 gives specific assumptions concerning the timing of the cash flows, and Table 15-4 shows the results of the NPV analysis ($k = 10\%$). According to these

Table 15-3 Argile Textiles: Existing and Proposed Credit Policies, 2003

	Existing Policy	Proposed Policy
I. General Credit Policy Information		
Credit terms	2/10 net 30	2/10 net 30
Days sales outstanding (DSO) for all customers[a]	43.2 days	34.9 days
DSO for customers who take cash discount (17%)	10.0 days	10.0 days
DSO for customers who forgo cash discount (83%)	50.0 days	40.0 days
II. Annual Credit Sales and Costs ($ million)		
Sales	$825.0	$823.0
Amount paid by discount customers[b]	$137.4	$137.4
Amount paid by nondiscount customers[b]	$684.8	$682.8
Variable operating costs (80% of sales)[c]	$660.0	$658.4
Bad debts	$ 0.0	$ 0.0
Credit evaluation and collection costs[c]	$ 8.0	$ 8.5
III. Daily Credit Sales and Costs ($ thousand)[d]		
Sales	$2,291.7	$2,286.1
Amount paid by discount customers	$ 381.8	$ 381.8
Amount paid by non-discount customers	$1,902.1	$1,896.5
Variable operating costs (80% of sales)	$1,833.3	$1,828.9
Bad debts	$ 0.0	$ 0.0
Credit evaluation and collection costs	$ 22.2	$ 23.6

[a]With the existing policy, 17 percent of the customers take the cash discount and pay on Day 10; the remaining customers (83 percent) pay on average on Day 50. Thus the DSO for all customers is 43.2 days = 0.17(10 days) + 0.83(50 days).

[b]Currently, 17 percent of Argile's customers pay on Day 10, taking advantage of the 2 percent cash discount. As a result, the amount expected to be paid by this group of customers is $137.4 million = 0.17 × (1.0 − 0.02) × $825.0 million. Customers who take the discount will not be affected by the credit policy changes that are aimed at delinquent customers; thus the amount paid by customers who take the discount will be the same under either credit policy—$137.4 million. Consequently, the $2 million decrease in total sales associated with the proposed credit policy will reduce the amount paid by customers who do not take the discount from $684.8 million to $682.8 million.

[c]The variable operating costs are paid at the time of the credit sale. Fixed operating costs are not included in the analysis, because the amount does not change if the credit policy is changed. Expenses related to credit sales (evaluation and collection costs) are also paid at the time of the credit sale. These assumptions are made to simplify the analysis.

[d]Daily figures are required to evaluate whether the proposal should be adopted. See Table 15-4 for the actual analysis. For consistency, we use a 360-day year to compute the daily figures.

results, the NPV for the existing credit policy is $401,100 per day, whereas the NPV for the proposed credit policy is $403,700 per day. If the company changes its credit policy, the change in the daily NPV (NPV in Section III of Table 15-4) is $2,600. Given the assumptions we have stated previously as well as the assumptions given in Table 15-3, we would expect that this change will have a permanent, or continuing, effect on the firm. Thus the $2,600 change represents a daily perpetuity, which, according to Section III of Table 15-4, will increase the value of the firm by $9.36 million. Clearly, then, the proposed changes should be made.

The analysis in Table 15-4 provides Argile's managers with a vehicle for considering the effects of credit policy changes on the firm's value. They must apply a great deal of judgment to the final decision, however, because both customers' and competitors' responses to credit policy changes are very difficult to gauge. Nevertheless, this type of analysis is essential.

Table 15-4 Argile Textiles: NPV Analysis of Credit Policies ($ thousand)

I. Existing Credit Policy

Cash Flow Time Line

0	k = (10% ÷ 360)	10	. . .	50 Days
(1,833.3) (22.2) (1,855.5)		381.8		1,902.1

$$\text{NPV}_{\text{Existing}} = (1{,}855.5) + \frac{381.8}{\left(1 + \frac{0.10}{360}\right)^{10}} + \frac{1{,}902.1}{\left(1 + \frac{0.10}{360}\right)^{50}}$$

$$= (1{,}855.5) + 380.7 + 1{,}875.9 = 401.1$$

II. Proposed Credit Policy

Cash Flow Time Line

0	k = (10% ÷ 360)	10	. . .	40 Days
(1,828.9) (23.6) (1,852.5)		381.8	1,896.5	

$$\text{NPV}_{\text{Proposal}} = (1{,}852.5) + \frac{381.8}{\left(1 + \frac{0.10}{360}\right)^{10}} + \frac{1{,}896.5}{\left(1 + \frac{0.10}{360}\right)^{40}}$$

$$= (1{,}852.5) + 380.7 + 1{,}875.5 = 403.7$$

III. Effect on Firm's Value if Proposal Is Adopted

$$\Delta\text{NPV on a daily basis} = \$403.7 - \$401.1 = \$2.6$$

$$\Delta\text{ Value} = \frac{\$2.6}{\left(\frac{0.10}{360}\right)} = \$9{,}360.0$$

SELF-TEST QUESTIONS

What are the four credit policy variables? Describe how each variable affects sales and profitability.

Define days sales outstanding (DSO). What can you learn from it? How is it affected by sales fluctuations?

What is an aging schedule? What can you learn from it? How is it affected by sales fluctuations?

Describe the procedure used to evaluate a change in credit policy.

INVENTORY MANAGEMENT

If it could, a firm would prefer to have no inventory. After all, while products are in inventory, they do not generate returns and must be financed. Nevertheless, most firms find it necessary to maintain inventory in some form for two reasons: Demand cannot be predicted with certainty, and it takes time to get a product ready for sale. While excessive inventories can be costly to the firm, so are insufficient inventories—customers might purchase from competitors if products are not available when demanded, and future business could be lost.

Although inventory models are covered in depth in production management courses, it is important to understand the basics of inventory management. Proper management requires coordination among the sales, purchasing, production, and finance departments. Lack of coordination among these departments, poor sales forecasts, or both can lead to financial ruin. This section briefly describes the concepts of inventory management.

Types of Inventory

An inventory item can be classified according to its stage of completion:

raw materials The inventories purchased from suppliers, which ultimately will be transformed into finished goods.

work-in-process Inventory in various stages of completion. Some work-in-process is at the very beginning of the production process, whereas other work-in-process is at the end of the process.

finished goods Inventories that have completed the production process and are ready for sale.

stockout A situation in which a firm runs out of inventory *and* customers arrive to purchase the product.

1. **Raw materials** include new inventory purchased from suppliers; a firm purchases these materials so it can transform them into finished products for sale. As long as the firm has an inventory of raw materials, delays in ordering and delivery from suppliers will not affect the production process.
2. **Work-in-process** refers to inventory items that are at various stages of completion. If a firm has work-in-process at every stage of the production process, then it will not have to completely shut down production if a problem arises at one of the earlier stages.
3. **Finished goods** inventory represents products that are ready for sale. Firms carry finished goods to ensure that orders can be filled when they are received. If there are no finished goods, the firm must wait for the completion of the production process before inventory can be sold, so demand might not be satisfied when it arrives. When a customer arrives and no inventory is available to satisfy that customer's demand, a **stockout** exists. In such a situation, the firm might lose the customer to its competitors, perhaps permanently.

Optimal Inventory Level

The goal of inventory management is to provide the inventories required to sustain operations at the lowest possible cost. The first step in determining the optimal inventory level is to identify the costs involved in purchasing and maintaining inventory. Next, we must determine at what point those costs are minimized.

carrying costs The costs associated with having inventory, which include storage costs, insurance, the cost of tying up funds, depreciation costs, and so on. These costs generally increase in proportion to the average amount of inventory held.

Inventory Costs We generally classify inventory costs into three categories: those associated with carrying inventory, those associated with ordering and receiving inventory, and those associated with running short of inventory (stockouts). First, let's look at the two costs that are most directly observable—carrying costs and ordering costs.

1. **Carrying costs** include any expenses associated with having inventory, such as rent paid for storage space, insurance on the inventory, and so forth. Carrying costs generally increase in direct proportion to the average amount of inventory carried.

ordering costs The costs of placing an order. The cost of each order generally is fixed, regardless of the average size of the inventory.

2. **Ordering costs** include those expenses associated with placing and receiving an order for new inventory, such as the costs of generating memos, fax transmissions, and so forth. For the most part, the costs associated with each order are fixed regardless of the order size.[9]

If we assume that the firm knows how much inventory it needs and sales are distributed evenly during each period, then we can combine the total carrying costs (TCC) and the total ordering costs (TOC) to find total inventory costs (TIC) as follows:

15-8

$$\begin{aligned}\text{Total inventory costs (TIC)} &= \text{Total carrying costs} + \text{Total ordering costs}\\ &= \begin{pmatrix}\text{Carrying cost}\\ \text{per unit}\end{pmatrix} \times \begin{pmatrix}\text{Average units}\\ \text{in inventory}\end{pmatrix} + \begin{pmatrix}\text{Cost per}\\ \text{order}\end{pmatrix} \times \begin{pmatrix}\text{Number of}\\ \text{orders}\end{pmatrix}\\ &= (C \times PP) \times \left(\frac{Q}{2}\right) + O \times \left(\frac{T}{Q}\right)\end{aligned}$$

The variables in the equation are defined as follows:

C = Carrying costs as a percentage of the purchase price of each inventory item
PP = Purchase price, or cost, per unit
Q = Number of units purchased with each order
T = Total demand, or number of units sold, per period
O = Fixed costs per order

According to Equation 15-8, the average investment in inventory depends on how often orders are placed and the size of each order. If we order every day, average inventory will be much smaller than if we order once per year and inventory carrying costs will be low, but the number of orders will be large and inventory ordering costs will be high. We can reduce ordering costs by ordering greater amounts less often, but then average inventory, and hence the total carrying cost, will be high. This tradeoff between carrying costs and ordering costs is shown graphically in Figure 15-3. Note from the figure that there is a point where the total inventory cost is ***minimized;*** this point is called the **economic (optimum) ordering quantity (EOQ).**

economic (optimum) ordering quantity (EOQ) The optimal quantity that should be ordered; the quantity that will minimize the total inventory costs.

The Economic Ordering Quantity (EOQ) Model The EOQ is determined by using calculus to find the point where the slope of the TIC curve in Figure 15-3 is

[9]In reality, both carrying and ordering costs can have variable and fixed cost elements, at least over certain ranges of average inventory. For example, security and utilities charges probably are fixed in the short run over a wide range of inventory levels. Similarly, labor costs in receiving inventory could be tied to the quantity received, and hence could be variable. To simplify matters, we treat all carrying costs as variable and all ordering costs as fixed.

Figure 15-3 Determination of the Optimal Order Quantity

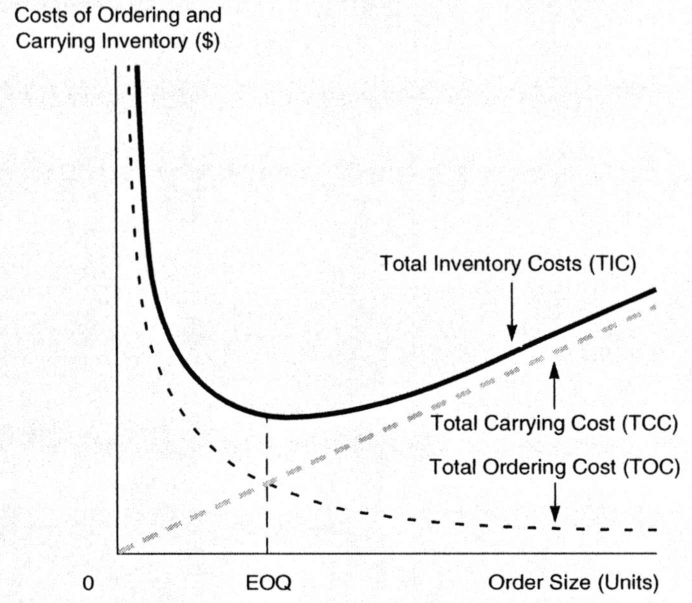

perfectly horizontal—that is, where the slope equals zero. The result is the following equation:

15-9

$$\text{Economic ordering quantity} = \text{EOQ} = \sqrt{\frac{2 \times O \times T}{C \times PP}}$$

EOQ model
A formula for determining the order quantity that will minimize total inventory costs.

The primary assumptions of the **EOQ model** given by Equation 15-9 are that (1) sales are evenly distributed throughout the period examined and can be forecasted perfectly, (2) orders are received when expected, and (3) the purchase price (PP) of each item in inventory is the same regardless of the quantity ordered.[10]

To illustrate the EOQ model, consider the following data supplied by Cotton Tops, Inc., a distributor of custom-designed T-shirts that supplies concessionaires at Daisy World:

T = 78,000 shirts per year
C = 25 percent of inventory value
PP = $3.84 per shirt (The shirts sell for $9, but this information is irrelevant for our purposes here.)
O = $260 per order

[10]The EOQ model can also be written as

$$\text{EOQ} = \sqrt{\frac{2 \times O \times T}{C^*}},$$

where C* is the carrying cost per unit expressed in dollars.

Substituting these data into Equation 15-9, we find an EOQ of 6,500 units:

$$\text{EOQ} = \sqrt{\frac{2(\$260)(78{,}000)}{(0.25)(\$3.84)}}$$
$$= \sqrt{42{,}250{,}000} = 6{,}500 \text{ units.}$$

investment banker
An organization that underwrites and distributes new issues of securities; it helps businesses and other entities obtain needed financing.

If Cotton Tops orders 6,500 shirts each time it needs inventory, it will place 78,000/6,500 = 12 orders per year and carry an average inventory of 6,500/2 = 3,250 shirts. Thus, at the EOQ amount, Cotton Tops' total inventory costs would equal $6,240:

$$\text{TIC} = (\text{C} \times \text{PP})\left(\frac{\text{Q}}{2}\right) + \text{O}\left(\frac{\text{T}}{\text{Q}}\right)$$
$$= [0.25(\$3.84)]\left(\frac{6{,}500}{2}\right) + \$260\left(\frac{78{,}000}{6{,}500}\right)$$
$$= \$3{,}120 + \$3{,}120 = \$6{,}240$$

Note the following two points:

- Because we assume that the purchase price of each inventory item does not depend on the amount ordered, TIC does *not* include the annual cost of purchasing the inventory itself, which is $299,520 = 78,000($3.84).
- As we see in Figure 15-3 as well as in the computation here, at the EOQ, total carrying cost equals total ordering cost. This property is not unique to our Cotton Tops illustration—it always holds with the assumptions outlined earlier.

Table 15-5 contains the total inventory costs that Cotton Tops would incur at various order quantities, including the EOQ level. As the amount ordered increases, the total carrying costs increase but the total ordering costs decrease, and vice versa. Also, if less than the EOQ amount is ordered, then the higher ordering costs more than offset the lower carrying costs. Conversely, if more than the EOQ amount is ordered, the higher carrying costs more than offset the lower ordering costs.

EOQ Model Extensions It should be obvious that some of the assumptions necessary for the basic EOQ to hold are unrealistic. To make the model more useful, we can apply some simple extensions.

reorder point
The level of inventory at which an order should be placed.

safety stocks
Additional inventory carried to guard against changes in sales rates or production/shipping delays.

First, if a delay occurs between the time when inventory is ordered and when it is received, the firm must reorder before it runs out of inventory. For example, if it normally takes two weeks to receive orders, then Cotton Tops should reorder when it has two weeks of inventory remaining. The firm sells 78,000/52 = 1,500 shirts per week, so its **reorder point** occurs when inventory drops to 3,000 shirts.

Even if Cotton Tops orders additional inventory at the appropriate reorder point, unexpected demand might cause it to run out of inventory before the new inventory is delivered. To avoid this problem, the firm could carry **safety stocks,**

Table 15-5 Cotton Tops, Inc.: Total Inventory Costs for Various Order Quantities

	Quantity	Number of Orders	Total Ordering Costs	Total Carrying Costs	Total Inventory Costs
	3,000	26	$6,760	$ 1,440	$ 8,200
	5,200	15	3,900	2,496	6,396
	6,000	13	3,380	2,880	6,260
EOQ	**6,500**	**12**	**3,120**	**3,120**	**6,240**
	7,800	10	2,600	3,744	6,344
	9,750	8	2,080	4,680	6,760
	13,000	6	1,560	6,240	7,800
	78,000	1	260	37,440	37,700

T = Annual sales = 78,000 shirts
C = Carrying cost = 25 percent
PP = Purchase price = $3.84/shirt
O = Ordering cost = $260/order

or additional inventory that helps guard against stockouts. The amount of safety stocks held by a firm generally *increases* with three factors:

- The uncertainty of demand forecasts
- The costs (in terms of lost sales and lost goodwill) that result from stockouts
- The chances that delays will occur in receiving shipments

The amount of safety stock *decreases* as the cost of carrying this additional inventory increases.

Another factor that a firm might need to consider when determining appropriate inventory levels is whether its suppliers offer discounts for purchasing large quantities. For example, if Cotton Tops' supplier offered a 1 percent discount for purchases equal to 13,000 units or more, the total reduction in the annual cost of purchasing inventory would be [0.01($3.84)] × 78,000 = $2,995.20. Looking at Table 15-5, we see that the costs of carrying existing inventory and ordering new inventory at 13,000 units equal $7,800, which is $1,560 = $7,800 − $6,240 greater than the costs at the EOQ level of 6,500 units. The net benefit of taking advantage of the **quantity discount** is $1,435.20 = $2,995.20 − $1,560.00. Therefore, in this case each time Cotton Tops orders inventory, it will be more beneficial to order 13,000 units rather than the 6,500 units prescribed by the basic EOQ model.

quantity discount
A discount from the purchase price offered for ordering inventory in large quantities.

In cases in which it is unrealistic to assume that the demand for the inventory will remain uniform throughout the year, the EOQ should not be applied on an annual basis. Rather, it would be more appropriate to divide the year into the periods within which sales are relatively constant—for example, the summer, the spring and fall, and the winter. The EOQ model can then be applied separately to each period.

Although we did not explicitly incorporate the extensions mentioned here into the basic EOQ, this discussion should give you an idea of how the EOQ amount should be adjusted to determine the optimal inventory level if any of these conditions exist.

Inventory Control Systems

red-line method
An inventory control procedure where a red line is drawn around the inside of an inventory-stocked bin to indicate the reorder point level.

computerized inventory control system
A system of inventory control in which a computer is used to determine reorder points and to adjust inventory balances.

just-in-time system
A system of inventory control in which a manufacturer coordinates production with suppliers so that raw materials of components arrive just as they are needed in the production process.

outsourcing
The practice of purchasing components rather than making them in-house.

The EOQ model can be used to help establish the proper inventory level, but inventory management also involves the establishment of an *inventory control system.* Inventory control systems run the gamut from very simple to extremely complex, depending on the size of the firm and the nature of its inventories. One simple control procedure is the **red-line method.** In this method, inventory items are stocked in a bin, a red line is drawn around the inside of the bin at the level of the reorder point, and the inventory clerk places an order when the red line becomes visible. This procedure works well for parts such as bolts in a manufacturing process or for many items in retail businesses.

Most firms employ some type of **computerized inventory control systems.** Large companies, such as Wal-Mart, often have fully integrated computerized inventory control systems in which the computer adjusts inventory levels as sales are made, orders inventory when the reorder point is reached, and records the receipt of an order. The computer records also can be used to determine whether the usage rates of inventory items have changed, and adjustments to reorder amounts can be made accordingly. Increased use of electronics technologies has allowed firms to better coordinate orders with suppliers, thereby enabling them to follow the **just-in-time system,** which was refined by Japanese firms many years ago. With this system, materials are delivered to the company at about the same time they are needed—perhaps only a few hours before they are used.

Another important development related to inventories is **outsourcing,** which is the practice of purchasing components rather than making them in-house. For example, if GM arranged to buy radiators rather than making them itself, it would be outsourcing. Outsourcing is often combined with just-in-time systems to reduce inventory levels.

Inventory control systems require coordination of the inventory policy with the manufacturing/procurement policies. Companies try to minimize *total production and distribution costs,* and inventory costs are just one part of these total costs. Nevertheless, they are an important cost, and financial managers should be aware of the determinants of inventory costs and ways to minimize them.

SELF-TEST QUESTIONS

What are the types of inventory?

What are the three categories of inventory costs?

What is the purpose of the EOQ model?

What are safety stocks, and why are they needed?

Describe some inventory control systems used in today's businesses.

MULTINATIONAL WORKING CAPITAL MANAGEMENT

For the most part, the methods used to manage short-term assets and liabilities in multinational corporations are the same as those used in purely domestic corporations. Multinational corporations face a far more complex task, however, because they operate in many different business cultures, political environments, economic conditions, and so forth. This section describes some of the differences between multinational and domestic working capital management.

Cash Management

Like a purely domestic company, a multinational corporation (MNC) wants to attain the following goals: (1) speed up collections and slow down disbursements where possible; (2) shift cash as rapidly as possible to those areas where it is needed; and (3) put temporary cash balances to work earning positive returns. Multinational companies use the same general procedures for achieving these goals as do their domestic counterparts, but because of the longer distances and more serious mail delays encountered by MNCs, lockbox systems and electronic funds transfers are even more important to them.

One potential problem faced by a multinational company is the chance that a foreign government will restrict transfers of funds out of the country. Such restrictions are intended to encourage domestic investment. Even if funds can be transferred without limitation, deteriorating exchange rates might discourage a multinational from moving these funds to its operations in other countries.

Once it has been determined what funds can be transferred out of the various nations in which a multinational corporation operates, it is important to get those funds to locations where they will earn the highest returns. Whereas domestic corporations tend to think in terms of domestic securities, MNCs are more likely to be aware of investment opportunities all around the world. Most multinational corporations use one or more global concentration banks, located in money centers such as London, New York, Tokyo, Zurich, or Singapore. They also work with international bankers to take advantage of the best rates available globally.

Credit Management

Credit policy generally is more important for a multinational corporation than for a purely domestic firm for two reasons. First, much U.S. trade takes place with poorer, less-developed nations; in such situations, granting credit is typically a necessary condition for doing business. Second, and in large part as a result of the first point, developed nations whose economic health depends on exports often help their manufacturing firms compete internationally by granting credit to foreign customers. In Japan, for example, government agencies help firms identify potential export markets and potential customers to arrange credit for purchases from Japanese firms. The U.S. government has implemented some programs that help domestic firms to export products, but it does not provide the degree of financial assistance that many multinationals based in other countries receive from their local governments.

When granting credit, the multinational firm faces a riskier situation than the purely domestic firm because, in addition to the normal risks of default, it must deal with two potential problems:

- Political and legal environments often make it more difficult to collect on defaulted accounts.
- The multinational corporation must worry about exchange rate changes between the time a sale is made and the time a receivable is collected.

Hedging can reduce the latter type of risk, albeit at a cost.

By pointing out the risks in granting credit internationally, we do not mean to suggest that such credit is bad. Quite the contrary—the potential gains from international operations far outweigh the risks, at least for companies that have the necessary expertise.

Inventory Management

Inventory management in a multinational setting is more complex than that in a purely domestic market because of the logistical problems associated with handling inventories. For example, if a firm concentrates its inventories in a few strategic centers located worldwide, it might minimize the total amount of, and hence the investment in, inventories needed to operate globally. Of course, the firm might also incur delays in getting goods from the central storage locations to user locations all around the world. It is clear that both working stocks and safety stocks must be maintained at each user location, as well as at the strategic storage centers.

Exchange rates can also significantly influence the MNC's inventory policy. For example, if a country's currency was expected to rise in value against the U.S. dollar, a U.S. company operating in that country would want to increase its stocks of local products before the rise in the currency, and vice versa.

Another factor that must be considered is the possibility of import or export quotas or tariffs. Quotas restrict the quantities of products that firms can bring into a country. Tariffs, like taxes, increase the prices of products that are allowed to be imported. Both quotas and tariffs are designed to restrict the ability of foreign corporations to compete with domestic companies. At the extreme, foreign products are excluded altogether.

Another danger in certain countries is the threat of expropriation, or government takeover of the firm's local operations. If the threat of expropriation is large, inventory holdings will be minimized, and goods will be brought in only as needed.

Taxes also must be considered when deciding on a multinational inventory management policy, for two reasons. First, countries often impose property taxes on assets, including inventories. Second, any such tax will be based on holdings as of a specific date. Such rules make it advantageous for a multinational firm to schedule production so that inventories are low on the assessment date. If assessment dates vary among countries in a region, the company could find it beneficial to hold safety stocks in different countries at different times during the year.

In general, then, multinational firms use techniques similar to those described in this chapter to manage working capital. Their job is more complex, however, because business, legal, and economic environments can differ significantly from one country to another.

SELF-TEST QUESTIONS

What are some factors that make cash management especially complicated in a multinational corporation?

Why is granting credit especially risky in an international context?

What are some factors that make inventory management in multinational firms more complex than in purely domestic firms?

SMALL BUSINESS

Growth and Working Capital Needs

Working capital is the requirement that entrepreneurs most often underestimate when seeking funds to finance a new business. The entrepreneur generally plans for research and development and for the plant and equipment required for production. Working capital, however, frequently comes as a surprise to the entrepreneur, who probably expects to develop a product that the market will immediately accept and for which customers will pay a substantial premium. This premium will, he or she assumes, lead to high profit margins, which will then "finance" all of the firm's other needs. As naive as this point of view seems, it is common among founders of new businesses.

Rick was one of the founders of a new microcomputer software company that began seeking venture capital to support its products in early 1995. When speaking with a venture capitalist, who was concerned about the low level of funding being sought, Rick explained that the company's products had such a high profit margin that the company essentially would be self-financing. According to Rick, the firm would not need financing once the marketing was under way, because the profits would generate more than enough cash to pay for new product development.

Sally, a venture capitalist approached by Rick, was disconcerted by Rick's reasoning. She explained to him that the selling price of his product would not be received fully by his company because distributors and wholesalers were involved. She also pointed out that most of the sales would be on credit, so the revenues received by his company initially would be added to accounts receivable—not received as cash—and probably not collected, on average, for 45 to 60 days. Meanwhile, Rick would have to write checks to pay for overhead, for high research and development expenses, for a marketing staff, for advertising, and so on. So instead of cash flowing in, the firm would be, on balance, paying cash out for the first few years of its life.

Rapid growth consumes cash; it does not generate cash. Rapid growth might generate profits, but profits do not pay the bills—cash does. Consider what a firm must do to sustain a high growth rate. If it is a manufacturer, the components of its assets include raw materials inventory, work-in-process inventory, finished goods inventory, and accounts receivable, as well as fixed assets. With the exception of fixed assets, these items all are components of gross working capital. When the firm produces a product, it makes an investment in each of these working capital items before it receives any cash from the collection of its receivables, assuming that all sales are credit sales.

Consider a small firm that finances its activities solely through internally generated funds. If the firm has a cash conversion cycle of 180 days, cash is "turned over" only twice per year. If the company earns, for example, 3 percent on its sales dollar, it has about 3 percent more money available after each cash cycle than before it. With two cycles per year, approximately 6 percent more is available for investment at the end of the year than at the beginning. Thus annual growth of approximately 6 percent can be supported internally. If this company is growing at a rate of 20 percent per year, it must either obtain funds externally or face enormous pressures.

Generally, a firm can fund more rapid growth internally either by raising the profit margin or by shortening the cash conversion cycle (increasing the number of cycles per year). To raise its profit margin, the company must raise prices, cut costs, or both. Raising prices might reduce growth (because customers will be less eager to buy at higher prices), but it might also bring growth and financial resources more into balance. Shortening the cash conversion cycle requires reducing inventory, collecting receivables more efficiently, or paying suppliers more slowly. For example, if the cash turnover changes to four times per year from two, internally fundable growth doubles (to 12 percent rather than 6 percent). Improving the cash conversion cycle and thus increasing the rate at which the firm can support growth internally reduces the firm's need for outside funds to a more manageable level.

For the small business with serious constraints on obtaining outside funds, these discretionary policies can help bring the firm's rate of growth into balance with its ability to finance that growth. Furthermore, such control on the part of management might impress bankers and others who have funds, which might ultimately help the firm get the outside financing it would have preferred all along.

ETHICAL DILEMMA

Money Back Guarantee, No Questions Asked

TradeSmart, Inc., operates 1,200 discount electronics stores throughout the United States. TradeSmart has been quite successful in a highly competitive industry, primarily because it has been able to offer brand-name products at prices lower than can be found at other discount outlets. Because of its size, the firm can purchase bulk inventory directly from manufacturers, and the economies of scale it derives from such purchases can be passed on to consumers in the form of lower prices.

In addition to low prices, TradeSmart offers an extremely liberal product return policy. Customers are permitted to return products for virtually any reason, with little regard to the time period covered by manufacturers' warranties. In fact, just a few days ago, a customer returned a digital pager that was more than two years old. TradeSmart gave the customer a full refund even though the pager appeared to have been run over by a car, which, if true, certainly would have voided the manufacturer's warranty. In another instance, a customer was given a refund when he returned the camcorder he had purchased three days earlier to record his daughter's wedding festivities. The customer could not describe the camcorder's malfunction—he said "it just didn't work right." The customer refused an offer to replace the camcorder; instead, he insisted on a full refund, which he was given. The manager of the customer relations department suspected that the customer had "purchased" the camcorder intending all along to return it after his daughter's wedding.

TradeSmart's return policy does not dissuade customers from this practice. According to Ed Davidson, vice-president of customer relations, TradeSmart is willing to stand behind every product it sells, regardless of the problem, because the company believes that such a policy is needed to attract and keep loyal customers in such a competitive industry. The company's motto—"Customer Satisfaction Is Our Business"—is displayed prominently throughout TradeSmart stores.

With such a liberal return policy, how does TradeSmart keep its prices so low? Actually, the firm ships the returned products back to the manufacturers as defective products, so the return costs are passed on to the manufacturers. According to manufacturers, only one out of every six products returned by TradeSmart is really defective. When manufacturers complain about returns of used products or products that have no mechanical problems, TradeSmart reminds them that the company does not have a service department, so its personnel are not knowledgeable concerning the technical circuitry of the products. Instead, the products are returned to the manufacturers with the customers' complaints attached. TradeSmart's inventory manager would contend that the company does not intentionally deceive or take advantage of the manufacturers' return policies and warranties.

Do you agree with TradeSmart's return policy? Is it ethical? What action would you take if you were one of TradeSmart's suppliers?

SUMMARY

This chapter examined working capital management, the relationship between working capital accounts, alternative ways of financing current assets, and ways to manage and evaluate the various working capital accounts. In addition, complexities faced by multinational firms when managing working capital in other countries were described. The key concepts covered in this chapter are listed below.

- **Working capital** refers to current assets, and **net working capital** is defined as current assets minus current liabilities. **Working capital policy** refers to decisions relating to the level of current assets and the way they are financed.

- The **cash conversion cycle** is the length of time between paying for purchases of inventory and receiving cash from the sale of finished goods. The cash conversion cycle can be calculated as follows:

$$\begin{matrix}\text{Cash}\\\text{conversion}\\\text{cycle}\end{matrix} = \left(\begin{matrix}\text{Inventory}\\\text{conversion}\\\text{period}\end{matrix} + \begin{matrix}\text{Receivables}\\\text{collection}\\\text{period}\end{matrix}\right) - \begin{matrix}\text{Payables}\\\text{deferral}\\\text{period}\end{matrix}$$

- The **inventory conversion period** is the average length of time required to convert raw materials into finished goods and then to sell them. The **receivables collection period** is the average length of time required to convert the firm's receivables into cash and is equal to the days sales outstanding (DSO). The **payables deferral period** is the average length of time between the purchase of raw materials and labor and the payment for them.
- Under a **relaxed current asset investment policy,** a firm holds relatively large amounts of each type of current asset. Under a **restricted current asset investment policy,** the firm holds minimal amounts of these items.
- **Permanent current assets** are those current assets that the firm holds even during slack times. **Temporary current assets** are the additional current assets that are needed during seasonal or cyclical peaks.
- The methods used to finance permanent and temporary current assets constitute the firm's current asset financing policy. A **moderate approach** involves matching the maturities of assets and liabilities so that temporary current assets are financed with short-term nonspontaneous debt whereas permanent current assets and fixed assets are financed with long-term debt or equity plus spontaneous debt. Under an **aggressive approach,** some permanent current assets and perhaps even some fixed assets are financed with short-term debt. A **conservative approach** would be to use long-term capital to finance all permanent assets and some of the temporary current assets.
- The advantages of short-term credit include the **speed** with which short-term loans can be arranged, increased **flexibility,** and the fact that short-term **interest rates** are generally **lower** than long-term rates. The principal disadvantage of short-term credit is the **extra risk** that the borrower must bear, because the lender can demand payment on short notice and the cost of the loan will increase if interest rates rise.
- **Short-term credit** is defined as any liability originally scheduled for payment within one year. Five major sources of short-term credit include the following: (1) **accruals,** which are continually recurring short-term liabilities, represent free, spontaneous credit; (2) **accounts payable** (also known as **trade credit**), which arise spontaneously as a result of purchases on credit from suppliers; (3) **bank loans,** which require the firm to sign a **promissory note** specifying the amount borrowed, the percentage interest rate, the repayment schedule, and any other conditions to which the parties have agreed; (4) **commercial paper,** which is unsecured short-term debt issued by large, financially strong corporations; and (5) **secured loans,** where the borrower pledges assets such as inventories or accounts receivable as collateral for loans.
- **Pledging** occurs when the firm uses accounts receivable as collateral for a loan. **Factoring** occurs when a firm sells its receivables to a financial organization.
- There are three basic arrangements when inventory is used as collateral for a loan. A **blanket lien** gives the lender a lien against all of the borrower's inven-

tories. A **trust receipt** is an instrument that acknowledges that goods are held in trust for the lender. **Warehouse receipt financing** is an arrangement under which the lender employs a third party to exercise control over the borrower's inventory and to act as the lender's agent.

- In general, the **effective cost** and the **annual percentage rate** of a short-term borrowing are computed as follows:

$$\text{Effective annual rate} = \text{EAR} = \left[1 + r_{PER}\right]^{m} - 1.0$$

$$\text{Annual percentage rate} = \text{APR} = r_{PER} \times m$$

where m is the number of borrowing (compounding) periods in one year. The interest rate per period, r_{PER}, is computed using the following equation:

$$\text{Interest rate per period (cost)} = r_{PER} = \frac{\text{Dollar cost of borrowing}}{\text{Amount of usable funds}}$$

- The **primary goal of cash management** is to reduce the amount of cash held to the minimum necessary to conduct business. The **transactions balance** is the cash necessary to conduct day-to-day business, whereas the **precautionary balance** is a cash reserve held to meet random, unforeseen needs. A **compensating balance** is a minimum checking account balance that a bank requires as compensation either for services provided or as part of a loan agreement. Firms also hold **speculative balances,** which allow them to take advantage of bargain purchases.
- **Effective cash management** encompasses the proper management of cash inflows and outflows. It entails five activities: (1) synchronizing cash flows, (2) using float, (3) accelerating collections, (4) determining where and when funds will be needed and ensuring that they are available at the right place at the right time, and (5) controlling disbursements.
- Two techniques that can be used to speed up collections are **lockboxes** and **preauthorized debits.** Also, a **concentration banking system** consolidates cash into a centralized pool that can be managed more efficiently than can a large number of individual accounts.
- Three techniques for controlling disbursements are **payables centralization, zero-balance accounts,** and **controlled disbursement accounts.**
- Firms can reduce their idle cash balances by holding **marketable securities,** which are investments that can be sold easily on short notice at close to their quoted market values. Marketable securities serve both as a substitute for cash and as a temporary investment for funds that will be needed in the near future.
- A firm's **credit policy** consists of four elements: (1) credit standards, (2) credit terms, (3) the collection policy, and (4) monitoring of receivables.
- Firms can use an **aging schedule** and the **days sales outstanding (DSO)** to keep track of their receivables position so as to help avoid a significant change in customers' payment patterns.
- **Inventory management** involves determining how much inventory to hold, when to place orders, and how many units to order.
- Inventory can be classified into three categories: (1) **raw materials,** (2) **work-in-process,** and (3) **finished goods.**

- **Inventory costs** can be divided into three types: carrying costs, ordering costs, and stockout costs. In general, carrying costs increase as the level of inventory rises, but ordering costs and stockout costs decline with larger inventory holdings.
- The **economic ordering quantity (EOQ)** model is a formula for determining the order quantity that will minimize total inventory costs:

$$\text{EOQ} = \sqrt{\frac{2 \times \text{O} \times \text{T}}{\text{C} \times \text{PP}}}$$

  Here O is the fixed cost per order, T is sales in units, C is the percentage cost of carrying inventory, and PP is the purchase price per unit.
- The **reorder point** is the inventory level at which new items must be ordered. **Safety stocks** are held to avoid shortages caused by two types of events: increases in demand and shipping delays. If suppliers offer **quantity discounts** to purchase materials, it might be beneficial for the firm to order more than the EOQ amount.
- Firms use inventory control systems such as the **red-line method,** as well as **computerized inventory control systems,** to help them keep track of actual inventory levels and to ensure that inventory levels are adjusted as sales change. **Just-in-time systems** and **outsourcing** are also employed to hold down inventory costs and, simultaneously, to improve the production process.
- **Multinational firms** use techniques similar to purely domestic firms to manage working capital, but they face more complex situations due to differences in the business, economic, legal environments of various countries.

Questions

15-1 Describe the relationships between accounts payable, inventories, accounts receivable, and the cash account by tracing the effects on these accounts of a product manufactured and sold by a company. Start with the purchase of raw materials, and conclude with the collection for the sale of the product.

15-2 Describe the cash conversion cycle. How can a financial manager use knowledge of the cash conversion cycle to better manage the firm's working capital?

15-3 What are the advantages of matching the maturities of assets and liabilities? What are the disadvantages?

15-4 What are the two principal reasons for holding cash? Can a firm estimate its target cash balance by summing the cash held to satisfy each of these reasons?

15-5 Why is it important for a financial manager to understand the concept of float to effectively manage the firm's cash?

15-6 Why would a lockbox plan make more sense for a firm that makes sales all over the United States than for a firm with the same volume of business but for which the sales are concentrated where the firm's corporate headquarters are located?

15-7 In general, does a firm want to speed up or slow down collections of payments made by its customers? Why? How does the same firm want to manage its disbursements? Why?

15-8 When selecting securities for portfolio investments, corporate treasurers must make a tradeoff between risk and returns. Is it true that most treasurers are willing to assume a fairly high exposure to risk to gain higher expected returns?

15-9 What are the four elements of a firm's credit policy? To what extent can firms set their own credit policies as opposed to having to accept policies that are dictated by "the competition"?

15-10 What are aging schedules, and how can the credit manager use them to more effectively manage accounts receivable?

15-11 Describe the three classifications of inventory, and indicate the purpose of holding each type.

15-12 "Every firm should use the EOQ model to determine the optimal level of inventory to maintain." Discuss the accuracy of this statement with respect to the form of the EOQ model presented in this chapter.

Self-Test Problems *(Solutions appear in Appendix B)*

Key terms

ST-1 Define each of the following terms:

a. Working capital; net working capital; working capital policy
b. Permanent current assets; temporary current assets
c. Cash conversion cycle; inventory conversion period; receivables collection period (DSO); payables deferral period
d. Relaxed current asset investment policy; restricted current asset investment policy; moderate current asset investment policy
e. Moderate (maturity matching) current asset financing policy; aggressive current asset financing policy; conservative current asset financing policy
f. Accruals; trade credit
g. Promissory note; line of credit; revolving credit agreement
h. Compensating balance (CB); commitment fee
i. Commercial paper; secured loan
j. Pledging receivables; factoring
k. Inventory blanket lien; trust receipt; warehouse receipt financing
l. Transactions balance; compensating balance; precautionary balance; speculative balance
m. Float; disbursement float, collections float, and net float
n. Lockbox plan; preauthorized debit
o. Marketable securities
p. Credit policy; credit terms; collection policy; aging schedule
q. Inventory carrying costs; ordering costs; total inventory costs
r. Economic ordering quantity (EOQ); EOQ model
s. Just-in-time system; outsourcing

Working capital policy

ST-2 The Calgary Company is attempting to establish a current assets policy. Fixed assets are $600,000, and the firm plans to maintain a 50 percent debt/assets ratio. The interest rate is 10 percent on all debt. The three alternative current asset policies under consideration are to carry current assets that total 40, 50, and 60 percent of projected sales. The company expects to earn 15 percent before interest and taxes on sales of $3 million. Calgary's marginal tax rate is 40 percent. What is the expected return on equity (ROE) under each alternative? (*Hint:* ROE is computed by dividing net income by the dollar amount of equity.)

Trade credit versus bank credit

ST-3 Gallinger Corporation projects an increase in sales from $1.5 million to $2 million, but it needs an additional $300,000 of current assets to support this expansion. The money can be obtained from the bank with a discount interest loan with a simple interest of 13 percent; no compensating balance is required. Alternatively, Gallinger can finance the expansion by no longer taking discounts, thereby increasing its accounts payable. The company makes purchases under terms of 2/10, net 30, but it can delay payment for an additional 35 days—paying in 65 days and thus becoming 35 days past due—without a penalty because of its suppliers' current excess capacity problems.

a. Based strictly on effective annual interest rate comparisons, how should Gallinger finance its expansion?
b. What additional qualitative factors should Gallinger consider before making a decision?

Change in credit policy

ST-4 The Boca Grande Company expects to have sales of $10 million this year under its current operating policies. Its variable costs as a percentage of sales are 80 percent, and its cost of short-term funds is 16 percent. Currently, Boca Grande's credit policy is net 25 (no discount for early payment), but its customers pay on average in 30 days. Boca Grande spends $50,000 per year to collect its credit accounts. It collects all receivables (that is, it has no bad debts), and its marginal tax rate is 40 percent. All costs associated with the manufacture of the product and with the credit department's operations are paid when the product is sold.

The credit manager is considering two alternative proposals for changing Boca Grande's credit policy. Should a change in credit policy be made?

Proposal 1: Lengthen the credit period by going from net 25 to net 30. Collection expenditures will remain constant. Under this proposal, sales are expected to increase by $1 million annually and the DSO is expected to increase from 30 to 45 days on all sales.

Proposal 2: Shorten the credit period by going from net 25 to net 20. Collection expenses will remain constant, but sales are expected to decrease by $1 million per year and the DSO is expected to decline from 30 to 22 days.

EOQ and total inventory costs

ST-5 The Homemade Bread Company buys and then sells (as bread) 2.6 million bushels of wheat annually. The wheat must be purchased in multiples of 2,000 bushels. Ordering costs are $5,000 per order. Annual carrying costs are 2 percent of the purchase price of $5 per bushel. The delivery time is six weeks.

a. What is the EOQ?

b. At what inventory level should the firm place an order for more wheat?

c. What are Homemade Bread's total inventory costs?

Problems

Disbursement float

15-1 The Garvin Company is setting up a new checking account with Barngrover National Bank. Garvin plans to issue checks in the amount of $1.6 million each day and to deduct them from its own records at the close of business on the day they are written. On average, the bank will receive and clear (that is, deduct from the firm's bank balance) the checks at 5 P.M. on the fourth day after they are written; for example, a check written on Monday will be cleared on Friday afternoon. The firm's agreement with the bank requires it to maintain a $1.2 million average compensating balance; this amount is $400,000 greater than the cash balance the firm would otherwise have on deposit. Garvin will make a $1.2 million deposit at the time it opens the account.

a. Assuming that the firm makes deposits at 2 P.M. each day (and the bank includes them in that day's transactions), how much must it deposit daily so as to maintain a sufficient balance once it reaches a steady state? (To figure out this answer, set up a table that shows the daily balance recorded on the company's books and the daily balance at the bank until a steady state is reached.) Indicate the required deposit on Day 1, Day 2, Day 3, and Day 4, if any, and on each day thereafter, assuming that the company will write checks for $1.6 million on Day 1 and each day thereafter.

b. How many days of float does Garvin carry?

c. What ending daily balance should the firm try to maintain (1) on the bank's records and (2) on its own records?

d. Explain how net float can help increase the value of the firm's common stock.

Lockbox system

15-2 Durst Corporation began operations five years ago as a small firm serving customers in the Denver area. Its reputation and market area grew quickly, such that today Durst has customers throughout the entire United States. Despite its broad customer base, Durst has maintained its headquarters in Denver and keeps its central billing system there. The firm's management is considering an alternative collection procedure to reduce its mail time and processing float. On average, it takes five days from the time customers mail payments until Durst is able to receive, process, and deposit them. Durst would like to set up a lockbox collection system, which it estimates would reduce the time lag from customer mailing to deposit by three days—bringing it down to two days. Durst receives an average of $1,400,000 in payments per day.

a. How many days of collection float now exist and what would this period be under the lockbox system? What reduction in cash balances could Durst achieve by initiating the lockbox system?

b. If Durst has an opportunity cost of 10 percent, how much is the lockbox system worth on an annual basis?

c. What is the maximum monthly charge that Durst should pay for the lockbox system?

Cost of bank loans

15-3 UFSU Corporation intends to borrow $450,000 to support its short-term financing requirements during the next year. The company is evaluating its financing options at the bank where it maintains its checking account. The financing alternatives offered by the bank include the following:

Alternative 1: A discount interest loan with a simple interest of 9.5 percent

Alternative 2: A bank loan with 10.5 percent interest that is paid at the maturity of the loan (at the end of the year)

Alternative 3: A $1 million revolving line of credit with interest of 9.25 percent paid on the amount borrowed at the end of the year and a 0.25 percent commitment fee paid on the unused balance

Compute both the APR and the effective cost of each financing alternative assuming that UFSU borrows $450,000. Which alternative should UFSU use?

Cost of bank loans

15-4 Gifts Galore, Inc., borrowed $1.5 million from National City Bank. The loan was made at an annual interest rate of 9 percent and a 20 percent compensating balance requirement. The loan was for a period of three months.

a. The approximate interest rate on the loan was 11.25 percent. What is the true effective rate?

b. What would be the effective cost of the loan if the note required discount interest?

Relaxing collection efforts

15-5 The Pettit Corporation has annual credit sales of $2 million. Current expenses for the firm's collection department are $30,000, bad debt losses are 2 percent, and the days sales outstanding is 30 days. Pettit is considering easing its collection efforts so that collection expenses will be reduced to $22,000 per year. The change is expected to increase bad debt losses to 3 percent and to increase the days sales outstanding to 45 days. In addition, sales are expected to increase to $2.2 million per year.

Should Pettit relax collection efforts if the opportunity cost of funds is 12 percent, the variable cost ratio is 75 percent, and its marginal tax rate is 40 percent? Assume that any costs associated with the manufacture and sale of the product (including credit costs) are made on the day of the sale.

EOQ and inventory costs

15-6 The following inventory data have been established for the Thompson Company:

(1) Orders must be placed in multiples of 100 units.
(2) Annual sales are 338,000 units.
(3) The purchase price per unit is $6.
(4) Carrying costs are 20 percent of the purchase price of goods.
(5) The fixed order cost is $48.
(6) Three days are required for delivery of orders.

a. What is the EOQ?

b. How many orders should Thompson place each year?

c. At what inventory level should an order be made?

d. Calculate the total cost of ordering and carrying inventories if the order quantity is (1) 4,000 units, (2) 4,800 units, and (3) 6,000 units. (4) What are the total costs if the order quantity is the EOQ?

Exam-Type Problems

The problems included in this section are set up in such a way that they could be used as multiple-choice exam problems.

Cash conversion cycle

15-7 The Saliford Corporation has an inventory conversion period of 60 days, a receivables collection period of 36 days, and a payables deferral period of 24 days.

a. What is the length of the firm's cash conversion cycle?

b. If Saliford's annual sales are $3,960,000 and all sales are on credit, what is the average balance in accounts receivable? (*Hint:* The accounts receivable balance should equal the average age of the receivables, which is the collection period, times the daily sales.)

c. What would happen to Saliford's cash conversion cycle if, on average, the length of time that products remain in inventory is shortened to 45 days?

Cost of bank credit

15-8 Susan Visscher, owner of Visscher's Hardware, is negotiating with First Merchant's Bank for a $50,000, 1-year loan. First Merchant's has offered Visscher the following alternatives. Calculate the effective interest rate for each alternative. Which alternative has the lowest effective interest rate?

a. A 12 percent annual rate on a bank loan with no compensating balance required and interest due at the end of the year

b. A 9 percent annual rate on a bank loan with a 20 percent compensating balance required and interest due at the end of the year

c. An 8.75 percent annual rate on a discount interest loan with a 15 percent compensating balance

Cost of credit

15-9 Boles Corporation needs to raise $500,000 for one year to supply working capital to a new store. Boles buys from its suppliers on terms of 3/10, net 90, and it currently pays on the Day 10 and takes discounts. It could, however, forego discounts, pay on Day 90, and obtain the needed $500,000 in the form of costly trade credit. Alternatively, Boles could borrow from its bank on a 12 percent discount interest rate basis. What is the effective annual interest rate of the lower-cost source of funds?

Computation of float

15-10 Clearwater Glass Company has examined its cash management policy and found that it takes an average of five days for checks written by the company to reach its bank and thus be deducted from its checking account balance (that is, disbursement delay, or float, is five days). On the other hand, it takes, on average, four days from the time Clearwater Glass receives payments from its customers until the funds are available for use at the bank (that is, collection delay, or float, is four days). On an average day, Clearwater Glass writes checks that total $70,000, and it receives checks from customers that total $80,000.

a. Compute the disbursement float, collection float, and net float in dollars.

b. If Clearwater Glass has an opportunity cost equal to 10 percent, how much would it be willing to spend each year to reduce collection delay (float) by two days? (*Hint:* Assume that any freed-up funds are invested at 10 percent annually.)

Receivables balance and DSO

15-11 Morrissey Industries sells on terms of 3/10, net 30. Total sales for the year are $900,000. Forty percent of the customers pay on Day 10 and take discounts; the other 60 percent pay, on average, 40 days after their purchases.

a. What is the days sales outstanding?

b. What is the average amount of receivables?

c. What would happen to the average receivables if Morrissey tightened its collection policy such that all nondiscount customers paid on Day 30?

Tightening credit terms

15-12 Helen Bowers, the new credit manager of the Muscarella Corporation, was alarmed to find that Muscarella sells on credit terms of net 50 days, whereas industrywide credit terms have recently been lowered to net 30 days. Muscarella's annual credit sales are $3 million. Bowers estimates that tightening the credit terms to 30 days would reduce annual sales to $2.6 million, but days sales outstanding would fall from 60 days to 35 days.

Muscarella's variable cost ratio is 70 percent, its marginal tax rate is 40 percent, and all costs associated with the production and sale of the product (including credit costs) are paid on the day of the sale. If the opportunity cost of funds invested in receivables is 11 percent, should Muscarella make the change in its credit terms?

EOQ

15-13 Green Thumb Garden Centers sells 240,000 bags of lawn fertilizer annually. The optimal safety stock (which is on hand initially) is 1,200 bags. Each bag costs Green Thumb $4, inventory carrying costs are 20 percent, and the cost of placing an order with the firm's supplier is $25.

a. What is the economic ordering quantity?
b. What is the maximum inventory of fertilizer?
c. What will Green Thumb's average inventory be?
d. How often must the company order bags of fertilizer?

Integrative Problem

Cash management

15-14 Ray Smith, a retired librarian, recently opened an outdoor recreation shop called Smitty's Sports Paradise (SSP). Ray decided that, at age 62, he wasn't quite ready to stay at home, living the life of leisure. It had always been his dream to open an outdoor recreation shop, so his friends convinced him to go ahead. Because Ray's educational background was in literature and not in business, he hired you, a finance expert, to help him with the store's cash management. Ray is very eager to learn, so he has asked you to develop a set of questions to help him understand cash management. Answer the following questions:

a. What is the goal of cash management?
b. For what reasons do firms hold cash?
c. What is meant by the terms "precautionary balance" and "speculative balance"?
d. What are some specific advantages for a firm in holding adequate cash balances?
e. How can a firm synchronize its cash flows, and what good would this effort do?
f. You have been going through the store's checkbook and bank balances. In the process, you discovered that SSP, on average, writes checks in the amount of $10,000 each day and that it takes approximately five days for these checks to clear. Also, the firm receives checks in the amount of $10,000 daily, but loses four days while they are being deposited and cleared. What is the firm's disbursement float, collections float, and net float?
g. How can a firm speed up collections and slow down disbursements?
h. Why would a firm hold marketable securities?
i. What factors should a firm consider in building its marketable securities portfolio? What are some securities that should be held and some that should not be held?

Credit policy

15-15 Ray now asks you to examine his company's credit policy to determine whether changes are needed. One of his employees, who graduated recently with a finance major, has recommended that the credit terms be changed from 2/10, net 30, to 3/20, net 45, and that both the credit standards and the collection policy be relaxed. According to the employee, such a change would cause sales to increase from $3.6 million to $4.0 million.

Currently, 62.5 percent of SSP's customers pay on Day 10 of the billing cycle and take the discount, 32 percent pay on Day 30, and 5.5 percent pay (on average) on

Day 60. If the firm adopts the new credit policy, Ray thinks that 72.5 percent of customers would take the discount, 10 percent would pay on Day 45, and 17.5 percent would pay late, on Day 90. Bad debt losses for both policies are expected to be trivial.

SSP's variable operating costs are currently 75 percent of sales, its cost of funds is 10 percent, and its marginal tax rate is 40 percent. None of these factors would change as a result of a credit policy change. All cash payments associated with the production and sale of products (including credit costs) are made on the day the products are sold.

To help him decide whether to adopt the new policy, Ray has asked you to answer the following questions.

a. What four variables make up a firm's credit policy? In what direction would each be changed if the credit policy were tightened? How would each variable tend to affect sales, the level of receivables, and bad debt losses?

b. How are the days sales outstanding and the average collection period related? What would the DSO be if SSP maintains its current credit policy? If it adopts the proposed policy?

c. What is the dollar amount of discounts granted under the current and the proposed credit policies?

d. Should SSP make the change?

e. Suppose the company makes the proposed change, but its competitors react by changing their own credit terms, with the net result being that SSP's gross sales remain at the $3.6 million level. How would this situation affect the company's value?

f. *(1)* What does the term "monitoring accounts receivable" mean?
(2) Why would a firm want to monitor its receivables?
(3) How might the DSO and the aging schedule be used in this process?

EOQ model

15-16 Now Ray asks you to look at the company's inventory position. He thinks that inventories might be too high as a result of the manager's tendency to order in large quantities. Ray has decided to examine the situation for one key product—fly rods that cost $320 each to purchase and prepare for sale. Annual sales of the product are 2,500 units (rods), and the annual carrying cost is 10 percent of inventory value. The company has been buying 500 rods per order and placing another order when the stock on hand falls to 100 rods. Each time SSP orders, it incurs a cost equal to $64. Sales are uniform throughout the year.

a. Ray believes that the EOQ model should be used to help determine the optimal inventory situation for this product. What is the EOQ formula, and what are the key assumptions underlying this model?

b. What is the formula for calculating total inventory costs?

c. What is the EOQ for the fly rods? What will the total inventory costs be for this product if SSP orders the EOQ amount?

d. What is SSP's added cost if it orders 500 fly rods rather than the EOQ amount? What if it orders 750 rods each time?

e. Suppose it takes three days for SSP to receive its orders and package the rods before they are ready for sale. Assuming certainty in production time and usage, at what inventory level should SSP order more fly rods? (Assume a 360-day year, that SSP is open every day, and that SSP orders the EOQ amount.)

f. Of course, there is uncertainty in SSP's usage rate as well as in order delays, so the company must carry a safety stock to avoid running out of the fly rods and having to lose sales. If SSP carries a safety stock of 50 rods, what effect would this policy have on total inventory costs?

g. For most of SSP's products, inventory usage is not uniform throughout the year, but rather follows some seasonal pattern. Could the EOQ model be used in this situation? If so, how?

b. How would the following factors affect the use of the EOQ model?
  (1) Use of "just-in-time" procedures.
  (2) The use of air freight for deliveries.
  (3) Computerized inventory control systems.

■ Short-term financing

15-17 Ray has asked you to review the company's short-term financing policies and prepare a report to help him with SSP's future working capital financing decisions. To assist you in getting started, he has prepared some questions that, when answered, will give Ray a better idea of the company's short-term financing policies.

a. What is short-term credit, and what are the major sources of this credit?

b. Is there a cost to accruals, and do firms have much control over them? What is trade credit?

c. Like most small companies, SSP has two primary sources of short-term debt: trade credit and bank loans. One supplier, which supplies SSP with $50,000 of materials each year, offers purchases on terms of 2/10, net 50.
  (1) What are SSP's net daily purchases from this supplier?
  (2) What is the average level of SSP's accounts payable to this supplier if SSP takes the discount? What is the average level if it does not take the discount?
  (3) What is the approximate cost if SSP does not take the discount? What is its effective annual cost?

d. In discussing a possible loan with the firm's banker, Ray has found that the bank is willing to lend SSP a maximum of $800,000 for one year at a 9 percent simple, or quoted, rate. Unfortunately, he forgot to ask what the specific terms would be.
  (1) Assume that the firm will borrow $800,000. What would be the effective interest rate if the loan required interest to be paid at the end of the year (not a discount interest loan)? If the loan had been an 8 percent interest loan for six months rather than for one year, would that change affect the effective annual rate?
  (2) What would be the effective rate if the loan were a discount interest loan? Assume the loan is a 1-year loan.
  (3) Assume that the bank requires interest to be paid at the end of the year and it requires the firm to maintain a 20 percent compensating balance. What is the effective annual rate on the loan? Assume that SSP does not have any funds in a checking account at the bank.

e. SSP is considering using secured short-term financing. What is a secured loan? What two types of current assets can be used to secure loans?

f. What are the differences between pledging receivables and factoring receivables? Is one type generally considered better?

g. What are the differences among the three forms of inventory financing? Is one type generally considered best?

12

The Financial Environment: Markets, Institutions, and Interest Rates

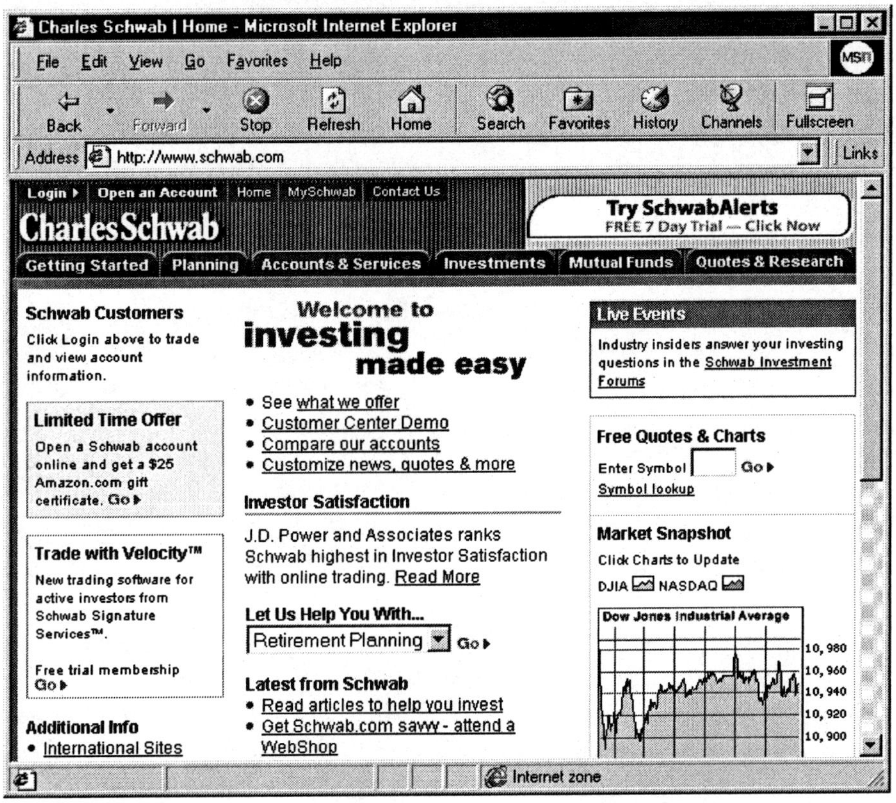

SOURCE: Accessed November 1999. © 1999 Charles Schwab & Co., Inc. www.schwab.com

To take a look at the online ventures of Charles Schwab and Merrill Lynch, check out their web sites at **http://www.schwab.com** and **http://askmerrill.ml.com.** You can test the Schwab customer experience or take a tour of Merrill Lynch Online.

SCHWAB AND MERRILL LYNCH COMPETE IN A CHANGING ENVIRONMENT

CHARLES SCHWAB AND MERRILL LYNCH

Financial managers and investors don't operate in a vacuum — they make decisions within a large and complex financial environment. This environment includes financial markets and institutions, tax and regulatory policies, and the state of the economy. The environment both defines the available financial alternatives and affects the outcomes of various decisions. Therefore, it is crucial that financial managers and investors have a good understanding of the environment in which they operate.

Good financial decisions require an understanding of the current direction of the economy, interest rates, and the stock market — but figuring out what's likely to happen is no trivial matter. Recently, the financial environment has been extraordinarily favorable to financial managers and investors: The economy has not seen a recession for nearly 10 years; interest rates and inflation have remained relatively low; and the stock market has boomed throughout most of the past decade. At the same time, the financial environment has undergone tremendous changes, presenting financial managers and investors with both opportunities and risks.

Consider Charles Schwab and Merrill Lynch. Benefiting from the strong stock market, traditional brokerage powerhouse Merrill Lynch has seen its stock rise more than 350 percent over the past five years. During this same period, Charles Schwab, the leader in online trading, has seen its stock rise by nearly 900 percent! The Internet has enabled online brokers such as Schwab, E*Trade, DLJDirect, and Datek to offer investors the opportunity to trade stocks at a small fraction of the price traditionally charged by full-service firms such as Merrill Lynch. While online trading was virtually nonexistent just a couple of years ago, there are now an estimated 160 online brokers serving more than 13 million customers. Some estimate that by 2003 there will be more than 40 million online accounts.

The same forces that dramatically affected the brokerage industry have had similar effects on other industries. Companies such as Barnes and Noble and Toys Я Us have been presented with new and aggressive competition from the likes of Amazon.com and eToys Inc. Likewise, changing technology has altered the way millions of consumers purchase airline tickets, hotel rooms, and automobiles. Consequently, financial managers must understand today's technological environment and be ready to change operations as the environment evolves. ■

PUTTING THINGS IN PERSPECTIVE

In earlier chapters we discussed financial statements and showed how financial managers and others analyze them to see where their firms have been and are headed. Financial managers also need to understand the environment and markets within which businesses operate. Therefore, this chapter describes the markets where capital is raised, securities are traded, and stock prices are established, as well as the institutions that operate in these markets. In the process, we also explore the principal factors that determine the level of interest rates. ■

THE FINANCIAL MARKETS

Businesses, individuals, and governments often need to raise capital. For example, suppose Carolina Power & Light (CP&L) forecasts an increase in the demand for electricity in North Carolina, and the company decides to build a new power plant. Because CP&L almost certainly will not have the $1 billion or so necessary to pay for the plant, the company will have to raise this capital in the financial markets. Or suppose Mr. Fong, the proprietor of a San Francisco hardware store, decides to expand into appliances. Where will he get the money to buy the initial inventory of TV sets, washers, and freezers? Similarly, if the Johnson family wants to buy a home that costs $100,000, but they have only $20,000 in savings, how can they raise the additional $80,000? If the city of New York wants to borrow $200 million to finance a new sewer plant, or the federal government needs money to meet its needs, they too need access to the capital markets.

On the other hand, some individuals and firms have incomes that are greater than their current expenditures, so they have funds available to invest. For example, Carol Hawk has an income of $36,000, but her expenses are only $30,000, and in 2000 Ford Motor Company had accumulated roughly $21 billion of cash and marketable securities, which it has available for future investments.

Types of Markets

People and organizations wanting to borrow money are brought together with those having surplus funds in the *financial markets*. Note that "markets" is plural — there are a great many different financial markets in a developed economy such as ours. Each market deals with a somewhat different type of instrument in terms of the instrument's maturity and the assets backing it. Also, different markets serve different types of customers, or operate in different parts of the country. For these reasons it is often useful to classify markets along various dimensions:

1. **Physical asset vs. Financial asset markets.** *Physical asset markets* (also called "tangible" or "real" asset markets) are those for such products as

wheat, autos, real estate, computers, and machinery. *Financial asset markets,* on the other hand, deal with stocks, bonds, notes, mortgages, and other *claims on real assets,* as well as with *derivative securities* whose values are *derived* from changes in the prices of other assets.

Spot Markets
The markets in which assets are bought or sold for "on-the-spot" delivery.

Futures Markets
The markets in which participants agree today to buy or sell an asset at some future date.

2. **Spot vs. Futures markets. Spot markets** are markets in which assets are bought or sold for "on-the-spot" delivery (literally, within a few days). **Futures markets** are markets in which participants agree today to buy or sell an asset at some future date. For example, a farmer may enter into a futures contract in which he agrees today to sell 5,000 bushels of soybeans six months from now at a price of $5 a bushel. In contrast, an international food producer looking to buy soybeans in the future may enter into a futures contract in which it agrees to buy soybeans three months from now.

Money Markets
The financial markets in which funds are borrowed or loaned for short periods (less than one year).

Capital Markets
The financial markets for stocks and for intermediate- or long-term debt (one year or longer).

3. **Money vs. Capital markets. Money markets** are the markets for short-term, highly liquid debt securities. The New York and London money markets have long been the world's largest, but Tokyo is rising rapidly. **Capital markets** are the markets for intermediate- or long-term debt and corporate stocks. The New York Stock Exchange, where the stocks of the largest U.S. corporations are traded, is a prime example of a capital market. There is no hard and fast rule on this, but when describing debt markets, "short term" generally means less than one year, "intermediate term" means one to five years, and "long term" means more than five years.

Primary Markets
Markets in which corporations raise capital by issuing new securities.

Secondary Markets
Markets in which securities and other financial assets are traded among investors after they have been issued by corporations.

4. **Primary vs. Secondary markets. Primary markets** are the markets in which corporations raise new capital. If Microsoft were to sell a new issue of common stock to raise capital, this would be a primary market transaction. The corporation selling the newly created stock receives the proceeds from the sale in a primary market transaction. **Secondary markets** are markets in which existing, already outstanding, securities are traded among investors. Thus, if Jane Doe decided to buy 1,000 shares of AT&T stock, the purchase would occur in the secondary market. The New York Stock Exchange is a secondary market, since it deals in outstanding, as opposed to newly issued, stocks and bonds. Secondary markets also exist for mortgages, various other types of loans, and other financial assets. The corporation whose securities are being traded is not involved in a secondary market transaction and, thus, does not receive any funds from such a sale.

Initial Public Offering (IPO) Market
The market in which firms "go public" by offering shares to the public.

The **initial public offering (IPO) market** is a subset of the primary market. Here firms "go public" by offering shares to the public for the first time. Microsoft had its IPO in 1986. Previously, Bill Gates and other insiders owned all the shares. In many IPOs, the insiders sell some of their shares plus the company sells new shares to raise additional capital.

Private Markets
Markets in which transactions are worked out directly between two parties.

Public Markets
Markets in which standardized contracts are traded on organized exchanges.

5. **Private vs. Public markets. Private markets,** where transactions are worked out directly between two parties, are differentiated from **public markets,** where standardized contracts are traded on organized exchanges. Bank loans and private placements of debt with insurance companies are examples of private market transactions. Since these transactions are private, they may be structured in any manner that appeals to the two parties. By contrast, securities that are issued in public markets (for example, common stock and corporate bonds) are ultimately held by a large number of individuals. Public securities must have fairly standardized contractual

TABLE 5-1 Summary of Major Market Instruments, Market Participants, and Security Characteristics

INSTRUMENT (1)	MARKET (2)	MAJOR PARTICIPANTS (3)	SECURITY CHARACTERISTICS: RISKINESS (4)	ORIGINAL MATURITY (5)	INTEREST RATE ON 12/29/00[a] (6)
U.S. Treasury bills	Money	Sold by U.S. Treasury to finance federal expenditures	Default-free	91 days to 1 year	5.7%
Bankers' acceptances	Money	A firm's promise to pay, guaranteed by a bank	Low degree of risk if guaranteed by a strong bank	Up to 180 days	6.3
Commercial paper	Money	Issued by financially secure firms to large investors	Low default risk	Up to 270 days	6.4
Negotiable certificates of deposit (CDs)	Money	Issued by major money-center commercial banks to large investors	Default risk depends on the strength of the issuing bank	Up to 1 year	6.3
Money market mutual funds	Money	Invest in Treasury bills, CDs, and commercial paper; held by individuals and businesses	Low degree of risk	No specific maturity (instant liquidity)	6.0
Eurodollar market time deposits	Money	Issued by banks outside U.S.	Default risk depends on the strength of the issuing bank	Up to 1 year	6.3
Consumer credit loans	Money	Issued by banks/credit unions/finance companies to individuals	Risk is variable	Variable	Variable
U.S. Treasury notes and bonds	Capital	Issued by U.S. government	No default risk, but price will decline if interest rates rise	2 to 30 years	5.5

[a] The yields reported on money market mutual funds and bankers' acceptances are from *The Wall Street Journal*. All other data are from the *Federal Reserve Statistical Release*. Money market rates assume a 3-month maturity. The corporate bond rate is for AAA-rated bonds.

features, both to appeal to a broad range of investors and also because public investors cannot afford the time to study unique, nonstandardized contracts. Their diverse ownership also ensures that public securities are relatively liquid. Private market securities are, therefore, more tailor-made but less liquid, whereas public market securities are more liquid but subject to greater standardization.

Other classifications could be made, but this breakdown is sufficient to show that there are many types of financial markets. Also, note that the distinctions among markets are often blurred and unimportant, except as a general point of reference. For example, it makes little difference if a firm borrows for 11, 12, or 13 months, hence, whether we have a "money" or "capital" market transaction. You should recognize the big differences among types of markets, but don't get hung up trying to distinguish them at the boundaries.

A healthy economy is dependent on efficient transfers of funds from people who are net savers to firms and individuals who need capital. Without efficient

TABLE 5-1 continued

			SECURITY CHARACTERISTICS		
INSTRUMENT (1)	MARKET (2)	MAJOR PARTICIPANTS (3)	RISKINESS (4)	ORIGINAL MATURITY (5)	INTEREST RATE ON 12/29/00[a] (6)
Mortgages	Capital	Borrowings from commercial banks and S&Ls by individuals and businesses	Risk is variable	Up to 30 years	7.1%
State and local government bonds	Capital	Issued by state and local governments to individuals and institutional investors	Riskier than U.S. government securities, but exempt from most taxes	Up to 30 years	5.1
Corporate bonds	Capital	Issued by corporations to individuals and institutional investors	Riskier than U.S. government securities, but less risky than preferred and common stocks; varying degree of risk within bonds depending on strength of issuer	Up to 40 years[b]	7.2
Leases	Capital	Similar to debt in that firms can lease assets rather than borrow and then buy the assets	Risk similar to corporate bonds	Generally 3 to 20 years	Similar to bond yields
Preferred stocks	Capital	Issued by corporations to individuals and institutional investors	Riskier than corporate bonds, but less risky than common stock	Unlimited	7 to 9%
Common stocks[c]	Capital	Issued by corporations to individuals and institutional investors	Risky	Unlimited	10 to 15%

[b] Just recently, a few corporations have issued 100-year bonds; however, the majority have issued bonds with maturities less than 40 years.

[c] Common stocks are expected to provide a "return" in the form of dividends and capital gains rather than interest. Of course, if you buy a stock, your *actual* return may be considerably higher or lower than your *expected* return. For example, Nasdaq stocks on average provided a negative return of 39.3 percent in 2000, but that was well below the return most investors expected.

Students can access current and historical interest rates and economic data as well as regional economic data for the states of Arkansas, Illinois, Indiana, Kentucky, Mississippi, Missouri, and Tennessee from the Federal Reserve Economic Data (FRED) site at **http://www.stls.frb.org/fred/**.

transfers, the economy simply could not function: Carolina Power & Light could not raise capital, so Raleigh's citizens would have no electricity; the Johnson family would not have adequate housing; Carol Hawk would have no place to invest her savings; and so on. Obviously, the level of employment and productivity, hence our standard of living, would be much lower. Therefore, it is absolutely essential that our financial markets function efficiently—not only quickly, but also at a low cost.[1]

Table 5-1 gives a listing of the most important instruments traded in the various financial markets. The instruments are arranged from top to bottom in

[1] As the countries of the former Soviet Union and other Eastern European nations move toward capitalism, just as much attention must be paid to the establishment of cost-efficient financial markets as to electrical power, transportation, communications, and other infrastructure systems. Economic efficiency is simply impossible without a good system for allocating capital within the economy.

ascending order of typical length of maturity. As we go through the book, we will look in much more detail at many of the instruments listed in Table 5-1. For example, we will see that there are many varieties of corporate bonds, ranging from "plain vanilla" bonds to bonds that are convertible into common stocks to bonds whose interest payments vary depending on the inflation rate. Still, the table gives an idea of the characteristics and costs of the instruments traded in the major financial markets.

RECENT TRENDS

Financial markets have experienced many changes during the last two decades. Technological advances in computers and telecommunications, along with the globalization of banking and commerce, have led to deregulation, and this has increased competition throughout the world. The result is a much more efficient, internationally linked market, but one that is far more complex than existed a few years ago. While these developments have been largely positive, they have also created problems for policy makers. At a recent conference, Federal Reserve Board Chairman Alan Greenspan stated that modern financial markets "expose national economies to shocks from new and unexpected sources, and with little if any lag." He went on to say that central banks must develop new ways to evaluate and limit risks to the financial system. Large amounts of capital move quickly around the world in response to changes in interest and exchange rates, and these movements can disrupt local institutions and economies.

With globalization has come the need for greater cooperation among regulators at the international level. Various committees are currently working to improve coordination, but the task is not easy. Factors that complicate coordination include (1) the differing structures among nations' banking and securities industries, (2) the trend in Europe toward financial service conglomerates, and (3) a reluctance on the part of individual countries to give up control over their national monetary policies. Still, regulators are unanimous about the need to close the gaps in the supervision of worldwide markets.

Derivative
Any financial asset whose value is derived from the value of some other "underlying" asset.

Another important trend in recent years has been the increased use of **derivatives.** A derivative is any security whose value is *derived* from the price of some other "underlying" asset. An option to buy IBM stock is a derivative, as is a contract to buy Japanese yen six months from now. The value of the IBM option depends on the price of IBM's stock, and the value of the Japanese yen "future" depends on the exchange rate between yen and dollars. The market for derivatives has grown faster than any other market in recent years, providing corporations with new opportunities but also exposing them to new risks.

Derivatives can be used either to reduce risks or to speculate. Suppose an importer's net income tends to fall whenever the dollar falls relative to the yen. That company could reduce its risk by purchasing derivatives that increase in value whenever the dollar declines. This would be called a *hedging operation,* and its purpose is to reduce risk exposure. Speculation, on the other hand, is done in the hope of high returns, but it raises risk exposure. For example, Procter & Gamble recently disclosed that it lost $150 million on derivative investments, and Orange County (California) went bankrupt as a result of its treasurer's speculation in derivatives.

The size and complexity of derivatives transactions concern regulators, academics, and members of Congress. Fed Chairman Greenspan noted that, in theory, derivatives should allow companies to manage risk better, but that it is not clear whether recent innovations have "increased or decreased the inherent stability of the financial system."

SELF-TEST QUESTIONS

Distinguish between physical asset markets and financial asset markets.

What is the difference between spot and futures markets?

Distinguish between money and capital markets.

What is the difference between primary and secondary markets?

Differentiate between private and public markets.

Why are financial markets essential for a healthy economy?

What is a derivative, and how is its value related to that of an "underlying asset"?

FINANCIAL INSTITUTIONS

Transfers of capital between savers and those who need capital take place in the three different ways diagrammed in Figure 5-1:

1. *Direct transfers* of money and securities, as shown in the top section, occur when a business sells its stocks or bonds directly to savers, without going through any type of financial institution. The business delivers its securities to savers, who in turn give the firm the money it needs.
2. As shown in the middle section, transfers may also go through an *investment banking house* such as Merrill Lynch, which *underwrites* the issue. An underwriter serves as a middleman and facilitates the issuance of securities. The company sells its stocks or bonds to the investment bank, which in turn sells these same securities to savers. The businesses' securities and the savers' money merely "pass through" the investment banking house. However, the investment bank does buy and hold the securities for a period of time, so it is taking a risk—it may not be able to resell them to savers for as much as it paid. Because new securities are involved and the corporation receives the proceeds of the sale, this is a primary market transaction.
3. Transfers can also be made through a *financial intermediary* such as a bank or mutual fund. Here the intermediary obtains funds from savers in exchange for its own securities. The intermediary then uses this money to purchase and then hold businesses' securities. For example, a saver might give dollars to a bank, receiving from it a certificate of deposit, and then the bank might lend the money to a small business in the form of a mortgage loan. Thus, intermediaries literally create new forms of capital—in this case, certificates of deposit, which are both safer and more liquid

FIGURE 5-1 **Diagram of the Capital Formation Process**

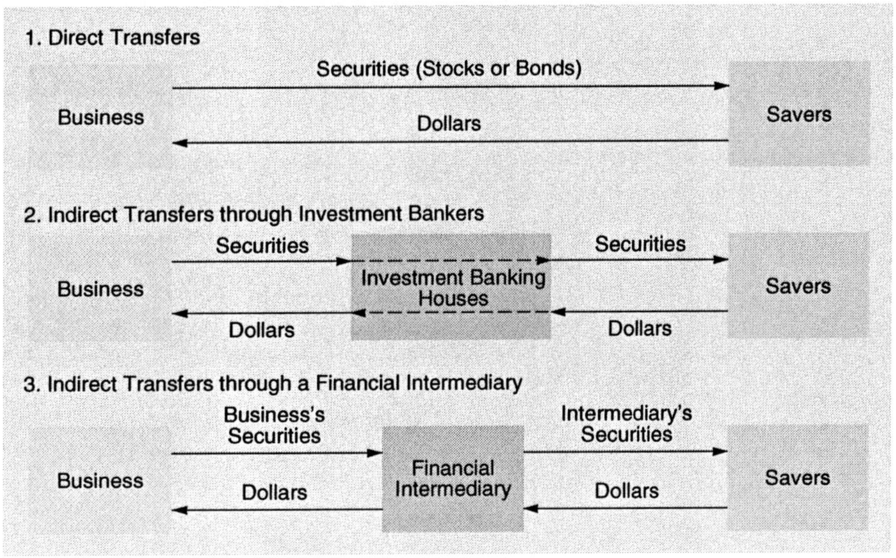

than mortgages and thus are better securities for most savers to hold. The existence of intermediaries greatly increases the efficiency of money and capital markets.

In our example, we assume that the entity needing capital is a business, and specifically a corporation, but it is easy to visualize the demander of capital as a home purchaser, a government unit, and so on.

Investment Banking House
An organization that underwrites and distributes new investment securities and helps businesses obtain financing.

Direct transfers of funds from savers to businesses are possible and do occur on occasion, but it is generally more efficient for a business to enlist the services of an **investment banking house** such as Merrill Lynch, Salomon Smith Barney, Morgan Stanley Dean Witter, or Goldman Sachs. Such organizations (1) help corporations design securities with features that are currently attractive to investors, (2) then buy these securities from the corporation, and (3) resell them to savers. Although the securities are sold twice, this process is really one primary market transaction, with the investment banker acting as a facilitator to help transfer capital from savers to businesses.

Financial Intermediaries
Specialized financial firms that facilitate the transfer of funds from savers to demanders of capital.

The **financial intermediaries** shown in the third section of Figure 5-1 do more than simply transfer money and securities between firms and savers — they literally create new financial products. Since the intermediaries are generally large, they gain economies of scale in analyzing the creditworthiness of potential borrowers, in processing and collecting loans, and in pooling risks and thus helping individual savers diversify, that is, "not putting all their financial eggs in one basket." Further, a system of specialized intermediaries can enable savings to do more than just draw interest. For example, individuals can put money into banks and get both interest income and a convenient way of making payments (checking), or put money into life insurance companies and get both interest income and protection for their beneficiaries.

In the United States and other developed nations, a set of specialized, highly efficient financial intermediaries has evolved. The situation is changing rapidly, however, and different types of institutions are performing services that were formerly reserved for others, causing institutional distinctions to become blurred. Still, there is a degree of institutional identity, and here are the major classes of intermediaries:

1. *Commercial banks,* the traditional "department stores of finance," serve a wide variety of savers and borrowers. Historically, commercial banks were the major institutions that handled checking accounts and through which the Federal Reserve System expanded or contracted the money supply. Today, however, several other institutions also provide checking services and significantly influence the money supply. Conversely, commercial banks are providing an ever-widening range of services, including stock brokerage services and insurance.
2. *Savings and loan associations (S&Ls),* which have traditionally served individual savers and residential and commercial mortgage borrowers, take the funds of many small savers and then lend this money to home buyers and other types of borrowers. In the 1980s, the S&L industry experienced severe problems when (1) short-term interest rates paid on savings accounts rose well above the returns being earned on the existing mortgages held by S&Ls and (2) commercial real estate suffered a severe slump, resulting in high mortgage default rates. Together, these events forced many S&Ls to either merge with stronger institutions or close their doors.
3. *Mutual savings banks,* which are similar to S&Ls, operate primarily in the northeastern states, accept savings primarily from individuals, and lend mainly on a long-term basis to home buyers and consumers.
4. *Credit unions* are cooperative associations whose members are supposed to have a common bond, such as being employees of the same firm. Members' savings are loaned only to other members, generally for auto purchases, home improvement loans, and home mortgages. Credit unions are often the cheapest source of funds available to individual borrowers.
5. *Pension funds* are retirement plans funded by corporations or government agencies for their workers and administered primarily by the trust departments of commercial banks or by life insurance companies. Pension funds invest primarily in bonds, stocks, mortgages, and real estate.
6. *Life insurance companies* take savings in the form of annual premiums; invest these funds in stocks, bonds, real estate, and mortgages; and finally make payments to the beneficiaries of the insured parties. In recent years, life insurance companies have also offered a variety of tax-deferred savings plans designed to provide benefits to the participants when they retire.
7. *Mutual funds* are corporations that accept money from savers and then use these funds to buy stocks, long-term bonds, or short-term debt instruments issued by businesses or government units. These organizations pool funds and thus reduce risks by diversification. They also achieve economies of scale in analyzing securities, managing portfolios, and buying and selling securities. Different funds are designed to meet the objectives

of different types of savers. Hence, there are bond funds for those who desire safety, stock funds for savers who are willing to accept significant risks in the hope of higher returns, and still other funds that are used as interest-bearing checking accounts (the **money market funds**). There are literally thousands of different mutual funds with dozens of different goals and purposes.

Money Market Fund
A mutual fund that invests in short-term, low-risk securities and allows investors to write checks against their accounts.

Mutual funds have grown more rapidly than any other institution in recent years, in large part because of a change in the way corporations provide for employees' retirement. Before the 1980s, most corporations said, in effect, "Come work for us, and when you retire, we will give you a retirement income based on the salary you were earning during the last five years before you retired." The company was then responsible for setting aside funds each year to make sure that it had the money available to pay the agreed-upon retirement benefits. That situation is changing rapidly. Today, new employees are likely to be told, "Come work for us, and we will give you some money each payday that you can invest for your future retirement. You can't get the money until you retire (without paying a huge tax penalty), but if you invest wisely, you can retire in comfort." Most workers know they don't know how to invest wisely, so they turn their retirement funds over to a mutual fund. Hence, mutual funds are growing rapidly. Excellent information on the objectives and past performances of the various funds are provided in publications such as *Value Line Investment Survey* and *Morningstar Mutual Funds*, which are available in most libraries.

Financial institutions have historically been heavily regulated, with the primary purpose of this regulation being to ensure the safety of the institutions and thus to protect investors. However, these regulations — which have taken the form of prohibitions on nationwide branch banking, restrictions on the types of assets the institutions can buy, ceilings on the interest rates they can pay, and limitations on the types of services they can provide — have tended to impede the free flow of capital and thus have hurt the efficiency of our capital markets. Recognizing this fact, Congress has authorized some major changes, and more are on the horizon.

The result of the ongoing regulatory changes has been a blurring of the distinctions between the different types of institutions. Indeed, the trend in the United States today is toward huge **financial service corporations,** which own banks, S&Ls, investment banking houses, insurance companies, pension plan operations, and mutual funds, and which have branches across the country and around the world. Examples of financial service corporations, most of which started in one area but have now diversified to cover most of the financial spectrum, include Merrill Lynch, American Express, Citigroup, Fidelity, and Prudential.

Financial Service Corporation
A firm that offers a wide range of financial services, including investment banking, brokerage operations, insurance, and commercial banking.

Panel a of Table 5-2 lists the ten largest U.S. bank and thrift holding companies, and Panel b shows the leading world banking companies. Among the world's 10 largest, only two (Citigroup and Bank of America) are from the United States. While U.S. banks have grown dramatically as a result of recent mergers, they are still small by global standards. Panel c of the table lists the 10 leading underwriters in terms of dollar volume of new issues. Five of the top underwriters are also major commercial banks or are part of bank holding com-

TABLE 5-2

10 Largest U.S. Bank and Thrift Holding Companies and World Banking Companies and Top 10 Leading Underwriters

Panel a	*Panel b*	*Panel c*
U.S. Bank and Thrift Holding Companies[a]	**World Banking Companies**[b]	**Leading Global Underwriters**[c]
Citigroup Inc.	Deutsche Bank AG (Frankfurt)	Merrill Lynch
Bank of America Corp.	Citigroup (New York)	Salomon Smith Barney
Chase Manhattan Corp.	BNP Paribas (Paris)	Morgan Stanley Dean Witter
Bank One Corp.	Bank of Tokyo-Mitsubishi Ltd. (Tokyo)	Credit Suisse First Boston
J. P. Morgan & Co.	Bank of America (Charlotte)	J. P. Morgan
First Union Corp.	UBS AG Group (Zurich)	Goldman Sachs
Wells Fargo & Co.	HSBC Holdings PLC (London)	Deutsche Bank
Washington Mutual Inc.	Fuji Bank Ltd. (Tokyo)	Lehman Brothers
Fleet Boston Financial Corp.	Sumitomo Bank Ltd. (Osaka)	UBS Warburg
SunTrust Banks Inc.	HypoVereinsbank AG (Munich)	Banc of America Securities

NOTES:
[a] Ranked by total assets as of June 30, 2000. SOURCE: Compiled by *American Banker* from bank and thrift holding company second quarter 2000 reports.
[b] Ranked by total assets as of December 31, 1999. SOURCE: "Top 50 World Banking Companies in Assets," *American Banker.com,* September 15, 2000.
[c] Ranked by dollar amount raised through new issues in 2000. For this ranking, the lead underwriter (manager) is given credit for the entire issue.

panies, which confirms the continued blurring of distinctions among different types of financial institutions.

SELF-TEST QUESTIONS

Identify three different ways capital is transferred between savers and borrowers.

What is the difference between a commercial bank and an investment bank?

Distinguish between investment banking houses and financial intermediaries.

List the major types of intermediaries and briefly describe the primary function of each.

THE STOCK MARKET

As noted earlier, secondary markets are those in which outstanding, previously issued securities are traded. By far the most active secondary market, and the most important one to financial managers, is the *stock market,* where the prices of firms' stocks are established. Since the primary goal of financial management is to maximize the firm's stock price, a knowledge of the stock market is important to anyone involved in managing a business.

While the two leading stock markets today are the New York Stock Exchange and the Nasdaq stock market, stocks are actually traded using a variety of market procedures. However, there are just two basic types of stock markets: (1) *physical location exchanges*, which include the New York Stock Exchange (NYSE), the American Stock Exchange (AMEX), and several regional stock exchanges, and (2) electronic dealer-based markets that include the Nasdaq stock market, the less formal over-the-counter market, and the recently developed electronic communications networks (ECNs). (See the Technology Matters box entitled, "Online Trading Systems.") Because the physical location exchanges are easier to describe and understand, we consider them first.

The Physical Location Stock Exchanges

Physical Location Exchanges
Formal organizations having tangible physical locations that conduct auction markets in designated ("listed") securities.

The **physical location exchanges** are tangible physical entities. Each of the larger ones occupies its own building, has a limited number of members, and has an elected governing body — its board of governors. Members are said to have "seats" on the exchange, although everybody stands up. These seats, which are bought and sold, give the holder the right to trade on the exchange. There are currently 1,366 seats on the New York Stock Exchange, and on April 25, 2000, a seat on the NYSE sold for $1.7 million, which was down from the previous high of $2.6 million.

Most of the larger investment banking houses operate *brokerage departments*, and they own seats on the exchanges and designate one or more of their officers as members. The exchanges are open on all normal working days, with the members meeting in a large room equipped with telephones and other electronic equipment that enable each member to communicate with his or her firm's offices throughout the country.

WWW You can access the home pages of the major U.S. stock markets by typing **http://www.nyse.com** or **http://www.nasdaq.com**. These sites provide background information as well as the opportunity to obtain individual stock quotes.

Like other markets, security exchanges facilitate communication between buyers and sellers. For example, Merrill Lynch (the largest brokerage firm) might receive an order in its Atlanta office from a customer who wants to buy shares of AT&T stock. Simultaneously, Morgan Stanley Dean Witter's Denver office might receive an order from a customer wishing to sell shares of AT&T. Each broker communicates electronically with the firm's representative on the NYSE. Other brokers throughout the country are also communicating with their own exchange members. The exchange members with *sell orders* offer the shares for sale, and they are bid for by the members with *buy orders*. Thus, the exchanges operate as *auction markets*.[2]

---

[2] The NYSE is actually a modified auction market, wherein people (through their brokers) bid for stocks. Originally — about 200 years ago — brokers would literally shout, "I have 100 shares of Erie for sale; how much am I offered?" and then sell to the highest bidder. If a broker had a buy order, he or she would shout, "I want to buy 100 shares of Erie; who'll sell at the best price?" The same general situation still exists, although the exchanges now have members known as *specialists* who facilitate the trading process by keeping an inventory of shares of the stocks in which they specialize. If a buy order comes in at a time when no sell order arrives, the

(footnote continues)

TECHNOLOGY MATTERS

ONLINE TRADING SYSTEMS

The forces described in the vignette that led to online trading have also promoted online trading systems that bypass the traditional exchanges. These systems, known as electronic communications networks (ECNs), use technology to bring buyers and sellers together electronically. Bob Mazzarella, president of Fidelity Brokerage Services Inc., estimates that ECNs have already captured 20 to 35 percent of Nasdaq's trading volume. Instinet, the first and largest ECN, has a stake with Goldman Sachs, J. P. Morgan, and E*Trade in another network, Archipelago, which recently announced plans to form its own exchange. Likewise, Charles Schwab recently announced plans to join with Fidelity Investments, Donaldson, Lufkin & Jenrette, and Spear, Leeds & Kellogg to develop another ECN.

ECNs will accelerate the move toward 24-hour trading. Large clients who want to trade after the other markets have closed may utilize an ECN, bypassing the NYSE and Nasdaq. The move toward faster, cheaper, and continuous trading obviously benefits investors, but it does present regulators, who try to ensure that all investors have access to a "level playing field," with a number of headaches.

Because of the threat from ECNs and the need to raise capital and increase flexibility, both the NYSE and Nasdaq plan to convert from privately held, member-owned businesses to stockholder-owned, for-profit corporations. This suggests that the financial landscape will continue to undergo dramatic changes in the upcoming years.

SOURCES: Katrina Brooker, "Online Investing: It's Not Just for Geeks Anymore," *Fortune*, December 21, 1998, 89–98; and "Fidelity, Schwab Part of Deal to Create Nasdaq Challenger," *The Milwaukee Journal Sentinel*, July 22, 1999, 1.

THE OVER-THE-COUNTER AND THE NASDAQ STOCK MARKETS

Over-the-Counter Market
A large collection of brokers and dealers, connected electronically by telephones and computers, that provides for trading in unlisted securities.

While the stocks of most large companies trade on the NYSE, a larger number of stocks trade off the exchange in what has traditionally been referred to as the **over-the-counter market (OTC).** An explanation of the term "over-the-counter" will help clarify how this term arose. As noted earlier, the exchanges operate as auction markets — buy and sell orders come in more or less simultaneously, and exchange members match these orders. If a stock is traded infrequently, perhaps because the firm is new or small, few buy and sell orders come in, and matching them within a reasonable amount of time would be difficult. To avoid this problem, some brokerage firms maintain an inventory of such

---

(Footnote 2 continued)
specialist will sell off some inventory. Similarly, if a sell order comes in, the specialist will buy and add to inventory. The specialist sets a *bid price* (the price the specialist will pay for the stock) and an *asked price* (the price at which shares will be sold out of inventory). The bid and asked prices are set at levels designed to keep the inventory in balance. If many buy orders start coming in because of favorable developments or sell orders come in because of unfavorable events, the specialist will raise or lower prices to keep supply and demand in balance. Bid prices are somewhat lower than asked prices, with the difference, or *spread*, representing the specialist's profit margin.

Special facilities are available to help institutional investors such as mutual funds or pension funds sell large blocks of stock without depressing their prices. In essence, brokerage houses that cater to institutional clients will purchase blocks (defined as 10,000 or more shares) and then resell the stock to other institutions or individuals. Also, when a firm has a major announcement that is likely to cause its stock price to change sharply, it will ask the exchanges to halt trading in its stock until the announcement has been made and digested by investors. Thus, when Texaco announced that it planned to acquire Getty Oil, trading was halted for one day in both Texaco and Getty stocks.

stocks and stand prepared to make a market for these stocks. These "dealers" buy when individual investors want to sell, and then sell part of their inventory when investors want to buy. At one time, the inventory of securities was kept in a safe, and the stocks, when bought and sold, were literally passed over the counter.

Dealer Market
Includes all facilities that are needed to conduct security transactions not conducted on the physical location exchanges.

Today, these markets are often referred to as **dealer markets.** A dealer market is defined to include all facilities that are needed to conduct security transactions not made on the physical location exchanges. These facilities include (1) the relatively few *dealers* who hold inventories of these securities and who are said to "make a market" in these securities; (2) the thousands of brokers who act as *agents* in bringing the dealers together with investors; and (3) the computers, terminals, and electronic networks that provide a communication link between dealers and brokers. The dealers who make a market in a particular stock quote the price at which they will pay for the stock (the *bid price*) and the price at which they will sell shares (the *ask price*). Each dealer's prices, which are adjusted as supply and demand conditions change, can be read off computer screens all across the world. The *bid-ask spread,* which is the difference between bid and ask prices, represents the dealer's markup, or profit. The dealer's risk increases if the stock is more volatile, or if the stock trades infrequently. Generally, we would expect volatile, infrequently traded stocks to have wider spreads in order to compensate the dealers for assuming the risk of holding them in inventory.

Brokers and dealers who participate in the over-the-counter market are members of a self-regulatory body known as the *National Association of Securities Dealers (NASD),* which licenses brokers and oversees trading practices. The computerized network used by the NASD is known as the NASD Automated Quotation System.

Nasdaq started as just a quotation system, but it has grown to become an organized securities market with its own listing requirements. Over the past decade the competition between the NYSE and Nasdaq has become increasingly fierce. In an effort to become more competitive with the NYSE and with international markets, the Nasdaq and the AMEX merged in 1998 to form the Nasdaq-Amex Market Group, which might best be referred to as an *organized investment network.* This investment network is often referred to as Nasdaq, but stocks continue to be traded and reported separately on the two markets. Increased competition among global stock markets assuredly will result in similar alliances among other exchanges and markets in the future.

Since most of the largest companies trade on the NYSE, the market capitalization of NYSE-traded stocks is much higher than for stocks traded on Nasdaq ($11.4 trillion compared with $3.6 trillion at year-end 2000). However, reported volume (number of shares traded) is often larger on Nasdaq, and more companies are listed on Nasdaq.[3]

Interestingly, many high-tech companies such as Microsoft and Intel have remained on Nasdaq even though they easily meet the listing requirements of the NYSE. At the same time, however, other high-tech companies such as Gateway 2000, America Online, and Iomega have left Nasdaq for the NYSE.

---

[3] One transaction on Nasdaq generally shows up as two separate trades (the buy and the sell). This "double counting" makes it difficult to compare the volume between stock markets.

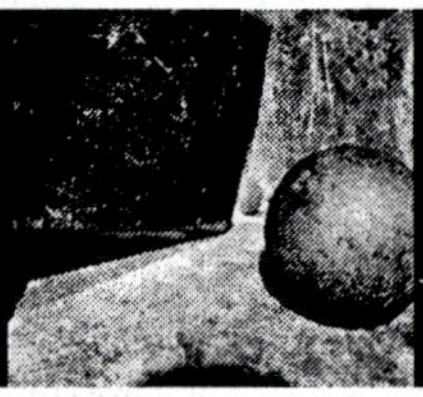

INDUSTRY PRACTICE

A VERY EXPENSIVE BEER

A few summers ago, two professors met for a beer at an academic conference. During their conversation, the professors, William Christie of Vanderbilt University and Paul Schultz of Ohio State University, decided it would be interesting to see how prices are set for Nasdaq stocks. The results of their study were startling to many, and they produced a real firestorm in the investment community.

When looking through data on the bid/asked spreads set by Nasdaq market makers, Christie and Schultz found that the market makers routinely avoided posting quotes that had "odd-eighths fractions," that is, $\frac{1}{8}$, $\frac{3}{8}$, $\frac{5}{8}$, and $\frac{7}{8}$. For example, if a market maker were to use odd-eighths quotes, he might offer to buy a stock for $10\frac{1}{2}$ a share and sell it for $10\frac{5}{8}$, thus providing a "spread," or profit, of $\frac{1}{8}$ point ($10\frac{5}{8} - 10\frac{1}{2} = \frac{1}{8}$). The spread between the two prices is the market maker's compensation for providing a market and taking the risk associated with holding an inventory of a given stock. Note that if he or she avoided odd-eighths fractions, then the offer price would be $10\frac{3}{4}$ (which is $10\frac{6}{8}$), so the spread would be $10\frac{6}{8} - 10\frac{1}{2} = \frac{1}{4}$, or twice as high as if he or she made an odd-eighths quote.

What amazed Christie and Schultz was the fact that this practice was so widespread — even for widely followed stocks such as Apple Computer and Lotus Development. The professors concluded that the evidence strongly suggested that there had to be tacit collusion among Nasdaq dealers designed to keep spreads artificially high. The National Association of Securities Dealers (NASD) originally denied the accusations. Others have come forward to provide a justification for the practice.

The publicity surrounding the study led the Securities and Exchange Commission (SEC) to investigate. Without admitting guilt, the NASD settled with the SEC, and, as part of the agreement, the dealers agreed to spend $100 million during the next five years to improve their enforcement practices. These allegations have also led to a civil class-action suit. In a dramatic development, several of the nation's largest securities firms have reached an agreement to pay more than $1 billion in damages — which is believed to be the largest antitrust settlement in history. All of this explains why the professors' beers turned out to be so expensive.

SOURCES: William Christie, "An Expensive Beer for the N.A.S.D.," *The New York Times,* August 25, 1996, Sec. 3, 12; and Michael Rapoport, "Securities Firms' Settlement Wins Backing from Judge," *The Wall Street Journal Interactive Edition,* December 30, 1997.

Despite these defections, Nasdaq's growth over the past decade has been impressive. In the years ahead, the competition will no doubt remain fierce.

SELF-TEST QUESTIONS

What are the differences between the physical location exchanges and the Nasdaq stock market?

What is the bid-ask spread?

THE COST OF MONEY

Capital in a free economy is allocated through the price system. *The interest rate is the price paid to borrow debt capital. With equity capital, investors expect to receive dividends and capital gains, whose sum is the cost of equity money.* The factors that affect supply of and demand for investment capital, hence the cost of money, are discussed in this section.

INDUSTRY PRACTICE

MEASURING THE MARKET

A *stock index* is designed to show the performance of the stock market. The problem is that there are many stock indexes, and it is difficult to determine which index best reflects market actions. Some are designed to represent the whole equity market, some to track the returns of certain industry sectors, and others to track the returns of small-cap, mid-cap, or large-cap stocks. We discuss below three of the leading indexes.

DOW JONES INDUSTRIAL AVERAGE

Unveiled in 1896 by Charles H. Dow, the Dow Jones Industrial Average (DJIA) provided a benchmark for comparing individual stocks with the overall market and for comparing the market with other economic indicators. The industrial average began with just 10 stocks, was expanded in 1916 to 20 stocks, and then to 30 in 1928. Also, in 1928 *The Wall Street Journal* editors began adjusting it for stock splits, and making substitutions. Today, the DJIA still includes 30 companies. They represent almost a fifth of the market value of all U.S. stocks, and all are both leading companies in their industries and widely held by individual and institutional investors.

S&P 500 INDEX

Created in 1926, the S&P 500 Index is widely regarded as the standard for measuring large-cap U.S. stock market performance. The stocks in the S&P 500 are selected by the Standard & Poor's Index Committee for being the leading companies in the leading industries, and for accurately reflecting the U.S. stock market. It is value weighted, so the largest companies (in terms of value) have the greatest influence. The S&P 500 Index is used by 97 percent of all U.S. money managers and pension plan sponsors, and approximately $700 billion is managed so as to obtain the same performance as this index (that is, in indexed funds).

NASDAQ COMPOSITE INDEX

The Nasdaq Composite Index measures the performance of all common stocks listed on the Nasdaq stock market. Currently, it includes more than 5,000 companies, and because many of the technology-sectored companies are traded on the computer-based Nasdaq exchange, this index is generally regarded as an economic indicator of the high-tech industry. Microsoft, Intel, and Cisco Systems are the three largest Nasdaq companies, and they comprise a high percentage of the index's value-weighted market capitalization. For this reason, substantial movements in the same direction by these three companies can move the entire index.

RECENT PERFORMANCE

The accompanying figure plots the value that an investor would now have if he or she had invested $1.00 in each of the three indexes on August 31, 1979. The returns on the three indexes are compared to an investment strategy that only invests in T-bills. Every year, the proceeds from that T-bill investment are reinvested at the current one-year T-bill rate. Over the past 20 years each of these indexes has performed quite well, which reflects the spectacular rise in the stock market. During this pe-

Production Opportunities
The returns available within an economy from investments in productive (cash-generating) assets.

Time Preferences for Consumption
The preferences of consumers for current consumption as opposed to saving for future consumption.

Risk
In a financial market context, the chance that an investment will provide a low or negative return.

The four most fundamental factors affecting the cost of money are (1) **production opportunities,** (2) **time preferences for consumption,** (3) **risk,** and (4) **inflation**. To see how these factors operate, visualize an isolated island community where the people live on fish. They have a stock of fishing gear that permits them to survive reasonably well, but they would like to have more fish. Now suppose Mr. Crusoe had a bright idea for a new type of fishnet that would enable him to double his daily catch. However, it would take him a year to perfect his design, to build his net, and to learn how to use it efficiently, and Mr. Crusoe would probably starve before he could put his new net into operation. Therefore, he might suggest to Ms. Robinson, Mr. Friday, and several others that if they would give him one fish each day for a year, he would return two fish a day during all of the next year. If someone accepted the offer, then the fish that Ms. Robinson or one of the others gave to Mr. Crusoe would constitute *savings;* these savings would be *invested* in the fishnet; and the extra fish the net produced would constitute a *return on the investment.*

riod the average annualized returns of these indexes ranged from 12.0 percent for the S&P 500 to 13.5 percent for the Nasdaq. The Nasdaq's relatively strong performance occurred primarily after 1992, reflecting the fact that it includes a large number of technology stocks, a sector that has performed extraordinarily well in recent years.

Growth of a $1 Investment Made on August 31, 1979

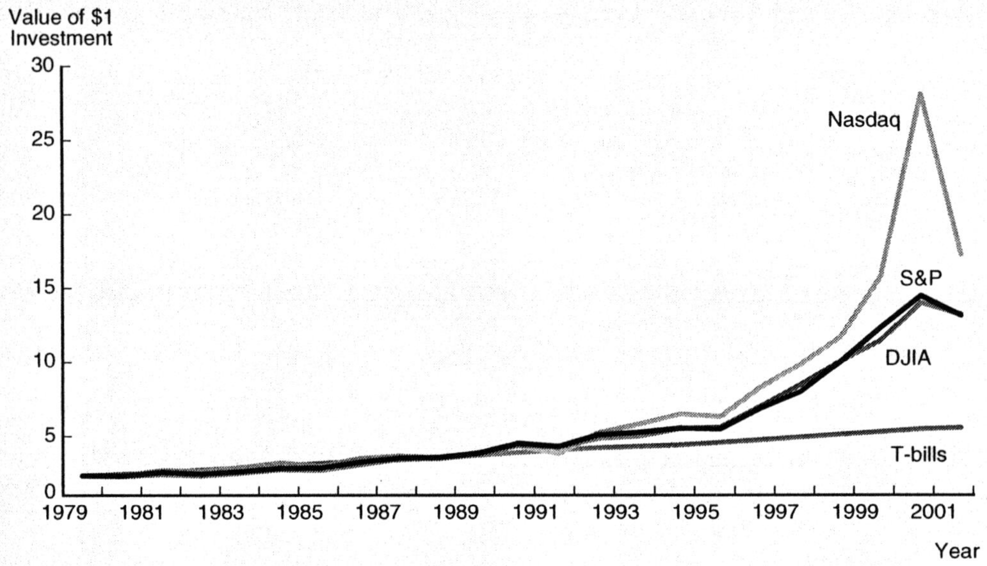

SOURCES: Yahoo! Finance, Nasdaq, and FRED Database.

Inflation
The amount by which prices increase over time.

Obviously, the more productive Mr. Crusoe thought the new fishnet would be, the more he could afford to offer potential investors for their savings. In this example, we assume that Mr. Crusoe thought he would be able to pay, and thus he offered, a 100 percent rate of return — he offered to give back two fish for every one he received. He might have tried to attract savings for less — for example, he might have decided to offer only 1.5 fish next year for every one he received this year, which would represent a 50 percent rate of return to Ms. Robinson and the other potential savers.

How attractive Mr. Crusoe's offer appeared to a potential saver would depend in large part on the saver's *time preference for consumption.* For example, Ms. Robinson might be thinking of retirement, and she might be willing to trade fish today for fish in the future on a one-for-one basis. On the other hand, Mr. Friday might have a wife and several young children and need his current fish, so he might be unwilling to "lend" a fish today for anything less than three fish next year. Mr. Friday would be said to have a high time preference for current consumption and Ms. Robinson a low time preference. Note also that if the entire population were living right at the subsistence level, time preferences for current consumption would necessarily be high, aggregate savings would be low, interest rates would be high, and capital formation would be difficult.

The *risk* inherent in the fishnet project, and thus in Mr. Crusoe's ability to repay the loan, would also affect the return investors would require: the higher the perceived risk, the higher the required rate of return. Also, in a more complex society there are many businesses like Mr. Crusoe's, many goods other than fish, and many savers like Ms. Robinson and Mr. Friday. Therefore, people use money as a medium of exchange rather than barter with fish. When money is used, its value in the future, which is affected by *inflation*, comes into play: the higher the expected rate of inflation, the larger the required return. We discuss this point in detail later in the chapter.

Thus, we see that the interest rate paid to savers depends in a basic way (1) on the rate of return producers expect to earn on invested capital, (2) on savers' time preferences for current versus future consumption, (3) on the riskiness of the loan, and (4) on the expected future rate of inflation. Producers' expected returns on their business investments set an upper limit on how much they can pay for savings, while consumers' time preferences for consumption establish how much consumption they are willing to defer, hence how much they will save at different rates of interest offered by producers.[4] Higher risk and higher inflation also lead to higher interest rates.

SELF-TEST QUESTIONS

What is the price paid to borrow money called?

What are the two items whose sum is the "price" of equity capital?

What four fundamental factors affect the cost of money?

INTEREST RATE LEVELS

Capital is allocated among borrowers by interest rates: Firms with the most profitable investment opportunities are willing and able to pay the most for capital, so they tend to attract it away from inefficient firms or from those whose products are not in demand. Of course, our economy is not completely free in the sense of being influenced only by market forces. Thus, the federal government has agencies that help designated individuals or groups obtain credit on favorable terms. Among those eligible for this kind of assistance are small businesses, certain minorities, and firms willing to build plants in areas with high unemployment. Still, most capital in the U.S. economy is allocated through the price system.

---

[4] The term "producers" is really too narrow. A better word might be "borrowers," which would include corporations, home purchasers, people borrowing to go to college, or even people borrowing to buy autos or to pay for vacations. Also, the wealth of a society and its demographics influence its people's ability to save and thus their time preferences for current versus future consumption.

FIGURE 5-2 **Interest Rates as a Function of Supply and Demand for Funds**

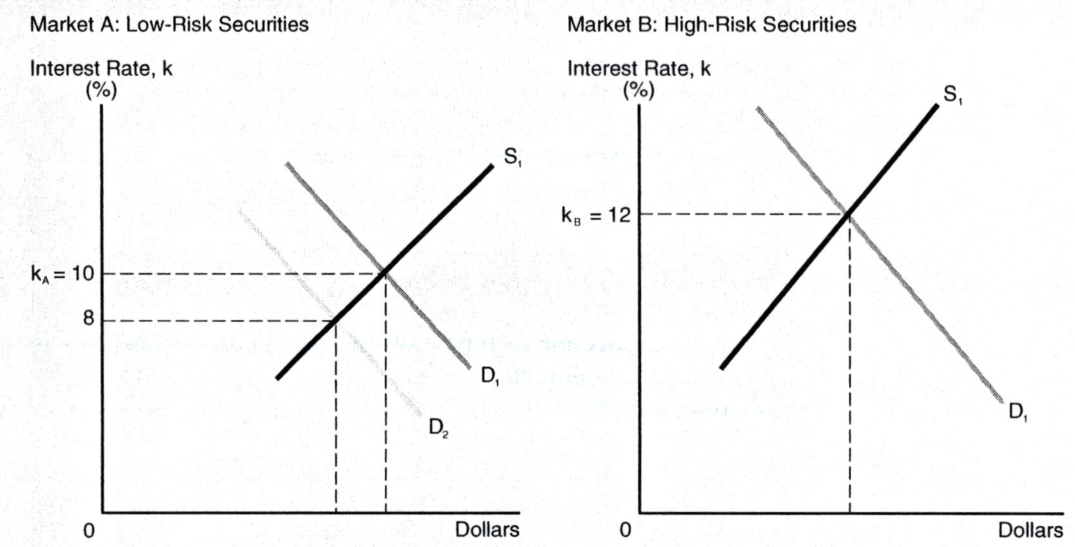

Figure 5-2 shows how supply and demand interact to determine interest rates in two capital markets. Markets A and B represent two of the many capital markets in existence. The going interest rate, which can be designated as either k or i, but for purposes of our discussion is designated as k, is initially 10 percent for the low-risk securities in Market A.[5] Borrowers whose credit is strong enough to borrow in this market can obtain funds at a cost of 10 percent, and investors who want to put their money to work without much risk can obtain a 10 percent return. Riskier borrowers must obtain higher-cost funds in Market B. Investors who are more willing to take risks invest in Market B, expecting to earn a 12 percent return but also realizing that they might actually receive much less.

If the demand for funds declines, as it typically does during business recessions, the demand curves will shift to the left, as shown in Curve D_2 in Market A. The market-clearing, or equilibrium, interest rate in this example declines to 8 percent. Similarly, you should be able to visualize what would happen if the Federal Reserve tightened credit: The supply curve, S_1, would shift to the left, and this would raise interest rates and lower the level of borrowing in the economy.

Capital markets are interdependent. For example, if Markets A and B were in equilibrium before the demand shift to D_2 in Market A, then investors were willing to accept the higher risk in Market B in exchange for a *risk premium* of $12\% - 10\% = 2\%$. After the shift to D_2, the risk premium would initially increase to $12\% - 8\% = 4\%$. Immediately, though, this much larger premium

[5] The letter "k" is the traditional symbol for interest rates and the cost of equity, but "i" is used frequently today because this term corresponds to the interest rate key on financial calculators. Therefore, in Chapter 7, when we discuss calculators, the term "i" will be used for the interest rate.

would induce some of the lenders in Market A to shift to Market B, which would, in turn, cause the supply curve in Market A to shift to the left (or up) and that in Market B to shift to the right. The transfer of capital between markets would raise the interest rate in Market A and lower it in Market B, thus bringing the risk premium back closer to the original 2 percent.

There are many capital markets in the United States. U.S. firms also invest and raise capital throughout the world, and foreigners both borrow and lend in the United States. There are markets for home loans; farm loans; business loans; federal, state, and local government loans; and consumer loans. Within each category, there are regional markets as well as different types of submarkets. For example, in real estate there are separate markets for first and second mortgages and for loans on single-family homes, apartments, office buildings, shopping centers, vacant land, and so on. Within the business sector there are dozens of types of debt and also several different markets for common stocks.

There is a price for each type of capital, and these prices change over time as shifts occur in supply and demand conditions. Figure 5-3 shows how long- and short-term interest rates to business borrowers have varied since the early

FIGURE 5-3 **Long- and Short-Term Interest Rates, 1961-2000**

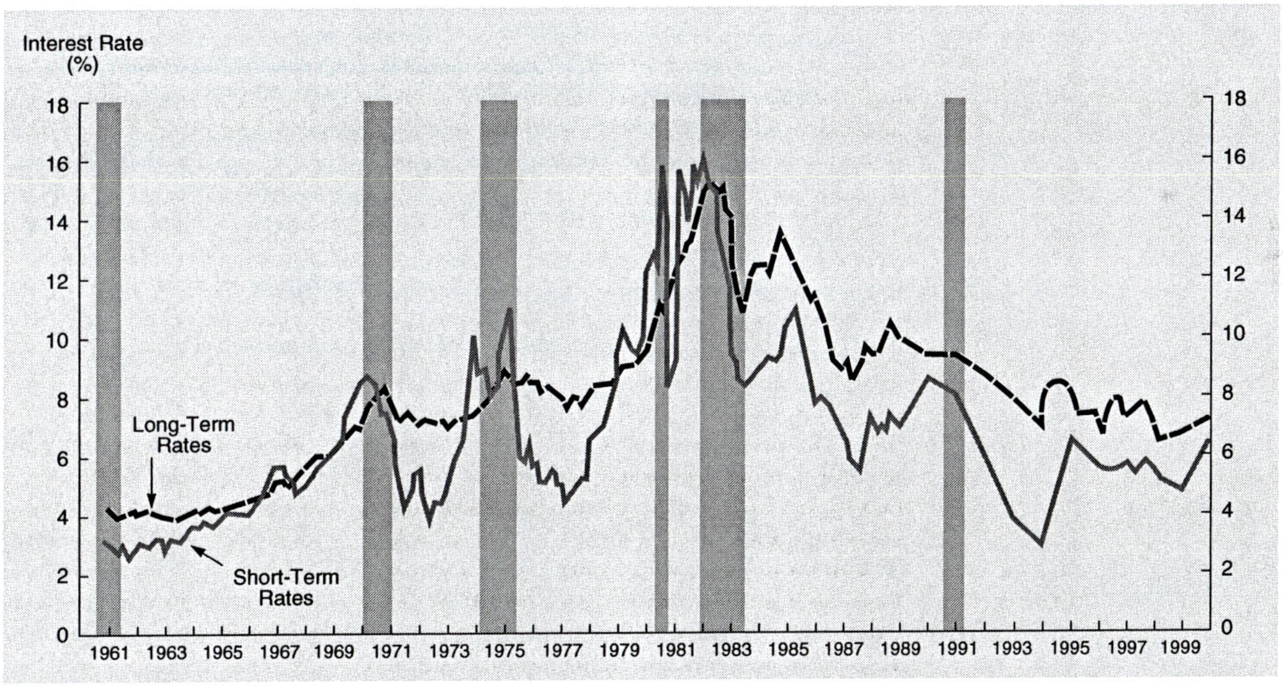

NOTES:

a. The shaded areas designate business recessions.

b. Short-term rates are measured by three- to six-month loans to very large, strong corporations, and long-term rates are measured by AAA corporate bonds.

SOURCE: *Federal Reserve Bulletin.*

1960s. Notice that short-term interest rates are especially prone to rise during booms and then fall during recessions. (The shaded areas of the chart indicate recessions.) When the economy is expanding, firms need capital, and this demand for capital pushes rates up. Also, inflationary pressures are strongest during business booms, and that also exerts upward pressure on rates. Conditions are reversed during recessions such as the one in 1990 and 1991. Slack business reduces the demand for credit, the rate of inflation falls, and the result is a drop in interest rates. Furthermore, the Federal Reserve deliberately lowers rates during recessions to help stimulate the economy.

These tendencies do not hold exactly—the period after 1984 is a case in point. The price of oil fell dramatically in 1985 and 1986, reducing inflationary pressures on other prices and easing fears of serious long-term inflation. Earlier, these fears had pushed interest rates to record levels. The economy from 1984 to 1987 was strong, but the declining fears of inflation more than offset the normal tendency of interest rates to rise during good economic times, and the net result was lower interest rates.[6]

The relationship between inflation and long-term interest rates is highlighted in Figure 5-4, which plots rates of inflation along with long-term interest rates. In the early 1960s, inflation averaged 1 percent per year, and interest rates on high-quality, long-term bonds averaged 4 percent. Then the Vietnam War heated up, leading to an increase in inflation, and interest rates began an upward climb. When the war ended in the early 1970s, inflation dipped a bit, but then the 1973 Arab oil embargo led to rising oil prices, much higher inflation rates, and sharply higher interest rates.

Inflation peaked at about 13 percent in 1980, but interest rates continued to increase into 1981 and 1982, and they remained quite high until 1985, because people were afraid inflation would start to climb again. Thus, the "inflationary psychology" created during the 1970s persisted to the mid-1980s.

Gradually, though, people began to realize that the Federal Reserve was serious about keeping inflation down, that global competition was keeping U.S. auto producers and other corporations from raising prices as they had in the past, and that constraints on corporate price increases were diminishing labor unions' ability to push through cost-increasing wage hikes. As these realizations set in, interest rates declined.

The gap between the current interest rate and the current inflation rate is defined as the "current real rate of interest." It is called the "real rate" because it shows how much investors really earned after taking out the effects of inflation. The real rate was extremely high during the mid-1980s, but it averaged about 4 percent during the 1990s.

In recent years, inflation has been running at about 3 percent a year. However, long-term interest rates have been volatile, because investors are not sure if inflation is truly under control or is getting ready to jump back to the higher levels of the 1980s. In the years ahead, we can be sure that the level of interest rates will vary (1) with changes in the current rate of inflation and (2) with changes in expectations about future inflation.

---

[6] Short-term rates are responsive to current economic conditions, whereas long-term rates primarily reflect long-run expectations for inflation. As a result, short-term rates are sometimes above and sometimes below long-term rates. The relationship between long-term and short-term rates is called the *term structure of interest rates*, and it is discussed later in the chapter.

FIGURE 5-4 **Relationship between Annual Inflation Rates and Long-Term Interest Rates, 1961-2000**

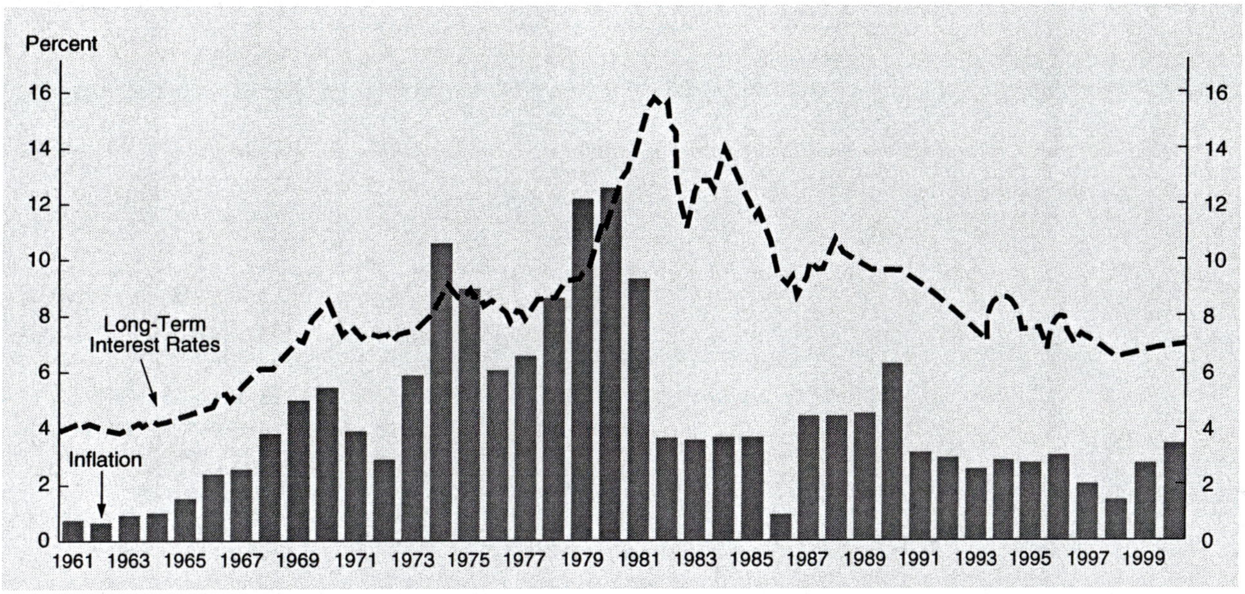

NOTES:

a. Interest rates are those on AAA long-term corporate bonds.

b. Inflation is measured as the annual rate of change in the Consumer Price Index (CPI).

SOURCE: *Federal Reserve Bulletin.*

SELF-TEST QUESTIONS

How are interest rates used to allocate capital among firms?

What happens to market-clearing, or equilibrium, interest rates in a capital market when the demand for funds declines? What happens when inflation increases or decreases?

Why does the price of capital change during booms and recessions?

How does risk affect interest rates?

THE DETERMINANTS OF MARKET INTEREST RATES

In general, the quoted (or nominal) interest rate on a debt security, k, is composed of a real risk-free rate of interest, k*, plus several premiums that reflect inflation, the riskiness of the security, and the security's marketability (or liquidity). This relationship can be expressed as follows:

$$\text{Quoted interest rate} = k = k^* + IP + DRP + LP + MRP. \qquad \textbf{(5-1)}$$

Here

k = the quoted, or nominal, rate of interest on a given security.[7] There are many different securities, hence many different quoted interest rates.

k^* = the real risk-free rate of interest. k^* is pronounced "k-star," and it is the rate that would exist on a riskless security if zero inflation were expected.

k_{RF} = $k^* + IP$, and it is the quoted risk-free rate of interest on a security such as a U.S. Treasury bill, which is very liquid and also free of most risks. Note that k_{RF} includes the premium for expected inflation, because $k_{RF} = k^* + IP$.

IP = inflation premium. IP is equal to the average expected inflation rate over the life of the security. The expected future inflation rate is not necessarily equal to the current inflation rate, so IP is not necessarily equal to current inflation as reported in Figure 5-4.

DRP = default risk premium. This premium reflects the possibility that the issuer will not pay interest or principal at the stated time and in the stated amount. DRP is zero for U.S. Treasury securities, but it rises as the riskiness of issuers increases.

LP = liquidity, or marketability, premium. This is a premium charged by lenders to reflect the fact that some securities cannot be converted to cash on short notice at a "reasonable" price. LP is very low for Treasury securities and for securities issued by large, strong firms, but it is relatively high on securities issued by very small firms.

MRP = maturity risk premium. As we will explain later, longer-term bonds, even Treasury bonds, are exposed to a significant risk of price declines, and a maturity risk premium is charged by lenders to reflect this risk.

As noted above, since $k_{RF} = k^* + IP$, we can rewrite Equation 5-1 as follows:

$$\text{Nominal, or quoted, rate} = k = k_{RF} + DRP + LP + MRP.$$

We discuss the components whose sum makes up the quoted, or nominal, rate on a given security in the following sections.

The Real Risk-Free Rate of Interest, k^*

Real Risk-Free Rate of Interest, k^*
The rate of interest that would exist on default-free U.S. Treasury securities if no inflation were expected.

The **real risk-free rate of interest, k^*,** is defined as the interest rate that would exist on a riskless security if no inflation were expected, and it may be thought of as the rate of interest on *short-term* U.S. Treasury securities in an inflation-free world. The real risk-free rate is not static—it changes over time depending on economic conditions, especially (1) on the rate of return corporations and other borrowers expect to earn on productive assets and (2) on people's time preferences for current versus future consumption. Borrowers'

[7] The term *nominal* as it is used here means the *stated* rate as opposed to the *real* rate, which is adjusted to remove inflation effects. If you had bought a 10-year Treasury bond in February 2001, the quoted, or nominal, rate would be about 5.2 percent, but if inflation averages 2.5 percent over the next 10 years, the real rate would be about 5.2% − 2.5% = 2.7%.

expected returns on real asset investments set an upper limit on how much they can afford to pay for borrowed funds, while savers' time preferences for consumption establish how much consumption they are willing to defer, hence the amount of funds they will lend at different interest rates. It is difficult to measure the real risk-free rate precisely, but most experts think that k* has fluctuated in the range of 1 to 5 percent in recent years.[8] The best estimate of k* is the rate of return on indexed Treasury bonds, which are discussed in a box later in the chapter.

The Nominal, or Quoted, Risk-Free Rate of Interest, k_{RF}

Nominal (Quoted) Risk-Free Rate, k_{RF}
The rate of interest on a security that is free of all risk; k_{RF} is proxied by the T-bill rate or the T-bond rate. k_{RF} includes an inflation premium.

The **nominal, or quoted, risk-free rate, k_{RF}**, is the real risk-free rate plus a premium for expected inflation: $k_{RF} = k^* + IP$. To be strictly correct, the risk-free rate should mean the interest rate on a totally risk-free security—one that has no risk of default, no maturity risk, no liquidity risk, no risk of loss if inflation increases, and no risk of any other type. There is no such security, hence there is no observable truly risk-free rate. However, there is one security that is free of most risks—an indexed U.S. Treasury security. These securities are free of default, maturity, and liquidity risks, and also of risk due to changes in the general level of interest rates.[9]

If the term "risk-free rate" is used without either the modifier "real" or the modifier "nominal," people generally mean the quoted (nominal) rate, and we will follow that convention in this book. Therefore, when we use the term risk-free rate, k_{RF}, we mean the nominal risk-free rate, which includes an inflation premium equal to the average expected inflation rate over the life of the security. In general, we use the T-bill rate to approximate the short-term risk-free rate, and the T-bond rate to approximate the long-term risk-free rate. So, whenever you see the term "risk-free rate," assume that we are referring either to the quoted U.S. T-bill rate or to the quoted T-bond rate.

Inflation Premium (IP)

Inflation has a major impact on interest rates because it erodes the purchasing power of the dollar and lowers the real rate of return on investments. To illus-

---

[8] The real rate of interest as discussed here is different from the *current* real rate as discussed in connection with Figure 5-4. The current real rate is the current interest rate minus the current (or latest past) inflation rate, while the real rate, without the word "current," is the current interest rate minus the *expected future* inflation rate over the life of the security. For example, suppose the current quoted rate for a one-year Treasury bill is 5 percent, inflation during the latest year was 2 percent, and inflation expected for the coming year is 4 percent. Then the *current* real rate would be $5\% - 2\% = 3\%$, but the *expected* real rate would be $5\% - 4\% = 1\%$. The rate on a 10-year bond would be related to the expected inflation rate over the next 10 years, and so on. In the press, the term "real rate" generally means the current real rate, but in economics and finance, hence in this book unless otherwise noted, the real rate means the one based on *expected* inflation rates.

[9] Indexed Treasury securities are the closest thing we have to a riskless security, but even they are not totally riskless, because k* itself can change and cause a decline in the prices of these securities. For example, between October 1998 and January 2000, the price of one indexed Treasury security declined from 98 to 89, or by almost 10 percent. The cause was an increase in the real rate on long-term securities from 3.7 percent to 4.4 percent. One year later, the real rate on long-term securities has dropped to 3.5 percent.

trate, suppose you saved $1,000 and invested it in a Treasury bill that matures in one year and pays a 5 percent interest rate. At the end of the year, you will receive $1,050—your original $1,000 plus $50 of interest. Now suppose the inflation rate during the year is 10 percent, and it affects all items equally. If gas had cost $1 per gallon at the beginning of the year, it would cost $1.10 at the end of the year. Therefore, your $1,000 would have bought $1,000/$1 = 1,000 gallons at the beginning of the year, but only $1,050/$1.10 = 955 gallons at the end. In *real terms*, you would be worse off—you would receive $50 of interest, but it would not be sufficient to offset inflation. You would thus be better off buying 1,000 gallons of gas (or some other storable asset such as land, timber, apartment buildings, wheat, or gold) than buying the Treasury bill.

Inflation Premium (IP)
A premium equal to expected inflation that investors add to the real risk-free rate of return.

Investors are well aware of all this, so when they lend money, they build in an **inflation premium (IP)** equal to the average expected inflation rate over the life of the security. As discussed previously, for a short-term, default-free U.S. Treasury bill, the actual interest rate charged, $k_{\text{T-bill}}$, would be the real risk-free rate, k*, plus the inflation premium (IP):

$$k_{\text{T-bill}} = k_{\text{RF}} = k^* + \text{IP}.$$

Therefore, if the real risk-free rate of interest were k* = 2.8%, and if inflation were expected to be 2 percent (and hence IP = 2%) during the next year, then the quoted rate of interest on one-year T-bills would be 2.8% + 2% = 4.8%. Indeed, in February 2001, the expected one-year inflation rate was about 2 percent, and the yield on one-year T-bills was about 4.8 percent, so the real risk-free rate on short-term securities at that time was 2.8 percent.

It is important to note that the inflation rate built into interest rates is the *inflation rate expected in the future*, not the rate experienced in the past. Thus, the latest reported figures might show an annual inflation rate of 3.3 percent, but that is for the *past* year. If people on the average expect a 6 percent inflation rate in the future, then 6 percent would be built into the current interest rate. Note also that the inflation rate reflected in the quoted interest rate on any security is the *average rate of inflation expected over the security's life*. Thus, the inflation rate built into a one-year bond is the expected inflation rate for the next year, but the inflation rate built into a 30-year bond is the average rate of inflation expected over the next 30 years.[10]

Expectations for future inflation are closely, but not perfectly, correlated with rates experienced in the recent past. Therefore, if the inflation rate reported for last month increased, people would tend to raise their expectations for future inflation, and this change in expectations would cause an increase in interest rates.

---

[10] To be theoretically precise, we should use a *geometric average*. Also, since millions of investors are active in the market, it is impossible to determine exactly the consensus expected inflation rate. Survey data are available, however, which give us a reasonably good idea of what investors expect over the next few years. For example, in 1980 the University of Michigan's Survey Research Center reported that people expected inflation during the next year to be 11.9 percent and that the average rate of inflation expected over the next 5 to 10 years was 10.5 percent. Those expectations led to record-high interest rates. However, the economy cooled in 1981 and 1982, and, as Figure 5-4 showed, actual inflation dropped sharply after 1980. This led to gradual reductions in the *expected future* inflation rate. In February 2001, as we write this, the expected inflation rate for the next year is about 2 percent, and the expected long-term inflation rate is about 2.5 percent. As inflationary expectations change, so do quoted market interest rates.

Note that Germany, Japan, and Switzerland have over the past 3.5 or so years had lower inflation rates than the United States, hence their interest rates have generally been lower than ours. Italy and most South American countries have experienced high inflation, and that is reflected in their interest rates.

Default Risk Premium (DRP)

The risk that a borrower will *default* on a loan, which means not pay the interest or the principal, also affects the market interest rate on a security: the greater the default risk, the higher the interest rate. Treasury securities have no default risk, hence they carry the lowest interest rates on taxable securities in the United States. For corporate bonds, the higher the bond's rating, the lower its default risk, and, consequently, the lower its interest rate.[11] Here are some representative interest rates on long-term bonds during November 2000:

	RATE	DRP
U.S. Treasury	5.8%	—
AAA	7.5	1.7%
AA	7.8	2.0
A	8.1	2.3
BBB	8.3	2.5

Default Risk Premium (DRP) The difference between the interest rate on a U.S. Treasury bond and a corporate bond of equal maturity and marketability.

The difference between the quoted interest rate on a T- bond and that on a corporate bond with similar maturity, liquidity, and other features is the **default risk premium (DRP).** Therefore, if the bonds listed above were otherwise similar, the default risk premium would be DRP = 7.5% − 5.8% = 1.7 percentage points for AAA corporate bonds, 7.8% − 5.8% = 2.0 percentage points for AA, 8.1% − 5.8% = 2.3 percentage points for A corporate bonds, and so forth. Default risk premiums vary somewhat over time, but the November 2000 figures are representative of levels in recent years.

Liquidity Premium (LP)

Liquidity Premium (LP) A premium added to the equilibrium interest rate on a security if that security cannot be converted to cash on short notice and at close to "fair market value."

A "liquid" asset can be converted to cash quickly and at a "fair market value." Financial assets are generally more liquid than real assets. Because liquidity is important, investors include **liquidity premiums (LPs)** when market rates of securities are established. Although it is difficult to accurately measure liquidity premiums, a differential of at least two and probably four or five percentage points exists between the least liquid and the most liquid financial assets of similar default risk and maturity.

---

[11] Bond ratings, and bonds' riskiness in general, are discussed in detail in Chapter 8. For now, merely note that bonds rated AAA are judged to have less default risk than bonds rated AA, while AA bonds are less risky than A bonds, and so on. Ratings are designated AAA or Aaa, AA or Aa, and so forth, depending on the rating agency. In this book, the designations are used interchangeably.

Maturity Risk Premium (MRP)

U.S. Treasury securities are free of default risk in the sense that one can be virtually certain that the federal government will pay interest on its bonds and will also pay them off when they mature. Therefore, the default risk premium on Treasury securities is essentially zero. Further, active markets exist for Treasury securities, so their liquidity premiums are also close to zero. Thus, as a first approximation, the rate of interest on a Treasury bond should be the risk-free rate, k_{RF}, which is equal to the real risk-free rate, k^*, plus an inflation premium, IP. However, an adjustment is needed for long-term Treasury bonds. The prices of long-term bonds decline sharply whenever interest rates rise, and since interest rates can and do occasionally rise, all long-term bonds, even Treasury bonds, have an element of risk called **interest rate risk.** As a general rule, the bonds of any organization, from the U.S. government to Continental Airlines, have more interest rate risk the longer the maturity of the bond.[12] Therefore, a **maturity risk premium (MRP),** which is higher the longer the years to maturity, must be included in the required interest rate.

Interest Rate Risk
The risk of capital losses to which investors are exposed because of changing interest rates.

Maturity Risk Premium (MRP)
A premium that reflects interest rate risk.

The effect of maturity risk premiums is to raise interest rates on long-term bonds relative to those on short-term bonds. This premium, like the others, is difficult to measure, but (1) it varies somewhat over time, rising when interest rates are more volatile and uncertain, then falling when interest rates are more stable, and (2) in recent years, the maturity risk premium on 30-year T-bonds appears to have generally been in the range of one or two percentage points.[13]

Reinvestment Rate Risk
The risk that a decline in interest rates will lead to lower income when bonds mature and funds are reinvested.

We should mention that although long-term bonds are heavily exposed to interest rate risk, short-term bills are heavily exposed to **reinvestment rate risk.** When short-term bills mature and the funds are reinvested, or "rolled over," a decline in interest rates would necessitate reinvestment at a lower rate, and this would result in a decline in interest income. To illustrate, suppose you had \$100,000 invested in one-year T-bills, and you lived on the income. In 1981, short-term rates were about 15 percent, so your income would have been about \$15,000. However, your income would have declined to about \$9,000 by 1983, and to just \$4,800 by 2001. Had you invested your money in long-term T-bonds, your income (but not the value of the principal) would have been stable.[14] Thus, although "investing short" preserves one's principal, the interest income provided by short-term T-bills is less stable than the interest income on long-term bonds.

---

[12] For example, if someone had bought a 30-year Treasury bond for \$1,000 in 1998, when the long-term interest rate was 5.25 percent, and held it until 2001, when long-term T-bond rates were about 5.5 percent, the value of the bond would have declined to about \$965. That would represent a loss of 3.5 percent, and it demonstrates that long-term bonds, even U.S. Treasury bonds, are not riskless. However, had the investor purchased short-term T-bills in 1998 and subsequently reinvested the principal each time the bills matured, he or she would still have had \$1,000. This point will be discussed in detail in Chapter 8.

[13] The MRP for long-term bonds has averaged 1.4 percent over the last 73 years. See *Stocks, Bonds, Bills, and Inflation: (Valuation Edition) 2000 Yearbook* (Chicago: Ibbotson Associates, 2000).

[14] Long-term bonds also have some reinvestment rate risk. If one is saving and investing for some future purpose, say, to buy a house or for retirement, then to actually earn the quoted rate on a long-term bond, the interest payments must be reinvested at the quoted rate. However, if interest rates fall, the interest payments must be reinvested at a lower rate; thus, the realized return would be less than the quoted rate. Note, though, that reinvestment rate risk is lower on a long-term bond than on a short-term bond because only the interest payments (rather than interest plus principal) on the long-term bond are exposed to reinvestment rate risk. Zero coupon bonds, which are discussed in Chapter 8, are completely free of reinvestment rate risk during their life.

INDUSTRY PRACTICE

A NEW, ALMOST RISKLESS TREASURY BOND

Investors who purchase bonds must constantly worry about inflation. If inflation turns out to be greater than expected, bonds will provide a lower-than-expected real return. To protect themselves against expected increases in inflation, investors build an inflation risk premium into their required rate of return. This raises borrowers' costs.

In order to provide investors with an inflation-protected bond, and also to reduce the cost of debt to the government, on January 29, 1997, the U.S. Treasury issued \$7 billion of 10-year inflation-indexed bonds. These initial bonds paid an interest rate of 3.375 percent plus an additional amount to offset inflation. At the end of each six-month period, the principal (originally set at par, or \$1,000) is adjusted by the inflation rate. For example, during the first six-month interest period, inflation (as measured by the CPI) was 1.085 percent. The inflation-adjusted principal was then calculated as \$1,000(1 + inflation) = \$1,000 × 1.01085 = \$1,010.85. So, on July 15, 1997, each bond paid interest of 0.03375/2 × \$1,010.85 = \$17.06. Note that the interest rate is divided by two because interest is paid twice a year.

By January 15, 1998, a bit more inflation had occurred, and the inflation-adjusted principal was up to \$1,019.69, so on January 15, 1998, each bond paid interest of 0.03375/2 × \$1,019.69 = \$17.21. Thus, the total return during the first year consisted of \$17.06 + \$17.21 = \$34.27 of interest and \$1,019.69 − \$1,000.00 = \$19.69 of "capital gains," or \$34.27 + \$19.69 = \$53.96 in total. Thus, the total return was \$53.96/\$1,000 = 5.396%.

This same adjustment process will continue each year until the bonds mature on January 15, 2007, at which time they will pay the adjusted maturity value. Thus, the cash income provided by the bonds rises by exactly enough to cover inflation, producing a real, inflation-adjusted rate of 3.375 percent. Further, since the principal also rises by the inflation rate, it too is protected from inflation. The accompanying table gives the inflation-adjusted principal and interest paid during the life of these $3\frac{3}{8}$ percent coupon, 10-year, inflation-indexed bonds:

DATE	INFLATION-ADJUSTED PRINCIPAL	INTEREST PAID
7/15/97	\$1,010.85	\$17.06
1/15/98	1,019.69	17.21
7/15/98	1,026.51	17.32
1/15/99	1,035.12	17.47
7/15/99	1,049.01	17.70
1/15/00	1,061.92	17.92
7/15/00	1,080.85	18.24
1/15/01	1,098.52	18.54

SOURCE: Bureau of the Public Debt's Online, Historical Reference CPI Numbers and Daily Index Ratios for $3\frac{3}{8}$%, 10-year note due January 15, 2007, at http://www.publicdebt.treas.gov/of/ofhiscpi.htm.

The Treasury regularly conducts auctions to issue indexed bonds. The 3.375 percent rate was based on the relative supply

SELF-TEST QUESTIONS

Write out an equation for the nominal interest rate on any debt security.

Distinguish between the *real* risk-free rate of interest, k*, and the *nominal,* or *quoted,* risk-free rate of interest, k_{RF}.

How is inflation dealt with when interest rates are determined by investors in the financial markets?

Does the interest rate on a T-bond include a default risk premium? Explain.

Distinguish between liquid and illiquid assets, and identify some assets that are liquid and some that are illiquid.

Briefly explain the following statement: "Although long-term bonds are heavily exposed to interest rate risk, short-term bills are heavily exposed to reinvestment rate risk. The maturity risk premium reflects the net effects of these two opposing forces."

and demand for the issue, and it will remain constant over the life of the bond. However, new bonds are issued periodically, and their "coupon" real rates depend on the market at the time the bond is auctioned. In January 2001, 10-year indexed securities had a real rate of 3.5 percent.

Federal Reserve Board Chairman Greenspan lobbied in favor of the indexed bonds on the grounds that they would help him and the Fed make better estimates of investors' expectations about inflation. He did not explain his reasoning (to our knowledge), but it might have gone something like this:

- We know that interest rates in general are determined as follows:

$$k = k^* + IP + MRP + DRP + LP.$$

- For Treasury bonds, DRP and LP are essentially zero, so for a 10-year bond the rate is

$$k_{RF} = k^* + IP + MRP.$$

  The reason the MRP is not zero is that if inflation increases, interest rates will rise and the price of the bonds will decline. Therefore, "regular" 10-year bonds are exposed to maturity risk, hence a maturity risk premium is built into their market interest rate.
- The indexed bonds are protected against inflation — if inflation increases, then so will their dollar returns, and as a result, their price will not decline in real terms. Therefore, indexed bonds should have no MRP, hence their market return is

$$k_{RF} = k^* + 0 + 0 = k^*.$$

In other words, the market rate on indexed bonds is the real rate.

- The difference between the yield on a regular 10-year bond and that on an indexed bond is the sum of the 10-year bonds' IP and MRP. The yield on regular 10-year bonds was 6.80 percent when the indexed bonds were issued, and the indexed bonds' yield was 3.375 percent. The difference, 3.425 percent, is the average expected inflation rate over the next 10 years plus the MRP for 10-year bonds.
- The 10-year MRP is about 1.0 percent, and it has been relatively stable in recent years. Therefore, the expected rate of inflation in January 1997 was about 2.425 percent (3.425% − 1.00% = 2.425%).

The interest received and the increase in principal are taxed each year as interest income, even though cash from the appreciation will not be received until the bond matures. Therefore, these bonds are especially suitable for individual retirement accounts (IRAs), which are not taxed until funds are withdrawn.

Keep in mind, though, that despite their protection against inflation, indexed bonds are not completely riskless. The real rate of interest can change, and if k^* rises, the price of the indexed bonds will decline. This just confirms one more time that there is no such thing as a free lunch or a riskless security!

SOURCES: "Inflation Notes Will Offer Fed Forecast Tool," *The Wall Street Journal*, February 3, 1997, C1; and *The Wall Street Journal*, January 6, 2000, C21.

THE TERM STRUCTURE OF INTEREST RATES

Term Structure of Interest Rates
The relationship between bond yields and maturities.

WWW Students can find current U.S. Treasury yield curve graphs and other global and domestic interest rate information at Bloomberg markets' site at **http://www.bloomberg.com/markets/index.html.**

The **term structure of interest rates** describes the relationship between long- and short-term rates. The term structure is important to corporate treasurers who must decide whether to borrow by issuing long- or short-term debt and to investors who must decide whether to buy long- or short-term bonds. Thus, it is important to understand (1) how long- and short-term rates relate to each other and (2) what causes shifts in their relative positions.

Interest rates for bonds with different maturities can be found in a variety of publications, including *The Wall Street Journal* and the *Federal Reserve Bulletin*, and on a number of web sites, including Bloomberg, Yahoo, and CNN Financial. From interest rate data obtained from these sources, we can construct the term structure at a given point in time. For example, the tabular section below Figure 5-5 presents interest rates for different maturities on three different

FIGURE 5-5 **U.S. Treasury Bond Interest Rates on Different Dates**

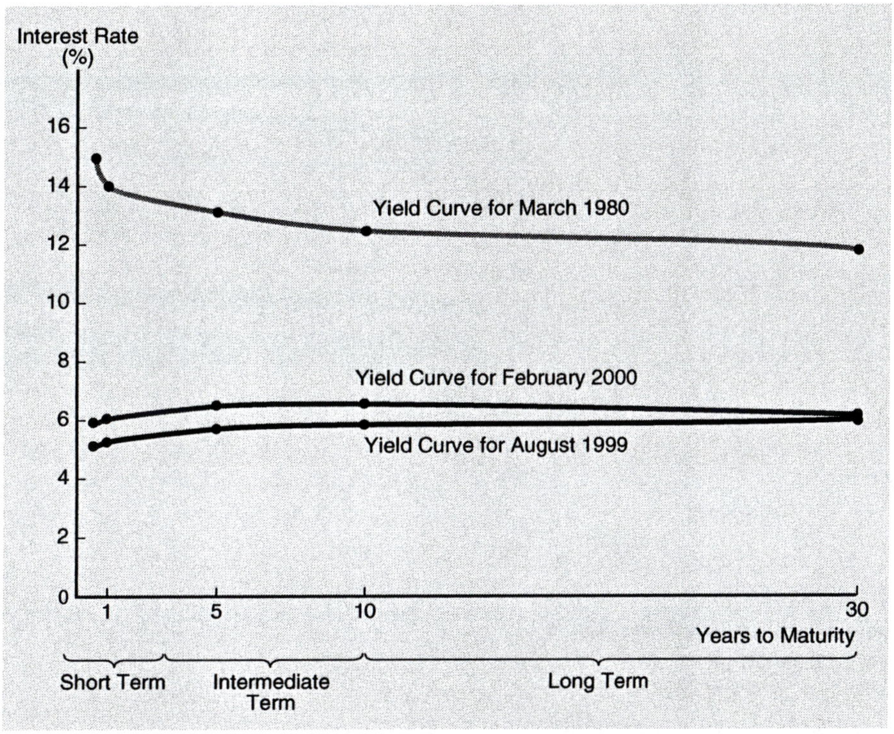

	INTEREST RATE		
TERM TO MATURITY	MARCH 1980	AUGUST 1999	FEBRUARY 2000
6 months	15.0%	5.1%	6.0%
1 year	14.0	5.2	6.2
5 years	13.5	5.8	6.7
10 years	12.8	5.9	6.7
30 years	12.3	6.0	6.3

dates. The set of data for a given date, when plotted on a graph such as that in Figure 5-5 is called the **yield curve** for that date.

Yield Curve
A graph showing the relationship between bond yields and maturities.

The yield curve changes both in position and in slope over time. In March 1980, all rates were relatively high, and since short-term rates were higher than long-term rates, the yield curve was *downward sloping*. However, by August 1999, all rates had fallen, and because short-term rates were lower than long-term rates, the yield curve was *upward sloping*. Six months later, in February 2000, all rates were higher, and the yield curve had become *humped*—medium-term rates were higher than both short- and long-term rates. If the current yield curve (February 2001) were graphed on Figure 5-5, it would be downward sloping for short-term securities but upward sloping for longer-term securities. The data points would plot close to the August 1999 yield curve.

Figure 5-5 shows yield curves for U.S. Treasury securities, but we could have constructed curves for corporate bonds issued by AT&T, IBM, Delta Airlines, or any other company that borrows money over a range of maturities. Had we constructed corporate curves and plotted them on Figure 5-5, they would have been above those for Treasury securities because corporate yields include default risk premiums. However, the corporate yield curves would have had the same general shape as the Treasury curves. Also, the riskier the corporation, the higher its yield curve, so Delta Airlines, which has a lower bond rating than either AT&T or IBM, would have a higher yield curve than those of AT&T and IBM.

"Normal" Yield Curve
An upward-sloping yield curve.

Inverted ("Abnormal") Yield Curve
A downward-sloping yield curve.

Humped Yield Curve
A yield curve where interest rates on medium-term maturities are higher than rates on both short- and long-term maturities.

Historically, in most years long-term rates have been above short-term rates, so the yield curve usually slopes upward. For this reason, people often call an upward-sloping yield curve a **"normal" yield curve** and a yield curve that slopes downward an **inverted,** or **"abnormal," curve.** Thus, in Figure 5-5 the yield curve for March 1980 was inverted and the one for August 1999 was normal. However, the February 2000 curve was **humped**, which means that interest rates on medium-term maturities were higher than rates on both short- and long-term maturities. We explain in detail in the next section why an upward slope is the normal situation, but briefly, the reason is that short-term securities have less interest rate risk than longer-term securities, hence smaller MRPs. Therefore, short-term rates are normally lower than long-term rates.

SELF-TEST QUESTIONS

What is a yield curve, and what information would you need to draw this curve?

Distinguish among the shapes of a "normal" yield curve, an "abnormal" curve, and a "humped" curve.

WHAT DETERMINES THE SHAPE OF THE YIELD CURVE?

Since maturity risk premiums are positive, then if other things were held constant, long-term bonds would have higher interest rates than short-term bonds. However, market interest rates also depend on expected inflation, default risk, and liquidity, and each of these factors can vary with maturity.

Expected inflation has an especially important effect on the yield curve's shape. To see why, consider U.S. Treasury securities. Because Treasuries have essentially no default or liquidity risk, the yield on a Treasury bond that matures in t years can be found using the following equation:

$$k_T = k^*_t + IP_t + MRP_t.$$

While the real risk-free rate, k*, may vary somewhat over time because of changes in the economy and demographics, these changes are random rather than predictable, so it is reasonable to assume that k* will remain constant. However, the inflation premium, IP, does vary significantly over time, and in a somewhat predictable manner. Recall that the inflation premium is simply the

FIGURE 5-6 **Illustrative Treasury Yield Curves**

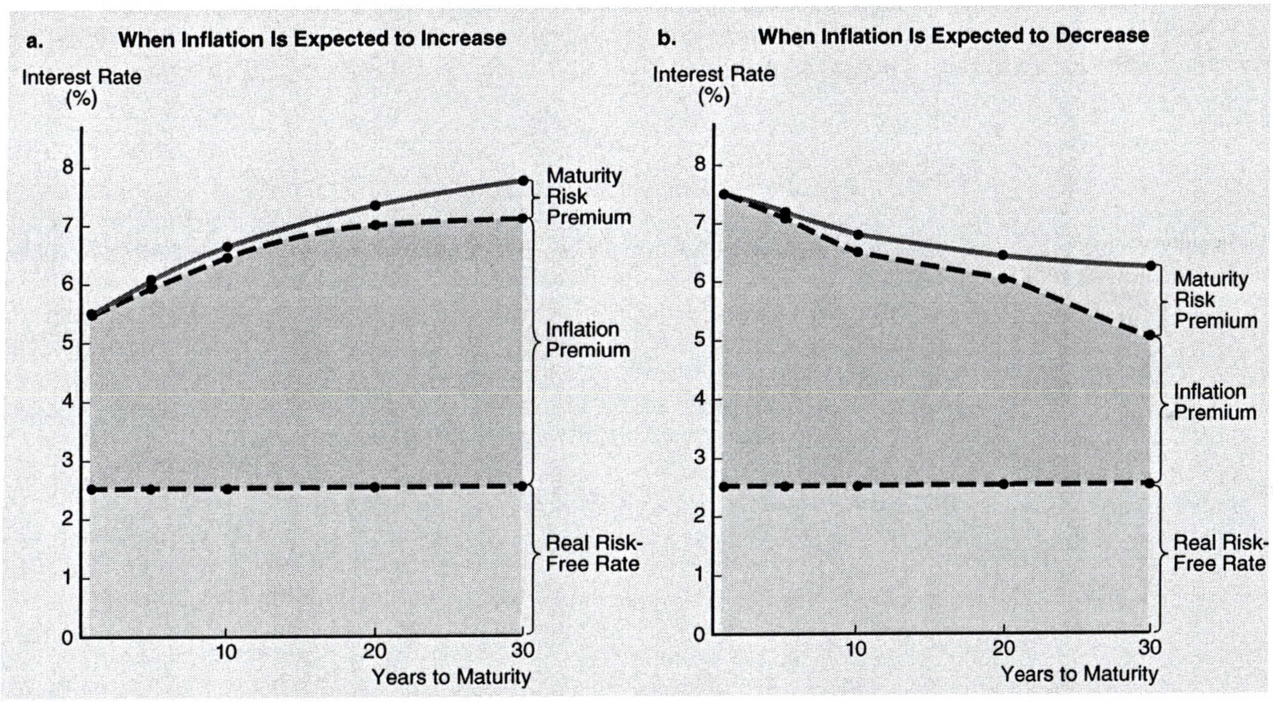

	WITH INCREASING EXPECTED INFLATION					WITH DECREASING EXPECTED INFLATION			
MATURITY	k*	IP	MRP	YIELD	MATURITY	k*	IP	MRP	YIELD
1 year	2.50%	3.00%	0.00%	**5.50%**	1 year	2.50%	5.00%	0.00%	**7.50%**
5 years	2.50	3.40	0.18	**6.08**	5 years	2.50	4.60	0.18	**7.28**
10 years	2.50	4.00	0.28	**6.78**	10 years	2.50	4.00	0.28	**6.78**
20 years	2.50	4.50	0.42	**7.42**	20 years	2.50	3.50	0.42	**6.42**
30 years	2.50	4.67	0.53	**7.70**	30 years	2.50	3.33	0.53	**6.36**

average level of expected inflation over the life of the bond. Thus, if the market expects inflation to increase in the future, the inflation premium will be higher the longer the bond's maturity. On the other hand, if the market expects inflation to decline in the future, long-term bonds will have a smaller inflation premium than short-term bonds. Finally, if investors consider long-term bonds riskier than short-term bonds, the maturity risk premium will increase with maturity.

Panel a of Figure 5-6 shows the yield curve when inflation is expected to increase. Here long-term bonds have higher yields for two reasons: (1) Inflation is expected to be higher in the future, and (2) there is a positive maturity risk premium. Panel b of Figure 5-6 shows the yield curve when inflation is expected to decline, causing the yield curve to be downward sloping. Downward sloping yield curves often foreshadow an economic downturn, because weaker economic conditions tend to be correlated with declining inflation, which in turn leads to lower long-term rates.

Now let's consider the yield curve for corporate bonds. Recall that corporate bonds include a default-risk premium (DRP) and a liquidity premium (LP). Therefore, the yield on a corporate bond that matures in t years can be expressed as follows:

$$k_C = k^*_t + IP_t + MRP_t + DRP_t + LP_t.$$

A corporate bond's default and liquidity risks are affected by its maturity. For example, the default risk on Coca-Cola's short-term debt is very small, since there is almost no chance that Coca-Cola will go bankrupt over the next few years. However, Coke has some 100-year bonds, and while the odds of Coke defaulting on these bonds still might not be that high, the default risk on these bonds is considerably higher than that on its short-term debt.

Longer-term corporate bonds are also less liquid than shorter-term debt, hence the liquidity premium rises as maturity lengthens. The primary reason for this is that, for the reasons discussed earlier, short-term debt has less default risk, so a buyer can buy short-term debt without having to do as much credit checking as would be necessary for long-term debt. Thus, people can move into and out of short-term corporate debt much more rapidly than long-term debt. The end result is that short-term corporate debt is more liquid, hence has a smaller liquidity premium than the same company's long-term debt.

Figure 5-7 shows yield curves for two hypothetical corporate bonds, an AA-rated bond with minimal default risk and a BBB-rated bond with more default risk, along with the yield curve for Treasury securities as taken from Panel a of Figure 5-6. Here we assume that inflation is expected to increase, so the Treasury yield curve is upward sloping. Because of their additional default and liquidity risk, corporate bonds always trade at a higher yield than Treasury bonds with the same maturity, and BBB-rated bonds trade at higher yields than AA-rated bonds. Finally, note that the yield spread between corporate bonds and Treasury bonds is larger the longer the maturity. This occurs because longer-term corporate bonds have more default and liquidity risk than shorter-term bonds, and both of these premiums are absent in Treasury bonds.

FIGURE 5-7 **Corporate and Treasury Yield Curves**

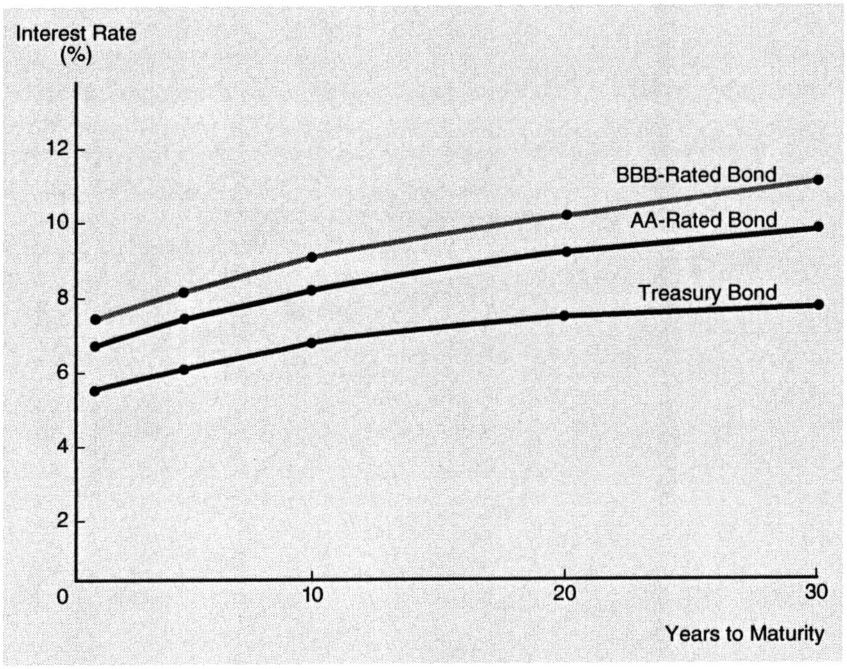

	INTEREST RATE		
TERM TO MATURITY	TREASURY BOND	AA-RATED BOND	BBB-RATED BOND
1 year	5.5%	6.7%	7.4%
5 years	6.1	7.4	8.1
10 years	6.8	8.2	9.1
20 years	7.4	9.2	10.2
30 years	7.7	9.8	11.1

SELF-TEST QUESTIONS

How do maturity risk premiums affect the yield curve?

If the rate of inflation is expected to increase, would this increase or decrease the slope of the yield curve?

If the rate of inflation is expected to remain constant in the future, would the yield curve slope up, down, or be horizontal?

Explain why corporate bonds' default and liquidity premiums are likely to increase with maturity.

Explain why corporate bonds always trade at higher yields than Treasury bonds and why BBB-rated bonds always trade at higher yields than AA-rated bonds.

USING THE YIELD CURVE TO ESTIMATE FUTURE INTEREST RATES[15]

In the last section we saw that the shape of the yield curve depends primarily on two factors: (1) expectations about future inflation and (2) the relative riskiness of securities with different maturities. We also saw how to calculate the yield curve, given inflation and maturity-related risks. In practice, this process often works in reverse: Investors and analysts plot the yield curve and then use information embedded in it to estimate the market's expectations regarding future inflation and risk.

This process of using the yield curve to estimate future expected interest rates is straightforward, provided (1) we focus on Treasury securities, and (2) we assume that all Treasury securities have the same risk; that is, there is no maturity risk premium. Some academics and practitioners contend that this second assumption is reasonable, at least as an approximation. They argue that the market is dominated by large bond traders who buy and sell securities of different maturities each day, that these traders focus only on short-term returns, and that they are not concerned with risk. According to this view, a bond trader is just as willing to buy a 30-year bond to pick up a short-term profit as he would be to buy a three-month security. Strict proponents of this view argue that the shape of the yield curve is therefore determined only by market expectations about future interest rates, thus their position has been called the *pure expectations theory* of the term structure of interest rates.

Expectations Theory
A theory which states that the shape of the yield curve depends on investors' expectations about future interest rates.

The pure **expectations theory** (which is sometimes simply referred to as the "expectations theory") assumes that investors establish bond prices and interest rates strictly on the basis of expectations for interest rates. This means that they are indifferent with respect to maturity in the sense that they do not view long-term bonds as being riskier than short-term bonds. If this were true, then the maturity risk premium (MRP) would be zero, and long-term interest rates would simply be a weighted average of current and expected future short-term interest rates. For example, if 1-year Treasury bills currently yield 7 percent, but 1-year bills were expected to yield 7.5 percent a year from now, investors would expect to earn an average of 7.25 percent over the next two years:[16]

$$\frac{7\% + 7.5\%}{2} = 7.25\%.$$

According to the expectations theory, this implies that a 2-year Treasury note purchased today should also yield 7.25 percent. Similarly, if 10-year bonds yield 9 percent today, and if 5-year bonds are expected to yield 7.5 percent 10 years from now, then investors should expect to earn 9 percent for 10 years

[15] This section is relatively technical, but instructors can omit it without loss of continuity.

[16] Technically, we should be using geometric averages rather than arithmetic averages, but the differences are not material in this example. For a discussion of this point, see Robert C. Radcliffe, *Investment: Concepts, Analysis, and Strategy*, 5th ed. (Reading, MA: Addison-Wesley, 1997), Chapter 5.

and 7.5 percent for 5 years, for an average return of 8.5 percent over the next 15 years:

$$\frac{9\% + 9\% + \cdots + 9\% + 7.5\% + \cdots + 7.5\%}{15} = \frac{10(9\%) + 5(7.5\%)}{15} = 8.5\%.$$

Consequently, a 15-year bond should yield this same return, 8.5 percent.

To understand the logic behind this averaging process, ask yourself what would happen if long-term yields were *not* an average of expected short-term yields. For example, suppose 2-year bonds yielded only 7 percent, not the 7.25 percent calculated above. Bond traders would be able to earn a profit by adopting the following trading strategy:

1. Borrow money for two years at a cost of 7 percent.
2. Invest the money in a series of 1-year bonds. The expected return over the 2-year period would be (7.0 + 7.5)/2 = 7.25%.

In this case, bond traders would rush to borrow money (demand funds) in the 2-year market and invest (or supply funds) in the 1-year market. Recall from Figure 5-2 that an increase in the demand for funds raises interest rates, whereas an increase in the supply of funds reduces interest rates. Therefore, bond traders' actions would push up the 2-year yield but reduce the yield on 1-year bonds. The net effect would be to bring about a market equilibrium in which 2-year rates were a weighted average of expected future 1-year rates.

Under these assumptions, we can "back out" of the yield curve the bond market's best guess about future interest rates. If, for example, you observe that Treasury securities with 1- and 2-year maturities yield 7 percent and 8 percent, respectively, this information can be used to calculate the market's forecast of what 1-year rates will yield one year from now. If the pure expectations theory is correct, the rate on 2-year bonds is the average of the current 1-year rate and the 1-year rate expected a year from now. Since the current 1-year rate is 7 percent, this implies that the 1-year rate one year from now is expected to be 9 percent:

$$\text{2-year yield} = 8\% = \frac{7\% + X\%}{2}$$

$$X = 16\% - 7\% = 9\% = \text{1-year yield expected next year.}$$

The preceding analysis was based on the assumption that the maturity risk premium is zero. However, most evidence suggests that there is a positive maturity risk premium, so the MRP should be taken into account.

For example, assume once again that 1- and 2-year maturities yield 7 percent and 8 percent, respectively, but now assume that the maturity risk premium on the 2-year bond is 0.5 percent. This maturity risk premium implies that the expected return on 2-year bonds (8 percent) is 0.5 percent higher than the expected returns from buying a series of 1-year bonds (7.5 percent). With this background, we can use the following two-step procedure to back out X, the expected 1-year rate one year from now:

Step 1: 2-year yield − MRP on 2-year bond = 8.0% − 0.5% = 7.5%.

Step 2: 7.5% = (7.0% + X%)/2

X = 15.0% − 7.0% = 8.0%.

Therefore, the yield next year on a 1-year T-bond should be 8 percent, up from 7 percent this year.

SELF-TEST QUESTIONS

What key assumption underlies the pure expectations theory?

Assuming that the pure expectations theory is correct, how are long-term interest rates calculated?

According to the pure expectations theory, what would happen if long-term rates were *not* an average of expected short-term rates?

INVESTING OVERSEAS

Investors should consider additional risk factors before investing overseas. First there is **country risk**, which refers to the risk that arises from investing or doing business in a particular country. This risk depends on the country's economic, political, and social environment. Countries with stable economic, social, political, and regulatory systems provide a safer climate for investment, and therefore less country risk, than less stable nations. Examples of country risk include the risk associated with changes in tax rates, regulations, currency conversion, and exchange rates. Country risk also includes the risk that property will be expropriated without adequate compensation, as well as new host country stipulations about local production, sourcing or hiring practices, and damage or destruction of facilities due to internal strife.

Country Risk
The risk that arises from investing or doing business in a particular country.

A second point to keep in mind when investing overseas is that more often than not the security will be denominated in a currency other than the dollar, which means that the value of your investment will depend on what happens to exchange rates. This is known as **exchange rate risk.** For example, if a U.S. investor purchases a Japanese bond, interest will probably be paid in Japanese yen, which must then be converted into dollars if the investor wants to spend his or her money in the United States. If the yen weakens relative to the dollar, then it will buy fewer dollars, hence the investor will receive fewer dollars when it comes time to convert. Alternatively, if the yen strengthens relative to the dollar, the investor will earn higher dollar returns. It therefore follows that the effective rate of return on a foreign investment will depend on both the performance of the foreign security and on what happens to exchange rates over the life of the investment.

Exchange Rate Risk
The risk that exchange rate changes will reduce the number of dollars provided by a given amount of a foreign currency.

SELF-TEST QUESTIONS

What is country risk?

What is exchange rate risk?

GLOBAL PERSPECTIVES

MEASURING COUNTRY RISK

Various forecasting services measure the level of country risk in different countries and provide indexes that measure factors such as each country's expected economic performance, access to world capital markets, political stability, and level of internal conflict. Country risk analysts use sophisticated models to measure it, thus providing corporate managers and overseas investors with a way to judge both the relative and absolute risk of investing in a given country. A sample of recent country risk estimates compiled by *Institutional Investor* is presented in the following table. The higher the country's score, the lower its estimated country risk. The maximum possible score is 100.

The countries with the least amount of country risk all have strong, market-based economies, ready access to worldwide capital markets, relatively little social unrest, and a stable political climate. Switzerland's top ranking may surprise you, but that country's ranking is the result of its strong economic performance. You may also be surprised that the United States was not ranked in the top five — it is ranked sixth.

Arguably, there are fewer surprises when looking at the bottom five. Each of these countries has considerable social and political unrest, and none has embraced a market-based economic system. Clearly, an investment in any of these countries is a risky proposition.

Top Five Countries (Least Amount of Country Risk)

RANK	COUNTRY	TOTAL SCORE (MAXIMUM POSSIBLE = 100)
1	Switzerland	95.6
2	Germany	94.6
3	Netherlands	94.5
4	Luxembourg	93.9
5	France	93.6

Bottom Five Countries (Greatest Amount of Country Risk)

RANK	COUNTRY	TOTAL SCORE (MINIMUM POSSIBLE = 0)
141	Sudan	8.7
142	Liberia	8.6
143	Afghanistan	6.5
144	Sierra Leone	6.4
145	North Korea	6.2

WWW

Students can access the home page of *Institutional Investor* magazine by typing **http://www.iimagazine.com.** Although the site requires users to register, the site is free to use. (Some data sets and articles are available only to subscribers.) The country risk rankings can be found by clicking on "Research and Rankings," shown on the top of the screen, and then clicking on "Country Credit" in the middle of the screen.

OTHER FACTORS THAT INFLUENCE INTEREST RATE LEVELS

In addition to inflationary expectations, other factors also influence both the general level of interest rates and the shape of the yield curve. The four most important factors are (1) Federal Reserve policy; (2) the federal budget deficit or surplus; (3) international factors, including the foreign trade balance and interest rates in other countries; and (4) the level of business activity.

Federal Reserve Policy

WWW The home page for the Board of Governors of the Federal Reserve System can be found at **http://www.federalreserve.gov/**. You can access general information about the Federal Reserve, including press releases, speeches, and monetary policy.

As you probably learned in your economics courses, (1) the money supply has a major effect on both the level of economic activity and the inflation rate, and (2) in the United States, the Federal Reserve Board controls the money supply. If the Fed wants to stimulate the economy, as it did in 1995, it increases growth in the money supply. The initial effect of such an action is to cause interest rates to decline. However, a larger money supply may also lead to an increase in the expected inflation rate, which, in turn, could push interest rates up. The reverse holds if the Fed tightens the money supply.

To illustrate, in 1981 inflation was quite high, so the Fed tightened up the money supply. The Fed deals primarily in the short-term end of the market, so this tightening had the direct effect of pushing short-term rates up sharply. At the same time, the very fact that the Fed was taking strong action to reduce inflation led to a decline in expectations for long-run inflation, which led to a decline in long-term bond yields.

In 1991, the situation was just the reverse. To combat the recession, the Fed took steps to reduce interest rates. Short-term rates fell, and long-term rates also dropped, but not as sharply. These lower rates benefitted heavily indebted businesses and individual borrowers, and home mortgage refinancings put additional billions of dollars into consumers' pockets. Savers, of course, lost out, but the net effect of lower interest rates was a stronger economy. Lower rates encourage businesses to borrow for investment, stimulate the housing market, and bring down the value of the dollar relative to other currencies, which helps U.S. exporters and thus lowers the trade deficit.

During periods when the Fed is actively intervening in the markets, the yield curve may be temporarily distorted. Short-term rates will be temporarily "too low" if the Fed is easing credit, and "too high" if it is tightening credit. Long-term rates are not affected as much by Fed intervention. For example, the fear of rising inflation led the Federal Reserve to increase short-term interest rates six times during 1994. While short-term rates rose by nearly 4 percentage points, long-term rates increased by only 1.5 percentage points.

Budget Deficits or Surpluses

If the federal government spends more than it takes in from tax revenues, it runs a deficit, and that deficit must be covered either by borrowing or by printing money (increasing the money supply). If the government borrows, this added demand for funds pushes up interest rates. If it prints money, this increases expectations for future inflation, which also drives up interest rates. Thus, the larger the federal deficit, other things held constant, the higher the level of interest rates. Whether long- or short-term rates are more affected depends on how the deficit is financed, so we cannot state, in general, how deficits will affect the slope of the yield curve.

Over the past several decades, the federal government routinely ran large budget deficits. However, in 1999, for the first time in recent memory, the government had a budget surplus, and further surpluses are projected on into the future. As a result, the government is buying back some of the outstanding Treasury securities. If these surpluses become a reality, the government would become a net supplier of funds rather than a net borrower of funds. All else equal, this would tend to reduce interest rates.

International Factors

Businesses and individuals in the United States buy from and sell to people and firms in other countries. If we buy more than we sell (that is, if we import more than we export), we are said to be running a *foreign trade deficit*. When trade deficits occur, they must be financed, and the main source of financing is debt. In other words, if we import $200 billion of goods but export only $100 billion, we run a trade deficit of $100 billion, and we would probably borrow the $100 billion.[17] Therefore, the larger our trade deficit, the more we must borrow, and as we increase our borrowing, this drives up interest rates. Also, foreigners are willing to hold U.S. debt if and only if the rate paid on this debt is competitive with interest rates in other countries. Therefore, if the Federal Reserve attempts to lower interest rates in the United States, causing our rates to fall below rates abroad, then foreigners will sell U.S. bonds, those sales will depress bond prices, and the result will be higher U.S. rates. Thus, if the trade deficit is large relative to the size of the overall economy, it may hinder the Fed's ability to combat a recession by lowering interest rates.

The United States has been running annual trade deficits since the mid-1970s, and the cumulative effect of these deficits is that the United States has become the largest debtor nation of all time. As a result, our interest rates are very much influenced by interest rates in other countries around the world (higher rates abroad lead to higher U.S. rates). Because of all this, U.S. corporate treasurers — and anyone else who is affected by interest rates — must keep up with developments in the world economy.

Business Activity

Figure 5-3, presented earlier, can be examined to see how business conditions influence interest rates. Here are the key points revealed by the graph:

1. Because inflation increased from 1961 to 1981, the general tendency during that period was toward higher interest rates. However, since the 1981 peak, the trend has generally been downward.
2. Until 1966, short-term rates were almost always below long-term rates. Thus, in those years the yield curve was almost always "normal" in the sense that it was upward sloping.
3. The shaded areas in the graph represent recessions, during which (1) both the demand for money and the rate of inflation tend to fall and (2) the Federal Reserve tends to increase the money supply in an effort to stimulate the economy. As a result, there is a tendency for interest

[17] The deficit could also be financed by selling assets, including gold, corporate stocks, entire companies, and real estate. The United States has financed its massive trade deficits by all of these means in recent years, but the primary method has been by borrowing from foreigners.

rates to decline during recessions. Currently, in early 2001, there are continued signs that the economy has begun to weaken. In response to these signs of economic weakness, the Federal Reserve has instituted a series of interest rate cuts. At the same time, there are also signs that inflation has begun to increase. These concerns about inflation may limit the Fed's ability to cut rates further.

4. During recessions, short-term rates decline more sharply than long-term rates. This occurs because (1) the Fed operates mainly in the short-term sector, so its intervention has the strongest effect there, and (2) long-term rates reflect the average expected inflation rate over the next 20 to 30 years, and this expectation generally does not change much, even when the current inflation rate is low because of a recession or high because of a boom. So, short-term rates are more volatile than long-term rates.

SELF-TEST QUESTIONS

Other than inflationary expectations, name some additional factors that influence interest rates, and explain the effects of each.

How does the Fed stimulate the economy? How does the Fed affect interest rates? Does the Fed have complete control over U.S. interest rates; that is, can it set rates at any level it chooses?

INTEREST RATES AND BUSINESS DECISIONS

The yield curve for August 1999, shown earlier in Figure 5-5, indicates how much the U.S. government had to pay in 1999 to borrow money for one year, five years, ten years, and so on. A business borrower would have had to pay somewhat more, but assume for the moment that we are back in August 1999 and that the yield curve for that year also applies to your company. Now suppose your company has decided (1) to build a new plant with a 30-year life that will cost $1 million and (2) to raise the $1 million by selling an issue of debt (or borrowing) rather than by selling stock. If you borrowed in 1999 on a short-term basis — say, for one year — your interest cost for that year would be only 5.2 percent, or $52,000. On the other hand, if you used long-term (30-year) financing, your cost would be 6.0 percent, or $60,000. Therefore, at first glance, it would seem that you should use short-term debt.

However, this could prove to be a horrible mistake. If you use short-term debt, you will have to renew your loan every year, and the rate charged on each new loan will reflect the then-current short-term rate. Interest rates could return to their previous highs, in which case you would be paying 14 percent, or $140,000, per year. Those high interest payments would cut into, and perhaps eliminate, your profits. Your reduced profitability could easily increase your firm's risk to the point where its bond rating would be lowered, causing lenders to increase the risk premium built into the interest rate they charge. That would force you to pay an even higher rate, which would further reduce your profitability, worrying lenders even more, and making them reluctant to renew your loan. If your lenders refused to renew the loan and demanded its repayment, as they would have every right to do, you might have to sell assets at a loss, which could lead to bankruptcy.

On the other hand, if you used long-term financing in 1999, your interest costs would remain constant at $60,000 per year, so an increase in interest rates in the economy would not hurt you. You might even be able to buy up some of your bankrupt competitors at bargain prices — bankruptcies increase dramatically when interest rates rise, primarily because many firms do use too much short-term debt.

Does all this suggest that firms should always avoid short-term debt? Not necessarily. If inflation falls over the next few years, so will interest rates. If you had borrowed on a long-term basis for 6.0 percent in August 1999, your company would be at a major disadvantage if it were locked into 6.0 percent debt while its competitors (who used short-term debt in 1999 and thus rode interest rates down in subsequent years) had a borrowing cost of only 3 or 4 percent.

Financing decisions would be easy if we could make accurate forecasts of future interest rates. Unfortunately, predicting interest rates with consistent accuracy is somewhere between difficult and impossible — people who make a living by selling interest rate forecasts say it is difficult, but many others say it is impossible.

Even if it is difficult to predict future interest rate *levels*, it is easy to predict that interest rates will *fluctuate* — they always have, and they always will. This being the case, sound financial policy calls for using a mix of long- and short-term debt, as well as equity, to position the firm so that it can survive in any interest rate environment. Further, the optimal financial policy depends in an important way on the nature of the firm's assets — the easier it is to sell off assets to generate cash, the more feasible it is to use large amounts of short-term debt. This makes it more feasible for a firm to finance its current assets such as inventories than its fixed assets such as buildings with short-term debt. We will return to this issue later in the book, when we discuss working capital policy.

Changes in interest rates also have implications for savers. For example, if you had a 401(k) plan — and someday you almost certainly will — you would probably want to invest some of your money in a bond mutual fund. You could choose a fund that had an average maturity of 25 years, 20 years, and so on, down to only a few months (a money market fund). How would your choice affect your investment results, hence your retirement income? First, your annual interest income would be affected. For example, if the yield curve were upward sloping, as it normally is, you would earn more interest if you choose a fund that held long-term bonds. Note, though, that if you choose a long-term fund and interest rates then rose, the market value of the bonds in the fund would decline. For example, as we will see in Chapter 8, if you had $100,000 in a fund whose average bond had a maturity of 25 years and a coupon rate of 6 percent, and if interest rates then rose from 6 percent to 10 percent, the market value of your fund would decline from $100,000 to about $64,000. On the other hand, if rates declined, your fund would increase in value. In any event, your choice of maturity would have a major effect on your investment performance, hence your future income.

SELF-TEST QUESTIONS

If short-term interest rates are lower than long-term rates, why might a borrower still choose to finance with long-term debt?

Explain the following statement: "The optimal financial policy depends in an important way on the nature of the firm's assets."

TYING IT ALL TOGETHER

In this chapter, we discussed the nature of financial markets, the types of institutions that operate in these markets, how interest rates are determined, and some of the ways interest rates affect business decisions. In later chapters we will use this information to help value different investments, and to better understand corporate financing and investing decisions. The key concepts covered are listed below:

- There are many different types of **financial markets.** Each market serves a different region or deals with a different type of security.
- **Physical asset markets,** also called tangible or real asset markets, are those for such products as wheat, autos, and real estate.
- **Financial asset markets** deal with stocks, bonds, notes, mortgages, and other claims on real assets.
- **Spot markets** and **futures markets** are terms that refer to whether the assets are bought or sold for "on-the-spot" delivery or for delivery at some future date.
- **Money markets** are the markets for debt securities with maturities of less than one year.
- **Capital markets** are the markets for long-term debt and corporate stocks.
- **Primary markets** are the markets in which corporations raise new capital.
- **Secondary markets** are markets in which existing, already outstanding, securities are traded among investors.
- A **derivative** is a security whose value is derived from the price of some other "underlying" asset.
- Transfers of capital between borrowers and savers take place (1) by **direct transfers** of money and securities; (2) by transfers through **investment banking houses,** which act as middlemen; and (3) by transfers through **financial intermediaries,** which create new securities.
- Among the major classes of intermediaries are **commercial banks, savings and loan associations, mutual savings banks, credit unions, pension funds, life insurance companies,** and **mutual funds.**

- One result of ongoing regulatory changes has been a blurring of the distinctions between the different financial institutions. The trend in the United States has been toward **financial service corporations** that offer a wide range of financial services, including investment banking, brokerage operations, insurance, and commercial banking.
- The **stock market** is an especially important market because this is where stock prices (which are used to "grade" managers' performances) are established.
- There are two basic types of stock markets — the **physical location exchanges** (like the NYSE) and the **electronic dealer-based markets** (that include the Nasdaq and the over-the-counter market).
- Capital is allocated through the price system — a price must be paid to "rent" money. Lenders charge **interest** on funds they lend, while equity investors receive **dividends and capital gains** in return for letting firms use their money.
- Four fundamental factors affect the cost of money: (1) **production opportunities,** (2) **time preferences for consumption,** (3) **risk,** and (4) **inflation.**
- The **risk-free rate of interest, k_{RF},** is defined as the real risk-free rate, k^*, plus an inflation premium, IP, hence $k_{RF} = k^* + IP$.
- The **nominal** (or **quoted) interest rate** on a debt security, **k,** is composed of the real risk-free rate, k^*, plus premiums that reflect inflation (IP), default risk (DRP), liquidity (LP), and maturity risk (MRP):

$$k = k^* + IP + DRP + LP + MRP.$$

- If the **real risk-free rate of interest and the various premiums were constant over time,** interest rates would be stable. However, both the real rate and the premiums — especially the premium for expected inflation — **do change over time, causing market interest rates to change.** Also, Federal Reserve intervention to increase or decrease the money supply, as well as international currency flows, leads to fluctuations in interest rates.
- The relationship between the yields on securities and the securities' maturities is known as the **term structure of interest rates,** and the **yield curve** is a graph of this relationship.
- The shape of the yield curve depends on two key factors: (1) **expectations about future inflation** and (2) **perceptions about the relative riskiness of securities with different maturities.**
- The yield curve is normally **upward sloping** — this is called a **normal yield curve.** However, the curve can slope downward (an **inverted yield curve**) if the inflation rate is expected to decline. The yield curve can also be **humped,** which means that interest rates on medium-term maturities are higher than rates on both short- and long-term maturities.
- Because interest rate levels are difficult if not impossible to predict, **sound financial policy** calls for using a mix of short- and long-term debt, and also for positioning the firm to survive in any future interest rate environment.

QUESTIONS

5-1 What are financial intermediaries, and what economic functions do they perform?

5-2 Suppose interest rates on residential mortgages of equal risk were 7 percent in California and 9 percent in New York. Could this differential persist? What forces might tend to equalize rates? Would differentials in borrowing costs for businesses of equal risk located in California and New York be more or less likely to exist than differentials in residential mortgage rates? Would differentials in the cost of money for New York and California firms be more likely to exist if the firms being compared were very large or if they were very small? What are the implications of all this for the pressure now being put on Congress to permit banks to engage in nationwide branching?

5-3 What would happen to the standard of living in the United States if people lost faith in the safety of our financial institutions? Why?

5-4 How does a cost-efficient capital market help to reduce the prices of goods and services?

5-5 Which fluctuate more, long-term or short-term interest rates? Why?

5-6 Suppose you believe that the economy is just entering a recession. Your firm must raise capital immediately, and debt will be used. Should you borrow on a long-term or a short-term basis? Why?

5-7 Suppose the population of Area Y is relatively young while that of Area O is relatively old, but everything else about the two areas is equal.
a. Would interest rates likely be the same or different in the two areas? Explain.
b. Would a trend toward nationwide branching by banks and savings and loans, and the development of nationwide diversified financial corporations, affect your answer to part a?

5-8 Suppose a new process was developed that could be used to make oil out of seawater. The equipment required is quite expensive, but it would, in time, lead to very low prices for gasoline, electricity, and other types of energy. What effect would this have on interest rates?

5-9 Suppose a new and much more liberal Congress and administration were elected, and their first order of business was to take away the independence of the Federal Reserve System, and to force the Fed to greatly expand the money supply. What effect would this have
a. On the level and slope of the yield curve immediately after the announcement?
b. On the level and slope of the yield curve that would exist two or three years in the future?

5-10 It is a fact that the federal government (1) encouraged the development of the savings and loan industry; (2) virtually forced the industry to make long-term, fixed-interest-rate mortgages; and (3) forced the savings and loans to obtain most of their capital as deposits that were withdrawable on demand.
a. Would the savings and loans have higher profits in a world with a "normal" or an inverted yield curve?
b. Would the savings and loan industry be better off if the individual institutions sold their mortgages to federal agencies and then collected servicing fees or if the institutions held the mortgages that they originated?

5-11 Suppose interest rates on Treasury bonds rose from 7 to 14 percent as a result of higher interest rates in Europe. What effect would this have on the price of an average company's common stock?

5-12 What does it mean when it is said that the United States is running a trade deficit? What impact will a trade deficit have on interest rates?

5-13 What are the two leading stock exchanges in the United States today?

5-14 Differentiate between dealer markets and stock markets that have a physical location.

SELF-TEST PROBLEMS (SOLUTIONS APPEAR IN APPENDIX B)

ST-1 Key terms

Define each of the following terms:
a. Money market; capital market
b. Primary market; secondary market; initial public offering (IPO) market
c. Private markets; public markets
d. Spot market; futures market

e. Derivatives
f. Investment banking house; financial service corporation
g. Financial intermediary
h. Mutual fund; money market fund
i. Physical location exchanges; dealer market; over-the-counter market
j. Production opportunities; time preferences for consumption; risk; inflation
k. Real risk-free rate of interest, k*; nominal (quoted) risk-free rate of interest, k_{RF}
l. Inflation premium (IP)
m. Default risk premium (DRP)
n. Liquidity; liquidity premium (LP)
o. Interest rate risk; maturity risk premium (MRP)
p. Reinvestment rate risk; country risk
q. Term structure of interest rates; yield curve
r. "Normal" yield curve; inverted ("abnormal") yield curve; humped yield curve
s. Expectations theory
t. Foreign trade deficit; exchange rate risk

ST-2 **Inflation rates** Assume that it is January 1, 2002. The rate of inflation is expected to be 4 percent throughout 2002. However, increased government deficits and renewed vigor in the economy are then expected to push inflation rates higher. Investors expect the inflation rate to be 5 percent in 2003, 6 percent in 2004, and 7 percent in 2005. The real risk-free rate, k*, is expected to remain at 2 percent over the next 5 years. Assume that no maturity risk premiums are required on bonds with 5 years or less to maturity. The current interest rate on 5-year T-bonds is 8 percent.

a. What is the average expected inflation rate over the next 4 years?
b. What should be the prevailing interest rate on 4-year T-bonds?
c. What is the implied expected inflation rate in 2006, or Year 5, given that Treasury bonds which mature in that year yield 8 percent?

STARTER PROBLEMS

5-1 **Expected rate of interest** The real risk-free rate of interest is 3 percent. Inflation is expected to be 2 percent this year and 4 percent during the next 2 years. Assume that the maturity risk premium is zero. What is the yield on 2-year Treasury securities? What is the yield on 3-year Treasury securities?

5-2 **Default risk premium** A Treasury bond that matures in 10 years has a yield of 6 percent. A 10-year corporate bond has a yield of 8 percent. Assume that the liquidity premium on the corporate bond is 0.5 percent. What is the default risk premium on the corporate bond?

5-3 **Expected rate of interest** One-year Treasury securities yield 5 percent. The market anticipates that 1 year from now, 1-year Treasury securities will yield 6 percent. If the pure expectations theory is correct, what should be the yield today for 2-year Treasury securities?

5-4 **Maturity risk premium** The real risk-free rate is 3 percent, and inflation is expected to be 3 percent for the next 2 years. A 2-year Treasury security yields 6.2 percent. What is the maturity risk premium for the 2-year security?

EXAM-TYPE PROBLEMS

The problems included in this section are set up in such a way that they could be used as multiple-choice exam problems.

5-5 **Expected rate of interest** Interest rates on 1-year Treasury securities are currently 5.6 percent, while 2-year Treasury securities are yielding 6 percent. If the pure expectations theory is correct, what does the market believe will be the yield on 1-year securities 1 year from now?

5-6 **Expected rate of interest** Interest rates on 4-year Treasury securities are currently 7 percent, while interest rates on 6-year Treasury securities are currently 7.5 percent. If the pure expectations theory is correct, what does the market believe that 2-year securities will be yielding 4 years from now?

5-7 **Expected rate of interest** The real risk-free rate is 3 percent. Inflation is expected to be 3 percent this year, 4 percent next year, and then 3.5 percent thereafter. The maturity risk premium is estimated to be $0.0005 \times (t - 1)$, where t = number of years to maturity. What is the nominal interest rate on a 7-year Treasury note?

5-8 Expected rate of interest

Suppose the annual yield on a 2-year Treasury bond is 4.5 percent, while that on a 1-year bond is 3 percent. k* is 1 percent, and the maturity risk premium is zero.

a. Using the expectations theory, forecast the interest rate on a 1-year bond during the second year. (Hint: Under the expectations theory, the yield on a 2-year bond is equal to the average yield on 1-year bonds in Years 1 and 2.)
b. What is the expected inflation rate in Year 1? Year 2?

5-9 Expected rate of interest

Assume that the real risk-free rate is 2 percent and that the maturity risk premium is zero. If the nominal rate of interest on 1-year bonds is 5 percent and that on comparable-risk 2-year bonds is 7 percent, what is the 1-year interest rate that is expected for Year 2? What inflation rate is expected during Year 2? Comment on why the average interest rate during the 2-year period differs from the 1-year interest rate expected for Year 2.

5-10 Maturity risk premium

Assume that the real risk-free rate, k*, is 3 percent and that inflation is expected to be 8 percent in Year 1, 5 percent in Year 2, and 4 percent thereafter. Assume also that all Treasury bonds are highly liquid and free of default risk. If 2-year and 5-year Treasury bonds both yield 10 percent, what is the difference in the maturity risk premiums (MRPs) on the two bonds; that is, what is MRP_5 minus MRP_2?

5-11 Interest rates

Due to a recession, the inflation rate expected for the coming year is only 3 percent. However, the inflation rate in Year 2 and thereafter is expected to be constant at some level above 3 percent. Assume that the real risk-free rate is k* = 2% for all maturities and that the expectations theory fully explains the yield curve, so there are no maturity risk premiums. If 3-year Treasury bonds yield 2 percentage points more than 1-year bonds, what inflation rate is expected after Year 1?

PROBLEMS

5-12 Yield curves

Suppose you and most other investors expect the inflation rate to be 7 percent next year, to fall to 5 percent during the following year, and then to remain at a rate of 3 percent thereafter. Assume that the real risk-free rate, k*, will remain at 2 percent and that maturity risk premiums on Treasury securities rise from zero on very short-term bonds (those that mature in a few days) to a level of 0.2 percentage point for 1-year securities. Furthermore, maturity risk premiums increase 0.2 percentage point for each year to maturity, up to a limit of 1.0 percentage point on 5-year or longer-term T-bonds.

a. Calculate the interest rate on 1-, 2-, 3-, 4-, 5-, 10-, and 20-year Treasury securities, and plot the yield curve.
b. Now suppose Exxon Mobil, an AAA-rated company, had bonds with the same maturities as the Treasury bonds. As an approximation, plot an Exxon Mobil yield curve on the same graph with the Treasury bond yield curve. (Hint: Think about the default risk premium on Exxon Mobil's long-term versus its short-term bonds.)
c. Now plot the approximate yield curve of Long Island Lighting Company, a risky nuclear utility.

5-13 Yield curves

The following yields on U.S. Treasury securities were taken from *The Wall Street Journal* in September 1999:

TERM	RATE
6 months	5.1%
1 year	5.5
2 years	5.6
3 years	5.7
4 years	5.8
5 years	6.0
10 years	6.1
20 years	6.5
30 years	6.3

Plot a yield curve based on these data.

5-14
Inflation and interest rates

In late 1980, the U.S. Commerce Department released new figures that showed that inflation was running at an annual rate of close to 15 percent. At the time, the prime rate of interest was 21 percent, a record high. However, many investors expected the new Reagan administration to be more effective in controlling inflation than the Carter administration had been. Moreover, many observers believed that the extremely high interest rates and generally tight credit, which resulted from the Federal Reserve System's attempts to curb the inflation rate, would shortly bring about a recession, which, in turn, would lead to a decline in the inflation rate and also in the interest rate. Assume that at the beginning of 1981, the expected inflation rate for 1981 was 13 percent; for 1982, 9 percent; for 1983, 7 percent; and for 1984 and thereafter, 6 percent.

a. What was the average expected inflation rate over the 5-year period 1981–1985? (Use the arithmetic average.)
b. What average *nominal* interest rate would, over the 5-year period, be expected to produce a 2 percent real risk-free rate of return on 5-year Treasury securities?
c. Assuming a real risk-free rate of 2 percent and a maturity risk premium that starts at 0.1 percent and increases by 0.1 percent each year, estimate the interest rate in January 1981 on bonds that mature in 1, 2, 5, 10, and 20 years, and draw a yield curve based on these data.
d. Describe the general economic conditions that could be expected to produce an upward-sloping yield curve.
e. If the consensus among investors in early 1981 had been that the expected inflation rate for every future year was 10 percent (that is, $I_t = I_{t+1} = 10\%$ for $t = 1$ to ∞), what do you think the yield curve would have looked like? Consider all the factors that are likely to affect the curve. Does your answer here make you question the yield curve you drew in part c?

SPREADSHEET PROBLEM

5-15
Analyzing interest rates

a. Suppose you are considering two possible investment opportunities: a 12-year Treasury bond and a 7-year, A-rated corporate bond. The current real risk-free rate is 4 percent, and inflation is expected to be 2 percent for the next two years, 3 percent for the following four years, and 4 percent thereafter. The maturity risk premium is estimated by this formula: $MRP = 0.1\%(t - 1)$. The liquidity premium for the corporate bond is estimated to be 0.7 percent. Finally, you may determine the default risk premium, given the company's bond rating, from the default risk premium table in the text. What yield would you predict for each of these two investments?
b. Given the following Treasury bond yield information from the September 27, 1999, *Wall Street Journal*, construct a graph of the yield curve as of that date.

MATURITY	YIELD
1 year	5.37%
2 years	5.47
3 years	5.65
4 years	5.71
5 years	5.64
10 years	5.75
20 years	6.33
30 years	5.94

c. Based on the information about the corporate bond that was given in part a, calculate yields and then construct a new yield curve graph that shows both the Treasury and the corporate bonds.
d. Using the Treasury yield information above, calculate the following forward rates:
(1) The 1-year rate, 1 year from now.
(2) The 5-year rate, 5 years from now.
(3) The 10-year rate, 10 years from now.
(4) The 10-year rate, 20 years from now.

CYBER PROBLEM

The information related to the cyberproblems is likely to change over time, due to the release of new information and the ever-changing nature of the World Wide Web. With these changes in mind, we will periodically update these problems on the textbook's web site. To avoid problems, please check for these updates before proceeding with the cyberproblems.

5-16 Financial environment

The yield curve is a graph of the term structure of interest rates, which is the relationship of yield and maturity for securities of similar risk. When we think of the yield curve we typically think of the Treasury yield curve as found each day in financial publications such as *The Wall Street Journal.* The yield curve changes in both level and shape due to a variety of monetary, economic, and political factors that were discussed in Chapter 5. The Federal Reserve is a useful site for obtaining actual economic and monetary data. Along with other data, you can obtain historical interest rates at this site to construct a yield curve and analyze changes in interest rates.

To access information from the Federal Reserve, you will be using FRED (the Federal Reserve Economic Database). First, you must connect to the Federal Reserve Bank of St. Louis web site, which can be found at **www.stls.frb.org.** From this web page, click on data (near the bottom of the screen), and then select monthly interest rates from the list of database categories. On this page, you will find links to all of the information needed for this cyberproblem.

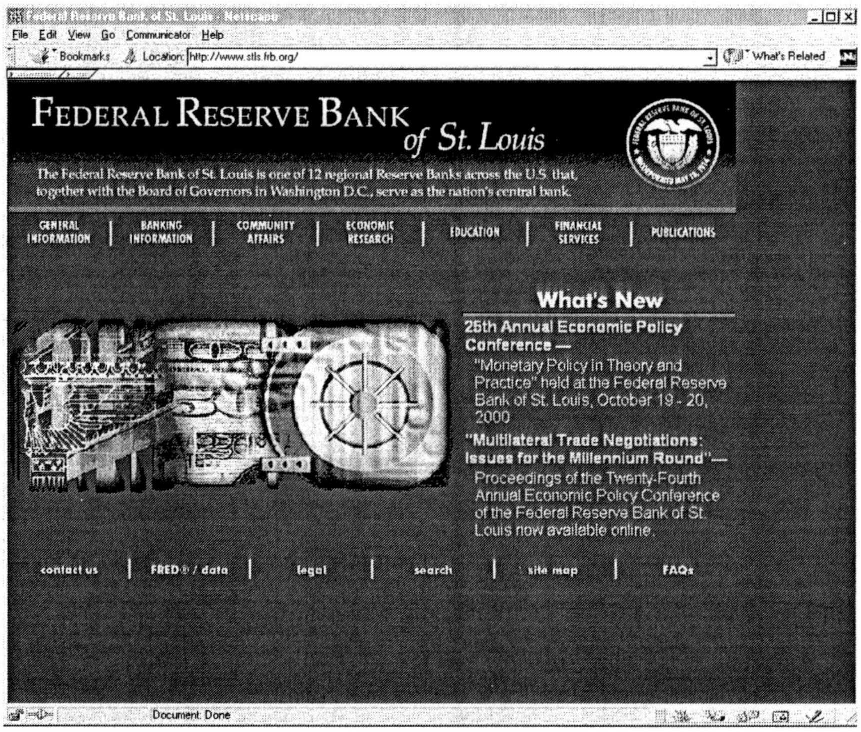

a. Construct four distinct Treasury yield curves using monthly interest rate data for February 1982, 1988, 1993, and 1998. Use the constant maturity interest rates for maturities of 3 months, 6 months, 1 year, 5 years, 10 years, and 30 years.
b. Examine the yield curves you have constructed. What could explain the large variation in the 3-month, risk-free rate over the different time periods?

c. (1) Contrast the slope of the February 1982 yield curve with that of February 1993. What do we call a yield curve that has the same shape as the 1982 yield curve? (2) Why might the 1982 yield curve be downward sloping? What does this indicate? (3) What does the 1993 yield curve illustrate about long-term versus short-term interest rates?

d. Contrast the yield curves of 1993 and 1998. Note that the 1998 yield curve is almost flat, while the 1993 yield curve has a very steep slope. What could account for this difference in slopes?

e. Pretend that you are an investor back in 1988, and you have no knowledge of future interest rates, except the information given in the yield curve. Use the 1988 yield curve to determine the expected yield on 5-year Treasury bonds five years from 1988 (or the 5-year bond rate in 1993). Then, compare that figure to the actual 5-year bond rate in 1993. Did investors under- or overestimate future inflation in 1988?

INTEGRATED CASE

SMYTH BARRY & COMPANY

5-17 Financial Markets, Institutions, and Interest Rates Assume that you recently graduated with a degree in finance and have just reported to work as an investment advisor at the brokerage firm of Smyth Barry & Co. Your first assignment is to explain the nature of the U.S. financial markets to Michelle Varga, a professional tennis player who has just come to the United States from Mexico. Varga is a highly ranked tennis player who expects to invest substantial amounts of money through Smyth Barry. She is also very bright, and, therefore, she would like to understand in general terms what will happen to her money. Your boss has developed the following set of questions that you must ask and answer to explain the U.S. financial system to Varga.

a. What is a market? Differentiate between the following types of markets: physical asset vs. financial markets, spot vs. futures markets, money vs. capital markets, primary vs. secondary markets, and public vs. private markets.

b. What is an initial public offering (IPO) market?

c. If Apple Computer decided to issue additional common stock, and Varga purchased 100 shares of this stock from Merrill Lynch, the underwriter, would this transaction be a primary market transaction or a secondary market transaction? Would it make a difference if Varga purchased previously outstanding Apple stock in the dealer market?

d. Describe the three primary ways in which capital is transferred between savers and borrowers.

e. What are the two leading stock markets? Describe the two basic types of stock markets.

f. What do we call the price that a borrower must pay for debt capital? What is the price of equity capital? What are the four most fundamental factors that affect the cost of money, or the general level of interest rates, in the economy?

g. What is the real risk-free rate of interest (k^*) and the nominal risk-free rate (k_{RF})? How are these two rates measured?

h. Define the terms inflation premium (IP), default risk premium (DRP), liquidity premium (LP), and maturity risk premium (MRP). Which of these premiums is included when determining the interest rate on (1) short-term U.S. Treasury securities, (2) long-term U.S. Treasury securities, (3) short-term corporate securities, and (4) long-term corporate securities? Explain how the premiums would vary over time and among the different securities listed above.

i. What is the term structure of interest rates? What is a yield curve?

j. Suppose most investors expect the inflation rate to be 5 percent next year, 6 percent the following year, and 8 percent thereafter. The real risk-free rate is 3 percent. The maturity risk premium is zero for bonds that mature in 1 year or less, 0.1 percent for 2-year bonds, and then the MRP increases by 0.1 percent per year thereafter for 20 years, after which it is stable. What is the interest rate on 1-year, 10-year, and 20-year Treasury bonds? Draw a yield curve with these data. What factors can explain why this constructed yield curve is upward sloping?

k. At any given time, how would the yield curve facing an AAA-rated company compare with the yield curve for U.S. Treasury securities? At any given time, how would the yield curve facing a BB-rated company compare with the yield curve for U.S. Treasury securities? Draw a graph to illustrate your answer.

l. What is the pure expectations theory? What does the pure expectations theory imply about the term structure of interest rates?

m. Suppose that you observe the following term structure for Treasury securities:

MATURITY	YIELD
1 year	6.0%
2 years	6.2
3 years	6.4
4 years	6.5
5 years	6.5

Assume that the pure expectations theory of the term structure is correct. (This implies that you can use the yield curve given above to "back out" the market's expectations about future interest rates.) What does the market expect will be the interest rate on 1-year securities one year from now? What does the market expect will be the interest rate on 3-year securities two years from now?

n. Finally, Varga is also interested in investing in countries other than the United States. Describe the various types of risks that arise when investing overseas.

CHAPTER 13

INSURANCE

MANY PRECAUTIONS CAN BE TAKEN to protect against the hazards of life. For example, an individual can wear a seat belt to protect against automobile injuries or install smoke detectors to guard against the risk of injury from fire. Of course, no one can predict whether an accident or a fire will ever occur, but individuals and businesses must establish plans to protect their personal and financial interests should some event threaten to undermine their security.

Insurance is a contract by which the insurance company (the insurer) promises to pay a sum of money or give something of value to another (either the insured or the beneficiary) in the event that the insured is injured or dies, or the insured's property sustains damage as a result of particular, stated contingencies. Basically, insurance is an arrangement for *transferring and allocating risk.* In many cases, **risk** can be described as a prediction concerning potential loss based on known and unknown factors. Insurance, however, involves much more than a game of chance.

Risk management normally involves the transfer of certain risks from the individual to the insurance company by a contractual agreement. We examine the insurance contract and its provisions in this chapter. First, however, we look at some basic insurance terminology and concepts.

SECTION 1

INSURANCE TERMINOLOGY AND CONCEPTS

Like other areas of law, the area of insurance has its own special concepts and terminology, a knowledge of which is essential to an understanding of insurance law.

INSURANCE TERMINOLOGY

An insurance contract is called a **policy;** the consideration paid to the insurer is called a **premium;** and the insurance company is sometimes called an **underwriter.** The parties to an insurance policy are the *insurer* (the insurance company) and the *insured* (the person covered by its provisions).

Insurance contracts are usually obtained through an *agent,* who ordinarily works for the insurance company, or through a *broker,* who is ordinarily an independent contractor. When a broker deals with an applicant for insurance, the broker is, in effect, the applicant's agent. In contrast, an insurance agent is an agent of the insurance company, not an agent of the applicant. As a general rule, the insurance company is bound by the acts of its agents when they act within the scope of the agency relationship (see Chapters 33 and 34). In most situations, state law determines the status of all parties writing or obtaining insurance.

THE CONCEPT OF RISK POOLING

All types of insurance companies use the principle of risk pooling; that is, they spread the risk among a large number of people—the pool—to make the premiums small compared with the coverage offered. Life insurance companies, for example, know that only a small proportion of the individuals in any particular age group will die in any one year. If a large percentage of people in this age group pay premiums to the company in exchange for a benefit payment in the event of death, there will be a sufficient amount of money to pay the beneficiaries of the policyholders who die. Through the extensive correlation of data over a period of time, insurers can estimate fairly accurately the total amount they will have to pay if they insure a particular group, as well as the rates that they will have to charge each member of the group so they can make the necessary payments and still show a profit.

CLASSIFICATIONS OF INSURANCE

Insurance is classified according to the nature of the risk involved. For example, fire insurance, casualty insurance, life insurance, and title insurance apply to different types of risk. Furthermore, policies of these types differ in the persons and interests that they protect. This is reasonable because the types of losses that are expected and the types that are foreseeable or unforeseeable vary with the nature of the activity. See Exhibit 52–1 for a list of various insurance classifications.

INSURABLE INTEREST

A person can insure anything in which he or she has an **insurable interest.** Without this insurable interest, there is no enforceable contract, and a transaction to insure would have to be treated as a wager. The existence of an insurable interest is a primary concern in determining liability under an insurance policy.

LIFE INSURANCE In regard to life insurance, one must have a reasonable expectation of benefit from the continued life of another to have an insurable interest in that person's life. The insurable interest must exist *at the time the policy is obtained.* The benefit may be pecuniary (related to money), or it may be founded on the relationship between the parties (by blood or affinity). Close family relationships give a person an insurable interest in the life of another. Generally, blood or marital relationships fit this category. A husband can take out an insurance policy on his wife and vice versa; parents can take out life insurance policies on their children; brothers and sisters, on each other; and grandparents, on grandchildren—as all these are close family relationships. A policy that a person takes out on his or her spouse remains valid even if they divorce, unless a specific provision in the policy calls for its termination on divorce.

Key-person insurance is insurance obtained by an organization on the life of a person who is important to that organization. Because the organization expects to receive some pecuniary gain from the continuation of the key person's life or some financial loss from the key person's death, the organization has an insurable interest. Typically, a partnership will insure the life of

EXHIBIT 52–1 ■ INSURANCE CLASSIFICATIONS

TYPE OF INSURANCE	COVERAGE
Accident	Covers expenses, losses, and suffering incurred by the insured because of accidents causing physical injury and any consequent disability; sometimes includes a specified payment to heirs of the insured if death results from an accident.
All-risk	Covers all losses that the insured may incur except those resulting from fraud on the part of the insured.
Automobile	May cover damage to automobiles resulting from specified hazards or occurrences (such as fire, vandalism, theft, or collision); normally provides protection against liability for personal injuries and property damage resulting from the operation of the vehicle.
Casualty	Protects against losses that may be incurred by the insured as a result of being held liable for personal injuries or property damage sustained by others.
Credit	Pays to a creditor the balance of a debt on the disability, death, insolvency, or bankruptcy of the debtor; often offered by lending institutions.
Decreasing-term life	Provides life insurance; requires uniform payments over the life (term) of the policy, but with a decreasing face value (amount of coverage).
Employer's liability	Insures employers against liability for injuries or losses sustained by employees during the course of their employment; covers claims not covered under workers' compensation insurance.
Fidelity or guaranty	Provides indemnity against losses in trade or losses caused by the dishonesty of employees, the insolvency of debtors, or breaches of contract.
Fire	Covers losses to the insured caused by fire.
Floater	Covers movable property, as long as the property is within the territorial boundaries specified in the contract.
Group	Provides individual life, medical, or disability insurance coverage but is obtainable through a group of persons, usually employees; the policy premium is paid either entirely by the employer or partially by the employer and partially by the employee.

each partner, because the death of any one partner will cause some degree of loss to the partnership. Similarly, a corporation has an insurable interest in the life expectancy of a key executive whose death would result in financial loss to the company. If a firm insures a key person's life and then that person leaves the firm and dies, the firm can collect on the insurance policy, provided it continued to pay premiums.

PROPERTY INSURANCE In regard to real and personal property, an insurable interest exists when the insured derives a pecuniary benefit from the preservation and continued existence of the property. That is, one has an insurable interest in property when one would sustain a pecuniary loss from its destruction. Both a mortgagor and a mortgagee, for example, have an insurable interest in the mortgaged property. So do a landlord and a tenant in leased property, a secured party in the property in which he or she has a security interest, a partner in partnership property, and a stockholder in corporate property. John or Jane Doe, however, cannot obtain fire insurance on the White House or auto insurance on the Andrettis' racing cars.

The insurable interest in property must exist *when the loss occurs*. In the following case, the insurance company claimed that the insured possessed no insurable interest in her former husband's house because she had deeded her interest to him one year before his death.

EXHIBIT 52–1 ■ INSURANCE CLASSIFICATIONS (CONTINUED)

TYPE OF INSURANCE	COVERAGE
Health	Covers expenses incurred by the insured resulting from physical injury or illness and other expenses relating to health and life maintenance.
Homeowners'	Protects homeowners against some or all risks of loss to their residences and the residences' contents or liability arising from the use of the property.
Key-person	Protects a business in the event of the death or disability of a key employee.
Liability	Protects against liability imposed on the insured resulting from injuries to the person or property of another.
Life	Covers the death of the policyholder. On the death of the insured, an amount specified in the policy is paid by the insurer to the insured's beneficiary.
Major medical	Protects the insured against major hospital, medical, or surgical expenses.
Malpractice	Protects professionals (doctors, lawyers, and others) against malpractice claims brought against them by their patients or clients; a form of liability insurance.
Marine	Covers movable property (including ships, freight, and cargo) against certain perils or navigation risks during a specific voyage or time period.
Mortgage	Covers a mortgage loan; the insurer pays the balance of the mortgage to the creditor on the death or disability of the debtor.
No-fault auto	Covers personal injury and (sometimes) property damage resulting from automobile accidents. The insured submits his or her claims to his or her own insurance company, regardless of who was at fault. A person may sue the party at fault or that party's insurer only in cases involving serious medical injury and consequent high medical costs. Governed by state "no-fault" statutes.
Term life	Provides life insurance for a specified period of time (term) with no cash surrender value; usually renewable.
Title	Protects against any defects in title to real property and any losses incurred as a result of existing claims against or liens on the property at the time of purchase.

CASE 52.1 Motorists Mutual Insurance Co. v. Richmond

Court of Appeals of Kentucky, 1984.
676 S.W.2d 478.

BACKGROUND AND FACTS *Linda Richmond and Eddie Durham were married, the parents of two children, and homeowners in Kentucky. When Richmond and Durham divorced, Richmond, the plaintiff, deeded her legal interest in the title to their home to Durham and moved out with their children. Shortly thereafter, Durham died, leaving the two children as his only legal heirs. Richmond returned to the home with the children. She had been living there and making the mortgage payments for more than one year when the home was totally destroyed by fire. Ten months prior to the fire, Richmond had secured fire insurance with the defendant, Motorists Mutual Insurance Company. She sought payment from Motorists for the destruction of the house, but Motorists refused to pay, claiming that she had no insurable interest in the house. The trial court awarded Richmond, her children, and the mortgage company $29,000. Motorists appealed.*

IN THE LANGUAGE OF THE COURT

CLAYTON, Judge.

* * * *

Linda Richmond, both before and after the death of her late former husband, made substantial monetary contribution to the maintenance and improvement of the destroyed residence. As natural guardian for her minor children, * * * she was obligated to provide for the care and custody of their offspring, including the duty to protect their home, of which the children became sole owners * * * upon the death of their father. Thus, when Richmond returned to the property following Durham's death she was not a surreptitious trespasser. Her offspring and she as their guardian were fully entitled to use and dominion over the premises. While not possessed of title, Richmond certainly possessed an insurable interest in the residence; first, by her status as natural guardian for the protection of her minor children's interest; and second, by her extensive pecuniary investment in the residence.

DECISION AND REMEDY

The state intermediate appellate court held that Linda Richmond had an insurable interest in the home, for which Motorists was required to pay.

SECTION 2 THE INSURANCE CONTRACT

An insurance contract is governed by the general principles of contract law, although the insurance industry is heavily regulated by the states. Customarily, a party offers to purchase insurance by submitting an insurance application to the insurance company. The company can either accept or reject the offer. Sometimes, the insurance company's acceptance is conditional—on the results of a life insurance applicant's medical examination, for example. For the insurance contract to be binding, consideration (in the form of a premium) must exist, and the parties forming the contract must have the required contractual capacity to do so.

APPLICATION FOR INSURANCE

The filled-in application form for insurance is usually attached to the policy and made a part of the insurance contract. Thus, an insurance applicant is bound by any false statements that appear in the application (subject to certain exceptions). Because the insurance company evaluates the risk factors based on the information included in the insurance application, misstatements or misrepresentations can void a policy, especially if the insurance company can show that it would not have extended insurance if it had known the facts.

EFFECTIVE DATE

The effective date of an insurance contract—that is, the date on which the insurance coverage begins—is important. In some instances, the insurance applicant is not protected until a formal written policy is issued. In other situations, the applicant is protected between the time the application is received and the time the insurance company either accepts or rejects it. Four facts should be kept in mind:

1. A broker is merely the agent of an applicant. Therefore, if the broker fails to procure a policy, the applicant is normally not insured. According to general principles of agency law, if the broker fails to obtain policy coverage and the applicant is damaged as a result, then the broker is liable to the damaged applicant-principal for the loss.
2. A person who seeks insurance from an insurance company's agent is usually protected from the moment the application is made, provided—in the case of life insurance—that some form of premium has been paid. Between the time the application is received and the time it is either rejected or accepted, the applicant is covered (possibly subject to certain conditions, such as passing a physical examination). Usually, the agent will write a memorandum, or **binder,** indicating that a policy is pending and stating its essential terms.
3. If the parties agree that the policy will be issued and delivered at a later time, the contract is not effective until the policy is issued and delivered or sent to the applicant, depending on the agreement. Thus,

any loss sustained between the time of application and the delivery of the policy is not covered.

4. Parties may agree that a life insurance policy will be binding at the time the insured pays the first premium, or the policy may be expressly contingent on the applicant's passing a physical examination. If the applicant pays the premium and passes the examination, then the policy coverage is continuously in effect. If the applicant pays the premium but dies before having the physical examination, then in order to collect, the applicant's estate normally must show that the applicant would have passed the examination had he or she not died.

Coverage on an insurance policy can begin when a binder is written; when the policy is issued; or, depending on the terms of the contract, after a certain period of time has elapsed.

In the following case, the court had to decide whether a requirement that an applicant be "still insurable" on the effective date of the policy should prevent the beneficiary from recovering.

CASE 52.2 Life Insurance Co. of North America v. Cichowlas

District Court of Appeal of Florida, Fourth District, 1995. 659 So.2d 1333.

HISTORICAL AND INTERNATIONAL SETTING *The United States leads the world in insurance coverage. Over 3,500 U.S. companies sell property insurance, and more than 2,200 offer life insurance. Thirty-three of these companies have been selling insurance for more than one hundred years and control more than half of the insurance market. In the 1980s, some of these companies tripled the amount that they took in annually in premiums. Despite these glowing figures, some insurers claim that they are losing money writing insurance in certain markets.*

BACKGROUND AND FACTS *Waldemar Cichowlas applied to Life Insurance Company of North America (LINA) for insurance, naming his wife, Ewa, as beneficiary. The application asked if he had been hospitalized during the past five years and if he had ever been treated for lung disease. An answer of yes would have affected his insurability. Waldemar truthfully answered no. The policy required that an applicant be "still insurable" on the effective date of the policy. Three weeks before the policy took effect, Waldemar was hospitalized with a lung disease. He did not tell LINA. When he died of other causes, LINA refused to pay Ewa. She filed a suit in a Florida state court against the insurer. The court ordered LINA to pay. The insurer appealed.*

IN THE LANGUAGE OF THE COURT

PER CURIAM [by the entire court].

* * * *

* * * Clauses requiring that an applicant remain insurable between the filing of the application and the delivery of the policy have traditionally been approved by Florida courts. They are generally in the form of statements that the policy shall not take effect unless it is delivered during the continued insurability or sound health of the applicant. Thus, as the evidence was uncontradicted that Mr. Cichowlas was not insurable on the effective date of the policy, the "still insurable" clause precluded recovery for [Ewa] pursuant to its terms.

DECISION AND REMEDY *The District Court of Appeal of Florida reversed the judgment of the lower court and remanded the case. The beneficiary could not recover because the applicant was not insurable on the effective date of the policy.*

PROVISIONS AND CLAUSES

Some of the important provisions and clauses contained in insurance contracts are defined and discussed in the following subsections.

PROVISIONS MANDATED BY STATUTE If a statute mandates that a certain provision be included in insurance contracts, a court will deem that an insurance policy contains the provision regardless of whether the parties actually included it in the language of their contract. If a statute requires that any limitations regarding coverage be stated in the contract, a court will not allow an insurer to avoid liability for a claim through reliance on an unexpressed restriction.

INCONTESTABILITY CLAUSES Statutes commonly require that a life or health insurance policy provide that after the policy has been in force for a specified length of time—often two or three years—the insurer cannot contest statements made in the application. This is known as an *incontestability clause.* Once a policy becomes incontestable, the insurer cannot later avoid a claim on the basis of, for example, fraud on the part of the insured, unless the clause provides an exception for that circumstance. The clause does not prohibit an insurer's refusal or reduction of payment for a claim due to nonpayment of premiums, failure to file proof of death within a certain period, or lack of an insurable interest.

COINSURANCE CLAUSES Often, when taking out fire insurance policies, property owners insure their property for less than full value. Part of the reason for this is that most fires do not result in a total loss. To encourage owners to insure their property for an amount as close to full value as possible, a standard provision of fire insurance policies is a coinsurance clause. Typically, a *coinsurance clause* provides that if the owner insures the property up to a specified percentage—usually 80 percent—of its value, he or she will recover any loss up to the face amount of the policy. If the insurance is for less than the fixed percentage, the owner is responsible for a proportionate share of the loss.

Coinsurance applies only in instances of partial loss. For example, if the owner of property valued at \$100,000 took out a policy in the amount of \$40,000 and suffered a loss of \$30,000, the recovery would be \$15,000. The formula for calculating the recovery amount is as follows:

$$\frac{\text{amount of insurance } (\$40{,}000)}{\text{coinsurance percentage } (80\%) \times \text{property value } (\$100{,}000)} = \text{recovery percentage } (50\%)$$

$$\text{recovery percentage } (50\%) \times \text{amount of loss } (\$30{,}000) = \text{recovery amount } (\$15{,}000)$$

If the owner had taken out a policy in the amount of \$80,000, then according to the same formula, the full loss would have been recovered.

APPRAISAL AND ARBITRATION CLAUSES Most fire insurance policies provide that if the parties cannot agree on the amount of a loss covered under the policy or on the value of the property lost, an *appraisal* can be demanded. An appraisal is an estimate of the property's value determined by suitably qualified individuals who have no interest in the property. Typically, two appraisers are used, one being appointed by each party. A third party, or *umpire,* may be called on to resolve differences. Other types of insurance policies also contain provisions for appraisal and arbitration when the insured and insurer disagree as to the value of a loss.

MULTIPLE INSURANCE COVERAGE If an insured has *multiple insurance coverage*—that is, policies with several companies covering the same insurance interest—and the amount of coverage exceeds the loss, the insured can collect from each insurer only the company's proportionate share of the liability, relative to the total amount of insurance. Many fire insurance policies include a pro rata clause, which requires that any loss be shared proportionately by all carriers. For example, if Grumbling insured \$50,000 worth of property with two companies, each of whose policies had a liability limit of \$40,000, then on the property's total destruction Grumbling could collect only \$25,000 from each insurer.

ANTILAPSE CLAUSES A life insurance policy may provide, or a statute may require a policy to provide, that it will not automatically lapse if no payment is made on the date due. Ordinarily, under an *antilapse provision,* the insured has a *grace period* of thirty or thirty-one days within which to pay an overdue premium. If the insured fails to pay a premium altogether, there are alternatives to cancellation:

1. The insurer may be required to extend the insurance for a period of time.
2. The insurer may issue a policy with less coverage to reflect the amount of the payments made.
3. The insurer may pay to the insured the policy's **cash surrender value**—the amount the insurer has agreed to pay on the policy's cancellation before the insured's death. (In determining this value, the following factors are considered: the period that the policy has already run, the amount of the premium, the insured's age and life expectancy, and amounts to be repaid on any outstanding loans taken out against the policy.)

When the insurance contract states that the insurer cannot cancel the policy, these alternatives are important.

INTERPRETING PROVISIONS OF AN INSURANCE CONTRACT

The courts are increasingly cognizant of the fact that most people do not have the special training necessary to understand the intricate terminology used in insurance policies. The words used in an insurance contract have their ordinary meanings and are interpreted by courts in light of the nature of the coverage involved. When there is an ambiguity in the policy, the provision is interpreted against the insurance company. When it is unclear whether an insurance contract actually exists because the written policy has not been delivered, the uncertainty is resolved against the insurance company. The court presumes that the policy is in effect unless the company can show otherwise. Similarly, an insurer must take care to make sure that the insured is adequately notified of any change in coverage under an existing policy.

CANCELLATION

The insured can cancel a policy at any time, and the insurer can cancel under certain circumstances. When an insurance company can cancel its insurance contract, the policy or a state statute usually requires that the insurer give advance written notice of the cancellation. Any premium paid in advance and not yet earned may be refundable. The insured may also be entitled to a life insurance policy's cash surrender value.

The insurer may cancel an insurance policy for various reasons, depending on the type of insurance. For example, automobile insurance can be canceled for nonpayment of premiums or suspension of the insured's driver's license. Property insurance can be canceled for nonpayment of premiums or for other reasons, including the insured's fraud or misrepresentation, gross negligence, or conviction for a crime that increases the hazard insured against. Life and health policies can be canceled because of false statements made by the insured in the application, but cancellation can only take place before the effective date of an incontestability clause. An insurer cannot cancel—or refuse to renew—a policy because of the national origin or race of an applicant or because the insured has appeared as a witness in a case brought against the company.

State laws normally impose specific requirements relating to insurance policy cancellations. In the following case, the plaintiff claimed that the insurer had not complied with the state's statutory requirements governing policy cancellation.

CASE 52.3 Clyburn v. Allstate Insurance Co.

United States District Court, District of South Carolina, 1993. 826 F.Supp. 955.

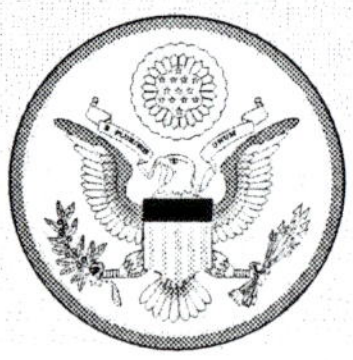

COMPANY PROFILE *Allstate Corporation sells life and property insurance in the United States, Puerto Rico, Canada, Japan, and South Korea. Allstate sells reinsurance (insurance for insurers) worldwide through Allstate Reinsurance Company in London. In the United States, Allstate also offers annuities, as well as other business and retirement benefits insurance. Allstate was started by Sears, Roebuck and Company in the 1930s to sell auto insurance through the mail and is today the second largest auto—and home—insurer in the United States.*

BACKGROUND AND FACTS *When William Clyburn's house burned to the ground, two years had passed since he had paid a premium on his policy with*

Allstate Insurance Company. Allstate refused to cover the loss of the house, and Clyburn brought suit against the insurer, claiming that the policy had not been legally canceled and that the insurer had therefore improperly denied coverage. Specifically, Clyburn argued that Allstate had not followed the state's statutory requirements governing policy cancellation. The relevant state statute required an insurer to send written notice to both the insured and the insurer's "agent of record"—the insurance agent who had issued the policy to the insured. Allstate argued that it had properly notified Clyburn in writing of the cancellation and that it had also sent its agent of record, Thomas Young, a computer diskette containing the cancellation notice. The jury found in Clyburn's favor, concluding that Allstate had sent written notice to Clyburn but not to Allstate's agent of record. Allstate made a motion for either a new trial or a judgment notwithstanding the verdict. The key issue before the court was whether notice sent via a computer diskette constituted "written" notice.

IN THE LANGUAGE OF THE COURT

BLATT, Senior District Judge.

* * * *

* * * As noted by the parties in the briefs submitted to the court, there is no case that could be located on this exact issue * * * . There have been some cases dealing with videotapes as a "writing" with regard to some states' rules of procedure. In addition, in other contexts, tape recordings have been deemed to be "writings."

Although * * * these cases arise in entirely different contexts and stem from different statutes or rules, the cases do suggest that other media forms are recognized as "writings." The storage of information on tape recordings and videotapes is not that much different from that on floppy diskettes for computers, but rather is more a difference in the devices used to read the information. The information can be retrieved and printed as "hardcopy" on paper. In today's "paperless" society of computer generated information, the court is not prepared, in the absence of some legislative provision or otherwise, to find that a computer floppy diskette would not constitute a "writing" * * * .

DECISION AND REMEDY

The court held that a notice on diskette could constitute written notice. The court granted Allstate's motion.

BASIC DUTIES AND RIGHTS

Essentially, the parties to an insurance contract are responsible for the obligations the contract imposes. These include the basic contractual duties discussed in Chapters 12 through 20 of this text, which cover contract law.

In applying for insurance, for example, the obligation to act in good faith means that a party must reveal everything necessary for the insurer to evaluate the risk. In other words, the applicant must disclose all material facts. These include all facts that would influence an insurer in determining whether to charge a higher premium or to refuse to issue a policy altogether.

Once the insurer has accepted the risk, and on the occurrence of an event giving rise to a claim, the insurer has a duty to investigate to determine the facts. When a policy provides insurance against third party claims, the insurer is obligated to make reasonable efforts to settle such a claim. If a settlement cannot be reached, then regardless of the claim's merit, the insurer must defend any suit against the insured. Usually, a policy provides that in this situation the insured must cooperate. A policy provision may expressly require the insured to attend hearings and trials, to assist in obtaining evidence and witnesses, and to assist in reaching a settlement.

DEFENSES AGAINST PAYMENT

An insurance company can raise any of the defenses that would be valid in any ordinary action on a contract, as well as some defenses that do not apply in ordinary contract actions. If the insurance company can show that the policy was procured through fraud or misrepresentation, for example, it may have a valid defense for not paying on a claim. (The insurance company may also have the right to disaffirm or rescind an insurance contract.) An absolute defense exists if the insurer can show that the insured lacked an insurable interest—thus rendering the policy void from the beginning. Improper actions, such as those that are against public policy or that are otherwise illegal, can also give the insurance company a defense against the payment of a claim or allow it to rescind the contract.

The insurance company can be prevented, or estopped, from asserting some defenses that are normally available. For example, if a company tells an insured that information requested on a form is optional and the insured provides it anyway, the company cannot use the information to avoid its contractual obligation under the insurance contract. Similarly, incorrect statements as to the age of the insured normally do not provide the insurance company with a way to escape payment on the death of the insured. Also, incontestability clauses prevent the insurer from asserting certain defenses. Some states follow the *concurrent causation doctrine,* which requires that the insurer pay on a claim when the accident was due to more than one cause, at least one of which was covered under the policy.[1]

In the following case, an insurance company attempted to avoid payment under a policy for life and disability insurance by claiming that the policy owner did not have an insurable interest, thus rendering the policy void from the outset.

1. This doctrine was enunciated by the California Supreme Court in *State Farm Mutual Automobile Insurance Co. v. Partridge,* 10 Cal.3d 94, 514 P.2d 123, 109 Cal.Rptr. 811 (1973). Subsequently, a number of other states, particularly in the Midwest, adopted the doctrine. But see *Vanguard Insurance Co. v. Clarke,* 438 Mich. 463, 475 N.W.2d 48 (1991), in which the Michigan Supreme Court rejected the doctrine.

CASE 52.4 Paul Revere Life Insurance Co. v. Fima

United States Court of Appeals, Ninth Circuit, 1997. 105 F.3d 490.

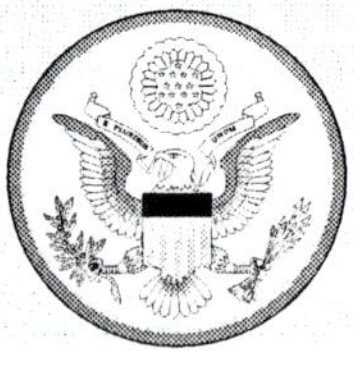

BACKGROUND AND FACTS *Raoul Fima applied to Paul Revere Life Insurance Company for a disability policy. On the application, Fima stated his income as $105,000 for the previous year and $85,000 for the current year. Fima's actual income for those years was $21,603 and $6,320, respectively. The policy included the following incontestability clause: "After your policy has been in force for two years, . . . we cannot contest the statements in the application." Three years later, when Fima filed a claim under the policy, Revere discovered the truth regarding Fima's income. Revere filed a suit in a federal district court against Fima, seeking to have the policy declared void* ab initio *(from the beginning) on the ground that he lacked an insurable interest. The court denied the request. Revere appealed.*

IN THE LANGUAGE OF THE COURT

BRUNETTI, Circuit Judge:

* * * *

Fima had an insurable interest under California Insurance Code [S]ection 10110 as a matter of law. Section 10110 states that "[e]very person has an insurable interest in the life and health of * * * [h]imself." Because Fima had an insurable interest under [S]ection 10110, his disability insurance policy was not void *ab initio.*

* * * *

* * * Because that policy is not void *ab initio* and because the period for contesting the policy has passed under the incontestability clause, Revere may not now challenge the terms of the policy or the extent of Fima's insurable interest.

DECISION AND REMEDY *The U.S. Court of Appeals for the Ninth Circuit affirmed the judgment of the lower court. Every person has an insurable interest in his or her own life and health.*

INTERNATIONAL CONSIDERATIONS **False Statements on Insurance Applications in the United Kingdom** *The United Kingdom has stricter rules than most states in the United States in regard to false statements made on insurance applications. In the United Kingdom, insurance applicants are held to a standard of* uberrima fides *(Latin for "the most abundant good faith"). Even an innocent (unintentional) misrepresentation on an insurance application makes the contract voidable at the option of the insurer.*

SECTION 3

TYPES OF INSURANCE

There are five general types of insurance coverage: life insurance, fire and homeowners' insurance, automobile insurance, marine insurance, and business liability insurance. We now examine briefly the coverage available under each of these types of insurance. In the course of our discussion, we point out certain features and provisions as they relate to the law, with special emphasis on life and fire insurance policies.

LIFE INSURANCE

There are five basic types of life insurance:

1. **Whole life** is sometimes referred to as straight life, ordinary life, or cash-value insurance. This type of insurance provides protection with a cumulated cash surrender value that can be used as collateral for a loan. Premiums are paid by the insured during the insured's entire lifetime, with a fixed payment to the beneficiary on death.
2. **Limited-payment life** might be a twenty-payment life policy. Premiums are paid for a stated number of years, after which the policy is paid up and fully effective during the insured's life. Naturally, premiums are higher than for whole life. This insurance has a cash surrender value.
3. **Term insurance** is a type of policy for which premiums are paid for a specified term. Payment on the policy is due only if death occurs within the term period. Premiums are less expensive than for whole life or limited-payment life, and there is usually no cash surrender value. Frequently, this type of insurance can be converted to another type of life insurance.
4. **Endowment insurance** involves fixed premium payments that are made for a definite term. At the end of the term, a fixed amount is to be paid to the insured or, on the death of the insured during the specified period, to a beneficiary. Thus, this type of insurance represents both term insurance and a form of **annuity** (the right to receive fixed, periodic payments for life or—as in this case—for a term of years). Endowment insurance has a rapidly increasing cash surrender value, but premiums are high, as payment is required at the end of the term even if the insured is still living.
5. **Universal life** is a type of insurance that combines some aspects of term insurance and some aspects of whole life insurance. Every payment, usually called a "contribution," involves two deductions made by the issuing life insurance company. The first one is a charge for term insurance protection; the second is for company expenses and profit. The money that remains after these deductions earns interest for the policyholder at a rate determined by the company. The interest-earning money in the policy is called the policy's cash value, but that term does not mean the same thing as it does for a traditional whole life insurance policy. With a universal life policy, the cash value grows at a variable interest rate rather than at a predetermined rate.

The rights and liabilities of the parties in life insurance are basically dependent on the insurance contract. A few features deserve special attention.

LIABILITY The life insurance contract determines not only the extent of the insurer's liability but, generally, whether the insurer is liable on the death of the insured. Most life insurance contracts exclude liability for death caused by suicide, military action during war, execution by a state or federal government, and even something that occurs while the insured is a passenger in a commercial vehicle. In the absence of exclusion, most courts today construe any cause of death to be one of the insurer's risks.

ADJUSTMENT DUE TO MISSTATEMENT OF AGE The insurance policy constitutes the agreement between the parties. The application for insurance is part of the policy and is usually attached to the policy. When the insured misstates his or her age in the application, an error is introduced, particularly as to the amount of premiums paid. Misstatement of age is not a material error sufficient to allow the insurer to void the policy. Instead, on discovery of the error, the insurer will adjust the premium payments and/or benefits accordingly.

ASSIGNMENT Most life insurance policies permit the insured to change beneficiaries. When this is the case, in the absence of any prohibition or notice requirement, the insured can assign the rights to the policy (for example, as security for a loan) without the consent of the insurer or the beneficiary. If the beneficiary's right is *vested*—that is, has become absolute, entitling the beneficiary to payment of the proceeds—the policy cannot be assigned without the consent of the beneficiary. The vast majority of life insurance contracts permit assignment and require notice only to the insurer to be effective.

CREDITORS' RIGHTS Unless insurance proceeds are exempt under state law, the insured's interest in life insurance is an asset that is subject to the rights of judgment creditors. These creditors generally can reach insurance proceeds payable to the insured's estate, proceeds payable to anyone if the payment of premiums constituted a fraud on creditors, and proceeds payable to a named beneficiary unless the beneficiary's rights have vested. Creditors, however, cannot compel the insured to make available the cash surrender value of the policy or to change the named beneficiary to that of the creditor. Almost all states exempt at least a part of the proceeds of life insurance from creditors' claims.

TERMINATION Although the insured can cancel and terminate the policy, the insurer generally cannot do so. Therefore, termination usually takes place only on the occurrence of the following:

1. Default in premium payments that causes the policy to lapse.
2. Death and payment of benefits.
3. Expiration of the term of the policy.
4. Cancellation by the insured.

FIRE AND HOMEOWNERS' INSURANCE

There are basically two types of insurance policies for a home—standard fire insurance policies and homeowners' policies.

STANDARD FIRE INSURANCE POLICIES The standard fire insurance policy protects the homeowner against fire and lightning, as well as damage from smoke and water caused by the fire or the fire department. Most fire insurance policies are classified according to the type of property covered and the extent (amount) of the issuer's liability. Exhibit 52–2 lists typical fire insurance policies.

EXHIBIT 52–2 ■ TYPICAL FIRE INSURANCE POLICIES

TYPE OF POLICY	COVERAGE
Blanket	Covers a class of property rather than specific property, because the property is expected to shift or vary in nature. A policy covering the inventory of a business is an example.
Floater	Usually supplements a specific policy. It is intended to cover property that may change in either location or quantity. To illustrate, if the painting mentioned below under "specific policy" were to be exhibited during the year at numerous locations throughout the state, a floater policy would be desirable.
Open	A policy in which the value of the property insured is not agreed on. The policy usually provides for a maximum liability of the insurer, but payment for loss is restricted to the fair market value of the property at the time of loss or to the insurer's limit, whichever is less.
Specific	Covers a specific item of property at a specific location. An example is a particular painting located in a residence or a piece of machinery located in a factory or business.
Valued	A policy in which, by agreement, a specific value is placed on the subject to be insured to cover the eventuality of its total loss.

As with life insurance, certain features and provisions of fire insurance deserve special mention. In reading the following, it is important to note some basic differences in the treatment of life and fire policies.

Liability. The insurer's liability is determined from the terms of the policy. Most policies, however, limit recovery to losses resulting from *hostile* fires—basically, those that break out or begin in places where no fire was intended to burn. A *friendly* fire—one burning in a place where it was intended to burn—is not covered. Therefore, smoke from a fireplace is not covered, but smoke from a fire caused by a defective electrical outlet is covered. Sometimes, owners add "extended coverage" to the fire policy to cover losses from "friendly" fires.

If the policy is a *valued* policy (see Exhibit 52–2) and the subject matter is completely destroyed, the insurer is liable for the amount specified in the policy. If it is an *open* policy, then the extent of actual loss must be determined, and the insurer is liable only for the amount of the loss or for the maximum amount specified in the policy, whichever is less. For partial losses, actual loss must always be determined, and the insurer's liability is limited to that amount. Most insurance policies permit the insurer either to restore or replace the property destroyed or to pay for the loss.

Proof of Loss. Fire insurance policies require the insured to file with the insurer, within a specified period or immediately (within a reasonable time), a proof of loss as a condition for recovery. Failure to comply *could* allow the insurance carrier to avoid liability. Courts vary somewhat on the enforcement of such clauses.

Occupancy Clause. Most standard policies require that the premises be occupied at the time of loss. The relevant clause states that if the premises become vacant or unoccupied for a given period, unless consent by the insurer is given, the coverage is suspended until the premises are reoccupied. Persons going on extended vacations should check their policies on this matter.

Assignment. Before a loss has occurred, a fire insurance policy is not assignable without the consent of the insurer. The theory is that the fire insurance policy is a personal contract between the insured and the insurer. The nonassignability of the policy is extremely important in the purchase of a house. The purchaser must procure his or her own insurance. If the purchaser wishes to assume the remaining insurance coverage period of the seller, consent of the insurer is essential.

To illustrate: Ann is selling her home and lot to Jeff. Ann has a one-year fire policy with Ajax Insurance Company, with six months of coverage remaining at the date on which the sale is to close. Ann agrees to assign the balance of her policy, but Ajax has not given its consent. One day after passage of the deed, a fire totally destroys the house. Can Jeff recover from Ajax?

The answer is no, as the policy is actually voided on the closing of the transaction and the deeding of the property. The reason the policy is voided is that Ann no longer has an insurable interest at the time of loss, and Jeff has no rights in a nonassignable policy.

HOMEOWNERS' POLICIES A homeowners' policy provides protection against a number of risks under a single policy, allowing the policyholder to avoid the cost of buying each protection separately. There are two basic types of homeowners' coverage:

1. *Property coverage* includes the garage, house, and other private buildings on the policyholder's lot. It also includes the personal possessions and property of the policyholder at home, in travel, or at work. It pays additional living expenses for living away from home because of a fire or some other covered peril.
2. *Liability coverage* is for personal liability in case someone is injured on the insured's property, the insured damages someone else's property, or the insured injures someone else who is not in an automobile.

Perils insured under property coverage often include fire, lightning, wind, hail, vandalism, and theft (of personal property). Personal property that is typically not included under property coverage, in the absence of a specific provision, includes such items as motor vehicles, farm equipment, airplanes, and boats. Coverage for other property, such as jewelry and securities, is usually limited to a specified dollar amount.

Liability coverage under a homeowners' policy applies when others are injured or property is damaged because of the unsafe condition of the policyholder's premises. It also applies when the policyholder is negligent. It does not normally apply, however, if the liability arises from business or professional activities or from the operation of a motor vehicle. These are subjects for separate policies. Also excluded is liability arising from intentional misconduct. Similar to liability coverage is coverage for the medical payments of others who are injured on the policyholder's property and coverage for property of others that is damaged by a member of the policyholder's family.

Renters, too, take out insurance policies to cover losses to personal property. Renters' insurance covers personal possessions against various perils and includes additional living expenses and liability coverage.

AUTOMOBILE INSURANCE

There are two basic kinds of automobile insurance: liability insurance and collision and comprehensive insurance.

LIABILITY INSURANCE Automobile liability insurance covers bodily injury and property damage liability. Liability limits are usually described by a series of three numbers, such as 100/300/50. This means that the policy, for one accident, will pay a maximum of \$100,000 for bodily injury to one person, a maximum of \$300,000 for bodily injury to more than one person, and a maximum of \$50,000 for property damage. Many insurance companies offer liability up to \$500,000 and sometimes higher.

Individuals who are dissatisfied with the maximum liability limits offered by regular automobile insurance coverage can purchase separate coverage under an *umbrella* policy. Umbrella limits sometimes go as high as \$5 million. Umbrella policies also cover personal liability in excess of the liability limits of a homeowners' policy.

COLLISION AND COMPREHENSIVE INSURANCE Collision insurance covers damage to the insured's car in any type of collision. Usually, it is not advisable to purchase full collision coverage (otherwise known as zero deductible). The price per year is relatively high, because it is likely that some small repair jobs will be required each year. Most people prefer to take out coverage with a deductible of \$100, \$250, or \$500, which costs substantially less than zero-deductible coverage.

Comprehensive insurance covers loss, damage, and destruction by fire, hurricane, hail, vandalism, and theft. It can be obtained separately from collision insurance.

OTHER AUTOMOBILE INSURANCE Other types of automobile insurance coverage include the following:

1. *Uninsured motorist coverage.* Uninsured motorist coverage insures the driver and passengers against injury caused by any driver without insurance or by a hit-and-run driver. Certain states require that it be included in all insurance policies sold to drivers.
2. *Accidental death benefits.* Sometimes referred to as *double indemnity*, accidental death benefits provide a lump sum to named beneficiaries if the policyholder dies in an automobile accident. This coverage generally costs very little, but it may not be necessary if the insured has a sufficient amount of life insurance.
3. *Medical payment coverage.* Medical payment coverage provided by an auto insurance policy pays hospital and other medical bills and sometimes funeral expenses. This type of insurance protects all the passengers in the insured's car when the insured is driving.
4. *Other-driver coverage.* An **omnibus clause,** or an *other-driver clause,* protects the vehicle owner who has taken out the insurance and anyone who drives the vehicle with the owner's permission. This coverage may be held to extend to a third party who drives the vehicle with the permission of the person to whom the owner gave permission.
5. *No-fault insurance.* Under no-fault statutes, claims arising from an accident are made against the claimant's own insurer, regardless of whose fault the accident was. In some cases—for example, when injuries involve expensive medical treatment—an injured party may seek recovery from another party or insurer. In those instances, the injured party may collect the maximum amount of no-fault insurance and still sue for total damages from the party at fault, although usually, on winning an award, the injured party must reimburse the insurer for its no-fault payments.

MARINE INSURANCE

Marine insurance developed as a means of protecting shippers and vessel owners from the inherent risks involved in transporting goods by water. The insured is protected from damage to or loss of a vessel or its cargo due to perils at sea (such perils include shipwrecks, as well as pirates). Marine insurance is of particular importance in the shipment of oil.

Marine insurance policies are often *valued*—that is, they are entered into for coverage up to a set amount (the established value of the freight or vessel insured). They may be voyage policies or time policies. A *voyage policy* covers the insured for the duration of the trip, regardless of how long it takes. The *time policy* lapses, or expires, at a specified time, regardless of whether the voyage has been completed. Policies may cover inland marine travel or ocean marine travel. *Inland marine* policies insure vessels navigating the inland waterways, such as the Great Lakes. *Ocean marine* policies, of course, insure vessels traveling on the oceans.

To acquire marine insurance for a ship or cargo, a vessel owner or a shipper warrants that the vessel is seaworthy. A seaworthy vessel can withstand ordinary weather conditions and has a competent captain of good moral character, a satisfactory crew, and suitable equipment on board. A breach of the warranty of seaworthiness would normally void the marine insurance policy.

BUSINESS LIABILITY INSURANCE

A business may be vulnerable to all sorts of risks. A key employee may die or become disabled; a customer may be injured when using a manufacturer's product; the patron of an establishment selling liquor may leave the premises and injure a third party in an automobile accident; or a professional may overlook some important detail, causing liability for malpractice. Should the first situation arise (for instance, if the company president dies), the firm may have some protection under a key-person insurance policy, discussed previously. In the other circumstances, other types of insurance may apply.

GENERAL LIABILITY Comprehensive general liability insurance can cover virtually as many risks as the insurer agrees to cover. For example, among the types of coverage that a business might wish to acquire is protection from liability for injuries arising from on-premises events not otherwise covered, such as company social functions. Some specialized establishments, such as taverns, may be subject to liability in individualized circumstances, and policies can be drafted to meet their needs. In many jurisdictions, for example, statutes impose liability on a seller of intoxicating liquor when a buyer of the liquor, intoxicated as a result of the sale, injures a third party. Legal protection may extend not only to immediately consequent injuries, such as quadriplegia resulting from an automobile accident, but also to the loss of financial support suffered by a family because of the injuries. Insurance can provide coverage for these injuries and financial losses.

PRODUCT LIABILITY Manufacturers may be subject to liability for injuries that their products cause, and product liability insurance can be written to match specific products' risks. Coverage can be procured under a comprehensive general liability policy or under a separate policy. The coverage may include expenses involved in recalling and replacing a product that has proved to be defective. (For a comprehensive discussion of product liability, see Chapter 8.)

PROFESSIONAL MALPRACTICE In recent years, professionals—attorneys, physicians, architects, and engineers, for example—have increasingly become the targets of negligence suits. Professionals may purchase malpractice insurance to protect themselves against such claims. The large judgments in some malpractice suits have received considerable publicity and are sometimes cited in what has been termed "the insurance crisis," because they have contributed to a significant increase in malpractice insurance premiums.

WORKERS' COMPENSATION Workers' compensation insurance covers payments to employees who are injured in accidents arising out of and in the course of employment (that is, on the job). Workers' compensation, which was discussed in detail in Chapter 35, is governed by state statutes.

TERMS AND CONCEPTS TO REVIEW

Questions and Case Problems

52–1. Insurable Interest. Adia owns a house and has an elderly third cousin living with her. Adia decides she needs fire insurance on the house and a life insurance policy on her third cousin to cover funeral and other expenses that will result from her cousin's death. Adia takes out a fire insurance policy from Ajax Insurance Co. and a $10,000 life insurance policy from Beta Insurance Co. on her third cousin. Six months later, Adia sells the house to John and transfers title to him. Adia and her cousin move into an apartment. With two months remaining on the Ajax policy, a fire totally destroys the house; at the same time, Adia's third cousin dies. Both insurance companies tender back premiums but claim they have no liability under the insurance contracts, as Adia did not have an insurable interest. Discuss their claims.

52–2. Insurer's Defenses. Patrick contracts with an Ajax Insurance Co. agent for a $50,000 ordinary life insurance policy. The application form is filled in to show Patrick's age as thirty-two. In addition, the application form asks whether Patrick has ever had any heart ailments or problems. Patrick answers no, forgetting that as a young child he was diagnosed as having a slight heart murmur. A policy is issued. Three years later, Patrick becomes seriously ill. A review of the policy discloses that Patrick was actually thirty-three at the time of application and issuance of the policy and that he erred in answering the question about a history of heart ailments. Discuss whether Ajax can void the policy and escape liability on Patrick's death.

52–3. Assignment of Insurance. Sapata has an ordinary life insurance policy on her life and a fire insurance policy on her house. Both policies have been in force for a number of years. Sapata's life insurance names her son, Rory, as beneficiary. Sapata has specifically removed her right to change beneficiaries, and the life policy is silent on right of assignment. Sapata is going on a one-year European vacation and borrows money from Leonard to finance the trip. Leonard takes an assignment of the life insurance policy as security for the loan, as the policy has accumulated a substantial cash surrender value. Sapata also rents out her house to Leonard and assigns to him her fire insurance policy. Discuss fully whether Sapata's assignment of these policies is valid.

52–4. Coinsurance Clauses. Fritz has an open fire insurance policy on his home for a maximum liability of $60,000. The policy has a number of standard clauses, including the right of the insurer to restore or rebuild the property in lieu of a monetary payment, and it has a standard coinsurance clause. A fire in Fritz's house virtually destroys a utility room and part of the kitchen. The fire was caused by an electric water heater's overheating. The total damage to the property is $10,000. The property at the time of loss is valued at $100,000. Fritz files a proof-of-loss claim for $10,000. Discuss the insurer's liability in this situation.

52–5. Multiple Insurance Coverage. Lori has a large house. She secures two open fire insurance policies on the house. Her policy with the Ajax Insurance Co. is for a maximum of $100,000, and her policy with Beta Insurance Co. is for a maximum of $50,000. Lori's house burns to the ground. The value of the house at the time of the loss is $120,000. Discuss the liability of Ajax and Beta to Lori.

52–6. Insurer's Defenses. On April 16, 1982, Frances and Michael Berthiaume made a written application for life insurance with the Minnesota Mutual Life Insurance Co. The policy sought was to provide $44,308.37 in insurance to cover the Berthiaumes' loan balance on the mortgage for their house, for a monthly premium of $12.42. Mr. Berthiaume did not take a physical examination for the policy, but in filling out the application, he answered no to a question asking whether he had ever been treated for, or had ever been advised that he had, high blood pressure. The answer Mr. Berthiaume gave was incorrect; in fact, he had been diagnosed as having hypertension four months before the application was made. In October 1982, Mr. Berthiaume became ill, and he died two months later. When his widow submitted a claim for the mortgage insurance, the insurance company denied payment, citing Mr. Berthiaume's inaccurate answer on the application. Minnesota Mutual sought summary judgment, which was granted by the trial court. Mrs. Berthiaume appealed. Discuss whether Mr. Berthiaume's inaccurate answer on the insurance policy application voided Minnesota Mutual's obligation to pay on the policy. [*Berthiaume v. Minnesota Mutual Life Insurance Co.*, 388 N.W.2d 15 (Minn.App. 1986)]

52–7. Effective Date of Coverage. Robert Gladney applied for disability insurance from Paul Revere Life Insurance Co., enclosing with the application a check for $3,100, which represented the first semiannual premium. The issuance of the policy was conditional on the insurance company's receipt of a medical form that was to be completed by Gladney's doctor following a physical examination. Gladney was a busy man and kept putting off the physical examination. Over a month later, Gladney submitted a second application, because the first one was too old. The insurance agent advised Gladney to leave the application undated so that if Gladney failed to have the physical examination within a month, he would not have to submit yet a third application. Gladney told the agent that he would notify him when the examination was completed. Soon thereafter, Gladney fell ill. His doctor examined him but did not conduct all the tests normally required by Paul Revere for disability insurance. A month later, Gladney was hospitalized and underwent heart surgery. Gladney never told the insurance agent about his visit to the doctor and the fact that the doctor had examined him. Gladney now claims that he is entitled to disability benefits under the policy because he paid the premium and would have been approved for insurance had he notified the insurance company of his examination. Will the court agree? Discuss fully. [*Gladney v. Paul Revere Life Insurance Co.*, 895 F.2d 238 (5th Cir. 1990)]

52–8. INSURER'S DEFENSES. Kirk Johnson applied for life insurance with New York Life Insurance Co. on October 7, 1986. In answer to a question about smoking habits, Johnson stated that he had not smoked in the past twelve months and that he had never smoked cigarettes. In fact, Johnson had smoked for thirteen years, and during the month prior to the insurance application, he was smoking approximately ten cigarettes per day. Johnson died on July 17, 1988, for reasons unrelated to smoking. Johnson's father, Lawrence Johnson, who was the beneficiary of the policy, filed a claim for the insurance proceeds. While investigating the claim, New York Life discovered Kirk Johnson's misrepresentation and denied the claim. The company canceled the policy and sent Lawrence Johnson a check for the premiums that had been paid. Lawrence Johnson refused to accept the check, and New York Life brought an action for a declaratory judgment (a court determination of a plaintiff's rights). What should the court decide? Discuss fully. [*New York Life Insurance Co. v. Johnson*, 923 F.2d 279 (3d Cir. 1991)]

52–9. INSURER'S DEFENSES. Jeffrey Duke purchased a life insurance policy on his own life from New England Mutual Life Insurance Co. Duke listed as his beneficiary his lover and business adviser, William Remmelink. On his insurance application, however, Duke described his beneficiary as merely his business partner. After Duke died of acquired immune deficiency syndrome (AIDS), New England Mutual brought an action against William Johnson, the executor of Duke's estate, to rescind (cancel) the insurance contract on the ground that Duke had "materially misrepresented his relationship with his beneficiary." Johnson claimed that New England Mutual's attempt to rescind the contract was in bad faith and asked for both punitive damages and attorneys' fees. During the trial, an underwriter with twenty-four years of experience testified that New England Mutual had never before rescinded a policy because of a misrepresentation regarding the relationship between the beneficiary and the insured. Did Duke mischaracterize his relationship with his beneficiary? If so, was such a misrepresentation material? How should the court decide? [*New England Mutual Life Insurance Co. v. Johnson*, 155 Misc.2d 680, 589 N.Y.S.2d 736 (1992)]

52–10. INTERPRETATION OF AN INSURANCE CONTRACT'S TERMS. RLI Insurance Co. issued an insurance policy to Richard Brown to cover his aircraft. One provision of the policy excluded coverage for a "resident spouse." A different provision included coverage for "any passenger." Richard was piloting the aircraft, with his wife, Janet, as a passenger, when it crashed. Richard was killed, and Janet was injured. At the time, Janet and Richard had been living together. Janet filed a suit in a federal district court to collect under the policy for her injuries. RLI claimed that the policy clearly excluded Janet. Janet argued that the policy was ambiguous. What will the court decide? Why? [*RLI Insurance Co. v. Drollinger*, 97 F.3d 230 (8th Cir. 1996)]

14

INTRODUCTION TO CONTRACTS

In Marina del Rey, California, Cassandra sits on the sunny deck of her waterside condominium, sipping a *mocha latte* while watching spinnakers fill with the warm Pacific wind. She has just received an offer of $1.7 million to buy her condominium. Cassandra has decided to counteroffer for $1.9 million. She is in high spirits because she assumes that at the very worst she has $1.7 million guaranteed, and that represents a huge profit to her. Cassandra plans to buy a cheaper house in North Carolina and invest her profits so that she can retire early. She opens the newspaper, notices a headline "Hard Body Threatens Suit," and turns the page, thinking that a corporate lawsuit in Ohio is of no concern to her. She is mistaken and may learn some hard lessons about contract law.

A year earlier, Jerusalem Steel had signed a contract with Hard Body, a manufacturer of truck and bus bodies. Jerusalem was to deliver 20,000 tons of steel to Hard Body's plant in Joy, Ohio. Hard Body relied on the contract, hiring 300 additional workers even before the steel was delivered, so that the plant would be geared up and ready to produce buses when the metal arrived. To help deal with the new workers, Hard Body offered a mid-level personnel job to Nicole. Hard Body told Nicole, "Don't worry, we expect your job to last forever." Nicole, in turn, relied on that statement to quit her old job in Minneapolis, move to Joy, and sign an

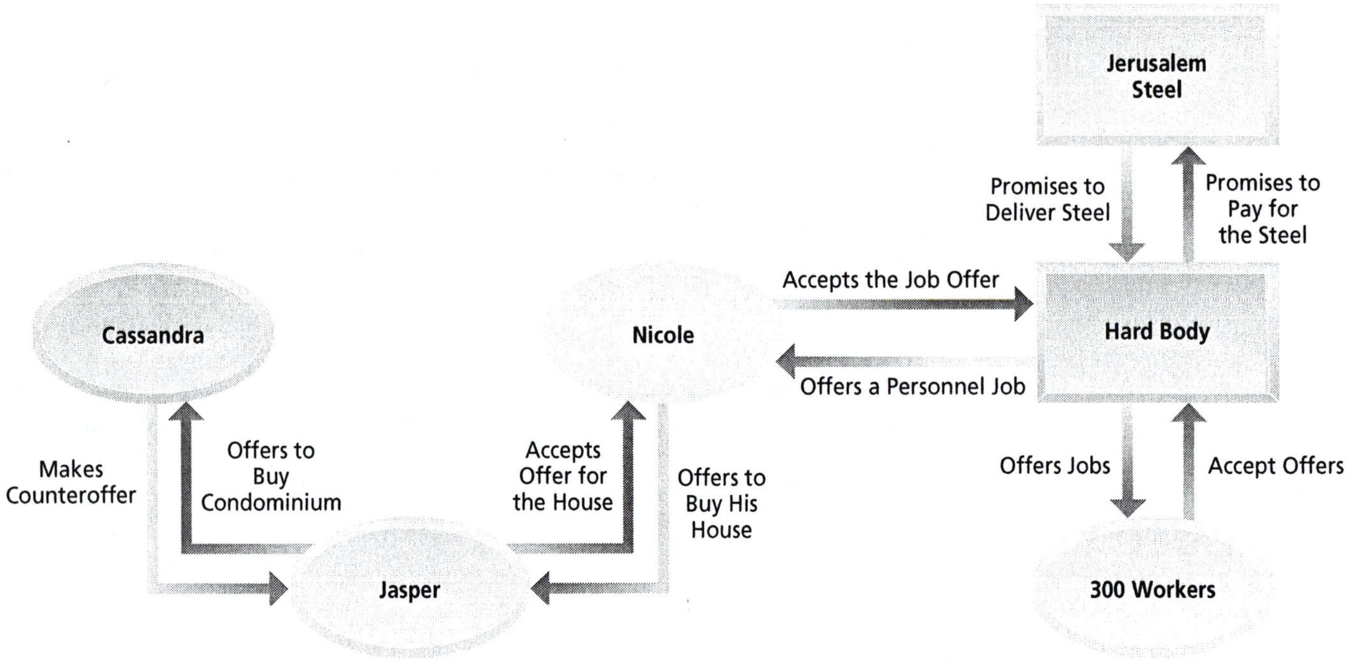

Exhibit 10.1

Contracts are intended to make business matters more predictable. Frequently, a series of contracts becomes mutually dependent.

agreement with Jasper to purchase his house for $450,000. Based on that sales contract, Jasper phoned his offer to Cassandra's real estate agent for $1.7 million. See Exhibit 10.1.

But in the year since Jerusalem signed its contract, the price of the specified steel has gone up 60 percent. Jerusalem now refuses to deliver the steel unless the price is renegotiated. Hard Body has insisted on the original contract price. Hard Body cannot afford to buy steel at the current price, which would make its deal to produce buses unprofitable. If Hard Body receives no steel, does it have a valid lawsuit against Jerusalem? May it force Jerusalem to deliver the steel? If it cannot get steel, may it lay off the newly hired workers? May it fire Nicole, or does she have a job for life? If Nicole loses her paycheck, will the law force her to buy a house she no longer wants? Jasper will never get such a good price from anyone else, because with no work at Hard Body property prices in Joy will plummet. May Jasper refuse to buy Cassandra's condo, or is he committed for $1.7 million?

Contracts

The Purpose of a Contract

Throughout this unit on contracts, we will consider issues like those raised in the Cassandra–Hard Body story. This long chain of mutually dependent people and companies exemplifies not only the law of contracts but the *purpose* of contracts. Parties enter into contracts attempting to control their future. **Contracts exist to make business matters more predictable.** Most contracts work out precisely as the parties intended because the parties fulfill their obligations. Most—but not all. In this unit we will study contracts that have gone wrong. We look at these errant deals to learn how to avoid the problems they manifest.

Judicial Activism versus Judicial Restraint

We will see that *the courts will not always do what we expect*. In most contract cases, it is true, judges do their best simply to enforce whatever terms the parties have agreed to. Even if the contract results in serious harm to one party, a court will generally enforce it. This is **judicial restraint**—a court taking a relatively passive role and requiring the parties to fulfill whatever obligations they agreed to, whether the deal was wise or foolish. Judges often say that it is not their job to rewrite a deal that the parties crafted. For example, if a real estate developer contracts with a builder to erect 10 expensive homes, but the housing market collapses before construction begins, the developer is still obligated to pay the builder for the houses, even though the expense will cause him devastating losses. Judicial restraint makes the law **less flexible but more predictable.**

On the other hand, some courts practice **judicial activism.** In contract law, this means that a court will ignore certain provisions of a contract, or an entire contract, if the judge believes that enforcing the deal would be unjust. Further, a court may be willing to artificially create a contract where none really existed, if the judge believes that is the only way to avoid injustice. Since judicial activism is always phrased in terms of "doing justice," it has an initial appeal. For example, when one party deceives the other with a misleading contract, it may be appropriate for a court to rewrite the agreement. But when a court practices judicial activism, it may diminish our ability to control our own future—which is the whole point of creating a contract. Judicial activism makes the law **more flexible but less predictable.** In this unit on contracts we look at many examples of both judicial activism and restraint.

Issues (and Answers)

The chain of contracts connecting Jerusalem Steel and Cassandra illustrates various contract problems. We consider each problem in detail in this unit, but here we briefly identify the issues and summarize the answers. **A contract has four elements:**

- **Agreement**. One party must make a valid offer, and the other party must accept it.
- **Consideration.** There has to be bargaining that leads to an exchange between the parties.
- **Legality**. The contract must be for a lawful purpose.
- **Capacity**. The parties must be adults of sound mind.

The chapters that follow cover each of the elements in sequence. Contract cases often raise several other important issues, which we examine in later chapters:

- **Consent**. Neither party may trick or force the other into the agreement.
- **Written Contracts**. Some contracts must be in writing to be enforceable.
- **Third Party Interests**. Some contracts affect people other than the parties themselves.
- **Performance and Discharge**. If a party fully accomplishes what the contract requires, his duties are discharged.
- **Remedies**. A court will award money or other relief to a party injured by a breach of contract.

When we apply these principles to the problem at this chapter's beginning, we see that Jerusalem Steel is almost certainly bound by its agreement. A rise in price is generally no excuse to walk away from a contract. Hard Body has made the bargain precisely to protect itself in case of a price rise. These are issues of offer and acceptance, consideration, and discharge. Can Hard Body force Jerusalem to deliver the steel? Probably not, as we learn in Chapter 18, on remedies. But Hard Body might be able to block Jerusalem from delivering the steel anywhere else. And Hard Body almost certainly is entitled to money damages if it is forced to buy steel at higher prices. If Hard Body is unable to obtain steel in the rising market, may it lay off its workers? Very likely, as Chapter 11, on agreement, indicates. Can it fire Nicole? The statement about expecting her job to last forever almost certainly creates no lifetime employment. In fact, even if Nicole has begun her job, the company can probably terminate her. What about the fact that she quit her job in reliance on this one? That raises an issue called promissory estoppel, which we discuss later in this chapter; it may or may not help Nicole, depending on the facts.

Must Nicole go through with her purchase of Jasper's house? Probably, as Chapters 15 and 18, on written contracts and remedies, will demonstrate. Do Jasper and Cassandra have a contract? No, because the agreement must be in writing to be enforceable. Even if there is no settled price, is Cassandra safe in assuming she has $1.7 million guaranteed? Not at all, as Chapter 11, on agreement, shows. If Cassandra had read this unit, she would be faxing a written contract to Jasper rather than waiting for her *latte* to cool.

All Shapes and Sizes

Some contracts are small. If you agree to sell your bicycle to your roommate for $75 at the end of the academic year, that is an enforceable agreement. But contracts can also be large. US Airways agreed to buy 400 narrow-body jets from Airbus Industrie, the European aircraft manufacturer. The value of the agreement? About $14 *billion*. Airbus was ecstatic, but not Boeing Aircraft Corp., its American competitor, which filed suit, claiming that US Airways had already signed a contract to purchase Boeing jets.

Many contracts involve public issues. When the owner of the Pittsburgh Pirates announced that he might sell the baseball team to out-of-town buyers, a group of local businesses banded together to buy the team and keep it in their city. The mayor publicly promised $25 million in city aid to enable the local businesses to make the purchase. But after the purchase, the city refused to honor the mayor's commitment. A court later ruled that the mayor's promise was unenforceable because he lacked the authority to make it. (The U.S. government contracts for more goods and services than any other organization in the world. To examine a few of the countless opportunities to sell things to Uncle Sam, browse through **http://www.fedmarket.com/**.)

Other contracts concern intensely private matters. Mary Beth Whitehead signed a contract with William and Elizabeth Stern, of New Jersey. For a fee of $10,000, Whitehead agreed to be impregnated with Mr. Stern's sperm, carry the baby to term, and then deliver it to the Sterns for adoption. But when little Melissa was born, Whitehead changed her mind and fled to Florida with the baby. The Sterns sued for breach of contract. Surrogacy contracts now lead to over 500 births per year. Are the contracts immoral? Should they be illegal? Are there limits to what one person may pay another to do? The New Jersey Supreme Court, the first to rule on the issue, declared the contract illegal and void. The court nonetheless awarded Melissa to the Sterns, saying that it was in the child's best interest to live with them. There will be many more rulings, in other states, before the legal status of surrogacy contracts is resolved.

At times we enter contracts without knowing it. Suppose you try to book a flight using your frequent flyer miles, but the airline tells you the terms of the frequent flyer program have changed and you must earn more mileage. According to the Supreme Court, you may well have an enforceable agreement based on the terms the airline quoted when you earned the miles.[1] At other times we may be stunned to learn that a contract we are relying on does not exist. Jerome Howard was the agent for rap recording star Domino. Howard was delighted that his contract gave him a long-term relationship with an artist whose most recent album sold at "platinum" levels. But Domino was unhappy with the arrangement and walked away from it—legally. Howard was not licensed by the state of California to work as a music agent. His contract with Domino was void.

Societal interests can shape contract law. For example, federal law requires that landowners clean up toxic waste on their property, a process that can cost millions of dollars. Suppose Klene Corp. wants to sell land that might have toxic chemicals underground. May Klene include a provision in its sales contract shifting the cost of any cleanup to the buyer? No, and yes. Regardless of what the contract says, federal statutes prohibit Klene from abandoning its own responsibility to clean up the waste. Yet the contract could make the buyer equally liable.

In turn, contract law can shape society. For example, California places a cap on the interest rate that a mortgage company may charge. Because of the cap, mortgage companies may not find it profitable to lend money to the most credit-risky customers, meaning that those people will be unable to borrow money. On the other hand (and the other coast), Virginia places no cap at all on mortgage rates. This enables low-income borrowers to obtain funds. But it also means they pay astronomical interest rates, sometimes over 50 percent. The result? Many end up losing their homes. This is a typical problem at the intersection of public policy and contract law.

Contracts Defined

Contract law is a study in promises. Did Hard Body promise a lifetime job to Nicole? Should the city of Pittsburgh be bound by the mayor's promise of $25 million? If a homeowner promises to pay a 45 percent interest rate, should the law enforce the deal, even to the point of throwing a family out of its home? In each case there is a promise, or at least someone's claim that a promise was made. Contract law determines which promises to enforce. **A contract is a promise that the law will enforce.**

As we look more closely at the elements of contract law, we will encounter some intricate issues. This is partly because we live in a complex society, which conducts its business in an infinite variety of ways. It is also due to the constant tug between predictability and fairness, described above. Remember, though, that we are usually interested in answering three basic questions of common sense, all relating to promises:

- Is it certain that the defendant promised to do something?
- If she did promise, is it fair to make her honor her word?
- If she did *not* promise, are there unusual reasons to hold her liable anyway?

---

[1] *American Airlines, Inc. v. Wolens*, 513 U.S. 219, 115 S. Ct. 817, 1995 U.S. LEXIS 690 (1995).

Development of Contract Law

Courts have not always assumed that promises are legally significant. As English judges were developing the common law in the twelfth and thirteenth centuries, they seldom used the term "contract," focusing instead on other issues in the case. Suppose a farmer and a horse dealer orally agreed that the dealer would deliver two draught horses to the farmer by April 1, and the farmer agreed to pay £100 for each. If the horse dealer never made any effort to fulfill his promise, the farmer could *not* sue. Even if he lost a year's crop because of the dealer's incompetence, he recovered nothing. The dealer's promise was never binding unless he made it *in writing and affixed a seal* to the document. This was seldom done, and therefore most promises were unenforceable.

Times change, but contract issues do not.

The common law changed very slowly, but by the fifteenth century courts began to allow some suits based on a broken promise. There were still major limitations. Suppose a merchant hired a carpenter to build a new shop, and the carpenter failed to start the job on time. Now courts would permit the suit but only if the merchant had paid some money to the carpenter. If the merchant made a 10 percent down payment, the contract would be enforceable. But if the merchant merely *promised* to pay when the building was done, and the carpenter never began work, the merchant could recover nothing.

In 1602, English courts began to enforce *mutual promises*, that is, deals in which neither party gave anything to the other but both promised to do something in the future. Thus, if a farmer promised to deliver a certain quantity of wheat to a merchant and the merchant agreed on the price, both parties were now bound by their promise, even though there had been no down payment. This was a huge step forward in the development of contract law, but many issues remained. Consider, for example, the following employment case from 1792, which raises issues of public policy that still challenge courts today.

Davis v. Mason

Court of King's Bench
Michaelmas Term, 33d George III, p. 118 (1792)

Facts: Mason was a surgeon/apothecary in the English town of Thetford. Davis wished to apprentice himself to Mason. The two agreed that Davis would work for Mason and learn his profession. They further agreed that if Davis left Mason's practice, he would not set up a competing establishment within 10 miles of Thetford at any time within 14 years. Davis promised to pay £200 if he violated the agreement not to compete.

Davis began working for Mason in July 1789. In August 1791, Mason dismissed Davis, claiming misconduct, though Davis denied it. Davis then established his own practice within 10 miles of Thetford. Mason sued for the £200.

Davis admitted promising to pay the money. But he claimed that the agreement should be declared illegal and unenforceable. He argued that 14 years was unreasonably long to restrict him from the town of Thetford, and that 10 miles was too great a distance. (Ten miles in those days might take the better part of a day to travel.) He added an additional policy argument, saying that it was harmful to the public health to restrict a doctor from practicing his profession: if the people needed his service, they should have it. Finally, he said that his "consideration" was too great for this deal. In other words, it was unfair that he should pay £200, because he did not receive anything of that value from Mason.

Issue: **Was the contract too unreasonable to enforce?**

Excerpts from Lord Kenyon's Decision: Here, the plaintiff being established in business as a surgeon at Thetford, the defendant wished to act as his assistant with a view of deriving a degree of credit from that situation; on which the former stipulated that the defendant should not come to live there under his auspices and steal away his patients: this seems to be a fair consideration. Then it was objected that the limits within which the defendant engaged not to practise are unreasonable: but I do not see that they are necessarily unreasonable, nor do I know how to draw the line. Neither are the public likely to be injured by an agreement of this kind, since every other person is at liberty to practise as a surgeon in this town.

Judgment for the Plaintiff.

The contract between Davis and Mason is called a **noncompetition agreement**. Today they are more common than ever, and frequently litigated. The policy issues that Davis raised have never gone away. Two hundred years later, a group of stockbrokers brought a class action suit, alleging that their employer had forced them to pay an excessive fee for taking their skills elsewhere.

NEWSWORTHY

Dean Witter Reynolds agreed to pay $1.8 million to settle a suit brought by 34 stockbrokers. The brokerage house had required new employees to sign a contract requiring them to repay the cost of training if they left the firm within two years. Evidence indicated that the firm generally sought recoupment of its training costs only from brokers who moved to a competitor. The plaintiff's attorney said that the repayment requirement was nothing but a noncompetition agreement, holding the employees in "involuntary servitude." Many Wall Street firms require similar agreements from employees.

You may well be asked to sign a noncompetition agreement sometime in your business or professional life. We look at the issue in detail in Chapter 12, on consideration. But note that in 1792 the court did in fact enforce the contract. In other words, the mutual promises seemed reasonable, and the court ordered the parties to live up to the deal.

That outcome was typical of contract cases for the next 100 years. Contracts were generally bargained between business people of roughly equal knowledge and power, and the law expected them to know what they were doing. Courts took a *laissez-faire* approach, declaring that parties had *freedom to contract* and would have to live with the consequences. Lord Kenyon saw Davis and Mason as equals, entering a bargain that made basic sense, and he had no intention of rewriting it. After 500 years of evolution, courts had come to regard promises as almost sacred. The law had gone from ignoring most promises to enforcing almost all.

By the early twentieth century, bargaining power in business deals had changed dramatically. Farms and small businesses were yielding place to huge corporations in a trend that accelerated throughout the century. Today multinational corporations span many continents, wielding larger budgets and more power than many of the nations in which they do business. When such a corporation contracts with a small company or an individual consumer, the latter may have little or no leverage. As the century progressed, courts increasingly looked at the basic fairness of contracts. In other words, they were more willing to play an *activist* role.

Noncompetition agreements are no longer automatically enforced. Courts may alter them or ignore them entirely because the parties have such unequal power and because the public may have an interest in letting the employee go on to compete. Davis's argument—that the public is entitled to as many doctors as it needs—is frequently more successful in court today than it was before Lord Kenyon.

It is not only the unequal bargaining power that causes courts to look closely at contracts. The issue of toxic waste illustrates how the public interest may be "read into" a contract. Environmental statutes assume that the public interest requires holding all owners of property liable to clean up toxic waste. So even when the seller of polluted land writes a contract placing cleanup responsibility on the buyer, the courts will simply ignore the provision, holding that the seller remains liable. This is socially sensible, because it ensures that our world will be cleaned up, but it diminishes a party's ability to control its future.

Legislatures and the courts limit the effect of promises in other ways. Suppose you purchase a lawn mower with an attached tag, warning you that the manufacturer is not responsible in the event of any malfunction or injury. You are required to sign a form acknowledging that the manufacturer has no liability of any kind. That agreement is clear enough—but a court will not enforce it. The law holds that the manufacturer *has* warranted the product to be good for normal purposes, regardless of any language included in the sales agreement. If the blade flies off and injures a child, the manufacturer is liable. This is socially responsible, but again, it interferes with a private agreement.

The law has not come full circle back to the early days of the common law. Courts still enforce the great majority of contracts. But the possibility that a court will ignore an agreement means that any contract is a little less certain than it would have been a century ago. That is all the more reason to understand contract principles and avoid agreements that fall afoul of the law.

TYPES OF CONTRACTS

BILATERAL AND UNILATERAL CONTRACTS

In a bilateral contract, both parties make a promise. Suppose a producer says to Gloria, "I'll pay you $2 million to star in my new romantic comedy, *A Promise for a Promise*, which we are shooting three months from now in Santa Fe." Gloria says, "It's a deal." That is a bilateral contract. Each party has made a promise to do something. The producer is now bound to pay Gloria $2 million, and Gloria is obligated to show up on time and act in the movie. The vast majority of contracts are bilateral contracts. They can be for services, such as this acting contract; they can be for the sale of goods, such as 1,000 tons of steel, or for almost any other purpose. When the bargain is a promise for a promise, it is a bilateral agreement.

In a unilateral contract, one party makes a promise that the other party can accept only *by doing* something. These contracts are less common. Suppose the movie producer says to Leo, "I'll give you a hundred bucks if you mow my lawn this weekend." Leo is not promising to do it. If he mows the lawn, he has accepted the offer and is entitled to his hundred dollars. If he spends the weekend at the beach, neither he nor the producer owes anything.

EXPRESS AND IMPLIED CONTRACTS

In an express contract, the two parties explicitly state all important terms of their agreement. Most contracts are express contracts. The contract between the producer and Gloria is an express contract, because the parties explicitly state what Gloria will do, where and when she will do it, and how much she will be paid. Some express contracts are oral, as that one was, and some are written. They might be bilateral express contracts, as Gloria's was, or unilateral express contracts, as Leo's was. Obviously, it is good business sense always to make express contracts. The clearer things are, the less chance there is of a dispute.

In an implied contract, the words and conduct of the parties indicate that they intended an agreement. Suppose every Friday, for two months, the producer asks Leo to mow his lawn, and loyal Leo does so each weekend. Then for three more weekends, Leo simply shows up without the producer asking, and the producer continues to pay for the work done. But on the twelfth weekend, when Leo rings the doorbell to collect, the producer suddenly says, "I never asked you to mow it. Scram." The producer is correct that there was no express contract, because the parties had not spoken for several weeks. But a court will probably rule that the conduct of the parties has *implied* a contract. Not only did Leo mow the lawn every weekend, but the producer even paid on three weekends when they had not spoken. It was reasonable for Leo to assume that he had a weekly deal to mow and be paid. Naturally, there is no implied contract thereafter.

NEWSWORTHY

Companies may have to be a little more careful about what they promise employees after a Summit County [Ohio] verdict involving a laid-off transportation analyst at Akron's General Tire Co. Thomas Brown on Thursday won a $107,042 jury verdict against General Tire because the company backed down from a promise to move him into a job based on seniority.

Brown, now a security guard in Las Vegas, had worked at General Tire since 1968 as a transportation analyst. He charged that the company long had a policy of allowing senior employees to replace those with less time when layoffs took place. Brown was not a member of a union and had no formal employment contract.

"After 12 years of using the bumping procedure, the company unilaterally changed policy and, two months later, laid off several senior employees, including Brown," said his lawyer, Andrew Margolius. Many of the employees had nearly 30 years of service with the company, when they would become eligible for life-time health care in retirement, he said. Officials of the company, which recently changed its name to Continental General Tire, could not be reached for comment yesterday.

"This appears to be the first time in Ohio that the implied contract doctrine was applied in an employment matter where no written contract or union agreement existed," Margolius said. He pointed out that similar cases were pending for others who were laid off by General Tire along with Brown. "We felt the understanding that seniority would provide some job security is an inducement for people to come to work at the company," Margolius said. "When the company decides on its own to change that, it constitutes the breach of an implied contract." He said the amount of the verdict was based on lost back pay and the fact that Brown had to take a job at reduced pay. Brown was earning $38,000 a year at General Tire and now was earning $8 an hour, or $16,640 a year, in Nevada.[2]

Today, the hottest disputes about implied contracts continue to arise in the employment setting. Many corporate employees have "at-will" contracts with their companies. This means that the employees are free to quit at any time and the company has the right to fire them at any time, for virtually any reason. Courts routinely enforce at-will contracts. But often a company provides its workers with personnel manuals that guarantee certain rights. The company may assure all workers that they will have a hearing and a chance to present evidence on their behalf before being fired. The legal issue then becomes whether the handbook *implies a contract* guaranteeing a right to a hearing or whether the company is still at liberty to fire any worker at will.

---

[2] Marcus Gleisser, "A Promise Is a Promise, Court Tells Tire Maker," *Cleveland Plain Dealer*, Jan. 17, 1995. Reprinted with permission from The Plain Dealer © 1995. All rights reserved. The appellate court affirmed the award. *Brown v. General Tire, Inc.*, 1996 Ohio App. LEXIS 767 (Ohio Ct. App. 1996).

You Be The Judge

FEDERAL EXPRESS CORP. v. DUTSCHMANN

846 S.W.2d 282, 1993 Tex. LEXIS 9
Supreme Court of Texas, 1993

Facts: When Marcie Dutschmann began working as a courier at Federal Express, she received an Employment Handbook and Personnel Manual stating that her employment was at-will and "would continue as long as it was mutually satisfactory to both parties." The manual specified that it created no contractual rights. But it also described a "Guaranteed Fair Treatment Policy" (GFTP). According to the GFTP, any employee who was terminated would have a hearing at a Board of Review, at which he could appear and present evidence.

Federal Express fired Dutschmann in October 1987, claiming that she had falsified delivery records. She responded that her termination was in retaliation for her complaints of sexual harassment. She attempted to appeal her termination through the GFTP, but Federal Express did not allow her the kind of hearing that the handbook described. Dutschmann was not allowed to present the documents that she offered, call her own witnesses, cross-examine the company witnesses, or discuss her claims of harassment.

Dutschmann sued. At trial, Federal Express argued that Dutschmann was an employee at-will and that the company was free to fire her at any time without a hearing. Dutschmann contended that the employee handbook and manual created an implied contract that she was entitled to a full, fair hearing. The jury found that the handbooks did create an implied contract and that Federal Express had not given her a fair hearing. The court of appeals affirmed. Federal Express appealed to the Texas Supreme Court.

You Be the Judge: Did the employee handbook and manual create an implied contract guaranteeing a fair hearing?

Argument for Federal Express: Your honors, when Federal Express created its employee manuals, it was well aware that some state courts have ruled that these handbooks *may* create an implied contract. So we studied the cases carefully and they are very clear: a booklet *does not* create any implied contract if it states that it does not. And that is why Federal Express wrote employee manuals including the following statements: "The employee's employment is at-will and will continue as long as it is mutually satisfactory to both parties." "This manual does not create any contractual rights. Its use is intended only as a reference." That manual states that it is intended "solely as a guide for management and employees and is not a contract of employment and that no such contract may be implied from its provisions." We think that language is about as clear as it is possible to be, but we didn't stop there. At the inception of Ms. Dutschmann's employment, she signed an agreement stating that she understood the employee manuals *did not constitute a contract*. Now, your honors, she is in court claiming that the booklets *did* create an implied contract.

At-will employment has existed for centuries. Freedom to contract means freedom, among other things, to create at-will employment. That is what both parties here voluntarily chose to do. Neither was obligated. Both understood their actions. Ms. Dutschmann signed an agreement saying she understood her position. What more can a company do to comply with the law?

Argument for Ms. Dutschmann: Your honors, the manuals do state that the employment is at-will. But those manuals then go on to say that *all employees are guaranteed* certain rights, including the rights to a fair, thorough termination hearing. The company refused to hear her evidence and refused to see her documents, because they knew she could prove sexual harassment. So they just fired her, pretending that there was no booklet and no guarantee of a hearing.

Federal Express is trying to have it both ways. The company creates these handsome, glossy booklets, filled with assurances of fair dealing. The booklets describe reasonable, sensible ways of treating employees and guarantee those rights to all employees. But then Federal Express comes into court and argues that those words don't really mean anything. They aren't a guarantee, says Federal Express, and a hearing is not a hearing.

When Federal Express distributed that booklet to all employees, the company intended the employees to read and rely on it. Federal Express knew that guaranteeing fair treatment was a proven way to attract and retain good employees. Would Ms. Dutschmann have gone to work for Federal Express if she had been told she might be sexually harassed and then fired without a fair hearing? Of course not. When a company hands out a booklet and tells employees to rely on it, the company must also keep its part of the bargain. Federal Express created an implied contract guaranteeing fair termination hearings, and Ms. Dutschmann is entitled to damages because the company broke its promise.

RIGHT & WRONG

Was it fair for Federal Express to include the termination procedure in its employee manual? Could the company have worded its manual differently to avoid misunderstanding?

Executory and Executed Contracts

A contract is **executory** when one or more parties has not fulfilled its obligations. Recall Gloria, who agrees to act in the producer's film beginning in three months. The moment Gloria and the producer strike their bargain, they have an executory bilateral express contract.

A contract is **executed** when all parties have fulfilled their obligations. When Gloria finishes acting in the movie and the producer pays her final fee, their contract will be fully executed.

Valid, Unenforceable, Voidable, and Void Agreements

A **valid contract** is one that satisfies all of the law's requirements. A court will therefore enforce it. The contract between Gloria and the producer is a valid contract, and if the producer fails to pay Gloria, she will win a lawsuit to collect the unpaid fee.

An **unenforceable agreement** occurs when the parties intend to form a valid bargain but a court declares that some rule of law prevents enforcing it. Suppose Gloria and the producer orally agree that she will star in his movie, which he will start filming in 18 months. The statute of frauds requires that this contract be in writing, because it cannot be completed within one year. If the producer signs up another actress two months later, Gloria has no claim against him.

A **voidable contract** occurs when the law permits one party to terminate the agreement. This happens, for example, when the other party has committed fraud or misrepresentation. Suppose that Klene Corp. induces Smart to purchase 1,000 acres of Klene land by telling Smart that there is no underground toxic waste, even though Klene knows that just under the topsoil lies an ocean of bubbling purple sludge. Klene is committing fraud. Smart may void the contract, that is, terminate it and owe nothing. If, for some reason, Smart still considers the land a bargain, he may go through with the sale. Klene has no power to void the contract.

A **void agreement** is one that neither party can enforce, usually because the purpose of the deal is illegal or because one of the parties had no legal authority to make a contract. When Jerome Howard agreed to represent the rapper Domino, the agreement was void from the start because Howard was not a licensed agent. He had no legal right to obtain employment for entertainers and therefore no lawful ability to sign a contract saying he would.

Remedies Created by Judicial Activism

Now we turn away from true contracts and consider two remedies created by judicial activism: promissory estoppel and quasi-contract. Each of these remedies has grown in importance over the last 100 years. In each case, a sympathetic plaintiff can demonstrate an injury. The harm has occurred in a setting where a contract might well have been made. But the crux of the matter is this: *There is no contract.* The plaintiff cannot claim that the defendant breached the contract, because none ever existed. The plaintiff must hope for more "creative" relief.

The two remedies can be confusingly similar. The best way to distinguish them is this:

- In **promissory estoppel** cases, the defendant made a *promise* that the plaintiff relied on.
- In **quasi-contract** cases, the defendant did not make any promise, but did receive a *benefit* from the plaintiff.

Promissory Estoppel

A fierce fire swept through Dana and Derek Andreason's house in Utah, seriously damaging it. The good news was that agents for Aetna Casualty promptly visited the Andreasons and helped them through the crisis. The agents reassured the couple that all of the damage was covered by their insurance, instructed them on which things to throw out, and helped them choose materials for repairing other items. The bad news was that the agents were wrong: the Andreasons' policy had expired six weeks before the fire. When Derek Andreason presented a bill for $41,957 worth of meticulously itemized work that he had done under the agents' supervision, Aetna refused to pay.

The Andreasons sued—but not for breach of contract. There *was* no contract, that was exactly the problem. The insurance contract had expired. So they sued Aetna under the legal theory of promissory estoppel: **Even when there is no contract, a plaintiff may use promissory estoppel to enforce the defendant's promise if he can show that:**

- The defendant made a promise knowing that the plaintiff would likely rely on it
- The plaintiff did rely on the promise; and
- The only way to avoid injustice is to enforce the promise.

Aetna made a promise to the Andreasons, namely, its assurance that all of the damage was covered by insurance. The company knew that the Andreasons would rely on that promise, which they did by ripping up a floor that might have been salvaged, throwing out some furniture, and buying materials to repair the house. Is enforcing the promise the only way to avoid injustice? Yes, ruled the Utah Court of Appeals.[3] The Andreasons' conduct was reasonable and based entirely on what the Aetna agents told them. Under promissory estoppel, the Andreasons received virtually the same amount they would have obtained had the insurance contract been valid.

Preventive Law

It appears that the Aetna agents responded quickly and in good faith to the Andreasons' emergency, yet clearly something went wrong. How could Aetna have prevented the agents' misstatements? Probably by keeping an easy-to-locate notation of every contract that has expired, so that no agent would make any promises without first checking to see the status of the policy.

Promissory estoppel is an important development of twentieth-century law. The doctrine provides opportunities for a court to do justice where no contract exists. Clearly, this is judicial activism, helping people by crafting new remedies.

[3] *Andreason v. Aetna Casualty & Surety Co.*, 848 P.2d 171, 1993 Utah App. LEXIS 26 (Utah App. 1993).

But, as is true whenever the rules are "bent," it means that the outcome of a particular case is less predictable. We will return to this flexible and powerful doctrine in Chapter 12, on consideration.

Quasi-Contract

Don Easterwood leased over 5,000 acres of farmland in Jackson County, Texas, from PIC Realty for one year. The next year he obtained a second one-year lease. During each year, Easterwood farmed the land, harvested the crops, and prepared the land for the following year's planting. Toward the end of the second lease, after Easterwood had harvested his crop, he and PIC began discussing the terms of another lease. While they negotiated, Easterwood prepared the land for the following year, cutting, plowing, and disking the soil. But the negotiations for a new lease failed, and Easterwood moved off the land. He sued PIC Realty for the value of his work preparing the soil.

Did Easterwood have an express contract? Clearly not. The lease was their contract, it had expired, and they failed to create a new one. Did he have an implied contract? No. The parties were actively trying to create a new express contract, so their conduct would not create any kind of an implied agreement. If he had neither an express nor an implied contract to pay him for the value of the work he has done, how could he make any legal claim? By relying on the legal theory of a quasi-contract: **Even when there is no contract, a court may use quasi-contract to compensate a plaintiff who can show that:**

- The plaintiff gave some benefit to the defendant
- The plaintiff reasonably expected to be paid for the benefit and the defendant knew this; and
- The defendant would be unjustly enriched if he did not pay.

If a court finds all of these elements present, it will generally award the value of the goods or services that the plaintiff has conferred. The damages awarded are called ***quantum meruit,*** meaning that the plaintiff gets "as much as he deserved." The court is awarding money that it believes the plaintiff *morally ought to have*, even though there was no valid contract entitling her to it. This again is judicial activism, with the courts inventing a "quasi" contract where no true contract exists. The purpose is justice, the term is contradictory.

Don Easterwood testified that in Jackson County, it was quite common for a tenant farmer to prepare the soil for the following year but then be unable to farm the land. In those cases, he claimed, the landowner compensated the farmer for the work done. Other witnesses agreed that this was the local custom. PIC Realty argued that it had no contract with Easterwood. The court ruled that indeed there was no contract, but that all elements of quasi-contract had been satisfied. Easterwood gave a benefit to PIC because the land was ready for planting. Jackson County custom caused Easterwood to assume he would be paid, and PIC Realty knew it. Finally, said the court, it would be unjust to let PIC benefit without paying anything. The court ordered PIC to pay the fair market value of Easterwood's labors.

Quasi-contract may require compensation even when no contract exists.

Almost all courts would agree with the result in the *Easterwood* case. But once again, if a court "invents" a contract where none existed, it may have opened the door to an infinite variety of claims. When would a defendant "reasonably know that the plaintiff expects compensation"? When is the enrichment "unjust"? The following case, from the same state, raises quasi-contract in the high stakes world of oil exploration. Notice that even within one court, judges can disagree about how far this doctrine should go.

VORTT EXPLORATION CO. v. CHEVRON U.S.A., INC.
33 Tex. Sup. J. 409, 787 S.W.2d 942, 1990 Tex. LEXIS 49
Supreme Court of Texas, 1990

Facts: A 160-acre tract of land in Texas contained valuable minerals. Both Vortt Exploration Co. and Chevron U.S.A. had rights to various sections of the land. Vortt's president proposed that the two companies enter a joint operating agreement to develop the minerals, and Chevron expressed some interest. For the next four years, the two companies negotiated but never reached an agreement. During the negotiations, Vortt provided Chevron with confidential seismic services, graphics, and maps, in an attempt to prod an agreement. Chevron used Vortt's information to locate and drill a producing well. Chevron then sued to invalidate Vortt's claim to mineral rights, and Vortt counterclaimed, seeking quasi-contract damages for the information it had provided Chevron.

The trial court found in favor of Vortt and awarded *quantum meruit* damages. But the court of appeals reversed, stating that Chevron could not know that Vortt expected to be paid for the information it divulged. Vortt appealed to the Texas Supreme Court.

Issue: **Is Vortt entitled to *quantum meruit* damages based on quasi-contract?**

Excerpts from Justice Hightower's Decision: *Quantum meruit* is an equitable remedy which does not arise out of a contract, but is independent of it. Generally, a party may recover under *quantum meruit* only when there is no express contract covering the services or materials furnished. This remedy is based upon the promise implied by law to pay for beneficial services rendered and knowingly accepted. Recovery in *quantum meruit* will be had when nonpayment for the services rendered could result in an unjust enrichment to the party benefited by the work.

Chevron knew that Vortt furnished the information with the expectation that a joint operating agreement would be reached. The parties had negotiated for over four years trying to achieve this end. At trial, Vortt's president testified that he shared the confidential seismic services, graphics, maps and other seismic information in the spirit of cooperation and that he would not have done so if he had not believed that a joint operating agreement would be reached. We hold that the trial court's findings of fact reflect that Chevron was reasonably notified that Vortt expected to be paid for the services and assistance which were rendered. [Vortt is entitled to money damages based on quasi-contract.]

Excerpts from Justice Hecht's Dissenting Opinion: Vortt tried for years to persuade Chevron to agree to develop jointly certain mineral interests, but Chevron refused to make such an agreement. At one point in the negotiations, Vortt decided to "share" seismic information with Chevron "in the spirit of cooperation," in hopes that Chevron would agree to jointly develop the mineral interests. Chevron's representatives never asked to see the information. Vortt's representative never told Chevron that Vortt expected anything in return for the information. Indeed, Vortt's representative never expected Vortt to be paid for the information, and absolutely the only thing Vortt expected to gain by giving the information to Chevron was favorable consideration of the proposed agreement. Under these circumstances, the Court says, Chevron should reasonably have expected to pay Vortt for the information. The information cost Vortt roughly $18,000. The trial court ordered Chevron to pay Vortt $178,750 for it.

Was ever fainter hope more richly rewarded? For not refusing to look at Vortt's information, Chevron must pay ten times its cost. The court's ruling today should be a tremendous encouragement to benefaction. A frustrated negotiator should never overlook this tactic in attempting to induce agreement. The recipient of such charity, however, should beware.

I would hold that Chevron could not reasonably have expected to pay when Vortt did not expect to be paid. Accordingly, I would affirm the judgment of the court of appeals.

Four Theories of Recovery

Theory	Did the Defendant Make a Promise?	Is There a Contract?	Description
Express Contract	Yes	Yes	The parties intend to contract and agree on explicit terms.
Implied Contract	Not explicitly	Yes	The parties do not formally agree, but their words and conduct indicate an intention to create a contract.
Promissory Estoppel	Yes	No	There is no contract, but the defendant makes a promise that she can foresee will induce reliance; the plaintiff relies on it; and it would be unjust not to enforce the promise.
Quasi-Contract	No	No	There is no intention to contract, but the plaintiff gives some benefit to the defendant, who knows that the plaintiff expects compensation; it would be unjust not to award the plaintiff damages.

Sources of Contract Law

Common Law

We have seen the evolution of contract law from the twelfth century to the present. Express and implied contracts, promissory estoppel, and quasi-contract were all crafted, over centuries, by appellate courts deciding one contract lawsuit at a time. In this country, the basic principles are similar from one state to another, but there have been significant differences concerning most important contract doctrines.

In part because of these differences, the twentieth century saw the rise of two major new sources of contract law: the Uniform Commercial Code and the Restatement of Contracts.

Uniform Commercial Code

Business methods changed quickly during the first half of the twentieth century. Executives used new forms of communication, such as telephone and wire, to make deals. Transportation speeded up. Corporations routinely conducted business across state borders and around the world. Executives, lawyers, and judges wanted a body of law for commercial transactions that reflected modern business methods and provided uniformity throughout the United States. That desire gave birth to the Uniform Commercial Code (UCC), created in 1952. The drafters intended the UCC to facilitate the easy formation and enforcement of contracts in a fast-paced world. The Code governs many aspects of commerce, including the sale and leasing of goods, negotiable instruments, bank deposits, letters of credit, investment securities, secured transactions, and other commercial matters. Every state has adopted at least part of the UCC to govern commercial transactions within that state. For our purposes in studying contract, the most important part of the Code is Article 2. The entire UCC is available online at **http://www.law.cornell.edu/ucc/ucc.table.html**.

UCC Article 2 governs the sale of goods. "Goods" means anything movable, except for money, securities, and certain legal rights. Goods include pencils, commercial aircraft, books, and Christmas trees. Goods do not include land or a house, because neither is movable, nor do they include a stock certificate. A contract for the sale of 10,000 sneakers is governed by the UCC; a contract for the sale of a condominium in Marina del Rey is governed by the California common law and its statute of frauds. Thus, when analyzing any contract problem as a student or business executive, you must note whether the agreement concerns the sale of goods. Most of the time the answer is clear, and you will immediately know whether the UCC or the common law governs. In some cases, as in a mixed contract for goods and services, it is not so obvious. **In a mixed contract, Article 2 governs only if the primary purpose was the sale of goods.** In the following case, the court had to decide the primary purpose.

PITTSLEY v. HOUSER
125 Idaho 820, 875 P.2d 232, 1994 Ida. App. LEXIS 71
Idaho Court of Appeals, 1994

Facts: Jane Pittsley hired Hilton Contract Carpet Co. to install carpet in her home. Hilton installed the carpet, but Pittsley complained that there were visible seams and gaps, that the carpet did not lie flat everywhere, and that it failed to reach the wall in certain areas. Hilton attempted to fix the problems but failed to satisfy Pittsley. She sued, seeking to rescind the contract, that is, to undo it. Pittsley asked for return of her money. Hilton responded by seeking the remaining $902 owed under the contract.

Under the UCC, a buyer who claims that goods are defective can *reject* them, that is, send them back to the seller. Further, a buyer who has accepted goods can later *revoke* that acceptance, essentially saying that she belatedly realized there were problems. Pittsley argued that she was entitled to reject the carpet because of the many problems, or, if she had accepted it, that she should be permitted to revoke her acceptance. But Hilton argued that she could do neither, because the UCC did not govern the contract. He asserted that their agreement was one for services, namely, his installation. Under the common law of contract, he argued, Pittsley had no right to reject or revoke except in an extreme case, which this was not. A magistrate agreed with Hilton, but the trial judge ruled that the UCC *did* govern the deal. Hilton appealed.

Issue: **Did the UCC or the common law of contract govern this contract?**

Excerpts from Judge Swanstrom's Decision: The single question upon which this appeal depends is whether the UCC is applicable to the subject transaction. Although there is little dispute that carpets are "goods," the transaction in this case also involved installation, a service. Such hybrid transactions, involving both goods and services, raise difficult questions about the applicability of the UCC. Two lines of authority have emerged to deal with such situations.

The first line of authority, and the majority position, utilizes the "predominant factor" test.

> The test for inclusion or exclusion is not whether they are mixed, but, granting that they are mixed, whether their predominant factor, their thrust, their purpose, reasonably stated, is the rendition of service, with goods incidentally involved (e.g., contract with artist for painting) or is a transaction of sale, with labor incidentally involved (e.g., installation of a water heater in a bathroom).

The second line of authority, which Hilton urges us to adopt, allows the contract to be severed into different parts, applying the UCC to the goods involved in the contract, but not to the non-goods involved, including services as well as other non-goods assets and property.

We believe the predominant factor test is the more prudent rule. Severing contracts into various parts, attempting to label each as goods or non-goods and applying different law to each separate part clearly contravenes the UCC's declared purpose "to simplify, clarify and modernize the law governing commercial transactions."

Applying the predominant factor test to the case before us, we conclude that the UCC was applicable to the subject transaction. The record indicates that the contract between the parties called for "165 yds Masterpiece #2122—Installed." It appears that Pittsley entered into this contract for the purpose of obtaining carpet of a certain quality and color. It does not appear that the installation, either who would provide it or the nature of the work, was a factor in inducing Pittsley to choose Hilton as the carpet supplier. On these facts, we conclude that the sale of the carpet was the predominant factor in the contract, with the installation being merely incidental to the purchase.

[The court remanded the case so that the lower court could apply the remedies available under the UCC. The court requested that the trial judge decide whether Pittsley had rejected the carpet or revoked acceptance, and if so, what her damages should be.]

The common law governs contracts for services, employment, real estate and certain other things, and so each chapter in this unit will analyze the relevant common law principles—of offer and acceptance, consideration, and so forth. But the sale of goods is obviously a major element in business nationwide, and therefore each chapter will also discuss appropriate aspects of Article 2.

Restatement (Second) of Contracts

In 1932 the American Law Institute (ALI), a group of lawyers, scholars, and judges, drafted the Restatement of Contracts, attempting to codify what its members regarded as the best rulings of contract law. Where courts had disagreed, for example, about when to enforce promissory estoppel, the drafters of the Restatement chose what they considered the wisest decisions. The Restatement was a treatise and never became the law anywhere. But because of the eminence of those who wrote it, the Restatement influenced many courts as they decided contract cases.

In 1979, the ALI issued a new version, the Restatement (Second) of Contracts. This revised version naturally reflects the changes in society, business, and judicial decisions in the half century since the first edition. Like its predecessor, the Restatement (Second) is not the law anywhere, and in this respect it differs from the common law and the UCC. But the Restatement (Second) influences lawyers as they draft contracts and judges as they decide cases; we, too, will seek its counsel throughout the chapters on contracts.

CHAPTER CONCLUSION

Contracts govern countless areas of our lives, from intimate family issues to multibillion dollar corporate deals. Understanding contract principles is essential for a successful business or professional career and is invaluable in private life. As we enter a new century, this knowledge is especially important because courts no longer rubber-stamp any agreement that two parties have made. If we know the issues that courts scrutinize, the agreement we draft is likelier to be enforced. We thus achieve greater control over our affairs—the very purpose of a contract.

CHAPTER REVIEW

A contract is a promise that the law will enforce. Contracts are intended to make business matters more predictable. Analyzing a contract generally involves inquiring into some or all of these issues:

1. What is the subject of the agreement?
   - If the contract is for the sale of goods, UCC Article 2 governs.
   - If the contract is for services, employment, or real estate, the common law governs.
2. Did the parties intend to contract?
   - If the parties formally agreed and stated explicit terms, there is probably an express contract.
   - If the parties did not formally agree but their conduct, words, or past dealings indicate they intended a binding agreement, there may be an implied contract.
3. If there is an agreement, is there any reason to doubt its enforceability?
   - An unenforceable agreement is one with a legal defect, such as an oral agreement that the law requires to be in writing.
   - A voidable contract occurs when one party has committed fraud, giving the other party the right to terminate the agreement, or when one party lacks capacity to make the contract and may escape liability.
   - A void agreement means that the law will ignore the deal regardless of what the parties want, typically because the purpose of the deal is illegal.
4. If there is no contract, are there other reasons to give the plaintiff damages?
   - A claim of promissory estoppel requires that the defendant made a promise knowing that the plaintiff would likely *rely*, and the plaintiff did so. It would be wrong to deny recovery.
   - A claim of quasi-contract requires that the defendant received a *benefit*, knowing that the plaintiff would expect compensation, and it would be unjust not to grant it.

PRACTICE TEST

1. What is the purpose of a contract?

2. Pennsylvania has contracted with Envirotests Systems, Inc., an Arizona company, to build 86 automobile emissions inspection stations in 25 counties, and operate them for seven years. This contract is worth hundreds of millions of dollars to Envirotest. But suddenly Pennsylvania legislators are opposing the entire system, claiming that it will lead to long delays and high expenses for motorists. These lawmakers are urging that Pennsylvania simply stop construction of the new system. Is Pennsylvania allowed to get out of the contract because its legislators now believe the whole system is unwise?

3. Central Maine Power Co. made a promotional offer in which it promised to pay a substantial sum to any homeowner or builder who constructed new housing heated with electricity. Motel Services, Inc., which was building a small housing project for the city of Waterville, Maine, decided to install electrical heat in the units in order to qualify for the offer. It built the units and requested payment for the full amount of the promotional offer. Is Central Maine obligated to pay? Why or why not?

4. Interactive Data Corp. hired Daniel Foley as an assistant product manager at a starting salary of $18,500. Over the next six years Interactive steadily promoted Foley until he became Los Angeles branch manager at a salary of $56,116. Interactive's officers repeatedly told Foley that he would have his job as long as his performance was adequate. In addition, Interactive distributed an employee handbook that specified "termination guidelines," including a mandatory seven-step pre-termination procedure. Two years later Foley learned that his recently hired supervisor, Robert Kuhne, was under investigation by the FBI for embezzlement at his previous job. Foley reported this to Interactive officers. Shortly thereafter, Interactive fired Foley. He sued, claiming that Interactive could only fire him for good cause, after the seven-step procedure. What kind of a claim is he making? Should he succeed?

5. The Hoffmans owned and operated a successful small bakery and grocery store. They spoke with Lukowitz, an agent of Red Owl Stores, who told them that for $18,000 Red Owl would build a store and fully stock it for them. The Hoffmans sold their bakery and grocery store and purchased a lot on which Red Owl was to build the store. Lukowitz then told Hoffman that the price had gone up to $26,000. The Hoffmans borrowed the extra money from relatives, but then Lukowitz informed them that the cost would be $34,000. Negotiations broke off and the Hoffmans sued. The court determined that there was no contract because too many details had not been worked out—the size of the store, its design, and the cost of constructing it. Can the Hoffmans recover any money?

6. **RIGHT & WRONG** You want to lease your automobile to a friend for the summer but do not want to pay a lawyer to draw up the lease. Joanna, a neighbor, is in law school. She is not licensed to practice law. She offers to draft a lease for you for $100, and you unwisely accept. Later, you refuse to pay her fee and she sues to collect. Who will win the lawsuit, and why? Apart from the law, was it morally right for the law student to try to help out by drafting the lease? Was she acting helpfully, or foolishly, or fraudulently? Is it just for you to agree to her fee and then refuse to pay it? What is society's interest in this dispute? Should a court be more concerned with the ethical issue raised by the conduct of the two parties or with the social consequences of this agreement?

7. Describe the role each of the following plays in contract law: the common law, the UCC, and the Restatement (Second) of Contracts.

8. **YOU BE THE JUDGE WRITING PROBLEM** John Stevens owned a dilapidated apartment that he rented to James and Cora Chesney for a low rent. The Chesneys began to remodel and rehabilitate the unit. Over a four-year period, they installed two new bathrooms, carpeted the floors, installed new septic and heating systems, and rewired, replumbed, and painted. Stevens periodically stopped by and saw the work in progress. The Chesneys transformed the unit into a respectable apartment. Three years after their work was done, Stevens served the Chesneys with an eviction notice. The Chesneys counterclaimed, seeking the value of the work they had done. Are they entitled to it? **Argument for Stevens:** Mr. Stevens is willing to pay the Chesneys exactly the amount he *agreed* to pay: nothing. The parties never contracted for the Chesneys to fix up the apartment. In fact, they never even *discussed* such an agreement. The Chesneys are making the absurd argument that anyone who chooses to perform certain work, without *ever discussing it* with another party, can finish the job and then charge it to the other person. If the Chesneys expected to get paid, obviously they should have said so. If the court were to allow this claim, it would be inviting other tenants to make improvements and then bill the landlord. The law has never been so foolish. **Argument for the Chesneys:** The law of quasi-contract was crafted for cases exactly like this. The Chesneys have given an enormous benefit to Stevens by transforming the apartment and enabling him to rent it at greater profit for many years to come. Stevens saw the work being done and understood that the Chesneys expected some compensation for these major renovations. If Stevens never intended to pay the fair value of the work, he should have stopped the couple from doing the work or notified them that there would be no compensation. It would be unjust to allow the landlord to seize the value of the work, evict the tenants who did it, and pay nothing.

9. Honeywell, Inc. and Minolta Camera Co. had a contract providing that Honeywell would give to Minolta various technical information on the design of a specialized camera lens. Minolta would have the right to use the information in its cameras provided that Minolta also used certain Honeywell parts in its cameras. Honeywell delivered to Minolta numerous technical documents, computer software, and test equipment, and Honeywell engineers met with Minolta engineers at least 20 times to discuss the equipment. Several years later, Honeywell sued, claiming that Minolta had taken the design information but failed to use Honeywell parts in its cameras. Minolta moved to dismiss, claiming that the UCC required lawsuits concerning the sale of goods to be filed within four years of the breach and that this lawsuit was too late. Honeywell answered that the UCC did not apply and that therefore Minnesota's six-year statute of limitations governed. Who is right?

10. Explain the difference between judicial restraint and judicial activism in contract law.

Internet Research Problem

Visit **http://www.law.cornell.edu/states/listing.html**. Select a state. Then click on *judicial opinions.* Search for a case concerning "quasi-contract." What are the details of the quasi-contract dispute? Who won and why?

You can find further practice problems in the Online Quiz at http://beatty.westbuslaw.com or in the Study Guide that accompanies this text.

15

WRITTEN CONTRACTS

Oliver and Perry were college roommates, two sophomores with contrasting personalities. They were sitting in the cafeteria with some friends, Oliver chatting away, Perry slumped on a plastic bench. Oliver suggested that they buy a lottery ticket, as the prize for that week's drawing was $3 million. Perry muttered, "Nah. You never win if you buy just one ticket." Oliver bubbled up, "O.K., we'll buy a ticket every week. We'll keep buying them from now until we graduate. Come on, it'll be fun. This month, I'll buy the tickets. Next month, you will, and so on." Other students urged Perry to do it and, finally, grudgingly, he agreed. The two friends carefully reviewed their deal. Each party was providing consideration, namely, the responsibility for purchasing tickets during his month. The amount of each purchase was clearly defined at one dollar. They would start that week and continue until graduation day, two and a half years down the road. Finally, they would share equally any money won. As three witnesses looked on, they shook hands on the bargain. That month, Oliver bought a ticket every week, randomly choosing numbers, and won nothing. The next month, Perry bought a ticket with equally random numbers—and won $52 million. Perry moved out of their dorm room into a suite at the Ritz and refused to give Oliver one red cent. Oliver sued, seeking $26 million, and the return of

an Eric Clapton compact disc that he had loaned Perry. If the former friends had understood the statute of frauds, they would never have slid into this mess.[1]

The rule we examine in this chapter is not exactly news. Parliament passed the original statute of frauds in 1677. The purpose was to prevent lying (fraud) in civil law suits. Jury trials of that era invited perjury. Neither the plaintiff nor the defendant was permitted to testify, meaning that the jury never heard from the people who really knew what had happened. Instead, the court heard testimony from people who claimed to have witnessed the contract being created. A plaintiff might concoct a fraudulent claim of contract, knowing that he would never be subjected to aggressive cross-examination, and then bribe witnesses to support his case. A powerful earl, seeking to acquire 300 acres of valuable land owned by a neighboring commoner, might claim that the neighbor had orally promised to sell his land. Although the claim was utterly false, the earl would win if he could bribe enough "reputable" witnesses to persuade the jury.

In order to provide juries with more reliable evidence that a contract did or did not exist, Parliament passed the statute of frauds. The statute required that in six types of cases, a contract would be enforced only if it were in writing. Almost all states of this country later passed their own statutes making the same requirements. It is important to remember, as we examine the rules and exceptions, that Parliament and the state legislatures all had a commendable, straightforward purpose in passing their respective statutes of fraud: *to provide a court with the best possible evidence of whether the parties intended to make a contract.*

Ironically, the British government has repealed the writing requirement for most contracts. Parliament concluded that the old statute, far from preventing wrongdoing, was *helping* people commit fraud. A wily negotiator could orally agree to terms and then, if the deal turned unprofitable, walk away from the contract, knowing it was unenforceable without written evidence.

Thus far, no state in this country has entirely repealed its statute of frauds. Instead, as we have often seen in the common law, courts have carved exceptions into the original statute to prevent unfairness. Some scholars have urged that state legislatures go further and repeal the law altogether, or repeal at least that part found in the Uniform Commercial Code (UCC), governing the sale of goods. The UCC *may* be the first place we will see the writing requirement eliminated. But again, these are only proposals for repeal. Some commentators defend the statute of frauds as a valuable tool for justice. They argue that, among other benefits, the requirement of a writing cautions people to be careful before making—or relying on—a promise. For now, the statute of frauds is a vital part of law. Sadly, Oliver will learn this the hard way.

The statute of frauds: A plaintiff may not enforce any of the following agreements, unless the agreement, or some memorandum of it, is in writing and signed by the defendant. The agreements that must be in writing are those:

- For any interest in **land**
- That **cannot be performed within one year**
- To pay the **debt of another**
- Made by an **executor of an estate**

[1] Based loosely on *Lydon v. Beauregard*, (Middlesex Sup. Ct., Mass., Dec. 22, 1989), reported in Paul Langher, "Couple Lose Suit to Share $2.8M Prize," *Boston Globe*, Dec. 23, 1989, p. 21.

- Made **in consideration of marriage; and**
- For the **sale of goods over $500.**

Unenforceable

In other words, when two parties make an agreement covered by any one of these six topics, it must be in writing to be enforceable. Oliver and Perry made a definite agreement to purchase lottery tickets during alternate months and share the proceeds of any winning ticket. But their agreement was to last two and one-half years. As the second item on the list indicates, a contract must be in writing if it cannot be performed within one year. The good news is, Oliver gets back his Eric Clapton disc. The bad news is he gets none of the lottery money. Even though three witnesses saw the deal made, it is unlikely to be enforced in any state. Perry the pessimist will probably walk away with all $52 million.[2]

But Not Void

Note that although the Oliver-Perry agreement is unenforceable, it is not void. Suppose that Perry does the right thing, agreeing to share the winnings with Oliver. Over the next 20 years, as he receives the winnings, Perry gives one-half to his friend. But then, having squandered his own fortune, Perry demands the money back from Oliver, claiming that the original contract violated the statute of frauds. Perry loses. **Once a contract is fully executed, it makes no difference that it was unwritten.** The statute of frauds prevents the enforcement of an executory contract, that is, one in which the parties have not fulfilled their obligations. But the contract is not *illegal*. Once both parties have fully performed, neither party may demand rescission.

RIGHT & WRONG

The law permits Perry to keep all of the lottery money. Is that right? Does Perry have a moral right to deny Oliver his half-share, when we know the two friends had agreed? Is the statute of frauds serving a useful purpose here? Remember that Parliament passed the original statute of frauds believing that a written document would be more reliable than the testimony of alleged witnesses. If we permitted Oliver to enforce the oral contract, based on his testimony and that of the witnesses, would we simply be inviting other plaintiffs to conjure up lottery "contracts" that had never been made?

Contracts That Must Be in Writing

Agreements for an Interest in Land

A contract for the sale of any interest in land must be in writing to be enforceable. Notice the phrase "interest in land." This means *any legal right* regarding land. A house on a lot is an interest in land. A mortgage, an easement, and a leased

[2] Div. Perry might also raise *illegality* as a defense, claiming that a contract for gambling is illegal. That defense is likely to fail. Courts appear to distinguish between the simple purchase of a legal lottery ticket, which friends often share, and the more traditional—and socially dangerous—gambling contracts involving horse racing or casino betting. See, e.g., *Pando v. Fernandez*, 118 A.D.2d 474, 499 N.Y.S.2d 950, 1986 N.Y. App. Div. LEXIS 54345 (N.Y. App. Div. 1986), finding no illegality in an agreement to purchase a lottery ticket, even where the purchaser was a minor! Since an illegality defense would probably fail Perry, it is all the more unfortunate that Oliver did not jot down their agreement in writing.

apartment are all interests in land. As a general rule, leases must therefore be in writing, although most states have created an exception for short-term leases. A short-term lease is often one for a year or less, although the length varies from state to state.

Kary Presten and Ken Sailer were roommates in a rental apartment in New Jersey, with a view of the Manhattan skyline. The lease was in Sailer's name, but the two split all expenses. Then the building became a "cooperative," meaning that each tenant would have the option of buying the apartment.[3] Sailer learned he could buy his unit for only $55,800 if he promptly paid a $1,000 fee to maintain his rights. He mentioned to Presten that he planned to buy the unit, and Presten asked if he could become half owner. Sailer agreed and borrowed the $1,000 from Presten to pay his initial fee. But as the time for closing on the purchase came nearer, Sailer realized that he could sell the apartment for a substantial profit. He placed an ad in a paper, and promptly received a firm offer for $125,000. Sailer then told Presten that their deal was off, and that he, Sailer, would be buying the unit alone. He did exactly that, and Presten filed suit. Regrettably, the outcome of Presten's suit was only too easy to predict.

A cooperative apartment is an interest in land, said the court. This agreement could be enforced only if put in writing and signed by Sailer. The parties had put nothing in writing, and therefore Presten was out of luck. He was entitled to his $1,000 back, but nothing more. The apartment belonged to Sailer, who could live in it or sell it for a large, quick profit.[4] (For sample leases, and other contracts in writing, see **http://www.kinseylaw.com/freestuff/FreeIndex.html#anchor339521**.)

Preventive Law

Suppose that you are interested in buying five expensive acres in a fast-growing rural area. There is no water on the property, and the only way to bring public water to it is through land owned by the neighbor, Joanne, who agrees to sell you an easement through her property. An easement is a legal right that an owner gives to another person to make some use of the owner's land. In other words, Joanne will permit you to dig a 200-foot trench through her land and lay a water pipe there in exchange for $15,000. May you now safely purchase the five acres? Not until Joanne has signed the written easement. You might ignore this "technicality," since Joanne seems friendly and honest. But you could then spend $300,000 buying your property, only to learn that Joanne has changed her mind. She might refuse to go through with the deal unless you pay $150,000 for the easement. Without her permission to lay the pipe, your new land is worthless. Avoid such nightmares: get it in writing.

Even sophisticated business people can run afoul of this ancient rule, as the following letter to an advice columnist indicates.

NEWSWORTHY

Dear Legal Advisor:

I have been a licensed real estate broker for 19 years. A friend who lives four blocks from me mentioned that she was going to put her house on the market. I did a free appraisal and then told her the house should sell for about $675,000. We agreed that I would be her exclusive agent for a three percent commission. I drew up a listing agreement, but she was out of town and never signed it. I showed the house to four potential buyers in two days. That weekend, while I was visiting my mother in a hospital, my friend agreed with one of the potential buyers to a sale

[3] Technically, the residents of a "co-op" do not own their apartments. They own a share of the corporation that owns the building. Along with their ownership shares, residents have a right to lease their unit for a modest fee.

[4] *Presten v. Sailer*, 225 N.J. Super. 178, 542 A.2d 7, 1988 N.J. Super. LEXIS 151 (N.J. Super. Ct. App. Div. 1988).

for $660,000. My commission should be $19,800, but my "friend" refuses to pay a penny. If I sue, will I win?

Dear Broker:

You will lose. In many states, including ours, the Statute of Frauds covers not only the contract to sell the house, but any broker's agreement as well. You cannot enforce your agreement unless it is in writing and signed by the owner. Don't waste money on a futile lawsuit.

Exception: Full Performance by the Seller

If the seller completely performs her side of a contract for an interest in land, a court is likely to enforce the agreement even if it was oral. Adam orally agrees to sell his condominium to Maggie for $150,000. Adam delivers the deed to Maggie and expects his money a week later, but Maggie fails to pay. Most courts will allow Adam to enforce the oral contract and collect the full purchase price from Maggie.

Exception: Part Performance by the Buyer

The buyer of land may be able to enforce an oral contract if she paid part of the purchase price *and either* entered upon the land *or* made improvements to it. Suppose that Eloise sues Grover to enforce an alleged oral contract to sell a lot in Happydale. She claims they struck a bargain in January. Grover defends based on the statute of frauds, saying that even if the two did reach an oral agreement, it is unenforceable. Eloise proves that she paid 10 percent of the purchase price and that in February she began excavating on the lot, to build a house, and that Grover knew of the work. Eloise has established part performance and will be allowed to enforce her contract.

This exception makes sense if we recall the purpose of the statute of frauds: to provide the best possible evidence of the parties' intentions. The fact that Grover permitted Eloise to enter upon the land and begin building on it is compelling evidence that the two parties had reached an agreement. But be aware that most claims of part performance fail. Merely paying a deposit on a house is *not* part performance. A plaintiff seeking to rely on part performance must show partial payment *and* either entrance onto the land *or* physical improvements to it.

Exception: Promissory Estoppel

The other exception to the writing requirement is our old friend promissory estoppel. **If a promisor makes an oral promise that should reasonably cause the promisee to rely on it, and the promisee does rely, the promisee *may* be able to enforce the promise,** despite the statute of frauds, if that is the only way to avoid injustice. This exception potentially applies to any contract that must be written, such as those for land, those that cannot be performed within one year, and so forth.

Maureen Sullivan and James Rooney lived together for seven years as husband and wife, although they never married. After renting for a few years, they decided to buy a house. The parties agreed that they would be equal owners of the house, but Rooney told Sullivan that in order to obtain Veterans' Administration financing he would have to be the sole owner on the deed. They each contributed to the purchase and maintenance of the house, and Rooney several times assured Sullivan that he would change the deed to indicate joint ownership. He never did. When the couple split up, Sullivan sued, seeking a 50 percent interest in the house. The Massachusetts high court ruled in her favor. The agreement of the parties was for an interest in land and should have been in writing. But Rooney had clearly promised Sullivan that she would be a half owner, and she had relied on the promise by contributing to the purchase and maintenance of the house. The statute of frauds was passed to *prevent* fraud, not to enable one person to mislead another and benefit at her expense.[5]

In the following case, the plaintiffs make three valiant efforts to evade the piercing grasp of the statute of frauds. They argue that their contract is not *really* for the sale of land, that they partly performed, and that they relied on the seller's promise.

HERSHON v. CANNON
1993 U.S. Dist. LEXIS 689
United States District Court, District of Maryland, 1993

Facts: Mary Drysdale and her husband, Simon Hershon, lived in Washington, D.C. They wanted to buy Tulip Hill, an eighteenth-century mansion located on 54 acres in Anne Arundel County, Maryland, property that was owned by an estate and managed by Jonathan Cannon. Drysdale and Hershon orally agreed with Cannon on a purchase price of $1.2 million. Cannon promised that while the lawyers were drafting the written purchase agreement, he would not seek offers from anyone else. Also, if he received an unsolicited offer, he agreed to give Drysdale and Hershon the opportunity to match it.

Drysdale and Hershon applied for a mortgage to buy Tulip Hill. They also met with the Maryland Historical Commission to discuss improvements to the property. Meanwhile, Cannon sold Tulip Hill to someone else. Drysdale and Hershon sued.

Issue: **Did Drysdale and Hershon have an enforceable contract for Tulip Hill?**

Excerpts from Judge Hargrove's Decision: The plaintiffs premise their suit upon alleged oral promises by Cannon. Plaintiffs make no allegation that they entered into a written contract regarding Tulip Hill, nor do they allege or present a writing of any sort. Clearly, the plaintiff's alleged oral agreements with respect to Tulip Hill are unenforceable under the statute of frauds.

Plaintiffs contend that their claim is not barred by the statute of frauds for two reasons. First, the plaintiffs argue that they do not seek to enforce an oral purchase agreement. To the contrary, they seek to enforce two other agreements with Cannon, namely Cannon's agreement not to solicit other offers for the property or to use their agreement as part of his marketing effort, and Cannon's agreement that if another offer arose, the plaintiffs would have the right of first refusal to purchase the property on the same terms and conditions as the new offer. The court finds this argument unpersuasive and believes that the promise the plaintiffs seek to enforce is indeed unenforceable under the statute of frauds, absent a sufficient "writing" or "memorandum."

Second, the plaintiffs contend that Maryland law recognizes exceptions to the statute of frauds where necessary to avoid injustice, including the doctrines of part-performance and estoppel. Part performance of oral agreements can remove the bar of the statute of frauds if the part performance consists of acts that would not have been done but for the existence of the contract. Even if the plaintiffs' allegations are taken as true, their activities are insufficient to create an issue of material fact as to part performance. While the plaintiffs' actions in meeting with officials from the Maryland Historical Trust, preparing design alternatives for Tulip Hill, applying for mortgages to finance the purchase, and liquidating assets, were consistent with the existence of the alleged agreements, they were also consistent with the absence of the alleged agreements. Plaintiffs' activities could have been undertaken in anticipation of a contract for the sale of Tulip Hill. Thus, the parties were not unequivocally in a position different from that which they would have

---

[5] *Sullivan v. Rooney*, 404 Mass. 160, 533 N.E.2d 1372, 1989 Mass. LEXIS 49 (1989).

been in had there been no agreements with the defendant. As conflicting inferences may be drawn from the plaintiffs' activities regarding the property, they do not raise an issue of material fact as to part performance.

[As to promissory estoppel] a court must determine if the plaintiff's action or forbearance is definite and substantial in comparison to the remedy sought. Cannon argues that in relation to the remedy which the plaintiffs seek, namely [enforcement of the contract to sell Tulip Hill, what] the plaintiffs allege is insufficient to support a claim under a theory of promissory estoppel. [In other words, Drysdale and Hershon's reliance was very slight. If the statute of frauds is enforced, and they are unable to buy Tulip Hill, they will not suffer any great injustice.] The court agrees and finds that the plaintiffs' claim based on promissory estoppel fails as a matter of law.

For the reasons discussed above, the motion to dismiss the amended complaint of Simon A. Hershon and Mary D. Drysdale, submitted by Defendant Jonathan Z. Cannon, is granted. It will be so ordered.

Agreements That Cannot Be Performed within One Year

Contracts that cannot be performed within one year are unenforceable unless they are in writing. This one-year period begins on the date the parties make the agreement. The critical phrase here is "*cannot be performed* within one year." If a contract *could* be completed within one year, it need not be in writing. Betty gets a job at Burger Brain, throwing fries in oil. Her boss tells her she can have Fridays off for as long as she works there. That oral contract is enforceable, whether Betty stays one week or five years. It *could* have been performed within one year if, say, Betty quit the job after six months. Therefore it does not need to be in writing.[6]

If the agreement will *necessarily* take longer than one year to finish, it must be in writing to be enforceable. If Betty is hired for three years as manager of Burger Brain, the agreement is unenforceable unless put in writing. She cannot perform three years of work in one year.

Type of Agreement	Enforceability
Cannot be performed within one year. *Example*: An offer of employment for three years.	Must be in writing to be enforceable.
Might be performed within one year, although could take many years to perform. *Example*: "As long as you work here at Burger Brain you may have Fridays off."	Enforceable whether it is oral or written, since the employee might quit working a month later.

In the following case, an employee did not insist on a written agreement. Was that a fatal mistake? You decide.

6 This is the majority rule. In most states, for example, if a company hires an employee "for life," the contract need not be in writing because the employee could die within one year. "Contracts of uncertain duration are simply excluded [from the statute of frauds]; the provision covers only those contracts whose performance cannot possibly be completed within a year." Restatement (Second) of Contracts §130, Comment a, at 328 (1981). However, a few states disagree. The Illinois Supreme Court ruled that a contract for lifetime employment is enforceable only if written. *McInerney v. Charter Golf, Inc.*, 176 Ill. 2d 482, 680 N.E.2d 1347, 1997 Ill. LEXIS 56 (Ill. 1997).

YOU Be The Judge

WIOR v. ANCHOR INDUSTRIES, INC.
669 N.E.2d 172, 1996 Ind. LEXIS 114
Indiana Supreme Court, 1996

Facts: Glenn Wior spent his adult life in the "needle trades," working for companies that sewed clothing and other textiles. Anchor Industries manufactured custom canvas and synthetic products for the outdoor recreation industry. Anchor offered Wior a job as plant supervisor at its factory in Evansville, Indiana. Wior did not want to leave his home and job in Indianapolis unless he had a long-term commitment. Allegedly, Anchor executives orally agreed to employ Wior for "20 plus years, until he retired." Wior accepted the offer, though the parties never put the agreement in writing.

Wior moved his family to Evansville, where he bought a home and began working for Anchor. Three months later, Anchor fired him, claiming that Wior did not "fit in." Wior filed suit, but the trial court granted summary judgment for the company because there was no writing to support the agreement. The appellate court reversed, holding that the contract *could* have been completed in one year. Anchor appealed to the state supreme court.

You Be the Judge: Does the statute of frauds bar enforcement of the oral agreement?

Argument for Anchor: Your honors, this is a very simple case. Wior claims that Anchor offered him a job that would last for at least 20 years. The statute of frauds is crystal clear that such an agreement, even if there had been one, must be in writing. This so-called deal was oral and unenforceable. We concede that if a company offered an employee a job "for life," with no time period specified, the agreement might be outside the statute of frauds. An employee could theoretically die within the first year, and thus the statute should not control. That isn't the case here. By Wior's own allegations, the supposed offer was for *at least* 20 years, until retirement. Neither the 20 years nor the retirement could theoretically occur within one year, and Wior, by his own allegations, has no case.

Argument for Wior: Your honors, this ancient rule was designed to prevent fraud, not to encourage it. Courts have interpreted the statute of frauds narrowly because of the injustice it might otherwise cause. Mr. Wior is hardworking, dedicated, and experienced in the industry, and Anchor wanted him. Wior was reluctant to leave Indianapolis for a smaller town, and a new job, unless he received a long-term commitment. Anchor gave it! The company knew it would never land a man of Wior's caliber unless it promised secure employment, so it offered a job until Mr. Wior retired. Wior accepted, sold his old home, bought a new one, and began work. For reasons we do not know, Anchor changed its mind and now wants to hide behind a technical rule of law. The court of appeals held that one technicality deserved another: the statute of frauds should not bar enforcement because the contract *could* have been performed within one year, had Mr. Wior died. This case should go to a jury, and a hardworking employee should have his chance to prove his damages.

PROMISE TO PAY THE DEBT OF ANOTHER

When one person agrees to pay the debt of another as a favor to that debtor, it is called a collateral promise, and it must be in writing to be enforceable. D. R. Kemp was a young entrepreneur who wanted to build housing in Tuscaloosa, Alabama. He needed $25,000 to complete a project he was working on, so he went to his old college professor, Jim Hanks, for help. The professor said he would see what he could do about getting Kemp a loan. Professor Hanks spoke with his good friend Travis Chandler, telling him that Kemp was highly responsible and would be certain to repay any money loaned. Chandler trusted Professor Hanks but wanted to be sure of his money. Professor Hanks assured Chandler that if for any reason Kemp did not repay the loan, he, Hanks, would pay Chandler in full. With that assurance, Chandler wrote out a check for $25,000, payable to Kemp, never having met the young man.

Kemp, of course, never repaid the loan. (Thank goodness he did not; this textbook has no use for people who do what they are supposed to.) Kemp exhausted the cash trying to sustain his business, which failed anyway, so he had nothing to give his creditor. Chandler approached Professor Hanks, who refused to pay (some professor!), and Chandler sued. The outcome was only too predictable.

When one party promises to pay the debt of another, the enforceability of that promise may depend upon whom the promisor intended to benefit.

Professor Hanks agreed to repay Kemp's debt *as a favor to Kemp*, making it a collateral promise. Chandler had nothing in writing, and that is exactly what he got from his lawsuit—nothing.

Exception: The Leading Object Rule

There is one major exception to the collateral promise rule. When the promisor guarantees to pay the debt of another and *the leading object of the promise is some benefit to the promisor himself*, then the contract will be enforceable even if unwritten. In other words, if the promisor makes the guarantee not as a favor to the debtor, but out of self-interest, the statute of frauds does not apply.

Robert Perry was a hog farmer in Ohio. He owed $26,000 to Sunrise Cooperative, a supplier of feed. Because Perry was in debt, Sunrise stopped giving him feed on credit and began selling him feed on a cash-only basis. Perry also owed money to Farm Credit Services, a loan agency. Perry promised Farm Credit he would repay his loans as soon as his hogs were big enough to sell. But Perry couldn't raise hogs without feed, which he lacked the money to purchase. Farm Credit was determined to bring home the bacon, so it asked Sunrise Cooperative to give Perry the feed on credit. Farm Credit orally promised to pay any debt that Perry did not take care of. When Perry defaulted on his payments to Sunrise, the feed supplier sued Farm Credit based on its oral guarantee. Farm Credit claimed the promise was unenforceable, based on the statute of frauds. But the court found in favor of Sunrise. The *leading object* of Farm Credit's promise to Sunrise was self-interest, and the oral promise was fully enforceable.[7]

Promise Made by an Executor of an Estate

This rule is merely a special application of the previous one, concerning the debt of another person. An executor is the person who is in charge of an estate after someone dies. The executor's job is to pay debts of the deceased, obtain money owed to him, and disburse the assets according to the will. In most cases, the executor will use only the estate's assets to pay those debts. The statute of frauds comes into play only when an executor promises to pay an estate's debts with her *own* funds. **An executor's promise to use her own funds to pay a debt of the deceased must be in writing to be enforceable.** Suppose Esmeralda dies penniless, owing Tina $35,000. Emeralda's daughter, Sapphire, is the executor of her estate. Tina comes to Sapphire and demands her $35,000. Sapphire responds, "There is no money in mamma's estate, but don't worry, I'll make it up to you with my own money." Sapphire's oral promise is unenforceable. Tina should get it in writing while Sapphire is feeling generous.

Promise Made in Consideration of Marriage

Barney is a multimillionaire with the integrity of a gangster and the charm of a tax collector. He proposes to Li-Tsing, who promptly rejects him. Barney then pleads that if Li-Tsing will be his bride, he will give her an island he owns off the coast of California. Li-Tsing begins to see his good qualities and accepts. After they are married, Barney refuses to deliver the deed. Li-Tsing will get nothing from a court either, since **a promise made in consideration of marriage must be in writing to be enforceable.**

7 *Sunrise Cooperative v. Robert Perry*, 1992 Ohio App. LEXIS 3913 (Ohio Ct. App., 1992).

What the Writing Must Contain

Each of the five types of contract described above must be in writing in order to be enforceable. What must the writing contain? It may be a carefully typed contract, using precise legal terminology, or an informal memorandum scrawled on the back of a paper napkin at a business lunch. The writing may consist of more than one document, written at different times, with each document making a piece of the puzzle. But there are some general requirements: **the contract or memorandum**:

- **Must be signed by the defendant, and**
- **Must state with reasonable certainty the name of each party, the subject matter of the agreement, and all of the essential terms and promises.**[8]

Signature

A statute of frauds typically states that the writing must be "signed by the party to be charged therewith," that is, the party who is resisting enforcement of the contract. Throughout this chapter we refer to that person as the defendant, since when these cases go to court, it is the defendant who is disputing the existence of a contract.

Judges define "signature" very broadly. Using a pen to write one's name, though sufficient, is not required. A secretary who stamps an executive's signature on a letter fulfills this requirement. Any other mark or logo placed on a document to indicate acceptance, even an "X," will likely satisfy the statute of frauds. Electronic commerce creates new methods of signing—and new controversies, discussed in the Cyberlaw feature later in the chapter.

Reasonable Certainty

Suppose Garfield and Hayes are having lunch, discussing the sale of Garfield's vacation condominium. They agree on a price and want to make some notation of the agreement even before their lawyers work out a detailed purchase and sales agreement. A perfectly adequate memorandum might say, "Garfield agrees to sell Hayes his condominium at 234 Baron Boulevard, apartment 18, for $350,000 cash, payable on June 18, 2003, and Hayes promises to pay the sum on that day." They should make two copies of their agreement and sign both. By doing that, they will avoid the problem that Drysdale and Hershon encountered when trying to purchase Tulip Hill, described above in *Hershon v. Cannon*. Notice that although Garfield's memo is short, it is *certain* and *complete*. This is critical because problems of vagueness and incompleteness often doom informal memoranda.

Vagueness

Ella Hayden owned valuable commercial property on a highway called Route 9. She wrote a series of letters to her stepson Mark, promising that several of the children, including Mark, would share the property. One letter said: "We four shall fairly divide on the Route 9 property. [sic]" Other letters said: "When the Route 9

[8] Restatement (Second) of Contracts §131.

Plaza is sold you can take a long vacation," and "The property will be sold. You and Dennis shall receive the same amount." Ella Hayden died, without leaving Mark anything. He sued, but got nothing. The court ruled:

> The above passages written by Ms. Hayden do not recite the essential elements of the alleged contract with reasonable certainty. The writings do not state unequivocally or with sufficient particularity the subject matter to which the writings relate, nor do they provide the terms and conditions of alleged promises made which constitute a contract. The alleged oral contract between Ms. Hayden and Mr. Hayden cannot be identified from the passages from Ms. Hayden's letters quoted above when applied to existing facts. In sum, Mr. Hayden's cause of action seeking an interest in the Route 9 property is foreclosed by the statute of frauds.[9]

Incompleteness

During Ronald McCoy's second interview with Spelman Memorial Hospital, the board of directors orally offered him a three-year job as assistant hospital administrator. McCoy accepted. Spelman's CEO, Gene Meyer, sent a letter confirming the offer, which said:

> To reconfirm the offer, it is as follows: 1. We will pay for your moving expenses. 2. I would like you to pursue your Master's Degree at an area program. We will pay 100% tuition reimbursement. 3. Effective September 26 you will be eligible for all benefits. 4. A starting salary of $48,000 annually with reviews and eligibility for increases at 6 months, 12 months and annually thereafter. 5. We will pay for the expenses of 3 trips, if necessary, in order for you to find housing. 6. Vacation will be for 3 weeks a year after one year, however, we do allow for this to be taken earlier. [Signed] Gene Meyer.

Spelman Hospital fired McCoy less than a year after he started work, and McCoy sued. The hospital's letter seems clear, and it is signed by an authorized official. The problem is, it is incomplete. Can you spot the fatal omission? The court did.

> To satisfy the statute of frauds, an employment contract—[or] its memorandum or note—must contain all essential terms, including duration of the employment relationship. Without a statement of duration, an employment at will is created which is terminable at any time by either party with no liability for breach of contract. McCoy's argument that the letter constituted a memorandum of an oral contract fails because the letter does not state an essential element, duration. The letter did not state that Spelman was granting McCoy employment for any term—only that his salary would be reviewed at six months, twelve months and "annually thereafter."[10]

These two lawsuits demonstrate the continuing force of the statute of frauds. In either case, if the promisor had truly wanted to make a binding commitment, he or she could have written the appropriate contract or memorandum in a matter of minutes. Great formality and expense are unnecessary. But the document *must be clear and complete*, or it will fail.

Because some merchants make dozens or even hundreds of oral contracts every year, the drafters of the UCC wanted to make the writing requirement less onerous for the sale of goods, to which we now turn.

---

[9] *Hayden v. Hayden*, Mass. Lawyers Weekly No. 12-299-93 (Middlesex Sup. Ct. 1994).

[10] *McCoy v. Spelman Memorial Hospital*, 845 S.W.2d 727, 1993 Mo. App. LEXIS 105 (Mo. Ct. App. 1993).

Sale of Goods

The UCC requires a writing for the sale of goods worth more than $500. This is the sixth and final contract that must be written, although the Code's requirements are easier to meet than those of the common law. **UCC §2-201,** the statute of frauds section, has three important elements: (1) the basic rule, (2) the merchants' exception, and (3) special circumstances. (To read the UCC online go to **http://www.law.cornell.edu/ucc/ucc.table.html**.)

UCC §2-201(1)—The Basic Rule

A contract for the sale of goods worth more than $500 is not enforceable unless there is some writing, signed by the defendant, indicating that the parties reached an agreement. The key difference between the common law rule and the UCC rule is that the Code does not require all of the terms of the agreement to be in writing. The Code looks for something simpler: an *indication that the parties reached an agreement*. The two things that *are* essential are the signature of the defendant and the quantity of goods being sold. The quantity of goods is required because this is the one term for which there will be no objective evidence. Suppose a short memorandum between textile dealers indicates that Seller will sell to Buyer "grade AA 100% cotton, white athletic socks." If the writing does not state the price, the parties can testify at court about what the market price was at the time of the deal. If the writing says nothing about the delivery date, the court will assume a reasonable delivery date, say, 60 days. But how many socks were to be delivered? 100 pairs or 100,000? The court will have no objective evidence. The quantity must be written. (A basic sale of goods contract appears at **http://www.lectlaw.com/forms/f124.txt**.)

Writing	Result
"Confirming phone conversation today, I will send you 1,000 reams of paper for laser printing, usual quality & price. [Signed,] Seller."	This memorandum satisfies UCC §2-201(1), and the contract may be enforced against the seller. The buyer may testify as to the "usual" quality and price between the two parties, and both sides may rely on normal trade usage.
"Confirming phone conversation today, I will send you best quality paper for laser printing, $3.25 per ream, delivery date next Thursday. [Signed,] Seller."	This memorandum is not enforceable because it states no quantity.

UCC §2-201(2)—The Merchants' Exception

When both parties are "merchants," that is, business people who routinely deal in the goods being sold, the Code will accept an even more informal writing. **Within a reasonable time of making an oral contract, if one merchant sends a written confirmation to the other, and the confirmation is definite enough to bind the *sender herself*, then the merchant who receives the confirmation will *also* be bound by it unless he objects in writing within 10 days.** This exception dramatically changes the rules from the common law. It only applies between two merchants, since the drafters of the Code assumed that experienced merchants are

The UCC gives merchants special leeway—and important responsibilities.

able to take care of themselves in fast-moving negotiations. The critical difference is this: a writing may create a binding contract even when it is not signed by the defendant.

Madge manufactures "beanies," that is, silly caps with plastic propellers on top. Rachel, a retailer, telephones her and they discuss the price of the beanies, shipping time, and other details. Madge then faxes Rachel a memo: "This confirms your order for 2,500 beanies at $12.25 per beanie. Colors: blue, green, black, orange, red. Delivery date: 10 days. [Signed] Madge." Rachel receives the fax, reads it while negotiating with another manufacturer, and throws it in the wastebasket. Rachel buys her beanies elsewhere and Madge sues. Rachel defends, claiming there is no written contract because she, Rachel, never signed anything. Madge wins, under UCC §2-201(2). Both parties were merchants, because they routinely dealt in these goods. Madge signed and sent a confirming memo that could have been used to hold her, Madge, to the deal. When Rachel read it, she was not free to disregard it. Obviously, the intelligent business practice would have been to promptly fax a reply saying, "I disagree. We do not have any deal for beanies." Since Rachel failed to respond within 10 days, Madge has an enforceable contract. In the following case, the merchant's confirmation contained a troubling ambiguity.

GPL TREAMENT, LTD. v. LOUISIANA-PACIFIC CORP.

323 Or. 116, 914 P.2d 682, 1996 Ore. LEXIS 34
Oregon Supreme Court, 1996

Facts: GPL manufactures and sells cedar shakes, which are wooden shingles that many homeowners use for their roofs. Louisiana-Pacific (L-P) often purchased shakes from GPL. Executives of the two companies negotiated over the telephone and allegedly agreed that L-P would buy 88 truckloads of shakes. GPL sent an "Order Confirmation" form that included this language:

> "CONDITIONS OF SALES: GPL LTD.
>
> "All orders accepted subject to strikes, labor troubles, car shortages or other contingencies beyond our power to control. Any freight rate increases, sales, or use taxes is for buyers account.
>
> "SIGN CONFIRMATION COPY AND RETURN BY: _______ THANK YOU"

L-P neither signed nor rejected the form. The company accepted 13 truckloads of shakes but about that time the market price of shakes dropped, and L-P refused to accept any more. GPL sued. A jury awarded the company its lost profits, and the court of appeals affirmed. L-P appealed, arguing that, because GPL's form required the buyer to sign, no acceptance was valid without a signature.

Issue: Was GPL's form sufficient to satisfy the merchants' exception to the statute of frauds?

Excerpts from Judge Van Hoomissen's Decision: GPL's order confirmation forms unambiguously identify the parties to the alleged oral contract and the prices and quantities of the goods being sold. Each form was signed by GPL and sent to L-P, which did not object within 10 days of receipt. GPL's forms would have been "sufficient" against GPL, the sender, if GPL had attempted to rescind the contract because, for example, the price of cedar shakes had gone up substantially. We are unpersuaded by L-P's argument that inclusion of the words "sign confirmation copy and return" on GPL's order confirmation forms indicate any intention on GPL's part that it was not bound until L-P signed and returned copies of the forms indicating its approval. We do not read GPL's order confirmation forms to require L-P to signal its acceptance of the terms and conditions of the parties' alleged oral agreement. Rather, we read the forms to be nothing more than a request for an acknowledgment of the receipt of GPL's forms. Thus read, GPL's "sign and return" clause and its "order accepted by" signature line were merely record keeping devices of GPL. We hold, therefore, that GPL's forms were sufficient to satisfy the merchant's exception of [UCC 2-201(2)].

The decision of the Court of Appeals and the judgment of the [trial] court are affirmed.

Preventive Law

Assume that you work for GPL. What change in the form should you make?

UCC §2-201(3)—Special Circumstances

An oral contract *may* be enforceable, even without a written memorandum, if:

- **The seller is specially manufacturing the goods for the buyer, *or***
- **The defendant admits in court proceedings that there was a contract, *or***
- **The goods have been delivered or they have been paid for.**

In these three special circumstances, a court may enforce an oral contract even without a memorandum.

Specially Manufactured Goods

If a seller, specially manufacturing goods for the buyer, begins work on them before the buyer cancels, and the goods cannot be sold elsewhere, the oral contract is binding. Bernice manufactures solar heating systems. She phones Jason and orders 75 special electrical converter units designed for her heating system, at $150 per unit. Jason begins manufacturing the units, but then Bernice phones again and says she no longer needs them. Bernice is bound by the contract. The goods are being manufactured for her and cannot be sold elsewhere. Jason had already begun work when she attempted to cancel. If the case goes to court, Jason will win.

Admissions in Court

When the defendant admits in court proceedings that the parties made an oral contract, the agreement is binding. The Nebraska Builders Co. claimed that it had entered into a binding contract to buy construction cranes from Industrial Erectors for $450,000. There had been extensive negotiations between Hawkins (Nebraska Builders) and Brennan (Industrial Erectors), and many letters back and forth, but the documents were unclear about what the parties had agreed to. At trial, Brennan first denied that he had agreed to anything. But then came cross-examination:

> Q. At the meeting on October 14th in Chicago you specifically told Mr. Hawkins, did you not, that Industrial Erectors would not perform or supply any cranes on this project unless it received compensation somewhere in the neighborhood of $150,000 more than that set forth in its bid, isn't that correct?
>
> A. I believe it was stated, if the order was to be as per specified with the electrical circuitry and everything else, that there would be an increase to the contract.

Fatal slip. After all, if the purpose of the statute of frauds is to obtain the clearest evidence of what the parties intended, nothing can speak louder than the defendant's admission that they had a contract.[11]

Goods Delivered or Paid For

If the seller has delivered the goods, or the buyer has paid for them, the contract may be enforced even with nothing in writing. Malik orally agrees to sell 500 plastic chairs to University for use in its cafeteria. Malik delivers 300 of the chairs, but then University notifies him that it will not honor the deal. Malik is entitled to payment for the 300 chairs, though not for the other 200. Conversely, if University had sent a check for one-half of the chairs, it would be entitled to 250 chairs.

CYBERLAW

Cheap Cheep sends an e-mail to Pet Chain, offering to sell 1,000 canaries for $25 each. Pet Chain responds electronically, accepting the offer. But when the birds fly up to the door, Pet Chain refuses delivery, and Cheap Cheep sues. The statute of frauds requires this contract to be in writing. Is it? The defendant must have signed the contract or memorandum. Did Pet Chain do so?

The dazzling growth of the Internet has created countless opportunities for electronic commerce, and businesses are taking advantage. Observers estimate that by the turn of the century, U.S. enterprises alone will do tens of billions of dollars worth of buying and selling over the Internet. But what happens to the writing requirement when there is nothing on paper? And without a traditional signature, how can the parties—or a court—be certain that the defendant agreed to the deal? Because electronic commerce is so new, there are no definitive answers to these questions, but we can highlight some of the basic issues and make a few cautious predictions.

First, electronic commerce is efficient and profitable, meaning it is here to stay. Legislatures and courts will adapt. Recall that the UCC itself sprang to life because twentieth-century commercial practices had rendered some common law contract principles obsolete. Business leads, and the law follows.

Second, in disputes over electronic contracts, courts will continue to focus on the questions that have always been at the heart of business litigation: Did the parties intend to make a deal? If so, what were the terms? What evidence is there that the defendant agreed to the deal? The present statute of frauds requires some sort of "signing" to ensure that the defendant committed to the deal. But even at common law, this requirement does not mandate a traditional pen-and-ink signature. As mentioned above, corporate stamps, seals, or other marks indicating an assent to the bargain are sufficient. Today, an "electronic signature" could theoretically mean any of the following: a name typed at the bottom of an e-mail message; a retinal or vocal scan; a name signed by electronic pen on a writing tablet; a magnetic card using a personal identification number; or a public-key digital signature, created by complex encryption software. Legislatures and courts will have some picking and choosing to do, as they decide which of these "signatures" are necessary and which are sufficient.

A new UCC article 2B will appear soon, attempting to resolve many issues raised by new technology. As with all UCC provisions, however, article 2B will be the law nowhere until state legislatures adopt it. The new article will probably include these provisions:

---

[11] *Nebraska Builders Products Co. v. Industrial Erectors*, 239 Neb. 744, 478 N.W.2d 257, 1992 Neb. LEXIS 4 (1992).

- The basic idea of a "writing" will be replaced with that of a "record," a term that includes most electronic messages or transmittals. The concept of "signing" will give way to that of "authenticating," which means placing almost any electronic identifier on the record. Thus an e-mail message (record) that contains some type of electronic identifier (authentication) will probably satisfy the statute of frauds.

- The drafters of the article will probably recommend limiting the UCC statute of frauds to contracts valued at over $20,000. Most Internet purchases are below that level, meaning that in a few years there may be no "record" or "signature" requirement for many contracts.

Congress is also considering national legislation for electronic transactions. And the United Nations Commission on International Trade Law (UNCITRAL) has published a Model Law for consideration by countries throughout the world. With so much legal uncertainty, what should an executive do who wants to take advantage *now* of the Internet's commercial opportunities? Several things.

First, business leaders must learn the basic advantages and risks of electronic commerce. The greatest advantages are speed and convenience: parties 8,000 miles apart can record an agreement in seconds. Risks include lost or intercepted communications, fraudulently altered documents, and difficulties in authenticating the source of an offer or acceptance. Executives would be wise to understand public-key digital signatures. This encryption-based software provides the greatest security in sending and authenticating documents.

Second, a company that engages in a high volume of electronic agreements with a limited number of companies should consider a "master agreement," that is, a paper contract that describes the nature of the electronic transactions and allocates risk. The master agreement can specify what authentication the parties accept, who bears the loss if electronic documents are altered or lost, how the parties decide disputes (for example, with mediation or arbitration), and what limits are placed on liability.

Third, a firm that makes a pricey agreement should *put it in an old-fashioned written, signed contract*. If the deal is big enough to cause serious financial harm, a company should be cautious. Let other firms have the honor of creating electronic contract law through years of costly litigation.

PAROL EVIDENCE

Tyrone agrees to buy Martha's house for $800,000. The contract obligates Tyrone to make a 10 percent down payment immediately and pay the remaining $720,000 in 45 days. As the two parties sign the deal, Tyrone discusses his need for financing. Unfortunately, at the end of 45 days, he has been unable to get a mortgage for the full amount. He claims that the parties orally agreed that he would get his deposit back if he could not obtain financing. But the written agreement says no such thing, and Martha disputes the claim. Who will win? Probably Martha, because of the parol evidence rule. To understand this rule, you need to know two terms. **Parol evidence refers to anything (apart from the written contract itself) that was said, done, or written before the parties signed the agreement or as they signed it.** Martha's conversation with Tyrone about financing the house was parol evidence because it occurred as they were signing the contract. The other important term is **integrated contract,** which means a writing that the parties intend as the final, complete expression of their agreement. Now for the rule.

The parol evidence rule: When two parties make an integrated contract, neither one may use parol evidence to contradict, vary, or add to its terms. Negotiations may last for hours, weeks, or even months. Almost no contract includes everything that the parties said. When parties consider their agreement integrated, any statements they made before or while signing are irrelevant. If a court determines that Martha and Tyrone intended their agreement to be integrated, it will prohibit testimony about Martha's oral promises.

Preventive Law

One way to avoid parol evidence disputes is to include an *integration clause*. That is a statement clearly proclaiming that this writing is the full and final expression of the parties' agreement, and that anything said before signing or while signing is irrelevant. For example, an art dealer may say to a prospective buyer, "Watteau's paintings have increased in value 10 percent every year for the last decade. They're going to continue to climb, I know it." Perhaps the dealer shows the customer an article on Watteau that claims that his paintings are still undervalued. When it is time to sign the contract, the dealer will not want these statements included, since they were meaningless puffery, and he has no intention of being bound by them. The dealer will include an integration clause, stating that the buyer is not relying on any promises, statements, or documents of any kind made or examined during negotiations, and that the written agreement is the complete expression of their contract.

Exception: An Incomplete or Ambiguous Contract

If a court determines that a written contract is incomplete or ambiguous, it will permit parol evidence. As a result, in parol evidence cases, the primary argument is often about whether or not the written contract is clear and complete. Consider the following case:

CHEYENNE MOUNTAIN SCHOOL DISTRICT NO. 12 v. THOMPSON
861 P.2d 711, 1993 Colo. LEXIS 889
Supreme Court of Colorado, 1993

Facts: Dr. Loren Thompson was Superintendent of Schools for the Cheyenne Mountain School District in Colorado. His contract provided for salary of $62,500 and 20 vacation days annually, of which he had to use at least 10 per year. He could accumulate the remaining days to a maximum of 60. The contract said nothing about whether Thompson was entitled to compensation for unused vacation days if he quit. When Thompson resigned from his job, he had accumulated 33 unused vacation days, worth a substantial amount of money. When the school district refused to pay him for the unused time, he sued. The trial court prohibited parol evidence about vacation compensation, stating that the contract was complete and unambiguous. Since the agreement was silent about vacation compensation, Thompson was entitled to none. Thompson appealed and the case reached the Colorado Supreme Court.

Issue: **May Thompson introduce parol evidence about vacation compensation?**

Excerpts from Judge Vollack's Decision: Based on the pleadings and the four corners of the employment contract, the trial court concluded that the contract was not ambiguous and construed it to deny Thompson compensation for his unused vacation. The court relied on the parties' failure to provide explicitly for the additional compensation in the contract; the paragraph fixing Thompson's compensation at $62,500 annually; and paragraph 17, which would have denied fringe benefits to Thompson if he had been terminated without cause by the school board.

We first address whether Thompson's employment contract is ambiguous on the issue of compensation for unused vacation time. To ascertain whether certain provisions of a contract are ambiguous, the language used therein must be examined and construed in harmony with the plain and generally accepted meaning of the words employed and by reference to all the parts and provisions of the agreement and the nature of the transaction which forms its subject matter. A document is ambiguous when it is reasonably susceptible to more than one meaning. Parol evidence is admissible to explain or supplement the terms of an agreement, but not to vary or contradict them. A court should use parol evidence only when the agreement is so ambiguous that the intent of the parties is not clear.

The contract is silent on the specific question of whether Thompson is entitled to compensation for unused vacation at the expiration of his contract. Silence does not by itself necessarily create ambiguity as a matter of law. Silence does create ambiguity, however, when it involves a matter naturally within the scope of the contract. Compensation for unused accrued vacation on expiration of Thompson's contract is a matter naturally within the scope of the contract.

Because Thompson's employment contract is ambiguous on the issue of compensation for unused vacation time, the parties will be free to introduce at trial evidence extrinsic to the four corners of the document. Parol evidence will be admissible to assist the trier of fact in determining whether the parties intended that Thompson be compensated for the unused vacation time.

RIGHT & WRONG

The employer normally drafts the employment contract. Was it ethical for the school district, having created the ambiguity, to litigate Thompson's claim all the way to the state's high court? How else might the parties have settled the dispute? Besides the money potentially owed to Thompson, what was the district worried about? What changes should the district make in future contracts?

Exception: Misrepresentation or Duress

A court will permit parol evidence of misrepresentation or duress. A. O. Smith manufactured and sold grain storage systems for farmers. Alfred and Martha Keller, farmers, bought two systems, which included specially constructed silos and unloading equipment, all designed to keep oxygen away from the stored grain so it would stay fresh. The sales contract included several integration clauses, stating that the Kellers agreed that "any advertisements, brochures, and other written statements which he may have read are not guarantees and he has not relied upon them as such," and that the Kellers "relied on no other promises or conditions" except statements in the contract itself. The systems failed. The grain went bad, cattle developed sores, watery eyes, and other ailments, and some died. The Kellers sued, claiming that A. O. Smith had misrepresented its product. Smith moved to dismiss the case, claiming that the parol evidence rule barred the Kellers from relying on the advertising brochures. The state supreme court found in favor of the Kellers. A claim of misrepresentation is an exception to the parol evidence rule. Such a claim is not really based on the contract itself, but on the discussions of the parties leading up to the contract. The Kellers were permitted to introduce evidence that A. O. Smith misrepresented its storage systems.[12]

Remember, however, that ambiguity and misrepresentation are both exceptions. The basic rule favors the written contract as the full expression of the parties' intentions. More often than not, the written contract is all that a court considers in determining the parties' intentions.

---

[12] The dispositive ruling came from the Colorado Supreme Court, in a case certified to it: *Keller v. A. O. Smith Harvestore Products, Inc.*, 819 P.2d 69, 1991 Colo. LEXIS 703 (Colo. 1991). The case was later remanded on the unrelated issue of prejudgment interest, 1991 U.S. App. LEXIS 31142 (10th Cir. 1991).

CHAPTER CONCLUSION

Some contracts must be in writing to be enforceable, and the writing must be clear and unambiguous. Drafting the contract need not be arduous. The disputes illustrated in this chapter could all have been prevented with a few carefully crafted sentences. It is worth the time and effort to write them.

CHAPTER REVIEW

1. Contracts that must be in writing to be enforceable concern:
   - The sale of any interest in land
   - Agreements that cannot be performed within one year
   - Promises to pay the debt of another
   - Promises made by an executor of an estate
   - Promises made in consideration of marriage; and
   - The sale of goods over $500
2. The writing must be signed by the defendant and must state the name of all parties, the subject matter of the agreement, and all essential terms and promises.
3. A contract or memorandum for the sale of goods may be less complete than those required by the common law.
   - The basic UCC rule requires only a memorandum signed by the defendant, indicating that the parties reached an agreement and specifying the quantity of goods.
   - Between merchants even less is required. If one merchant sends written confirmation of a contract, the merchant who receives the document must object within 10 days or be bound by the writing.
   - In the following special circumstances, no writing may be required: the goods are specially manufactured; one party admits in litigation that there was a contract; or one party pays for part of the goods or delivers some of the goods.
4. When an integrated contract exists, neither party may generally use parol evidence to contradict, vary, or add to its terms. Parol evidence refers to anything (apart from the written contract itself) that was said, done, or written before the parties signed the agreement or as they signed it.

PRACTICE TEST

1. **CPA QUESTION** Able hired Carr to restore Able's antique car for $800. The terms of their oral agreement provided that Carr was to complete the work within 18 months. Actually, the work could be completed within one year. The agreement is:

(a) Unenforceable because it covers services with a value in excess of $500

(b) Unenforceable because it covers a time period in excess of one year

(c) Enforceable because personal service contracts are exempt from the statute of frauds

(d) Enforceable because the work could be completed within one year

2. Richard Griffin and three other men owned a grain company called Bearhouse, Inc., which needed to borrow money. First National Bank was willing to loan $490,000, but insisted that the four men sign personal guaranties on the loan, committing themselves to repaying up to 25 percent of the loan each if Bearhouse defaulted. Bearhouse went bankrupt. The bank was able to collect some of its money from Bearhouse's assets, but it sued Griffin for the balance.

At trial, Griffin wanted to testify that before he signed his guaranty, a bank officer assured him that he would only owe 25 percent of *whatever balance was unpaid,* not 25 percent of the total loan. How will the court decide whether Griffin is entitled to testify about the conversation?

3. Donald Waide had a contracting business. He bought most of his supplies from Paul Bingham's supply center. Waide fell behind on his bills, and Bingham told Waide that he would extend no more credit to him. That same day, Donald's father, Elmer Waide, came to Bingham's store, and said to Bingham that he would "stand good" for any sales to Donald made on credit. Based on Elmer's statement, Bingham again gave Donald credit, and Donald ran up $10,000 in goods before Bingham sued Donald and Elmer. What defense did Elmer make and what was the outcome?

4. James River-Norwalk, Inc. was a paper and textile company that needed a constant supply of wood. James River orally contracted with Gary Futch to procure wood for the company, and Futch did so for several years. Futch actually purchased the wood for his own account and then resold it to James River. Do the parties have an agreement for services or for sale of goods? Why does it matter?

5. When Deana Byers married Steven Byers, she was pregnant with another man's child. Shortly after the marriage Deana gave birth. The marriage lasted only two months, and the couple separated. In divorce proceedings, Deana sought child support. She claimed that Steven had orally promised to support the child if Deana would marry him. Steven claims he never made the promise. Comment on the outcome.

6. CPA QUESTION Two individuals signed a contract that was intended to be their entire agreement. The parol evidence rule will prevent the admission of evidence offered to:

(a) Explain the meaning of an ambiguity in the written contract

(b) Establish that fraud had been committed in the formation of the contract

(c) Prove the existence of a contemporaneous oral agreement modifying the contract

(d) Prove the existence of a subsequent oral agreement modifying the contract

7. Lonnie Hippen moved to Long Island, Kansas, to work in an insurance company owned by Griffiths. After he moved there, Griffiths offered to sell Hippen a house he owned, and Hippen agreed in writing to buy it. He did buy the house and moved in, but two years later Hippen left the insurance company. He then claimed that at the time of the sale, Griffiths had orally promised to buy back his house at the selling price if Hippen should happen to leave the company. Griffiths defended based on the statute of frauds. Hippen argued that the statute of frauds did not apply because the repurchase of the house was essentially part of his employment with Griffiths. Comment.

8. RIGHT & WRONG Jacob Deutsch owned commercial property. He orally agreed to rent it for six years to Budget Rent-A-Car. Budget took possession, began paying monthly rent, and over a period of several months expended about $6,000 in upgrading the property. Deutsch was aware of the repairs. After a year, Deutsch attempted to evict Budget. Budget claimed it had a six-year oral lease, but Deutsch claimed that such a lease was worthless. Please rule. Is it ethical for Deutsch to use the statute of frauds in attempting to defeat the lease? Assume that, as landlord, you had orally agreed to rent premises to a tenant, but then for business reasons preferred not to carry out the deal. Would you evict a tenant if you thought the statute of frauds would enable you to do so? How should you analyze the problem? What values are most important to you?

9. Landlord owned a clothing store and agreed in writing to lease the store's basement to another retailer. The written lease, which both parties signed, (1) described the premises exactly, (2) identified the parties, and (3) stated the monthly rent clearly. But an appeals court held that the lease did not satisfy the statute of frauds. Why not?

10. YOU BE THE JUDGE WRITING PROBLEM Harrison Epperly operated United Brake Systems in Indianapolis, Indiana, and wanted to open a similar store in Nashville. He offered Kenneth Jarrett a job as manager, promising six months severance pay if the store was not profitable in six months, and 49 percent ownership if he managed the new store for 10 years. Jarrett agreed, but the two men never put the deal in writing. Under Jarrett's management, the Nashville branch grew dramatically. After four years of renting space, the company purchased the land and buildings it used. Epperly periodically acknowledged his promise to make Jarrett 49 percent owner of the Nashville branch, and from time to time he mentioned the arrangement to other workers. But after 10 years, Epperly sold United Brake, which had grown to 23 branches, to another company for $11 million. Jarrett sued Epperly for 49 percent of the Nashville branch. The trial court awarded Jarrett $812,000. Epperly appealed. Is Jarrett's contract with Epperly barred by the statute of frauds? **Argument for Epperly:** This alleged contract is unenforceable for two reasons. First, the agreement includes real estate, namely, the valuable land and buildings the company uses. A contract for the sale of any interest in land is unenforceable unless written. Second, the contract could not have been performed within one year. If there was a deal, then by Jarrett's own words the parties intended it to last 10 years. Ten years' work cannot be performed in one year. **Argument for Jarrett:** The agreement had nothing to do with land. Jarrett and Epperly agreed that Mr. Jarrett would obtain a 49 percent ownership of the *Nashville branch.* At the time they made that agreement, the Nashville branch had no real estate. There is no rule saying that a valid contract becomes invalid because a corporation acquires some land. The "not in one year" argument also misses the point. The primary obligation was to open the branch and manage it for six months. If it was not profitable, Mr. Jarrett would immediately receive six months' severance pay, and the contract would be fully performed by both parties in less than a year. Finally, Epperly made a binding commitment and Mr. Jarrett relied. Promissory estoppel prohibits Mr. Epperly from using deceit to profit.

11. Mast Industries and Bazak International were two textile firms. Mast orally offered to sell certain textiles to Bazak for $103,000. Mast promised to send documents confirming the agreement, but never did. Finally, Bazak sent a memorandum to Mast confirming the agreement, describing the goods, and specifying their quantity and the price. Bazak's officer signed the memo. Mast received the memo but never agreed to it in writing. When Mast failed to deliver the goods, Bazak sued. Who won?

Internet Research Problem

Examine the lease at **http://www.kinseylaw.com/freestuff/leaseten/ResLease.html.** Is it important for a lease to be in writing? Who probably drafted the lease, a landlord or a tenant? How can you tell? Should any other provisions be included?

You can find further practice problems in the Online Quiz at http://beatty.westbuslaw.com or in the Study Guide that accompanies this text.

16

REMEDIES

Anybody can wrestle an alligator. But Freddie could wrestle an alligator and a python *simultaneously*. Kira watched Freddie clamp the snake on the gator's back and pin them both to the hard red soil; and when the small roadside crowd screamed approval, she knew she was looking at profit. She immediately signed Freddie to a two-year contract, promising him $500 per week plus room and board. They agreed that Rasslin' Reptiles would start its tour in a month, as soon as Kira had everything ready. Kira then spent $20,000 on a used mobile home and paid $8,000 for two more alligators and another python. Next, she hustled out on the road, drumming up business. Country bars and suburban malls were intrigued by her promotional pitch, though slow with guarantees.

Some suggested they would pay her $500 to put on a show, if and when she arrived. Others promised to rent space to her, allowing her to charge admission. Everything was looking great, and Kira went back to collect her star performer. But Freddie had met the girl of his dreams.

Breaching the Contract

The young woman had read Freddie one of her original sonnets, and the wrestler had fallen in love with poetry. He planned to enroll in State University's creative writing program. Kira hissed and thrashed to no avail, and finally sued. Freddie had certainly breached his contract. **Someone breaches a contract when he fails to perform a duty, without a valid excuse.** When the case gets to trial, a court will declare that Freddie is in breach of the agreement. But what will Kira's *remedy* be? **A remedy is the method a court uses to compensate an injured party.** How will a court help Kira? Should the court force Freddie to return to rasslin'? **An order forcing someone to do something, or refrain from doing something, is an injunction.** Courts seldom grant injunctions to compel a party to perform a job, since that would force two antagonistic people to work together. The court could prohibit Freddie from working elsewhere, and perhaps from going to school. Is that sensible?

The most common remedy, used in the great majority of lawsuits, is money damages. If the court decides to award Kira damages, how much money should she get? Kira may claim that she could have performed 8 to 10 shows a week, at $500 per show, for a total of $4,000 to $5,000 per week. Lost profits are considered ***expectation* damages**. Freddie will respond that all of the "shows" were hypothetical, since not one penny of income had been guaranteed. If Kira is not entitled to lost profits, should she receive the money spent on tour preparations? Such a remedy is called ***reliance* damages**.

How to help an injured party, without unfairly harming the other person, is the focus of remedies. Courts have struggled with remedies for centuries, but we will master them in one chapter. Kira will not obtain an injunction forcing Freddie to wrestle. An order barring him from college is also unlikely. And she will be hard-pressed to prove lost profits, since she had no guarantee of earnings. She should win something for her reliance on Freddie's deal since she spent $28,000 on major purchases. But she may not get that full amount because in losing Freddie's services she also shed the expense of an unproven road tour. The questions and issues created by Kira's broken road tour are typical remedy problems.

RIGHT & WRONG

Though a court may have several alternative remedies available, it is important to note that almost all of them have one thing in common: the focus is on *compensating the injured party, rather than punishing the party in breach.* A court must decide whether to give Kira her lost profits or her expenses, but it will not consider sending Freddie to jail or assessing damages to punish him.

Critics argue that someone who willfully breaches a contract should pay a penalty. In Kira and Freddie's case, the stakes are modest. But what if a retail company deliberately breaches a $50 million deal with a manufacturer. That could cost the manufacturer hundreds or thousands of jobs; it might require closing a plant, and that in turn could damage an entire community. Should a remedy reflect morality? In this chapter we will see very few instances in which a court punishes unethical conduct. In most disputes, judges focus on compensating the injured person, not on punishing the party in breach.

Identifying the "Interest" to Be Protected

The first step that a court takes in choosing a remedy is to decide what interest it is trying to protect. An **interest** is a legal right in something. Someone can have an interest in property, for example, by owning it, or renting it to a tenant, or lending money to buy it. He can have an interest in a *contract* if the agreement gives him some benefit. There are four principal contract interests that a court may seek to protect:

- *Expectation Interest*. This refers to what the injured party reasonably thought she would get from the contract. The goal is to put her in the position she would have been in if both parties had fully performed their obligations.
- *Reliance Interest*. The injured party may be unable to demonstrate expectation damages, perhaps because it is unclear he would have profited. But he may still prove that he *expended money* in reliance on the agreement and that in fairness he should receive compensation for the expenses.
- *Restitution Interest*. The injured party may be unable to show an expectation interest or reliance. But perhaps she has conferred a *benefit* on the other party. Here, the objective is to restore to the injured party the benefit she has provided.
- *Equitable Interest*. In some cases, money damages will not suffice to help the injured party. Something more is needed, such as an order to transfer property to the injured party (specific performance) or an order forcing one party to stop doing something (an injunction).

In this chapter, we look at all four interests.

Expectation Interest

This is the most common remedy that the law provides for a party injured by a breach of contract. **The expectation interest is designed to put the injured party in the position she would have been in had both sides fully performed their obligations.** A court tries to give the injured party the money she would have made from the contract. If accurately computed, this should take into account all the gains she reasonably expected and all the expenses and losses she would have incurred. The injured party should not end up better off than she would have been under the agreement, nor should she suffer serious loss.

William Colby was a former director of the CIA. He wanted to write a book about his 15 years of experiences in Vietnam. He paid James McCarger $5,000 for help in writing an early draft and promised McCarger another $5,000 if the book was published. Then he hired Alexander Burnham to co-write the book. Colby's agent secured a contract with Contemporary Books, which included a $100,000 advance. But Burnham was hopelessly late with the manuscript and Colby missed his publication date. Colby fired Burnham and finished the book without him. Contemporary published *Lost Victory* several years late, and the book flopped, earning no significant revenue. Because the book was so late, Contemporary paid Colby a total of only $17,000. Colby sued Burnham for his lost expectation interest. The court awarded him $23,000, calculated as follows:

	$100,000	advance, the only money Colby was promised
	– 10,000	agent's fee
	= 90,000	fee for the two authors, combined
divided by 2	= 45,000	Colby's fee
	– 5,000	owed to McCarger under the earlier agreement
	= 40,000	Colby's expectation interest
	– 17,000	fee Colby received from Contemporary
	= 23,000	Colby's expectation damages, that is, the amount he would have received had Burnham finished on time[1]

1 *Colby v. Burnham*, 31 Conn. App. 707, 627 A.2d 457, 1993 Conn. App LEXIS 299 (Conn. App. Ct. 1993).

The *Colby* case presented an easy calculation of damages. Other contracts are complex. Courts typically divide the expectation damages into three parts: (1) compensatory (or "direct") damages, which represent harm that flowed directly from the contract's breach; (2) consequential (or "special") damages, which represent harm caused by the injured party's unique situation; and (3) incidental damages, which are minor costs such as storing or returning defective goods, advertising for alternative goods, and so forth. The first two, compensatory and consequential, are the important ones. We look at them one at a time.

Compensatory Damages

If a star walks off, who pays for the damage?

Compensatory damages are the most common monetary awards for the expectation interest. Courts also refer to these as "direct damages." **Compensatory damages are those that flow directly from the contract.** In other words, these are the damages that inevitably result from the breach. Suppose Ace Productions hires Reina to star in its new movie, *Inside Straight*. Ace promises Reina $3 million, providing she shows up June 1 and works until the film is finished. But in late May, Joker Entertainment offers Reina $6 million to star in its new feature, and on June 1 Reina informs Ace that she will not appear. Reina has breached her contract, and Ace should recover compensatory damages.

What are the damages that flow directly from the contract? Ace obviously has to replace Reina. If Ace hires Kween as its star and pays her a fee of $4 million, Ace is entitled to the difference between what it expected to pay ($3 million) and what the breach forced it to pay ($4 million), or $1 million in compensatory damages. Suppose the rest of the cast and crew are idle for two weeks because of the delay in hiring a substitute, and the lost time costs the producers an extra $2.5 million. Reina is also liable for those expenses. Both the new actress and the delay are inevitable.

Reasonable Certainty

The injured party must prove the breach of contract caused damages that can be quantified with reasonable certainty. What if *Inside Straight*, now starring Kween, bombs at the box office. Ace proves that each of Reina's last three movies grossed over $60 million, but *Inside Straight* grossed only $28 million. Is Reina liable for the lost profits? No. Ace cannot prove that it was Reina's absence that caused the film to fare poorly. The script may have been mediocre, or Kween's co-stars dull, or the publicity efforts inadequate. Ace *hoped* to gross over $60 million, but mere hopes create "speculative damages," worth zero. Because Ace cannot demonstrate a quantifiable box office loss directly attributable to Reina, it will get nothing for the disappointing ticket sales.

Consequential Damages

In addition to compensatory damages, the injured party may seek consequential damages or, as they are also known, "special damages." **Consequential damages are those resulting from the unique circumstances of *this injured party*.** The rule concerning this remedy comes from a famous 1854 case, *Hadley v. Baxendale*, which all American law students read. Now it is your turn.

HADLEY v. BAXENDALE
9 Ex. 341, 156 Eng. Rep. 145
Court of Exchequer, 1854

Facts: The Hadleys operated a flour mill in Gloucester. The crankshaft broke, causing the mill to grind to a halt. The Hadleys employed Baxendale to cart the damaged part to a foundry in Greenwich, where a new one could be manufactured. Baxendale promised to make the delivery in one day, but he was late transporting the shaft, and as a result the Hadleys' mill was shut for five extra days. They sued, and the jury awarded damages based in part on their lost profits. Baxendale appealed.

Issue: **Should the defendant be liable for profits lost because of his delay in delivering the shaft?**

Excerpts from Judge Alderson's Decision: Where two parties have made a contract which one of them has broken, the damages which the other party ought to receive in respect of such breach of contract should be such as may fairly and reasonably be considered either arising naturally, i.e. according to the usual course of things, from such breach of contract itself, or such as may reasonably be supposed to have been in the contemplation of both parties, at the time they made the contract, as the probable result of the breach of it. Now, if the special circumstances under which the contract was actually made were communicated by the plaintiffs to the defendants, and thus known to both parties, the damages resulting from the breach of such a contract, which they would reasonably contemplate, would be the amount of injury which would ordinarily follow from a breach of contract under these special circumstances so known and communicated. But, on the other hand, if these special circumstances were wholly unknown to the party breaking the contract, he, at the most, could only be supposed to have had in his contemplation the amount of injury which would arise generally, and in the great multitude of cases not affected by any special circumstances, from such a breach of contract.

Now, in the present case, if we are to apply the principles above laid down, we find that the only circumstances here communicated by the plaintiffs to the defendants at the time the contract was made, were, that the article to be carried was the broken shaft of a mill, and that the plaintiffs were the millers of that mill. But how do these circumstances shew [sic] reasonably that the profits of the mill must be stopped by an unreasonable delay in the delivery of the broken shaft by the carrier to the third person? Suppose the plaintiffs had another shaft in their possession put up or putting up at the time, and that they only wished to send back the broken shaft to the engineer who made it; it is clear that this would be quite consistent with the above circumstances, and yet the unreasonable delay in the delivery would have no effect upon the intermediate profits of the mill. It follows, therefore, that the loss of profits here cannot reasonably be considered such a consequence of the breach of contract as could have been fairly and reasonably contemplated by both the parties when they made this contract.

[The court ordered a new trial, in which the jury would *not* be allowed to consider the plaintiffs' lost profits.]

The rule from *Hadley v. Baxendale* has been unchanged ever since: **the injured party may recover consequential damages only if the breaching party should have foreseen them.**

Let us return briefly to *Inside Straight*. Suppose that, long before shooting began, Ace had sold the film's soundtrack rights to Spinem Sound for $2 million. Spinem believed it would make a profit only if Reina appeared in the film, so it demanded the right to discharge the agreement if Reina dropped out. When Reina quit, Spinem terminated the contract. Now, when Ace sues Reina, it will also seek $2 million in consequential damages for the lost music revenue. If Reina knew about Ace's contract with Spinem when she signed to do the film, she is liable for $2 million. If she never realized she was an essential part of the music contract, she owes nothing for the lost profits. (Because damage calculation can be complex, there are companies that specialize in doing the work on behalf of litigants or other interested parties. One such firm explains its services at **http://www.ei.com/concentrations/damages.htm**.)

Does the plaintiff in the following case deserve consequential damages?

LAWRENCE v. WILL DARRAH & ASSOCIATES, INC.

445 Mich. 1, 516 N.W.2d 43, 1994 Mich. LEXIS 890
Supreme Court of Michigan, 1994

Facts: Benjamin Lawrence purchased a tractor-trailer for long-distance hauling. He obtained an insurance policy covering theft from the Will Darrah agency. The policy noted that Lawrence would use the vehicle to haul freight. Two months after Lawrence bought the truck it was stolen, and he reported its theft to Will Darrah. The tractor-trailer was worth about $19,500.

The insurer delayed paying the claim. After several months, the agency agreed to pay $19,500, but by then Lawrence requested money covering profits he had lost as a result of the insurer's delay. The company refused to pay for lost profits, noting that the policy did not cover them.

Lawrence sued. The adjusters who worked for Will Darrah and handled the claim acknowledged that the company knew that Lawrence, like many of its customers, was a one-truck enterprise, with the vehicle his only source of income. The jury awarded Lawrence $70,800, representing the value of his truck and lost profits. The insurer appealed, claiming that Lawrence was entitled only to the truck's value. The appeals court reversed, stating that lost profits were not a foreseeable consequential damage. Lawrence appealed to the Michigan Supreme Court.

You Be the Judge: Under the insurance contract, were lost profits a foreseeable harm, entitling Lawrence to consequential damages?

Argument for Lawrence: Your honors, Will Darrah knew perfectly well that Mr. Lawrence operated a small trucking outfit with only one truck. The agency knew that without the truck he could make no money. The company understood that the longer it delayed payment, the more money its customer would lose.

Under the rule of *Hadley v. Baxendale*, foreseeability is the key. The insurer here could easily foresee everything that happened after the truck was stolen. The whole purpose of theft insurance is to enable the owner to buy a replacement vehicle quickly and get back on the road. It is true that the contract did not provide for lost profits but that was because the parties assumed the insurance benefits would be paid promptly. There is no rule that says consequential damages must be stated in the contract. The damages must simply be foreseeable, and these were. It's time for Will Darrah to pay.

Argument for Will Darrah: Your honors, we agree that foreseeability is the key to this case. We also think that it is easy to determine what the parties foresaw as Mr. Lawrence's potential losses. *They foresaw the things they listed in the contract.* The contract covered theft, fire, accident, and a few other losses. It did not cover lost profits. Why not? Because Mr. Lawrence chose not to insure lost profits, that's why. He might have insisted on covering lost profits, or numerous other potential problems. He didn't cover them, he didn't pay premiums based on them, he didn't mention them. The parties did not foresee them, and the insurer owes nothing but the value of the truck.

In *Hadley v. Baxendale* the court held that Baxendale could reasonably have assumed that the Hadleys had another shaft. Here, the insurers could reasonably have believed that Lawrence had other means to finance a new truck, and that some delay in paying the benefits would cause no particular harm. If a delay would prove critical, the burden was on Lawrence to inform the insurers of that when they drafted the contract, not after the loss occurred. The Hadleys' failure to notify Baxendale of their special circumstances cost them any claim of consequential damages, and Lawrence's failure should have the same result. We ask you to affirm the judgment of the appeals court.

Incidental Damages

Incidental damages are the relatively minor costs that the injured party suffers when responding to the breach. When Reina, the actress, breaches the film contract, the producers may have to leave the set and fly back to Los Angeles to hire a new actress. The travel cost is an incidental damage. In another setting, suppose Maud, a manufacturer, has produced 5,000 pairs of running shoes for Foot The Bill, a retail chain, but Foot The Bill breaches the agreement and refuses to accept the goods. Maud will have to store the shoes and advertise for alternate buyers. The storage and advertising costs are incidental expenses, and Maud will recover them.

Sale of Goods

Under the Uniform Commercial Code (UCC), remedies for breach of contract in the sale of goods are similar to the general rules discussed throughout this chapter. UCC §§2-703 through 2-715 govern the remedies available to buyers and sellers.[2]

Seller's Remedies

If a buyer breaches a sale of goods contract, the seller generally has at least two remedies. She may resell the goods elsewhere. If she acts in good faith, she will be awarded **the difference between the original contract price and the price she was able to obtain in the open market.** Assume that Maud, the manufacturer, had a contract to sell her shoes to Foot The Bill for $35 per pair and Foot The Bill's breach forces her to sell them on the open market, where she gets only $28 per pair. Maud will win $7 per pair times 5,000 pairs, or $35,000, from Foot The Bill.

Alternatively, the buyer may choose not to resell and settle for the difference between the contract price and the market value of the goods. Maud, in other words, may choose to keep the shoes. If she can prove that their market value is $28 per pair, for example, by showing what other retailers would have paid her for them, she will still get her $7 each, representing the difference between what the contract promised her and what the market would support. In either case, the money represents compensatory damages. Maud is also entitled to incidental damages, such as the storage and advertising expenses described above. But there is one significant difference under the UCC: **Most courts hold that the seller of goods is *not* entitled to consequential damages.** Suppose Maud hired two extra workers to inspect, pack, and ship the shoes for Foot The Bill. Those are consequential damages, but Maud will not recover them because she is the seller and the contract is for the sale of goods.

Buyer's Remedies

The buyer's remedies under the Code are similar to those we have already considered. She typically has two options. First, the buyer can "cover" by purchasing substitute goods. To **cover** means to make a good faith purchase of goods similar to those in the contract. The buyer may then obtain **the difference between the original contract price and her cover price.** Alternatively, if the buyer chooses not to cover, she is entitled to the difference between the original contract price and the market value of the goods.

---

[2] We discuss these remedies in greater detail in Unit 3, on commercial transactions.

Suppose Mary has contracted to buy 1,000 six-foot Christmas trees at $25 per tree from Elmo. The market suddenly rises, and in the spirit of the season Elmo breaches his deal and sells the trees elsewhere. If Mary makes a good faith effort to cover but is forced to pay $40 per tree, she may recover the difference from Elmo, meaning $15 per tree times 1,000 trees, or $15,000. Similarly, if she chooses not to cover but can prove that $40 is now the market value of the trees, she is entitled to her $15 per tree.

Under the UCC, **the buyer *is* entitled to consequential damages provided that the seller could reasonably have foreseen them.** If Mary tells Elmo, when they sign their deal, that she has a dozen contracts to resell the trees, for an average price of $50 per tree, she may recover $25 per tree, representing the difference between her contract price with Elmo and the value of the tree *to her*, based on her other contracts.[3] If she failed to inform Elmo of the other contracts, she would not receive any money based on them. The buyer is also entitled to whatever incidental damages may have accrued.

We turn now to cases where the injured party cannot prove expectation damages.

Reliance Interest

George plans to manufacture and sell silk scarves during the holiday season. In the summer, he contracts with Cecily, the owner of a shopping mall, to rent a high-visibility stall for $100 per day. George then buys hundreds of yards of costly silk and gets to work cutting and sewing. But in September, Cecily refuses to honor the contract. George sues and easily proves Cecily breached a valid contract. But what is his remedy?

George cannot establish an expectation interest in his scarf business. He *hoped* to sell each scarf for a $40 gross profit. He *planned* on making $2,000 per day. But how much would he actually have earned? Enough to retire on? Enough to buy a salami sandwich for lunch? He has no way of proving his profits, and a court cannot give him his expectation interest. Instead, George will ask for *reliance damages*. **The reliance interest is designed to put the injured party in the position he would have been in had the parties never entered into a contract.** This remedy focuses on the time and money the injured party spent performing his part of the agreement.

George should be able to recover reliance damages from Cecily. Assuming he is unable to sell the scarves to a retail store, which is probable since retailers will have made purchases long ago, George should be able to recover the cost of the silk fabric he bought and perhaps something for the hours of labor he spent cutting and sewing. But reliance damages can be difficult to win because *they are harder to quantify*. Courts prefer to compute damages using the numbers provided in a contract. If a contract states a price of $25 per Christmas tree and one party breaches, the arithmetic is easy. Judges become uncomfortable when asked to base damages on vague calculations. How much was George's time worth in making the scarves? How good was his work? How likely were the scarves to sell? If George has a track record in the industry, he will be able to show a market price for his services. Without such a record, his reliance claim becomes a tough battle, as the following case demonstrates.

[3] As we discuss in the section on mitigation, later in the chapter, Mary will get only her consequential damages if she attempts to cover.

SULLIVAN v. OREGON LANDMARK-ONE, LTD.
122 Or. App. 1, 856 P.2d 1043, 1993 Or. App. LEXIS 1193
Oregon Court of Appeals, 1993

Facts: Russell and Jean Sullivan wanted to start a restaurant-bookstore. They had no experience running either kind of business. They spoke with an agent for Oregon Landmark-One about renting space. The Sullivans explained that they were new to these businesses and would be doing a great deal of preparatory work. The parties reached an agreement for the Sullivans to rent space. Landmark-One agreed to make specified improvements to the building at its own expense and then lease the space.

The Sullivans spent countless hours preparing to run their new business. They studied books on operating a restaurant, tested recipes, obtained financing, and purchased equipment. Since they were partly responsible for remodeling, they spoke with designers, reviewed building codes, and negotiated with contractors. Their expenses included equipment and supplies, interest on loans, license and legal fees, and office expenses.

Eight months after the parties signed their lease, Landmark-One told the Sullivans that it would not perform the renovations because the work would cost twice what it had calculated. The Sullivans sadly abandoned their project, sold much of their equipment, paid off their loans—and filed suit.

The Sullivans sought reliance damages. The jury awarded $2,502 for out-of-pocket expenses and $17,230 for the hours of work the Sullivans expended. The trial judge reduced the "hours" damages to $5,998 and awarded a total of $8,500. Landmark-One appealed, claiming that there was no evidence to support the money for the Sullivans' services.

Issue: Are the Sullivans entitled to reliance damages for the hours of work they performed?

Excerpts from Judge Landau's Decision: Reliance interest damages put the injured party in the position he or she would have been in had the contract not been entered. They may include out-of-pocket expenses incurred in reliance on the agreement, particularly those expenses that were necessary to prepare for performance of the contract.

The only evidence of [the plaintiffs'] loss, however, was their own opinion testimony concerning the value of their services. That evidence, by itself, is insufficient to establish that plaintiffs suffered any losses in reliance on the lease agreement. There is no evidence that plaintiffs quit their jobs to spend time preparing to operate the new restaurant. Plaintiffs were, in fact, unemployed when they entered into the agreement. There is, likewise, no evidence concerning the amount of money plaintiffs would have made elsewhere, had they not invested their time in preparing to operate the restaurant. Plaintiffs' opinion testimony concerning the value of their time is just that, and nothing more. It does nothing to establish that they actually would have been paid anything for their time had they not relied on their lease agreement with defendant. They have, in short, failed to produce any evidence of damages that would place them in the position they would have been in had the lease agreement never been executed.

We agree with defendant that the trial court erred in permitting any recovery of hours expended damages. We do not agree, however, that the trial court erred in allowing recovery of the out-of-pocket expenses. There was testimony that plaintiffs informed defendant's property manager that they intended to do substantial work in preparation for performance and that he knew of plaintiffs' efforts. There also was evidence of the amount of expenses plaintiffs actually incurred. That evidence is sufficient to support the award of the out-of-pocket expenses.

[The court affirmed the award of $2,502 in out-of-pocket expenses but denied all other damages.]

RIGHT & WRONG

The Sullivans acted entirely in good faith, and Landmark-One willfully broke the agreement. Was the court right to adjudicate this case without considering those facts? Notice that the court allows the Sullivans nothing for the hours they spent on preparations. This illustrates how reluctant courts are to award damages that are hard to quantify. Is the result fair? How would you have ruled?

Reliance Damages and Promissory Estoppel

In several earlier chapters of this unit, we have seen that a plaintiff may sometimes recover damages based on promissory estoppel even when there is no valid contract. The plaintiff must show that the defendant made a promise knowing that the plaintiff would likely rely on it, that the plaintiff did rely, and that the only way to avoid injustice is to enforce the promise. **In promissory estoppel cases, a court will generally award only *reliance damages*.** It would be unfair to give expectation damages for the full benefit of the bargain when, legally, there has been no bargain.

Costas works as a chef in Philadelphia, making $40,000 per year. Lou greatly enjoys Costas's curried shrimp and wanders back into the kitchen. "Fabulous food," Lou gushes. "You ought to come out to Los Angeles. I'm part owner of a terrific restaurant, with several friends. I'll double your salary, if not more—guaranteed." Costas takes Lou at his word, quits his job, and travels out west—where no job awaits him. Costas cannot sue Lou based on a contract because none exists. Costas gave no consideration, since there was no exchange of bargaining or promises, and in any event, the terms of the offer were too vague to be enforceable. But Lou should have expected Costas to rely on his promise, and the only way to avoid injustice is to give Costas something. He will *probably* receive the value of his reliance on Lou's promise. If Costas is out of work six months, he may get $20,000 (six months of his *former* salary), plus his travel expenses and any additional living costs. But he will not receive any expectation interest, which would have been an annual salary of $80,000 or more.

Costa's predicament and the losing battle fought by the Sullivans demonstrate one fact of contract life: an injured party is much better off if he can prove an expectation interest in a valid contract. Reliance damages will generally be less and may be impossible to recover at all.

Law and Equity

Expectation and reliance interests are considered **legal remedies.** The other interests we will examine are equitable remedies. The difference is largely historical but still may affect a plaintiff's ability to obtain help from a court. As we saw in the textbook's introductory chapter, the common law developed in England, very gradually, over many centuries. English *law* courts gave money damages to the plaintiff, so money damages became known as "legal remedies."

In some cases, an English law court might refuse to hear a case, claiming that it lacked jurisdiction. Or the injured plaintiff might want more than mere money damages. For example, a plaintiff who had a contract to buy land might want the property itself, not money damages. When a law court would not or could not help, a plaintiff often took his case to the Chancellor in London. There was no jury in a Chancery case, but the Chancellor did have broader, more flexible powers than the law judges. The Chancellor's powers came to be known as **equitable remedies**. In the United States today, trial courts of general jurisdiction have the power to grant legal *and* equitable remedies. We now turn to an equitable remedy called restitution.

Restitution Interest

Lillian and Harold Toews signed a contract to sell 1,500 acres of Idaho farmland to Elmer Funk. He was to take possession immediately, but would not receive the deed until he finished paying for the property, in 10 years. This arrangement enabled him to enroll in a government program that would pay him "set-asides" for *not* farming. Funk kept most aspects of his agreement. He did move onto the land and did receive $76,000 from the government for a year's worth of inactivity. (Nice work if you can get it.) The only part of the bargain Funk did not keep was his promise to pay. The Toewses sued. Funk had clearly breached the deal. But what remedy?

The Toewses still owned the land, so they did not need it reconveyed. Funk had no money to pay for the farm, so the Toewses would never get their expectation interest. And the Toewses had expended almost no money based on the deal, so they had no reliance interest. What they had done, though, was to *confer a benefit* on Funk. They had enabled him to obtain $76,000 in government money. The Toewses wanted a return of the benefit they had conferred on Funk, a remedy called restitution. **The restitution interest is designed to return to the injured party a benefit that he has conferred on the other party, which it would be unjust to leave with that person.** The Toewses argued that they had bestowed a $76,000 benefit on Funk and that it made absolutely no sense for him to keep it. The Idaho Court of Appeals agreed. It ruled that the Toewses had a restitutionary interest in the government set-aside money and ordered Funk to pay the money to the Toewses.[4]

Restitution is awarded in two types of cases. First, the law allows restitution when the parties have reached a contract and one of them breaches, as Funk did. In such cases, a court may choose restitution because no other remedy is available or because no other remedy would be as fair. Second, courts may award restitution in cases of quasi-contract, which we examined in earlier chapters. In quasi-contract cases, the parties never made a contract but one side did benefit the other. We consider each kind of restitution interest in turn.

Restitution in Cases of a Valid Contract

Restitution is a common remedy in contracts involving fraud, misrepresentation, mistake, and duress. In these cases, restitution often goes hand-in-hand with **rescission,** which means to "undo" a contract and put the parties where they were before they made the agreement. Courtney sells her favorite sculpture to Adam for $95,000, both parties believing the work to be a valuable original by Barbara Hepworth. Two months later, Adam learns that the sculpture is a mere copy, worth very little. A court will permit Adam to rescind the contract on the ground of mutual mistake. At the same time, Adam is entitled to restitution of the purchase price. Courtney gets the worthless carving and Adam receives his money back.

The following case involved fraud in the sale of a valuable property.

PUTNAM CONSTRUCTION & REALTY CO. v. BYRD
632 So. 2d 961, 1992 Ala. LEXIS 1289
Supreme Court of Alabama, 1992

Facts: Putnam Construction & Realty Co. owned the University Square Business Center (USBC), an office complex with several major tenants, including McDonnell-Douglas, TRW, and the Army Corps of Engineers. William Byrd and some partners (the "buyers") entered into a contract to buy USBC for slightly over $17 million. They financed the purchase with a $16.2 million loan from

[4] *Toews v. Funk*, 129 Idaho 316, 924 P.2d 217, 1994 Idaho App. LEXIS 75 (Idaho Ct. App. 1994).

Northwestern Mutual Life. Northwestern's loan was secured with a mortgage on the USBC, meaning that if the borrowers failed to repay the loan, Northwestern would own the property. Shortly after the sale closed, Byrd learned that several of the major tenants were leaving. The buyers sued Putnam, seeking rescission of the contract and restitution of their money. The trial court found that Putnam (the "sellers") had committed fraud. It rescinded the sales contract, returning the property to the sellers. It ordered the sellers to assume full liability for the mortgage. The trial court did not, however, order restitution of the buyers' expenses, such as the closing costs. The sellers appealed—which proved to be a big mistake.

Issue: **Were the buyers entitled to rescission and/or restitution?**

Excerpts from Justice Steagall's Decision: As early as December 1988, the sellers were aware that the Corps of Engineers was planning to build its own facility and eventually move into it. In spite of this knowledge, the sellers repeatedly told the buyers that the Corps of Engineers had no intention of leaving USBC and that it would probably agree to lease even more space. In May or June 1989, the sellers learned that McDonnell-Douglas was definitely going to move some of its personnel to new facilities, but did not report this information to the buyers. [The court concluded that the sellers had committed fraud.]

With the departure of its major tenants, the USBC does not have the profit potential the buyers bargained for and is, in fact, a liability to them. While the buyers could receive money damages to approximate the value of the lost leases, such an award would be speculative at best and would not abrogate the fact that the buyers now have a property that operates at an increasing loss. The equitable remedy of rescission, while difficult to execute, would more completely provide the buyers with the compensation they seek. The jury was, therefore, correct in determining that rescission is the proper remedy to be applied in this case.

We agree with the trial court that a reconveyance of USBC to the sellers, subject to the mortgage, "constitutes the most equitable result which can be achieved." Accordingly, we affirm those portions of the court's order relating to the reconveyance of USBC subject to the mortgage. We must also recognize, however, that the buyers incurred other substantial out-of-pocket costs to finance a transaction that was born out of the sellers' fraud. After carefully considering the evidence in this case, we conclude that repayment of the following costs is necessary to more equitably restore the buyers to the position they occupied before the sale: $483,006.75 in closing costs on the purchase of USBC; $121,000 in interest payments they paid to the sellers on the $1.5 million note; and the $500,000 in nonrefundable fees the buyers paid to Northwestern to obtain the loan. We remand this case for the trial court to enter a judgment ordering repayment of these costs.

RIGHT & WRONG

Imagine that you are the officer from Putnam in charge of negotiating the sale of USBC to the buyers. You learn that several major tenants are soon to depart and realize that if the buyers learn this they will lower their offer or reject the deal altogether. Your boss insists you tell the buyers that all tenants will be staying. What will you do?

Restitution in Cases of a Quasi-Contract

George Anderson owned a valuable 1936 Plymouth. He took it to Ronald Schwegel's repair shop, and the two orally agreed that Schwegel would restore the car for $6,000. Unfortunately, they never agreed on the word "restore." Anderson thought the term meant complete restoration, including body work and engine repairs, whereas Schwegel intended body work but no engine repairs. After doing some of the work, Schwegel told Anderson that the car needed substantial engine work, and asked for Anderson's permission to allow an engine shop to do it. Anderson agreed, believing the cost was included in the original estimate. When the car was finished and running smoothly, Schwegel demanded $9,800. Anderson refused to pay more than the $6,000 agreed price, and Schwegel sued.

The court held that there was no valid contract between the parties. A contract requires a meeting of the minds. Here, said the court, there was no meeting of the minds on what "restore" included, and hence Schwegel could not recover either his expectation or his reliance interest, since both require an enforceable agreement. Schwegel therefore argued "quasi-contract." In other words, he claimed that even if there had been no valid agreement, he had performed a service for Anderson and that it would be unjust for Anderson to keep it without paying. **A court may award restitution, even in the absence of a contract, where one party has conferred a benefit on another and it would be unjust for the other party to retain the benefit.** The court ruled that Schwegel was entitled to the full $3,800 above and beyond the agreed price because that was the fair market value of the additional work. Anderson had asked for the repairs and now had an auto that was substantially improved. It would be unjust, ruled the court, to permit him to keep that benefit for free.[5]

Preventive Law

Of all the disputes in this unit, the one between Anderson and Schwegel was the easiest to prevent. The parties needed only a few lines on an estimate sheet, listing exactly which repairs would be included for $6,000 and which would not. Indeed, it is remarkable that the parties were able to discuss the matter on several occasions *without* specifying whether Schwegel would repair the engine. Which party is in the better position to ensure a clear agreement? If there was no meeting of the minds, whose fault was it?

Other Equitable Interests

In addition to restitution, the other three equitable powers that concern us are specific performance, injunction, and reformation.

Specific Performance

Leona Claussen owned Iowa farmland. She sold some of it to her sister-in-law, Evelyn Claussen, and, along with the land, granted Evelyn an option to buy additional property at $800 per acre. Evelyn could exercise her option anytime during Leona's lifetime or within six months of Leona's death. When Leona died, Evelyn informed the estate's executor that she was exercising her option. But other relatives wanted the property and the executor refused to sell. Evelyn sued and asked for *specific performance*. She did not want an award of damages; she wanted the land itself. The remedy of specific performance forces the two parties to perform their contract.

A court will award specific performance, ordering the parties to perform the contract, only in cases involving the sale of land or some other asset that is unique. Courts use this equitable remedy when money damages would be inadequate to compensate the injured party. If the subject is unique and irreplaceable,

[5] *Anderson v. Schwegel*, 118 Idaho 362, 796 P.2d 1035, 1990 Idaho App. LEXIS 150 (Idaho Ct. App. 1990).

money damages will not put the injured party in the same position she would have been in had the agreement been kept. So a court will order the seller to convey the rare object and the buyer to pay for it.

Historically, every parcel of land has been regarded as unique, and therefore specific performance is always available in real estate contracts. Evelyn Claussen won specific performance. The Iowa Supreme Court ordered Leona's estate to convey the land to Evelyn, for $800 per acre.[6] Generally speaking, either the seller or the buyer may be granted specific performance. One limitation in land sales is that a buyer may obtain specific performance only if she was ready, willing, and able to purchase the property on time. If Evelyn had lacked the money to buy Leona's property for $800 per acre within the six months' time limit, the court would have declined to order the sale. The following article illustrates a very human mistake that will invoke specific performance.

NEWSWORTHY

Dear Attorney:

We foolishly listed our home for sale last April. Our realty agent did a fine job and found a buyer by mid-May. The closing was supposed to be June 30. My husband and I bought a Florida condo in February and thought we wanted to move there to live year-round. But in May, after we agreed to sell our home, we went to visit our new condo for a week and encountered terrible heat and humidity. We instantly decided we only want to live in Florida in the winter.

The first week of June we notified our real-estate agent and the buyer that we changed our minds and wanted to cancel the sale. We immediately refunded the buyer's $5,000 deposit. But the buyers refused to take the money. A few weeks later we were served with legal papers for a lawsuit involving something called "specific performance." The buyers really want our house. What can we do to get out of this sale?

Answer: Unless there is a loophole in the sales contract, your home buyers will probably win their specific performance lawsuit to force you to honor the agreement and deliver the deed as you promised to do. Disliking the summer heat and humidity in Florida is not a legal reason for breaching your real estate sales contract.[7]

Other unique items, for which a court will order specific performance, include such things as rare works of art, secret formulas, patents, and shares in a closely held corporation. Money damages would be inadequate for all these things since the injured party, even if she got the cash, could not go out and buy a substitute item. By contrast, a contract for a new Jeep Cherokee Laredo is not enforceable by specific performance. If the seller breaches, the buyer is entitled to the difference between the contract price and the market value of the car. The buyer can take his money elsewhere and purchase a virtually identical auto.

Injunction

You move into your new suburban house on two acres of land, and the fresh air is exhilarating. But the wind shifts to the west, and you find yourself thinking of farm animals, especially pigs. It turns out that your next-door neighbor just started an organic bacon ranch, and the first 15 porkers have checked in. You check out the town's zoning code, discover that it is illegal to raise livestock in the neighborhood, and sue. But money damages will not suffice, because you want

6 *In re Estate of Claussen*, 482 N.W.2d 381, 1992 Iowa Sup. LEXIS 52 (Iowa 1992).

7 Robert Bruss, "Compound Mistakes," *Chicago Tribune*, Nov. 5, 1995, p. 7P.

the bouquet to disappear. You seek the equitable remedy of injunction. **An injunction is a court order that requires someone to do something or refrain from doing something.**

The court will order your neighbor immediately to cease and desist raising any pigs or other farm animals on his land. "Cease" means to stop, and "desist" means to refrain from doing it in the future. The injunction will not get you any money, but it will move the pigs out of town, and that was your goal.

Injunctions are usually stated in the negative. Look, for example, at noncompetition agreements, where the seller of a business might promise the buyer that he will not open a competing activity in a specified area. If the seller breaches the agreement by opening an identical enterprise across the street, the court will order him *not* to compete within the specified area. In a copyright violation, a court will order a television producer *not* to make a movie-of-the-week based on a copyrighted script owned by someone else.

In the increasingly litigious world of professional sports, injunctions are commonplace. In the following basketball case, the trial court issued a **preliminary injunction,** that is, an order issued early in a lawsuit prohibiting a party from doing something *during the course of the lawsuit*. The court attempts to protect the interests of the plaintiff immediately. If, after trial, it appears that the plaintiff has been injured and is entitled to an injunction, the trial court will make its order a **permanent injunction**. If it appears that the preliminary injunction should never have been issued, the court will terminate the order. The Web site **http://www.kinseylaw.com/ATTY%20SERV/civil/complaints/injunction.html** provides a sample complaint requesting an injunction.

WORLD VIEW

For several years, political activists in the United Kingdom have campaigned against British Aerospace, Europe's largest defense contractor, seeking to deter the company from manufacturing military weaponry. In response, British Aerospace has obtained injunctions prohibiting demonstrators from its property. The protesters vividly present their view of the political issues and resulting injunctions at **http://dialspace.dial.pipex.com/town/terrace/gdn22/BAe/index.html**. Not surprisingly, the company sees things differently, as it explains on its homepage, **http://www.bae.co.uk/html/if.html**.

BOSTON CELTICS LIMITED PARTNERSHIP v. SHAW

908 F.2d 1041, 1990 U.S. App. LEXIS 12117
United States Court of Appeals for the First Circuit, 1990

Facts: In 1989, Brian Shaw, an American basketball player, signed a two-year contract to play with the Italian team Il Messaggero Roma. The team agreed to pay him $800,000 per year and permitted Shaw to cancel the second year if he returned to the United States to play in the National Basketball Association (NBA).

In January 1990, Shaw signed a five-year contract to play for the Boston Celtics of the NBA. The Celtics agreed to pay him a $450,000 signing bonus and more than $1 million per year. In turn, Shaw agreed to cancel the second year of his contract with Il Messaggero.

In June 1990, Shaw told the Celtics that he had changed his mind and would play for Il Messaggero after all. The Celtics sought immediate arbitration, and the arbitrator ordered Shaw to play for the Boston club. He refused, and the Celtics filed suit. The trial court granted a preliminary injunction, ordering Shaw to rescind the contract with Il Messaggero and ordering him not to play for any team but the Celtics. In other words, like most injunctions, this one was stated in the negative. The court would not order Shaw to play for the Celtics, because that would force two antagonists to work together. But it prohibited him from playing elsewhere. Shaw appealed.

Issue: **Did the trial court improperly issue a preliminary injunction?**

An injunction can halt play as quickly as a referee's whistle.

Excerpts from Chief Judge Breyer's Decision:[8] The only legal question before us is whether the district court acted outside its broad equitable powers when it issued the preliminary injunction. That is to say, did the court improperly answer the four questions judges in this Circuit must ask when deciding whether to issue a preliminary injunction. They are: (1) have the Celtics shown a likelihood of success on the merits? (2) have they shown that failure to issue the injunction would cause the Celtics "irreparable harm?" (3) does the "balance of harms" favor Shaw or the Celtics? and (4) will granting the injunction harm the "public interest?" Our examination of the record has convinced us that the court acted well within the scope of its lawful powers.

To begin with, the Celtics have shown a clear likelihood of success on the merits. The arbitration award is lawful, and courts have authority to enforce lawful arbitration awards. The Celtics also have demonstrated irreparable harm. Without speedy relief, they will likely lose the services of a star athlete next year, and, unless they know fairly soon whether Shaw will, or will not play for them, they will find it difficult to plan intelligently for next season.

Further, the court could reasonably find that the "balance of harms" favors the Celtics. Of course, a preliminary injunction, if ultimately shown wrong on the merits, could cause Shaw harm. He might lose the chance to play in the country, and for the team, that he prefers. [But that harm is offset by his $5 million contract with the Celtics.]

Finally, the court could properly find that issuing a preliminary injunction would not harm the public interest. Indeed, as we have pointed out, the public interest favors court action that effectuates the parties' intent to resolve their disputes informally through arbitration.

Shaw makes an additional argument. He notes that courts will not provide equitable relief such as an injunction to a party with "unclean hands," and he argues that the Celtics' hands are not clean. To support this argument, he has submitted an affidavit saying, in effect, that he signed the contract in a weak moment. His trip to Italy had made him "homesick"; he was "depressed" by what he viewed as undeserved and "negative criticism" in the Italian press; [and] he was not represented by an agent.

Other evidence in the record, however, which Shaw does not deny, shows that he is a college graduate; that he has played under contract with the Celtics before; that the contract is a standard form contract except for a few, fairly simple, rather clear, additions; that he had bargained with the Celtics for an offer that increased from $3.4 million (in December) to $5.4 million (less than one month later); that he looked over the contract before signing it; [and] that he told the American consul in Rome (as he signed it) that he had read and understood it.

Given this state of the record, the district court could easily, and properly, conclude that the Celtics' hands were not "unclean."

Affirmed.

Reformation

The final remedy, and perhaps the least common, is **reformation**, a process in which a court will partially "re-write" a contract. Courts seldom do this, because the whole point of a contract is to enable the parties to control their own futures. But a court may reform a contract if it believes a written agreement includes a simple mistake. Suppose that Roger orally agrees to sell 35 acres to Hannah for $600,000. The parties then draw up a written agreement, accidentally describing

[8] Chief Judge Breyer has since become a Justice of the United States Supreme Court.

the land as including 50 additional acres that neither party considered part of the deal. Roger refuses to sell. Hannah sues for specific performance, but asks the court to *reform* the written contract to reflect the true agreement. Most but not all courts would reform the agreement and enforce it.

A court may also reform a contract to save it. If Natasha sells her advertising business to Joseph and agrees not to open a competing agency in the same city anytime in the next 10 years, a court may decide that it is unfair to force her to wait a decade. It could reform the agreement and permit Natasha to compete, say, three years after the sale. But some courts are reluctant to reform contracts and would throw out the entire noncompetition agreement rather than reform it. Parties should never settle for a contract that is sloppy or overbroad, assuming that a court will later reform errors. They may find themselves stuck with a bargain they dislike or with no contract at all.

Special Issues of Damages

Finally, we consider some special issues of damages, beginning with a party's obligation to minimize its losses.

Mitigation of Damages

A party injured by a breach of contract may not recover for damages that he could have avoided with reasonable efforts. In other words, when one party perceives that the other has breached or will breach the contract, the injured party must try to prevent unnecessary loss. A party is expected to **mitigate** his damages, that is, to keep damages as low as he reasonably can.

Malcolm agrees to rent space in his mall to Zena, for a major department store. As part of the lease, Malcolm agrees to redesign the interior to meet her specifications. After Malcolm has spent $20,000 in architect and design fees, Zena informs Malcolm that she is renting other space and will not occupy his mall. Malcolm nonetheless continues the renovation work, spending an additional $50,000 on materials and labor. Malcolm will recover the lost rental payments and the $20,000 expended in reliance on the deal. He will *not* recover the extra $50,000. He should have stopped work when he learned of Zena's breach.

Mitigation and the Sale of Goods

The UCC emphasizes the importance of mitigation. As mentioned earlier in the chapter, when a seller breaches, a buyer has the option of obtaining cover. If the buyer fails to cover, she will generally be *denied* consequential damages. Mary has a contract to buy 1,000 Christmas trees from Elmo for $25 each. The market value is $40 per tree, but Mary has arranged various contracts to resell the tress at $50 each. If Elmo breaches, Mary should try to cover. If she makes no effort to cover, the court will award her $15 per tree, representing the difference between the contract price and market value, but will not award her the consequential damages based on her own expectation of $50 per tree.

Nominal Damages

Nominal damages are a token sum, such as one dollar, given to a plaintiff who demonstrates that the defendant breached the contract but cannot prove damages. A school board unfairly fires Gemma, a teacher. If she obtains a teaching job at a better school for identical pay the very next day, she probably can show no damages at all. Nonetheless, the school wrongfully terminated her, and a court may award nominal damages.

Liquidated Damages

It can be difficult or even impossible to prove how much damage the injured party has suffered. So lawyers and executives negotiating a deal may include in the contract a **liquidated damages clause, a provision stating in advance how much a party must pay if it breaches.** Assume that Laurie has hired Bruce to build a five-unit apartment building for $800,000. Bruce promises to complete construction by May 15. Laurie insists on a liquidated damages clause providing that if Bruce finishes late, Laurie's final price is reduced by $3,000 for each week of delay. Bruce finishes the apartment building June 30, and Laurie reduces her payment by $18,000. Is that fair? The answer depends on two factors: **A court will generally enforce a liquidated damages clause if (1) at the time of creating the contract it was very difficult to estimate actual damages, *and* (2) the liquidated amount is reasonable.** In any other case, the liquidated damage will be considered a **penalty** and will prove unenforceable.

We will apply the two factors to Laurie's case. When the parties made their agreement, would it have been difficult to estimate actual damages caused by delay? Yes. Laurie could not prove that all five units would have been occupied or how much rent the tenants would have agreed to pay. Was the $3,000 per week reasonable? Probably. To finance an $800,000 building, Laurie will have to pay at least $6,000 interest per month. She must also pay taxes on the land and may have other expenses. Laurie does not have to prove that every penny of the liquidated damages clause is justified, but only that the figure is reasonable. A court will probably enforce her liquidated damages clause.

On the other hand, suppose Laurie's clause demanded $3,000 per day. There is no basis for such a figure, and a court will declare it a *penalty clause*, and refuse to enforce it. Laurie will be back to square one, forced to prove in court any damages she claims to have suffered from Bruce's delay.

Note that merely using the phrase "liquidated damages clause" does not make the provision enforceable. As the following case illustrates, when there is a dispute, a court will decide whether the clause is a valid liquidated damages clause or an unenforceable penalty clause.

Lake Ridge Academy v. Carney

66 Ohio St. 3d 376, 613 N.E.2d 183, 1993 Ohio LEXIS 1210
Supreme Court of Ohio, 1993

Facts: In March, Mr. Carney reserved a spot in the fourth grade class at Lake Ridge Academy for his son, Michael. He paid a $630 deposit and agreed in writing to pay the balance of the tuition, $5,610, later that year. The contract permitted Carney to cancel the agreement and withdraw his son with no further obligation provided he did so before August 1. If he failed to notify the school before that date, he became liable for the full tuition.

Carney wrote a letter notifying Lake Ridge that Michael would not attend. He dated the letter August 1, mailed it August 7, and the school received it August 14. Lake Ridge demanded its full tuition, Carney refused, and the school sued. One of the disputed issues was whether the liquidated damages clause was a penalty. The trial court found for Carney, but the court of appeals reversed, finding that the clause was valid. Carney appealed to the state's highest court.

Issue: **Was the liquidated damages clause enforceable?**

Excerpts from Judge Wright's Descision: Contracting parties may provide in advance for damages to be paid in the event of a breach as long as the provision does not disregard the principle of compensation. Determining whether stipulated damages are punitive or liquidated is not always easy. It is necessary to look to the whole instrument, its subject-matter, the ease or difficulty of measuring the breach in damages, and the amount of the stipulated sum, not only as compared with the value of the subject of the contract, but in proportion to the probable consequences of the breach.

We conclude that the damages in this case are liquidated damages [and thus enforceable].

When Carney and Lake Ridge entered into their contract the damages that Lake Ridge might suffer as a result of a breach by Carney were "uncertain as to amount and difficult of proof." Lake Ridge goes through a long budgeting process which begins each year in January and ends in the fall. The tuition money paid by students is pooled and goes towards staff salaries and benefits, department budgets, student materials, maintenance, improvements, and utilities. Trial testimony reveals that the school budget process is often an uncertain science; it is quite clear that Lake Ridge would be unable to calculate and prove the precise damages caused by the loss of one student's tuition.

Nor is the contract as a whole unreasonable. The headmaster testified that August 1 was chosen as the day before which notice of cancellation had to be given simply because the school had to know in order to meet its financial commitments. Carney had almost five months after he signed the contract to decide whether to cancel it. Because Lake Ridge's financial commitments became more firm as the school year approached, it is reasonable to assume that by August 1 the school was relying on Carney's full tuition payment.

NEWSWORTHY

For the latest in liquidated damage developments, watch cable television news—or simply your cable television *bill.* To obtain this service, consumers sign an agreement that often includes an automatic fee of $5 or more for any bills paid late. Cable companies claim that the charges are reasonable liquidated damages, but consumer advocates—and now some courts—consider the fees to be illegal penalties, out of all proportion to the minor damage caused when a customer fails to pay on time. In a class action in Baltimore, the judge declared that, in setting its $5 late fee, the cable company had been "haphazard, cavalier, careless and presumptuous." He ordered the cable provider to repay customers $5.4 million for the exorbitant charges and to reduce future late fees to a maximum of 50 cents. Consumers won similar sums in a class action in Washington, D.C., and lawsuits aimed at the late fees are pending in many other states.

Punitive Damages

We have seen that courts devote little time to morality when granting remedies for breach of contract. In most cases, a party who deliberately breaks its promise is treated the same as one who attempts but fails to honor its bargain. Occasionally, though, a court *will* take into account the question of what is morally right and order a breaching party to pay extra money damages because his conduct was socially intolerable.

Punitive damages are designed not to compensate the injured party but to punish the breaching party. The courts grant punitive damages *in addition* to the usual expectation, reliance, or restitution monies. The goal is to prevent the unethical party from repeating its offense and to deter others in society from similar behavior. Bear in mind that these are exceptional cases. In a contract case, courts will consider a punitive damages claim only when the breach of contract involves conduct such as fraud or bad faith.

How much money may a jury award to penalize a defendant? That question has produced a series of hotly contested cases, but no definitive answer. The United States Supreme Court has given some guidance on the issue in a case arising from Alabama, a state that has historically allowed relatively high punitive awards. After Ira Gore purchased a new BMW automobile, he discovered that the car had been repainted. When he sued, BMW admitted that it never told customers about minor predelivery repairs. The company had sold about 1,000 repainted cars nationwide. The jury concluded that BMW had engaged in gross, malicious fraud and awarded Gore compensatory damages of $4,000 and punitive damages of $4 million. The Alabama Supreme Court reduced the award to $2 million, but the United States Supreme Court said that sum was still too high. The justices declared that **in awarding punitive damages, a court must consider three "guideposts":**

- The reprehensibility of the defendant's conduct
- The ratio between the harm suffered and the award; and
- The difference between the punitive award and any civil or criminal penalties used in similar cases.

The Supreme Court concluded that BMW had shown no evil intent and that Gore's harm had been merely economic, not physical. The Court also found that the ratio between punitive and compensatory damages—500 to 1—was excessive, although it declined to set a proper ratio. On remand, the Alabama Supreme Court reduced the punitive damages award to $50,000.[9]

In the following case, the same two courts again wrangled over a large punitive award.

LIFE INSURANCE COMPANY OF GEORGIA v. DAISEY L. JOHNSON

701 So.2d 524, 1997 Ala. LEXIS 368
Alabama Supreme Court, 1997

Facts: Daisey L. Johnson, an 84-year-old woman with a third grade education, had spent her life as a domestic worker. Over a 25-year period, she purchased various insurance policies from Life Insurance Company of Georgia. The company's agent, Barbara Holt, came to Johnson's house monthly to collect premiums. On one visit, she recommended that Johnson purchase a "Medicare supplement policy," explaining that if Ms. Johnson were hospitalized, the policy would pay for bills not covered by Medicare. What Holt did not explain was that Ms. Johnson was already fully protected since she was enrolled in *Medicaid*, a separate government program for poor people. Before long, Ms. Johnson was paying about $103 per month for the new policy, almost one-third of her small fixed income.

Johnson sued Life of Georgia, alleging that the company had fraudulently sold her a worthless policy. The jury awarded her $250,000 in compensatory damages and $15 million in punitive damages. The Alabama Supreme Court lowered the punitive award to $5 million. The United States Supreme Court ordered the Alabama Supreme Court to reconsider whether the $5 million was reasonable in light of the three newly established "guideposts" from *BMW v. Gore*.

---

[9] *BMW of North America, Inc. v. Gore*, 517 U.S. 559, 116 S. Ct. 1589, 1996 U.S. LEXIS 3390 (1996).

Issue: Was the award of $5 million punitive damages reasonable?

Excerpts from Justice Shores's Decision: [A] former Life of Georgia agent, James Russell Clark, testified that his training could be summed up in three words: "Get the money." Life of Georgia's corporate officers testified during the plaintiff's presentation of her case that Life of Georgia had done nothing to try to prevent the sale of Medicare supplement policies to unqualified persons even though in 1992 Life of Georgia had been faced with trial in Mobile County and had experienced an adverse verdict of $1 million. The company continued its history of noncompliance, giving rise to the conclusion that even a million-dollar sanction against the company was not sufficient to deter its misconduct.

Applying the first guidepost, the reprehensibility of the defendant's conduct, we conclude that the evidence was sufficient to permit the jury to conclude that Life of Georgia's egregiously improper conduct was sufficiently reprehensible to give rise to tort liability and was sufficient to establish the high degree of culpability that warrants a substantial punitive damages award. Life of Georgia was aware that its actions or omissions were causing harm, but it did not change its policy. It consciously disregarded the rights of old, indigent, and uneducated citizens of Alabama.

[The court then focused on the second guidepost.] Unlike Dr. Gore and other BMW purchasers, who the United States Supreme Court concluded were not threatened with any additional potential harm by BMW's nondisclosure policy, the plaintiff here proved that there was a sizable group of Alabama citizens who were put at risk by the defendant's wrongful conduct. She proved that over 116,000 Alabamians have both Medicare and Medicaid; given the Medicare and Medicaid eligibility standards, we can conclude that these Alabamians are both old and poor.

Applying the Supreme Court's second guidepost, we conclude that following the remittitur of punitive damages to $3 million, as we order today, the ratio of exemplary damages to the compensatory damages of $250,000 will bear a reasonable relationship, given the facts in this case.

[As to the third guidepost, the court concluded that Alabama law provided no civil or criminal penalties to compare to this award. The court lowered the punitive award to $3 million, and affirmed.]

CHAPTER CONCLUSION

The powers of a court are broad and flexible and may suffice to give an injured party what it deserves. But problems of proof and the uncertainty of remedies demonstrate that the best solution is a carefully drafted contract and socially responsible behavior.

Chapter Review

1. Someone breaches a contract when he fails to perform a duty, without a valid excuse.
2. A remedy is the method a court uses to compensate an injured party.
3. An interest is a legal right in something, such as a contract. The first step that a court takes in choosing a remedy is to decide what interest it is protecting.

4. The expectation interest puts the injured party in the position she would have been in had both sides fully performed. It has three components:
   (a) Compensatory damages, which flow directly from the contract.
   (b) Consequential damages, which result from the unique circumstances of the particular injured party. The injured party may recover consequential damages only if the breaching party should have foreseen them.
   (c) Incidental damages, which are the minor costs an injured party incurs responding to a breach.
5. The reliance interest puts the injured party in the position he would have been in had the parties never entered into a contract. It focuses on the time and money that the injured party spent performing his part of the agreement. If there was no valid contract, a court might still award reliance damages under a theory of promissory estoppel.
6. The restitution interest returns to the injured party a benefit that she has conferred on the other party, which it would be unjust to leave with that person. Restitution can be awarded in the case of a contract created, for example, by fraud, or in a case of quasi-contract, where the parties never created a binding agreement.
7. Specific performance, ordered only in cases of land or a unique asset, requires both parties to perform the contract.
8. An injunction is a court order that requires someone to do something or refrain from doing something.
9. Reformation is the process by which a court will—occasionally— rewrite a contract to ensure that it accurately reflects the parties' agreement and/or to maintain the contract's viability.
10. The duty to mitigate means that a party injured by a breach of contract may not recover for damages that he could have avoided with reasonable efforts.
11. Nominal damages are a token sum, such as one dollar, given to an injured plaintiff who cannot prove damages.
12. A liquidated damages clause will be enforced if and only if, at the time of creating the contract, it was very difficult to estimate actual damages *and* the liquidated amount is reasonable.
13. Punitive damages are designed not to compensate the injured party but to punish the breaching party.

PRACTICE TEST

1. Mr. and Ms. Beard contracted for S/E Joint Venture to build a house on property it owned, and then sell the completed house to the Beards for $785,000. S/E was late with construction and ultimately never finished the house or conveyed anything to the Beards, who sued. Evidence at trial demonstrated that S/E had clearly breached the contract and that the Beards had spent about $32,000 in rent because of the delay. There was testimony that the market value of the house as promised would have been about $100,000 more than the contract price, but this point was not clearly established because the trial judge considered it irrelevant. The judge awarded only the rental payments. Both sides appealed. Is the market value of the house, as it should have been built, relevant? How much money are the Beards entitled to?

2. Lewis signed a contract for the rights to all timber located on Nine Mile Mine. He agreed to pay $70 per thousand board feet ($70/mbf). As he began work, Nine Mile became convinced that Lewis lacked sufficient equipment to do the job well and forbade him to enter the land. Lewis sued. Nine Mile moved for summary judgment. The mine offered proof that the market value of the timber was exactly $70/mbf, and Lewis had no evidence to contradict Nine Mile. The evidence about market value proved decisive. Why? Please rule on the summary judgment motion.

3. Twin Creeks Entertainment signed a deal with U.S. JVC Corp. in which JVC would buy 60,000 feature film videocassettes from Twin Creeks over a three-year period. JVC intended to distribute the cassettes nationwide. Relying on its deal with JVC, Twin Creeks signed an agreement with Paramount Pictures, agreeing to purchase a minimum of $600,000 worth of Paramount cassettes over a two-year period. JVC breached its deal with Twin Creeks and refused to accept the cassettes it had agreed upon. Twin Creeks sued and claimed, among other damages, the money it owed to Paramount. JVC moved to dismiss the claim based on the Paramount contract, on the ground that Twin Creeks, the seller of goods, was not entitled to such damages. What kind of damages is Twin Creeks seeking? Please rule on the motion to dismiss.

4. Bingo is emerging as a rock star. His last five concerts have all sold out. Lucia signs a deal with Bingo to perform two concerts in one evening in Big City, for a fee of $50,000 for both shows. Lucia then rents the Auditorium for that evening, guaranteeing to pay $50,000. Bingo promptly breaks the deal before any tickets are sold. Lucia sues, pointing out that the Auditorium seats 3,000 and she anticipated selling all tickets for an average of $40 each, for a total gross of $120,000. How much will Lucia recover, if anything?

5. Racicky was in the process of buying 320 acres of ranch land. While that sale was being negotiated, Racicky signed a contract to sell the land to Simon. Simon paid $144,000, the full price of the land. But Racicky then went bankrupt, before he could complete the *purchase* of the land, let alone its sale. Which of these remedies should Simon seek: expectation, restitution, specific performance, or reformation?

6. Ambrose hires Bierce for $25,000 to supervise the production of Ambrose's crop, but then breaks the contract by firing Bierce at the beginning of the season. A nearby grower offers Bierce $23,000 for the same growing season, but Bierce refuses to take such a pay cut. He stays home and sues Ambrose. How much money, if any, will Bierce recover from Ambrose, and why?

7. Parkinson was injured in an auto accident by a driver who had no insurance. Parkinson filed a claim with her insurer, Liberty Mutual, for $2,000 under her "uninsured motorist" coverage. Liberty Mutual told her that if she sought that money, her premiums would go "sky high," so Parkinson dropped the claim. Later, after she had spoken with an attorney, Parkinson sued. What additional claim was her attorney likely to make?

8. **CPA QUESTION** Master Mfg., Inc. contracted with Accur Computer Repair Corp. to maintain Master's computer system. Master's manufacturing process depends on its computer system operating properly at all times. A liquidated damages clause in the contract provided that Accur would pay $1,000 to Master for each day that Accur was late responding to a service request. On January 12, Accur was notified that Master's computer system had failed. Accur did not respond to Master's service request until January 15. If Master sues Accur under the liquidated damage provision of the contract, Master will:

(a) Win, unless the liquidated damages provision is determined to be a penalty

(b) Win, because under all circumstances liquidated damage provisions are enforceable

(c) Lose, because Accur's breach was not material

(d) Lose, because liquidated damage provisions violate public policy

9. **CPA QUESTION** Kaye contracted to sell Hodges a building for $310,000. The contract required Hodges to pay the entire amount at closing. Kaye refused to close the sale of the building. Hodges sued Kaye. To what relief is Hodges entitled?

(a) Punitive damages and compensatory damages

(b) Specific performance and compensatory damages

(c) Consequential damages or punitive damages

(d) Compensatory damages or specific performance

10. **YOU BE THE JUDGE WRITING PROBLEM** John and Susan Verba sold a Vermont lakeshore lot to Shane and Deborah Rancourt for $115,000. The Rancourts intended to build a house on the property, but after preparing the land for construction, they learned that a wetland protection law prevented building near the

lake. They sued, seeking rescission of the contract. The trial court concluded that the parties had reached their agreement under a "mutual, but innocent, misunderstanding." The trial judge gave the Verbas a choice: they could rescind the contract and refund the purchase price, or they could give the Rancourts $55,000, the difference between the sales price and the actual market value of the land. The Rancourts appealed. Were the Rancourts entitled to rescission of the contract? **Argument for the Rancourts:** When the parties have made a mutual mistake about an important factual issue, either party is entitled to rescind the contract. The land is of no use to us and we want our money back. **Argument for the Verbas:** Both sides were acting in good faith and both sides made an honest mistake. We are willing to acknowledge that the land is worth somewhat less than we all thought, and we are willing to refund $55,000. The buyers shouldn't complain—they are getting the property at about half the original price, and the error was as much their fault as ours.

11. RIGHT & WRONG The National Football League owns the copyright to the broadcasts of its games. It licenses local television stations to telecast certain games and maintains a "blackout rule," which prohibits stations from broadcasting home games that are not sold out 72 hours before the game starts. Certain home games of the Cleveland Browns team were not sold out, and the NFL blocked local broadcast. But several bars in the Cleveland area were able to pick up the game's signal by using special antennas. The NFL wanted the bars to stop showing the games. What did it do? Was it unethical of the bars to broadcast the games that they were able to pick up? Apart from the NFL's legal rights, do you think it had the moral right to stop the bars from broadcasting the games?

Internet Research Problem

You represent a group of neighborhood residents in a large city who are protesting construction of a skyscraper that will violate building height limitations. Draft a complaint, requesting an appropriate injunction. You may use the sample injunction complaint found at **http://www.kinseylaw.com/ATTY%20SERV/civil/complaints/injunction.html**.

You can find further practice problems in the Online Quiz at http://beatty.westbuslaw.com or in the Study Guide that accompanies this text.

Glossary

A

Accelerated depreciation method. A depreciation method that provides for a high depreciation expense in the first year of use of an asset and a gradually declining expense thereafter. (396)

Account. The form used to record additions and deductions for each individual asset, liability, owner's equity, revenue, and expense. (46)

Account form. The form of balance sheet with the assets section presented on the left-hand side and the liabilities and owner's equity sections presented on the right-hand side. (18, 245)

Account payable. A liability created by a purchase made on credit. (13)

Account receivable. A claim against a customer for services rendered or goods sold on credit. (14, 314)

Accounting. The process of identifying, measuring, and communicating economic information to permit informed judgments and decisions by users of the information. (6)

Accounting cycle. The sequence of basic accounting procedures during a fiscal period. (149)

Accounting equation. The expression of the relationship between assets, liabilities, and owner's equity; it is most commonly stated as Assets = Liabilities + Owner's Equity. (11)

Accounting period concept. An accounting principle that requires accounting reports be prepared at periodic intervals. (100)

Accounting system. The methods and procedures used by a business to record and report financial data for use by management and external users. (180)

Accounts payable subsidiary ledger. The subsidiary ledger containing the individual accounts with suppliers (creditors). (187)

Accounts receivable subsidiary ledger. The subsidiary ledger containing the individual accounts with customers (debtors). (187)

Accounts receivable turnover. The relationship between credit sales and accounts receivable. This ratio is computed by dividing net sales on account by the average net accounts receivable. (327, 650)

Accrual basis. A basis of accounting in which revenues are recognized in the period earned, and expenses are recognized in the period incurred in the process of generating revenues. (100)

Accrued expenses. Expenses that have been incurred but not paid. Sometimes called accrued liabilities. (102)

Accrued revenues. Revenues that have been earned but not collected. Sometimes called accrued assets. (102)

Accumulated depreciation account. The contra asset account used to accumulate the depreciation recognized to date on plant assets. (109)

Acid-test ratio. A ratio that measures the "instant" debt-paying ability of a company. Also known as quick ratio. (649)

Activity base. The measure used to allocate factory overhead. Also known as allocation base, or activity driver. (696)

Activity drivers. An activity that is thought to cause a cost to be incurred. Used in analyzing and classifying cost behavior. (770)

Activity-based costing. A cost allocation method that identifies activities causing the incurrence of costs and allocates these costs to products (or other cost objects) based upon activity bases (drivers). (697, 957)

Adjusted trial balance. The trial balance which is prepared after all the adjusting entries have been posted. Used to verify the equality of the total debit balances and total credit balances before preparing the financial statements. (113)

Adjusting entries. Entries required at the end of an accounting period to bring the ledger up to date. (101)

Adjusting process. The process of updating the accounts at the end of a period. (101)

Administrative expenses (general expenses). Expenses incurred in the administration or general operations of a business. (242)

Aging the receivables. The process of analyzing the accounts receivable and classifying them according to various age groupings, with the due date being the base point for determining age. (320)

Allowance method. A method of accounting for uncollectible receivables, whereby advance provision for the uncollectibles is made. (317)

Amortization. The periodic expense attributed to the decline in usefulness of an intangible asset. (407)

Annuity. A series of equal cash flows at fixed intervals. (542, 989)

Appropriation. The amount of a corporation's retained earnings that has been restricted and therefore is not available for distribution to shareholders as dividends. (518)

Assets. Physical items (tangible) or rights (intangible) that have value and that are owned by the business entity. (11, 46)

Available-for-sale security. A debt or equity security that is not classified as either a held-to-maturity or a trading security. (520)

Average cost method. The method of inventory costing that is based on the assumption that costs should be charged against revenue in accordance with the weighted average unit costs of the items sold. (361)

Average rate of return. A method of evaluating capital investment proposals that focuses on the expected profitability of the investment. (985)

B

Balanced scorecard. A set of financial and nonfinancial measures that reflect multiple performance dimensions of a business. (914)

Balance of the account. The amount of difference between the debits and the credits that have been entered into an account. (49)

Balance sheet. A financial statement listing the assets, liabilities, and owner's equity of a business entity as of a specific date. (16)

Bank reconciliation. The analysis that details the items responsible for the difference between the cash balance reported in the bank statement and the balance of the cash account in the ledger. (289)

Betterment. An expenditure that increases operating efficiency or capacity for the remaining useful life of a plant asset. (398)

Bond. A form of interest-bearing note employed by corporations to borrow on a long-term basis. (550)

Bond indenture. The contract between a corporation issuing bonds and the bondholders. (552)

Book value. The amount at which an asset or liability is reported on the balance sheet. Also called basis or carrying value. (395)

Book value of a fixed asset. The difference between the balance of a fixed asset account and its related accumulated depreciation account. (110)

Boot. The cash balance owed the seller when an old asset is traded for a new asset. (402)

Bottleneck. An important consideration influencing production volumes and prices. Occurs at the point in the process where the demand for the company's product exceeds the ability to produce the product. (958)

Break-even point. The level of business operations at which revenues and expired costs are equal. (779)

Budget. An outline of a business's future plans, stated in financial terms. A budget is used to plan and control operational departments and divisions. (818)

Budget performance report. A report comparing actual results with budget figures. (869)

Business. An organization in which basic resources (inputs), such as materials and labor, are assembled and processed to provide goods or services (outputs) to customers. (2)

Business entity concept. The concept that accounting applies to individual economic units and that each unit is separate from the persons who supply its assets. (10)

Business stakeholder. A person or entity that has an interest in the economic performance of the business. (4)

Business transaction. The occurrence of an economic event or a condition that must be recorded in the accounting records. (13)

C

Capital expenditures. Costs that add to the usefulness of assets for more than one accounting period. (398)

Capital expenditures budget. The budget summarizing future plans for acquiring fixed assets. (835)

Capital investment analysis. The process by which management plans, evaluates, and controls long-term capital investments involving property, plant, and equipment. (984)

Capital leases. Leases that treat the leased assets as purchased assets in the accounts. (404)

Capital rationing. The process by which management allocates available investment funds among competing capital investment proposals. (996)

Carrying amount. The amount at which a long-term investment or a long-term liability is reported on the balance sheet. (561)

Cash. Coins, currency (paper money), checks, money orders, and money on deposit that is available for unrestricted withdrawal from banks or other financial institutions. (280)

Cash basis. A basis of accounting in which revenue is recognized in the period cash is received, and expenses are recognized in the period cash is paid. (100)

Cash budget. One of the most important elements of the budgeted balance sheet. It presents the expected receipts (inflows) and payments (outflows) of cash for a period of time. (832)

Cash dividend. A cash distribution of earnings by a corporation to its shareholders. (488)

Cash equivalents. Highly liquid investments that are usually reported on the balance sheet with cash. (293)

Cash flows from financing activities. The section of the statement of cash flows that reports cash flows from transactions affecting the equity and debt of the entity. (591)

Cash flows from investing activities. The section of the statement of cash flows that reports cash flows from transactions affecting investments in noncurrent assets. (590)

Cash flows from operating activities. The section of the statement of cash flows that reports the cash transactions affecting the determination of net income. (590)

Cash payback period. The expected period of time that will elapse between the date of a capital expenditure and the complete recovery in cash (or equivalent) of the amount invested. (986)

Cash payments journal. The special journal in which all cash payments are recorded. (195)

Cash receipts journal. The special journal in which all cash receipts are recorded. (192)

Cash short and over account. An account which has recorded errors in cash sales or errors in making change causing the amount of actual cash on hand to differ from the beginning amount of cash plus the cash sales for the day. (282)

Chart of accounts. The system of accounts that make up the ledger for a business. (46)

Closing entries. Entries necessary to eliminate the balances of temporary accounts in preparation for the following accounting period. (141)

Common-size statement. A financial statement in which all items are expressed only in relative terms. (645)

Common stock. The basic ownership class of corporate stock. (481)

Comprehensive income. All changes in stockholders' equity during a period, except those resulting from dividends and stockholders' investments. (519)

Consolidated financial statements. Financial statements resulting from combining parent and subsidiary company statements. (526)

Consolidation. The creation of a new corporation by the transfer of assets and liabilities from two or more existing corporations. (525)

Continuous budgeting. A method of budgeting that provides for maintaining a twelve-month projection into the future. (822)

Contra accounts. Accounts that are offset against other accounts. (109)

Contra asset. An account that affects an asset account, such as the allowance for uncollectible accounts receivable or accumulated depreciation. (317)

Contract rate. The interest rate specified on a bond; sometimes called the coupon rate of interest. (553)

Contribution margin. Sales less variable costs and variable selling and administrative expenses. (776)

Contribution margin ratio. The percentage of each sales dollar that is available to cover the fixed costs and provide an operating income. (777)

Controllable expenses. Costs that can be influenced by the decisions of a manager. (906)

Controllable variance. The difference between the actual amount of variable factory overhead cost incurred and the amount of variable factory overhead budgeted for the standard product. (876)

Controller. The chief management accountant of a business. (689)

Controlling account. The account in the general ledger that summarizes the balances of the accounts in a subsidiary ledger. (187)

Conversion costs. The combination of direct labor and factory overhead costs. (691)

Copyright. The exclusive right to publish and sell a literary, artistic, or musical composition. (407)

Corporation. A separate legal entity that is organized in accordance with state or federal statutes and in which ownership is divided into shares of stock. (4)

Cost. A disbursement of cash (or a commitment to pay cash in the future) for the purpose of generating revenues. (689)

Cost accounting system. A system used to accumulate manufacturing costs for financial reporting and decision-making purposes. (691)

Cost allocation. The process of assigning indirect cost to a cost object, such as a job. (696)

Cost behavior. The manner in which a cost changes in relation to its activity base (driver). (770)

Cost center. A decentralized unit in which the department or division manager has responsibility for the control of costs incurred and the authority to make decisions that affect these costs. (904)

Cost concept. The basis for entering the exchange price, or cost, into the accounting records. (11)

Cost method. A method of accounting for an investment in common stock, by which the investor recognizes as income its share of cash dividends of the investee. (523)

Cost of goods sold. The cost of the manufactured product sold. (692)

Cost of goods sold budget. A budget in which the desired ending inventory and the estimated beginning inventory data are combined with data from direct materials budget, direct labor budget, and factory overhead cost budget. (830)

Cost of merchandise sold. The cost of merchandise purchased by a merchandise business and sold. (227)

Cost of production report. A report prepared periodically by a processing department, summarizing (1) the units for which the department is accountable and the disposition of those units and (2) the costs incurred by the department and the allocation of those costs between completed and incomplete production. (743)

Cost per equivalent unit. The rate used to allocate costs between completed and partially completed production in a process costing system. (741)

Cost price approach. An approach to transfer pricing that uses cost as the basis for setting the transfer price. (918)

Cost variance. The difference between actual cost and the flexible budget at actual volumes. (866)

Cost-volume-profit analysis. The systematic examination of the relationships among selling prices, volume of sales and production, costs, expenses, and profits. (776)

Cost-volume-profit chart. A chart used to assist management in understanding the relationships among costs, expenses, sales, and operating profit or loss. (783)

Credit. (1) The right side of an account; (2) the amount entered on the right side of an account; (3) to enter an amount on the right side of an account. (48)

Credit memorandum. The form issued by a seller to inform a buyer that a credit has been posted to the buyer's account receivable. (234)

Cumulative preferred stock. Preferred stock that is entitled to current and past dividends before dividends may be paid on common stock. (482)

Currency exchange rate. The rates at which currency in another country can be exchanged for U.S. dollars. (996)

Current assets. Cash or other assets that are expected to be converted to cash or sold or used up, usually within a year or less, through the normal operations of a business. (140)

Current liabilities. Liabilities that will be due within a short time (usually one year or less) and that are to be paid out of current assets. (141)

Current ratio. A financial ratio that is computed by dividing current assets by current liabilities. (151, 648)

Currently attainable standards. Standards that represent levels of operation that can be attained with reasonable effort. (867)

D

Debit. (1) The left side of an account; (2) the amount entered on the left side of an account; (3) to enter an amount on the left side of an account. (48)

Debit memorandum. The form issued by a buyer to inform a seller that a debit has been posted to the seller's account payable. (230)

Decentralization. The separation of a business into more manageable operating units. (902)

Declining-balance depreciation method. A method of depreciation that provides declining periodic depreciation expense over the estimated life of an asset. (395)

Deferred expenses. Items that are initially recorded as assets but are expected to become expenses over time or through the normal operations of the business. Sometimes called prepaid expenses. (101)

Deferred revenues. Items that are initially recorded as liabilities but are expected to become revenues over time or through the normal operations of the business. Sometimes called unearned revenues. (101)

Deficit. A debit balance in the retained earnings account. (480)

Defined benefit plan. A pension plan that promises employees a fixed annual pension benefit at retirement, based on years of service and compensation levels. (451)

Defined contribution plan. A pension plan that requires a fixed amount of money to be invested for the employee's behalf during the employee's working years. (450)

Depletion. The cost of metal ores and other minerals removed from the earth. (406)

Depreciation. In a general sense, the decrease in usefulness of fixed assets other than land. In accounting, refers to the systematic allocation of a fixed asset's cost to expense. (109, 391)

Depreciation expense. The portion of the cost of a fixed asset that is recorded as an expense each year of its useful life. (109)

Differential analysis. The area of accounting concerned with the effect of alternative courses of action on revenues and costs. (945)

Differential cost. The amount of increase or decrease in cost expected from a particular course of action as compared with an alternative. (945)

Differential revenue. The amount of increase or decrease in revenue expected from a particular course of action as compared with an alternative. (945)

Direct labor cost. Wages of factory workers who are directly involved in converting materials into a finished product. (690)

Direct labor rate variance. The cost associated with the difference between the standard rate and the actual rate paid for direct labor used in producing a commodity. (873)

Direct labor time variance. The cost associated with the difference between the standard hours and the actual hours of direct labor spent producing a commodity. (873)

Direct materials cost. The cost of materials that are an integral part of the finished product. (689)

Direct materials price variance. The cost associated with the difference between the standard price and the actual price of direct materials used in producing a commodity. (871)

Direct materials purchases budget. A budget that uses the production budget as a starting point for determining the quantities of direct materials to purchase. (828)

Direct materials quantity variance. The cost associated with the difference between the standard quantity and the actual quantity of direct materials used in producing a commodity. (871)

Direct method. A method of reporting the cash flows from operating activities as the net income from operations adjusted for all deferrals of past cash receipts and payments and all accruals of expected future cash receipts and payments. (592)

Direct write-off method. A method of accounting for uncollectible receivables, whereby an expense is recognized only when specific accounts are judged to be uncollectible. (317)

Discontinued operations. The operations of a business segment that has been disposed of. (513)

Discount. The interest deducted from the maturity value of a note. (434); The excess of the face amount of bonds over their issue price. (553); The excess of par value of stock over its sales price. (484)

Discount rate. The rate used in computing the interest to be deducted from the maturity value of a note. (434)

Dishonored note receivable. A note that the maker fails to pay on its due date. (325)

Dividends per share. The cash dividends per common shares commonly used by investors in assessing alternative stock investments, computed by dividing dividends by the number of shares of stock outstanding. (657)

Dividend yield. The rate of return to stockholders in terms of cash dividend distributions. (490)

Division. A decentralized organizational unit that is structured around a common function, product, customer, or geographical territory. Divisions can be cost, profit, or investment centers. (902)

Doomsday ratio. The ratio of cash and cash equivalents to current liabilities. (294)

Double-entry accounting. A system for recording transactions, based on recording increases and decreases in accounts so that debits always equal credits. (52)

Drawing. The account used to record amounts withdrawn by an owner of a proprietorship. (47)

E

Earnings per share (EPS) on common stock. The profitability ratio of net income available to common shareholders to the number of common shares outstanding. (515, 657)

Effective interest rate method. One method of amortizing a bond discount. Also known as the interest method. (558)

Effective rate of interest. The market rate of interest when bonds are issued. (553)

Electronic funds transfer (EFT). A payment system that uses computerized information rather than paper (money, checks, etc.) to effect a cash transaction. (285)

Elements of internal control. The control environment, risk assessment, control activities, information and communication, and monitoring. (182)

Employee fraud. The intentional act of deceiving an employer for personal gain. (182)

Employee's earnings record. A detailed record of each employee's earnings. (445)

Equity method. A method of accounting for investments in common stock, by which the investment account is adjusted for the investor's share of periodic net income and dividends of the investee. (526)

Equity security. A security that represents ownership in a business, such as stock in a corporation. (520)

Equivalent units of production. The number of units that could have been completed within a given accounting period with respect to direct materials and conversion costs. Equivalent units are used to allocate departmental costs incurred during the period between completed units and in-process units at the end of the period. (739)

Ethics. The moral principles that guide the conduct of individuals. (7)

Expenses. Assets used up or services consumed in the process of generating revenues. (14, 47)

Extraordinary items. Events or transactions that are unusual and infrequent. (514)

Extraordinary repair. An expenditure that increases the useful life of an asset beyond the original estimate. (398)

F

Factory overhead cost. All of the costs of operating the factory except for direct materials and direct labor. (691)

FICA tax. Federal Insurance Contributions Act tax used to finance federal programs for old-age and disability benefits (social security) and health insurance for the aged (Medicare). (439)

Financial accounting. The branch of accounting that is concerned with the recording of transactions using generally accepted accounting principles (GAAP) for a business or other economic unit and with a periodic preparation of various statements from such records. (9, 686)

Financial Accounting Standards Board (FASB). An authoritative body for the development of accounting principles. (10)

Finished goods inventory. The cost of finished products on hand that have not been sold. (692)

Finished goods ledger. The subsidiary ledger that contains the individual accounts for each kind of commodity or product produced. (700)

First-in, first-out (FIFO) method. A method of inventory costing based on the assumption that the costs of merchandise sold should be charged against revenue in the order in which the costs were incurred. (354, 737)

Fiscal year. The annual accounting period adopted by a business. (149)

Fixed assets. Physical resources that are owned and used by a business and are permanent or have a long life. (109, 390)

Fixed costs. Costs that tend to remain the same in amount, regardless of variations in the level of activity. (772)

Flexible budget. A budget that adjusts for varying rates of activity. (823)

FOB (free on board) destination. Terms of agreement between buyer and seller whereby ownership passes when merchandise is received by the buyer, and the seller pays the transportation costs. (236)

FOB (free on board) shipping point. Terms of agreement between buyer and seller whereby ownership passes when merchandise is delivered to the freight carrier, and the buyer pays the transportation costs. (236)

Free cash flow. The amount of operating cash flow remaining after replacing current productive capacity and maintaining current dividends. (587)

Fringe benefits. A variety of employee benefits that may take many forms, including vacations, pension plans, and health, life, and disability insurance. (449)

Future value. The estimated worth in the future of an amount of cash on hand today invested at a fixed rate of interest. (554)

G

General journal. The two-column form used for entries that are otherwise not recorded in special journals. (189)

General ledger. The primary ledger, when used in conjunction with subsidiary ledgers, that contains all of the balance sheet and income statement accounts. (187)

Generally accepted accounting principles (GAAP). Generally accepted guidelines for the preparation of financial statements. (10)

Goal conflict. Occurs when an employee's self-interest differs from business objectives. (821)

Goodwill. An intangible asset of a business due to such favorable factors as location, product superiority, reputation, and managerial skill. (408)

Gross pay. The total earnings of an employee for a payroll period. (437)

Gross profit. The excess of net sales over the cost of merchandise sold. (227)

Gross profit method. A means of estimating inventory based on the relationship of gross profit to sales. (367)

H

Held-to-maturity securities. Investments in bonds or other debt securities that management intends to hold to their maturity. (566)

High-low method. A technique that uses the highest and lowest total costs as a basis for estimating the variable cost per unit and the fixed cost component of a mixed cost. (773)

Horizontal analysis. Financial analysis that compares an item in a current statement with the same item in prior statements. (71, 642)

I

Income from operations (operating income). The excess of gross profit over total operating expenses. (243, 909)

Income statement. A summary of the revenues and expenses of a business entity for a specific period of time. (16)

Income Summary. The account used in the closing process for transferring the revenue and expense account balances to the retained earnings account at the end of the period. (141)

Indirect method. A method of reporting the cash flows from operating activities as the net income from operations adjusted for all deferrals of past cash receipts and payments and all accruals of expected future cash receipts and payments. (592)

Inflation. A period when prices in general are rising and the purchasing power of money is declining. (996)

Intangible assets. Long-lived assets that are useful in the operations of a business, are not held for sale, and are without physical qualities. (407)

Internal controls. The detailed policies and procedures used to direct operations, ensure accurate reports, and ensure compliance with laws and regulations. (181)

Internal rate of return method. A method of analysis of proposed capital investments that focuses on using present value concepts to compute the rate of return from the net cash flows expected from the investment. (991)

Inventory shrinkage. Loss of inventory due to shoplifting, employee theft, or errors in recording or counting inventory. (244)

Inventory turnover. A ratio that measures the relationship between the volume of goods (merchandise) sold and the amount of inventory carried during the period. (368, 651)

Investment center. A decentralized unit in which the manager has the responsibility and authority to make decisions that affect not only costs and revenues but also the fixed assets available to the center. (909)

Investments. The balance sheet caption used to report long-term investments in stocks or bonds not intended as a source of cash in the normal operations of the business. (522)

Investment turnover. A component of the rate of return on investment, computed as the ratio of sales to invested assets. (991)

Invoice. The bill provided by the seller (who refers to it as a sales invoice) to a buyer (who refers to it as a purchase invoice) for items purchased. (228)

J

Job cost sheet. An account in the work in process subsidiary ledger in which the costs charged to a particular job order are recorded. (693)

Job order cost system. A type of cost accounting system that provides for a separate record of the cost of each particular quantity of product that passes through the factory. (691)

Journal. The initial record in which the effects of a transaction on accounts are recorded. (49)

Journal entry. The form of recording a transaction in a journal. (50)

Journalizing. The process of recording a transaction in a journal. (50)

Just-in-time processing. A processing approach that focuses on eliminating time, cost, and poor quality within manufacturing and nonmanufacturing processes. (747)

L

Last-in, first-out (LIFO) method. A method of inventory costing based on the assumption that the most recent merchandise costs incurred should be charged against revenue. (354)

Ledger. The group of accounts used by a business. (46)

Leverage. The tendency of the rate earned on stockholders' equity to vary from the rate earned on total assets because the amount earned on assets acquired through the use of funds provided by creditors varies from the interest paid to these creditors (655)

Liabilities. Debts owed to outsiders (creditors). (11, 47)

Long-term liabilities. Liabilities that are not due for a long time (usually more than one year). (141)

Loss from operations. The excess of operating expenses over gross profit. (243)

Lower-of-cost-or-market (LCM) method. A method of valuing inventory that reports the inventory at the lower of its cost or current market value (replacement cost). (364)

M

Managerial accounting. The branch of accounting that uses both historical and estimated data in providing information that management uses in conducting daily operations, in planning future operations, and in developing overall business strategies. (9, 686)

Managers. Individuals who the owners have authorized to operate the business. (4)

Manufacturing businesses. A type of business that changes basic inputs into products that are sold to individual customers. (3)

Manufacturing cells. A grouping of production processes where employees are cross-trained to perform more than one function. (748)

Margin of safety. The difference between current sales revenue and the sales at the break-even point. (789)

Market price approach. An approach to transfer pricing that uses the price at which the product or service transferred could be sold to outside buyers as the transfer price. (916)

Markup. An amount that is added to a "cost" amount to determine product price. (953)

Master budget. The comprehensive budget plan encompassing all the individual budgets related to sales, cost of goods sold, operating expenses, capital expenditures, and cash. (825)

Matching concept. The concept that expenses incurred in generating revenue should be matched against the revenue in determining the net income or net loss for the period. (18, 101)

Materiality concept. A concept of accounting that accounts for items that are deemed significant for a given size of operations. (68)

Materials inventory. The cost of materials that have not yet entered into the manufacturing process. (692)

Materials ledger. The subsidiary ledger containing the individual accounts for each type of material. (693)

Materials requisitions. The form or electronic transmission used by a manufacturing department to authorize materials issuances from the storeroom. (693)

Maturity value. The amount due (face value plus interest) at the maturity or due date of a note. (324)

Merchandise inventory. Merchandise on hand and available for sale to customers. (227)

Merchandising businesses. A type of business that purchases products from other businesses and sells them to customers. (3)

Merger. The combining of two corporations by the acquisition of the properties of one corporation by another, with the dissolution of one of the corporations. (525)

Minority interest. The portion of a subsidiary corporation's stock that is not owned by the parent corporation. (527)

Mixed cost. A cost with both variable and fixed characteristics, sometimes called a semivariable or semifixed cost. (772)

Multiple-step income statement. An income statement with several sections, subsections, and subtotals. (240)

N

Natural business year. A year that ends when a business's activities have reached the lowest point in its annual operating cycle. (149)

Negotiated price approach. An approach to transfer pricing that allows managers of decentralized units to agree (negotiate) among themselves as to the transfer price. (917)

Net income. The amount by which revenues exceed expenses. (18)

Net loss. The amount by which expenses exceed revenues. (18)

Net pay. Gross pay less payroll deductions; the amount the employer is obligated to pay the employee. (437)

Net present value method. A method of analysis of proposed capital investments that focuses on the present value of the cash flows expected from the investments. (990)

Net realizable value. The valuation of an asset at an amount equal to the estimated selling price less any direct cost of disposal. (365)

Nonparticipating preferred stock. Preferred stock with a limited dividend preference. (481)

Notes receivable. A written promise to pay by the maker, representing an amount to be received by the payee. (140, 314)

Number of days' sales in inventory. A measure of the length of time it takes to acquire, sell, and replace the inventory. (368, 651)

Number of days' sales in receivables. An estimate of the length of time the accounts receivable have been outstanding. (327, 650)

Number of times the interest charges are earned. A ratio that measures the risk that interest payments to debtholders will continue to be made if earnings decrease. (566, 653)

O

Objectivity concept. Requires that the accounting records and reports be based upon objective evidence. (11)

Operating leases. Leases that do not meet the criteria for capital leases and thus are accounted for as operating expenses. (404)

Operating leverage. A measure of the relative mix of a business's variable costs and fixed costs, computed as contribution margin divided by operating income. (789)

Opportunity cost. The amount of income forgone from an alternative use of cash or its equivalent. (950)

Other expense. An expense that cannot be traced directly to operations. (243)

Other income. Revenue from sources other than the primary operating activity of a business. (243)

Outstanding stock. The stock that is in the hands of stockholders. (480)

Overapplied factory overhead. The amount of factory overhead applied in excess of the actual factory overhead costs incurred for production during a period. (697)

Owner's equity. The owner's right to the assets of the business after the total liabilities are deducted. (11, 47)

P

Paid-in capital. The capital acquired from stockholders. (479)

Par. The monetary amount printed on a stock certificate. (480)

Parent company. The company owning a majority of the voting stock of another corporation. (526)

Partnership. An unincorporated business owned by two or more individuals. (4)

Patents. Exclusive rights to produce and sell goods with one or more unique features. (407)

Payroll. The total amount earned by employees for a certain period. (436)

Payroll register. A multicolumn form used to assemble and summarize payroll data at the end of each payroll period. (442)

Period costs. Those costs that are used up in generating revenue during the current period and that are not involved in the manufacturing process. These costs are recognized as expenses on the current period's income statement. (701)

Periodic inventory system. A system of inventory accounting in which only the revenue from sales is recorded each time a sale is made. The cost of merchandise on hand at the end of a period is determined by a detailed listing (physical inventory) of the merchandise on hand. (227)

Perpetual inventory system. A system of inventory accounting in which both the revenue from sales and the cost of merchandise sold are recorded each time a sale is made, so that the records continually disclose the amount of the inventory on hand. (227)

Petty cash fund. A special cash fund used to pay relatively small amounts. (292)

Physical inventory. The detailed listing of merchandise on hand. (227, 351)

Pooling-of-interests method. A method of accounting for an affiliation of two corporations resulting from an exchange of voting stock of one corporation for substantially all the voting stock of the other corporation. (526)

Post-closing trial balance. A trial balance prepared after all of the temporary accounts have been closed. (148)

Posting. The process of transferring debits and credits from a journal to the accounts. (54)

Postretirement benefits. Rights to benefits that employees earn during their term of employment for themselves and their dependents after they retire. (451)

Predetermined factory overhead rate. The rate used to apply factory overhead costs to the goods manufactured. The rate is determined by dividing the budgeted overhead cost by the estimated activity usage at the beginning of the fiscal period. (696)

Preferred stock. A class of stock with preferential rights over common stock. (481)

Premium. The excess of the sales price of stock over its par amount. (484, 553)

Prepaid expenses. Purchased commodities or services that have not been used up at the end of an accounting period. (13)

Present value. The estimated worth today of an amount of cash to be received (or paid) in the future. (553)

Present value concept. A concept in which cash to be received (or paid) in the future is worth less than the same amount of money held today. (988)

Present value index. An index computed by dividing the total present value of the net cash flow to be received from a proposed capital investment by the amount to be invested. (990)

Present value of an annuity. The sum of the present values of a series of equal cash flows to be received at fixed intervals. (555, 989)

Price-earnings ratio. The ratio, often called the P/E ratio, computed by dividing the market price per share of common stock at a specific date by the company's earnings per share on common stock. (528, 657)

Prior-period adjustments. Corrections of material errors related to a prior period or periods, excluded from the determination of net income. (519)

Proceeds. The net amount available from discounting a note. (434)

Process cost system. A type of cost accounting system that accumulates costs for each of the various departments or processes within a manufacturing facility. (692, 734)

Process manufacturers. Manufacturers that use machines to process a continuous flow of raw materials through various stages of completion into a finished state. (734)

Product cost concept. A concept used in applying the cost-plus approach to product pricing in which only the costs of manufacturing the product, termed the product cost, are included in the cost amount to which the markup is added. (954)

Product costs. The three components of manufacturing cost: direct materials, direct labor, and factory overhead costs. (691)

Production budget. A budget of estimated production. (827)

Profitability. The ability of a firm to earn income. (647)

Profit center. A decentralized unit in which the manager has the responsibility and the authority to make decisions that affect both costs and revenues (and thus profits). (906)

Profit margin. A component of the rate of return on investment, computed as the ratio of income from operations to sales. (911)

Profit-volume chart. A chart used to assist management in understanding the relationship between profit and volume. (785)

Promissory note. A written promise to pay a sum in money on demand or at a definite time. (322)

Property, plant, and equipment. Fixed, or plant, assets that include equipment, machinery, buildings, and land. (140)

Proprietorship. A business owned by one individual. (4)

Purchase method. The accounting method employed when a parent company acquires a controlling share of the voting stock of a subsidiary other than by the exchange of voting common stock. (526)

Purchases discounts. An available discount taken by a buyer for early payment of an invoice. (229)

Purchases journal. The special journal in which all items purchased on account are recorded. (193)

Purchases returns and allowances. Reductions in purchases, resulting from merchandise being returned to the seller or from the seller's reduction in the original purchase price. (230)

Q

Quick ratio. A financial ratio that measures the ability to pay current liabilities within a short period of time. (452)

Quick assets. The sum of cash, receivables, and marketable securities. (649)

R

Rate earned on common stockholders' equity. A measure of profitability computed by dividing net income, reduced by preferred dividend requirements, by common stockholders' equity. (655)

Rate earned on stockholders' equity. A measure of profitability computed by dividing net income by total stockholders' equity. (655)

Rate earned on total assets. A measure of the profitability of assets, computed as net income plus interest expense divided by total average assets. (654)

Rate of return on investment (ROI). A measure of managerial efficiency in the use of investments in assets, computed as income from operations divided by invested assets. (910)

Ratio of fixed assets to long-term liabilities. A financial ratio that provides a measure indicating the margin of safety to creditors. (409, 652)

Ratio of liabilities to stockholders' equity. The relationship between the total claims of the creditors and owners. (652)

Ratio of net sales to assets. A profitability measure that shows how effectively a firm utilizes its assets. (653)

Receivables. All money claims against other entities, including people, business firms, and other organizations. (314)

Receiving report. The form or electronic transmission used by the receiving personnel to indicate that materials have been received and inspected. (693)

Relevant range. The range of activity over which changes in cost are of interest to management. (770)

Report form. The form of balance sheet with the liabilities and owner's equity sections presented below the assets section. (18, 245)

Residual income. The excess of income from operations over a "minimum" amount of desired income from operations. (913)

Residual value. The estimated recoverable cost of a depreciable asset as of the time of its removal from service. (393)

Responsibility accounting. The process of measuring and reporting operating data by areas of responsibility. (904)

Responsibility center. An organizational unit for which a manager is assigned responsibility for the unit's performance. (820)

Retail inventory method. A means of estimating inventory based on the relationship of the cost and the retail price of merchandise. (366)

Retained earnings. Net income retained in a corporation. (479)

Revenue. The gross increase in owner's equity as a result of business and professional activities that earn income. (13, 47)

Revenue expenditures. Expenditures that benefit only the current period. (398)

Revenue journal. The special journal in which all sales of services on account are recorded. (189)

Revenue recognition concept. The principle by which revenues are recognized in the period in which they are earned. (100)

S

Sales budget. One of the major elements of the income statement budget that indicates the quantity of estimated sales and the expected unit selling price. (826)

Sales discounts. An available discount granted by a seller for early payment of an invoice; a contra account to Sales. (233)

Sales mix. The relative distribution of sales among the various products available for sale. (787)

Sales returns and allowances. Reductions in sales, resulting from merchandise being returned by customers or from the seller's reduction in the original sales price; a contra account to Sales. (234)

Selling expenses. Expenses incurred directly in the sale of merchandise. (242)

Services businesses. A business providing services rather than products to customers. (3)

Service department charges. The costs of services provided by an internal service department and transferred to a responsibility center. (907)

Single-step income statement. An income statement in which the total of all expenses is deducted in one step from the total of all revenues. (243)

Sinking fund. Assets set aside in a special fund to be used for a specific purpose. (560)

Slide. The erroneous movement of all digits in a number, one or more spaces to the right or the left, such as writing $542 as $5,420. (69)

Solvency. The ability of a business to pay its debts. (151, 647)

Special journals. Journals designed to be used for recording a single type of transaction. (188)

Standard cost. A detailed estimate of what a product should cost. (866)

Standard cost systems. Accounting systems that use standards for each element of manufacturing cost entering into the finished product. (866)

Stated value. A value approved by the board of directors of a corporation for no-par stock. Similar to par value. (480)

Statement of cash flows. A summary of the major cash receipts and cash payments for a period. (16, 590)

Statement of owner's equity. A summary of the changes in the owner's equity of a business that have occurred during a specific period of time. (16)

Statement of stockholders' equity. A summary of the changes in the stockholders' equity of a corporation that have occurred during a specific period of time. (519)

Static budget. A budget that does not adjust to changes in activity levels. (822)

Stock. Shares of ownership of a corporation. (476)

Stock dividend. Distribution of a company's own stock to its shareholders. (489)

Stock split. A reduction in the par or stated value of a share of common stock and the issuance of a proportionate number of additional shares. (487)

Stockholders. The owners of a corporation. (476)

Stockholders' equity. The equity of the stockholders of a corporation. (479)

Straight-line depreciation method. A method of depreciation that provides for equal periodic depreciation expense over the estimated life of an asset. (394)

Subsidiary company. The corporation that is controlled by a parent company. (526)

Subsidiary ledger. A ledger containing individual accounts with a common characteristic. (187)

Sum-of-the-years-digits depreciation method. A method of depreciation that provides for declining periodic depreciation expense over the estimated life of an asset. (410)

Sunk cost. A cost that is not affected by subsequent decisions. (944)

T

T account. A form of account resembling the letter T, showing debits on the left and credits on the right. (48)

Target cost concept. A concept used to design and manufacture a product at a cost that will deliver a target profit for a given market-determined price. (957)

Taxable income. The base on which the amount of income tax is determined. (511)

Temporary accounts. Revenue, expense, or income summary accounts that are periodically closed; nominal accounts. (141)

Temporary differences. Differences between income before income tax and taxable income created by items that are recognized in one period for income statement purposes and in another period for tax purposes. Such differences reverse, or turn around, in later years. (511)

Temporary investments. Investments in securities that can be readily sold when cash is needed. (520)

Theoretical standards. Standards that represent levels of performance that can be achieved only under perfect operating conditions. (867)

Theory of constraints (TOC). A manufacturing strategy that attempts to remove the influence of bottlenecks (constraints) on a process. (958)

Time tickets. The form on which the amount of time spent by each employee and the labor cost incurred for each individual job, or for factory overhead, are recorded. (695)

Time value of money concept. The concept that an amount of money invested today will earn income. (985)

Total cost concept. A concept used in applying the cost-plus approach to product pricing in which all the costs of manufacturing the product plus the selling and administrative expenses are included in the cost amount to which the markup is added. (953)

Trade discounts. Special discounts from published list prices offered by sellers to certain classes of buyers. (235)

Trade-in allowance. The amount a seller grants a buyer for a fixed asset that is traded in for a similar asset. (402)

Trademark. A name, term, or symbol used to identify a business and its products. (408)

Trading security. A debt or equity security that management intends to actively trade for profit. (520)

Transfer price. The price charged one decentralized unit by another for the goods or services provided. (915)

Transposition. The erroneous arrangement of digits in a number, such as writing $542 as $524. (69)

Treasury stock. A corporation's issued stock that has been reacquired. (485)

Trial balance. A summary listing of the titles and balances of the accounts in the ledger. (67)

Two-column journal. An all-purpose general journal. (55)

U

Uncollectible accounts expense. The operating expense incurred because of the failure to collect receivables. (317)

Underapplied factory overhead. The amount of actual factory overhead in excess of the factory overhead applied to production during a period. (698)

Unearned revenue. The liability created by receiving cash in advance of providing goods or services. (47)

Unit contribution margin. The dollars available from each unit of sales to cover fixed costs and provide operating profits. (777)

Unit of measure concept. A concept of accounting that requires that economic data be recorded in dollars. (11)

Units-of-production depreciation method. A method of depreciation that provides for depreciation expense based on the expected productive capacity of an asset. (395)

Unrealized holding gain or loss. The difference between the fair market values of the securities and their cost. (521)

V

Variable cost concept. A concept used in applying the cost-plus approach to product pricing in which only the variable costs are included in the cost amount to which the markup is added. (955)

Variable costing. The concept that considers the cost of products manufactured to be composed only of those manufacturing costs that increase or decrease as the volume of production rises or falls (direct materials, direct labor, and variable factory overhead). (776)

Variable costs. Costs that vary in total dollar amount as the level of activity changes. (770)

Vertical analysis. An analysis that compares each item in a current statement witha total amount within the same statement. (114, 645)

Volume variance. The difference between the budgeted fixed overhead at 100% of normal capacity and the standard fixed overhead for the actual production achieved during the period. (876)

Voucher. A document that serves as evidence of authority to pay cash. (283)

Voucher system. Records, methods, and procedures used in verifying and recording liabilities and paying and recording cash payments. (283)

W

Working capital. The excess of the current assets of a business over its current liabilities. (151, 648)

Work in process inventory. The direct materials costs, the direct labor costs, and the applied factory overhead costs that have entered into the manufacturing process, but are associated with products that have not been finished. (692)

Work sheet. A working paper used to summarize adjusting entries and assist in the preparation of financial statements. (138)

Y

Yield. A measure of materials usage efficiency; it measures the ratio of the materials output quantity to the materials input quantity. Yields less than 1.0 are the result of materials losses in the process. (746)

Z

Zero-based budgeting. A concept of budgeting that requires all levels of management to start from zero and estimate budget data as if there had been no previous activities in their unit. (822)

Glossary

abandoned property Personal property that has been deliberately left in a location without the intention to retrieve it.

acceptance Final step necessary to form a legal contract. A demonstration of agreement to all of the terms of the contract that has been offered.

actus reus Element of physical conduct necessary to commit a criminal act.

administrative agency Government office enabled by the legislature and overseen by the executive branch. The purpose of such agencies is to apply certain specified laws created by the legislature.

administrative branch Administrative agencies created pursuant to legislation and overseen by the executive branch to administer and define statutes.

administrative law Regulations and decisions issued by administrative agencies that explain and detail statutes.

administrative law judge Judicial officer assigned to preside over cases between individuals or entities and government administrative agencies.

Administrative Procedure Act Congressional enactment applied to all federal administrative agencies requiring them to follow certain procedures in the issuance of administrative law.

adverse possession When title to real property is acquired without purchase or voluntary transfer of title. Ordinarily, one who obtains title by adverse possession must openly and continuously exercise possession and control over the entire property inconsistent with the interest of the current owner and all others who claim rights to the property for a period of time specified by statute.

affirm Approve. When an appellate court affirms the result in the original court, that result is approved and can be enforced.

agency Relationship in which one party, known as the agent, acts on behalf of another party, known as the principal. In a valid agency relationship, the agent can legally bind the principal; e.g. an agent can enter into a contract on behalf of a principal.

ancillary jurisdiction Authority of a court over issues in a case subject to the court's authority on grounds unrelated to the issues.

annulment Legal relationship declared invalid in which the parties to the relationship are treated as if the relationship never existed, e.g., marriage.

antenuptial agreement Agreement between parties prior to a marriage that states the terms for distribution of assets and liabilities in the event the marriage relationship ends.

appellate jurisdiction Authority of one court to review the actions in another court for the purpose of identifying an abuse of discretion. See *Discretion*

arraignment Stage of a criminal proceeding in which the accused is formally charged.

articles of incorporation Document filed with the state at the time of incorporation to state the purpose of the corporation and define the corporate structure.

assignment A grant of rights to a third party an original party is entitled to under a contract.

assumption of risk Defense to negligence on the basis that the plaintiff knew of, appreciated, and voluntarily encountered the danger of the defendant's conduct.

attorney Individual who has completed the necessary requirements of education and training to receive a license to practice law in a jurisdiction.

bailment Temporary relinquishment of control over one's personal property to a third party.

bench trial Trial in which the judge determines which law will be applicable and applies the law to the facts of the case.

bilateral contract Contractual agreement between two or more persons in which each party promises to deliver performance in exchange for the performance of the other.

bill Proposed law presented to the legislature for consideration.

bylaws Document of a corporation that details the methods of operation, such as officers and duties, chain of command, and general corporate procedures.

case law Law that is created judicially when a legal principle of common law is extended to a similar situation.

cases Judicial opinions that are common law or case law and that interpret statutory and administrative law.

civil law Law that governs the private rights of individuals, legal entities, and government. See *Criminal Law*

Code of Federal Regulations Publication that contains all current administrative regulations.

codification Process of incorporating newly passed legislation into existing publication of statutes.

common law Judicially created legal principles or standards. The judiciary has the authority to create law in situations where none currently exists.

comparative negligence Degree of plaintiff's own negligent conduct that was responsible for plaintiff's injury.

compensatory damages An award of money payable to the injured party for the reasonable cost of the injuries.

complaint (also known as petition) Document that apprises the court and the defendant of the nature of the cause of action by the plaintiff.

concurrent jurisdiction When more than one court has authority to hear a case.

contract Legally binding agreement that obligates two or more parties to do something they were not already obligated to do or refrain from doing something to which the parties were legally entitled.

contractual capacity Ability to enter into and be bound by a legal contract, which ability has not been diminished by age of minority or adjudicated incompetence.

contributory negligence Doctrine that maintains that a plaintiff who, in any way, contributes to his/her injury cannot recover from a negligent defendant.

consideration That which one party provides to another party as inducement to enter into a contractual agreement. The benefit a party receives as the result of entering a contract with another party.

corporation Entity legally recognized as independent of its owners, known as shareholders. A corporation can sue or be sued in its own name regarding its own rights and liabilities.

criminal law Law created and enforced by the legislature for the health, welfare, safety, and general good of the public.

criminal procedure Law created to assist in the fair and efficient enforcement of criminal law.

critical stage Stage of a criminal proceeding in which the presumed innocence of the accused is in jeopardy and thus the accused is entitled to representation of counsel.

damage Financial, physical, or emotional injury.

deposition Written or oral questions submitted to a party or witness in a lawsuit in which the answers are given orally and under oath, then transcribed into writing.

defendant Party against whom a lawsuit is instituted.

delegation Transfer of one's contractual obligations to a third person.

delegation doctrine Principle that Congress may not assign its authority to create statutory law, nor may any other government entity assume such authority.

discovery Court-supervised exchange of evidence and other relevant information between parties to a lawsuit.

discretion Limits of authority. Abuse of discretion occurs when one's authority is exceeded or improperly used; e.g., abuse of discretion by a judge or jury is grounds for appeal.

dissolution of marriage End of a marriage relationship.

diversity of citizenship Method of achieving federal jurisdiction over a matter. It is necessary that all parties be diverse; i.e., no plaintiff and defendant can be domiciled in the same state. The second requirement of diversity of citizenship is that the amount in dispute between the parties be in excess of the minimum amount stated by federal statute.

double jeopardy Being placed on trial for the same crime twice.

due process That which is necessary to fundamental fairness in the American system of justice.

enabling act Congressional enactment that creates the authority in the executive to organize and oversee an administrative agency.

equity Functional legal remedy sought when money damages would be inadequate as a method of compensating the injured party. Actions in equity ask the court to order performance or nonperformance of certain acts.

estate All material assets of an individual or legal entity, including liquid assets (cash or items that can readily be converted to cash) and nonliquid assets.

evidence Testimony, documentation, or tangible items admissible in court to support a party's claims or defenses in a lawsuit.

exclusive jurisdiction Authority of a court to hear a case, which authority is superior to all other courts.

excusable behavior Behavior by one who, under the color of authority, is considered to be innocent of otherwise criminal behavior.

exhaustion of remedies Requirement that anyone having a dispute with an administrative agency must first follow all available procedures to resolve the dispute within the agency before taking the issue before the judiciary.

federal court A court that is part of the United States courts.

federal question Method of achieving jurisdiction of the federal courts over a dispute between parties. It is necessary that a significant part of the dispute arise from the Constitution or a federal law.

fee simple Absolute ownership of property in American law.

felony Serious crime punishable by imprisonment in excess of one year and/or other significant penalties.

fixture Item of personal property that has been so affixed to real property that it cannot be removed without damage to the real property. A fixture is personal property that essentially becomes part of the real property.

forced share Legal right of a surviving spouse to receive a certain percentage of the estate of the deceased spouse, superior to the terms of a will or other rights of inheritance by heirs.

forum non conveniens (inconvenient forum) Applied when a court with jurisdiction over a matter determines that another court, which also has jurisdiction, would be the more appropriate forum.

freehold estate Interest in real property that involves certain rights of ownership. See *Nonfreehold estate*

grand jury A number of individuals (usually more than 20) who review the evidence to determine whether defendant could be convicted of the crime if charged and tried.

in personam jurisdiction Authority of a court over an individual and all of his/her assets.

in rem jurisdiction Authority of a court over a person's real or personal property.

intentional tort Act that the actor knows or should know with substantial certainty will cause harm to another.

interrogatories Questions submitted by one party in a lawsuit to the opposing party. Said questions must pertain to the dispute between the parties and must be answered within a specific time and under oath. A method of discovery.

intestate succession Method of distributing an estate of one who died without a valid will.

joint custody Sharing of responsibility for upbringing of children of the joint custodians. In some cases, joint custody also involves shared physical custody of the children.

joint tenancy Form of multiple property ownership in which the property owners have fee simple and share four unities. Each owner shares in the right of survivorship.

judge Judicial officer who presides over cases in litigation within a court system.

judiciary Appointed or elected officials (judges, magistrates, justices of the peace) who preside in the courts over disputes among citizens and the government.

jurisdiction (1) Authority of a court over parties and subject of a dispute. (2) Geographical boundaries of the area and citizens over which a court has authority.

justifiable behavior Behavior by one who, under the circumstances, is considered to be innocent of otherwise criminal behavior.

law clerk Lawyer, law student, or paralegal who conducts legal research and writing and various other duties but who does not represent individual clients as a licensed attorney.

lawyer See *attorney.*

legal analysis Process of examining precedent in detail to predict its effect on future similar circumstances.

legal separation Legal document that establishes the property rights of the parties without effecting a dissolution of the actual marriage relationship.

legal standard Law created by one of the three sources of government, including the legislature, executive branch or the judiciary.

legislative branch Members of a congress elected by the citizens of a jurisdiction to represent their interests, e.g., senator or representative.

liability Legal responsibility resulting from an act or failure to act when there was a legal obligation to do so.

life estate Right to possess and use real property for the duration of one's life, with limited ownership rights.

limited partnership Partnership of two or more persons in which the limited partner can be held liable for partnership debts only to the extent of his or her investment and cannot take part in general management and operation of the partnership business.

lobbyist Individual representing interested parties who meets with legislators about proposed laws.

long-arm jurisdiction Authority of the government of one jurisdiction to reach into another jurisdiction for the purpose of exercising control over a particular citizen.

lost property Property unintentionally left by the owner in a place no longer known to the owner.

maintenance Financial assistance from a divorced spouse to the other divorced spouse to be used for necessary living expenses and income.

material evidence Evidence necessary to a fair and informed decision by the trier of fact.

mens rea Mental state required as an element necessary to commit a criminal act.

misdemeanor Criminal offense punishable by a fine or imprisonment of less than one year.

mislaid property Property that was intentionally placed by the owner and later forgotten.

modern balance Goal of lawmaking authorities to balance the need for consistency and stability against the need for a flexible and adaptive government.

motion Formal request by a party to a lawsuit for court-ordered action/nonaction.

naturalist theory Philosophy that all persons know inherently the difference between right and wrong.

negligence Act or failure to act toward another when (1) a duty was owed to the other person; (2) the act or failure to act was less than a reasonable person would have done under the circumstances; (3) the act or failure to act was the direct cause of injury to the other person; and

(4) the injury caused measurable financial, physical, or emotional damage to the other person.

negotiable instrument Document recognized by law as an exchange for legal tender and that meets all legal requirements, including that the document be (1) written, (2) signed, (3) for a specified amount, (4) payable on a certain date or on demand, (5) written with words that indicate whether the document is payable to a stated person (bearer), (6) required that no additional acts are to be performed before payment.

nonfreehold estate Interest in real property that is limited in duration and involves the right of possession but not ownership. See *Freehold Estate*

note Negotiable instrument that involves two parties: the "payor" promises to pay an amount to the "payee" on a specified date.

offer A party presents an agreement for acceptance or rejection by a second party, which agreement includes all necessary requirements and elements of a legal contract.

original jurisdiction Authority of a court to rule in a lawsuit from commencement through the conclusion of trial.

overrule Judicial action that states that a legal standard previously recognized is no longer effective as law. Distinguished from reversal (see below).

par value Legal value of stock (percentages of ownership) in a corporation. Par value is determined by the board of directors of the corporation.

paralegal/legal assistant One who has legal training and education and performs tasks in the law office traditionally performed by the attorney, with the exception of advocacy and giving of legal advice. In some geographical areas, these terms are used interchangeably, while in others, they imply distinct levels of professional ability.

partnership Agreement of two or more parties to engage in business or enterprise, with profits and losses shared among all parties.

pendant jurisdiction Occurs when a case involves multiple issues and the court in which the case is filed has actual authority over some but not all of the issues, in which case, the court has the option to exercise authority over those issues it could not ordinarily decide, thus exercising pendant jurisdiction.

per capita Distribution in equal shares, with each person representing one share.

per stirpes Distribution in equal shares to one level or class of persons; if a member of this level or class is deceased, the member's heirs divide the share.

permanent injunction Court order that permanently orders a party to act or refrain from acting in a particular manner.

personal property Movable items that are not land or permanently affixed to land. Personal property includes tangible (physical) and intangible items, such as rights of ownership in property held by others, e.g., bank accounts, or rights of ownership in legal entities, e.g. stock. It does not include rights to bring legal action against others, commonly known as a chose in action.

positivist theory Political belief that there should be a superior government entity not subject to question or challenge.

precedent Existing legal standards that courts look to for guidance when making a determination of a legal issue.

preliminary injunction Court order that orders a party to act or refrain from acting in a particular manner for a specified period of time.

probable cause Legal concept of suspicion supported by facts necessary before a search or arrest can be conducted by law enforcement officers.

probate Process of paying creditors and distributing the estate of one who is deceased. Probate courts also often administer the estates of living persons who are incapable of managing their own affairs.

procedural law Law used to guide parties fairly and efficiently through the legal system.

promoter One who is hired as a fiduciary to recruit investors in a proposed corporation.

property settlement agreement Agreement as to the property rights and obligations of co-owners/co-debtors, such as parties to a marriage.

proximate cause Direct cause sufficient to produce a result. No other intervening force can occur independently and prior to the result that is also sufficient to produce the result.

quasi in rem jurisdiction Authority of a court to alter a person's interest and/or ownership in real or personal property.

real property Land or anything permanently affixed to land and no longer movable.

reasonable conduct That action or nonaction that is appropriate under the circumstances when all risks and benefits are taken into account.

reasonable man One similar in age, intelligence, and experience to the party alleged to be at fault who perceives and appreciates all dangers and benefits of action or nonaction and who acts in the most careful manner.

recision Legal termination of a contract prior to its completion. Cancellation.

relevant evidence Evidence that tends to establish an essential fact in the dispute.

remand Action of one court that returns a case to the court where it originated, e.g., following a reversal or improper transfer.

removal Transfer of a case to federal court that was originally filed in state court.

request for production Written request from one party in a lawsuit to the opposing party that seeks to copy and/or inspect documentary evidence relevant to the dispute. A method of discovery.

res ipsa loquitur "The thing speaks for itself." Method of proving negligence when (1) the injury would not ordinarily have occurred without negligence, (2) the instrument causing injury was in the exclusive control of the defendant, and (3) the plaintiff in no way contributed to the injury.

respondeat superior Liability of an employer for the acts of an employee who caused damage to a third party while acting within the scope of employment.

reverse The action of an appellate court used to invalidate a decision by a court of original jurisdiction. The parties to the lawsuit are affected accordingly.

right of survivorship Characteristic associated with multiple property ownership in which the ownership interest transfers automatically to co-owners upon death.

session law Published statutes passed during a specific session of the legislature.

shareholder One who owns stock representing an ownership interest in a corporation.

slip law Individual statute not yet published with other statutes.

slip opinion Individual court opinion that is not yet published with other opinions.

sociological theory Doctrine that follows the principle that government should adapt laws to reflect the current needs and beliefs of society.

sole proprietorship Individual ownership of a business entity. The individual is personally liable for debts of the business.

specific performance Court order to complete performance as stated in a contract. Allowed in certain cases of equity where the performance is unique and cannot be imitated or compensated by the payment of money.

stare decisis "Let the decision stand." Method used by the judiciary when applying precedent to current situations.

statute of frauds Statutory law that specifies what contracts must be in writing before they will be enforced.

statutory law A statute. Law that is created by the legislature.

strict liability Liability without fault. Applied in situations where the intention or neglect of the party is immaterial. The mere performance of the act or omission will result in liability.

subject matter jurisdiction Authority of a court to determine the actual issue between the parties.

substantive law Law that creates and resolves the issue between the parties. Legal standard that guides conduct and is applied to determine whether or not conduct was legally appropriate.

summary judgment Determination prior to trial of the rights and obligations of the parties. This is granted only when there is no significant fact left to be decided on the basis of the evidence. The greatest weight of the evidence supports only one result.

temporary restraining order Court order that orders a party to act or refrain from acting in a particular manner for a short time until the court has the opportunity to consider a more permanent ruling.

tenancy in common Form of multiple ownership of property in which each tenant (owner) shares with the other(s) an undivided interest in the property.

tenancy by entirety Form of multiple ownership of property between spouses that includes right of survivorship.

testate succession Method of distributing the estate of a deceased person in accordance with the terms of a valid will.

third-party beneficiary One who, as the result of gift or collateral agreement, is entitled to the contractual performance owed another.

tort Civil wrong by a party, other than breach of contract, that results in injury to the private rights or interests of another party.

traditional balance Goal of the judiciary to allow maximum personal freedom without detracting from the welfare of the general public.

trial court Court of original jurisdiction with authority to hear evidence of parties and render a verdict.

unilateral contract Contractual agreement in which one party makes a promise to perform upon receiving the actual performance of the other party.

venue Proper individual court within a jurisdiction to determine a dispute between parties.

veto Presidential power to invalidate law passed by a majority of Congress (2/3 majority of each house needed to override).

INDEX

A

C

D

E

F

G

H

I

Y

Z